# A History of Fine Arts in India and the West

# A History of Fine Arts in India and the West

by

EDITH TOMÖRY F. MM. Ph.D.
*Formerly Head of the Department of Fine Arts,*
*Stella Maris College, Madras.*

Orient BlackSwan

A HISTORY OF FINE ARTS IN INDIA AND THE WEST

**ORIENT BLACKSWAN PRIVATE LIMITED**

*Registered Office*
3-6-752 Himayatnagar, Hyderabad 500 029, Telangana, India
E-mail: centraloffice@oreientblackswan.com

*Other Offices*
Bengaluru, Chennai, Guwahati, Hyderabad, Kolkata,
Mumbai, New Delhi, Noida, Patna


First published by Orient Longman Pvt. Ltd., 1982
Reprinted 1989, 1992, 1995, 1997, 1999, 2000, 2002, 2003, 2004, 2006, 2007
First Orient Blackswan impression 2010
Reprinted 2011, 2012, 2013, 2015, 2017, 2018, 2019, 2020, 2022, 2024, 2026

*Maps by*
Sangam Books (India) Private Limited
Hyderabad

*The following are applicable for the map(s) in this book:*
Government of India, Copyright 2017.
The responsibility for the correctness of internal details rests with the publisher.
The territorial waters of India extend into the sea to a distance of twelve nautical miles measured from the appropriate base line.
The external boundaries of India agree with the Record/Master Copy certified by the Survey of India.
The spellings of names have been taken from various sources.

ISBN : 978 81 250 0702 9

041951

*Prinnted in India at*
B. B. Press
Tronica City Ghaziabad (UP) 201 102

*Published by*
Orient Blackswan Private Limited
3-6-752 Himayatnagar, Hyderabad 500 029, Telangana, India
E-mail: info@orientblackswan.com

# PREFACE

In order to bring the fascinating riches of artistic development within the reach of college and university students as well as general readers, the Fine Arts Department of Stella Maris College—the staff, graduates and students—have collaborated in compiling this present volume, aided by the precious advice and help of numerous friends and experts in relevant fields.

In this desire to bring the superabundant wealth of art within the means of students and the general public we could do no more than select some of the most distinctive and outstanding contributions in the long development of art in our own vast country, together with a survey of the growth of art in the West, trusting that this will arouse interest in the artistic contributions of other cultures as well.

Stress has been laid on India's most distinctive role in world art—its development of rock-cut architecture and its immense wealth of stone carvings, illustrated by many line drawings contributed by the Stella Maris Fine Arts Department.

Since a better appreciation of Indian art requires also an understanding of its conventions and vocabulary, these have been especially explained in the glossary and illustrations of the symbolic gestures have been provided.

Since so-called facts always remain open to further discoveries and different points of view, no really conclusive statements are possible in the field of art, subject as it is to personal tastes and stages of understanding.

In the choice of subjects and works, emphasis has been laid chiefly on those that contributed to original development. For this reason some have received more coverage. Moreover, where comprehensive literature is not easily available on topics like rock-cut architecture and modern world art, these have received more attention.

# ACKNOWLEDGEMENTS

The following illustrations in this book are reproduced by kind permission of the institutions and individuals here named: Archaeological Survey of India: Plates 1.1-3; 2.1–2; 3.1–2; 4.1–3; 5.1–3; 5.5; 6.6–7; 7.1–3; 8.1–3; 9. 1–4; 10.1–4; 11.1; 11,4; 12.1–2; 13.1–3; 14.1–5; 15.1–2; 16.1–3; 17.1–3; 18.3; 18.2; Figure 222. Y.M.C.A. Publishing House, Calcutta: Plates 20.2; 20.1. Victoria and Albert Museum, London: Plates 17.4; 18.1. Museo Nacional del Prado, Madrid: Plates 47.2; 56.4. L. Grote, Munich: Plates 49.1; 49.3; 51.2–4. Methuen & Co., London, from G. F. Hill, One Hundred Masterpieces of Sculpture: Plates 24.2–3; 24. 6–7; 27. 2–3; 55. 2–4; 41.3; and by courtesy of the photographs and copyright permission: Museum of Fine Arts, Boston (through the U.S.I.S. Madras): Plates 11.3; 19.1–2. Philadelphia Museum of Art (through the U.S.I.S. Madras): Plate 38.3 (from the Wilstach Collection). Metropolitan Museum of Art, New York (through the U.S.I.S. Madras): Plate 20.3 (Rogers Fund 1927), Plate 23.2 (Fletcher Fund 1932). Plate 57.1 (Bequest of Mrs. H.O. Havemeyer 1929, The H.O. Havemeyer Collection). N. V. Philips Gloeilam-penfabriken, Holland (through Philips India Ltd.): Plates 41.1–2; 45.1; 48.2; 51.2; 52.1; 53.1; 54.4; 55.3; 57.2; 58.1–2; 59.1; 61.1–2; 64.1–2. Embassy of Belgium, New Delhi Plate 62.1. Embassy of Spain, New Delhi Plates 56.1–3; 58.3; 59.3–4. Embassy of the United Arab Republic in India: Plate 22.1–2. Consulate General of the Federal Republic of Germany, Madras: Plate 50. 2–4. The Fine Arts Department of Stella Maris College, Madras, for all their line drawings.

Every effort has been made to contact owners of copyright material. The publishers would be glad to hear from those from whom we have had no response yet so that due acknowledgement is made in the next and future editions.

Special mention must be made of the following for their valuable contributions: to Louise Oeser for the text of 'Modern Architecture, Painting and Sculpture' and to Rama Prabhakaran for the text of 'Indian Murals and Rajput Paintings'; to Greta Bestall, former Professor in Drawing and Painting, for most of the line drawings, as well as to Suchi and to K. Mangala Gowri for a number of line drawings; to Louise Oeser and Teresa Fennessey for typing; to Ashrafi Sabbhir and Sheila Balaji for helping to collect material; to M. Alamelu and M. Yashodara for practical assistance; to Rama Prabhakaran and Rama Narayana for help with the Sanskrit, as well as to Mrs. Saroja, Sanskrit lecturer, for her advice; to Sri K. R. Srinivasan, Retired Deputy Director-General of Archaeology for making himself available for consultation in case of doubt and for his useful suggestions and clarifications; to S. Mallika, N.S. Svapna, N. Rajalakshmi and Prabha for helping to prepare the index; and to Louise Oeser for helping to correct and edit the entire text.

# CONTENTS

**THE WEST**

ANCIENT ART



MEDIEVAL ART



RENAISSANCE ART



MODERN TRENDS

# FIGURES

# MAPS

# MUDRAS I–IV

Chin mudra
Suci mudra.
Dhyana mudra.
Vismaya mudra.
Varada mudra.
Katyavalambita.
Dharmachakra mudra.
Katakamukha.
Kartarimukha.
Anjali.
Pataka mudra.
Tripataka mudra.
Abhaya mudra.
Chatura mudra.
Sukhasana.
Maharaja-Lilasana.
Sopasaryana
Padmasana.
Kirita makuta.
Jewellery worn by a male figure in sculpture.
Jewellery worn by a female figure in sculpture.
Atibhanga.
Tribhanga.
Samabhanga

# PLATES

PLATE 1

1. Great bath, Mohenjo-Daro.
2. Stambha, Laurya-Nandangarh.
3. Stupa I, Sanchi.

PLATE 2

1. Northern torana, stupa I, Sanchi.
2. Chaitya, interior, Karle.
3. Ajanta caves, general view.
4. Cave I, Ajanta (wooden model).

PLATE 3

1. Muktesvara temple, Bhuvanesvar.
2. Lingaraja temple, Bhuvanesvar.

PLATE 4

1. Kandarya-Mahadeva temple, Khajuraho.
2. Surya temple, Osian.
3. Surya temple Modhera.

PLATE 5

1. Five athas, Mamallapuram.
2. Dharmaraja ratha, Mamallapuram.
3. Brihadisvara temple, Tanjavur.
4. Vitthala temple, Vijayanagar.
5. Southern gopura, Meenakshi temple, Madurai.

PLATE 6

1. Kailasa, Ellora.
2. Kesava temple, Somnathpur.

PLATE 7

1. Qutb-Minar, Delhi.
2. Alai Darwaza, Delhi.
3. Humayun's tomb, Delhi.

PLATE 8

1. Jama Masjid, Fatehpur-Sikri.
2. Buland Darwaza, Fatehpur-Sikri.
3. Taj-Mahal, Agra.

PLATE 9

1. Bull capital from Rampurva, National Museum, Delhi.
2. Lion capital from Sarnath, Archaeological Museum, Sarnath.
3. Yaksa Supavasa, Bharhut stupa, Indian Museum, Calcutta.
4. Parts of vedika and eastern torana, Bharhut stupa, Indian Museum, Calcutta.

PLATE 10

1. Chaddanta Jataka, southern torana, stupa I Sanchi.
2. Siege of Kusinagara, southern torana, stupa I, Sanchi.
3. Great departure from Kapilavastu, eastern torana, stupa I, Sanchi.
4. Lotus frieze, northern torana, stupa I, Sanchi.

PLATE 11

1. Standing Buddha from Hoti Mardan.
2. Seated Buddha from Takht-i-Bahai, Berlin Museum.
3. Standing Bodhisatva, Museum of Fine Arts, Boston.
4. Seated Bodhisatva, Indian Museum, Calcutta.

PLATE 12

1. Great renunciation, Indian Museum, Calcutta.
2. Parinirvana, Indian Museum, Calcutta.

PLATE 13

1. Kanishka, Archaeological Museum, Mathura.
2. Buddha dedicated by bhiksu Bala, Archaeological Museum, Sarnath.
3. Drum slab with stupa representation from Amaravati, Government Museum, Madras.

PLATE 14

1. Veneration of the Buddha's begging bowl from Amaravati, Government Museum, Madras.
2. Standing Buddha from Mathura, National Museum, Delhi.
3. Seated Buddha from Sarnath, Archaeological Museum, Sarnath.
4. Nagaraja, cave 19, Ajanta.

PLATE 15

1. Descent of the Ganga or Kiratarjunya, Mamallapuram.
2. Ravana shaking Mount Kailasa, Ellora.
3. Siva Mahesamurti, Elephanta.

PLATE 16

1. Horse court, Ranganathaswami temple, Srirangam.
2. Siva Nataraja from Tiruvalangadu, Government Museum, Madras.

PLATE 53

1. Rembrandt: Night watch, Rijksmuseum Amsterdam.
2. Rembrandt: Syndics of the cloth hall, Rijksmuseum Amsterdam.

PLATE 54

1. Rembrandt: Simeon in the temple, Mauritshuis, The Hague.
2. Rembrandt: Supper at Emmaus, Louvre Museum, Paris.
3. Pieter de Hooch: In the bedroom, Staatliche Kunsthalle, Karlsruhe.
4. Ter Borch: The concert, former Kaiser Friedrich Museum, Berlin.

PLATE 55

1. Vermeer: Girl with a pearl necklace, former Kaiser Friedrich Museum, Berlin.
2. Ruisdael: The mill at Wijk, Rijksmuseum, Amsterdam.
3. Hobbema: Avenue of Middelares, National Gallery, London.

PLATE 56

1. Entrance to the university of Salamanca.
2. Escorial, near Madrid.
3. El Greco: the burial of the Count of Orgaz, church of Santo Tome, Toledo.
4. El Greco: Resurrection, Prado Museum, Madrid.

PLATE 57

1. El Greco: Storm over Toledo, Metropolitan Museum of Art, New York.
2. Velasquez: Surrender of Breda, Prado Museum, Madrid.

PLATE 58

1. Velasquez: Las Meninas, Prado Museum, Madrid.
2. Velasquez: Infanta Margarita, Prado Museum, Madrid.
3. Velasquez: Crucifix, Prado Museum, Madrid.

PLATE 59

1. Murillo: Immaculada, Louvre Museum, Paris.
2. Murillo: Vision of St. Francis .
3. Goya: The family of Charles IV, Prado Museum, Madrid.
4. Goya: Josefa Bayeu, Prado Museum, Madrid.

PLATE 60

1. Wren: St. Paul's Cathedral, London.
2. Hogarth: Marriage a la mode, 2nd scene, Tate Gallery, London.
3. Hogarth: Shrimp girl, National Gallery London
4. Reynolds: Dr. Samuel Johnson, National Gallery, London.

PLATE 61

1. Reynolds: Age of innocence, Wallace Collection Landon
2. Gainsborough: Blue boy, Huntington Art Gallery, San Marino, California
3. Constable: Hay wain, National Gallery, London

PLATE 62

1. Turner: Fighting Temeraire, National Gallery, London.
2. Perrault: Eastern facade, Louvre, Paris.

PLATE 63

1. The Palace of Versailles
2. Houdon: St. Bruno, Church of Santa Maria degli Angeli, Rome
3. Poussin: Arcadian shepherds, Louvre Museum, Paris
4. Claude Lorrain: Landscape with Amor and Psyche, Wallraf Richartz Museum, Cologne'

PLATE 64

1. Chardin: Saying grace, Louvre Museum, Paris
2. Watteau: Gilles, Louvre Museum, Paris
3. Millet: Angelus (destroyed by a recent fire)

# SANSKRIT PRONUNCIATION GUIDE

| | | | | | | | | | | | | | |
|---|---|---|---|---|---|---|---|---|---|---|---|---|---|
| अ | a | ङ | ṅ | प् | p | ऐ | ai | ड् | ḍ | व् | v |
| आ | ā | च् | ch | फ् | ph | आ | au | ढ् | ḍh | श् | ś |
| इ | í | छ् | chh | ब् | b | i (अनुस्वर) | ṁ | ण् | ṇ | ष् | ṣ |
| ई | ī | ज् | j | भ् | bh | : (विसर्ग) | ḥ | त् | t | स् | s |
| उ | u | झ् | jh | म् | m | क् | k | थ् | th | ह् | h |
| ऊ | ū | ञ् | ñ | य् | y | ख् | kh | द् | d | ऌ | lṛ |
| श्रृ | ṛ | ट् | ṭ | र् | r | ग् | g | ध् | dh | क्ष | kṣ |
| ए | e | ठ् | ṭh | ल् | l | घ् | gh | न् | n | ज्ञ | jñ |

*Note:*

For popular names of rivers, places, birds, demons, sages, rulers and dynasties, as well as literary works, no diacritical marks have been used. Common terms in Sanskrit, such as the Buddha, linga, nandi, rishis, have no diacritical marks either.

# INTRODUCTION

By nature, human beings love to beautify themselves and their surroundings; and they also like to share their feelings and ideas with other people. This tendency shows itself in every place and age. Even primitive men decorated their earthenware pots with lines or colours for the sheer delight of seeing them—although these have no practical use. When civilisation progressed and people had more means and time at their disposal to make things beautiful or artistic, they produced many works of art, such as imposing buildings with ornamental gardens, paintings and sculpture. In fact, art holds an honoured place in every great civilisation since beauty serves to enrich our souls with spiritual joy.

Beauty appears primarily in nature—in a pretty flower, a rugged mountain or a glorious sunset. This is natural beauty—the divine creation. Artistic beauty proceeds from man—a fine painting, a graceful statue, an elegant home, soul–stirring music. Works of art show great variety because human beings differ in their tastes or appreciation of beauty.

This appreciation or feeling for beauty results from the cooperation or working together of a number of powers. First, our senses, especially our eyes and ears, perceive or notice something beautiful outside us. Artists usually have more sensitive and penetrating powers of perception. The mind, however, plays the most important part, for it alone recognises the beauty that lies beyond what we see, hear or feel. The memory stores up these impressions, until the creative imagination conceives them in a new order, ready to give birth to artistic expression. Since the appreciation and creation of art comes chiefly from the human gift of reflection, and because beauty arouses joy, great art can and should bring spiritual enchantment. Art harmonises well with human nature since all of man's powers can come into play. It starts from something tangible or concrete, perceived by the senses, and leads on to spiritual understanding by the mind and enjoyment by the heart or soul. Thus it helps a great deal to educate—to lead the human spirit from material perception to spiritual understanding and love through the attraction of joy in beauty—or, as the philosophers would say, from beauty to truth and goodness.

The arts are sometimes divided into 'art in time', like music which lasts only as long as we hear the tune; 'art in space and time' like dancing which exists in space but only for a time; and 'art in space', namely the visual or spatial arts formed out of some permanent material.

To produce the visual arts, one needs not only a keener sense to perceive or notice the beauty around, a more penetrating mind to understand its hidden attraction or meaning, and a creative imagination to communicate and interpret the enjoyment to others, but also the skill to imprint one's feelings on permanent material like wood, stone, metal or canvas. An artist needs the ability to organise the few basic elements of his material—line, colour, light and shade, texture, area, mass and volume—and to put them into the right relationships so that they will give birth to something beautiful. To achieve this loveliness, the work must have unity in variety, balance, coherence and correct emphasis. The essential meaning or message must stand out clearly, enhanced by the less important details but not smothered by them.

Great art serves not only as a means of self-expression but of communication. The artist has discovered something worthwhile, some good which he desires to share with others. For his part, the onlooker must learn the language of art—he requires some training to observe, recognise and understand the meaning of true beauty.

The visual arts, commonly referred to as fine arts, include architecture, sculpture, painting and the minor arts.

The term fine arts sometimes includes literature, music, dance and drama, but in this book, it is restricted to the more common meaning of the spatial arts only.

Architecture or building art pertains to the construction of houses, places of worship, factories and many other structures, consisting usually of walls and roofs enclosing space, to serve man's needs of habitation and civil life. The plan or form of the building conforms to its purpose. The materials for its construction may be wood, stone, brick, tile, concrete, steel, glass and many others. The site or location of the edifice also has great influence on the planning of its shape. There will be differences according to whether the building stands in a crowded city or in the countryside amidst gardens, whether in a flat or hilly terrain, or in a cold or hot climate. Engineering, or the mechanical activity in building, provides the stability needed so that the fabric does not collapse. In addition, aesthetic considerations help to make the edifice beautiful.

Sculpture is the art of producing statues by cutting, carving or hewing them out of a block of wood or stone or some other hard substance, or by modelling them out of some plastic material. According to the derived form, sculpture may be in the round, like a standing or seated statue, or relief sculpture where the carved figures stand out from the background to which they remain attached. High reliefs and low reliefs depend on the degree of their projection. Relief sunk into the surface came into use in Egypt. In low relief the background has the same level as the height of the figures. In the intaglio or cut-in process, used for gems, all the parts that usually protrude in a relief are incised deeply so that the impression produces the relief image.

Painting is the art of making pictures by applying colours to a flat surface like wood, canvas, wall or paper, in order to create a two-dimensional image or to give the illusion of three dimensions by making the figures appear round and giving the impression of depth. To make them adhere to the surface, the colours or pigments must be mixed with some binding material, called the medium. The most common media are water-colour, tempera, oils and fresco.

The minor arts include various processes by which craftsmen create objects that combine beauty with utility, such as pottery, metal work, textiles and many others.

# INDIA

# 1. INDIAN ART

## GENERAL SURVEY

The early history of India is well known to the student, and since, except for the entirely distinct remains of the Indus Valley civilisation, the records of the artistic achievements of any period before the third century B.C. are very scanty, we need not dwell on the earlier centuries, except to trace briefly the significant religious developments, Hinduism, Jainism and Buddhism, which were served by the artists of later times.

Hinduism as it is now known, is the product of the fusion of the Aryan culture with the Dravidian, which may possibly include that of the Indus Valley. The Aryans had gods personifying natural powers like the king of gods, Indra (rain), Varuṇa (ocean), Vāyu or Marut (wind), and others. Through fusion with the earlier inhabitants, they adopted their gods: chiefly Viṣṇu and Śiva; while some of the older deities lost their importance. Later, the different castes chose their own gods to whom the cult of bhakti, personal devotion, was offered. Hence arose the two main sects, Vaiṣṇavites and Śaivites. In art, this division is important since each god came to have his own symbol: Śiva the trident, the bull and within the temple, the lingam; Viṣṇu the disc above the śikhara, and within, a statue of the god. Similarly, particular gestures came to have special significance and were therefore stereotyped, as the varada mudrā, the abhaya mudrā, etc.

Though Jainism and Buddhism were in one sense a revolt against Brahmin domination by Kṣatriyas, and both arose in a region which was still only partly Aryanised, in another sense, both were developments from the philosophy of the forest-dwelling rishis, and roots of both can be found in the Upanishads.

Jainism is attributed to Vardhamana Mahāvirā, a Kṣatriya prince, who laid emphasis on ahimsa (respect for all forms of life or nonviolence), and the power of asceticism to liberate the soul completely. His followers were divided into yatis or sadhus forming the sangha (community of the strict followers) and upasakas (laity); but the latter were more closely bound to the sangha than in Buddhism. In later times, they split into two sects: the digambaras and the svetāmbaras. Each has its own canon of Jain scripture, and each has contributed to the development of the regional language and to Indian art.

Buddhism developed from the teachings of Gautama, the Buddha (enlightened one). For him the way of salvation was moderation, not rigorous asceticism; nor did he believe in the efficacy of rituals and formulas. The final release of the soul, according to him, was to be nirvāna, which should be attained by the individuals following the eight-fold path. He organised his followers in the sangha. The lay disciples or upasakas were not so closely linked with the sangha as were those of Mahāvirā. The Buddhists deified their master after his death, and also gradually developed a cycle of legends about him. A division also arose between the earlier Hīnayāna (meaning Lesser Vehicle) sect, and the later Mahāyāna (meaning Greater Vehicle) sect, which is quite important for the student of art, since the former did not represent the Buddha in human form. But the first evidence of the existence of Mahāyānism is precisely the appearance of statues of the Buddha.

The period in which these religions developed was that in which the earliest kingdoms grew up among the Aryans of north India; and during the Maurya empire religious art is found in a mature form. Alexander's invasion in 326 B.C. had served a double purpose, even if not the one he had intended: by crushing the strong kingdoms of the north-west, such as that of the Paurava, he made the extension of the Maghadha empire over their ruins by Chandragupta Maurya much easier; and, though Greek control of the Punjab and Sind lasted for barely eight years, he established a contact between India and the West which continued to bear fruit for many years after his empire had broken up.

Chandragupta Maurya successfully asserted his claim to Aria and Arachosia (in modern Afghanistan) as well as to the whole of northwest India, against Seleucus Nicator; his son Bindusara extended the empire southwards into the Deccan; and his grandson, Ashoka, beginning a similar career of conquest with a successful war against Kalinga (a strong non-

Aryan kingdom on the east coast) turned aside from it by horror at the bloodshed thus caused, became a convert to Buddhism, and thenceforward sought, not universal dominion by force of arms, but universal spiritual conquest through the teaching of the dharma. What he meant by dharma can be discovered from the examination of the rock-edicts and the pillar-edicts which he had carved in different parts of his empire, and which are among the most important sculptural remains of the post-Vedic period in India.

Not long after the death of Ashoka, his empire fell to pieces: the outlying provinces, such as Andhra and Kalinga, reasserted their independence, and Magadha itself came under the rule of the Sungas. During the later part of the Sunga period (185–72 B.C.) Buddhist art, of the Hīnayāna sect, reached a high peak of achievement, especially in the sculptural decoration of the Bhārhut stūpa and the carving of the Chaitya halls of Bhaja, Karle etc., while in central and southern India a new Dravidian dynasty, the Andhras, in the first century B.C., continued to develop Hīnayāna art on *stūpa no. I* at *Sānchi*, which enclosed what was probably an Aśokan stūpa.

The early Christian era saw the establishment of foreign rule in north-western India, first by Seleucid Greeks from Bactria, and later by Scythian tribes: the Sakas, who settled in southern Sind, and afterwards the Yueh-chi, known in Indian history as the Kushans, who succeeded in displacing both the last of the Greek rulers and their own kinsfolk, the Sakas. It was during the confused Scytho-Parthian period that the first Christian, St. Thomas the Apostle, one of the twelve intimate disciples of Jesus Christ, came to India. History and legend are mixed together in the ancient account of his journey, but it refers to a six-month stay in the territory of King 'Gondophernes' (the Greek form of the name of Gundophar, the last Parthian king of Sind); and a persistent tradition in Travancore describes him establishing local Christian churches there; while his tomb has always been venerated in Mylapore. Certainly, from early times there has always been a body of Christians calling themselves 'Thomas Christians' in that region. In the fourth century, Syrian Christians established themselves on the west coast, and their spiritual descendants are still active.

During the Kushan period the Mahāyāna Buddhists were favoured with royal patronage, and two distinct art-styles flourished at different places under Kanishka and his successors (2nd century A.D. onwards): the Greco-Roman style of Gandhara, and the truly Indian art of Mathura. The invasion of White Huns at the end of the fifth century probably put an end to artistic activity in Gandhara; but that at Mathura continued into the Gupta period. At the same time, the Andhras continued to patronise Buddhism in the Deccan, and though they had trading contacts by sea with the Romans, with Burma and with China, their art remained more purely Indian than that of the north, as the remains at Amarāvati, and elsewhere prove.

The fourth century A.D. saw the creation of a new empire in the north, that of the Guptas. This has been called the Indian Golden Age, and with reason, for between the fourth and sixth centuries, not only was the political ideal of unity once more realised in the north, but all the arts, literary, pictorial, sculptural, architectural, and musical reached a rich maturity. It was indeed Indian art at its best. During the Gupta age, under the patronage of the imperial house, Hinduism and in particular the cult of Viṣṇu received a new impetus; and while Buddhism did not yet disappear (in fact Buddhist art continued to flourish at Mathura, Sārnāth and in the Ajantā caves), it was becoming more and more like a branch of Hinduism, and was eventually re-absorbed into the older religion. Meanwhile for the first time in Indian history, Hindu temples were built of stone instead of wood, as was the case during the earlier period, of which the monuments have perished.

After the fall of the Gupta empire, about 600 A.D., the separate kingdoms which were set up in different parts of India were mostly Rajput, and some of them are very important from the artistic point of view, such as the Chālūkya kingdom of the Deccan, in whose territories the Ajantā caves are found, as well as the large group of Hindu temples at Aihole, built during the Gupta Age. Orissa also became a centre of temple building, of the northern style, as at Bhuvaneśvar; and so too were Rājputāna and Gujarat, under the Solanki dynasty.

In the south, Dravidian dynasties were established, such as the Pallavas, from the seventh to the ninth centuries, on the east coast; and the Rashtrakutas of the Deccan from the eighth to tenth centuries, creators of the great Kailāśa at Ellora. The great Chola dynasty, during the tenth and half of the eleventh century, ruled most of peninsular India as far north as the Ganges, and the architectural style named after them influenced all south-eastern Asia. Meantime, in Mysore, the Hoysala dynasty (during the 12th and 13th centuries) was promoting an architecture which has affinities with both the northern and southern styles. The last great Hindu dynasty to resist Muslim invasion, that of Vijayanagar (early fourteenth to late sixteenth centuries), built their capital in a style of exuberant richness.

While these Hindu dynasties flourished in the south, from the eighth century onward, the north was troubled by Muslim invasions. The first assault, that of Mohammed bin Qasim in 712 A.D., had no permanent results; but in the eleventh and twelfth centuries, first the Ghaznavids, then the Ghoris invaded; and by 1206 Muhammad of Ghor's successor established his capital at Delhi. From that date, until 1526, is the period known as the Delhi Sultanate. Five dynasties of sultans succeeded each other at that time: the Mamluk (or Slave) dynasty, the Khaljis, the Tughluqs, the Sayyids and the Lodis. The political history of the time does not concern us, but the period is important for introducing a Muslim element into Indian art. The Delhi style of architecture which they evolved had some foreign elements, but was nonetheless sufficiently influenced by Hindu art to give it an especially Indian character. The buildings of the provincial sultanates either show close imitation of the Delhi style, or follow the Hindu tradition in art.

The Mughal period (1526–1857) marks yet another new element in Indian art and architecture. All the early Mughal rulers were men of artistic taste, as their memoirs indicate, even when, as in the case of Babur, they had no time to leave solid proof of it; and the development of the Mughal style can be traced not only in their own buildings, but also in the influence they had on later Hindu palace-building and decoration. During the early part of the Mughal period, the Rajput school of miniature painting flourished side by side with Mughal painters at Hindu courts.

Indian art did not develop under the British, but they helped both directly and indirectly to rediscover Indian cultural heritage. The British rule and the spirit of nationalism which came in its wake made the Indian leaders probe deep into their history, which has resulted in an appreciation and revival of the past.

# PROTOHISTORIC PERIOD

## THE HARAPPA CIVILISATION

The Indus Valley or Harappa civilisation, the first great city or urban culture known in India, flourished during the third millenium B.C., contemporaneously with the ancient Sumerian culture. Its existence came to light through unexpected archaeological discoveries from 1924 onwards at Harappa in the Punjab and Mohenjo-daro in Sind. Until that time, art historians considered the Cyclopean walls of Rāj agriha (6th century B.C.) as the earliest architectural remains; and a continuous history of India reached back only to the Macedonian invasion in the 4th century B.C.

The first discoveries of this civilisation were made in the valley of the Indus river and in the Punjab, but later excavations prove that this civilisation had a far greater extension because sites have been found scattered from the North-West Frontier and the foot of the Himalayas down to Gujarat and eastward as far as the Ganges Valley—from the north of Sind to Saurashtra in the south, and from Baluchistan in the west to the Ganga-Yamuna Doab in the east. Many settlements have been discovered, of which the most important remain those first unearthed—the two great cities, Harappa excavated by Madho Sarup Vats in the Punjab and Mohenjo-daro by Sir John Marshal on the Indus river (Map I). In both places several cities lay buried one beneath the other. The other settlements were smaller towns belonging to the central, western, eastern and southern provinces, which were divided in this manner by S. R. Rao for the sake of clarity.* They are Jhukar, Kot-Diji, Chanhudaro and Surkotda belonging to the central province, Sutkagen-dor and Sotka-koh in the western province, Alamgirpur, Kalibangan and Rupar in the eastern province and Lothal, Rangpur and Surkotda in the southern province.

Indus Valley seals, beads and other objects found in Mesopotamian towns such as Lagash, Ur, Tel-Asmar and other places indicate some communication and commercial intercourse between the Indus Valley or Harappa civilisation and that of Sumeria. Until recent, more scientific methods of dating, scholars attempted

* Mohenjo-daro and Harappa belonging to the central provinces

a chronology of the Indus Valley civilisation by comparing it with the Sumerian. But until further evidence is discovered, the full flowering of the Harappan culture may be placed between 2500 and 1700 B.C.

## Architecture

The perfection of *town planning* constitutes the most striking feature of the excavated cities of Harappa civilisation. That some central authority directed the construction of the towns according to a master plan, appears evident from the extraordinary similarity in the arrangement of the various parts of the cities in sites separated from each other by many kilometres. For instance, Harappa and Mohenjo-daro lie 640 km apart, yet the general principles of layout show strict adherence to a preconceived arrangement. These cities, therefore, did not result from straggling villages growing in size and importance through accretion of buildings and extended areas of habitation; rather they were built up directly as urban centres planned as integrated units. Both at Harappa and Mohenjo-daro an interspace separated two distinct units. On the west of both cities rose the citadel with fortified walls enclosing big buildings, probably used for some public, royal or religious purposes—assembly halls, granaries, baths and what may have been some form of temples. These buildings rested on high mud-brick platforms.

The lower city on the east was laid out on the gridiron pattern (Fig. 1), with main streets nearly-ten metres wide, running almost exactly in the north-south and east-west directions and intersecting each other at right angles—unlike the meandering streets at Ur in Mesopotamia. These main streets divided the area into regular squares or rectangular blocks, containing dwelling houses, shops and factories, with access; to smaller, less orderly streets and lanes. The houses always opened on these alleys and side streets.

The building materials and methods of construction, like the general layout of the different parts of the city, also show remarkable uniformity. Kiln-burnt bricks went into the construction of defence works, important buildings and the walls of houses; while they generally employed sun-dried mud bricks to raise platforms and to fill in floor areas and courtyards inside the houses. The bricks, cemented together with mud mortar, were laid in the so-called

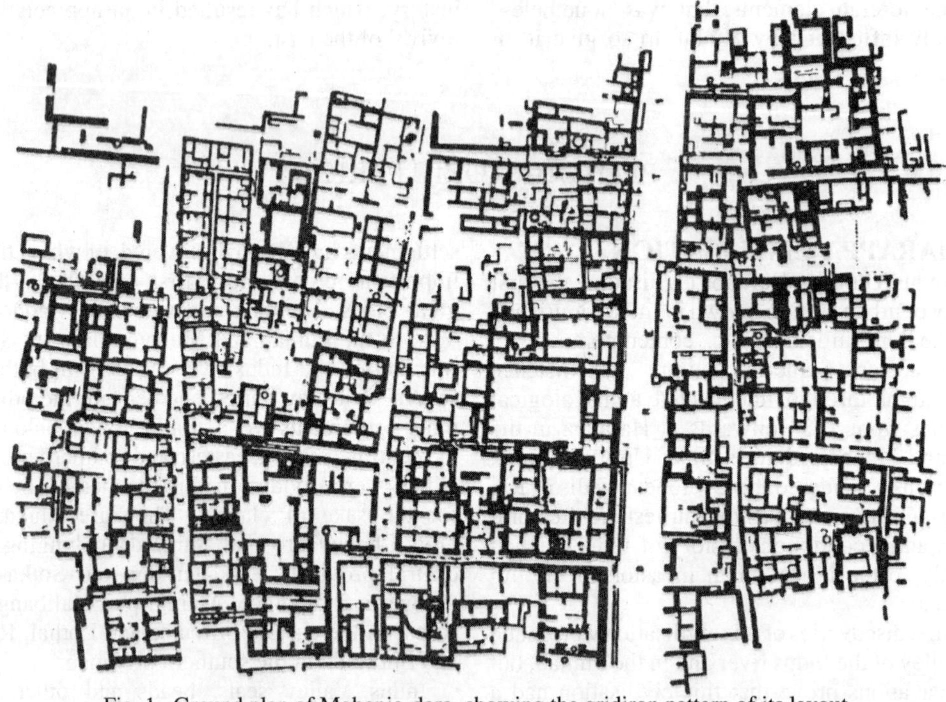

Fig. 1. Ground plan of Mohenjo-daro, showing the gridiron pattern of its layout.

'English bond', that is, a course of stretchers alternating with a course of headers. Mud plaster usually covered the inner walls. No finds have substantiated the use of stucco for outer surfaces. Traces of a decorative bond make it unlikely that a layer of plaster covered it.

All the excavated remains reveal only ground floors, but the abundance of staircases and drain pipes descending from the top of walls as well as the thickness of the bearing walls themselves, suggest a wide prevalence of upper storeys. Probably constructed of wood, they perished long ago, together with the roofs of which no trace remains.

Lintels normally spanned the openings since they had not discovered the principles of the true arch. Wherever they needed a rounded architectural form they used corbelling, as in the main drain of the great bath at Mohenjo-daro.

The drainage and water supply system show a very great advance for such an early age. For instance, in Mohenjo-daro most houses had their own private bathrooms and privies, supplied with soakage jars as well as pipe drains to dispose of waste. The bathroom floors, paved with burnt bricks, sloped into one corner, from where the house drain carried the soiled water to the street conduits, which were thirty to sixty centimetres deep, and covered with bricks stone (Figs. 2, 3). At regular intervals

Fig. 2. Covered drain, Mohenjo-daro

they had provided traps for inspection and also manholes for cleaning purposes. The street channels opened into bigger corbel-vaulted sewers that emptied into the river. According to Sir Mortimer Wheeler, this excellent sanitation system is 'unparalleled in pre-classical times, and unapproached in the non-westernised

Fig. 3. A drain in a narrow lane showing a right-angled turn, Mohenjo-daro

world of today' (Fig. 4). Each house had a tube well, and often there was a public well (Fig· 5) on the street between two houses.

Fig. 4. Privy, Mohenjo-daro

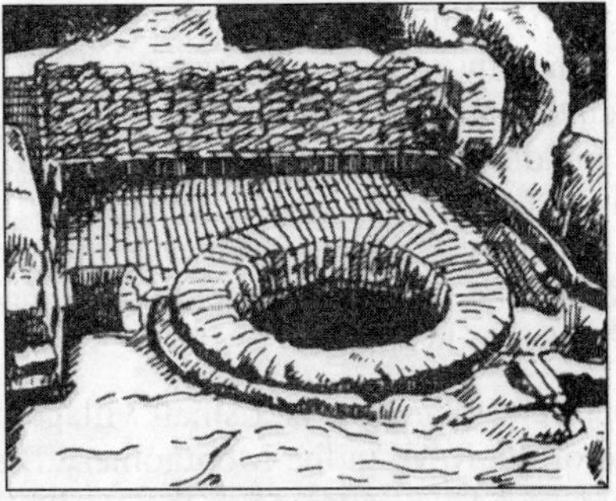

Fig. 5. A typical well, Mohenjo-daro

The high standard of town planning and sanitation, with sufficient water supply and drainage system, makes the Indus Valley or Harappan culture outstanding among all the ancient cultures. We find it not only in the larger cities, but it reached even the distant outposts of Harappan culture. To a lesser extent the idea of a place of public importance being separated from the residential area had penetrated even into the Harappan villages which far outnumber the cities. At Hasan and Amiliano, in the Malir river area, two such village sites show the remains of a building erected on the highest part of the site, serving perhaps as the focus for the communal life of the surrounding villages.

The *dwelling houses* were of different sizes. Some, with many spacious apartments, also resembled palaces, while the small ones had only a partition. In general, the houses had an air of comfort, with rooms of good sizes. They ranged around an open courtyard, having doors and windows opening into the court. The rooms of the typical house unit were enclosed by a thick outer wall, and had only one door that opened on the side lane—never onto the main roads. These exterior walls must have looked monotonously plain, for no trace of stucco or painted decoration has been found and windows too, were rare. It can be only assumed that painted or carved superstructures and mat screens on the upper storeys provided at least some decoration. The thickness of the outer walls measured nearly ninety centimetres. The remains of stairways, water pipes and chutes, as mentioned earlier, indicate that most houses did have an upper storey, probably made of wood and supplemented by reed mats and light screens. Impressions of such reed mats have been found in Kot-Diji. The houses and courtyards usually had brick floors. The kitchen was in the corner of the courtyard. A small room, usually near the doorway, may, according to Wheeler, have served as the porter's lodge. One of the rooms contains a well to supply water. The regular planning of these private dwellings speaks of a well ordered civic administration. A flourishing upper middle class, who could afford to employ servants and whose domestic activity centred around the courtyard—as even now in many parts of Sind and the Punjab, appears to have made their homes in these dwellings.

At present, *Harappa* is a small village near the old bed of the Ravi, in the Montgomery District of the Punjab. As yet, even after the twelve seasons of excavations, archaeologists have not succeeded in getting an overall picture of the city as it existed in the heyday of the Harappan civilisation. Large-scale robbing of bricks by railway constructors previous to the excavations have frustrated their work. The excavations conducted so far exposed the citadel and areas of the upper city; but the mound comprising the lower city has still to be systematically excavated.

The citadel formed a rough parallelogram 415 × 193 m, with a north-south axis (Fig. 6).

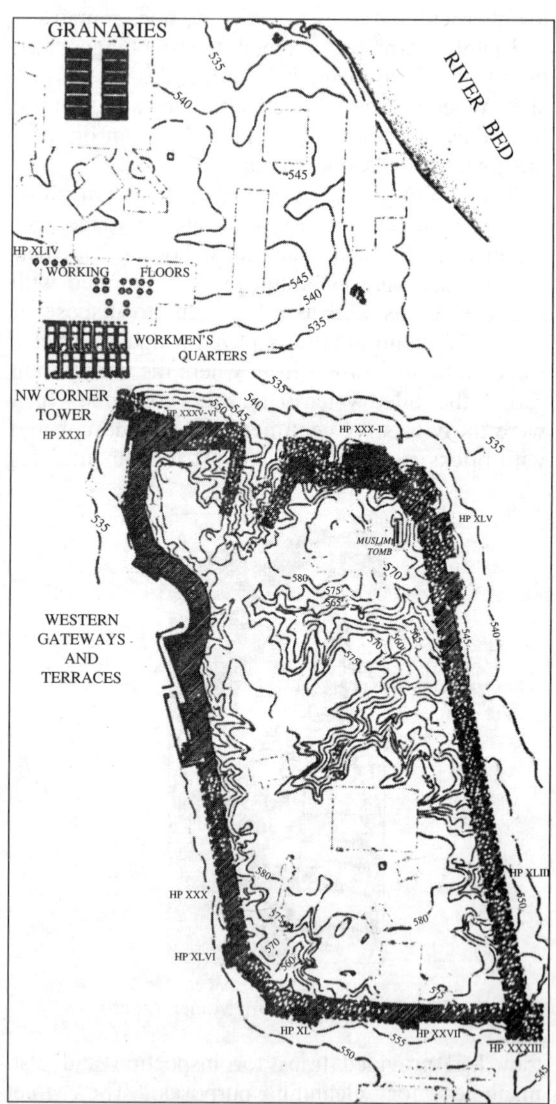

Fig. 6. Site plan showing the layout of Harappa

Parts of the fourteen-metre-thick, battered walls have been discovered, along with a few defensive bastions at intervals. The main entrance faced north, while to the west rose another network of bastions, ramps and terraces approached by gates overlooking guardrooms on the west, in a curved re-entrant on the encircling wall.

To the north of the citadel ran a double line of barrack-like dwellings, on a north-south axis, sixteen furnaces as well as a twin file of granaries and five rows of circular platforms. Wheeler calls the first of these 'coolie-lines'—presumably workmen's quarters. Each line forms an oblong of 18 × 8 m, with each house consisting of two rooms and a courtyard, with partly brick-paved floors.

On a higher level nearby, stand a row of sixteen furnaces—probably used for smelting bronze or copper. Hence, those who lived in the barracks may have been coppersmiths as well as labourers connected with the granaries.

North of the workmen's quarters lie eighteen round platforms made of brick. Five concentric rows of bricks were laid on the edge around a hole in the centre, provided for the insertion of a wooden pestle. They served for a large-scale pounding of the grain stores in the nearby granaries, as shown by remaining fragments of charred wheat, barley, straw and husk.

The granaries consist of twelve units, about 15 × 6m each, laid in two rows, six on each side, with a central passage seven metres wide. They stand on a platform of packed earth edged with baked bricks and walls now in ruins. The floors of the individual units rest on sleeper walls, with air-ducts to keep the grain dry. Since the granaries lie near the river bank, the grain was probably transported by boat.

The granary complex, with its pounding platform as well as the supposed workmen's quarters, reinforced the view that agriculture formed the main occupation of the Indus Valley people, and that they employed some form of forced or paid labour to collect and store the grain. A similar economy based on grain as a source of civic wealth prevailed both at Ur and in Upper Egypt, but nowhere else in the pre-classical world have we found such imposing granaries, specially designed and endowed with monumental dignity.

*Mohenjo-daro*, a modern Sind word meaning 'place of the dead', lies in the Larkhan district of Sind. The general plan of the city is almost identical with that of Harappa (Fig. 7). It has a circuit of about 4.82 km. Here as in Harappa, the citadel rises on the west and the lower city lies to the east—apparently separated in ancient times by a canal or branch of the Indus.

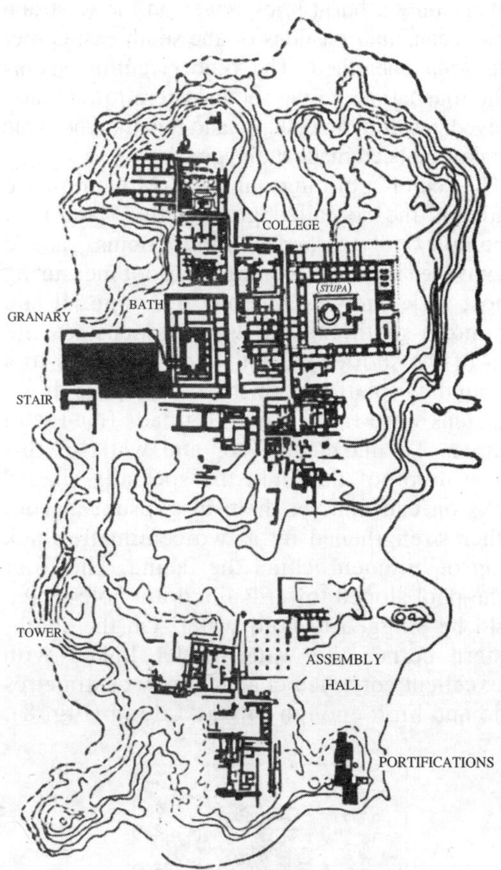


Fig. 7. Ground plan of Mohenjo-daro, showing the various structures.

On the northern part of the citadel mound a Buddhist stūpa was built in the second century A.D. Excavations in the area south of this stūpa have revealed seven strata of habitation, but because of the high water table, more layers may lie underneath, inaccessible to archaeologists. The citadel tumulus, which rises from six metres in the south to twelve metres in the north, has been cut into two by floods which still form an annual threat to engineers and archaeologists, even though the nearest branch of the Indus itself now flows about five kilometres away.

As usual a high mud-brick platform with fire-brick revetment raised the citadel area. To protect it from floods they built massive bunds or embankments which bear evidence of repeated repairs. The rectangular space occupied by the citadel measures roughly 360 × 180m. Of the system of bastions, enclosure walls and gates which originally formed the defence network only a burnt-brick tower on the west and a few rectangular bastions on the south-east corner have been unearthed. The timber reinforcements in the foundations of the south-eastern towers later decayed, resulting in collapse and repairs. The same mistake had been made in the granary.

The chief buildings in the Mohenjo-daro citadel is the so-called great bath (Plate 1.1), a complex of verandahs and rooms ranged around the sides of a rectangular pool measuring almost 12 × 7 m with a depth of 2.44m, all laid on a north-south axis. A flight of steps set into each of the shorter sides of the pool leads to a surrounding platform thirty centimetres high. The steps were furnished with treads fixed with bitumen. To make the floor and walls of this tank waterproof they laid the specially shaped bricks on end and set them in gypsum mortar, further strengthened by a two-centimetre-thick lining of bitumen behind the facing. The floor of the pool sloped towards the drain hole which could be plugged to hold water. On the south-western corner the water outlet linked with an excellent corbelled channel sixty centimetres wide and high enough to walk along (Fig. 8).

Fig. 8. Drain of the great bath, Mohenjo-daro.

Another remarkable feature was a man-hole, about 60 × 105 cm, accessible both from the tank and the corbelled drain. The water supply came from a double-ringed well in a room to the east.

A pillared verandah surrounded all four sides of the pool, with rooms beyond except on the west. On the south, two entrances led to a paved vestibule, with a drain at the eastern extremity. At either end this vestibule terminated in two small apartments of unknown function. A series of rooms, perhaps used for dressing, extend on the east. The one which contains the well has an entrance from the street. On the north the original arrangement of rooms is not clear because at a later stage, due to floods, they raised the level by filling in the units.

To the north of the great bath lie two rows of bathrooms on either side of a lane containing a drain. Each bathroom measures about three by two metres (2.9 × 1.8 m), and has brick-paved floors. Each had a staircase presumably leading to a now extinct upper storey. The excavators believe that these may have been reserved for priests who lived upstairs and came down at specific intervals for ritual bathing, while the laymen used the main bathing pool. The doors of these bathrooms were staggered to ensure privacy.

Immediately to the west of the great bath, Sir Mortimer Wheeler's methodical excavations revealed a structure of immense significance, namely the granary (Fig. 9). It consists of a

Fig. 9. A conjectural drawing of the granary, Mohenjo-daro. (After Sir Mortimer Wheeler)

high podium of massive proportions (46 × 23 m) with battered walls and a crisscross of passages inside serving as air-ducts. The storage area may have had a superstructure of which no trace remains. An alcove on the northern side of the outer wall, having straight inner sides, probably served for hauling up sheaves of grain. Since its foundation was reinforced by timber, as in parts of the bastions, the granary seems to be contemporary with them and earlier than the great bath.

The discovery of this structure strengthens the view that in a Bronze Age economy, granaries corresponded to state banks or treasuries. Its situation inside the citadel and its design as an essentially single building with formidable battered walls adds to its importance. At Harappa, however, as mentioned earlier, the granary consists of a dozen separate Units situated outside the citadel and near the river bank, but the combined storage space of these equalled that of Mohenjo-daro.

To the north-east of the great bath lie the remains of a building often referred to as the 'college of the priests'. Probably of public importance, but without further excavations, the actual significance of this network of walls, drains, Stairways and an open court cannot be ascertained.

On the southern mound of the great citadel stood a great pillared hall about 127 m square and opening to the north. Twenty square pillars divided the floor space into five aisles. At a later date it was paved with strips of brick. Since the general plan resembles an Achaemenian 'apadana' or audience hall, this may have served as a place of assembly also.

The overall picture presented by the great bath, the imposing granary, the so-called college and the assembly hall inside a well-fortified encircling wall indicates a stable seat of power. We do not know whether a political ruler or priest king directed the administration, since no palace or building of definite religious importance has been discovered as yet, even though scholars suspect that a temple may lie beneath the stūpa.

The lower city at Mohenjo-daro, protected from floods by bunds, extended over an area of 2.6 square miles. The plan resembled a grid, (Fig. 1) with a broad main thoroughfare running north-south and smaller streets going in east-west direction, thus dividing it into regular blocks of houses and commercial buildings. Seven such blocks have been excavated.

In a room of one of these houses we find a row of conical pits lined with wedge-shaped bricks. Perhaps they supported dying vats, and the dyers may have lived in the two adjoining rooms.

A curious oblong structure 16 × 12 m with an imposing gateway approached by a pair of symmetrical stairways on the south stood among the dwelling houses in the HR area (Fig. 10). A circular brickwork 1.22 m in diameter lies within the inner courtyard. Did it have some connection with tree worship? Did the building serve some public function? The singular occurrence of two

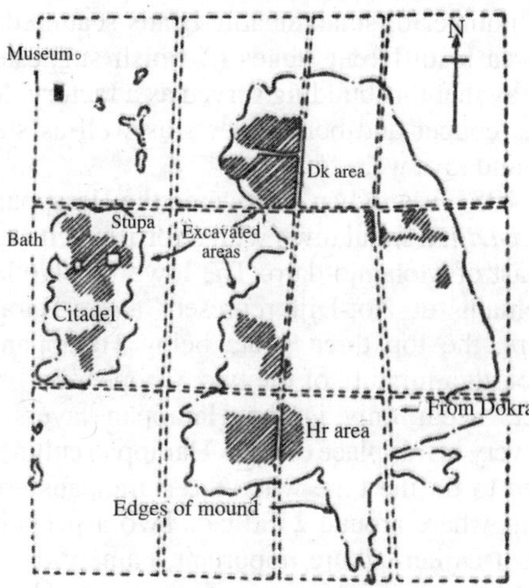


Fig. 10. Mohenjo-daro plan showing the various areas of excavations.

of the rare Harappan sculptural remains (a bearded man and the fragments of a seated figure) inside this edifice, lends weight to the view that it possessed some public importance or even served as a temple. However we have no evidence as yet either of a cult figure used for worship or an altar, and no congregational hall.

In the Mohenjo-daro area too, a row of barracks-like quarters similar to the 'coolie-lines' at Harappa suggest regimented labour. They consist of sixteen two-roomed units with a paved bathing floor in one room, provided with drainage. Two wells nearby supplied water.

Remains of later dwellings show degenerations as well as evidence of floods, havoc and subsequent repairs of inferior quality. In all likelihood the city had begun to decay before it came to a sudden end.

*Chanhudaro*, discovered by Majumdar in 1931 and excavated on a large scale by Mackay, lies about 129 km south of Mohenjo-daro. Five strata of habitation have been found here, the lower three being of Harappan culture, while the upper two belong to the Jhangar and Jhukar cultures. Being a smaller town, Chanhudaro has no citadel but the city plan follows the traditional grid, with burnt brick houses and well planned drainage. Mud-brick platforms represent later endeavours to protect the town from floods. The importance of the site lies in the commercial aspects of its finds. Many of its inhabitants seem to have been craftsmen

Mackay unearthed a large rectangular building containing a criss-cross of brickwork flues overlaid with a thin layer of bricks with compartments. The large number of small steatite beads scattered over the area in different stages of finish suggested to Mackay that this building served as a factory. Many shells, copper and bone objects as well as steatite seals and toys were found.

In 1957 F. A. Khan discovered the Harappan site of *Kot-Diji*, a small town with a fortified citadel, 40 km east of Mohenjo-daro. The lower twelve layers of remains at Kot-Diji represent a pre-Harappan culture, the top three strata being Harappan and the fourth a mixture of the two. Copper and bronze objects occur only in the Harappan layers. The discovery in this place of a pre-Harappan culture, has helped to fix the time when the Harappans arrived at somewhere around 2100 B.C. Two aspects make the Kot-Dijian culture important, namely the scale pattern already used in its pottery prior to Harappa, and the occurrence of the typical Harappan terracotta 'cakes'. Whether they used these 'cakes' for ritual or toilet purposes remains unknown.

More than eightyfive sites of the late Harappan period have been brought to light after a large scale archaeological survey of Saurashtra and Gujarat. The intermingling of a red and black pottery, the use of ceramic motifs affiliated with Central Indian Chalcolithic types, together with the typical Harappan-ware in Rangpur, Lothal and other Saurashtrian sites, shows that this culture represents a provincial offshoot of the metropolitan mature Harappan culture. During the latter half of third millenium B.C. the Harappans probably migrated southwards, either to enlarge their maritime trade operations or as a result of the coastal uplift of the lower Indus Valley. Whether they took an overland route or went by sea remains a matter of dispute among scholars. Though Rangpur was first to be explored in depth, *Lothal* discovered by S. R. Rao in 1954, has the most significance. This town situated at the head of the Gulf of Cambay near the estuaries of the Sabarmati and Bhigawo rivers, flourished as a seaport around 2440 B.C. (Map II). It encompasses six phases of habitation.

Though it follows the traditional scheme of a citadel raised on a higher level and overlooking the township, at Lothal the citadel lies on the south-east corner of a walled enclosure. A mud-brick wall surrounds the whole site, which is roughly rectangular with a north-south axis. The excavator believes that a palace of the 'ruler' existed on top of the citadel platform, along with other public buildings—all provided with excellent water supply and drainage facilities. A strange substructure on the south-east corner of the acropolis consisted of criss-cross ducts running between sixtyfour blocks, and measuring 3.6 sq. m. Sir Mortimer wheeler took it to be a granary, whereas S. R. Rao asserted that it functioned as a warehouse handling an enormous amount of trade because of its proximity to the dock and its great size—the floor area being 1930 sq. m.

A massive terraced platform which may have supported another public building faces the warehouse on the west. But the so-called dock, a rectangular depression measuring 214 × 36m. is the most important find at Lothal (Fig. 11).

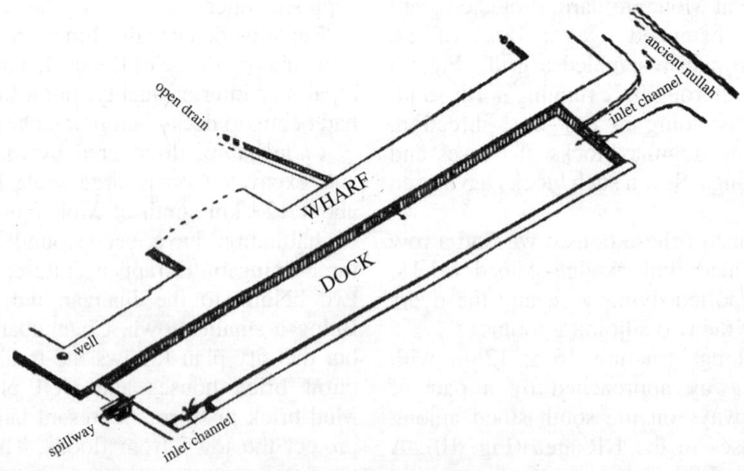


Fig. 11. Lothal dock.

The sides revetted by kiln-burnt bricks are absolutely vertical to facilitate the berthing of ships. The water level at low tide must have been two metres, and three and half metres at high tide. A channel, one metre wide, on the south wall, served as a spillway for excess water. Wooden sluice-gates probably acted as a water-locking device and insured a minimum water level inside the dock. The ships floated into the dock over a gap twelve metres wide on the northern side. Rao based his contention that this served as a dock and not a tank on the following points: the use of fired bricks—not necessary for a tank, the absence of steps, the existence of a loading platform and of post holes in the side of the wails for tying up ships, the discovery of anchor stone in the basin itself, the salinity of the silt which also contains marine deposits, and the worthlessness of salty water either for drinking or irrigation. However Leon Leshnik refutes these points.*

If this structure actually functioned as dockyard it was an astonishing feat of scientific engineering in the ancient world, taking into consideration the direction and force of the current, the water-thrust and other problems, in addition to its unique water-locking device. As such not only was it the largest dockyard built by any Bronze Age community but it surpassed in design and execution those of Phoenicia and Rome.

The township of Lothal lies to the north-west of the citadel and occupies three-quarters of the total area of the walled enclosure. It was subdivided into blocks in the typical Harappan fashion, with main streets running in the cardinal directions. The blocks so far excavated include a bazaar area in the north (block A), industrial quarters to the west (blocks E and F), and the residential sectors on the north-west (block G) (Figs. 12 and 13).

* *American Anthropologists* Vol. 70. No. 5, October, 1968, p. 911.

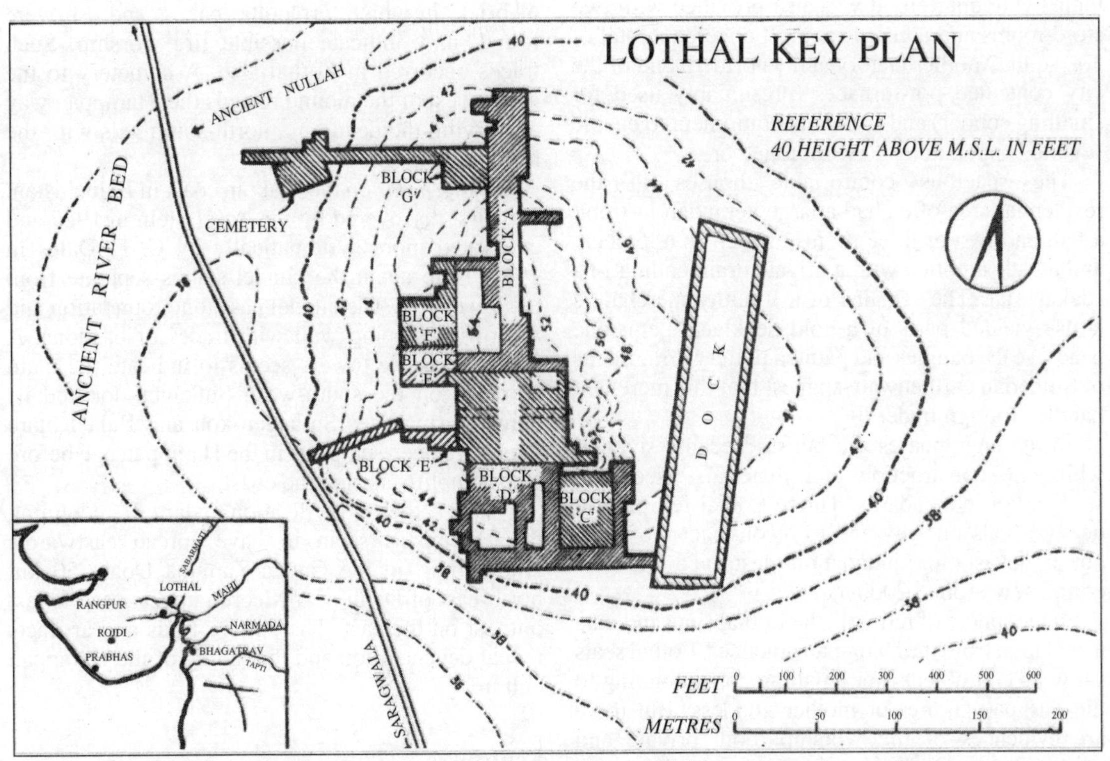


Fig. 12. Lothal key plan.

On the main bazaar street the houses of merchants and craftsmen adjoined the shops. Anvils and ovens, crucibles and muffles, the drills and chisels of metal workers and bone carvers came to

Fig. 13. Life in Lothal four thousand years ago.

light in this area as well as a bead factory producing works in carnelian, agate, opal, crystal and other stones. It had a platform or working area for the lapidaries with rooms ranged around it to serve as their living quarters. It was also provided with two store-rooms and a guard-room. It covered a total of 500 sq.m. Another factory at the northern end of the city contained pot-furnaces (presumably used for smelting copper) and sufficient equipment to enable several coppersmiths to work together.

The spacious comfortable houses in the residential area often had a large verandah in front, a hall and two or three rooms as well as a kitchen, and a bath supplied with a private drain ending in a soakage jar. The remains of a wealthy merchant's house yielded parts of a gold necklace, gemstone beads, seals, bangles and painted pottery. Fragments of Sumerian earthenware suggest that this merchant handled foreign trade.

In the later phases the houses became smaller, while the construction and materials used also show a fall in standards. Thrice Lothal fell prey to heavy floods but city and to reconstruct the dock, but a devastating inundation destroyed the city completely around 2000 B.C.

In the sphere of religion, the Lothal finds indicate a deviation from the Harappan practices. Lothal seals show no cult objects nor anything corresponding to the Paśupati figures or mother goddess. But there are evidences of fire worship: both private and public altars with brick enclosures containing the ash of triangular terracotta 'cakes' and potsherds have been found.

A large number of protohistoric sites have been discovered in the Bikaner district of Rajasthan. In ancient times the rivers Sarasvati and Drishadvati flowed through it and made it more fertile. These rivers have dried up. Kalibangan, the most important of these sites, lies beside the arid bed of the Sarasvati, now known as the Chaggar river. Ghosh explored it in 1953 and B. B. Lal and Thapur excavated it extensively later on. In plan it conforms to type: a fortified citadel on the west and on the east an open city with a grid pattern with modular blocks of houses and rectilinear streets. Here mud bricks rather than burnt bricks formed the common building material even for the sloping enclosure walls of the citadel. The underground and overground ovens found in the houses as well as the use of decorative tiles for paving the floor attract special archaeological interest. On the other hand some of the houses in this place had private baths, drains and soakage jars, and the absence of street drains show a deterioration in the civic standards. The citadel mound reveals a pre-Harappan occupation by a Chalcolithic or Bronze Age folk. Small oval or rectangular blocks made of brick, in which terracotta 'cakes' and ash were found, may indicate possible fire worship. Such traces occurred in Lothal also. A cemetery to the north-west of the mound reveals the Harappan way of burying the dead on a north-south axis with the head to the north.

*Sutkagen-dor* on the Makran coast in Baluchistan, was first discovered by Sir Aurel Stein in 1927 and excavated more systematically by C. F. Dales in 1960. Here again the citadel stands separate from the lower city. The citadel has stone foundation and a fortified sloping wall with traces of bastions. A pair of massive towers seems to indicate the main entrance on the south-west. Sutkagen-dor and its neighbouring sites Sutkagen-koh and Bala Kotare may have been sea-ports in the Harappan age before coastal uplifts shifted the coast.

When their civilisation started declining the Harappans seem to have spread eastwards. Alamgirpur, in the Ganga-Yamuna Doab, 50 km north-east of Delhi near Meerut, appears as the last outpost on the east. The pottery finds and artifacts reveal degeneration and the fading of the Harappan culture.

## Sculpture

Sculptural remains at Harappan sites, apart from the well-known seals and terracotta figures, are confined to Mohenjo-daro and Harappa. Since the rendering of the human and animal forms on the seals exhibit advanced artistry and technical proficiency, sculpture on a large scale may have been produced in perishable materials which did not survive the ravages of time. Further excavations may bring to light other sculptural remains, but only eleven pieces have been unearthed so far, all from the upper strata at Mohenjo-daro. In Mohenjo-daro whatever sculpture was found, was only in the upper strata.

Very few statues have been found, and the biggest of these is only 42 cm high. They are made of steatite, alabaster or limestone. Most of them represent elderly men with beards and wearing loose garments. They seem to be early attempts at portraiture. The most important of the statues from Mohenjo-daro is the *bearded man* (Fig. 14), a limestone statuette measuring 17.5 cm. His half closed eyes belong to the long type. The tip of the flattish nose has been broken off. The lips are unusually thick. As in Mesopotamian figures, the upper lip is shaven. The ears, beard and hair are conventionalised or stylised—the ears resembling a two-edged shell with a hole in the centre, while parallel grooves indicate the hair and beard. A narrow ribbon or fillet with a circle in front surrounds his head. He wears a draped cloth decorated with big trefoil patterns like the clover leaf. It covers his left shoulder and passes under the right arm. The so-called 'temple' at Harappa has yielded another head of a bearded man 17.5 cm high. It too has wavy hair tied with a fillet, shell-like ears with holes, a beard and a moustache. The eyes have hollows left for the inlay of shells or faience. Here the lips look less grim and the face appears more like an attempted portrait.

Fig. 14. Bearded man, Mohenjo-daro.

Four other pieces of statuary resemble a squatting figure—perhaps a priest. One of these, 40 cm high and made of alabaster, has the right knee slightly raised and the hands resting on the knees. A skirt-like garment covers the lower body. The details of the bearded face have been worn away. As usual a fillet encircles the head and the face is too big for the skull.

The most important among the bronze statues is the *dancing girl* now in the National Museum, New Delhi (Fig. 15). She stands in a dancing pose, her right hand on her hip. Heavy bangles cover her left arm from the shoulder down to the wrist. The fact that the Indus Valley knew how to smelt bronze shows how well advanced they were in metalwork. Another but more inferior figure was also found as well as a fragmentary foot with anklet. Bronze figures of animals occur quite frequently.

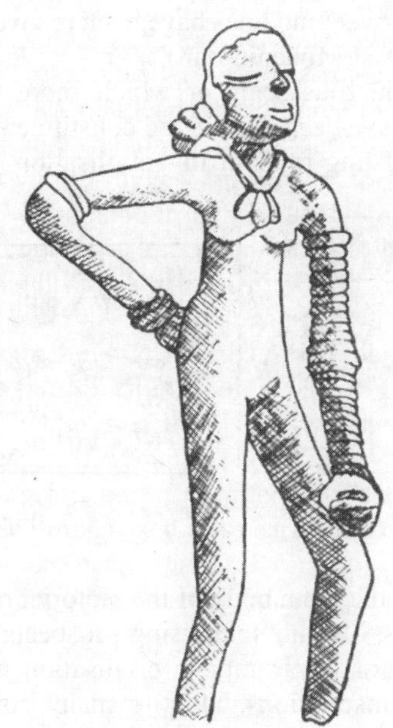

Fig. 15. Dancing girl, Mohenjo-daro.

Terracotta sculpture is more numerous than either stone or metal in the Indus Valley and

Lothal, and animal figures far outnumber human representations, and show greater realism as well. The torso of a woman from Lothal, similar to the Harappan torso of a dancing figure in stone, shows better modelling. Many terracotta figures, perhaps of a mother goddess, with pinched nose, pellet eyes and elaborate headdress have been unearthed. To make the lips, the ornate necklets and girdles, they pressed strips of day into the figure before baking. At Lothal the figures of women do not show elaborate jewellery.

Animal figures include cattle, sheep, dogs, pigs, monkeys, elephants, rhinoceros and birds. A terracotta *horse* at Mohenjo-daro and two more at Rangpur and Lothal and Surkotda refute the view that horses were unknown to the Harappans. Although no cows are shown either at Mohenjo-daro or Harappa and only a few were found at Lothal, yet the most common animal representation is the bull. Two fine examples of an *ox* and *buffalo* with bold, sweeping lines have been recovered from the remains at Mohenjo-daro.

The numerous seals of which more than two thousand have been discovered constitute one of the most interesting finds of this civilisation (Fig. 16). clay or wax, are cut into the surface of the seal, so that when it is pressed upon the plastic substance, the impression stands out in relief. Many of these seal impressions have been found in Lothal along with weights and measures, indicating that the seals were used to stamp export cargo.

On the right side, the seals represent one or more animals or human and mythological figures, with short inscriptions on top.

The seals were generally made of steatite, but occasionally also of copper, agate, faience and terracotta. Square or rectangular in shape, the seals have a pierced boss at the back for threading or holding. The seals measure about two or three centimetres in size. A few cylindrical seals also occur.

The tiny animals incised in these seals are exquisite. The artists chose the essential characteristics of the creatures and imbued the figures with an extraordinary vitality. Short-horned and humped bulls, antelopes, elephants, rhinoceros, tigers and crocodiles are depicted in their most typical poses, or at times parts are shown in their most expressive form. For instance zebu or the humped bull (Fig. 16), one of the most frequently represented animals, appears in side view with the

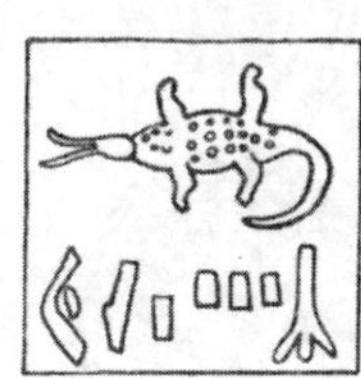

Fig. 16. Seals, Mohenjo-daro.

They form the main body of the pictorial records of those times, offering tantalising prospects of better knowledge of the Harappan civilisation with their intriguing inscriptions. Despite many attempts to decipher the script, no acceptable interpretation has been found until now. The pictographs consist of some four hundred signs in all, of which around two to eight occur on each seal. The writing goes from right to left, and if there is a second line it runs from left to right. The vast majority of these seals come from the sites of Harappa, Mohenjo-daro and Lothal.

One or more animals or human and mythological figures are incised under the pictographic inscription. The carving is done in the intaglio technique—all the parts that must stand out in relief when the seal has been pressed upon soft material like

horns in front view. Mythological figures were also represented as mentioned before. Many seals show a curious standard or incense burner in front of the animal depicted.

These seals offer a few noteworthy clues to the religious practise of those remote times, but their full significance will be known only when the script has been definitely deciphered. Sir John Marshall found three seals of similar design at Mohenjo-daro. The best of these shows a deity sitting on a platform (perhaps a throne) flanked by wild animals, a rhinoceros and buffalo on the right and an elephant and tiger on the left, and a pair of goats or antelopes below. Marshall calls it a prototype of Śiva in the aspect of Pasupati or lord of beasts. Bangles cover the deity's arms, and the face is painted. He wears a buffalo-horn head-dress, a V-shaped necklace or collar and a girdle.

Some seals hint at animal and human sacrifice. One of these shows a divinity standing inside the fork of a tree with a kneeling human figure in front and a ram behind him. Below appear seven people wearing clothes and long pigtails. Common in the lower levels of Harappa are many miniature seals without knobs and showing simple motifis like a swastika, crosschecks or circles indicating that they derive from an earlier date.

Jewellery was found in great abundance and variety: gold, silver and jade necklaces, earrings with pendants, belts and bangles. Beads of faience are very common besides others of precious metals and semi-precious stones. These exquisite jewels and beads may have served largely for export trade. Household pottery, some pieces having geometric patterns painted on them, came in a variety of shapes like ceramic rattles, and toy ox-carts with solid wheels (Fig. 17). Two of these carts are made of copper, the rest of them are in terracotta. Other terracotta finds include whistles shaped like hollow birds, rattles, spindles, gamesmen and dice.

Though pottery finds constitute a great help to archaeologists for estimating the dates of ancient cultures—and there is no dearth of these in the Indus Valley sites—as yet no definite chronological sequence has been formulated, and problems of origins and influence still remain unsolved.

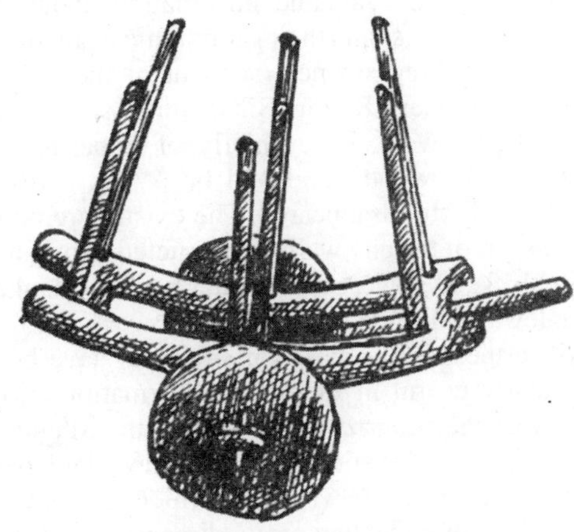

Fig. 17. A toy terracotta cart, Mohenjo-daro.

Face masks with horns were also common as well as grotesque figures. Mythological figures were created such as fighting tigers with horns, three-headed animals, many examples of a unicorn-like animal, or human figures with the horns, ears, hoofs, and tails of bulls. These appear most commonly on seals.

# HISTORIC PERIODS

## Architecture

Obscurity shrouds the period between the decline of the Harappa civilisation and the definite historic period starting with the Mauryas. The only known sources of information are the early Vedic texts, beginning with the Rig Veda (c.1000 B.C.). These mention the names of various geographical areas and of tribes who usually settled near some river. The Rig Veda alone contains some twenty-five of the thirty-one names of rivers appearing in the Vedas—the Saraswati and the Indus being the most frequently mentioned. The tribes include the Sudas (whose chief priest was Vishwamitra), the Bharatas and a score of others. In the Dasarajña (War of the Ten Kings), an important historical event recorded in the Vedas, the Bharatas emerged as the victors and gave their name to the whole country, i.e. Bharata-varsha. As the years passed, more and more people colonised various regions of this vast land. Eventually the small early settlements grew to form the Kosala, Videha, Magadha and other kingdoms.

Based on the information gleaned from the Vedic texts, various excavations have been undertaken. These brought to light the ruins of several ancient cities. For example Ahichchatra, capital of Panchala, revealed city walls some twelve metres high, made of burnt brick. A moat surrounded these walls. Through gateways at the four cardinal points, roads led to the centre of the city. The exact lay-out probably followed that described in Kautilya's 'Arthasastra', which speaks of a well-planned town consisting of a market-place, crossroads, public squares, parks, etc.

Other than these texts, accounts of foreign travellers provide valuable information about the appearance of cities and their geographical positions. For example Megasthenes' account of the city of Rajagriha (modern Rajgir, Bihar State) shows that the buildings were made chiefly of impermanent materials like wood, mud and brick. As a result they have all but disappeared. The existing remains include part of the city walls, constructed of massive uncut blocks of stone. Semicircular bastions flanked the gateways of these cyclopean walls.

Megasthenes' and Fa-Hien's records have been particularly useful in supplying information about the city of *Pāṭaliputra*, the capital of the Maghada country. The excavations at Patna have laid bare huge wooden *palisades* (Fig. 18), which substantiate to some extent the herculean dimensions of Fa-Hien's accounts of the city. Further excavations at *Kumrahar*, near Patna, have disclosed some ruins. Here the main structure is a palace, consisting of a large *pillared hall* built on a wooden substratum (Fig. 19). The pillars, aligned in regular rows, divide the main hail into square bays. The

Fig. 19. Pillared hall, Kumrahar, near Patna.

Fig. 18. Wooden palisade, Patna.

remains include a *capital* (Fig. 20) and some fragmentary stone columns as well as an almost complete one with a round, tapering and polished shaft. This bright polish indicates the Mauryan and particularly Ashokan connections of these buildings.

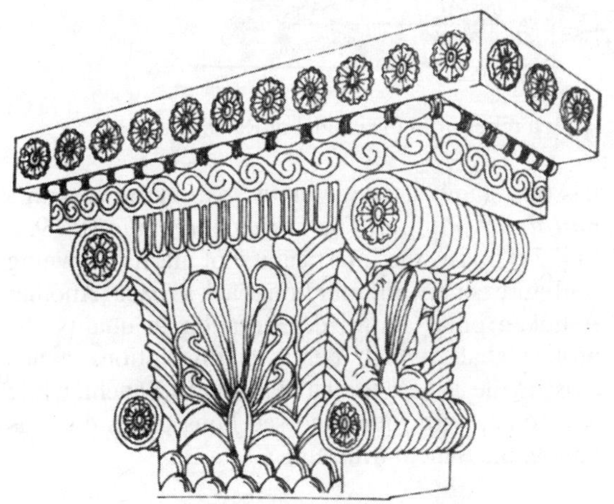

Fig. 20. Mauryan capital from pillared hall, Kumrahar, near Patna.

Ashoka, the grandson of Chandragupta Maurya, was one of the greatest emperors of the Maurya dynasty. Distressed at the killing and violence of the Kalinga (Orissa) war, he embraced Buddhism. His name is connected with the initial development of religious (predominantly Buddhist) architecture. The main architectural types appear very early—the stambha, the stūpa and the rock-cut chambers—the prototypes of chaitya and vihāra.

An idea of the *appearance of ancient cities* can also be derived from the representation of various types of buildings in the reliefs of Bhārhut and *Sanchi* (Fig. 21). Copings or *battlements* (Fig. 22) crowned the city walls. The wide entrances, accessible to chariots and elephants, had the same height as the walls and were flanked by lofty gatehouses.

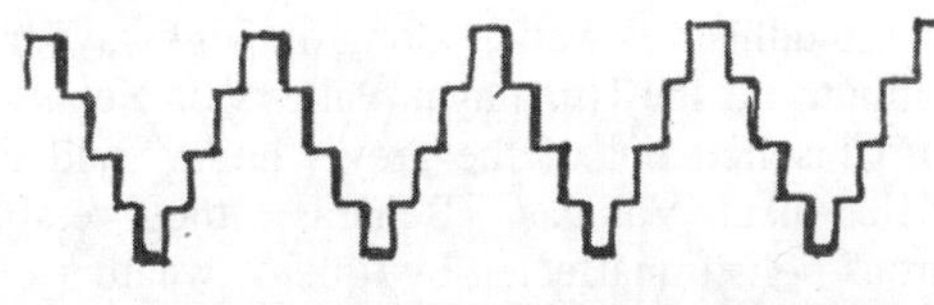

Fig. 22. Battlements.

Fig. 21. Conjectural reconstruction of the main gateway to Kusinagara, from a bas-relief on the southern torana, Sanchi.

Fig. 23. Mode of transporting a stone pillar, after a relief from the citadel of Raichur.

STAMBHA

Stambhas (pillars) characterise all the ages and styles of Indian architecture (Fig. 23). Ashoka set up at least thirty free-standing pillars, ten of which have his edicts engraved on them. One of these pillar-edicts states that 'his gracious majesty the king' ordered them to be inscribed twenty-six years after his consecration in order to convey to his subjects the teaching of the dharma. The extant examples show that they were set up at places sacred to the Buddhists as well as along the highways from Pataliputra to the Himalayan valleys of Nepal (Pl. 1.2). Chiselled out of the grey Chunar sandstone quarried near Varanasi (Benaras), they retain a lustrous polish unaffected by time or weather even after so many centuries.

A *stambha* (Fig. 24, p. 21) consists of a shaft and capital upholding a statue. The shaft, circular in section and tapering slightly towards the summit, is monolithic—carved out of a single stone. The gracefulness of the column depends on the proportion between the height and the tapering of its width. Not all the Ashokan stambhas are equally graceful. The capital, decorated with gently curved lotus petals, resembles an inverted lotus—often called the Persepolitan bell. This member, together with the abacus and the crowning sculpture in the round, were carved out of another single stone. Sculptures in relief often adorn the sides of the circular or rectangular abacus. The statue on the top comprises one or more animal figures— usually lion, bull or elephant, or four lions sitting back to back.

We can trace the development of these stambhas. The *Basarh Bakhira* (Fig. 25) and the *Laurya Nandangarh* (Pl. 1.2) pillars show a striking contrast. While the former has a rather clumsy, ill-proportioned shaft terminating in a somewhat crude lion capital, the graceful Laurya Nandangarh column shows a surprising progress in a short time. This pillar, in the Champaram district of Nepal, rises almost ten metres high. The shaft, 89 cm in diameter at the base, tapers to a width of 56 cm at the top. The inverted lotus capital bears a round, carved abacus supporting a seated lion. *Rampurva* has two stambhas, one with a *lion*, the other with a *bull finial* (Pl. 9.1). The *Sarnath stambha* (Pl. 9.2; Fig. 24) boasts the finest capital of all. Its crowning sculpture consists of four lions back to back. Another Ashokan pillar shows deterioration in quality. Its broken shaft, which bears an inscription, stands close to the eastern toraṇa of stūpa I at Sanchi, while its capital, with four addorsed lions on its crest, is now in the Sanchi Museum.

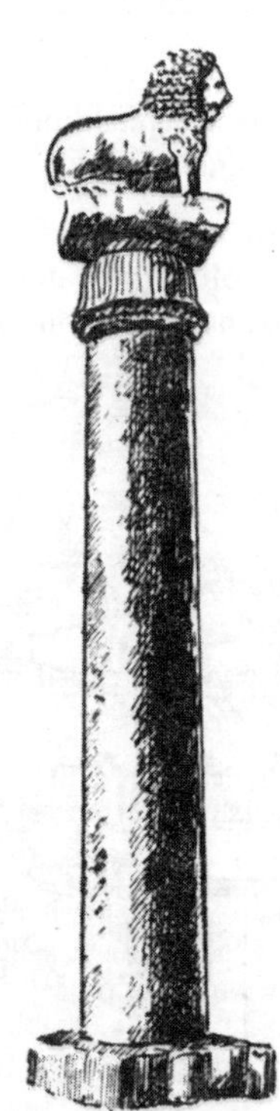

Fig. 25. Stambha with a lion capital, Basarh Bakhira.

Like the Buddhists, the Hindus too had columns. The most famous of these is the *Garuda pillar* at *Besnagar*, erected by Heliodorus, an envoy from the Bactrian king. Similarly the Jains constructed many detached columns, especially in the Karnataka district. Though it belongs to a later date, mention must also be

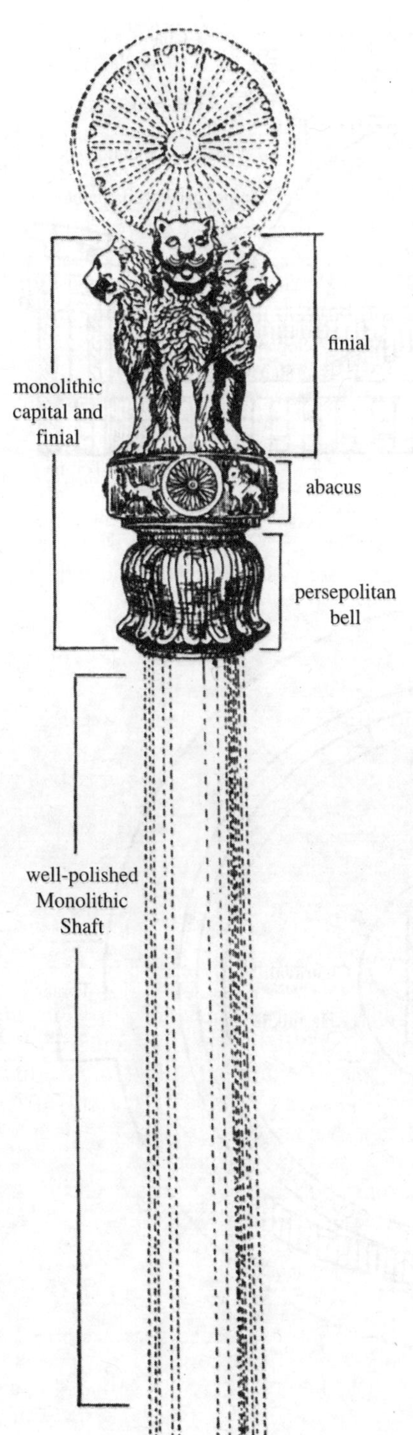


Fig. 24. Reconstruction of the Sarnath stambha, indicating the various parts of a stambha.

made of the famous *iron pillar* from the Gupta period, first erected perhaps in Bihar, but now adorning the Qutb at *Delhi.* In spite of exposure to rain and storm through many centuries, it remains smooth and unrusted, a wonder of Indian metal-casting.

### Stupa

The stūpa obviously evolved from the simple prehistoric burial heap or tumulus under which the ashes of the dead were buried. Many such funeral mounds—low, circular elevations of earth ringed by huge boulders—can be seen in the Deccan and South India. Though the Jains too built stūpas, this kind of monument appears most frequently in Buddhist art. Sometimes another circle of stones surrounded the first, and the space between the two served as a processional path.

At the death of the Buddha his remains were enshrined under such artificial mounds of earth and brick—the famous Eight Great Stūpas mentioned in Buddhist texts but destroyed since then. A few early stūpas have been discovered but it remains uncertain whether they belong to the pre-Ashokan period. We know, however, that the emperor Ashoka built a great number of them and may have instituted the stūpa cult.

The chief purpose of the stūpa was to enshrine śārīrika (body relics, usually in the form of small pieces of calcinated bone) of the Buddha or of Buddhist teachers, or their pāribhogika (personal belongings). Preserved in reliquaries of crystal, gold or other materials and enclosed in a stone box, they were placed in a small chamber during the time of building so that the solid masonry of the stūpa enclosed them securely. Sometimes they built stūpas to commemorate uddeśika (some event) at places sacred to the Buddhists. Besides being the symbol of the Buddha's parinirvāṇa (death), the stūpa itself became an object of veneration, as for instance the rock-cut stūpas in chaityas. Later on they considered the donation of small stūpas a meritorious act—from this originate the numerous votive stūpas around the large ones. Diminutive stūpas were also built over the ashes of the sangha members.

The stūpa (Fig. 26) consists of a solid hemisphere or dome called the aṇḍa (egg-mound). It stands on a medhi (circular or square base) and on its flattened top rests a kind of kiosk, usually called harmikā. Originally an umbrella was firmly implanted into the brickwork of the dome, with a dwarf railing or vedikā around it. The supporting mast was called the yaṣṭi;

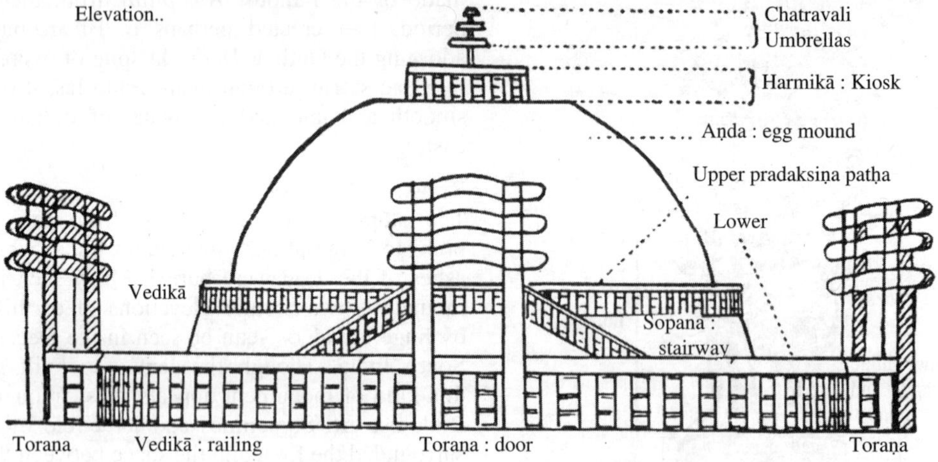

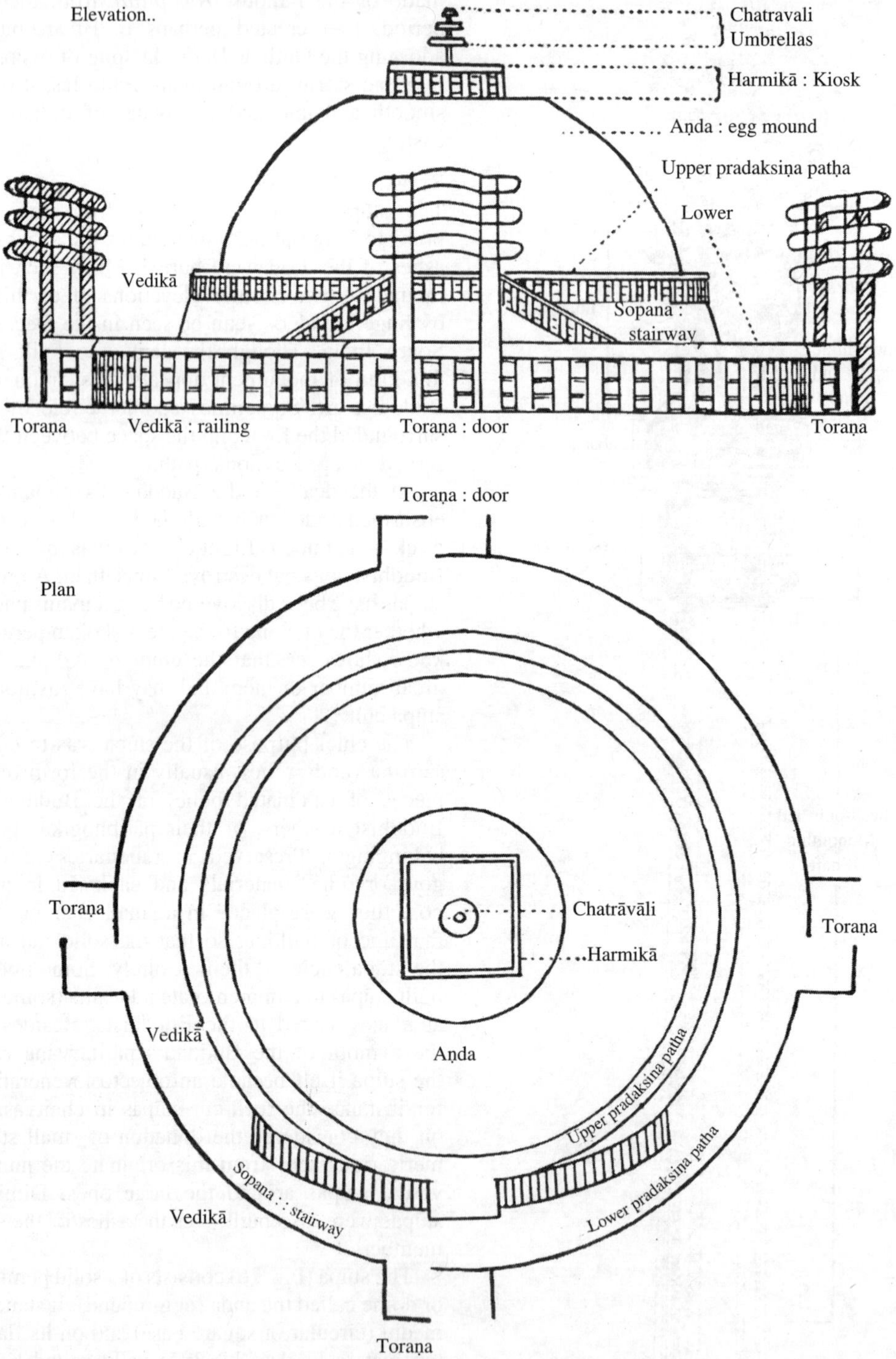

Elevation..
Chatravali
Umbrellas
Harmikā : Kiosk
Aṇda : egg mound
Upper pradaksiṇa paṭha
Lower
Vedikā
Sopana :
stairway
Toraṇa
Vedikā : railing
Toraṇa : door
Toraṇa
Toraṇa : door
Plan
Toraṇa
Chatrāvāli
Harmikā
Toraṇa
Vedikā
Aṇda
Upper pradaksina patha
Lower pradaksiṇa patha
Sopana : : stairway
Vedikā
Toraṇa

Fig. 26. Stupa I, Sanchi: elevation, plan.

the umbrella, the chatra; and the whole, the chatrāvali.

Since the ancient Indian customarily enclosed sacred buildings with a wooden fence or balustrade, the Buddhists too surrounded their stūpas with a vedikā, which became a characteristic feature of the stūpa. Later they made it of stone but gave it all the features of a wooden railing. The principal vedikā surrounded the structure and enclosed the lower pradakṣiṇa-pātha(the processional path on which the Buddhists walked, keeping their right shoulders turned towards the stūpa as a sign of reverence). Another vedikā surrounded the medhi or base, which included the upper pradakṣiṇa-pātha and was reached by means of the sopāna (staircase).

The vedikā (Fig. 27) was either plain or richly decorated with sculptured figures and lotus patterns. It rested on an ālambana (base) on which stood upright posts called thāba (from the Sanskrit word stambha). These were connected to each other by sūci (horizontal bars) and an uṣṇīṣa (continuous rounded coping stone). Toraṇa (gateways) (Fig. 28) faced each of the cardinal points. Their design—a pair of high posts crossed near the top by one to three slightly arched bars—resembles stone copies of wooden village gates. Often these toraṇas were richly carved.

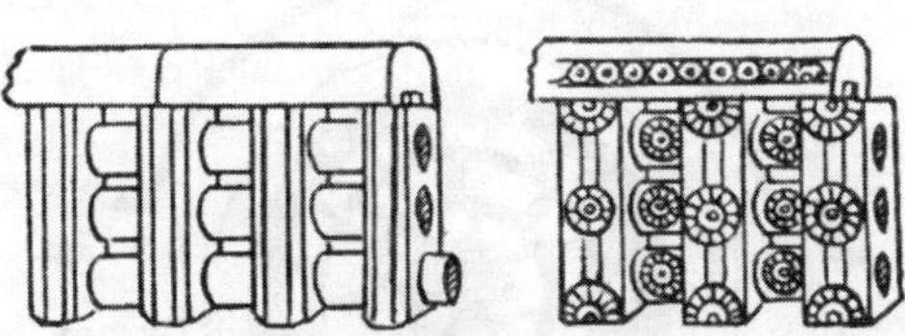

Fig. 27. Vedikas.

The aṇḍas of the stūpas were made of large unburnt bricks and rubble, covered with a thick layer of white plaster usually coated with colour and gilt. Festoons, flowers and drapery, hung on a row of wooden pegs fixed in the brickwork halfway up the dome, adorned the stūpa during festivals, and colourful fluttering banners added to the gaiety of the whole (Fig. 29).

*Sānchi* (in Madhya Pradesh) has the best-preserved remains of the large type of stūpa and of a whole Buddhist settlement. Several stūpas and ruins of other buildings have been found on the top of the hill. The *great stūpa I* (Pl. 1.3), the most notable monument of the site, was first constructed during the Maurya period as a brick tumulus surrounded by a wooden railing. A century later, under the Sungas, it was greatly enlarged and a terrace built around it. A stone vedikā encircled both the stūpa and the terrace. During the second half of the first century B.C., the new conquerors, the Andhras or Satavahanas, erected the beautifully carved toraṇas (Pl. 2.1), one at each of the cardinal points of the vedikā. This stūpa I is a classical example of its type, for it shows all the parts clearly. Moreover, the numerous relief representations of stūpas, carved on the four toraṇas, provide valuable material for the study of the early stūpas, as well as many interesting details regarding their decoration.

*Sānchi stūpa II,* built on the hillside, has no toraṇas, but the vedikā is richly carved. *Stūpa III* was destroyed but has been reconstructed. Of its four toraṇas only the southern one remains and its surrounding vedikā no longer exists.

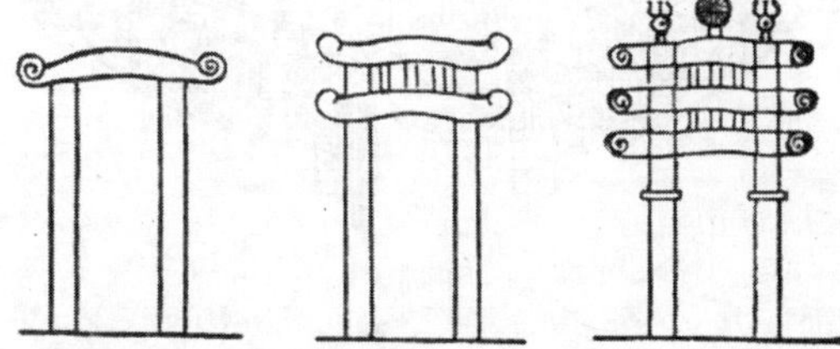

Fig. 28. Toranas.

A *stūpa* built under the Sunga dynasty in *Bhārhut* (modern Satna in Madhya Pradesh), was demolished by neighbouring villagers who took away the bricks and stones for building

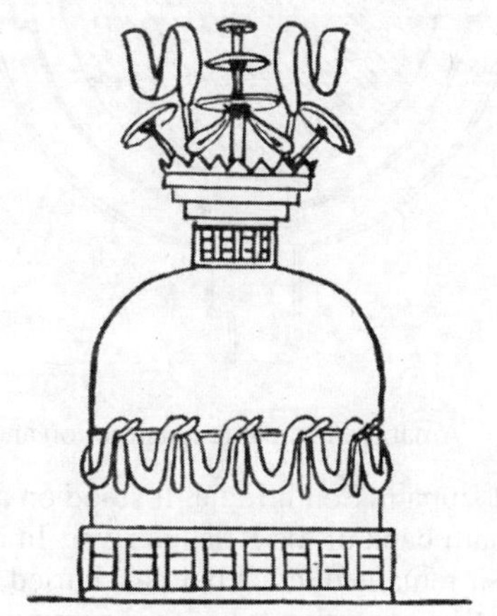

Fig. 29. Decorated stupa, from a carving, Amaravati stupa.

purposes. Sir Alexander Cunningham recovered some parts of the vedikā (Pl. 9.4) and southern toraṇa (Indian Museum, Calcutta).

*Amaravati* (the ancient capital of the Later Andhra kingdom) had the largest of the big *stūpas* (Fig. 30) and the finest example of a

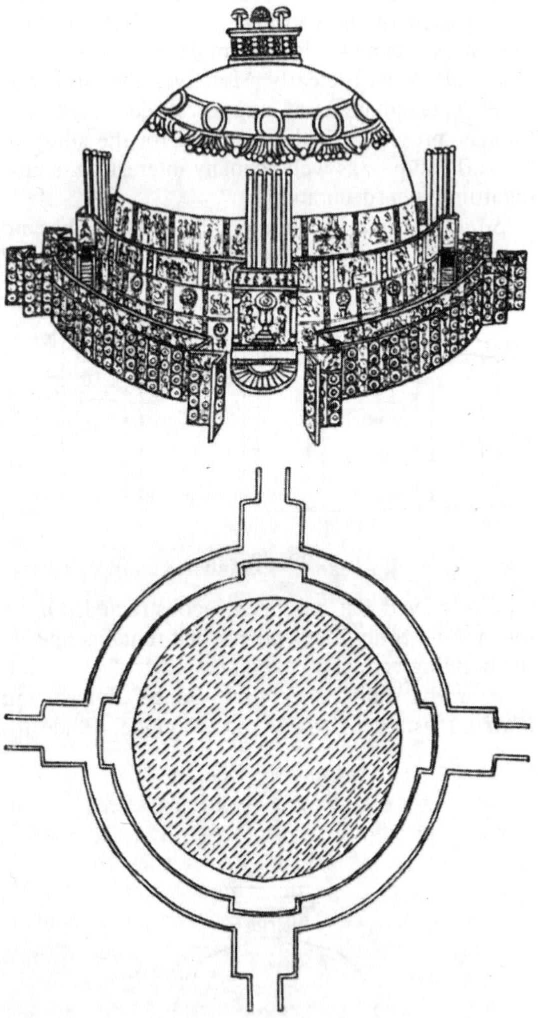

Fig. 30. Amaravati stupa: reconstruction and plan.

Buddhist stūpa in South India. It stood on a low hill on the south bank of the Krishna river. In its lonely isolation it remained intact but half buried under an accumulation of earth until a local zamindar during the last quarter of the eighteenth century selected a nearby site to construct his mansion. He found the stūpa a convenient source of building materials and razed it to the ground. He even burned some of the beautifully carved marble slabs in order to make lime, but fortunately quite a number of these slabs as well as some railing carvings were rescued. Numerous pieces were sent to the British Museum in London and a few to the Indian Museum in Calcutta but the chief collection of the remains now constitutes one of the glories of the Madras Museum. Some of these slabs give valuable information because copies of the original stūpa are carved on them.

The other important remains of South Indian stūpas are those at *Nagarjunakonda* (Fig. 31), *Jaggayapetta* and *Ghantasala* Unlike the earlier stūpas which were built solid, the stūpa at Nagarjunakonda had a core formed of cross walls, resulting in a compartment at the centre. From here masonry walls radiated outward

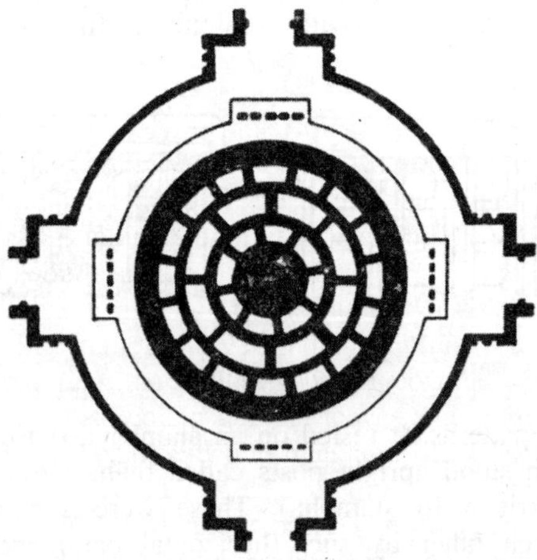

Fig. 31. Stūpa, Nagarjunakonda: plan.

like the spokes of a wheel. The intervening spaces between the masonry walls were filled with earth or alternate layers of earth and concrete. In this way they needed fewer bricks while at the same time they secured the strength required for the foundation of the stūpa.

The *monolithic stūpa* in each of the rock-cut chaityas at *Karle*, *Ajanta* and other places is merely symbolic. The one at Karle still retains the ancient wooden umbrella—the only surviving example in India.

Around certain stūpas, for example in *Bodh Gaya, Gandhara* and *Nepal*, pilgrims placed small *votive stūpas*—miniature stone replicas of the large ones. Some of these were hollow and contained a statue of the Buddha. Sometimes modest stūpas were erected over the ashes of ordinary Buddhist bhikshus. Quite a number of these may still be seen in South India and Sri Lanka.

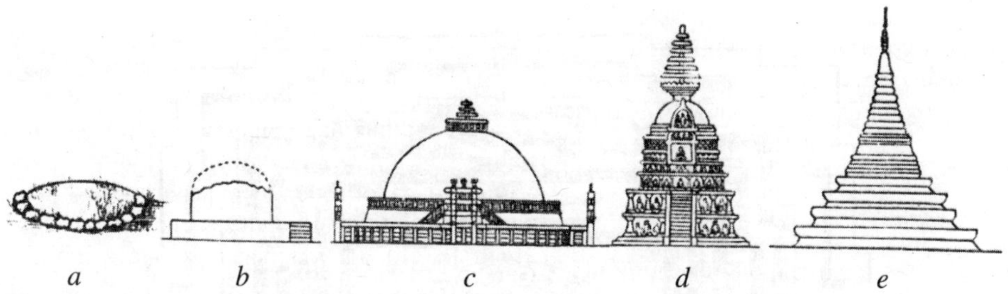


Fig. 32. Development of the stupa : *a*. prehistoric tumulus, *b*. early stupa of Ashoka's time, *c*. Stupa I, Sanchi, *d*. stupa at Takhti-Bahai, *e*. Tawyagyaung stupa, Mandalay.

It is interesting to trace the development of the stūpa (Fig. 32 a–e) from the prehistoric tumulus (Fig. 32 a) to the mighty structures of later ages. The simple stūpa of Ashoka's time (Fig. 32 b) consisted of aṇḍa set on a simple medhi. From this evolved the classical form, best represented by stūpa I at Sanchi (Fig. 32 c) which contains all the components that from then onward form an integral part of the stūpa. The aṇḍa predominates, while the medhi and the harmikā, with the chatrāvali on the top, are proportionately subordinated.

The stūpas at *Gandhara* show a further step in the development—well seen in the stūpa at *Takht-i-Bahai* (Fig. 32 d). The base, which has become very high, consists of two square blocks forming a terrace for circumambulation. On this rest the four round drums, diminishing in size, which carry the proportionately small aṇḍa. The latter supports the harmikā, which bears a huge stone chatrāvali consisting of six umbrellas diminishing in size—thus giving a top-heavy impression. The whole has a spire- like form. No vedikās or toranas surround this stūpa. All the sculptural decoration was carved on the stūpa itself, especially on the high base.

The tendency towards a structural, towerlike form is evident also in the development of the stūpas in the rock-cut chaityas. While the earlier ones were very simple, the later type shows a like tendency towards increasing the height of the finial, as in *cave* 19 at *Ajanta* (Fig. 33), where it resembles a tall steeple reaching to the roof.

Fig. 33. Rock-cut stupa in chaitya no. 19, Ajanta.

The whole structure looks like a high ornamental tower.

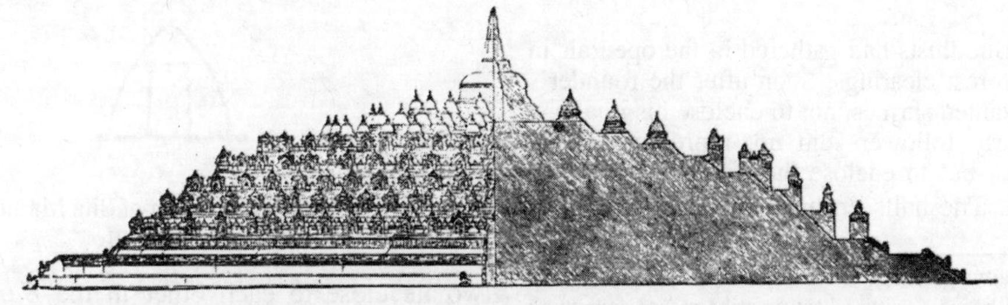

Fig. 34. Elevation and section of stupa, Borobodur.

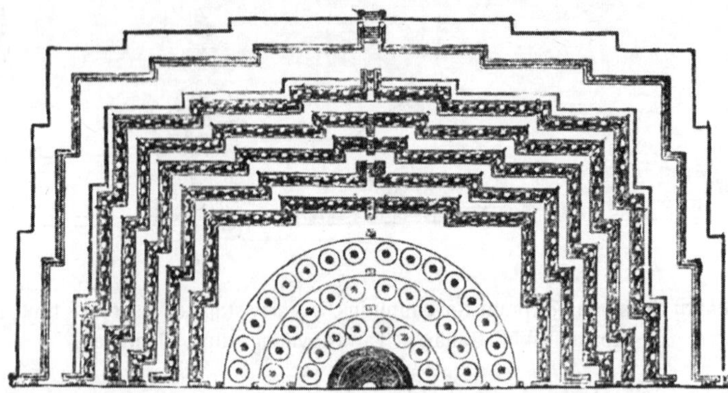

Fig. 35. Half-plan of stupa, Borobodur.

The stūpa reached the last stage of its development, not in India but in Burma and Indonesia, particularly in Java. These structures bear little or no resemblance to the original humble brick tumuli. Numerous receding terraces and chatras increased the height of the stūpa to such an extent that the mound itself became insignificant. The *Tawyagyaung stūpa* in *Mandalay* (Fig. 32 e) stands on three terraces, all elaborately decorated. The square harmikā has disappeared, replaced by a tall ringed one topped by a metal umbrella. The *stūpa* of *Borobudur* (stūpa of the many Buddhas) in *Java* (Figs. 34, 35) reveals a further development. Above the first three square terraces rise three more diminishing circular ones, each crested with a number of small stūpas—seventy-two in all. The central main stūpa, rising high above, forms the crowning pinnacle of the entire structure. A steep flight of steps, and ornate arched openings give entrance to sculpted galleries depicting various religious scenes. These run all along the terraces. Although different from other towerlike stūpas, a close study reveals that the silhouette of the multiple terraces has the shape of a flattened hemisphere—an outline similar to that of the early stūpas.

### The Chaityas*

At first the Buddhists had gathered in the open air in groves and forest clearings. Soon after the founder's death they wanted shrines, not to enclose his image—since his early followers did not represent him in human form—but to enclose the stūpa, a symbol of his nirvāṇa. The halls enshrining these stūpas are usually called chaityas. On these they centred their devotion. The inscriptions often refer to chaitya ghara, thūpa ghara and rarely to gaha thūpa (griha stūpa).

To early architecture Ashoka contributed not only the stambhas and stūpas but also the eight rock-cut halls or chambers in the Barabar and Nagarjuni hills and the one near Rajgir. He dedicated them to the Ājīvika sect of the Jaina monks. The hard quartzose gneiss rock out of which these halls were hewn produced brightly polished walls. These chambers, which resembled the wooden buildings of that period, became the prototypes of the later more sophisticated rock-cut chaityas. The best-known among them are the *Lomas Rishi*, the *Sudama*, and the *Sītā Marhi* (Fig. 36) caves. The first

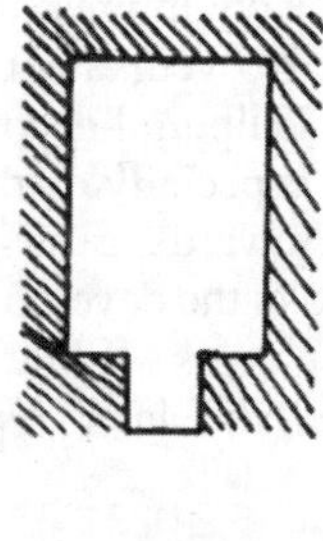

Fig. 36. Plan and section of Sita Marhi cave, Nagarjuni Hills

two lie close to each other in the *Barabar hills* and the third is in the *Nagarjuni hills*. The axes

* The word chaitya probably derives from the Sanskrit root cita, a funeral pyre; hence a caitya ghara or griha means something containing the cita.

of the two caves lie parallel to the rock face, with the entrance at the side (Fig. 37), unlike the later ones where the axes run at right angles to the surface (Fig. 38)—probably because these caves represent the first experiments in rock cuttings. The façade of the Lomas-Rishi cave (Fig. 39) shows an imitation of construction in wood. The door has two vertical poles—a version of wooden struts in stone. At the sides they slope inwards as if to resist an outward thrust of the arching beam above. Curved rafters join the upper ends of these jambs or poles. Subsidiary rafters, parallel to them, form lunettes. The by the rafters, resembles a thatched hut. A finial crowns the top. Short tie-rods hold the lower ends of the roof in place to prevent their springing back. The square-headed doorway at the side gives entrance to the rectangular hall, at one end of which lies a separate circular chamber resembling an inserted round building. Originally this probably housed the object of worship but is now empty.

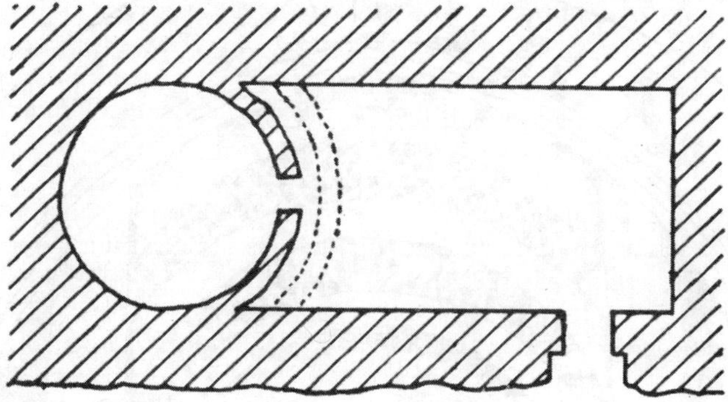

Fig. 37. Ground plan of Sudama cave, Barabar Hills, lying parallel to the rock face.

Fig. 38. Ground plan of Ajanta cave no. 26, with the axis at right angles to the surface.

The Sudama cave resembles the Lomas-Rishi in plan (Fig. 37). Both the halls and circular chamber have vaulted ceilings. The exterior wall of this round apartment has grooves imitating wooden planks or bamboo.

The earliest known *structural chaitya* is the one situated on a small hill called *Bijak-ki-Pahadi* in *Bairat* in Rajasthan (Fig. 40). This chaitya may be ascribed to Ashoka for the following reasons: firstly, the presence of inscribed bricks; secondly, fragments of Chunar sandstone pillars and a polished stone umbrella found nearby, as also two edicts of Ashoka, one of which prescribes for study certain passages of Buddhist texts. The early structural chaityas followed the round contour of the stūpa for the purpose of circumambulation. At Bairat the round central chamber is made of wedge-shaped bricks alternating with octagonal wooden pillars. A pradakvṣiṇa pātha, enclosed by an outer wall, surrounds the chaitya. The entrance on the east is in direct line with the portico of the central building. The oblong wall around the entire structure belongs to a later date. The superstructure, no longer there, may have been domical and tiled. We may infer this from a bas-relief on the railing of the Bharhut stūpa, which shows a domed building, and thus gives

Fig. 39. Facade of the Lomas-Rishi cave, Barabar Hills.

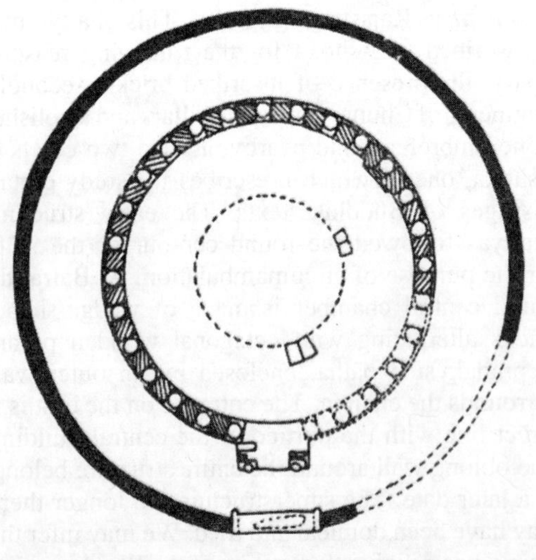

Fig. 40. Ground plan of the structural chaitya, Bairat.

an idea of how the free-standing round buildings may have looked (Fig, 41, p. 30).

Remains of other structural chaityas exist in Andhra Pradesh, Gujarat, Gandhara and elsewhere. The one at *Guntapalle* (Fig. 42, p. 30), Andhra Pradesh, also circular, has a projection for a passage or porch on the west. Slabs of stone pave its pradakṣi ṇa pātha. The walls of the sanctuary, composed of mud and mortar and plastered on both sides, have no wooden pillars in between. The *chaitya* at *Salihundam*, similar in plan, also has a rectangular porch.

While the exterior of the outer wall of *temple* 40 at *Sānchi* (Fig. 43) was rectangular, the inside of this chaitya was apsidal. The wooden superstructure has disappeared entirely, but the stone foundation of the apsidal inner wall remains. The original structure belonged to the Mauryan period. By the time of the Sungas, pillars were built over the foundation.

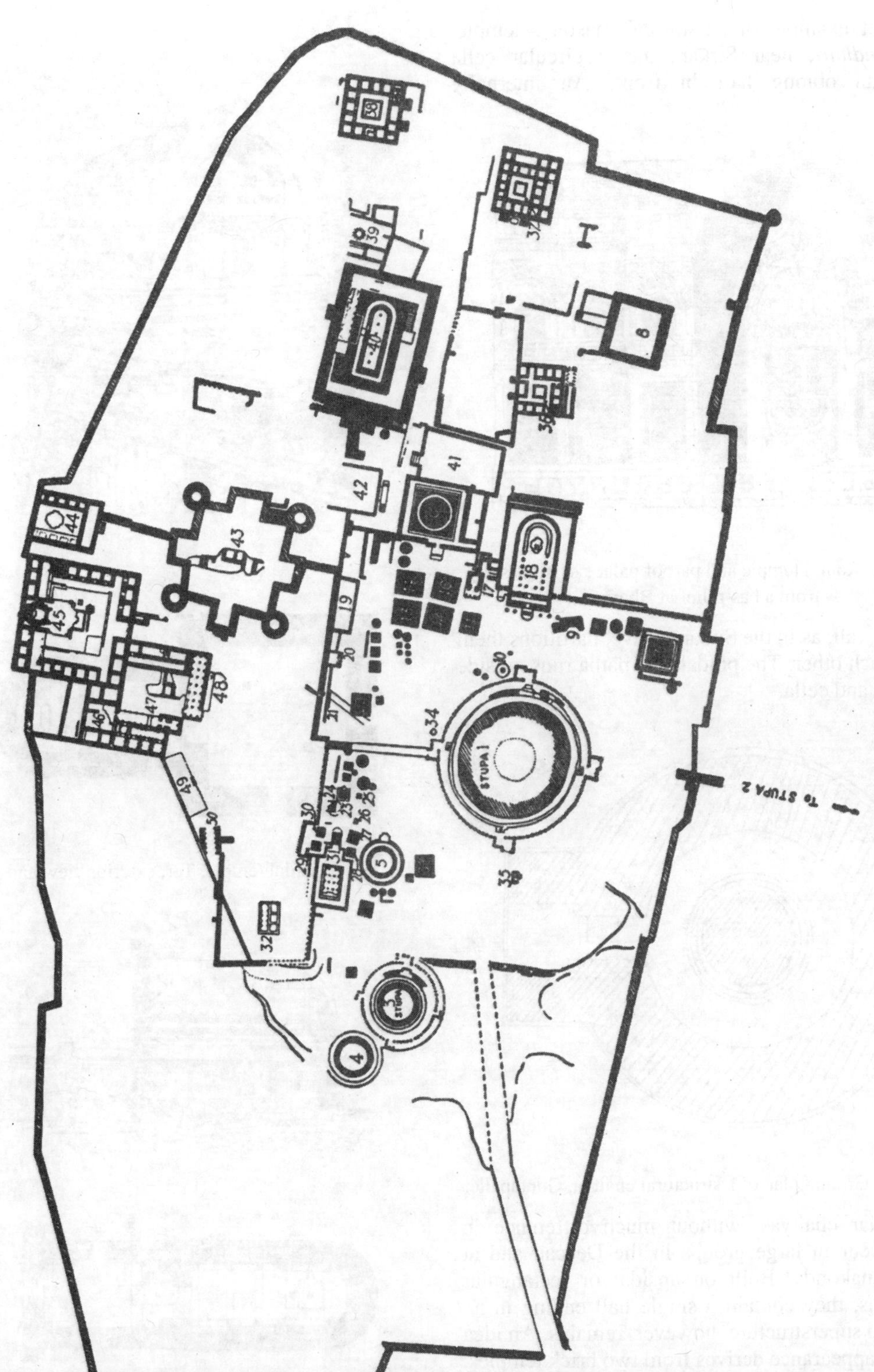


Fig. 43. Ground plan of Buddhist settlement, Sanchi.

Another example of an apsidal masonry temple, at *Gandhara* near Sirkap, has a circular cella with an oblong hall in front. An internally curved wall, as in the Sudama cave, partitions them from each other. The pradakṣiṇa pātha runs outside the hall and cella.

Fig. 41. Round temple and part of palace or monastery, from a bas-relief at Bharhut.

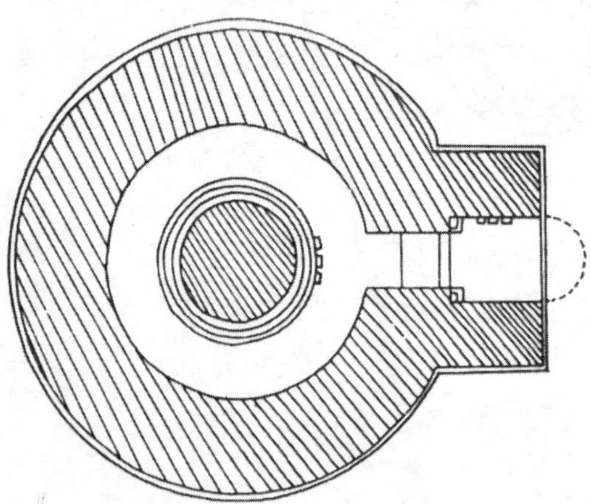

Fig. 42. Ground plan of a structural chaitya, Guntapalle.

Similar chaityas, without much difference in plan, occur in large groups in the Deccan and at Nagarjunakonda. Built on apsidal or rectangular platforms, they contain a single hall ending in an apse. No superstructure, however, remains. An idea of their appearance derives from two brick temples, now in Brahmanical use, one at *Ter* in *Maharashtra* (Fig. 44), and the other at *Chejarla* in *Andhra Pradesh*

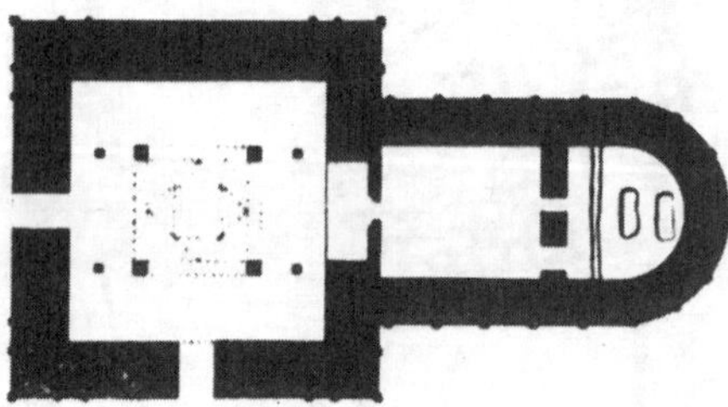

Fig. 44. Apsidal temple, Ter, exterior view and plan.

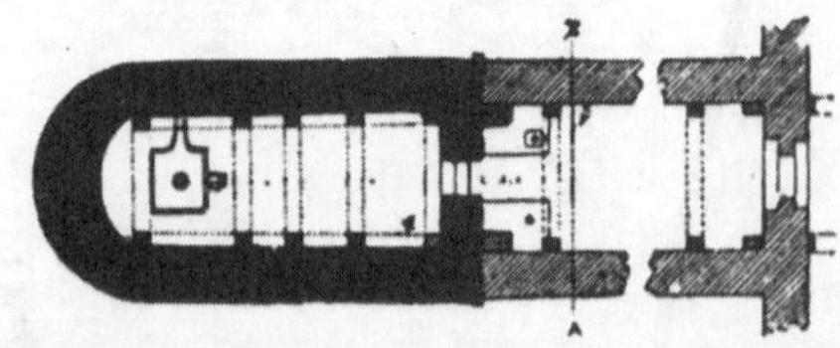

Fig. 45. Apsidal temple, Chejarla, elevation and plan.

(Fig. 45). They have gabled fronts and an arched motif above the doorway. The interior at Chejarla has a flat ceiling which obstructs the inside view of the roof, while at Ter the vault is corbelled.

From the early caves of the Sudama and Lomas-Rishi in the Barabar hills developed the final form of rock-cut architecture which spread all over India and constitutes one of the greatest movements in Indian art. Examples of this art have been discovered in Andhra Pradesh, at Kathiawar in Gujarat, in the trap rock of the Deccan plateau from Chalisgaon to Karad, but mainly in the Western Ghats and at Ajanta and Ellora, where almost a thousand specimens exist. The rock formations at these places suited this type of architecture spiendidly. The hills consist of horizontal strata of amygdaloidal and similar rock of uniform texture and thickness. The alternating layers of hard and soft rock prevents moisture from seeping inside. Out of these rocks the artists shaped reproductions in stone of existing timber, brick or even thatched structures. Though all the three faiths—Buddhist, Hindu and Jaina—practised this art, the Buddhists developed it to its fully mature form.

Hollowing out the rocky hillsides for these halls presented a sculptural rather than an architectural problem. First a perpendicular rock wall had to be cut down and smoothened, and on this the outlines of the façade and entrance were indicated. Then a window was cut, through which tunnelling could begin from the front to the rear. After completion, this window was covered with a wooden framework. As may be seen from certain unfinished caves at Ajanta, the workmen began by tunnelling into the cliff at the level of the height indicated for the interior vault. After completing the ceiling, the workmen continued quarrying downwards, removing the debris of rock through the open façade. In this way they required no scaffolding since they worked from top to bottom, disengaging the columns and the carved stūpa at the back of the cave. The debris served for erecting courts outside.

People accustomed to wood and other perishable material became impressed by the permanency of the stone architecture and by the grand scale of the buildings. Unlike the structural method, rock-cut architecture cost much less since it did not require a nearby quarry to supply the stone and necessary transport of the material, nor the hewing and dressing of stone, nor the preparation of columns, slabs and corner-stones.

As few experimental specimens have been found, rock-cut architecture appears almost in its matured form with few signs of trial and error. Everywhere the walls are straight and angles true, with smooth and polished surfaces. Though the craftsmen must have had a long period of apprenticeship, no traces of it remain. Rock-cut architecture represents sculpture on a large scale rather than the true building art. The imitation of wooden structural details (Fig. 46) such as ribs, pillars and decorative motifs resulted in irrelevant forms with

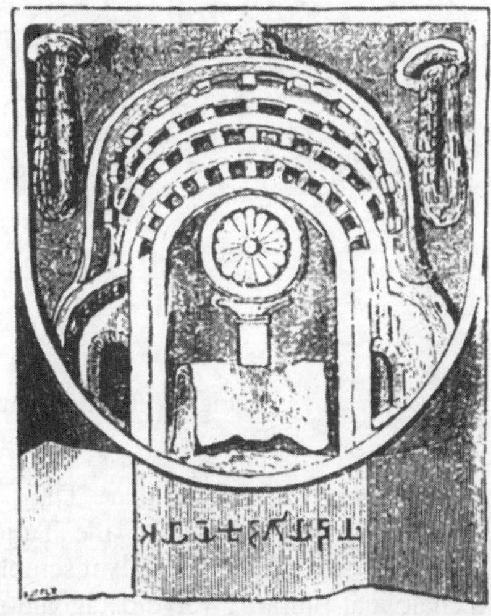

Fig. 46. Front of a chaitya hall, from a bas-relief at Bodh-Gaya, with imitation of wooden structural details.

no functional value. At *Kondane*, for instance, the broken pillars remain hanging from the roof, without any base.

Before describing the mature chaityas of the Western Ghats, mention must be made of some more primitive caves at *Kondivte*, *Guntapalle* and *Junnar*, closely resembling the Ashokan excavations. The Kondivte example contains a circular cella without columns. It has a flat ceiling, with a long flat-roofed hall in front, unlike the Sudama caves where both the halls are vaulted. A square doorway flanked by two jali (lattice or perforated) windows connects the outer hall and inner cella. The plan looks as though a round building stands at one end of a rectangular hall.

The *Guntapalle* cave (Fig. 47), also astylar, has a domical ceiling, formed by a network of rafters imitating the wooden or bamboo framework used in building huts. The roof has overhanging eaves. Above the doorway of the narrow porch is an arch, shaped like a horseshoe.

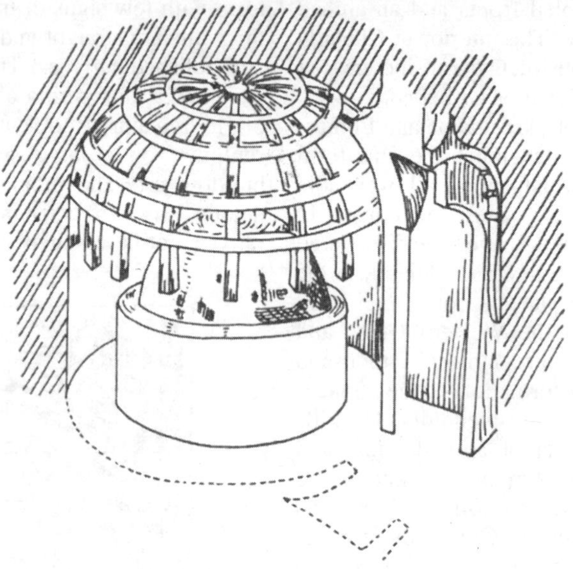

Fig. 47. Interior view of the rock-cut chaitya, Guntapalle

The rock-cut *chaitya* at 'Junnar Dt., Pune, Maharashtra'. (Fig. 48) belongs to the Tulja-lena group. Of a slightly later date, it closely resembles the structural chaitya at Bairat. Twelve octagoanl pillars form the central arrangement surrounding the stupa.

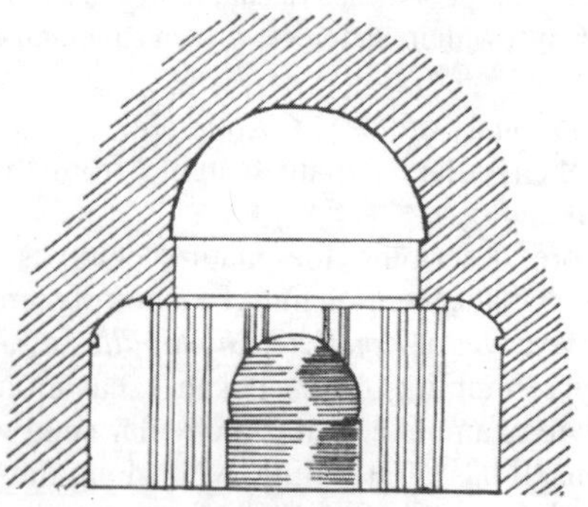

Fig. 48. Rock-cut chaitya, Junnar, setion and plan.

On the architraves above the pillars rests a domical ceiling. The roofing over the aisles, lower in height, forms a half arch which rests on the circle of pillars. The wooden rafters of the ceiling have disappeared. The pot-shaped members, both at the base and capitals of the pillars on the facade and interior of this chaitya, produce a rather clumsy appearance. The pillars rest on stepped bases.

The chaityas belonging to this early Hīnayāna period, opposed as it was to the representation of the Buddha in human form, often presented an austere interior, although the exterior was often ornate with animal and human figures. With the coming of the Mahāyāna phase, Buddha images were added to many of these early chaityas to suit the tenets of the new creed, as for example at Karle and Kanheri.

Through the numerous rock-cut chaityas in the Western Ghats one can follow the varying fortunes of Buddhism from very early times till its decline in India. They also provide the best examples of the development of the chaitya. The main ones occur at *Bhaja, Kondane, Pitalkhora, Ajanta, Junnar, Nasik, Bedsa, Karle, Kanheri* and especially the Mahāyānic chaityas of *Ajantā* and *Ellora.*

In the early caves, imitation of wooden constructions as well as the use of timber predominated, as seen in the *Bhaja* example (Fig. 49), where the presence of mortice holes indicates that the façade was probably of wood

Fig. 49. Facade of the rock-cut chaitya, Bhaja.

which has disappeared entirely, giving a wide open look to the interior. Chaitya window motifs above railing patterns as well as perforated windows flank the sides of this widemouthed chaitya arch. The decoration imitates existing wooden structures (Fig. 50), comprising a balcony or balustrade resting on a beam with rectangular mortices or cavities. Through these holes pass the joists or rafters of the floor. The ends of the rafters, called tenons, chiselled to fit the rectangular openings, project from the mortices. Those morticed beams in front of the window produce the illusion of carrying the parapet of the balcony. The form of this parapet resembles the vedikā or railing of the stūpa. The entablature above the window, in the form of inverted steps, also rests on a morticed beam. Another beam with merlons surmounts the entablature, and on top of it rests the horseshoe arch. In the interior of the hall, the ribs of the roof and the chatra of the stūpa were all of wood originally. In one case such a curved wooden rib was found *in situ* with a Brahmi inscription, indicating its early date. The chatra no longer exists—the mortice hole on the top of the stūpa proves its former presence. A colonnade surrounds the stūpa (Fig. 51) and divides the hall into a nave and aisles. The octagonal pillars, without bases or capitals, taper upwards. The chaitya arch on the face of the *Kondane* cave (Fig. 52) has a firmer outline, slightly constricted at the base, and the posts flanking the façade are partly of stone. Double arches decorate both sides of the chaitya window. In the interior a number of columns have broken and their remains seem to hang from the roof. Some of the wooden ribs still remain in the vault.

At *Pitalkhora* (Fig. 53) and *Ajanta cave no. 10* (Fig. 54) the façade has disappeared. Stone replaces the woodwork in the aisles. The octagonal pillars remain plain, with no base. A slight elongation characterises the two-tiered drums and hemispherical aṇḍa of the stūpa.

At *Nasik* (Figs. 55-57) the unique feature is the *façade*. Quite unlike the chaityas mentioned so far, it has no traces of timber, only imitation of wood technique. The chaitya arch over the rectangular entrance encloses decorative motifs. Above this rises the chaitya window, flanked by pillars with addorsed animal capitals alternating with decorative stūpas in front of trellises.

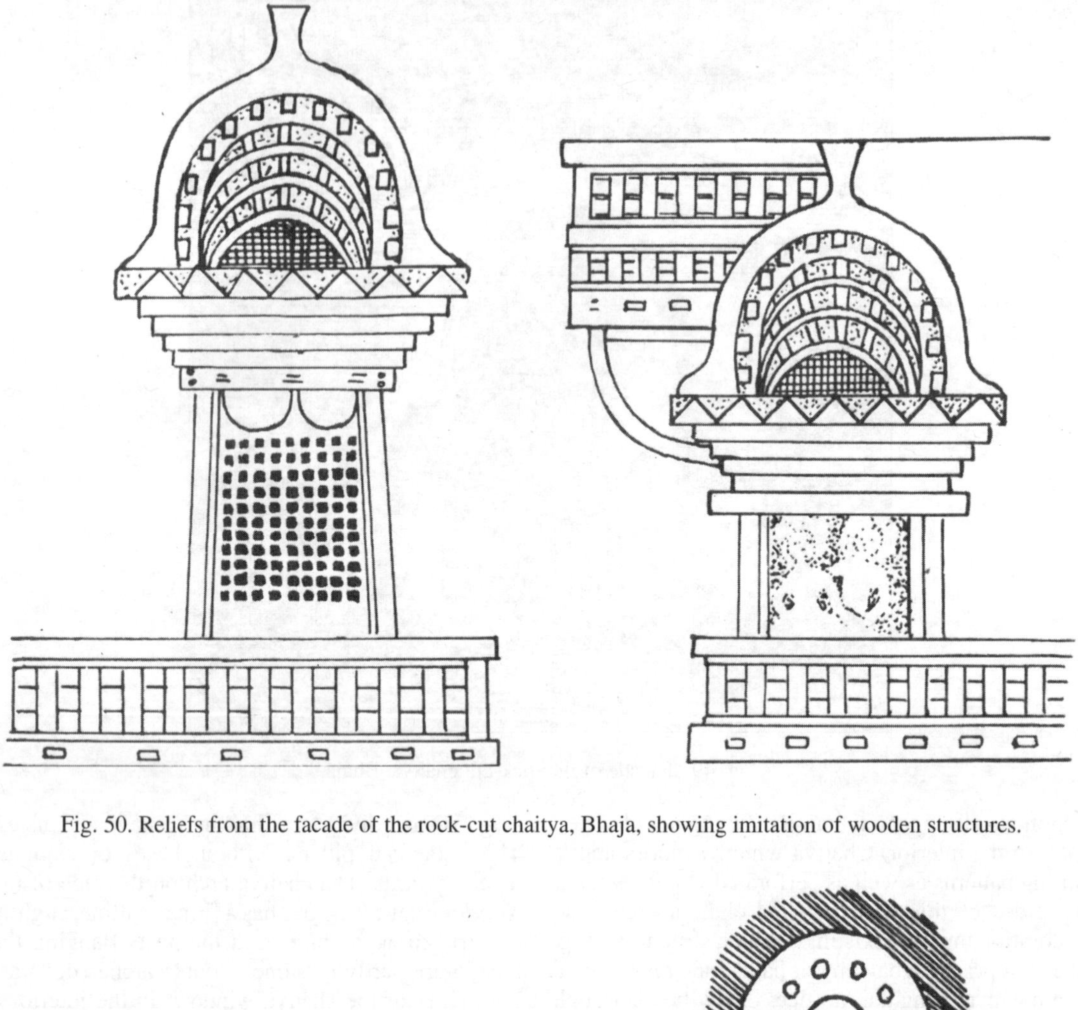

Fig. 50. Reliefs from the facade of the rock-cut chaitya, Bhaja, showing imitation of wooden structures.

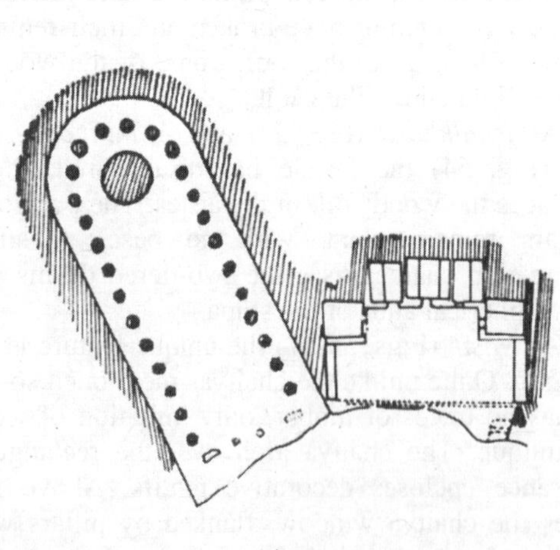

Fig. 51. Chaitya and vihara, Bhaja.

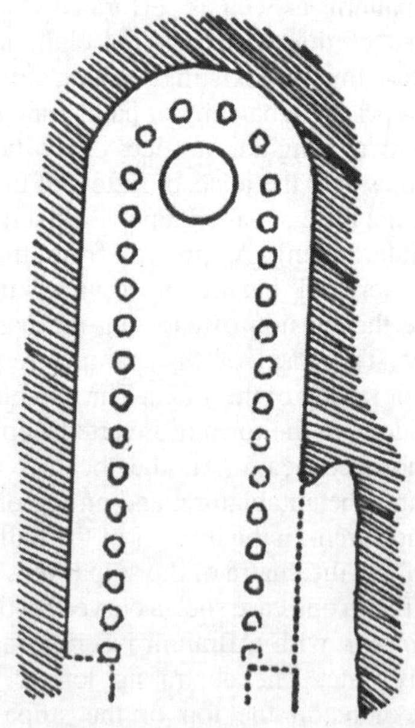

Fig. 52. Rock-cut chaitya, Kondane.

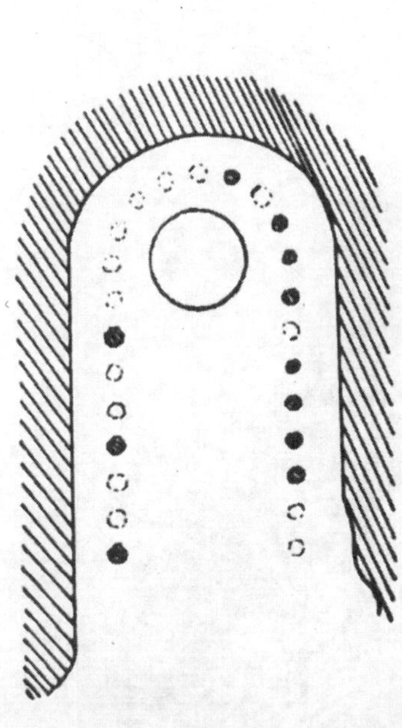

Fig. 53. Rock-cut chaitya, Pitalkhora.

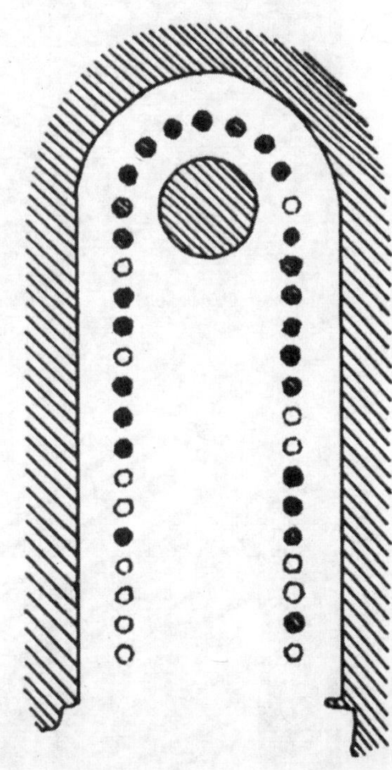

Fig. 54. Rock-cut chaitya no. 10, Ajanta.

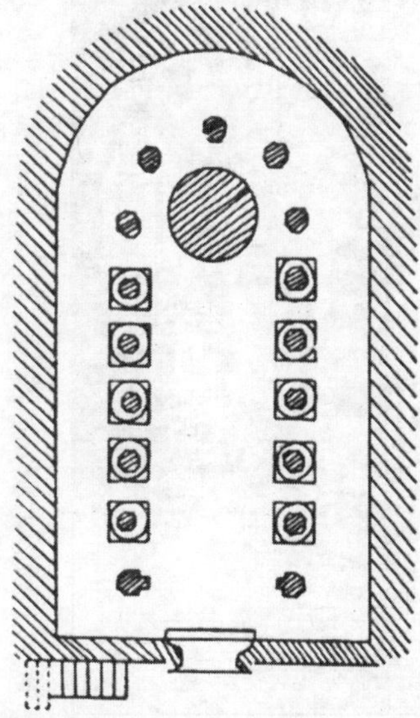

Fig. 55. Pandu-lena chaitya, Nasik, plan.

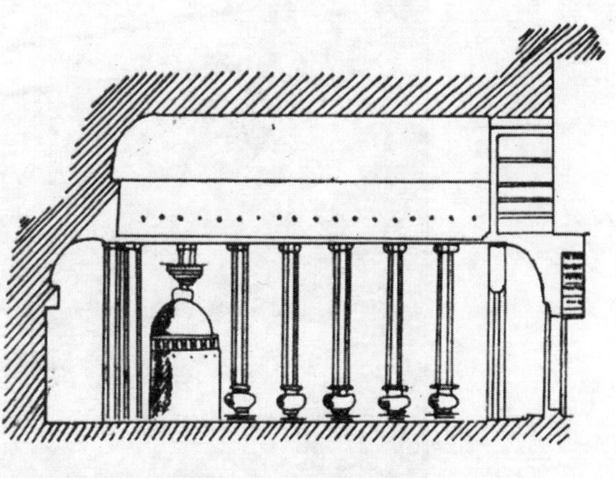

Fig. 56. Pandu-lena chaitya,Nasik, longitudinal section.

Fig. 57. Pandu-lena chaitya, Nasik, facade.

A unique feature of *cave no.* 9 at *Ajanta* (Fig. 58) is the rectangular plan of the interior, with plain octagonal pillars forming the apse around the stūpa. Wooden ribs continue in the nave, although stone replaces them in the aisles.

Fig. 58. Ground plan, rock-cut chaitya no. 9, Ajanta.

The façade has no wooden attachments. The usual chaitya arch and rail motifs flank the finial of the main chaitya window, with a row of chaitya arches below, just above the doorway.

At the vestibule of the *Bedsa chaitya* (Fig. 59), beautifully proportioned columns rise from pot bases. Fluted members, not unlike the Ashokan Persepolitan bell, crown these pillars, with āmalakas above in box-like coffers, and abaci in the form of inverted steps. These in turn support the capitals, consisting of addorsed animal pairs. The chaitya window is inside the portico. From the portal, cells lead out at the sides. Around the doorways of these are rhythmic patterns of large and small chaitya arch motifs and vedikā patterns.

While woodwork has completely disappeared from the façade, which is carved entirely in stone, the interior contains much timber, such as the ribs of the nave. In contrast with the ornate exterior,

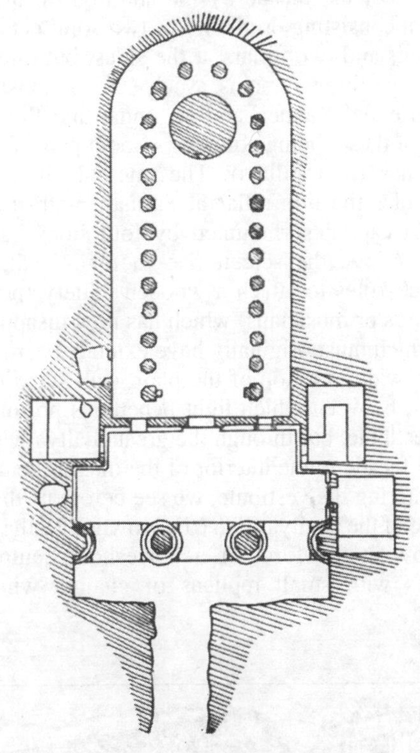

Fig. 59. Chaitya, Bedsa.

the interior looks plain and austere, with octagonal pillars having no base.

The *Karle chaitya* (Fig. 60; Pl. 2. 2), an archi-

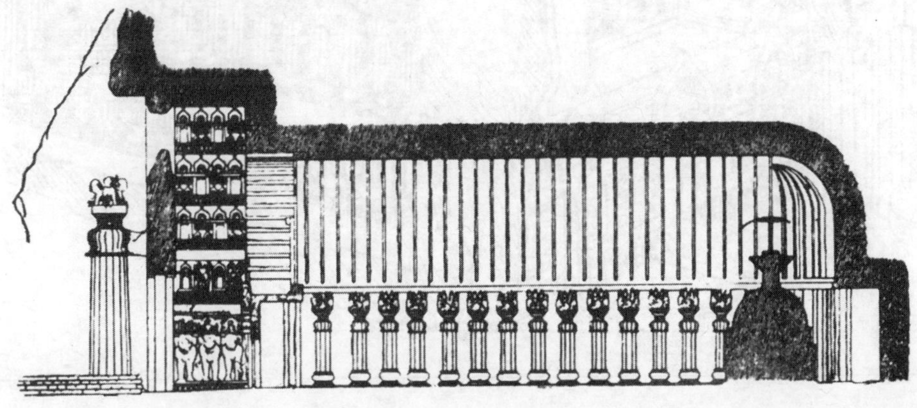

Fig. 60. Chaitya, Karle, longitudinal section.

tectural gem, shows the usual nave divided from the side aisles by pillars and terminating in the apse containing the stūpa. A vestibule has been formed in front of the façade by the addition of an outer screen, consisting originally of two solid octagonal columns and two pillars at the sides, but only half of the partition remains. Such screens exist only at Karle and Kanheri and at Junnar and Bedsa. In front of these facing columns stood a pair of simha stambhas (lion pillars). The one which remains resembles the lion pillar at Sarnath, with its bell-shaped capital surmounted by four lions back to back. Above the screen rises a plain wall, with mortice-holes to attach a wooden gallery (perhaps for bards or musicians) which has now disappeared but which must originally have extended across the whole width. On top of the plain wall stand dwarf pillars, between which light penetrates not only to the vestibule, but through the great chaitya window of the façade to the interior of the magnificent hall. On entering the vestibule, we see before us the real façade of the chaitya (Fig. 61), crowned by the great window in the form of a horseshoe. Sculptured figures with small replicas of chaitya windows and railings above them adorn the rest of the rock surface. Three entrances lead into the hall: the central one, meant for the members of the sangha, had a raised pathway into the nave (37.8 ×13.9 × 14 m); the other two open into the aisles (2.7 m wide).

Thirty-seven pillars adorn the interior of the hall (Fig. 62), thirty of them belonging to the pot-based type, richly carved. Each stands on a stepped base of diminishing squares. On this rests the pot-like base which appears to hold the bottom of the pillar—a reminder of wood and bamboo constructions where this device served as a protection against termites. An inverted lotus capital, with the ribbed element placed inside a box above it, crowns the octagonal columns. The abacus, which repeats the forms of the stepped base but in reverse order, supports finely sculptured groups of figures mounted on elephants and horses (Fig. 63), probably representing lay merchant devotees. A high barrel vault, with ribs formed of separate pieces of wood fixed by plugs into the rock, covers the nave. The seven remaining pillars, without base and capitals, stand in the apse at the far end around the back of the stūpa, which rests on an ornamental base with

Fig. 61. Chaitya, Karle, diagram in perspective showing exterior and interior.

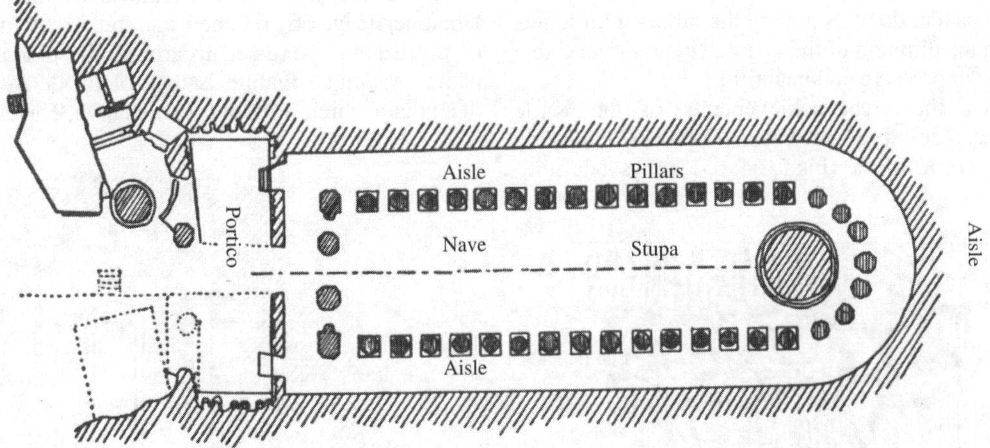


Fig. 62. Chaitya, Karle, ground plan.

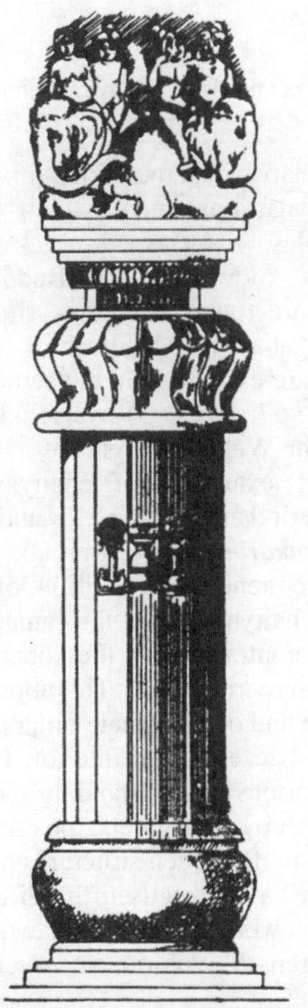

Fig. 63. A pillar from chaitya, Karle.

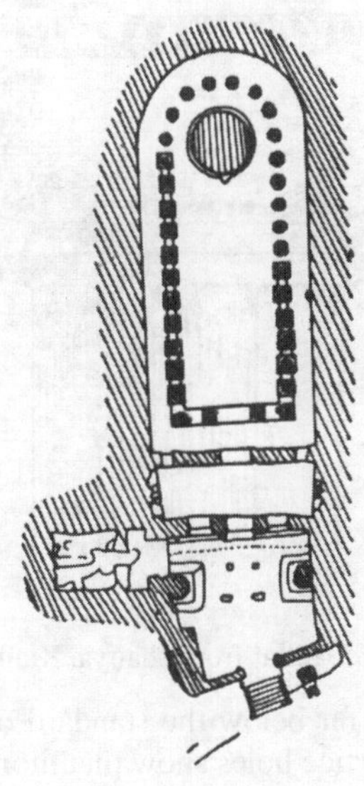

Fig. 64. Chaitya, Kanheri, ground plan.

railing motifs. A massive harmikā with a wooden umbrella in the form of a lotus—the only wooden umbrella that remains—crowns the stūpa. A semi-dome overhangs this apse.

The great chaitya window at the entrance, the only source of light, is specially arranged to subdue and diffuse the fierce glare of the sun throughout the hall. First the light passes between the dwarf pillars of the outer screen and then through the chaitya window, so that the filtered light falls with a softened radiance on the stūpa and diffuses among the pillars until it gets lost in the dimness of the aisles. This lighting effect is very impressive and beautiful.

After the great achievements of the Kārle chaitya, the style declines. The last Hīnayāna *chaitya at Kanheri* (Figs. 64, 65) shows a definite

Fig. 65. Pillar from chaitya, Kanheri.

deterioration, far below the standard of Karle. The numerous mortice holes show that more timber was used, almost reverting to the earlier practise of using wood instead of stone. The two lion pillars are no longer free-standing but attached to the façade. The colonnade in the interior consists of squat pillars, only a few of which are ornamented, betraying decadence of style and technique.

The latest phase of the Hīnayāna period appears at *Kolvi* and *Dhamner*, on the borders of Rajasthan and Madhya Pradesh. At Kolvi, a Buddha image carved on the rear wall and converted into a shrine by two short parallel walls attached to the back of the stūpa, reveals the popular, Mahāyāna influence. As at Kolvi, the Hīnayāna bhikshus of Dhamner (Fig. 66) retained the stūpa, but images of the Buddha were set up around the pradakṣiṇā pātha. A unique feature is the colonnade in front of a vihāra which surrounds the chaitya. The closest

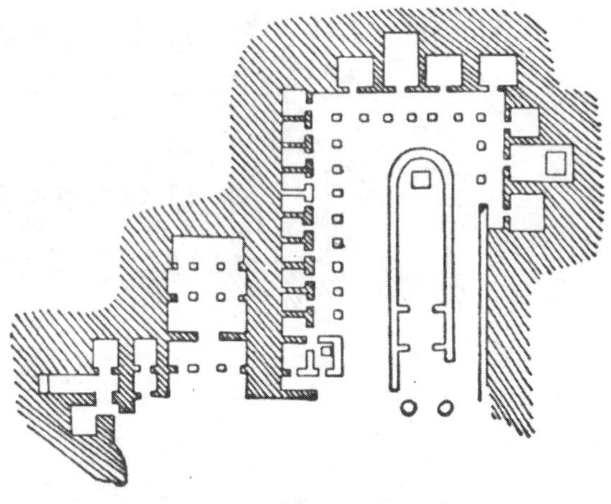

Fig. 66. Cave no. 12, Dhamner, chaitya combined with vihara.

affinity, perhaps, may be found in the structural vihāra at Nagarjunakonda, which encloses two apsidal temples.

The best known of the Buddhist rock-cut monuments are found at Ajanta, situated 109 km from Aurangabad in Maharashtra State. All the thirty caves are excavated in the semicircular scarp of rock (Fig. 67; P1. 2. 3) overlooking the valley watered by the Waghora river.

The chief examples of chaityas during the Mahāyāna period are *caves no.* 19 and 26 at *Ajanta*, and the *Viśvakarmā cave* (*cave no.* 10) at Ellora. Although the general disposition of the various parts of the chaitya remains the same, exhuberance of sculpture contrasts with the sober architectural treatment of the earlier caves. This appears especially on the façade and on the ornate pillars, brackets and surmounting friezes of the interior. Figures of the Buddha in various poses, standing with or without canopies, occupy prominent positions. By that time, imitation of wooden structures had decreased, the workmen having realised the difference in the material they were handling. The quality of the stone, its strength, volume and weight received more emphasis.

Two pillars uphold the porch in front of

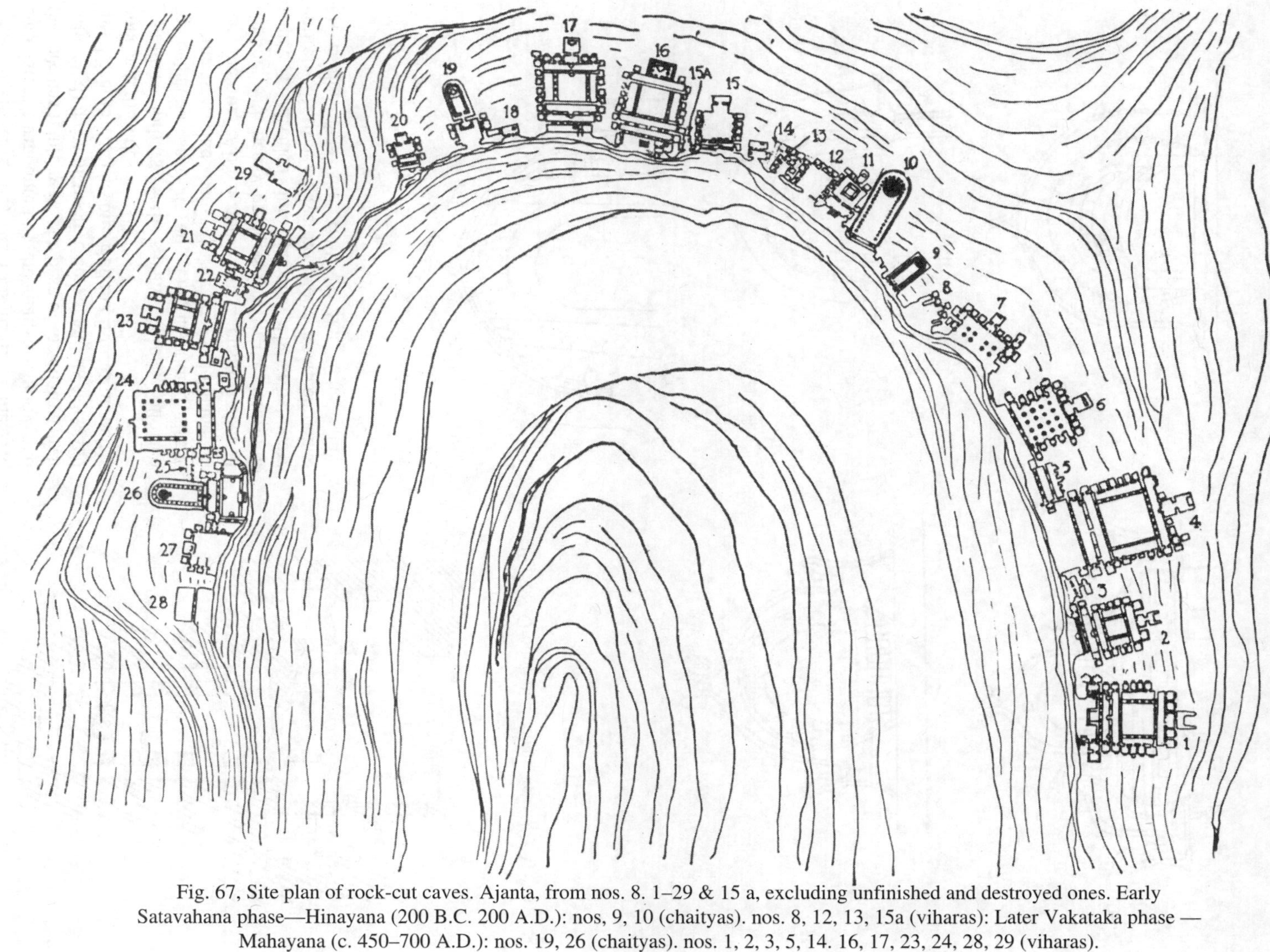


Fig. 67, Site plan of rock-cut caves. Ajanta, from nos. 8. 1–29 & 15 a, excluding unfinished and destroyed ones. Early Satavahana phase—Hinayana (200 B.C. 200 A.D.): nos, 9, 10 (chaityas). nos. 8, 12, 13, 15a (viharas): Later Vakataka phase — Mahayana (c. 450–700 A.D.): nos. 19, 26 (chaityas). nos. 1, 2, 3, 5, 14. 16, 17, 23, 24, 28, 29 (viharas).

*cave no*. 19 (Fig. 68). Its roof forms a massive entablature surmounted by the chaitya window and the yakshas flanking it. The base of the chaitya arch (Fig. 69 d) has a distinctive curve, and its sides and finial bear ornate carving. Buddha figures in niches appear at the sides.

Fifteen pillars with square bases, followed by octagonal sections and circular fluted shafts having traceried belts, form the colonnade in the interior. Above the shafts, cushion-shaped capitals with heavy brackets rise to the triforium, which is divided into panels. The ribs, now entirely of stone, have no wooden attachments. Over the aisle the roof is flat. The stūpa

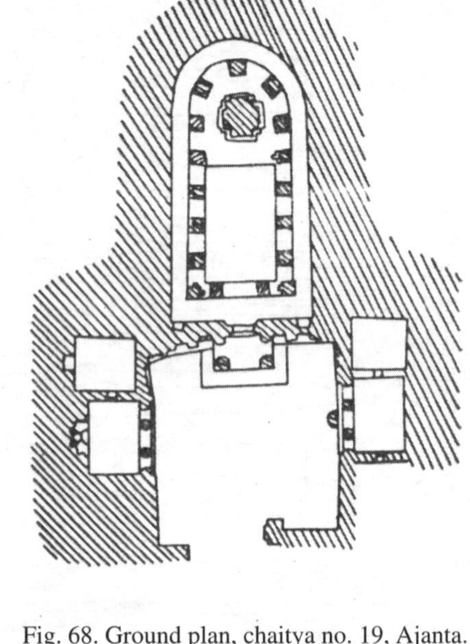

Fig. 68. Ground plan, chaitya no. 19, Ajanta.

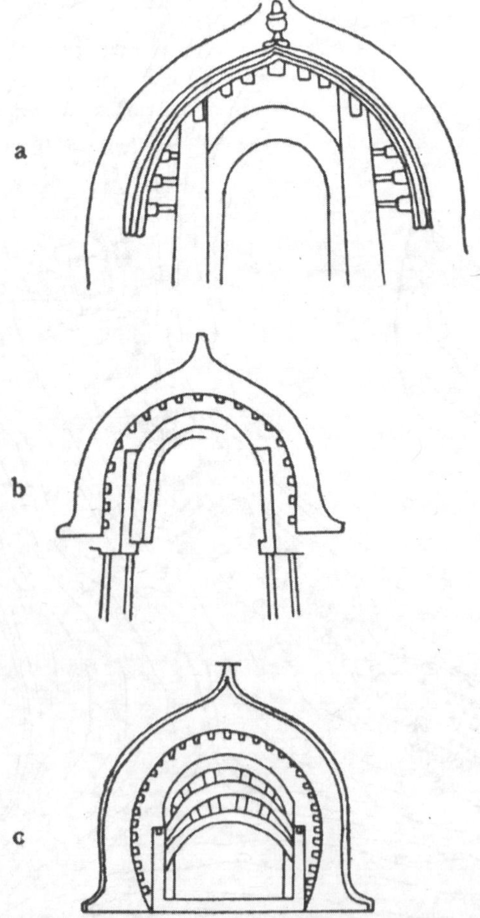


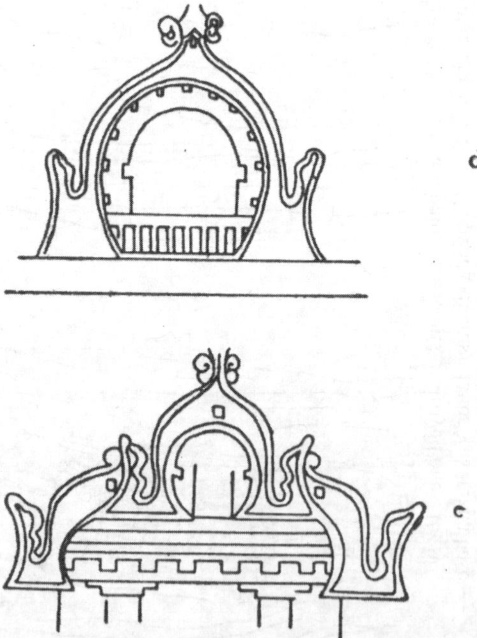


Fig. 69. Shape of chaitya arches in the facade of cave temples : *a*. Lomas-Rishi, *b*. Bhaja, *c*. Karle *d*. Ajanta no. 19, *e*. Visvakarama, Ellora.

Fig. 70. Chaitya no. 19, Ajanta, rock-cut stupa.

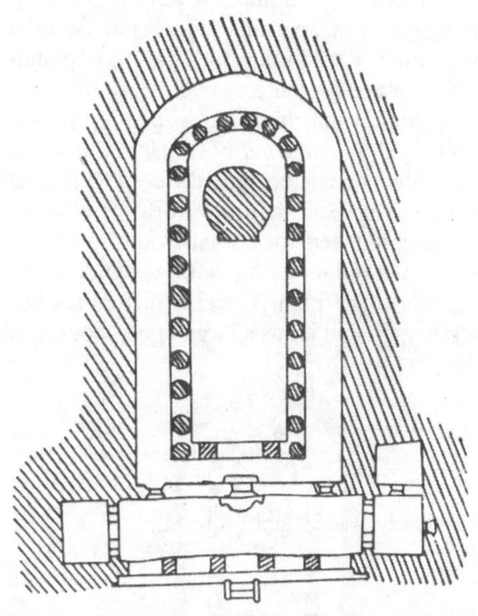

Fig. 71. Ground plan, chaitya no. 26, Ajanta.

at the rear (Fig. 70) has a low pedestal and an elongated drum. Before it stands a figure of the Buddha enclosed by a pair of columns supporting an arch. Tiers of harmikā and chatra soar above the dome of the stūpa.

*Cave no*. 26 (Fig. 71), similar in plan to cave no. 19, also has a porch—later destroyed by a landslide—but the bases of the four pillars remain. It is also richly ornamented with carvings. The chaitya arch window, flanked by numerous panels with Buddha figures, is larger and more constricted at the base. Voluted floral motifs decorate the finial. Two smaller doors on either side of the central one lead to the aisles. The frames of all three of them are decorated with figure sculptures.

The interior (20.1 × 11 × 9.3 m) resembles cave no. 19 architecturally, but it is even more ornate. Panels with Buddha figures fill the triforia and capitals. The stūpa contains a niche with a seated figure of the Buddha framed by a pair of pillars. The wall of the left aisle

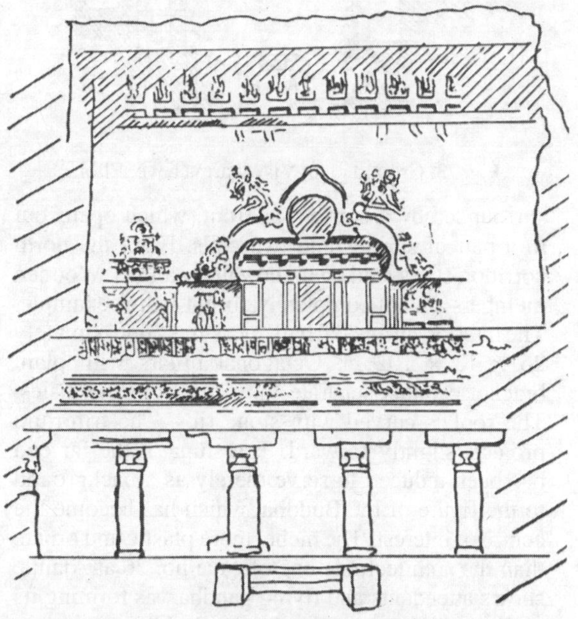

Fig. 72. Visvakarma cave, Ellora, facde showing chaitya window.

has a large piece of sculpture, seven metres long, representing the Mahāparinirvāṇa of the Buddha. The stone cutter's technique has now completely replaced that of the carpenter.

The only Mahāyāna chaitya at *Ellora* is *cave no.* 10, the so-called *Viśvakarmā cave*. Here the whole design of the façade has become different (Fig. 72). The usual chaitya window in the form of a horse-shoe has been reduced to a small round porthole, rising above two pillars with openings which admit light (Fig. 69a). The plan (Fig. 73) differs slightly from the others in that it has a large open courtyard

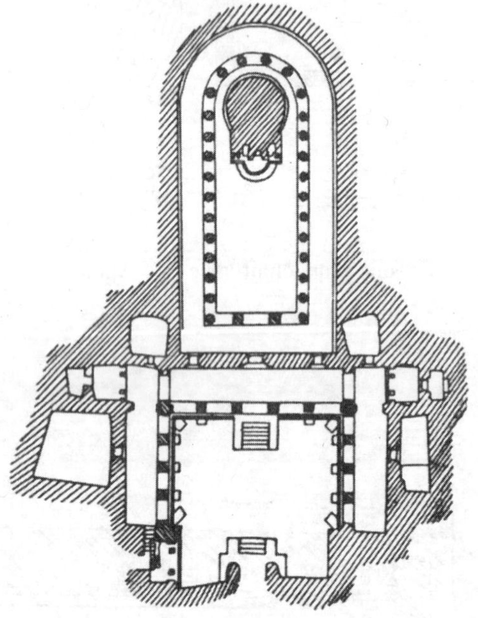

Fig. 73. Ground plan, Visvakarma cave, Ellora.

surrounded by a corridor in front, which opens out to a pair of shrines and two cells. From the north corridor, stairs lead on to the gallery above. Wooden members are not completely absent in this example. The interior, an apsidal hall, measures approximately 26 × 13 × 102 m. Octagonal pillars with plain bracket capitals separate the nave from the aisles. The roof is carved with stone ribs. The triforium projects slightly forward. The stūpa at the far end has been reduced to serve merely as a background to the figure of the Buddha, which has become the centre of interest. The niche, more plastic and ornate than the architectonic one of cave no. 26 at Ajanta, shows attendants and flying gandharvas forming its outline which curves around the Buddha.

### Viharas

The early Buddhist bhikshus were mainly parivrajakas (mendicants) with no fixed abode except during the varsha (rainy season). This custom changed even during the lifetime of the Buddha, for we hear of his accepting lands for vihāras—e.g. the Jetavana given by the merchant Anathapindika, and the sixty dwelling-places donated by another merchant at Raja griha.

The first types of vihāras were obviously free-standing structures made of wood and later of stone. The wooden buildings have disappeared and even those built in stone have fallen into ruin—only their foundations remain visible at Sanchi and Gandhara. From these remains, however, we can see that the structural vihāras consisted of cells built around a central courtyard, which was entered through a doorway in the vestibule.

The vihāras soon developed from primitive thatched huts into large saṅghārāmas. The site for the structural vihāras had to fulfill two conditions—firstly, proximity to some village from where the bhikshus could receive alms, and secondly, enough seclusion to ensure the proper atmosphere for meditation. In the beginning the size of the vihāras was specified so that they should not degenerate into luxury buildings.

According to the Pali texts, the fully- developed vihāra included vihāras (living rooms), pariveṇas (private dwellings), maṇḍapas (halls), upatthāna śālās (service corridors), aggi śālās (halls with fireplaces), koṭṭhakas (porches), chaṅkamas (promenades), chaṅkamas śālās (rooms with promenade), kappiya kuṭis (storehouses outside the vihāra), vaccha kuṭis (privies), jantā ghara (bathing rooms), jantā ghara śālās (passages attached to the bathing rooms), udapānas (wells), udapāna śālās (sheds attached to wells) and pokkharaṇi (tanks).

In course of time the saṅghārāmas developed into educational institutions and centres of Buddhist learning, such as those at Nalanda, Vikramasila, Somapura.

Like the chaityas, vihāras were later hewn out of rock, and it is in these examples that we can study their development. The rock-cut vihāra (Fig. 67; Pl. 2.4) hewn into the mountain side, could no longer have a central courtyard. There was instead an inner hall with surrounding cells opening into it, each provided with raised stone beds. This change, however, resulted in a dearth of ventilation and light. A pillared verandah provided entrance

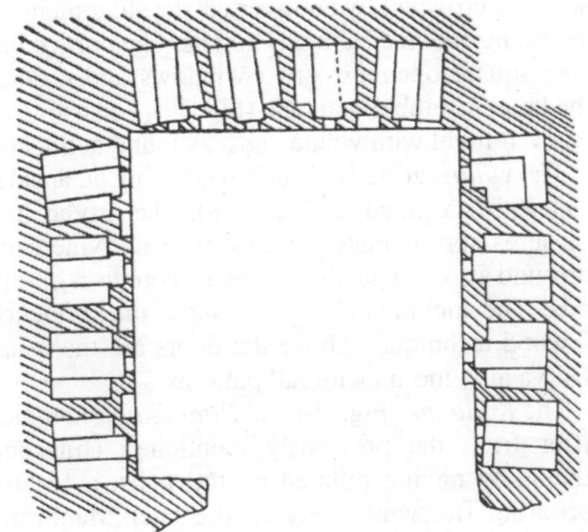

Fig. 74. Vihara no. 12, Ajanta.

into the central hall through one or more doors. The method of excavation, the same as that used in the chaityas, shows that the workers had great skill in this specialised form of quarrying. Hīnayāna vihāras occur in the *Western Ghats*, *Ajanta, Ellora* and in the *Orissan hills* near the east coast. At *Ajanta*, they include *caves no.* 8, 12, 13 and 15*a*. All have a similar plan, with an astylar central hall and cells around it. Chaitya arch motifs with rail patterns below were the main decoration, as seen in *cave no.* 12 (Fig. 74). Here the square central hall measures approximately 10.87 m and a dozen cells lead from it. All except one have double beds with raised stone pillows.

Hīnayāna vihāras in the *Western Ghats* include those at *Nasik, Bedsa, Kondane* and *Pital khora. Caves no.* 3, 8 and 15 at *Nasik*, belonging to the first century A.D., contain pillared porticos and astylar halls. Most of the cells have stone beds. High decorative façades constitute the important feature in these caves. The earliest is probably *cave no.* 8 (*Nahapana cave*). Its façade consists of four pillars, a variation of which occurs in the *Junnar cave no.* 7 of the *Ganesalena group*, which has six pillars in front of a short wall. In the *Gautamiputra cave*, the short wall behind the pillars resembles a railing. Here, as in the other caves, the pillars consist of octagonal shafts supporting a bell-shaped member (Figs. 75,76). Above this rests a ribbed stone

Fig. 75. Pillar in vihara no. 8 or Nahapana cave, Nasik.

Fig. 76. Pillar in vihara no. 3 or Gautamiputra cave, Nasik.

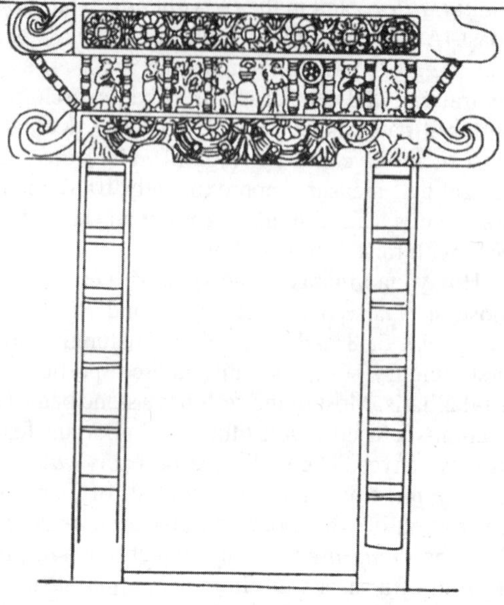

Fig. 77. Door of Gautamiputra cave, Nasik.

in a box, crowned by an inverted step-like member upholding addorsed animal capitals. The portico has three square openings—two windows and a door. The latter resembles a toraṇa (Fig. 77), consisting of a curved lintel with volute ends, as found at Sanchi.

The *vihāra* at *Bedsa* is unique, having an apsidal plan with a vaulted roof (Fig.78). The astylar hall measures approximately 5.45 × 9.73 m. Nine cells surround it, most of them having double rock-cut beds. The inclining doorposts show the influence of wood technique. Above the doors are the usual chaitya arch motifs with rail patterns.

The *Kondane* (Fig. 79) and *Pitalkhora* examples differ from the previously mentioned Hīnayāna vihāras by having pillared central halls, a feature appearing frequently only in the later Mahāyāna vihāras. At Kondane, the portico that once stood in front has disappeared. A pair of windows flank the doorway. A colonnade, now badly damaged, runs all round the hall which measures about 6.90 × 8.70 × 2.5 m. Beams and rafters, copies of timber construction, adorn the ceiling. The usual chaitya arches, connected by rail patterns and string

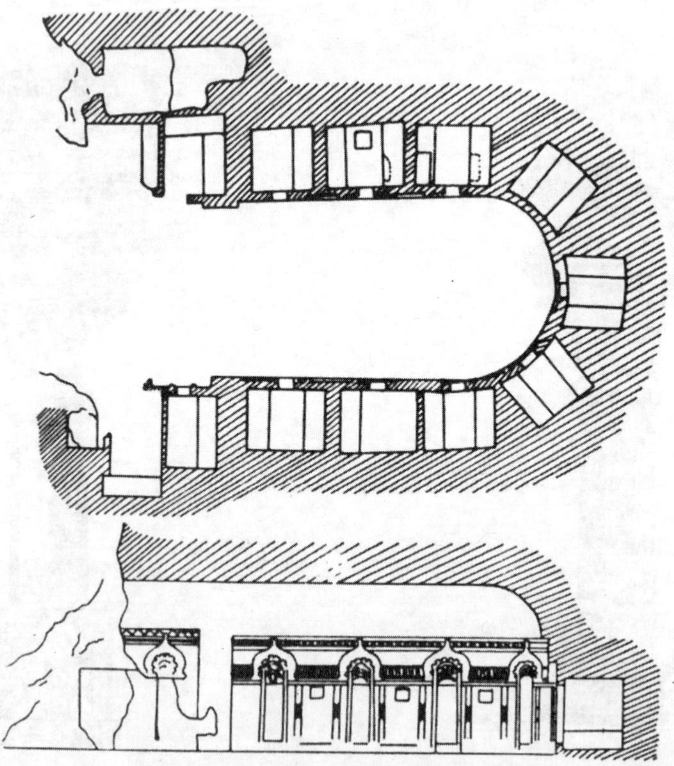

Fig. 78. Plan and section, vihara, Bedsa.

courses, appear above the lintels of the cell doorways. The cells have stone beds.

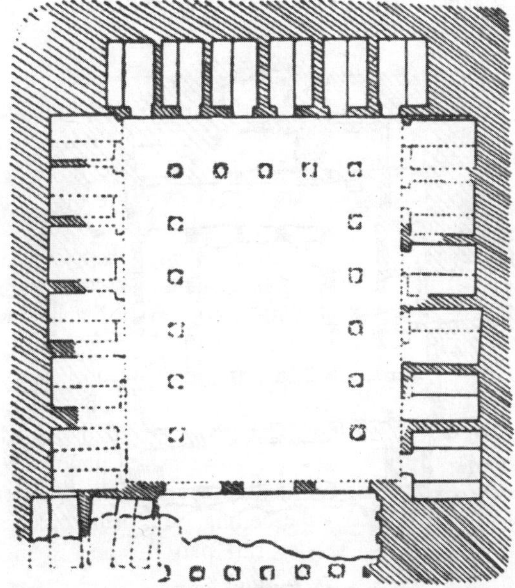

Fig. 79. Rock-cut vihara, Kondane.

Only a few cells and fragments of the colonnade remains of the badly damaged *vihāra* at *Pitalkhora*. Here the cells have vaulted ceilings, and lattice windows pierce the walls.

The caves in the *Udaigiri* and *Khandagiri* hills in *Orissa* date back to the same period (c. second century B.C.), but belong to the Jaina sect. In these Orissan caves the cells overlook an open courtyard. Here the workmanship shows less refinement, due probably to the rough sandstone material. The cells lead out from pillared verandahs. The square pillars have bracket capitals, sometimes with carved struts resembling those in cave no. 3 at Badami. The chaitya arch is semi-circular, the unconstricted lower ends resting on pilasters. Some cells have a ledge, like a continuous bench, resembling the āsanas of medieval temples. The cells in this case are rectangular, not square, and some resemble a dormitory with many doors. The floor slopes upward about 1.20 m, probably to form a couch instead of the usual stone beds.

The façade of the *Tiger cave* resembles a tiger's head (Fig. 80). It contains a single cell, and according to an inscription it belonged to a bikshu named Sabhuti.

Dramatic reliefs on the upper floor of the two-storeyed *Rāni Gumpha* indicate that it probably served as an open-air theatre for pageants.

Fig. 80. Tiger cave, Udaigiri.

The colonnade around the courtyard supports a terrace, above which stands a throne with arms and foot-rest, probably used by the head of the monastery. The cells overlook an open quadrangle (Figs. 81, 82).

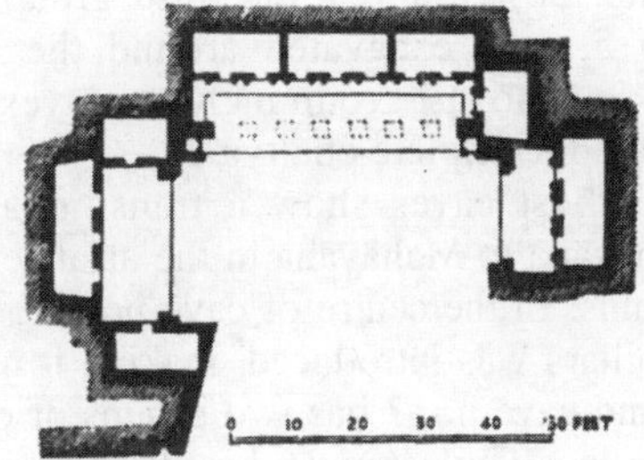


Fig. 81. Ground plan, lower storey of Rani Gumpha cave, Orissa.

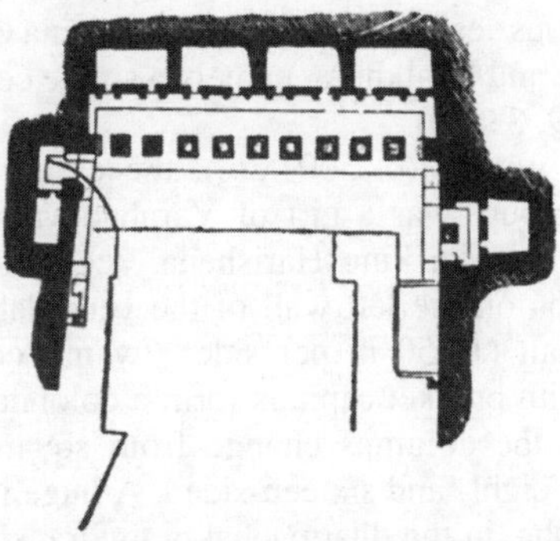

Fig. 82. Plan, upper storey, Rani Gumpha cave, Orissa.

With the coming of Mahāyāna Buddhism, the new sect appropriated many existing vihāras and chaityas. They converted the central cell of the back wall into a shrine enclosing the image of the Buddha, often flanked by attendants or by Avalokiteśwara and Maitreya. Here the vihāra combined the functions of both sanghārāma and chaitya. Instead of a stūpa, the image of the Buddha became the object of worship. At times shrines flanked the sides of the verandah. But the basic plan of the vihāra remained unchanged, consisting of a pillared central hall with cells leading out of it. Decorations began to proliferate especially on the façade and porch. Most of the central halls have pillars. Some double-storeyed vihāras exist, such as *no*. 6 at *Ajanta* and *nos*. 11 and 12 at *Ellora* (Fig. 83).

The development of the Mahāyāna vihāra can be traced only at Ajanta (Fig. 67) (c. fifth and sixth centuries A.D., under the Vakataka dynasty). Caves no. 11, 7 and 6 belong to the earliest group. When the number of bhikshus increased they added caves no. 15 to 20 (except cave no. 19 which is a chaitya) in order to provide more accommodation. Numbers 21 to 25 (including chaitya no. 26) comprise the third group. Caves no. 1 to 5 were excavated around the seventh century A.D. The last group includes caves no. 27, 28 (and the incomplete chaitya 29).

The earliest caves show a transitional phase from Hīnayāna to Mahāyāna in the arrangement of the columns. In the centre of cave no. 11, a group of four pillars was introduced, making it resemble a shed; and cave no. 7 has two groups of columns in the portico. The verandah has disappeared from the lower floor of *cave no*. 6. The interior hall (16 × 16.45 m), embodying sixteen pillars in four rows, looks rather overcrowded. A staircase on the right leads to the first floor, which retains the harmonious design of the earliest Hīnayāna vihāras at Kondane and Pitalkhora, namely a single colonnade (Figs. 79, 83a, b).

*Cave no*. 16 (c. 500 A.D.), the earliest of the second group, was a gift of Varahadeva, minister of the Vakataka king Harishena, according to an inscription on the left wall of the verandah. In the square hall (19.50 m per side), twenty octagonal pillars with bracket capitals form a colonnade. The bases of the columns change from square at the centre to eight- and sixteen-sided. A huge image of the Buddha, in the dharmachakra mudrā, sits in the pralambapāda āsana at the back wall of the shrine. Sixteen cells lead out of the hall. The rafters on the ceiling of the front aisles imitate wood.

The fluted pillars in the verandah of *cave no*. 17 (Fig. 84), square at the bottom and top, have carved floral bands in the middle. In the

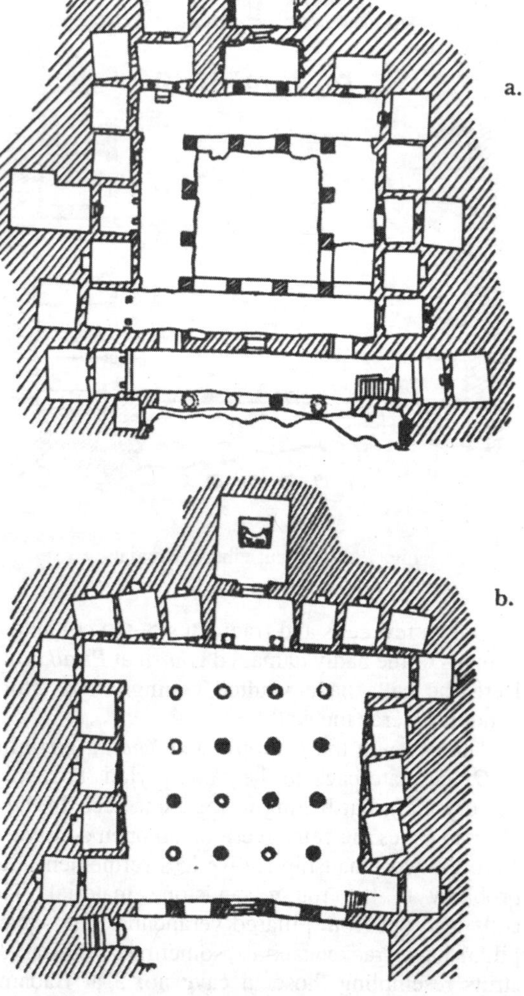


Fig. 83. Vihara 6, Ajanta, ground plans: *a*. upper floor, *b*. lower floor.

large hall (19.20m per side), the twenty pillars have square pedestals followed by eight and sixteen-sided sections. Bands of floral carvings adorn the shafts. The bracket capital has three parts.

The elaborately carved façade constitutes the most notable feature of *cave no*. 1 (Fig. 85). The plan is typical in having cells all around

(Pl. 2.4) cut into the matrix of the rock, and the central hall has twenty pillars forming a square. The front portico has disappeared. The pillars of the façade have elaborate square pedestals and octagonal, sixteen-sided or fluted shafts with beautiful tracery patterns. Each pillar upholds a ribbed cushion-like member. Above this rises the bracket capital divided into three parts, the centre having a figure of the Buddha.

Fig. 84. Pillar from vihara no. 17, Ajanta.

*Cave no.* 2 shows an improvement in the symmetrical alignment of the cells. The hall (14.23 × 14.5 m) has pillars similar to those of cave no. l.

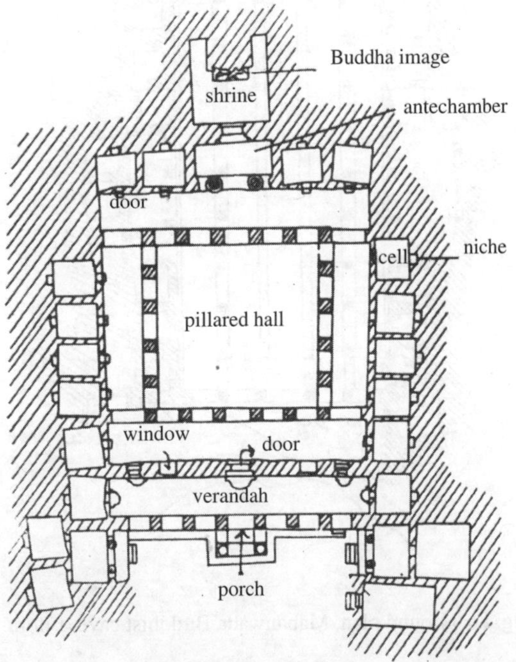


Fig. 85. Ground plan, vihara no. 1, Ajanta.

Though *cave no.* 24 remains incomplete, the decoration of the pillars shows a masterly touch in the ornate vase and foliage capitals. The octagonal upper portion of the pillar has circular medallions containing figures.

Ellora reveals another phase of Mahāyāna rock-cut architecture. Of the twelve Buddhist caves, *nos.* 1 *to* 5 belong to the early *Dhedwada group*; caves *no.* 6 *to* 12 originated later. *Cave no.* 5, the *Mahānwāda* (Fig. 86), has an uncommon rectangular hall (17.55 × 35.10 m), divided into nave and aisles by twenty-four pillars with cushion capitals. A transverse vestibule appears at the rear with the shrine at the very end. The cells and two recesses lead out from the aisles. A pair of low narrow platforms runs through the middle of the nave. As in Sikkim and Tibet, the bhikshus probably sat in two rows facing each other while the head of the sangha had the shrine behind him.

Of the later group, the *Do* Tal (*no.* 11) and *Tin Tal* (*no.* 12) are three-storeyed vihāras. The latter, almost fifteen metres high, has a verandah on each storey, supported by eight

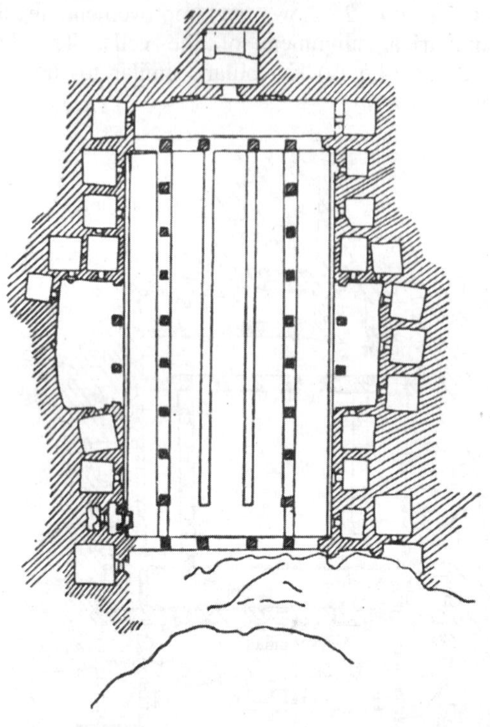

Fig. 86. Ground plan, Mahanwada Buddhist cave, Ellora.

pillars. Three rows of eight pillars divide the hall on the ground floor (Fig. 87) into three aisles. Six more pillars lead to the shrine. Square cells adjoin this hall. From one of these a staircase goes up to the first floor which has another hall with two rows of pillars and a seated figure of the Buddha at the rear. The topmost floor of the cave is a large hall divided into aisles by four rows of eight pillars, each aisle ending with a figure of the Buddha. The plain exterior contrasts with the richly sculptured interior.

The plan of the *nine caves* at Bagh in Madhya Pradesh (fifth and sixth centuries A.D.) resembles the Mahāyāna examples at Ajanta in many respects. The cells and shrine of *cave no.* 2 show symmetrical arrangement. A group of four pillars stand on circular moulded bases in the centre of the colonnade. This additional group of pillars was probably added to support the roof, as the rock here is soft. Instead of the Buddha image, the shrine at the back contains a stūpa.

At the centre of *cave no.* 3, eight octagonal pillars alternate with four square piers. This cave gives entrance to *cave no.* 4 (Fig. 88), through the so-called śālā (schoolroom) which probably served as a dharmaśālā, like the Darbar cave at Kanheri. Twenty-eight pillars, with four square piers in the middle, support

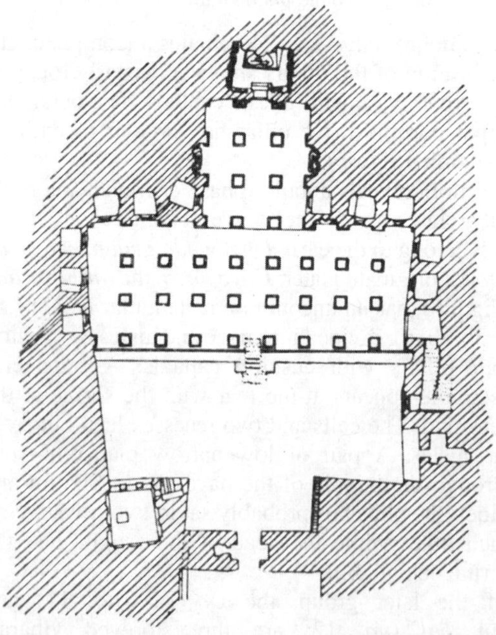

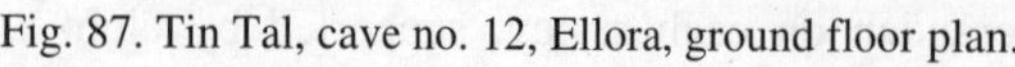

Fig. 87. Tin Tal, cave no. 12, Ellora, ground floor plan.

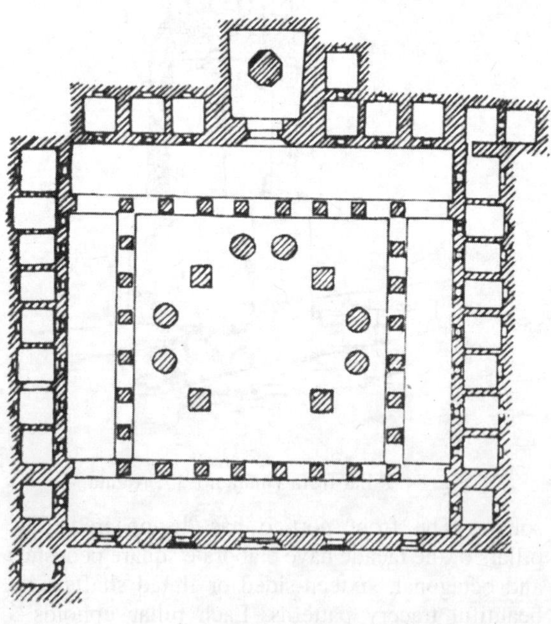

Fig. 88. Cave no. 4, Bagh.

the central hall. Ornate porches with deep entablatures, projecting from the middle of the three sides and supported by two pillars each, give it a distinctive feature. Both this cave and the previous ones were elaborately painted, a fact which probably accounts for the name Rangamahal given to cave no 4.

The Buddhist vihāras at *Aurangabad* (c. sixth or seventh centuries A.D.) seem to represent the last phase of Buddhist rock-cut architecture, beginning to verge on its Hindu counterpart. The *vihāras* 3 and 7 are the best examples. *Cave no.* 3 resembles those at Ajanta, except that the shrine at the rear is cut deep into the rock. The cells, and large recesses with two pillars in front, lead out of the central hall. Elaborate carvings of foliage and figures adorn the pillars.

*Cave no.* 7 influenced the later development of Hindu rock-cut vihāras. The shrine, placed in the centre of the main hall, has a circumambulatory passage around it—an unusual design. The pillars combine bracket, vase and foliage design. Reliefs adorn the pillars and superstructures—the high relief sculptures seem almost statues in the round.

Of the structural vihāras, the *Jivakāmravana* at *Rajgir* seems the earliest, probably dating from the Buddha's time. Only the foundations remain. They reveal four long elliptical halls three of them with the opening on the long side.

As time went on, vihāras with one or more storeys became popular. The cells overlook a quadrangle. The plan probably derived from existing houses seen even now in Bengal. Sometimes a pillared maṇḍapa stood in the courtyard, as at Nagarjunakonda where rows of cells, with raised verandahs in front, surrounded three sides of the courtyard. The same vihāra complex also includes two apsidal temples, one housing a stūpa and the other an image of the Buddha.

At *Gandhara*, architecture was chiefly structural, the main buildings being stūpa and sanghārāma. The latter included temples, houses for bhikshus, votive stūpas, etc. The best example is found at Takht-i-*Baha*i, while others include those at *Dharmarajika*, *Jamal- garhi* (Fig. 89), *Charsada* and *Manikyala*.

The sanghārāma at *Takht-i-Bahai* (Fig. 90), the best example of Gandhara architecture, is laid out in an axial plan although the ground has various levels. A rectangular wall (about sixty m long) encloses the main buildings, the stūpa court in the south, and the vihāras in the north. The terrace in between held votive stūpas and small shrines. West of the vihāra stood an assembly hall. The other structures may have served as the kitchen, refectory and other utility buildings. Due to the difference in the ground levels, steps connected the stūpa court with the vihāra. The latter has the usual

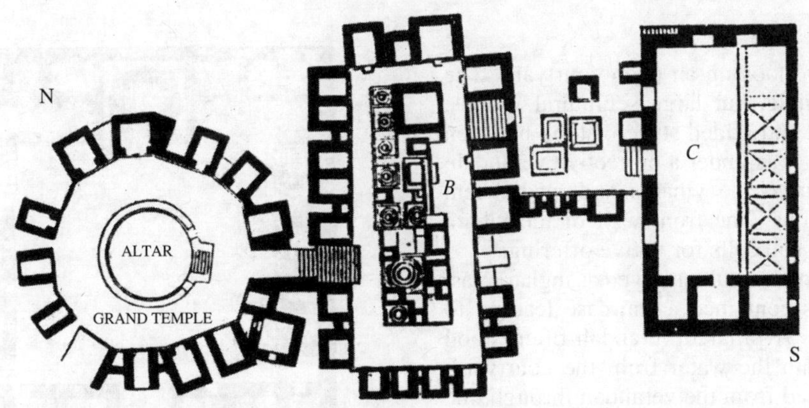


Fig. 89. Ground plan, vihara Jamalgarhi.

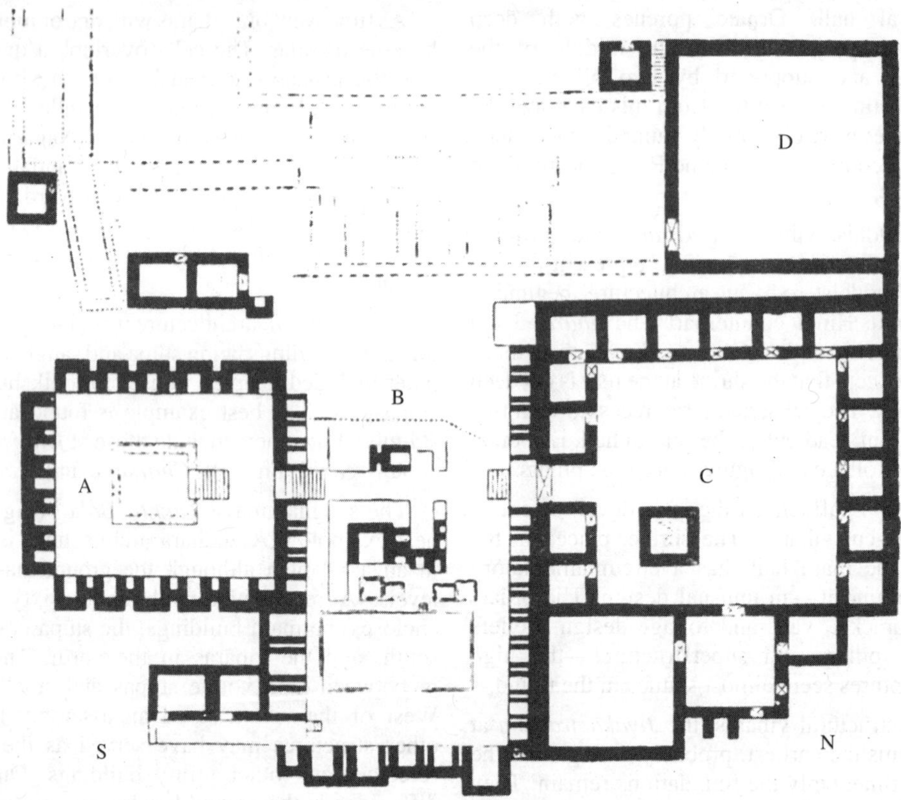


Fig. 90. Ground plan, vihara. Takht-i-Bahai.

plan of cells overlooking an open courtyard. The rooms were simple, but large sculptural groups, often in painted and gilded stucco, stood between the walls of the cells under a protective verandah. This lent colour to the vihāras and made them resemble museums. The front wall of the vihāra facing the stūpa had cells for votive offerings.

In the complex multistoreyed saṅghārāmas, one of the cells contained a staircase leading to the floor above. A pillared verandah often stood in front. To drain the water from the courtyard, covered drains led from the verandah through one of the cells. Both at Nalanda and Sanchi, sloping buttress-like members abutted either side of the entrance.

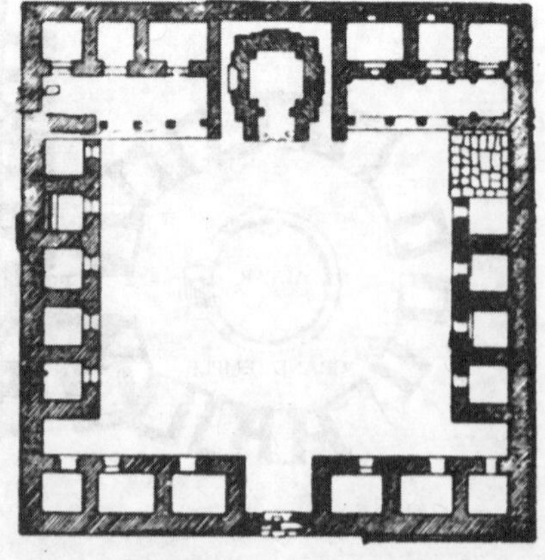

Fig. 91. Vihara 45, Sanchi.

In *vihāra* 45 at *Sanchi* (Fig. 91) the position of the shrine, in the middle of the back wall opposite the entrance, heralds the plan of the more developed sanghārāmas. A high wall, with two screened windows on the east for light, forms a circumambulatory passage. The plan of *sanghārāma* 51 at *Sanchi* resembles that of vihāra 45.

The *Somapura-Mahāvihāra* at Paharpur (Fig. 92), illustrates the fully developed structural sanghārāma. Numerous cells overlook the central courtyard. The temple in the centre, pancharatha in plan, rises in three tiers. The north side is elongated to accommodate the staircase connecting the ground and first floor. A square enclosure, measuring about 246.60 m, surrounds the whole complex.

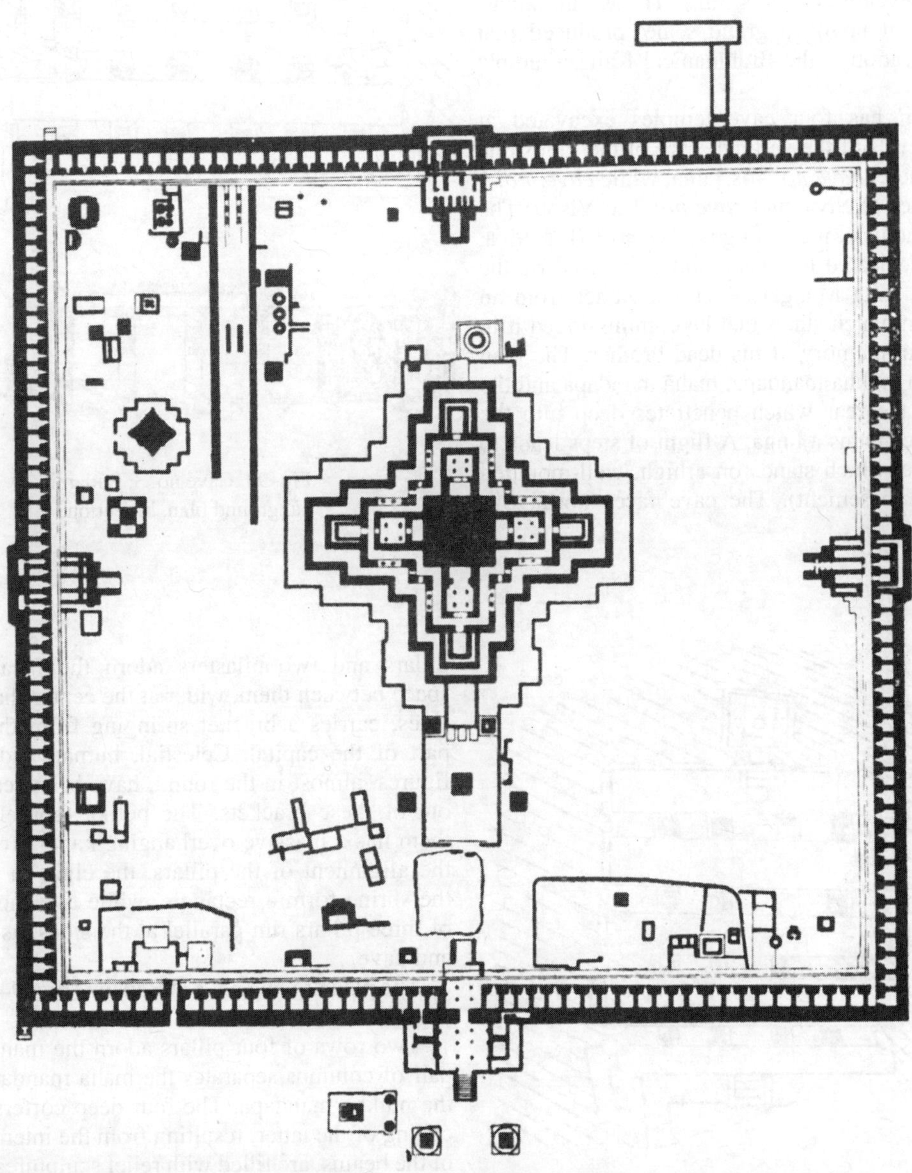

Fig. 92. Somapura-Mahavihara, Paharpur.

## HINDU AND JAINA ROCK-CUT ARCHITECTURE

Soon after the Buddhists had initiated the method of hewing caves out of the rock to suit their purpose, Hindus and Jainas started to imitate them mainly at Badami, Aihole, Ellora, Salsette, Elephanta, Aurangabad and Mamallapuram, under the patronage of the Chalukyas and the succeeding Rashtrakutas and contemporary Pallavas (in the sixth to seventh centuries A.D.). The Rashtrakutas, who took it up on a grand scale, produced that superb creation —the Brahmanical Kailāsa temple at Ellora.

*Badami* has four cave temples excavated at various levels of the vertical scarp of the sandstone hill. Of these, *cave no*. 4 is Jaina, while *cave. no*. 1 is dedicated to Śiva, and *cave no*. 2 to Viṣṇu. The earliest and most interesting is *cave no*.3 (Fig. 93 a, b), also dedicated to Viṣṇu, and patronised by the Chalukya King Mangalesa, as we gather from an inscription which states that he commissioned it in 578 A.D. in memory of his dead brother. The plan includes a mukha maṇḍapa, mahā maṇḍapa and the shrine at the rear which penetrates deep into the rock and contains a linga. A flight of steps leads to the temple, which stands on a high, well-moulded adisṭhāna (basement). The cave faces north. Six pillars and two pilasters adorn the façade. The space between them, wider at the centre than at the sides, carries a bracket springing from the lower part of the capital. Celestial, human and animal figures, almost in the round, have been sculptured out of these brackets. The potikā (corbel) above them has a massive overhanging kapōta (eave). In the alignment of the pillars, the eight in front of the shrine form a rectangle, while two more rows of three pillars run parallel at the sides, as in aisle and nave.

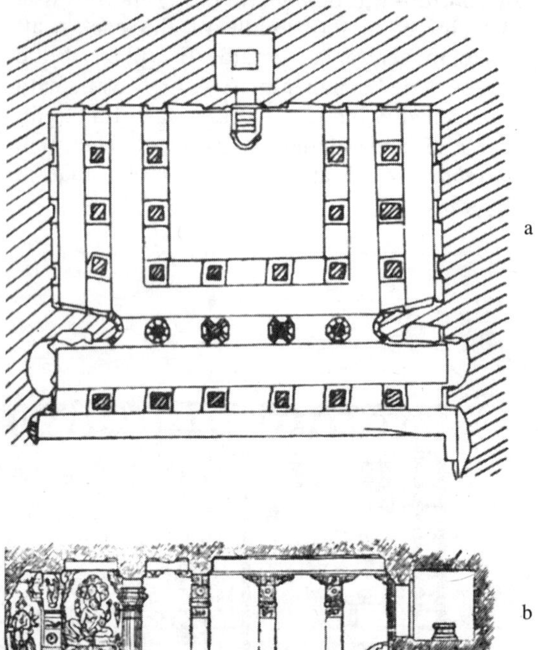


Fig. 93. Cave no. 3, Badami
a. ground plan, b. section.

The plan of *cave no*. 1 at Badami (Fig. 94) differs slightly from cave no. 3

Two rows of four pillars adorn the maṇḍapa. A pair of columns separates the mahā maṇḍapa from the mukha maṇḍapa. The four deep coffers on the ceiling of the latter, resulting from the intercrossing of the beams, are filled with relief sculptures. *Caves no*. 2 and 4 resemble cave no. 1. They differ only in a more varied sculptural representation.

Fig. 94. Cave no.1, Badami, ground plan.

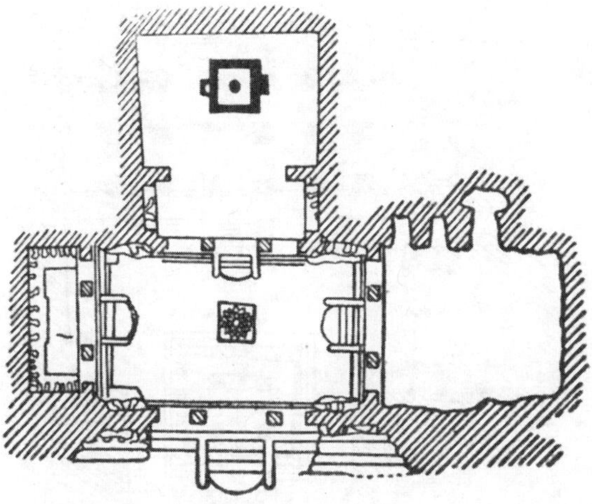

Fig. 95. Ravana-Phadi cave temple, Aihole, ground plan.

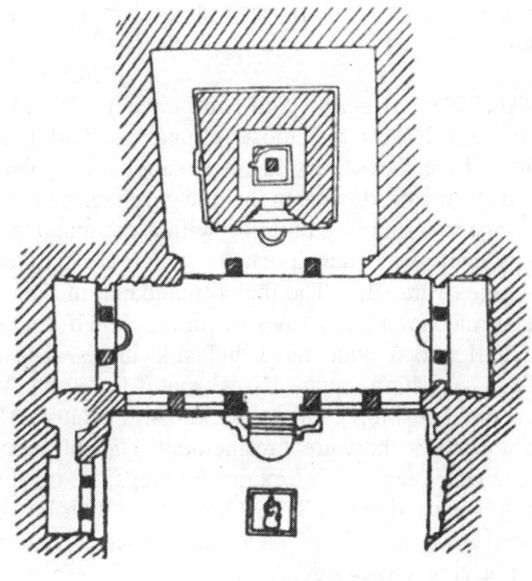

Fig. 96. Ramesvara cave temple no. 21, Ellora, ground plan.

*Aihole* has two rock-cut temples, one Jaina, and the other Brahmanical and known as the *Rāvaṇa-Phadi* (Fig. 95). Though smaller than those at Badami, their plan, design and sculpture are more elaborate. The main shrine of the Rāvaṇa-Phadi cave temple is almost the same size as the square maṇḍapa before it. Connecting the maṇḍapa to the shrine is an antarāla (antechamber). The ceiling of this antarāla has three large circular carvings: Viṣṇu on Garuḍa, a central lotus, and Indra on Airā- vata. Two more shrines are excavated on either side of the maṇḍapa, the one on the left dedicated to forms of Śiva, and the other on the right to the Saptamātrikas.

The Jaina temple at Aihole, partly rock-cut and partly structural, is larger than the one at Badami. It has a rectangular maṇḍapa in front, with a cella at the rear containing the image of Tīrthankara.

At Ellora the Brahmanical caves number seventeen in all (nos. 13 to 29). Of these the *Rāmeśvara* or *cave no.* 21 (Fig. 96), dedicated to Śiva, is the earliest. The courtyard in front has a naṇdi shrine. Four short pillars, resting on a wall sculpted with dwarfs, adorn the façade beyond. The plan includes a mukha maṇḍapa (portico), with a pair of cells excavated transversely at its extreme end. Cushion-type pillars adorn the mahā maṇḍapa (main hall). The temple, having a circumambulatory passage all around the garbhagriha, belongs to the

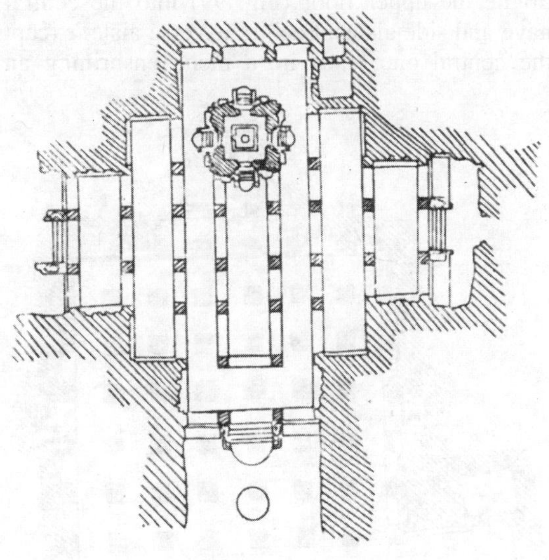

Fig. 97. Dhumarlena cave no. 29, Ellora, ground plan.

sāndhara type. Sculpture abounds in this temple.

The *Dhumarlena* or *Sitā Nani* cave no. 29 (Fig. 97) is the largest and most refined excavation at Ellora. Like the Rāmeśvara it is sāndhara in plan, but it shows an advance in that the garbhagriha is an entirely free-standing building within the maṇḍapa. Steps lead to its four doorways which are flanked by huge dvārapālas. The mahā maṇḍapa, in which the shrine stands, has rows of pillars which divide the hall into a wide nave and side aisles. These pillars have high square bases, round fluted shafts and fluted cushion capitals of exquisite beauty. All the sculptures show great refinement. The entrances to the cave, each with ornamental steps, lie on the south, west and north. Seated lions, with their heads turned inwards and one paw raised, seem to guard the portal on either side.

The *Dasāvatār* or *cave no*. 15 has a two- storeyed façade. Within its court is a naṇdi pavilion, with four pillars and flights of steps at the front and rear. The square pillars of the façade resemble the arrangement at Tin Tal. The fourteen pillars of the ground floor (Fig. 98) lead to the four cells cut into the rock at the far end. Six rows of seven pillars divide the upper floor (Fig. 99) into the central nave and side aisles. Each transverse aisle, except the central one, ends in a niche enshrining an image of a deity. The central aisle connects a pair of shrines, one at each end, containing lingas. Two pillars at the far end of the central aisle form a vestibule in front of the main shrine.

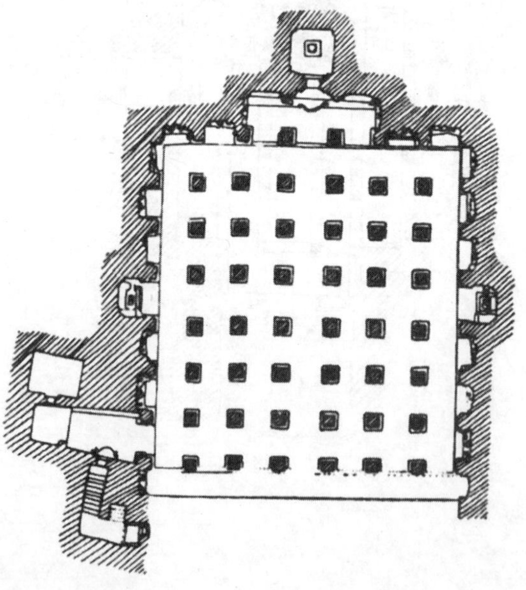

Fig. 98. Dasavatar cave no. 15, Ellora, upper floor plan.

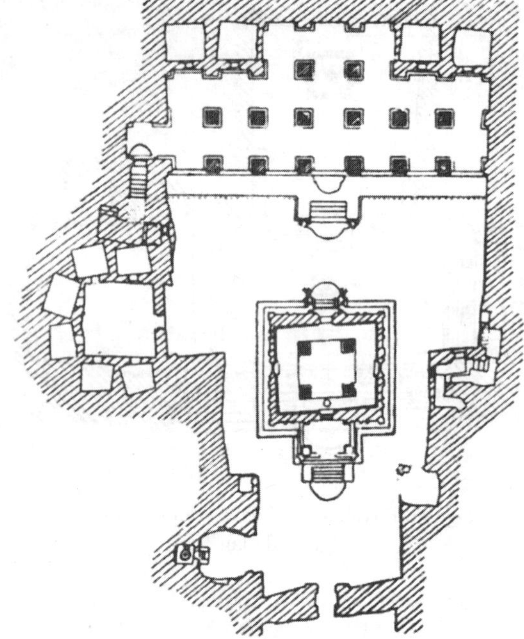

Fig. 99. Dasavatar cave no. 15, Ellora, ground floor plan.

The *Kailāśa* or *cave no*. 16 (Pl. 6.1; Fig. 100), a magnificent and unique monolithic temple complex, was excavated under the patronage of the Rashtrakuta king Krishna I. The method consisted initially in scooping three huge trenches out of the hillside at right angles, and continuing vertically through the rock till the required depth of the hill was reached. This outlined the shape of the rectangular courtyard, measuring 90 × 60 m. At the same time they isolated a mass of rock (60 × 30 × 30m.) that remained standing in the middle. On this rock they marked off the various parts of the temple to be carved out. Since the sculptor immediately followed the rock carver, each part of the *Kailāśa* was finished in its artistic detail.

Four components (Figs. 101,102) comprise the scheme of the *Kailāśa*. The actual body of the temple, the naṇdi shrine and the entrance gateway all three of which stand on a high platform, thus raising the temple to a higher

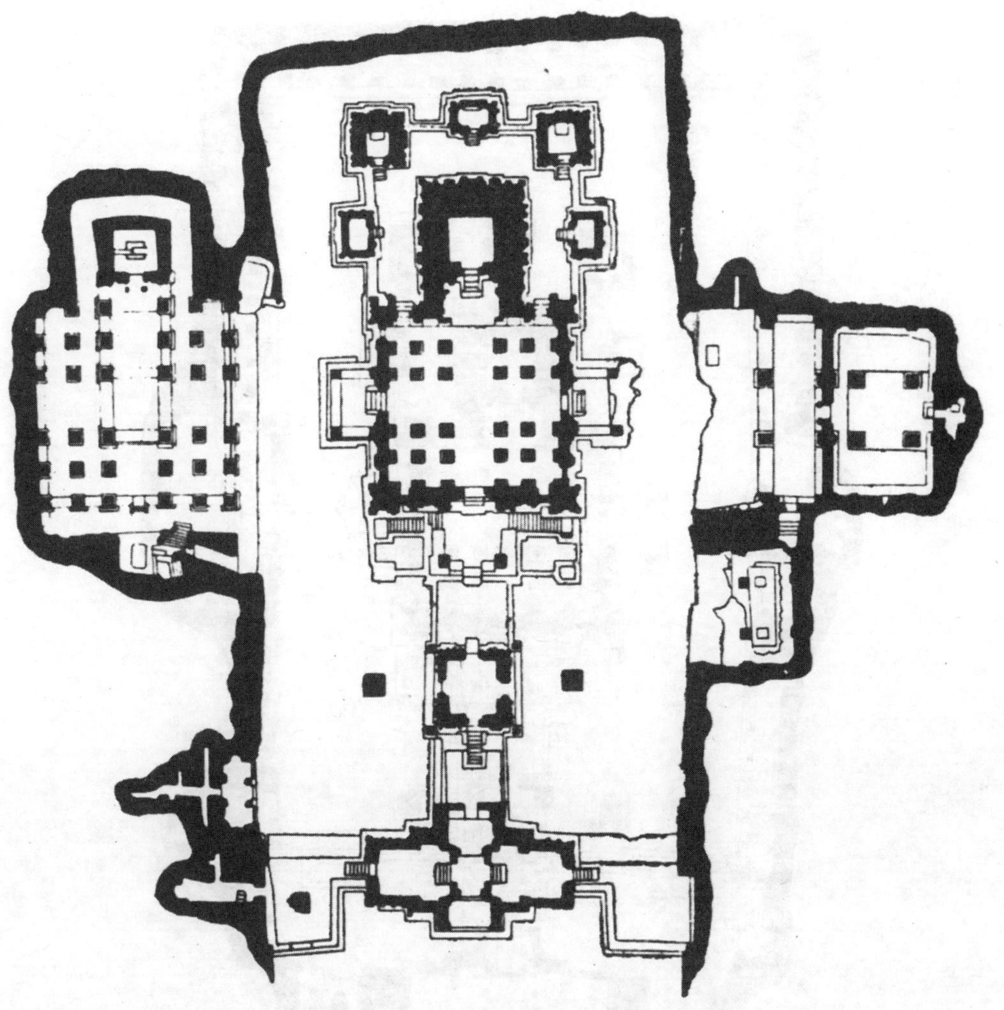

Fig. 100. Kailasa rock-cut temple, cave no. 16, Ellora, plan and upper storey of rock-cut side shrines.

level. The fourth component of the temple is in two parts: *a*) the ground floor cloisters and the surrounding courtyard as well as some minor excavations on both sides of the hill; *b*) on the level of the three temple components, the Lankeśvara and or other minor excavations hewn into both sides of the hill. The temple faces west. The entrance gateway, a double-storeyed oblong gopuram with a śalā śikhara (barrel vault), has an opening in the middle of its lower part to provide access to the court in front. This forecourt, at a lower level than the rest, has a pair of huge elephants on the north and south sides. The southern one is now considerably mutilated. A bridge connects the upper storey of the gopuram with the floor of the naṇḍi maṇḍapa. The lower part of the latter has no function except to serve as a high platform for the upper storey which houses the naṇḍi. A pair of dvajastambhas (monolithic columns), beautifully carved, flank the sides of the naṇḍi maṇḍapa.

The main part of the temple beyond consists of the sanctuary, with an antarāla and a

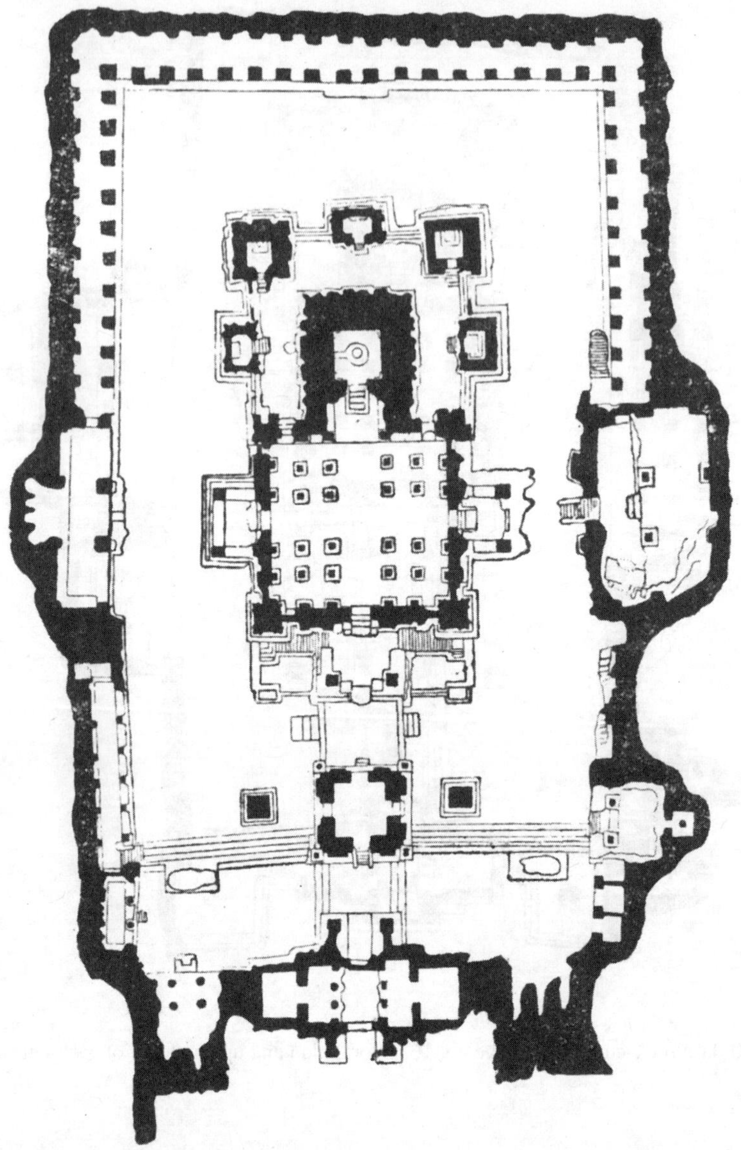

Fig. 101. Kailasa temple, Ellora, plan, with lower storey of side shrines and colonnade.

closed mahā maṇḍapa aligned axially in front. Boldly carved elephants, lions and a number of mythological figures appear to support the high, richly ornate platform. The mahā maṇḍapa has two pillared porches on its north and south sides. A large multi-petalled lotus upholds the base of the finial over the centre of its flat roof. Five detached sub-shrines jut out over the edge of the platform. A śukanāsikā (an arched forward projection from the lower storey of the vimāna, forming a roof over the vestibule before it) juts out in front over the antarāla of the four-storeyed vimāna—a characteristic feature of the Chalukya temples and of its lineal successors. Four bulls occupy the corners of the topmost storey which has no hāras. The

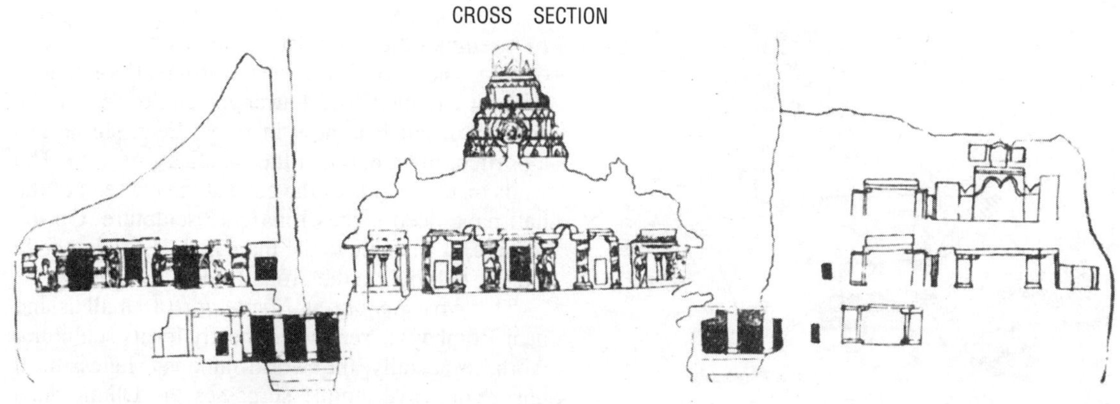


Fig. 102. Kailasa rock-cut temple, Ellora.

majority of the cells surrounding the temple complex have been left unfinished.

Of the six Jaina excavations (*nos*. 30 *to* 35) at *Ellora*, the most important are the Chota Kailāsa, the *Indra Sabhā* and the *Jagannāth Sabhā*. The *Chota Kailāsa* or *cave no*. 30 imitates in miniature its great Brahmanical namesake, but its śikhara looks quite stunted and remains unfinished.

The *Indra Sabhā* (*cave no*. 32) and *Jagannāth Sabhā* (*cave no*. 33), which stand close together, surpass the Chota Kailāsa. The *Indra Sabhā* excavation (the so-called "court of Indra") has a monolithic shrine in its forecourt, dedicated either to Riṣabanātha, the first of the twenty-four Tīrthankaras, or to Mahāvīra, the last. It belongs to the southern type. The shrine stands in the centre of the courtyard in front of the cave. The elaborate sculptures on three sides of the courtyard make it appear like a two-storeyed façade. A broad entablature, profusely carved, surmounts the first and second storey of the cave. The one over the upper storey represents a series of shrines with images of Tīrthankaras, while the lower one has elephants alternating with rampant lions, each figure set between a pair of pilasters. Only the upper storey (Fig. 103) was finished. It has a navaranga (nine-bayed maṇḍapa) preceded by a portico. A shrine projects at each of the extreme ends of the portico. The bay in the centre of the maṇḍapa is elevated for the Jaina chaumukh, i.e. a stele with four images back to back, the faces looking towards the cardinal points. A carved lotus adorns the ceiling. A pillared verandah gives entrance to the main hall of the unfinished lower storey, which remains blocked out for carving. A number of cells had been planned to open from the main hall. Beyond this hall stood a shrine containing a figure of the Mahāvīra on a lion throne.

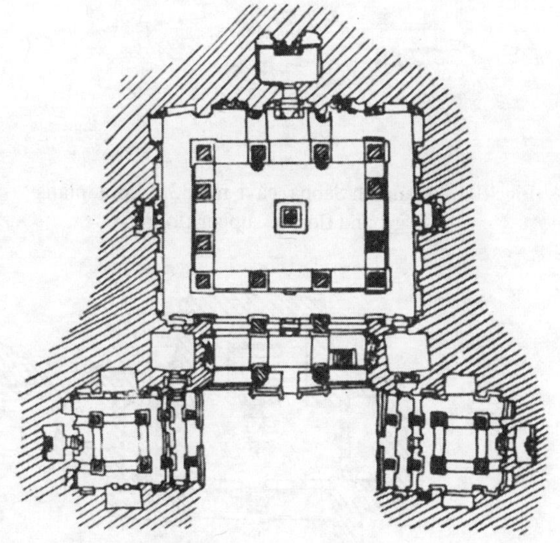

Fig. 103. Indra Sabha, cave no. 32, Ellora, upper hall plan.

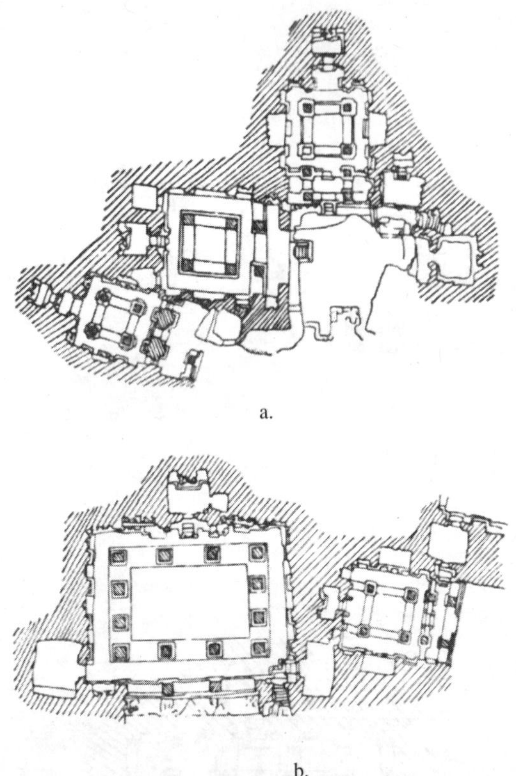

Fig. 104. Jagannath Sabha, cave no. 33, Ellora, plans: a. ground floor, b. upper floor.

The *Jagannāth Sabhā* or *cave no*. 33 (Fig. 104 *a b*) resembles the Indra Sabhā but lacks its regularity of plan. The three shrines on the ground floor, placed without any methodical arrangement, open into the courtyard which is now in ruins. Each shrine has a portico, main hall and the sanctuary beyond. The walls on either side of the cella at the rear end of the hall have deep niches for figure sculpture. On the outside, at an angle to the main hall, is another cella similar to those on the ground floor.

The *cave temple* at *Elephanta* (a small island near Bombay) is renowned mostly for its sculptural work, especially the world-famous Maheśamūrti bust. This cave temple surpasses the Dhumarlena in the refinement of its sculpture and beauty of its pillars. The temple faces east. On the western side, immediately behind the main shrine, an open courtyard has been formed by cutting away the rock. Like the Dhumariena cave temple at Ellora, this temple has a free-standing garbhagriha with the linga (Fig. 105). Massive dvārapālas guard the four entrances to the shrine. Twenty heavy pillars support the mahā maṇḍapa. The pillars have round fluted shafts, and the fluted cushion capitals have attained their most exquisite development. On its northern side, the mahā maṇḍapa has a projection, divided by pillars into the mukha and ardha maṇḍapa. The latter has a façade of two pillars and pilasters. The

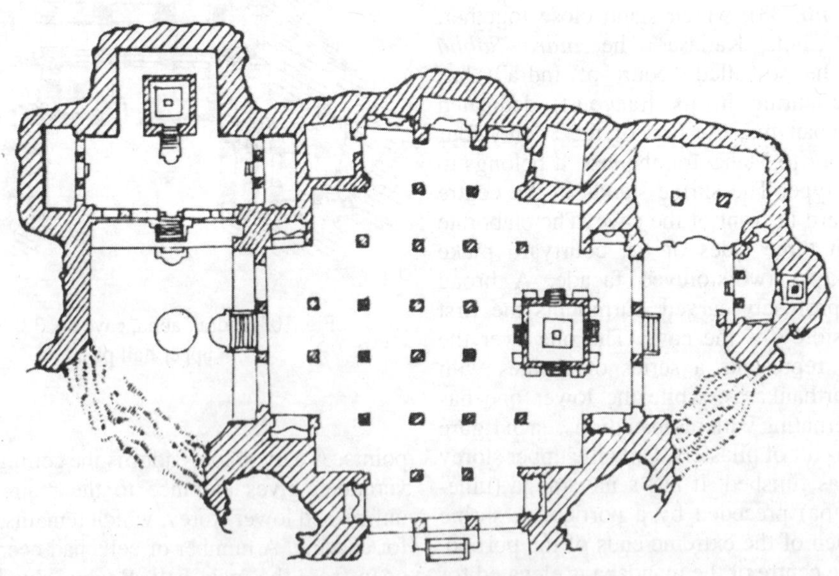

Fig. 105. Rock-cut cave temple, Elephanta.

former, immediately behind it, is a little longer. Opposite to this, on the southern side, is the enormous niche adorned with the Maheśamūrti. In the eastern court stands a circular pedestal, perhaps for a naṇdi. On the southern side of this court a temple dedicated to Durga was excavated.

The *Jogeśwari cave* at *Salsette*, also near Bombay, is much larger than the one at Elephanta though it resembles it very much in plan. Both have a mukha maṇḍapa and a shrine surrounded by a row of pillars. The maṇḍapa itself, on a lower level than the shrine, has entrances on the east, west and south—the latter comprising three door openings in a line. The main shrine in the centre has elaborately ornate overdoors, flanked as usual by dvāra pālas. The entrance in the centre of the longer eastern side, while not as imposing as a gopuram, is larger than an ordinary doorway. On either side of the entrance stand a pair of maṇḍapas, one of them housing an image of Gaṇeśa. Like the great Kailāśa at Ellora, this temple was excavated by initially trenching all around a rectangular mass of rock and isolating it.

The *Bhokardan cave* near *Aurangabad* possesses an unusual plan, with five shrines instead of one at the rear of the maṇḍapa, each shrine having an independent entrance. The maṇḍapa is divided into the mukha and ardha maṇḍapa, the former serving as entrance to the temple. Figure sculpture adorns the semicircular walls of the maṇḍapa.

The Great Pallavas of Kanchi rose to power in the latter half of the sixth century. Their coming marks an important epoch in the history of South Indian architecture. Politically and geographically they dominated the southern region continuously until the ninth century A.D.

Mahendravarman I (c. 580–630 A.D.) inherited from his father Simha Viṣṇu a vast empire extending from the river Pennar as far as the Kaveri. To him is attributed the initiation of rock-cut architecture in the south. Unlike the Chalukyas, the Pallavas did not use soft sandstone but hard rock such as granite, gneiss and basalt because sandstone cliffs were not available and hard rock would be more durable.

In the history of rock-cut architecture, the only other examples of excavations out of hard stone are the eight Ājīvika caves in the Barabar, Nagarjuni and Sitamarhi hills in Bihar, commissioned by Ashoka and his grandson Dasa-ratha. After a span of almost a thousand years, the Pallavas started once more to hew into hard rock as Ashoka had done, but they did not give it a high polish. This distinguishes Pallava art and architecture from its contemporaries.

This use of hard rock imposed considerable limitations on the size of the caves as well as on the sculpture, which consists only of large-size figures in relief—a marked contrast to the Chalukya caves of that time which were larger and more elaborately carved.

The first rock-cut architecture of Mahendravarman I was the *Lakṣitāyatana Trimūrti cave temple* at *Mandagapattu*, hewn out of granite. The inscription in this cave states: "This brickless, timberless, metalless and mortarless abode of Laksita was caused to be made by King Vicitracitta for Brahma, Iśvara and Viṣṇu.*

King Mahendra caused nine more temples, simllar to the *Lakṣitāyatana cave temple* at *Mandagapattu*, to be excavated. They are:

- the *Pañcha Pāṇḍava cave* at *Pallavaram*
- the *Rudravaliśvaram* or *cave temple no.* 2 at *Mamandur*
- the *Kal maṇḍapam* at *Kuranganilmuttam*
- the *Vasamteśvara* or the larger cave temple at *Vallarn*
- the *Mahendra Viṣṇugriha* at *Mahendravadi*
- the *Viṣṇu cave temple* at *Mamandu*
- the *Lalitāṅkura Pallavesvara griha* (upper cave) at *Tiruchirapalli*
- the *Śatrumalleśvarālaya* at *Dalvanur*
- and the *Avinabhājana Pallaveśvara griha* at *Siyamangalam*

These cave temples imitated the interiors of structural buildings made out of more perishable materials like wood. The maṇḍapa is divided into the mukha and ardha maṇḍapa. A row of equally-spaced pillars (a Chalukya system), four, six, or eight in number, and terminating with pilasters at both ends, serves as a façade, in front of the mukha maṇḍapa. A similar arrangement of the pillars behind, parallel to the façade, comprises the ardha maṇḍapa. If no pillars separate the sections, then varying floor levels or celling heights indicate the demarcation. The massive pillars are divided into three sections (Fig. 106): square sadurams at the top and bottom, with an octagonal kaṭṭu in the middle. Sometimes the profile of the huge potikā (corbel) above the pillars resembles a series of rolls (taranga),

*The Sanskrit inscription reads:
Etad—an-istakam-a-druma (m-a-l-o)
ham-a-sudham (Vicitrachi) ttena
nirmrnapitam-nripe (na) Brahma-E-
svara-Visnu-Laks it ayatanam.

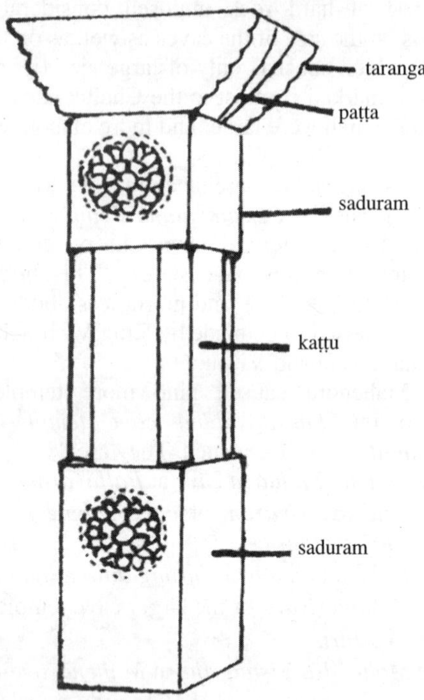


Fig. 106. Mahendra style pillar.

Fig. 107. LakSitayatana cave temple, Mandagapattu, first example of a prastara: the primitive kapota consists of a straight line cut into the rock.

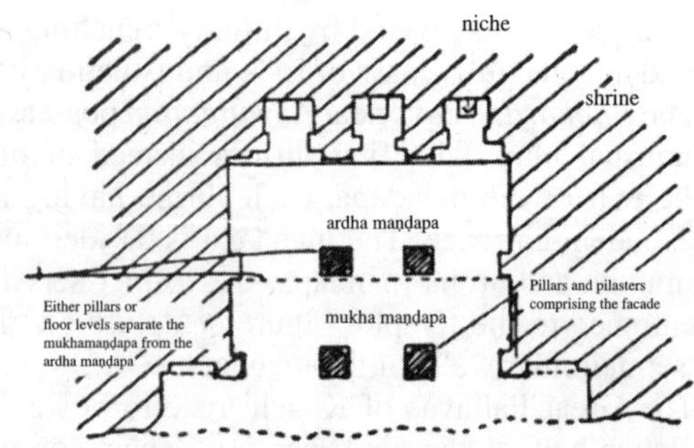


Fig. 108. Laksitayatana cave temple, Mandagapattu, ground plan.

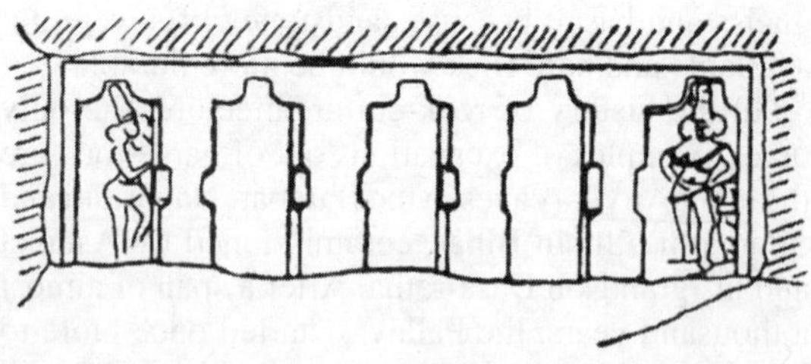

Fig. 109. Laksitayatana cave temple, Mandagapattu, facade.

with a paṭṭa (flat median band) running along the centre of the taranga. Ornamentations like lotus medallions often decorate the square sadurams of the pillars. The prastāra (entablature) is not yet developed. The kapōta (cornice) consists of a straight line cut into the rock (Fig. 107). In the early Mahendra style cave temples the dvārapāla figures stood guard at either end of the façade, while in the later ones they also flanked both sides of the shrine, as in the Viṣṇu cave temple at Mamandur, the Lalitāṅkura-Pallaveśvara griha (upper cave) at Tiruchirapalli, the Śatrumalleśvarālaya cave temple at Dalvanur, and the Avanibhājana Pallaveśvara griha cave tempie at Siyaman- galam.

The *LakSitayatana cave temple* which, as mentioned earlier, bears an inscription of King Mahendravarman I, faces east. Its plan (Fig. 108) includes an ardha and mukha maṇḍapa separated by the lower floor level of the latter, as well as by a row of two pillars and pilasters. The façade (Fig. 109) too has a line of pillars and pilasters. Beyond them, on either side, a pair of recesses were hewn out for dvārapālas. The potikā (corbels) have a curved profile, but without any taranga ornamentation. Plain rectangular niches in the back wall of the ardha maṇḍapa occupy the space between four pilasters. Sockets at the bottom of these niches probably served as receptacles for the bas-relief panels of Brahma, Viṣṇu and Śiva, which are now absent. Traces of thick plaster on the back wall indicate that the objects of worship were originally painted and that the bas-relief panels came later. Except for the dvārapāla figures on the façade, the absence of any other sculpture shows the early date of the temple.

The *Pañcha Pāṇḍava cave temple* at *Pallavaram* (Fig. 110), later converted into a dargah (Muslim tomb), differs by being oblong in plan. The five shrine cellas on the back wall of the ardha maṇḍapa face south—somewhat unusual for a Hindu cave temple. The central one, which projects slightly more than the rest, has a low adiṣṭ hāna. Originally it had a flight of three steps, with a chandraśila (moonstone) in front of it.

The *Rudravailśvaram* at *Mamandur* has a similar plan (Fig. 1ll), but only three shrine cellas, each with a moulded adiṣṭhāna and a short flight of steps with curved parapets. According to the inscription, the central shrine was dedicated to Śiva, the other two to Brahma and Viṣṇu.

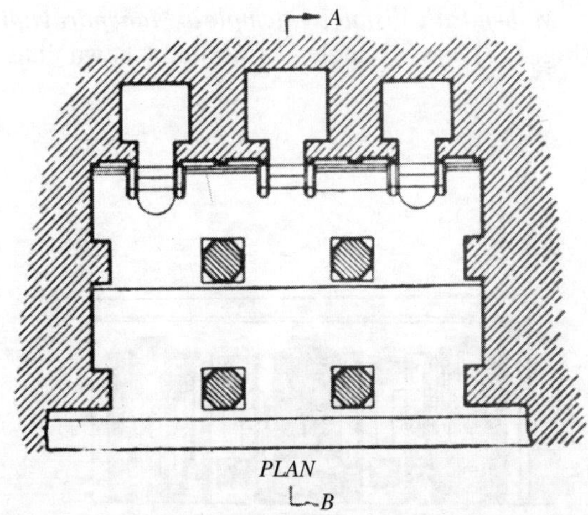


Fig. 111. Rudravalisvaram cave temple no. 2, Mamandur.

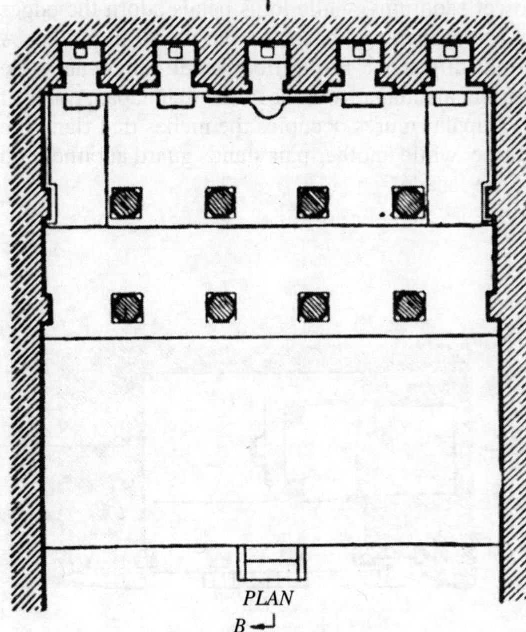


Fig. 110. Panchapandava cave temple, Pallavaram.

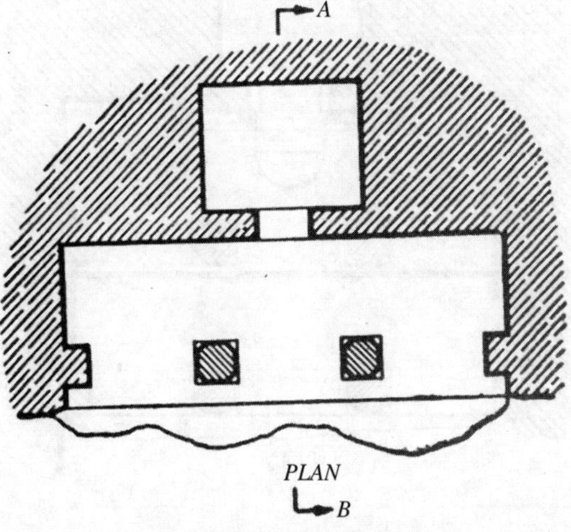


Fig. 112. Vasantesvara cave temple no. 1, Vallam.

The *Vasanteśvara*, the largest of the group at *Vallam*, is a typical example of the Mahendra style (Fig. 112). The plan includes only an oblong ardha maṇḍapa, and a cubical cella hewn into the rear wall at a slightly higher level than the ardha maṇḍapa. The two niches on either side of the shrine contain dvārapālas in profile. The massive potikā, no longer angular, has assumed a curved profile. The façade pillars have three inscriptions on the front.

*Mahendra's Viṣṇu cave temple at Mahendravadi* (Fig. 113) has a single shrine cella hewn into the rear wall of the ardha maṇḍapa. A row of two pillars and pilasters as well as a slightly higher floor level of the ardha maṇḍapa separate the mukha and ardha maṇḍapa. A lotus medallion adorns each of the four upper sides of the sadurams of the façade pillars but only three sides of the lower sadurams; while the inner row of pillars lack this ornamentation altogether. A pair of shallow niches, containing the dvārapālas in identical poses, flank the shrine entrances. Remains of painting on the back wall of the shrine show that the deity was originally painted.

Since the *Śatrumalla cave temple* at *Dalvanur* (Fig. 114) faces north, the shrine is cut into the western side of the maṇḍapa in order to face east. It stands on a roughly-moulded adisṭhāna, with a square-pillared porch in front, forming an antarāla maṇḍapa. A chandraśila (moonstone) is cut in the floor before it. The façade is composed of two intricately ornamented pillars and pilasters. Its well-finished prastāra (entablature) with a curved kapōta adorned with five kūdu arches (Fig. 115) is the first of its kind. An elaborate makara toraṇa (Fig. 116), spanning the centre of the façade, adds beauty to this picturesquely-set cave temple. Two flights of four steps, carved laterally, give entrance to the mukha maṇḍapa. Full-blown lotus medallions, in very high relief, decorate all the faces of the upper and lower sadurams, while lotus petals adorn the edges of the projecting abacus on the top of the pillar. A slight difference in the floor level demarcates, the mukha maṇḍapa from the ardha maṇḍapa. A pair of dvārapāla figures occupies the niches that flank the shrine, while another pair stands guard at either end of the façade.

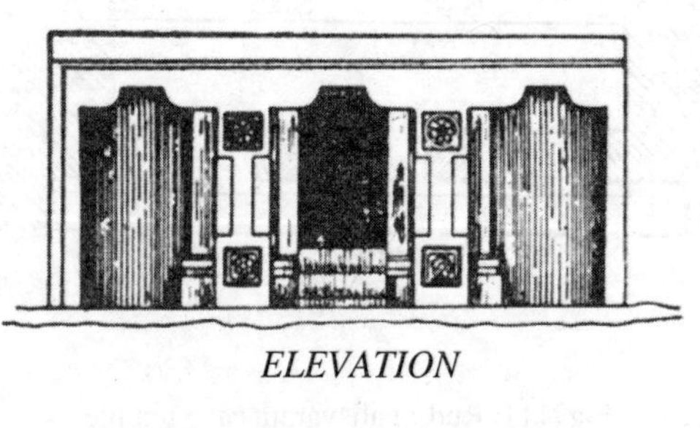


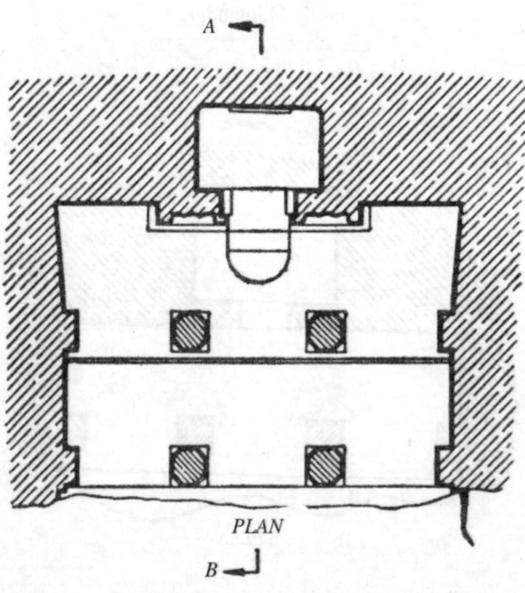


Fig. 113. Mahendra's Visnu cave temple, Mahendravadi.

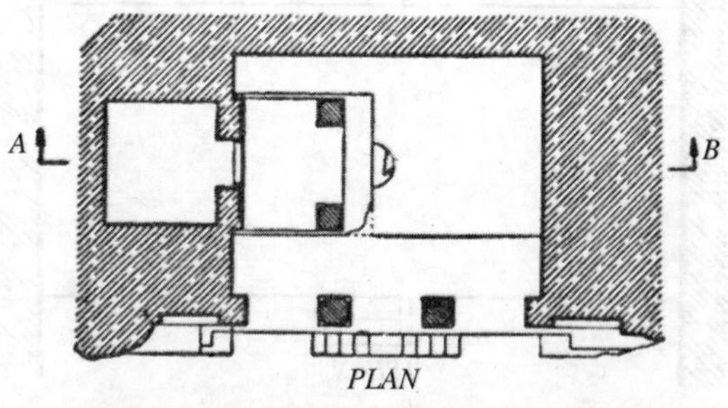


Fig. 114. Satrumalla's cave temple, Dalavanur, plan.

Fig. 115. Satrumalla's cave temple, Dalavanur, further development of the prastara: a curved kapota with kudu arches.

Under the patronage of the successors of Mahendravarman I, namely Narasimhavarman I Mamalla, Paramesvaravarman I, and Narasimhavarman II Rajasimha, a series of cave temples were excavated. Since they follow Mahendra's style rather closely, they are designated as belonging to the Post-Mahendra style. They differ only in a few aspects (Fig. 117). While the general layout of the cave temple remains unchanged in having a mukha and ardha maṇḍapa with a shrine behind, the latter projects more into the ardha maṇḍapa. The pillars are rectangular, tall and more slender. Two pillars and pilasters, with wider spaces between them, form the façade. The Sōmāskanda relief panel begins to make its appearance.

Fig. 116. Satrumalla's cave temple, Dalavanur, makara torana on the façade.

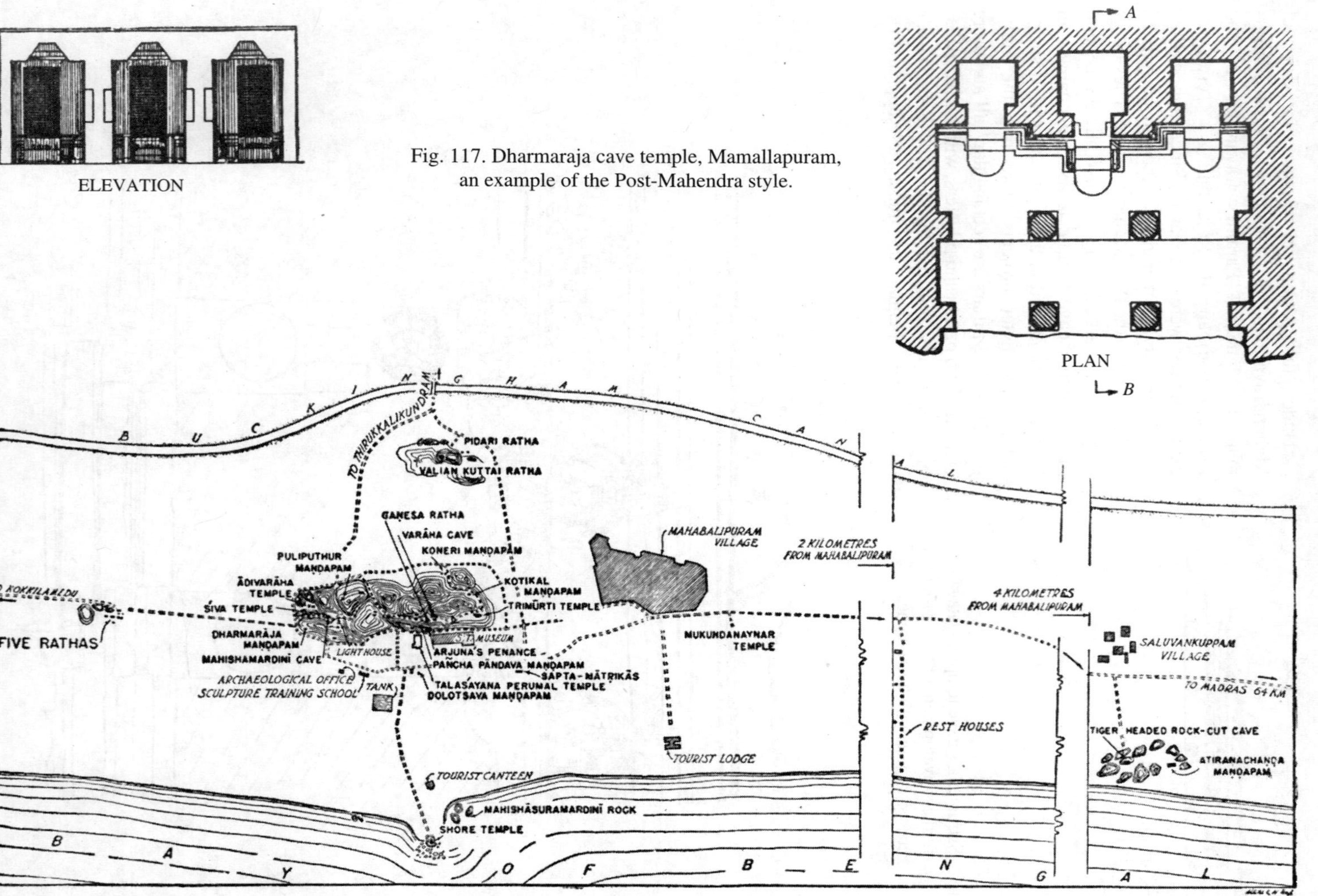


Fig. 117. Dharmaraja cave temple, Mamallapuram, an example of the Post-Mahendra style.

Fig. 118. Mamallapuram, site plan.

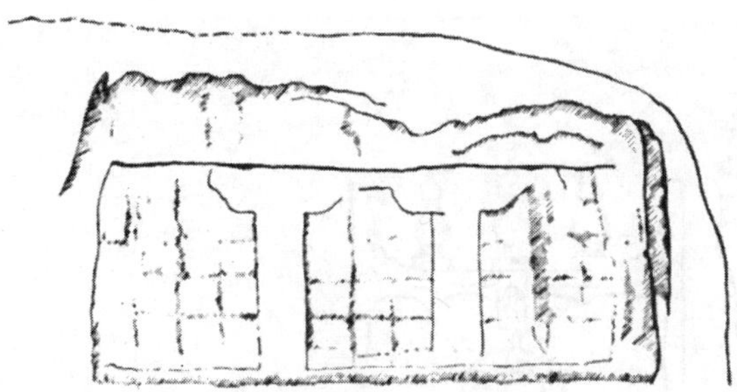

Fig. 119. Mamallapuram, technique of excavating a cave temple.

Fig. 120. Mamallapuram, an unfinished ratha, showing the process of excavation.

Hitherto only traditional paintings on stucco relief, or carved wooden panels, covered the rear wall of the sanctuary.

The Post-Mahendra cave temples include:

the *Orukal maṇḍapam* at *Tirukkalukunram*
the *Koṭikal maṇḍapam* at *Mamallapuram*
the *Narasimha cave temple* at *Singaperumal Kovil*
the *Ranganātha cave temple* at *Singavaram*
the *Dharmarāja maṇḍapam* at *Mamallapuram*
and the *Atiraṇchanda maṇḍapam* at *Saluvankuppam*

Narasimhavarman I Mamalla (630–668), the successor of Mahendravarman, built the new coastal town 51 kms south of Madras, named after him as Mamallapuram (Fig. 118). He realised the advantage of naval power, and soon had emissaries sent to countries further east, like Cambodia, Java, Borneo and Sumatra, where Indians settled and introduced Indian culture. Contacts with Sri Lanka influenced its culture too. In architecture, he continued the tradition of rock-cut temples (Fig. 119) but under his patronage they became more elaborate. Moreover, he introduced a completely novel method of hewing out temples —the monolithic vimānas or rathas, all at Mamallapuram (Fig. 120).

The Mamalla style cave temples display many changes in the design of the interior, such as the introduction of more profuse relief sculpture and the development of the pillars, as well as the fuller representation of the façades.

The entablature on the façade of the maṇḍapa reached full development in the Mamalla style. The kapōta has kūdu motifs (horseshoe arches) (Fig. 121). Above it runs a line of śālās

Fig. 121. Development of the kudu:

a. origin, sun window of chaitya;
b. Pallava (7th – 8th C. A.D.);
c. Chola (11th C.);
d. Pandya (13th C.);
e. Vijayanagar (15th C.);
f. Madurai (18th C.).

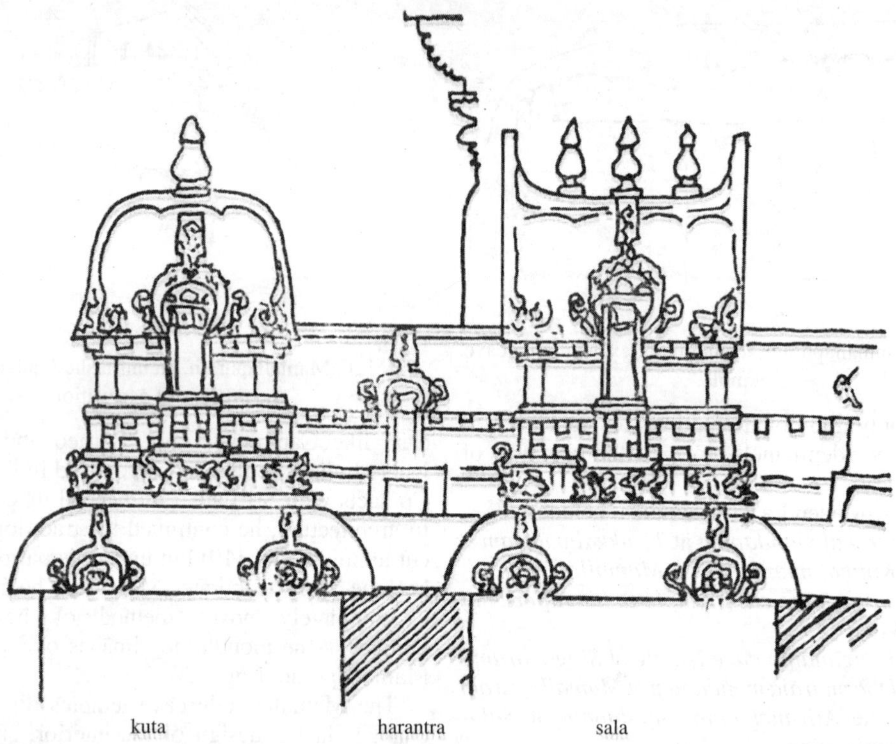


Fig. 124. hara, with Fig. 123 kuta, Fig. 122 sala, and with harantara in between the two.

(diminutive shrines), oblong in plan with a barrel-vaulted roof (Fig. 122). In later temples, this row of śālās terminates at either end with kūtas (miniature shrines), square in plan with a domical roof (Fig. 123). The whole, called hāra (Fig. 124), has hārāntaras (interconnecting cloisters). The adiṣṭhāna (basement) of the cave façade is often moulded.

The pillars derive from wooden prototypes (Fig. 148). They are taller and more slender. In section they are circular, octagonal or fluted. Their bases resemble crouching vyālas (lions). The shaft of the pillar has a decoration of mālāsthāna (loops of garlands), above which is a broad band of padmabandha (lotus petals) which demarcates the shaft from the capital. The latter has various carved members, namely kalaśa (vase), tāḍi (shaped like a saucer), kumbha (bulbous member), pālī (resembling a lotus but without any scalloped petals), and the phalaka (abacus). On the phalaka rests the potikā (corbel), circular at the edges with taranga ornamentation, and a paṭṭa (flat median band).

The number of shrines varies from one to five. They project boldly into the ardha maṇḍapa. The elevation of the shrine is in three angas (parts), namely the adiṣṭhāna (basement), the kudya stambhas (pilasters) with their capitals, and the prastāra (entablature) with its developed kapōta decorated with kūdu arch motifs. The shrine tends to be more centrally placed and has a sopāna (staircase) in front. The sanctuary has no figure sculpture but a rock-cut platform for stucco relief or shallow square sockets at the appropriate height in order to fix carved wooden plaques.

Mamalla style cave temples, all at Mamallapuram, and in varying stages of completion, include:

- the *Kōneri maṇḍapam,*
- the *Mahiṣamardini or Yamapuri maṇḍapam*
- the *unfinished cave temple next to the Kōneri maṇḍapam,*
- the *Pañchapāṇḍava maṇḍapam,*
- the *Adivarāha cave temple,*
- the *Mahāvarāha Viṣnugriha,*
- the *Rāmānuja maṇḍapam,*

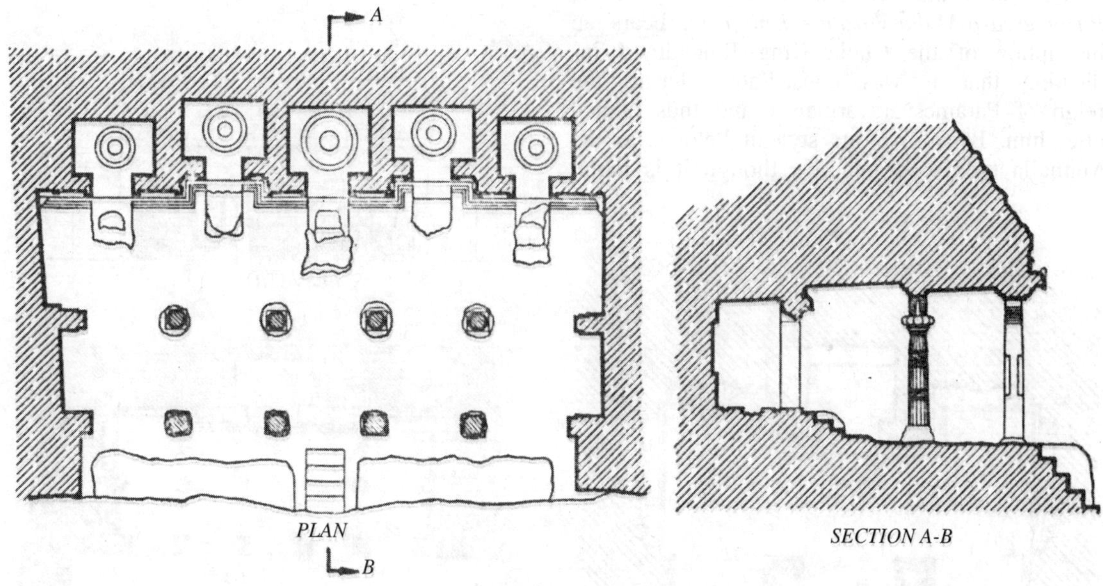


Fig. 125. Koneri mandapam, Mamallapuram.

The earliest of the series, the *Kōneri maṇḍapam* (Fig. 125), dedicated to Śiva, combines the features of both the Mahendra and Mamalla styles. It has five shrines (Fig. 126).

The *Varāha maṇḍapa* (Fig. 127) faces west. It consists of the maṇḍapa in front, and a square shrine behind projecting boldly into the maṇḍapa. Dvārapālas, in half profile, occupy the niches on either side. The shrine rests on a well-moulded adiṣṭhāna, with a flight of steps cut into the middie. Their curved parapets seem to issue from the mouths of vyālas. Kūdu arches with human heads adorn the kapōta above the shrine, while below it geese turn their heads in various directions. The façade consists of two pillars and pilasters, with characteristic vyālas (lion socles) resting on well-moulded oma (bases). The potikās have taranga ornamentations, and the kapōta is decorated with six kūdu arches, the insides of which have lotus ornamentations instead of the usual human heads.

The *Mahiṣamardini* or *Yamapuri cave* (Fig. 128) is a three-shrined Śaiva temple facing east. Its interior shows more finish than the exterior. The boldly-projected central shrine contains a large and slightly later Sūmāskanda panel. A pair of dvārapālas in niches flank the entrance to the shrine. A porch, resting on a well-moulded adiṣṭhāna, projects far out from the central shrine. Two pillars, with vyāla bases and circular shafts and capitals, support its flat roof. Five kūdu motifs adorn the well- finished kapōta. The façade, consisting of four pillars and two pilasters, has been left unfinished. The kūdus on the kapōta have been no more than indicated, while the hāra elements above it are merely blocked out. The Mahiṣāsuramardini, the best-sculptured panel in the Pallava tradition, occupies the northern wall of the maṇḍapa.

Fig. 126. Koneri maṇḍapam, Mamallapuram, showing the almost full development of the kapota.

The *Adivarāha cave temple* (Fig. 129), or the *Parameśvara-Mahā-Varāha-Viṣṇugriha*, bears an inscription of the Chola King Rajendra I indicating that it was consecrated during the reign of Paramesvaravarman I and thus named after him. Because of its style it belongs to the Mamalla type cave temples, though it is much

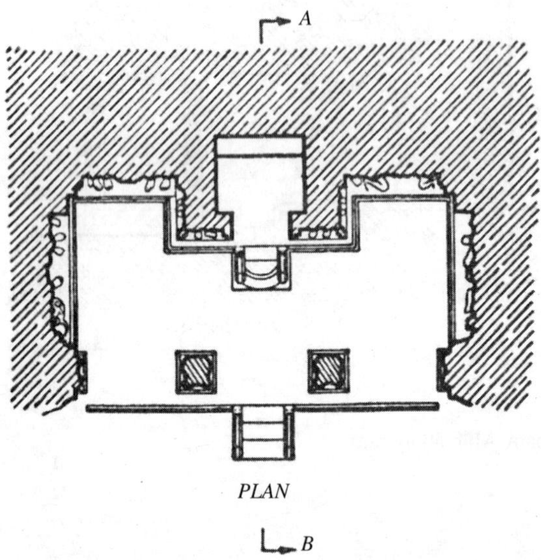


Fig, 127. Varaha mandapam, Mamallapuram.

ELEVATION

A

PLAN

A

Fig. 129. Adivaraha cave temple, Mamallapuram.

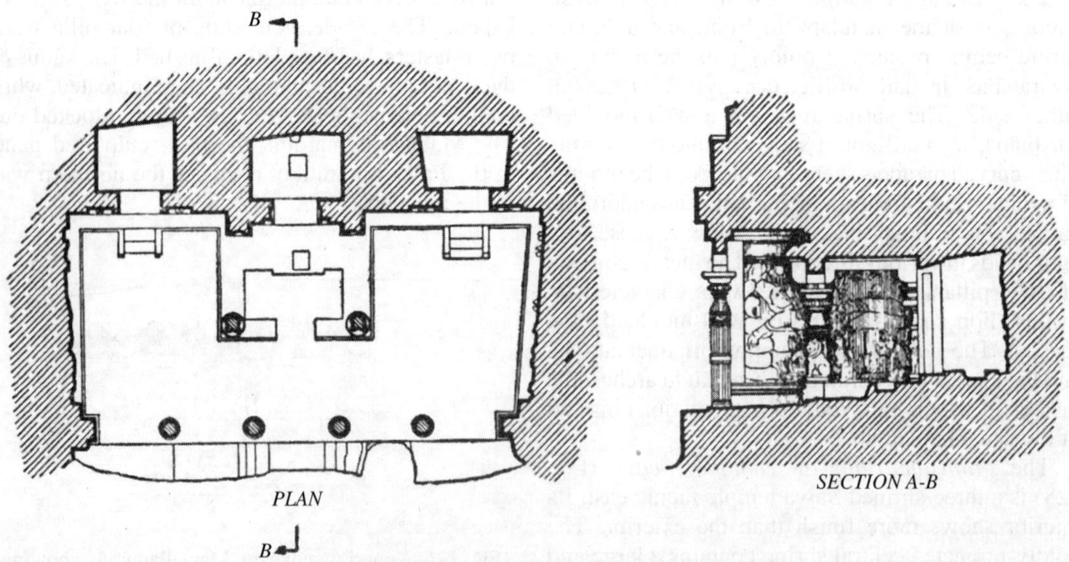


Fig. 128. Mahisamardini or Yamapuri mandapam, Mamallapuram.

more elaborate and shows advanced features. The plan consists of an oblong maṇḍapa and shrine facing West. Two rows of pillars demarcate the maṇḍapa into the mahā maṇḍapa in front and the ardha maṇḍapa before the shrine. The oblong projecting shrine stands on a well-moulded adiṣthāna. The sanctuary, flanked by dvārapālas on the exterior, contains a bas-relief panel of Varāha as Bhūvarāha or Ādivarāha. The other maṇḍapa walls bear relief panels. Crouching vyālas (lions) on an oblong oma (base) adorn the four pillars and two pilasters of the façade. While the vyālas of the pillars look straight ahead, those of the pilasters are in profile, facing north-south. The apex of the shaft has a row of padmabandha (lotus petals), with mālāsthāna (looped strings of beads and pearls) below. The capital consists of a kalaśa (vase), tāḍi (saucer-shaped member), kaṇṭha (necking), kumbha (bulbous member). The potikā, decorated with ten kūdu arch motifs, upholds five śālās connected by hārāntara (lengths of cloister) .

Narasimha Varman Mamalla continued to excavate cave temples, but he went one step further in the evolution of rock-cut architecture by initiating the carving of free-standing monolithic vimānas—or rathas, as they are popularly called. These were chiselled out of the hard granite and gneiss boulders at Mamallapuram. As with the cave temples, the stonecutters imitated contemporary brick and timber structures. Not only did they carve out the superstructure but all the parts of the temple from the finial to the base. Then a small antarāla (vestibule) or ardha maṇḍapa was cut in front of it. They had to choose suitable rocks and to reduce them to manageable proportions by cutting away the extraneous material, beginning at the top and working down. The necessary horizontal portions served at the same time as footing for the workmen, since no scaffolding was employed. As the work proceeded they used the rock not yet cut as footing. At the top they could not shape the stūpi (finial) first, since the ritual of temple building prescribed that the stūpi could be installed only at the consecration of the finished temple during the kumbhābhishekam ceremony. They may have left the top portion of the rock to form the stūpi later or they carved it separately and put it into position at the consecration ceremony.

The simplest form of the monolithic vimāna had six parts in its vertical direction from base to top, namely the adiṣthāna (basement), pāda (pillar) and bhitti (wall), prastāra (entablature), grīva (clerestory), śikhara (ultimate roof- covering over the grīva), and the stūpi (finial) crowning the top of the śikhara. This simple shadanga (six-sided) structure, known as an alpavimāna, is ekatala (single-storeyed). For a dvitala (two-storeyed) vimāna, a new element called hāra was inserted between the prastāra (entablature) and the grīva (clerestory). This hāra or tier of miniature shrines surrounding each tala (storey) is the most characteristic feature of the Southern vimāna. Of the three types of hāra, the kūta or karṇakūṭa (Fig. 123), placed at the corners, is square with a domical roof and a single stūpi (finial); the śalā (Fig. 122), between the kūtas, is oblong with a barrel vaulted roof crowned by a row of stūpis (finials) on the ridge; and the nida or panjara (apsidal-ended) which appear between śālās, or kūtas and śālās.*

The hārāntara (a sort of balustrade simulating cloisters) acts as a connecting link between the hāra. A kṣuḍranāsikā (arched kūdu motif on a pilaster) projects from the middle of the hārāntara.

Besides the ekatala and dvitala (single- and double-storeyed) vimānas, there are also tritala and chatushtala (three- and four-storeyed) vimānas. These are known as jāti vimānas. Larger ones with panchatala (five storeys) or even more—sometimes reaching sixteen—are designated as mukya vimānas in the Śilpa texts. Each time a new storey was added, another hāra had to be inserted between the prastāra (entablature) and the grīva (clerestory).

Each superimposed tala (storey) must necessarily be smaller than the lower one. In this way the vimāna resembles a stepped pyramid, each step composed of a hārmya (back wall) and prastāra (entablature) smaller than the one before. Thus the vimāna is a one- or multi- storeyed building of diminishing size. An understanding of this gives a clearer conception of the somewhat confused impression that one gets on seeing a many-storeyed vimāna especially when crowded with sculpture.

In the southern architectural canons, vimānas are classified according to their shape from base to finial: Nagara if four-sided, square or oblong; Dravida if six or eight-sided; Vesara if circular, ellipsoidal or apsidal. Pure types, however, are rarely found; in most cases we

* At Mamallapuram the nida or panjara hara appear only on the first tala of the Dharmaraja ratha and the second tala of the Nakula-Sahadeva ratha.

meet with a mixed variety. If the body of the vimāna differs from the grīva śikhara in plan, it is usually accepted that the plan of the latter is taken into consideration for classification.

There are nine monolithic vimānas, popularly known as rathas, all at Mamallapuram, and named after the Pandavas of the Mahabharata:

in the north-west: Valayankuttai ratha
Northern Pidari ratha
Southern Pidari ratha

in the south: Draupadi ratha
Arjuna ratha
Bhima ratha
Dharmarāja ratha
Nakula-Sahadeva ratha

in the north: Gaṇesha ratha

All these represent the different types of vimānas. Besides these there are small replicas of vimānas in bas-reliefs, as well as the façade of the Trimūrti cave temple which is a full-scale example. Taken all together—the nine

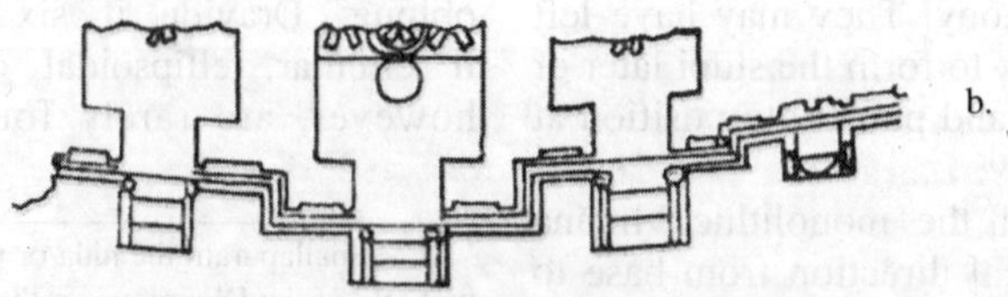


Fig. 130. Trimurti cave temple, Mamallapuram, a. frcade, b. ground plan.

monolithic vimānas, the eight relief representations, and the Trimūrti cave façade—they constitute the richest variety of all vimāna forms, and all in the same place, Mamallapuram. As stone copies of contemporary wood and brick vimānas, they preserve not only the main types and forms but even the minute details of wood and metal work. They also exemplify the rules contained in the Āgama, Śilpa and Vastu Śāstras, where all the details were laid down. These stone buildings became models for the architects of later times, and they constitute the most important dossiers for the study of South Indian architecture.

The *Trimūrti cave temple* (Fig. 130) at Mamallapuram has only the façade of the vimāna without the maṇḍapa in front. Each of its three shrines, dedicated to Śiva, Viṣṇu and Brahma Sāsta, is a finished unit, consisting of the adiṣṭhāna with a flight of steps in front, an excavated shrine, and a prastāra (architrave) on top. Its kapōta is decorated with kūdu arch motifs, with a row of hāras over it. No superstructure appears above, as the second tala behind the hāra has been reached. Dvārapālas flank each of the shrine entrances. However, further elaboration of the talas was not attempted in the three because the top of the rock had already been attained.

On the left side of the *Arjuna's Penance* relief appears a small *bas-relief* model of an ekatala (single-storeyed) vimāna belonging to the Nagara order (Fig. 131). It has all the six angas (parts): the adiṣṭhāna (basement), bhitti and pāda (wall and pillars), prastāra (architrave), grīva (clerestory), śikhara and stūpi (finial).

The bas-reliefs on either side of the façade of the *Rāmānuja maṇḍapam* show a vimāna (Fig. 132) of similar character as the bas-relief on Arjuna's Penance. The *relief* on top of the *Nakula-Sahadeva ratha* façade (Fig. 133) portrays a model of the Dravidian order, hexagonal in plan from base to finial. Those of the *Bhima* (Fig. 134) and *Gaṇeśa rathas* illustrate the Vesara order, with circular grīva and śikhara, though over a square body. The former is a simple ekatala vimāna.

At the southern end of Mamallapuram stand the *Draupadi, Arjuna, Bhima, Dharmarāja* and *Nakula-Sahadeva rathas* (Pl. 5. 1). The first four, in axial alignment, have been carved out of a section of a single whale-back rock facing southwest, while the Nakula-Sahadeva ratha was formed out of a smaller rock near the Bhima ratha. The Draupadi and Arjuna rathas stand on a common platform.

The small *Draupadi ratha* (Fig. 135), facing west and dedicated to Durga, is the simplest and most elegant of the group. Shaped like a kūtaghara (hut), it is very much a stone model of the wooden original. In its elevation it shows only four of its six angas (parts), namely the adiṣṭhāna, the pāda and bhitti, the śikhara and the stūpi. It lacks an ardha maṇḍapa in front. On its four lower corners the domical śikhara has carved scroll ornamentations (Fig. 136) very similar to embossed metal designs. A vaseshaped finial, made separately and now placed in front of the ratha, at one time crowned the śikhara. Dvārapālikas (female counterparts of the dvārapālas) stand in niches on either side of the entrance, which is surmounted by a makara toraṇa. Similar makara toraṇas adorn the middle of the other three exterior sides. While having its own adiṣṭhāna, the Draupadi ratha stands on the same upapitha (platform) as the Arjuna ratha. Crouching lions and elephant fronts, now very much eroded by the saline air, decorate this upapitha, while a freestanding, rock-cut lion seems to guard the western side of this ratha.

The *Arjuna ratha* (Fig. 137), dedicated to Śiva, stands next to the Draupadi ratha. It also faces west. It has a dvitala (two-storeyed) vimāna of the Dravida order. The two pillars of the ardha maṇḍapa in front are modern additions replacing the lost originals. Cushionshaped capitals surmount the two octagonal pilasters at the corners. Diminutive rampant lions, springing from the abacus of the capital, support the corbel bracket over the capital. Gaṇas (goblins) adorn the underside of the kapōta, while its curved outer surface has three pairs of kūdu arches with human heads. Over the prastāra (entablature) is the hāra of small shrines, namely karna kūtas at the corner and śalās in between, Connected by hārāntara (lengths of cloister). The hāra over the ardha maṇḍapa is smaller than that over the vimāna. The shrine behind the ardha maṇḍapa has not been fully excavated. Due to lack of wall space, the dvārapāla figures do not appear at either end of the façade but at the angles of the side and back walls. The underside of the kapōta of the upper storey has a frieze of haṁsas (geese).

The śikhara crowning the upper storey is octagonal, and its wooden origin is very clear. The crossbeams supporting the base of the śikhara resemble the spokes of a wheel. Their square ends jut out of the mahā-nāsikā arch, which has a projected dormer-like shape from each facet of the octagon. In addition to this mahā-nāsikā, the śikhara has an ornamentation

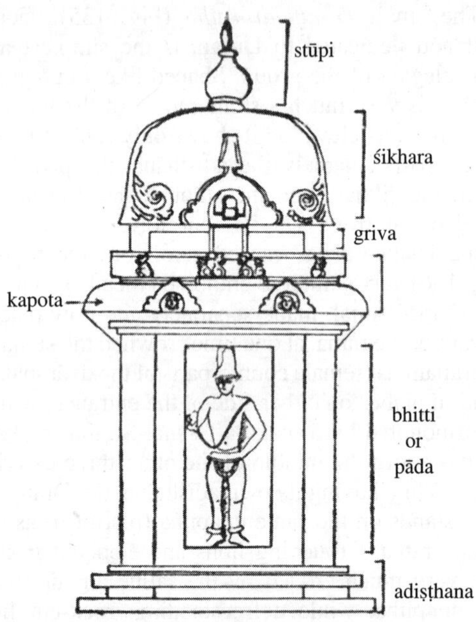


Fig. 131. A bas-relief in Arjuna's Penance, Mamallapuram, showing a miniature ekatala vimana of the Nagara order.

Fig. 133. Relief on the inside of the front sikhara arch of the Nakula-Sahadeva ratha, Mamallapuram, showing a miniature ekatala Vimana of the Dravidian order (polygonal).

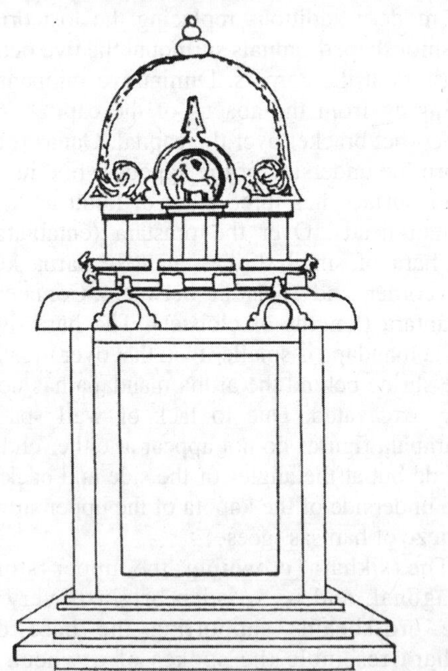

Fig. 132. Relief on either side of the Ramanuja mandapam, Mamallapuram, showing a miniature ekatala vimana of the Nagara order (four-sided).

Fig. 134. Relief on the arched ends of the wagon-top śikhara of the Bhima ratha, Mamallapuram, showing a miniature ekatala vimana of the Vesara order (curved).

Fig. 135. Draupadi ratha, Mamallapuram.

similar to the one bracing the corners on the Draupadi ratha—essentially a creeper design. The stūpi (finial), which now stands on the ground in front of the temple, formerly crowned the śikhara. Figure sculptures abound in this ratha.

The central section of the original whale-back rock formed an ideal situation for the rectangular *Bhima ratha* (Fig. 138), an ewkatala (one-storeyed) vimāna with a śalā type wagon roof. A row of stūpis (finials) crowned its ridge. The ratha remains unfinished and its basal parts uncarved, still attached to the parent rock on the north and south. Though incomplete, the aditala (ground floor) indicates that the original design included a rectangular maṇḍapa going all around it. The façade of this peripheral maṇḍapa has four vyāla-based pillars and two pilasters on each of the four cardinal faces. The solid walls appear only at the corners, while pillars and pilasters stand on the middle of each side. The kapōta over the potikā has seven pairs of kūdu arches, or alpanāsikās with human heads. The hara consists of śālās between the karnakūtas (kūtas at the corners). In order to make its wooden origin more obvious, the sculptors carved square-headed transverse beams to support the curved rafters of the roof on the tall grīva. On each of the two long sides of the grīva śikhara are five well-projected nāsikās in three sizes: the one in the centre is the biggest, those on either side of it the smallest, and the ones at the extreme ends of middling size. The largest nāsikā in the centre is known as the mahā nāsikā. It consists of a pillared niche surmounted by a cornice over which is a kūdu- shaped member. The middling-sized ones at the extreme ends, known as the alpa nāsikās, resemble the mahā nāsikās in their parts, but in the pillared niche they are very shallow. The smallest, named kṣuḍra nāsikās, have no cornice over the pillars and both the space between the pillars as well as the depth is more restricted. Each of the gable ends of the śikhara has a miniature bas-relief of a two-storeyed vimāna. Crowning the śikhara are the bases of about eighteen finials, now lost. Their sockets indicate that they were carved separately but never installed.

The *Dharmarāja ratha* (Pl 5.2; Fig. 141), a tritala (three-storeyed) vimāna, square in its talas (storeys) but octagonal in the grīva śikhara region, faces west. In style it resembles the Arjuna ratha. Its ground storey (Fig. 139), like those of the other rathas, remains incomplete. It was intended to have a sanctuary in the centre, surrounded by an ambulatory passage. An ardha maṇḍapa stands in front. The solid walls of this peripheral maṇḍapa appear only at the corners, since pillars and pilasters are hewn out at the middle of each of the four sides. Plain rectangular niches, cut into these walls, enclose figure sculpture, with Sanskrit titles of the king inscribed on top of

Fig. 136. Draupadi ratha, Mamallapuram, corner decoration on the roof.

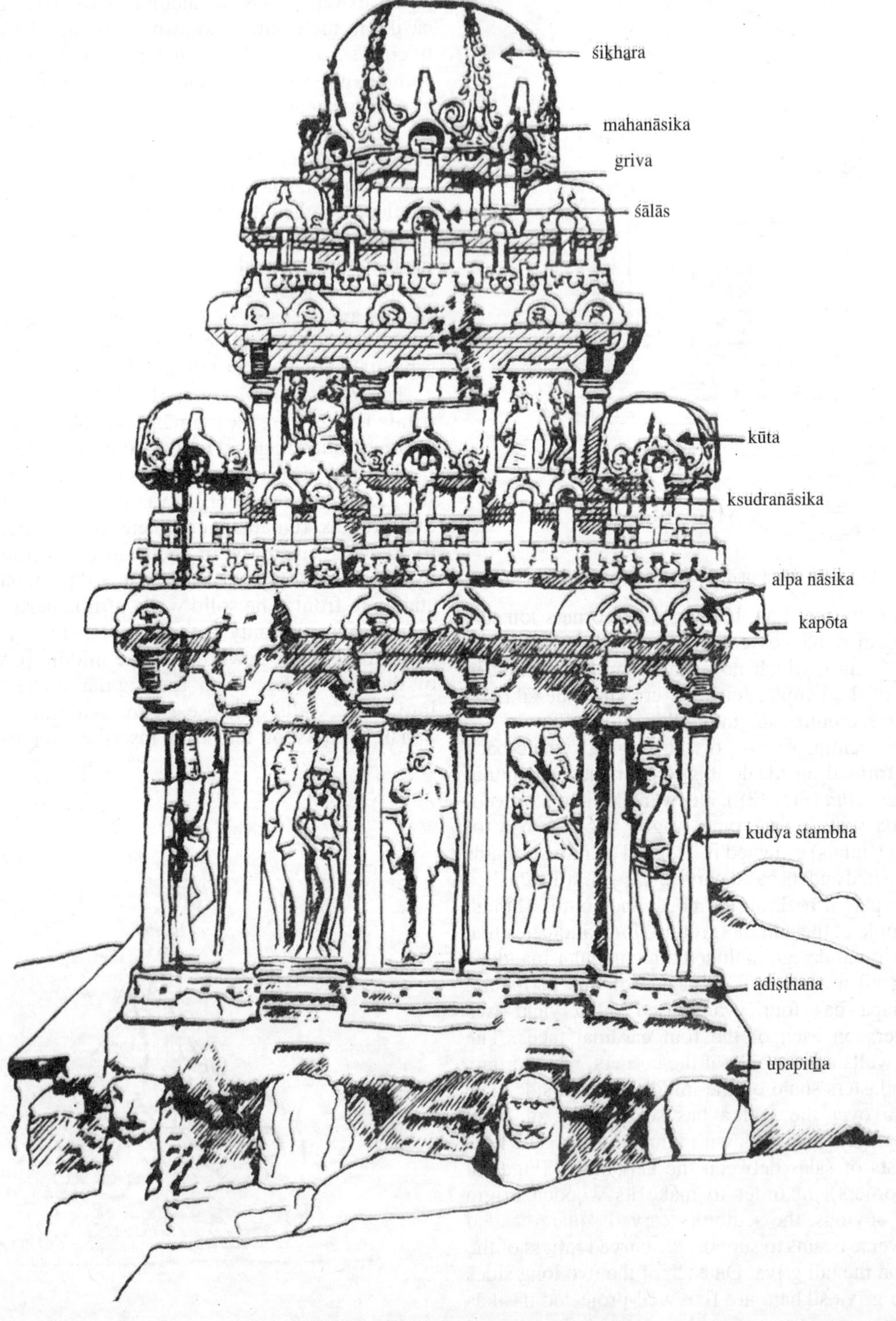


Fig. 137. Arjuna ratha, Mamallapuram.

Fig. 138. Bhima ratha, Mamallapuram.

each niche. The pillars are typical, with crouching lion bases and simple capitals. The well-formed kapōta above them has kūdu arches. Human and animal heads between arches serve as gargoyles, but these have not been finished on all the sides. Garland-bearing gaṇas adorn the underside of the western kapōta, while a simple frieze of gaṇas runs along the remaining sides. Animal motifs decorate the well-moulded adiṣṭhāna on which the temple stands.

Of the *Dharmaraja ratha* (Fig. 140) the

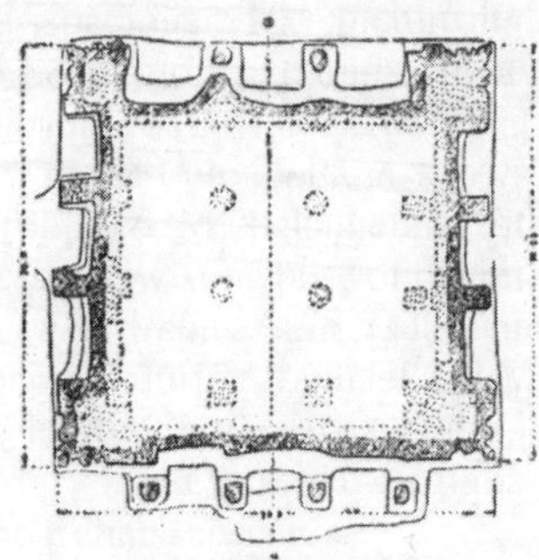

Fig. 139. Dharmaraja ratha, Mamallapuram, ground plan.

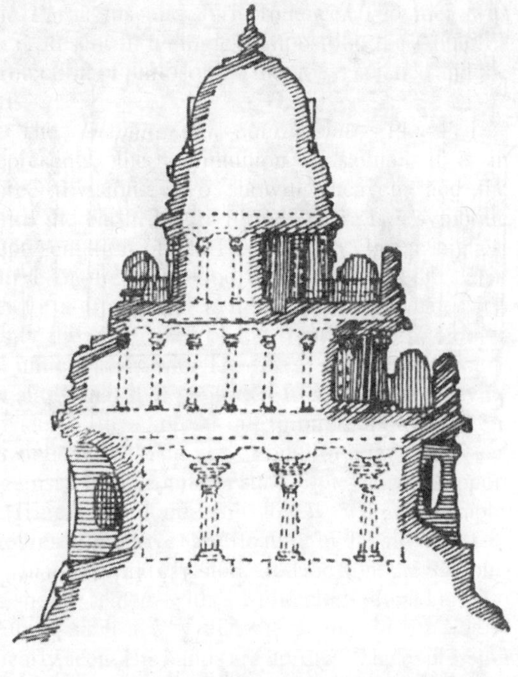

Fig. 140. Dharmaraja ratha, Mamallapuram, section, with conjectural internal arrangement.

Fig. 141. Dharmaraja ratha, Mamallapuram.

different storeys were meant to be functional since each tala makes provision for a shrine. These, however, have been left incomplete except on the topmost storey which has a finished shrine containing a Sōmāskanda panel flanked by dvārapālas at its entrance. The hāras surrounding each tier belong to a class known as the anarpita, for they are not attached to the body of the storey but leave a passage all around between the hāra line and the hārmya wall. As usual, the hāras consist of the śālās in between and the kūtas at the corners. For the first time a third member makes its appearance in the hāra over the ardha maṇḍapa, namely the panjara or nida, a miniature apsidal-ended shrine. The octagonal śikhara, very similar in style to that of the Arjuna ratha, was meant to be crowned by a separately- carved vase-shaped finial which remains unfinished and stands on the ground behind the ratha. The Dharmarāja ratha, replete with sculptural decoration, illustrates the various features of early Pallava iconography.

The *Nakula-Sahadeva ratha* (Fig. 142), carved out of an independent boulder, stands near the Arjuna ratha and faces south. It has a dvitala (two-storeyed) vimāna with an apsidal end in both its storeys, crowned by a wagon-vaulted roof also with an apsidal end. The base remains incomplete. An ardha maṇḍapa

Fig. 142. Nakula-Sahadeva ratha, Mamallapuram.

(Fig. 143) projects in front, its roof supported by a pair of lion-based pillars. The shrine cut out behind remains incomplete. The pilasters flanking it have elephant

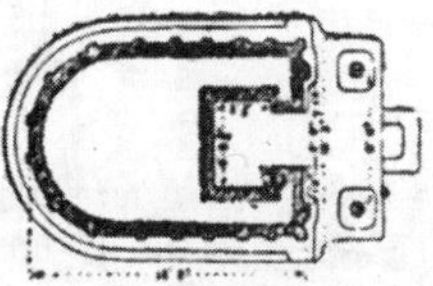

Fig. 143. Nakula-Sahadeva ratha, Mamallapuram, ground plan.

bases. Nine pairs of square pilaster, with capitals corresponding in position to the kūtas and śālās of the first storey, adorn the apsidal walls. On the western side and round the apse, the pilasters are more finished. A flexed cornice, decorated with kūdu arches, runs around the tops of two talas. The hāra over the ardha maṇḍapa consists of kūdus at the corners, śālās in between, and panjaras on either side of the śālās. The gable of the wagon-vaulted roof has a miniature bas-relief of dvitala (double-storeyed) vimānas. A monolithic elephant, carved out of the same boulder, stands at the eastern side of the ratha, indicating, perhaps, that the shrine was dedicated to Indra.

The *Dharmarāja* and *Arjuna rathas*, which influenced the later forms and development of southern temple architecture, are the most important rathas.

The monolithic *Gaṇeśa ratha* (Fig. 144) is the most finished and ornate of all the rathas. This dvitala (two-storeyed) vimāna, hewn from a free-standing boulder near the northern end of the main hill at Mamallapuram, resembles the Bhima ratha with its wagon-vaulted roof and three nāsikās the one in the centre large and the two at the extreme side small. According to its inscription, the temple was dedicated to Śiva. It faces west. The ardha maṇḍapa in front has the same size as the shrine behind. Vyāla-based pillars and pilasters adorn the façade. On either side stand a pair of dvārapāla figures in simple rectangular niches. The remaining three sides of the ground floor have pilasters on the exterior. A series of stūpis (finials) crowns the edge of the roof. They form

Fig. 144. Ganesha ratha, Mamallapuram.

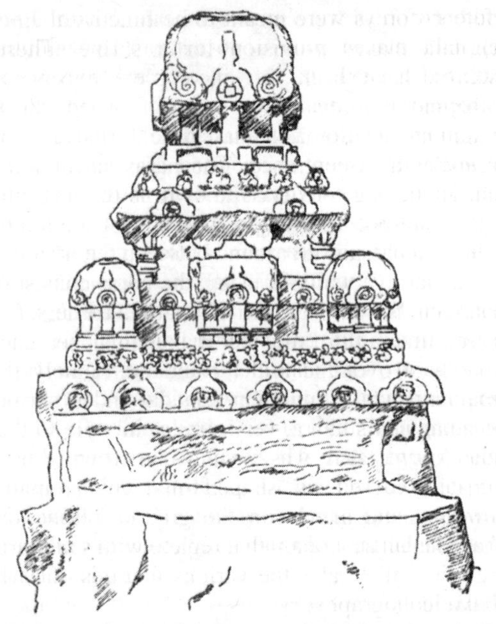

Fig. 145. Northern Pidari ratha, Mamallapuram

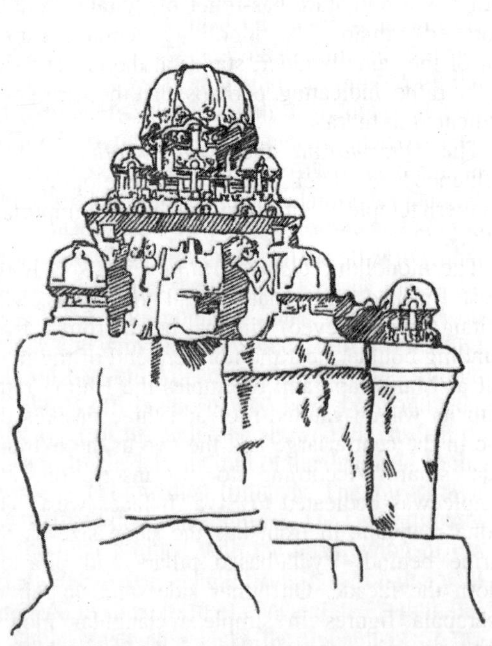

Fig. 146. Southern Pidari ratha, Mamallapuram.

Fig. 147. Valaiyankuttai ratha, Mamallapuram.

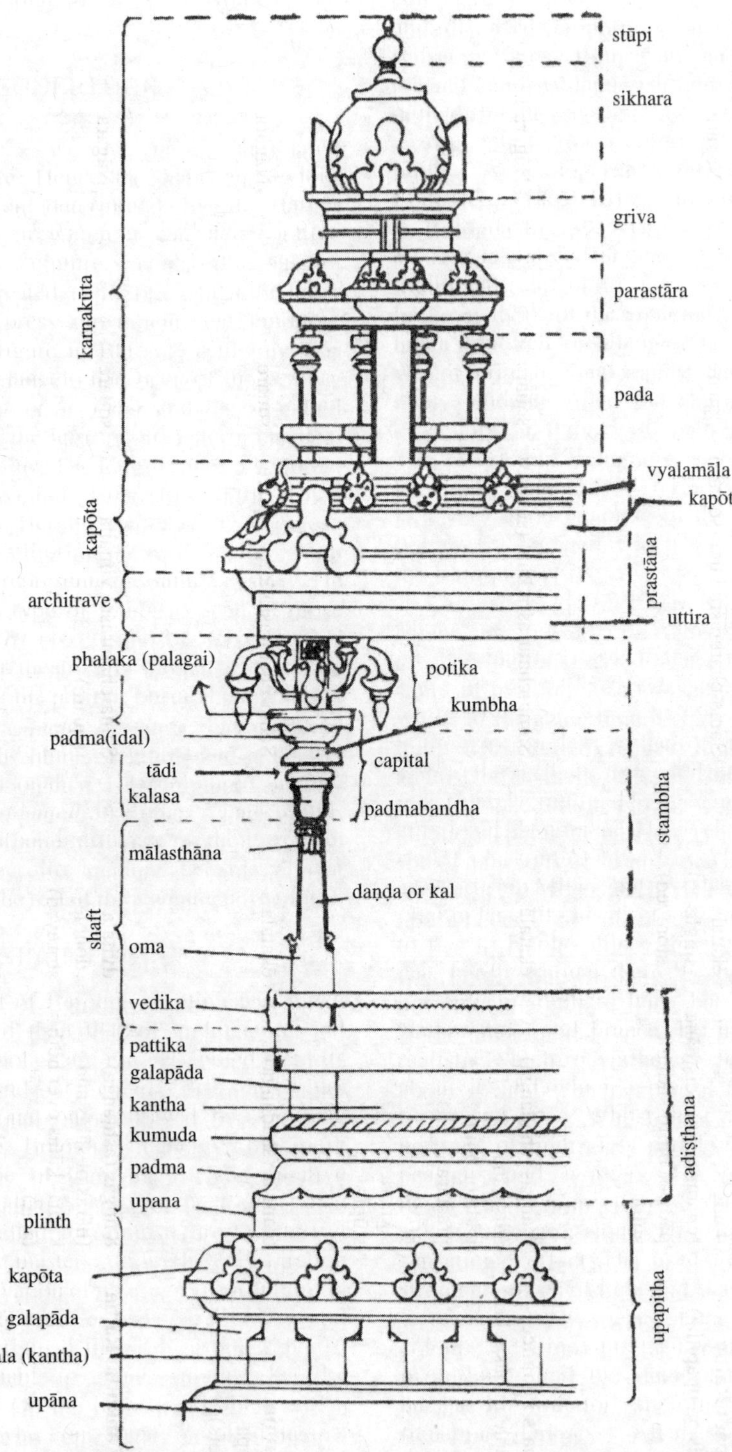


Fig. 148. Dravidian order.

Fig. 149. NAGARA, VESARA AND DRAVIDA STYLES AS SEEN AT MAMALLAPURAM.

| NAME OF RATHA | PARTS (ANGAS) | NO. OF STOREYS | FORM OF VIMANA | FORM OF SIKHARA | ORDER |
|---|---|---|---|---|---|
| **Draupadi Ratha** (Stands on upapitha) | 4 angās (chāturvarga) adiṣṭhāna pāda or bhitti sikhara stūpi | ēkatala (single-storeyed) | Sama-chaturaśra kūṭa (square) | square | Nagara |
| **Arjuna's Penance** (1 temple in bas relief) | 6 angās (shaḍanga) adiṣṭhāna<br>pāda or bhitti<br>prastāra<br>grīva<br>śikhara<br>stūpi | ēkatala | Sama-chaturaśra kūṭa (square) | square | Nāgara |
| **Ramanuja** Maṇḍapa (2 reliefs) | 6 angās (shaḍanga) | ēkatala | Sama-chaturaśra kūṭa (square) | square | Nāgara |
| **Valaiy ankuttai Ratha** | 8 angās (ashṭanga) (hāras of śālās and karṇa- kūṭas over both talas) | dvitala (double-storeyed) | Sama-chaturaśra vimāna (square) | square | Nāgara |
| **Northern Pidari Ratha** | 8 angās (ashṭanga) (prastāra of second storey has no hāra) | dvitala | Sama-chaturaśra vimāna (square) | square | Nāgara |

| | | | | | |
|---|---|---|---|---|---|
| **Southern Piḍari Ratha** | 8 angās (ashṭanga) (hāras of śālās and karṇa-kūṭas over both talas) | dvitala | Sama-chaturaśra vimāna (square) | octagonal | Drāviḍa (composite variety) |
| **Arjuna Ratha** | 8 angās (ashṭanga) (hāras of śālās and karṇa- kūṭas over both talas) | dvitala | Sama-chaturaśra vimāna (square) | octagonal | Drāviḍa (composite variety) |
| **Dharmaraja Ratha** | 10 angās (hāra of mukha maṇḍapam having karṇakūtas, śālās and nidas) | tritala (three-storeyed) | Sama-chaturaśa vimāna (square) | octagonal | Drāviḍa (composite variety) |
| **Nakula Sahadeva Ratha** (1 relief on toraṇa mukha patti) | 6 angās (shaḍanga) | ēkatala | hexagonal | hexagonal | Drāviḍa |
| **Bhima Ratha** | 6 angās (shaḍanga) | ēkatala | Āyatāśra (oblong) vimāna or koshṭa or śālā type | oblong | |
| **Ganesha Ratha** | 8 angās (ashṭanga) | dvitala | Āyatāśra (oblong) vimāna or koshṭa or śālā type | oblong | |
| **Nakula Sahadeva Ratha** | 8 angās (ashṭanga) (hāra with niḍas karṇakūṭas and śālās) | dvitala | Dvayaśra (apsidal) gaja or hasti prishṭa | elliptical | Vēsara |
| **Bhima Ratha** (2 reliefs) | 6 angās (shaḍanga) | ēkatala | square (up to prastara) | circular | Vēsara |
| **Ganesha Ratha** (2 reliefs) | 8 angās (ashṭanga) | dvitala | column-lik vimāna (circular) | circular | Vēsara |

an integral part of the monolith since they were not carved separately to be installed later. A triṣula (trident) surmounts the gable end of the śikhara.

The *Bhima* and *Gaṇeśa rathas* may have served as models for the form and development of the gopurams (temple gateways)—the most characteristic feature of the South Indian temple complex.

The two *northern* and *southern Piḍari rathas*, both dvitala (two-storeyed), are carved from free-standing boulders at Mamallapuram. The *northern Piḍari ratha* (Fig. 145) which faces north, belongs to the Nagara order. It remains incomplete. Its second tala', which has no hāra elements, heralds a feature which became a permanent characteristic of South Indian temples in subsequent epochs. The fine toraṇa, carried on two pilasters, which adorns the eastern wall, serves as a good example of a bhitti toraṇa. The ratha has an ardha maṇḍapa in front. Over the well-finished kapōta is a hāra of kūtas and śālās interconnected by hārāntaras.

The smaller *southern Piḍari ratha* (Fig. 146), also incomplete, faces east. It too has an ardha maṇḍapa in front; but hāra elements appear on its second tala as well.

The *Valaiyankuttai ratha* (Fig. 147), situated further south and carved out of another freestanding boulder, is a dvitala vimāna facing east. A pair of bay niches, projecting from each exterior wall of the shrine, gives it distinction. In front stands an ardha maṇḍapa.

The Pandyas, contemporaries of the Pallavas, also excavated rock-cut temples from the middle of the seventh century, and continued this activity for over three hundred years until they were overthrown by the Cholas of Thanjavur. Their cave-shrines, sixty in all, scattered in the southern half of Tamil Nadu and Kerala, outnumber the Pallava excavations. Hewn out of the hard local rocks, they bear resemblance to the Mahendra-style caves in plan and design.

Each consists of a maṇḍapa, with one or more shrine cells excavated either at its rear or at the side. The façade has massive pillars divided into three sections, the base and top being square and the middle octagonal. A heavy potikā (corbel) with an angular profile usually crowns the pillar. In a few examples, however, the potikā has a curved profile with taranga ornamentation. None of these cave temples havo a well-defined kapōta (cornice), nor do all of them have a maṇḍapa before the shrine. Sometimes only shrine cells have been scooped directly into the rock-face.

A beautiful and well-known example of the Pandyan rock-cut temple is the *Vettuvankoil* at *Kalugumalai*—a half-finished, free-standing monolith. In its architoctural arrangement and ornamental decoration, it recalls the Dharmarāja ratha at Mamallapuram. As for the Kailāsa at Ellora, the excavation began from the top downwards, but for some unknown reason the work was abandoned when it was almost half finished.

The temple faces east. Its front porch has no ornamentation other than a long frieze of rearing gaṇas. The rest of the facade remains roughly cut and unfinished. Kūdu motifs, alternating with lion and shovel-heads, embellish the octagonal śikhara of the vimāna. The kūdu motifs are elaborately sculpted with beautiful, minute details. The unfinished sanctuary now has a modern image of Gaṇeśa.

## GUPTA ARCHITECTURE

The Hindu temple was not meant for large congregational worship. It was considered to be the sacred abode on earth of the 'Ruler of the Universe'. Hence the word prasada, (originally meaning 'palace') probably applied to the temple. This also explains the presence of accessory halls for offering and entertainment in the temple precincts, as well as sculpture representing receptions fit for a king's palace.

According to rituals of Hindu worship, a temple should comprise a garbhagriha (literally meaning 'the womb')—an inner chamber to house a deity or symbol of a deity. This forms the nucleus of the temple—dark and secluded —where each individual offers his worship. Above the garbhagriha, a high śikhara tapers upwards to the crowning finial. The term śikhara, meaning 'mountain peak', may indicate that it signified Meru, the world-mountain or Kailāsa, sacred to Śiva. Very often a processional or circumambulatory passage surrounded the garbhagriha.

The maṇḍapa, usually a pillared assembly hall to provide shelter for the devotees, formed another essential part of the temple unit. An antarāla (vestibule) connected it to the garbhagriha (cella). In order to make a strong impression on the mind of the devotee before he reached the cella, it often had elaborate sculptural figures of various minor deities. An ardha maṇḍapa (porch) frequently preceded the maṇḍapa. Besides these three, accessory structures like the nāṭya maṇḍapa (hall of dance), and bhog maṇḍapa (hall of offering) occur in Orissan and other temples. Together with the main temple unit, these ancillary structures constitute an organic whole.

The regular building of structural temples in brick and dressed stone started in the reign of the Imperial Guptas, who by the first quarter of the fourth century A.D. had established their sovereignty over almost the whole of northern India. It is from the Gupta era that we can trace a clear and continuous chronological record of the political history of India. Under their rule of more than two centuries, the country enjoyed unbroken unity, peace and prosperity. Being Brahmanical in belief, they gave impetus to the renaissance of Hinduism. With their personal interest in arts and letters, they ushered in a resurgence of cultural activity and heralded India's greatest effloresence. A high watermark was reached in all phases of art, science and literature. Gupta ideals served to inspire generations long after the empire had perished. The period under their immediate patronage fully deserves the name 'the Golden Age' of Indian art and culture. Aesthetic principles of architecture, sculpture and painting were formulated during this period.

Prior to the Gupta age, small structural shrines had been erected like the one at Bairat (Fig. 40) belonging to the Mauryan period (third century B.C.), as well as the two elliptical structures at Besnagar and Nagari and temple number 40 at Sanchi (Fig. 43), a stone edifice on an apisdal plan. During the Gupta period, the Hindu temple evolved, and according to inscriptions of that time, a great number were erected. Since this age marked the beginning of structural temples, experiments in different types were made. The basic one consisted of the cella, the maṇḍapa and the vestibule.

In the field of architecture, an innovation of great significance was the use of dressed stone in building construction. Instead of imitating the wooden prototypes of the preceding age, the architects grappled with the fresh problem of stability, proportion and balance arising from the use of this new material.

The Gupta temples display a wide variety of types and forms, the results of creative experimentation. The simplest and most popular temple forms consist of a plain square flat-roofed garbhagriha to house the image of the deity and a low pillared maṇḍapa in front to shelter the worshippers. The inner shrine has only one door and no windows. The lower part of the pillar is plain and square and gives the impression of a pedestal. Many sides, sometimes eight, sometimes sixteen, transform the stubby shafts into cylinders. Their capitals resemble broad conventional vases, and a lion finial surmounts the massive abacus. The inter-columniation is wider between the two central pillars than between those of the sides. The architrave continues as a string course around the whole building. Over the decorated doorway is an 'over-door'—a survival of the timber age when a wooden beam surmounted the opening, extending beyond the top of the side parts to give extra strength and stability. This simple plan of the early period developed until it crystallised into the classical temple plan, with its regional differences. The basic arrangement, as well as its variants may be studied in existing examples spread over a wide area of northern India. The first addition was the covered pradakṣiṇa pātha (circumambulatory passage), and the garbhagriha was crowned by a square śikhara. Next, minor shrines placed around the main one created a composite unit.

Gupta temples may be classified into different groups: the first square and flat-roofed with a shallow porch in front, like temple number 17 at Sanchi; the second, with a covered ambulatory all around the cella, a very good example being the Pārvati temple at Nachna Kuthara; the third, with a short śikhara above the garbhagriha, such as the brick temple at Bhitar- gaon and the Dasāvatāra at Deogarh. The last- named exemplifies the final structure of the basic Hindu temple, reached towards the end of the Gupta period. The śikhara, now missing, may have had a straight edge and there may have been angle amalakas at the corners. No trace of the finial remains. The classic square cella, with triratha projections or porticos on three sides, seems to foreshadow the triratha plan of the temples in Orissa as they developed there. In the Bhitargaon temple, the śikhara continues the projections on the body of the cella, but the top elements have disappeared.

*Temple* number 17 at *Sanchi* (Fig. 150), though modest in proportions, provides a good example of the early Gupta style, with a plain square cella fronted by a pillared verandah (Fig. 151). It shows an independent handling of material without any imitation of wooden prototypes. The flat roof, provided with water spouts for drainage, rests on walls built of ordinary dressed stone closely set without mortar. The maṇḍapa has four pillars, with typical Gupta inter-columniation, wider at the centre and narrow at the sides. A pair of pilasters flanks the doorway. The ornamentation is restricted to the pillars and to a moulding which surrounds the whole building, prolonging the line

Fig. 150. Temple no. 17, Sanchi, perspective view.

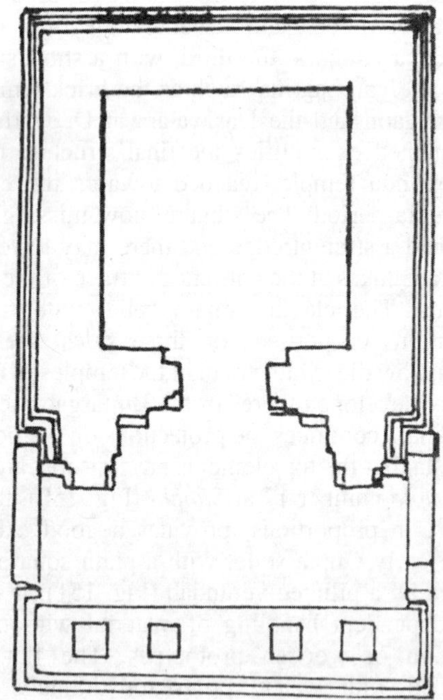

Fig. 151. Temple no. 17, Sanchi, ground plan.

of the architrave over the maṇḍapa columns. The pillars rise square at the base, succeeded by octagonal and then sixteen-sided sections, and culminate in a bell-shaped capital. Scholars like Cunningham deduce the chronology of Gupta temples by a study of this 'bell capital'. At Sanchi, it represents the last occurrence of the traditional Ashokan campani-form capitals, thus revealing some Mauryan influence on the temple.

The *temple* of *Kankali Devi* at *Tigawa*, Jabalpur district, probably the earliest instance of the true Gupta order, has vase-like capitals called pūrna-kalaśa (bowl of plenty). This continued to form a graceful part of all subsequent Indian architecture, even till the present. Lions keep guard on the massive abacus. The other characteristically Gupta feature of this temple is the ornamentation of the portal. The extended lintel on the top of the doorway, reminiscent of wooden construction, is enriched with river goddesses—transmutations of yakṣiṇīs embracing trees on Buddhist toraṇas. In the temple at Tigawa for example, Ganga stands on a makara (crocodile) and Yamuna on a kurma (tortoise). In later Hindu temples this representation occurs at the base of the door. The portals of the more mature Gupta style have other figures besides, such as gaṇas (dwarfs), mithunas (amorous couples), flying vidyadharas (celestials) and dvārapālas (doorkeepers). A significant aspect of the companion figure of the presiding deity of the temple is represented in the middle of the lintel. Otherwise, with its modest proportions (the cella is 3.75 $m^2$ externally, while the inner sides measure 2.4 m), flat roof and overhanging eaves, it resembles temple no. 17 at Sanchi. The maṇḍapa, with four pillars, has a wider intercolumniation in the centre than between the side pillars. Each pillar has a square firm base and a short, many-sided shaft. On stylistic grounds, V. A. Smith has ascribed the temple of Tigāwa to the period of Samudragupta.

The *temples of Viṣṇu* and *Varāhā* at *Eran*, similar in plan and proportions, probably belong to a somewhat later period. In the Viṣṇu temple we see the first instance of buttress-like projections on three sides of the cella, corresponding to the doorway extensions in front. A further development of these vertical divisions led to ornate light and shade effects, and contributed to the richness of decoration found in the fully developed temples, not only in India but in South-East Asia also.

The importance of the *Pārvati temple* at *Nachna Kuthara* (Fig. 152) in the Panna district lies in the addition of the covered pradakṣiṇa pātha (circumambulatory passage) around the garbhagriha. Lattice-work on each of the three sides provides lighting. The inner cella also has trellises in two of its walls. Another notable feature is the upper storey, supported by the cella, and set back from the pradakṇiṇa pātha—the first indication of the vertical elaboration which culminated in the magnificent śikharas of later temples. The building, standing on a platform (10.5 × 14.10 m), has the usual pillared portico in front, with a projecting flight of steps. Rich sculptures surround the doorway, as well as some elegantly carved panels on the sides.

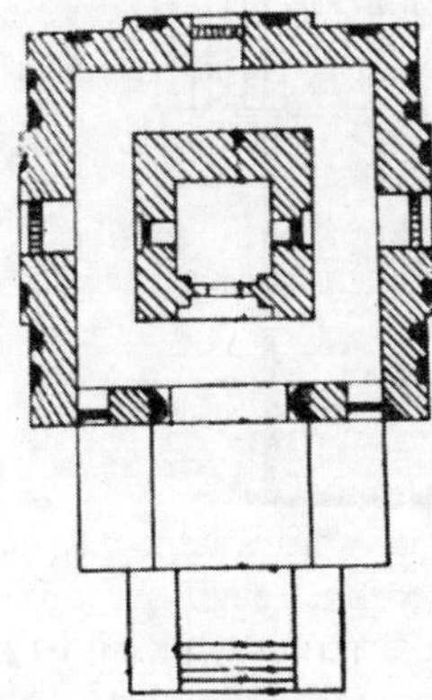

Fig. 152. Parvati temple, Nachana Kuthara, ground plan.

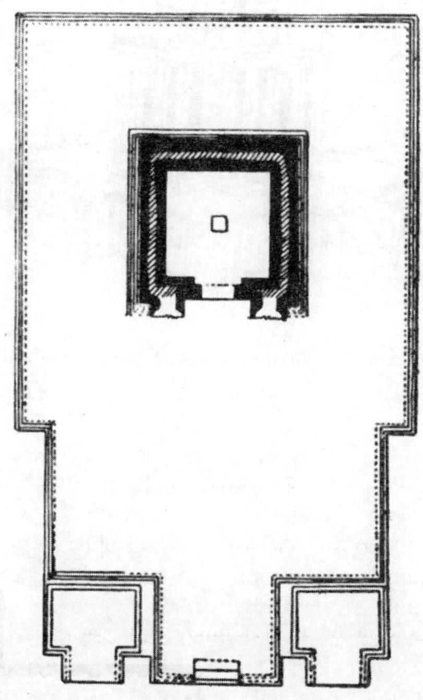

Fig. 153. Shiva temple, Bhumara, ground plan.

The *Śiva temple* at *Bhumara* (Fig. 153), Panna district, shows a further step in the evolution of the temple plan in the two minor shrines on either side of the stairway. Though in a very ruined condition, the remains of the temple found lying there—carved stones with exquisite floral motifs etc. showing excellent plastic modelling and infused with spiritual movement —recall the best murals of Ajanta.

The *Dasāvatāra temple* at *Deogarh* (Fig. 154) in the Jhansi district, dating from the fifth or early sixth centuries, exemplifies the finial form of the basic Hindu temple, reached towards the end of the Gupta period. It has three outstanding characteristics. In the first place, it is the earliest known example of a śikhara over the garbhagriha, further elevated by a square terrace 1.5 m high, with steps in the middle of each side, giving majesty to the whole structure. Secondly, flat-roofed porticos projecting from each side give a stage effect to the dramatic

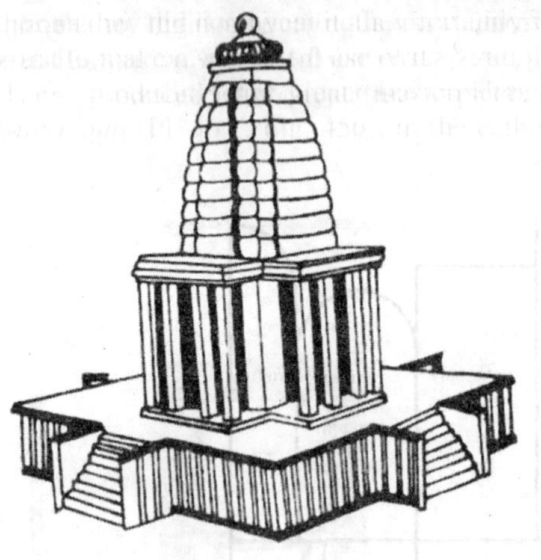

Fig. 154. Dasavatara temple. Deogarh, conjectural view.

high-relief sculptured panels on three sides of the cella. Thirdly, so many decorations have been given to the doorway that they almost obscure the characteristic projecting lintel. Plain surfaces enhance these decorations even more. Further, the scenes from the Rāmāyaṇa in the continuous frieze around the platform of the temple represent the first examples of motifs popular in later Javanese art. All the parts, well-ordered and serving a practical use, have a high degree of artistic refinement.

Though inscriptions prior to this period refer to buildings with lofty spires, figuratively spoken of as reaching to the sky or as high as the sacred mount Kailāsa, this is the first concrete example of a śikhara, which in later times reached glorious heights to satisfy the aspirations for verticality common to most religions. Its original appearance is largely conjectural because of its ruined condition. The śikhara may have reached a height of twelve metres. The contours were perhaps straight-edged, with diminishing tiers of stone courses continuing the

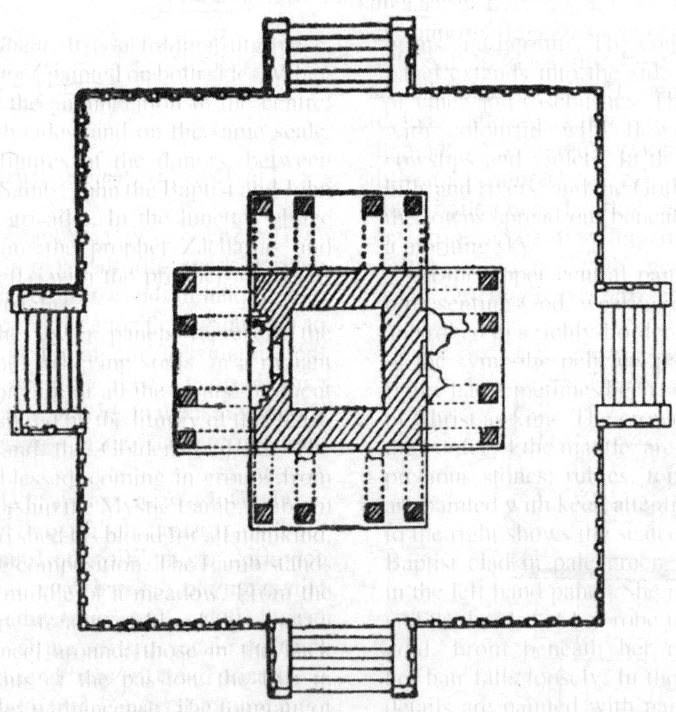

Fig. 155. Dasavatara temple, Deogarh, ground plan.

wall projections right up to the top. Besides there may have been angle āmalakas at the corners. No trace of the finial remains. Despite its dilapidated condition, it gives sufficient proof of excellence in architectural composition, technical skill and elegant sculptural ornamentation to be considered a gem of Gupta architecture. In plan (Fig. 155) the temple has a classic square cella, each side measuring 5.15 m, with a projection on three sides and a vestibule in front. Each of the four sides had flat-roofed, four-pillared porticos with a wider space between the middle pillars. The temple stands on a high basement decorated with sculptured niches on all four sides. Evidence points to a minor shrine at each corner, making it a pañchāyatana. The walls end in a double cornice with a frieze of small arched niches. Over this rise parts of the original śikhara.

Each of the triratha projections of this most ornate of the Gupta temples has a sculptured panel enclosed between richly carved pilasters and topped by an architrave with superbly chiselled foliage scrolls and lion heads. The main doorway, no less impressive, is framed by pilasters of varying shaft designs, and an elaborately carved architrave, displaying chaitya motifs, leafy scrolls, and lion heads, among other things.

Experiments with other types of temples were also attempted during the same period. For example, the *Mundeśvari temple* (*Bihar*) has an octagonal plan, while the *Maniyar Math* (*Rajgir*) is circular.

Many shrines continued to retain the prevailing pian of Buddhist chaitya halls. Some of these had actually been chaitya halls, later transformed into Hindu temples. Two such structures, as we have seen, occur in Ter (Fig. 44) near Sholapur, and at Chejarla (Fig. 45) in Andhra. This type, however, soon lost popularity and was superseded by the square plan with its variations.

In dealing with temple architecture during the Gupta period, mention must be made of the shrines built of brick. The use of brick for free-standing monuments dates from very early times. With a few exceptions it was largely replaced by stone during the Gupta period. The most important of these brick temples are the Bhitargaon in Kanpur district, the original Mahābodhi temple at Bodh Gaya, and the Lakṣmaṇa temple at Sirpur.

The *temple* at *Bhitargaon* has a triratha pian (Fig. 156), with projections on all sides. The entrance porch has a round arch made of bricks in the form of radiating voussoirs, but placed edge to edge, in what Cunningham designates

Fig. 156. Bhitargaon brick temple, ground plan.

Fig. 157. Bhitargaon brick temple, elevation.

as the 'Hindu fashion'. The outer walls have a strong basement moulding (Fig. 157), on top of which the main wall decorations consist of alternating pilasters and terra-cotta panels. The double cornice on top has a carved frieze remarkable for its beautiful finish and fresh and lucid motifs typical of the Gupta style. On top of the cornice rises the badly damaged śikhara, in receding tiers of brickwork, decorated with chaitya heads, busts, and even figures of gods. The wall projections also continue upwards at an angle indicating that the śikhara could have a risen to a height of 20 metres. Its ruined state, however, gives no clue regarding the shape or style of the finial or crowning element.

In its original form during the Gupta period, the *Mahābodhi temple* at *Bodh Gaya* resembled the Bhitargaon both in plan and vaulted ceilings. The present shrine is the result of many restorations and additions. The pyramidal pañcharatha śikhara, subdivided into seven storeys with the introduction of bhūmi-āmalakas at each level, now rises to a height of 55 m. Niches decorate the walls. A large arched opening on the east serves as an entrance. The four turrets at the corners of the high basement were later additions.

Such corner towers, however, existed even earlier, as shown by the excavations at Nalanda. *Temple* No. 3 at *Nalanda* was also a brick structure, rebuilt and restored seven times. The fifth phase shows a shrine on a lofty plinth, approached by an imposing staircase. It has four comer towers, embellished with niches containing stucco figures of Buddhist themes. According to Hiuen Tsang, the Nalanda temple also had an imposing tower, but nothing remains of this superstructure.

Most of these early temple towers had straight edges, but later śikharas curved inward slightly at the top, as seen in the *Mahādeva temple* at *Nachna Kuthara*, probably belonging to the seventh century A.D. The crowning element is an āmalaka.

The *Lakṣmaṇa temple* at *Sirpur*, in the Raipur district, also belonging to the late seventh century, presents the fully-developed form of brick temple. It has the usual square plan, with a projecting porch on the east and a high basement. The walls, however, have a number of projections which produce a rich light and shade effect. The firm horizontal string courses balance the vertical pilasters and the receded false windows. This reveals considerable skill and long experience in building construction and design. The chastely ornamented carved panels and imitation windows, patterned like lattice-work, were added after the completion of the walls. The bricks (measuring 42.6 × 22.5 × 7.5 cm) were carefully smoothed, and the whole wall was treated as an unbroken slab on which the carvings were executed. Unfortunately, the tower is mostly in ruins, and one can only surmise that it may have resembled that of the Mahādeva temple at Nachna Kuthara. With its balanced proportions, perfect harmony of parts and elegant carvings, this temple holds a very important position among the early śikhara temples of India.

## NORTHERN TEMPLES

The centuries following the fall of the Imperial Guptas witnessed a tremendous progress and development in the traditional temple styles. There is such a rich variety that the classification becomes an intricate problem. The Indian Silpasastras divide the temples into the Nagara, Dravida and Vesara types. In North India the temples belong mostly to the Nagara type. But this classification cannot be done on a strictly geographical basis since the Northern or Nagara order is found further south as well. For the sake of simplicity we shall divide them into the Northern, Southern and Deccani temples.

The chief characteristics of the North Indian temple lie in their plan and elevation. In the interior the shrine is always square, but on the outside projections adorn each of the four sides. The forerunner of such an outline may be traced back to the panels at the centre of each side of the cella wall in the Dasāvatār temple at Deogarh (Fig. 155), dating from the sixth century A.D. Such a plan is called triratha if there is one extension on each side, pañcharatha if two projections, saptaratha if three, and navaratha if four (Fig. 158). As these

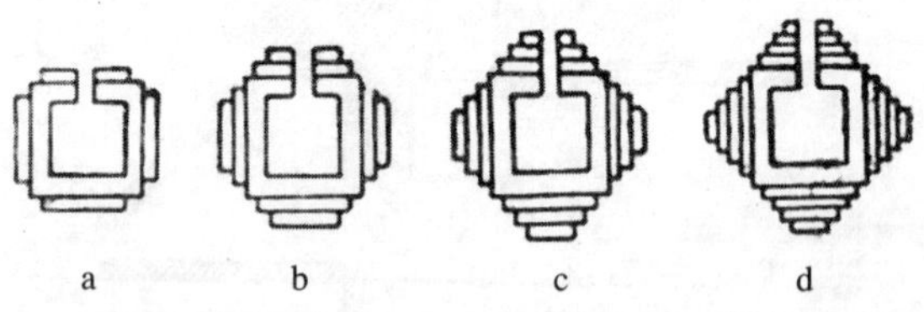


Fig. 158. Nagara or Northern temple plans, comprehensive diagrams showing the different projections: *a*. triratha, *b*. pancharatha, *c*. saptaratha, *d*. navaratha.

extensions increase in number, the plan becomes cruciform in shape, until finally it can be included in a new square. Although all these projections alter the outer face of the sanctuary entirely, the form and position of the inner cella and the place of the door do not change, even though the entrance is at the angles of the new cruciform shape. However, this is not so conspicuous, because the portal of the garbhagriha opens into the antarāla (vestibule) and the assembly hall attached to it.

The projections occur not only on the walls of the cella, but continue along the height of the śikhara. The edges of the latter are rounded or curvilinear. The top of the śikhara always has a crowning element, of which the most conspicuous part is the āmalaka (huge ribbed stone disc) which, together with the curvilinear outline of the śikhara, is the most outstanding and characteristic part of the Northern temple.

The common denominator of the medieval North Indian temples is the cruciform plan, the continuation of the offsets of the plan on the entire elevation, and the curvilinear spire. Regional tendencies, influenced by powerful dynasties, appeared by the seventh century. During the ninth and tenth centuries they became fully matured and established. The finest specimens of this temple style may be found in Orissa, Central India, Rajasthan and Gujarat.

## ORISSA

Orissa possesses the most remarkable Northern temples. To a certain extent they represent a pure form of the original Nagara style. Of the numerous temples erected from the seventh to the thirteenth centuries A.D., many still remain in a relatively well-preserved condition. Because of the remote position of Orissa, the monuments there were not razed to the ground by devastating raids of Muslim conquerors. They can be divided into two groups, namely the early form of Nagara temples and the later evolution of the same in the fully developed Orissan type.

Bhuvaneshvar, a sacred city with many tanks and a good number of well-preserved temples, is the main centre of Orissan architecture. The good condition of the temples, ranging over a period of nearly four centuries, makes it fairly easy to investigate the evolution of the type. Two other assets facilitate the study of this architectural mode, namely the preservation of some ancient texts of the Orissan canons of architecture, containing names and measurements of the different parts of the temple and the oral traditions kept alive among some living families of sthapatis, descendants of the ancient śilpins who built these places of worship.

The Orissan temple (the prāsāda) is composed of the usual two main buildings (Fig. 160), namely the shrine proper (according to local terminology, the rekhā deul) and its adjoining maṇḍapa (called the jagamohana or bhadra or piḍhā deul). The rekhā and piḍhā deul, similar up to the cornice, differ mainly in the shape and form of the śikhara. That of the former (Fig. 159) has a straight edge, gradually inclining inwards, and demarcated into a number of bhūmis (planes or sections) by means of bhūmi āmlā (ribbed elements) at the corners. All the crowning features, collectively known as the mastaka, are circular, composed of the beki (neck) overtopped by āmlā (flat circular ribs at the edge) together with the domical khapuri (literally 'skull') carrying the kalaśa (water jar), an important element in Hindu ritual. Crowning them all appears the āyudha (emblem) of the particular deity to whom the temple is dedicated.

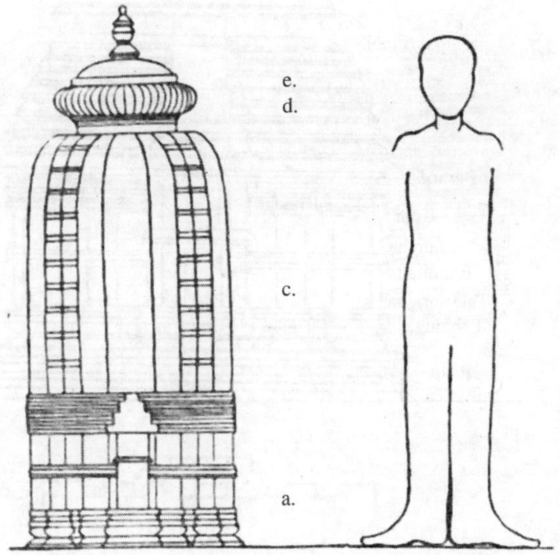


Fig. 159. Orissan temple, rekha deul segments named after parts of the human body:

*a.* pabhaga (pada; foot),

*b.* jangha (shin),

*c.* gandi (trunk),

*d.* mastaka (head),

*e.* khapuri (kapala; skull).

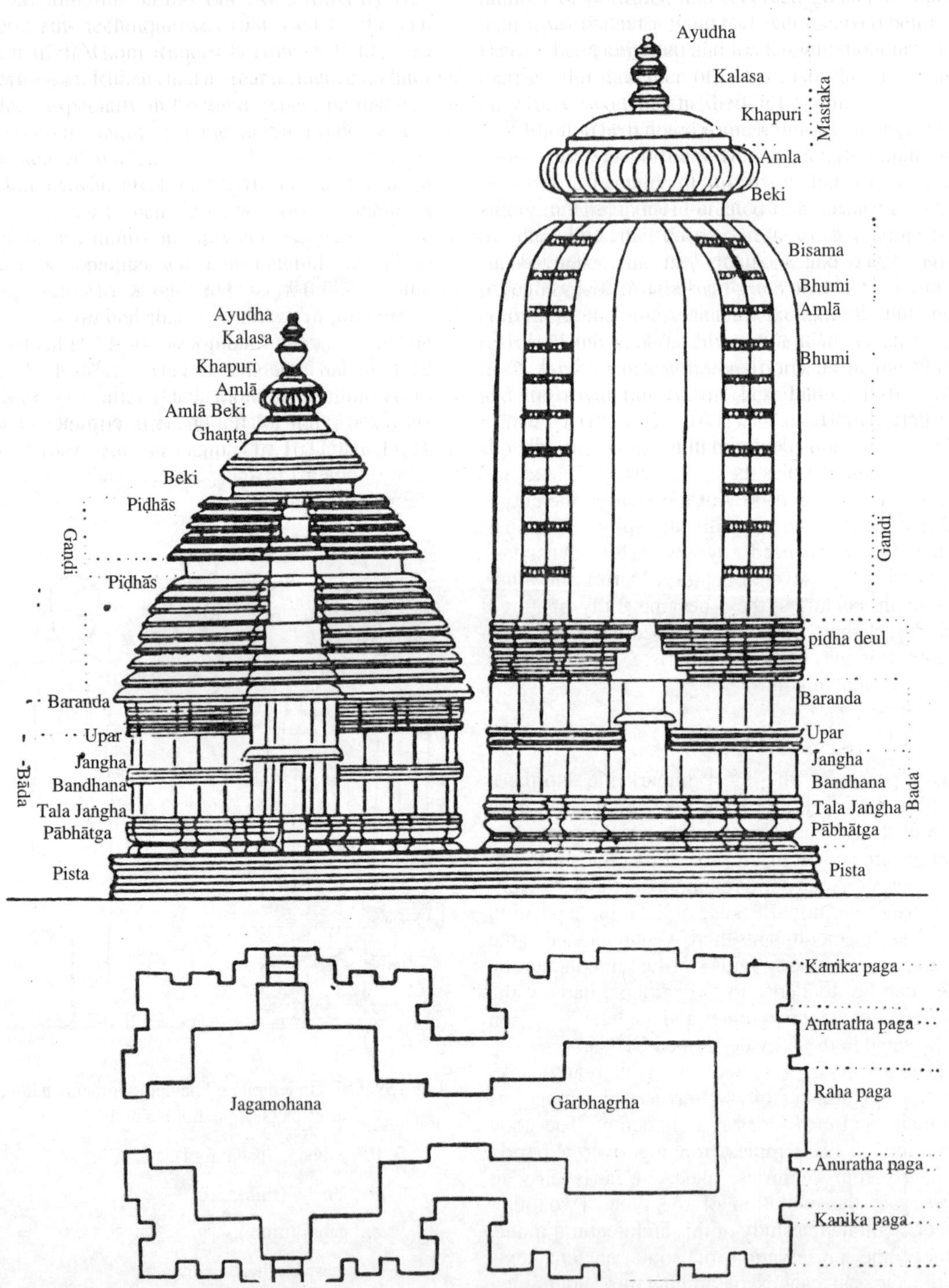


Fig. 160. Lingaraja temple, Bhuvaneshvar, Orissa, plan and elevation of the rekha deul and pidha deul.

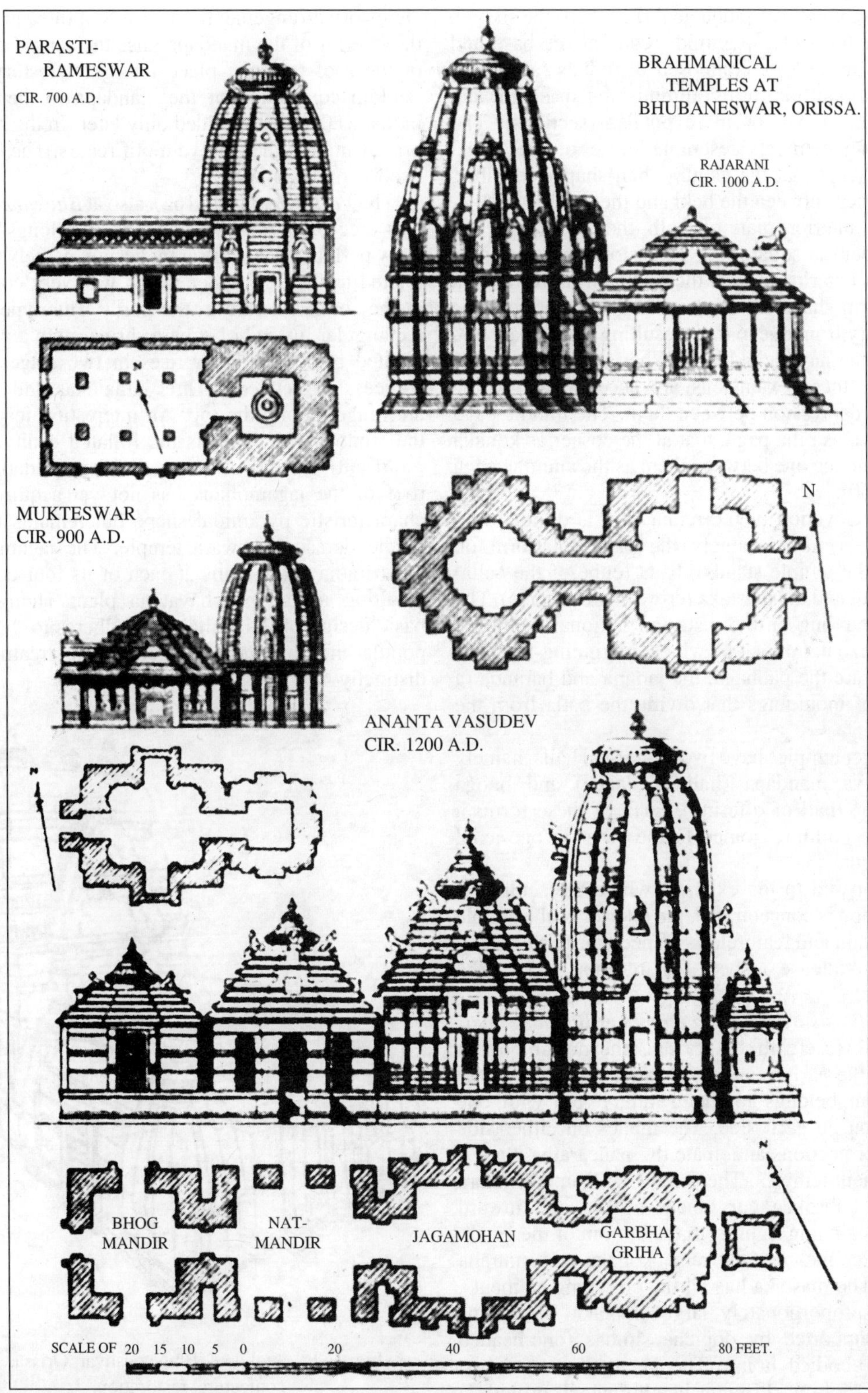
PARASTI-
RAMESWAR
CIR. 700 A.D.
BRAHMANICAL
TEMPLES AT
BHUBANESWAR, ORISSA.
RAJARANI
CIR. 1000 A.D.
N
MUKTESWAR
CIR. 900 A.D.
ANANTA VASUDEV
CIR. 1200 A.D.
BHOG
MANDIR
NAT-
MANDIR
JAGAMOHAN
GARBHA
GRIHA
SCALE OF 20 15 10 5 0 20 40 60 80 FEET.

In the bhadra or piḍhā deul (Fig. 160) the śikhara has the form of a pyramid, broad at the base and narrow at the top, composed of piḍhās (a number of horizontal platforms) diminishing in height and arranged in two or more potalas (sections). The crowning elements resemble those of the rekhā deul, except that the gaṇṭā, a bell-shaped member, intervenes between the beki and the āmlā.

The interior plan of both the rekhā and the piḍhā deul is square, but extensions in the middle of each exterior face of the garbhagriha result in a cruciform shape on the outside. These projections may vary from one to four, resulting in tri-, pañcha-, sapta- and navaratha plans. When continued on the śikhara, these extensions are accentuated by the narrow depression between them. The middle pāga is known as rāha pāga, that at the corner as konaka pāga, and the one between them as the anurāha pāga (Fig. 160).

The elevation of the rekhā deul is divided into distinct sections, namely the piṣṭa (platform on which the temple stands), bāda (cube of the cella) the gāṇḍī and the mastaka (crowning elements). The bāda, standing on the piṣṭa (an optional member), has horizontal divisions which, beginning from the bottom are the pābhaga, the jangha and baranda (a series of mouldings that divide the bāda from the gāṇḍī).

Bigger temples have two additional halls, namely the nāṭya maṇḍapa (hall of dance) and bhoga maṇḍapa (hall of offering). Each of these forms a separate building, joined to the other in one axial alignment.

Compared to the exterior, where the sculptural decoration is concentrated, the interior of the temple looks plain and featureless—a peculiarity stemming from an intense respect for tradition among the builders.

The *Paraśurāmeśwara temple* at *Bhuvaneshvar* (Fig. 161) (c. eighth century A.D.), the most important among the early temples, is fairly well preserved. The plan belongs to the triratha type, with one extension on each side. The niches on either side of the projections anticipate the pañcaratha plan of subsequent temples. The somewhat stunted śikhara has an unbroken curvilinear profile, the inward curve beginning right from the bottom of the gāṇḍī. The latter includes the rāha, konaka and anurāha pāgas. The mastaka has all the crowning elements. The disproportionately large āmalaka śila seems to be supported by dopicha simhas (one-headed and two-bodied lions). The jagamohana has two sloping roofs of different heights which provide a clerestory arrangement. Two rows of three pillars in the interior of the maṇḍapa raise the central portion of the roof to make place for the clerestory. The random connection of the maṇḍapa to the shrine indicates that it was added only later. In the surface ornamentation the chaitya motif recurs. The temple itself is rather small.

The *Vaitāl deul* (Fig. 162), also at *Bhuvaneshvar*, was erected in 850 A.D. Though it belongs to the early period, it has a different design, namely a form related to the deul order which was very common in the south but rare in the north. This type has a rectangular instead of square shrine, with a wagon-vaulted roof. The latter rises in two stages, with a recess in between. Three āmalakas and finials are ranged along the top. An interesting feaure on the front of the gāṇḍī is the foliated chaitya arch motif jutting out over the roof of the maṇḍapa. The roof of the jagamohana has not yet acquired the characteristic pyramidal shape but remains flat as in the Paraśurāmeśwara temple. The jagamohana has triratha rekhā deuls at each of its four corners, resulting in the pañchāyatana plan. Though the basic design of the Vaitāl deul adheres to the style popular in South India, its architectural treatment is distinctly North Indian.

Fig. 162. Vaital deul, Bhuvaneshvar, Orissa, a conjectural restoration.

An important landmark in the architectural development in *Bhuvaneshvara* is the small *Mukteśvara temple* on the outskirts of the city, dating from 950–975 A.D. It marks the end of the first phase and anticipates the second. The proportions of this temple are so balanced and its decoration so harmonious that the Mukteśvara is considered 'a gem of Orissan architecture'. A wall, with rich sculptures on the outside surface, encloses the temple (Pl. 3.1) which is entered through an exquisitely carved toraṇa consisting of an arch supported by a pair of columns. The well within the enclosure is called marīchi-kuṇḍa. The plan of the rekhā deul (Fig. 161) belongs to the full-fledged pañcharatha type, with two extensions on each side. Both the rekhā and piḍhā deul stand on a low platform. The pidhā deul has a pyramidal roof typical of the Orissan style, but the richly sculpted interior is not characteristic of Orissan temples. Figures of the Saptamātrikās and Virabhadra decorate the ceiling. Lacy chaitya motifs, intricately carved, adorn the surface of the tower. Softened outlines result from the rounded corners of the gāṇḍī and pāgas.

All these buildings, simple at the beginning, gradually became more elaborate through richer sculptural decoration and the multiplication of divisions both horizontally and vertically. In course of time the plan enlarged from the triratha to the navaratha, and the sections of the bāda increased from three to five. A bandhana (moulding) around the middle portion of the bāda divides the jangha into the tala (lower) jangha and the upāra (upper) jangha. The mouldings on the pābhaga and baranda increased as well. By adding more and more bhūmis, the śikhara became taller and more slender. While the ratio between the height of the śikhara and the length of the cella is three to one in the early temples like the Paraśurāmeśwara), those of the middle period have a ratio of five to one, and still later examples (e.g. the Sun temple at Konarak) seven to one. On the anurāhapāgas, miniatures shrines known as angaśikharas make their appearance. Above the bisāma, figures usually known as deul chāraīs appear to support the āmalakaśila, somewhat in the manner of the caryatids. The rampant figure of a lion on an elephant projects from the rāha pāga of the gāṇḍī. These features, characteristic of the later Orissan types, mark the final development of temple architecture in this region.

The temple of *Brahmeśvara* in *Bhuvaneshvar* erected, according to an inscription, in the eleventh century, belongs to the pañchāyatana (five-shrined) class, with four lesser shrines at the corners of the platform. Enclosed by an inner and outer wall, it has a tank on the southern side which forms an attractive feature and adds to the beauty of the composition. In its architectural characteristics and details of ornamentation it is typical of the Orissan form but lacks proportion and the finished appearance of temples like the Lingarāja.

The typical example of the fully matured Orissan temple, and the most important among all the *Bhuvaneshvar* group, is the great *Lingarajā temple* (Figs. 160, 163; Pl. 3.2) dating from 1000 A.D. Measuring about 158 by 142 m, and surrounded by many small shrines contributed by devotees, it stands in a walled enclosure with an entrance on the eastern side. All the four structures of the great Orissan temples, the rekhā and piḍhā deul, the nāṭya and bhoga maṇḍapa, lie along the same axis. The rekhā the piḍhā deul are divided into four divisions along the vertical axis: the piṣṭa (basement), the bāda including the sanctuary, the gāṇḍī (curvilinear tower) and the crowning mastaka (finial). The rekhā deul, the piṣṭa and bāda are similar, while the two upper parts differ.

The gāṇḍī of the rekhā deul rises to a height of 45 m, almost straight in the beginning, then gradually bending in a convex arc (Fig. 160) This inward curve is obtained by corbelling, a system where each successive block of stone extends a little bit īnward beyond the previous one, until the four sides come so near each other that the opening can be closed with one slab. Ten bhūmis are superimposed along the edges of the konaka pāgas while anga-śikharas (miniature replicas of the śikhara) extend along the anurāha pāgas. The rekhā deul forms an organic whole; the various parts are named after the different members of the human body (Fig. 159).

Dopicha simhas (lions) keep guard at the four corners of the bisāma. A variation of these, the gaja simha (a rampant lion on a crouching elephant) often adorned the body of the śikhara, especially the middle section of the rāhapāga (Fig. 163). A foliated chaitya arch, sometimes in an off-set panel, frequently decorates the rāhapāga just above the roof of the maṇḍapa. The horizontal beam over the doorway to the garbha-griha takes the form of a sculptured panel, traditionally representing the nine planets, while personifications of the river goddesses Ganga and Yamuna embellish the jambs—a practice maintained from the Gupta period.

The tower is a well-proportioned structure,

Fig. 163. Lingaraja temple, Bhuvaneshvar, Orissa, plan and section.

with the vertical lines of the anga-śikhara balanced by the horizontal mouldings on the body of the gāṇḍī, thus creating a rich harmony. Though profuse, the carvings on the exterior of the temple show orderly arrangement. By way of contrast, the interior looks austere with no more than four decorated columns upholding the roof, while the projecting rows of inward corbelling form the ceiling itself. We can no more than surmise why the same builders who decorated the outside of the temple so lavishly, left the inside so pure and simple. Though the ancillary halls, the nāṭya and bhoga maṇḍapa form later additions, their architectural treatment blends harmoniously with the older structures.

Fig. 164. Surya temple, Konarak, Orissa, entrance and plan.

The smaller *Anantha Vāsudeva temple* (Fig. 161), also at *Bhuvaneshvar*, resembles the Lingarāja both in layout and decorative scheme. Among the group of Śaivite temples, this is the only one dedicated to Viṣṇu. An Ornate piṣṭa with bold mouldings replaces the simple one. The roofs of the different parts of the temple (the bhoga and nāṭya maṇḍapa, the piḍhā and rekhā deul) are lined in a clearly ascending manner, spectacular to the eye.

The *Rājarāni* (Fig. 161) at Bhuvaneshvar, a fine example among Orissan temples, has two rows of anga śikharas, one above the other. The temple derives its name from the yellow stone, called rājarānia, of which it is built. Mellowed by time, the glowing amber of the stone complements the architectural splendour. Basically, the temple forms one architectural mass. While the anga śikharas appear only on the anurāha pāgas of the Lingarāja temple, they surround the whole body of the Rājarāni tower, with an accent on the lower section, thus making the rekhā deul more heavy and massive.

The *Sūrya* or *Sun temple* at *Konarak*, constructed from 1238–64 A.D., and known as the black pagoda from its dark colour, marks the climax

Fig. 165. Surya temple, Konarak, Orissa, plan and section designed to explain the construction of Hindu temples; conjectural restoration of rekha deul.

of Orissan architecture in its excellent proportions and the example of architect and sculptor working in unison. It resembles a chariot with exquisitely carved wheels (Fig. 164). Spirited horses, prancing in front, seem to draw the chariot alongside the basement which upholds both the rekhā and piḍhā deul. The nāṭya maṇḍapa, in front of the temple and aligned with the sanctuary, enhances the layout. It stands on a separate richly carved piṣṭa, approached by a flight of steps on each side. The plan of both the rekhā and piḍhā deul (Figs. 165, 166) is pañcharatha. The superstructure of the' rekhā deul was probably left incomplete or it may have fallen off A huge āmalaka crowns the pyramidal roof of the piḍhā deul. The latter is composed of three potalas (Fig. 167). Two distinct friezes adorn the bāda. Of all the structures, only the piḍhā deul, a beautiful piece of architecture, remains intact. A monolithic Aruṇa stambha stood in the courtyard next to the nāṭya maṇḍapa. Now it stands in front of the eastern gate at Puri.

The *Jagannath temple* at *Puri*, like the Lingarāja, has the sanctuary shrines aligned in the same axis. In this case, however, the enclosure has three outer walls (a feature typical of South Indian temples) and four gateways. It resembles the Lingarāja, but its greater size is enhanced even more by being erected on elevated ground dominating the whole landscape. The very ornate and conventionalised decoration as well as the structures themselves, clearly indicate that the style had become stagnant and decadent. Repeated renovations, carried out with no respect for the original, added to the deterioration. Many of the parts have been lime-washed. Unlike the Lingarāja, this temple does not impress the onlooker despite its imposing size and location and its prominence as a pilgrimage centre.

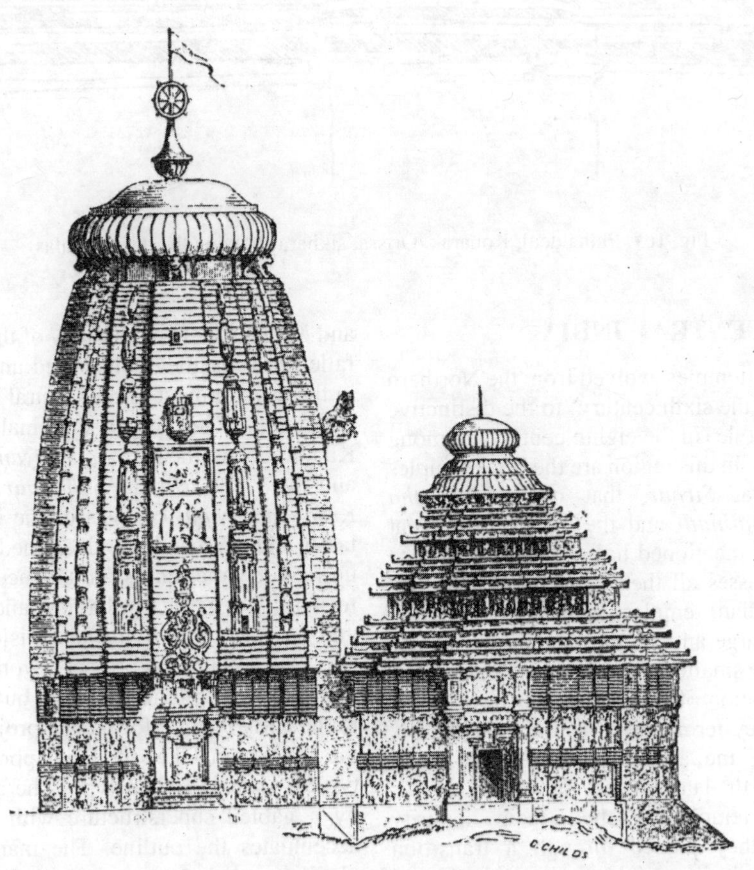


Fig. 166. Surya temple, Konarak, Orissa, a conjectural restoration.

Fig. 167. Pidha deul, Konarak, Orissa, sikhara showing the three potalas.

## CENTRAL INDIA

In Central India, temples evolved from the Northern Nagara type (in the sixth century) to the distinctive Central Indian style (in the eighth century). Among the early temples in this region are the brick temples of *Lakṣmaṇa* at *Sirpur*, that of *Vaidyanātha Mahādeva* at *Baijnath* and the *Sikara temple* at *Baroli*. The last-mentioned has special importance because it possesses all the distinctive features of the Central Indian temples, namely the double āmalakas, one large and another small, placed one over another, the smaller one supporting the kalaśa; and the continuation of the rāha pāgas beyond the gāṇḍī, where they terminate in a triangular shape, almost reaching the āmalaka. From these early temples evolved the later ones at Khajuraho.

Before the temples reached their maturity at Khajuraho, they passed through a transition phase. A number of beautiful temples had adorned Amarkantak, very sacred in the ancient times as the reputed source of the rivers Narmada, Son and Mahanadi. Though many of these temples have fallen to ruin, they constituted an important phase in the development of the Central Indian types. The two temples leading to the final development of Khajuraho are the *Keśavanārāyaṇa* at *Amarkantak* and the *Virāteśvara* at *Sohagpur*. The plan of the *Keśavanārāyaṇa* consists of the garbha-griha, antarāla and the maṇḍapa, all aligned in one axis. This unified scheme marks an advance over the earlier forms. The garbha-griha is pañcharatha in plan and has the same five-fold division in its vertical axis. The rāha pāgas project beyond the gāṇḍī (Fig. 168), and though the unbroken outline still belongs to the early Nagara forms, the projecting pāgas and the double āmalakas show an approach towards the typical Central Indian type. The antarāla, covered by a gabled superstructure with a straight edge, accentuates the outline. The maṇḍapa, square in plan, has kakṣāsanas and chajjas (overhanging eaves).

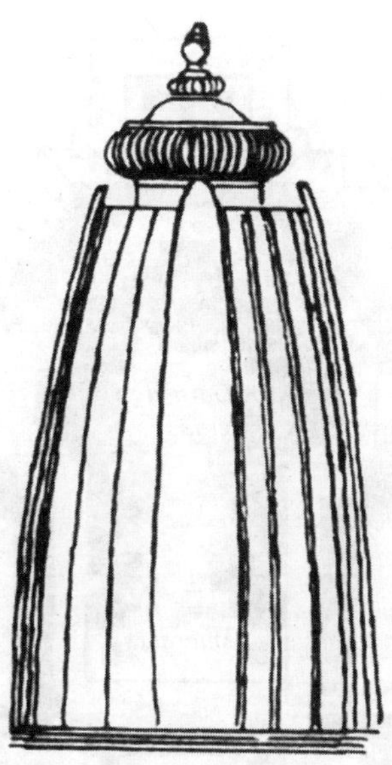

Fig. 168. A Central Indian sikhara, showing the double amalakas and the raha-pagas projecting beyohd the gandi.

The *Virāteśvara temple* at *Sohagpur*, in the old Rewa State, represents another step in the evolution of the distinctively Central Indian types. The plan of the temple consists of the garbha-griha, antarāla, maṇḍapa and ardha maṇḍapa, all aligned in one axis. The whole stands on a common platform. The addition of the ardha maṇḍapa characterises the typical form of the Central Indian temple complex. The garbha-griha, usually saptaratha in plan, has the same divisions in its vertical axis. Two bandhanas divide the jangha into three sections. The rāha pāgas project beyond the gāṇḍī, and three instead of two āmalakas crown the top.

The zenith of the typical Central Indian temple types and sculpture was attained at Khajuraho, the capital of the Chandellas, who ruled from the middle of the tenth to the twelfth century. They were great temple builders and connoisseurs of art. To construct most of the temples at Khajuraho they used the fine-grained variety of sandstone in different shades ranging from buff to pink or pale yellow, quarried at Panna on the east coast of the river Ken. The *Chausaṭh-Yogini*, *Lālguān-Mahādeva* and *Brahmā temples*, however, were made either wholly or partially of granite. Some twenty-five temples or shrines, large and small, still remain at Khajuraho in various stages of preservation. They can be divided into the western, eastern and southern groups.

Although they belong to the Śaivite, Vaiṣṇavite and Jaina sects, architecurally there is little distinction between the style of these temples. The variations appear only in certain details. These compact, lofty structures, saptaratha in plan, have no enclosure wall. They stand on a jagatī (high platform), which gives added height and prominence, while at the same time making provision for an open ambulatory around the temple, and at times for four shrines, thus making the temple pañchāyatana.

From the point of view of elevation they can be divided into temples with anga-śikharas (here called ūruśringas) (Fig. 169) around the main śikhara, and temples without anga-śikharas. As far as their plan is concerned, they are divided again into temples without a

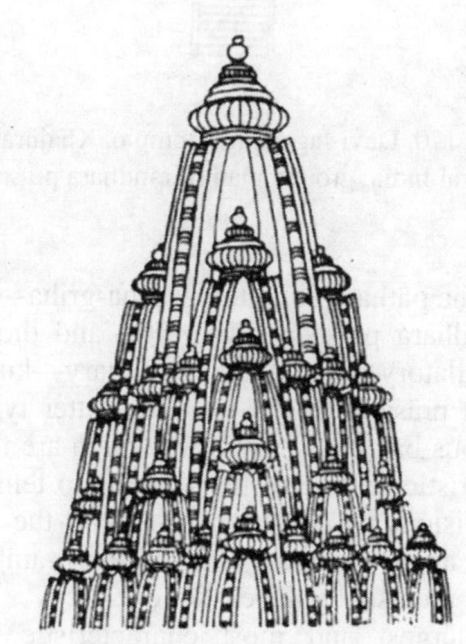

Fig. 169. Kandariya Mahadeva temple, Khajuraho, Central India, śikhara with urusringas.

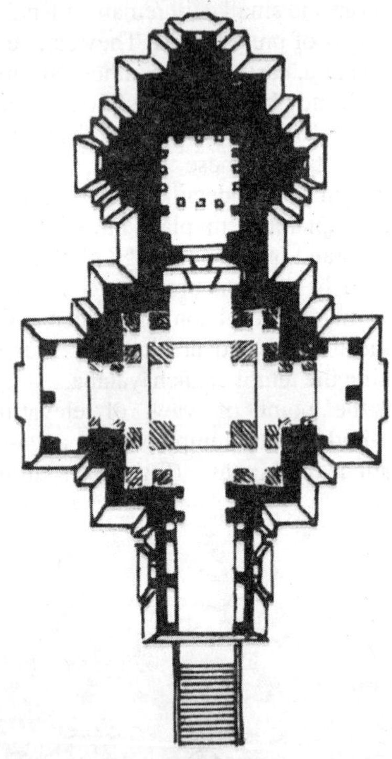

Fig. 170. Devi Jagadamba temple, Khajuraho, Central India, ground plan (nirandhara prasada).

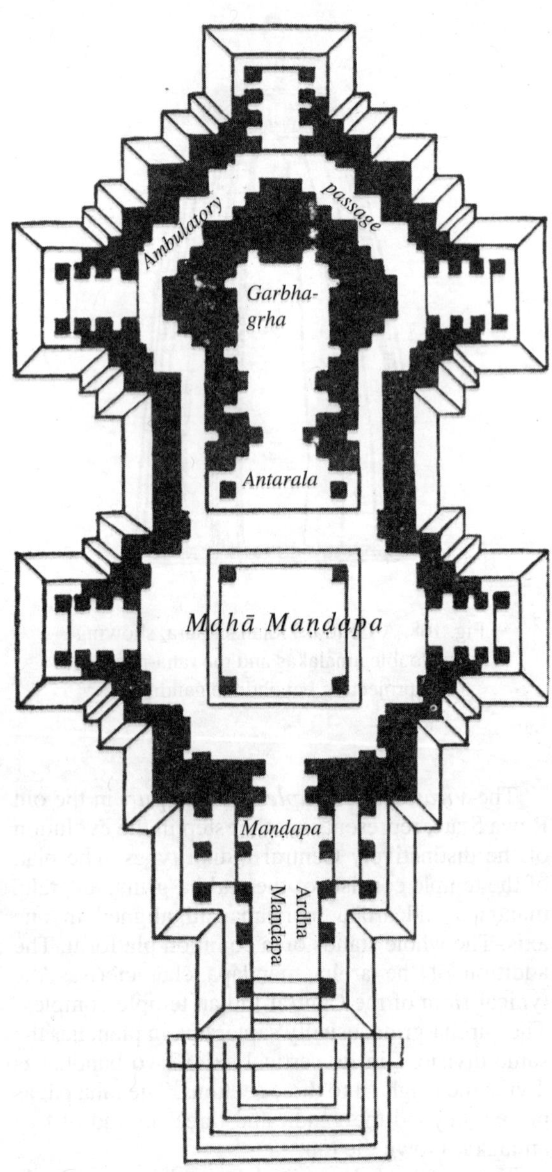


Fig. 171. Khandariya Mahadeva temple, Khajuraho, Central India, ground plan (sandhara prasada).

pradakṣiṇa pātha around the garbha-griha— known as nirandhara prāsāda (Fig. 170), and those with an ambulatory around the sānctuary—known as sāndhara prāsāda (Fig. 171). The latter type have the famous balconied windows which are the most characteristic feature of the Khajuraho temples. In both divisions of elevation and plan, the temples without anga śikharas and without ambulatory passages are usually the earlier ones.

The largest and most characteristic temples are the *Lakṣmana, Parsvanātha, Viśvanātha* and *Kandāriyā Mahādeva temples*. All of them illustrate the typical parts of the Khajuraho temples. A flight of steps and a doorway decorated with an ornate makara toraṇa leads into the interior. Aligned in one east-west axis, the various compartments of the temple are united both internally and externally, but each element has its own roof.

The ardha maṇḍapa is a verandah open on three sides. Pillars support the roof and uphold the overhanging chajja (eave). The ardha maṇḍapa is surrounded by kakṣāsanas which serve both as seats on the inside and as low decorative walls on the outside, with their outward sloping lean-backs and fence-like ved below. The ardha maṇḍapa enlarges into the mandapa, which in the bigger temples is a continuation of the same balconied open verandah, with kakṣāsanas on both sides and pillars carrying the roof.

In the larger temples, namely the Lakṣmaṇa, Viśvanātha and Kandariya Mahādeva, a new element makes its appearance, namely the mahā maṇḍapa, an enclosed hall with balconies (Fig. 172) attached on both sides, for

Fig. 172. Kandariya Mahadeva temple, Khajuraho, Central India, balcony with chajja.

which the thickness of the wall had to be opened to give entrance to these balconies. This gives the plan a cruciform shape. In the case of the abovementioned temples the plan is sāndhara, so three more balconies are attached to the ambulatory around the garbha-griha—one at each side of the passage and another at the back. This gives the plan the shape of a double- armed Latin cross. Generally these extensions are designated as transepts, but technically this is not quite correct since it is not a question of a hall crossing the main hall, but the cross shape results from the addition of the balconies to the rectangular hall. And in the passage around the garbha-griha these balconies do not cross anything at all. These balcony openings into the ardha maṇḍapa, maṇḍapa, mahā maṇḍapa and the pradakṣiṇa-pātha not only supply air and light to the interior, but aesthetically they are the most beautiful elements of the Khajuraho temples. These balconies are composed of two pillars holding the roof and chajja (eave) and are surrounded by kakṣāsanas which serve the double purpose of seats on the inside and low ornamental walls on the outside, with their outward sloping backs and fence-like vedis underneath.

The mahā maṇḍapa has not only the pillars of the verandah, but four columns in the centre hold the architraves which support the ceiling. The stability of the dome required underpinning by means of these additional pillars, since it was built with oversailing courses (corbelling), —the true arch had not yet been introduced. The pillars and rich decoration distinguish these temple interiors from those of Orissa, where they are astylar and plain.

The antarāla, with one or more chandraśilas (moonstones) and a flight of steps, leads from the mahā maṇḍapa up to the garbha-griha. All the interior parts of the temple, even those which have no proper lighting, are richly decorated.

The elevation of the Central Indian temple developed on similar lines to the Orissan. The process of dividing the exterior of the temple, both horizontally and vertically, is maintained in this region. The elevation, like the saptaratha plan, has very distinctive and rich features. In addition to the jagati, which provides a common platform, the temple stands on a high adiṣṭhāna subdivided into a series of ornamental mouldings with an outward slope. Over this rises the bāda (temple wall), on which the jangha is divided by two bandhanas, thus raising the usual five sections of Orissa to seven segments called saptānga-bāda.*

The saptaratha plan of the sanctuary, and the seven vertical segments bn the bāda (sap- tānga-bāda) are the highest achievement in Indian architectural design. The increased jangha sections provide the background for the rich sculptural decorations which alternate with the balconied windows. These latter stand out from the body of the temple and rest on the projecting adiṣṭ hāna. Their rectangular box-like form, with small flat pilasters and the outward-sloping backs of the kakṣāsanas to-

---

* *Bada divisions*

| *In Orissa*: | *In Khajuraho*: |
|---|---|
| 1. pābhaga | 1.pābhaga |
| 2. tala jangha | 2. jangha |
| 3. bandhana | 3. bandhana |
| 4. uparjangha | 4. jangha |
| 5. baranda | 5. bandhana |
| | 6. jangha |
| | 7. baranda |

upholding the overhanging eave, provide a calm tectonic contrast to the exuberance of the jagatī portions. The light and shade effects of the open balconies all around the building add a tranquil note to the architectural orchestration.

Above the saptānga bāda rise the superstructures. As in Orissa, each element of the temple has its own roof. The lowest appears over the ardha maṇḍapa, the higher one over the maṇḍapa, one higher still over the mahā maṇḍapa, while the lofty crowning śikara covers the garbha-griha. These ascending heights symbolise Mount Kailāsa or Meru. Horizontal tiers in receding stages cover the maṇḍapa—similar to the Orissan but much richer in decoration. In the majority of these maṇḍapas the profile of the superstructure looks rounded or domical.

The tall graceful śikhara over the garbha- griha has a curvilinear design. The rāha pāgas continue beyond the śikhara and terminate in a triangular form reaching almost to the āmalaka. Around the main śikhara are grouped a series of its replicas, known as ūruśringas (Fig. 169) and equivalent to the Orissan anga śikharas. They project boldly and create an impression of restless movement. Over the beki (necking) rest two āmalakas, one large and another small. The smaller one supports the kalaśa, over which appears the āyudha. All these form distinctively characteristic features of Central Indian temples.

From the earliest to the latest, all the existing temples at Khajuraho reveal some of the typical characteristics peculiar to the structures of this region. The *Chausaṭh-yogini temple*, made entirely of rough granite, is one of the earliest. It has an extraordinary design, with sixty-four plain minuscule shrines forming an open-air quadrangle. Only thirty-five of these remain. Each has a primitive curvilinear śikhara. The largest of these shrines, in the back wall opposite the entrance, was the main sanctuary. Even in its archaic form, it shows some of the basic features of the Khajuraho style in the high platform, and the division of the jangha into two sections.

The *Lālguān-Mahādeva temple*, constructed partly of granite and partly of sandstone, shows a transitional phase. Originally it had two components—a sanctuary and a portico—but the latter is fully ruined while the rest of this modest structure is quite dilapidated too. The pyramidal superstructure consisted of diminishing tiers of the piḍhā. A naṇḍī stands on its west front.

The *Brahmā temple* resembles the Lālguān-Mahādeva temple in plan, building material, design and decoration, but it varies in a few details. Its pyramidal roof is better preserved. The receding piḍhās, with ribbed ganṭa, two āmalakas and a kalaśa on the top show a step forward in the evolution of these early temples.

The *Mataṅgeśvara temple*, one of the earliest, has three canopied balconies. It is the only temple in Khajuraho where worship is still conducted.

Also interesting from the point of view of roofing are the Varāha and Naṇdi shrines. These open shrines manifest interesting architectural details. The *Varāha shrine* stands on a high plain jagatī. Pillars uphold the pyramidal roof composed of receding tiers, with a ganta, āmalakas and a kalaśa on top. The more developed *Naṇdi shrine* stands on a high jagatī with well-formed adiṣṭhāna mouldings. Here too pillars hold up the roof of the open verandah, but in this case kakṣāsanas form a parapet all around. And the roofing has become more complex—smaller roofs covering the projecting balconies surround the central pyramidal roof with piḍhās, hanging eaves shade the entire building.

Among the nirandhara temples, mention must be made of the following. The *Vāmana temple* has a balconied entrance portico, a closed maṇḍapa with a pair of balconied windows, and a ruined śikhara without ūruśringas. At the *Javāri temple*, the open ardha maṇḍapa and maṇḍapa show the fully developed box-like balcony with sloping backs of kakṣāsanas. Two pillars uphold the hanging eave. The roofs of these two structures are very richly treated, in contrast to the more sober śikhara which has only a few ūruśringas. Being nirandhara, there are no balconies around the śikhara.

The *Devi Jagadambi temple* has a large ardha maṇḍapa with three pillars on the sides to uphold the hanging eave. The closed maṇḍapa, with the saptānga bāda and a pair of three- pillared balconies, give the temple a monumental aspect. The śikhara, with more ūruśringas, has a richly carved base.

The Jaina temples have their enclosure on the eastern side. The largest of them is the *Pārśvanātha temple* (c. 1002). It has an ardha maṇḍapa and a closed maṇḍapa, followed by a śikhara with ūruśringas. It does not have balconies, but the closed inner ambulatory around the garbha-griha is provided with lattice windows to admit light and air.

No more than the sanctuary and vestibule remain of the smaller Jaina *Adinātha temple*, immediately north of the Pārśvanātha. This nirandhara temple resembles the Vāmana temple in sculptural elegance. They differ only in the decoration of the topmost line of the outer wall, where the Adinātha has a lively band of vidyādharas flying about, as in the Javāri temple. Its śikhara indicates a higher evolution in its finer proportions than the

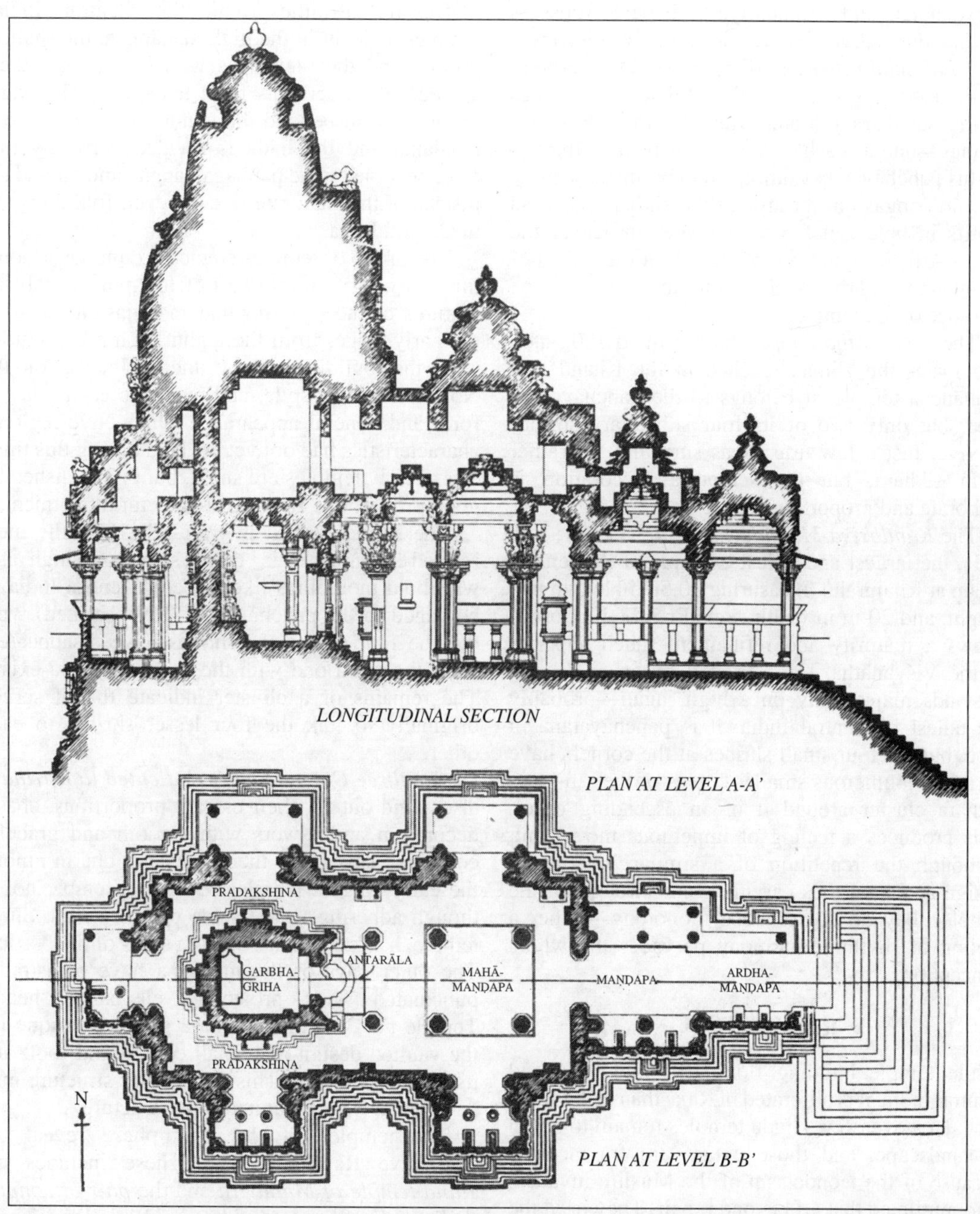


Fig. 173. Laksmana temple, Khajuraho, Central India.

heavier stumpy one of the Vāmana. Its sculpture too shows greater delicacy. The vestibule roof of this temple is noted for its elegant decoration and design.

All these temples have some of the typical Khajuraho elements, but only the Lakṣmaṇa, Viśvanātha and Kandāriyā-Mahādeva possess all the distinctive features as already described. The *Lakṣmaṇa temple* (Fig. 173), built around 950 a.d., the best preserved of this style, belongs to the sāndhara prāsāda type. All the subsidiary shrines—one at each corner and a fifth in front—of this pañchāyatana complex remain intact. Only a few ūruśringas cluster around the śikhara. Chaitya motifs in bold relief ornament the surface of the latter. Artistic figure sculptures adorn the pillars of the mahā maṇḍapa. A makara toraṇa beautifies the entrance of the temple.

The *Viśvanātha temple*, built around 1002 a.d., anticipates the climax reached in the Khandāriyā Mahādeva temple. It belongs to the pañchāyatana type, but only two of its four subsidiary shrines survive. Just a few ūruśringas surround the rather plain śikhara, but the sculptural decoration is elaborate and proportionate.

The *Kandariya-Mahādeva temple* (Pl. 4.1; Fig. 171), the largest and tallest example of the temple group at Khajuraho (measuring 30.5m in length and height, and 20 m in width excluding the platform), shows a maturity and refinement much superior to the Viśvanātha. Unobstructed by an enclosure, it stands majestically on a high jagatī—probably the tallest in Central India. It is pañchāyatana in type, but the four small shrines at the corners have perished. Numerous smaller copies of the tall main śikhara cluster around it in an ascending order. This produces a feeling of impetuous movement. Although the repetition of a similar ornamental design and luxurious carving recur throughout the temple, they do not produce monotony—rather a feeling of rhythmic harmony pervades the whole conception.

## RAJASTHAN

While temple building flourished in Orissa and Central India, it proliferated in Rajasthan at the same time. However, few Hindu temples remain to adorn its landscape, and those extant are fragmentary because of the iconoclasm of the Muslim invaders who mutilated that art beyond repair. They used the material of these temples to erect fortifications in order to consolidate their conquests. The ruins of nearly twenty-seven temples went into the Quwwat-ul-Islam mosque of Delhi, where the pillars give an idea of the art of Rajasthan in the early periods of the building phase, namely the eighth and ninth centuries. These remains illustrate that pillared halls were prominent features in the early temples.

Despite affinities with the Central Indian temples, evident in the high mahāpiṣṭa, the shallow portico and the maṇḍapas with kakṣāsanas, there are definite diversions from that style. The pāgas do not extend beyond the gāṇḍī, there is only one āmalaka, and the bāda is divided vertically into three sections— the pābhaga, jangha and baranda—instead of the elaborate five-or seven-fold divisions in Central India.

The group of temples erected around Osia, some thirty-two miles north-west of Jodhpur, reveals the features of the style popular in Rajasthan. During the early stage, from the eighth or ninth centuries a.d., the buildings show the influence of the Northern temple style, and resemble each other in form and general appearance. Distinctive regional characteristics had not yet evolved during this time. These early temples are small, but distinguished by good proportions and rich architectural treatment.

The *Sūrya temple* in *Osia* (PI. 4.2), the most refined example of this_ group, stands on a high piṣṭa with bold mouldings like those of Central India. It belonged to the pañchāyatana (five- shrined) type, but the four subsidiary shrines have disappeared. Only the main one with the open maṇḍapa exists. The remains of a cloister indicate that it served originally to link the four lesser shrines to each other.

*The three Osian temples dedicated to Harihara* also stand out for their elegant proportions, chaste decoration and towers with smooth and graceful contours. This gives them a special charm among the early Nagara temples. Of these, temple no. 2, though adhering to the same pattern as the Sūrya temple, has kakṣāsanas on both sides of the portico. The outer bays of the maṇḍapa have balustrades punctuated with projecting elephants' heads. Temple no. 3 of this Harihara group is unique for the vaulted design of its hall ceiling and roof, and its simple platform. This rectangular structure may have had a wagon-vaulted superstructure.

The temples of the later phase reveal the distinctive Rajasthan type. These includes the *Jaina temple of Mahāvira* and the *pair of temples dedicated to Saciya Mathiya and Pipla Devi*. These temples, identically laid out, bear more resemolauce to those of Gujarat than the Central Indian. Though proportionately small, the angaśikaras project more prominently—a characteristic feature of the Rajasthan temple. The boldly projecting chajjas that shade the bāda and its niches also distinguish the temple architecture of both Rajasthan and Gujarat. The most typical, however, is the layout of the interior where profusely carved pillars, arranged in a circle, form a nave in the central maṇḍapa. They also uphold the architrave, which is laid along an octagon and carries a shallow central dome. Only in Rajasthan and Gujarat do we find pillars of this form and circular arrangement, and toraṇas fronting the entrance. This disposition of the pillars anticipates the support of the colossal dome at Mount Abu. The sculptural arrangement on the piṣṭa resembles that of Gujarat. Though highly ornate, the columns have no distinct parts. This results in confusion and indicates that the art has deteriorated.

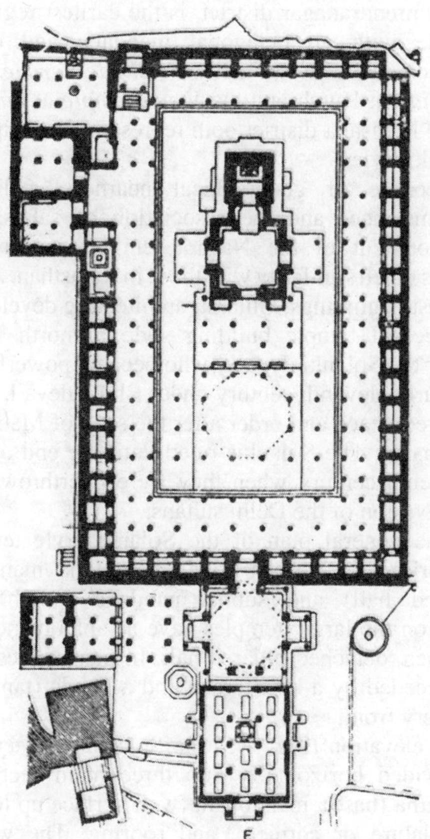


Fig. 174. Vimala Vasahi temple, Mount Abu, Rajasthan, plan.

The temple of *Neminātha* at *Khumbaria* (eleventh century) resembles those of Rajasthan in some features, but its śikhara has two āmalakas, and its maṇḍapa has a row of richly carved pillars in the centre supporting a shallow dome.

In the twelfth century the temple art of Rajasthan, like that of Gujarat, flourished under the Solanki rulers. At *Mount Abu*, the Jain temple complex of *Dilwara*, most notably the *Vimala Vasāhi* and *Lūna Vasāhi*, show an advance in the Rajasthan style.

*The temple of Vimala Vasāhi* (Fig. 174), consecrated to Adinātha, stands within a quadrangle, with the entrance from the east. The halls, one rectangular and the other square, are placed axially. The plan is composed of four structures, named according to Jain terminology the mūlagarbho (inner shrine), gūdha maṇḍapa (maṇḍapa), sabhā maṇḍapa (portico) and devakūlika (colonnaded portico) of image cellas. The sanctuary of this temple is made of black stone. North-east of it lies the *Lūna Vasāhi temple* dedicated to Nemināṭha. Exquisite ornate halls form the most characteristic feature of both these temples. Their focal point is the octagonal nave supporting the shallow trabeated dome, supported by eight richly sculpted pillars. A small bracket at each angle of the pillar converts the octagon into a circle, until the apex is reached. At this point the dome culminates in a beautiful pendant.

The twelfth century *Jaya stambha* at Chitor in Rajasthan shows that the builders did not confine themselves to the temple designs. This tower, with eight alternately receding and expanding storeys, shows a fine blend of utility and beauty. On the top is an open pillared pavilion covered by a pyramidal roof. There is unity within the animated variety of balconied windows, turrets and mouldings.

## GUJARAT

A natural artistic talent and good taste together with the affluence that came from its being on the trade route between east and west made this region and its environs one of the richest and most prolific artistic centres of art in India. Unfortunately the ravages of climate, invasions and a destructive earthquake early in the nineteenth century have ruined and destroyed many of its architectural monuments.

In 1025 the iconoclastic Afghan ruler Mahmud of Ghazni ravaged many temples, in particular the famous Somanātha temple in Kathiawar. Under the powerful Solanki rulers peace and prosperity were quickly restored and the temples were not only repaired but many others of excellent quality were added. This Śaivite dynasty ruled not only in Gujarat but also in Kathiawar, Kutch and much of Rajasthan. Their capital lay near modern Patan, north-west of Ahmedabad.

Although these rulers inspired many of the temples, others were patronised by governors and ministers, often Jains, like the brothers Vastupala and Tejapala (first half of the thirteenth century). However, much more than the inspiration of one man, these temples expressed the spontaneous faith of the people in general. Everyone took a personal interest in the building and each one shared according to his ability in a system of offerings initiated by the head men. This created an interest in art among the common people. They had an inborn feeling for beauty, for structural fitness and efficiency.

The salats (lay artisans and hereditary masons) in particular cultivated this innate aesthetic sense. Without models, drawings or plans they followed their śilpas (rules of the craft) but at the same time they showed versatility and inventive power, and always in good taste.

The conquest by the Delhi sultans at the end of the thirteenth century destroyed much of this great art, although the salats and their senas (builder's guilds) continued to work for the new Muslim overlords.

Gujarat architecture is divided into the pre-Solanki buildings and the Solanki style. The pre-Solanki temples, attributed to the Mait- rakas of Valabhi, are very simple and small. The oldest known structural building is the *temple of Gop*, in the Barda hills of Jamnagar district in Kathiawar. It dates from the sixth century A.D. This ruined structure stands on a basement of two terraces. The upper, slightly smaller level may have served as a pradakṣiṇa-pātha. The temple consists only of the sanctuary. Its bare walls have a tower-like appearance, with no more than two grooves at the top to relieve their plain severity. The pyramidal superstructure consists of stepped courses, the lower one decorated with two chaitya dormers and the upper course with one. A domical finial crowns the whole. More than fifty such temples, with the roof comprising three to five tiers, have been found in the coastal region of Gujarat. The last of this type, dating from the seventh century, A.D., the *Bileśwar temple* in the Junagadh district, has a pyramid of six tiers, with a cupola-like finial. It is the most evolved of this class.

The temples of the late seventh and early eighth centuries, such as the *Varāha temple* at *Kadwar*, near Prabhas Patan in the Junagadh district, and the *Sūrya temple* at *Sutrapada*, exhibit a transition to the northern type with a rudimentary śikhara in the triratha form, a garbha-griha with a pradakśiṇa-pātha, and a closed maṇḍapa with a porch and a sloping roof. They retain the chaitya ornaments of the Gop type.

The temples of the late eighth century reveal the next step in the evolution. For example the *Roda temples* have triratha or pañcaratha śikharas over the garbha-griha, entrance porches, and occasional maṇḍapas with simple pyramidal roofs. The *Hariś chandra-ni-Chori* at *Shamlaji*, of the same period, has a ranga (open) maṇḍapa. The celebrated *Ranakadevi temple* at *Wadhwan* (ninth century) exhibits a further step in the evolution in the exquisite workmanship and proportions of its śikhara. The *Muni-Bawa temple*, near *Than* in the Sunrendranagar district, is the earliest regional temple with an octagonal maṇḍapa and eight vidyādhara brackets. Finally the *Bhadeśvara temple* at *Anjar* in Kutch and the *Viṣṇu temple* at *Sander* in the Mehsana district both represent the incipient Solanki style.

Because of geographical nearness, political circumstances and the association of salats, the development of the Nagara temples in Gujarat shows much similarity with those in Rajasthan. After modest beginnings, Gujarati architecture developed the richest temple building style in north India under the Solanki dynasty who became powerful in the early eleventh century under Bhimadeva I, who restored peace and order after the sack of Mahmud of Ghazni. The Solankis ruled until the end of the thirteenth century when they were overthrown by the invasion of the Delhi sultans.

The general plan of the Solanki style temple comprises the garbha-griha, the gūḍha maṇḍapa (closed hall) and subha maṇḍapa (porch). In addition the larger temples have a sabhā maṇḍapa, an open, detached pillared hall. In many cases this is preceded by a kirti toraṇa and a kuṇḍa (tank) in the very front.

In elevation (Fig. 175) the Solanki type temple is divided horizontally into three main sections: the pitha (base), mandovara (wall surface up to the entablature or cornice), and roofing. The whole temple stands on a khara- śila (paved terrace). The pitha is composed of a series of mouldings and string courses with repeating motifs arranged in fixed order: rākṣasās (horned heads) on the garaspaṭṭi (lowest band), elephant fronts on the gajapitha just above the former, and horses on the aśvathara higher up. The narathara (top row) is adorned with human figures. The upper, surface of the pitha forms the floor of the building.

This basement supports the second or middle division, the mandovara, which corresponds to the Orissan bāda. Its vertical wall face is reserved exclusively for figure sculpture—deities in bas relief enshrined in niches all around the building, in most cases.

The maṇḍapas are covered by a low pyramidal roof composed of horizontal courses, diminishing as they rise, and terminating in a vase-shaped finial. A samvarana roof is a special type consisting of a pyramidal composition of diagonally arranged rooflets crowned by bell- members. Urusringas, almost in the round, surround the lower portion of the śikhara over the garbha-griha. This śikhara is the most distinctive feature of the western temples.

The most splendid example of Solanki architecture and the earliest datable building

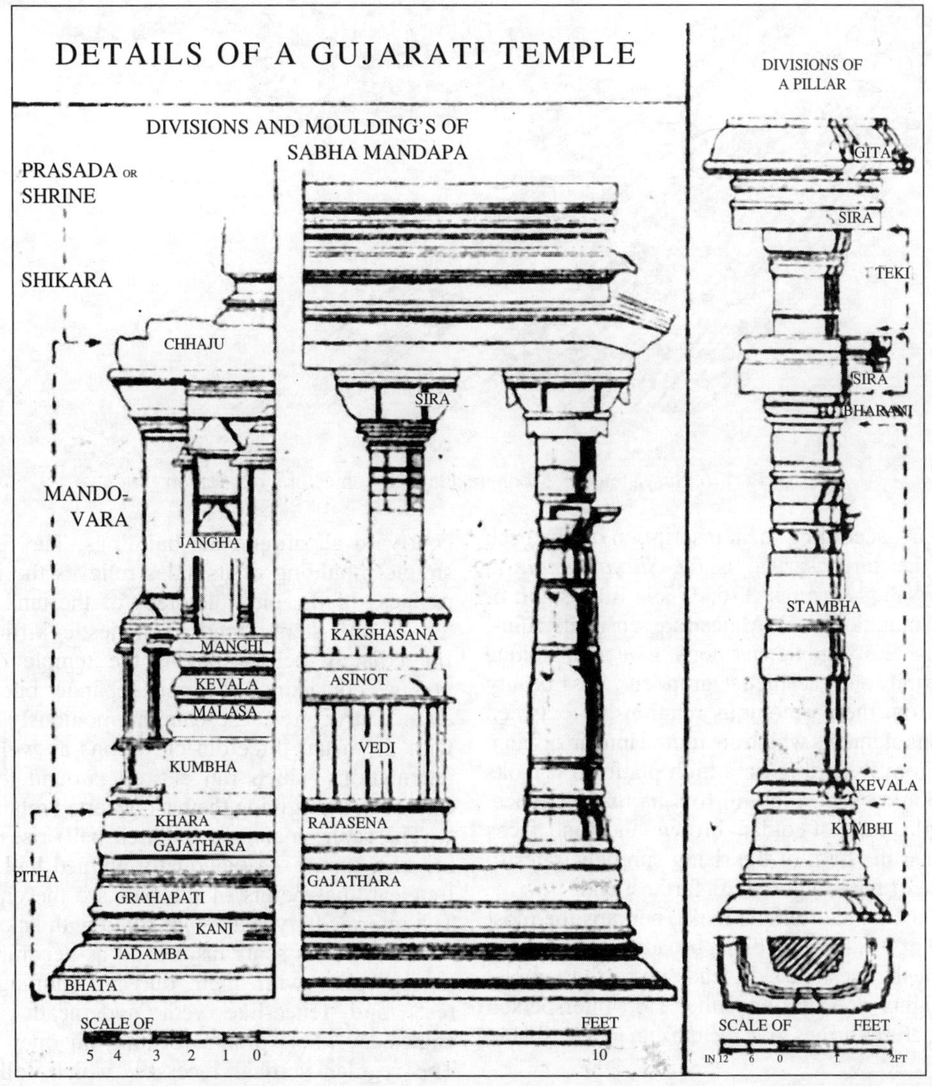


Fig. 175. Elevation of Solanki type temples, Gujarat.

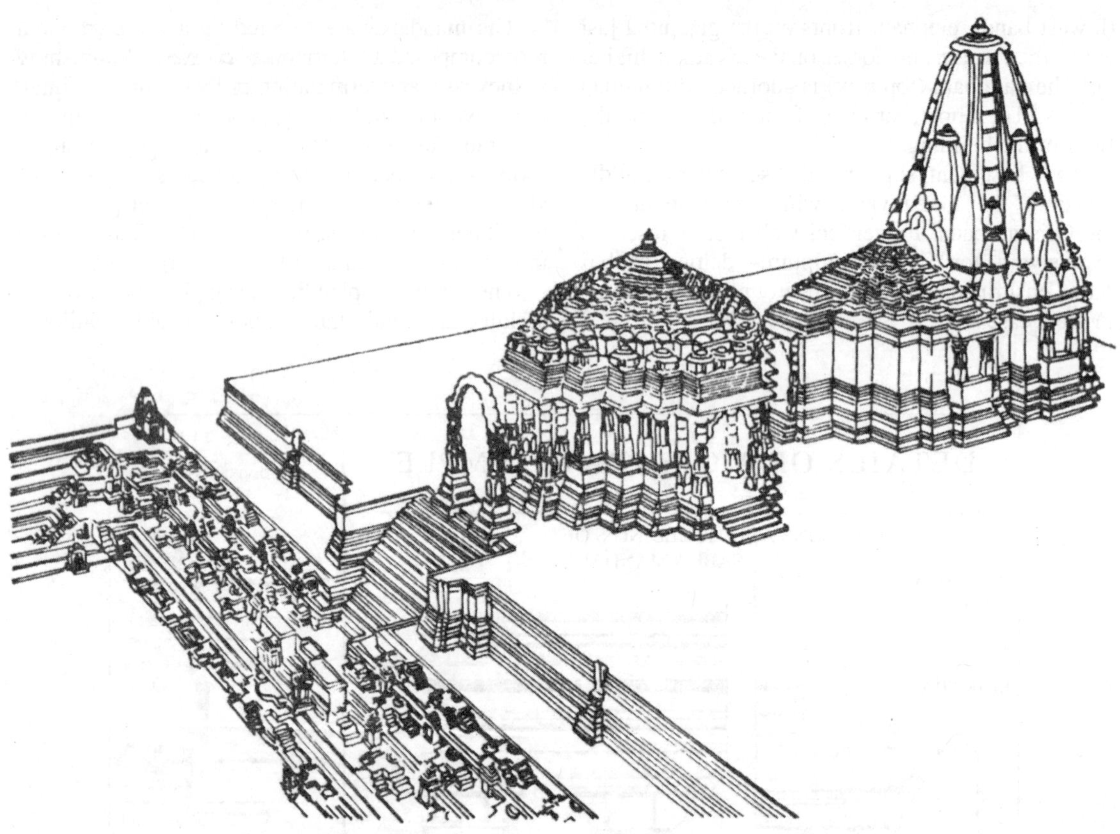

Fig. 176. Surya temple, Modhera, Gujarat, conjectural restoration.

(1026 A.D., according to an inscription on the back wall of the garbha-griha) is the *Sūrya temple* at *Modhera* (Pl. 4, 3; Figs. 176, 177) a little south of the old Solanki capital. Majestic even in its ruins, its setting and organic harmony give it a unique architectural and aesthetic grandeur. Its beauty derives from the harmonious relationship between the various elements which are united into an organic whole. From its setting on a high platform it looks down upon a tank which mirrors its magnificence. The temple, made of golden- brown sandstone, faces east so that the light of the rising sun penetrates to the shrine of the sun god in its farthest end.

From the kuṇḍa (temple tank), perhaps the most beautiful of its kind in India, a broad stairway in the middle of the western side leads up to the temple. Small flights of steps on either side interspersed with miniature shrines give the tank an indescribable elegance.

The kharaśila (broad terrace), constructed of solid brick faced with stone, forms an imposing courtyard all around the buildings. The relatively simple moulding of its sides relieves the intricate richness of the multiple steps of the tank. At the top of the steps stands a majestic kirti toraṇa. Immediately behind begins the temple complex proper, consisting of three separate but axially aligned structures. These are harmoniously blended with the usual threefold elevations as well as the indentations which run entirely around the three elements, thus giving them a concerted relationship.

The sabhā maṇḍapa (pillared hall) rises behind the kirti toraṇa—a diagonally aligned hall. At the four cardinal points of the hall are the entrances. The intermediary spaces are filled with kakṣāsanas, which serve as seats inside and as decorative low outer walls, with their outward sloping back-rests and fence-like vedi underneath. At the angles are short pillars forming an open arcade. The regular vertical recesses, which follow the angles of the plan, give a fluted appearance to the sides of the building. A wide continuous chajja

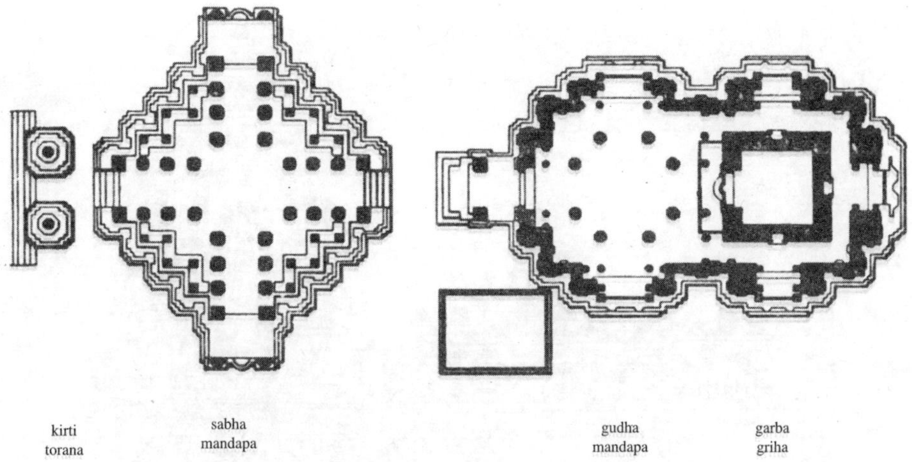


Fig. 177. Surya temple, Modhera, Gujarat.

projects all around the lowest part of the roof, and has a triple cornice above it. The ruins of the roof indicate that it was probably a low stepped pyramid, with numerous small finials breaking up the horizontal lines.

Inside the sabhā maṇḍapa, tall pillars form cross-shaped aisles with an octagonal nave in the centre. To uphold the domical roof while keeping the same size of the pillars, small tekis (attic pillars) each with its own sira (bracket) is superimposed on the sira of the eight central pillars to form an attic storey.

The pillars, richly carved from the kumbhi (moulded base) to the barani (capital), have stainbhas (shafts) with bands of sculpture, each belt a little smaller and narrower than the one below it. Small toraṇa arches separate the figure sculptures on these bands. This toraṇa arch motif runs throughout the temple, from the kirti toraṇa and cusped toraṇas at the entrances to the alternating semi-circular and triangular toraṇas which cross the pairs of pillars around the central nave. With the top attached to the architrave, their ends rest on the brackets of the pillars. The carvings, especially those on the pillars, are so deep and fine that they could have been done only by the laborious process of abrasion rather than by cutting. The joints of the overlapping courses forming the ceiling are so well hidden by delicate carving that it seems to be made all of a piece.

Close behind the sabhā maṇḍapa stands the gūdha maṇḍapa (closed hall), which forms one unit with the garbha-griha and the pradakṣiṇa-pātha around it. This building is much simpler than the sabhā maṇḍapa, but here too vertical indentations give a fluted appearance to the sides. The mandovara (wall) has niches in every bay containing figures of the sun-god. The superstructure has fallen to ruin. A portico covers the sole entrance to the gūdha maṇḍapa on the east. Balconied windows with side pillars project from the northern and southern sides of both the gūdha maṇḍapa and the pradakṣiṇa-patha, which has a third balconied window projecting from the western side as well.

The interior of the gūdha maṇḍapa has fewer pillars, but here too the over-all arrangement resembles that of the sabhā maṇḍapa, with aisles and octagonal nave, and attic pillars above the central ones to uphold the ceiling.

The temple has a sāndara plan. The ambulatory is lit by balconied windows. Horizontal bands, similar to those decorating the pillars, adorn the doorway to the garbha-griha, thus giving harmony to the decoration. Here the figures look somewhat stiff and crowded.

The harmony of the whole temple complex shows that a mastermind conceived and planned it.

The treatment of the interiors of the Northern temples reveals interesting variations, while everywhere the exterior decoration shows no restraint. For example in Orissa the interiors are almost completely plain. In Khajuraho on the other hand the interiors are more richly carved, while in Gujarat only the dark innermost chambers and passages have no ornament.

*The Rudreśvara temple* at *Prabhas Patan*, built shortly after the Modhera temple, does not have the octagonal design of the maṇḍapa.

The *Nilakanta-Mahādeva* temple at *Sunak* (Fig. 178), in the Mehsana district, is the most developed and best preserved among the late

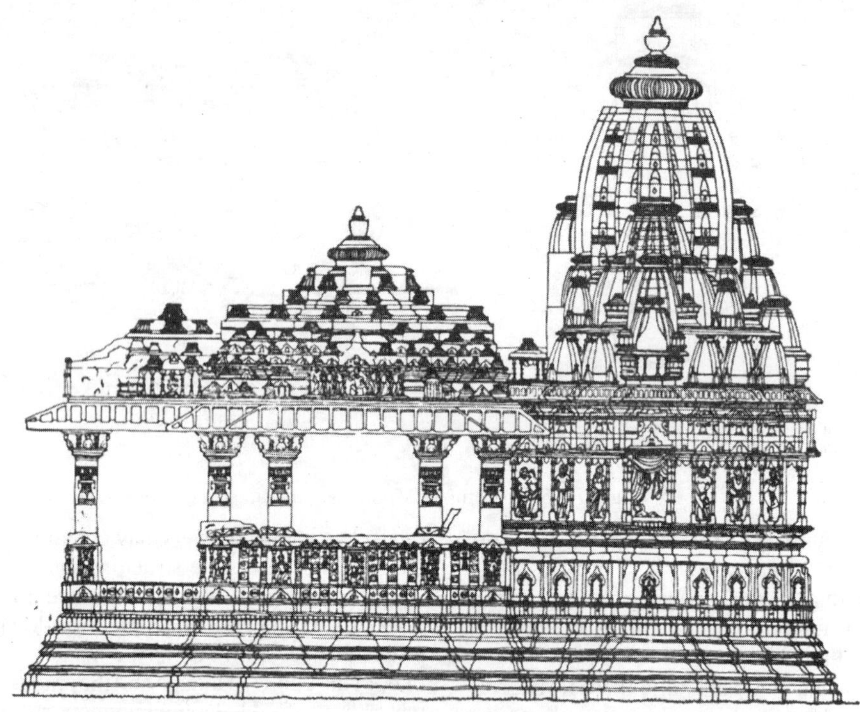

Fig. 178. Nilakantha-Mahadeva temple, Sunak, Gujarat.

eleventh century Solanki temples, and provides a good understanding of the triple elevation of the Solanki type temples, namely of the pitha, mandovara and roofing. It consists of an open portico, maṇḍapa and garbha-griha. The śikhara, with three rows of ūruśringas each with a double āmalaka similar to that of the main śikhara, has one of the most graceful outlines. The saṁvarana roof of the maṇḍapa is another outstanding feature. Twelve bracket figures of celestial nymphs adorn the maṇḍapa ceiling.

The *Navalakha temple* at *Sejakpur*, in the Surendranagar district, dating from the middle of the eleventh century, is nirandhrara in plan, having no ambulatory. The garbha-griha has a foliated plan. Around the base of the śikhara the ūruśringas are closely grouped. The gūdha maṇḍapa, with pillars, has the typical projections and recesses.

During the twelfth century, the Solanki rulers Siddharaja Jayasimha and Kumarapala patronised many grandiose buildings, but already they foreshadow a decline from the beauty of the previous cenutry. The *Rudra-mālā temple* at *Sidhpur*, now a colossal ruin, was one of the biggest and most richly decorated temples of this period. An exaggerated description of it survives in a Gujarati ballad. The few remaining fragments reveal the rich character of its design. The maṇḍapa may have had more than one storey. Of the *temple* at *Vadnagar*, an elaborately carved kīrti toraṇa makes us presume that this temple may have been even larger than the *Rudra-mālā* temple. The present ruin of the *Somanatha temple* at *Prabhas Patan* is similar to the Rudra-mālā and almost as large The original part of this temple, dating from the tenth century, has been almost obliterated by successive demolitions and reconstructions. After the sack of Mahmud of Ghazni in 1025 it had been rebuilt by Bhima I; and in the latter half of the twelfth century king Kumarapala enlarged it into the greatest temple of his reign.

In the thirteenth century the elegance of form and decoration of the eleventh century Solanki temples had declined. These structures have little architechtural interest. Among them, the *Nilakanṭa-Mahādeva* temple at *Miyani*, dated 1204, has a well-proportioned śikhara and a plain ranga-maṇḍapa. The *Navalakha temple* at

*Ghumli*, of the same period, is an ambitious, highly ornamented building with a two-storeyed maṇḍapa.

Besides temples, this vigorous Solanki art produced semi-religious and civic structures as well, such as temple archways, city gates and water reservoirs and sluices. The kirti toraṇa(temple archways), generally outside the temple entrance, were erected on the same principles as the temple design but much more ornate: with spreading base, figured shaft, bracket capital and covered superstructure, all in graceful proportions. Among the best examples are the ones at *Vadnagar* (where the temples have entirely disappeared), and the more complete one at *Rewah*, where a pair of heavy elaborate columns uphold a wide, richly decorated architrave. These toraṇas were used for the hindola (ceremony of swinging the image of the god) or for weighing rulers against gold, as well as other purposes.

The *city gates* combine utility and beauty, protection and a welcoming approach. They form the most artistic part of the fortifications of the towns. All of them were double, but in most cases only the inner gateway remains. Though in stone, they preserve the elements of their wooden prototypes. Rich and lively sculpture adorns the lintels of the archways. The best examples are the four at Dabhoi in Baroda, built in the twelfth century and altered in the thirteenth. One occupied the centre of each of the four walls. Three of them resemble the general type seen also at *Ghumli* in the *Rampola gate*, and the complete set of four at *Jhinjuwada*. The fourth or main gate at *Dabhoi*, the Hira or Diamond gate, is unique. It is very wide and so thick that it contains a number of rooms for guards in its wings, and a temple on either side. The *Kalika Mātā temple* within the thickness of the northern side of the wall of the gateway is quite large and resembles a Greek cross. While the exterior is plain, on the interior it is one of the most ornate buildings in the city. Here the imagination of the artists, unrestricted by any convention, had free play. No regulations inhibit either the architecture or decoration.

Gujarat has the most artistic of all the *tanks*, *wells* and *conduits* of India, where water plays an essential role in religious and economic life. The *sluice* of the *Khan Sarovar tank* at *Anihila-pattana*, with its elegant eleventh century vase and foliage pillars, shows that even water gates were works of fine art. The *wavs or baoli* (a special kind of public well in western India) combine utility and beauty. The passages to the well form a series of narrow galleries connected by flights of steps. Groups of pillars adorn each bay, while pillared kiosks and pavilions give beauty to the mouth of the draw- well and to the entrance, with the two passages provided with skylights. One of the largest and most elegant, judging by a remaining pillar, is the ruined *Rāni wav* at *Anihilapattana,* dating from the middle of the eleventh century, but the *Vethiya wav* near *Mukhana* (eleventh century) and the *Vayad* in *old Baroda* (thirteenth century) are better preserved. The latter is well proportioned and has four galleries. These wavs were fore-runners to the pillared courts constructed underground in the time of the Muslims to provide refreshment from the hot sun above.

## TEMPLES IN THE DECCAN

## EARLY WESTERN CHALUKYAS

A distinctive style of structural Hindu temple emerged in the Deccan during the sixth to eighth. centuries A.D This was due largely to the religious zeal of the Early Western Chalukyas of Badami who ruled over parts of the Kanarese and Maharashtrian regions. Until the Rashtrakutas vanquished them, they had their capital successively at Aihole, Vātāpi (Badami) and Pattadakal—all in the Bijapur district of Mysore. At Aihole, their first capital on the banks of the Malaprabha river, they erected thirty temples within its walls and forty in its outskirts. Some fifty of them are still extant, though Aihole itself is little more than a village at present.

This style flourished chiefly in its formative centres—Aihole, Badami with its close neighbour Mahakutesvar, and Pattadakal. For all these temples they used the locally available sandstone of fine grain and quality. Since it was easily manageable, it could be used not only for making large building blocks but also for delicate sculpture. This alone enabled them to erect bigger structures richly adorned with figure sculpture.

The simplest form can be seen in the so- called maṇḍapa type temples at Aihole. These resemble the cave temples to some extent. They consist of a simple cella in an open construction—a sort of verandah. Gradually this developed into the mature prasāda and vimāna forms of temple, having a mukha maṇḍapa, a closed sabhā maṇḍapa, an antarāla (antechamber) and a pradakṣiṇa pātha. Both types of the śikhara, the pyramidal and curvilinear, may be seen here.

The Konti-gudi group of temples and the Ladh Khan are usually regarded as the simplest type of temples in Aihole.* Whatever their chronological priority may be, the *Kontigudi* group looks more primitive. Of the three temples in this group, one faces east and the other west. They stand one in front of the other (Fig. 179), while the third one stands near the one facing east. The *temple facing*

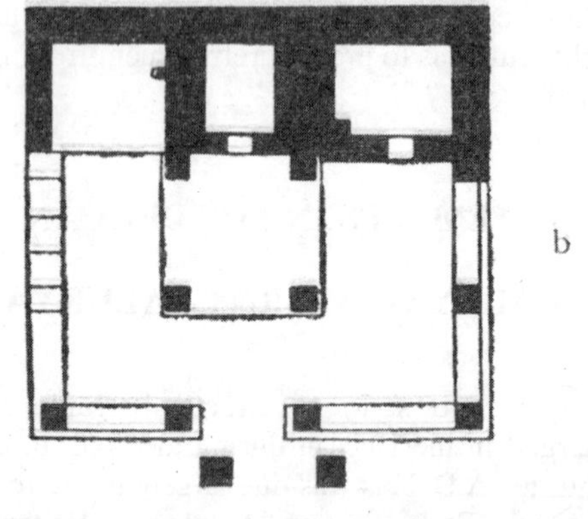


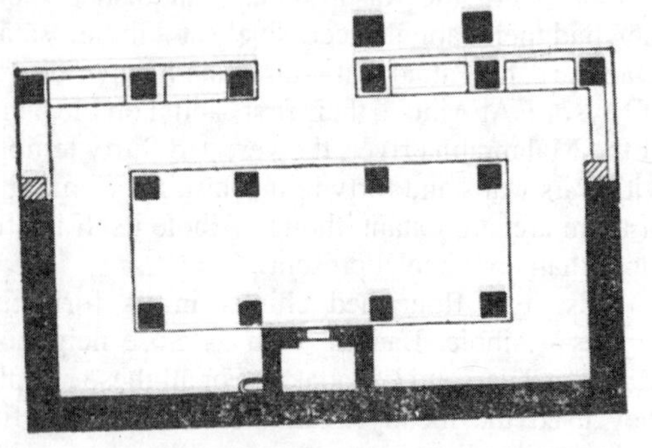


Fig. 179. Konti Gudi temples, Aihole, plan,

a. temple facing east,

b. temple facing west.

*east* has an oblong plan, with the entrance in the centre of a long open verandah. This unclosed side at the east has six pillars, while solid walls encompass the other three sides. Eight more pillars stand on a platform in the centre of the building The garbha griha adjoins the rear wall on the west. A flat-roofed porch with four pillars unites this temple with the one before it.

This second *temple facing west* (square in plan) has another open verandah in front. Its garbha griha too abuts the rear wall. But the square, platform-like structure on top of the sabhā maṇḍapa is a novel feature. It may be an embryonic form of the śikhara.

The *third temple*, adjacent to the one facing east and resembling it with its oblong plan and the six pillars in front of the verandah, seems to be the latest of the group. Here we see for the first time a kind of screen formed by connecting the four front pillars of the eight pillars in the centre by means of a latticed wall. This may be the first step towards enclosing the garbha griha. Here the garbha griha is still attached to the back wall of the temple.

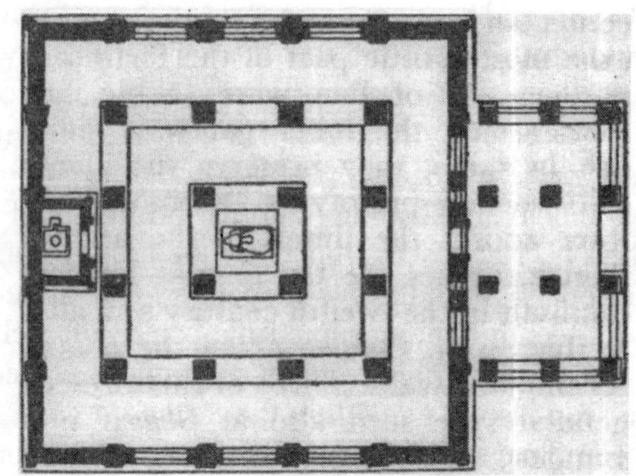

Fig. 180. Lad Khan temple, Aihole, plan.

The *Lad Khan* (Fig. 180) is a large maṇḍapa-type temple at Aihole. It stands on a moulded adiṣṭhāna. Sixteen pillars, arranged into two squares—one inside the other—support the roof. In this way they form a double aisle all around the central Naṇḍī shrine. The four pillars in the middle are somewhat higher. The pillars of the third concentric square forming the outer periphery of the temple have been transformed into pilasters by closing the intercolumnar space with wall screens, each consisting of a single massive slab set on edge, except at the entrance on the middle of the eastern side. The three slabs in the middle of the southern and northern sides were perforated to serve as windows providing light and air. The western wall, adjoining the garbha griha, was left blank. This closing in of

* Opinions differ regarding the dating of these temples.

the walls with slabs between the pillars has led to the supposition that this temple may originally have been an open secular meeting hall, perhaps a santhagara, described in ancient writings as open, flat-roofed structures without walls.

The roofing is unusual, consisting of large flat sloping slabs arranged in two tiers. Long narrow stone strips covering their entire length protect the joints of these slabs. The third temple of the Konti-gudi group has similar roofing. This system continued for a long period.

On the roof of the Ladh Khan, just above the middle of the hall, stands another small shrine with images sculpted on the outer walls. Again, as already seen at Konti-gudi on the temple facing west, this may be an embryonic form of śikhara. A stone ladder attached to the porch gives access to this rooftop shrine.

The mukha maṇḍapa (porch) stands in front of the sabhā maṇḍapa on the same moulded adiṣṭhāna. Rectangular in form, it is wider than deep. A dozen pillars, set in rows of three, uphold the roof which is similar to that of the sabhā maṇḍapa. These pillars have beautiful sculpted images of Yamuna standing on a tortoise and Ganga with a pair of dwarfs and flying figures.

Kakṣāsanas make their first appearance here. These serve both as seats and as low ornamental outer walls between the pillars, with outward sloping backs and a fence-like vedi underneath, decorated with dwarf pilaster and ornamental sculpture including the pūrṇa-kalasa (bowl of plenty).

The pillars have plain square shafts with bracket capitals. But on the exterior angles of the sabhā maṇḍapa the pillars taper slightly at the upper ends. Cushion capitals with an open flower abacus uphold the bracket. Here again we see for the first time a typical form of capital used almost everywhere in South India in the Dravidian style.

The *Durgā temple* (Fig. 181), one of the finest of the Early Chalukyan buildings, shows a development in temple structure. Apsidal in plan, it bears resemblance to a Buddhist chaitya. However, it is not the first experiment of its kind. Twenty miles away, the Chikka Mahākūtā temple near Badami, also apsidal in plan, probably influenced the planning of the Durgā temple. Other examples of the kind exist also at Chejarla, and at Ter where the Trivikrama temple was orginally a Buddhist structural chaitya later adapted to Hindu worship. But the temple at Ter was made of brick while the Chikka Mahākūtā temple was constructed of stone without the use of binding mortar (cf. Figs. 44, 45).

The Durgā temple stands on a high well- moulded base. The temple includes a mukha maṇḍapa, sabhā maṇḍapa and garbha griha with a pradaksiṇa pātha all around it. Short massive square pillars on top of the adiṣṭhāna form a colonnaded passage. These pillars, decorated with figure sculptures, show much more elegance than those of the Ladh Khan or the Konti-gudi. An amusing frieze of dwarfs adorns the high adiṣṭhāna. The squat pyramidal śikhara over the garbha griha appears out of harmony with the rest of the building. Two flights of steps leading to a portico give entrance to the temple on the eastern side. Four square pillars support the ceiling of the mukha maṇḍapa from which a highly ornate doorway leads into the sabhā maṇḍapa, which is divided into a central nave and two side aisles by two rows of pillars. The sloping roof of the aisles is lower than the flat roof of the nave, which is raised over a sort of clerestory. Niches

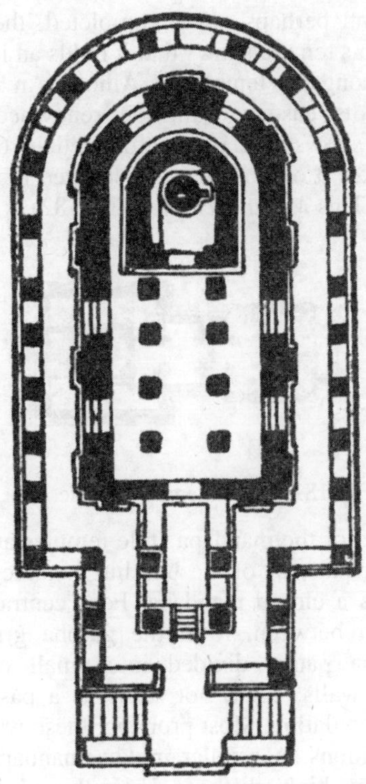

Fig. 181. Durga temple, Aihole, plan.

enclosing bold figure sculpture adorn the walls of the sabhā maṇḍapa and garbha griha along the pillared corridor.

The temple is not dedicated to Durgā, but the name derives from the fact that till the early nineteenth century it formed part of a fortification, also called durga.

The *Huchchimalli-gudi temple* has a novel feature making its appearance for the first time—namely the antarāla, obtained in a primitive manner by building a masonry wall between the pillars of the nave closest to the garbha griha, to which a doorway in the centre of this wall gives access. Besides the garbha griha and antarāla, the rectangular plan of this temple includes a pradakṣiṇa pātha, mukha maṇḍapa and sabhā maṇḍapa. The śikhara was added at a later date. The kakṣāsanas on both sides of the portico have an exceptionally elegant ghata pallava (vase and foliage) design signifying the bowl of plenty symbolic of prosperity.

Meguti, meaning the temple on high, derives its name from the graceful Jaina temple built on an imposing hill overlooking Aihole. Though partly ruined and perhaps never completed, the ground plan of this temple shows that it holds an important place among the temples at Aihole. An inscribed slab on its eastern wall, the renowned Aihole praśasti, shows that it was founded in 634 A.D. This makes it one of the earliest dated monuments in India. This *Meguti temple* (Fig. 182) is the most

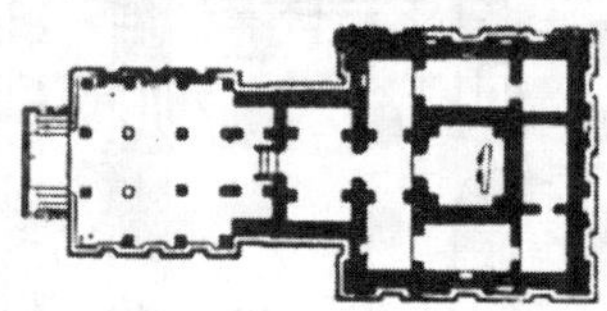

Fig. 182. Meguti temple, Aihole, plan.

developed of the maṇḍapa style temples at Aihole. The principal part of the building, square in plan, resembles a closed maṇḍapa. Four central pillars, walled in between, form the garbha griha. The pradakṣiṇa pātha, divided into small chambers by cross walls, could not serve as a passage for circumambulation. Most probably these walls were later additions. A smaller mukha maṇḍapa stands on the same high adiṣṭhāna. From this adiṣṭhāna up the pilastered walls to the parapet on top, the outer surface of the main part of the building forms a rhythmic pattern of projections and recesses.

*Badami*, the second capital of the Early Chalukyas, was a picturesque town formerly known as Vātāpi, nestling at the foot of steep cliffs beside a small lake or tank. With its close neighbour Mahākuteśvar, Badami possesses the first examples of the Dravidian order or style. Here we see the first known examples of the vimāna temples of the Early Western Chalukyas, namely the upper Śivālaya high on the main hill, the lower Śivālaya, and the Malegitti Śivālaya perched on an outer crag of the Badami hills.

The *Upper Śivālaya*, although partly ruined, still dominates the city below from its majestic eminence within the Fort of Badami. A closed pradakṣiṇa pātha surrounds its sāndara vimāna and extends forward to encompass a pillared maṇḍapa. Now only one side of this wall remains. Pilasters with recesses in between adorn the external walls of the maṇḍapa and vimāna, and kūdus decorate the chajjas (eaves). The square vimāna rises in diminishing tetragonal storeys. Nāsikas embellish each of the four sides of the square grīva and śikhara.

The *Lower Śivālaya* (so called for want of any other name) differs from the Malegitti Śivālaya only in being sāndhara and smaller. All the talas (storeys) of the vimāna have the hāra elements, while the octagonal grīva and śikhara have kūtas.

Surmounting a towering sandstone boulder overlooking the town, and constructed of the same material, the *Malegitti Śivālaya* temple seems almost part of the rock on which it is built. Massively constructed to bear the brunt of the elements in its exposed position, the nirandhara vimāna shares a common moulded base with the closed maṇḍapa in front of it, which has almost the same width. An open four-pillared porch precedes it. It has better proportions and unity than the Upper Śivālaya temple. The hāra of the lowest tala (storey) of the vimāna has karṇakūtas and śālās, and extends over the maṇḍapa. Nāsikas adorn the four cardinal faces of the grīva. A heavy dome covers the octagonal śikhara.

*Mahākuteśvar*, on the outskirts of Badami, also possesses typical early temples of the Chalukyas. Here a group of prasāda (Northern) and vimāna (Southern) style temples stand side by side in the same walled enclosure. The main temple, called the *Mahākuteśvara* temple, displays the Southern temple style as conceived by the Early Western Chalukyas. Whitewash and modern additions have partly disfigured it. The vimāna is sāndhara. Pierced stone windows admit light to the pradakṣiṇa pātha around the garbha griha. The circumbulatory passage leads to a large columned maṇḍapa. A separate Naṇḍī hall stands on an axis with the entrance porch. The temple rests on an elaborately carved adiṣṭhāna. Double sets of pilasters, flanking niches with sculpture, enrich the temple walls.

The *Saṇgameśvara temple*, one of the best preserved Northern style temples in the enclosure, stands close to the Mahākuteśvara temple. It has a garbha griha preceded by a portico. The former carries a massive stumpy śikhara.

At *Pattadakal*, the third Chalukyan capital about 16 km from Badami, we see the final stage in the development before the traditions of the styles became fully established. Here too examples of both the Northern and Southern styles stand side by side. The four main temples at Pattadakal are the Pāpanāth, Saṇgameśvara, Virūpakṣa, and Mallikārjuna. Of these, the first-named is more Northern in character while the others show more Southern characteristics, as crystallised in the Pallava temples.

The *Pāpanāth temple* (Fig. 183 a, b), erected before the end of the seventh century, reveals inexperience in architectural design. The plan lacks correct placement of the main parts and a logical interrelationship between them. The śikhara at the eastern end of the building is too short and undersized for the long, low building; and the antarāla is too big. It looks more like a square assembly hall than a vestibule, more like a maṇḍapa than an antechamber to the sanctuary. Both the plan and elevation do not harmonise. The massive

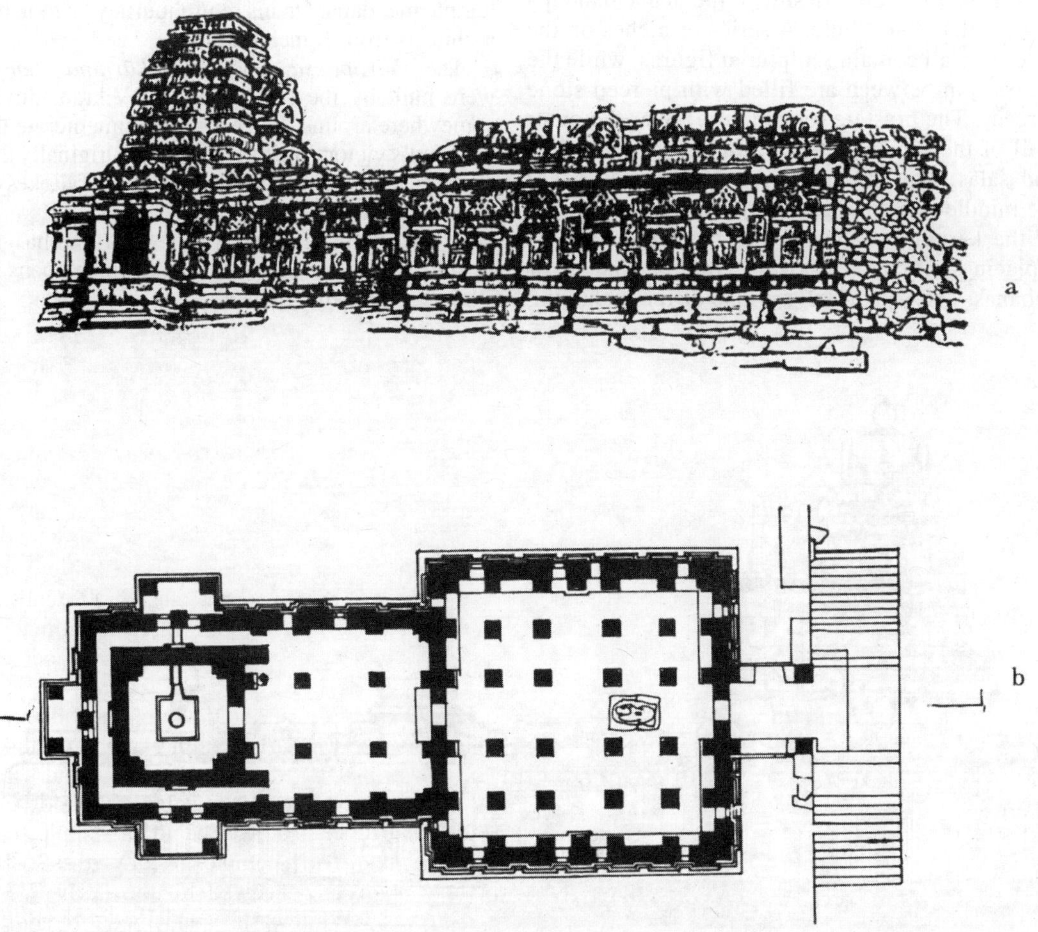


Fig. 183. Papanath temple, Pattadakal; a. elevation, b. plan.

interior still bears the influence of rock-cut architecture. The string courses surrounding the building resemble strong braces holding the structure together. The decoration of the outer surface, consisting of repetitions of bas-relief shrines in a triangular pattern on the canopies, shows little understanding of architectural ornamentation.

The earliest of the three temples displaying Southern influence is the *Saṇgameśvara* built by Chalukya Vijayaditya. Like the Pallava temples it has no sukhanāsika, while. Chalukyan temples have it. Square from the base to the śikhara, it rises in three storeys. With its closed pradakṣiṇa pātha around the garbha griha it belongs to the sāndhara mode. The outer wall of the sanctuary extends forward to enclose the ardha maṇḍapa and the mahā maṇḍapa, standing on a common adiṣṭhāna. The northern side of the mahā maṇḍapa has a pillared vestibule. A series of niches on the exterior wall contain sculptured figures, while the recesses in between are filled with pierced stone screens. The prastāra (entablature) over the outer wall of the vimāna carries a hara of karṇa kūtas and śālās. The third storey has only śālās over the middle of four sides. In this case the absence of the karṇa kūtas marks the first step towards replacing the hara itself by the lanchanas or vāhanas. The Saṇgameśvara also differs in having cellas dedicated to Durgā and Gaṇeśa at the two ends of the ardha maṇḍapa.

The earliest extant temple complexes are the larger Virūpakṣa and the smaller neighbouring Mallikārjuna. They are almost identical. In their plan and sculptural representation they bear resemblance to the Kailāsanātha temple at Kanchi. The reason was that during the reign of Mamalla, the Pallavas scored a significant victory over the Chalukyas and occupied the latter's capital Vātāpi (Badami) for twelve years. One of the later kings of this early dynasty, Vikramaditya II, to avenge the dishonour of his forefathers, victoriously entered the city of Kanchi. However instead of ransacking the city, he gave large amounts of gold to the Kailāsanātha temple and to the Brahmans of that city. A record of his magnanimity can be seen in one of the inscriptions on the pillar of the Kailāsanātha temple maṇḍapa. On his return journey he took back architects from Kanchipuram.

The *Virūpakṣa* and *Mallikārjuna temples* were built by the two queens of Vikramaditya II somewhere around 740 A.D. to commemorate their husband's victory over the Pallavas. Originally these temples were named Lokeśvara and Trailokeśvara after these queens.

In plan both temples consist of a garbha griha surrounded by a pradakṣiṇa pātha, which opens into a large columned maṇḍapa.

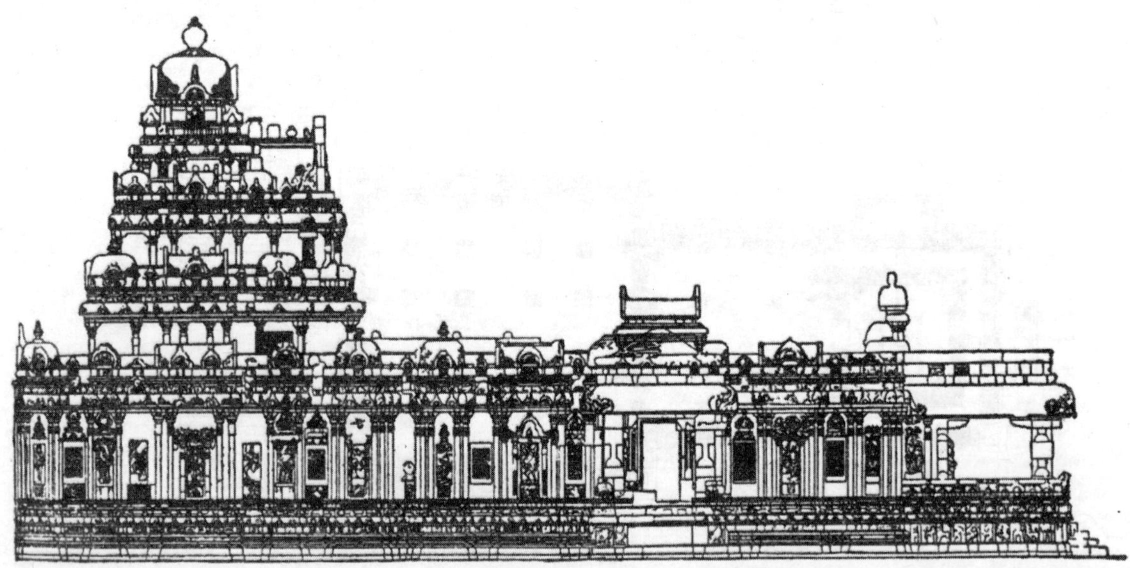

Fig. 184. Virupaksha temple, Pattadakal, elevation

The latter has three entrances. In the Virūpakṣa the maṇḍapa is wider than the sanctuary and circumambulatory passage. A Naṇḍī shrine stands in front of both temples, and an enclosure wall surrounds each temple. The enclosure walls of these two temples interlock by a diagonal arrangement which is unique in Indian temple architecture. The elevation of both temples shows Southern characteristics.

The Virūpakṣa temple has a tall vimāna (Fig. 181) of the sāndhara type, square in plan from base to śikhara, and rising in four storeys. Five bays adorn its outer walls. On all sides, except the western, porches lead to the multi-pillared hall. Over the parapet at the rear of each porch rises an embryonic gopuram, which resembles an additional storey over the entrances to the maṇḍapa. From the third storey of the vimāna projects the sukanāsika.

Sculptural decorations, perfectly blended with the architecture, relieve the heavy solidity of the structure. Perforated windows alternate with niches. The canopy of the latter, consisting of a chaitya arch, shows much more maturity than the multiple decorative arches on the Pāpanāth. One or two pilasters separate the niches from the windows. These pilasters, constricted just below the capital, like a neck and shoulder under the head, are among the first examples of the characteristic Dravidian order. The kūtas and śālās on the coping of the compound wall of the temple complex bear resemblance to the Shore temple at Mamallapuram.

The harmonious blending of the elements of this temple shows that it results from much thought both for the whole and for every little detail. The stones, though old and grey, seem to vibrate with the feeling and spirit that shaped them. It is one of those rare buildings where the original inspiration of the builders lives on in their creation.

In the Mallikārjuna temple the hāras have been completely left out on the fourth storey of the vimāna, thus exposing the circular grīva and śikhara with their cardinal nāsikas. From its second, third and fourth storeys project sukanāsikas. Whereas the wall fillings of the Virūpakṣa have double pilasters, on the Mallikārjuna they are triple. Though smaller, the Mallikārjuna shows greater stylistic progress relative to the Virūpakṣa, especially in the finely carved windows which alternate with sculptured panels, and its interior carving seems to be the most advanced in Early Western Chalukyan art.

## LATER WESTERN CHALUKYAS

Under the Later Western Chalukyas (eleventh to thirteenth century A.D.), this particular style of architecture reached its full maturity. In the numerous temples erected under their patronage, particularly at the northern boundary of Mysore, in the upper valleys of the Tungabhadra, Bhima and Krishna rivers, they turned from the traditional sandstone to the softer and more tractable chloritic schist. This resulted in less massive architecture and in finer, more delicate sculpture.

About a hundred of these temples remain. With one exception, all these structures are rectangular, and have no pradakṣiṇa pātha. Instead the adiṣṭhāna extends far beyond the walls to provide a processional path around the whole structure. Often the main entrance is at the sides rather than the front, while on the eastern side another cella, shrine or pillared portico was added on.

In most temples in sunny India, where sufficient light comes through the doorways, few windows are provided so that there is much wall space inviting decoration. Besides, the darkness enhances the sense of mystery. Most of the ornamentation of the wall was exuberant without much consideration for order or restraint. During this period, however, greater experience, taste and charm are evident. These temples, outstanding for more appropriate decoration, continue a tradition begun at Pattadakal. The pilasters are more slender and better spaced. They alternate with buttress-like half-pillars which harmonise in design with the pillars in the open hall in front. At suitable spaces, there are ornamental shrines or niches overshadowed by wide eaves and a canopy which echoes the form of the śikhara. An inborn gift for sculptural decoration is shown also by graceful reliquary-like designs which uphold ornaments similar to creepers wherever they fit artistically into the space they occupy. A section of moulding just below the capital juts out sharply like a knife-edge. The doorways are specially contrived to focus attention on the shrine.

The *Jain temple* at *Lakkundi* near Gadag is the first example of a building made entirely of the softer chloritic schist. It probably dates from the middle of the eleventh century. It is the most majestic of its group at Lakkundi, distinguished by a high central storey in the śikhara and by a greater curve on the top of the tower. In all, the vimāna has five storeys, square from the base to the śikhara. The navaraṅga has a square bay at the centre, flanked by eight smaller ones. A sukhanāsika projects in front; and tall nāsika fronts, between pairs of slender pilasters, adorn the walls.

A new architectural feature appears. Up to this period the cornice was bulky owing to its rock-cut origin which in turn simulated the overhanging thatch of primitive wooden buildings. Such a cornice, however, did not protect the structural temples from heavy monsoon rains nor from the strong sun. Towards the end of the eleventh century a wide eave, sometimes straight but often double-curved and projecting far out, makes its first appearance. It combines both beauty and utility. Such eaves became characteristic of the Later Chalukyan style.

One of the first examples of this style is the *Mukuteśvara* (around the end of the eleventh century) at *Chaudadampur* on the bank of the Tungabhadra river. Here we see the new kind of eave, together with a more mature form of śikhara, where profuse sculptural ornamentation obscures the outlines of the storeys. Though otherwise plain and asymetricai, the temple is elegant.

The finest examples of this new development are the Kāsiviśveśvara at Lakkundi, the Mahādeva at Ittagi, and the Mailikārjuna century.

Lakkundi became the Hoysala capital in 1193. The *Kāsiviśveśvara* temple at *Lakkundi*, Dharwar, has a shrine at both ends and a tower over each, both partly destroyed. Near the centre of its layout is an open court, with different compartments extending axially on both sides. In elevation it shows power and vitality. It is richly decorated. Its plan consists of four squares of different sizes aligned together. In places the pillars are embossed with an intricate design as delicate as metalwork. The bold decoration of the vimāna contrasts aesthetically with the refined carving of the doorways. A striking feature of the ornamentation is a large, prominent niche with a canopy in the middle of each side. Above it is a trefoil design which is repeated along the middle of the śikhara, becoming smaller as it rises. Like the Baroque, the decoration is voluptuous but under control. The doorways, each a masterpiece, are the principal feature. Mouldings frame rectangular openings supported by strong pilasters. Over the moulded lintel is a sculptured cornice and an overdoor. Elephants anointing Lakshmi constitute the central motif of the heavy keystone. The southern doorway looks even richer with the rugged surface of its relief sculpture. On the S-shaped curves of the cornice over the door to the sanctuary a lively battle between riders on elephants and horses is depicted. In the minute detail of technique it resembles ivory carving.

The *Mahādeva temple* at *Ittagi*, east of Gadag, is the only temple that remains intact among a group of religious buildings erected on a terrace (Fig. 185). Although the śikhara is partly gone and and the roof damaged, it retains a harmonious beauty. The various parts are grouped simply and appropriately, with pleasing proportions. The decoration shows balance and order, and is well planned and distributed. The gently curving tower has no more storeys, only tiers covered completely with sculpture. The ceiling of the maṇḍapa is coffered, with delicate figures and scrolls of foliage. The pair of rectangular recesses on each wall of the navaraṅga have a kind of table and pedestal. On the front of the tower is a round niche to change images when desired.

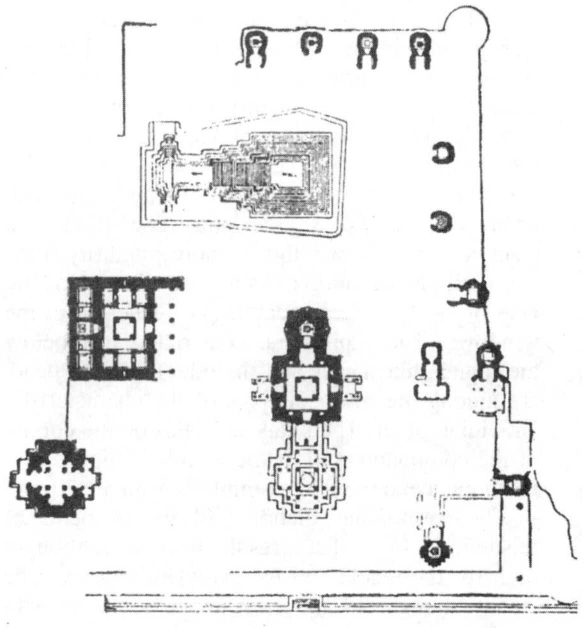

Fig. 185. Temples at Ittagi, ground plans.

The *Mallikārjuna* at *Kuruvatti*, on the Tungabhadra river, has a symmetrical plan and complete śikhara. Here the decoration is less crowded and more controlled. The toraṇa at the entrance to the vestibule of the sanctuary has a heavy lintel on a pair of free-standing pillars, all with elaborate carvings. The sculpture on the brackets of the upper portion of the pillars is more delicate.

The *Someśvara* at *Gadag* (Fig. 186), at one time belonging to a group of three temples, differs from the Dravidian tradition in the decoration of the walls. At the centre of the exterior wall we find the beginnings of figure sculpture in niches, as in the Hoysala temples. Each niche resembles a stele and contains a figure in high relief. This new decoration replaces the pilasters around the temple. But the decoration tends to confusion and loss of vitality, showing decline.

The *Dodda Basappa* at Dambal (around the end of the twelfth century) is the only star-shaped temple in this region. But while the Hoysala temples have star-shaped sanctuaries, here the navaraṅga too has a stellate plan. By joining the twenty-four pointed sanctuary with the thirty-four pointed navaraṅga, the points are reduced to nineteen and twenty-one respectively. This star plan continues to the top of the structure, giving the temple an unusual appearance of projecting angles with a sharp light-and-shade effect. This impression of strength, given by the vertical angles, gets lost when the verticals begin to intersect with the horizontal string-courses of the śikhara, for the pattern becomes too minute for architectural effect. The fluted pillars of the porch harmonise with the angularity of the building, but the consistency seems to be exaggerated. In the offsets of the vimāna, however, forms alternate with designs and designs with forms, gracefully tapering so that the whole resembles walls with tracery or buttresses with panels.

Fig. 186. Someshvara temple, Gadag.

## THE HOYSALAS

The Hoysalas rose to power in the eleventh century after defeating the Chalukyas. They formed an independent kingdom in Mysore for two and a half centuries, and erected over a hundred temples—a very great achievement for the limited area and time of their rule.

Hoysala temples are made of very finegrained and close-textured greenish-grey chloride schist (soapstone) which is much easier to work with than granite or sandstone because it is quite soft when first quarried but turns very hard after it is exposed to the air. It can be carved fairly easily and lends itself to sculpture with minute details and deep undercutting.

The Hoysala temple consists of the usual three parts: the vimāna containing the garbha griha, the śukhanāsikā (antarāla) and the navaraṅga (maṇḍapa). Often a separate mukha maṇḍapa (open pillared pavilion) stands in front of it. Sometimes three vimānas, each fronted by their antarālas, group around the same navaraṅga instead of the usual single one. Such a temple is called trikutachala. Many Hoysala temples are double, with all their parts duplicated. At times there are even triple, quadruple and quintuple ones.

Hoysala temples usually stand in an enclosure. The surrounding walls frequently have cellas with a pillared verandah in front. The plan of the temples is usually aṣthabadra (star-shaped) obtained by a number of rotated squares.

The decorations of the wall surface run in horizontal bands. The navaraṅga (maṇḍapa) is divided into two main zones, namely the adiṣṭhāna and the pillared maṇḍapa. The vimāna has three main zones—the same adiṣṭhāna mouldings, the vimāna wall surface with statue decorations, and the śikhara.

The high upapitha (platform) on which the temple stands harmonises with the buildings in shape but is much wider, providing a terrace all around for circumambulation. It serves as an open pradakṣiṇa pātha.

The elevated adiṣṭhāna of the Hoysala temples has lively bands of running designs all around the whole building. Generally the lowest band has a procession of elephants to give the impression of stability and strength. A band of horsemen just above may signify speed. A strip with spiralling foliage separates the horsemen from a frieze having vividly detailed scenes from the epics. The next strip has yālis (scaly monsters similar to a hippopotamus, or hippogryphs) with spiralling creepers coming out of them. Finally on the top band appear hamsas (legendary gooselike birds), which according to the poets 'swim in the minds of the great'. Above this decorative moulded adiṣṭhāna are kakṣāsanas (sloping seat-backs).

The second zone of the navaraṅga is the pillared hall. Originally it was an open maṇḍapa, but with the addition of pierced stone screens through which the light filters into the interior, it became a closed maṇḍapa. Lathe-turned pillars and capitals, resembling a baluster with rounded mouldings, uphold the ceiling of the maṇḍapas. The base of the pillars remains square. Most of them have a bell-like portion at the lower end of the shaft. They reveal an early type of mass-production. A sloping strut-like bracket, attached to the capital by sockets, has well-finished madanakai figures (figures with halos of leaves).

The carved adiṣṭhāna continues around the vimāna. The walls of the vimāna are sharply dentated—the alternately recessed and projected angles forming a pattern of light and shade. Each surface has the sculptured figure of a deity surrounded by foliage which serves as a niche with a superstructure above.

The crowning śikhara strikes the keynote of this style. A wide eave jutting far out separates it from the vimāna wall yet the star-shape continues up, resulting in a fluted appearance all the way up the vimāna elevation. Balanced by horizontal mouldings, these vertical lines produce an orderly arrangement of diminishing tiers, crowned at the top by an umbrella-like finial. Small shrines and niches decorate the spaces between the horizontal and vertical lines, forming a beautiful texture from the sculptural point of view.

The Hoysala style of temples seems to indicate that the architecture and sculpture were adapted to metalwork and the carving of sandalwood and ivory. As in sandalwood art, each figure on the vimāna wall is a distinct image in its own setting. The madanakai brackets resemble ivory work, and the strap patterns under the eaves imitate metalwork. The profuse simulated jewellery on the figures recalls the work of goldsmiths, while the fine relief resembles silver filigree. Each artist seems to have created an individual masterpiece in stone and added it to the temple, without regard to the other contributions. The builders of these temples recounted in detail the dramatic scenes from mythology familiar to all.

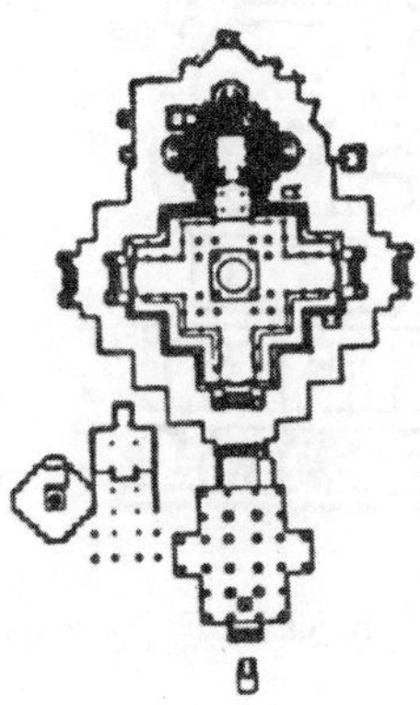

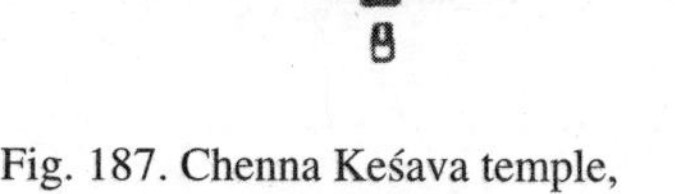

Fig. 187. Chenna Keśava temple, Belur, plan.

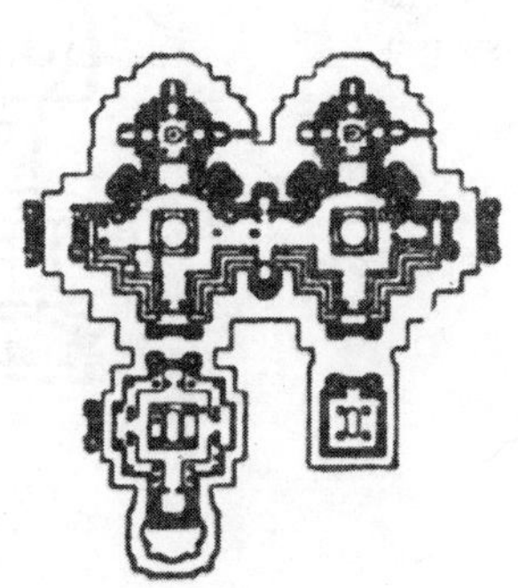

Fig. 188. Hoysaleshvara temple, Halebid, plan.

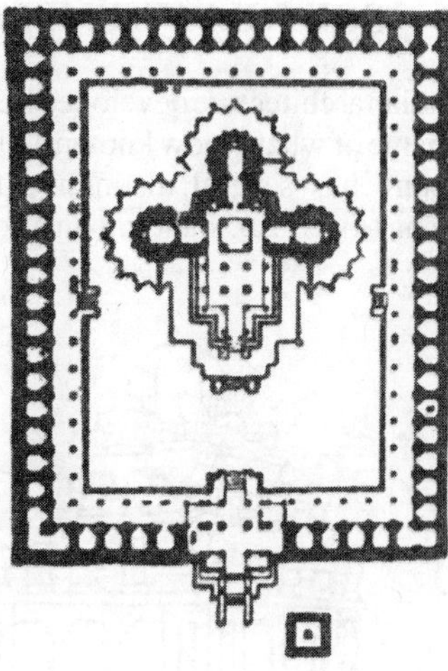

Fig. 189. Kesava temple, Somnathpur, plan.

The *Chenna Keśava temple* (Fig. 187) at *Belur* in the Hassan district, built in 1117 A.D. by king Vishnuvardhana, is noted for its lavish carvings. Though the superstructure is gone it has aesthetic values. The artists were still unrestricted in placing the sculpture on the exterior and had more freedom in arranging the ornamentation of the adiṣṭhāna. One of its distinctions lies in the lively sculptural figures on ten of the twenty grilles between the pillars of the maṇḍapa. They illustrate Puranic stories. In the interior the cruciform aisles crossing in the middle produce a central nave. The temple looks overcrowded and lacks a sense of spaciousness, repose and control. The pillars huddle too close together and there is too much carving. All the pillars except the four in the centre have different designs, producing variety and astonishing complexity as if each were produced by a separate team as a distinct masterpiece. One of these, called the Narasimha pillar, has a repeated design of niches with an image in every one. The whole pillar can be easily turned. Inscriptions in the temple show that each artist contributed an example of his work.

The most lavish example of this style is the *Hoysaleṣvara temple* (Fig. 188) at *Halebid* (1120—1182). Inscriptions on the temple bear the names of its chief builders. Its superstructure is missing too, like that of the Chenna Keśava. It has profuse sculptural adornment.

The plan consists of two cruciform vimānas connected to each other by their transepts. Repeated angles and projections break up the exterior, where contrast is obtained by the different forms of the stellate vimāna and the surface of the navaraṅga. Every detail of this temple is intricately carved but many of the figures look rather stiff and conventional. On either side of the doorways stand huge dvārapālas in the tribhanga attitude (with the head, trunk and legs at different angles). They are richy attired in the symbols of their office. The ornate lintel has scenes from mythology.

Though the temple shows deep religious awareness, imagination and skill, it does not rank high as a composition. Its appeal is sensuous rather than structural. The large pillars of its complex interior crowd too closely together and every part is overloaded with decoration. It represents a climax of lavish sculpture and of systematised confusion.

The last of the Hoysala temples, built in 1268 A.D., is the *Keśava* at *Somnathpur* (Pl 6.2; Fig. 189) in the Mysore district. The temple proper stands on a terrace in the middle of a courtyard. Its plan belongs to the trikūṭāchala (three-shrined) type, with the main shrine facing east and the other two north and south. Each cella consists of a garbha griha and a sukanāsika (vestibule). The chief shrine, opposite the entrance, once contained an image of Keśava, after whom the temple was named, but the image no longer exists. Three elegantly carved śikharas, identical in design and execution, surmount the three cellas. These, together with their towers, as well as the mukha maṇḍapa (front hall) adjoin the navaraṅga. With its three towers, the front of the temple presents an imposing appearance.

## SOUTHERN TEMPLES

South Indian architecture developed in Dravidadesha, the old name of what is now known as Tamilnad. This architecture has several distinctive features. Here the vimāna (Fig. 190), standing on a square base, is a

Fig. 190. South Indian vimana, comprehensive diagram.

high pyramidal tower obtained by superimposing diminishing storeys. Hāras (rows of miniature shrines) composed of kūtas and śālās (Fig. 191 a, b) around each of these storeys form the most characteristic feature of the South Indian vimāna. On the comprehension of this fact depends the understanding of these sometimes seemingly bewildering structures.

Fig. 191 a. Kuta or karnakuta.

Fig. 191 b. Sala.

The other typical building of the South Indian temple complex is the *gopuram* (Fig. 192) or temple gateway. The Sansk rit word denotes the village cow-gates of the Vedic age, which developed into city and temple gates. Its plan is oblong. The storey on the ground floor has vertical walls. The passage leads through its centre. Pilasters and niches usually adorn these walls. They simulate two storeys separated from each other by a horizontal moulding. Like the vimāna it has a pyramidal superstructure divided into storeys surrounded by hāras (rows of shrines), and like the plan it is oblong. It is crowned by a barrel vault, with a row of stūpis (finials) along it ridge.

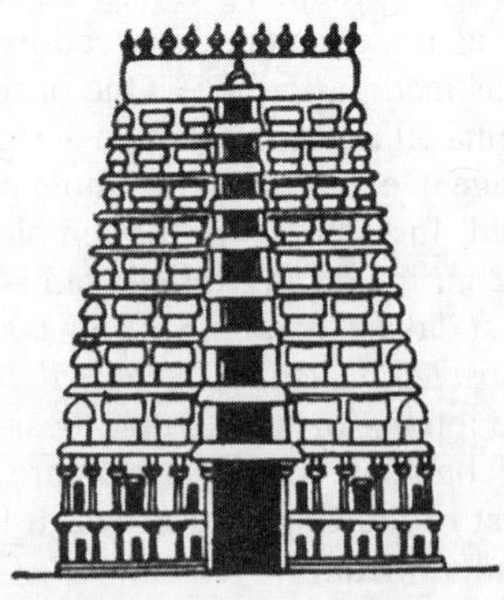

Fig. 192. South Indian gopuram, comprehensive diagram

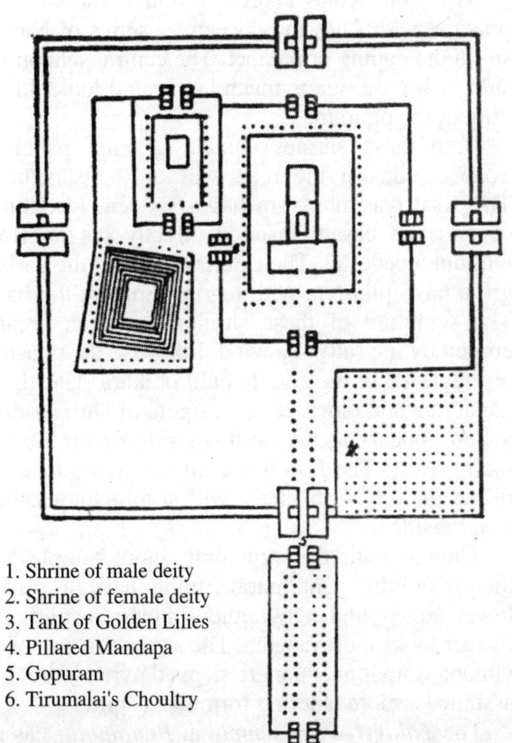


Fig. 193. South Indian temple plan, Meenakshi temple, Madurai, showing the prakaras and gopurams.

Another essential part of the South Indian temple is the prakāra (Fig. 193) or enclosure wall, sometimes simple but frequently with a series of cells attached to it. At times there are several of these prakāras—the shrine at Srirangam has seven. They enclose not only the main shrine but other smaller ones, as well as bathing pools and shaded porticoes, not common in the north but necessary in the hot climate of the south.

The southern type of architecture underwent a long evolution in its details. It can most conveniently be divided into five periods, which coincide with the ruling dynasties in South India, since here as elsewhere, architecture developed under royal patronage. These are the:

Pallava (A.D. c. 550-900)
Chola (900-1150)
Pandya or Later Chola (1100-1350)
Vijayanagara (1350-1565)
Madurai (from 1600 onwards)

## PALLAVAS

In addition to excavating rock-cut maṇḍapas and carving out monolithic vimānas, the Pallavas also erected structural temples at their port town of Mamallapuram and in their capital at Kanchipuram. Narasimha- varman II Rajasimha (700-728 A.D.) began this mode of construction which did not restrict the choice of the location to places where boulders or hillocks were available.

Experiments were first made with different kinds of stones like grey-white granite in the Olakkanneśvara temple, a harder blackish leptinite in the Shore temple, and the hard red- or pinkish gneiss in the Mukundanāyanār and the Talagirīśvara—the three former at Mamallapuram and the last-named at Panamalai. King Rajasimha, realising that building with these hard stones was time-consuming, resorted to the inferior soft local sandstone in order to compete with his rivals. He used the hard varieties only for slabs and for the top and bottom courses of the adiṣṭhāna.

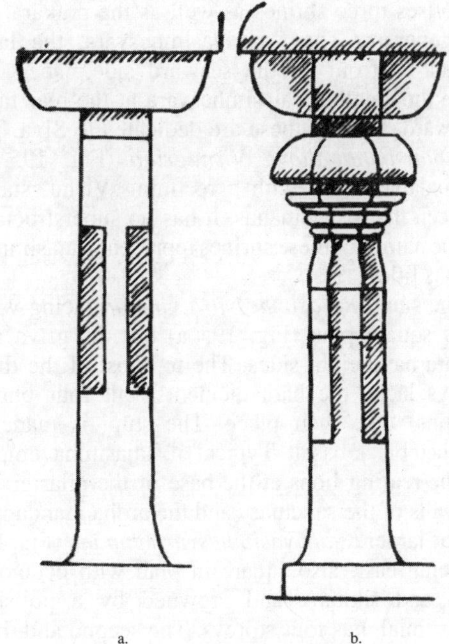


Fig. 194. Pillars of the early phase of the Dravidian order, Pallava period, imitation of originall timber and brick features;

a. Mamallapuram, 620 A.D.,

b. Tirurhirapalli, 625 A.D.

Unlike the earlier maṇḍapa excavations, Rajasimha's temples were not mere experiments, but developed forms of the typical South Indian temples as far as their plan and elevations were concerned. The characteristic features of South Indian temples evolved out of the experience gained from many years of maṇḍapa excavations, above all from the chiselling out of the monolithic vimānas. As a result, the structural temples show more elegance and better proportions, through skilful imitation of the features of timber and brick originals (Fig. 194 a, b).

Rajasimha built at least five temples, three of them at Mamallapuram (the Olakkaneśvara, Mukundanāyanār and Shore temple), the Talagiriśvara at Panamalai in the South Arcot district and the Kailās anātha at Kanchipuram. The Shore temple, the Kailāśanātha of Rajasimha and the Vaikuṇṭha Perumāl built by Naṇdivarman illustrate a stage, not only in the matter of style, but also in the development of the temple formation as such.

The *Shore temple* at *Mamallapuram* (Fig. 195), constructed out of the hard, blackish leptinite, comprises three shrines as well as the prakāra and the gopuram. The Kṣatriyasimheśvara, the large vimāna in front on the seaward side, faces east while the smaller Rājasimheśvara at the rear faces westward. Both of these are dedicated to Śiva. The *Narapatisimhapallava Viṣṇugriha* (Fig. 195 b), a maṇḍapa shrine with a reclining Viṣṇu, stands between the two vimānas. It has no superstructure. All the names of these shrines represent Rajasimha's various titles.

The small *Rājasimheśvara vimāna* facing west, has a square plan (Fig. 195 a) but the grīva and śikhara have eight sides. The topmost of the three storeys lacks the hāra elements, but four bhūtas (goblins) take their place. The stūpi is made of polished black basalt. Typical of Rajasimha temples are the rearing lions at the base of the pilasters on the walls of the sanctuary and the ardha maṇḍapa.

The larger *Kṣatriyasimheśvara vimāna* (Fig. 195 c) facing east, also square in plan with octagonal grīva and śikhara, and crowned by a polished basalt finial, has four storeys. The second and third storey each have a hāra of kūtas and śālās, while four squatting bhūtas blow conches on the topmost storey. Four crouching lions adorn the top corners of the āditala (first storey). A very close-set prakāra, much lower than the wall of the sanctuary, gives the appearance of an additional storey when viewed from outside. It also enlarges he base in relation to its height. Kūtas adorn the four corners of this prakāra, with śālās in between. A series of Naṇdīs sit on the coping or parapet. The central śālā on the side facing the sea is much larger and looks like a miniature gopuram.

Both these shrines contain a relief panel of Somāskanda on the rear wall of the sanctuary. The Kṣatriyasimheśvara has a sixteen-sided linga of polished basalt, inserted directly on the floor without a pedestal. The exterior walls of the garbha griha have pilasters with rearing lions at the base. The sculpture of these shrines has been greatly eroded by the salty sea wind. Likewise the pilasters or the inside of the closely built prakāra. They have nāga, ram and other bases. A figure of Durgā riding a lion appears at the northern side of the temple facing west. The lion has a little square niche cut in the middle of its chest, with a miniature Durgā relief inside it.

Though both the structural Shore temple and the monolithic Dharmarāja ratha have a square lower storey and a pyramidal superstructure, the former looks more elegant. The superstructure of its vimāna is no longer a mere stepped pyramid but has assumed a more tapering form like a spire.

The *Talagiriśvara temple* at *Panamalai* has an unusual plan. On its exterior walls, a two- storeyed oblong sanctuary is attached to the middle of each side of the central shrine right from the adiṣṭhāna level. The western one serves as an antarāla to the shrine proper and has a passage through the middle. From base to kapōta the temple is built of pinkish granite. The original superstructure was later replaced by one made of brick and plaster. The vimāna has four storeys. The hāras of the attached shrines merge into those of the main one. The pilasters at the corners of the main sanctuary, as well as the attached shrines, have the usual rearing lions at the base. The main sanctuary has a Somāskanda relief panel, while the side shrines are dedicated to Śiva. The one on the north contains remnants of Pallava painting. The pillared maṇḍapa in front of the sanctuary is a much later addition.

At *Kanchipuram*, their capital, the Pallava kings, Rajasimha and his son Mahendravarman III,erected the *Kailāsanātha temple* (Figs. 196,197 a, b, c.). A Pallava inscription, eulogising Rajasimha in twelve Sanskrit verses, runs outside the main shrine, while a Kanarese inscription of the Chalukyan king Vikramaditya II is found on a pillar in the maṇḍapa. Built with the local variety of weak sandstone, its plan elaborates the features of the Tālagirīśvara.

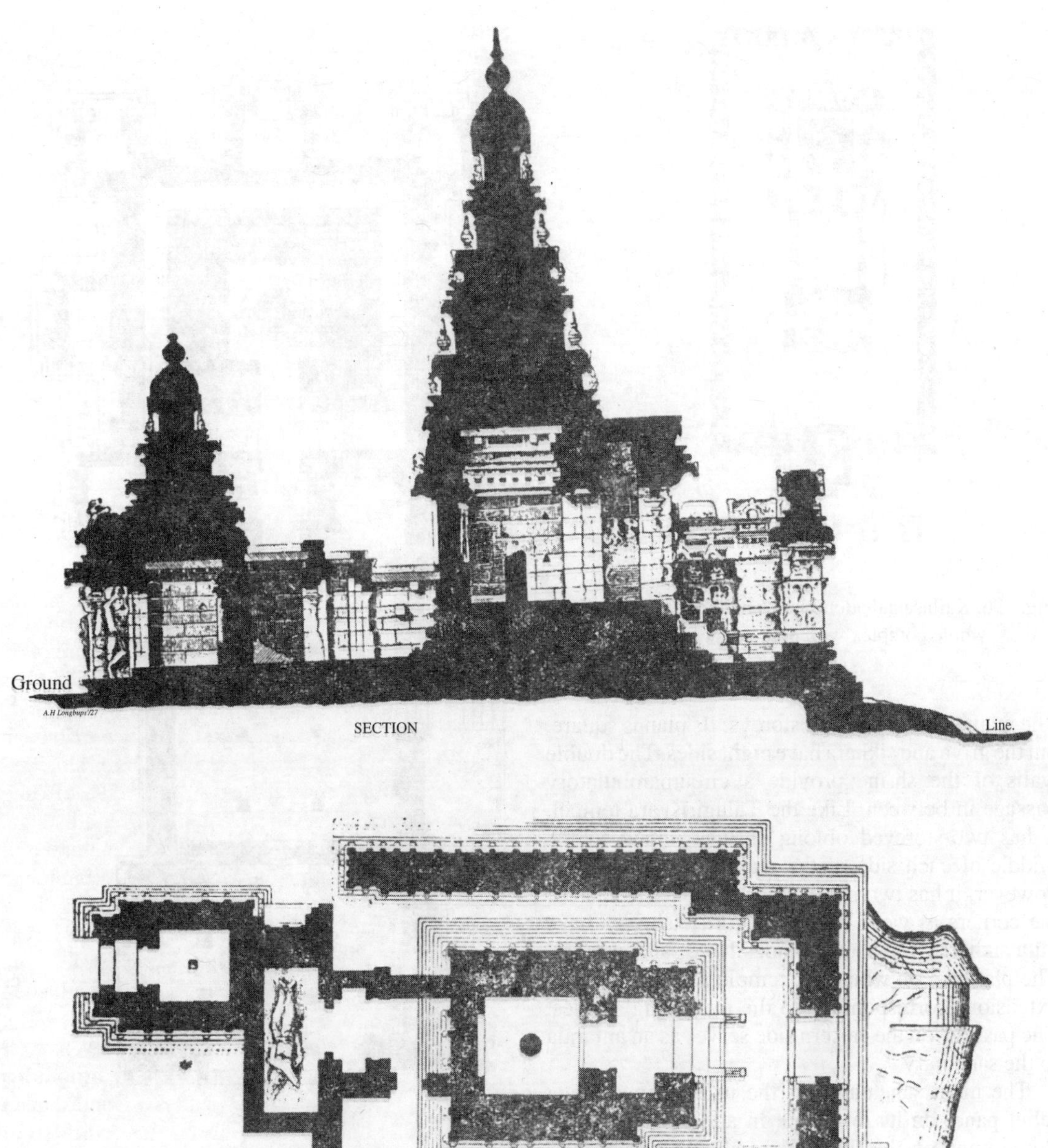


Fig, 195. Shore temple, Mamallapuram, section and plan:

a. Rajasimheshvara, b. Narapatisimhapallava Vishnigriha, c. Kṣatriyasimheshvara.

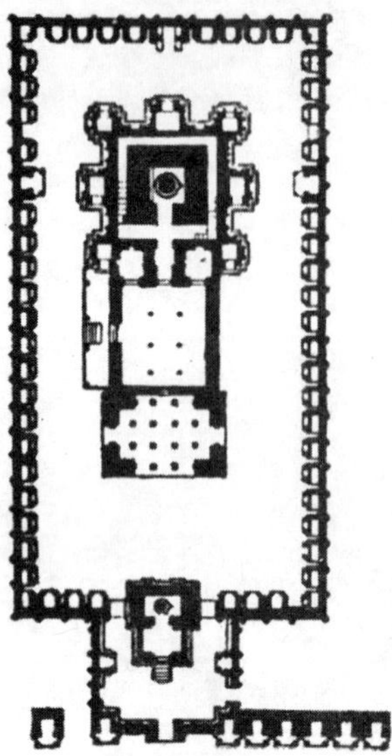

Fig. 196. Kailasanatha temple, Kanchipuram, plan of the whole complex with prakara and shrines.

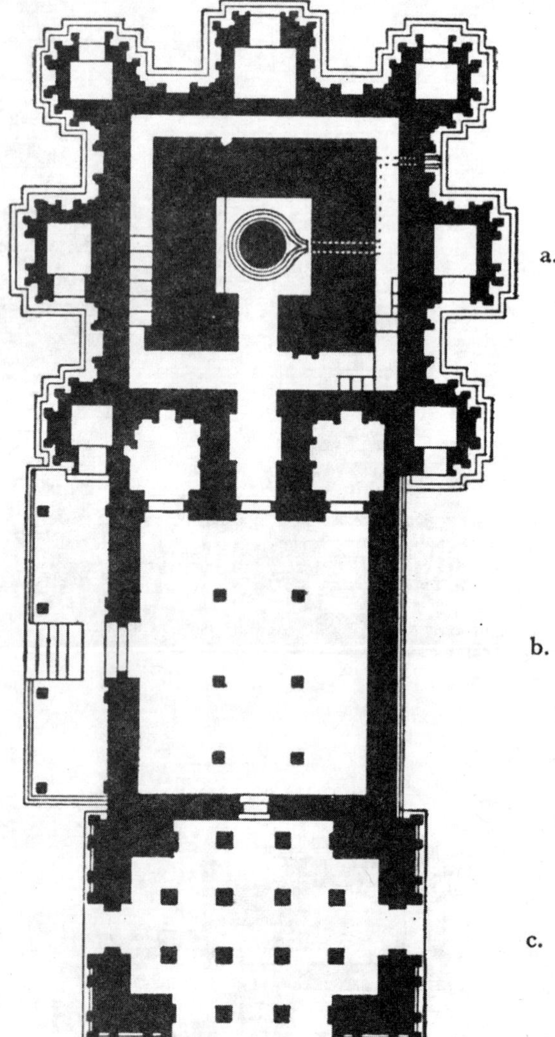


Fig 197. Kailasanatha temple, Kanchipuram, plan:

a. vimana,

b. hall added later,

c. maṇḍapam.

The main vimāna has four storeys. Its plan is square, but the grīva and śikhara have eight sides. The double walls of the shrine provide a circumambulatory passage in between. Like the Tālagirīśvara tempel, it has two-storeyed oblong shrines joined to the middle of each side of the main one. In addition, however, it has two-storeyed square ones at each of the corners as well. While the corner shrines have kūta śikharas, those at the sides have śālā śikharas. The platform on which the temple rests has similar extensions corresponding to the projecting shrines. The passage on the eastern side serves as an antarāla to the sanctuary.

The main sanctuary has the usual Somāskanda relief panel on its rear wall, in addition to a large fluted linga on the floor. The cells of the abutting shrines contain forms of Śiva. Though the inner walls have no sculpture, those parts of the exterior wall visible between the adjoining shrines have profuse carvings of various gods and goddesses.

While the first and third talas of the vimāna have only kūtas and śālās, the hāra of the second one has panjaras as well. Naṇḍīs adorn the four corners of the top storey. The exterior walls of the vimāna and shrines have the usual pilasters with rearing vyāla at the base, so characteristic of Rājasimha tempies.

In front of the main shrine stands an oblong independent multipillared maṇḍapa. A later structure connects the shrine with the maṇḍapa, detracting from the beauty of the original design. A prakāra surrounds the whole complex. On the eastern side, in front of the maṇḍapa, is an oblong two-storeyed śālā-type vimāna called Mahendravarmeśvara, with an ardha maṇḍapa, giving it the appearance of a gopuram when viewed from afar. No hāra elements appear on either of the talas of this vimāna. The main entrance on the east is a gopuram with a śālā superstructure. Along the inner side of the prakāra extend a series of small dvitala vimanās. A rich variety of sculptures, both Śaivite and Vaiṣṇavite, adorn the exterior. Granite was used only for the top and bottom courses of the adiṣṭhāna, while the rest of the temple was built of sandstone.

The *Vaikuṇṭha Perumal temple* (Figs. 198, 199), also at *Kanchipuram*, was erected by Naṇdi-varman Pallavamalla (731-796 A.D.) and dedicated to Viṣṇu. Built of sandstone, it stands on a well-moulded adhisthāna with granite for its top and basal courses. Square in its lower talas, the temple becomes octagonal in its grīva and śikhara. Three walls, one within the other, surround the main shrine. The innermost wall rises to the height of the third storey, the intermediate one to the second, and the outermost to the first tala. Thus, a pair of covered pradakṣiṇa pāthas surround the ground floor. At the rear, the inner circumambulatory also provides access

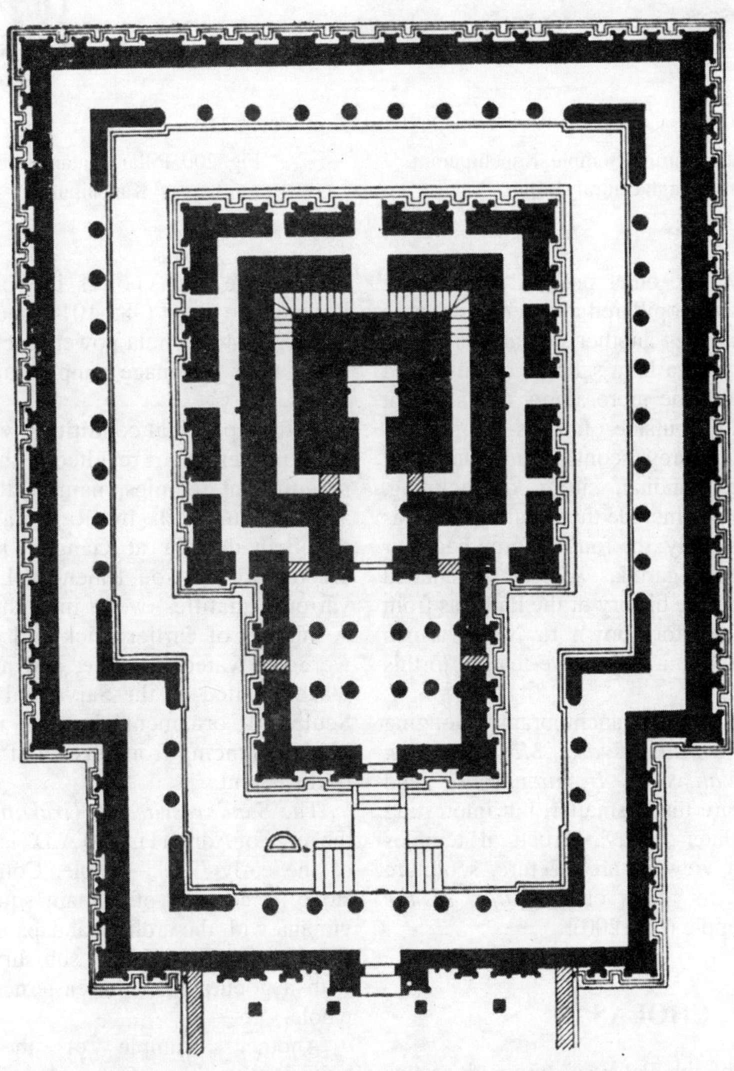

Fig. 198. Vaikuntha Perumal temple, Kanchipuram, plan.

Fig. 199. Vaikuntha Perumal temple, Kanchipuram, section through central shrine.

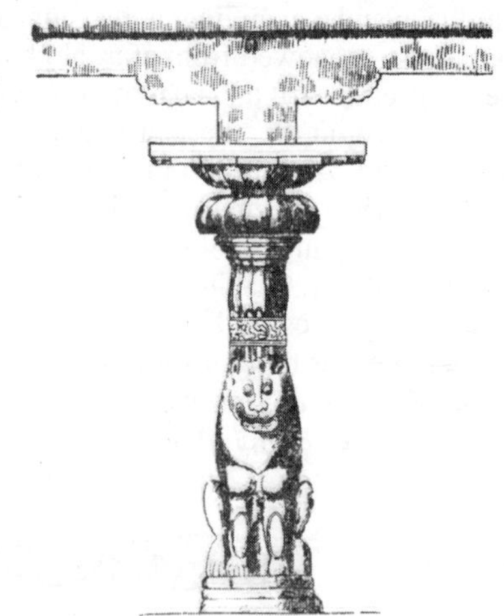

Fig. 200. Pillar, Matangesvara temple, Kanchipuram.

to the first storey. The outer prakāra surrounding the whole temple has a pillared cloister raised on a platform. This provides another pradakṣiṇa pātha. The prakāra, carrying a hāra scheme of kūtas and śālās, seems to add one more storey to its height when viewed from outside. In this temple, all the superimposed storeys contain a cella, each enshrining Viṣṇu, standing, sitting or reclining. The first three storeys include the usual kūtas, śālās and panjaras. Originally, the fourth storey had four lions, now replaced by garuḍas. A series of panelled sculptures narrating the history of the Pallavas from their legendary ancestors down to Naṇḍīvarman II Pallava - malla give a distinctive feature to this temple.

The other temples at Kanchipuram belonging to this period, the *Mukuteśvara, Mataṅgeśvara, Airāvateśvara, Valiśvara, Iravataneśvara* and *Piravataneśvara* are much smaller, but interesting as examples of later Pallava structural temples from the point of view of architecture, sculpture and iconography, as seen on a *pillar of the Maṭangeśwara* temple (Fig. 200).

## CHOLAS

After the fall of the Pallavas, minor dynasties kept up the cultural traditions until the Cholas became the chief power in South India. Under Rajaraja the Great (985-1014) and his son Rajendra I (1012-1044), Chola power reached its zenith and under their patronage temple building attained its peak.

Settled political conditions, vast resources and great interest in art resulted in the creation of two magnificent temples, namely the Bridhadīśvara at Tanjavur built by Rajaraja the Great, and the Brihadīśvara at Gangai- kondacholapuram erected by his son Rajendra I. Hard stones of various qualities went into their construction. A number of earlier brick and timber structures were renovated in stone, and new ones built in places visited by the Śaiva and Vaiṣṇava saints. Sculptural ornaments became more ornate and bold, advancing from bas-relief to figures almost in the round.

The *Sundareśvara* at *Tirukattalai*, built during the reign of Aditya I in 873 A.D., is a typical example of the early Chola temple. Completely made of stone, it consists of a main square two-storeyed vimāna with the ardha maṇḍapa surrounded by the aṣthaparivārālaya (eight sub-shrines). A prakāra with a gopuram on the eastern side encloses the whole.

Another example of the early temple built in the time of the Imperial Cholas is the *Vijayālaya Choleśvaram* at *Narttamalai*, named

Fig. 201. Chola entablature and pillar,
a. Phalaka (abacus),
b. padmabandham and kalasa.

Fig. 202. Dravidian order under Cholas,
a. pilasters and niches,
b. adisthana.

after Vijayalaya, the first great ruler of the dynasty. The shrine has an unusual plan, a circular chamber surrounded by a square circumambulatory passage. Other details however retain typical Pallava and Chalukya elements like the pillared maṇḍapa, the storeyed vimāna, the exterior- walls of the maṇḍapa relieved by pilasters and recesses, and the maṇḍapa carrying a hāra in continuation of the āditala hāra.

The *Korṅganātha* at *Srinvasanallur*, built during the time of Parantaka I, displays a new phase in the development of the South Indian temples and marks a transition from the Pallava to the Chola style. The plan consists of a cella and maṇḍapa like the Pallava examples, but the exterior walls have been greatly simplified and not encumbered with details. Some new features make their appearance in this temple. The yāli type of pillars have gone (Fig. 200); the padmabandham and kalaśa (Fig. 201 a,b), now more ornate, appear in the capital, and the phalaka (abacus) is very much extended. Pilasters divide the exterior of the walls into niches containing some excellent relief sculpture. The adiṣṭhāna has a row of griffins (Fig. 202 a,b).

In the Brihadiśvara temples at Tanjavur and Gangaikondacholapuram the South Indian temple attained its full development. They combine all that is best in South Indian architecture.

Rajaraja I conceived the *Brihadiśvara temple* at *Tanjavur* (Pl. 5.3) as a whole complex on a very grand scale and completed the major part during his reign. Constructed out of large blocks of granite from the neighbourhood, this temple has the loftiest known vimāna, rising to a height of sixty-six m and standing on a base 30 $m^2$ (Figs. 203, 204). In front of the sanctuary stands the antarāla with flights of steps on its northern and southern side, leading from the mahā maṇḍapa to its raised floor. The latter, a large enclosed hall, has an entrance on the east with a central nave and two raised aisles. The whole temple stands on a bold ornate basement, covered all over with inscriptions. The detached Naṇḍī maṇḍapa in front—for the large mono-

Fig. 203. Vimana, Brihadishvara temple, Tanjavur.

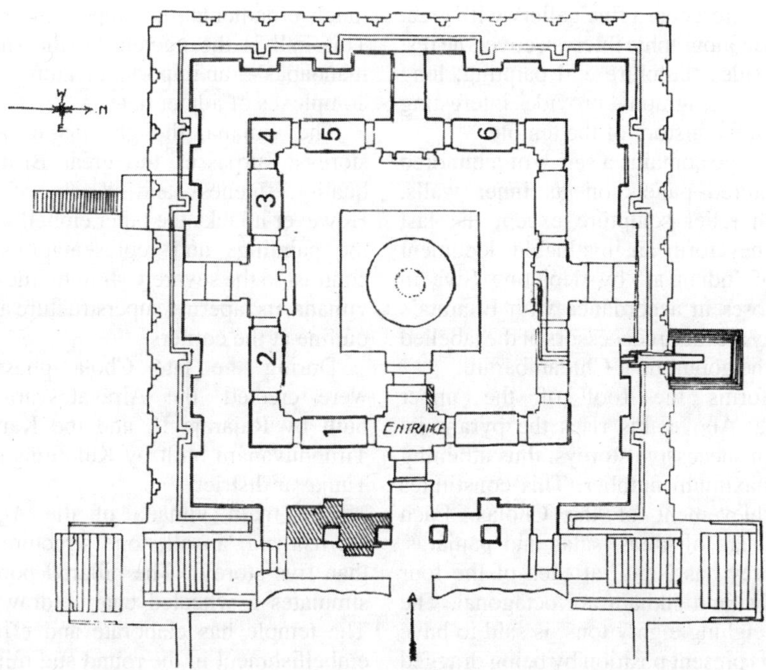


Fig. 204. Vimana, Brihadishvara temple, Tanjavur, ground plan.

lithic bull on a pedestal—belongs to a later date.

A prominent moulding divides the lower part of the vimāna wall into two storeys. Pilasters and niches containing statues decorate the exterior walls of each storey. Between the regular pilasters are decorative pilasters, an early form of the kumbha-panjaras (Fig. 205).*

A two-storeyed pradakṣiṇa pātha separates the outer wall of the vimāna from the inner wall of the garbha griha. The latter, also two-storeyed, encloses a colossal linga standing on a large pedestal. A door in the centre of the north, south and west walls of both storeys of the vimāna leads to the pradakṣiṇa pātha. These, with the larger opening on the east, make it a chaturmukha, i.e. a sanctuary having entrances on all the four sides.

In the middle of the exterior face of the inner wall of the garbha griha are life-size statues of the seated Śiva on the south, the dancing Śiva on the west and Devī on the north. They overlook the lower ambulatory.

Fig. 205. Decorative pilaster, early form of kumbha-panjaram

* Kumbha-panjaras arc pilasters with foliage rising from kumbhas (vases). The later ones were crowned by a panjara motif. They symbolise abundance.

The famous Chola frescoes, a fine gallery with great artistic merit and iconographic interest, cover the rest of the walls. Besides sculpture and painting, long and well-inscribed epigraphs provide interesting information about the history of the temple.

The upper passage contains a series of a hundred and eight sculptured panels on its inner walls, all finished with relief sculpture except the last twenty-seven. They form an invaluable document in the history of Indian art by depicting Śiva in various dance poses in accordance with Bharata's Nāṭyaśāstra. They are the predecessors of the labelled dance poses on the gopuram at Chidambaram.

Corbelling forms the roof of the upper pradakṣiṇa pātha. Above this rises the pyramidal vimāna in sixteen successive storeys, thus attaining the traditional maximum number. This constitutes the greatest achievement of the Cholas. Each storey carries a hāra of kūtas, śālās and panjaras. The topmost storey has Naṇdī at each of the four corners. The grīva and śikhara are octagonal. The śikhara stone, weighing eighty tons, is said to have been hoisted to its present position by being dragged up on a ramp which had its beginnings four miles away.

A compound wall surrounds the broad open court. On its eastern side it has a wide but short all-stone gopuram; and inside it is a continuous two-storeyed cloister. In front of the gopuram stands a larger outer one— the only remnant of an outer prakāra. In addition to the inner gopuram on the east three smaller entrances of the toraṇa variety pierce the compound wall. The Chandikeśvara, a smaller vimāna, adjoins the large gargoylelike water spout to the north of the main vimāna. Such water spouts became characteristic of post-Pallava temples. The other structures within the court, such as the Amman shrine and the Gaṇeśa and Subramaṇya temple, belong to later periods.

Another magnificent structure is the *Brihadiśvara temple*, built by Rajendra I Chola (1012–44) in his new capital *Gangaikonda-cholapuram*, to commemorate the conquest of the northern territories. Like its predecessor, the great Brihadiśvara at Tanjavur, this temple was enclosed within an immense prakāra of which much has now disappeared— its stones were used to construct the river dam near by.

The temple stood in the centre of this enclosure, facing east. The entire plan forms a rectangle. The main doorway at the east leads to an assembly hall. A hundred and fifty slender pillars without much ornamentation support the roof of this hall. This hall is the nucleus of the ‹thousand-pillared maṇḍapas'—an important feature in all large temple complexes of a later date.

The vimāna, though smaller and having few storeys, surpasses the great Brihadīśvara in the quality, fineness and variety of bold sculpture. However it lacks the other embellish ments, namely the paintings and representations of dances. In contrast to the severely straight lines of the Tanjavur vimāna, its tapering superstructure assumes a curved outline at the corners.

During the late Chola phase two temples were erected, the Airāvateśvara at Darasuram built by Rajaraja II, and the Kampahareśvara at Tirubhuvanam built by Kulottuñga III, both in the Tanjavur district.

The main vimāna of the *Airāvateśvara*, at *Darasuram*, an all-stone structure, rises no more than five storeys. The pillared porch on the south simulates a wheeled chariot drawn by elephants. The temple has elaborate and effusive sculptural embellishment in the round and miniature narrative panels in relief. Black polished basalt-like stone, a new medium, was used for the large sculptures. The *Kampahareśvara* at *Tirubhuvanam* closely resembles the Airāvateśvara, including its wheeled porch.

The temples of this and subsequent periods incorporate a new, significant addition, nameiy the Amman shrine or tirukkamakottam dedicated to devī, consort of the principal god (Śiva, Viṣṇu or others as the case may be). The gopuram (entrance gateway) also assumed a dominant role, either singly or in a series, and became a major feature of the southern temples.

## PANDYAS

In the twelfth century the Chola power began to wane and the Pandyas gradually supplanted them. In the thirteenth century the Chola dynasty collapsed, and for a time the Paṇḍyas gained supremacy in the south.

The Paṇḍyas, unlike the Cholas, were not prolific temple builders like their predecessors. In addition to the few vimānas built during their reign, they concentrated mainly on the gopurams (gateways)—the most imposing element of the South Indian temple complex. In this respect they changed the tradition of lavishing the greatest attention and skill on the vimāna, the most sacred part of the temple.

The characteristic pyramidal tower of the gopuram rests on a single or two-storeyed oblong base. A doorway provides entrance in the middle of its longer side. The lower vertical part, made of solid stone masonry, provides a strong foundation. Lighter materials like brick, timber and plaster usually go into the pyramidal superstructure. Like the ground plan, the wagon-vaulted roof is oblong. A row of stūpis (finials) crowns the whole.

In general these principal designs of the gopuram were maintained fairly consistently, but differences in appearance and surface treatment makes it possible to categorise the gopurams into two broad types. One has the sloping sides more or less straight and the surface decoration is mainly architectural, consisting of pillars, pilasters and niches. In the other type the sloping sides are curved, mostly concave, sometimes convex, thus giving it a soaring appearance, and the surface decoration is plastic, with floral decorations and figure-subjects representing a wide range of the Hindu pantheon.

A typical example from this period is the Sundara Paṇḍya gopuram added to the Jambukeśvara temple around the middle of the thirteenth century. The gopuram on the eastern side of the Chidambaram temple (Fig. 206) bears an inscription with the name of the Pandyan ruler Sundara. It rises to a height of forty m. Except that the lower storey is more elaborate, it does not differ from the late Chola types. The surface decoration shows some further development as well as new elements. For example the nāgabandham (snake motif) makes its appearance where the square portion of the pillar turns into the octagonal form. The idaḷ, under the phalaka (abacus), has spiked indentations. New forms appear in the kūdū (Fig. 207 A,B,C) A shrine motif or kūdū crowns the kumbapanjaram (Fig. 208a); while a shrine, such as śālā, kūtā, etc., surmounts the devakosta (niche) (Fig. 208b).

Fig. 206. Eastern gopuram. great temple, Chidambaram.

Fig. 207 A. Pillar with nagabandham. and idal with spiked identations; B & C. Kudus.

Fig. 208a. Kumbhapanjaram.

Fig. 208b. Devakoshta surmounted by a sala.

## VIJAYANAGAR

Vijayanagar power, which dominated almost the whole of the Peninsula, had risen in response to the vital need of stemming the Muslim invasion of the South during the middle of the fourteenth century. These rulers continued the tradition inherited in their northern domain from the Chalukyas, Kakatiyas and Hoysalas, while in the south they took up almost from where the Later Cholas and Pandyas had left off. They introduced their preferences for building in hard stone even to the Chalukyan area, where soft stone had generally been used before. An abundance of temples adorn their once magnificent but now ruined capital, Vijayanagar (modern Hampi) on the Tungabhadra river in the Bellary district. Their subsequent capitals at Penukonda, Chandragiri, Vellore and other places from the Godavari to Kanyakumari contain numerous temples large and small. During this period more places of worship arose than during Chola times.

One of the main contributions of the Vijayanagar period were the tall massive gopurams (raya gopurams), sometimes eleven storeys high as in the Ekāmbaranātha temple at Kanchipuram. The other contributions were the multiple maṇḍapas. Unlike the unified composition of Chola times the Vijayanagar temple complex contains a greater number of moderately sized buildings including maṇḍapas, pillared halls, shrines and bathing tanks at fixed places around the central shrine dedicated to a god. The shrine of his consort (Amman shrine) usually lies a little behind it to the north-west. This Amman shrine is another characteristic feature of the Vijayanagar temple. The most typical building however of this style is the kalyāṇa maṇḍapa. generally to the left before the east entrance. This open pillared pavilion with an elevated platform in the centre is generally the most highly decorated of all the buildings, though all the structures are richly adorned, sometimes verging on exuberance and even extravagance. Yet they remain highly artistic.

The largest mapas, the so-called thousand pillar variety, serve as protection from the hot sun. The richly carved pillars, sometimes most complicated pieces of art with different types of ornamentation, give the Vijayanagar temples their intricate decorative richness.

The pillars, fronted by statues such as rearing simhas (lions), yāḷis (lions with elephant trunks) are naturally the most conspicuous.

The early Pallava pillars, formed of sadurams (squares) alternating with kattu (polygonal) shafts have become much more enriched and common during the Vijayanagar period (Fig. 209).

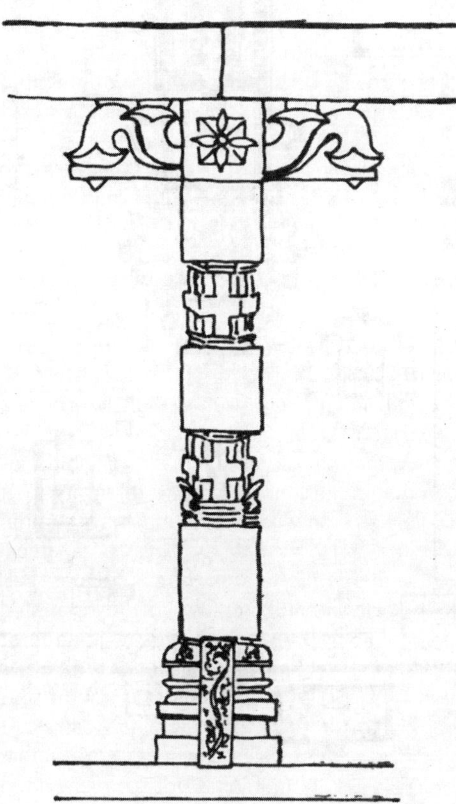

Fig. 209. Vijayanagar style pillar, Ekambaranatha temple, Kanchipuram, a rich development of Early, Pallava pillars, with 3 sadurams and 2 kattus decorated with a cross; the potika developed into the pushpapotika

Sometimes small pillars cluster all around the larger columns and are carved out of the same block of stone (Fig. 210). Another kind of pillar is composed of small shrines superimposed one on the other. The lion-based pillars of the Pallava period reappear again.

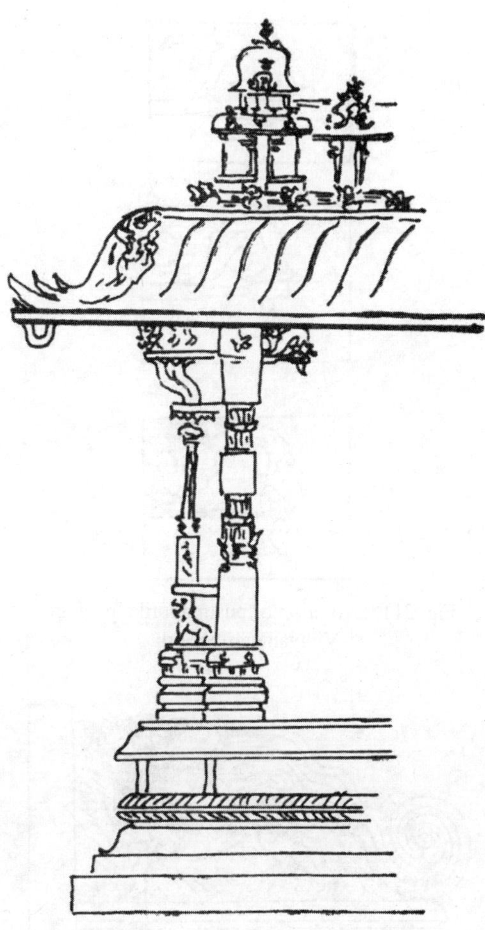

Fig. 210. Maṇḍapam with double-flexed kapotal (cornice) and clustered pillar, Vijayanagar period, Hampi.

The potikā on the top of the pillars shows a further evolution. It has the form of a volute with a hanging lotus bud (called puṣpapotikā); but the whole is still attached to the main body by a rod (Fig. 211). The cornice of the maṇḍapa (Fig. 210) is no longer a quarter circle but double flexed. Up to this time it was thick and curved down; now it is thin with a double flexure and it exends forward, often showing underneath the stone imitation of the wooden ribs of the supporting frame carrying it.

The steps leading to the maṇḍapa have sculptured ramps decorated with mythical

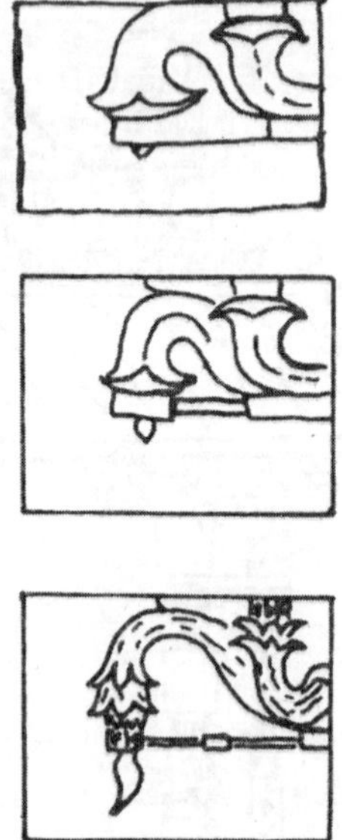

Fig. 211. Evolution of pushpapotika pendant, Vijayanagar period.

Fig. 212. Hybrid animal, ramp of staircase leading to maṇḍapam, Vijayanagar period, Hampi.

Fig.213 a. Kumbhapanjaram, Vijayanagar period, b. Kudu, Vellore. Tanjavur.

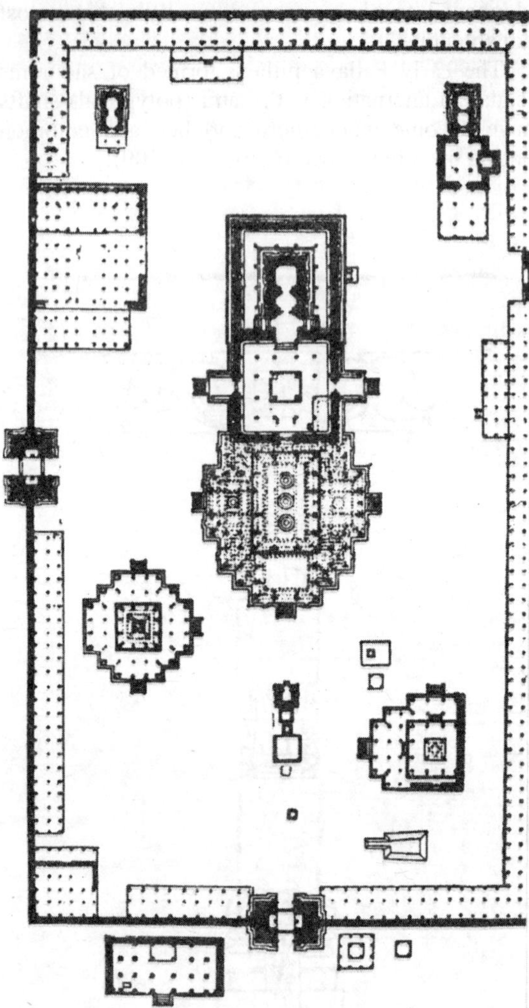

Fig. 214. Vitthala temple, Vijayanagar, ground plan.

animals of hybrid form (Fig. 212). The kumbhapanjara has become more ornate and elaborate (Fig. 213a). So has the kūdū (Fig. 213b).

The most important temple at *Vijayanagar* is the *Viṭṭhala* (Fig. 214). In 1513 Krishnadeva Raya began this beautiful and artistic piece of architecture; but after the fall of the Vijayanagar empire in 1565 it remained incomplete. The rectangular enclosure (150 × 93m.) embraces six distinct structures. The most important of these, the main temple in the centre dedicated to Viṣṇu in the form of Viṭ ṭhala, is a long squat building because the superstructure either could not be completed or fell into decay. It consists of the ardha maṇḍapa in front, the closed mahā maṇḍapa in the middle and the garbha griha at the rear. The first-named, distinguished by a range of pillars, is the most characteristic with its exuberant sculpture. Each pillar, fashioned out of a single large block of granite, comprises an entire sculptured group in itself. The garuda maṇḍapa (Fig. 215) in front of the court assumes the form of a chariot with stone wheels. It had a śikhara as superstructure which no longer exists.

The Hazāra Rāma temple, probably begun earlier and completed by Krishna Deva Raya, lacks the characteristic gopuram. The mahā maṇḍapa, with its four central pillars—square, polished and embellished with sculpture and carvings—bears the Chalukyan navaranga character. The walls of the main vimāna, as well as those of the adjoining Amman shrine and the enclosure, teem with panel sculptures. More characteristic is the śukha nāsikā projected from the superstructure.

Fig. 215. Garuda maṇḍapam, resembling temple car, Viṭṭhala, Swami temple, Vijayanagar.

## NAYAKS

After the fall of the central power, the Vijayanagar viceroys in the southern regions (Nayaks) assumed independent rule at Gingee, Tanjavur, Vellore and Madurai in Tamil Nadu and at Ikkeri in north-west Karnataka. Of these, the Madurai and Tanjavur Nayaks probably contributed more to architecture than the other two lines.

The Nayaks further elaborated the maṇḍapas of the hundred or thousand pillared type. During this period the gopurams reached full development, as seen in the southern one of the Madurai temple. With its projecting section at the centre, its slightly inward curving outlines, and its innumerable stucco statues creating a rich surface pattern, it is one of the most graceful and ornate gopurams of South India.

*Srivilliputtur* has the tallest gopuram, with an even greater number of plastic stucco figures.

Fig. 216. Front of pillar, horse court, Ranganathaswami temple, Srirangam.

The number of enclosures around the sanctuary also increased, for the *Raṅganātha temple* at *Srirangam* has seven prakāras. Another distinctive feature is the long corridors. They result from the closed ambulatory flanked by massive columns. These columns have elaborately corbelled brackets which span the gap above and almost reach across to each other. The pradakṣiṇa pātha in the *temple* at *Rameswaram* serves as a good example.

Other valuable contributions of the Nayaks are the kalyaṇā maṇḍapas at Vellore and a similar one in the northern prakāra of the *Raṅganātha temple* at *Srirangam* (Fig. 216). Here the facade columns carry full-size monolithic sculptures of rearing horses with riders and retinue and other animal figures. Also of Nayak origin, the large *complex* of *Madurai* (Fig. 193), includes great maṇḍapas and lofty gopurams on the four sides. The *Subramaṇya temple*, a fine vimāna (Fig. 217) with ardha and mahā maṇḍapas standing in the *Brihadiśvara temple court* at *Tanjavur*, exemplifies the ornate variety of the Nayak temple. Constructed of fine-textured granite, its typical features include the puṣpapotikā, kumbhapanjara and the double flexed cornice. In accordance with the six-faced ṣaṇmukh form of the Subramaṇya housed in the sanctuary, the grīva and śikhara over the square vimāna are hexagonal. The mouldings of the adiṣṭhāna and the pillars display refined, intricate work.

Fig. 217. Subramanya temple, Tanjavur.

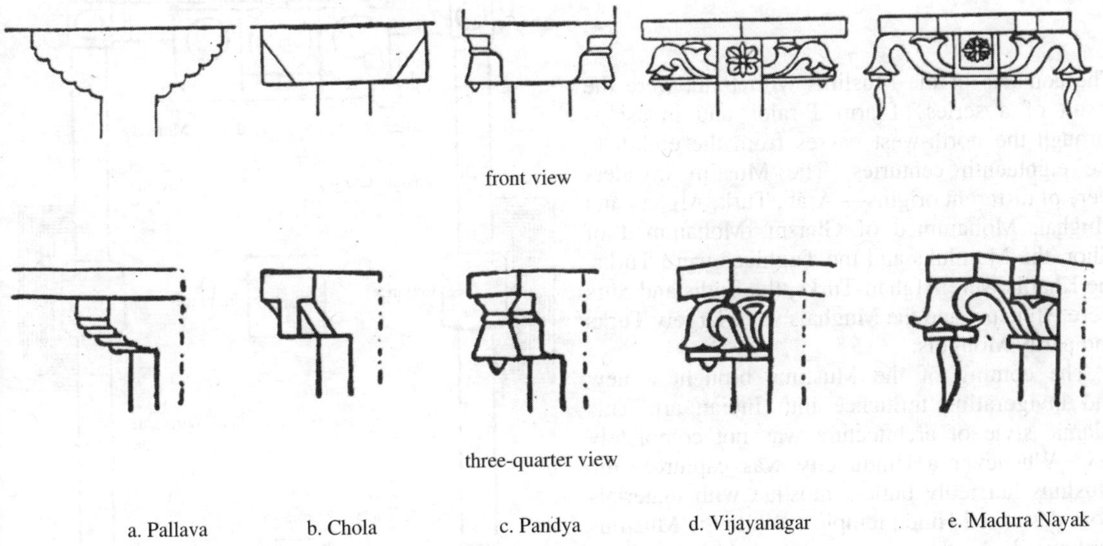


Fig. 218 A. Evolution of potika (cornice)

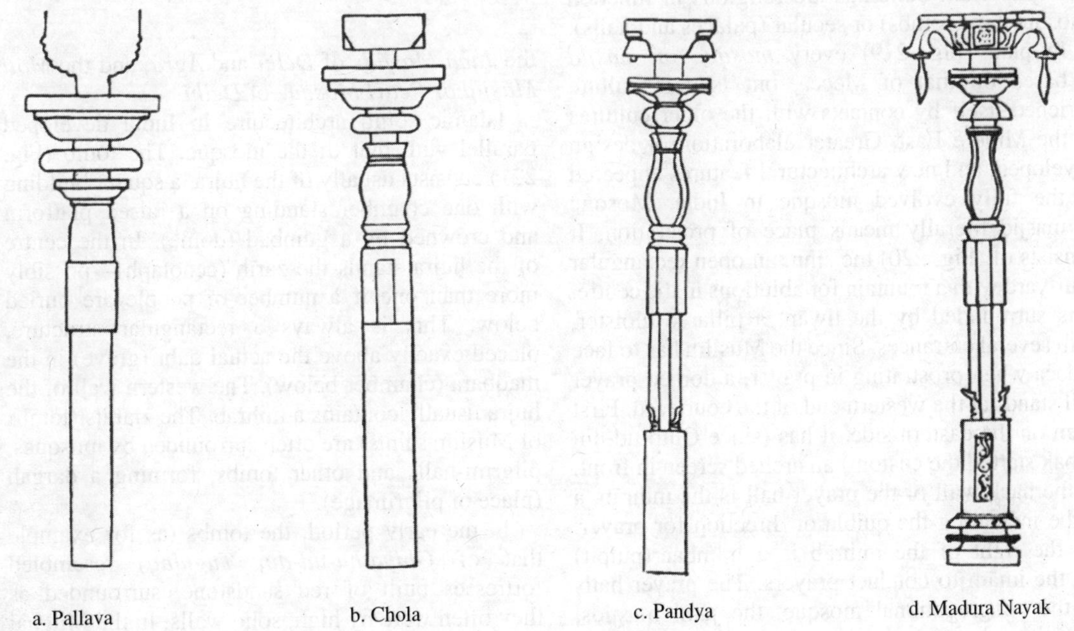


Fig. 218 B. Evolution of column.

## INDO-ISLAMIC ARCHITECTURE

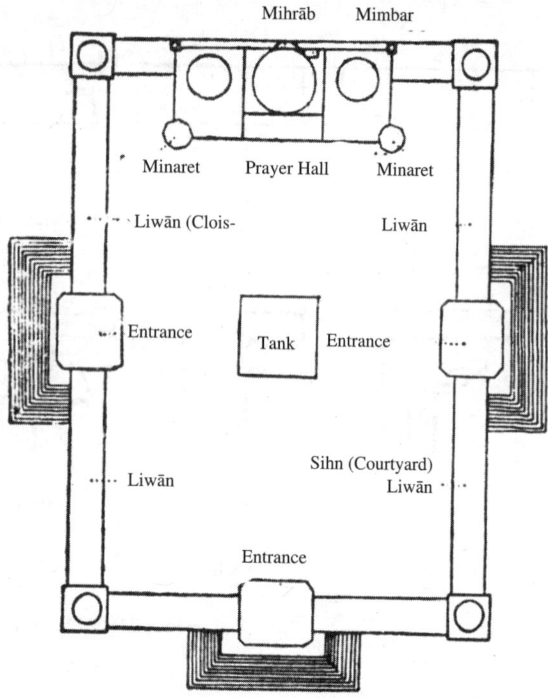


Fig. 219. Indian mosque, plan.

The contacts of the Muslims with India were the result of a series of armed raids and invasions through the north-west passes from the eighth to the eighteenth centuries. The Muslim invaders were of different origins— Arab, Turk, Afghan and Mughal. Mohammed of Ghazni, Mohammed of Ghor, the Mamluks and the Tughlaqs were Turks; the Khaljis were Afghan-Turks, the Lodis and Surs were Afghans; and the Mughals were largely Turks and partly Mongols.

The coming of the Muslims brought a new and invigorating influence into Indian art. This Islamic style of architecture was not completely new. Whenever a Hindu city was captured, the Muslims hurriedly built a mosque with materials from destroyed Hindu temples. While the Muslims supervised—as they were mainly soldiers and not artists— the Hindus did the actual work. Therefore traces of Hindu influence can readily be detected in these monuments from the very beginning. Yet the design of the architecture was truly Islamic and strikingly contrasted with the Hindu art. The most important buildings are religious in function (mosques and tombs) or secular (palaces and halls).

In plan (Fig. 219) every *mosque or masjid* is based on that of Mecca, but Islamic culture enriched itself by contacts with the older cultures of the Middle East. Greater elaboration of design developed, and new architectural features appeared in the fully evolved mosque in India. Mosque or masjid literally means place of prostration. It consists of (Fig. 220) the sihn, an open rectangular courtyard with a fountain for ablutions in the centre. It is surrounded by the liwān, a pillared cloister, with several entrances. Since the Muslim has to face Mecca when prostrating in prayer, a domed prayer hall stands at the western end of the courtyard. First open on the eastern side, it has (since Qutb-ud-din Aibak started the custom) an arched screen in front. In the back wall of the prayer hall is the miḥrāb, a niche indicating the quibla or direction for prayer. To the right of the mihrāb is a mimbar (pulpit) for the imām to conduct prayers. The prayer halls of the congregational mosque, the jami masjids, sometimes have a section screened off for women. From the minār, a high slender tower, the mu'azzin calls the faithful to prayer. Fine examples of mosques can be seen in many parts of India, notably the *Jami Masjids* of *Delhi* and *Agra*, and the *Moti Masjid or Pearl Mosque* of *Delhi*.

Islamic tomb architecture in India developed parallel with that of the mosque. The tomb (Fig. 221) consists usually of the ḥujra, a square building with one chamber standing on a raised platform and crowned by a gumbad (dome). In the centre of the ḥujra stands the zarīḥ (cenotaph)—possibly more than one if a number of people are buried below. This is always a rectangular structure, placed exactly above the actual qabr (grave) in the maqbara (chamber below). The western wall of the ḥujra usually contains a miḥrāb. The ziarats (tombs of Muslim saints) are often surrounded by mosques, pilgrim-halls and other tombs, forming a dargah (place of pilgrimage).

In the early period, the tombs (as for example that of *Ghiyathu-ud-din Tughlaq*) resembled fortresses built of red sandstone, surrounded as they often were by high, solid walls. In the Mughal period however they were set in splendid gardens and became much more refined in structure. Finally marble replaced red sandstone. Notable among the tombs of the early Mughal period is that of *Humayun*

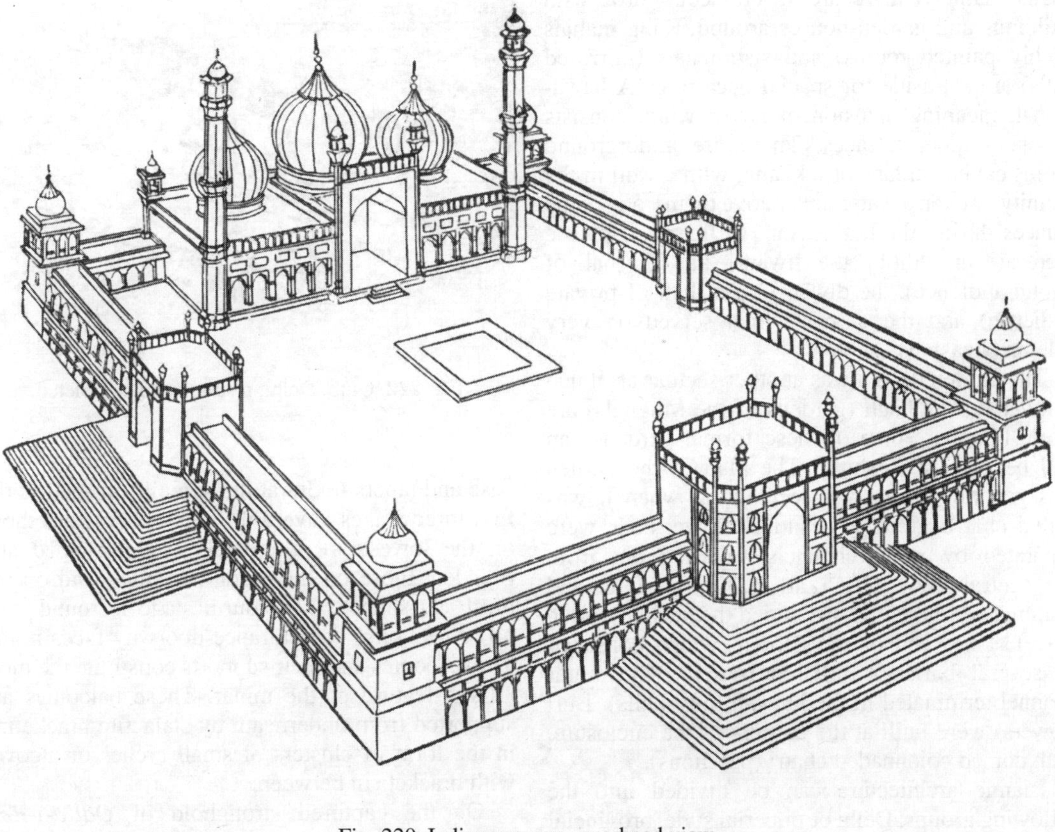

Fig. 220. Indian mosque, overhead view.

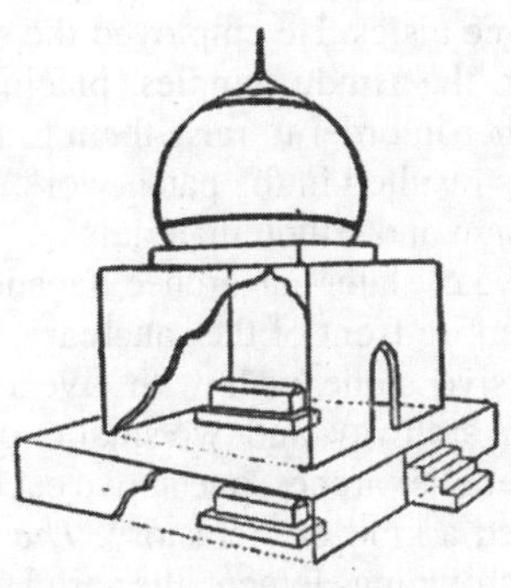

Fig. 221. Islamic tomb, comprehensive diagram of exterior and interior.

in Delhi, while among the later marble edifices, the most outstanding is the *Tāj Mahal* at *Agra*.

Minor religious buildings are the idgah and the madrasa. The idgah is actually a large open space (meant to accommodate the large crowds which gather for common prayer on the day of Id-ul-Fitr), with a long wall on the side facing Mecca, containing prayer- niches and perhaps a pulpit. The madrasa is a school or college for the teaching of Islamic doctrine. It resembles the mosque from which it originates, except that the central hall and most of the entrances are replaced by lecture-halls.

Secular buildings are based on the khāna (house) which has a central courtyard around which are aiwans (halls) with dalan (verandas) all facing inwards. The madrana (men's quarters) are always separated from the haram or zanana (women's habitation). A mahal is a building for rich people and a sarai, a royal palace. The plan of these consists of the multiplication of the simple khāna: namely, there are several courtyards with buildings and garden-houses around. Rang maḥals (richly painted rooms) and sishmaḥals (mirrored halls) are set aside for special occasions. A hawa-maḥal, meaning mansion of air or wind, consists of open upper terraces. There are underground rooms called sardabs or takhana, with a well in the vicinity or even a water tank above them, to cool the palaces during the hot season. In the royal palace there are in addition the dīwan-i-'ām (the hall of public audience), the dīwān-i-khās (hall of private audience) and the darbar which served on very solemn occasions.

The garden design was another secular art much cultivated. The bagh (gardens of the Mughals) are world-famous. Some of these formal gardens can still be seen in Kashmir. The plan of the garden was generally square or rectangular when it was called char-bagh. The beautiful flower-beds were separated by water channels radiating out from the central pool. Often artificial waterfalls and illuminated fountains surrounded the kushk (garden place) at the end of the garden, which consisted of several baradari (pillared rooms). The water channel terminated in the bhavan (airy halls). Burj (towers) were built at the corners of the enclosure, with domed colonnaded chatri (pavilions).

Islamic architecture can be divided into the following groups: Delhi or imperial style, provincial styles and Mughal architecture. The Delhi style developed under the Mamluk or Slave dynasty in the late twelfth century, not long after the conquest of North India by the Turks, and continued in use until the sixteenth century when it was replaced by the Mughal style.

## DELHI OR IMPERIAL STYLE

The most important monument erected under the Mamluk dynasty (1191-1246) is the *Quṭb* of *Delhi* (Figs. 222, 223), named from Quṭb-ud-Din Aibak the first ruler of the dynasty who made Delhi his capital. At the end of the thirteenth century he began the famous *Quṭb Minār* (Pl. 7.1) in order to proclaim to the world the power and greatness of Islam from this gigantic tower. It was also the minār belonging to the Quwwat-ul-Islam mosque. It consists of four diminishing storeys, each division fringed with a projecting balcony. The circular tower measures 13.20m at the

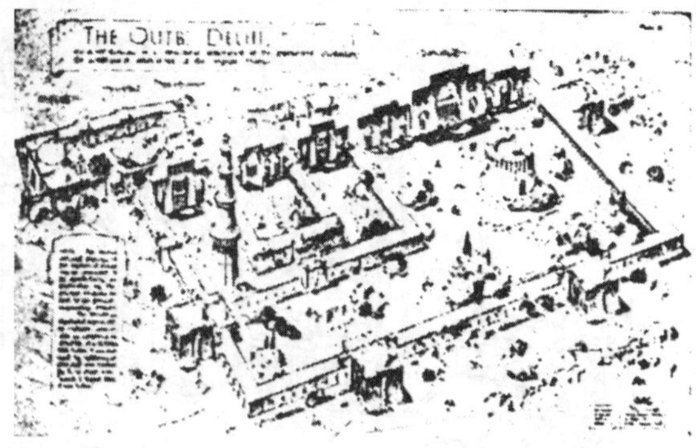

Fig. 222. Quṭb. Delhi, restored and completed.

base and tapers to 3m at the summit. In section the first three stages have a different projection: those on the lowest are alternately wedge-shaped and rounded, those on the second circular, and on the third star-shaped. The fourth stage is round with no projections. The entrance doorway faces north. The balconies and their supports constitute the most artistic feature of the minār. These balconies are supported from underneath by stalactite bracketing in the form of clusters of small arches or alcoves with brackets in between.

On the captured stronghold of *Qal'a-i-Rai-Pithaura* which became the first of the seven cities of Delhi (Fig. 224), Quṭb-ud-Din erected huge stone buildings. He demolished the Hindu temple in the centre of the citadel and gave the local workmen the plan of the mosque Quwwat-ul-Islam, consisting of a courtyard surrounded by a liwan (pillared cloister) forming three aisles. He employed the short carved pillars from the Hindu temples, placing them one over the other in order to raise them to the required height. This resulted in the patch-work effect of the Islamic design and Hindu materials.

A few years later an arched façade was built across the entire front of the sanctuary. This screen was a massive stone wall with five openings—a large central archway, and two smaller ones on each side. Four smaller arches, one above each of the side ones, formed a kind of clerestory. *The iron pillar*, without its crowning element, the garuda, was placed in front of the sanctuary. The primitive method of corbelling the arch, unmistakably Indian, and the shape of the arches reveal that the workmanship of this mosque was Hindu.

Iltutmish, the next great Mamluk ruler,

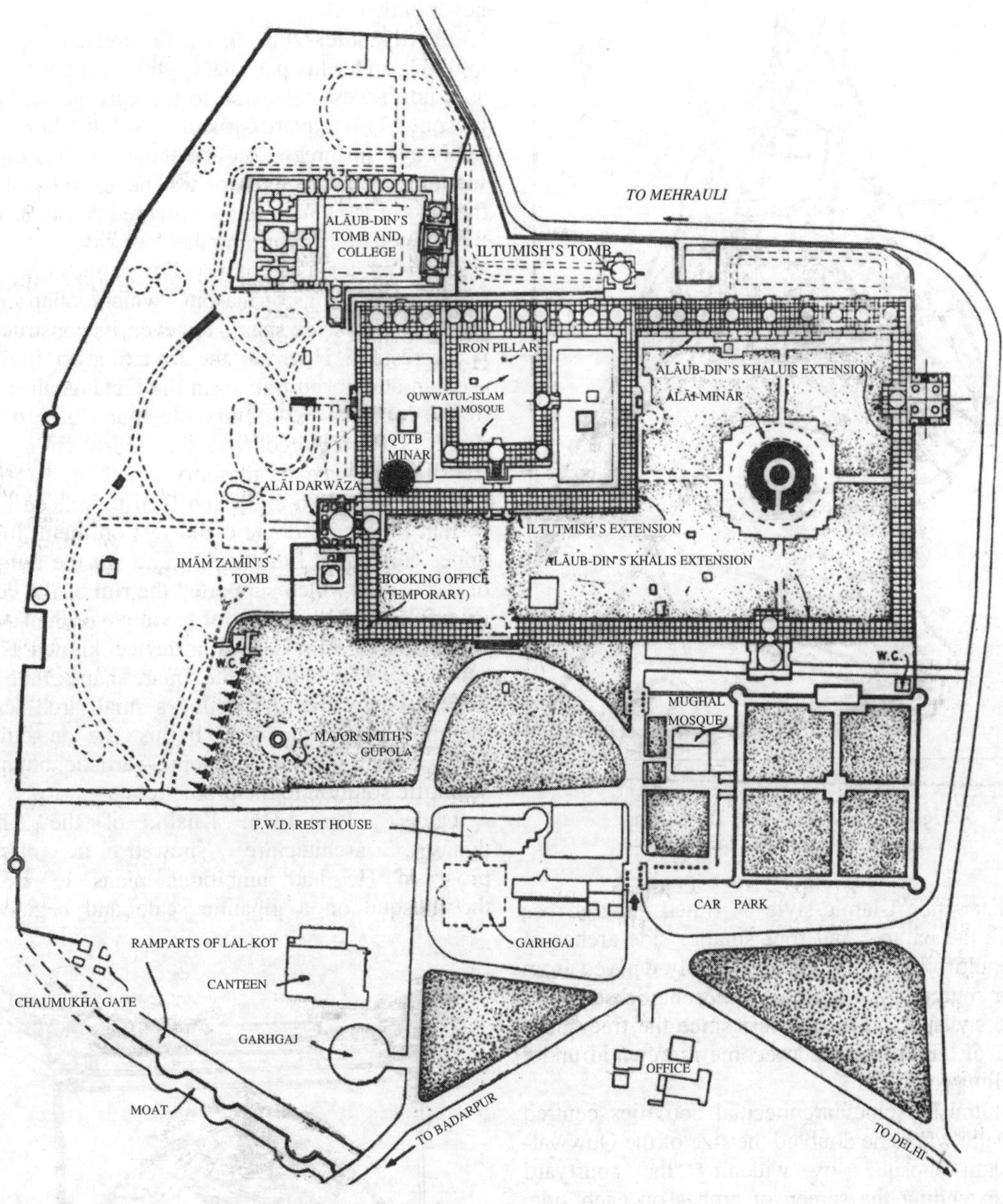


Fig. 223. Area of Qutb.

erected four important works—the addition of the façade to the Ajmer mosque, the extension of Quṭb-ud-Din's mosque at Delhi, the building of his son's tomb and his own tomb at Delhi.

Adding the façade of the *Ajmer mosque* (*Arhai-din-ka-Johmpara*) was obviously an imitation of Quṭb-ud-Din's doing the same for the Delhi mosque some twenty-five years earlier. The advance made in architecture during those years is especially noticeable in the curves of the arches. They are more of the four-centred type, the shape that became characteristic of

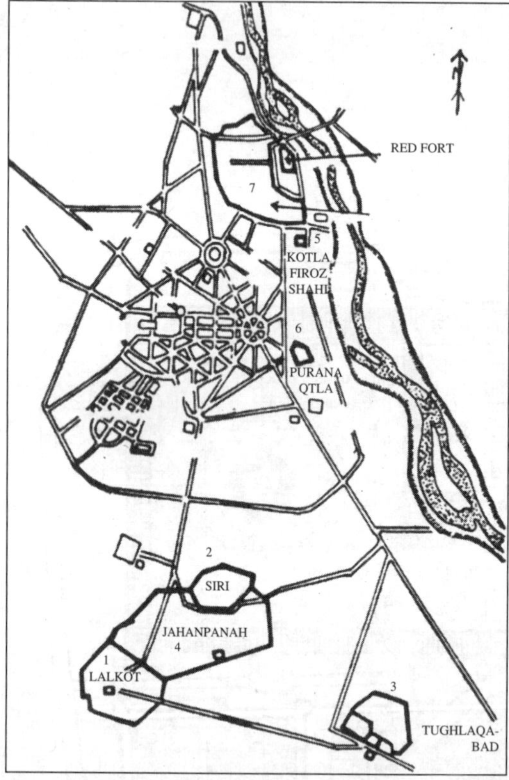


Fig. 224. Seven cities of Delhi, map.

the later Indo-Islamic style. A fluted minaret rose above the parapet and four smaller side arches of the multifoil pointed type—probably derived from Arab sources. The surface ornamentation appears more stylised and mechanical since the free hand-work of the Hindus had become more rigid under Muslim prohibition.

Iltutmish's chief architectual activities centred on Delhi where he doubled the size of the Quwwat-ul-Islam mosque, by widening the courtyard and extending the screen of arches on each side, conforming himself to the same type of architecture.

In *Delhi* he built the first monumental *tomb* in India, namely that of his son *Nasir-ud-Din Mohammed*. It consists of a square courtyard surrounded by a wall. In the centre is an octagonal platform which forms the roof of the sepulchral chamber below. There is a feeling of incompleteness about this unoccupied platform; probably it was designed to support a pillared pavilion with a pyramidal roof which has now disappeared or was never built at all.

Shortly after this *Iltutmish* erected the last building under his patronage—his own tomb, built as a north-west extension to the Quwwat-ul-Islam mosque. This square structure, solidly built, has doorways on three sides and three mihrābs on the western flank. The exterior was never finished and the only ornamentation is a patterned border around the pointed arches forming the doorway.

The roof consisted of a shallow dome composed of concentric rings of masonry which collapsed on account of its wide span. However, its construction is interesting. Here for the first time in India is seen an attempt to transform the rectangualr shape of the room so as to carry the round base of the dome. This required first the construction of a transitional piece of masonry which transformed the four sides into eight and then to sixteen sides so that the round dome could rest on them. In the upper corners of Iltutmish's tomb are the remains of the device which supported the rim of the dome (Fig. 225) at the crossing of the angle of the square hall it roofed. This particular device, known as the squinch system, changes the square shape of the hall into an octagon by projecting a small arch across the upper part of the angle. In this case the squinch forms a small vault or half dome—artistic, but not a scientific solution to the problem.

Under Alau-ud-Din Khalji, of the Khalji dynasty, architecture showed a marked progress. He had ambitious plans to extend the mosque on a gigantic scale and began the

Fig. 225. Squinch, tomb of Iltutmish, Delhi.

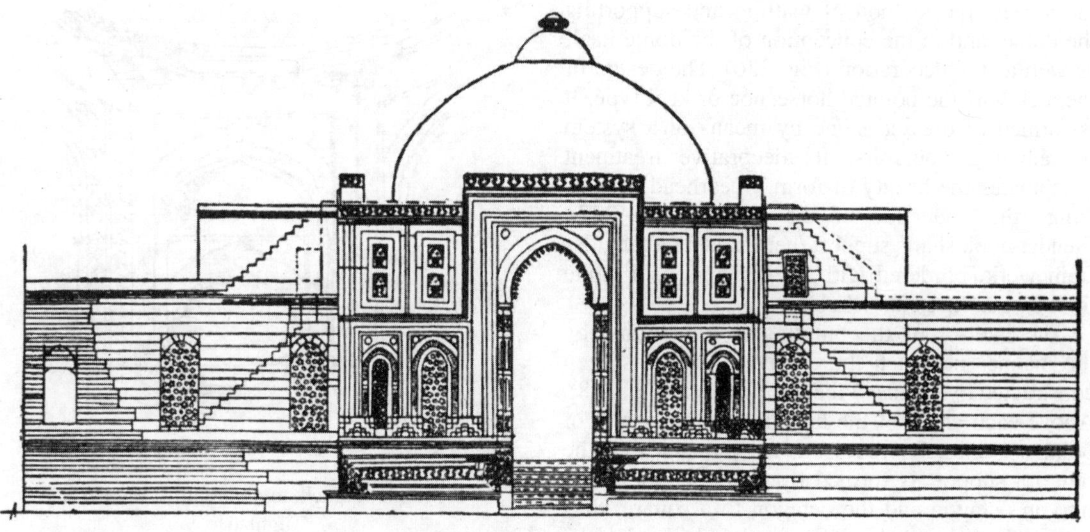

Fig. 226. Alai Darwaza, front elevation.

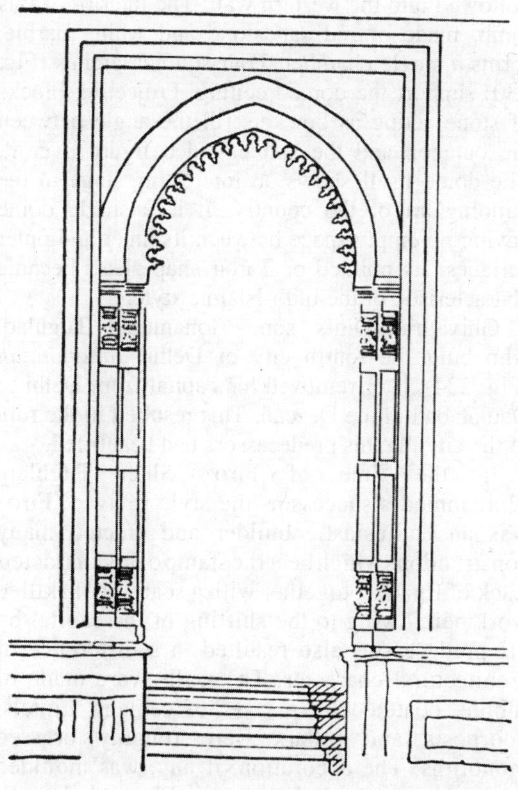

Fig. 227. Alai Darwaza, Delhi, a doorway.

Fig.228. Squinch, Alai Darwaza, Delhi.

erection of Alāi Minār, but very little had been accomplished by the time of his death. The principal record of his architectural ambition lies in a small structure known as the Alāi Darwāza (P1. 7.2), the only gateway of his huge plan that he managed to finish. That some new influence was at work is clear from its mature style and method of construction. The work shows a more thorough and expert understanding of architecture particularly noticeable in the shape and design of the arches, the method of walling and supporting the dome, and in the conception of the dome itself as well as the decoration (Fig. 226). The design of the arch was the pointed horseshoe or keel type. It is formed of dressed stone by means of a system of radiating voussoirs. Its decorative treatment accentuates the beauty of form. Spearhead designs fringe the underside of the arches (Fig. 227). Slender nook shafts support them, and a rectangular framework, bordered with an inscription in white marble, embraces the whole.

The interior of the building is remarkable by the manner in which the domed ceiling has been constructed by means of the squinch arch (Fig. 228). Above each angle of the hall rises a semi-vault of pointed arches. By recessing these one within the other, a support is formed by changing the circle into an octagon and the octagon to a square, thus gracefully and completely conveying the load of the dome to the ground.

Alau-ud-Din built other constructions, one of the chief being the city of *Siri*, the second of the seven cities of Delhi (Fig. 224). The ruins of these are in such a crumbling state that they are not of much value.

Architecture continued to develop under the Tughlaq dynasty. One of the greatest citadels or fortresses of India was *Tughlaqabad* near Lalkot, third of the seven cities of Delhi (Fig. 224) erected by *Ghiyath-ud-Din Tughlaq*. In addition he built a *tomb* for himself (Fig. 229) on an island in an artificial lake. The plan of this forms an irregular pentagon with a spreading bastion at each angle. Its uncommon form was occasioned by the rough uneven ground on which it was built. The courtyard follows the same unsymmetrical outline; and in order to place the tomb in the right position, facing the direction of Mecca, it was built diagonally at the widest part of the enclosure. The tomb

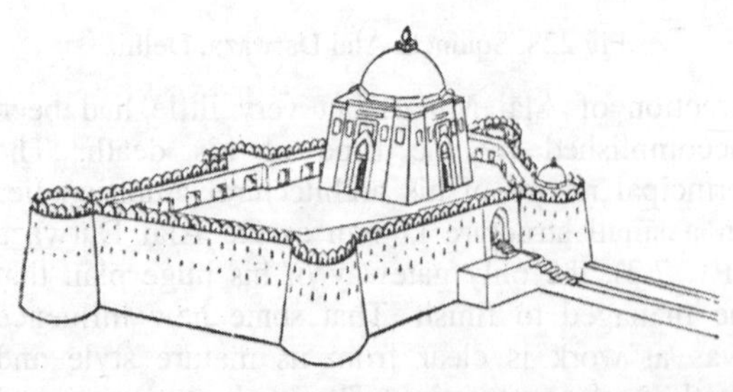

Fig. 229. Tomb of Ghiyath-ud-Din Tughlaq, Tughlaqabad.

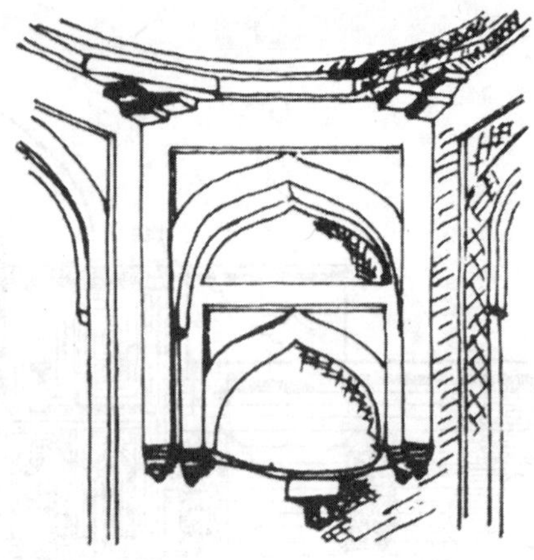

Fig. 230. Squinch, tomb of Ghiyath-ud-Din Tughlaq.

proper is square in plan and its walls have a determined slope. A tall doorway provides entrance in the centre of three sides, while the miḥrāb is hollowed into the western wall. The interior of this tomb, made of red sandstone and white marble, forms a single chamber. Four squinch arches (Fig. 230) support the domed ceiling. Projecting blocks of stone acting as brackets fill the angle between the octagon and the sixteen-sided figure over it. The dome itself shows an interesting stage in the building art of the country. It is a single dome having no empty space between its inner and outer surfaces. Its pointed or Tartar shape later became characteristic of the Indo-Islamic style.

Ghiyath-ud-Din's son, Mohammed Tughlaq, who built the fourth city of Delhi, *Jahanpanah* (Fig. 224), later removed his capital from Delhi to Daulatabad in the Deccan. This resulted in the ruin of the city that his predecessors had beautified.

In the time of Firoz Shah Tughlaq, Mohammed's successor, the style revived. Firoz was an enthusiastic builder and erected many constructions which bear the stamp of his character. Lack of finance, together with a scarcity of skilled workmen, owing to the shifting of the capital by his predecessor, also resulted in a difference of architectural character. The walls were made of rubble, coated with a layer of cement. Lintels, doorposts and pillars were roughly dressed monoliths. The decoration, if any, was moulded in piaster not carved in stone. Firoz Shah built at least four cities, including *Firozabad* (*Kotla*

*Firoz Shah*) the fifth city of Delhi (Fig. 224). He also erected numerous mosques and many tombs.

The *tomb* of his minister, *Khan-i-Jahan Tilangani*, though modest, is important since it shows the development of the tomb building style which influenced this form of architecture during the next two centuries. An innovation in design occurs in the building both in its plan and elevation. The tomb, although similar to the earlier fortified ones, no longer has the defensive character. Instead of the usual square, the plan is now octagonal in its elevation. It has an octagonal verandah pierced with three Tudor arches on each side. Above this is the wide chajja. The parapet over it has eight cupolas, one on each side.

Architectural activity suffered decline in the troubled times of the Sayyid dynasty and of the Lodis. The only buildings erected were tombs—notably the three royal tombs of *Mubarak Sayyid* (Fig. 231), *Mohammed Sayyid* and *Sikander Lodi*. These royal tombs were octagonal in plan, surrounded by an arched colonnade and one storey high, wit a a projecting eave. The other type of tomb was square (Fig. 232) without an eave, and two or even three storeys in height. Both these forms had a surmounting dome, often with a range of pillared kiosks rising above the parapet, square at the corners and octagonal at the sides.

Fig. 231. Tomb of Mubarak Shah Sayyid, Delhi.

## PROVINCIAL STYLES

Daring the Imperial period, a variety of Provincial styles of Indo-Isiamic architecture flourished in different provinces. The Delhi style influenced those centres which were in fairly close contact with the capital; others, more remote, reveal the influence of arts indigenous to their own locality. Another decisive influence on Provincial art was the fact that foreign craftsmen were sometimes employed.

There were eight Provincial styles. The centres of the *Punjab* style—Multan and Lahore show Persian influence. In *Lahore* they used mainly brick and wood—of a ber (jujube) kind, now rare. The doorways were carved with distinctive designs ending in tassels and knotted fringes—probably inspired by cloth hangings.

Of the five tombs at *Multan*, that of the Muslim saint *Rukhn-i-Alam* is the most important. An imposing monument of distinct character and solemn grandeur, its style synchronises three cultures—Arab, Iranian and Indian. Partly inlaid glazed tiles and bands of carved timber enhance the finely chiselled brickwork. The octagonal plan is perhaps the first of this type in the Punjab.

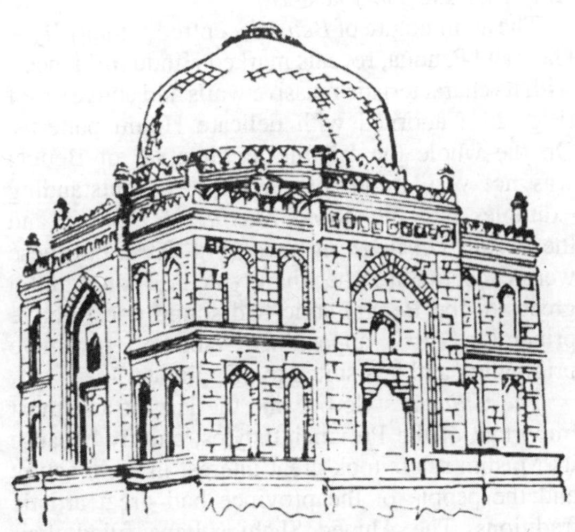

Fig. 232. Shish Gumbad, Delhi.

Jaunpur and Malwa were both close enough to Delhi to show the influence of the Imperial style. At *Jaunpur*, the Sharqi sultans produced a number of fine buildings, the *Atāla Masjid* being the most notable. The name derives from the Hindu temple of Atāla Devī, on the site of which it was built. Its sanctuary, displaying considerable skill and originality, constitutes the most important feature. This masjid shows the influence of Delhi, particularly in the beam and bracket system supporting the arches, and in the tapering turrets on the quoins of the western wall. The last of the Sharqi dynasty built the large Jaunpur mosque, which marks the end of the Jaunpur style.

Dhar and Mandu, the two chief cities exemplifying the provincial style in Malwa, also reveal the influence of the Imperial style because of their proximity to Delhi. Their chief innovations were first the combination of the arch, post and lintel system, and secondly mosques built on high plinths ascended by majestic flights of steps. They used colour in the decorations, produced by tinted stones and marbles and encaustic tiles. The outstanding monument of the Malwa style, the Jami Masjid at Mandu, is an impressive structure raised on a lofty plinth. The elegantly carved mimbar, together with the colour decoration, forms the only ornamentation of the stately interior. Its beauty lies in this quiet simplicity and sober austerity.

The architecture of *Bengal*, centred principally at Gaur and Pandua, reveals marked Hindu influences, with its characteristic massive walls and convex roof (Fig. 233) adorned with delicate Hindu patterns. On the whole the Islamic architecture of Bengal was not very impressive, except for outstanding examples like the *Adina Masjid* of *Pandua* and the *Dakhil Darwāza* in *Gaur* (Fig. 234), but these were exceptional rather than typical. Though not a great art, the Bengal style had sound constructive principles. Its appearance shows inventive originality, and it is suited to the climate.

The *Gujarat* style became the largest and most important of the Provincial styles, chiefly because its Muslim rulers took great interest in architecture and the people of the province had great artistic traditions. The Ahmed Shahi sultans filled their cities with splendid constructions in order to impress others with their power and wealth. Cultural tendencies did not inspire them. The aesthetic sense of the builders themselves contributed more than

Fig. 233. Tomb of Fath Khan, Bengal.

Fig. 234. Dakhil Darwaza, Gaur, Bengal.

anything else to the fine results. The rulers employed skilful native artisans and workmen. For this reason the Gujarat style became the most Indian of all its Provincial modes. It flourished from the fourteenth to the end of the sixteenth century. During the latter half of the fifteenth and the early part of the sixteenth century, it reached its zenith, a typical example being the *Jami Masjid* at *Champaner*—a finished architectural achievement. The most striking feature of the interior is the three-storeyed nave.

On the other hand, the buildings erected in *the Deccan* under the Bahmani rulers show very little indigenous influence. Here the Persian inspiration predominates because many of the Muslim invaders of the early middle ages were Persians and the first independent ruler of the Deccan—Alau-ud-Din Hassan Bahman Shah, who established the Bahmani dynasty in Gulbarga, also came from Persia. The shifting of the capital also brought strong currents of ideas from Delhi. The *Jami Masjid* is in the best state of preservation of what remains of the building activities in *Gulbarga*. The wide plain surfaces of the exterior, relieved by the aerial effect of the stilted dome, gives the impression of quiet greatness. *Gol-Gumbad* in *Khandesh*, not far from the Bahmani kingdom of Bijapur, was a centre of minor Provincial styles.

In *Kashmir*, the indigenous tradition continued as basis of the new Provincial style, with Islamic structural forms and decorative motifs grafted on to the native Kashmiri wooden architecture, producing a distinctive blend of Hindu and Muslim culture.

Fig. 235. Tomb of Sher Shah Sur, Sasaram, Bihar.

## MUGHAL STYLE

The Mughal architecture which replaced the Imperial style around the middle of the sixteenth century stands out as the golden age of Islamic architecture. All the Mughal rulers were cultured men who took great interest in the building art and filled their capitals with magnificent structures until the time of Aurangzeb.

In the first years of the Mughal conquest of north India, unsettled conditions did not allow much architectural activity; but when their rule became firmly established, the distinctive type of Mughal art started to evolve into one of the most important styles of architecture in India.

The great development of architecture and the excellence of the productions over so long a period resulted chiefly from the wealth and might of the empire, together with the exceptional aesthetic taste of the Mughal rulers themselves. Five successive emperors took keen interest in building and the allied arts— Babur, Humayun, Akbar, Jahangir and Shah Jahan. The period may be divided into two phases: at first, in Akbar's time, red sandstone was used; later Shah Jahan employed white marble.

Babur (1526-1530), though keenly interested in architecture, had no opportunity to develop it because of political troubles. For the same reason Humayun (1530-1556) too had little chance to build. During his time, the usurper *Sher Shah Sur*, who interrupted the Mughal rule, built the *Purānā Qilā or Old Fort*, which became the sixth city of Delhi (Fig. 224) with the Qilā-i-Kuhna masjid and his famous *mausoleum* in the lake at *Sasaram* (Figs. 235, 236). Situated in the centre of the great artificial

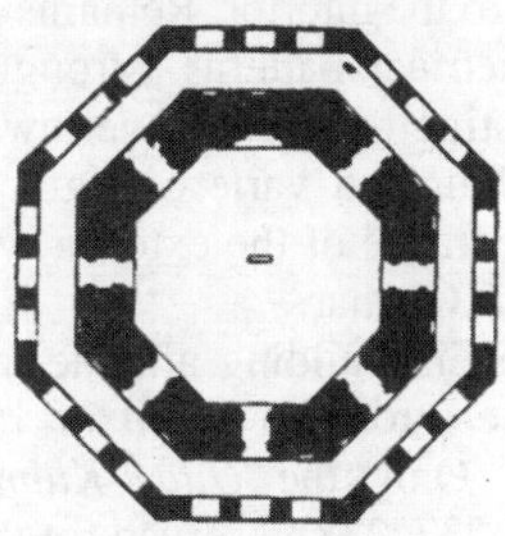

Fig. 236. Tomb of Sher Shah Sur, Sasaram, Bihar, ground plan.

lake, the exquisite setting enhances the beauty of his mighty tomb. It has five storeys, the two lower ones square in plan. The stepped basement rises out of the water and the lofty terrace above forms a wide courtyard with a pillared pavilion at each corner. Inside the courtyard stands the tomb building, an octagonal structure in three diminishing stages, crowned by a low broad dome. In this mausoleum the transition from the square to the octagon is treated more simply. The eight sides of the tomb are changed into a circle by the beam and bracket method,

Fig. 237. Qila-i-Kuhna mosque. Purana Qila, Delhi, constructed under Sher Shah Sur.

with an arched niche at each angle corresponding to a squinch. Doorways on the north, south and east give entrance to the interior. Remains of glazed and painted geometrical patterns, strongly marked in boldly contrasting reds, blues, yellows and whites, show that colour and variety originally enhanced the outer appearance of the exterior walls, made of sandstone from Ghunar.

Sher Shah's first building, after he had established himself on the throne of Delhi in 1540, was the *Purānā Qila.* Only the *Qilā-i-Kuhna* the royal mosque (Figs. 237, 238) reserved for the private use of the Sur ruler remains. It is an architectural gem, containing in itself much that was later developed by the Mughals. Its chief attraction is the façade with five archways and recessed central arch, all exquisitely designed. The white marble additions to the sandstone material and the coloured inlaid parts serve to enhance its charm even more. The building shows the same elegance inside as outside. The mihḥrābs have an exceptional beauty with their decorated imposts, foliated major arches and delicately inscribed border round the rectangular frame.

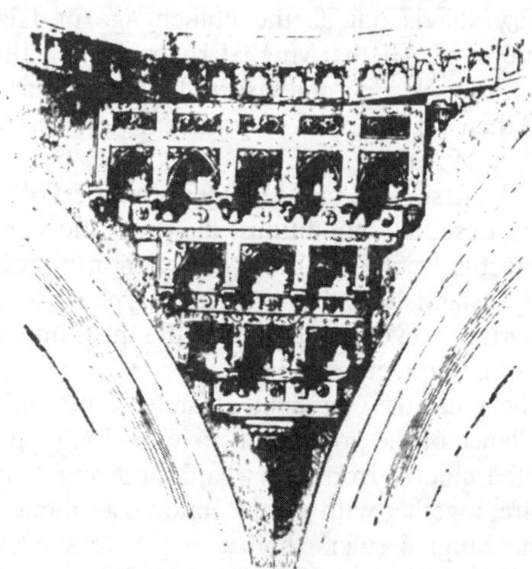

Fig. 238. Squinch, Qila-i-Kuhna mosque, Purana Qila, Delhi.

Humayun spent fifteen years in exile after Sher Shah usurped the throne. He died within a few months after regaining power in 1556. Through him Persian influence entered into the architecture of north India. His widow built *Humayu's tomb* in *Delhi* (Pl. 7.3) the first to be placed in a garden setting and one of the finest

Fig. 239. Tomb of Humayun, Delhi.

examples of early Mughal art in India a very important landmark in the development of the style. Persian influence reveals itself in various parts. The great arched alcove of the façade as well as the dome show obvious Persian extraction in shape and construction. The kiosks, however, with their elegant cupolas, are typically Indian; and the stone masonry, skilfully and artistically blended with marble, could have been produced by Indian masons. On the other hand the complex of rooms and corridors in the interior was a characteristic of Persian tombs, never before used in India. Certain features moreover were quite original: a lofty and imposing gateway built in the middle of each of the four sides with the main entrance facing west, and a spacious garden surrounding the tomb—the layout of the park forming an integral part of the architectural composition.

The tomb stands in the centre of a square sandstone terrace (Fig. 239). Small chambers breach the sides of this platform. The four sides of the tomb, practically the same in elevation, have a rectangular fronton with an arched recess, flanked by wings with arched openings. Above the central arch rises the great dome. The interior of the tomb chamber consists of a group of rooms instead of one hall. The largest one in the centre contains the emperor's cenotaph, while the smaller rooms at each angle accommodate those of his family. The beauty of the building lies in the perfect harmony and skilful presentation of all its necessary parts, especially in the relation between the plan and design of both exterior and interior, and in the understanding of architectural principles.

Akbar (1556-1605), keenly interested in art, became the first of the great Mughal builders. He gathered architects from all over north India to plan out his many splendid constructions. Akbar preferred the Indian system of architecture to the Persian style. Indigenous craftsmen still maintained their ancient traditions, and under Akbar's patronage produced buildings of red sandstone with insertions of white marble. They used the trabeated order of construction and the tudor arch for decorative arcading. Bracket capitals and many-sided shafts became typical of the period. The ornamentation consisted of carved and inlaid patterns, and painted designs on the interior walls and ceilings.

The first example of the Akbari style of architecture, the *fortress palace at Agra* (Fig. 240), was constructed with great ingenuity, the stones being linked so closely with iron rings that they appear to be solidly welded. According to the Ain-i-Akbari, the interior of the fort consisted of more than five hundred buildings. Later, Shah Jahan demolished many of them to make way for his new structures in marble. One of Akbar's palaces, the *Jahangiri Maḥal*, which still remains, was the first of its type to be erected as its experimental planning shows. The southern gateway of the fortified walls served as a private entrance; but the Delhi gate, the main entrance on the west, designed to harmonise with the dignified aspect of the rampart, was one of the best works of Akbar's reign, showing a freshness and spontaneity that marked the beginning of a new era.

Akbar built two more of these fortress palaces, one at Lahore and the other at Allahabad. The *Lahore fort* (Fig. 241) has a more regular plan than the Agra one and in its general outline it forms a parallelogram, enclosed in a high bastioned wall. The same red sandstone material was used as at Agra, but the designs on its

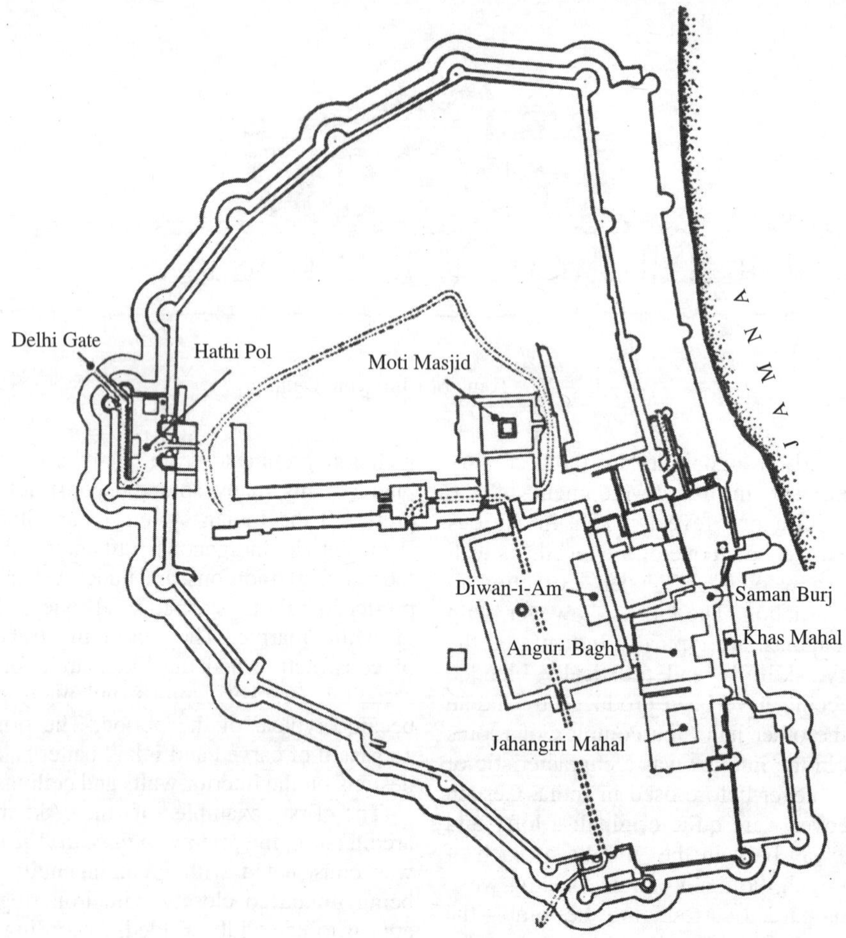


Fig. 240. Fortress palace, Agra.

brackets and most of the carving show much more imaginative skill. The exterior wall of the northern angle is covered with decorations in glazed tile work. The *Allahabad fortress* is wedge-shaped, because of its position at the junction of the Ganges and Jamuna. It is the largest example built by Akbar, but is now in a ruined condition.

Akbar's greatest and most ambitious architectural achievement was the construction of his new capital, *Fatehpur Sikri* (Figs. 242,243), a site 36 km west of Agra—a most spectacular production with its palatial, residential, official and religious buildings. A city without streets, Fatehpur Sikri was an arrangement of broad terraces and courtyards, with palaces and pavilions all grouped around them—all of them elegant and rich in their architectural treatment. The most impressive of all the structures are the religious buildings—the Jami Masjid (great mosque) with its triumphal gateway, the Baland Darwāza and the tombs of Salim Chisti and Islam Khan. The *Jami Masjid* (Pl. 8.1; Fig. 244) the principal building constructed in 1571, is one of the largest of its kind in India. It has the usual wide open courtyard, with pillared cloisters on three sides and the sanctuary on the western one. Its chief beauty lies in the planning and execution of the sanctuary. The façade consists of a large rectangular fronton, in the centre of which is the spacious alcove. On either side a pillared arcade forms the wings. A large dome rises behind the rectangular fronton with smaller domes over each wing. Along the parapets are pillared kiosks. The exterior feature harmonises

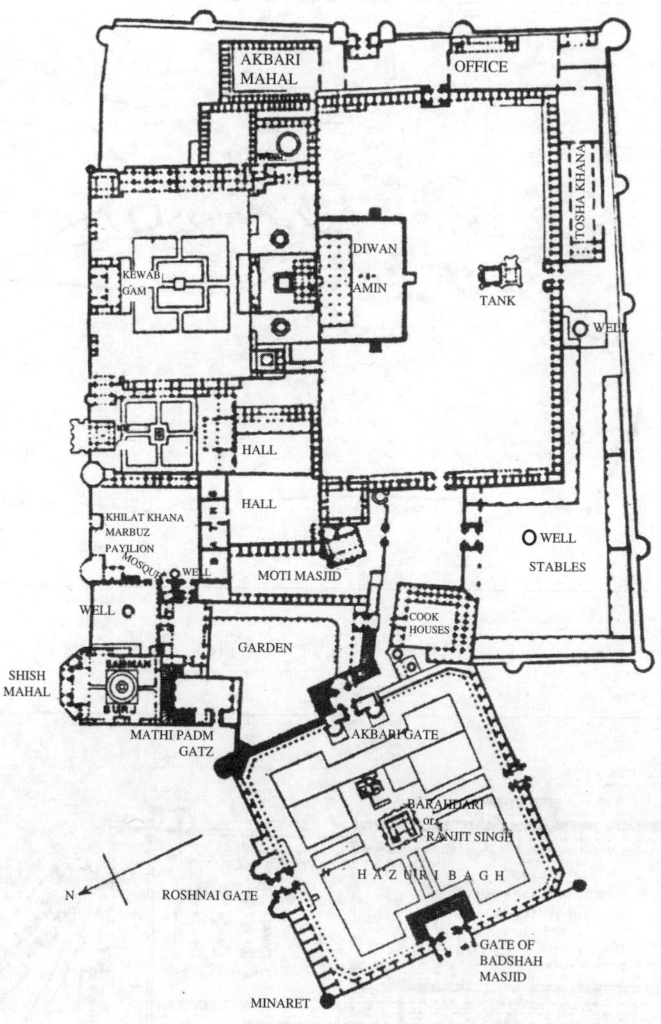


Fig. 241. Fort, Lahore, ground plan.

with the interior arrangement, which consists of a nave with three doorways. The aisles on each side correspond to the broad arcaded wings of the façade. The open spaces of the nave and side chapels contrast with the pillared aisles, thus giving a pleasing variety.

The *baland darwāza* (gate of magnificence; Pl. 8.2; Figs. 245, 246), the southern gate of the Jami Masjid, commemorates Akbar's victorious campaign in the Deccan. Its dominating bulk of masonry draws attention to itself rather than the mosque. The façade of the gateway has a large central face with two narrow ones at each side receding at an angle. The central rectangular face has an arched entrance. The narrow wings on the sides are divided into three storeys. Above the façade is a parapet crowned with cupolas, with a range of kiosks rising behind. The rear portion of the gateway is less imposing than the front. The wide border, the chief element of its composition, emphasises its rectangular shape. It also provides much space for the ornamental inscriptions so characteristic of most Mughal architecture. It makes its appearance in the façade of the first mosque in Delhi. In the Baland Darwāza, which Akbar erected near the end of his life, this decorative border becomes

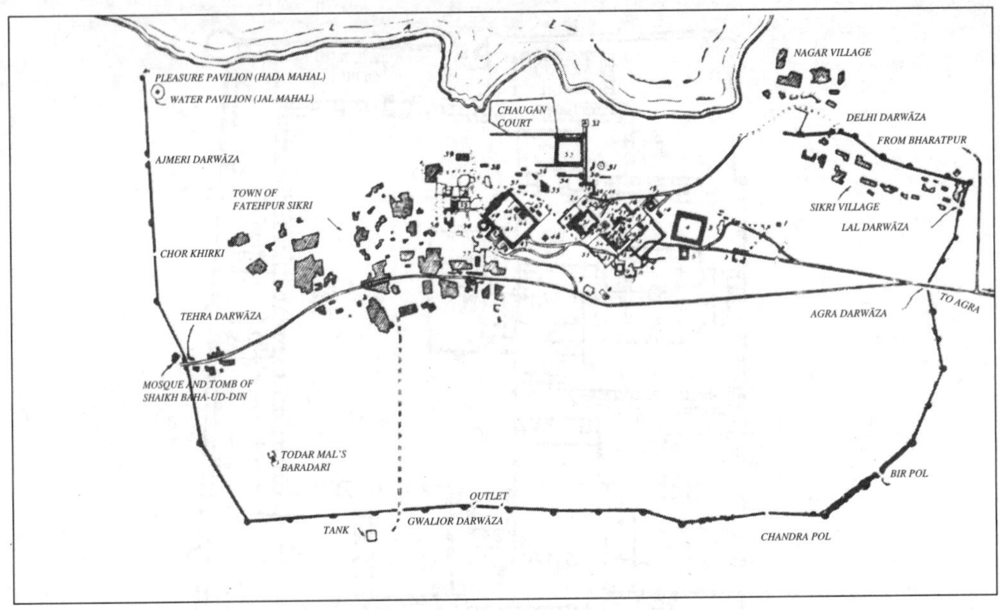


Fig. 242. Fatehpur Sikri, plan.

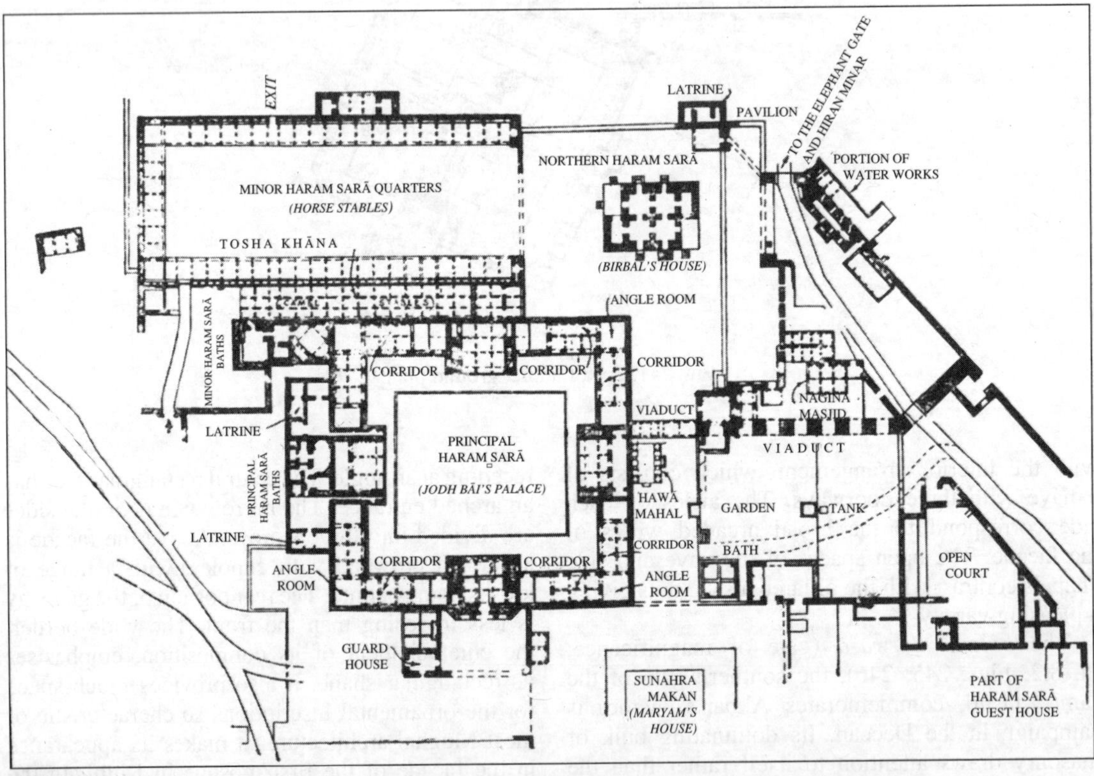

Fig. 243. Fatehpur Sikri, plan of palatial and residential buildings.

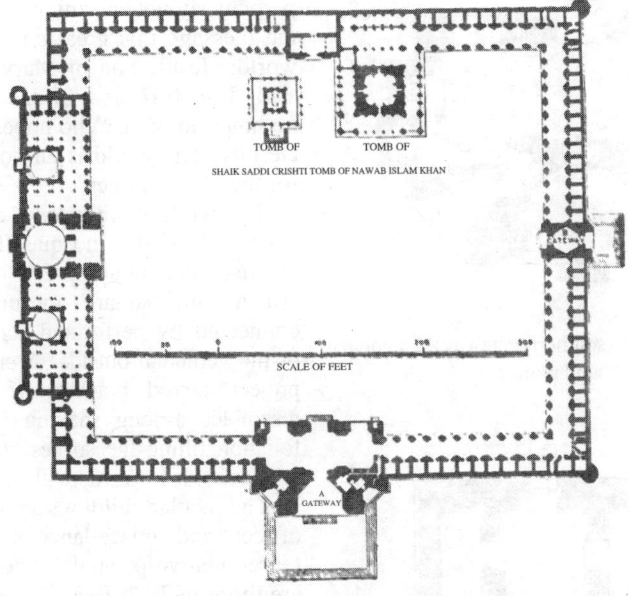


Fig. 244. Great mosque, Fatehpur Sikri, ground plan.

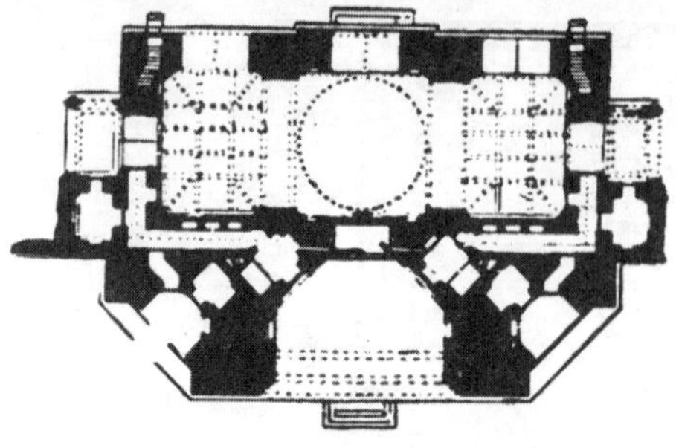

Fig. 246. Baland darwaza (southern gateway), Fatehpur Sikri, ground plan.

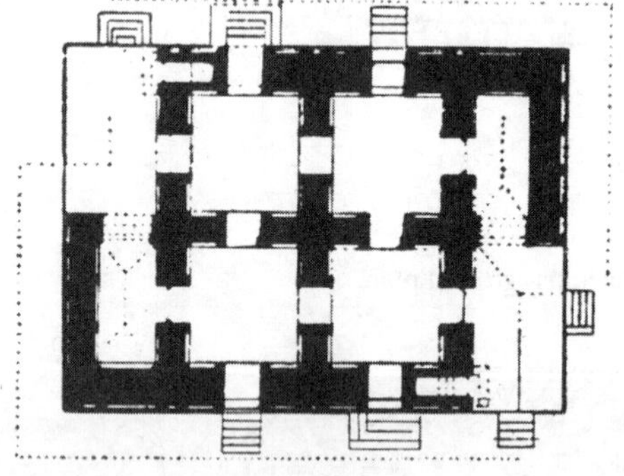

Fig. 247. Raja Birbal's house, Fatehpur Sikri, ground plan.

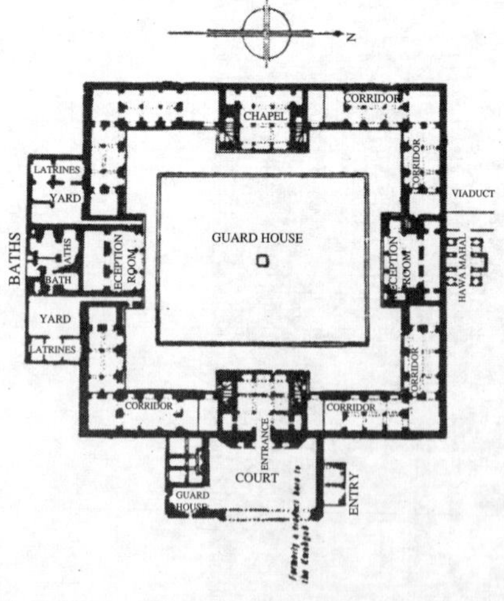


Figl 248. Jodh Bai's palace, Fatehpur Sikri, ground plan.

particularly noteworthy not only for *its* size but for the message this great emperor proclaimed to the world: 'Jesus, Son of Mary, (on whom be peace) said: The world is a bridge. Pass over it but build no house upon it. Who hopes for an hour hopes for eternity. The world is an hour. Spend it in prayer, for the rest is unseen'.

The white marble *tomb* of *Salim Chisti*, in the courtyard of the mosque (Pl. 8.1), possesses an exquisite beauty and purity of design. A low dome crowns the square mortuary chamber. Pillars connected by perforated screens support the roof of the verandah outside. Around the whole building project carved brackets of unique design. Each resembles a long snaking volute, with perforated foliation filling the spaces between the curves. The whole design looks more like carved ivory than marble.

The secular buildings are of three kinds: palaces, offices and miscellaneous buildings. The most representative palatial residences in Fatehpur Sikri are those of Jodh Bai, Miriam, the Sultana and the so-called *Raja Birbal house* (Fig. 247). *Jodh Bai's palace* (Fig. 248), the most complete in design and arrangement, has a distinctive style of its own. In its carved decoration it resembles temple architecture, especially in the design of the niches and brackets with volute forms, and in the shape of the pillar shafts. The builders were probably artisans from Gujarat. The chief buildings attached to the inner side of the surrounding high plain wall face an inner courtyard. Staggered doorways ensure complete seclusion. The enclosure incorporates a private chapel and screened roof terraces for promenades.

The principal official administrative building, the *Diwān-i-Khās* (hall of private audience) (Fig. 249) is relatively small, rectangular in plan,

Fig. 249. Diwan-i-Khas, Fatehpur Sikri, section

Fig. 250. Diwan-i-Khas, Fatehpur Sikri, view of pillar from below.

Fig. 251. Diwan-i-Khas, Fatehpur Sikri, upper section of pillar.

with two storeys, and a flat terraced roof enriched by a pillared kiosk at each corner. Its interior, consisting of a single unusual hall, has a large solid pillar (Fig. 250) supporting a circular stone platform with its great capital. Stone bridges (Fig. 251) extend from this platform along each diagonal of the hall to join hanging galleries surrounding the upper portion. This strange construction, where he sat on a throne listening to representatives of different faiths, may have signified Akbar's 'dominion over the four quarters'.

Jehangir (1605-1627) showed greater interest in painting than architecture. The tombs of Akbar and I'timad-ud-Daulah, his father-in-law are the chief monuments of his reign. *Akbar's tomb* (Fig, 252), an enormous work at *Sikandra* near Agra, took eight years to complete. The plan of the central building is square, enclosed by walls with an entrance to the south and a false gateway in the middle of each wall. Though the building was intended to be innovative, to depart from set structures, it turned out to be retrograde, much inferior to Humayun's tomb erected half a century earlier. The massive terrace of the lower portion has great beauty and may have been erected during Akbar's time. The next storey however, composed of light and whimsical rows of sandstone pavilions, is out of harmony with the sturdy ground floor. Again the upper story, composed of white marble, looks out of place with the red sandstone of the two lower storeys. The composition lacks unity and coherence.

The *tomb of I'timad-ud-Daulah* (Fig. 253), built for the father of Jehangir's queen Nur Jahan, is small but exquisitely finished. It stands in a garden—a suitable setting for the beautiful white marble structure. Square in plan, the tomb comprises a central structure, with broad octagonal towers resembling minarets at each angle, and a small pavilion rising above the roof. Each side has three arched openings. The ground floor of the interior, consisting of a series of rooms and passages round the central chamber containing the cenotaph, corresponds to an enclosed verandah. The walls of the square pavilion are traceried marble screens. On its shining, patterned floor stands the yellow porphyry cenotaph. The white marble enhances the beauty of the design. The decoration consists of an inlaid work known as pietra dura, in which hard, rare stones like lapis lazuli, onyx, jasper, topaz etc., were embedded in the marble, forming graceful foliate designs. Thus the tomb of I'timad-ud-Daulah heralded the sumptuous phase of white marble studded with gold and precious stones which marked the zenith of the Mughal style.

Under the patronage of Shah Jahan (1628–1658), Mughal architecture reached the heights of its grandeur. Instead of using red sandstone, he changed the building material to white marble and erected splendid mosques and palaces in many cities of north India, spending enormous sums on his architectural schemes.

With the change of material there also followed the corresponding change of techniques. The marble used by Shah Jahan was obtained from the quarries of Makrana in Rajasthan. The graining was very delicate and the ornamentation judiciously applied, for too much of it would spoil its beauty of appearance. The change in technique also brought about a change in certain elements of the style, especially the arch. Its curves were now more foliated by means of nine cusps, so that graceful white arcades of engrailed arches became the chief characteristic of the period. The dome was also changed; the bulbous Persian type with the constriction at the neck became popular.

Shah Jahan replaced the red stone buildings by marble ones at different periods of his reign, not all at once. At Agra Fort he rebuilt the original sandstone structures of Akbar in marble. He did the same at Lahore.

Shah Jahan shifted the imperial capital from Agra to Delhi where he proceeded to build the city of *Shahjahanabad or Red Fort* (Fig. 254) which became the seventh city of Delhi (Fig. 224). It consisted of a palace fortress surrounded by the city and was the last of the great citadels which represented the Mughal power in India. This fort at Delhi measures 488 × 351m and is aligned from north to south. The main entrance, called Lahore Gate, faces west; the eastern side lies near the river.

The interior of the fort has a very formal

Fig. 252. Akbar's tomb, Sikandra.

Fig. 253. Tomb of I'timad-ud-Daula, Agra.

and regular layout. The splendid palaces, the finest of the period, were aligned on the eastern side and rose above the rampart walls, giving the exterior a very picturesque appearance with their balconies and oriel windows crowned with gilt cupolas.

Besides these palaces there were other buildings, among them the *Diwān-i-Khās* and Rang-Maḥal being the largest and most luxuriant. These two buildings resemble each other in their general character. They are single-storeyed pavilions with engrailed arches and a wide eave. Above the eave rises a parapet with a graceful kiosk at each corner. Engrailed arcades divide the interior into bays and present at the same time a perspective of arches and flowing curves. Inlaid patterns, consisting of roses, lilies, poppies and other flowers in traceried foliations ornament the walls and arches.

The *Rang-Maḥal* is most splendid and decorative. Piers divide the interior into bays. A sunken marble basin with a carved lotus flower adorns the centre of the hall. Scented water gurgled out from a fountain in the form of a lotus bud in the middle of the pool.

The *Diwān-i-Am* (the hall of public audience), another notable structure enclosed by an ornamental garden, occupied the centre of the fort. The original plan consisted of a square courtyard surrounded by a colonnade, with this hall on the eastern side; but as it exists all the other structures have disappeared and only the hall remains.

For public worship in Delhi, Shah Jahan bullt the great *Jami Masjid*, the most impressive of all mosques in India. The lofty plinth on which it stands contributes a great deal to its majestic appearance. Three splendid gateways dominated the surroundings, thus adding to the lofty dignity of the exterior. The conventional plan includes a large paved sihn surrounded by liwans and sanctuary on the western end. The exterior view of the sanctuary presents a wide central archway. An arcade of five engrailed arches on each side of the central arch forms the wings. Three bulbous domes crown the centre and wings. The treatment of architecture and decoration harmonises perfectly with the imposing size of the building. There is balance of light and shade and even minor elements are well proportioned. Yet aesthetically the structure does not give a pleasing impression and lacks artistic appeal. It seems too rigid—no movement is created through difference of texture and many details such as merlons and inlaid panels are multiplied to the point of monotony. Hence the general effect is one of calculated and almost mechanical precision.

The *Taj Maḥal* at *Agra* (Pl. 8.3) is undoubtedly Shah Jahan's finest achievement and the most exquisite of all Mughal buildings. In its flawless beauty it ranks among the most perfect monuments in the world. It was erected to the memory of his beloved queen, Arjumand

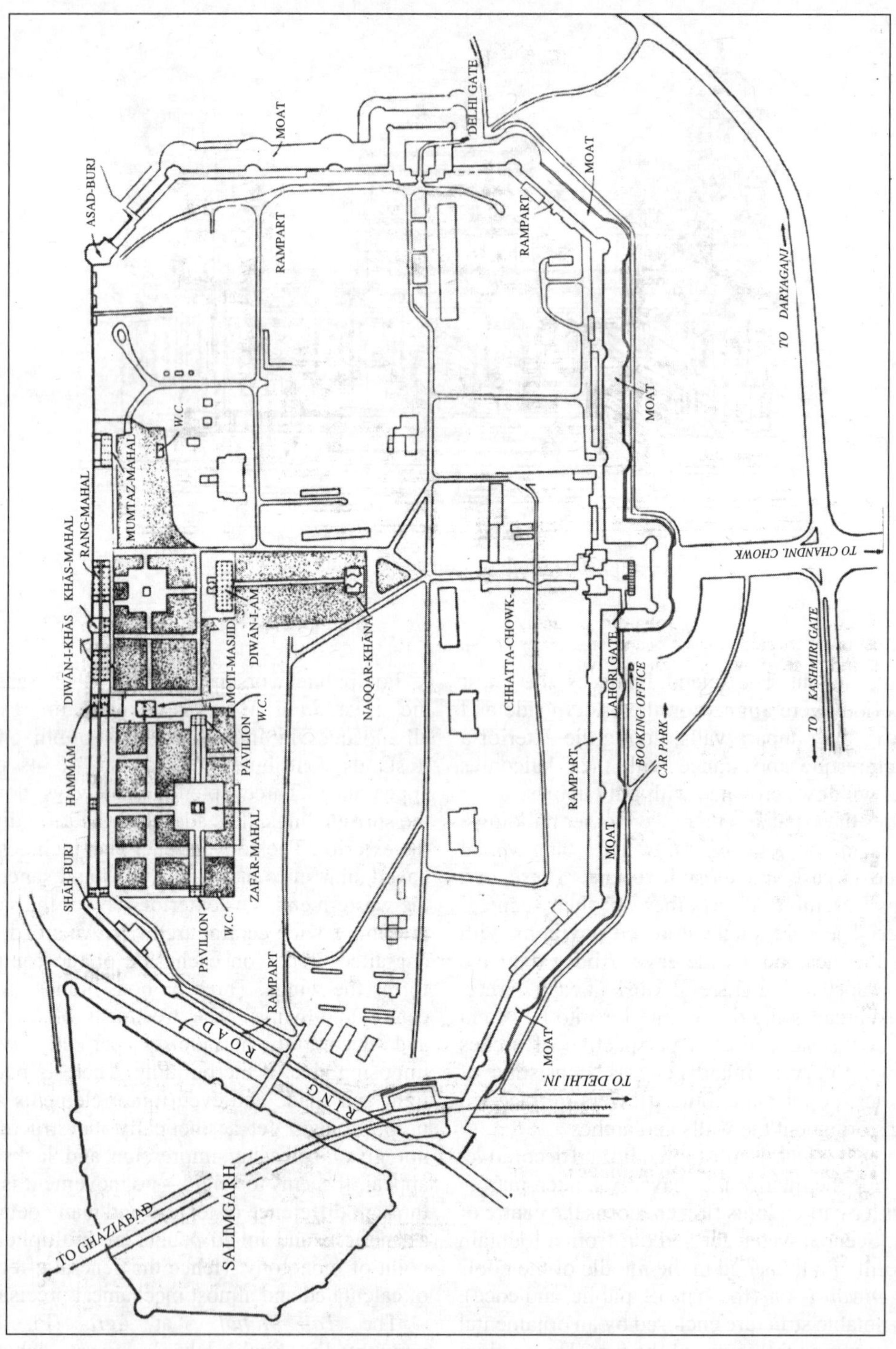


Fig. 254. Red Fort, Delhi.

Banu Begum, called Mumtaz Maḥal (exalted of the palace) or Taj Maḥal (crown of the palace). A year after her death in 1631 he began the Taj and it took twenty-two years to complete.

The Taj Maḥal stands in a walled enclosure measuring around 580 × 305m. The red sandstone gateway at the south leads to a spacious ornamental garden (305 sq.m). Near the river Jamuna on the northern side of the enclosure, a low red stone terrace extends from one end of the wall to the other, terminating on both sides in a red sandstone building. That on the west is a mosque, and the eastern one—its jawab (answer)—serves as mihmān-khāna (guest-house) or as majlis khāna (assembly hall).

In the centre, on a white marble platform almost seven metres high, is the rauza (Fig. 255)

Fig. 255. Taj Mahal, Agra, simplified section.

in glittering white marble, with four minarets at the corners of the plinth. The bevelled angles give this cubicle structure the shape of an irregular octagon. The elevation, equal on all four sides, is typically Islamic in design. In the centre it has a magnificent arched recess framed by a rectangular wall that rises above the parapet of the roof. Smaller arched recesses in two storeys flank the main arch and are echoed in the narrower bevelled wall surfaces. These arched recesses contain the doors and windows. Perforated marble screens, so delicately carved that they resemble lacework, fill the windows. Floral designs, inlaid with semiprecious stones, decorate the spandrels of the arches. The large frame surrounding the door arches bears carved inscriptions from the Koran—marvels of Persian calligraphy.

The greatest elegance of the Taj lies in its beautiful white marble dome (Fig. 256) surrounded by four chatrīs (smaller domed pavilions). The dome rests on a low drum. Lotus petals encircle its restricted base. It curves up gently to the pointed top, covered with radiating petals. While the dome reveals Persian influence, the four chatrīs are purely Indian.

The interior of the Taj (Fig. 257) has several

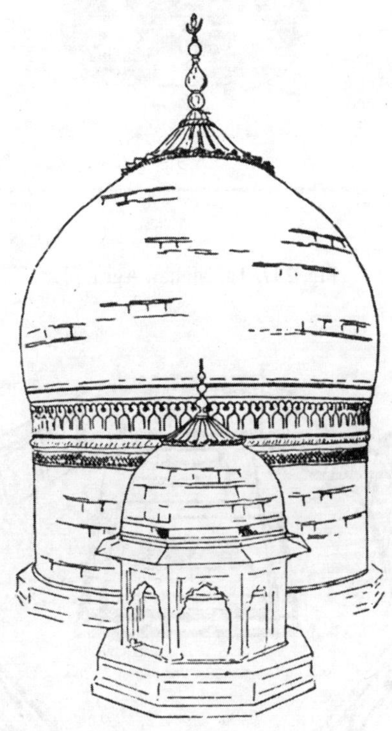

Fig. 256. Taj Mahal, Agra, central dome and one chatri.

octagonal and square rooms that surround the central octagonal hujra (hall) containing the zarīḥs (cenotaphs; Fig. 258) of Mumtaz Maḥal in the centre and Shah Jahan's on one side of it. Both are surrounded by the splendid muhajjar (perforated marble screens). Steps lead down to the underground maqbara with the qabrs (graves).

Delicacy and grace characterise the beauty of the Taj. As Helen Gardner observes, this effect 'results from at least four elements: the material, the control of light and dark, the open design, and the setting in a larger design of contrasting elements'.

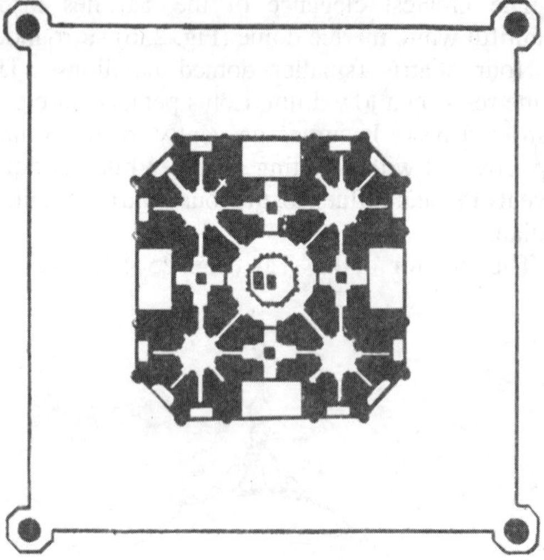

Fig. 257. Taj Mahal, Agra, plan.

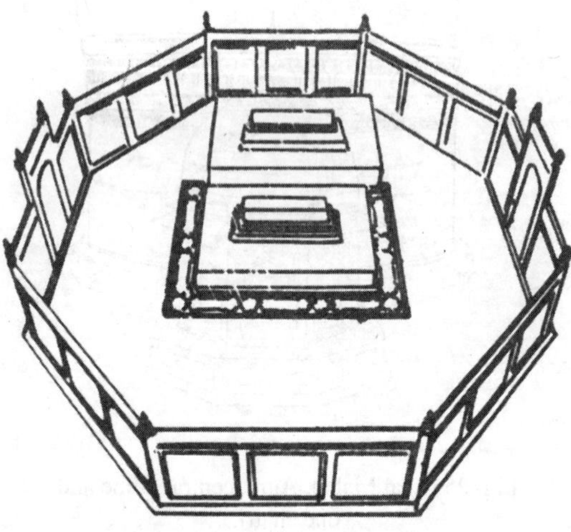

Fig. 258. Taj Mahal, inlaid cenotaphs of Mumtaz Mahal and Shah Jahan, surrounded by marble screen.

The white marble from the Makrana quarries has a texture of the finest quality. It shows subtle variations in colour with every change of light: dazzling white in the noonday sunshine, tinted pale rose at sunset, and gleaming like a pearl in the moonlight. Light and shade are cleverly arranged. There are no outstanding parts producing sharp contrasts of light and shadow; the shadows are soft and delicate. The arched recesses of doors and windows are just deep enough to bring out their pointed shape. This softness of shadows is one of the great charms of the Taj.

The lovely tomb building together with the four minarets, detached from it yet united by means of the common platform, form a harmonious open design. The setting too fits such a lovely masterpiece. A pair of buildings in red sandstone flank the glittering white edifice. Before it lies a spacious garden laid out in a conventional plan, forming a carpet of green lawns and flower beds as well as of streams, fountains and lotus pools whose clear waters mirror the beauty of the Taj. The contrast of the dark green trees and red sandstone buildings enhances its white loveliness all the more.

Shah Jahan had planned to build another tomb for himself exactly like the Taj, but in black marble, on the opposite side of the river, and connect the two by a bridge, but he could not realize this plan. None of his other buildings equals the Taj, although all are splendid and rich in architectural decoration. Because of their delicacy and refined ornamentation, his buildings have been described as 'jewellery on a large scale'.

Another characteristic of the Mughal architecture was the love of *formal gardens* exemplified by picturesque parks laid out by the Mughal rulers on selected sites. This was very much a Persian derivative, brought to India by Babur who after his first victory at Panipet laid out a garden called *Kabul Bagh*.

But the most typical example is the one created by Shah Jahan at *Lahore*, known as the *Shalimar Bagh*. The design of the garden forms a series of descending terraces in order to maintain the flow of water through the fountains, basins, pools and cascades. The layout, very conventional and symmetrical, provides no rhythm. A high wall surrounds the entire garden to ensure privacy.

After the golden age of Mughal architecture under Shah Jahan, decline set in under Aurangzeb (1658-1707) who had no interest in art or building. The few mosques and tombs erected during his time betray a decay in style and construction. The *mausoleum* of the emperor's wife *Rabia Daurani* at Aurangabad is an obvious imitation of the Taj Mahal but considerably less than half its size.

In the *Red Fort* at *Delhi* Aurangzeb erected his private mosque known as the *Moti Masjid* or *Pearl Mosque* (Fig. 259), constructed out of white marble The domes of this mosque are too rounded in their contours and lack flowing grace of form.

Fig. 259. Moti Masjid, Red Fort, Delhi.

The Mughal empire collapsed following the death of Aurangzeb in 1707 and the few buildings erected show decadence of the style. The centre of power was shifted to Lucknow, where the Nawabs of Oudh became the most important rulers. After the fall of the empire under the Nawabs of Oudh, came the last dying phase of the Mughal style. The numerous remains of this period in Lucknow prove that, despite the quantity, the quality had degenerated. Since the Mughals had reached the highest perfection in architecture, the workers of Oudh could advance no further. They tried therefore to elaborate and repeat the elements on a larger scale, but lack of funds obliged them to make these larger buildings of brick on rubble foundations, and to face them with stucco instead of stone and marble. Only the technical skill of the builders and the fine workmanship of the decoration give artistic value to these buildings.

# SCULPTURE

## THE MAURYAS

At its peak, the Mauryan empire (c. 324 B.C. to c. 188 B.C.), founded by Chandragupta, extended northwards almost to Persia, the heart of Achaemenid power and culture, thus initiating an era of more intimate cultural connections between India and the Achaemenid and Seleucid empires. Hellenic influences became more pronounced with the increase of social contacts, matrimonial alliances and trade between them. This foreign influence may have inspired the royal patrons of India to erect structures which were monumental.

The most important sculptural remains of the Mauryan period are the capitals and the crowning animal figures on the Ashokan pillars. Some of the Ashokan edicts were carved on already existing pillars, as for example the *Basarh-Bakhira* (ancient Vaisali) *lion pillar* (Fig. 25) where the workmanship is crude and rough. On stylistic grounds, the figures can be divided into two groups: the sophisticated but conventional lion and the cruder but very powerfully modelled representations of the bull and elephant. The one at Basarh-Bakhira marks the earliest stage in their development. A lion crouching above the plain square abacus shows the primitive beginnings of an art which culminated in the lion figures of Lauriya Nandangarh and Sarnath.

The *elephant* at *Sankasya* and the Rampurva bull illustrate the transition from the Basarh-Bakhira lion to the Lauriya Nandangarh capital. The Sankasya pillar itself shows an improvement in the change from a square to a round abacus, thus making the transition from the capital to the animal more harmonious. The decoration on the abacus and the manner of filling the space between the legs are rather primitive—probably copies of wooden models.

The *Rampurva bull capital* (Pl. 9.1) shows stylistic similarities with the Sankasya capital. The bull bears a striking resemblance to those on the Indus seals. Though the technique is less sophisticated than in the lion figures, the modelling and form of the animal appear vigorous. The volume, following closely the anatomical details, reveals keen observation of nature and understanding on the animal form. Unfortunately, this naturalistic representation of the bull does not harmonise with the conventional patterns on the abacus. The decoration on the abacus, consisting of rosettes and honeysuckle, appears a little rough.

The lion capitals at Rampurva and Lauriya Nandangarh are chronologically close to the Rampurva bull capital. The *Rampurva lion capital* resembles an inverted lotus with the petals clearly marked. It retains some of the lustrous polish. A line of geese adorns the round abacus. The crowning statue on top represents a seated lion, with muscles, veins and paws skilfully carved. The uniform curls of the mane show the schematic repetition of the same design. The whole is represented in a conventional way. On the tall and graceful pillar of *Lauriya Nandangarh* we see another *seated lion* (P1. 1.2). This frequent use of the lion figure could be due to the fact that it symbolised one of the cardinal directions. The lion seems to be uncomfortably fitted into the round abacus, with parts of the body projecting beyond it.

The quadripartite *lion capitals* of *Sarnath* and *Sanchi* mark the last stage in the evolution. At *Sarnath* (P1. 9.2; Fig. 260) we find for the first time four lions grouped together instead of a single figure as in the earlier examples. This capital consists of an inverted lotus with gently curved petals. On the round abacus above it are high relief carvings of a lion, a galloping horse, an elephant and a bull, separated from each other by a wheel. These animals represent the four points of the compass: the lion north, the horse south, the elephant east, and the bull west, for the Buddhists believed them to be the guardians of the four cardinal points. In this abacus, they symbolise the continuous movement and unceasing progress of the dharma-chakra (wheel of the law), destined to spread throughout the world. The freshness and naturalism of the animal figures on the abacus contrast strongly with the four conventionalised lions above. Sitting back to back on top of the abacus, they echo the essential shape of the stylised lotus. Though the rippling curls of the mane, the upturned whiskers and the shape of the lips are conventionalised, the snarling mouth and bared teeth look very real. The leg muscles and paws are powerfully modelled also, and the curved claws seem to express all the native ferocity of the animals. Originally, the lions supported a dharmachakra, the remains of which are still visible on the backs of the animals. The lion heads, with incised parallel lines representing the muzzle, and eyes in a triangular shape, resemble Persian lion figures. Though the sophisticated conception seems to confirm the Achaemenid influence, only experience could have resulted in

Fig. 260. Lion capital, Sarnath.

the advance to naturalism seen in these animals. The Sarnath lion capital now serves as the emblem of the Indian Republic.

The *Sanchi capital*, resembling the one at Sarnath, is even more conventional and stylised. The higher and narrower relief of the abacus frieze eases the transition from the capital to the crowning figures better than at Sarnath.

Fig. 261. Elephant, Dauli, Orissa.

Besides these animal figures on the pillars, another piece of sculpture, the *elephant* at *Dhauli* (Fig. 261), carved out of the living rock, strikes an essentially indigenous note quite different from the art traditions of the capitals. The voluminous mass shows plasticity and knowledge of the animal form. The slightly raised right leg and flowing trunk accentuate the animal's forward movement. Compared with this elephant, the lion figures seem too conventional. Stylistically it does not come much later than the elephant capital at Sankasya. The unconventional Dhauli elephant as well as the Rampurva bull and Sankasya elephant seem to belong to a different artistic tradition—perhaps that of the Indus Valley. These animal forms are not schematic— nascent life seems to stir within them. This indigenous quality saw further development in the subsequent periods of the Sunga and Early Andhra dynasties.

But before we discuss the art under these dynasties, let us consider those sculptures which are supposedly Mauryan in character since they are carved in the same grey Chunar sandstone as the animal figures. These consist mainly of yakṣa and yakṣinī figures. All the yakṣas have certain general characteristics such as a powerful physique, an earthy quality, frontal conception, strong rounded legs, and a contrast between the flat back and rounded arms, chest and abdomen. Their crudeness and directness indicate native spirit. The pot-bellied appearance, found here and in many later sculptures, is meant to represent prāṇa (yogic breath control). The lower garment clings like a wet cloth, and the tight girdle, with its ends hanging down the centre, is treated as a separate volume. The folds are marked by incised parallel lines, forming convex ridges in between. These traits can be seen in the two *Patna yakṣas,* the *Parkham yakṣa* (Fig. 262) and the *yakṣa Manibhadra* from *Pawaya.* The last two are slightly cruder than the Patna yakṣas in their frontal poses, the slightly bent legs and the treatment of the drapery. This is especially apparent when we compare the girdle cloths of the Maṇibhadra and Parkham yakṣas with those of the Patna yakṣas. In the modelling of the body, the pair of nude *Jaina torsos* from *Lohanipur* resemble the Patna yakṣas. They have the same powerful thighs and broad shoulders.

Fig. 262. Parkham yaksha

Fig. 263. Didarganj yakshini.

*The Didarganj yakṣiṇī* (Fig. 263) shows an almost complete contrast to the crudeness of these figures. The bright polish of Mauryan sculptures still appears on the whole figure, while only the upper half of the Patna yakṣas is polished. According to some authors this may indicate the decline of the Mauryan court art. The statue of the yakṣiṇī is fully round, finished on all sides, unlike the yakṣas which were meant to be seen only from the front. The treatment of the ornaments and drapery is the same as that of the yakṣas. Her form recalls the sophisticated female figures immortalised in later Indian art and literature. The sensuous curves of the body and heavy mass of hair bring to mind the later yakṣiṇīs of Mathura. A catulatilakamaṇi (crest jewel) adorns her forehead. The upper part of her body shows a slight forward incline. A hrīnmālā (long necklace) hangs rhythmically between her full breasts which curve down to a narrow waist. The broad hips taper gradually to the slim ankles which bear heavy ornaments. The body is sensitively modelled, particularly the eyes, chin and abdomen.

These statues, as mentioned before, belong to a tradition more indigenous than the capitals of the pillars, showing the art of the people— not reflecting as the capitals do, the ideas and culture of royalty alone. With the overthrow of the Mauryas by the Sungas, the court art died a natural death, while new life was given to folk art, an art which belonged to the people, and with which the people also identified themselves.

## THE SUNGAS

The exact cause of the rapid decline of the Maurya dynasty (within fifty years of Ashoka's reign) is not known. Many factors must have contributed to the final overthrow. One reason could be that Ashoka, in his enthusiasm, typical of the newly converted, to follow the tenets of Buddhism, issued a new set of rules for the public, such as the ban on animal sacrifices, samājams (social gatherings) and other popular pastimes and festivals. This deprived the people of the freedom to worship in the customary manner their favourite deities especially the grāma devatas (village gods). Furthermore, those who carried out Ashoka's orders in the various provinces were strict to the point of tyranny: so that - even during Ashoka's reign we hear of rebellions being put down. This repression of the local social customs ended with the assassination of the Mauryan King Brihadratha by his commander- in-chief Pushyamitra Sunga, a Brahman of the Bharadvaja dan.

With the Sungas on the throne (c. 188 B.C.–76 B.C.), the people could return to their old customs and honour their village and nature deities, whom they represented with much skill and tender care, as seen in the monuments at Bharhut and Bodhgaya. Perhaps this accounts for the profusion of yakṣa and yakṣiṇī figures so soon after the fall of the Mauryan empire. The Sungas, although Brahmans by faith, did not persecute the Buddhists, with the result that many Buddhist monuments were erected during this period. The people now relied on their own resources for answers to their artistic problems. Achaemenid influence, so obvious in Mauryan art, disappeared. The dense overcrowding of the reliefs with human figures contrasts almost completely with the Mauryan art where relatively few examples of human figures exist.

The sculptures of the Sunga period show the evolution from an archaic phase to one of maturity. The sculptural remains of this period consist of those on the stone vedikās and toraṇas of Sanchi stūpa no. 2, Bharhut and Bodhgaya.

The carvings on *Sanchi stūpa no.* 2, probably the earliest examples of Sunga art, are found on the thābas (uprights): mainly lotus medallions or rectangular panels with a figure or motif such as a donor or mithuna couple. In one such panel, below a mithuna couple, a *rampant lion attacks a turbaned man* holding a shield and dagger. The figures on the two top panels stand on rock bases resembling cushions, seen also at Jaggayepeta. The flat, low reliefs are cut perpendicular to the background thus forming a line of shadow around each figure, making it stand out. This shadow around them gives a semblance of depth to the composition. Being the earliest examples of the sculptures of this period; they retain a certain diffidence in their representation. But the flowing rhythm, so typical of Sunga art, is already evident. A good example is on the *Prasenajit pillar* from *Bharhut.* A spiralling curve binds the *dance of the absaras* and draws attention repeatedly to two of the four central ones, Alambusha, Misrakesi, Padmavati and Subhadra.

The extant remains of the *stūpa* of *Bharhut*, now preserved in the Indian Museum, Calcutta, are *parts of* the *vedikā* (Pl. 9.4) and the *eastern toraṇa*, all elaborately carved. The scenes narrated mainly the stories from the life of the Buddha in square, rectangular, round and half-round panels. These are interspersed with lotus medallions, beautifully carved. One particular example on the uṣṇīsa (coping stone) of the railing (Fig. 264; Indian Museum, Calcutta) shows open *lotus flowers on a winding stem.* On the other side of the relief, the same winding stem forms partitions for various scenes, alternating with jewel garlands and leaves. Some of the railing *medallions* are developed as open lotus flowers, several with *turbaned human head* in the centre (Fig. 265).

Fig. 264. Lotus frieze, Bharhut vedika, Indian Museum, Calcutta.

Fig. 265. Lotus medalliion with human head, Bharhut vedika, Indian Museum, Calcutta.

On the upright pillars of the gateways and some of the railing pillars are life-size standing figures of yakṣas and yakṣiṇīs, easily identified by inscriptions below each one in Kharoshti script, giving the name of the person represented e.g. Yakṣa Supāvasa (Pl. 9.3).

Fig. 266. Chulakoka yakshini, Bharhut.

Flowing lines characterise the *Sudarsana* and *Chulakoka yakṣiṇīs* at *Bharhut.* The latter (Fig. 266) embraces a tree, as if caressing it to coax it into bloom. This symbolism goes back to a period when trees were associated with fertility rites. There are many legends relating the power of women and yakṣiṇīs to bring trees to flower by an embrace or a mere touch of their feet. The figure is fully rounded, the sensuous ness enhanced by the flowing line running from the tree trunk to the bending branches, through the raised arm of the yakṣiṇī and on to the left interlocked arm, and then to the left foot. The contrast between this and the sharpness of the precisely carved jewelled ornaments is striking. The channavira (bandoleer) appears for the first time, with five medallions at the shoulders, chest and hips. The dress in conventionalised, with long parallel pleats bordered with chevron folds.

Compared to the swaying movement of the Chulakoka yakṣiṇī, the *Kuvera yakṣa* (Fig. 267) at *Bharhut*, with right leg slightly bent and raised and with hands folded, appears rather stiff and flat. The treatment of the drapery, here as well as in the Chulakoka devata, is flat with an emphatic definition of the borders.

Fig. 267. Kuvera yaksha, Bharhut.

A *soldier* (Fig. 268) at *Bharhut*, with his hair curling out below and above the headband, is another interesting figure. He holds a sword in one hand and a flower with leaves in the other. He appears in the same rigid frontal manner as the Kuvera yakṣa. The drapery, indicated by parallel lines, has scalloped edges to represent folds.

Instead of the vivacity found in the usual

Fig. 268. Soldier, Bharhut.

Jātaka or other stories, some of the scenes in the quadrangular panels from *Bharhut* show practically no movement. For instance on the so-called *Ajatasatru pillar*, everything seems to be transfixed, motionless. The densely-packed figures stand rigidly erect, hands folded. Only the contrast of light and shade relieves the solemnity.

The Bharhut reliefs appear flat, without any suggestion of depth in the background. They look like plasticine figures on a flat board. Though the artist showed the human form in all sorts of poses, he did it defectively—the body seems like an accumulation of its details rather than an organic whole. But everywhere we admire a naive freshness of vision as well as keen interest and delight in every manifestation of life. The stories are told with all their minute details, with nothing left out. The scenes depicted show the ways of life in ancient India. We see the customs, daily occupations, festivals, houses and palaces, dresses and ornaments of the people of the past displayed on these stone carvings—constituting a most precious documentation for

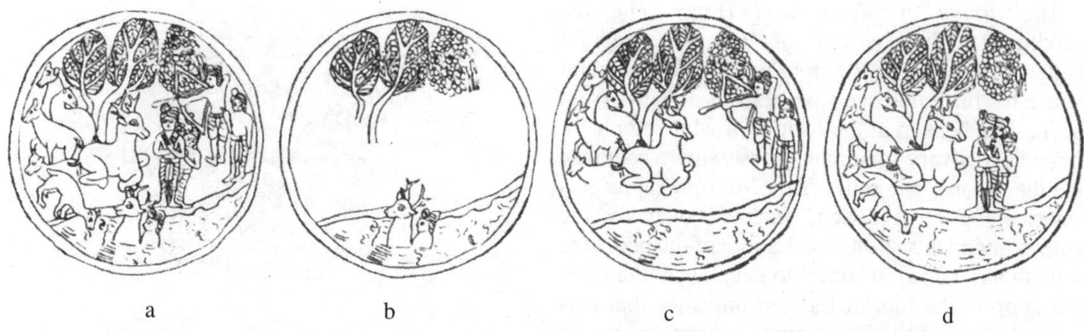


Fig. 269. Mriga or Ruru Jataka, Bharhut vedika medallion, Indian Museum, Calcutta: a. complete representation, b. first episode, c. second episode, d. third episode.

Indian history. A closer observation of some scenes will help us to understand some particular features of early Indian sculpture in general.

In the *Mṛga* or *Ruru Jātaka,* a medallion from the *Bharhut* vedikā (Fig. 269), the method of continuous narration has been used. This means that the various episodes of a story, which occurred at the same place but at different periods, are represented in a single carving. The Ruru Jātaka takes place in a forest near the river Ganga where lived the golden ruru (stag). The three successive episodes appear on the same round panel. The first is at the bottom, where the son of a merchant, in the act of drowning himself in the river, is rescued by the golden stag which carries him to the bank on its back. The second episode, on the right upper half, shows this ungrateful youth pointing out the stag to the king of Varanasi who has promised a reward to the one who would reveal the whereabouts of this precious animal seen in a dream by his queen. The king is shown in the act of taking aim with his bow to shoot the deer. In the centre we see the last episode where the king, having dropped his bow, listens with awe and admiration to the eloquent speech of the deer.

On another medallion from *Bharhut* is an interesting carving—that of the *Mahākapi Jātaka* (Fig. 270). The theme is a supposed previous existence of the Buddha as prince of an immense herd of monkeys who had their home on the banks of the river Ganga beside a mango tree with excellent fruit. Having heard of these delicious mangoes, King Brahmadatta of Varanasi went there with his soldiers intending to kill the monkeys and carry off the tree. Thereupon the Bodhisatva, holding on to the tree, stretched himself across the river and seized a tree on the opposite bank, so enabling his fellow monkeys to escape to a place of safety across the bridge thus formed by his body. This heroic act cost the Bodhisatva his life, for Devadatta, his cousin and bitter enemy, jumped so violently on his back that he injured him mortally. Brahmadatta, deeply moved by the self-sacrificing spirit of the Bodhisatva, nursed him devotedly. In return for his kindness, the dying Bodhisatva discoursed with the king beneath a tree and gave him useful advice regarding his duties as king. In this relief there are two scenes and the monkey appears twice.

Fig. 270. Mahakapi Jataka, Bharhut.

Fig. 271. Dream of Maya Devi, Bharhut vedika medallion, Indian Museum, Calcutta.

The *dream of Maya Devi* (Fig. 271), the Buddha's mother, is one of the most popular themes. According to the story, queen Maya dreamt before his birth that she saw her son descend from the Tushita heaven in the form of a white elephant, 'huge as a silvery mountain, possessing a radiance like the moon'. The relief from *Bharhut* represents her sleeping on a couch, watched over by the women attendants sitting on the side of the bed. One of them has a cowtail chauri to keep away the flies. The lamp at the foot of the bed indicates that it is night. The elephant Bodhisatva, whose enormous bulk dominates the scene, descends from above.

Fig. 272. Descent from the Trayatrimsa, Bharhut vedika, Indian Museum, Calcutta.

Another legend of the Buddha's life is the *descent from the Trayatrimsa* (abode of the thirty-three gods; Fig. 272). In the centre of the *Bharhut* relief stands a triple ladder with a footprint of the Buddha on the highest and lowest rung to represent his descent from the Trayatrimsa where he was believed to have gone to preach the law to his mother. Other symbols of the Buddha appear on the left, namely a throne, an umbrella and a sacred tree. On the right devotees stand close to each other in superimposed rows. Spirits fly about on the upper part of the relief.

The *purchase of the Jetavana park* (Fig. 273) tells how the banker Anathapindika gifted the Jetavana park to the Buddha. The park had been the property of prince Jeta, who consented to sell it only on condition that the buyer give him as many gold coins as it would take to cover the ground. A single medallion from *Bharhut* depicts the two distinct parts of the episode. In the right half two men lay out the coins on the ground. Anathapindika stands beside the bullock cart which carried the gold. He appears again to donate the park to the Buddha. Characteristic of ancient Indian tradition, Anathapindika holds a pot to pour

Fig. 273. Purchase of the Jetavana park, Bharhut vedika, Indian Museum, Calcutta.

water over the recipient's hands. Although a number of witnesses are portrayed, the Buddha's figure is not represented, (cf. Fig. 278).

All these reliefs at Bharhut show certain peculiar features more or less common to all early sculptures. At the beginning of Buddhism the Buddha's figure was never shown. Symbols such as a vacant throne, an umbrella or *pāduka* (footprints; Fig. 274) indicate his presence, as in the purchase of the Jetavana park and the descent from the Trayastrimsa.

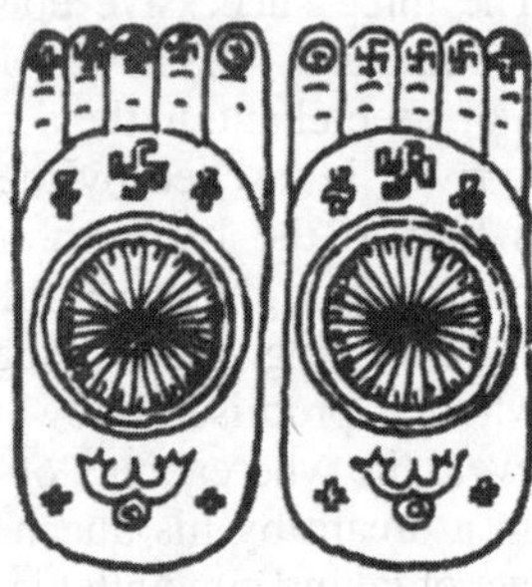

Fig. 274. Paduka (the Buddha's footprints.

Another symbol, the *triratna* (three jewels; Fig. 275) indicates not only the Buddha but also the sangha (his order) and the dharma (his teaching). In depicting a story, the artist paid no heed to time. Hence a single relief may group together incidents which occurred at different times but at the same place, with a repetition of the main figures as often as necessary, as for example in the Ruru Jātaka.

The visualisation of the third dimension is another feature of early Indian art. The artists did not depict objects as they saw them but as they actually are. They tried to represent what they knew to be true rather than what their eyes observed. In other words, they did not consider the laws of perspective. In looking at

Fig. 275. Triratna (three jewels) : symbol of the Buddha, sangha and dharma.

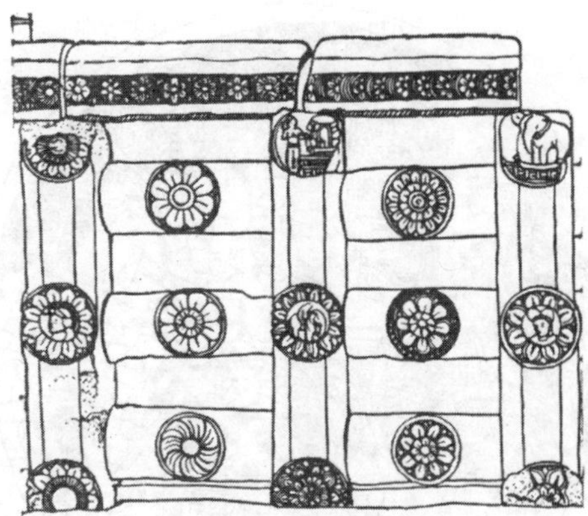

Fig. 276. Vedika around the bodhi tree (detail), Bodh Gaya.

an object we do not see it from all angles at the same time. Some parts remain hidden since they are out of our view. The early artists, however, did not surmise the third dimension, but tilted into view figures that would, according to the laws of perspective, be only partly visible or entirely hidden by others in front of them. So he would raise the top of a throne, not visible otherwise; or in representing crowds, where only the first row is seen, he put those in the rear above the ones in the front—sometimes only the heads, at times the full figures seem to stand on top of each other.

Nor did the artist regulate the size of the figures by distance but by the importance of the main persons or objects. Accordingly he depicted them in a size befitting their greatness without any regard for the actual proportions of the respective figures.

At *Bodhgaya*, sacred to Buddhists as the place of the Buddha's enlightenment, there is a remnant of a *vedikā* (Fig. 276) *round the bodhi tree* (ficus religiosa). This railing has carvings similar to those at Bharhut: on the coping, a lotus frieze; on the thābas and sūcis, lotus medallions, some of which bear in the centre a human head or bust or even an animal figure. The Jātaka stories on the half medallions of the thābas are represented with lesser details and the human bodies show more natural movements, an advance over those at Bharhut.

There is an interesting *relief of* the *bodhi tree* (Fig. 277-a) enclosed by a railing and flanked on either side by an umbrella and a garland. The artist has used three eye-levels in the same composition: the railing is seen below the eye- level (Fig. 277-b); the two umbrellas are shown above the eye-level (Fig. 277-c); the bodhi tree and the two garlands are on the eye-level of the spectator (Fig. 277-d).

On one of the thābas at *Bodhgaya* is the figure of *Sūrya riding a chariot* drawn by four rearing horses, two facing left and two to the

a.

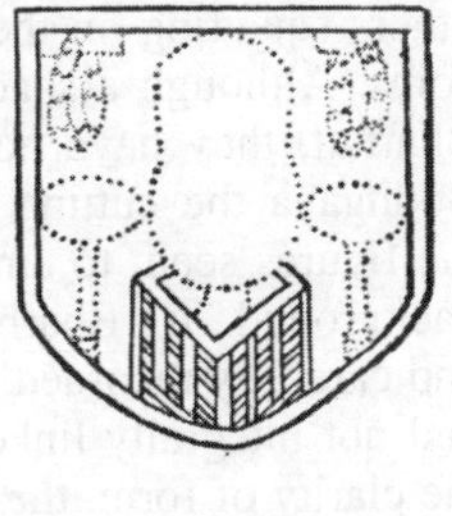

b.

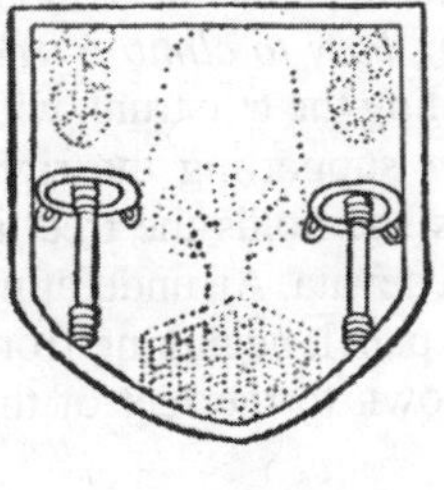

c.

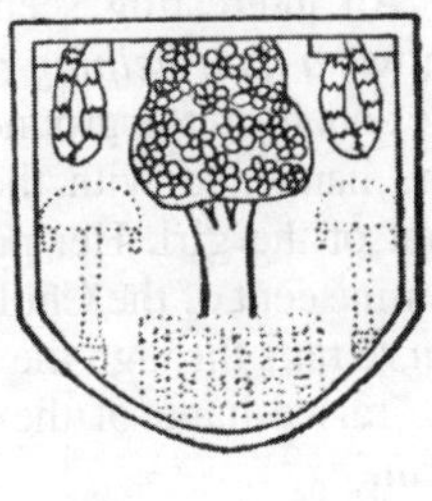

d.

Fig. 277. The bodhi tree, Bodh Gaya vedika relief: a. complete relief, b. parts seen below the eye level, c. parts seen above the eye level, d. parts seen on the eye level.

Fig. 278. The Jetavana park, Bharhut relief, Indian Museum, Calcutta.

Fig. 279. Relief of the Jetavana park, Bodh Gaya raililng.

right. This symmetrical balance is followed not only in the placing of the horses but also in the two women with bows and arrows seated on either side of Sūrya, and in the two demons falling one on each side. Depth is suggested by overlapping the horses and demons.

Another Vedic deity, *Indra,* is represented at *Bodhgaya* on a thāba. He stands on a crouching animal, with his left leg placed rather precariously on its rump. This positioning of the leg, accentuated by the very deep carving, seems to impel the figure forward. The modelling of the body, its fleshy fullness, is typical of the period.

An interesting scene from a panel on a thāba shows *a man helping a young lady to climb a tree.* He squats on the ground, holding the tree trunk with one hand and with the other supporting the right foot of the girl. Her pose, as she holds the tree, is reminiscent of the Chulakoka devata. An undulating curve runs through the entire panel, beginning from the raised hand of the girl down to the feet of the man.

The artists at Bharhut were reticent in their representation of emotion and drama. The figures seem detached from their surroundings; an air of sobriety pervades the narratives. The presentation looks unsophisticated and often diffident. At Bodhgaya, on the other hand, the method of narration appears more elegant and confident. By that time the Jātaka stories were well known and there was no need to depict them in detail. Not only are they abbreviated but there are no more labels to indicate the stories. A comparison of the *Jetavana scenes* from both places (Figs. 278, 279) shows this clearly. While at Bharhut every detail of the story is clearly shown, at Bodhgaya the scene is reduced to just three figures—at the back a man carrying the gold coins in a vessel, with two others squatting on the ground to pave it with the coins. Although a shadow separates the figures at Bharhut, they have no rhythmical connection. At Bodhgaya the cutting is at a slight angle so that the figures seem to emerge from a uniformly dark background. At Bharhut every detail is patiently and carefully recorded, but each part seems distinct and not integrally linked; at Bodhgaya, in spite of the clarity of form, the figures interconnect harmoniously and rhythmically.

## THE EARLY SATAVAHANAS OR ANDHRAS

The first century B.C. witnessed the rise of the Satavahana dynasty (also known as the Andhras) which dominated in the Deccan till the third century A.D. Their empire included parts of northern Maharashtra and the adjoining eastern and western regions, ruled over from their capital Pratishthana (modern Paithan in the Aurangabad district, Maharashtra state). Some of the inscriptions in the Nanaghat cave (Pune district) record eight names of the early members of this dynasty, including that of queen Nayanika (Nagannika), the wife of Satakarni I, who ruled around the end of the first century B.C.

Under these Early Satavahana rulers, the art phase which began in Bharhut and Bodhgaya reached its culmination at *Sanchi*, in the vicinity of Vidisa, Madhya Pradesh. The sculptures appear mainly on the *four toraṇas of the great stūpa* no. 1 and the *single toraṇa of stūpa no.* 3, executed during the reign of king Satakarni I. The top architrave of the south gateway bears an inscription stating that a gift was made by Ananda, the foreman of the artisans who worked for Satakarni. The earliest toraṇa is the southern one, followed by the northern, eastern, and western respectively. Not more than fifty years elapsed between the erection of these four toraṇas, since a man named Balamitra, the pupil of Aya Chuda, gave both the right pillar of the western toraṇa and the middle architrave of the southern toraṇa. Again, a native of Kurara, Namapiya by name, made a gift of the south pillar of the eastern toraṇa and the north pillar of the northern toraṇa.

These richly carved toraṇas, where no empty space is left on the jambs, capitals and crossbars,

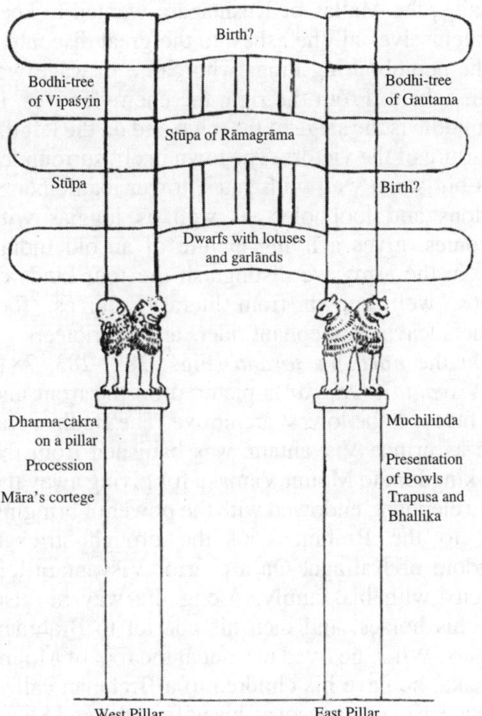


Fig. 280. Front face of southern torana, Great Stupa, Sanchi.

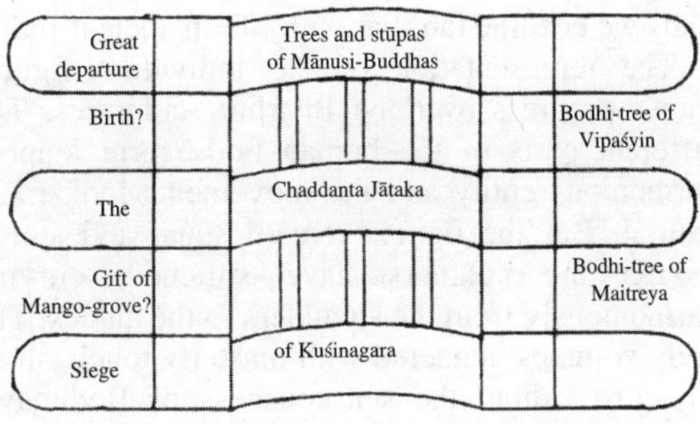


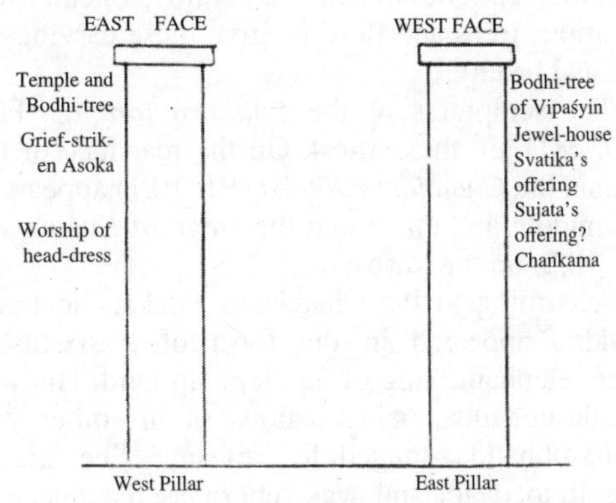


Fig. 281. Rear face of southern torana, Great Stupa, Sanchi.

create a beautiful contrast of lavish decoration with the bare simplicity of the plain, unbroken stūpa before which they stand. The carvings are no longer flat, as at Bharhut', but in high relief. The compositions are more crowded, so that the shadows of the figures cover each other, resulting in a dark background from which the carvings stand out more clearly in the bright sun. The figures are now grouped together in well-defined spaces.

The scenes represent Jātaka stories or episodes from the life of the Buddha and other Buddhist events. They are carved on the jambs of the toraṇas in rectangular partitions and in the upper part on the cross bars, where the long surfaces proved to be more suitable for continuous narration than the round medallions at Bharhut. The stories are told in an easy and cheerful way with all the minute details recorded. The artist's love is centred on all the minutiae of the material world. Nothing in contemporary life escapes his observation, from the life of the court with its festive and military pageants in palaces and fortified cities, down to the modest country life with its simple occupations and huts. Thus we become familiar with life in ancient India.

The representation of the individual figures shows progress over the Bharhut sculptures. The different parts of the human body form a more harmonious entity and the movements look more natural. But the figures remain squat and sturdy though the contours have softened, curving harmoniously from the shoulders to the ankles. The body volumes, rendered with masterly touch, show strength without the sensuousness of Bodhgaya. The animal forms display keen observation of nature together with a deep feeling for the animal's own life. Varieties of beasts and birds, together with luxurious trees and flowers, give these carvings an unusual beauty.

The sculptures of the *southern toraṇa,* (Figs. 280, 281) are the earliest. On the rear face of this toraṇa, the *Chaddanta Jātaka* (P1. 10.1) appears on the middle architrave and the *siege of Kuśinagara* (Pl. 10.2) on the lowest one.

According to the Chaddanta Jātaka, the future Buddha appeared in the form of a six-tusked white elephant, king of an elephant herd. His wife Chullasubhadda, being jealous of his other wife Mahasubhadda, longed for revenge. She starved herself to death and was reborn as the queen of Varanasi. Feigning illness, she told her husband that only the royal elephant's tusks would cure her. At once the hunter Sonuttara was sent to satisfy her desire. Disguised as a bhikṣu he approached the herd and shot the royal elephant with a poisoned arrow. The dying elephant not only took no revenge on his aggressor but hearing on what mission he had been sent, tore out his own tusks with his bleeding trunk and passed them over to the assassin. When Sonuttara returned to Varanasi, the queen, on seeing the bleeding tusks, died of a broken heart. Here only those incidents of the story dealing with the life of the elephants in the wilderness are represented. On the left side, the king elephant (recognisable by his six tusks and the royal emblems—the umbrella and the chauri held over him) bathes in the lotus pond. A tree divides the scenes. At the right side the six-tusked elephant appears twice: walking towards the place where the hunter lies in ambush, and in the corner he appears just when the hunter draws his bow.

In the *siege of Kuśinagara* (Pl. 10.2) the sculptors show their ability to depict representations of war with the same facility as forest scenes. After the cremation of the Buddha's mortal remains, the Mallas of Kuśinagara wanted to keep for themselves all the ashes, to the great discontent of the neighbouring kings who came to wage war against them. From the right the enemy arrives, in the middle is the siege of the town and on the left the departure of the victors. The town itself, surrounded by a big stone wall with gates, tower, battlements, merlons and loopholes, as well as loggias with balconies, gives a living picture of an old Indian city. In the army we distinguish the four kinds of troops, well known from literary sources: foot soldiers, cavalry, elephant riders and charioteers.

On the *northern toraṇa* (Figs. 282, 283, 284) the *Visvantara Jātaka* is pictured on the front and rear faces on the lowest architrave. The Bodhisatva, born as prince Visvantara, was banished from the Sibi kingdom to Mount Vamaka for giving away the white elephant, endowed with the power of bringing rain, to the Brahmans of the drought-stricken kingdom of Kalinga. On a chariot Visvantara left the city with his family. Along the way he also gave his horses, and then his chariot to Brahman beggars. While he lived in a hut at the foot of Mount Vamaka, he gave his children to a Brahman called Jūjaka. He even gave away his wife to the god Sakra who came disguised as a Brahman. The god, pleased by his generosity, gave back his wife and restored the prince to his kingdom. The prince's father ransomed the children from Jūjaka. The story begins on the front face of the lowest architrave: the prince appears on an elephant behind a battlemented rampart. With his family on a chariot he takes leave outside the city gate after his banishment. In the foreground he gives away his chariot, while in the background he gifts his horses. At the left projecting end of the architrave, he walks with Madri, his wife, and their children. On the rear face of the architrave the Jātaka continues: in the centre they live at an ashram, on the extreme right the family reaches the forest. Then the prince gives away his children to Jujaka, while his wife is away in the forest collecting a basket of fruit. In the next scene he gives away his wife. This is followed by their reunion and the journey back to his father's house.

On the *eastern toraṇa* (Figs. 285, 286) the artist excelled themselves, making it the most

Fig. 283. Triratna symbol, northern torana, Sanchi.

FRONT FACE

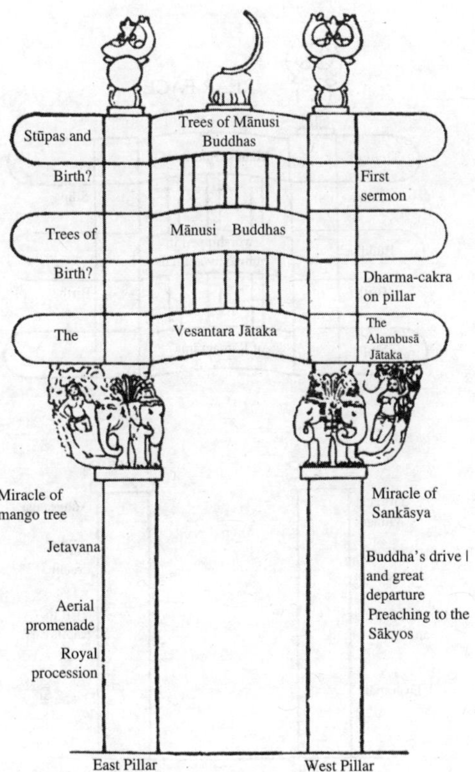


Fig. 282. Front face of northern torana, Great Stupa, Sanchi.

REAR FACE

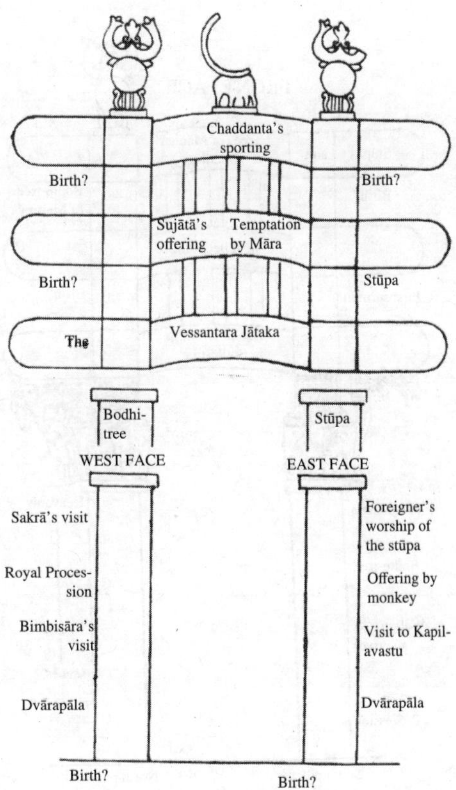


Fig. 284. Rear face of northern torana, Great Stupa, Sanchi

notable sculptural creation at Sanchi. The stūpas represented on the outer face of the topmost architrave symbolise the Buddhas of past ages. In the centre appears the great departure from Kapilavastu, and at the bottom Ashoka's visit to the bodhi tree. The remaining areas contain richly carved lions, elephants and peacocks. On the front face of the left pillar of the toraṇas we see the bodhi tree, the Buddha walking on the river, and a royal procession. The front face of the right pillar shows scenes of the heaven of Brahmā and the thirty-three gods.

In *the great departure from Kapilavastu* (Pl. 10.3), the walled city with balconies full of spectators rises at the left side. A toraṇa with one cross bar forms the gateway. The horse Kanthaka, on which the prince took flight from his father's palace, appears five times to indicate its advance. Nowhere, however, does the rider appear. Only the umbrella held by his faithful servant Chandaka symbolises his presence. At the hermitage on the right side, two footprints with the dharmachakra motif in the centre (Fig. 274) show that the prince has dismounted. Now the umbrella appears above the footprints before which Chandaka kneels. The horse returns riderless—the umbrella no longer appears. The precision of the carving here and in the other panels confirms the inscription on the western toraṇa which states that the artists were ivory carvers from Bhilsa, a nearby town.

The carvings are no longer flat as at Bharhut, but project, being done in high relief; and the compositions are more crowded so that the shadows of the figures cover each other. This results in a dark background from which the figures stand out more clearly in the bright sun. This, together with the dramatic poses, the strong feeling of volume and the well-marked outlines, give vitality and energy to these reliefs.

Mention must be made of the remaining *yakṣiṇī* on the *eastern toraṇa* (Fig. 285) which

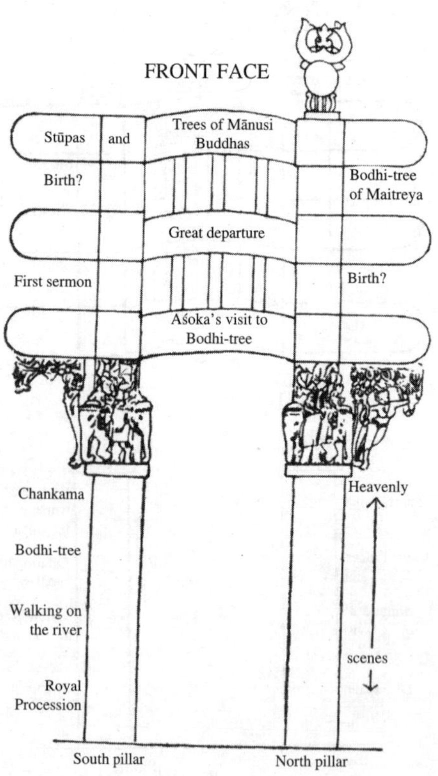


Fig. 285. Front face of eastern torana, Great Stupa, Sanchi.

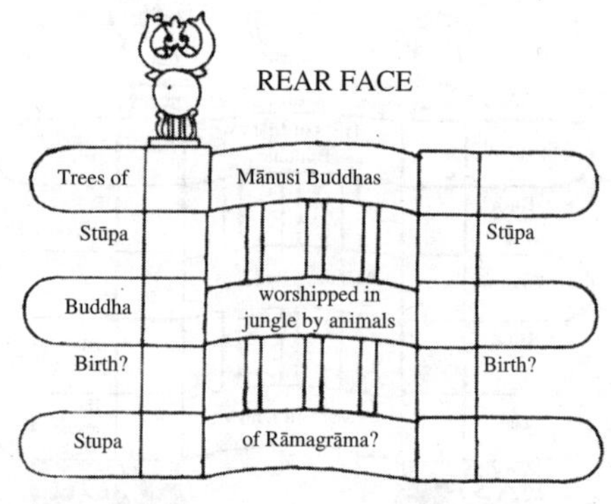


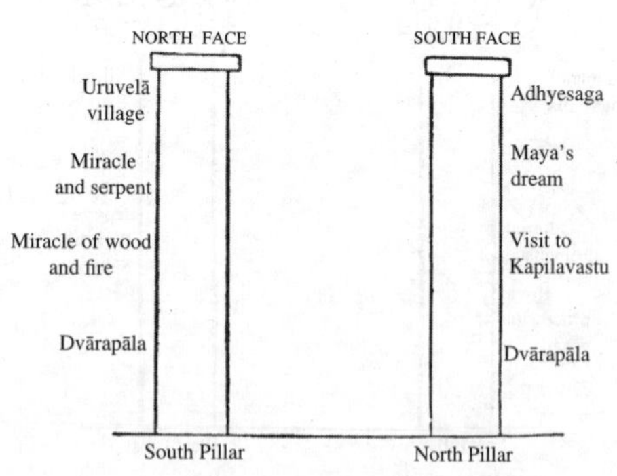


Fig. 286. Rear face of eastern torana, Great Stupa, Sanchi.

joins the north pillar diagonally to the lowest architrave. Originally one stood on either side. The remaining one shows tremendous improvement when compared with the Chulakoka devata. The thrust of the body and limbs harmonises beautifully with the architecture. Here the yakṣiṇī clasps a mango tree. Her legs press hard against its trunk to signify that this touch had made the tree to flower and bear fruit. Her form is both plastic and full of movement. The soft moulding and smooth contours suggest living flesh. The contrast between the round breast and tight belt encircling her waist and the tubular arms and legs enhances this further. The line of the tree repeats the sweep of the figure. This frankly erotic portrayal of the Sanchi yakṣiṇī illustrates the mixture of the sensual and spiritual in Indian art.

The *western toraṇa of the great stūpa* (Figs. 287, 288) is the last one. On the outer face of the lowest architrave appears the *Chaddanta Jātaka.* Here jungle life receives more emphasis—with numerous elephants crowding round the tree in the centre. Only the hunter at the extreme right gives a clue to the story. The elephants look natural, in poses typical of them. The Sanchi artists show confidence in handling animal figures.

While in the southern gateway the bodies are modelled flat within a sharp contour line, on the western toraṇa they are powerfully projected, and its Chaddanta Jātaka looks more convincing. Here the symmetrical arrangement of the big animals and smaller trees imparts a great strength from both sides, while the movement swells rhythmically from the sides towards the centre. Were it not for the figure of the hunter, the composition would give the impression of worship of the bodhi tree. The narrative has become subordinate to decoration: the whole composition shows to what extent the story can be veiled for the sake of the decorative scheme, while on the southern toraṇa there is no focal point, no really organised composition, and the narrative takes precedence over the decoration.

In the siege of *Kuśinagara* on the rear face of

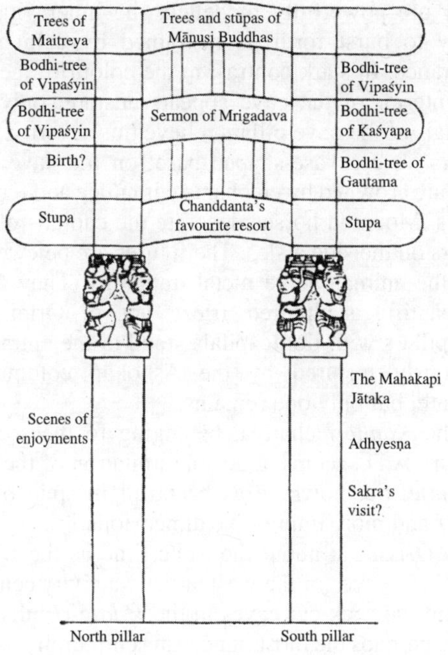


Fig. 287. Front face of western torana, Great Stupa, Sanchi.

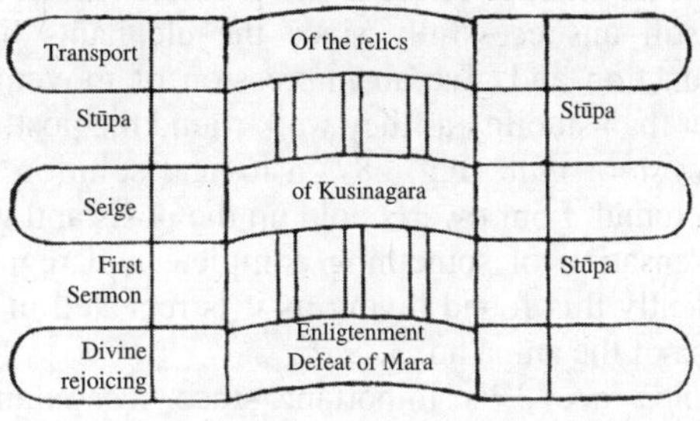


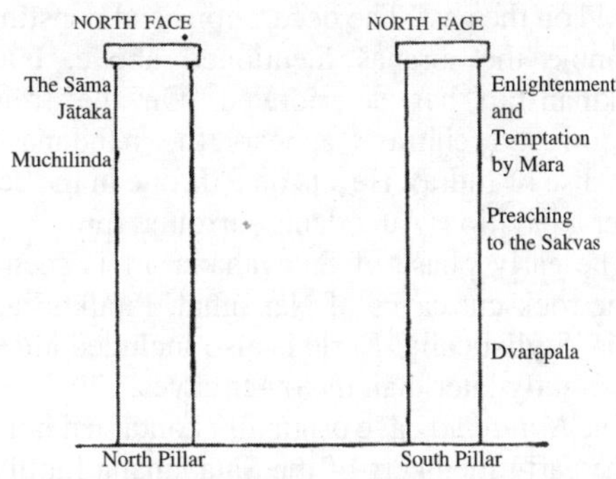


Fig. 288. Rear face of western torana, Great Stupa, Sanchi.

central architrave on the western gateway, the theme is arranged with one large design running over the entire cross bar. The shape and contents correspond one to the other, and the result is decorative. On the southern gateway, however, the scheme lacks organisation. It is verbiage in stone, as at Bharhut. The narrative is scattered in disconnected scenes. The story predominates over the art.

Decorations, mainly floral, abound on the Sanchi toraṇas. The most beautiful, perhaps, is the *lotus frieze* on the bottom of the lowest cross bar of the *northern toraṇa* (Pl. 10.4). Carvings adorn the pillars too, one example being the scene of the *Syama Jātaka* on the top panel of the rear face of the left pillar of the *western toraṇa.*

An interesting development can be traced in the *capitals of the pillars* supporting the architraves of the toraṇas. On the *southern toraṇa* (Fig. 280), the earliest, are four lions placed back to back. The upper post rests on their sloping backs. This gives the impression that the posts are on the point of slipping down, an aesthetic defect, because they should be firm in appearance as well as in reality. On the *northern gate* (Fig. 282) the same defect reappears in the four elephants. The *eastern toraṇa* (Fig. 285) shows an attempt to solve the problem differently but still unsuccessfully since the elephants have no function and give an impression of movement rather than stability as they walk round the post. On the *western gate* (Fig. 287) a logical solution has been found. Four dwarfs hold up the posts and give the sensation of something complete and regular. Evidently this found favour as it is repeated in the toraṇa of the stūpa no. 3.

*Stūpa no.* 3 is important since it contained the relics of Sariputra and Maudgalyayana, the Buddha's most important disciple. It has only one *toraṇa* on the east. The decorations and constituents resemble the toraṇas mentioned above, but the workmanship has deteriorated. On the front of the lowest architrave appears the nandana vana (paradise of Indra). He sits on a throne in the centre, under a pavilion. Attendants surround him.

The early phase of Satavahana art is seen also in the rock-cut caves of Nanaghat, Pitalkhora, and Bhaja. Stylistically, Karle is also included although it is slightly later than the other caves.

The *Nanaghat* cave originally contained portraits of the early members of the Sātavahana family but now only portions of turbans and jewellery, together with the inscriptions bearing the names of the persons portrayed remain. The elaborate ornaments are clearly carved.

The *Bhaja* carvings consist of panels. On the sides of the eastern doorway Sūrya and Indra face each other, one on a four-horse chariot and the other on an elephant. Sūrya symbolises the Buddha as the spiritual ruler of the universe, one who lightens the darkness of the world. Indra, the king of the gods, denotes the temporal power of the Buddha. The Indra panel is rich in detail. At the left centre stands a tree surrounded by a railing and bearing on its branches the bodies of those sacrificed to the deity of the tree. Below, a dancing girl performs before a seated king. On the lower right appears the horse-headed yakṣiṇī, the aśvamukhi, whom the Buddha converted. Continuous narration is the method used, with the figures chiselled in the same way as at Bharhut.

At *Pitalkhora*, inscriptions of the second and first century B.C. have been found. One relief shows a royal couple with attendants. Despite the overcrowding the details are precisely carved, such as the fur cover of the seat. The sensuous bodies resemble those at Sanchi.

The *Karle* chaitya, although of a later period, continues these stylistic trends. The façade is richly carved with six mithuna figures—probably donors. They are powerfully modelled: the inner vitality, ready to burst forth, is restrained by calm self-assurance. In stark contrast to the colourful façade, the interior of the cave appears austere: only the capitals of the nave pillars relieve this severity. The pillars have a vase-shaped base; on the nave side they are crowned by elephants with male and female riders. Mounted horses decorate the capitals of the pillars on the side aisles. The figures are bejewelled and the animals have metal trappings. They form a beautiful sculptured frieze above. Originally two pillars with lion capitals stood at the entrance, obviously inspired by the Ashokan column at Sarnath, but only one remains.

The *Kanheri* chaitya, belonging to the second century A.D., seems almost an imitation of the one at Karle, but nowhere as beautiful in spite of its larger and more impressive dimensions.

In *Orissa*, at about the same time as the Bhaja and Karle caves of the west, artistic activity centred around the rock-cut caves in the *Udaigiri* hills. Of these, perhaps the most important sculpturally, is the *Rani Gumpha* (queen's cave)—a double-storeyed vihāra of the second century B.C. All around the walls of the upper floor runs a long frieze with dramatic figures in many interesting scenes, such as a hunter stalking a deer.

## THE KUSHANS : GANDHARA PHASE

The term 'Gandhara art' brings to mind a mixture of Hellenistic and Buddhist forms. This art developed from the first century B.C. under the patronage of the Kushan rulers (c. 78-200 A.D.), and continued till the fifth century A.D. when much of Gandhara was invaded by the white Huns or Ephthalites who destroyed many Buddhist monuments. Gandhara included the west bank of the Indus, comprising the valleys of Peshawar, Swat, Buner and Bajaur. These valleys came under various foreign influences, the earliest being the Achaemenid empire of Persia, then occupation by Alexander's armies, followed by Chandragupta Maurya. A century later the Seleucid Greeks came into power, then the Sakas, Parthians and Kushans. Then in the third century A.D., the Persians came back again. The inroads by these various peoples, as well as its geographical position, made Gandhara truly cosmopolitan in outlook as well as in art and language. The people spoke Prakrit while they used the Kharoshti script employed by Ashoka in his edicts as well as by the Persians. With all this intermingling of languages, customs and races, inevitably each conqueror brought with him his pantheon of gods, as seen in the Kushan coins of the second century A.D. which depict a bewildering galaxy of deities. These include many Persian ones such as Mioro (sun), Mao (moon), Oado (wind); as well as the Greek Helios, Selene and Herakies; the Babylonian Anahita under the name of Nana or Nanaia; and from India Śiva, Skanda, Viśākha, to mention only a few.

Gandhara was one of the provinces Ashoka converted to Buddhism and it had many prosperous Buddhist settlements. Chinese pilgrims among them Fa-Hien who travelled to Gandhara between the fourth and seventh centuries, impressed by the great monuments and centres of Buddhism, have left valuable information in their chronicles. Thus Gandhara, having received western influences, became in turn a centre of inspiration for Asia, affecting chiefly the art of China and to a somewhat lesser degree that of Japan. The numerous sculptures found there are almost entirely Buddhist in subject.

The dating and classification of the Gandhara remains caused many difficulties to archaeologists, but excavations at Taxila, carried out by the late Sir John Marshall, permitted him to establish a chronology with more certainty. According to him, the so-called Gandhara art consisted of two schools: the early one flourishing in the Peshawar valley and areas west of the Indus where the statues were carved of fine-grained local stone, and the later school which extended over a much greater area, namely from Taxila to ancient Bactria and the Oxus river. It probably developed in Afghanistan, not in Gandhara. Here the sculptors used lime-stucco or clay, sometimes fired into terracotta. The early school, which flourished during the first and second centuries A.D., came to its maturity during the time of the Kushans and ended abruptly during the reign of Vasudeva, one of the last Kushan kings. The later school came into being in the latter half of the fourth century and lasted until the end of the fifth century A.D.

Gandhara art was not homogeneous, often because of the local differences in skill and the type of influence prevailing in that particular area. The examples from Sirkap in Taxila may be the earliest: toilet trays of grey schist, steatite and slate, mainly with erotic dancing and drinking scenes. Hellenistic influences are quite obvious.

Many Buddhist sculptures have been unearthed. Reliefs with drinking scenes have been found, adapted to Buddhist monuments by substituting flowers or stalks for wine cups. One such from *Takht-i-Bahai* is labelled *the presentation of the bride to Siddhartha* (British Museum, London). The dress of both men and women is obviously Hellenistic: the women wearing long chiton caught at the waist by a twisted band and a hemation (shawl) draped over the left shoulder and covering the body round the hips and legs. Ornaments are mainly bangles and necklets.

This Hellenistic character in art soon became more Indianised as the artists tried to reconcile Greek and local ideas and to create an art suitable to the Buddhist creed.

The most important contribution of the Gandhara school was the creation of the Buddha image. With the change from the Hinayāna to the Mahāyāna Buddhism, in compliance with common demand, the Buddha image appeared simultaneously in Gandhara and Mathura; but while the Mathura artist drew his inspiration from the yakṣa figures of the earlier centuries, the Gandhara artist turned to the Hellenistic world for a model.

In the *gift of the Jetavana garden* (Fig. 289) from *Mardan* (Peshawar Museum) we see the Buddha represented for the first time in human form. A halo identifies him. Beside him stands the merchant Anathapindika holding a water

Fig. 289. Gift of the Jetavana park, Mardan.

pot. These Jātaka themes, represented with vigour in the early Indian style of Bharhut and Sanchi, are shown at Gandhara with greater dignity and repose but with less imagination and vivacity.

The reliefs no longer use the continued narrative method: each episode is now confined to a single scene, and each succeeds the other chronologically from right to left, in conformity with the direction of the pradakṣiṇa pātha. In the long panels scenes are separated by short columns with pseudo-Corinthian capitals of acanthus leaves.

Of the same date as the Jetavana garden is the oldest *parinirvāṇa* scene from *Mardan* (Peshawar Museum). The Buddha seems to sleep as he lies on his side. Sorrow and grief are written on the faces of the Malla chiefs and monks. Vajrapani stands near the head of the Buddha. In the faces of the mourners the artist differentiated between the crude Mallas on one hand and the dignified monks and Vajrapani on the other. In the *parinirvāṇa* scene from *Nathu* (Indian Museum, Calcutta), the figures, including the Buddha, smile as if they assisted at a marriage rather than a funeral. In the sculptures of this group the artist had difficulty in depicting the eyes and drapery.

Parts of these spontaneous representations contrast with the *parinirvāṇa* scene from *Swat* (Pl. 12.2; Indian Museum, Calcutta) of a century later. Here the figures form a stylised conventional pattern of light and shade. The work, imitative of miniature carvings, was probably influenced by the ivory work of this period. Mahakasyapa, staff in hand, stands on the extreme left while Ajivika, who brought the news of the Buddha's death, appears in the nude. Anuruddha raises the kneeling Ananda. Conventionalism has replaced the spontaneity of the earlier period.

In Bharhut and Sanchi the reliefs were crammed with details, the artist taking delight in representing animals and forest scenes. At Gandhara the narration is concise and the human figure holds the centre of interest. The compositions show little movement, the artist concentrating chiefly on direction and balance, thus giving a stabilising effect.

Although Jātaka scenes were summarily treated, episodes from the life of the Buddha found more favour here. One such is the *birth of the Buddha.* Maya, supported by her sister, stands in the Lumbini garden under a sala tree, holding it with her right arm. The child, coming from the right, is received by Indra accompanied by Brahmā.

Among the individual figures are standing and seated Boddhisatvas, Buddha figures and deities such as Pañcika and Hārīti. A good example is the *standing Buddha* from *Hoti Mardan* (Pl. 11.1) near Peshawar. The head, with its adolescent features and rich hair, as well as the pose of the body slightly inclined, the weight leaning on one leg—resembles the Greek Apollo type. The sanghati (Buddhist mantle) looks like a Roman toga, covering the whole body with deep heavy folds. The halo or disc of light behind the head is of Hellenistic origin. The uṣṇīṣa (skull protruberance), considered to be the distinguishing mark of every Buddha, appears here as a tuft of hair on top, similar to the krobylos (top knot) of the Greek sun-god. Some of the other lakṣaṇas (signs) like the elongated ear-lobes and the ūrṇa on the forehead are also shown. The arms of this statue are missing but on other standing Buddhas the right hand is raised in the abhaya mudrā (gesture of protection).

The standing Buddha of the *great miracle* from *Paitava* (Museum, Dar-ul-Aman, Kabul) looks more Indian and quite unclassical. The rounder face lacks expression. Ridges suggest the drapery. This linear treatment of the garment is found on the Buddhist sculptures of China and Japan as well.

The seated figures of the Buddha adopt the padmāsana pose. Usually the hands are in the abhaya, dhyāna or dharmachakra mudrā. The clothing of the upper part of the body resembles that of the standing figures, but the lower half varies: the pleats are gathered in the middle where the cloak falls in decorative waves, accentuating the curves in the centre.

A typical example of the *seated Buddha* is that from the *vihāra* at *Takht-i-Bahai* (Pl.11.2; Berlin Museum). The padmasana pose, unknown in the Hellenistic world, is Indian, but the representation of the Buddha resembles the standing examples. We see the same Apollo-like facial type with the krobylos on top of the head and the halo behind, and a heavy deeply-pleated mantle worn like the Roman toga. The figure sits on a simhāsana (lion throne). The robe covers the upturned soles. From the position of the broken arm we may conclude that the right hand was in the abhaya mudrā. Probably because it was meant for a niche, the figure is more a relief than a statue in the round.

Fig. 290. Head of the Buddha, Gandhara.

The *head of* these *Buddha* statues is usually classical (Fig. 290): oval in shape with regular features, eyes half closed to show meditation and introversion, eyebrows arched over the straight nose, and wavy hair in a tuft (krobylos). Tne thirty-two lakṣaṇas were closely followed, as seen in the uṣṇīṣa, the elongated ears, and the ūrṇa (sometimes made hollow to hold a stone). The best work in Gandhara created a Buddha image conforming to the spiritual requirements of the Buddhist doctrine. The serene passive face expresses benevolence towards all.

A long period of development preceded the attainment of this ideal, but as time went on this art became too conventional and it degenerated. The faces began to look heavy and inexpressive—almost mask-like; and the limbs and hair appear dull. Short snail-shell curls characterise the later figures. The drapery varies in treatment from period to period. The best has supple pleats, the material following the line of the body. The body however has a flexible appearance because it rests more on one leg than the other—often on the left.

The Gandhara school is also credited with inventing the statue of the *Bodhisatva.* These princely figures, dressed like rājas, show the same Hellenistic type. They may be standing (Pl. 11.3) or seated (Pl. 11.4).

The Bodhisatva figure offered greater opportunities to the Gandhara artists since the exuberance of jewellery, ornaments and drapery could be fantasised. Pearls or fillets often threaded the hair styles. Sometimes precious stones were added too. If short, the hair covered the forehead; if long it fell behind, spreading over the shoulders. The dress was that of the Indian royalty: the upper part of the body remained nude while drapery, held in place by a girdle knotted in front, covered the lower part. The uttariya (top cloth) hung over the left shoulder down to the hips and legs while the other end fell over the left arm. Often the Bodhisatvas, like the *Bodhisatva Maitreya* from *Sahri Bahlol,* wear a moustache—certainly not Indian in origin.

Continuous narration was abandoned, each episode becomes a separate composition. These sculptures consists mainly of reliefs. In the time of the early school—according to Sir John Marshall—they were set on the surface of the smaller votive stūpas. These reliefs usually show scenes from the Buddha's life. Jātaka stories are rare; and the *Visvantara, Sibi and Shyama Jātākās*, where the Bodhisatva appears in a human form are preferred to the animal stories of the early period. Not only have the separate compositions for each scene replaced the continuous narrative but a classical restraint and balance in composition supplants the joyous exuberance of the Sanchi sculptures. The Buddha, represented in human form rather than by symbols, now takes the central place, often dominating all the others by his proportionately greater size. The many little details of a Jātaka story are given up—only the essentials being represented.

Besides these Buddhas and Bodhisatvas there are figures of *Pañcika,* the senapati (commander-in-chief) of Kuvera (god of riches), and of his consort *Hariti*, the goddess of fertility. In one example from Sahri-Bahlol (Peshawar Museum) both sit side by side. The corpulent Pañcika lacks the belligerence of strength required by his post as commander-in-chief. The statue, dull and uninspired, is typical of a period which produced many works with a uniformly precise but superficial in finish and lacking originality. Even the children and the

Bacchic revelry at the base are conventional. The vigour of the early school had disappeared and the art had degenerated into mere copies.

Unusual in Indian art, but serving as examples of the later school of Buddhist art spread throughout central Asia, are two *colossal statues of the Buddha*, cut out of the living rock at *Bamiyan.* These two seem to embrace the whole Buddhist centre built in the valley between. The eastern one, 36½ m high, may be around a century earlier than that of the west, rising to c.53 m, but the basic construction of each remains the same. Only the nucleus of the figure was cut in the rock. This was then covered over with a plaster made of mud mixed with chopped straw in which the features and the folds of the clothing were moulded, and then coated with lime plaster. In the larger figure the folds of the robe were obtained by means of ropes fixed to the stone core of the figure by wooden pegs, then coated with the mud plaster—no doubt an attempt to imitate on a large scale the late Gandhara style. The statues were finished by applying colours or metal leaf.

Quite a large amount of metal sculpture must at one time have been produced by the Gandhara school or its imitators since the few surviving pieces show a wide divergence of skill over a long period of time. The two most important examples of this art are *Kanishka's relic-box* (Fig. 291; Indian Museum, Calcutta) made of an alloy of precious metals, and the gold *Bimaran reliquary* (Fig. 292; British Museum, London). Both are small drumshaped boxes with relief carving around the side. The lid of the Bimaran reliquary has not been preserved but Kanishka's relic-box is complete and topped by three free-standing statuettes: the Buddha in the centre with Indra and Brahma on either side. The drum of this reliquary has figures around, standing in niches formed by classic columns and topped by pointed arches reminiscent in form of the chaitya windows. There is a great difference between the two boxes in the standard of craftsmanship: Kanishka's relic-box looks crude in contrast to the refinement of the Bimaran reliquary.

The early school preferred stone suited for fine carving. The subjects chosen were Jātakas and stories of the Buddha. Patronage came chiefly from the Kushan court of Kadphises and his successors. The works show originality, often with an exaggerated expression of vigour, and reveal an evident Greek influence.

As mentioned earlier, stucco, sometime fired into terracotta, was used more often in

Fig. 291. Kanishka's relic box. Indian Museum, Calcutta.

Fig. 292. Bimaran reliquary, British Museum, London.

the later school. The figures included mainly Buddhas and Bodhisatvas in niches separated by short Corinthian pillars. The *terracotta head of a Bodhisatva* from the *Kalawan monastery*, *Taxila* (National Museum of Pakistan, Karachi) shows serene dignity and compassion. This later school, unlike the earlier one, succeeded in making matter come to life.

The *stucco* products of this later period were often painted in brilliant colours. Perhaps one of the best examples is the *head of the Bodhisatva* (Museo Nazionale d'Arte Orientale, Rome). It has the purity of the classical profile, seen in the well-arched eyebrows and the straight sharp nose. The elaborate turban is rendered with great restraint. The *head of a donor or deva* (Central Museum, Lahore) is another example of stucco work. Both belong to the fourth or fifth century A.D. The colours are well preserved. The headdress and ear ornaments are gilt, the hair and lips reddish. These bright colours enlivened the bare plain stūpas which they decorated.

## THE KUSHANS : MATHURA PHASE

The Kushans (first century A.D. to third century A.D.) were a branch of the well- known Yueh-Chi tribe of China. Expelled from their native land by another clan, they finally settled near Bactria and divided the land into regions, of which Kushan was one. Almost a century later, one of the Kushan chiefs, Kujula (Kadphises), overthrew the other chiefs and declared himself king. His son, Vima Kadphises (Kadphises II), brought Kushan rule to India. Under Kanishka, the greatest of the Kushan rulers in India, their empire stretched from Khotan in the north to Bihar in the east and as far as Malwa in the south. He patronised art and literature, and Buddhist philosophers like Ashvaghosha and Vasumitra found favour with him.

As we have seen, one phase of Kushan art centred at Gandhara in the north-western region. The other converged around Mathura, fifty miles south-east of Delhi on the Jamuna river. In the first three centuries of the Christian era Mathura was a great hub of culture. It owed its importance chiefly to its situation at the junction of great trade routes which linked the Gandhara commercial centres in the north-west with Pataliputra in the east and part of Bharukkachcha on the west coast.

Literary and archaeological evidence prove its importance also as a religious centre. The remains of Jaina, Buddhist and Brahmanical shrines and images have been found there. Jainas, Buddhists and Hindus have contributed to an artistic tradition common to India as a whole.

The art of Mathura carried on the early tradition found at Bharhut and Sanchi. The few remaining fragments from the early period show a close connection with the art of these places. The middle period, during the first centuries A.D., coincides with the rule of the Kushans. The later period, under the Guptas, belongs to that school of art.

It is easy to identify statues belonging to the Mathura school since all are carved in the red spotted sandstone from the quarries of Sikri, marred by yellow and white veins, streaks and spots which disfigure its surface. The artists tried to overcome this defect by painting or gilding the statues.

The Mathura workshops became commercialised and served as factories, suppling images over a wide area of north India. The growth of the Mahāyāna Buddhist sect created a demand for images which the Hinayānas had never used.

An important contribution of Mathura is portrait-sculpture—the only examples of the type in ancient India. True, some Gandhara reliefs represented the figures of donors but these seem more generalised than realistic portraits. The making of portrait statues may have been due to foreign influence. Perhaps the Kushans knew of the Roman practice of erecting statues in the likeness of the Caesars, or of the Parthian representations of their chiefs. The group of statues found at Mat, near Mathura, includes portraits of *Kanishka*, of his predecessor *Vima Kadphises* and of *Chastana*, satrap of Sind.

A Prakrit inscription on the *statue of Kanishka* (Pl. 13.1; Archaeological Museum, Mathura) incised in Brahmi script across the bottom of the mantle and skirt, identifies the personage as 'Mahārāja Rājādhirāja devaputro Kaniṣko' (the king of kings, his majesty Kanishka). The monarch stands in a bold, rigid posture, entirely in frontal position, holding a sword and mace in his hands. The head and arms are missing, but a comparison of the remaining parts of this statue with the monarch's figure on his coins shows such a close resemblance between the two that we may justly complete the present statue with a rather massive, bearded head, wearing a peaked cap. The dress consists of a tunic with a flat belt, a heavy mantle and enormous felt boots (a costume quite unsuited for the heat of Mathura) supposedly brought along from the original home of the Kushans and retained for ceremonial purposes. The folds of the garments are represented in a primitive way by undulating lines incised on the tunic and by straight radiating lines on the mantle. The whole figure looks flat—more like a relief without background than a three-dimensional statue— but the arrogantly rigid posture infuses it with an impression of power and authority.

*Vima Kadphises* (Archaeological Museum, Mathura) sits on a lion throne in a strictly frontal position. He wears a short tunic and heavy felt boots similar to Kanishka's. Here too the head is missing. The ornamental border of the cloth draping the throne is precisely carved.

The greatest contribution of Mathura art is the creation of an entirely Indian type of the Buddha figure. During the early period only symbols indicated his presence since the Hinayāna sect opposed any anthropomorphic representation of the Buddha. With the Mahāyāna sect the human figure replaced the symbols.

The earliest *standing* statue of the *Buddha* was *dedicated by* a certain *bhikshu Bala* (Pl. 13.2; Archaeological Museum, Sarnath) in the third year of Kanishka's reign, about 131 or 147 A.D. Though it was discovered at Sarnath, the red spotted sandstone of Sikri from which it is carved proves that it came from Mathura. The figure stands stiffly on both legs. His garments are made of thin material: the dhoti tied with a girdle, the robe covering only the left shoulder leaving the right one bare. The drapery, arranged in schematic folds, clings to the body. With the left hand he holds the hem of the robe while the right arm, now missing, was originally raised. His full cheeks and smiling lips give the face on open, radiant expression. A small lion between the legs indicates that the statue represents the Sakya simha (the lion of the Sakya race), the historical Buddha, here probably as a Bodhisatva before his enlightenment. Though carved in the round, the statue is meant to be seen from the front only. The figure, clearly related to the yakṣas of the Maurya period, represents an outgrowth of the ancient Indian school.

There are many *seated* figures. A typical example is the *Buddha from Katra* (Fig. 293; Museum of Archaeology, Mathura). In style it resembles the standing Buddha of bhikshu Bala. The Buddha sits in the padmāsana (cross- legged yogi position with the soles turned upwards). The face has the same smiling, friendly expression which characterises all the Mathura Buddhas. The ends of the shorn hair curl to the right in a single spiral and form a sort of snail shell on top of the head—the way in which the early Mathura artists represent the uṣṇīṣa. Later on the head was covered with many short tight curls all turned to the right. Other lakṣaṇas —like the ūrṇā on the forehead between the eyebrows, the wheel on the right palm and the soles of the feet—are scrupulously represented. Behind the Buddha's head is a halo with a scalloped edge. Beside him stand two attendants, one on each side—an early example of representing three figures together. Here the two attendants may be identified as

Fig. 293. Seated Buddha, Katra.

Fig. 294. Head of the Buddha, Mathura.

Indra and Brahma; in later examples they were replaced by two Bodhisatvas, the Vajrapani and the Padmapani.

A comparison of the *Buddha's head* (Fig. 294) from *Mathura* with the one from *Gandhara* (Fig. 290; formerly Spink and Son, London) shows the difference between the two schools. In the latter the uṣṇīṣa resembles the Greek krobylos, while in Mathura it looks like a cranial protruberance in the form of a spiralling snail shell. The Gandhara head combines the abstract and the real: the upper part of the face appears hard while the lower part is modelled more softly. This gives the face an inconsistent mask-like character. The Mathura head is completely abstract with the features moulded gently into the round face. The main concern of the artist was the whole volume rather than the details of anatomy. There is inner beauty and spirituality in the smile, emphasised by the curving cheeks, jaw, eyebrows and eyelids.

A comparison of the *Buddha* from *Paitava* with the seated Buddha from *Katra* shows a striking similarity: both have rounded faces, but while the Gandharan example has a rather cold, mask-like expression, that of Mathura has the typical smile. Both figures have a firm solid physique and their drapery is treated as a system of strings and ridges. The Mathura style reveals no western influence while it shows up strongly in the Gandharan example.

Besides these Buddhist figures there are images of *yakṣiṇīs*, the best known examples being those on rail pillars from a Jaina stūpa at *Bhutesar.* They continue the Bharhut and Sanchi trend but at Mathura they appear more sensuous and frankly erotic. Complete mastery is shown in the articulation of the members of these solid figures. The body bends along its axis, giving the impression of sinuous movement. Two of these yakṣiṇīs are in the Mathura Museum and three in the Indian Museum at Calcutta. The ornaments are many, including numerous bangles. The heavy anklets emphasise the slimness of the legs.

On a railpillar, a *yakṣiṇī* (Mathura Museum) appears coming out of her bath, wrapping her dress around, half covering and half revealing the contours of the body. All these yakṣiṇīs have large breasts, narrow waists and wide hips, emphasising their connections with fertility spirits. Characteristic of these yakṣiṇīs are the broad girdles, like rows of circular discs joined together with round floral clasps in the centre.

Fig. 295. Yakshini with a parrot, Mathura.

In an example at the Indian Museum, Calcutta, a *yakṣiṇī converses with a parrot* (Fig. 295) seated on her left shoulder. She holds a cage in her right hand, smiling charmingly as he tilts her had towards the bird. Above some of these panels there are couples; sometimes the man holds up a mirror to his beloved.

At Mathura the iconography of the Brahmanical figures shows interesting features. *Sūrya*, squatting down, wears kavacha (armour) and boots; *Gaṇeśa* is nude and has only two arms; *Viṣṇu*, instead of holding the gada, merely rests his hand on it while he thrusts the lower left hand into a conch held horizontally. The turbans of the deities are very elaborate. Only Indra wears a crown.

Indian and Asian art are indebted to the Kushans who patronised the flourishing school at Gandhara where the representation of the Buddha came into being, as well as the school at Mathura where the first mature style of genuinely Indian Buddhist art developed.

## THE LATER ANDHRAS OR SATAVAHANAS, AND THE IKSHVAKUS

Amaravati was the centre of artistic activity of the later Satavahana rulers (c. 124-225 A.D.). After being repulsed from the Deccan, they had moved eastwards along the Krishna and Godavari valleys as far as the coastline. In north India they traded with the Kushans, and outside the country with the Far East as well as the West. Ptolemy mentions Roman trading posts both on the western and eastern coasts of India. At Arikamedu-Virapatnam, near Pondicherry, excavations brought to light the Roman commercial port 'Poduke Emporium', which was near the Andhra domain.

Amaravati is the ancient Dhanyakataka in the Krishna valley, where Buddhist monks had settled around the close of the third and the beginning of the second century B.C. It lay in the vicinity of Pallavabhogga, the modern Palnad in the Guntur district of Andhra Pradesh. Mahadeva, one of the Buddhist missionaries sent out by Ashoka, had been assigned to Mahishamandala and had travelled as far east as Pallavabhogga. Traces of Buddhist settlements have been found, with ruins of stūpas and vihāras, particularly at Amaravati, as well as at Bhattiprolu, Jaggayyapeta, Gummidurru, Pedda Maddur, Pedda Ganjam Gudivada, Ghantasala, Nagarjunakonda and Goli—to mention only a few.

Under the patronage of this enterprising and wealthy Satavahana dynasty, Indian art entered a glorious period in the south. These kings, especially Satakarni and Gautamiputra Satakarni (beginning of the second century A.D.), patronised artisans of great genius whose works inspired the Pallavas, who in their turn carried this tradition to the Far East. Unfortunately frequent wars weakened their power considerably.

The Ikshvakus (c. first quarter to end of third century A.D.) overthrew the Satavahanas. This dynasty, founded by Santamula I, ruled from the city of Vijayapuri, near Nagarjunakonda. Although Santamula was Brahmanical in faith, his immediate successors and particularly the female members of the family, favoured Buddhism. Santamula's son Mathari- putra Virapurushadatta, succeeded to the throne and records of his reign have been found at Amaravati, Jaggayepeta and Nagarjunakonda. In the last-named place, inscriptions record donations by royal members to the Mahāchaitya. This dynasty ceased to exist as an independent power, having succumbed to the rising Pallavas at the end of the third century A.D.

The great stūpa at Amaravati is the most outstanding artistic monument representing the later Satavahana style. The sculptures at Amaravati (mainly reliefs surrounding the aṇḍa of the stūpa) may be separated into four stages. The first period coincides with that of Bharhut—the works show many similarities. During the second period, around 100 A.D., the remaining pieces consist mainly of a series of casing slabs. The third and fourth periods (150-250 A.D.) show stylistic affinities with the carvings of Mathura in the Kushan era.

Of the sculptures of the first period only a few fragmentary examples remain. These statues look rigid and awkwardly posed without bodily flexions—even the fingers have an unnatural stiffness. The faces, with slightly slanting eyes, show little expression and the lips look rather coarse. The ornaments adhere clumsily to the figures. While the men at Bharhut and elsewhere used a sash tied like a ribbon, at Amaravati they wore a thick, corded waistband. Double lines at intervals indicate the folds of the clothing which usually covered the thighs. The women however seem almost nude. The *conversion of the Jatilas* or Kasyapas (Madras Museum) reveals some typical characteristics of this period. It depicts a few men with jatila (matted hair), hands joined and looking heavenward. Parallel lines above represent rain.

Fig. 296. Mandhata as chakravartin, Jaggayapeta panel.

The panel from the stupa at *Jaggayepeta* depicting *Mandhata as chakravartin* or universal monarch (Fig. 296; Madras Museum) also belongs to the first period of Amaravati. Having conquered the Trayatrimsa heaven, the king, tall and slim, stands in the centre surrounded by the seven gems— wife, prince, minister, elephant, horse, jewel and wheel. He holds one hand close to his chest while raising the other. On the left stands the svelte figure of the queen, resembling the yakṣiṇīs of Mathura. Cushion-like rock bases, similar to those on the panels of the vedikā of stūpa no. 2 at Sanchi, uphold all the figures.

In the early period of the Amaravati sculptures symbols represent the Buddha but later on he appears as a man, retaining his curls while the other monks appear with their heads closely shaven. This makes him look like a prince in monk's garb. Usually the left hand grasps the upper part of the garment while the right is held lower down in the abhaya mudrā.

A *head of the Buddha* (Fig. 297; Musée Guimet, Paris) gives a good idea of the Buddha image at *Amaravati*. In its fullness and warmth it shows some connection with the Kushan images at Mathura but the face is more narrow and oval, not as rounded as in the Mathura

Fig. 297. Head of the Buddha, Amaravati.

Fig. 298. Maya bathing in the Anotata lake, Amaravati.

examples. The hair has snail-shell curls, all of them turning to the right. The soft, plastic modelling does not place so much emphasis on the lines of the features. The eyelids are less heavy but the same amiable smile persists.

The second period at Amaravati (100 A.D.) forms a transition phase. In the sculptural remains from the casing slabs of the stūpa— usually showing scenes from the Buddha's life— his figure has become more graceful, with a supple form and clothing. The representations have lost their stiffness.

The low relief carving depicting *Maya bathing in water from the Anotata lake* (Fig. 298; Madras Museum) belongs to this period. She stands in the centre combing her hair. The other four ladies close by, holding water pots in their hands, represent the consorts of the four devas. A blossoming lily indicates the lake. Continuous narration is used: the same lady filling the pot with water at the pond appears once again near Maya. The wasp- waisted figures, wearing heavy rings on their slim ankles, recall the yakṣiṇīs of Mathura. According to the story, Maya bathed and dressed on the last day of a yearly festival celebrated at Kapilavastu. As she lay on her couch she dreamed that the gods of the four quarters took her up and placed her under a sāl tree where the consorts of the gods bathed her with the waters of the Anotata lake and then dressed her in beautiful clothes. After this the gods themselves escorted her to a palace and made her lie on a beautiful couch. As she lay there the Bodhisatva appeared with a lotus in his hand, went round her thrice and entered her womb.

Fig. 299. Disposal of the Buddha's relics, from Amaravati vedika, Government Museum, Madras.

The sculptures of the third period (150 A.D.), appearing mainly on the vedikā (rail), display great softness and a delicate touch. In this outstanding sculptural phase at Amaravati, foreshortening and perspective have been successfully introduced and the planes have been differentiated—the most distant figures in low relief, the nearer ones in slightly higher relief and those in the foreground in very high relief. Tne scenes on the coping stone of the vedikā depicting the *disposal of the Buddha's relics* (Fig. 299; Madras Museum) belong to this time. After the Buddha's cremation ceremonies the Malias of Kuśinagara wanted to keep all his remains for themselves, to the great displeasure of the neighbouring rulers. But on the advice of the Brahman Dona (Drona) they consented to share them. The composition is first divided into two parts, with the city gateway set across the middle. The lower part of the right side shows the funeral dance. The scene on the upper right represents the Mallas refusing to give the relics, and the upper left depicts the division of the relics into eight parts. On the left half of the composition seven elephants leave the city gateway with small relic caskets on their heads. The carving shows the lower part of the gatehouse and of the wall in brick, and the upper part of the gatehouse in wood. The rectangular lattice windows are surmounted at the gable ends by horseshoe-like windows that fit the barrel roofs. A square hut stands on top of the wall turret beside the gatehouse.

Another composition, highly dramatic in character, is the *subduing of the mad elephant Nalagiri* (Fig. 300; Madras Museum). Devadatta had set it loose in order to kill the Buddha. The medallion shows two episodes of the story. On the left the beast attacks the terror-stricken people. After knocking down one unfortunate victim, it grips the legs of another with its trunk. Nearby a frightened woman clings to her friend. The people at the windows of a neighbouring house however, feeling themselves in safety, gape at the spectacle. On the right the same elephant, now subdued by the appearance of the Buddha, prostrates before him. He is no longer visible because this edge of the medallion is worn away.

*The veneration of the Buddha's begging bowl* (Pl. 14.1; Madras Museum) shows a crowd in wild agitation rising almost to frenzy. Nagas, garuḍas and other spirits dance while yakṣas provide the music. The swaying movement of

Fig. 300. Subduing the mad elephant Nalagiri, medallion from Amaravati vedika, Government Museum Madras.

each character surges through all the groups of the composition which fits well into the medallion.

The figures of the fourth period (200-250 A.D.) look taller and slimmer. The yajñopavīta (sacred thread), made fully of pearls and worn by both men and women, appears for the first time. Pearl ornaments occur frequently in the sculptures of this time.

The great stūpa at Amaravati (Fig. 30), built in the second century B.C., was gradually enlarged and renovated during the next four centuries. A marble vedikā surrounded it and richly-carved marble slabs covered the aṇḍa (dome). Unfortunately the stūpa itself has been destroyed— only the ground plan and a number of carvings survive. The *drum slab with stūpa representation* from *Amaravati* (Pl. 13.3; Madras Museum) gives some notion of its appearance. The aṇḍa, decorated with carved marble slabs all around, rose from a high medhi (base). Relief decorations made of stucco adorned the upper part of the aṇḍa since it was difficult to cut plates of marble to fit a round surface. A square harmikā with chatras crowned the whole. The high medhi jutted out at the four cardinal points and each of these projections carried five āyaka or āryaka pillars. An empty throne with a dharma- chakra pillar is carved on the vertical wall surface of the āyaka projections facing the entrances. The richly decorated vedikā around the lower circumambulatory passage, composed of the usual thābas and uṣṇīṣas, has four sūcis instead of the usual three. Along the top of this drum slab runs a frieze, while a pair of richly carved pillars with the wheel of the law decorate the sides. These carvings have special interest, combining as they do both the Hinayāna method of representing the Buddha by symbols and the anthropomorphic Mahāyāna portraiture.

These sculptors have shown great skill in giving unity to compositions, in depicting lively scenes and in arranging light and shade. The Amaravati reliefs had a very great influence on later Indian art, particularly on the dynamic carvings of the Hindu dynasties that succeeded the Andhras in the south.

Though the subjects of the Amaravati reliefs are purely Buddhist, they show great enjoyment and fondness for the material world—in contrast with the Buddhist ideal of renunciation and moral discipline. The representation of nature has lost its importance although we still find some animals—both true to life and mythical—mainly elephants, horses, bulls, deer and a few others. Here they form part of a design or serve decorative purposes, especially in the Jātakas. Plants and animals no longer display such rich exuberance as at Sanchi. Human forms now hold the centre of interest. They appear tall and slender, with delicately modelled bodies and extremely tenuous legs in every position of movement or repose— sitting, standing, bending, flying or dancing with an amazing elasticity. The compositions, mostly in circular frames, show beautiful balance, great vitality and a sense of rapid movement highly dramatic in character, rising at times to a sort of frenzy. These carvings, finished with ivory-like delicacy and great precision, count among the most refined specimens of Indian sculpture.

Nagarjunakonda, named after the Buddhist saint Nagarjuna who started the Madhyamika school of Buddhism, was the centre of the Ikshvaku school of art. The artistic productions of the Ikshvakus concur with the later period of Amavati.

In subject matter, composition and arrangement of figures, the Nagarjunakonda sculptures show slight differences from those at Amaravati. In spite of the human representation of the Buddha, the use of symbols persisted. Stylistically the works maybe divided into two periods. The earlier ones, belonging to the reign of Santamula, include memorial pillars and drum slabs. On the *memorial column of Santamula,* showing scenes of his life, the figures still look somewhat rigid. The art has not yet attained the vigour and confidence of Amaravati, due perhaps to the instability after the decline of the Satavahanas until the Ikshvakus gained full control.

In the *Mandhata Jātaka* at *Nagarjunakonda* the figures have become more delicate and show subtle expressions. Attended by the seven gems, the king crushes the nāgas who oppose him and conquers the Trayatrimsa heaven where he shares the throne with Indra. But he desires everything for himself. This evil thought causes his downfall. A comet in the sky at the top right corner signifies the fall of the king from heaven.

The sculptures of the later period date from about the eighth year of Virapurushadatta's reign. Examples of these include the great renunciation and the breaking of the news of Siddhartha's departure. In *the great renunciation* from *Nagarjunakonda* (National Museum, New Delhi). Siddhartha sits on a horse with Indra holding the royal umbrella. The four devas carry the legs of Kanthaka, the horse. These

Fig. 301. Breaking the news of Siddharta's departure, Nagarjunakonda.

figures look so vibrant that we can almost visualise the arimal moving forward. The two men in front of the horse almost dance—especially the one at the extreme left—whereas at Amaravati the men march staidly forward holding spears. In the *breaking of the news of Siddhartha's departure* (Fig.301; Nagarjunakonda Museum), Sudhodana raises his hand to his head and Yasodhara begins to swoon. Thus the artists skillfully depicted mingled astonishment and grief.

These sculptors were equally adroit in showing amorous and combative scenes. A *panel* in the Museum at *Nagarjunakonda* depicts a rider on a rearing horse pursued by a ferocious animal—each figure dramatic in its actions. On the left side of the panel, men with weapons raised high repel an attack by horse and elephant riders. Strength and vigour imbue the whole composition. The mithuna couple, separated from the scene by a kūḍu-bearing pillar, provides a balancing contrast. Mythical animals support the sculptured frame. A comparison with a similar setting at Amaravati shows the stylistic affinity of the two places— the same, almost aggressive movement but intensified even more at Nagarjunakonda.

Another battle scene represents *Saka soldiers*, recognisable by their long Scythian smock, hip boots and caps, as well as their features. The numerous *mithuna panels*, separating the scenes, skillfully portray coquetry, frowns and caresses, particularly in the scene where beautiful maidens surround Siddhartha in accordance with his father's orders to keep him ignorant of the world outside.

Of the Buddha images found at *Nagarjunakonda,* that of the headless *standing Buddha*

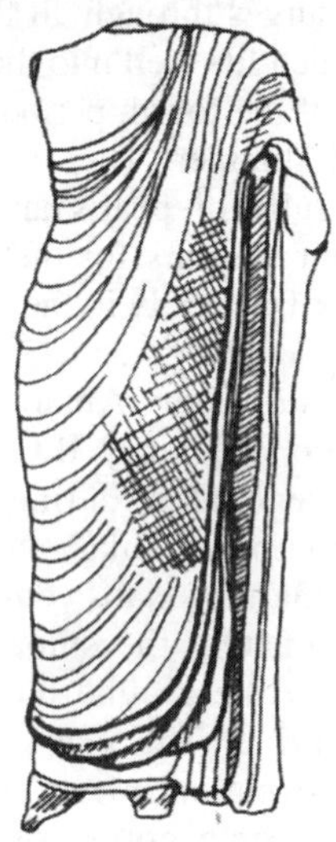

Fig. 302. Standing Buddha, Nagarjunakonda.

(Fig. 302; National Museum, New Delhi) is a good example. Massively conceived, the figure faces directly forward. He wears the saṅghāti, with the right shoulder bare, the drapery shaped by combining incised lines and overlapping seams. A characteristic peculiar to this region is the way the mantle falls above the ankles in a heavy fold.

Stylistically the sculptures of the village of Goli, in the Palnad taluk of Guntur district, resemble those of Amaravati and Nagarjunakonda. The scenes too show great similarity, with some differences in the details. Generally the figures have less refinement—already revealing a decline in the art of this area. The stūpa too has diminished in size. The style, height and width of the friezes as well as the use of the three knobs (neatly carved like a full-blown lotus) to separate the scenes all resemble closely the Amaravati slabs belonging to the fourth period. The relief panels are usually rectangular.

The art of this region slowly gave way to the productions of the south Indian dynasties that followed, but it made itself felt by the continuing influence it exerted on them.

## THE GUPTAS

The Golden Age of the Imperial Guptas (fourth to sixth century A.D.) begins with the founder Srigupta. At the zenith of their power the Guptas controlled the whole Ganges valley from Ujjain to Orissa. Such a vast tract of land united under one authority contributed to the artistic heights reached during this period.

During the Gupta era Indian sculpture, architecture and painting reached their highest perfection—the flowering after centuries of slow growth under the influence mainly of the earlier Indian style of Mathura and the Gandhara school. It is not a rebirth but the logical outgrowth of several continuous traditions.

Relatively few artistic remains of the Gupta period have survived because of destructive Muslim invasions. Though Gupta temples are scarce, fortunately more statues have been preserved.

The main centres of artistic activity seem to have been Mathura and Sarnath. But the Gupta influence spread out much farther. Even in the Western Ghats we find carvings so close to the Gupta style that we have to include them in Gupta art although these caves were produced under the patronage of the Vakatakas, allies of the Guptas.

These sculptures include standing and seated figures—Buddhist, Hindu and Jaina. Although a period of Hindu revival, both Buddhism and Jainism flourished throughout the Gupta empire, and Indian art was never sectarian.

A study of the standing Buddhas found at Mathura (now housed in different museums—mainly Calcutta, Mathura, New Delhi and London) shows that the Gupta specimens have special, advanced features in comparison with the early Mathura types. The Gupta style Buddhas are entirely clad with the saṅghāti— this may be of Gandharan influence. While the previous Mathura statues had ridges indicating the folds of the saṅghāti, the Gupta examples have a series of strings instead. They cover the garment in parallel lines and follow the form of the body. Thus the former stiff conventionalisation of the drapery has become a rhythmic pattern which creates a pleasing contrast to the rather static columnar mass of the body. This is the iast step in the linear treatment of the drapery.

The representation of the human body is fully Indian, showing a feeling for plastic volume and mass, as in the early Kushan Buddhas, but the crudeness has given place to an awesome dignity. Gupta sculptures have acquired great mastery of technique and refinement. The treatment of the Buddha figures in particular reveals a new awareness of the supremacy of man's spiritual powers over material values. Whereas the solidity of earlier images gave the impression of purely physical strength, the Gupta figures, with their delicate modelling, finer proportions and emphasis on the facial expression of thoughtfulness and serenity, show that the material body is dominated from within by the powers of the soul.

This effect of great refinement is obtained in various ways. The actual proportions of the body are finer and more smoothly curved, suggesting asceticism. With its lowered eyelids the whole face has a recollected air. In the Buddha and Bodhisatva figures, however, the transition from the forehead to the eyes is still rather sharp. The necks are modelled with deeply incised lines. The ūrṇa is absent. The hair and uṣṇīṣa is usually curly and close- cropped.

The statues have a halo. Exquisitely carved with concentric bands of floral motifs, these halos became the most beautiful elements of Gupta statues, although they had lost the original meaning, namely to represent a disc of light.

The two *standing figures of the Buddha from Mathura* (now in the *Indian Museum, Calcutta)* illustrate the emergence of the Gupta style. Made of Chunar sandstone, they stand erect in the samabhanga pose. The left hands hold the garment while the right, now broken, may have been in the abhaya mudrā. A rhythmic pattern of string courses indicates the scant, simple drapery. Through the transparent robe the massive shoulders, round arms and broad chest stand out. The faces show a fusion of Indian and Gandharan style. The features are softened, the faces warm and full. The artist followed the Buddhist canons in representing the uṣṇīṣa (skull protruberance), the hanging earlobes, and in marking the wheel and other symbols on the palms. Spiritual dignity and inner repose breathe from these figures with seem to be in deep meditation with their lowered eyelids.

The face of the *standing Buddha* in the *Mathura Museum* resembles the two in the Indian Museum, Calcutta. With his eyes fixed on the tip of his nose, he too appears deeply recollected.

One of the finest examples of the *standing Buddha* is another one *from Mathura* (Pl. 14.2), now in the *National Museum, New Delhi.* The left hand holds the hem of the robe; the right is broken away. The delicate folds of the transparent robe are treated decoratively, like string courses. Concentric bands of floral designs alternating with conventional motifs cover the halo. With half-closed eyes he appears in the bliss of contemplation.

The great monastic complex at Sarnath seems to have been the most flourishing centre of Buddhist sculpture in the Gupta period. Many standing or seated Buddha images in Chunar sandstone were recovered during the excavations. They show a stylistic departure from the Gandhara and Mathura Buddhas. The thin drapery seems to cling to the body like wet material. It is indicated merely by a hem at the wrists and ankles, and reveals completely the form of the body beneath. All indication of folds has disappeared. Even the string courses of Mathura have been eliminated.

The *standing Buddha* from *Sarnath* (National Museum, New Delhi) demonstrates this new style of drapery. Moreover his body shows a slight bend or broken axis which gives him a more flexible and natural appearance than the more rigid, columnar Buddha figures of Amaravati and Mathura.

The *seated Buddha* preaching the first sermon (PL 14.3; Archaeological Museum, *Sarnath)* is a masterpiece not only of Gupta sculpture but of Indian art. The refined graceful figure is typical of Sarnath, the body combining beauty and strength as set forth in the lakṣaṇas. It illustrates most exquisiteiy the metaphorical idea of Buddha statues with the bow-like eyebrows and lotiform eyes in the perfectly oval face. The hair, in small curls, has the uṣṇīṣa on top. The ear-lobes are long. His face, with half-closed eyes, looks serene and kindly, with that spiritual expression characteristic of all Buddha images during the Gupta period. Only a line at the neck, wrists and ankles indicates the robe. The rear slab represents the throne, decorated on both sides with rampant yālis (leogryphs) and makara. (crocodile) heads above. The wide halo, artistically adorned with floral motifs between two rows of pearls, has a flying gandharva on each side.

In this Sarnath sculpture we see the last step in the representation of the Buddha story. In the earlier ones all the figures had the same size and were grouped around the Buddha. Here the story is indicated merely at the base, where three of his followers kneel on either side of the dharmachakra (wheel of the law) which his first sermon set into motion. A pair of deer in front allude to the deer park in Varanasi where this first sermon was preached. Above them sits the Buddha, greatly enlarged, in the padmāsana posture with upturned soles and with the hands in the dharmachakra (wheel-turning) mudrā to represent the event.

Gupta artists did not favour narrative scenes with details from the Buddha's life nor Jātaka tales. The dominating figure is that of the Master himself with the narrative scenes relegated to the base as in the seated Buddha just described. The Sarnath reliefs do not have the dramatic movement and passion found at Amaravati nor the love of narrative as revealed in the early period at Bharhut and Sanchi., The figures look more calm, seemingly detached from the surroundings. One relief, a *stele* (Archaeological Museum, *Sarnath)*, depicts the four principal events in the Buddha's life: jāti (birth), sambodhi (enlightenment), dharma- chakrapravartana (first sermon) and nirvāṇa (death). On the bottom panel Maya stands under a tree while the Buddha issues from her right side, received by Sakra. A little to the left the Buddha stands on a lotus (signifying the seven steps) with a pair of nagas above him on either side performing ritual ablutions. Though all these scenes are combined in one panel they do not overcrowd the relief. In the panel just above this Mara and his daughters try to tempt him just before his enlightenment, while the Buddha sits in deep meditation in the padmāsana pose with his right hand in the bhūmisparśa mudrā. In the third panel the Buddha preaches his first sermon. Under his seat is the dharmachakra with devotees on both sides. The long fourth panel shows his death. Another *stele* (Archaeological Museum, *Sarnath)* shows eight scenes from the Buddha's life. The principal events, the same as on the abovementioned stele, occupy the four corners of the slab. The other four, in two rows between them, show a monkey giving honey to the Buddha, his taming of the mad elephant Nalagiri, his descent from the Tushita heaven, and the thousandfold multiplication of his form in the miracle of Srāvastī.

The treatment of the *Bodhisatva figures* at *Sarnath* resembles that of the Buddha, but their bodies look more massive. In these statues the artists contrasted the richly-carved headdress and armlets with the bare torso in order to relieve the heaviness of the figures.

In the *Avalokitesvara* from *Sarnath* (Indian Museum, Calcutta) the inclination of the torso from the waist upward is more pronounced than on the standing Buddha from Sarnath, in the National Museum, New Delhi. The Buddha still stands firmly on two legs while the Avalokitesvara's left leg steps forward thus giving his slim, graceful body a rhythmic movement.

Fig. 303. Copper Buddha, from Sultanganj, Birmingham Museum.

A *copper Buddha* found at *Sultanganj* (Fig. 303; Birmingham Museum) is the only large piece of metal sculpture surviving from the Gupta period. The style resembles that of the stone sculptures of Mathura during the fifth century in the slenderness of the body and the tubular smoothness of the long limbs. The treatment of the transparent robe lies midway between that of Mathura in which the folds of the robe were clearly shown by string courses, and that of Sarnath, where there are none. Here the sculptor has merely indicated the folds by means of faintly incised curves in the smooth surface. The dignity of the figure has been enhanced by the flow of the robe which in its sweeping lines also heightens the impression of movement created by the posture which is slightly off balance.

The Brahmanical sculptures resemble the Buddhist figures. In the panel showing *Viṣṇu of Vaikuṇṭha* (Fig. 304; Museum of Fine Arts, Boston) the smooth body has the same massive proportions as the Buddha statues and his face resembles them so much that without the Narasimha (lion) and Varāha (boar) avatāra heads close to his own, it would be hard to identify it as Hindu sculpture. The elaborate crown, resting on a fillet-like band, contrasts with the plain body. The only other ornaments are kuṇḍalas (earrings), a single necklet, armlets, the yajñopavīta (sacred thread) with a floral clasp and a vanamālā (broken garland).

The finest example of Brahmanical sculpture of the Gupta period, a statue of *Viṣṇu* (Archaeological Museum, *Mathura)*—identified as a Bodhisatva by some scholars—is a standing torso of red sandstone, with the legs and forearms missing. The upper part of the body is nude, the lower half clad in a waistcloth held by a cord. The figure wears a jewelled crown. A vanamālā (long garland of flowers) passes over the shoulders and arms near the elbow. Other details are necklaces, armlets, ear ornaments, the sacred cord knotted over the left breast, and part of a halo still visible from behind.

The best known, perhaps, of Gupta sculptures are the *gandharva and apsara reliefs* from *Sondani* near Gwalior (Archaeological Museum, Gwalior). They are shown flying, which is convincingly portrayed by the position of their legs, and accentuated by the wind-swept

Fig. 304. Vishnu of Vaikuntha, with heads of Narasimha (lion), and Varaha (boar), Mathura.

look of the billowing cloth tucked in at the hips of the apsaras, with the ends blown towards the right. In spite of the ponderous headdress, the bodies seem light and airy. The feet just brush the steps and do not rest on them, to give the impression of floating.

After the Imperial Guptas, the Gupta style or tradition extended both geographically and chronologically. Of the later or so-called post-Gupta sculptures those from the *Das- Avatār temple* at *Deogarh* surpass all the others in beauty and refinement. The temple has panels on three sides of the vimāna. One of these panels shows *Viṣṇu as Anantaśāyin* resting his leg on the lap of Bhūmidevī who holds it with both her hands. Near her are the standing āyudha purusas (personified weapons), in this case a gada (mace) and dhanus (bow). Above Viṣṇu, Brahma with three heads sits on a lotus issuing from Viṣṇu's navel. He holds a kamaṇḍalu or water pot in his left hand, the right being held in the chīn mudrā (the tips of the thumb and forefinger held together to form a circle, the other three fingers opened, and the palm facing the chest). A deer skin drapes his body in the upavīta fashion (over the left shoulder and below the right arm), with the deer's head falling over the shoulder on to the chest. Other gods such as Indra, Kārtikkeya, Śiva and Pārvati appear above. On the base below. Lakṣmī stands at the right corner. At the extreme left appear the personifications of the chakra (wheel), śankha (conch), and khadga (sword). This last moves forward belligerently to fight the two demons Madhu and Kaitabha.

Another panel shows *Nara and Nārāyaṇa*, previous incarnations of Arjuna and Kriṣṇa who performed severe penances in the Himalayas. The sculpture shows them sitting under the badari tree in the lalitāsana and wearing jaṭamakuṭas (crowns of matted hair). In one of his four hands Nārāyana holds an akṣamālā (string of prayer beads), while another is in the chīn mudrā (indicating instruction by silence or contemplation). The lower left hand holds a kamaṇḍalu (water vessel of riṣis). He wears a clinging transparent garment which moulds with the body. Above, flying apsaras intersperse with the badari tree. On the top is Brahmā on a lotus, flanked by flying couples. Deer and lions below the seat of Nara and Nārāyana indicate the forest.

On the third panel the gajendra mokṣa (Viṣṇu rescuing the elephant) is represented. On the fourth side figures of Ganga and Yamuna flank the elaborately carved doorway.

Gupta art appears also in the Ajanta caves, in some reliefs at Karle and in the Udayagiri caves near Bhopal. *Cave no.* 19 at *Ajanta*, a chaitya, has a particularly beautiful façade. On either side of the chaitya window *dwārapalas*, rather stocky in appearance, stand in a slight abhanga posture. Below, to the left of the door, appears a *Buddha* in the varada mudrā (gesture of giving), with a devotee prostrate at his feet. One of the finest pieces of sculpture is the panel of a *nāgarājā* or snake king (Pl. 14.4) on the left wall, a familiar figure in Buddhist legends. As in other reliefs of the period, a box-like frame encloses the nāgarājā and his queen. Sitting in the sukhāsana pose, suggestive of ease and comfort, the snake king rests idly, with his right hand on the raised knee, the left shoulder hunched up, and the arm stiff as he leans on it. His hoods spread out like a great halo above his jewelled crown. His queen, holding a lotus in her left hand, sits to his left looking up at him. To his right, balancing the figure of the queen, is a chauri-bearer in vismaya mudrā (suggesting astonishment), standing on one leg and resting the other knee on the block which serves as a seat for the royal pair. On the front wall, right of the entrance, stands the *Buddha with a begging bowl,* with small figures of Yasodhara and Rahula, his wife and son, to his right. On the right side wall, another *Buddha in the dharmachakra mudrā,* similar to the seated Buddha from Sarnath, sits on a lotus. But in the Ajanta figure the knees are not so far apart, while the body looks more massive and less slim. A pair of ganas fly above him. Buddha figures in various attitudes frame the whole panel.

When the Mahāyāna Buddhists used the existing Hinayāna chaitya at *Karle*, they added figures of the Buddha. One of the panels shows an *apotheosis of the Buddha.* Flanked by the bodhisatvas Avalokitesvara and Maitreya, the Buddha sits on a lotus throne supported by the nether world of nagas. Here in Karle as well as at Ajanta the style, though probably derived from Sarnath, is less refined.

*Udayagiri,* near Bhopal in Madya Pradesh, has the most monumental of Gupta carvings, namely the *Varāha avatāra* (boar incarnation) *of Viṣṇu.* With his tusks he holds Prithvi whom he rescued from the sea where the demon Hiranyaksha had concealed her. His left leg rests on a naga. He wears a vanamāla (huge garland). The style resembles that of Ajanta and Karle.

After the fall of the Guptas, the Vardhanas came to power for a short period. Harshavardhana

Fig. 305. Bust of a lady, from Gwalior, National Museum, New Delhi.

of Thaneswar was the most remarkable king of this dynasty. Both Hiuen-Tsang, the Chinese traveller, and the Sanskrit poet Bana have left valuable records of this great monarch. The style of this period follows closely the Gupta tradition, as seen in the *bust of a lady* from *Gwalior* (Fig. 305; National Museum, New Delhi). Gupta influence is seen particularly in the modelling of the eyebrows and the dreamy eyes with the pupils clearly marked. Pearls surround the kuntalā (turban-like hair style). Curls peep out beneath an elaborate ornament below the kuntalā. The modelling of the neck, with deeply incised lines, resembles that of the Buddhas of Mathura and Sarnath. She wears diaphanous drapery with embroidered edges at the neck and falling over her left shoulder. A thick cord of pearls adorns her throat.

## THE EASTERN GANGAS

The Eastern Ganga dynasty in present-day Orissa (eighth to thirteenth century A.D.) were probably connected in some way with the Gangas of Mysore. The later kings of this dynasty, often referred to as the Greater or Imperial Gangas, came under the influence of the Gholas, who invaded the Kalinga territory under the leadership of Rajaraja Chola (c. 985- 1016). They are said to have employed Chola officials, anu intermarried. However, with the coming of Anantavarman Dhodaganga, the Gangas asserted their independence by 1090. Anantavarman is also known as the founder of the magnificent Jagannātha temple at Puri (c. 1100). Another ruler, Narasimha I, was largely responsible for the Sun temple at Konarak (c. 1250). The Gangas established their capital at Kalinga, modem Mukhalingam, in the Ganjam district of Orissa state.

The temples of this region, uniformly of the northern nagara type, have intricate exteriors embellished by numerous sculptures. Of the many temples, we consider here the sculptures of the Paraśurāmeśwara and Vaital Deul (both belonging to the early period c. 750-900 A.D.), the Lingarāja (middle period c. 900-1100 A.D). and the Rājarāni and Konarak temples (later period c. 1100-1250 A.D.).

The earliest of these temples is the *Paraśurāmeśwara.* Images of various forms of Śiva filled the niches of the outer wall. However only *Gaṇeśa* and *Kārttikeya* in the southern and eastern walls remain. The corpulent four-armed Gaṇeśa sits on a simhāsana (lion throne). His trunk reaches out to the bowl of modakas (sweetmeats) in his lower left hand, while the upper left grasps a parasū (axe).

In the *Vaital Deul*, divine and mithuna figures occupy the niches above its baranda. One of these, the skilfully carved panel of *Mahiṣāsuramardinī*, depicts the goddess vanquishing the mahiṣā (buffalo demon). With her right leg on his body, she forces his head back with her left arm, forming a curving line that draws the eye from the tilted tip of her head through the bend of her arm and on to the twisted head of the animal. Thereby the Orissan artists portrayed tremendous energy and power. She pierces the demon's chest with a triśūla (trident). Each of her eight arms holds various weapons and attributes. This panel is flanked by two smaller ones with mithuna figures.

The *Lingarāja temple*, architecturally the most complete of the Orissan temples, combines both architecture and sculpture harmoniously since the decoration does not distract from the main architectural lines but forms a part of it, subtly emphasising the vertical lines. Most of the figure sculptures occur on the upper jangha. Among these *Pārvati* is a beautiful example. Tall, slender and bending slightly in the abhanga pose, she anticipates the devis (goddesses) of the Chola period. Though both hands are broken, this does not detract from her beauty. The transparent drapery reaches down to the ankles. Minute and precise attention has been paid to the details of the ornaments.

The masterpiece of the *Lingarāja temple* is a *nāyikā* (lady). The play of light and shade as well as the transparent drapery give her an ethereal look. Her shy smile, as she looks down to tie her lower garment, makes her a quite charming piece of sculpture. The sweep of her left arm as it bends to hold the diaphanous material accentuates the curving lines of her face and body. The slender arms and long graceful fingers have remarkable delicacy.

The *Rājarāni temple* may owe its name to the local word for the type of sandstone used in its construction, the rajarania. Particularly conspicuous in this temple are *alasakānyas* (graceful maidens) and *dikpālas* (guardians of the directions) carved on the corner projections of the lower jangha. The tall slender figures appear in different poses, the most popular being the abhanga, with one of the legs raised and bent. The *lady slipping on her anklets* illustrates this particularly well. She stands under a tree (a motif seen already at Bharhut) resting one hand langorously on a branch while the other coaxes the anklet over her left foot. The hair, combed back from the forehead, forms a round coil at the side. Bands of jewels encrust the girdle. Instead of the usual U-shaped ūrudāmas (thigh ropes), here we have small diamond-shaped pendants attached to a short string of pearls.

The sculptured faces of this region are usually full and round, with short, broad noses. The brows form a cupid's bow above the smallish eyes. While the earlier figures are rather short, the later ones are slightly taller with longer limbs, their arms reaching almost to the knees. Very often, the short drapery, both plain and patterned, ends far above the knees. While the men usually wear simple pearl necklets, the women have rows of kanṭhis and hārās. The hair, in the dhammīla style—flat in the front and decorated with rows of jewels—forms a large round coil at the back or side. Sometimes the kuṇḍalas (large round earrings) have figures carved in the centre. Two chains resembling the channa- vīra (like a double sacred thread crossing at the centre of the chest) issue from the pearl necklets. These figures are relatively less overladen with jewellery.

At *Konarak* the sculptures represent yet another stage of development reached by the Orissan artists. The *Sūrya temple* assumes the form of a ratha (chariot) drawn by horses. Twelve huge *wheels* seem to form the base of the temple. Intricately carved, each has sixteen spokes, some narrow and grooved alternating

Fig. 306. Soldier leading a horse, Konarak,

with broader decorated ones, bearing circular reliefs. At the hub of one wheel, where all the spokes meet, concentric bands of floral motifs lead to the round projecting panel at the centre, adorned with a horse. The rim of each wheel has a decorative band with circular motifs of animal figures, mainly elephants.

In the courtyard around the temple stand colossal figures of *horses and elephants* in the round, robust and full of life, their plastic forms dynamically modelled. In one example, a warrior, unable to restrain the horse, falls beneath the powerful hooves. The soldier leading the steed (Fig. 306) finds it hard to check its urge to gallop forward. Parallel lines along the horse's neck indicate the mane. A quiver full of arrows hangs beside the saddle, held in place by jewelled straps. An elephant, left leg bent, marches forward holding the lifeless body of an unfortunate victim in its trunk. The animals look true to life, the artist having captured their natural majesty and strength. Bands of reliefs on the plinth of the temple depict hunting scenes. The niches above contain very erotic sculptures, but the carvings have artistic value. While certain parts and ceremonies in a temple are considered too sacred for the uninitiated lest they be profaned by those who do not appreciate their meaning and value, and while for the same reason people generally veil life's most intimate mysteries from the common gaze so that they may not be desecrated by irreverence, here the latter are openly revealed.

*Ladies in various dance poses*, some holding musical instruments, adorn the pillars of the

Fig. 307. Dholak player, Konarak.

nāṭ mandir (dance hall), in front of the main temple. They stand with half-bent legs, a posture used even today in Bharatanatyam. Strangely enough most of these figures look rather heavy and buxom with robust limbs seemingly quite unsuited for dancers. They have an earthy sensuousness as they sway to the music of their own making, as for example the *woman clashing cymbals*. Her round smiling face has a low hair line decorated with a head band. She wears rows of necklets as well as simple keyuras (armlets) and nūpuras (anklets). The folds of her clothing, represented by closely incised wavy lines, resemble a chauri. The lower garment ends just above the knees. The *lady playing the dholak* or drum (Fig. 307) holds the drum gracefully with her forefinger and thumb. Her large round earrings have figures carved in the centre, while small bells hang from the outer rim. Scalloped edges indicate the clothing tied with a kaṭisūtra (tight girdle).

From the architectural point of view the sculptures of this edifice do not detract from the main lines of the building. The dancers of the nāṭ mandir lead on to the jagamohana with its bands of reliefs. On three sides of the jagamohana are figures of *Sūrya* placed within niches. In one of the niches the god stands in

Fig. 308. Surya, Surya temple, Konarak.

the samabhanga pose (Fig. 308). The composition has perfect balance with one side almost a replica of the other. Unlike the material used for the rest of the temple, Sūrya is carved out of a greenish chlorite stone. A trefoil halo and two lotuses surround his rotund face. His ornaments look flat and stylised. Rings hang from Sūrya's elongated ear lobes. Both hands are broken off just below the bracelets. The elaborate girdle is minutely carved. Near his arms stand a pair

Fig. 309. Aruna the charioteer, detail of Surya's pedestal, Surya temple, Konarak.

of ladies and below them swordsmen and bearded figures.

A diminutive figure of *Aruṇa* or dawn (Fig. 309) sits on the pedestal below holding the reins of the rearing horses which draw Sūrya's chariot across the sky. These restless steeds give a feeling of movement to an otherwise static composition.

## THE GURJARA PRATIHARAS

The disintegration of the vast Gupta empire threw the whole of northern India into a political maelstrom—with various tribal chieftains and feudatory kings fighting for power. Without a stable political atmosphere, artistic activity almost came to a standstill until the seventh century when Harsha Vardhana of Thaneswar restored political unity and solidarity to India. But at his death (around 647 A.D.) northern India again split up into many kingdoms large and small. From the eighth to the tenth century the Gurjara Pratiharas predominated in parts of northern India. Mihira Bhoja (circa ninth century) stands out as the most capable king of this dynasty. During this same period the Palas became powerful in the east and the Rashtrakutas overran the Chalukya territory in the south.

The artistic influence of the Gurjara Pratiharas extended even beyond their own territory. Some of the most outstanding examples of this art have been found at *Kanauj,* the *Viśvarūpa Viṣṇu* being one of the finest. The central eight-armed figure of Viṣṇu stands in a slight abhanga pose, holding in his hands various attributes, such as the śankha (conch), the chakra (wheel), kheṭaka (shield) and khaḍga (sword). The upper part of the panel, near Viṣṇu's head, represents the Brahmaloka (heavenly abode), while near his feet, on the lower part, crouch the nagas, representing the nether world. Around his head appear his incarnations such as Matsya (fish), Kūrma (tortoise), Varāha (boar) and Narasimha (man-lion). Above, encircling the crown, are the incarnations of Paraśurāma, Rāma and Kalkī. The various deities surrounding Viṣṇu are Saraswati, Kārtikkeya, the eleven Rudras on his sight and the twelve Sūryas on his left. On the top of all these towers Brahmā, while the eight Bhairavas, larger in size than the others, act somewhat as a frame. The shape of Viṣṇu's flat-crowned makuṭa and the muktayajñopavīta (sacred thread made of pearls) indicate Gupta influence, as also the features and the slim, almost feminine body. Instead of holding the sankha (conch) and chakra (wheel) in the right and left hands, as in most Viṣṇu figures, here the left hands hold both. The expression on the face, together with the abhaya mudrā of the right hand, represent Viṣṇu as protector.

The best-known piece of sculpture of this period is perhaps the *Surasundarī* (Fig. 310; Gwalior Museum). The head ornaments and necklaces frame the face. The slight tilt of the ornaments is repeated in the curve of the hips and emphasised by the swinging line of the tasselled garland. The diagonal line of the left thigh sets off the intermingling curves of the trunk. She wears a patterned cloth around her hips.

Other examples of this style include a head of Viṣṇu as Vaikuṇṭha flanked by the Narasimha and Varāha heads, Maheswari with attendants, and the marriage of Śiva and Pārvatī. In the *Viṣṇu* panel (Prince of Wales Museum, Bombay) the ornamented makuṭa, with the curls of hair arranged uniformly below, certainly shows Gupta influence. The representation of Viṣṇu as Vaikuṇṭha recalls the Viṣṇu figure now in the Museum of Fine Arts,

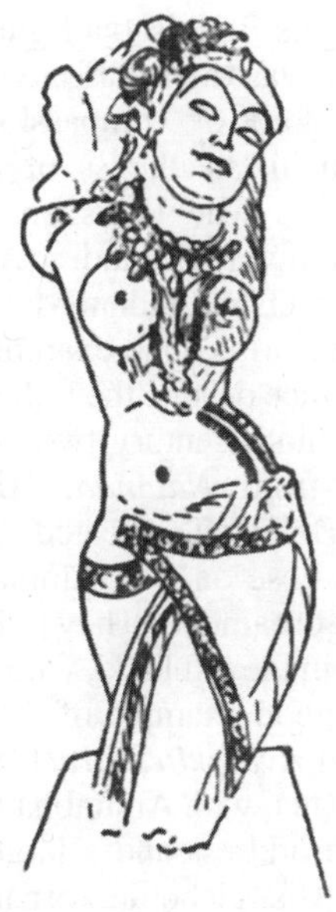

Fig. 310. Surasundari, Gwalior Museum.

Boston. The difference between the earlier and later examples can be seen in the headdress, the facial expression of the animals, and the placing of these incarnations on either side of Viṣṇu.

The *marriage of Śiva and Pārvati* panel at *Kanauj*, although not as full of movement as the one at Elephanta, still forms a charming composition. Śiva holds Pārvatī's right hand in his. Compared to her stance, his stiff pose emphasises his authority and masculinity. His ornaments include a pearl yajñopavīta, necklets of rudrākṣa, and sarpa kuṇḍalas (snakes used as ear ornaments). Pārvatī stands at a respectable distance and looks down bashfully. Her dhammila (headdress) consists of two rows of pearls with a central catulati-lakamaṇi (crest jewel) while a ring of pearls encircles the huge bulbous coil of hair at the back of her had. On her right stands an insignificant looking Viṣṇu, who may have performed the kanyā dānam (giving away the bride). The gods above sit on their respective mounts: Indra on his elephant, Nṛiti on a human figure, Yama on his buffalo, and Varuṇa on a makara (crocodile). They bring to mind the panels at the Deogarh temple where celestials often fly above the clouds and look down upon the scene below.

The figure of the *dancing Śiva* from *Ujjain* (Gwalior Museum) shows a lively composition. The feeling of movement given by the various poses of the ten arms and the position of the legs has rarely been excelled. Śiva dances in the lalita mode, to the music provided by gaṇas holding musical instruments.

Compared with this dynamic figure of Śiva Nataraja of Ujjain, *Maheśvari* (National Museum, New Delhi) seems rather static. She stands stiffly, the straight tubular legs revealed by the diaphanous lower garment. Finely carved lines indicate folds, and scalloped edges form a wavy line between the legs. The delicate carving of the drapery contrasts with the rather stern, awe-inspiring figure of Maheśwari, surrounded by celestials and attendants.

Certain features make the sculptures of this period recognisable, such as long, thin highly arched eyebrows converging at the bridge of the nose. The transition from the forehead to the eyes is not as sharp as in the Gupta or Vardhana statues. The elongated eyes usually remain half closed, while the sharp nose broadens at the base. The lower lip is slightly thicker, and the chin fleshy. The faces look broad and full, and the necks rather short. Thinly carved wavy or straight lines usually indicate the hair. A favourite way of dressing the hair seems to be a bulky round coil at the back, while the front is combed flat so that the head ornaments may be correctly placed.

## THE PALAS AND SENAS

Gopala, the founder of the Pala dynasty (c. eighth to tenth century A.D.), was chosen by the leaders of Bengal to restore order and stability in the eastern regions of India after more than a century of anarchy. His son Dharmapala built up the empire to include not only Bengal and Bihar, but made Kanauj (U.P.) a close dependency and received vassalage from the Punjab, the western hill states and Nepal. Their rule over Magadha gave them mastery of the greatest Buddhist mahā-vihāras (universities), especially Nalanda. The Palas followed the Buddhist faith and their reign gave a fresh lease of life to the waning Buddhist art and culture in India. Dharmapala not only rebuilt ruined Buddhist monasteries but founded new ones. A revival of Brahmanism in the south and invasions in the north had almost destroyed Buddhism in the country of its origin, but through the Palas it survived in Bengal until the Muslim invasions of the thirteenth century wiped it out almost completely in

India. Dharmapala also sponsored overseas trade especially with south-east Asia and thus certain elements of Javanese art found their way into India.

When the Palas declined under unmilitary rulers, much of their territory fell to the Senas (end of tenth to the twelfth century A.D.). Apparently they were of southern origin from the Kannada regions. They were Śaivites and introduced the worship of SadāŚiva to Bengal. Their seal bore the emblem of the five-faced, ten-armed Śiva, representing his various aspects. Theirs was a worldly court and they encouraged a voluptuous, sensuous art which smothered the religious inspiration. Despite the elegance and animation it degenerated into a rigid mechanical lavishness and frivolous, exaggerated decoration.

The art of this period marks the final phase of the classical Indian tradition. It prolongs the Gupta style of Sarnath in a degenerate form. The workmanship, though precise and refined, lacks the creative genius of fifth and sixth century Gupta art. The sturdy figures of ninth century sculpture became more vigorous in the tenth. The eleventh century figures, though more elegant, have stiffer legs; and by the twelfth century they became even more petrified with heavy column-like legs, while lavish ornaments and elaborate decorative details almost smothered the figures. They became voluptuous without spiritual significance, choked by material luxuriousness. A few rare specimens of creativeness do show dignity in spite of the rich ornamentation. The ideal form was soft fleshiness within definite outlines. The style wavered between the real and the abstract.

The Bengal artists excelled more in bronze or octo-alloy (aṣṭa dhatu) sculpture than in stone carving since the region has little stone. Most of the stone figures, made of black chlorite (kaṣṭi-pāthar) of coarse or fine grain, are cut in imitation of metal work, with the clear sharp outlines of metallic modelling. In metal work the ornamentation is more precise and fine. During that period more attention was paid to decorative details such as jewellery than to the essential bodily form. Because stone was rare, terra-cotta decorations were inter-persed with stone carvings, for example on the Paharpur stūpa. Nalanda produced imposing yet delicate stucco figures, such as the Buddha begging with a bowl at his wife's gate and gazing compassionately on his son.

Of the numerous Bodhisatva figures of this time the most popular was the Bodhisatva Lokanatha or Avalokitesvara (lord of compassion) recognized by the image in his headdress of Amitabha (the compassionate lord who looks on while in deep meditation). The numerous standing Avalokitesvaras in the Patna Museum and Indian Museum, Calcutta, have up to twelve arms. One example, outstanding for dignity and grace despite the rather heavy, thick-set body, is the ninth century two-armed *standing Avalokitesvara* from *Nalanda*, Bihar (National Museum, New Delhi). The seated figures, usually in the lalitāsana pose on a mahāmbuja (big lotus), wear all kinds of ornaments. They hold the stalk of a full-blown lotus in the left hand, with the right in the varada pose. A good example of the *seated* figure is the two-armed *Avalokitesvara* from *Bishenpur-Tandawa* (Fig. 311), with Amitabha in the centre of his jaṭamakuta headdress and a large lotus against the back slab. His elaborate ornaments include armlets and pearl anklets, a broad necklace, valayas

Fig. 311. Avalokitesvara, Bishenpur-Tandawa.

(bangles), yajñopavīta (sacred thread) and an elaborate mekhalā (girdie). He sits in the ialitāsana pose, his right hand held in the abhaya mudrā, with the auspicious mark of the wheel on the palm. The whole torso, inclined to his left, gives a graceful movement to the figure. The left arm rests on the raised left leg, and hangs rather limply in the front. Double lines, running diagonally and reaching to the ankles indicate the drapery. The *Avalokitesvara Padmapani* from *Nalanda* (National Museum, New Delhi) also ranks among the best stone sculptures of Pala times. It stands out for poise and charm and delicacy.

The masterpiece, however, of Pala sculpture, so distinctive that it is often ascribed to the Gupta period, is the so-called *Sanchi torso* (Victoria and Albert Museum, London). However, the antelope skin worn across the body like a scarf, points to the Pala period since this emblem identifies the Kasarpana Avalokitesvara, whose worship started only after Tantrism infiltrated into Buddhism during the Pala period. Unlike other Pala sculptures, this masterpiece keeps a proper balance between the exquisitely refined details and the modelling of the body by contrasting the hard metal accessories with the softness of the flesh which rises in a welt above the constriction of the belt. Breaking the line of the body on its axis gives it an athletic suppleness.

By contrast the *seated Buddha* (Museum of Fine Arts Arts, Boston) shows the more typical art of the period. The royal crown and jewels look out of place since the Buddha had renounced these worldly attributes. But the Mahāyāna Buddhists deified him and to show his power as chakravartin (universal monarch) they adorned him with crown and jewels to indicate the transformation he attained at his enlightenment.

Another example of the *seated Buddha* (Indian Museum, Calcutta), tall and slim, sits erect in the padmāsana pose with his hand pointing to the earth. Like all the Buddha figures of this period he is adorned with crown and necklace. The uttarīya (upper cloth), indicated by double lines with a slight scallop on the right side to signify folds, appears flat—almost part of the body. The lower garment reaches down to the ankles. The undulating double line just below the kirīṭa (crown) emphasises the heart-shaped face. There is very little space between the brow and the eyes, unlike the Pratihara images. The slightly slanting eyes resembles the far-eastern sculptures—understandable from the cultural contacts of the Palas with Malaysia and Indonesia. Buddha effigies in various attitudes surround the central image, while no more than the reposing figure of the Buddha represents the mahāpiraṇirvāṇa scene above.

One of the few examples of *Maitreya* (the Buddha of the future) includes the statue from *Bishenpur-Tandawa*. He is usually recognised by the small stūpa in his crown or beside him and by a bunch of nagakeshvara flowers. It almost mirrors the Lokanatha figure except that the left hand, instead of resting on the legs, touches the ground in order to support the body. But the posture, style of ornaments and drapery almost coincide with the Lokanatha image.

The large number of bronze figures, both Buddhist and Brahmanical, produced in Nalanda and Kurkehar and now in the Dacca and Patna Museums, have greater artistic value. Most of them continued the Sarnath style of the Gupta period. The precise details suited metal more than stone. Moreover they show more clearly the changes in Buddhism from Mahāyāna to Tantric forms, which were exported to south-east Asia and to Nepal and Tibet as well as to Kashmir. One example of these bronze figures is the Buddha's descent from the Tushita heaven by a jewelled ladder with Indra and Brahmā on either side.

When the Senas came to power, the Śaivites who were a minority under the Palas, asserted themselves. This resulted in an exuberance of Brahmanical sculptures. In facial features these statues resemble the Buddhist ones: the heart-shaped face, small tip-tilted eyes and smiling lips. And all of them, both male and female, have a tilaka (mark on the forehead) just like Buddhist images. The drapery has been reduced to shallow, wavy double lines. A few of these, running diagonally across the torso, indicate the uttarīya (upper cloth), while those running over the thighs and ending above the knees denote the lower garment. The palms bear the auspicious mark of the wheel. They wear rich jewels: an ornate kirīṭa (crown), patra kuṇḍalas (earrings), hāras (necklaces), keyūras (armlets), valayas (bangles), muktayajñopavīta (sacred thread of pearls) mekhalā (elaborate girdle) and nūpuras (anklets).

A different type of dancing Śiva or *Narteśvara* figure, with ten or twelve arms, evolved in Bengal, unlike the four-armed Natarājas famous in Chola sculpture. The one from *Sankarbandha* (Dacca Museum), ecstatically dancing on his nandī's back, is the most typical. The upper part of the body with the ten arms holding various weapons gives the figure a top-heavy look. This makes the composition rather incongruous considering that Śiva is performing the dance of destruction. Nor does the hair—it is ornately dressed not streaming behind as in the earlier examples—harmonise with the theme. Various adoring figures appear below on either side, with a pair of ladies in the foreground.

By contrast the tall beautiful *Pārvati* (Indian Museum, Calcutta) has good proportions. She stands gracefully on a lotus pedestal decorated with a lion, the devi's vehicle. Celestial beings worship her above. A band of wavy lines represents the clouds. Her attendants on either side are smaller in scale than Pārvati. Her jewels include an elaborate kirīṭa, ear ornaments, necklaces, pearl yajñopavīta, keyūras, valayas and an intricate girdle from which hang peari ūru-dāmas.

A masterpiece of Sena art is the finely carved bracket figure of *Ganga* (National Museum, New Delhi). She stands under a tree holding a pitcher in her hand. The upper part of the body is graceful unlike the some what stiff heavy legs. During this time mother and child figures, serving as charms for the protection of children, were very popular.

Of the sculptures of Viṣṇu in the Indian Museum, Calcutta, two stand out for the elegant poise and movement of the devis on either side of the central deity. Of these the *Viṣṇu* image discovered in the *Sunderban* district (Fig. 312) is a typical example of the art of this period. His left hands hold the chakra (wheel) and śankha (conch), while the upper right grasps the gadhā (mace) and the lower is in the varada mudrā. Viṣṇu stands stiffly on a full-blown lotus with a double row of petals. Rampant yālis (mythical animals) form the background. Devas above hold garlands (a borrowing from the Gupta period). A lion face, flanked by flying vidyādaras on either side, peers out right on top. Two women in graceful pose appear below near Viṣṇu's feet, the one on the left holding a chauri while the other on the right has a musical instrument. Small figures with crowns adjoin these ladies. Gaṇa, floral motifs and a winged being (probably Garuḍa—Viṣṇu's vehicle) adorn the pedestal.

Fig. 312. Standing Vishnu. Indian Museum, Calcutta.

Other than the images of Viṣṇu, there exist many examples of his avataras, such as Varāha, Narasimha and Trivikrama. In the *Varāha* panel, from the *Murshidabad* district, he lifts his face to indicate his effort to bring Prithvī, the earth, out of the ocean. Between his legs appear small figures of Varāha and Prithvi showing the former in the act of rescuing the earth. His right foot rests on a lotus while the left steps on a lotus held by a naga. Adoring figures appear on either side.

The art of this period reflects the religious syncretism of the time, with composite and fused deities. For instance they combined the Natarāja and Vīṇā Dakṣiṇāmūrti forms in Bengal as seen in the Narteśvara with vina in Ballalabadi and the Natghar in Brahmanbari. During this age the indefinite number of Viṣṇu avatārs were reduced to ten. All in all the art produced at this time resembles a religious art exhibition without unity or coherence.

## THE CHANDELLAS

The Chandellas or Chandratreyas (c. 950-1203 A.D.) rose to power with the break-up of the Pratihara empire. They ruled over central India from their capital at Khajuraho, about the same time as the Palas and Senas had control over the eastern regions of India.

By this time the various norms and codes of sculpture had become almost fully established—a great drawback since the artists lost originality and inspiration by following them almost verbatim. Thus began the slow but sure decline of Indian art. Sculptural works became stereotyped, monotonously resembling each other. While keeping within these codes, some artists did manage subtly to express some originality and individuality.

While they have a mechanical elegance and technical allure, the actual modelling of the Khajuraho sculptures has petrified into lifeless forms. They resemble puppets more than living beings, violently jerked into unnatural movements to compensate for the lack of inner vitality, to give a semblance of animation to the dull, mask-like facial expressions. The bodies twist unnaturally around their axis and the tubular limbs are wrenched almost to breaking-point at their joints. Often while the bodies turn towards the wall, the upper part is contorted in such a way that the face appears in profile. The bawdy poses lack dignity and self-respect. The round faces have elongated eyes and brows, long straight noses, with a kind of smirk on the thin pouting lips, and rounded chins. Slightly wavy double lines indicate the drapery, diaphanous and clinging to the legs almost like a second skin. A girdle, from which hang various pearl ornaments including ūru-dāmas, holds the lower garment. Necklaces, anklets, armlets, and various head ornaments abound. The male figures usually wear a kirīṭa makuta.

Decorative carvings literally cover the Khajuraho temples. Figure sculpture appears mostly on the badas. On the nirandhara temples, like the

Fig. 313. A lady playing with a ball, Khajuraho Museum.

Chitragupta and Devī Jagadambi temples, sculptural decoration surrounds the whole vimāna; whereas the balconies of the sāndhara type, like the Kandariya Mahādeva and Lakṣmaṇa temples, interrupt the figure ornamentation. Sometimes, as on the Lakṣmaṇa temple, a frieze surrounds the plinth. At times niches with statues adorn the base. On the bādas the figures usually stand on projecting platforms with sculptured canopies above them.

Other than statues of deities, figures of men and women without any religious significance abound as well, such as *a lady playing with a ball* (Fig. 313; *Khajuraho* Museum). She turns back, her face in profile, holding the ball in her right hand while her left arm bends, the elbow facing the observer. The graceful fingers, the curve of the body, and the feet slightly raised, give this statue artistic value. Other examples from the region of Khajuraho are a *lady looking into a mirror,* and *a mother and child* both in the Indian Museum, Calcutta. The latter, holding her baby and looking at it with tender affection, is beautifully and naturally represented. The mother bends her head towards the child who responds by smiling up at her. The lady's hair is indicated by wavy lines, flat and loosely coiled at the back. She looks more plump and maternal than the lady playing with a ball. In the other example, the profile of a lady looking into a mirror while adjusting her headdress, she stands under a tree, the curve of which is repeated in her right hand raised to her forehead. The hair style, with the group of curls at the side above the temple, resembles the previous example.

Some of the faces do show expression, as for example that of the *lady writing a letter.* The thoughtful look on her face—puckering her fine brows as she wonders what to write —-is skilfully portrayed. She turns away from the observer, showing only the profile. Another *lady playing a flute* has her back fully turned to the observer. Her body seems to sway to the music she produces. Besides these individual figures, mithunas appear everywhere. These representations profane and desecrate the sacred mystery of life and insult human dignity and decency.

## THE SOLANKIS OR CHAULUKYAS

The Solankis or Chaulukyas (eleventh to thirteenth century A.D.) ruled over Gujarat and western Rajasthan, including Mount Abu and Chitor. Thus these regions formed a cultural unit and represent the western branch of the post-classical art of India. Among the earliest and main targets of Muslim iconoclasm, almost all of the numerous temples of Gujarat were ravaged from time to time, and climatic conditions and earthquakes added to the destruction. Only their ruins give some idea of the wealth of architecture and sculpture in this region.

These remains show profuse and lavish carvings mainly on the pillars, ceilings, friezes and brackets. Niches with figure sculptures adorn the pillars and walls. As in other parts of India at this time, the originality and plastic creativeness of the classical period had congealed into set mechanical forms. In these regions the figures appear to move with vehement strain, their poise disturbed by angular poses rather than graceful curves. Gradually they begin to look more thin and flat with sharpened edges and exaggerated movements of the slender limbs. This nervous strain is less evident in Rajasthan where the movements are still more fluid. Rather than reproducing the actual bodily shape they emphasised sharp and pointed angles both of the limbs and features while they made the curves more and more concave. The compositions lack unity—they give a fragmentary impression with the stress on lines.

The workmanship display great skill but lacks tcreative spontaneity. The deeply undercut figures and elaboration of minute and delicate details must have required much patient labour, but they make the compositions look heavy and crowded. The sharp edges produce a pronounced contrast of light and shade.

The sculptures of the Sūrya temple at Modhera and the Dilwara group of temples at Mount Abu illustrate the general characteristics of Solanki sculptures in Gujarat and Rajasthan. In the sabhā maṇḍapa of the Sūrya temple at Modhera profuse figure sculptures, standing in niches, adorn the pillars, while the toraṇas or cusped arches over the entrance and garlanding the tops of the columns in the interior have beautiful motifs as ornaments.

The Vimala Vasāhi and Lūna Vasāhi temples are the chief Jaina shrines of the Dilwara group of temples on Mount Abu in Rajasthan. The Vimala Vasāhi, dedicated to Adinātha, the first Tirthankara (pathfinder on the way to nirvāṇa) was built by the minister of Bhimadeva I, Vimala Shah in 1032. Across the courtyard of this temple lies the Lūna Vasāhi temple, built in 1231 by the two philanthropic brothers Vastupala and Tejapala in memory of rheir dead brother Luniga, and dedicated to Nemināthа, the twenty-second Tirthankara. Both temples are built of white marble which is well maintained by wealthy merchants and bankers from Gujarat. All the visible surfaces are delicately carved in filigree, worked with a file rather than a chisel. Most of the sculptures and reliefs repeat a few basic forms. Though individually of little artistic value, as part of the architectonic scheme their limitations go unnoticed. Exuberant detail characterises the decoration, with the same motif repeated over and over again. This wealth of ornament together with the rich material tends to fatigue the eyes.

Eleven concentric rings, supported by sixteen brackets with figures of the goddess of knowledge, adorn the dome of the Vimala Vasāhi temple. These rings are filled with patterns of human and animal figures, elephant processions and countless dancers, with repeated statues in niches. A group of pendants adorn the apex, and conventional ornaments decorate the spaces between the rings of figures.

Some of the marble images show remnants

of colour, for example the sculptural panel on the ceiling of the second bay of the *Vimala Vasāhi temple*. It represents *Chakreśvari Devi* (Fig. 314). The eight-armed goddess sits on a stool in the lalitha pose, with one leg hanging down and the other tucked under her on the seat. Garuḍa, her vāhana (vehicle), seen in human form on a smaller scale, supports her leg. Two female chauri-bearers stand on either side of her.

Over the second outer bay of the *Vimala Vasāhi temple*, four *Vidyādevis* (goddesses of knowledge), each seated in the lalitāsana pose on her vehicle, are arranged on the diagonals of a square. The four arms of each carry an attribute. Two attendants flank each devī. These stylised figures do not represent human portraits but serve as part of a skilfully arranged decorative pattern.

These compositions, with the figures adjusted into circular, rectangular or square panels, form geometrical arrangements of fine decorative patterns.

In the sculptural ceiling panel representing the *Narasimha* avatāra of Viṣṇu in the *Vimala Vasāhi temple*, the group of Narasimha killing the demon Hiranyakasyapu is carved on a round lotus in the centre in very high relief and on a much larger scale than the other figures which are very small and almost flat. Through this juxtaposition of different scales and heights of reliefs they obtained splendid decorative effects.

The Lūna Vasāhi, built two centuries later, is the last great example of the Solanki style. It shows less creativity and more mechanical perfection. A striking feature is the dome, resting on eight pillars, with its pendants

Fig. 314. A Jaina Chakreshvari with attendants, Vimala Vasahi temple, Mount Abu.

Fig. 315. Ceiling panel (detail), Luna Vasahi temple, Mount Abu.

resembling clusters of half open lotuses so delicately and accurately carved that they resemble crystal chandeliers more than solid marble.

Some of the ceilings before the thirty-nine cells have elaborate carvings. Those in the porticos have scenes from Neminātha's life. One panel shows the reason for his conversion— the sight of the cattle to be killed for his marriage so filled him with pity and the vanity of human life, that he renounced marriage and the world. His bride followed his example. The portico ceiling of one cell has picturesque scenes both of army life and repose at home. Beautiful screen work encloses the elephant room with ten elephants in marble, their trappings delicately carved, showing the knotted ropes and ornamental drapery.

The *ceiling panel* on the low cupola over the dancing hall of the *Lūna Vasāhi temple* is outstanding for beauty (Fig. 315). From the central floral motif concentric bands of lacelike patterns ripple out in ever wider and more varied patterns, forming a delicate canopy for the sixteen Vidyā devīs standing each in a niche in various poses and radiating from the centre. A simpler background to these figures sets them off more beautifully. Under the pedestal of each figure, with a more elaborate background between them, are sitting and crouching figures in different poses.

## THE EARLY WESTERN CHALUKYAS OF BADAMI

The Chalukyas of Badami (sixth to eighth century A.D.) succeeded the Vakatakas in the Deccan. Obscurity shrouds the origin of this dynasty—like that of many other ancient royal families of India. Constant power struggles with the Pallavas sapped much of their strength, but these wars led to an exchange of artistic influences between the two domains. Chalukyan caves and structural temples cluster mainly in the small towns of Badami, Aihole, Pattadakal, Alampur and Mahakutesvar.

In the Deccan a new kind of art evolved from a tradition very different from the ethereal classical art of Sarnath, with its serene, compassionate, and unearthly blissful figures. From the live rock of the sixth century Badami caves more elemental, earth-born figures emerge from the dark, deep recesses, with powerful, massive bodies, heavy impersonal features completely self-absorbed, ready to burst with dynamic energy. The simple, generalised modelling of the huge principal figures, which cover the entire relief panels from wall to wall, adds to their majestic strength. The minor figures, much smaller and completely subordinated to the main one, show more refined workmanship and better modelling. Tall crowns, worn low over the forehead, appear to symbolise the burden of greatness that weighs upon the main figures. They wear elaborate clothing. The movement of the figures goes in a diagonal direction rather than straight ahead, and each one is self-absorbed, taking no notice of what the others are doing. Though both this art and that of Sarnath start with yogic concentration, the method and result are very different. From this new spring flowing from the Deccan another influence entered into the mainstream of Indian culture.

An artistic effusion swept over the Deccan in the seventh and eighth centuries, with experimental structural temples and sculptures wherein two different streams began to mingle. The carvings on the structural temples at Aihole differ very much from the contemporary rock-cut sculptures at Badami. This new stream, with tall, slender figures precisely modelled, may be traced to the Krishna-Godavari basin near Amaravati which the Chalukyas had conquered. But they retain the strength of the Badami rock-cut images. Gradually the sculptures became more and more refined and varied.

These experiments reached near perfection in the eighth century temples at Pattadakal, notably those of the Virupakṣa and Mallikārjuna, and in the temples at Alampur and Mahakuta. At this time of the artistic freshet from the Deccan, the classic Gupta art had dried up in other parts of India. These figures at Pattadakal show a blend, not yet completely successful, of the powerful rock-cut figures with the slender and supple elegance of the style flowing in as a result of contacts with Pallava culture. Greater technical experience resulted in a wider variety of themes. The diagonal direction continues but the movements have become more graceful, with the figures arched like a bow, and the chest and horizontal shoulders slightly flexed, as for example in the Natarāja and Mahiṣamardinī figures. Light and shade effects are put to fullest use, according to the subject and his state of mind, with graded reliefs and deep, dark recesses. Here the crown, lightly placed on the head, stresses the tendency towards height. Scroll work is used more aesthetically in the perforated stone windows. Thus the energy ready to burst out of the Badami sculptures was channelled into a novel artistic style which opened new vistas to Indian art. But the seed of Buddhist art, though planted in this region, never look deep root and gradually died out.

Of the seventy-odd temples at *Aihole*, the *Durgā temple* stands out both for its architecture and sculpture. The carvings occur mainly in the niches of the outer wall of the shrine, on the pillars of the ardha or mukha maṇḍapa, on the doorway leading to the inner hall, and on the ceiling. An example of a popular ceiling decoration, a *flying couple* from the Durgā temple, is now in the National Museum, New Delhi. The billowing clothes represent their swift flight. Floral motifs with sculptured medallions and graceful mithunas form the main decoration of the pillars. The figures reveal the typical Ghalukyan face—oval, with short pointed nose and full smiling lips.

For those walking in clockwise direction along the pradakṣiṇa pātha of the *Durgā temple* at *Aihole*, three statues in three of the numerous niches on each side include Śiva as Vṛṣabha- vāhana, Narasimha, and Viṣṇu on Garuḍa on one side, and on the other Varāha, Harihara and *Mahiṣāsuramardini* (Fig. 316)—the most

Fig. 316. Mahishasuramardini, Durga temple, Aihole.

dynamic of them all. Her serene expression contrasts with her act of destroying Mahiṣasura (the buffalo demon). With her eight arms raised and bearing the attributes of Śiva and Viṣṇu and of the other gods, she has planted her left foot on the demon's body, lying vanquished at her feet but still alive. By her side stands her vāhana (vehicle), a diminutive lion whose snarling lips and bared fangs express her mood of contempt for the defeated enemy. Formidable yet beautiful, she manifests both power and grace. The statue still reflects its original splendour although three of the left arms and the raised left leg with which she steps on the demon are broken away, though her foot remains visible on its back. Her dynamic figure occupies almost all of the niche in which she stands. A kirīṭa makuṭa with a halo behind crowns her head. With her trident she pierces the relatively puny buffalo, which raises its right front leg and mouth in agony.

Mention must be made of the *Varāha panel*, in the same *Durgā temple*, since innumerable examples exist of this avatāra of Viṣṇu, popular with the Chalukyas probably because they were originally Vaiṣṇavites and had the varāhalāñchana or boar crest as their symbol. In the Varāha panel the god holds Prithvī (earth) whom he has rescued from the demon Hiranyaksha, who had hidden her in the depths of the ocean. The firm right leg, planted on the body of the naga representing the nether world, emphasises the diagonal movement of the main figure. His raised head directs attention to Prithvī, who appears comfortably seated on his arm.

The *Varāha* representation is found also on the wall of *cave no.* 3 at *Badami*, but it lacks the dynamism of the previous example. The setting looks overcrowded with the addition of the devas above blessing the scene, female attendants on the left, and a naga in the middle and on the right side. Here Varāha holds Prithvī in his lower left hand. Other sculptures in this cave include those of Narasimha, Viṣṇu as Virāta puruṣa, and Viṣṇu on Ananta. Numerous mithunas adorn the brackets of the pillars. They stand gracefully under trees, some of them resting their hands on their companions or leaning on them. Richly ornamented with jewellery, they wear beautifully patterned garments, sometimes ending just above their knees and sometimes falling to the ankles. The sculptures of cave no. 2 at Badami resemble those of cave no. 3. On the lintels of this second cave appear stories of the amrita manthana (churning of the milk ocean) and stories of Kṛṣṇa's childhood.

The temples at Pattadakal, especially the Virupakṣa and Mallikārjuna, not only show the highest development of Early Chalukyan art but they are also the most richly adorned monuments of their time in India. Southern influence appears in these temples as well as in the Saṇgameśvara temple, built half a century before the Virupakṣa and Mallikārjuna temples. Already in the Saṇgameśvara temple pilasters flank the sculptured panels, and perforated stone windows fill the wall surface between the base and cornice. In the Saṇgameśvara temple these remain mostly unfinished, but the same decoration, much perfected, reappears on the Virupakṣa and Mallikārjuna.

Inscriptions bearing the name of the architect appear above the mithuna scenes on the eastern gate leading into the Virupakṣa temple from the Malaprabha river. The nandi pavilion inside the spacious courtyard has figures carved on the exterior walls. Mithuna couples and single figures of women, tall and slender, adorn the jambs of the openings on each of the four sides. The most beautiful of these is a lady standing near a column and holding a bird. Another lady, standing on the outer wall of the nandi pavilion, has an umbrella-like disc over her head—a very unusual representation. The Virupakṣa temple itself has carvings on the porches and outer walls as well as inside. These include the Lingodbhavamūrti on the eastern wall; and on the southern wall two representations of the Nrittamūrti Śiva, as well as Narasimha and Hiranyakasyapu, and a dramatic moment in Jatayu's attack on Ravana. The figures on the northern wall are better preserved. The best of these are the Vṛṣabhavāhana and Harihara. Viṣṇu in his Varāha and Trivikrama incarnations stands in niches flanked with pilasters, alternating with beautifully carved lattice windows. Projecting porches flank the temple on the eastern, southern and northern sides. The dvārapālas on either side of these deserve special mention. The remaining dvārapāla on the southern porch turns sideways—an uncommon posture—with one leg bent. A snake coils round the mace in his hand. A crown and rich jewellery give him a very distinguished appearance. On the eastern porch massive dvarapalas, also richly bejewelled, lean on their maces. The dignified pair on the northern porch, however, inspire the most awe, with their four arms, crowns and jewels, including the yajñopavīta studded with gems. They lean on their decorated maces. The one on the left stands on one leg. The other leg, once lifted, is broken away. The south porch has carvings of Ravana trying to lift the Kailasa with his twenty hands, his figure so twisted that while his heads turn forward, the front part of his body turns in the opposite direction. Śiva and Pārvati appear above, surrounded by ganas or bhūtagaṇas. The ceiling panels on the eastern porch include an elaborate carving of Sūrya standing on his chariot drawn by horses and driven by Aruṇa. The ceiling of the northern porch has Śiva sitting on a canopy, and the southern ceiling shows Brahma in a circular composition.

The exquisitely carved windows and interior sculptures of the Mallikārjuna temple reveal stylistic progress over the Virupakṣa temple. The dvārapālas on the porch, the reliefs on the columns, the carved beams and ceiling panels show the versatility, energy and the highest achievement of Early Western Chalukyan sculpture. The carved panels on the outer walls, however, which alternate with the beautiful windows, remain cruder than those of the Virupakṣa and are a bit smaller.

The *Pāpanāth temple,* some distance away, belongs to the north Indian tradition. Along its outer walls run scenes from the Ramayana, such as the fight between Rāma, Lakṣmaṇa and the demons Khara and Dushana, and the battle between Rāma and Ravana—identifiable by inscriptions in the Kanarese script below each panel. The porches, except for the one at the main entrance, are merely decorative, having blind entrances adorned with figures of Śiva dancing the Tāṇḍava. On the pillars of these porches are scenes like the Gajendramokṣa (Viṣṇu rescuing the elephant) and Tripurāntakamūrti (Śiva destroying the three cities of the demons).

Compared with the Virupakṣa and Mallikārjuna, the interior of the Pāpanāth temple looks rather plain. Mithuna figures decorate the pilasters of the maṇḍapa. The men wear something like a short skirt, and their hair is dressed in a coil at the side of the head. Some hold various musical instruments such as a Vīṇā and flute.

How far the influence of Early Western Chalukya art extended is hard to estimate, but we do know that when the Rashtrakutas overran the Chalukya territory, so impressed were they by its temples, especially by the Virupakṣa, that they imitated it in the Kailāsa at Ellora—a crowning tribute to the ancient artists of this region.

## THE RASHTRAKUTAS

The Rashtrakuta dynasty (eighth to tenth century A.D.), from being a feudatory of the Chalukyas of Badami, soon rose to become one of the supreme powers in the Deccan under the able leadership of Dantidurga, defeating the Chalukyas around 752 A.D. and ruling much of their territory and beyond. They initiated a period of Śaivite revivalism—the numerous caves at Ellora and Elephanta bearing ample testimony to the faith and fervour of these rulers. Of the many rock-cut temples at Ellora, the Kailāsa, carved entirely out of one rock during the reign of Krishna I (c. 758 A.D.), stands out as the most remarkable monument. Among the many other temples, those of Rāvaṇa-ka-khai, Dasāvatāra, Lankeśvara and Rāmeśvara contain the most numerous sculptures.

The rock-cut Kailāsa temple at Ellora and the rock-cut caves at Elephanta are the highest sculptural achievements in the Deccan during the eighth century. The marvellous carvings in the Kailāsa temple reveal the final artistic synthesis of the powerful, heavy forms of the Deccani tradition with the slender grace of southern sculpture, thus releasing the pent-up energy of the former in free and vigorous movement. Every composition catches the most dramatic moment of the story and expresses it with a passion rarely equalled in art. All life's varied moods—tender love and destructive fury, the speed of flight and controlled movement of dance find expression in creative realism. But the greatest merit of this sculpture lies in the detailed, individualised modelling of each figure. The clever arrangement of light and shade helps to increase the emotional effects. Deep cavities form the stage for the action. From these the figures appear to emerge from various depths of reliefs, in accordance with the mood of the dramatic moment. This artistic arrangement of the different elements imparts to these compositions a highly spectacular note. Centuries of experiments in the rock-cut tradition in the Deccan culminated in the perfection attained in the sculptures of the monolithic Kailāsa temple at Ellora.

The carvings of the Kailāsa (cave no. 16) are the most typical sculptures of this period. Among the numerous decorations of this temple mention can be made only of the most important. A pair of exquisitely carved monolithic dvaja-stambhas (flagstaff's) which bore

Śiva's triśūla stand at the entrance near the naṇḍī maṇḍapa. Bands of scenes from the Ramayana adorn the wall beside the naṇḍī maṇḍapa. The high plinth on which the temple stands resembles a ground storey. This base is divided into three sections, with an imposing frieze of vigorously carved elephants and lions between simple, heavy mouldings above and below. Vibrant with dynamism and shown in different poses, they appear to support the edifice on their backs.

The niches around the *Kailāsa temple* contain beautiful carvings, such as Ravana shaking the mountain, the kidnapping of Sītā, the Tripurāntaka murti and Mahiṣāsuramardini. *Ravana shaking the mountain.* (Pl. 15.1) shows the ten-headed demon imprisoned in a cave in the nether world under Mount Kailāsa as a punishment for abducting Rāma's wife Sītā. Śiva appears above as god over other gods, with his consort and other celestial beings hovering in the air. Ravana exerts all the power of his twenty arms to destroy the great mountain on which Śiva sits enthroned. In this relief the artist stresses the unconquerable serenity of the divine over the world-shaking exertions of evil. Unmoved, Śiva merely presses down his foot to foil the demon's efforts. Parvatī, in a graceful half-reclining posture, has felt the tremors and fearfully shrinks towards Śiva, grasping his arm while her terrified maid-servant flees into the darkness of the background. Yet a feeling of deep security prevails in the composition. The gestures of the figures rather than their facial expressions manifest the drama of the scene. Set in a double-storeyed stage within a deep niche, the scene gives an impression of living reality acted out on a spacious stage by figures of stone with natural proportions, rather than mere decorative symbols.

The *fight between Ravana and Jatayu* (Fig. 317) from the story of Sita's abduction, is artistically set in a deep niche with a bare surface to represent the scene of the battle high in the air. According to the story the demon king Ravana had lured Rāma away from his wife to pursue a golden deer, the disguise of one of Ravana's suite. Left unprotected in her hermitage in the wilderness of the Vindhya mountains, Sītā was kidnapped by Ravana and carried away in his magic flying chariot. Jatayu, the powerful king of vultures, to whose faithful care Rāma had entrusted his wife, came to her rescue upon hearing her cry but proved unequal to the fight. Ravana killed him and carried Sīta off to his native Lanka.

Fig. 317. Fight between Ravana and Jatayu, Kailasanatha temple, Ellora.

The sculpture shows her crouching in the chariot, but her figure has been damaged. The intact form of the vigorous Ravana emerges boldly from the niche, in very high relief. The dramatic posture catches the haste of his flight on the one hand and his violent backward turn as he threatens with uplifted arm to strike the large Jatayu behind him who is pecking his thigh. At Ellora Ravana's face looks calm and the bird appears rather quiet, while in the Chalukyan example in the Virupakṣa temple at Pattadakal, anger contorts Ravana's face and Jatayu attacks fiercely with its strong beak. At Pattadakal the puṣpaka vimānam (flying chariot) rises high above, but at Ellora it comes only to Ravana's shoulders and is drawn by horses, contrary to the Ramayaṇa version.

In the *Tripurāntaka mūrti*, on the outer wall of the *Kailāsa temple*, Śiva appears as the destroyer of the three Asura fortresses. He stands in his horse-driven chariot with Brahmā holding the reins while Viṣṇu in the form of a white bull stabilises the chariot in front. This piece of sculpture, from the second half of the eighth century, shows a more pronounced southern influence in the energy shown by the shoulders thrown back and the tense curve of the outlines, but the powerful chest retains the Deccani tradition.

In the *Mahiṣāsuramardini relief* the tense dramatic clash between the goddess and giant demon has been selected in the representation. Brandishing weapons of all kinds in her eight hands which form a halo around her head, Durgā attacks the bull-shaped giant. While her lion mount springs at the enemy and her attendants beneath join in the assault, Durgā has just shot three arrows at once. The demon has been cornered but the battle still remains undecided. Tense yet confident of Durgā's final victory, the gods who had been dethroned and who have gathered in the sky just above the battle, look on with anxious hope to be restored to their thrones.

One of the walls of the *Lankeśvara cave* (hewn out of the hillside beside the Kailāsa) has a particularly graceful image of *Śiva dancing* in the nādānta mode (Fig. 318). Though the panel has been severely damaged, the central figure remains complete enough to provide a good idea of the whole. Steadying himself on his left foot, he thrusts forward the right (now broken), twisting the body so that the hip appears in profile and the chest in complete frontal view as he tramples the demon Apasmara. The whole body curves in the atibhanga pose. The sense of movement and grace, stressed by the powerful curves of the body, proclaim him to be the lord of dance and divine harmony. The artist has successfully used the movement of the hands and body to stress rhythm and balance. The tilt of the head, framed by two of his arms, matches that of the hips, while the left leg repeats the forward thrust of the torso. He wears an ornate jaṭamakuṭa from which hang three loops of pearls. The edges of the cloth flow rhythmically on either side moving with the swaying body. Below him one musician plays the flute and another cymbals. A lady sits at the right, with Bhringi (the skeletal figure) behind her and Gaṇapathy standing near them.

Fig. 318. Dancing Shiva, ceiling, Lankeshvara cave, Ellora.

At Ellora innumerable sculptures adorn the walls of the Rāvaṇa-ka-Khai, Rāmeśvara, Dhumarlena and Dasāvatāra caves—the latter being so called as it contains many avatāras of Viṣṇu. The only two-storeyed Hindu cave temple, the Dasāvatāra cave was probably Buddhist originally and later given over to Brahmanical use under the Rashtrakutas, whose rule withessed a revival of Śaivism, as they were staunch adherents of this cult.

A beautiful panel of *Śiva dancing* in the lalita mode in the *Rāvaṇa-ka-khai* temple (*cave no.* 14, at *Ellora*) shows him with eight hands holding a damaru (drum), paraśu (axe) and triśūla (trident) in three hands while the others are in the patāka, tripatāka, simhakarṇa and gajahaṣṭa poses. The body bends to the right and rests on the toes. Behind him appears the skeletal figure of the rishi Bhringi. Pārvati, with a small dwarf beside her, stands gracefully watching the dance of her lord with an expression of awe. A pair of musicians, one with two drums before him, appears on the left below. Gods and other celestial beings look down from above and bless the scene.

The *Narasimha panel* in the *Dasāvatāra temple* (*cave no.* 15, *Ellora*) depicts the many-armed god with bared fangs pursuing the terror-stricken Hiranyakashyapu. The composition manifests extraordinary power. With brandished sword Narasimha pounces on the demon who is taken unawares. The god's left leg interlocks Hiranyakashyapu's right and one hand clutches his shoulder. The mane streams behind with the force of Narasimha's forward movement, his sheer appearance instilling fear. Hiranyakashyapu, with head and one hand turned away from Narasimha, tries to pull away but without success. The artist, has chosen the exact moment when the god springs out of the pillar which the demon had kicked in his pride and anger, or in reaction to this unexpected appearance. It is an interesting study in psychology, well illustrated by the Rashtrakuta artists.

Of the many sculptures in the *Rāmeśvara* (*cave no.* 21, *Ellora*), that of a *saptamātrikā* (one of the seven mother-goddesses) is among the best. She sits casually resting her hand on the ground. Her slim limbs and well-modelled body are particularly beautiful.

*Cave no.* 29, at *Ellora* commonly known as the *Sitā Nani or Dumarlena,* has a powerful *Andhakāsuravadhamūrti panel,* perhaps of an earlier date. Śiva thrusts his right leg on the ground, raises his left higher and lunges forward with his sword, piercing Andhakasura (the demon of darkness) right through, so deeply that the-point of the weapon comes out of the demon's back. Śiva's open mouth, bared teeth, and glaring eyes show his urge to kill. The frightened Pārvatī, sitting on the right, serves as a contrast to this ferocity. She holds one hand to her breast, gazing fearfully at this dreadful form of her lord. A chauri bearer stands beside her.

Five *Jaina caves* also belong to this period. One of these, cave no. 39, called the Choṭā (small) Kailāsa, resembles the Kailāsa, as its name implies, but does not equal it in beauty. An impressive figure here is *Chakreśvari,* originally with twelve hands, but many of them are destroyed. In her left hands she holds a lotus, wheel, conch and mace. The only remaining right hand brandishes a sword. She sits in the padmāsana on her vāhana.

Cave no. 32, the Indra sabhā, has a particularly beautiful panel of the Jaina goddess *Siddhaiki* sitting on a lion in the lalitāsana, with one hand resting on her lap. The other is broken. Foliage with monkeys, parrots and cranes forms a canopy over her. Attendants stand beside her.

Elephanta island (ancient Puri) discloses another phase of Rashtrakuta art. While the sculptures in Ellora reveal southern influence, the carvings in the Elephanta caves near Bombay show the highest perfection reached by the native Deccani tradition unaffected by any outside influence. The massive, powerful forms remain simple and generalised, within firm outlines and deeply self-absorbed. The rounded volumes give the impression of dynamic vigour controlled by a dignified serenity.

The sculptures, found mainly in the large cave at *Elephanta*, include the Maheśamūrti Śiva, Kalyanasundaramūrti, Natarāja and Andhakāsuravadhamūrti. The most awe-inspiring is the figure of *Śiva Mahesamūrti* (Pl. 15.2) opposite the northern entrance. Set in a deep niche, like some of the Ellora reliefs, the bust seems to emerge from the darkness of another world. The central face is that of the supreme Śiva who preserves—majestic, impassive,serene. On the left is the face of the Śiva who destroys —wrathful and angry. And on the right is the young and peaceful image of the Śiva who creates. The other reliefs, all relating to the various aspects of Śiva, reveal the skill of the sculptors in expressing a whole range of emotions from terror to bliss.

The *Andhakāsuravadhamūrti* at *Elephanta* shows all the terror and power of this theme. With protruding fangs, Śiva gathers in a cup the falling blood-drops of the demon he pierced through. Above him, two hands hold up a canopy made of elephant skin.

The *Elephanta* panel depicting the *marriage of Śiva* and *Pārvati* is one of the most graceful examples of Kalyāṇasundaramūrti Śiva. Śiva's smile reflects his happiness. He reaches out his right hand to receive Pārvaū's hand.* A halo appears behind the jaṭamakuṭa on his head. A cloth, tied at the left, crosses his hips. To his right stands the slim figure of Pārvati, looking down shyly, her head inclined towards Śiva. On the right are Brahmā as officiating priest and Viṣṇu, while a tall, well-built figure appears on the left—probably Himavān, the bride's father. Flying mithunas bless the divine couple from above. Mention must also be made of the *Gangādharamūrti,* showing the Ganga flowing down onto Śiva's mighty head.

The sculptural panels at Elephanta resemble a picture gallery relating the stories of Śiva's life to the worshippers—a fitting theme for a temple dedicated to this deity. The sculptures seem to move with the changing light and have a dramatic effect as the images emerge from the uniformly dark background.

Generally these figures have broad faces and foreheads, eyebrows curved and joined together, thick lips, and fleshy jaws and chins. The ornaments consist of a jaṭamakuṭa (crown), matted hair dressed and piled above the head,

* The name 'Parvati' derives from 'parvata', meaning 'mountain'; hence 'Parvati' means 'mountain-born'.

patra or sarpa kuṇḍalas (ear discs) or serpents as ear ornaments), single broad necklace, yajñopavīta or muktayajñopavīta (plain or pearl sacred thread), udara bandha (waist band), mekhalā (girdle), kaṭi bandha (band encircling the hips) and valayas (bangles) and keyūras (broad armlets). Anklets appear on some figures. The plain diaphanous garment worn by the ladies reaches down to the ankles while the men wear it short (ending at the knees) or long. In some figures of Śiva a snake is used as a kaṭi bandha, and as a valaya known as bhujanagavalaya (snake bangle).

## THE LATER CHALUKYAS

The Later Chalukyas of Kalyan (tenth to twelfth century A.D.) re-established their sovereignty in the Deccan when Taila II dethroned the Rashtrakuta king Karkka II in 973 A.D. The most powerful of these later Chalukya rulers were Someswara I and his son Vikramaditya VI. Both engaged in strenuous battles against the Cholas who were asserting their supremacy in the south, and against their neighbours, the Hoysalas.

The decorative and conventionalised sculptures patronised by this dynasty belong mainly to the eleventh and twelfth centuries. Scroll designs and over-ornamentation characterise this style. The bold designs, geometric or foliate, carved even to the minutest detail on the porous black hornblende, cover ceilings, pillars, niches and doorways, so much so that sculpture and architecture merge almost completely. Niches adorned with volute designs, curving inwards, enclose the rather voluptuous figures, usually of medium height. Draperies, indicated by diagonal double lines, reach down to the ankles. The most elaborate ornamentation centres around the crown, headdress and necks. The yajñopavīta (sacred thread) is now made entirely of pearls.

The temples belonging to this period include the Kalleśvara at Bagali, the Veṇugopālaswāmi at Magala, the Katteśvara at Hirahadagalli, the Mallikārjuna at Kuruvatti, and many others spread all over the state of Karnataka. The *Narasimha panel* in the *Bagali temple* shows a stylised twelve-armed man-lion tearing the entrails of the demon Hiranyakashyapu. Such a scene would require great power and movement, but here the god seems unaware of what he does as he stares vaguely out in front, so that even his bared fangs appear meaningless. Three rows of stylised parallel lines indicate his mane. On either side below, small figures of devotees look up in awe at the god.

The *Veṇugopālasubāmi temple* at *Magala* has some of the most intricate *ceiling designs* in this region, consisting mainly of concentric bands of cusped arches and volutes culminating in the central lotus flower. Jewels cover the image in the shrine shown in the samabhanga posture. The lower garment, gracefully draped, flows rhythmically on either side. Profuse floral and leaf designs adorn the niche above.

Fig. 319. Mahishasuramardini panel, Kattesvara temple, Hirahagalli.

The *Mahiṣāsuramardinī panel* (Fig. 319) in the *Katteśvara temple* at *Hirahadagalli* shows the eight-armed goddess with a quiver full of arrows at her back. Her right leg rests on the head of a small figure beside the diminutive demon Mahiṣāsura. On the right, a man fights a rearing lion. The drapery, represented by the usual twin diagonal lines, reaches to her ankles. Bands of necklaces cover the whole neck. The four-armed *Saraswatī*, in the same temple, is stylistically similar. She sits on a throne supported by a haṁsa and covered with U-shaped ornamental bands in front. An elaborate voluted niche encircles the ornate crown.

## THE HOYSALAS

The Hoysalas (eleventh to fourteenth century A.D.), originally feudatories of the Later Chalukyas, soon became independent. Under the able Bittiga, converted to Vaiṣṇavism by Ramanuja in the twelfth century and renamed Vishnuvardhana, the dynasty gradually assumed power. The Hoysalas patronised many temples, such as those at Halebid, Belur and Somnathpur. These were literally covered with sculptural decorations. The local stone, which has the double advantage of being soft when first quarried but hardening on exposure to air, enabled the Hoysala craftsmen to produce from it a profusion of detailed carvings.

The characteristic features of this sculpture are the elevated basements (Fig. 320) with band upon band of carved friezes each having its symbolic meaning as well as its position in the decorative scheme: elephants usually at the bottom, horsemen, scrollwork, yālis, haṁsas (geese sacred to Brahmā) and Purana stories. Above the friezes, statues of the gods are set in niches. The detailed carving and still more the general design of the decoration display remarkable skill.

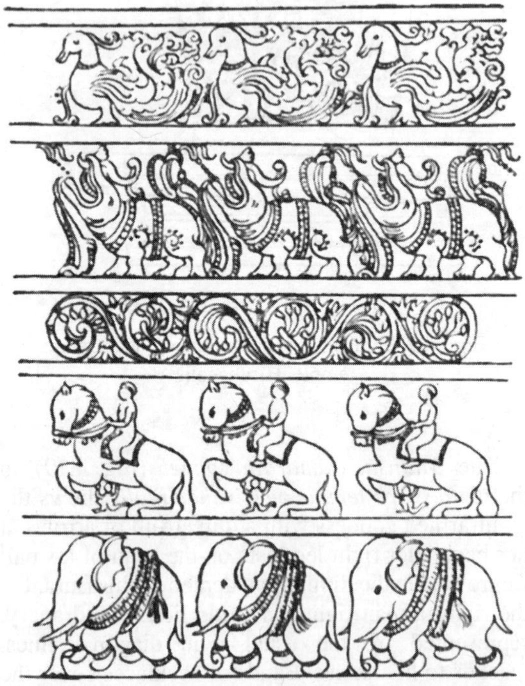

Fig. 320. Basement decoration (detail), Hoysaleshvara temple, Halebid.

A *Śiva* from the *Hoysaleśvara temple* at *Halebid* typifies this style. Short and squat, the figure as in most examples) stands in slight abhanga pose. His huge elaborate headdress resembles a niche above his head. Scrollwork fills the niche above—a motif typical of this period, and possibly influenced by the Later Chalukya style, as we see in the temples of Gadag and Belgaum belonging to that period. Śiva no longer appears as the god of destruction; in fact he is barely visible under the exuberance of ornamentation. The facial expression, however, remains fierce, and the arched eyebrows, broad flat nose, glaring eyes, protruding fangs and firm cleft chin express his power.

Innumerable jewels almost clothe the figures of this style. Particularly noticeable are the kirīṭas (crowns)—ornate and so encrusted with jewels that they resemble elaborate trellises. Other items of jewellery include long and short necklets, skaṇḍamālās (broad shoulder bands), keyūras (armlets), waist bands, and pādasaras encircling the feet below the anklets. In fact, jewellery covers almost all the parts of the body which could possible be adorned. The short figures with all their ornaments give an impression of heaviness, relieved to some extent by the delicate craftmanship.

The *Mahiṣāsuramardinī panel* from the *Hoysaleśvara temple* at *Halebid* does not sport as much ornamentation as the Śiva statue yet, notwithstanding this comparative sobriety, it fails to depict the mood of the goddess destroying the buffalo demon, unlike the earlier panels at Aihole and Mamallapuram which bring out her inner power in the conquest of evil. The Halebid devī, posing like a dancer, does not show any interest in her act of destroying the demon. Mahisha, considerably smaller and relegated to the bottom right corner of the panel, looks cowed down and so different from the belligerent earlier examples. He seems to have lost all desire to resist.

The feeling of movement, lacking in the Mahiṣāsuramardinī, is more apparent in the *viṇādhara Saraswatī* (Fig. 321) in the *Hoysaleśvara temple, Halebid.* The eight-handed figure holds the musical instrument in the right and left hands. She dances, resting on the right leg, slightly bent, while raising the left. The line of the body seems to move with the tilt of the head, the gesture of the arms and the bend

Fig. 321. Vina-dhara Saraswati, Hoysaleshvara temple, Halebid.

of the raised leg. Saraswatī's vāhana, the haṁsa, near her feet, is so highly stylised that it resembles a decorative motif more than a life-like representation of a bird.

In the *Chennakeśava temple* at *Belur* we find a similar mode of sculpture. Three dancing figures, belonging to the twelfth century, represent *Śiva* in like dance poses. In all of them he raises one leg and bends it so that it almost rests on the other. One of the images standing on the demon Apasmara-purusha, slants his head to the right and holds up a sword. Scrollwork, commonly seen here, appears above the niche. The next panel shows a calmer figure playing a Vīṇā. The third represents Śiva with fangs protruding dancing as ferociously on the Apasmāra-puruṣa as in the first panel.

Contrasting with the movement of the dancing Śivas, the *Garuḍa* in the *Chennakeśava temple* at *Belur* stands rather stiffly in the sama- bhanga pose. His joined hands, wings spread out at the back, and folds of cloth round his waist falling in graceful curves on either side give the panel symmetrical balance. His large eyes, looking heavenward, and his well-curved brows represent Garuḍa in the act of worshipping his master Viṣṇu. Serpents encircle his arms and wrists and bands of jewellery surround his waist and girdle.

## THE PALLAVAS

The Greater Pallavas (c. sixth to tenth century A.D.), beginning with Simhavisnu Avanisimha (lion of the earth), established themselves in south India, with their capital at Kanchipuram, near modem Madras in Tamil Nadu State. Their territory extended from the Krishna river in the north (including parts of the Andhra country) to the Kaveri river in the south. The innumerable monuments scattered over the southern region show that this dynasty patronised the arts generously.

Since their rule extended to the Andhra territory, they absorbed and carried on the Amaravati tradition and evolved an artistic style with far-reaching influence. One of the most outstanding monarchs of this dynasty, Mahendravarman I (c. 580-630 A.D.) liberally patronised different arts, as evidenced by his titles Vicitracitta (myriad-minded), Cetthakāri (temple-builder) and Citrakārappuli (tiger among artists). He promoted an energetic art movement in his domains. His son Narasimhavarman I Mamalla (630-668) started the novel method of carving out shrines from freestanding monoliths, and produced exquisite sculptures like the huge rock-cut open-air representation of the so-called Kiratarjuniya or Descent of the Ganga. Dravida sculpture rests on these solid, creative foundations laid down in the time of the Pallavas.

Pallava sculptures retain the same elongated, slender, pliant and graceful forms seen at Amaravati but the figures have become more sublime and disciplined. The Pallavas lay greater stress on natural simplicity, which gives their carvings an immediate charm. They do not rely on subtleties such as deep mysterious caves with their strong play of light and shade as in the Ellora sculptures of the same period. Everything is clear and open in these Pallava carvings on the face of rocks and shallow cavities. Everything looks so natural, especially the animal figures which reveal great love and understanding of the different species and a keen observation of the world around, combined with a sense of humour. For instance the cat in the Descent of the Ganga mimics the ascetic while the mice frolic around, a monkey cleans his mate's fur while she nurses her young, a stag scratches his nose with his hind foot, elephant calves find shelter between the legs of their elders, and an elegant pair of deer watch the scene from a cave on the other side.

The human and divine figures show an impersonal, dignified reserve verging on aloofness. Their long, thin, almost tubular limbs make them look even taller. The female figures usually lean on their tall, broad-shouldered partners and look very submissive, whether they are human or goddesses. They are much slighter, with narrow chests and shoulders, and very slender waists. Both their ornaments and clothing are scant.

The earliest individual Pallava statues are found at Mandagapattu, but the first narrative relief is the *Gangādhara* panel in the upper rock-cut cave at *Tiruchirapalli*—a noble creation of Pallava art. It portrays the majestic Śiva nonchalantly receiving the mighty river on only two of his locks.

The most famous achievement of Pallava sculpture, belonging to the Mamalla period, is the *Kiratarjuniya, known also as the descent of the Ganga* (Pl. 14.5) at *Mamallapuram.* It is sculpted out of two huge boulders in the hillside, separated by a narrow vertical cleft. Tnis rock wall, covered with more than a hundred figures, measures twenty-seven metres in length and about nine metres in height.

This so-called Kiratarjuniya (Arjuna's penance) is taken by some to represent a story from the Mahabharata, namely the hero's ascetic practices so that Śiva would favour him with the pāśupata weapon. Wearing deer skin and emaciated by starvation, Arjuna stood on the tip of one toe with arms joined over his head and gazed into the sun. At the time when this carving was made, this story was very popular and found expression in other forms of art. The Mamallapuram sculpture, however, does not depict the most important element of the story, namely Arjuna's fight with Śiva in the disguise of a hunter. For this reason others believe that the Mamallapuram carving may represent the austerities of Bhagiratha, and Śiva granting his wish to let the Ganga flow through his locks. The Mamallapuram scene pictures the river flowing down from the mountain while adoring gods look on ecstatically. For this reason the carving is sometimes called the Descent of the Ganga. A tank at the bottom of the cleft and a number of channels on the ledge above the cleft prove that at least on festive occasions the cleft was used to let water fall down to a cistern below. Unfortunately the opening of the cleft on top has been filled up with brick and cement because of an erroneous restoration. This fact as well as the similarity of the Mamallapuram carving with the Ganga monument at Anuradhapura in Sri Lanka lends more weight to the belief of several scholars that the scene represents the descent of the Ganga rather than Arjuna's penance.

According to. the story in the Ramayana, Bhagīratha obtained through his austerities the favour of the Ganga's descent to earth in order to purify the ashes of his ancestors, the sinful sons of the Solar race. Lest the force of the river's descent from heaven destroy the earth, Bhagiratha asked Śiva to let it fall on his adamantine head and to slow down its impetuous rush by entangling it in the jungle growth of his matted hair. So the waters came down to the Himalayas from Śiva's head and from thence watered the plains.

The central episode (Fig. 322) of the great carving is the descent of the celestial stream through the vertical cleft. Water divinities, notably a giant nāgarāja and his queen, surge up from the depths, lost in wonder at the world-refreshing event. All creation, represented by gods, demons, men and animals, have gathered from both sides to witness the spectacle and to plunge into the stream.

On the lower level to the left, a group of yogis have gathered around an exquisite little Pallava temple. One of them sits at the door in yoga posture with two others a little further away. It is a realistic picture of ascetic life.

Near the top of the cleft, also to the left, the emaciated Bhagiratha stands on one leg in pillar-like rigidity with the fingers of both hands interlocked above his head. The gigantic, fourarmed Śiva stands before him with the lower left hand in the varada mudrā (gift-bestowing posture). A mass of matted hair covers his head. Gaṇa accompany him.

The remainder of the rock-face is covered with different forms of life: divine, titanic, human and animal—all perfectly differentiated and shown in truly typical attitudes of movement or repose. All either hurry to witness the great event or peacefully contemplate it. On the right side of the cleft is a very striking elephant family, with the giant bull followed by the smaller cow while the calves shelter between their legs as they proceed to the river. Another rather droll scene shows a wily cat with upstretched paws pretending to do penance while the unsuspecting mice dance around. Distinct from the rock but associated with the scene is a pair of monkeys in outline but without detail. The skill of Indian sculptors in giving the impression of life is nowhere more evident than in this interesting and beautiful piece of sculpture on the open hillside of Mamallapuram.

Other examples of Pallava sculpture, also belonging to the Mamalla period, can be seen in the rock-cut temples at *Mamallapuram*, such as the beautiful panels in the Mahiṣāsura maṇḍapa. A large panel showing Durgā as *Mahiṣāsuramardinī* occupies the whole of the wall at the northern end of the cave. It shows the most famous exploit of the unconquerable goddess in the mardinī (crushing) of the buffalo (mahiṣa) demon (asura), thus rescuing the world from his tyranny. The plucky young warrior-goddess, astride on her fierce lion-mount, attacks the wily-looking buffalo demon, much bigger than herself and stronger than all the gods. In the scene the outcome of the battle hangs in the balance. The demon stands ready to strike with his great iron club, as he eyes his opponent waiting for the opportune moment. The umbrella of universal rule still hangs over his giant body and he retains his crown. It seems an uneven battle with the slender diminutive goddess playfully shooting her arrows over the demon's head and not even looking at him as she advances with drawn sword and other weapons in her eight arms. Only the ferocity of her mount and the confident attitude of her attendants, while the demon's followers cringe and flee, indicate

Fig. 322. Kiratarjuniya (Descent of the Ganga), Mamallapuram.

the outcome of the battle. With discreet restraint the artist shows the superiority of courage and trust in a higher power, as she looks upwards, over cunning and brute strength.

Pallava artists had a special gift for hinting at the significance of their themes by means of overtones. They never represented their subjects in dramatically decisive scenes.

The same Mahiṣāsuramardini cave also has a deep relief of *Viṣṇu Śeṣaśāyī* or Yogaśayanamūrti reposing on his serpent-couch as in yoganidrā. While the two-armed Viṣṇu sleeps peacefully the asuras at his feet, Madhu and Kaitaba, plot to strike him dead with their weapons. Near them Bhū Devī kneels with her hands in the anjali posture, while the pair of handsome young men in front of her, Sudarśana and Naṇdaka, keep guard. Above Viṣṇu fly another pair of figures, supposedly Pañcajaṇya as a dwarf gaṇa and Kaumodaki in the form of a beautiful warrior maiden.* Earlier writers had supposed that Kaumodaki would appear as the personification of yoganidrā (contemplative sleep) in order thus to enter into Viṣṇu to make him lapse into a mixture of sleep and contemplation at the end of the yuga. At the threat of Madhu and Kaitabha and in response to Brahmā's prayer, Kaumodaki withdrew and Viṣṇu woke up to kill the asuras. In this carving the sculptor has skilfully reproduced the peace of a face in deep sleep. The serpent Śeṣa too looks very tranquil here, while at Tirumayam he rages at the asuras with poison coming from his tongues in the form of flames. The calm figure of Viṣṇu contrasts with the manly energy of Durgā in the opposite panel.

The *Varāha maṇḍapa*, at the back of the Descent of the Ganga, contains four panels: Varāha lifting the earth out of the ocean, Gaja-Lakṣmī bathed by elephants while she sits on a lotus, a four-armed Durgā, and Trivikrama defeating Bali, the king of demons.

In the *Varāha panel* he holds Prithvī (earth) very gently in two hands, while the other two bear the śankha and chakra. His right leg rests on the hood of a worshipping naga. Scalloped lines depict waves. Brahmā, with three heads, stands on the right in the abhanga pose, holding a kamaṇḍalu (water vessels of riṣis). Near him is a bearded attendant, probably a riṣi and on his left stand two devotees, a man and a woman. As a mark of respect the man has bared his right shoulder while the lady joins her hands and bends her legs a little. A pair of celestial beings looks down on this scene from above.

In the *Gaja-Lakṣmī panel* the goddess wears the typical Pallava crown and suvarṇavaikākṣa (a garland crossing the body). As in most early Indian sculpture the apparent nudity of the figures is intended to indicate diaphanous clothing. The position of Lakṣmī's hands shows that they were meant to hold lotuses. Lotus leaves at the bottom of the panel suggest the pool. A pair of nymphs at either side of the goddess fetch water for her bath in pots which the two elephants pour over her. The outlines of their trunks and ears reveal close observation of nature.

In the *Durgā panel* the goddess, standing between a lion and an antelope, holds a wheel and discus in her upper hands, while the lower are held in the abhaya and kaṭyavalambita mudrās. The umbrella above her symbolises her universal rule. Śiva-gaṇa gambol above, while one of the pair of devotees at her feet is about to cut off his head to offer it to her.

In the *Trivikrama panel,* the eight-handed god holds a śankha (conch), chakra (wheel), dagger, sword, shield and bow. The upper right hand rests on the top (signifying the roof of the world) in order to balance himself as he measures the two worlds with his legs. The upper left hand and the toe of the outstretched leg turn attention to Brahmā seated on a lotus. A flying figure with a boar's head (of unknown significance) faces Brahmā. On the top left appears Śiva, also seated on a lotus, with Sūrya and Chandra (sun and moon) below to the left and right. A falling figure near Chandra seems to represent Bali as he plunges down to the nether world. Four seated figures below, one of whom shows fright and shock, may depict Bali and his retinue.

In front of another rock-cut relief, carved out of a hillside boulder, they erected the *Krsṇa maṇḍapa.* The sculpture represents *Kṛṣṇa lifting Mount Govardan* in order to protect the gopas and gopīs (male and female cowherds) from a heavy rainstorm. A cow to the left affectionately licks her calf while a gopa sits milking her.

The compact group of *five monolithic rathas* has rich and interesting sculptural decorations. The square *Draupadi ratha*, furthest to the north, has ghanadvāras (false doors) surmounted by makara toraṇas on three of its sides. They serve as niches for standing Durgā statues. On the eastern side she

* They are the four ayudha purusas of Vishnu: Sudarsana (discus), Nandaka (Sword), Kaumodaki (club) and Pancajanya (conch).

steps on the severed head of Mahisasura, the buffalo demon. Dvārapālikās (female doorkeepers) in niches flank the entrance to the sanctuary on the western side. A makara toraṇa adorns the door of the cella containing the statue of a four-armed Durgā. Two men kneel in worship at her feet. One of them wields his sword in order to cut off his head in offering to the goddess. Four dwarf gaṇas fly overhead. In front of the ratha stands a lion, Durgā's vāhana (vehicle), carved out of a free-standing boulder.

Not all the carvings on the rathas have the same high quality. The *Arjuna ratha* possesses some of the best and most refined. The ground floor of three of its sides has panels framed by pilasters, with dvārapālas standing guard at each corner. In the central panels Viṣṇu leans on Garuḍa on the northern side, Indrā rides Airāvata on the eastern side, and the Vṛṣabhānthikavāhana (Śiva leaning on the naṇḍī) appears on the southern side. Among the most delicate carvings of the rathas are the royal couples and ladies, shown either in full or in three-quarter profile. They adorn the first and second talas. On the latter the panels are found on either corner of the harmya wall, although it is an arpita (a non-functional hārā). On the western front is the entrance to the now empty cella. Each of the two pilasters on this side has a lion base while the pillars remain unadorned. A row of gaṇas (dwarfs) appears between the capitals and the kapōta (hanging eave); while a line of haṁsas (geese) adorns the upper storey. A seated bull, Śiva's vāhana, carved from a boulder behind Arjuna's ratha, remains unfinished. Lion and elephant busts hold up the common platform on which the Draupadi and Arjuna rathas stand.

The *Bhima ratha* has lion-based pillars. On each of the gable ends of its śālā-type waggon roof appear bas-reliefs each showing a miniature ekatala vimāna of the Vesara (curved) order (Fig. 134).

The *Dharmarāja ratha*, the southernmost and tallest of the group, is an anarpita vimāna, i.e. the hārās are not attached to the harmyas, thus leaving a circumambulatory passage behind. This permitted niches with sculptures on the harmya wall. Figures decorate all of its three talas, which were meant to have sanctuaries (Fig. 140). The āditala (ground floor) was intended to consist of a sanctuary surrounded by a pradakṣiṇa pātha, with closed walls only at the four corners while the centre of each side was to have open pillared façades, each side having a pair of lion-based pillars and two pilasters. The āditala (ground floor) has eight sculptured panels. Two figures of Śiva, each with four arms, face west. Brahmā (with three of his four heads) and Harihara face north. Śiva Ardhanārī and Skaṇda as Gurumūrti face east. A four-armed Śiva and a royal figure (Narasimhavarman) face south.

On the madhya tala (second storey) the unfinished sanctuary with its portico occupies the centre of the western side. It is flanked by a pair of dvarapālas, a woman devotee with offerings, and Śiva Kaṅkāḷamūrti. The other sculptures of the same tala, following the clockwise circumambulation, are: Śiva Vīṇādhara, a four armed Śiva with Taṇḍu, Śiva and Chaṇdeśa, Śiva Gangādhara (holding Ganga), Viṣṇu leaning on Garuḍa, Śiva Kalārimūrti, Śiva Vṛṣabhāntika—all facing north; a stāvaka (bard), svayampāki (cook), parichāraka (keeper), and an archaka (temple priest)—all facing east; Śiva, Śiva Aṇdhakāri, Śiva Vīṇādhara, Viṣṇu, Śiva with naṇḍī, Kāliya Kṛṣṇa and Śiva—all facing south.*

Fig. 323. Somaskanda panel, early version, Dharmaraja ratha, Mamallapuram.

The most important relief panel, *Śiva as Somāskaṇda* (Fig. 323), appears on the uparitala (third storey) on the rear wall of the shrine in the western face. Śiva as Sōmāskaṇda (Śiva with Umā and Skaṇda or Kārtikeya) is perhaps most characteristic and common of the Pallava sculptures. The early Sōmāskaṇda panels, both at Mamallapuram and belonging to the Mamalla style, include the one in the Dharmarāja ratha, and the damaged one, of which only a rough outline remains, in the Rāmānuja maṇḍapam. The panel in the Dharmarāja

* Since the upper storeys are not accessible to the general public, K. R. Srinivasan's *The Dharmaraja Ratha and its Sculptures, Mahabalipuram*, which contains reproductions of all the panels, will be of great help.

ratha at Mamallapurm shows Śiva seated in the lalitāsana pose, with the right leg dangling down. His headdress, moderately tall, consists of the jaṭamakuṭa. Only a single band crosses his chest. The lower left hand rests on his thigh while the lower right is held in the chīn mudrā. Umā or Pārvatī also sits in the lalitāsana, with her right leg folded and her left one hanging down. Her body appears in profile. Her face inclines slightly as she looks tenderly down at her son, the infant Skanda whom she holds on her lap. Her back almost rests on the side of the niche. Brahmā and Viṣṇu stand outside the niche to the left and right.

The other niches on the third floor include two devotees on the western side, Chandra with four devotees on the northern, Sūrya with four more devotees on the eastern, and Śiva with the same number of devotees on the southern side.

The *Nakula-Sahadeva ratha* has a bas-relief on the front gable end of the waggon-vaulted roof, showing a miniature ekatala vimāna of the Dravidian (polygonal) order (Fig. 133). This ratha has no other figure carvings. Near it stands a monolithic elephant, suggestive of the gajapṛṣṭākāra (elephant back) form of the apsidal temple.

The *Adivarāha cave* at *Mamallapuram*, carved in the western side of the hill, remains locked most of the time. Its facade is disfigured and hidden by a modem building. The cave has a large hall with four pillars in the front and two pilasters supported by seated lions. In the back row are two pillars without lions. A cell has been cut in the back wall for Varāha. To his right are a dvārapāla, Viṣṇu, Ādiśeṣa, Gajalakṣmi, a king sitting on a simhāsana with his two queens, and Śiva Gangādhara. To his left are another dvārapāla, Harihara, an attendant, Durgā, a king pointing to the shrine with two of his queens, and Brahmā. Two inscriptions in grantha characters permit the identification of the royal personages as Simhavishnu (seated) and Mahendravarman I (standing). The latter's two queens are very beautifully carved.

In the *Shore temple at Mamallapuram*, built by Narasimha II Rajasimha, Sōmāskaṇda reliefs appear again both in the Rājasimheśvara shrine (facing west) and in the Kṣatriyasimheśvara shrine (facing east). As usual in Pallava temples they form the background to the Śiva-linga; and in the latter shrine they adorn both walls of the porch. The *Somāskanda panel* (Fig. 324) in the Kṣatriyasimheśvara shrine is characteristic of the later period. It shows certain differences from the earlier one in the Dharmarāja ratha. The panel in the Shore temple depicts Śiva sitting in the same lalitāsana pose but with the left leg dangling, instead of the right as in the earlier version. His lower right hand, not in the chīn mudrā, is stretched out horizontally while the lower left is in the dhyāna mudrā. The number of diagonal bands across the chest has increased from the single one of the early style. The headdress towers above the face. Umā, seated in the same pose, turns her body and faces the observer directly. She supports herself on her left arm. The other arm encircles the baby Skaṇda. A fillet-like member, pinched in the middle, appears beneath her tall headdress. The ornaments include necklets and a diagonal string crossing her body. The number of anklets has increased from the single one of the early period. Flying gaṇa are no longer present. Instead Brahmā and Viṣṇu have now been included within the panel, the former on the left near Śiva, the latter behind Śiva and Umā. As usual, rampant lions divide the sculptured panels on the outer walls

Fig. 324. Somaskanda panel, later version, Shore temple, Mamallapuram.

of the temple. Continuous sea-spray has almost effaced many of them.

The structural temples, such as the Shore temple at Mamallapuram and those at Panamalai and Kanchipuram, belong to the Rajasimha period. The *Kailāsanātha temple* at *Kanchipuram* is not only the oldest and most characteristic of the Pallava structural temples, but also the richest in sculptural adornment. The temple complex consists of the main shrine (formerly called Rājasimheśvara, now Kailāsanātha), its detached multi-pillared mahā maṇḍapa (now united to it by a later hall built in between), and the Mahendravarmeśvara shrine near the entrance. The last-named has a śālā type vimāna with an ardha maṇḍapa attached to it. Fifty-eight small dvitala vimānas, addorsed to the inner side of the surrounding prakāra (wall), line the courtyard. An embryonic form of the gopuram forms the entrance at the eastern side. Near it, outside the walls, stand eight small shrines, six towards the north and two to the south. At some distance from the whole temple complex, on the eastern side, a *naṇdi* reclines on a raised platform. Sculptures adorn all the buildings that make up the temple.

On the wall behind the sixteen-sided linga in the garbha griha of the main vimāna (or Kailāsanātha proper) is a *Sōmāskaṇda* of a later type. On either side of Śiva, but behind him, stand Brahmā and Viṣṇu. Umā sits facing forward, holding Skaṇda on her lap. The garbha griha of the Mahendravarmeśvara shrine has a similar representation.

Devakoṣtas (niches), flanked by bulging pillars based on rearing vyāḷas, adorn the walls of the vimānas and maṇḍapa. They enshrine Śaivite figure sculptures framed by elaborate makara toraṇas, with running floral decoration on their jambs. Makaras (crocodiles), facing inward with open jaws, and spiralling foliage behind them, flank the lintel.

A niche on the southern wall of the garbha griha in the Kailāsanātha temple, Kanchipuram, enshrines a beautiful figure of *Yoga Dakṣiṇāmūrti*. A yogapaṭṭa (band to hold the legs in the meditation pose) binds Śiva's left leg— resting on the seat beside him in jackknife bent—to his body. He holds his front right hand in the yoga mudrā pose and the front left in the abhaya mudrā. The back right hand holds an akṣamālā (prayer beads) while the back left bears agnī (fire) or a lotus bud. One of the two deer under his seat locks up at him affectionately. Under Śiva's lower right elbow a cobra raises its hood. The tranquil shade of a banyan tree in the upper part of the panel forms the setting. Four gaṇa look down from under its lowest branches. The carving of Śiva's jaṭabhāra (matted locks) makes them look like strings of beads. He wears beaded jewellery around his upper arm, elbows, wrists and ankles, and large rings in his ears.

The *Lingōdhbhavamūrti* appears on the southern wall of the garbha griha of the Kailāsanātha temple, Kanchipuram. A crescent moon crowns Śiva, who stands in the middle of the open linga which resembles a diamond-shaped frame around the figure. The eight-handed god holds a śūla (trident), paraśu (axe) and akṣamālā (prayer heads), among other items. One hand is held in blessing. On top of the linga Brahmā rides on his haṁsa vāhana while Viṣṇu in the form of Varāha burrows into the earth underneath, in a vain attempt to discover Śiva's limits. Gaṇa fly above the dvārapālas flanking the niche.

In one of the niches on the northern wall of the Kailāsanātha garbha griha at Kanchipuram a ten-armed *Durgā* sits in the alīdhāsana pose on her lion vāhana. In accordance with the Āgamas each hand, except the lowest right which is in the kaṭyavalambita mudrā, holds a weapon donated by the various gods. She wears little jewellery. Her headdress resembles that of the GajaLakṣmī panels in Mamallapuram. The snake hood appears here as in the Yoga Dakṣiṇāmūrti panel.

The row of shrines forming the mālika (chain) along the prakāra of the Kailāsanātha temple, are all dedicated to Śiva, except the two at the north and south, in line with the garbha griha. These are dedicated to Brahmā and Viṣṇu, the other two deities of the Hindu Trimūrti. The panels on the external walls of these mālika shrines contain a variety of figures belonging to both the Śaivite and Vaiṣṇavite iconography, such as Gaṇeśa, the saptamātrikas, Chaṇḍeśa and other subsidiary deities. However, to preserve the inferior sandstone out of which these figures were carved, they were crudely plastered over near the beginning of the twentieth century.

Some of the better preserved panels of these mālika shrines include a representation of *Śiva cutting off one of Brahmā's four heads* and holding it in one of his left hands together with his broken symbols. Brahma sits despondently just below, while beside him, right under Śiva, sits a devotee in an attitude of amazement. The deep carving, not too much plastered over, reveals fine light and shade effects.

*The Tripurāntakamūrti* in the Kailāsanātha

temple, Kanchipuram, shows Śiva riding his chariot after defeating the Asuras who live in three forts. He sits in the alidhāsana pose, but his eight arms hold no weapons. Brahmā, here with three faces, acts as charioteer. The four horses, telescoped together and only partly shown, represent the four Vedas.

Among the beautiful dancing images of Śiva, that of *Śiva dancing in the tālasamsphoṭita mode* holds particular interest. While his left leg rests on the ground, the right is raised knee-high. The dance poses of his hands include the patāka mudrā, abhaya mudrā and the gajahasta. From the flow of his matted hair issues Ganga, seen on the top right with her hands in the anjali pose (hands joined together). Pārvati sits at the right, resting on her hand. The various poses and the halo of hair give a feeling of movement.

An *Alīdhanṛttamūrti Śiva,* one of the most graceful images found here, appears many times on the exterior wall of the temple as well as in the subsidiary shrines attached to the temple, half seated in the alīdha pose. Three of his hands assume the chatura, patāka and gajahasta poses while the other five hold various weapons such as a trident, axe and snake. The long arms and high makuṭa add to the god's dynamic and majestic impression. The kaṭisūtra (girdle cloth) streams out decoratively at the sides.

Here the figures are tall and slim, and have heart-shaped faces. In the early ones ornamentation is kept to the very minimum—a single anklet, plain yajñopavīta, kaṇṭhi worn close to the neck, and kuṇḍalas on elongated ear lobes. The headdress varies, ranging from medium height to very tali. Below the kirīṭa they often wear a fillet-like member, which in the later period is pinched or constricted in the centre. The ladies' clothes usually consist of an ankle-length lower garment, or at times of a kucha bandha (band tied across the breast), as in the Durgā panel in the Mahiṣāsura maṇḍapa. Sometimes the kucha bandha have shoulder straps.

The *Vaikuṇṭha Perumal temple* at *Kanchipuram* has a form of Viṣṇu in the sthānaka (standing), āsana (sitting) and śayana (reclining) posture in each of the superimposed cells.* The walled enclosure of the temple has a pillared verandah around it. Bas-relief panels, some with inscriptions, cover its walls. A narrow moulding divides the panels into two rows. This flat moulding was meant for titles to explain the sculptures which represent the genealogy of the Pallavas from mythical beginnings, their rise to power through battles, as well as coronation and court scenes, portraits of kings, illustrations of sacrifices and the like. Inscriptions on the south-east corner explain the election of Nandivarman II to the Paliava throne, his entry into Kanchipuram and his coronation.

## THE CHOLAS AND PANDYAS

The Cholas (ninth to twelfth century A.D.) who came into power under Vijayalaya, united almost the whole country south of the Tungabhadra. The early Chola temples, built under the patronage of Vijayalaya and his son Aditya I, may be found all over the Tanjavur district and the neighbouring areas. Since the Cholas were fervent Śaivites, the majority of the sculptures are Śaivite. Sculptural decorations consist mainly of mouldings and images of deities in niches both on the outer temple walls and in the interiors.

Though Chola art evolved out of Paliava and Early Pandyan forms it has certain characteristics of its own, which as yet have not been sufficiently studied by scholars. Generally speaking Chola art shows greater movement and rhythmic freedom of action within well-formed outlines. The human figures appear less abstract. The Cholas differentiate between the representation of gods and human portraits. The latter reveal distinctive individuality and character rather than an idealised type as in the case of the gods. Decorative details, however, have become more elaborate. While the Pallavas carved in low relief, the Chola statues stand out in bold high relief or in the round. Most of them face forward—profiles are seldom shown. In Chola sculpture the minor figures flank the devakoṣtas (niches) in the earlier period. Later they are incorporated within the large compositions.

The earliest sculptures, belonging to the time of Vijayalaya, include the Mātrikās (mother goddesses) in the temple of *Vijayalaya Choliśvaram* in *Narttamalai* (Tiruchirapalli district). Seated in the virāsana, *Vaiṣṇavī* (Government Museum, Pudukkottai) holds the śankha (conch) and chakra (wheel) in her two upper hands while the lower left rest on her lap and the right assumes the abhaya mudrā. The tall kirīṭa makuṭa adds to her height. Her lower garment reaches down to her ankles. Lines indicate the drapery folds.

* However, A. H. Longhurst's Paliava Architecture Part III, No. 40, Memoir of the Archaeological Survey of India, PI. VII shows the reclining between two seated figures of Visnu in the cells.

The keyūras (armlets) are very broad—a type common in Chola sculptures.

A *viṇādhara Dakṣiṇāmūrti* (Government Museum, Pudukottai) of the same *Vijayalaya Choliśvaram temple* in *Narrtamalai*, sits holding a vina in the two lower hands. The upper hands hold a triśūla (trident) and an akṣamālā (prayer beads). The hair, a mass of curls, resembles a large wig. As in the Vaiṣṇavī figure, the kaṭisūtra (cloth tied across the hips) falls in the centre. These very early figures look a bit stocky.

The later sculptures, especially the Chola bronzes, have a more ethereal appearance. They greatly exaggerate the length of the body and limbs in proportion to The head.

The *Koraṅganātha temple* at *Srinivasanallur* contains two niches with beautiful figures of *a man and woman.* The gently moulded curves of their well-proportioned bodies makes them look alive. With his right hand in the abhaya mudrā, the man stands with, the right foot a little bent. His smiling face, modelled with extraordinary delicacy, bespeaks compassion and understanding. Undistracted by many ornaments, the artist modelled the lady's body to perfection (Fig. 325). She looks down,

Fig. 325. A lady, Koranganatha temple, Srinivasanallur.

smiling shyly. The slender limbs contrast with the curving body.

In the *Brihadiśvara temple* at *Tanjavur*, the greatest example of Chola art, the architectural design generally takes precedence over lavish, detailed decoration. Unfortunately the images on the outer walls of the garbha griha were at a later date covered with a layer of stucco, thus hiding much of the features and attributes of The original carvings. They are distributed in two tiers of devakoṣṭas divided by a prastāra which demarcates the lower and upper section of the vertical wall of the vimāna. Each devakoṣṭa alternates with a decorative pilaster. The upper tier or section has figures of *Śiva Tripurāntaka* in different poses, in niches corresponding to those of the lower tier, all of which enshrine various forms of *Śiva,* except those on either side of the four entrances of the vimāna which are flanked by dvārapālas.

The *Kalārimūrti*, an interesting panel on the southern wall of the garbha griha of the *Brihadiśvara temple* at *Tanjavur* portrays Śiva trampling Yama, the god of death. The whole figure shows lively movement. With left leg raised he points his toes for a kick. The pupils of his eyes give him an awesome appearance. With the motion of his body, the ear ornaments dangle forward—this detail being carefully represented. The lower garment hangs in folds between the thighs. Bells adorn his left anklet, Śiva's hair appears above his elaborate headdress.

The *Śiva Natarāja* on the southern wall of the garbha griha of the *Brihadiśvara temple*, *Tanjavur*, displays the characteristic Dravidian combination of dynamism with massivity, but this whirling movement is more easily expressed in the metalwork. On top of the niches some of the deities are carved in small round panels. The interesting innovation is the small-scale synoptic narration of the stories connected with the various forms of Śiva in the niches. They appear in the spaces on either side of the kumbapanjarams (Fig. 208; decorative pilasters) which alternate with the devakoṣṭas. The rear half of the exterior wall of the maṇḍapa has similar niches in two tiers enshrining deities like Gaṇeśa, Viṣṇu with consorts, GajaLakṣmī, Sarasvatī, Mahiṣāsuramardinī, Bhairava etc.

*Dvārapālas* flank all the various entrances— in all nine pairs of imposing and powerful figures with elaborate headdresses. They symbolise the power of the Cholas.

Inside the vimāna, on the outer faces of the inner walls of the garbha griha, opposite the entrance to the pradakṣiṇa pātha, are recesses framed by huge pilasters enshrining more than life-size figures. There is one on each cardinal direction. The entrance to the garbha griha is on the eastern side. The southern side has a fierce seated Śiva carrying a sword and trident; the western side has a ten-armed dancing Śiva with Viṣṇu playing the drum. On the northern side Devī sits on a lotus in the padmāsana pose, with akṣamālā (prayer beads) in one hand.

The second storey of this inner pradakṣiṇa pātha has an interesting set of one hundred and eight square panels running all around like a belt. Each panel contains a four-armed Śiva in different karaṇas (dance postures), thus giving a clear documentation of the karaṇas mentioned in Bharatha's Nāṭyaśāstra. All except twenty-seven of the hundred and eight panels have been completed. This is a precedent to a similar series on the gopurams of the temple at Chidambaram where ladies perform the karaṇas.

The Chola king Rajendra, son of Rajaraja Chola, built the *Brihadiśvara temple* at *Gangaikondacholapuram.* Proud of his victories, he wished to immortalise them by erecting a temple to house the god of gods, Mahādeva. The sculptures here are monumental in conception—one of the reasons perhaps for its incomplete state. The layout of its sculptures imitates that of the Brihadiśvara temple at Tanjavur. The carvings include forms Śiva, such as Natarāja, Kalārimūrti, Gangādhara, as well as forms of Viṣṇu and Brahmā. The sculptures are bold and excel in fineness those of its their model.

Fig. 326. Chandeshanugrahamurti, Tanjavur.

In the *Chaṇḍeśānugrahamūrti panel* (Fig. 326), Rajendra has himself portrayed as the fortunate Chaṇḍeśa, crowned by Śiva himself. As the god covers his crown with a long garland of flowers, Chaṇḍeśa, on the lower left, bows in adoration. The happiness at this high honour conferred on him by the god radiates from his face. Majestic in bearing, tall and sturdy, yet smiling, Śiva dominates the other figures. Pārvatī sits close to him, with her right foot raised and her right hand close to his left arm while her left hand rests on her lap. Gaṇas fly about in the background.

The *Airāvateśvara temple* at *Darasuram* (of slightly later date than the Brihadīśvara temple at Gangaikondacholapuram) has some exquisite sculptures of goddesses, attendants and various forms of Śiva. The most renowned of these is Śiva as *Bikṣātana with Riṣi Patnī* (Tanjavur Art Gallery). In the temple itself an outstanding piece of sculpture is a *Mohini* in polished blacks tone.

Together with the Cholas, the Pandyas (1100–1350) were the main ruling families of south India. The early art of the latter dynasty closely resembles that the Pallava cave temples. For. example in the *temple* at *Tirumalaipuram,* sculptures of *Brahmā, Śiva, Viṣṇu* and *Gaṇeśa* recall the early Pallava figures in simplicity of ornamentation and detail of carving. The *rock temple* at *Kalugumalai* contains other examples of this art. On its vimāna is a heavy seated figure of *Śiva* in the lalitāsana, flanked by fat gaṇa. His florid smiling face and the meagre ornamentation are characteristic of this period. The drapery falls loosely on his lap. Similar to Śiva is the figure of *Viṣṇu,* seated in the vīrāsana. Here the drapery covers the legs fully. The artist has given particular attention to delineating the plump limbs and the ornaments of the gaṇas on either side.

*One hundred and eight karaṇas of Bharata's Nāṭyaśāstra* with explanations above each one in grantha writing, flank the gateways of the *eastern and western gopurams* at *Chidambaram.* Of mixed late Chola, Paliava and Pandyan origin, they being to the later Pandyan style. These figures may have been installed in the period of Kopperunjinga, who assumed the title 'Bharatam Vailan' and took the credit for building the superstructure of the gopuram; or they may have originated earlier in the time of Kuiottunga II.

## THE VIJAYANAGAR PERIOD AND THE NAYAKS

When the Cholas fell, South Indian artists lost their generous patronage. However they found support in the rising Vijayanagar empire (1335-1565) founded by Harihara, Kampa and Bukka, the sons of Sangama. Though the Vijayanagar rulers encouraged the various arts, quality was sacrificed to quantity of output and variety of subject-matter. Since these rulers favoured Vaiṣṇavism, most of the sculptures of this period represent Viṣṇu's ten avatāras, Kṛṣṇa's pranks and scenes from the great epics. These appear in reliefs on the pillars in the maṇḍapas and elsewhere in the temples.

During this period the custom established by the Guptas in North India of placing statues of the river goddesses Gangā and Yamunā at the entrances of temples was introduced in the South. In bold relief and mounted on their vāhanas, they flank the entrances under the gopurams. Thick foliage rises from each vāhana's mouth, entwines its body and rises above it in circles which frame reliefs of Viṣṇu's ten avatāras.

Many Vijayanagar sculptures represent social activities such as hunting scenes, dances and koiattam. Great numbers and varieties of birds and animals, represented realistically in groups occupy some of the panels. Flowers and creepers decoratively arranged also form much of the sculptural adornment during this time. They appear on pilasters and pillars in very bold relief or completely in the round. The portraits of the Vijayanagar period revert back to types and no longer show individual characteristics.

The conventionalised Vijayanagar sculpture has lost the natural charm of Pallava and Chola carvings. The figures look rigidly stiff and formal, the features lack expression and the noses are pointed. The clothing, ornaments and decorations have become even more elaborate than in the later Ghola period.

Some of the most outstanding contributions of the Vijayanagar empire are the Hindu monuments of that once mighty city of Hampi (near modern Hospet, Karnataka). But when the empire fell beneath the onslaught of the Muslim invaders these works were almost completely annihilated. An idea of the magnificence of Hampi can be had from the glowing accounts of the Portuguese traveller Paes, who visited the country during the reign of the greatest Vijayanagar monarch, Krishnadevaraya. An enlightened king, statesman as well as patron of art and literature, he is credited with the construction of many buildings, both religious and secular. The only remains at present include the Hazāra Rāma temple, the Viṣṇhala temple, and parts of the royal palace buildings such as the havā mahal and the bath. These secular buildings already reflect Islamic influences, not only in the use of the cusped arches but in its basic conception which is entirely Muslim.

The *Viṭṭhala temple* at *Hampi* (Pl. 5.4) consists of the cella, maṇḍapa, kalyāṇa maṇḍapa and the *stone ratha* (chariot; Fig. 215), a freestanding structure in the courtyard. Floral motifs decorate the four wheels of this chariot, and the projecting hub of each terminates in a lotus flower. The wheels rest on a base encircled by a broad band of carving with hunting scenes. A pair of lively elephants, delightfully modelled with raised trunks guard the entrance to the stone ratha.

Rows of narrative reliefs, mainly. hunting scenes, adorn the base of the *throne platform*, one of the secular structures at *Hampi.* Because the artists used hard, brittle granite the sculpture had necessarily to be less refined than at Belur or elsewhere, where soft stone enables intricate and deep carving. In spite of this basic drawback, the artists produced some remarkably fine works full of life. In the relief showing the *hunting of deer*, one of the pair of hunters at the far right draws his bow, ready to discharge the arrow. The deer flee before them, but one unfortunate animal has been wounded, while another turns its head to look back. The flight of the deer and their instinctive fright have been realistically represented. Above this is an undulating floral motif with peacocks placed at intervals, and above this lotuses alternative with haṁ sas (geese).

Another scene shows *men training horses.* In this relief one horse tries to throw its rider, while another, with a man holding a stick behind it, walks calmly in front. At the extreme left a man pulls another horse forward with a rope. Scenes of deer *hunting* appear below. One man pierces a hart, while another has just discharged an arrow. Two more hunters show up in the background. On the right, a man holding a whip leads a deer forward.

In *Kanchipuram* the Vijayanagara kings contributed to temples by way of additional maṇḍapas of exquisite craftsmanship. The hundred-pillared maṇḍapam of the *Varadarāja temple* has *rearing horses and hippogryphs with riders* decorating the pillars. *Monolithic stone chains*, yet another proof of the sculptor's skill, adorn the corners of this maṇḍapa.

The kalyāṇa maṇḍapa of the *Jalakanteśvara* in the *fort temple* at *Vellore* is another cioyingly rich example of the Vijayanagar period. The pillars have *yālis*, and *rearing horses* with riders in different hunting poses. Their charging forward with raised weapons on agitated animals and the wounded beasts depict the wild hunt.

After the battle of Talikota in 1565 and the fall of the Vijayanagar empire, many of the chieftains, such as the Nayaks (sixteenth to eighteenth century A.D.) established small kingdoms. The *horse court* in the Raṅganāthaswāmi temple at *Srirangam*, an example of Nayak art in the far south, has a whole row of columns fronted by monumental *horses rearing up* (Fig. 216; Pl. 16.1). With their open mouths and metal trappings, they look ferocious and awe-inspiring. Their riders, smaller by comparison, brandish swords. Below, men thrust swords at men or animals beneath the horses' feet. Warriors carrying swords or just standing with one arm raised nonchalantly, or rearing animals, or men sitting on warriors' shoulders, uphold the raised hoofs of the horses. The sides of the bases of the pillars supporting these horses have small panels with various religious images or scenes from the Puranas.

A shrine in the *Raṅganāthaswāmi temple* at *Srirangam*, known as the *Veṇugopālaswāmi sannidhi*, possesses some beautiful sculptures in the niches of its outer walls, including slim, delicate *maidens* holding various musical instruments, while one carries a parrot. Particularly arresting is the figure of *Veṇugopāla*, with his legs crossed and playing the flute.

One of the finest pieces of Nayak sculpture in the *thousand-pillared maṇḍapam* of the *Meenāksi temple complex*, *Madurai*, is the so-called *Saraswatī*, goddess of learning and music. Her oval face, typical of this period, tilts to her left, revealing the large coil of hair on her right side. She holds a vīṇā in her hands. The parrot sitting on her right shoulder makes some scholars suppose that the statue represents Rājamātangi who is described as list- tening to a parrot talking while she plays the Vīṇā. She seems to step forward with her right leg. Fine wavy lines, vertical at the top and oblique around the legs indicate the drapery. She wears many ornaments not only on the lobes but on the outer edges cf the ears as well. Three large rows of gems reach almost to her knees, while jewelled bands encircle her shins and ankles.

In the *pudu maṇḍapam* (or Tirumal Nayak's choultery), *Meenākṣi temple complex*, *Madurai*, stands the well-known *Meenākṣi-Sundareśvara marriage group* (or Meenākṣī's kalyanam). This piece of sculpture, dating from Tirumal Nayak's time, shows the marriage of Śiva and Parvati, with Viṣṇu, the bride's brother according to Hindu mythology, performing the kanyā dānam or kannikadāma (giving away of the bride) ceremony by pouring water out of the kamaṇḍalu (water vessel) while Śiva reaches out his right hand to receive the bride. Placing her right hand in his, she looks down demurely with a shy smile on her lips. She is much smaller than the two gods whose height is greatly increased by their tall kirīṭas. She wears a bulbous headdress which curves to her left. All three figures are heavily laden with jewellery.

The *Kambattadi maṇḍapam* in the Meenākṣi temple complex, Madurai, has another *Meenākṣi-Sundareśvara marriage group* (Fig. 327) of a much later date which some consider in some ways superior, though the latter appears almost like a copy of the earlier model except that it has a sculptured tree behind the group instead of the garland-like decoration back of the one in the pudu maṇḍapam.

The *portrait statue of Tirumal Nayak* with his four queens in the *pudu maṇḍapam*, *Meenākṣi temple complex*, *Madurai*, has been defaced by inartistic painting over the sculpture, without consideration for the features which the original had faithfully reproduced. The aṣtaṣakti maṇḍapam has another of his portraits which has not been painted over. Even so the one in the pudu maṇḍapam still shows individuality, with his nose which is not sharp like those of his predecessors, his somewhat slanting eyes, compressed lips, and small chin between wide jaws. Over his body, stout like that of the other Nayaks, he wears rich brocade clothing, and many necklaces, rings and armlets. A tight cap covers his forehead almost to the eyebrows. A pair of queens with a lady attendant flank him on either side.

Fig. 327. Meenakshi-Sundareshvara marriage group, Kambattadi mandapam, Meenakshi temple complex, Madurai.

The *Rāmaswāmi temple* at *Kumbakonam* also has sculptures belonging to this period, as for example *a lady* (Fig. 328) whose large staring eyes in her round face recall the Tirumal Nayak group. With her left arm on her hip, she holds a lotus bud in her right hand. The hair is parted at the centre and combed flat. Rows of pearls encircle her neck, and a longer pearl chain with a square pendant reaches below her breast. Delicate lines indicate the lower garment, tied high up on the waist. Rows of ornaments, starting with a broad floral band bordered by pearls and followed by alternating motifs of leaves and bells, surround her hips right down to her thighs.

Fig. 328. A lady, Ramaswami temple, Kumbakonam.

The figures of this period generally look rather stiff, with oval faces, wide staring eyes and deeply curving pencil line brows. Sometimes the nose looks almost like a flat triangular piece fixed on the face. The upper lip is usually narrower than the lower. Broad shoulders and sturdy legs are other noticeable features. The drapery is diaphanous and often tied high at the waist.

## SOUTH INDIAN BRONZES

Although metal sculpture was practised all over the country during the post-Gupta era, the South Indian bronzes, the finest specimens of which were cast during the Chola period, need special mention. The Chola images were made of bronze with an unusually high percentage of copper. The statues were cast by the 'cire perdue' (lost wax) process, of which two methods were practiced in India from earliest times. In the first method, they prepared a wax model. Over this they made a clay mould. When this mould became hard, they melted the wax out and poured liquid metal into the clay mould. When the metal had cooled, they broke the mould and gave the image the final chasing and burnishing.

In the second method, they first made a clay model and coated it with a layer of wax to reproduce exactly all the details of the form. Then they covered the wax with a thin layer of fine clay. When this dried, they added more layers until a thick outer shell had formed. This is called the negative. Then they heated the statue until the wax melted and ran through openings, leaving a space between the clay mould and the negative. Into this space they poured liquid metal to replace the wax and reproduce ail the details of the figure. When the metal had cooled and hardened, they broke away the outer shell. Then the figure was chased with a chisel and polished. The first method gave a solid figure, the second a shell.

In various Indian manuscripts especially in the Mānasāra—an ancient text-book on image-making—there is a fairly detailed description of the process for solid figures. The highly specialised craftsmen who made these images were organised in guilds known as the sthapathis. The larger bronze figures, called utsava-devas (festival idols), varying from about 30 cm to 1.5 m in height, were made especially for carrying in ceremonial processions because the dhruva-devas (main shrine images of a temple), usually made of stone or wood, are too large and heavy to be borne. In addition many smaller bronze images were made for private use.

The chief patrons, the Chola emperors, generally encouraged Śaivaite images since they were staunch tfaivites themselves. Various versions of Śiva Natarāja are the most popular figures cast in bronze. Other subjects range from different Hindu deities to Śaivite saints.

The *Śiva Natarāja* from *Tiruvarangulam* (National Museum, New Delhi), dancing in the chatura pose, dates from the tenth century. Its beauty lies in the springy poise of the body and the harmonious movements of the limbs. Their near symmetry provides both balance and variety. The upper arms and left forearm echo the position of the thighs. The legs almost form a diamond under the trunk which rises straight on its axis. The back arms bend upward at right angles from the elbows, while the front arms bend forward. It combines graceful gestures with the portrayal of the geometrical perfection of human proportions.

From the aesthetic point of view this is considered the most outstanding bronze statue in the National Museum.

The best known *Śiva Natarāja* (Pl. 16.2) from *Tiruvalangadu* (Madras Museum), dates from the eleventh century. This four-armed and three-eyed figure dances with the right foot resting on the prostrate demon Apasmara. His front left arm reaches across the body to point at the left leg raised in a dancing movement. The right front hand is in abhaya mudrā. A cobra, now missing, originally coiled around the forearm. The back right hand holds a kettle drum between the second finger and the thumb. The back left hand holds the flame. The hair is tied into a knot at the top. Originally an elliptical aureole with prabhāmaṇḍala (arch of flames), which is now missing, surrounded the figure. Though there are many bronze statues of Śiva Natarāja with the same ico- nometric details, none of them has the same graceful elasticity embodying the idea of dance. Its fame has spread ail over the world. The great French sculptor Rodin declared it 'the most perfect representation of rhythmic movement in art'.

The *Natarāja* from *Velankanni* (Government Museum, Madras) is a good example of a Natarāja with the prabhāmaṇḍala (arch of flames) completely preserved.

Of the other forms of Śiva in bronze, the *Kalyāasundara* from *Tiruvelirkkudi* (Ar Gallery, Tanjore) shows Parvati being given in marriage to Śiva by Viṣṇu and Lakṣmi.

The *Sōmāskaṇda* from *Tiruvangadu* (National Museum, New Delhi) is particularly well modelled, with a four-armed Śiva sitting beside Pārvatī. Both wear elaborate crowns. Unfortunately little Skaṇda's figure is broken away.

Almost unmatched for grace and beauty of form among the known Chola bronzes is the *Vṛṣabhavāhana* (Pl. 16.3) from *Tiruvengadu* (Art Gallery, Tanjore). It dates from 1011. This beautiful standing figure represents Śiva leaning against the naṇḍī, but the figure of the bull has been lost. Śiva's right arm was made to rest gracefully on the animal's back, and his elbow seems to lean on the naṇḍī's head while his fingers caress its forehead. The posture, with bent torso and crossed right leg resting on the tip of the toe, is most graceful and artistic. His hair, skilfully arranged in the jaṭabhāra manner, can hardly be distinguished from the snake coiled among his locks.

The eleventh or twelfth century South Indian bronze *Pārvati* (Freer Gallery, Washington), with its greatly elongated body and limbs, combines a certain dignity and liveliness despite the rather primitive features. Lugs at the base for inserting poles show that it was meant to be borne in processions.

Popular from the eleventh century onwards, bronze images of Śaivite saints personify the idea of bhakti (devotion) by showing through posture and gesture the enraptured readiness to listen and respond to divine inspiration. One of the best loved of these saints was *Sundaramurtiswami*, called on his wedding day to become Śiva's disciple. The image in Kansas City *(James Baldwin Collection)*, standing in the tribhanga pose as though suddenly arrested by a rapturous vision of Śiva, may represent this Hindu bard. The figure combines a sense of tranquillity and movement in the ecstatic gesture of the hands and fingers, and the breathless expression of the face. The features and proportions are exaggerated, as seen in the lotiform eyes and lithe, eiongated limbs and torso.

Though most of these exquisite bronzes have been scattered in museums both in India and abroad, an unexpected discovery not long ago has revealed *eighty bronze statues* that lay hidden away in a dark room in the *Chidambaram temple.* Most of these are twelfth and thirteenth century Chola bronzes, but some date from the tenth century and others belong to more recent times. This collection of early bronzes in a single temple is unique. The most beautiful specimen among them is perhaps the 80 cm statue of Umā (Pārvati), dated 917 A.D.

## PAINTING

Judging from literary evidence, the art of painting must have flourished in India from very early times.Indian painting may be divided into murals and miniatures. All paintings consist of the paint, the ground and the support. The pigments in the paint need a binding substance which preserves it and prevents it from flaking. In murals, the paint

Fig. 329. Chaddanta Jata

ka, cave No. 10, Ajanta.

unites itself to the ground (lime plaster) which is applied to a durable support (e.g. stone or rock). Murals (generally wall paintings as the name implies) are naturally bigger than miniatures, where the name itself implies smallness. The support of these miniatures is more perishable and smaller in size than in the case of murals.

## MURALS

Leaving to specialised treatises the complete enumeration of murals in India with only scanty remnants, we shall mention only those with sufficient remains, namely the Ajanta caves under the Satavahanas and the Vardhanas (contemporary to the Guptas), the Bagh caves (also of the Gupta era), the Badami caves under the Early Western Chalukyas, the Ellora caves under the Rashtrakutas, the Kailasanatha. temple in Kanchipuram, the Talagirīśvara temple in Panamalai and the Jaina cave in Sittanavasal (Pudukottai district) under the Pallavas, the Brihadiśvara temple in Tanjavur under the Cholas, the Virupaksa temple in Hampi and the Virabhadra temple in Lepakshi under the Vijayanagar rulers, and the Jain temple in Tiruparutikundram during the Nayak period.

### AJANTA

The Ajanta caves lie about a hundred and six km by road north of Aurangabad, cradled in the precipitious face of the Maharashtra plateau set like a huge amphitheatre. Below this splashes the little stream Waghora, after leaping down in seven precipitious steps from the highlands above, forming little pools at each step and cutting a deep crescent-like ravine at the base before coming out into the open valley. To this idyllic sylvan setting, so conducive to meditation with the peaceful grandeur of its natural surroundings, sheltered from the wind, but filled with the music of running water, the singing of birds and the voices of animals, and fresh with the smell of sun-kissed greenery, came the Buddhist monks in the second century B.C. In order to seek shelter from the rains during the monsoon, they scooped caves out of the volcanic rock of the mountain side.

Since the caves are not far from the ancient trade routes, in course of time they attracted travellers and pilgrims. Merchants and princes hoped to attain salvation by contributing to the construction of Buddhist temples. Pictures and inscriptions show that pilgrims and traders came here from far and near; and the art style was diffused as far as China and Japan.

In order to proclaim the message of the Buddha to these pilgrims, the monks employed artists who turned the stone walls into picture books of his life and teaching, Representations from the Jātaka tales illustrate his intelligence, noble character, selfless service and compassion by means of legends from his previous births. Though the pictures depict stories related to the Buddha, the artists portrayed at the same time the costumes and customs of their own epoch, especially the extravagance of court life. Nor did they overlook life's comedy and tragedy, its pathos and humour. The main theme of the stories seems to be the enduring teachings of the Buddha as against the impermanence and vanity of life, hanging precariously like the thin coat of paint on the rocky durability of the walls.

The paintings cover not only the walls and ceilings of the caves, but also a time-span of seven hundred years, thus showing changes in style. The monastery, one of the oldest in the world, first reveals the Hinayāna period (200 B.C. to 200 A.D.), where the Buddha is represented only by symbols, or in his supposed previous existences as related in the Jātaka stories. We see this chiefly in the chaityas of cave No. 10 (second century B.C.) and cave No. 9 (first century B.C.). Near the end of the fifth century A.D. (c. 450-650 A.D.) the Mahāyāna influence took over, as seen in caves No. 16, 17, 2 and 1. This brought with it the portrayal of the Buddha in human form.

Soon a decline set in, both in the style and in the importance of the caves. The latter may have resulted from a new trade route. Except for a mention of the caves by a Chinese traveler, Huien Tsang, in the first half of the seventh century, nothing more was known of them till they were rediscovered by some army officers in the early nineteenth century.

The paintings reveal a well-developed technique right from the earliest caves, but we know nothing about its development nor about the artists themselves. While they were restricted to the representation of Buddhist motifs on the walls, they were more free to use their initiative and imagination on the ceilings.

Because of their remote location, these

works of art have been fairly well preserved from human vandalism. Unfortunately, some weakness in the technique as well as the ravages of time have led to their deterioration. To discover the means of preserving them, the archaeologists have studied the technique in great detail.

The caves, having been chiselled out of porous volcanic trap rock, provided the requisite rough surface to hold the plaster. This, however, having been made of mud and vegetable fibres instead of lime and gypsum, was not very durable. Though they strengthened the mud plaster, the vegetable fibres were subject to attack by insects and to bacterial decay. The medium of the Ajanta painting was tempera. They applied the mud plaster in two coats—the first was rough, to fill in the pores of the rocks and cover the chisel strokes, and then they laid a fine coat of lime plaster over it. Generally they allowed the entire ground to dry before applying the colours.

The painting was done in the following way: first they drew the outlines in red ochre. Afterwards they applied the colours and renewed the contours in brown, deep red or black. The pigments of the paint came mainly from the local volcanic rock—various shades of ochre and green resulting from the weathering of the basalt. The only organic colour used was lamp black. Later on, expensive lapis lazuli was imported and ground to make blue pigment. The other colours were vermilion, terra-verde and ultramarine. However, since they bonded the colours chiefly with animal glue and vegetable gums, these too suffered from insects, oxidation and water seepage. As a result, many of the paintings have been spoiled by blistering and flaking. As they used only tempera technique, employing a glue to bind the colour, the paint did not fuse into the plaster as would have been the case if they had tried the true fresco method, applying pigments mixed with water on wet plaster.

In the early paintings at Ajanta, like those found in caves No. 9 and 10, the contours of the figures do not stand out as boldly as they do in the later paintings under Mahāyāna Buddhism, where the artists wanted to produce perfection in whatever they created. They used deep colour washes and laid emphasis on the outline. By patches of light colours they highlighted the facial expressions. The human and animal forms reveal a variety of graceful poses.

Various methods helped to create the illusion of depth. For the backgrounds they used cool or deep colours which produce a shadowy impression, while warm or light colours make the figures stand out distinctly. At times they used spots of black to intensify the colours further, as for instance the golden brown head of the Bodhisatva in cave No. 1 stands out in relief against the speckled dark green background.

With their attenuated poses, supple limbs and artistic features, the paintings at Ajanta bear close resemblance to the sculptures at Amaravati—due, perhaps, to some artistic traditions based on religious beliefs common to Amaravati and Ajanta which influenced both groups.

The Ajanta paintings show a great variety of dhammilas (hair styles)—from the simplest to the most elaborate. Never left plain, the hair was decorated with pearl strands and diverse gold jewellery, and the women wore ear and finger rings, hanglesand armlets, necklaces, tiaras and diadems of various patterns.

The earliest paintings were those of *caves No. 9 and 10* under the patronage of the powerful Satavahana kings who ruled in Maharashtra and Andhradesa and who were also responsible for excavating the famous caves at Nauaghat, Nasik, Bedsa, Bhaja, Karle and Kondane. These caves are chaityas—excavated during the Hinayāna phase of Buddhism. Paintings illustrating scenes from the life of Buddha, Jātaka and Avadānas (life stories) interspersed with floral and animal motifs, cover the walls, pillars and ceilings. The extraordinarily well-developed style testifies to a continuity of tradition started centuries earlier, perhaps in the painted decorations of the royal palaces of the Nandas, Mauryas and Sungas of northern and eastern India. Undoubtedly, these murals are the work of a well-trained guild of painters skilled in draughtsmanship, and not of bhiksus, as thought by many scholars. One notices striking resemblances between the headgear, jewellery and facial features of these paintings and the Satavahana sculptures at Bharhut and Sanchi.

On the left wail of *chaitya No.* 9 at *Ajanta* is a mural representing a group of votaries approaching a stupa with strips of cloth entwined in their hair. The figures are grouped naturally and their movement is convincingly portrayed. The design of their jewellery and the folds of the clothes have been artistically rendered. The next scene shows a profusely *decorated stūpa, surrounded by a wall with two gates*, one of which resembles those at Sanchi.

Musicians beating a drum and blowing a trumpet and a conch appear near the toraṇa on the right side of the court. Outside the enclosure, towards the right, stand a pair of trees and beyond them a barrel-vaulted vihāra. The final scene shows the *devotees on their home-ward journey*, indicated by an apsara flying towards a house where several ladies seem to await them. This painting shows the artists' love of variety in the position of the devotees' hands.

The paintings in cave No. 10 show the Chaddanta Jātaka, the Syāma Jātaka and the arrival of a raja with his retinue to worship the bodhi tree.

The Chaddanta Jātaka in cave No. 10 (Fig. 329) is an excellent example of the earlier phase of Ajanta painting. Since the anthropomorphic representation of the Buddha was not permitted during the early or Hinayāna period, they selected a Jātaka dealing mainly with the life of the Buddha in a previous incarnation as an elephant. According to the story, in one of his former incarnations the Buddha appeared as Chaddanta, an enormous, six- tusked elephant. With his two wives, Mahā-subhaddā and Chulla-subhaddā, he lived in a golden cave near a lotus lake fringed by a thick forest. Having heard that a grove of sal trees was in full bloom, he went there accompanied by his wives and sportingly shook the branches of a tree. But while flowers and leaves fell on Mahā-subhaddā, only dry twigs and ants rained on Chulla-subhadda. The latter did not take this as a mere coincidence. Holding him guilty of favouritism, she nursed a grudge against the royal elephant and starved herself to death, praying to be reborn as a beautiful queen of Varanasi. Her prayer was granted. After she had gained the affection of the king as his wife, she feigned a great illness and said she would die unless the six tusks of the famed elephant were brought to her. In order to save her life the king sent two hunters, Sonutara and a companion to kill him. Following the queen's directions, the hunters reached his abode. With a poisoned arrow Sonutara shot the elephant, who (being a Bodhisatva) realised immediately that the queen of Varanasi had once been his wife. He went so far as to help the hunters pull out his tusks. When the queen saw the tusks, she died overcome with guilt and grief.

The painter of this mural grouped the forest episodes and those in the royal court separately but without adequate consideration for chronological sequence. The different scenes run from left to right on the wall of the right aisle, behind pillars 2 to 12. The first scene shows a group of elephants in their forest habitat. On the extreme left, a python, partly encircling a tree, has caught in its coils the hind leg of an elephant which struggles to free itself while several other elephants rush to its help. Another elephant tramples a crocodile to death. Further to the right appears the royal elephant with six tusks and white hide, with clearly marked pink spots to represent the flower petals which had fallen on him. He appears on a larger scale, and his shape is superbly drawn. His erected tail and the raised trunks of his attendants who precede him show that they have sensed danger. Altogether some fifty elephants, painted in different poses, show the artists' skill in boldly handling these bulky forms even in back and head-on views.

The next scene shows him after being shot, lying down and dying yet helping the hunter to cut off his tusks. Even though this part of the painting has been damaged, the hunter in striped clothes sawing through three tusks is clearly visible, as well as his companion tying up the tusks. The next scene shows Sonutara carrying them in slings hung from a pole on his shoulders.

Further to the right, another group of elephants bathe in a lotus lake with their leader Chaddanta. An attendant had presented the lotus to the Bodhisatva, who gives it to Mahā-subhaddā after sprinkling its pollen on his own head. This lake scene shows the painter's great skill in drawing the elephants so true to life in various poses. Even in such a restricted area, one feels that the huge creatures have ample room to move about. A variety of lotus flowers in different stages of bloom fill the background.

The pictures of the elephants in the wilderness are followed by the palace settings. These too do not follow a strict chronological order. The first scene of the story comes more to the right, with the queen asking the king for the tusks. Then going from right to left we see the king giving the order to the hunters to bring them. The next scene shows the hunters returning and the queen dying of remorse. Her cot with its lathe-turned legs and the pair of brass ewers on the floor are noteworthy because such shapes continue in use even today. In the last scene, the king and queen with attendants go in procession to worship at a vihāra. It seems to depict an episode immediately after the king's wedding when the queen tried to gain his confidence by her charm.

The entire mural, with its extraordinarily detailed representations of the Jātaka story, exemplifies all the characteristics of the early Ajanta period and may be compared to a similar relief at Sanchi (Pl.10.1). The outlines are firmly drawn. The ornaments and details of the costumes date it to the period between the second and third century B.C.

Fig. 330. Shyama Jataka, cave No. 10, Ajanta.

The *Śyāma Jātaka* (Fig.330) in *cave No.* 10, also belonging to the Hinayana period, illustrates the Bodhisatva's love for his blind parents in a previous incarnation as Śyāma. The scene on the left shows Piliyakka, the king of Varanasi, accompanied by ten attendants, wearing the turban characteristic of Bharhut, and armed with spears and bows. Three of them have rhinoceros-skin shields of unusual shape. The king's horse follows him, and like similar examples at Ajanta, the rather clumsy drawing of the animal contrasts with the skillful treatment of the ruler himself, whose pose, as he draws the bow, is very cleverly portrayed. Two plantain trees stand on the right, and from the top of one of them a male figure, no doubt a forest spirit, signals to the king, but too late, that he should not shoot.

In the next scene, set between the plantain trees, the king's arrow pierces Shyama through the heart as he carries a pitcher of water. The ruler, seen beside the dying boy, repents of his hasty shot and vows to take care of Shyama's blind parents as if they were his own. The third setting shows the restoration of Shyama's life and of his parent's sight through their prayers to the goddess Bahusodari. Shyama, thus restored, addresses the king, whose astonishment is manifested by the stoop of his body and the lowering of his arms. Another figure close to the ruler may be the forest spirit of the first scene. An interesting feature of the mural is the skillful drawing of the deer which, according to the legend, tamely followed Shyama about the forest. They gallop to his cottage after he has been shot as if to inform his parents.

In the last scene Shyama sits on a deerhide in front of his cottage, teaching the ten duties of a ruler and the five precepts to the king who listens attentively to the Bodhisatva. A buck and doe in front of Shyama gaze at him with devotion. The design of the cottage, which stands by a pond, holds interest for a student of architecture. It is circular in plan and has a vaulted roof. The framework of the wall consists of upright wooden posts ringed both in the middle and at the top by circular bands as of cane or bamboo, while the panels between are filled with leaves. The door has a curved lintel, similar to the architraves of the toraṇas leading to the religious buildings of that time.

The mural in *cave No.* 10 entitled *the arrival of a rājā with his retinue to worship the bodhi tree* shows a king, surrounded by attendants and soldiers, apparently at prayer before the bodhi tree. The central group of this mural (Fig. 331) includes the raja with ten ladies and a child. Instead of a crown the raja wears a band of jewels resembling a serpent's hood at the right side of his head. And only in this mural do we see ladies covering their heeds and backs with veils or scarves (cf. square No. 1 in the middle of the figure). Over the raja's heed a lady holds an umbrella, a sign of royalty.

Fig. 331. Arrival of a king with his retinue to worship the bodhi tree, cave No. 10, Ajanta.

Another great wave of artistic activity spread over Ajanta between 450-650 A.D. At this time the monastery was governed by the Mahāyāna order of Buddhists and patronised by the Vakataka rulers. The absence of examples during the intervening period both here and elsewhere does not preclude the existence of paintings on more perishable materials like wood and plaster.

The paintings in caves No. 16 and 17, as well as in 2 and 1, are believed to have been completed at this time. From an inscription in cave No. 16, wnich states that Varahadeva, the minister of the Vakataka king Harisena (475-510 A.D.) dedicated it to the Buddhist order, it is inferred that its execution took place in the later half of the fifth century A.D. Cave No. 17 too belongs to the same period, being a donation by a feudatory of king Hari- sena. On stylistic grounds, caves No. 1 and 2 may be assigned to the first half of the sixth century A.D., towards the end of the Vakataka rule.

These later paintings differ in two important aspects from those of caves No. 9 and 10. A certain attempt at memory portraits has been made, since the faces show individual characteristics. Secondly, the important personalities have been emphasised by difference in size, as in the painting of mother and child (cave 17) and the Buddha preaching in the Tuṣita heaven (cave 17).

The Vakataka period occurred at the same time as the Golden Age of the Guptas. Since a marriage alliance existed between the two dynasties, it appears quite likely that ideas and techniques were exchanged. The style of the later murals at Ajanta reveals a merging of two streams of art: the Satavahana and Ikshvaku of Andhradesa, and the Gupta art of northern India. This resulted in the classical style, which had a far-reaching influence on all the painting of the country for centuries to come. It was essentially a narrative mode, admirably suited to the purpose of illustrating scenes from the life of the Buddha, Jātakas and Avadānas (life stories) and thereby propagating the religious beliefs of Buddhism.

A higher degree of craftsmanship, incorporating all the rules laid down by ancient Indian treatises on painting and aesthetics, marks the execution of these religious themes. One finds here, for instance, the six saḍāngas (limbs) of painting as enumerated in the Vishnudhar- mottara (a text on aesthetics), such as rūpabheda (differentiation of forms and proportions), pramāṇam (line and its quality), bhāva- yojana (expression of emotions), lāvaṇya-yojana (creation of grace and lustre), sadṛśya (portrayal oflikeness) and varṇikābhanga (harmony of colours).

Though these elements were present already in the earlier period, we see a greater crystallisation of conventions in the later phase. Draughtsmanship and brushwork reach a peak of perfection. One notices a fascinating mastery of fluid yet firm lines, the basis of all painting. Long sweeping brushstrokes outline the graceful contours, while short, skillful ones achieve a certain plasticity of form. Though they had not yet discovered the laws of perspective and shading to create three-dimensional modelling, yet by subtle gradations in the same colour, and by highlighting the nose, eyelids, lips and chin, the figures come to life and emerge from the flat wall surface. The variations of tone have been accomplished within a limited palette of earth colours—ochres, reds and browns for warm flesh tones, green for the lush vegetation, White for the gleaming pearl jewellery, and black for the hair, accentuated by a judicious use of lapis lazuli blue.

Male and female figures conform to the traditional standards of beauty, with their arched eyebrows, long almond-shaped eyes, straight noses, full lips and slightly pointed chins. Minute changes in the poses, gestures and direction of the faces create variety, so that, surprisingly, there is neither obviousness nor monotony. The aristocratic elegance of the male representations is matched by the sinuous grace of the justly famous and beautiful female figures.

The artist seems to delight in story-telling and, in an eclectic manner, provides a contemporary setting for the episodes. The Ajanta murals present a vast and lively panorama of the life of those times: kings and queens with their royal entourage in all its pomp and splendour, dancers, musicians, hunters and tradesmen, people of all professions and castes, scenes from everyday life, religious ceremonies and political intrigues—all these faithfully reflect contemporary life and customs. The artists show a keen interest in worldly affairs and joyous appreciation of nature. Animals, birds, trees and flowers are lovingly pictured with an eye to their beauty of form—so that they are a joy to behold. Heavenly beings and creatures of fantasy, such as kinnaras (half bird, half man), fish-tailed animals and legendary birds intermingle freely with terrestrial creatures. In the midst of this fascinating array of things real and imaginary, the compassionat e Buddha and the benevolent Bodhisatvas fulfill their roies. The true genius of the artist infuses the scenes with serenity and inspires reverence for the Buddha.

The paintings in cave No. 16, patronised by the Vakataka king Harisena in the last quarter of the fifth century A.D., include the conversion of Nanda, the conception and scenes from the Buddha's early life, such as the visit of the sage Asita, the young prince at school, and the practice of archery, as well as other scenes from his life, such as the Tusita heaven.

The *conversion of Nanda* above the second and the third cells of *cave* 16 shows him sitting on the floor. The inclination of his head may indicate his being shaved by a barber. This is conjectural because the top part of the mural, which may have shown the barber at the task, has disappeared. Back of this scene, towards the right, is a pavilion with round pillars where Nanda sits among a number of monks, his face a picture of sadness (probably because of the separation from his beautiful wife. The Buddha observes Nanda's melancholy from between the two pillars at the extreme right.

The *conception scene* in the corridor above the first and second ceil doors of *cave* 16 tells of Māyā's dream about her future son appearing in the form of a white elephant. This scene is badly damaged. In the second scene, which shows her telling the dream to king Suddodhana in the royal chamber, the figures of the king and queen have faded considerably. The skill of the artists, however, remains discernible in the graceful poses of the eight women in the round pavilion next to the bedroom. The expressions of their attractive features are natural and lively, and their postures show an elegance typical of Indian women.

The *scenes from the early life of the Buddha, namely the visit of the sage Asita*, the *young prince at school* and his *practice of archery* adorn the top of the first and second cell doors of *cave* 16. In the visit of the sage, Asita holds the baby in his arms, recognising his future greatness. The young prince at school is shown in a classroom with three other boys, and a teacher with half-shaven head. The young prince's attire looks somewhat Persian, with his conical hat and profusely embroidered coat. Below the school scene is an open court, where one of the four boys draws a bow, while another stands aside under a banyan tree watching the skill of the future Buddha.

The paintings in cave No. 17, also patronised by Harisena, but a quarter of a century later than the works of cave No. 16, portray Indrā and apsaras, apsaras and gandharvas adoring the Buddha, the Haṁsa Jātaka (the story of the golden goose), the mother and child before the Buddha, the Mātrpoṣ aka Jātaka (the story of the elephant who had blind parents), the Viśvantara Jātaka (the story of the prince devoted to alms-giving), the Buddha preaching in the Tuṣitā heaven and the toilet scene.

Fig. 332. Indra with apsaras, and a kinnara couple (square LX), cave No. 17, Ajanta.

The back wall of the verandah to the left of the door of cave No. 17 shows *Indrā with apsaras* (Fig.332) flying amidst the clouds. With his group of musicians Indrā appears frequently in Buddhist legends. Profuse jewellery, a magnificent crown and fair complexion identify the figure of Indrā. The bent knees, and strands of pearls across his chest flying backwards, suggest movement forwards. A dagger and sword hang from his belt. To Indra's left appears a crudely featured gan- dharva with iarge wide nose and small sunken eyes. He carries an ektara (stringed musical instrument). Two beautiful apsaras, both holding cymbals in their hands, accompany Indrā on his right. One has a swarthy complexion while the other is ruddy. Their bodies are modelled in the round. The artist has adorned them with a profusion of jewellery. By the impasto technique he emphasised the pearls and sapphires. The delineation of the clouds is very conventional. At the top right of this scene (square LX) appears a kinnara couple.

Exquisite figures of *flying gandharvas* and *apsaras* adorn the back wall of the verandah of *cave* 17. The best known, the *apsara* (PI. 17.3) with the turban-like headgear and wearing a rich necklace, earrings and anklets, has a very refined face. Her eyes are half closed and her left hand rests upon her breast—a masterpiece in itself. The sharply delineated fingernails accentuate the elegance of the graceful fingers curving around the cymbals she holds.

The first episode of the *Haṁsa Játaka* (Fig.333) in cave 17 represents the capture of the golden goose, while the second scene shows the haṁsa sitting on the throne before the king

Fig. 333. Hamsa Jataka, cave No. 17, Ajanta

preaching the law to the royal couple and court attendants. The artist produced delightful pictures of women in different attitudes and poses, and rendered the various details faithfully, especially the king's crown and the jewellery of the women. The flock of birds in the first episode looks very natural, with the geese in different stages of flight (cf. rectangle LXVIII at right of figure). This Jātaka theme seemed to be a favourite of the Ajanta artists, as it appears not only here but also at Boro- bodur.

*The mother and child before the Buddha* (Pl. 17.2), another wall painting in *cave* 17, presents a sublime and intensely human theme based on stories in the Buddhist texts regarding the visit of Gautama to Kapilavastu at the invitation of his father, King Suddodhana: how he begs for alms from door to door, how Yasodhara, his wife, adorns herself and takes her son to meet him, and how at last both she and her son Rahula join the sangha. The painters have shown the Buddha's visit to his wife and to their home. Fully adorned, she had come out with her child to meet him. The artist tried to express the human emotion and love in the heart of the woman, and the Buddha's indifference to worldly attachments, his mission being to point out the path of truth to humanity at large. The Buddha appears on a larger scale to indicate his spiritual superiority over ordinary human beings. The mother and child look very small by comparison. However, the Buddha's head inclines significantly towards her, showing compassion mingled with love. The features have become obliterated, but the eyes remain clear and their meditative gaze suggests the mind's absorption in high thoughts. A green halo surrounds the Buddha's head, and a vidyādhāri holds an umbrella (a symbol of sovereignty) above it, while flower- garlands fall from the sky.

Below, near the door, stand the Buddha's wife and son, the latter looking up at his father with mingled affection and awe, and (at his mother's suggestion) asking for his inheritance. His outstretched hands and expectant gaze reveal his plea. The Buddha replies, 'The wealth he asks for is liable to change and to cause trouble; I will give him instead the seven-fold noble wealth which I received at the foot of the bodhi tree and make him the owner of an inheritance beyond this world'.

The Buddha's wife has been shown with all the charm of natural beauty, but far more striking is the appealing gaze she casts on her husband, with feelings of affection mingling with reverence. This picture is one of the finest portrayals of feminine emotions and elegance. The colour-scheme, too, shows refined taste. The orange robe of the Buddha contrasts with the dark background, while the pale green halo accentuates the golden-brown head. The light tones of her dress and complexion bring out the young woman's femininity.

The *Matṛposaka Jataka*, the story of the elephant who nurtures his blind parents, in *cave* 17, is divided into two sections, one above the other. The upper part depicts the events at the royal court, the lower the forest scenes: the capture and return of the white elephant. The upper left shows a pillared hall, where a king presides on his throne, while his pose suggests ease of mind. His face, especially the eyes, indicate deep thought. A pair of chauri- bearing maids stand behind the throne on either side. Near the one on the left is a beautiful, richly-clad lady (perhaps a queen) with a servant sitting on the ground adjusting her anklet and another attendant on her left. The maid to the right holds a flower and a dish of fruits. Behind her appears a man, either the guard or forester who brought the news of the noble elephant. In front of the king sits another man, perhaps a minister, gazing attentively at his master.

This upper section deals mainly with the attempted feeding of the elephant after his capture. The king sits under a shamiyana (canopy) with four attendants, one carrying a tray of food, another attentively awaiting orders, and a third receiving something from the ruler. Below, two short-

Fig. 334. Matriposhaka Jataka, cave No. 17, Ajanta

statured aborigines sit by a tub of food prepared for the elephant beside which stands a small carriage loaded with laddus (sweet-balls). To the right, a servant bows under the load of grass he carries.

A group of hunters armed with spears appear on the right, while a pair of elephants, used as decoys in the hunt, occupy the extreme upper right-hand comer. Below stands the captured elephant, whose unusual colour and immense size accord with the words of the Jātaka, 'All white he was, a magnificent beast'. His inaction and refusal of food lead the king to order his release after the reason has been explained.

The lower part of the painting is still more striking (Fig. 334). The capture scene shows the great elephant bound by strong ropes around the hind legs and trunk, and goaded to a fast stride by the trained elephant-hunters armed with spears. Before him two officers ride on horseback, and behind a prince, similarly mounted, carries a spear like the hunters.

The elephant's return to his blind parents after his release appears above the capture scenes. His trotting gait suggests his joy. A prince on horseback, attended by four guards, follows to witness the reunion, while three spearsmen run ahead to clear the way to the pool, indicated by lotus flowers, and a masonry wall to signify its edge. The elephant pours water over his mother's head while the blind parents caress him.

The *Viśvantara Jātaka* (Fig. 335), the story of the generous prince, appears on the wall of the left corridor of *cave* 17. The first episode shows Prince Visvantara in his royal chamber breaking the news of his exile to his young beautiful wife Madri (of square LVIII at right of figure), who accepts it with the grave

Fig. 335. Visvantara Jataka (breaking the news and departure through the palace garden), cave No. 17, Ajanta.

expression characteristic of her noble breed. The next scene shows their departure through the garden of the palace (cf rectangle LVII of the figure). Above the first and third cell door they take their leave in an ornamental chariot drawn by four horses while a big crowd looks on.

In the course of his journey Visvantara gives his horses to four Brahmins. Then he donates his chariot to another near Mount Vamaka, the place of his exile. The delineation of this Brahmin—scantily clad, with a shaven head and dangling moustache—is a masterpiece of Ajanta art, very much a realistic portrayal.

The painting between the third and fourth cell doors is well preserved. It represents several incidents. The one at the bottom left corner (Fig. 336) shows Visvantara relinquishing his children to the rapacious Jujaka. The indignation depicted on the children's faces and the portrayal of Jujaka reveal the artist's skill in understanding and reproducing human emotions and character. Jujaka has a goatlike beard and wiry hair covers his head. His boldly defined limbs seem to move with a rhythmic sweep. The square umbrella over his head to protect him from the sun appears like a touch of humour added to the grim story. In the next scene (of square LXXI at right of figure) Jujaka appears in the court of Visvantara's father, King Sanjay, demanding a ransom for the release of the children. Jujaka's sinister character is artistically pictured in the parrot-like nose, small vicious eyes and broken teeth, revealed by the glee on his face at the jingle of money being poured into his scarf. Beside the king sits the queen with one of the children—perhaps Jali—and in front of him, seated on cushions, appear a few crowned figures, one of them having a greenish complexion.

On the right hand comer below the court scene is a lake with birds and lotus flowers in full bloom. Their leaves cover the entire surface of the water, and with the white lilies and the birds' feathers give the mural a bracing freshness amid the sordid human scenes.

Cave No. 2, though a small vihara without much architectural significance, displays a rich wealth of decoration in sculpture and painting in its interior. Exuberantly sculpted motifs decorate the pillars while the walls have murals such as the birth of the Buddha, the Buddha in various attitudes, votaries bringing offerings.

*Votaries bringing offerings* in *cave No.* 2 has been compared to Botticelli's Spring or Primavera, but the technique, ideals and the feelings are typically Indian. The composition includes five ladies, scantily dressed in diaphanous

Fig. 336. Visvantara Jataka, (giving away the children and ransoming them from Jujaka), cave No. 17, Ajanta.

cholis (blouses) and short saris. This contrasts vividly with the rich head-gear and elaborate hair-styles. The figures are modelled in dark pink and outlined in a lighter shade. Since no other tints have been added, the complexion looks dark.

Architecturally, *cave No.* 1 is the finest in Ajanta and its paintings and sculptures possess excellent workmanship and beauty. Numerous paintings adorn this cave, the major ones being: the Sibi Jātaka, Māra's temptation of the Buddha, Bodhisatva Padmapāṇi, the offering of the lotus to the Bodhisatva, a bhikṣu at a palace door, a king going out to attend a hermit's sermon, a king conferring with his wife and a Persian embassy.

The *Śibi Jātaka* (the story of the pigeon) adorns the wall of the front aisle between the main doorway and the window to the left of *cave No.* 1. The tale concerns a pigeon which took refuge with King Sibi when chased by a hawk. He compensated the hawk by giving it the pigeon's weight of his own flesh. In the first episode, the king, depicted much larger than life-size to show that the story revolves around him, sits on a long throne decorated with a canopy and jewellery. He reveals surprise at the blue and white pigeon which has just alighted on his lap by the unnatural position of his left hand and by turning the pupils of his eyes to one side. The next scene to the right depicts the king standing in an open courtyard beside a pair of scales. His open hand hanging low indicates that he offers a sacrifice. In the third episode, below the first two, peacocks dance with joy at the king's generosity, while a man and a number of yogis on the left watch them. The contrast of colours in the painting reveals exquisite taste. Both the modelling and brushwork are excellent. Intricate details such as jewellery have been beautifully rendered.

In *Mārā's temptation of the Buddha* in *cave* 1, the Buddha, conventionally represented, sits in the centre practising austerity. Mara's army, a mixed crowd including his ravishing daughters, as well as grotesque dwarfs and mischievous imps, surround the Buddha to distract him from his meditation. The delineation of all the faces reveals a keen observation of human nature.

The *Bodhisatva Padmapani* (Pl. 17.1) in *cave No.* 1 is unanimously considered the masterpiece of Indian art. The Bodhisatva, called Padmapāṇi because of the blue lotus in his right hand, dominates the, composition by his colossal size. The other figures seem to revolve around him. From the waist he inclines slightly to the right. This suggestion of grace continues through the tilt of his head and the gesture of his hand. The elegant features, high forehead and downcast eyes produce an impression of dignity and serene meditation. The highlights on cheek, nose and chin, as well as on the arms and breast, together with the warm colours and inward shading of the outline, give fullness to his appearance. The high sapphire crown indicates his royal birth. Here jewellery is not profuse but select. He wears a pearl and sapphire necklace. The long strings of pearls over the left shoulder, across the chest and falling over the right arm are highly artistic. The scanty dress may perhaps suggest an ascetic life, but at Ajanta kings generally have no upper garment. The cloth round the loins resembles a dhoti of striped silk worn in an ascetic style.

To enhance the Bodhisatva's pearl-grey complexion, the artist placed a swarthy princess beside him. A highlight on the lips and nose animates her face. The modesty, serenity and purity of her eyes reflect those of the Bodhisatva. She wears a fine gauze bodice and short skirt over her exquisitely modelled limbs. The lotus in her hand may indicate that she is his wife. She turns slightly away from him, as was the custom of Indian women when appearing in public with their husbands. Behind the pair stand a maid and a chauri-bearer with a long blue coat and a conical hat with upturned flaps, in the manner of the Scythians. Many of these had settled in the Deccan and became Buddhists at this time. The mace-bearer on the Bodhisatva's right raises one finger to show his watchful readiness. Near him stand two other dark attendants. Conventional red bands indicate a background of hills, where frolicking monkeys, a pair of peacocks and human and semi-divine beings watch the Bodhisatva. Their vivacity contrasts with the serene dignity of the central figures. The graceful contrast of colours heightens the general rhythm: the pale green foliage blending with the scarlet of the bird's feathers, and the drapery and jewellery enlivening the sober flesh tints. The name and history of the artist of this wonderful mural will never be known, but the fading painting will tell the story of his genius and skill in most eloquent terms as long as it survives.

## BAGH

At Bagh, in Madhya Pradesh, another flourishing Buddhist monastery existed in the fifth and sixth centuries A.D. In their heyday the nine caves were real storehouses of paintings and one of the viharas was in fact named Kalayana (abode of art). Unfortunately, little remains now except fragments and blotches of colour which continue to decay with every passing day. Luckily, artists made many copies of them. From these, and the best preserved murals in cave No. 4 we can see that the paintings of Bagh resembled the best works of Ajanta in style. Here too the earth pigments were enriched by the brilliant blue of lapis lazuli. As Bagh lay on a trade route, it may be that this colour was first introduced here and travelled to Ajanta later on.

On one of the pilasters of *cave No.* 4 at *Bagh* we find an interesting figure of *Bodhisatva Padmapani*, remarkably akin in pose and ornamentation to the famous Bodhisatva Padmapāṇi at Ajanta. On stylistic grounds, scholars consider lt as the forerunner of the great masterpiece in cave No. 1 at Ajanta.

On the outer wall of the verandah of *cave No.* 4 appear many scenes as yet unidentified either from a Jātaka or Avadāna. Particularly interesting is the *hallisālasya* (folk dance) in which women playing musical instruments form a double ring around a pair of male dancers. The pulsating rhythm in the poses and gestures of the figures is complemented by the judicious use of colours. There is also a procession of people riding elephants and horses as magnificent as any such theme found at Ajanta. Birds and flowers too are delineated with exquisite charm.

## BADAMI

The splendid caves and temples at Badami in the Deccan were commissioned by King Mangalesa of the Western Chalukya dynasty. On the evidence of an inscription, the Vaiṣṇava *cave No.* 3 at *Badami* can be assigned to around 578 A.D. The same inscription shows that the court painters of Mangalesa continued the excellent tradition of Ajanta, even though only fragmentary paintings survive on the inside of the cave. The *court scene* depicts a dark prince, possibly King Kirtivarman, Mangalesa's elder brother.

## ELLORA

Remnants of mural paintings at Ellora are found in the Kailāsa, Lankeśvara, Indra Sabhā and Gaṇeśa Lena temples, but only in the Kailāsa they are less decayed. The porch celling of the second story of the *Kailāsa temple* has the most important of these murals. The first series of paintings were made at the same time as the excavations, while the second series was done several centuries later. The earliest paintings show *Viṣṇu and Lakṣmi* borne through the clouds by garuḍas. Clouds fill the background of the panel. The thin sinewy figures have sharp features and long pointed noses. The protruding eye typical of the later Gujarati style appears for the first time in Ellora. In the later series the main composition shows a procession of *Śaiva holy men.*

Though the *Jaina rock temples* at *Ellora* were also profusely painted, only few remains survive. The flying *apsaras* are quite graceful but the repetition of *Tirthankaras* lacks vitality.

In south India wall paintings have been found both in the early rock-cut caves and later structural temples. They were executed under the royal patronage of the Pallavas, Pandyas, Cheras and Cholas during the course of many centuries. Unfortunately, most of the examples are very fragmentary.

## PANAMALAI, KANCHIPURAM

The Pallavas were great patrons of all art forms. A noteworthy example of Pallava painting is the graceful figure in the *Talagiriśvara temple* at *Panamalai* of *a goddess* in an Ajanta- like post. Vestiges of a group of *Śiva*, *Pārvati* and the infant *Skaṇda* as well as other paintings remain in the *Kailasanatha temple* at *Kanchipuram* but because of their extreme deterioration a critical appraisal of the technique and style of other Paliava paintings can scarcely be made.

## SITTANAVASAL

The earlier examples of Jaina painting in the south are found in the *Sittanavasal cave* in the Pudukottai district. The name Sittanavasal literally means the abode of the siddhas (Jaina saints who have won their spiritual freedom). Originally the cave temple was completely adorned with mural decorations, but what

Fig. 337. Gandharva, Sittanavasal.

survives today are the remnants on the ceiling, capital and the upper parts of the pillars. These paintings resemble the Ajanta murals. They were discovered by Professor Jouveau Dubreuil* On the ceiling we find a beautiful scene showing a *lake with lotuses in bloom*, with fish, geese, buffaloes and gandharvas sporting about. On the two pillars of the façade are the *two dancing apsaras*, but only one has been well preserved. The figure of the apsara is drawn with considerable grace and charm, with broad hips and slender waist. The upper part of the body is bare except for some jewellery. The figure of a *gandharva* (Fig. 337) has a quite austere appearance. His fishshaped eyes, however, have a rather softened look. The face is in three-quarter profile. In one hand he holds a lotus bud while the

* There are two layers of paintings. The earlier one is assigned to the ninth century.

other hand assumes the simhakarṇa mudrā. The colours are subdued, the contours flowing, the curves sinuous and the facial features elegant. All these characteristics echo the Ajanta masterpieces.

## TANJAVUR

Fig. 338. Rajaraja I and his guru Karuvurar, Brihadishvara temple, Tanjavur.

Under the powerful rulers of the Chola dynasty there was great budding activity during the tenth and eleventh centuries. The magnificent *Brihadiśvara temple* at *Tanjavur* reflects the glory of the Chola emperor Rajaraja I. Originally the entire wall and ceiling of the dark passages around the garbha griha were painted on a scale befitting the architectural grandeur of this great temple. These were over-painted during the Nayak period. Careful removal of this later layer has revealed parts of the exquisite original paintings, mainly on the western and northern walls.

The Tanjavur paintings were applied to a surface of soft lime plaster made gleaming white by using powdered conch shell and mother-of-pearl. On this surface the painters drew the outlines and filled them with flat colours to indicate the skin and drapery. Finally they added the details with a delicate brush. They used a wide range of colours such as yellow and red ochre, black, brown earth, terra-verde and the blue of lapis lazuli.

On the *western wall* Śiva appears as *Toga Dakṣiṇāmūrthy,* majestically seated on a tiger skin and watching the dance of two apsaras. Present also are the other gods and celestial beings playing musical instruments. Some royal personages form the audience in the foreground while Cheraman (saint) Sundara and a Chola chieftain approach on an elephant and horse. A little further on, *a Chola-style temple* with Natarāja enshrined in it is depicted. Beyond this they painted a huge *Natarāja* with priests and devotees on one side, and the royal family (including the Rajaraja and his three queens with followers) on the other side. A little further on they portrayed *Rajaraja I and his guru Karuvurar* (Fig 338). Lower down they pictured an *episode from the life of Cheraman Sundaramūrthy.*

The masterpiece of Chola painting, on the *northern wall,* shows Śiva as *Tripurāntaka*—a gigantic eight-armed warrior riding a chariot driven by Brahmā. Kārtikeya and Vināyaka, riding their respective vehicles the peacock and mouse, face the demons aggressively while

Fig. 339. Dancer, Brihadisvara temple, Tanjavur

their wives cling to them. With fluid lines, warm flesh tones and deep colours, this painting is a remarkably skillful composition portraying the emotions of vīra (courage), rudra (anger), karuṇa (pity), vismaya (wonder) and hāsya (humour). Tripurāntaka's alīdha pose follows the Pallava tradition. But here, in the typical Chola fashion, he stands in the abhanga pose, crushing the demon Apasmara (lion) with one foot. This heroic stance might well symbolise the zenith of Chola power.

The women in these murals soften the mood considerably. Their facial features are delicately modelled, with lustrous elongated eyes, straight noses and full sensitive lips. The hair is elaborately dressed with flowers, strands of pearls and star-shaped ornaments. They wear scanty clothes: a band across the breast and a diaphanous patterned ankle-length skirt. The figure of a *dancer* (Fig. 339) in the pṛṣṭaswastika pose has a supple form and slender waist. The head tilts slightly. The lines revealing the sensuous curves are firmly drawn, while the colours have a subdued tone.

## HAMPI, LEPAKSHI

The Vijayanagar paintings mirrored the great revival of Hindu religion and art in South India. Wall-paintings, which had yielded in importance to ornate sculptural decorations in the temples until the fifteenth century, now made a comeback. At Hampi, under the rule of Krishnadeva Raya (1511-1528 A.D.), the magnificent Vijayanagar (city of victory) sprang up with temples, palaces and bazaars.

The important examples of paintings in the Vijayanagar style survive in the Virupakṣa temple at Hampi and the Vīrabhadraswāmi temple at Lepakshi, and some fragments in various other South Indian temples that had been enlarged under Vijayanagar rule. But nothing remains of any paintings in the palatial buildings since the Muslim invaders razed their brick and timber superstructures to the ground after the Battle of Talikota in 1565.

The *Virupakṣa temple* at *Hampi* has murals representing episodes from the Mahabharata and Ramayaṇa, the exploits of Śiva and dynastic history. The series of paintings on the ceiling of its maṇḍapa needs repairs and cleaning. One of the scenes shows *Vidyaranya* (Fig. 340), the guru of Harihara and Bukka, the founders of the Vijayanagar empire, being carried on a palanquin and followed by a retinue. The composition shows a rhythmic forward movement and does not look overcrowded.

The *Vīrabhadra temple* at *Lepakshi* contains the best-preserved paintings of this style. During the time of Achyuta Raya, two nobles who were brothers (Virupanna and Viranna) undertook the erection and painting of this temple. Originally paintings covered the ceilings of many of the maṇḍapas and corridors which form the temple complex but now they are partially damaged.

Beams supporting the roof divide the ceiling of its mukha or ranga maṇḍapa. The longest of these shows an *episode from the life of King Manunitikanda Chola*, who granted justice to a cow whose calf was run over by his son's chariot. He sacrificed the prince under the chariot wheels, but Śiva restored life to both the victims and praised the king's sense of justice.

The same ceiling has scenes from Draupadi's wedding, Kirātārjunīya (Arjuna's penance) with a view to obtain pāśupatāstara from Śiva, and the story of Bhukailāsa. The adjacent panels of Vatapatraśāyī and Vīrabhadrānu- grha exemplify the spirit of tolerance. Vaṭapatraśāyī is the aspect of Krṣṇa as a baby lying on a banyan leaf floating over the primordial waters. Since the eyes are painted in full front view, they seem to follow the viewer wherever he goes.

Next to this panel comes an interesting one showing *Virūppanna and Viranna* with their sons and guards, all standing with clasped hands. They wear long white, full-sleeved robes, with a printed cloth tied round the waist. Their conical caps belong to the same type as the one on the statue of Krishnadeva Raya in Tirupati.

Fig. 340. Vidyaranya, Virupaksha temple, Hampi.

Fig. 341. Maids attending on parvati, Virabhadra temple, Lepakshi.

Another panel from the same ceiling depicts *maids in attendance on Pārvati* (Fig. 341). The composition reveals easy movement and charming grace. The textile patterns of the sarees reveal not only the skill of the artists but also the craftsmanship of the weavers of that period. Textile designs form the borders of the paining.

Different aspects of Śiva adorn the long narrow ceiling of the ardha maṇḍapa. A colossal *Virabhadra* standing in an awe-inspiring pose, occupies the ceiling of the maṇḍapa of the main shrine.

The ceiling of the maṇḍapa of the Raghu-nāthālaya, a temple inside the Vīrabhadra temple complex, shows the first seven avatāras of Viṣṇu.

Even though the subject matter of these paintings consists mainly of mythological legends of Śiva and stories from the epics— the costumes, jewellery, hair-styles and other elements represent the life and customs of the great Vijayanagar empire.

In general, the Lepakshi paintings are highly decorative. They are no more than line drawings with no attempt at modelling in the round. Human faces usually appear in profile or three- quarter view. The figures stand with a slight tilt, both feet pointing in the same direction like the leather puppets that constitute popular folk art in the area. Most of the ladies have the same type of hair-do, but the turbans and hair-styles of the men and riṣis vary a great deal. The most noteworthy feature of these paintings lies in the exquisite textile designs both for the clothing of the figures as well as for the borders and backdrops of the scenes. Few colours have been used — chiefly earth- red, yellow-ochre, green, black and grey on a brilliant white background. Blue is missing and is replaced by green wherever necessary.

The Vijayanagar style is not a direct development of classical painting, but it serves its decorative purpose exceptionally well with its undercurrent of folk art discernible in the tableau-like placing of flat figures against a patterned background. Historically its importance lies in its influence on the later Muslim painting in the Deccan kingdoms.

## TIRUPARUTEKUNDRAM

In a Jaina temple of the fourteenth century at Tiruparutikundram we see perhaps the last remains of the mural tradition in Indian painting. The technique is tempera on lime plaster and the subject matter is both Jaina and Hindu.

Two technical details in this mural style continued a long time in the history of Indian painting. First, to represent trees, the area of foliage is covered with a single greenish colour and the leaves and branches are drawn over this in fine lines and filled in with white. This method was used later in Central Indian painting and from there it passed on to Rajasthani painting. Second, they used raised white dots of solid paint to represent the jewellery. This occurs also in Mewar, Bundi and Basohli painting.

Other than that the style has nothing worthy of note. The figures, mostly in profile, stand in a row just above the base line, without any attempt to create visual space. Only the bare facts of a story are narrated.

## MINIATURES

From literary works we know that besides murals other forms of painting also existed in India from early times but since they were done on cloth, wooden boards and other objects which do not survive, we have definite proofs of illustrated manuscripts only from the eleventh century A.D. After this period Jaina and Buddhist texts were written on palm leaves and covered with painted wooden boards. From these beginnings Indian miniature painting developed.

## BENGAL, BIHAR, ORISSA

Under the Pala kings in *Bengal, Buddhist manuscripts* were illustrated in a style reminiscent of Ajanta but adapted to the miniature scale. The sombre hues, firm lines, simplicity of composition and graceful attitudes of the figures have an appeal of their own. Painted on palm leaves, they usually represent Buddhist deities and scenes from the life of the Buddha.

Many of these works were undertaken by bhikṣus in the Buddhist universities of Nalanda and Vikramasila and show their natural aptitude for this type of painting. These leaf manuscripts, which bear a striking similarity to Pala and Sena sculpture, illustrate mainly the Vajrāyana form of Buddhism with its elaborate iconography. This ṣtyle continued in Nepal, Tibet and Burma and travelled on to the Far East with some variations.

The text most popularly chosen for illustration was the *Prajna Pāramitā Sūtra*, according to which nothing in the universe is real but all is illusion. This prajña (wisdom) was personified as the female deity Prajña Pāramitā, and the manuscript itself was considered sacred and worshipped. Many illustrated versions of this text were made in Bihar, Bengal and Orissa between the eleventh and fifteenth centuries. Some fine examples still survive.

## GUJARAT

In *Gujarat* numerous illustrated manuscripts of *Jaina texts* were produced around the same period. They usually deal with canonical subjects such as *Kalpasūtra* and *Kālakācārya-kathā.* The illustrations recall the rather stylised and somewhat monotonous paintings in the Jaina caves at Ellora. But the floral motifs, animals and birds on the wooden outer covers are quite fascinating. Most probably the style of these pātlis was inherited by the artists from their ancestors who had painted murals in the Ajanta tradition. By the middle of the twelfth century these pātlis became less interesting and their production waned.

In the fourteenth century paper became popular for miniatures. The style, however, was no longer as elegant as before. The highly artificial rendering of the pointed nose and farther eye projecting into space in profiles had become an established feature (Fig. 342). The colouring is so rich that it becomes cloying. Since wealthy Jainas commissioned the manuscripts to acquire spiritual merit they did not give prime importance to aesthetic value. It is not surprising, therefore, that the style deteriorated into set formulae monotonously repeated.

In the middle of the fourteenth century a strange element appears in the portrayal of the popular story of *Kālakācārya* — the tale of the Jaina monk Kālakā who takes revenge on a wicked king who had wronged his sister. In the illustrations of this story, while the other personages appear in the conventional style, the face and costume of the Shāhī king, who helped the monk, show borrowing from Persian manuscripts. Even the convention of the projecting farther eye has been eliminated in this case. The drawing of the horses and cloud formations also reveals the Persian influence, which entered through the Muslim sultans who ruled Gujarat in the fourteenth century and who admired Persian art and culture. Since the two countries carried on much trade, the painters employed by the rich Jaina merchants doubtlessly came into contact with Persian miniatures. This Jaina manuscript style of mixed Indian and Persian elements spread to other centres like Mandu and Jaunpur.

## MANDU

Because of its location in Central India, many styles merged in Mandu: the Jaina manuscript conventions of Gujarat, Muslim elements from Jaunpur and Oudh in the east, the Rājput idiom of the north, and the Deccani mode from the south.

At Mandu noteworthy deviations from The Gujarat style appear in the illustrations of the Jaina scripture Kalpasūtra. Instead of the strictly conventional attire, maintained for almost four centuries in Gujarat, in these places the contemporary costumes were depicted.

In the fifteenth century the strong Khalji dynasty ruled Mandu and encouraged contacts with Persia. The Nimat-nama (Book of Delicacies), painted during this period, shows a strong Persian influence of the Turkoman school. In the latter part of that century several Persian texts were illustrated in other parts of North India in a middle-class style which combined Persian and Indian elements. Though this period coincides with the Lodi rule in Delhi, there was no court or royal school of painting as such in that city.

Meanwhile in Mandu itself a new development took place under the rule of Baz Bahadur. The illustration of secular and romantic themes came into vogue, as exemplified by the Laur Chanda and Chaurapañchāsika series, as well as an early example of a Rāgamālā series.

Thus central India withessed the infusion of

Fig. 342. Illustration from Kalpasutra, showing the further eye, Mandu.

fresh and invigorating elements into the stylised and unimaginative works of the Gujarati school. After several centuries of stagnation, Indian painting started on a new course which benefited from the many changes introduced by the coming of the Mughal school.

## MUGHAL PAINTING

Inspired by Persian art, the Mughal emperors introduced a new type of painting which bears their name. They descended from Timur (Tamerlane), a Turk from Central Asia. He sacked Delhi in 1398 but his descendents conquered India only in the sixteenth century. Although a despot, Timur patronised musicians, poets and philosophers in Samarkhand, his capital. During the rule of his son, Shah Rukh, we have the first record of support given to painters.

Towards the end of the fifteenth century, Timur's power diminished and the lead fell to the Safavid kings who ruled with much splendour at Tabriz, a centre of learning and art. Here a brilliant school of Persian painting developed and the best talents were engaged to work on book illustrations for the royalty.

Babur, a descendent of Timur through his father and of the Chagtai Turk, Chingy Khan (Genghis Khan) through his mother, also inherited his ancestor's love for the arts. He had visited Herat, the capital of Timur's son, Shah Rukh, while it was at the height of its splendour as a centre of Islamic culture. There he saw the famous paintings of Bhizad Shah Musavir and his followers. During the four years of his rule in India (1526-1530), Babur longed for the familiar artistic splendour of Herat. This nostalgia of his did not permit him to understand and appreciate the art of India, his newly-conquered domain. At the same time he had to strengthen his political position which gave him little or no time for art.

Humayun (1530-1556) inherited his father's artistic inclination but lacked his greatness of character and administrative talent. Unable to consolidate his position, he was driven into exile by the Afghan usurper Sher Shah Sur in

1540. He took refuge at the court of the Persian Safavid ruler, Shah Tahmasp, where he could admire the collection of illuminated manuscripts and see the artists at work. During his fifteen years of exile, Humayun travelled extensively. At Tabriz he met two young painters, Mir Sayyid Ali and Abd-al-Samad (or Khwajah Abdus Samad), to whom he gave hope of future employment in case he regained his kingdom. Shah Tahmasp assisted Humayun in setting up a small court in Kabul in 1550. The latter invited the painter Mir Musavvir to become the chief of his book illustrators. Later on his son Mir Sayyid Ali of Tabriz and Abd-al-Samad of Shiraz joined him in Kabul and the latter gave drawing lessons to little Akbar. Humayun regained his kingdom in 1555 but died within a year.

Akbar (1556-1605) who succeeded him at the age of thirteen ruled for almost half a century. Helped at first by his regent Bairam Khan and later on his own, Akbar conquered vast territories, and by shrewd diplomacy married Rājput princesses and won the support of the proud and faithful Rājputs. By 1570 he ruled an extensive and prosperous empire and built a new capital, Fatehpur Sikri, as well as the fortress of Agra. Around him he gathered administrators, generals, artists, poets and musicians of high caliber and pre-eminence in their respective fields. Fired by a sense of history, pride of ancestry and consciousness of the role of his dynasty, Akbar took extraordinary personal interest in the religion and way of life of his Hindu subjects; and in order to make his Persian and Turkish administrators well acquainted with Indian concepts, he had the Hindu epics and religious texts translated into Persian and illustrated.

Though illiterate, Akbar had great thirst for knowledge and commissioned the illustrations of several literary and religious texts. A peaceful rule and wealth enabled him to give a free outlet to his love of art. Already prepared by the training received at Kabul, once on the throne he favoured the development of painting and called a great number of artists to his court. Going by their names, the majority of these seemed to be Hindu. He showed much interest in their work and rewarded them according to merit. He also took great care to furnish the imperial atelier with the best equipment obtainable. Thus Akbar became the real founder of the Mughal school of painting.

The royal atelier gave steady employment to many artists. A hundred and fifty or so are known since the illustrations in the manuscripts produced during Akbar's reign bear the names of the artists; not their signatures, however, since their designations were put there by clerks (munshis) employed at the court or at the imperial library. Because some were often deleted and others inscribed on them, these inscriptions do not appear very reliable. This resulted from the fact that several painters usually collaborated on one picture. Rarely do we find a work by one artist alone, this being the procedure in nearly all Indian crafts, painting included. During Akbar's reign two or more artists worked together, but not more than four or five. One made the tarrah (sketch), another the aml (painting). Occasionally a third did the chira numa (portrait) and very rarely a fourth made the surat (figure drawing). A few inscriptions name a fifth artist who undertook the rangamezi (colouring). Such a system suggests that Mughal painting was a craft more than a fine art. In the workshop the head man gave out various orders while the chief artist did the actual composition or layout. After this, lesser artists executed the various parts, one drawing the figures, another painting the background and so on until the whole was finished. In all likelihood the patron selected the artists in order to get the best results. The chief painters were Mir Sayyid Ali, Abd-al-Samad (already in the service of Humayun) and Bashawan, a Hindu.

Mir Sayyid Ali and Abd-al-Samad drilled the craftsmen in all the technical details of Persian miniatures. Many Indians such as Bashawan, Miskina and Daswanth attained great positions as court artists and Abu'l Fazl in his Ain-i-Akbari (biography of Akbar) bestows high praise on them. Bashawan is mentioned in twelve of the best miniatures illustrating the *Razmnama* (*Mahābhārata*), which originally contained a hundred sixty-nine full page illustrations. In this and the *Persian version of the Rāmāyaṇa*, Indian artists could introduce some of their cherished figure types and details of landscape. Many paintings of these two series are now in the Jaipur Royal Collections.

Under the supervision of Mir Sayyid Ali and Abd-al-Samad the imperial atelier of painters and calligraphers took shape. Their first endeavour was to complete the pictures for the earliest Mughal illustrated manuscript, the *Dastan-i-Amir Hamza* (South Kensington and Vienna Museums). Begun in 1550 under Humayun, it took twenty-five years to finish. All of the 1375 paintings, however, show consistency in style because Mir Sayyid Ali had from the start planned out the whole work in the

Safavid style, though other artists, either Persian or Indian, assisted him in the actual painting.

These early illustrations followed the Persian Safavid mode, a two-dimensional, decorative way of painting without shading or perspective, eminently suitable for manuscripts. Like most oriental arts, it made excellent use of calligraphic line-drawings filled with brilliant enamel-like colours. Usually hilly landscapes with a lofty horizon formed the background of the pictures, with the sky either in gold or pure lapis lazuli. They loved flowers, which they enlarged out of all proportions, as seen in Persian carpets and canopies. The human figures, often in stereotyped poses, were shown in three-quarter profile.

To please aristocratic tastes, the artists of Akbar's atelier illustrated classical Persian literature such as Nizami's *Khamsa*, Sa'di's *Gulistan* (moral tales), Hafiz's *Diwan* and Jami's *Baharistan.* The perfect combination of exquisite calligraphy, beautiful painting, highly decorative and elegant borders interspersed with gilding make these an aristocratic art and the delight of book lovers.

Although the Persian school of painting gave a vast stimulus to the birth of the Mughal, its influence did not last. Indians learned from it the use of brilliant colours and refinement of lines. In the animal representations, the Indian genius manifested itself with that intimate knowledge and love which characteristises it.

The *Hamzanama* series, illustrating a popular romance interwoven with many legends of the prophet Mohammed's uncle, shows the difference between the work of Mir Sayyid Ali, who maintained the Persian Safavid conventions, and the more original Abd-al-Samad who succeeded him as chief artist in the atelier when the former left for Persia in 1574 never to return. The earlier symmetrical compositions show litfle movement but the colours are warm and vivid. Ornate patterns in the architecture and costumes modify the rather coarse lines. The later pages supervised by Abd-al-Samad, show more dynamism and resemble murals, with some figures in the foreground represented only by head and shoulders. In many paintings the giant Zamurad effectively fills the space of the unusually large-size pictures (67.5 × 50 cms) on cotton cloth. Being not only a miniaturist but also a mural painter with a sense of originality, Abd-al-Samad conceived novel ways of filling the painting and also invented many bizarre characters. Thus a new style took shape under his direction, though he continued to base himself on the Persian style while modifying it to suit his subject matter. Completed in 1582, the Hamzanama series consists of fourteen volumes, each containing a hundred pictures, but hardly a tenth survive.

In 1580 Akbar received in his court the first Jesuit priests who presented him with a copy of the Polyglot Bible illustrated with Flemish engravings. The emperor ordered his painters to copy them. Soon other European paintings were brought to his court and studied with interest. Coloured versions of Dürer's engravings were also done. As a result, Mughal artists began to use perspective, to employ light and shade, to lower the horizons in the pictures, and to represent the sky more realistically with cloud arrangements and brilliant sunsets. After 1595 Mughal paintings reveal the assimilation of western techniques: modelling of three dimensional figures by means of shading and a limited adaptation of perspective.

Western influence may be seen in the fables, another favourite topic of Akbar's atelier. Here, the characteristically Indian outlook and love of animals as well as the conventional painting of water, combine with a Persian rendering of rocks and a westernised portrayal of trees and sky. The *Tutinama* (the parrot's tale) and *Anwari Suhailt* show each bird and animal with detailed realism. The paintings of the latter series are treasured in the school of Oriental and African Studies in London. One page shows seven black Kashmiri bears and a monkey rendered with keen perception of their anatomical proportions and movements. This portrayal of animals foreshadows the perfection attained under Jahangir.

Illustrations of historical manuscripts became the distinctive contribution of Akbar's atelier. These included *Tarkh-i-Alfi* (history of the world), *Jami-ut-'Tawankh* or *Jami-al-Tawarikh* (history of the Mongols by Rashid-ud-Din), *Darabnama*, *Shahnama*, *Timurnama, Babur nama*. Artists who contributed to the Jami-al-Tawarikh included Bashawan, Lal, Bhim Gujarati, Dharm Das, Madhu and Surdas Gujarati; but the most typical work belongs to Miskina, who did scenes of lamentation and dancing with westernised figures set in Indian landscapes. Together with Nanha, Burah, Saravana and Kanha (who were famillar with European art), Miskina contributed to the Darabnama.

In *Akbar trying to control a wild elephant* (Pl 17.4) which rushes on to a bridge of boats on the Jhelum we have an excellent example of diagonal arrangement used by the artist Miskina. The painting also shows that vigorous and restless energy which characterised not only the chiperor but also the illustrations of his time.

In spite of western influences in figures and shading, the colours remain enamel-like and do not blend softly, as seen in *Akbar receiving the news of Salim's birth* (Pl. 18.1) where strong colours adjoin each other. The picture shows the palace. In the queen's room on the upper storey, the maidens take care of the new-born infant. Outside the zenana but within the palace walls, musicians blow trumpets and beat drums. Servants bring food to distribute to the poor gathered outside the palace walls. They also receive money. A small landscape peers through the top right-hand corner.

The Chester-Beatty Library in Dublin has another series of sixty-one illustrations of the Akbarnama, perhaps a later version (c. 1605). The artists mentioned here include Shankar, Daulat, Govardhan, Inayat and Pidarat. Less dramatic, these compositions have an air of greater surety, as for example Balchand's *the building of Fatehpur Sikri* which appears much more restrained and less spectacular than Miskina's *construction of the Red Fort at Agra* where strong diagonals and vibrant colours predominate.

The spiritual works illustrated during Akbar's reign include *Yoga Vashisht* (Hindu Vedanta philosophy) and *Nafhat-ul-Uns* (breaths of fellowship), a prose treatise by Jami on Sufi saints. Of the thirty miniatures only seventeen survive, preserved in the British Museum. Some of these pictures contain lively glimpses of Indian villages, life and customs.

Akbar also stimulated the painting of realistic portraits—a notable contribution to Indian art. Except for some rare individual faces pictured from memory at Ajanta, Indian artists had always depicted well-defined types and ideals. Persian influence set the art of portraiture on a course of perfection rivalling that of Persia itself. Under Akbar's orders artists painted the likeness of all the important personages in his court with exquisite skill and delicate but sure lines. This exerted a great influence on later Rajput painting.

Unlike his forceful, energetic father, Jahangir (1605-27) was a man of sensibility and aristocratic tastes. Thanks to the energy and administrative talent of his father he enjoyed a peaceful rule. And with an adroit and competent wife, Nur Jahan, at the helm of political affairs, he could indulge in his hobbies. He had a prediction for the art of painting which he cultivated much more than architecture. During his residence at Allahabad as prince Salim, he had already employed a number of painters, notably Aqa Riza, a master of the Safavid style of the 1550's, whose son Abu'l Hasan later served under Jahangir. Other renowned painters of his time included Bishan Das, Madhu, Anant, Manohar, Govardhan and Ustad Mansur, through whom Mughal painting reached its zenith. The co-operation of several painters on one work continued, but Jahangir could distinguish which part each artist had contributed.

During this period European influence manifested itself more and more. The colours became softer and less enamel-like than in the previous period. They melt harmoniously together, especially in the more naturalistic representation of landscapes. The custom of copying European paintings and engravings continued. By that time book illustrations become outdated except for the representation of fables, for examples *Iyar-i-danish* and *Anwar-i-Suhaili.*

The portrayal of officers also continued. Jahangir preferred group portraits as well as court scenes and different episodes of his life. *Jahangir embracing Shah Jahan* shows the same careful portrayal as in Akbar's time. It represents the emperor bidding farewell to his son at his departure for the Deccan. The elephant in the front right has been superbly depicted. This unfinished picture gives an insight into the working method: how after drawing the first delicate outlines the painter finished the faces and other details.

Paintings which faithfully record the pomp and splendour of the Mughal empire are typical of this period. An excellent example is the *Emperor Jahangir celebrating the festival of Gulab-Pashi* (Pl. 18.2), a Persian festival celebrated by sprinkling ab-pashi (water) in memory of a rain that ended a terrible famine. As time went on rose water replaced ordinary water. One would expect vitality in a scene of this kind but in this painting the emperor sits on his throne in the centre, surrounded by courtiers almost all in full profile. Each of these, however, carefully portrays individual character.

Soon after his accession he ordered *muraqqa* (albums) composed of mounted pictures of uniform size (40 × 24 cm). Completed around 1618, each folio has either one or several paintings on one side and on the other exquisite calligraphy. Arabesques or floral and animal motifs around the borders, all richly interspersed with gold, frame these paintings beautifully.

The original idea of decorated borders came from Persia around 1570, but it attained perfection in Jahangir's time. The calligraphy pages, with light-coloured figures in the margins, give a glimpse into contemporary life and activities: hunting, crafts, occupations, sometimes even portraits of the calligraphers, artists and courtiers.

A new type of painting, born of the emperor's great love of nature, produced the most delightful pictures of his time, namely the animal and flower representations. His painters used to accompany him on his outings and often the emperor asked them to paint the lovely blossoms, plants, birds and animals he noticed. These masterpieces show much fresher inspiration than the countless court scenes and constitute the highest achievement in the paintings of his reign. They illustrate the emperor's charming memoirs, known as *Tuzuk-i-Jahangiri* which record many episodes from his daily life. Unfortunately very few examples of this series remain. With the utmost care and detail the painters depicted whatever caught the ruler's fancy.

The *turkey cock* (Pl. 18.3; Indian Museum, Calcutta) for instance, shows the majestic bird in glowing colours, feathers ruffled and flap hanging down. The pale background enhances the effect. Exquisite decorative bands frame the picture. Other outstanding examples are the *chameleon* and *zebra* by Mansur, and *squirrels on a chenar tree*—a masterpiece approaching pure landscape, attribute to Abu'l-Hasan Nadir-al-Zaman, a painter whom the emperor esteemed very highly. The gold background, the orange-coloured leaves on the tree, and the deer strongly recall the Persian style but the squirrels scrambling up for safety as well as the frightened birds show a characteristically Indian perceptiveness and sympathy for nature.

During the last ten years of Jahangir's reign Mughal paintings reveal a change: an increased predilection for symbolism and genre, as well as a few glimpses of the zenana. The aging emperor, who indulged in fantasies of being a world-ruler, loved to be shown as a superman. Mysticism also attracted him so he entertained and visited Sufi holy men and ascetics. *Jahangir preferring a Sufi shaikh to kings*, an allegory painted by Bichitr around 1625 (Freer Gallery of Art, Washington) shows the emperor sitting on a big hourglass on which two cherubs write that the Shah may live a thousand years. He hands a book to a shaikh, most probably Shaikh Hussain, the head of the shrine of Khwaja Mu'in-ud-Din Chishti in Ajmer. Next to him, the Ottoman sultan humbly folds his hands, while below him waits James I king of England. The artist himself, holding a framed picture in his hands, occupies the bottom corner on the left; he has humbly signed his name on the footstool. The huge halo around the emperor's head, composed of the sun and the moon, alludes to his title Nur-ud-Din (light of religion); while the footstool, supported by an atlas-like figure, refers to his title Jahangir (world-seizer). In spite of all the allusions to glory, however, the emperor's face looks haggard and embittered by personal and political sorrows.

In the field of portraiture Jahangir perfected another genre initiated by Akbar. The early portraits show the persons standing or seated either in front of the buildings or inside. The mature Jahangiri portrait however depicts the full-length subjects standing against a plain turquoise or green background, either in profile or three-quarter view. Many of these were copied for nobles, so it is hard to identify the originals. In the *portrait of Inayat Khan* (c. 1680; Bodleian Library, Oxford), a masterpiece of fine draughtsmanship and keen insight into character, the artist has caught both the outer appearance of an aristocrat in face of death— his body debilitated by a life of pleasure and his inner anguish.

Shah Jahan (1627-1658), though interested mainly in architecture, continued to patronise painting. Though the high quality of craftsmanship continued, the inner vitality started to disappear. The paintings of this time lack both the dynamic energy of Akbar's time and the keen love of nature shown by Jahangir. Even the splendid court scenes became more and more stylized and rigid, though the costumes had an elegant, reserved style: white muslins, pastel shades, delicate gold embroidery. The visit of the emperor with his nobles and royal ladies to ascetics and dervishes constitutes a predominant theme of this period. Many night scenes were also painted for the first time in the Mughal period. Subdued emotion, unknown in the earlier, objective style of Mughal painting, often pervades these scenes. A new technique, consisting of fine, delicate line drawings slightly tinted with washes of pale colours and gold, and known as Siyahi Qalam became fashionable.

*Emperor Shah Jahan on the peacock throne* (Pl. 18.4; Baron Rothschild Collection, Paris), one of the best known Mughal miniatures, has a double interest. On the one hand it shows the famous peacock throne—now lost, but much admired by contemporaries and described by the French traveller Bernier. On the other hand, it typifies the portraits of this time. The emperor sits in strict profile, a halo behind his head and a flower in his right hand.

Aurangzeb (1658-1707), a fanatic with a puritanical outlook, did not patronise any arts. Culture lost its vitality and finally declined. Perhaps during his waning years he may have consented to have his portraits painted, for there are surviving examples where he is shown either as a bearded old man hunting or holding a copy of the Koran in his hand.

## THE POPULAR MUGHAL SCHOOL

The well organised imperial atelier at Delhi attracted hundreds of artists from all over northern India. Those who could not meet the exacting standards of craftsmanship and proficiency expected of them by the Persian ustads (master-artists) and supervisors, managed to find employment at the palaces of the grandees of the realm.

Many Hindu aristocrats also considered it a matter of prestige to employ artists. Their favourite themes naturally derived from the Rāmāyaṇa, Mahābhārata, Naḷa-Damayantī, Rāgamālā and other religious and secular Hindu literature. The illustrations to the incomplete *Mādhavanala*, *Kāmakanḍala* series (Collection of the late Sir Cowasji Jahangir, Bart., Bombay) exemplifies this so-called Popular Mughal School of Painting.

Though these miniatures could not compete with the refinement of line, harmony of colours and technical excellence of the product of the imperial atelier, yet they have a certain charm and vitality derived from a more characteristic Indian influence. Many 'standard' themes, however, were repeated.

## THE PROVINCIAL MUGHAL SCHOOL

From the various provinces young artists came to Delhi just to learn the basic characteristics of the Imperial style and then return to their native place. Together with other artists who had grown old in the service of the royalty, they spread the Mughal manner far and wide. Thus the so-called Provincial Mughal Schools came into existence through an interaction between the Mughal and local idioms. The main centres of this style were Lucknow, Faizabad, Murshidabad, Hyderabad and Oudh.

## DECCANI ISLAMIC PAINTING

In the Deccan the powerful Islamic kingdom of the Bahmanis had been established in 1347 A.D., with its capital at Bidar. Later it subdivided into five sultanates, namely Bidar, Berar, Ahmednagar, Bijapur and Golconda. Their rulers, of Persian or Afghan origin, patronised distinctive architectural styles besides encouraging painting and music. Since they engaged in feuds and squabbles among themselves, the great Vijayanagar emperors who championed Hinduism could easily block their passage southwards until 1565, when the sultans united against the Vijayanagar emperor and won the decisive battle of Talikota. The conquerors adopted many cultural ideas from their enemies. Painting flourished at Ahmednagar, Bijapur and Golconda—often executed by Hindu artists trained in the Vijayanagar style of Hampi and Lepakshi.

Sultan Hussain Nizam Shah I of *Ahmednagar* had been in the forefront of the combined war against Vijayanagar. After his death his widow commissioned an illustrated manuscript in praise of his valour. This work, called *Tarif-i- Hussain Shahi*, combines Persian elements found in the Nimatnama of Mandu with Indian figures, especially women in their indigenous costumes. The *Dohad scene* exemplifies this well: Indian women set against Persianised trees, and the beautiful girl kicking a tree to make it blossom—an old Indian belief.

The *Vasanta Rāga* (c. 1575), a more mature painting, shows a prince and lady sitting on a swing while two maids on the right shoot coloured water at them. A third, holding a musical instrument, seems ready to sing. The stylised pond in the foreground and the conventional trees in the background recall the Nimatnama, while the transparent veils of the girls resemble those in the early Rajasthani Chaurapañchāsika series.

In the field of portraiture Ahmednagar artists depended more on Mughal examples and absorbed a certain European naturalism and three-dimensional effect. *The lord of the Deccan*, an early seventeenth century painting, shows an indolent prince reclining under a tree, attended by his minions. The luxurious utensils and costly jewellery suggest prosperity. If the idle prince really was the puppet king Murtaza II, his prosperity did not last long. The portrait of *Burhan Nizam Shah II* also shows Mughal influence.

In *Bijapur*, artistic activity was more intense and paintings more numerous. The Sultan, Ali Adil Shah I (1558-1580), commissioned the illustrated manuscript *Najum-ul-ulm* (stars of the sciences). These illustrations show a marked influence of the mural paintings at

Hampi and Lepakshi in the human figures, but the tufts of grass in the background as well as the architectural details belong to the Deccan of that period while the format is Persian. The fine calligraphy of course derives from Persia.

The Bijapur court, which encouraged music during the reigns of Ali Adil Shah I and Ibrahim Adil Shah II, adopted Indian classical music and produced the earliest series of Rāgamālā paintings. According to some art historians, the very idea of depicting musical modes in painting originated in Bijapur.

Some excellent examples of these and other Bijapur paintings belong to the Bikaner Royal Collections—due to the fact that Raja Anup Singh (1669-1698) of Bikaner, who campaigned in the Deccan with the Mughal army, was later appointed governor of Bijapur. Thus many royal treasures and paintings from Bijapur and Adoni found their way to Bikaner.

One such masterpiece is the *Dhanaśri Rāgiṇi* (c. 1570), which demonstrates the fusion of Indian motifs with Persian techniques. Three lines of a Sanskrit poem on the top followed by two lines of Persian calligraphy, describes the heroine of the rāgiṇī. The next horizontal portion shows a lady in a red sari writing a letter to express her distress. One maid sits on the left, while another, in a white Lepakshi- type sari with a gold pallav, stands to the right fanning the princess with a scarf. Below are three miḥrab arches, with the side ones latticed in Persian style. The middle arch encloses a fan-tailed peacock—a frequent symbol of love and yearning.

The most famous of the Bijapur paintings, the portrait of *Ibrahim Adil Shah II* (Fig. 343), produced somewhere between 1590-95, is another prized possession of the Bikaner Royal Collection. Ibrahim II (1580-1626), who succeeded his uncle Ali Adil Shah I at the age of nine, was a very cultured prince, himself a master of calligraphy, a singer and a poet. In this miniature the artists achieved a delicate fusion of varied elements. The composition centres on the prince—his fine sensitive features and his flowing robes. The arrangement of the group of attendants or courtiers behind him expresses movements and depth. The clouds on the top and the grass at the bottom provide a richly- patterned contrast to the white middle ground, and also contribute to a sense of space and receding planes. The refined draughtsmanship owes much to the Safavid style. The faces of two of the attendants reveal a tentative exercise in modelling. Portuguese influence from Goa probably had something to do with this, but it does not compare with the influence that European art exerted on Later Mughal painting.

Fig. 343. Portrait of Ibrahim Adil Shah II, Bijapur.

In the *Golconda* sultanate, painting also enjoyed effective patronage. The portraits of this school owed much to Mughal influence. In that of *Abul Hasan Qutb Shah* (c. 1666), the exquisite profiles of the prince and his two attendants, as well as the manner of composition, are typically Mughal; while the trees and plants, though borrowed from the Mughal idiom, have a distinctly Deccani flavour. Golconda also contributed to the emergence of sub-schools in Hyderabad, Sholapur, Cudappah, Kurnool and Wanparthy.

## RAJPUT PAINTING

The Rajputs descend from the Gurjaras, Pratiharas, Hunas and other central Asian tribes who invaded India in the fifth and sixth centuries A.D., and brought about the disintegration of the Gupta empire. They ensured their right to rule by concocting legends of divine origins, and in time they won acceptance as overlords in a feudal and martial society.

The credit for discovering the school of Rajput painting goes to the pioneer scholar of Indian art history, Dr. A. K. Coomaraswamy. In his monumental work of two volumes, he puts forth the thesis that Rajput painting was a completely indigenous school, essentially religious and Hindu in character, which owed nothing to the secular and foreign style of the imperial Mughal court. Such a rigid attitude has lost its validity in the light of extensive research undertaken by both Indian and foreign scholars during the last five decades. Unfortunately, the bulk of this study is devoted to the later phases of Rajput painting; hence a continuous history of this style from its beginning has as yet not been fully reconstructed.

Rajput painting can be broadly classified into two styles, based on geographic and stylistic differences: the Rajasthani school and the Pahari school, each of which is a composite unit comprising many sub-schools.

## RAJASTHANI PAINTING

The term Rajasthani is applied to the schools which flourished between the sixteenth and early nineteenth centuries in the principalities of Rajasthan. Rajasthan (the abode of princes) is divided into two regions by the Aravalli hills which run roughly north to south. On the west are the desert states of Jodhpur, Bikaner and Jaisalmer, reaching up to the Indus river. To the east of the Aravailis lie the more temperate regions that stretch as far as the Chambal river. These were divided into many feudal states, among which the most important, from the viewpoint of painting, are Mewar, Bundi, Jaipur, Kishangarh and Kotah.

Chronologically however the same order is not followed. Painting in Rajasthan started first in Mewar and then spread to Bundi. The next phase saw the predominantly Mughal art patronised in Jaipur, Jaisalmer and Jodhpur. A sudden spurt of indigenous flowering of a distinctive style is seen in Kishangarh in the second half of the eighteenth century. The hunting scenes of Kotah bring to a close the history of Rajasthani painting.

From the eighth century onwards the Rajput chieftains fell prey to Muslim invaders. Though their chivalry and courage became legendary, their woeful lack of unity and internecine feuds allowed the Islamic invaders to get a foothold in India and to establish their supremacy later on by subtle diplomacy or by sheer force, so that the Rajput states were swallowed up one by one in the Mughal empire.

Rajasthani painting owes its existence to two major factors: the economic prosperity enjoyed by the commercial community of Rajasthan, and the growth of Vaiṣṇavism. In the late Mughal period Rajasthan lay on the trade route connecting the Mughal headquarters with Ahmedabad and Surat on the west coast, and the Rajput chiefs could levy taxes on goods passing through their cities. The resulting inflow of wealth was conducive to the patronage of literature, music and the arts.

The rivival of Vaiṣṇavism and the growth of the Bhakti cult also played a dominant role in the cultural milieu of medieval Rajasthan. As champions of Hindu faith and culture and as guardians of their country, the Rajputs had to lead a life of great courage and hardship. Even the women were called upon for the supreme self-sacrifice of 'jauhar' in order to preserve their chastity. Apparently they sought relief from the tensions of this stern and puritanical way of life by resorting to a religion of intense devotion to a personal deity—Sri Rāma or Lord Kriṣṇa. The latter especially appealed to their romantic temperament. This predilection for romance and fantasy is reflected in their choice of subject matter for painting.

Of the religious themes the most important are illustrations from the Rāmāyaṇa and Mahābhārata, works belonging to the Kriṣṇa cult such as the Gīta Govinda, Bhāgavata Purāṇa, the works of Surdas, Keshava Das and Bihari Lal. The theme of Rādhā and Kriṣṇa is the most profusely illustrated.

The prepondering theme is love, treated in a variety of ways, as in the illustrations for the Rāgamālā (musical modes), the Bārāmasa (12 months i.e. seasons) and the Nāyaka- Nāyikābheda (classification of heroes and heroines).

Folk-lore and ballads (from such literary works as the Dhola-Māru, Mādhavāṇaḷa- Kāmakandalā Hammīra-hatha, Sohni-Mahinwal, and Pañchatantra stories) as well as Sanskrit classics (like the Kādambari by Banabhatta, and Naiṣadhachanta by (Sriharsha, which deals with the Mahābhārata episode of Naḷa and Damayanti) Were also illustrated.

To these themes were added court scenes and royal portraits, a fashion set by the Mughals. The custom of employing court artists and maintaining an atelier, however small, became a matter of prestige among the feudal lords of the late Mughal times.

The general style of Rajasthani painting is characterised by primitive vigour, bold outlines and brilliant colours set into harmonious patterns. Regional idioms, in the treatment of facial types, local scenery and technical details can be discerned in the different sub-schools.

There is a controversy on the problem of

the interrelation between Rajasthani and Mughal styles. It is a fact that the few early Rajasthani paintings which survive are lifeless—no more than a slightly improved version of the central Indian style, whereas later, in the middle of the seventeenth century, it blossomed into great beauty and vigour. This could not have happened in a state of isolation. It was precisely at that early period of art that the Rajput states were engulfed one by one within the Mughal empire. Contact with Mughal court art was inevitable, but the proud Rajput would not yield in spirit to the alien master. The sophisticated and impersonal court style was too foreign to appeal to the Rajput taste. The native artist took only a few basic technical elements of composition and fluid outlines, and used them to revitalise his bold and independent artistic attempts. His pictures reflect his zest for life, his delight in nature and his love for romance and fantasy. In vibrant, glowing colours, highly decorative designs and competent technique, they recount the mischievous pranks of the cowherd Kriṣṇa, the entrancing love Rādhā showed him and the legendary episodes of devotion and courage, dear to the heart of nobleman and peasant alike.

## MEWAR

Mewar's contribution to the history of Rajasthani painting holds paramount importance. Quite a number of the pictures bear the names of the artists and can be dated. As a result the development of the style may be traced from the sixteenth century onwards. One can see clearly the progress made by indigenous art before it came into contact with the Mughal painting.

A *Chaurapañchāsika series* (N. C. Mehta Collection, Bombay) may represent the earliest phase of Rajasthani painting. On the basis of style, scholars have assigned it to various dates, ranging from 1550 to 1600 A. D. The evidently prosperous social conditions, reflected in the details of architecture and clothing in the paintings, point to a Hindu court art. Therefore the majority opinion holds that this series originated in Mewar during the period of its glory in the mid sixteenth century.

This Chaurapañchāsika (Fifty Stanzas of of the Thief), by the Kashmiri poet Vilhana (late eleventh or early twelfth century), was a favourite theme of Rajput painters. It deals with a thief's nostalgic reminiscences of his secret love for a princess whom he is eventually allowed to marry. The miniature depicting *the meeting of the poet* (thief) *with his beloved* contains many elements of the Central Indian style which resulted from the fusion of the Western Indian Jaina manuscript style with Persian influences. The colours remain bold, the features angular, the proportions rather awkward; but gone is the unsightly projecting eye. The figures stand out distinctly from the black background. Champāvatī the heroine wears a diaphanous odhani (veil fringed with tassels) over a tight choli and skirt. Her hair is plaited long and the jewellery is profuse. She presents a picture of coquetry—advancing with her feet, but turning her head away in coy retreat. The man wears a kulah (conical cap), a long four-pointed muslin coat, churidar pyjamas and pointed shoes, and his stance bespeaks sheer vanity. The same type of cap and coat appear in several other medieval paintings—but it has not been definitely established whether the Mughals set the fashion or whether they adopted it from a pre-Mughal culture. (The Gīta Govinda series of 1590, Prince of Wales Museum, Bombay, and several other paintings from dispersed sets also display this kulah or cap. Hence this paintings are collectively referred to as the Kulahdar group).

A typical Mewar product, in the painting, is the checked bedspread, found in many of these pictures. At times it served as a skirt, as in the case of Champāvatī in another painting. The overall refinement of technical details together with a new animation in the expressive gestures show a definite improvement on the Central Indian style.

During the formative period, the earliest dated example of Mewar painting is the *Rágamālā series* made in Chawand (earlier capital of Mewar) in 1605 by Nasiruddin (sometimes called Nasiradi). Some believe he came from Jaunpur. The painting shows a close relationship with the Chaurapañchāsika series mentioned above. This Rāgamālā (Necklace of Musical Modes) is a unique Indian invention. It gives a definite pictorial form to the rāgas (musical modes of classicāl music) by personifying them. The six principal ragas are considered to be male modes, each wedded to five female counterparts called rāginīs, making a total of thirty-six. Further elaboration brings forth janyarāgas (children modes) derived from the main rāgas. Particular rāgas and rāginīs have been assigned to the mood or sentiment of particular seasons and times of the day and night. As depicted in painting, they also represent love in union and love in separation. These pictures were widely prevalent in medieval Rajasthan and the Punjab.

The *Dipak rāga* of the Chawand series (G. K. Kanoria Collection, Calcutta) is essentially a two-dimensional composition filled in with flat areas of colour, mainly red, yellow and black. The red background, a Central Indian tradition, symbolises passion. The sky and landscape are also conventionally treated. The pavilion on the right is in strict frontal view, with no attempt at perspective. A man and woman, seated to the left, listen to music played by a figure sitting on the extreme left. The facial features resemble the Chaurapañchāsika type. The stark simplicity of detail undoubtedly results from the unsettled condition of the Mewar ruler at this time. A rustic vigour, apparent in the treatment of the figures, foretells a period of maturity in the near future.

The period of maturity was ushered in during the reign of Jagat Singh I (1628-1652). The paintings of this period are characterised by bright colours, lush vegetation treated decoratively, scant perspective to represent the simple architectural details, and a definite facial type—oval faces, narrow foreheads, prominent noses, fish-like eyes and small mouths. While horses and elephants are painted more naturalistically, the birds and other animals still follow the Western Indian idiom.

All these features can be discerned in another *Rāgamālā series* (1628) by Sahibdin, a prolific and accomplished master, who transformed Mewar painting from a primitive folk-style into a sophisticated art. The commissioning of Muslim artists by Hindu patrons and vice versa was quite common in these days. Not all the Muslim artists in Rajasthan were necessarily trained in the Mughal court; some of them may have come from Central India after the sack of Mandu in 1561. They could have felt the Mughal influence only indirectly by contact with paintings and artists, absorbing the essentials of composition, refinement of drawing, and competent use of a varied palette.

One of this Rāgamālā series, the *Vasantha Rāgini* (c. 1650) exemplifies the typical mature Mewar style. Flanked by three gopis Krişņa dances under flowering trees with many birds and two peacocks. The vivid lacquer red of the background forms the dominant colour. The gopi on the left plays a drum while the one on the right holds cymbals. The third one has a gun for spraying coloured powder at the time of the Holi festival. Below are vessels and a dish holding two more spray guns. A blue sky edged by a white wavy line crowns the scene. The picture conveys the exhilarating mood of the coming of spring. Krişņa's transparent coat with tight churidar pyjamas reflects Mughal influence.

Sahibdin was the greatest master of the mature Mewar style. His profuse output includes a *Nāyaka-Nāyikābheda* (classification of heroes and heroines) series, a *Bhāgavata Purāņa* (1648), *yuddhakāņḍa* of the Rāmāyaņa (1652), and *Sukar Ksetra Māhātmya* (1655). In his best compositions a backdrop of forest scenery helps to unify the figures in front. He makes clever use of the famous textile designs of Mewar to clothe his figures which he groups in a masterly fashion.

By the beginning of the eighteenth century the style degenerated to routine copying, particularly in the service of the Vallabhacharya sect of Vaişņavism centred at Nathadvara in Mewar. The large quantity of pictures produced during this century lacks the charming quality of the previous century. Thus the glory of Mewar lost its vigour.

## BUNDI

In the early period the paintings of Bundi and Kotah cannot be distinguished since Bundi formed a unified state with Kotah till the second quarter of the seventeenth century. From the middle of that century Bundi became the only other state in Rajasthan to exhibit a genuine style of painting. Its glorious productions reflect its picturesque landscape of hills, thick jungles, flowing rivers, lotus ponds and lakes alive with water-birds.

A dispersed Rāgamālā series can be assigned to the earliest and formative period of Bundi paintings (c. 1625-1640). The *Bhairavi Rāgiņi* (Allahabad Museum) belongs to this series. It shows a lady worshipping a lingam inside a domed shrine. The lotus pond in front teems with fish and waterbirds. The lady's rounded chin, her eyes and other features, as well as the dark colours, recall the Mewar style, while the trees in the background and the lotus pond reflect the Bundi landscape. The rendering of the lotus pond however may also derive from Mandu. A Rāgamālā set in the Bharat Kala Bhavan, Varanasi, also belongs to this period.

Many paintings of high quality were produced in the mid seventeenth century when the Bundi style matured. Human figures still conform to a regular type. They usually have a reddish-brown complexion. The ladies, with pinched waist, prominent nose and almond- shaped eyes, wear odhani (veils), choli (blouses)

Fig. 344. Vasanta Ragini, Bundi, Krishna dancing with girl musicians.

and ghaghra (skirts) in Indian fashion, while the men wear the Muslim type jamas (long transparent coats) over churidar pyjamas, and Mughal-type turbans occasionally adorned with a feather. A profusion of black tassels and pearls adorn both men and women.

Usually the setting is a landscape which at times incorporates domed pavilions and interiors with alcoves. The doors and windows have rolled-up curtains beneath chajjas (overhanging eaves). A curious feature, occurring between 1675-1680, is the use of receding lines to indicate perspective. This results in obtuse angles reminiscent of the Akbar style which had become outdated sixty years earlier in Delhi. This device was not employed in Mewar, where the architecture usually appears in frontal view. Bundi painting of the mature period also incorporates many Deccani elements —formal gardens with floral beds and fountains, architectural features and the figures of women handled as cylindrical forms. These influences may have come from the fact that Bundi rulers served the Mughal emperors as governors in the Deccan.

The illustrations for the Bhāgavata Purāṇa (c. 1640; Kotah Museum, Kotah), as yet unpublished, furnish an excellent example of the style in the early stages of its maturity. In *Kriṣṇa subduing the snake Kāliīa,* a band of masonry running horizontally divides the picture space into two. The lower part shows Kriṣṇa standing on the serpent's hood and playing the flute. Snake maidens on both sides join their hands in prayer for the nāga's release. A tree flanked by a group of figures forms the central motif of the upper area. To the left a party of musicians sit in front of a house. On the right milkmaids express wonder and gratitude through their gestures. The whole composition embodies a well-knit design. The facial type has been given its final shape—namely soft rounded cheeks, almond eyes and firm tight-lipped mouths.

The *Vasantha Rāgini* (Fig. 344; c. 1660; G. K. Kanoria Collection, Calcutta) typifies the

Bundi style at the height of its glory. It shows Krisṇa with the usual dark blue complexion dancing beside a lotus pond with a pair of gopis to his right. Another one on his left beats a drum. The lively rhythmic gestures contrast with the conventional treatment of the rippling waters of the pond, the grass, trees and flowers. These enhance the romantic mood of the scene. The lotus pond with birds characterises the Bundi style.

Because it provides the artist's signature and date of execution, the picture two *lovers in a grove* (Prince of Wales Museum, Bombay), signed by Mohan in 1689, holds great interest for a student of art. In addition it exemplifies a well-knit composition with a rich brocadelike texture. Standing on a stool, the figures gaze rapturously at the crescent moon. The trees and creepers burst with many coloured flowers and present a perfect forest setting infused with tropical warmth and that feeling of stillness peculiar to the twilight hour. The vibrant yellows of the stool, the lady's skirt and the turban contrast brilliantly with the cool greens of the scenery. The faces are reddish- brown.

Towards the end of the seventeenth century, the Bundi style underwent further changes. The faces become more refined and have a flesh-pink colour. Water is stylised into wavy White lines rippling on a dark indigo background. Vivid colours in various shades enrich the landscape. Orange, blue, white, grey and gold clouds hang in the sky. In the early eighteenth century these developments gave rise to a soft style of delicate charm combined with hard outlines and violent movements. Special mention should be made of the Bundi artists' special gift of portraying elephants. Undaunted by the bulk of these huge animals, they tackle them with confident, fluid, outlines. The painting *summer elephant* (Fig. 345; c. 1750; Prince of Wales Museum, Bombay) glows with hot colours—red, orange and yellow—effectively portraying the scorching summer heat.

The favourite themes of this period are Rāgamālā, Bārāmāsā and Rasikapriyā. Krisṇa was the beloved of the people of all classes. In the *hour of cowdust* (Prince of Wales Museum, Bombay), he drives the cattle home while the gopis await him on their balconies. One can almost hear the tinkle of the cowbells and stamping of hooves as the cows jostle each other on the narrow lanes of Gokula. Dramatic clouds fill the sky and even the gods have come out to share the magic of the moment.

A gradual decline set in towards the end of the eighteenth century. Quality suffered even though production was profuse. The only notable Work was the mural decoration of the Chitraśālā of the Bundi palace, dealing with the Krisṇa legend, hunting scenes and royal processions.

Fig. 345. Summer elephant, Bundi.

## JAIPUR

Jaipur was the first Rajasthani state to fall in line with the Mughal policy of empire-building, and the rulers became faithful generals and administrators of the Mughal emperors. Strong, mutual cultural contacts existed between Delhi and Amber. The indigenous architecture of the Amber palace, with its exquisitely carved doors and windows and mirrored walls, influenced to a great extent the early Mughal architecture at Fatehpur Sikri and Agra. In the field of painting, however, the Mughal influence was overwhelming. A flourishing school of court painters was patronised at Jaipur, and pictures of pomp and splendour and royal portraits were commissioned. Only in the late eighteenth century, when Mughal influence was thrown off, did a genuine

Jaipur style emerge. Under the personal inspiration of the ruler, Pratap Singh, many pictures devoted to the Kriṣṇa theme were executed. Over fifty artists worked under him.

The *ring dance* (c. 1800; Jaipur Museum) shows Kriṣṇa performing a folk dance as described in the Prēma Sāgara (Ocean of Love). Under a clear autumn sky bathed in the cool light of the moon, Kriṣṇa called the gopis with his enchanting music and danced with them. Standing with his favourite in the centre of concentric rings of gopis, his brilliant form rivals that of the moon and the light radiates all around on the sand. The gods come out to enjoy the beauty of the scene and shower blossoms on the dancers below. The gopis in the inner circle wear red and orange, those in the middle ring green, while the ones in the outer rings have black clothes. The profusion of gold dots and borders gives the painting a jewel-like quality.

## THE DESERT KINGDOMS

After Bikaner and Jaisalmer accepted Mughal sovereignty in 1750 a number of artists from Aurangzeh's court migrated to Bikaner which became an important centre of painting with a high Mughal character. Ali Raza who worked for Karan Singh and painted portraits in the Shah Jahan style was an important master.

Usted Hamid Ruknuddin's *ladies' party* (1666; Lalbagh Palace, Bikaner) is a typical genre scene. Two ladies sitting on a dais in a formal garden and attended by maids converse with each other. The painting shows refined draughtsmanship, fine blending of colours and superb technical mastery.

Ruknuddin's son Shahadin painted one of the finest Bikaner masterpieces *Kriṣṇa supporting Mount Govardhan* (c. 1690; British Museum, London). Serenely Kriṣṇa holds up the mountain to provide shelter for the cowherds, threatened by a cosmic downpour instigated by Indra. Semi-transparent clouds cover the mountain peaks. Indra looks on from his white elephant at the top corner to the right. The shepherds and cowherds gaze in wonder and rapture at their protector while the unruffled cattle display complete trust. The fine drawing, the clever use of jewel-like colours, landscape details and treatment of cattle derive from the Deccani style of Golconda. This comes as no surprise since the Bikaner prince Anūp Singh had served in the Deccan and acquired a fine collection of paintings, including a portrai of Ibrahim II of Bijapur. Towards the end of the eighteenth century, Bikaner painting adopted the mannerisms of the late Jodhpur style and ended as a lifeless craft.

## JODHPUR

Jodhpur is the largest state of Rajasthan and the home of the Rathore clan of Rajputs, claiming descent from Rāma. Originally the Rathores ruled in Central India, with their capital at Kanauj in the twelfth century. After Muhammed Ghori defeated Jai Chand in 1194 his nephew and followers migrated to Rajasthan. In 1459 Rao Jodha founded Jodhpur; and Bika, one of his sons, carved out for himself the state of Bikaner. Because of its forbidding terrain, Jodhpur is also called Marwar (the region of death).

During the fifteenth and sixteenth centuries Jodhpur painting followed the Jaina style of Western India since the patrons were usually Jaina merchants. Contact with the Mughals started in 1581 when Udai Singh gave his sister Jodh Bai in marriage to Akbar. Later his daughter married Prince Salim. In the seventeenth century, Jaswant Singh served the Mughals as viceroy in Malwa, Gujarat and the Deccan. The Jodhpur Palace Collections contain many portraits of this ruler done in the Mughal style. His successors too favoured this mode for their portraits.

A true Jodhpur style developed only between 1760 and 1780, during the reign of Bijai Singh, when the Rajasthani preference for rhythmic lines and jewel-like colours asserted itself. The Mughal influence however shows up in the graceful and romantic figures of the women silhouetted against a dark background. Depicted usually as playing with birds or flying kites they present a picture of charming simplicity. Their beautifully long uplifted eyes are a notable feature of the Jodhpur style. A good example of this genre is the *lady flying a kite.*

This refined style of painting reached its zenith during the reign of Man Singh (1803-1843). When the British took over in Jodhpur in 1818 Man Singh freed himself from the powerful hold of Deb Nath, the head of a religious sect. Thereafter Man Singh devoted all his time to patronising painting and literature. His own poem 'Kriṣṇa Vilas' as Well other stories from the Śiva Purāṇa, Nalacharita, Durgācharita, and Pañchatantra were profusely illustrated. A series of a hundred and twenty-one paintings (c. 1820) recounted the Dhola Mārvāni ballad. This miniature showing *Dhola and Mārvāni* (Jodhpur Palace Library) riding their favourite camel Māru is an exquisite example of a highly decorative design. The uplifted head and angular legs of the animal give a sense of movement. The outlines of the riders echo the main curves of the camel's body, while Mārvāni's odhani (veil) and the camel's tail take up a minor rhythm. The colours sparkle like enamel on a neutral blue background.

## KISHANGARH

In most of the Rajasthani states painting had come to a close by the end of the eighteenth century, but a sudden spark of genius lit up a new school of painting in the small state of Kishangarh. Its ruler Raja Sawant Singh (1748-1757), a great devotee of Krişņa, wrote many poems under the pen-name Nagari Das. He fell in love with a maid in his stepmother's entourage, called Bani Thani (meaning 'smart and well-dressed'). She too was well-versed in poetry. In 1757 she accompanied him to Brindavan where he died seven years later. Soon after his death the best Kishangarh paintings were produced. Their hall-mark is a new and beautiful type of Rādhā and Krişņa figures. The artist Nihal Chand is credited with the creation of this distinctive type, with Bani Thani as Rādhā and Sawant Singh as Krişņa.

Fig. 346. Portrait of Bani Thani as Radha, Kishangarh.

In the *portrait of Bani Thani as Rādhā* (Fig. 346) her long eyes, narrower than the Jodhpur type and tinged with a lotus-pink hue, curve upwards. This Rādhā face is unique in the exaggerated arch of the eyebrows, the decorative curl of hair spiralling down the cheek in front of the ear, the long straight nose, thin lips and pronounced chin. Krişņa's sharp features give him an aristocratic air. His orange-coloured turban decorated with pearls complements the pale blue of his complexion. *Krişņa presenting flowers to Rādhā* (National Museum, Delhi) and *Krişņa gathering lotuses in a lake* show that the main figures, generally small, are set within a large area occupied by wide expanses of water, an architectural setting and other figures. The silvery grey of the water and the lacy white of the marble terraces enhance the mysterious enchantment of these paintings.

## KOTAH

The final scene in the unfolding of Rajasthani painting is set in the hilly tracts of Kotah. Here alone Indian painting has represented the excitement of the chase. Kotah was ruled by Ummed Singh, a puppet in the hands of a powerful regent, Zalim Singh. From the age of ten he whiled away his time in hunting expeditions. Kotah painting of this period reflects this obsession with the chase, which became a social ritual akin to foxhunting in eighteenth century England. Even ladies took part in the royal forays into the jungle and were expert shots. The Kotah artists' contribution to the world of painting is unique. The real theme of their work is the jungle with its wild life; the hunters play only a minor role. The thrill of adventure pervades the silent, eerie moonlit nights, and 'the terrible sweet smell of the tiger', as Jim Corbett called it, seems to waft up to the hunter lying in wait on top of a tree. *Raja Ummed Singh shooting tigers from a tree* (c. 1790; Victoria and Albert Museum) is an excellent example of this style. The Rajasthani love of boldly simplified forms, as opposed to the Mughal love of detail, stands out in the treatment of jungle vegetation, hunters and animals. The handling of jungle scenery has a superficial resemblance to the paintings of Henri

Rousseau. The forms employed by these artists have no ulterior meaning. While the buffalo and tiger are locked in life and death struggle, an eerie stillness haunts the scene.

In the nineteenth century this bold clarity gave way to delicate refinement of forms and delight in picturing flora and fauna as in Jahangir's time. Rajasthani painting drew to a close on this note of keen interest in nature and the typically Indian feeling of oneness with all creation.

## PAHARI PAINTING

The term Pahari refers to the mountainous region watered by the five rivers of the Punjab, and divided into numerous small and isolated states each under its own hereditary chieftain. 'Pahari painting' therefore includes the work of all these states because it expresses the common spirit of the various schools. Within the limited space of this book we mention only the most important states—Basohli, Guler, Jammu, Kangra and Garhwal. Controversy makes a precise analysis of the dates, origins and styles of the Pahari school impossible. Scholarly research shows that Pahari miniature painting is a hybrid—a distinctive, creative composite of pre-existing elements of the Gujerati style of manuscript illustration, the Mughal style of the Aurangzeb period (1658-1707) and of the Rajasthani school of the first half of the seventeenth century—the last-named itself resulting from the influence of the Akbar, Jahangir and Shah Jahan schools on the static, over-conventionalised Gujerati manuscript illustrations. Add to these ingredients the possible influence of the quasi-historical folk element, and the result is a new art of exuberant expressive power and amazing technical finesse.

With Aurangzeb's prohibition of the arts, the provincial artists working at the courts of Hindu nobles were forced to seek refuge in the hills. Many of them converged on the small but important state of Basohli ruled by Sangram Pal (1635-1673). Abandoning the imitation of the weakened Mughal style and inspired by their indigenous love of colour, the Basohli artists recreated their celebrated themes in a new range of expressions—from the tempered primitivism of Basohli with its wild-eyed intensity, throbbing chromatic patterns and animated figures to the increasing softness of Guler with its finer drawing, mellower colouring and deliberate physical charm, to the clarity of the Jammu style with its simplicity and penchant for candid individualisation and human interest, to the lyrical rhythms of the Kangra school with its graceful women in flowing, musical contours and soft colour harmonies that celebrate the tenderness of love, and finally to Garhwal where linear sensualism reaches perfection, giving a sinuous delicacy to the figures, trees and landscapes, each element interacting with the other to glorify the theme of love.

### BASOHLI

Basohli, a small state in the Jammu territory of the present Jammu and Kashmir state, is now generally accepted as the cradle of Pahari style painting, a unique form of miniature painting which emerged in the late seventeenth century and spread to other states. Legends and quasi-history shroud its actual history. The Basohli rājās were called balaurias after Balor or Vallapura, their ancient capital.

The Basohli style resulted from the fusion of a deeply religious art rooted in folk tradition with the basic elements of the Mughal technique. During Sangram Pal's reign (1635-1673) the ruling family of Basohli adopted Vaiṣṇavism. Sangram Pal probably came into contact with Mughal painters during his visit to Delhi in Shah Jahan's reign. Though the strong warm colours, the treatment of trees and profusion of jewellery in Basohli art resemble Mewar painting, no historical evidence supports contact between the two states.

The early paintings of around 1660-70 reflect the conflicts involved in the change-over from Śaivism. While some of them depict Devī or Pārvatī, a major series illustrates Rasamaṇjari, apparently a secular work on love, but in this case the hero is identified with Krişṇa—a sly intrusion of Vaiṣṇavism which was as yet not firmly enough established to warrant a forthright illustration of a regular religious work belonging to this sect.

In addition to the special slant on religion this series also exemplifies all the characteristics of early Basohli painting. Though vigorous, this style does not have as yet the subtlety or sophistication of the later Kangra Kalam. The use of strong brilliant colours reinforces its spirited approach to both the secular and religious themes. Usually the borders are bright red to symbolise passion. At times they are yellow or blue. Very often parts of the scenes overflow into the borders, or objects and figures are cut off ruthlessly to fit into the picture. This shows that the artist still thought in terms of the wider spaces of wall murals.

The borders often contain inscriptions normally in Tākri script.* Sometimes excerpts from Sanskrit texts which the paintings illustrate are written on the back in Devanagiri script.

Except for isolated trees and architectural pavilions the background is flat, the figures being set against a vivid expanse of red, yellow, blue, orange and other bright colours of uniform tonality. The horizon is placed high. A narrow blue strip flecked with clouds indicates the sky.

A characteristic facial type distinguishes the Basohli school: the high, prominent nose often runs in a straight line with the receding forehead, and the lotus-shaped eyes almost pop out in the intensity of their gaze.

The female type has three variations: the first, a peasant type with sharp, intense expressions; the second, a more refined type dressed in Mughal costume; and the third, with a pronounced protuberance on the back of the head. These women sometimes wear the Rajput ghaghra (skirt), choli (blouse) and odhani (veil), and at other times the Mughal type of salvar (tight pyjamas), choli and a long over-garment of thin material called pesvaj, which was tied in front of the breast and allowed to hang free down to the ankles —a fashion during the Shah Jahan and Aurangzeb period. The male dress is more often the Mughal style of the time of Aurangzeb. Commoners wear the local clothing.

The architecture resembles that of the Akbar period and the early Rajasthani style: arched niches and inlay panels. The interiors show blue and white crockery, gold dishes, vases and plates, hukkas and wine flasks. There is no furniture other than cots and stools. Very often the people sit on rich carpets provided with masnats (bolsters).

The landscape is stark and conventionalised. Though highly stylised, the various kinds of trees can easily be identified by botanists. The rhododendron, with its brilliant red flowers, is a favourite of the Basohli artist. Other trees include the weeping willow, mango, horsechest- nut and cypress as well as purely imaginative trees. The cattle are of a nondescript breed— thin, with wide-open eyes and large ears.

The profusion of jewellery worn by the Basohli figures enhances the rich ornamental texture of the paintings. Pearls occur in abundance, depicted as raised blobs of opaque white paint. To represent emeralds, Basohli painters resorted to the unique method of using the green wing- cases of beetles which give a flashing brilliance and have endured to the present day.

Pahda Kunj Lal, a descendant of the royal physicians of the Basohli rajas, presented to the Dogra Art Gallery, Jammu, thirty-five paintings of the Rāsamañjari series cited above. This fact enhances the importance of the series because it is a rare case of known date and origin. Other paintings of this series are scattered in various museums and private collections.

One picture of this series, for instance, is in the Victoria and Albert Museum, London. Called the *resourceful Rādhā* from the Tākri inscription at the top which reads: Kriya vidagdha (the act of the resourceful mistress), it has a Sanskrit verse from the Rāsamañjari on the back which says that the lady's husband had ordered the servant to cut down her ber tree under which she used to meet her lover, but she took the axe from the servant and threw it into the pond. The text does not mention Kriṣṇa at all but the artist, in keeping with the rest of the illustrations, interpolated the figure of Kriṣṇa on the assumption that he came to the house after the husband had left; and the lady is taken to represent Rādhā. The picture shows a pavilion on the right with the eave projecting into the thin grey margin bordered with red.

*The lady and the herd of deer* (N. C. Mehta Collection, Ahmedabad) shows a garden scene against a yellowish-green background. Under a narrow strip of blue and white sky the branches of three slender trees flecked with white and pink flowers bend over a lady dressed in Mughal- type pyjamas, transparent overgarment and light blue veil. She holds a kerchief or scarf in her right hand and a sheaf of grass in her left. Behind her stands a maid with a peacock- feather fan and a bottle of rosewater. On the left a black-buck, a pair of does and a tiny fawn approach the lady, their necks craning forward. A pond with water-birds, lotus flowers, buds and leaves occupies the foreground.

A series of Bhāgavata Purāṇa, started around 1675, was probably never completed. *The earth appealing to Visṇu* (Chandigarh Museum), the opening scene of the tenth book, shows the second female type—tall and slim with almond complexion and dressed in Mughal costume.

The *forest fire* (Khandalavalạ Collection, Bombay), the only surviving example of a second Bhāgavata Purāṇa series painted somewhere between 1680-85 reveals a further step in the

* Dr. A. K. Coomaraswamy wrongly assumed that the script was of Jammu origin only and therefore all pictures with Takri inscriptions were assumed to belong to the Jammu school.

development of the Basohli style. The expression of the faces has softened and the flames look more natural. While seven cowherds close their eyes in dread and the nine cows, of varied hues, stare in wide-eyed terror whereas the wild animals flee for safety, Krisṇa stands within a circle of fire drawing the swirling flames into his mouth. He wears a long white floral garland and a red dhoti. Common conventions in the earlier Basohli style are the outer circle of stylised trees to represent the forest, the usual narrow band of sky on top, the Warm colours and tight grouping of figures.

Under the patronage of Kirpal Pal (1678- 1693), many of whose portraits have come down to us, two series of Rāsamañjari illustrations were undertaken. Since Vaiṣṇavism was Well established by now and the Bhāgavata Purāṇa was painted as a religious text there was no longer any need to camouflage the religious leanings of the ruling family under a secular garb.

The last series contains a rare Sanskrit inscription in Devanagari script. It states that Raja Kirpala in the Vikrama year 1752 (1695 A. D.) commissioned Devidasa to paint this Rāsamañjari series in the town called Vishnusthali (modern Basohli) on the banks of the river Airāvatī (Ravi) in order to see God's creation and realise the hollowness of the world. The inscription does not refer to Viṣṇu or Ṡiva but mentions God in a general way. Both Ṡaivite and Vaiṣṇavite marks appear on the heroes. This shows that Vaiṣṇavism, though popular, had not yet completely supplanted the earlier Ṡaivism.

This series of paintings conforms to the earlier traditions in the depiction of architecture (decorated porticoes with projecting eaves, turrets, and the peculiarly Basohli feature of monster heads at the base of the plinth), and in the continuation of red borders, high horizons, flat backgrounds and conventional landscapes. However, the richness of details has given way to simplicity of design and bolder composition. The figures show better modelling and there is a perceptible leaning towards more naturalism. Fashions have also changed: the gallants wear longer jamas (coats).

Nothing further is known about Devidasa, the painter mentioned in the inscription. The very fact that he is mentioned by name— a rarity—shows that he was either exceptionally talented or an outsider or both. His style differs markedly from that of earlier Basohli painters though the main elements of composition and iconography remain similar.

The *Gita Govinda,* painted in the mature Basohli style of the early eighteenth century, is another series of great importance. It is known to have originated in Basohli; and its date (A. D. 1730) is mentioned in the Sanskrit inscription on tne face of the final picture. This inscription, in chaste Sanskrit and legibly written, has aroused a welter of controversy among scholars because of an ambiguity in interpretation. It is believed that a lady devoted to Viṣṇu had this illustration of the Gīta Govinda painted and embellished with fine calligraphy by the artist Manaku, who probably came from Guler. Since the series displays a lavish use of beetle wing-cases and was acquired from Basohli by the Lahore Museum, it may be safe to conclude that the patroness was a Basohli rāni. Historical facts attest to the Vaiṣṇavite leanings of the ladies of the Basohli royal household.

Although Manaku is the only painter mentioned, scholars notice the hand of an assistant. This second artist shows less skill and lacks the confidence of a master artist. As many as a hundred pages of this series exist, over fifty of which were acquired by the Lahore Museum. The main elements of the Basohli style—a vibrant palette, flat backgrounds, architectural features, interior views and use of beetle wing- cases—-all conform to the 1690-1700 period. However, the monster-heads have been eliminated from the architectural plinths, the faces show better modelling, the gaze of the large eyes is less intense and the landscape has become more complex. The Guler predilection for lush scenery and greater fluency of line seems to have crept into Basohli art, leading to the supposition that Manaku hailed from Guler. For example, *Rādhā and Kriṇṇa watching a storm* shows Guler idioms in the treatment of nature but the architecture still protrudes into the border. In the scene *enter the bower of love* (Fig. 347 ; National Museum, New Delhi) Rādhā's friends urge her to overcome her shyness in meeting Krisṇa who awaits her in a clump of trees.

About thirty years after the Gīta Govinda series, i.e., around 1760, a large set of *Bhāgavata Purāṇa* paintings were done at Basohli. The sheets are now dispersed among various museum collections. Their importance from the viewpoint of style lies in the appearance and incorporation of Guler elements and the final disappearance of the Basohli style as a distinctive phenomenon. The palette looks

Fig. 347. Enter the bower of love (detail), Gita Govinda series, Basohli.

cooler, the figures less intense and angular, and beetle wing-cases are no longer used. The background remains flat but the colours are restricted to red and orange as in Guler. The conscious adoption of Nainsukh's style presupposes that the painter of its series enjoyed access to the paintings of Nainsukh who came to Basohli on a pilgrimage. Even though he may not have been the principal artist of this series, he seems to have painted *the house of the Pandavas is set on fire*—a magnificent scene of a star-spangled night ablaze with leaping flames.

The Basohli style continued in full vigour till the middle of the eighteenth century and became a standard in many of the hill states— Mankot, Nurpur, Kulu, Mandi, Suket, Bilaspur Nalagarh, Chamba, Guler and Kangra— with local variations. In some states it lasted even after the refined Kangra painting had emerged in Kangra and Guler and in Basohli itself.

## KULU

Kulu is a distinctive variant of the Basohli style. The ruling family of Kulu was a senior branch of the Rajput clan, while a junior branch founded Basohli. Naturally therefore the two states shared many cultural elements including free exchange of painters. The Kulu rājās too were ardent Vaiṣṇavites, and around 1650 an image of Raghunāth or Rāmā was brought from Ayodhyā or Oudh, and installed in their capital. They made over the whole kingdom to this presiding deity and ruled thereafter as vice-regents of Sri Raghunāth.

Like the Basohli painting of 1660-1680 the Kulu style shows the same lively colours,

Fig. 348. Departure of Rama and Lakshmana for the forest, Ramayana series, Kulu.

dress and hairstyles, conventionalised trees and flat background. But the harsh climate and rough, rocky terrain surrounding the Kulu Valley seems to have given a restless and violent mood to the thick-set figures. The compositions show less order. A large Rāmāyaṇa set, the so-called *Shangri Rāmāyana* (Fig.348) said to have been painted by a family of Kashmiri Brahmins, provides excellent examples of typical Kulu features.

*The hermitage of Vālmiki*, an illustration of a scene in Part V of Uttarakāṇḍa, shows two light yellow huts against a flat deep yellow background. Sītā sits in front of the smaller hut in the top centre supervising the lessons given to her sons Lava and Kuśa by the sage Vālmīki, seated in the bigger hut on the left. On the right stand three trees with intertwining creepers, and parts of other trees appear above the larger hut. The striped shorts worn by the boys, the bright colours, and the foliage treated as patterns in varied hues of blue, maroon and green, represent the Basohli idiom; but the twisted and gnarled trunks of the trees (the pine tree was a favourite with Kulu artists), the three-dot pattern on Sitā's veil as well as the facial features are peculiar to Kulu.

## GULER

Renowned as the birthplace of the beautiful Kangra style of Indian painting, tiny Guler was founded in 1405 by Raja Hari Chand. He had been lost in a hunting expedition. His wives, believing him dead, committed sati and his younger brother took the throne. About a month later a merchant saved Hari Chand but instead of returning to Kangra he went to Guler and founded a new kingdom. Even though Kangra was larger and more powerful Guler always took precedence as the senior branch of the Katoch family. Haripur, the capital, and Guler town face each other across the Bun Ganga river which winds along the Sewaliks mountain range. The horseshoe bend of Ban Ganga which joins the Beas further to the south is often depicted in Guler paintings as well as the pavilions and terraces of the picturesque fort perched on the flanks of the Sewaliks. To the north-west of Guler lies Kangra, and beyond rise the snowy peaks of the Himalayas.

Thus situated at the entrance of the Kangra Valley, with the safe and secluded hill kingdoms beyond, it was easily reached from the Punjab plains by artists fleeing from the terrors of Nadir Shah in 1739. During Dalip Singh's reign (1695-1741) a chitera (colony of artists) seems to have existed in Haripur. A number of early portraits including those of Dalip Singh indicate both a royal interest in painting and the influence of the late Mughal style of the Mohammad Shah period. It is now known that Pandit Seu hailed from Guler and some members of his family probably worked there.

In the beginning of the eighteenth century Guler had no pretence to military or political power. This fact itself prompted the growth of painting since Govardhan Chand could devote all his time to patronise art and letters. His only battle resulted from a quarrel over his favourite horse with Adina Beg, the Mughal governor of Jalandar. In 1730 he married a Basohli princess and gave his own sister in marriage to the Basohli ruler, his wife's brother. This double wedding strengthened the cordial relations that had always prevailed between the two kingdoms. Some scholars surmise that for this grand occasion the Gīta Govinda series of paintings was commissioned in Basohli and painted by Manaku, who may have been sent from Guler. Manaku, the son of Pandit Seu and elder brother of Nainsukh, took service under Amrit Pal of Basohli after the death in 1763 of his patron Balwant Singh of Jammu.

No signed paintings of artists, assignable to the Govardhan Chand period, are known. The family style of Pandit Seu has been identified only from distinctive characteristics: a keen interest in capturing likenesses, experiments with varied postures and gestures, firm control of fluid lines and a general air of easy naturalism.

An early example of Guler painting, the *yuddhakāṇḍa series* from the Rāmāyaṇa, holds unique place in Pahari painting on account of its large-sized pictures—60 X 82.5 cm on the average. The reason for this unusual size is unknown. Many of the pictures remain unfinished and numerous drawings uncoloured. It appears that the series was commissioned around 1725 and abandoned a few years later owing to the new popularity gained by the Kriṣṇa cult at Guler.

One of the finished paintings depicts the *arrest of the first spies* (PI. 19.1 Museum of Fine Arts, Boston). The walls of Rāvaṇa's fort rise to the left from a low hill with trees— including many plantains and cypresses. To the right lies a bigger hill ridged with trees full of monkeys. Inside a circular clearing Vibhīṣana denounces to Rāmā two of Rāvaṇa's spies who had adopted the guise of monkeys. This hill with its ridges and the water in front bears great resemblance to Haripur fort and the curve of the Ban Ganga river as viewed from the south-west. This use of local scenery with its abundant plantain trees and hills rising in wavy ridges is one of the hall-marks of later Guler painting as also the plain background (often red), the use of gold, the naturalistic treatment of animals, and birds in pairs. In this particular painting the background is a flat orange-red with a rim of blue and white sky at the top.

The earliest known portrait (c. 1745) of the Guler raja *Govardhan Chand* shows him *listening to musicians* (Chandigarh Museum). Wearing a yellow jama and scarlet scarf he sits in Muslim fashion on a flowered rug holding the stem of a hukka in one hand. Before him lies a sword. Behind him stand a pair of attendants and to his right a group of six courtiers sit in a row. Five musicians are seated in front of them with a pair of unfinished figures standing directly behind them. The reds, yellows, greens and blues of their clothing contrast clearly with the white background. Trees, with faint indications of leaves, cover the foreground of the setting. A white terrace overlooks an expanse of grey water, with green ridges of gently curving hills beyond. Towards the top left comer appears a curious grey parallelogram with gold borders left Unfinished.

In style this picture shows a mixture of two strains. One conforms to convention in the depiction of flat grey water, plain hills, angular architecture with no perspective, and figures lined up in a row. The other reveals a new love for naturalism in the representation of the foliage of the trees in the foreground and in the poses of the musicians, rendered with a deft command of fluid lines. This second element indicates the hand of a competent artist.

*A princess listening to girl-musicians* (c. 1750; Mittal Collection, Hyderabad) has an astonishing resemblance to the previous painting. Probably done five years later, it has the same three planes; foreground with realistic trees, middle area occupied by a terrace (here grey, with railings), and beyond it the expanse of grey water with lotus leaves and flowers. The hills in the background have trees and a tiny white building. The grey parallelogram of the previous picture has been converted into a canopy under which an aristocratic lady sits on a gold chair holding a hawk in her right hand and the stem of a hukka in her left. Two maids stand behind her. To her right sits an old lady, and a young woman a little lower down. A pair of girls bow to the princess in Muslim fashion. Behind them are two maids and a male attendant. In the right foreground a girl sits strumming a tambura. On account of the similarity of her features with another portrait inscribed with the words 'the portrait of the exalted Balauri Rani' the princess is presumed to be the Basohli rani of Raja Govardhan Chand.

The organisation of planes, grouping of figures, delineation of facial features and naturalistic treatment of landscape details indicate the hand of a master-painter. Since Nainsukh worked in Jammu at this time, this painting may have been done by a member of his family or by an unrelated Guler artist who conformed to the same style.

Inspired by the picturesque scenery of Guler, delight in nature shows itself in good measure in the *princess out hawking with her maids* (c. 1750; National Museum, New Delhi). An aristocratic lady riding a magnificent pale brown horse holds a falcon in her right hand. She wears a long full-sleeved dress and an elegant plumed turban. A half dozen maids accompany her. The one in front, dressed in male garb, holds a sword. The undulating hills, the trees with thick foliage, the pond rimmed with delicate grasses and filled with lotuses and water-birds—all reveal an obvious enjoyment of nature and show a marked departure from the earlier convention of flat backgrounds.

Masterly representation of the beauty and grace of women characterises all the masterpieces. For example in the *Vipralabdha Nāyika* (c. 1750-1755; Victoria and Albert Museum, London) the confident posture and delicate modelling of the lady's face, her elegant clothes and chaste jewellery bespeak high finesse and artistry. The heroine, disappointed that her lover has not appeared, throws her jewels away. She wears a yellow semi-transparent veil over a light brown choli and a mauve skirt. A slender tree with chocolate-brown trunk, slim delicate branches and pink flowers—a recurring feature of later painting—appears here for the first time. The grey hill, however, and dull white sky with stars and a full moon show a reversion to the flat background. On the right stand three trees with a winding creeper.

The lovely idealisation of Guler women, looking serene and graceful, appears also in *the prince seated with three ladies* (c. 1760; Allahabad Museum). The three ladies sit in a pavilion in front of a seated prince. He wears a green flowered jama and patterned turban.

Behind him, with head slightly inclined, is another graceful woman with the typical Guler skirt, having multicoloured horizontal bands. The deep grey wall sets off the delicately modelled faces. One of the three trees to the left shows the characteristic type—slender dark brown branches with white flowers against a pale blue sky. A bed of white lilies, which grow well in Guler, adorns the foreground.

The portrayal of Rādhā in *lover's quarrel* (Chandigarh Museum), another noteworthy example of picturing women with pronounced delicacy, shows her curled up in obvious disdain while Krișṇa walks away in despair. Their orange clothes stand out against the white architectural background.

The unfinished *bending of the bow* (c. late 1770's; British Museum, London) recalls Mughal painting in the facial types and the skillfully outlined forms of the spectators who Watch Rāmā bending his bow in order to win Sītā's hand. The group of ladies on the left shows an unusual variety of faces. Vishvamitra, Lakshmana and some ascetic characters appear on the right and a row of courtiers below. The atmosphere is serene and unemotional. The yellow, red and orange hues produce a warm contrast to the predominantly white background of palace architecture.

Fig. 349. Lament of separation, Guler.

The mature Guler style, which has effectively assimilated Rajput and Mughal types, emerged in full vigour during the late eighteenth century. Superb examples of this notable phase are the *lament of separation* (Fig. 349) and *the divine pair,* both in the Captain Sunder Singh Collection. The first is an exquisite portrayal of a beautiful lady in a long flowing white dress and red veil, strumming a musical instrument. The slight incline of her head finds an echo in the delicately arched branches of a slender tree behind her. A magnificent black buck listens, enchanted by the music. These two figures stand out clearly against a background, light green at the bottom, merging into yellow ochre in the major middle portion, and topped by a white and azure band of sky. The composition is simple, the colours few, the details sparse, yet the brush of a genius has transformed them into a picture of aesthetic enchantment.

*The divine pair* is another simple composition. Enraptured by the music of Krișṇa's flute Rādhā looks at him ecstatically. He stops playing to gaze at her. This moment of magic has been captured in the painting. Krișṇa in yellow dhoti, and Rādhā in a long flowing orange dress stand in the middle flanked by a dancing cowherd on either side. The green terrain slopes gently upwards behind them. A tree spreads its lush foliage above them and a quiet stream runs below.

## JAMMU

Jammu was a powerful feudal state, and from around 1720 to 1750 its sovereignty extended over Bhoti, Bhadu, Basohli, Mankot and Bandralta. Jammu's claim to a place in the history of Pahari painting stems mainly from a series of portraits of Raja' Balwant Singh (1724-63). Though he was only the fourth son of Raja Dhruv Dev, with little hope of becoming a ruler, he received the title of raja perhaps as a mark of respect in his capacity as chief minister. His name became famous because of his passionate interest in painting. At least fourteen finished portraits of Balwant Singh exist, and another twenty-seven drawings and unfinished pictures—most of them painted by Nainsukh, the second son of Pandit Seu of Guler.

Pandit Seu apparently came from the Mughal court. Through careful research, enough information has been collected regarding his family to assert that it belonged to Guler from where various members emigrated to other states to practice their art. Their surname Raina seems to indicate that they were originally Kashmiri Brahmins. Pandit Seu's two sons Manaku and Nainsukh and many of his grandsons were instrumental in evolving a superb style.

With his genius for sensitive drawing, astute insight into character, precise delineation of facial features, softly modulated colouring and simple but elegant settings Nainsukh, the great painter of Jammu, infused an original freshness into Pahari painting. Together with the other outstanding members of his family he banished the lingering violence, primitive passions and hot colours of the Basohli school.

In 1744 Nainsukh entered the service of Balwant Singh and until his patron's death in 1763 he painted a series of his portraits which record his daily activities. *Raja Balwant Singh of Jammu examining a picture presented by the artist Nainsukh* (signed by Nainsukh, c. 1747) shows the patron dressed in a plain jama, seated on an ornate gold chair holding the stem of a hukka in one hand and a painting in the other. Behind him stands the artist. In front of the raja appear a courtier, attendant and a group of musicians. The setting is a white terrace with a long verandah at the back. This verandah has a door at each of the narrow sides, a low railing on the farthest side and open arches supported by slim pillars. The painting shows that Balwant Singh wished to maintain an independent court, to appropriate imperial manners and to play the role of a great patron of art and music. Nainsukh with hands folded, reflects an eagēr expectation of approval. That he succeeded in pleasing the raja and was accepted as a personal artist is attested by the ensuing series of portraits.

*Raja Balwant Singh of Jammu listening to his singing girls and musicians at Jasrota* (1748) is important because it has an inscription in Tākri, elegantly written in two lines above a band of clouds, indicating that the painting was done by Nainsukh at Jasrota. It also gives the date and patron's age. The inclusion of a line of music implying a pun on the word manu (lover) and Mannu (the Mughal viceroy of Lahore) lends itself to various interpretations but it shows clearly Balwant Singh's taste for music. This painting shows Nainsukh's maturity of style, his flair for capturing likenesses, his keen insight into character, command of fluid line and deft grouping of figures. Balwant Singh, wearing a white jama and plumed turban, sits on a low chair. In one hand he holds a flower, in the other a hukka stem. In the foreground is part of another turbanned figure. In front of the raja is the musical party of men and women. Behind them stands a servant holding a torch and oil can. The moon in the dark rim of sky above the interior setting indicates that it is night.

Nainsukh excelled in depicting night scenes. A fine example is the *fireworks display* (c. 1751; Victoria and Albert Museum, London). In the foreground two groups of figures watch a pair of servants lighting fireworks in the middle. The raja appears as a tiny figure sitting at a window on the first floor of the palace. Dark shadows and a night sky above sprinkled with stars form the background.

*Nainsukh's self-portrait* (c. 1746 when he was about twenty) shows him in profile. The shapely eyebrows, meditative eyes, beautiful nose and thin moustache give youthful elegance to the finely modelled face. He wears a plain white double-breasted coat and Kangra-type turban. The caste mark on his forehead is Śaivite.

After Balwant Singh's death in 1763, Nainsukh accompanied the ashes of his patron to Haridwar where they were immersed in the Ganga. The fact that this visit was part of a pilgrimage undertaken by Amrit Pal of Basohli suggests that Nainsukh migrated to Basohli after 1763.

## KANGRA

Amid the natural beauty of the Kangra Valley, Pahari painting developed into an art of great charm and delicacy under the influence of its own early traditions as well as refined Guler and Mughal styles. In the late eighteenth century Kangra became the most powerful hill state at the time when the patronage of painting declined in Guler after Govardhan Chand's death. Though Raja Sansar Chand (1775-1823) came to the throne of Kangra when he was only ten years old, before long he set about expanding his domains. In 1786 he recaptured the prestigious Kangra fort from Mughal hands with the help of a highly trained mercenary army, and he enlarged his dominions by annexing various neighbouring states. In the three joint capitals of Kangra—Sujanpur Tira, Sujanpur and Alampur, all on the banks of the Beas river—Sansar Chand built splendid palaces, embellished with ornamental gardens, terraces and fountains. During the winter months the ruler resided in Nadaun lower down near the plains. Sansar Chand's personality combined love of military power and feudal splendour with a keen sensitivity to his cultural milieu. Early in life he already displayed an absorbing interest in poetry, music and painting. A series of portraits of himself show his early interest in painting. The *young Raja Sansar Chand celebrating the 'rain of roses' with his courtiers* is an important historical document since the inscription on the reverse gives the date (March-April 1778) and because it belongs to the ancestral collection of the Lambargaon, descendants of Sansar Chand's brother. With his courtiers around him the adolescent Sansar Chand, dressed in white, sits on the left. A row of seven 'opponents' on the other side, including rulers of friendly states, throw rose petals at each other. A pair of dancing girls with Nurpur type profiles appear below. This active scene is a departure from earlier studies of rulers and reflects Sansar Chand's. lively character.

Through a doorway, in *Sansar Chand of Kangra at Nadaun* (Mian Ram Singh Collection), we get an early glimpse of the Beas river and its bank. *Young Raja Sansar Chand of Kangra with courtiers looking at pictures* (c. 1785) gives farther proof of his devotion to painting even in his youth. He sits towards the right, flanked by Wazir Labha and his younger brother. A child seated in the middle appears to hand out pictures from a green portfolio to the courtiers who admire them. The dark sky as well as the torch bearers show that it is night. In a later painting of the same theme, the pictures in the hands of Sansar Chand, his brother and the courtiers depict romantic scenes.

Lured by his wealth and fame as a generous patron, painters flocked to his court. Artists from the neighbouring state of Guler naturally migrated to Kangra since it was ruled by the same family of Katoch Rajputs and since Sansar Cnand made it pay tribute to him. The court favourite among these artists seemed to be Manaku's son Kausala. Other artists known by name are Nainsukh's son Gaudhu, Fattu, Purkhu, and Bassia.

These Kangra artists produced numerous miniatures inspired by Sansar Chand's devotion to the Kriṣṇa cult and his love for romantic literature. The Rāmāyaṇa and Mahābhārata, the Bhāgavata Purāṇa, Jayadeva's Gīta Govinda, Rasikapriya of Kesava Das, the Sat Sai of Bihari Lal, the Bārāmāsā (cycle of seasons) and the Rāgamālā (musical modes) provided abundant subject matter.

The technique used resembles that of mural painting. First they prepared the carrier, made of several sheets of handmade paper gummed together to get the required thickness. Their favourite paper was called sialkoti (from Sialkot, the place of its manufacture). Sanganeri and Kashmiri papers were less popular. Sometimes a new sheet was used for the top layer while the lower ones consisted of discarded accounts sheets. Then they glazed the top sheet if this had not been done already during manufacture. On this carrier paper they drew the black and red outlines of the composition with a fine brush. Usually they did this freehand though at times they used a pounce to transfer the designs by means of a fine powder. After this they applied white priming either by covering the whole, or part by part. Through this thin coating the outlines remained visible and were reinforced by a second drawing in black or blood red. Now the picture was ready for burnishing to make it smooth by laying the paper face down on a sheet of glass or marble slab and rubbing it with a rounded stone in a quick back-and-forth movement. The rubbing stone, called gholti, was either agate, ivory, marble or the common smooth stones found along the banks of the Beas. Finally they applied colours. Each master had his own method. Often this was done by pupils who followed the notes on colour in the master's sketches. Such sketches have been preserved in the family heirlooms. The colours, mostly mineral, were mixed individually. Usually a gum served as the medium. Gold and silver were added last. They applied several coats of the same colour with burnishing in between to get that richness of tone which has not diminished in brilliance even after two hundred years.

Like all Indian painting the Kangra style is based on line. Nowhere, however, are the lines so fluid, so refined and deceptively free. By means of thin squirrel-hair brushes they succeeded in painting extremely fine lines to depict rain, jewellery and other details.

Though the Kangra artists never mastered the complexities of perspective, the richness of their varied colouring, their mastery of line and sensitive portrayal of nature more than compensates for this.

Inspired by the experiments in Guler—lovely faces and graceful forms, gracious poses and gestures, a harmonious blending of choice colours and the inclusion of nature in its varied moods—the Kangra artists gave eloquent expression to the Rajput ideals of beauty. In their paintings music and poetry, romance and religion are intertwined.

Their fertile output includes two main themes. The first records the royal activities and the second depicts the finest religious and romantic compositions ever painted in India. Above all they created an idealised type of feminine beauty—the focal point of all Kangra art. The most favoured pose was a slightly inclined head. The dress and veil, forming a curve as though filled by a gentle breeze, suggest a graceful forward movement. The stiff architectural forms, mostly of dazzling white marble, help to emphasise the lithe rhythm of the human figures and the delicate colouring of their features.

Scholars have identified two main types of faces. Generally they have long narrow eyes, a sharp nose almost in a straight line with the forehead and a mass of black hair. The unusual distance between the point of the chin and the throat gives the impression of width. In the second so-called Bhāgavata type, because it occurs in the Bhāgavata Purāṇa series, the face is more delicate and discerningly shaded, and the hair painted with fine strokes. The head is longer, the nose small and slightly upturned. This facial type always goes with good overall draftsmanship and is found in the Gīta Govinda, Bhāgavata Purana, Rāgamālā, Sat Sai and Bārāmāsa.

A *Gīta Govinda series,* comprising more than a hundred and forty paintings of which many formed part of the Tehri Garhwal Royal Collections, exemplifies the mature Kangra styles in every way. The Gīta Govinda, celebrating in Sanskrit lyrics the ecstatic love of Rādhā and Kriṣṇa, was generally sung at Weddings. This series may have been commissioned for Sansar Chand's marriage around 1781, and have come to Tehri Garhwal through his two daughters who married Raja Sudarshan Shah of Tehri Garhwal in 1829. Sansar Ghand's son, Anirudh Chand, who fled from the Sikhs to Haridwar in 1828, took with him many valuables. In the following year he may have given the Gīta Govinda paintings which he had inherited from his father as part of the dowry for his sisters. The Garhwal family tradition confirms this view. The style and general composition as well as the inscription on one of the leaves show that it came from Kangra.

Further proof comes from a set of a hundred and fifty-one drawings of a Gīta Govinda series. In 1730 Manaku had painted a Gīta Govinda series for Lady Malini. Manaku's two sons Khushala and Fattu, together with Nainsukh's son Gaudhu became Sansar Chand's court painters. Manaku's sons were well acquainted with the Basohli version. This younger generation of the Raina family, especially Kushala, were entrusted with the painting of the later series. The inscription served perhaps to pay tribute to their illustrious father Manaku.

To increase the devotee's emotional participation in the adventures of their god, the Kangra artists transformed lush groves and orchards of their countryside into the sacred land of Brindavan. The river Beas, its emerald green waters laced with White foam as it winds along between Sujanpur and Alampur, becomes the holy Jamuna. Kriṣṇa himself resembles a handsome Pahari prince and Rādhā a lovely young hill princess, while the local maidens and villagers were changed into idealised gopis and companions of the mischievous young god.

*Rādhā with Dūtikā* (N. C. Mehta Collection, Bombay) has a horizontal arrangement. Meadows slope gently down to both sides of the river fringed by slender trees with dark green leaves. Birds perch on their branches. Sprays of white and pink flowers on the creepers and trees as well as tiny varicoloured blossoms among the grass enrich the decorative quality of the painting. Rādhā wears a golden skirt while her friend's is a deep violet one. Both have orange veils. Heads turned to the right as if hearing his soft footsteps or the magical notes of his flute, they await Krisna's arrival.

*The blindman's buff* (c. 1780; Tehri Garhwal Collection), closely resembling the Gīta Govinda in style, may have come to Garhwal from Kangra on the same occasion. An inscription on the reverse reads 'Māṇak ki likhi' (painted by Manak), but it does not seem to be contemporary with the execution of the painting. It shows Kriṣṇa as a boy, dressed in striped shorts, and yellow scarf, crouching in the centre of the hillock. A cowherd covers Kriṣṇa's eyes while his companions try to find a hiding place. A stream flows in the foreground and cattle rest and graze on its banks. Two thick trees, entwined with flowering creepers, are depicted with great skill. Other trees form a loose circle around the playful boys.

*Rādha and Kriṣṇa in the grove* (c. 1780; Victoria and Albert Museum, London) is a masterpiece with rich scenic beauty, poetic charm and symbolic imagery. Like the creeper and tree beside them, Rādhā and Kriṣṇa, dressed in yellow-orange clothes, sit entwined on a bit of land skirted by a river. Absorbed in each other, they do not seem to notice their beautiful surroundings—delicate plants with pretty blossoms, pink sprays of bloom on the creepers, fresh green branches of trees with birds, lotus flowers swaying in the quiet stream, egrets craning about, and the clear blue sky beyond.

*The hour of cowdust* (Pl. 19.2; c. 1780-1800;

Fig. 350. Worship of Mount Govardhan, Kangra.

Museum of Fine Arts, Boston), probably a work of Sansar Chand's court painters, is outstanding for skillful composition and colouring. This miniature depicts Krișṇa returning in the evening with the cows. The artist shows the movement of the herd jostling and pressing towards the town gate. The herd-boys around the young god and the maidens in the windows above all gaze upon Krișṇa with admiration. The successive strata of architecture and the landscape in the distant background recall the Mughal style. The herd with Krișṇa and his companions enters from the right foreground. The upturned heads and long backs of the cattle, delineated with expert delicacy of line, suggest a convergent movement toward the village gate. Some of the animals have already passed through to an open courtyard beyond. The soft tones of the ladies' dresses and the colouring of the individual cows below them are admirably set off by the chalky whiteness of the buildings. The life and charm of the work come chiefly from the detailed drawing.

*The Bhāgavata Purāṇa paintings* (c. 1780), depicting the story of Krișṇa's incarnation, formed a sequel to the Gīta Govinda series which illustrates his love for Rādhā. Both series count among the greatest achievements of Kangra painting for colour harmony, flowing outlines, skillful composition and beautiful style. The easy naturalism and artistic combination of figures in varied poses seem to indicate that the master painter of the Bhāgavata Purāṇa series was a descendant of Nainsukh— perhaps his son Gaudhu who worked in Sansar Chand's court. The shaded outlines and clear tone, however, make others believe it was Purkhu who, though a native of Kot Kangra, may have adopted the Guler style from artists who had come to Kangra. Since these paintings invariably depict a moonlit scene, their author is usually called 'the master of the moonlight'.

*The worship of Mount Govardhan* (Fig. 350; J. K. Mody Collection, Bombay) is a fine example of the so-called Bhāgavata Purāṇa style. According to the story, Krișṇa told the people of Gokula, who had offered the god Indra special yearly sacrifices, to worship instead the trees and hills on which they depended for a livelihood. When they offered worship to the nearby mount Govardhan, Krișṇa showed himself on its peak while retaining his other form as an ordinary cowherd. The painting focuses on mount Govardhan, its towering peaks of violet and pink crags tinged with greenish shadows. Krișṇa and Balarāma stand in the middle at the foot of the mountain. Three animals rest at the left corner. A cowherd points in wonder at the small figure of Krișṇa seated on the mountain top. His companion stands with folded hands, while a turbanned figure just below bows in deep reverence. Women and cattle approach from the right. A group of musicians occupies the background behind them. Beyond them trees lift their greenery to the pale blue sky with white clouds drifting across. The wizened face of the old man just behind the animals in the foreground forms a charming contrast to the soft features of the child in his arms. He wears a loin cloth, and the black shawl covering his head falls down over his shoulders. The face of the young man in front of him reveals a strong character, showing that the artist portrayed sketches from life. The grouping of the figures, the easy poses, steady lines and harmonious combination of vividly clear and pleasing tones reveal the hand of a genius.

*Indra drowning Gokula* (National Museum, New Delhi) shows Indra's fury at this departure from custom. In revenge he tried to destroy Gokula with continuous torrential rains. Riding his white elephant and holding a thunderbolt, he commands the dark clouds to drown the people of Gokula. The heavy downpour, represented by thin white diagonal lines, bears down upon the trees behind the thatched huts which serve as a background to the agitated figures. The people and cattle rush to Krisṇa for protection. With his foster- father Nanda and brother Balarāma, he sits calmly in a hut on the left.

*Makhan-Chor* or *Krisṇa stealing butter* (F. D. Wadia, Pune) reflects the simple ways of village life, as seen in the curd pot, the methods of churning, and earthenware vessel hung from the ceiling. The painting reverts back to the old Indian tradition of continuous narration by showing Yaśodha twice—running towards a pot boiling over on the extreme right and again churning butter. While she is thus preoccupied, the mischievous Krisṇa steals some butter.

*Gopis waiting for Krisṇa* (F. D. Wadia, Pune) and *Krisṇa and gopis* (Madhuri Desai Collection, Bombay) are typical of the 'master of the moonlight'. The first shows the gopis sitting under trees on a river bank. Their faces reflect sorrow and anxiety when Krisṇa disappeared suddenly after pride had intoxicated them because he had danced with them on the night of the Rās Maṇḍala. In the second picture they meet him again on the river bank. The light of the full moon, shining brightly in the clear autumn sky, gives both paintings an ethereal atmosphere—ghostly white hillsides, pallid blue water and figures resembling porcelain figurines which seem to move as in a trance.

The Pahari version of the Rāgamālā usually consists of eighty-four illustrations. An incomplete Kangra *Rāgamālā* set of eighty paintings (National Museum, New Delhi) testifies to Sansar Chand's interest in music.

Fig. 351. Illustration from Vasanta Raga, Kangra.

In the *Vasanta rāga* (Fig. 351), a simple yet elegant composition, Vasanta (Spring), personified as a boy, dances on a river bank to the music of a drum and cymbals played by two girls dressed in orange and yellow, blue and pink. Vasanta wears a crown of lotuses and peacock feathers, a pink scarf and yellow dhoti. The setting is a green meadow with trees, some dark green and others completely covered with pink and white flowers.

*Ladies at chess* (Mian Chattar Singh Collection) reveals another of Sansar Chand's pastimes. The owner of the painting, a relative of the raja of Arkhi, states that a family tradition assigns the picture to Fattu, the second son of Manaku, who worked for Sansar Chand. With this painting began a convention of using white oval frames with a decorative outer border. This focused attention on the principal figures. These frames became very popular in Kangra between 1785-1820. 'Ladies at chess' has a plain white oval frame and a margin patterned in blue, red and gold. An aristocratic lady, wearing a pale mauve skirt, light brown choli and gold veil, sits with her companion in a marble pavilion, absorbed in a game of chess. The terrace opens out on a view of meadow, a grove of trees, a flowing stream beyond and another hill with a palace on the farther bank. The scenery resembles the view of Alampur as seen from Sujanpur.

*Along the roadside* (Pl. 20.1), one of the scenes from everyday life produced by the Kangra artists, realistically depicts the midday rest of a band of travellers who have gathered around a well under a banyan tree. A tired porter in the foreground stretches out his bedding, while a guard gratefully accepts a drink from a woman at the well. The master reclines at ease, fanned by one maid while another massages his travel-worn feet and a servant prepares his hukka. The whole scene, completely natural, reveals keen power of observation.

In *around the campfire* (Pl. 20.2), another of these everyday scenes, a group of people sit warming themselves near a fire which lights up their faces and a hut nearby while the rest is in shadow under a starry sky. There is an attempt at producing double lighting effects from two light sources.

A more dynamic theme handled by the Kangra school is that of *Kriṣṇa subduing Kāliya nāga* (Pl. 20.3), now in the New York Metropolitan Museum of Art. Though the whirlpool looks unrealistic, the landscape reveals a serious attempt at perspective, and as in other Kangra paintings the figures show real movement. In the main group, the god grips the serpent's tail and his foot crushes its many hoods while the nāga maidens grouped around plead for the life of their lord. The artist has depicted their unanimity of feeling by a striking variety of gestures. The same individuality and expressiveness had been given to the gopis on the river bank who fear for their hero. The desperate look of his old foster-father provides a focal point for this group just as the supremely self-confident young hero is the pivot of the other.

The *Bihari Sat Sai,* though found in Tehri-Garhwal, undoubtedly originated in Kangra. All the pictures in this series have the typical oval frame. A great calm and serenity, indistinguished feminine types and angular architecture generally characterise these simple compositions. Here too glimpses of scenery resemble landscapes of Alampur on the Beas. These traits point to Fattu as the artist but we have no proof.

Similar in shape and technique is the admirable *Bārāmās a* (twelve months) *series* belonging to the Lambargaon ancestral collection. Here again blue, red and gold designs fill in the corners of the oval format while the outer border is yellow. The Bārāmāsa, written by Kesavadas, with its spirited description of the seasons and the various activities of people, provides wonderful subjects for painters, and the artists of Kangra have illustrated them admirably. The portrayal of Sujanpur scenery makes the Lambargaon set especially charming. All the paintings of this series resemble each other in composition and format. Rādhā and Kriṣṇa occupy the foreground, with a scenic background showing the activities typical of the various seasons. Despite the simplicity of technique, the naive perspective and stereotyped faces and figures, these miniatures have a unique charm of their own and a graceful play of curves and clear tones similar to the refrains and harmonies of music which appeal to the emotions more than the mind.

In the *month of Phāgun* (mid-February to mid-March) Kriṣṇa stands on a white terrace with Rādhā, as spring awakens the earth with its warm touch. He looks at her lovingly as he encircles her shoulder with his arm. He wears a long yellow jama and turban and she a gold skirt and white veil. Her delicate hands are dyed with henna. A pear tree behind them has started to flower. The township and sloping hill in the background resemble Sujanpur. A group of people celebrate Holi, the spring festival, by squirting each other with coloured water and powder.

In *Kriṣṇa and the milkmaids* (W. G. Archer Collection, London) Kriṣṇa stands on the bank of the Jamuna embracing Rādhā with one arm while the other stretches across one gopi to touch another. The eyes of the lovers meet while all nature—lotus flowers, trees and cattle —stand enchanted.

At least three series of paintings, apparently commissioned in Kangra, illustrate the *Naiṣadha-charita*, a twelfth century story-poem dealing with a couple tried by misfortunes soon after their marriage, but finally attaining happiness. The unfinished condition of all three sets indicates the unsettled state of Kangra under the Gurkha occupation (1806-1809) and the subsequent decline of Sansar Chand's prosperity. To this late Kangra period (c. 1820-1825) also belongs a Gīta Govinda set (in the ancestral collection of Lambargaon) and a Rasika-priya series (in the Victoria and Albert Museum, London).

As in all examples of a great style, so here too decoration eventually took the place of real vitality and spontaneous grace. The technique became stereotyped and the postures appear artificial, as for example in *Kriṣṇa braiding Rādhā's hair* (Lambargaon Collection). They sit on a black rug, a product of Kangra often seen in these paintings. Krişṇa's yellow dupaṭṭa (scarf) and dhoti contrast with his mauve complexion. She wears an orange veil and golden skirt. A pair of trees flank them and another stands in the foreground. The individual leaves, the branches and trunks of the trees, the three peacocks as well as the lotus flowers and leaves in the stream are drawn in clear, hard outlines. The clouds look more like scrolls. All in all the main subjects seem to get lost among minor details.

## GARHWAL

Garhwal, a small and none too thriving feudal state in the seventeenth century, lies on the north-east fringes of the Punjab Hills. In 1658 a nephew of Aurangzeb sought refuge at Srinagar, the capital of Garhwal, in order to escape his uncle's wrath. With him he brought a painter and his son who settled down there and continued to ply their trade for many generations. Molaram, one of their descendants in the late eighteenth century, painted in the mannerisms of the late decadent Muslim style. However, after 1770 A.D. a number of Garhwal paintings were produced in a superior style surpassing that of Kangra in imaginative content, renewed delicacy and sensitivity of workmanship and design which harmonised with the predominantly romantic subjects.

This exotic style has raised several fascinating problems. Its sudden appearance and short duration of about thirty years suggests that immigrant artists produced it, and Molaram's verses on the back of some of his paintings reveal his bitterness at the encroachment of outsiders. So we know that the Garhwal masterpieces cannot be ascribed to him even though some of them were found in the family collection of his descendants among sketches and line drawings of his own signed works.

Where these artists came from remains to be solved. In spite of close similarity to the Kangra style, Garhwal painting has an individuality of its own. It seems unlikely that artists would have emigrated there from Kangra because Kangra was emerging during this period of Sansar Ghand's prosperity. Most probably both the Kangra and Garhwal styles drew their inspiration from the same source—most probably Guler. Two historical factors strengthen this view. Firstly, Raja Pradhyumna Shah of Garhwal (1785-1804) married a Guler princess and later gave his daughter in marriage to Hari Singh of Guler, who became his courtier and administrator. Secondly Guler artists were threatened by Sikh marauders in 1783 and mav have sought refuge in the secluded state of Garhwal which already had marriage ties with Guler.

Thus the basic idioms of Guler came to a new setting. and evolved into a distinctive style at Garhwal. The typical Garhwal landscapes, with the swirling Alaknanda bathing the feet of the twin hills of Nar and Narayan, are depicted in these paintings.

A further thrust was given to painting in Garhwal when the British made Sudarshan Shah (1815-1859) ruler of a portion of Garhwal with his capital at Tehri. He married two sisters of Sansar Chand and received a number of excellent Kangra miniatures with their dowry. When he gave asylum to Anirudh Chand, his brother-in-law, some Kangra artists may have accompanied the latter.

*Lovers in a moonlit retreat* (c. 1765–c.1775; Kasturibhai Lalbhai Collection, Ahmedabad) exquisitely portrays tender emotions in a tranquil atmosphere. The lover, the renowned Baz Bahadur of Mandu, could not save Rupmati, his beloved. The Garhwal artist has pictured the lovers in a beautiful, secluded retreat in the foothills of the Himalayas. Baz Bahadur, wearing a flowered pink jama and a yellow sashanda pugree (turban) over his delicately modelled features, looks affectionately at Rupmati, dressed in a brown choli with a white transparent skirt over patterned trousers. The red carpet and saddle add a touch of passion to the soft cool shades of undulating hills, lotus pond and pale sky with stars and crescent moon. The predominance of horizontal lines in the reclining figure of Rupmati, the softly curving branches and hills produce the feeling of repose while the vertical lines of tree trunks, the splendid pair of Marwar horses tethered in the left lower corner and the seated figure of Baz Bahadur add a note of strength.

A series of *Nayika paintings* probably derive from the same master artist. Their keenly alert faces differ from the Guler and Kangra type. They have a more aristocratic appearance, with slender figures, delicate wrists and long tapering fingers. Yet they look quite at home in the seclusion of the hill forests.

*Vipralabdha Nāyikā* (Prince of Wales Museum, Bombay) shows her frustration because her beloved did not show up at the appointed place. Wearing a yellow veil, brown choli and bright pink skirt, she throws off her jewels in anger and disappointment. In the foreground flows a smooth grey stream. The lady stands between a bed of fresh green leaves to the right and a slender tree with clusters of leaves on the left. In the background, trees entwined with creepers rise against a pale sky with a few grey clouds and a full moon.

The beautiful *Utkanthita Nāyikā* (Kasturbhai Lalbhai Collection, Ahmedabad) waits for her lover at the bank of a river, unmindful of the fearful darkening jungle in the background. Glimpses of pale sky with crescent moon and stars appear beyond the dense thicket. Flower sprays and white birds add touches of colour to the gloomy thicket. Wearing a bright blue veil with white dots and a dark red skirt, she sits on a bed of yellow-green leaves. In the foreground egrets and ducks revel in the greyish water. A deer stands nearby.

Undaunted by the lightning and storm of a rainy night, the *Abhisārika Nāyikā* (Fig. 352; British Museum, London) ventures out to meet her lover. The snakes gliding about in the foreground suggest the hazards lurking in the gloomy shadows of the forest around her. The sharp lines of her veil and the zigzag hem of her skirt which she grasps with one hand indicate the turmoil of mingled eagerness and fear within her.

The Krișņa story as well as romantic love poetry became very popular in Garhwal, but

Fig. 352. Abhisarika Nayika, Garhwal.

the rulers showed a decided bias for Śaivism and the Śaivite Ghandan tilaka (crescent mark of sandalwood paste on the forehead) was applied to all figures of Garhwal painting whether the subject matter was Śaivite or Vaișņavite.

Of the existing versions of *Kaliya Damana*, the first has a vertical arrangement, acquired by Mukandi Lal from Molaram's descendent, who attributed it to Molaram. The painting illustrates the first verse of the Gīta Govinda, calling upon Krișņa as the conqueror of the snake Kaliya which had polluted the Jamuna and tormented the people of Brindavan. The boyish Krișņa, with bluish-grey complexion, dances on the snake's hood. The five nāginīs implore him to spare their lord. The importance of this painting lies in the representation of Garhwal scenery: the Nar and Narayan hills in the background with royal palaces and the swirling Alaknanda river—a characteristic idiom of Garhwal.

The first two pictures illustrating the Krișņa-Sudama story show the touch of a master painter while the nine other paintings of the series come from a less skillful artist. The technique and general composition of *Sudamds hovel* (Fig. 353; c. 1775-1790; Victoria and Albert Museum, London) bring to mind the Abhisārika and Utka Nāyikā with their spear-shaped sprays of flowers. And the delicate features of Sudama's wife look like Rupmati's. The painting shows Sudama's wife, wearing a patched brown skirt and faded veil, begging her husband to go to his boyhood friend Krișņa to seek freedom from their poverty. Sudama, in his olive-green tatters, looks half-scandalised as he listens to her suggestion. A row of saplings on the left support the thatched roof gaping with holes. The broken spinning wheel and basket show their miserable condition. By way of contrast, the roofs of big houses beyond a wall in the background rise against a dark blue sky.

The dignified beauty of the *Varśa Vihara* (Museum of Fine Arts, Boston) is a Garhwal masterpiece with its artistic contrast of fresh and dark colours, and its deceptively delicate yet vigorous outlines. Under great dark clouds streaked with lightning and in a heavy downpour indicated by fine parallel lines, Krișņa and Rādhā take shelter in a cowherd's dark blanket used as a cloak. A pair of trees protecting two yellow birds and a peacock spread their foliage above them. Two gopis carrying pitchers on their heads leave in haste towards the left. While one cowherd sits inside a hollow tree, the other uses a lotus leaf as an umbrella.

Fig. 353. Sudama's hovel, Garhwal.

Their three cows have dispersed in different directions. Seven white cranes fly up into the sky.

The greatness of Garhwal painting rests on the early masterpieces. Though they lack some of the lively animated grouping characteristic of mature Kangra painting they have a rhythmic curving of lines, and the aristocratic women, beautiful and elegantly arranged in tableau-like compositions, summarise by means of line and colour the Indian attitude to love. These gems of painting bring to mind nostalgic ideals of bygone days, of security and love in idyllic landscapes among the Himalayan foothills.

Other than Molaram who, besides his own commonplace creations, made poor imitations of many Kangra masterpieces, the name of Chaitu is associated not only with a Rāmāyaṇan series but is also written in Nagari script on the back of an illustration from the Mahābhārata of the abduction of the Yadava women. Believed to have been a descendent of Manaku of Guler, he may have migrated to Tehri during the reign of Sudarshan Shah (c. 1817). His supple contours, warm colours—particularly yellow and red to set off white—characterise his paintings. The late Kangra style continued in Tehri until the middle of the nineteenth century.

## MODERN INDIAN PAINTING

Indian painting reached almost a dead end towards the close of the nineteenth century. The Late Mughal and Pahari schools had both exhausted their vitality. In short, an arid lack of spirit and mere formalism pervaded Indian art at that time.

In reaction, Indian creativity began to stir again in the late nineteenth and early twentieth centuries. It was not yet the beginning of a new national art, but at least an interpretation of Indian life and vision through Indian eyes. The champion of this first renaissance was *Raja Ravi Varma* (1848-1906), famous for his mythological and epic works such as Rāvaṇa and Jaṭāyu has been criticised for standing at the threshold of Indian art as a historic failure: his heroes seem little more than the bourgeois, his gods badly dressed-up yatra actors, his lovers look cloyingly sentimental and his tragic scenes lack the dignified self-restraint of genuine heroic art. However, it will always stand to his credit that he re-introduced Indian subjects and cherished national ideals and visions.

The next step forward, from national themes to a national style, proved to be more difficult. To a certain extent this was achieved by establishing *government schools of art* in the presidency towns of Madras, Calcutta, Bombay and Lahore. The coming of E. B. Havell as principal of the Calcutta School of Arts infused a vital element into Indian painting. He was the first Englishman to appreciate Indian art for its own values.

Rajput miniatures and Ajanta murals, hitherto little known, were at last published. Sir Alexander Cunningham, James Fergusson and others began to survey the monuments of the artistic past. In 1902 the *Archaeological Survey of India* was founded and its reports did much to awaken in Europe as well as India an appreciation of the beauties of Indian art and the ideals which inspired it. At the same time Indian artists turned for inspiration to the truly native tradition.

The Bengal School originated with the work of Abanindranāth Tagore in 1895, and soon became national. The name *Bengal School* applies to a style rather than a regional development or period of time. This school represents the first important art movement in modern India.

*Abanindranath Tagore* (1871-1951) was born at Jorasanko, the Tagore residence in Calcutta. Creative activity formed a part of daily life in the Tagore household. The presence of Rabindranath Tagore probably exercised the greatest influence and the poet's encouragement meant a great deal to Abanindranath. When Shantiniketan was well established, Rabindranath introduced the teaching of art as a separate department called Kala Bhavan.

Abanindranath's formal education consisted of some years spent at the Sanskrit College (1881-1890). From this stems his understanding and love of Indian classics. At this stage he also came across a few Irish illustrations and an album of Mughal miniatures, and between these two trends of art, one foreign and the other partly indigenous, Abanindranath's discerning eye found some strange affinity, and a new gate to the world of art opened wide before him. Thereupon, he created a new series of Rādhā-Krisṇa paintings, born out of this fresh enthusiasm.

Abanindranath's teaching methods were widely appreciated. He was tolerant but insisted that the students should have a sound knowledge of their own historic culture.

In a way, Abanindranath's career as an artist began after he came into contact with Havell who inspired him to pursue the technique followed in the Mughal miniatures. By the time he had achieved artistic maturity both in ideas and execution, he became acquainted with the noted Japanese connoisseur, Okakkura, through whom he got an opportunity to understand the art and culture of China and Japan. The impact of Japanese influence on his works shows up quite often in extraneous decoration. A study of his techniques in the *death of Shah Jahan* reveals the evolution of his style. From the Mughal tradition he inherited the qualities of line and sensitive modelling. But these never formed the technical base exclusively, for his technique has the transparent, liquid quality of an aquarelle or water colour. In support of the statements made above, the paintings on *Omar Khayyam* (Fig. 354; 1905-1907) serve as examples. In this series, inspired by a literary theme, his genius reveals itself in the way he handles colour. His light casts no shadows and his space is organised without any conventional perspective.

Fig. 354. Abanindranath Tagore : Omar Khayyam.

Abanindranath showed signs of further development between 1920 and 1930 when he did a number of pastel portraits and a series of mask drawings. However, the most important of his paintings during this period were his *landscapes* (1926-27). Their appeal lies primarily in the colouring.

His genius probably reached its zenith when he illustrated the series on the *Arabian nights* (1930) in which, despite the theme, he depicted the experience of his own time, thereby bridging old Baghdad and modern Calcutta so imaginatively that his own city stands out convincingly against the Arabian subject.

In his *Kabi Kankan* and *Krișņa Mangai* series (1938) he embarked on a new treatment. These works show an altogether novel atmosphere—colour now becomes subservient to form, which gets full stress. He uses only a few primary colours, usually flat and sometimes graded; but his contours, in black, are bold and heavy. Though the subject-matter remains traditional, he adopts some features of the folk style also. In *Krișņa slaying the horse Kesu,* the dynamic quality is notable and the animals, birds and people stand out in straightforward simplicity.

After 1940, he found a new interest in creating toys or works of sculpture, called katum-katum (bizarre forms), made out of shoots from trees, fruit seeds, bits of paper and similar insignificant materials.

When he died in 1951 his pioneering efforts had given a new direction to Indian art, ably carried on by his students.

After Abanindranath, *Nandalal Bose* (1883-1966) is acknowledged as the major painter of the Bengal School. He had great respect for the Indian tradition not only in art but also in life, and so he treated mythological themes more realistically. His constant reference to reality gives added vigour to his paintings. In 1910 he visited Ajanta and the Bagh caves. His best work is undoubtedly rooted in Indian art in spite of his many eclectic paintings. At first he adopted the wash-technique of Abanindranath—for example in *Śiva drinking poison Pārthasarāthi* and *return of the Buddha*—but a new reality breathes in these paintings if we compare them with those of his master.

He adopted a second style, based on linear expression and the reinterpretation of traditional forms, as for instance in the *Veena player* (Fig. 355). In *Ardhanārīśwar*, strong clear lines enclose an idealised figure against a background of some simple shape, and filled in with colourful decorative patterns. His *murals for Kala Bhavan* and the *panels for the Haripura Congress* belong to another category. Here the subject-matter was genre, depicting the life of the people. These paintings, such as *mother and child,* exhibit boldness, vigour and strong decorative qualities.

Fig. 355. Nandalal Bose: veena player.

Another method of his emphasised brush-work—*fishermen at Gopalpur* shows a close link with far-eastern technique—the brush strokes are visible, the bare paper appears between the strokes and no details distract from the main theme.

His subject-matter was either noble or rustic —the former suggesting the majesty of the gods and the latter the tranquility of an ideal, unspoiled country life. In his vision of nature he perceived something hardy and dependable which comes through in his art.

*Kshitindranath Majumdar* (1891-1975) one of Abanindranath's early followers, shows an impressive simplicity in his pictures which reflect the joys and sorrows, the customs and gatherings, the religious leaders and the people of the rural Bengal where he grew up. The spirituality of his simple and austere childhood remained with him and permeated his work, such as his depiction of the life of *Sri Chaitanya* and *Sri Kriṣṇa.*

Employing the wash technique of Abanindranath Tagore, Kshitindranath's skill manifests itself in the emotive quality of his line: geometric, angular and tight where austerity is required as in *Sri Chaitanya*; or exuberant, swirling and sensuous where vivacity and abandon are portrayed as in *Rādhā embracing the Tamal Vriksha.* His artistic talent will always be cherished for its naive realism and gentle Indian flavour.

*K. Venkatappa* (1887-1965), a pure traditionalist, lacks the clarity of style of his master Abanindranath Tagore. His strength, however, lies in an unaffected and deeply religious tone which infuses his paintings. This, together with the naive enchantment of his work established a personal style. An aura of mysticism predominates in his *mad after veena* and Mahā-*sivrātri.* Wnen representing stories he aimed chiefly at depicting them vividly. His *landscapes*, painted in the southern hill stations, show naturalism, fine craftsmanship and bright colours.

*Asit Kumar Haidar* (1890-1964), a distinguished disciple of Abanindranath Tagore, differed from his colleagues in his wealth of style and subject-matter. Early in his career he made numerous copies of the paintings at Ajanta, Bagh and Jogimara. His own *meeting of Rāma and Guha* and the *worship of the ashoka tree* show a strong impress of the ancient murals.

For his medium he used tempera, oil or water colour according to the requirement of the subject. In addition he discovered a special technique—lacquered painting on wood (or lacsit). This lacsit painting of his is mainly allegorical, like *veils of day and night.*

A discussion of the general characteristics of the Bengal School may help to make it more understandable. The personal style of its originator Abanindranath had a great influence on it. His subjects are mostly literary, and this has led writers to value them only as illustrations. He turned to the format and size of the Mughal miniatures and this smallness became characteristic of the school.

The Bengal School observed two major techniques. The first, a personal invention of Abanindranath, is usually called the wash, an alternative process of applying water colour and dipping in a basin of water till the desired shade comes out. This produces a hazy or misty atmosphere. Finishing touches are added by heightened details, highlights or even gold. Tempera, however, was more popular with the school.

The colours, one of the most important elements in their work, possess a sharp luminosity. Some paintings have one dominant hue, with its shades or values providing variety. Perspective too, is employed only when it contributes something to the painting, and space is usually treated rather ambiguously, although there is structural arrangement.

Though nearly always naturalistic, the figures usually have an ethereal beauty about them. Other painters, however, opted for a bolder and more rugged beauty, though none of them show extravagant gestures or movements. Though Abanindranath took an interest in portraits, his followers did not show much love for this field. Their representations of the gods are poetic renderings, not images for worship.

The early style of the school, dominated by Abanindranath Tagore, took the lead till about 1930. Later many hardy versions replaced the gentle, charming, somewhat feminine style of the originator. Even during the first half of the twentieth century a number of painters remained independent of the Bengal School, among them Gaganendranath Tagore, Rabindranath Tagore, Amrita Sher Gil and Jamini Roy. They took greater interest in the folk arts and in the potential of rural India as subjects for painting.

*Gaganendranath Tagore* (1867-1938), an elder brother of Abanindranath, started painting quite late in life merely for his own pleasure. His works reveal versatility in choice of subjects and their interpretation. He was the first in India to caricature social facts and evils. In *priest and pilgrim* he comments on the exploitation of the common man by religious personages. He also did a large number of portraits with a brush-drawing technique. His landscapes, in monochrome or soft dull shades, are the most naturalistic of his works. In his later semi-abstract works he portrays the exteriors of houses, silent and uninhabited, such as the *desolate house*. Abstraction takes over completely in his cubist work where the elements cannot be recognised. Small angular shapes are manipulated in such a way as to create the impression of movement on the canvas. In *laughter*, small geometric facets ripple across the canvas to represent the quality of laughter in abstract terms.

If the rising generation of politicians were inspired to alleviate the lot of the peasants, the aim of a whole group of young and promising artists was to express their dignity in order to help others see the fundamental grace of these emaciated bodies and of the spirit still unbroken by centuries of depressing poverty.

The real stimulus to creation came from the rediscovery of the village by educated Indians early in the twentieth century.

*Amrita Sher Gil* (1913-1941) was undoubtedly the greatest among these rising young artists. Of mixed Sikh-Hungarian parentage, she was trained in Paris and master therefore of western technique. Wholly Indian in spirit, she declared on her return to India in 1934, 'I realised my real artistic mission: to interpret the life of Indians and particularly the poor Indians pictorially; to paint those silent images of infinite submission and patience,...to reproduceon canvas the impression their sad eyes created in me'.

However the artists whose work influenced her most were not Indians. From Cezanne she learnt to strive for 'simplified naturalism', and from Gauguin, not his sensuality (though this has an affinity with ancient Indian art) but rather his melancholy.

Strongly reminiscent of Cezanne yet thoroughly Indian, is the *child wife*, one of her best pictures. The subject sits in the familiar Indian pose: one knee up, the other leg lying sideways, sharply bent at the knee. By elongating the limbs so that the raised knee is almost at the shoulder level, the artist gives the impression of childish thinness, further accentuated by the straightness of the startlingly white blouse. The face of this child appears inexpressibly sad. The large eyes look out from under the straight long hair. The title explains the sadness. The thick lips, strongly highlighted, express an almost sulky resentment— not generally found among older women, in India, accustomed as they are to have their fate decided for them by others.

*Hill men* (Fig. 356), painted in 1935, shows a group whose straight vertical lines heighten the over-riding melancholy of the theme. Two turbaned men stand half facing each other, While a woman, no less melancholy, sits at their feet, the outline of arm and knee no more than suggested under the smooth clothing, just as the form of the men is merely hinted at under their enveloping shawls. Here too the artist arrests the eye by a bold use of pure white in the turban and the pyjama of the younger man, in order to relieve and at the same time to emphasise the deliberately featureless dull browns and blues of the main colour areas.

Another melancholy group, painted at the same period, is *hill women.* They wear the kameez and tung pyjama of the Simla region, but details are obscured, as in the former, by the dupatta (upper cloth) draped over the head and across the body, so that all the main lines of the composition are again vertical. In the figure on the right the treatment of the transparent dupatta resembles that of the Buddha's clothing in the Mathura statues: almost perfectly regular sweeping lines of white serve to indicate the folds.

Fig. 356. Amrita Sher Gil : Hill men.

Other young artists, in reaction to the Bengal School, turned to the villages not only for their subjects but also for their technique. Such, in Bengal, was *Jamini Roy* (1887-1972). He was bom in a West Bengal village and received his art training in the Calcutta School. He grew dissatisfied with the academic style and with city life and turned to the folk-art of Bengal for his inspiration. At first the bazaar paintings of Kalighat, a suburb of Calcutta, drew his attention. From about 1925 he started painting in the glowing colours and flowing curves of this style, those subjects that really mattered to him. Yet while the manner was daringly simple, the composition had all the subtlety of the mature artist. He left academic portraiture for the painting of village scenes, especially among the Santals. Disgust with the sordidness of city life led him to return to the simple virtues of this primitive tribe remembered from his childhood.

From 1931 onwards he replaced the sweeping curves of Kalighat for the angular forms

Fig. 357. Rabindranath Tagore: design.

and harsh lines of patuas (village artists), and in place of western colours he adopted the local dyes. At first he continued painting village subjects, but the magnificent physique of the Santals no longer concerned him. Though not a Christian, he turned to the theme of Christ's life. Later he returned to his earlier style and to the subject-matter of Bengal village art.

Another individual artist should be mentioned, namely the poet *Rabindranath Tagore* (1861-1941), who took up the brush instead of the pen in his old age—he was over sixty-five. Completely untrained, his style is all his own, though it had been compared to that of Paul Klee because both had a strong sense of rhythm which informed their painting as much as their writing, and also because with both of them painting expressed subconscious impulses—for the picture came first, the subject second, and the title if any, last. In fact it was only with reluctance that Tagore gave names to his pictures at all. 'I do not draw after thinking of a subject', he said, 'accidentally the form of something of unknown family and characterises at the point of my moving pen—'like the birth of Sīta at the point of Kmg Janak's ploughshare' (Fig. 357). Though much of his later work does not attain the standard of that produced between 1928 and 1930, his best picture have three essential features in common: they are unmistakably modern in style and feeling, entirely individual, and at the same time very Indian.

Before and since the attainment of Independence, various groups of painters have grown up in different cities. They must be mentioned, though a detailed examination of the artists involved must be left to the art critic, for their development is too recent for the art historian to obtain a true perspective. In Calcutta, besides Jamini Roy, Rathin Maitra, Pradosh Das Gupta, Gopal Ghose, N. Majumdar and others have been experimenting in evolving an individual style.

In Bombay, K. K. Hebbar, S. Ghavda, V. S. Gaitonde, Akbar Padamsee, F. N. Souza, Raza, M. F. Hussain and others are developing their individuality.

Krishna Hebbar (1911-1996) came from a scenic village in South India. From his childhood days he had a predilection for village festivals which were enriched with folk culture. This is reflected in his art. During his formative years his style was electic, being a mixture of Impressionism, Indian Mughal, Rajput and Ajanta painting.

Lines are the chief means of expression for Hebbar and these are sensitively rendered. A good example is the *Bali dance*. His subjects are mainly village scenes and for this reason his works are filled with builders, farmers, fisher- folk etc. The people in his paintings never pose but are always natural like the artist himself.

Shiavax Ghavda (1914-1990) came from Gujarat and studied in Bombay at Sir J. J. School of Art. From his childhood he was familiar with the Indian way of life. He always studied the characteristics, features, postures and movements of people as well as animals. All these are rendered with the bare minimum of lines, simple shading and with very little colour combination. The sensitivity and the

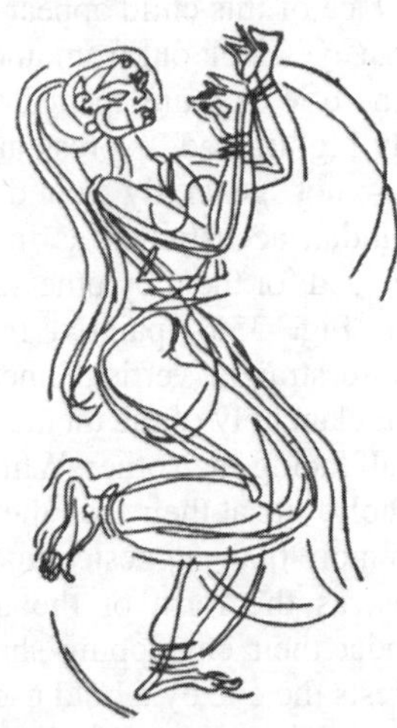

Fig. 358. Shiavax Chavda : Bharatha Natyam dancer.

vitality with Which he rendered the dancers is superb. A very good example is *the Bharata Natyam dancer* (Fig. 358). Not only are his dancing figures rendered masterfully but also his animal sketches reveal the same vigour, energy and muscularity. The art of Chavda lies in his rendering of lines.

In Baroda, N. S. Bendre (1910-1992) is one of the most promising younger artists. Born at Indore, in Madhya Pradesh, he had his schooling in art at the State School of Art, Indore. Before he settled down to his teaching profession at Baroda, Bendre travelled all over India. His early paintings were mainly landscapes with rustic Indian scenes done in a mixed style of wash and gouache. His brush strokes are bold and the colours brilliant and rich. He also has a predilection for lines and these together with the colours are the vital elements of his works throughout.

Bendre's restlessness led him to experiment with various techniques and he soon grew away from his early subjects of landscapes. He was also influenced by Cubism, and the feature which struck him most in this movement was the reduction of the three-dimensional world to conform with the two-dimensional surface of the canvas. Some of his most striking works are *boats, cow and calf, sunflower and thorn.*

In Delhi the most prominent painters are Satish Gujral, Ram Kumar, Sailoz Mukerjee, K. S. Kulkami and Kanwal Krishna.

*Sailoz Mukerjee* (1907-1960), born in Calcutta, was influenced by the Bengal School.

Fig. 359. Sailoz Mukerjee: windy day

His main medium of painting is oil. His subject matter is always very clear and includes landscapes, women at work, rustic scenes.

Sailoz Mukerjee uses the medium of oil with great understanding. He applies colour very finely, not thick as in impasto. The colours are luminous and his combinations show great skill. In his landscapes he creates space by the artistic use of colours rather than by perspective. His arrangement of the entire Work is usually asymetrical but well balanced—a good example being *the windy day* (Fig. 359).

Fig. 360. K. Srinivasulu: Krishnalila.

In the South, especially in Madras, we have K. C. S, Paniker, K. Madhava Menon, P. L. Narasimhamurthy, K. Srinivasuiu and Kokkapati Krishna Murthy.

K. C. *S. Paniker* (1911-1978), bom at Coimbatore, developed the Southern School. He had a passion for rich and pure colours and this became a characteristic feature of his work. His figures are not conceived as masses but rendered continuously, having a rhythmic movement. His red *interior* reminds one of Matisse with its rich exuberance of colours and its composition. Although there appears to be a massing of colours, they are delicately superimposed. Paniker was undoubtedly a great master of colour.

*K. Srinivasulu* (1923-1995) was born in Madras. His father was an amateur toy maker and this influenced him a great deal in his art. Srinivasulu also had an opportunity to copy the murals at Lepakshi and this too proved to be another influencing factor. He also copied Jaina miniatures, and the beauty of their designs and rich colours left an indelible mark on him. Jamini Roy's simplicity of design also influenced him. A good illustration of the various influences is the *Krişņa lila* (Fig. 360). Here we find the simplicity of design of Jamini Roy, the rich colours of Jaina miniatures and the toy-like rendering of the figures. The rich overall design of the whole composition reflects the Lepakshi murals.

Maqbool Fida Husain (1915-2011) of Sholapur belongs to the Progressive Artist Group. Early in life he began making portraits and in the evenings he painted landscapes by lantern light. With these landscape paintings he developed a sharp memory and an uncanny feeling for colour.

Husain is also a fine draughtsman, and for him line is never a separate element but exists side by side with form and colour. His figure types derive from wooden toys, which he distorts for greater expression.

His medium is mainly oil, but he also makes pen and ink sketches. His paintings include *1 came across*, *Padmini*, *green song* and *village life.*

# THE WEST

ANCIENT ART

# 2. EGYPTIAN ART

## GENERAL SURVEY

Egypt, in north-east Africa, had one of the oldest great civilizations which developed a magnificent art. The country consists of two long strips of fertile land, on either bank of the river Nile. It is not blessed with rain, but depends for its water on the periodic heavy downpours in Ethiopia, where the river takes its source. Then it overflows its banks, and spreads out to the high cliffs hemming it in on both sides. After the waters recede, the ground is covered with a fine black mud, or alluvial soil, which fertilizes it. For this reason, the early Egyptians called their country Kemet or Kemi, meaning black earth. The present name is a corruption of Homer's word for the country and its river. In this fertile land, primitive peoples settled down and planted grain. Soon they realized the need of working out an irrigation system to get the full benefit of the inundations. Before 3000 B.C., they also developed a sort of picture-writing called hieroglyphics, invented the calendar, and found new metals.

Small states formed which slowly merged into two kingdoms : Upper Egypt (in the south) and Lower Egypt (the delta of the Nile, in the north), both ruled by pharaohs. Around 3200 B.C., Menes united the two kingdoms. He assumed supreme power, appropriating the land, and enslaving the bulk of the people.

This earliest period of a strong government in Egypt is usually known as the Old Kingdom (about 4000-2280 B.C.). The capital was Memphis, almost at the delta of the Nile. This period was remarkable for the building of the pyramids and achievements in early sculpture. After an interval of decadence the Middle Kingdom arose (about 2065-1783 B.C.). The rulers set up their capital at Thebes, and excelled mainly in building temples. Instead of pyramids, they preferred rock-cut tombs penetrating deep into the cliffs along the Nile. Sculpture also flourished. Finally came the New Kingdom or Empire (from 1580-1085 B.C.).

Out of the complicated aspects of Egyptian religion, one point had the greatest bearing on art. namely their idea of the future life. They considered it as an extension of earthly existence, with all its requirements. Therefore they preserved the body by mummification, so that the ka, its spiritual double, could re-enter it. Offerings of food and other material satisfactions and comforts were put into the tomb to permit a normal continuation of physical life in the world of spirit. Statues and painted reliefs of servants filled the burial chambers, to be at the beck and call of their deceased masters, who could restore them to life by a word of incantation.

Near the end of the Middle Kingdom, however, the attitude became more mature. They realized that a happy after-life could be secured only by justice, truth, and righteousness in this life. When Egypt became an empire ruling over other peoples, the need of a universal god for all men was seen by a few, notably Amenophis IV, who introduced the worship of one god, Aton. He changed his own name to Akhenaten and composed beautiful hymns in his honour. But after his death the priests and people returned to polytheism and the practice of magic.

## ARCHITECTURE

When we study the buildings of the Old Kingdom, one feature strikes us : we find mainly one kind of monument, imposing tombs. The Egyptians lavished all their energy, engineering skill, and artistic talent on creating safe abiding places for their dead. The most impressive example by its combination of massive grandeur and simple form, is the pyramid, or royal tomb, the climax of a long evolution.

In very remote times, as far as we can ascertain, the Egyptians may have buried their dead in pits on which they heaped sand and stones. Slowly they built solid masonry over it, in the form of a truncated pyramid. This kind is called a mastaba, a modern Arab word meaning bench, because the workmen engaged in the excavation works saw a resemblance. The top is flat and the sides slope over a grave or burial chamber deep under the ground, which after the mummified body had been lowered, was walled up, and the shaft leading down to it was filled with rubble and carefully concealed to make it as inaccessible as possible. The mastaba (Fig. 361) contained the serdab, a chamber with one or several statues of the deceased. It was inaccessible from the outside, but according to Egyptian belief, the ka, being spiritual, could pass through solid masses. The effigies of the dead were put there so that if the mummified body were destroyed, they could replace it, and the soul could enter them instead. There was also a mortuary chapel in the mastaba, which could be entered from the outside. Inside there was a false or imitation door for the ka, who could pass through it to fetch the offerings put there. The walls of these and other accessory rooms (frequent in later mastabas) were covered with painted reliefs with ritual scenes or people doing everyday work. These were meant to help the spirit, who could call them to life by incantations, and so surround himself with hordes of servants to provide for the necessities and enjoyments of life.

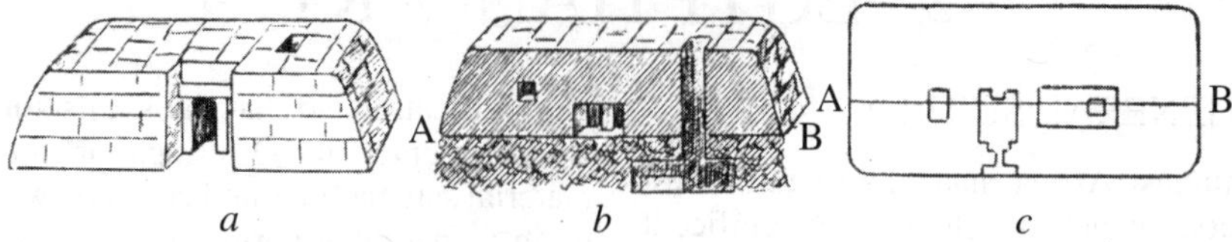


Fig. 361 Mastaba: *a*. bird's- eye view, *b*. section, *c*. plan.

The mastaba was not only an early form of the pyramid, but even in later times it remained the burial place of the nobles, sometimes surrounding the great pyramids reserved for the pharaohs. Some powerful rulers may have piled mastaba upon mastaba, to form the *step pyramid* (Fig. 362), of which several are extant.

Fig. 362 Step pyramid.

That of *Zoser* at *Saqqâra* , belonging to the Third Dynasty, is a good example. By filling up the steps of this kind of monument, the pure pyramidal form took shape. With the help of the existing remains, this seems a logical theory to draw concerning its development.

The pyramid (Fig.363) is the most characteristic of the Egyptian tomb buildings during the Old Kingdom. Its massive form is a simple geometrical pattern : four triangular sloping sides stand on a square base and unite in a point at the top. It has the same parts as the mastaba, but placed in a different way. The latter is a single composite building, while the pyramid conceals no more than the burial chamber, which is no longer deep under the ground but in the centre at a certain height. Galleries

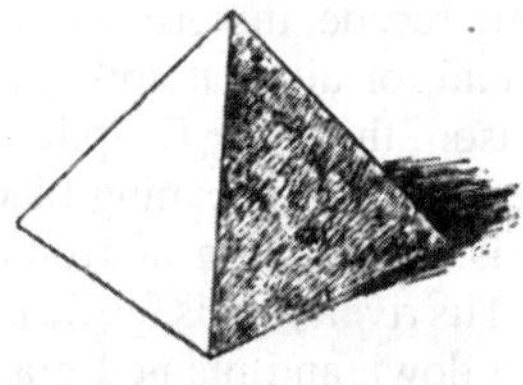

Fig. 363 Pyramid.

or corridors lead there from the entrance, which faces north. After the funeral, this opening was carefully hidden. A mortuary temple, for statues and offerings, corresponding to the serdab and chapel of the mastaba, stood at the eastern side of the pyramid.

Not far from Memphis, on the western bank of the Nile, is *Gizeh*, the most interesting *pyramid field*, with three great pyramids : those of *Khufu* (Cheops), *Khafre* (Chefren), and *Mycerinus* (Menkure) (Pl. 21.1 ).

The *pyramid of* the pharaoh *Khufu* is the largest structure man ever erected. Its square base is about 236 metres on each side, and it covers some 5¼ hectares. The original height was about 147 metres. The whole is a solid bulk, composed of some 2,300,000 blocks of limestone, each weighing about 2,540 kgm. These came from the eastern cliffs, where they were first roughly hewn, then floated across the river at the time of high Nile, to the building site on the western plateau. There the cutting was finished with great precision, by means of very primitive instruments such as knotted ropes. This was done entirely by human labour. Thousands of slaves were engaged in this colossal work of shaping, dragging and raising the huge blocks on temporal ramps made of sand heaps, and putting them into place in decreasing courses of layers, thus forming a step pyramid. After reaching the top, the angles were filled in, and the whole was covered with sheets of polished marble for the double purpose of decorating the whole and of completely hiding the entrance. These sheets are now missing from this pyramid but traces of them can be seen on the top of another, that of Khafre.

The interior of the pyramid of Khufu (Fig.364 can be reached from the northern entrance.

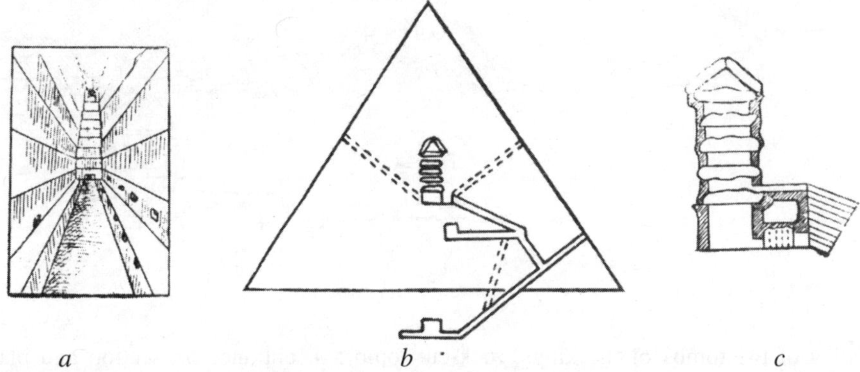


Fig. 364 Pyramid of Khufu, interior : *a*. great gallery: *b*. section of the pyramid with king's burial chamber in the centre: *c*. ceiling of king's burial chamber. Gizeh.

Passages, of which the last one is called the great gallery (Fig. 364*a*) because of its size, lead up to the king's burial Chamber (Fig. 364b*)* Here the mummy or embalmed body of the pharaoh was placed in a sycamore coffin within a granite sarcophagus. The place is ventilated by two air-shafts, on opposite sides, leading to the outer face of the pyramid. The ceiling (Fig. 364*c*) is elaborately constructed of stone slabs, One above the other, separated by blocks and resting on the solid masonry, to support the enormous weight above. Under this room is the queen's chamber; below the ground level there is another crypt, perhaps a well.

Every pyramid was surrounded by additional buildings, which have perished in most cases, but they are sufficiently well preserved around the *pyramid* of *Khafre* (Fig. 365), the middle one at Gizeh, to enable us to study them. The mortuary temple was built on the eastern side. It contained apartments for the statues, and storerooms for linen, grain, honey, oil and other donations of food and drink, together with the ceremonial vessels. Since gifts had to be brought frequently, a closed passage was built leading up from the valley, to avoid the tiresome climb over the sandy desert in the hot sun. At its entrance near the Nile, a flat-roofed vestibule was provided, which is wrongly called the valley temple. These were the additional buildings that surrounded the pyramids, and the whole is called the pyramid complex.

Fig. 365 Pyramid of Khafre, Gizeh.

The pharaohs of the Middle Kingdom did not build any more pyramids, not because their belief in the future life had changed, but they realized that in such a conspicuous position the mummy was not safe. In reality none of these great tombs has been found intact, thieves having penetrated everywhere. The rulers now chose a rocky hill on the western side of the Nile, not far from their new capital Thebes, and tunnelled their tombs deep into the rock. This place is called *the valley of the tombs of the kings (F*ig. 366). To keep the place hidden, and also because of its inaccessibility, the temple was no longer built near the tomb, but at a distance on the river bank. Care was taken, however to see that they were on the same axis, or in line with each other. During the pharaoh's lifetime, it was dedicated to the gods, but after his death it became his mortuary temple. The most wonderful example is that of queen Hatshepsut (about 1500 B.C.) at Deir-el-Bahri.

During the Middle Kingdom many temples were erected exclusively for the worship of the gods. The most famous and gigantic of them are those at *Luxor* and *Karnak* on the eastern side of the Nile, facing Thebes. At first they were simple, but to the original buildings additions were made later by successive pharaohs, obstructing and complicating the clarity of the original plan.

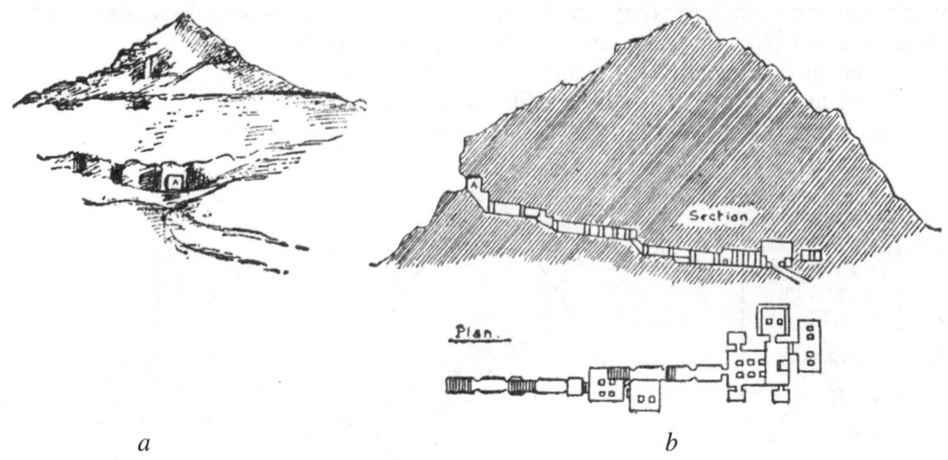


Fig. 366. Valley of the tombs of the kings, rock-cut tomb : *a*, entrance, *b*. section and plan. Thebes.

The smaller examples are more suitable for the study of the different parts. One such is the well-preserved *temple* at *Edfu* (Fig. 367), although it belongs to a later date. A long avenue, bordered on both sides by a row of recumbent animal figures, leads to a pair of colossal seated figures of the pharaoh. Before these are two high monoliths with pointed tops, called obelisks, meaning roasting sticks. They are inscribed with the king's glorious accomplishments. Directly behind stands the monumental gateway or pylon (Fig. 368), which consists of two huge rectangular sloping walls with a broader base and narrowing top, ending in a concave or outward-bending moulding. Between these is the entrance, surmounted by a lower architrave with the same concave moulding on the top. It opens on a large open courtyard with colonnades on three sides. Beyond this the common people were not permitted to go into the hypostyle hall, still less into the sanctuary beyond. This is a low, dark, mysterious room with the statue of the deity. Here only the royal family and priests could enter. A girdle-wall surrounds three sides, the front is closed with the pylon.

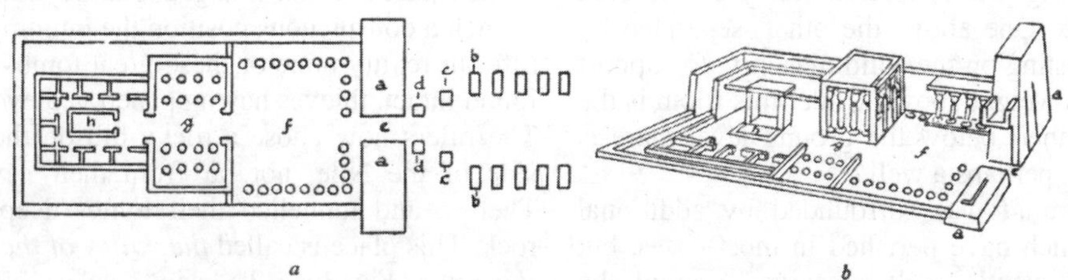

Fig. 367. Temple at Edfu : *a*. plan, *b*. bird's eye view half open.

The Egyptians used the post and lintel system. To roof their halls, they put inside them rows of square pillars or round columns, on the top of which they laid heavy stone beams, in such a way

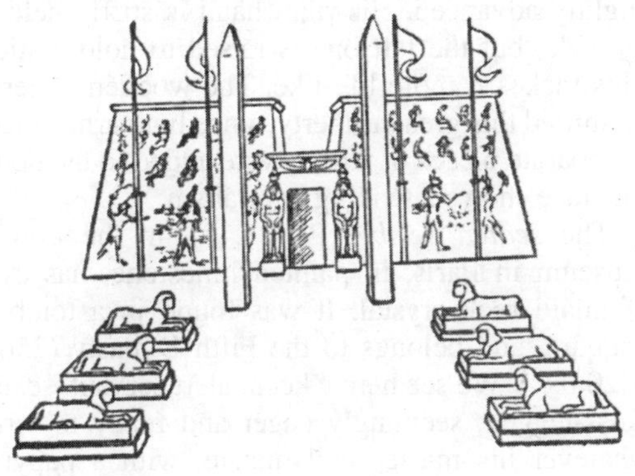

Fig. 368. Pylon.

that their ends joined over the centre of the piers. On these, stone slabs were placed crosswise to form the ceiling. Naturally these supports had to be close enough to be bridged with stone lintels, because these are brittle and liable to crack. This is why the *hypostyle hall* of the great *Amon temple* at *Karnak* (Fig. 369), one of the

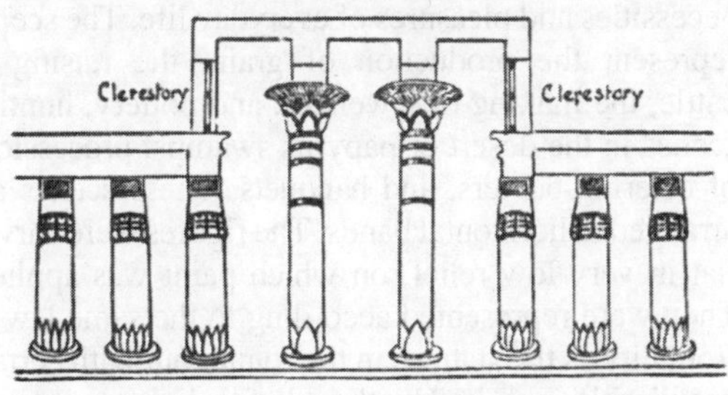


Fig. 369. Clerestory, hypostyle hall, Amon temple, Karnak.

greatest stone-roofed halls in the world (being about 150 metres long and 53 metres wide), had to contain 134 columns to support the roof. They were arranged in rows lengthwise, dividing it in a wider nave at the centre, and several aisles on both sides, so that the interior was literally obstructed by them.

An interesting feature is how they secured light for this immense hall : the two rows of columns and the ceiling of the central nave were higher than those of the aisles, so that between the two levels there was space for a vertical wall, which was filled with perforated stone slabs through which light penetrated into the nave. This raised part of the building, with windows that open above the roofs of the lower parts so as to give light to the nave, is called clerestory or clearstory.

## SCULPTURE

Egyptian sculpture, like its architecture, was also concerned with life after death. As we have seen, mastabas and pyramid temples contained one or more effigies of the deceased to assure his existence in the future life, and those of working people, to serve him in the after life. That is why Egyptian sculpture, mostly of stone, developed very early. Limestone and sandstone were obtained from the cliffs bordering the Nile valley; granite was found at the cataracts or water-falls, and diorite in the desert. Occasionally wood, clay, and bronze were also used.

During the Old Kingdom the sculptural remains can be divided into two main groups : statues in the round, and relief sculpture. The Egyptian artist, whether he represented figures in a standing, sitting or kneeling position, had to conform to the strictest geometrical rules, which meant a symmetrical arrangement of limbs and body on both sides of an imaginary vertical central line called the axis, neither of which bend or turn as in the case of moving figures in real life. This rigid symmetrical facing forward is called the Egyptian law of frontality.

A good example of royal statues to illustrate this rigidity is that of *Ranofer* (Fig. 370), in

Fig. 370. Ranofer, Cairo Museum.

painted limestone, preserved in the Cairo Museum. It belongs to the Fifth Dynasty (2565-2420 B.C.). We see this pharaoh standing in a strictly frontal position so that the body could be divided into two equal parts by a central line. With head erect, he is looking forward; his hanging arms press closely to the body, and his feet rest flat on the ground with the left one somewhat advanced. He wears a wig, and his dress consists only of a linen kilt around his loins, which was the usual dress during the Old Kingdom. In spite of these stiff conventions, the whole statue has an intense vitality. The erect head and the stiff bearing confer stateliness and royal dignity.

The seated statue of *Khafre* (Pl. 21.2 ), also in the Cairo Museum, was found in the so-called valley temple of Khafre's pyramid. It is life-sized and carved out of diorite, an extremely hard stone. It belongs to the Fourth Dynasty (2680-2565 B.C.). The pharaoh is seated on a throne decorated with lotus and papyrus plants intertwined, a symbol of United Egypt, and the head of a sphinx on each side. His posture is erect with shoulders against the back of the seat and the hands resting on his lap. Knees and legs are pressed firmly together, without the slightest movement. His garment consists of the simple kilt around his loins, leaving the upper part of the body bare. The soft linen head-gear falls on both shoulders. The long false ceremonial beard, which the pharaohs used to wear, is here partly broken away. Perched on his shoulders is a hawk, enveloping his head with its wings in token of protection, to show that he is a semidivine being. In spite of the rigid posture, it is an excellent piece of portraiture. The imperturbable calm produces the effect of pharaonic majesty, dignity and power similar to Ranofer's standing statue.

The seated statues of *Rahotep* and *Nofret* (Pl. 21.3 ), in the Cairo Museum, have the same rigid frontal pose as Khafre. Rahotep wears a similar kilt, while Nofret, his wife, has a tightiy fitting transparent linen garment, a broad collar necklace, and the usual wig beneath which appears the natural hair smoothly parted over the forehead. The eyes are of rock crystal. Both statues are entirely painted. The complexion of Rahotep is a dark reddish colour and that of Nofret is yellowish, because Egyptian ladies lived a more secluded indoor life than men, whose skin was tanned by the burning sun.

A typical example of statues of the lower classes is that of the *Sheik el-Beled (*Pl. 21. 4), in the Cairo Museum. It is made of wood, and cloth was originally glued to it, to which the colours were applied. It represents a round-faced, rather fat, self-satisfied man, perhaps an overseer. He stands in the same rigid frontal position, with the left foot slightly advanced. His right hand is stiffly held to the side, but the left one is raised to hold a stick. This makes it more life-like. The wooden material permitted this greater liberty, since both arms, made of separate pieces of wood, were added to the body. The face shows a striking naturalism.

The *seated scribe* (Pl. 21. 5), in the Louvre Museum in Paris, in painted limestone, has eyes of inlaid rock crystal. It was found in a tomb at Saqqâra, and belongs to the Fifth Dynasty (2565-2420 b.c.). We see here a keen, alert servant, seated cross-legged, seemingly eager and ready to write whatever his master will dictate, with a papyrus scroll in his left hand and a pen, no longer there but evident from the position of the fingers, in the right. His piercing gaze, so fitting to his bony face, the square jaws and thin closed lips make him an ideal secretary. Although wholly built according to the rigid frontal device of Egyptian art, the chest, shoulders, and head appear more life-like.

The numerous relief carvings on the walls of the mortuary chapels reveal the every-day life of the Egyptians. Like the statues of the lower classes, these were intended to serve the dead, providing them with necessities and pleasures of everyday life. The scenes represent the production of grain, the raising of cattle, the making of jewellery, and pottery, hunting scenes in the desert or papyrus swamps, processions of offering-bearers, and banquets. These scenes are arranged in horizontal bands. The figures were carved flat in very low relief, on which paint was applied. They were represented according to the same law of frontality as the statues, in the round, but with certain peculiarities required by the relief technique : namely the head and the legs were shown in profile, while the torso and the eyes were represented in front view.

The *panel of Hesire* (Fig. 371), dating from about 2780 B.C., has been found in his mastaba at Saqqâra, and is now in the Cairo Museum. This wooden painted relief is a good illustration of the Egyptian law (or, convention) of frontality applied to relief sculpture. Hesire is seen standing alone; his head and feet are represented from the side, while his eye and shoulders are entirely in front view. The whole relief, however, reveals high artistic qualities. The face shows individual distinction, with high cheek bones and firm closed lips. The modelling of neck, shoulders, arms and legs is perfect, especially the knees. Although the figure is not placed in the middle, there is balance in the composition by representing the left hand stretched out, holding the staff and writing equipment.

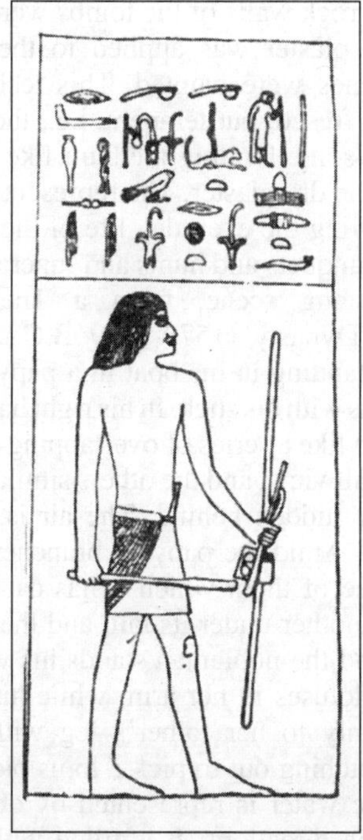

Fig. 371. Panel of Hesire, Cairo Museum.

An artist capable of such perfection could certainly represent the whole figure in a naturalistic way, but the conventional method established in early times had a more powerful influence on him.

Among the reliefs found in the mastaba of Ti at Saqqâra, one shows a *harvesting* scene, with reaping, threshing and stacking; the other represents *Ti hunting in the papyrus marsh.* It is interesting to note that Ti, standing in his boat, is carved on a much bigger scale than the people with him, because they were his social inferiors. There is more naturalism in the figures of the lower classes and animals than in the representation of the higher classes.

During the empire, colossal statues were made. Noteworthy examples are the *Memnon statues* at *Luxor* (Pl. 22.1). Originally they were in front of a pylon which has disappeared. In the Amun temple at Luxor, 7 metre-high figures of Ramesses II stand between the columns in the great court. At Abu Simbel, at the entrance of the rock-cut temple of Ramesses II, the seated statues of the pharaoh are about 20 metres high.

On the outer walls of the pylon temples, we see sunk reliefs (Pl. 22.2). First the outlines were chiselled, then the figures were rounded out and details were carved, but the background was not removed, so these images do not stand out from the wall since their highest point is level with it. This gave the reliefs more protection.

The monotheistic faith of Aton, sole creator of all life, was introduced during the religious revolution of Akhenaten (Amenophis IV). He ignored all the old gods of the Egyptian pantheon and turned the minds of men to nature, thus giving art a more realistic tendency. The sculptor Tuthmosis worked according to the new trend in Tell-el-Amarna. The conventional rigidity has disappeared during this period. The pharaoh is now seen in everyday informal actions; for instance, he is shown leaning on a stick, whilst his wife offers him flowers. Realism, and true likeness, were stressed. The *portrait of Akhenaten*, a painted sandstone statue now in Berlin, shows the head of a thinker and idealist, without any stress on stateliness and pharaonic dignity. The sculptured head of his wife *Nofretete* (Fig. 372), also preserved in Berlin, is

Fig 372. Nofretete, Berlin Museum.

outstanding for its beauty and extreme delicacy. The refined face rests on a slender curving neck. The big conventional headdress, of a geometrical form, helps to set off, by well balanced contrast, the distinctive characteristics of the natural countenance. The rich necklace, also in a geometrical pattern, harmonizes with the head-gear. Her lips, eyebrows and eyes are painted on the sandstone out of which the figure was chiselled.

But this period of religious and artistic revival was short-lived. It was contrary to vested interests and customs of centuries. After the death of Akhenaten, his weak son-in-law Tutank-hamon, under the pressure of the priests of Thebes, restored polytheism, and with it the rigidity of conventional representation in art.

We can study the effects of the naturalistic tendency of the Tell-el-Amarna school and the return to the rigid conventions in two reliefs. In the *wild bull hunt* in *Thebes*, among conventional representations, like the pharaoh in his chariot, a strong naturalistic tendency prevails. This is seen in the flight and agony of the animals, which certainly appear very true to life. The second relief of *Osiris and the goddesses*, in the temple of Seti, is represented in the old conventional way. It shows the reaction of the priestly class, who controlled not only the subject but also the manner of representation.

## PAINTING

During the Old Kingdom, painting was almost always associated with sculpture, that is, the reliefs on the walls of the rooms and corridors of the funerary chapels were first hewn out and then painted; the same applied to the statues in the round. An exception to this rule was a painted panel found in a mortuary chapel near *Meidum*, representing geese in exact symmetry of lines, but in great variety of colours.

During the Middle Kingdom and Empire, the rough, hard rock walls of the tombs were no longer carved, but plaster was applied to them, and on this the scenes were painted. This technique was not the true fresco, but tempera, i.e., the pigments, mixed with some binding medium like gum, were applied on the dry plaster. The representations were varied, showing the everyday life of the Egyptians, especially banquets and hunts and funeral offerings. In the fowling scene, from a Theban tomb, Eighteenth Dynasty (1570-1349 B.C.), we see a nobleman standing in his boat in a papyrus swamp chasing birds with his stick. In his right hand he holds three, shown like a series of overlapping silhouettes, the first in full view, and the others similar in outline but partially hidden behind. The air is filled with flying birds. Amid the papyrus branches sits a cat, holding three of them which it has caught, one in its mouth, another under its tail, and the third in its paws. Behind the nobleman stands his wife, with a bouquet of lotuses in her arm; while his little girl, holding firmly to her father's leg with her right hand, is stretching out to pick a lotus blossom with her left. The water is represented by oblique lines in alternating directions. It is filled with fat fishes and open flowers. The figures are painted in the conventional method, but the fishes, birds, and especially the cat are drawn in a naturalistic way.

# 3. GREEK ART

## GENERAL SURVEY

Greek or Hellenic art developed in the Greek peninsula, on the islands of the Aegean sea, and on the shores of Asia Minor. Colonists carried it to southern Italy, Sicily, north Africa, southern France and Spain, as well as to the Balkans and Crimea. Alexander the Great and his successors extended its influence to Syria, Egypt, Mesopotamia, Iran and India. Hellenic art lies at the foundations of Roman and Byzantine art.

The geography of the peninsula played a great role in the development of Hellenic civilization. The wooded country was divided by many low mountains that formed countless small, easily-defended valleys, and made communication difficult. This led to the separation of the inhabitants into small groups, resulting in the famous city-state organization. Another most important geographical feature was the deeply-indented coastline of the peninsula which formed many natural harbours. This fact is perhaps responsible for the triple character of the Greeks : they were good sailors, merchants and colonizers. They soon began to colonize the numerous islands in the Aegean sea. Later their adventurous character carried them further to establish colonies in the west and in the east. The chief mineral wealth of the country was the beautiful marbles, found chiefly in the mountains and islands.

The climate was intermediate between rigorous cold and relaxing heat. It influenced the character of the population which was energetic and intelligent, inclined to science and philosophy, and sensitive to beauty and art. The moderate weather also favoured outdoor life; and consequently, the administration of justice, dramatic representations, and most public ceremonies took place in the open air.

The inhabitants of Greece called themselves Hellenes, and their country Hellas. The Romans gave them the name Greeks. They were a mixture of different races. The aborigines probably had their centres among the islands called Cyclades. Around 3000 B.C., the Cretans became dominant. About 1400 B.C. came the Achaean invasion. These new invaders had their chief centre in Mycenae. The Cretan and Mycenaean civilizations together are often called Aegean culture. The life of the twelfth century Achaeans is pictured in the poems of Homer, but they contain some historical inaccuracies here and there. In 1100 B.C., the Dorians invaded the peninsula from the north. In course of time, these mingled with the original inhabitants. Their descendants are known as the Hellenes.

The Greek gods were generally nature personifications, who assumed human forms. Each city chose a patron divinity. The municipal authorities built temples, and organized processions, festivals and sacrifices to obtain divine favour. The people were expected to take part in these public demonstrations. There was no priestly class, but certain citizens had the honourable charge of supervising the actual services. The city officials took care of the conservation of temples, and administered the money spent for the ceremonies. There was no definite creed, all that mattered was that the prescribed rites should be properly carried out. They believed that the gods manifested their will through natural signs and oracles, the most famous of which was that of Apollo at Delphi.

Although the gods were supposed to be guardians of justice, the mythological stories about them are often immoral. There was no strong belief in a future life where virtue would be rewarded. But the people had a practical standard of conduct, of which the keynote was 'nothing in excess'. A man was expected to practise self-control by not giving way to extremes of emotion, by being brave without being rash, by acting always according to good taste. They felt that by observing this ideal they distinguished themselves from the barbarians.

In philosophy the Greeks showed great penetration into the causes and nature of things. Plato, influenced by Socrates, taught that there was one Supreme Being, source of all matter and life, and that man's spiritual soul, which makes him superior to all material things, is immortal, assuring him of a better life in the future. For this reason, he valued virtue and wisdom, by which man strives towards God, rather than all worldly possessions. His pupil, Aristotle, versed in the learning of his age, and basing his deductions on direct observation and experiment, systematized nearly every aspect of human knowledge. He inspired many later philosophers.

The aim of Greek education was to develop

good citizens through the training of mind and body, but the city-states were slow to organize systematic instruction. Sparta gave the lead, but concentrated almost exclusively on physical exercise. In Athens the children were taught at home until the age of seven, and then attended private schools until they were fourteen. There was very little that would resemble college until after the Peloponnesian War. But later there were centres where young men could learn politics, literature, science and oratory.

The importance they gave to athletic sports distinguished the Hellenistic societies most from those of the East. Physical education and sports were conducted in the gymnasium. A peculiar custom of theirs was the holding of competitions in honour of the gods, because for the Greeks athletics meant the giving of one's best efforts. Every city held games of this sort, but some were associated with particular places and open to competitors from all over the Hellenic world. The most ancient and famous were the Olympic games; the first Olympiad was held in 776 B. C.

The division of art history into periods is always arbitrary, because the development of styles is a continuous and gradual process, but it is a help to the student who wants to follow this development in all its phases. Greek art is often divided into : Pre-Hellenic, including chiefly the Cretan and Mycenaean (about 3000 to 1100 B. C.); Hellenic, subdivided into the archaic period (1200 to 450 B.C.), classical (from the second half of the fifth to the fourth century B. C.), and Hellenistic (from the third century B.C. to the Christian era).

Except for a few little statues or idols found on the Cyclades islands, not far from Athens, little is known of art in Greece before 3000 B.C. That which developed on the island of Crete is also called Minoan, after the mythological king Minos, who kidnapped Greek youths to fight his terrible bull, the minotaur. Cretan frescoes and carvings show that bullfighting was a favourite sport. The most important monuments are at Knossos (c. 2000 B. C.). Other places are Phaistos and Hagia Triada. They are chiefly gaily-painted palaces, a few tombs, but no religious buildings. There is no logical planning in the complex stone construction of rooms, courts, porticoes and stairways of the palace (hence perhaps the legend of the labyrinth). The existence of highly perfected drainage and plumbing shows an advanced material civilization, and the wall paintings in the true fresco medium as well as the beautiful pottery remains reveal great artistic development.

About 1500 B.C., the civilization of Crete passed to the mainland, where Mycenae and Tiryns are the most important art centres known to us. This is called Mycenaean art. In Crete the position of the island itself had provided protection and so there were no fortifications. But on the mainland we find fortress-palaces, the walls of which, at Tiryns, are twenty feet thick. They are constructed of unhewn stones, a method called by the later Greeks cyclopean, from the name of mythical giants whom they had believed to be the builders. The most important part was the great central hall, called megaron, a rectangular room with an open hearth. Four columns supported its roof. The megaron is the prototype of the Greek temple. At *Mycenae* the fortress palace has a monumental entrance, the *lion gate* (Fig. 373). Frescoes, interesting pottery and metalwork have also come down to us in sufficient numbers.

Fig. 373 Lion gate, Mycenae

Around 1100 B.C. the Dorian invaders destroyed the Aegean civilization, but what survived contributed to the formation of Hellenic or Greek art proper.

## ARCHITECTURE

The Greeks developed a simple but splendid architecture, unsurpassed in later ages : excellent building material, a simple but logical system of construction, refinement of proportions and details being the keynotes.

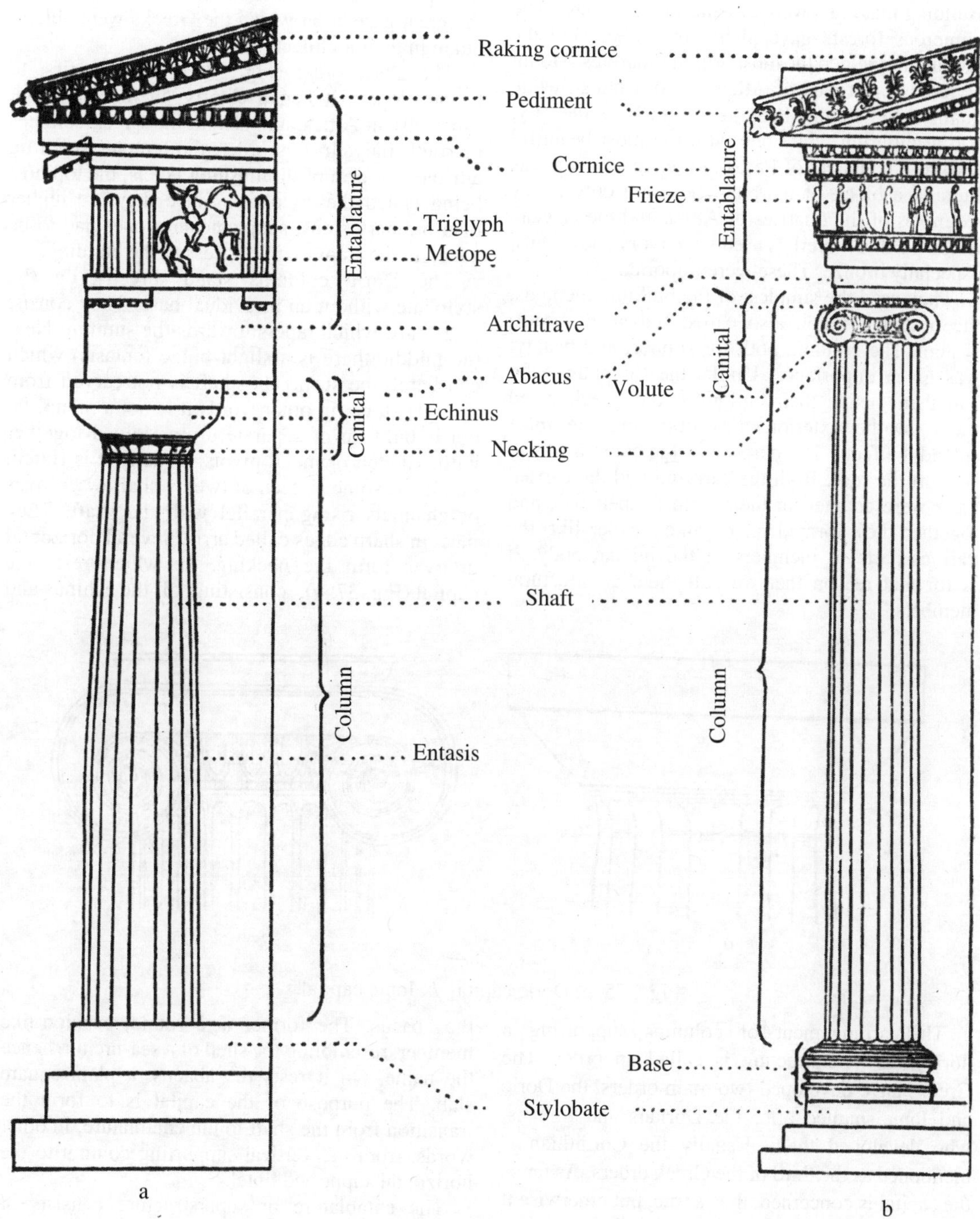


Fig. 374. *a*. Doric order, *b*. Ionic order.

Building materials were at hand in abundance. The numerous forests gave plenty of timber, and the mountains yielded the most brilliant marbles. Mount Hymettus, just east of Athens, had a bluish-white quality; and mount Pentelikos, north of the city, had a glittering white one with the most beautiful texture. The island of Paros in the Aegean sea was literally a block of marble. These are only a few examples of the quarries of Attica and the Aegean islands. Other materials used were ivory and metals, especially bronze. These were imported.

They used the simplest of the building methods, the post and lintel, also called trabeated (beam) system. The column, both for support and beauty, was given importance. Unlike the Egyptians who had them inside their buildings, the Greeks used them on the exterior, thus obtaining the most splendid effects. The purpose of the column was to support the roof. Both the carrying and the carried parts were adapted in their form to their use, and together they formed an organic whole, like the various parts or members of the human body. It is for that reason that we call them architectural members.

their proportions and details. Here lies the secret of the great perfection which the Greeks were able to attain in their architecture.

The Doric order (Fig. 374*a*) was the first to be developed. It began chiefly on the mainland, especially in Attica, and also in the Greek colonies of south Italy. In this order, the temples stand on a triple platform of diminishing levels, the topmost being called the stylobate. Since they are higher than ordinary steps, supplementary ones had to be added in the front to give access to the building.

The Doric columns stand directly on the stylobate without an individual base. They consist of a shaft, which tapers towards the summit. Near the middle there is a slight bulge (entasis) which can barely be seen. The shaft is not carved from a single stone, in other words it is not a monolith, but is built up of separate drums joined together with wooden or metal pivots. Usually it is fluted, i.e., it has some sixteen or twenty shallow grooves or channels rising parallel with the shaft. They meet in sharp edges called arris. Several horizontal grooves form the necking, on which rests the capital (Fig. 375*a*), consisting of the echinus and

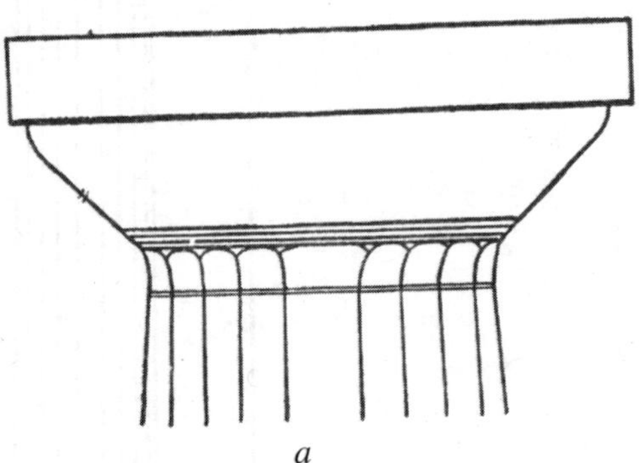

*a*

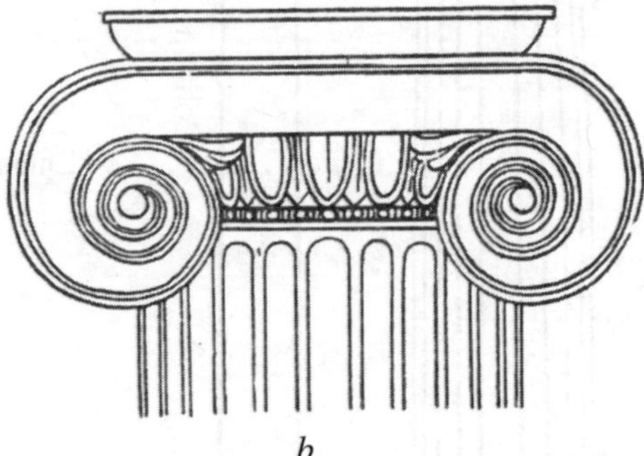

*b*

Fig. 375. *a*. Doric capital, *b*. Ionic capital.

This arrangement of columns supporting a horizontal superstructure is called an order. The Greeks have developed two main orders, the Doric and Ionic, named after the Dorians and Ionians, who developed them. Usually the Corinthian is mentioned as the third of the Greek orders. As far as the capital is concerned, this is true, but otherwise it is very similar to the Ionic order, and it is sometimes looked upon as being merely a later variation of it. Each order is easily recognized by its capital.

Once the orders were formulated, they did not change them any more, but continued refining on

the abacus. The former is a round, cushion-like member, resembling the shell of a sea-urchin, hence the name. On it rests the abacus, a plain square slab. The purpose of the capital is to form the transition from the shaft to the entablature, in other words, from the vertical supporting column to the horizontal supported lintel.

The entablature or superstructure consists of three horizontal parts. The architrave is entirely plain. It is formed of closely-joined beams, of which each bridges the span between two columns (inter-columniation). The frieze is composed of triglyphs (three vertical grooves), with metopes (square stone slabs) in between. These are often carved. Roughly two triglyphs correspond to one column. The boldly projecting cornice, called corona, completes the design and serves as a protection against rain. Over the slopes of the gable is the racking cornice or cymatium, which is a gutter-moulding. The triangular field of the gable is called the pediment, or tympanum, or tympanon.

Ornament plays an important part in the architectural design, and is concentrated on the upper part of the building, especially in the metopes and pediments. This decoration is basically sculptural. It is not in the natural colour of the stone, but gaily painted in red and blue, with touches of green and yellow, black, and perhaps a little gold. The unpainted parts may have been rubbed with wax. By the use of colour the artist could bring out more clearly the relationship of the parts, could soften the glitter of the stone, and could provide a background to set off the figures.

It is believed generally that the Doric order is derived from wooden prototypes (Fig. 376). The

Fig. 376. Wooden prototype of the Doric order.

triglyphs look like the ends of the beams which were put across the walls to form the ceiling, and which were grooved and chamfered to decorate the otherwise unpleasing aspect of cut wood. This leads also to the supposition of the wooden origin of the entablature. Pausanias, a Greek historian of the second century A.D., one of the best sources of information for modern archaeologists about traces of ancient monuments, states that the Doric Heraeum, or temple of Hera at Olympia, had originally timber columns.

In general, the Ionic order (Fig.374*b*) has more slender proportions, greater elegance and grace, and more richly-carved decoration than the Doric. It has the same triple platform, but the columns do not stand directly on the stylobate. Each one has an individual base, made of concave and convex mouldings. The shaft is more slender, and has little or no enthasis. It has some twenty-four grooves or channels, which do not meet in sharp edges, but have a narrow strip in between, which is called fillet. Sometimes there is a honey-suckle band around the necking. The capital (Fig.375*b*) is the most conspicuous part of the Ionic order. It is composed of an echinus decorated with bead and reel, and egg and dart mouldings. On this rests a band which ends on both sides in scrolls called volutes. The grace and beauty of the capital depends on the form of the volutes and the sweep of the connecting band. Over this is a narrow abacus. The architrave consists of three plain beams, and above it the frieze is continuous, not interrupted with triglyphs and metopes. Sometimes it is decorated with relief sculpture. The cornice has great beauty.

The Corinthian order (Fig.377) was fully developed and amply used by the Romans. The Greeks themselves, who preferred simplicity, did

Fig. 377. Corinthian capital.

not employ it much. It is a sort of late outgrowth of the Ionic order developed by the more cosmopolitan citizens of Corinth. Here the entablature was the same, and the base and shaft of the column differed only slightly. The capital, however, was new. According to Vitruvius, Callimachus designed it. There is nothing historical about the charming story that he may have been inspired by acanthus foliage growing around a basket covered with a square wooden lid, and placed on the tomb of a young girl. The capital has a core resembling an inverted bell. It is decorated all around with acanthus leaves arranged in one or two rows. The frail stalks of the plant rise in pairs, spiraling and meeting at the corners to sustain the abacus.

Although the Greeks developed different types of buildings, they centred almost all their artistic skill and noblest aspirations on the temple, the function of which was to shelter the statue of the deity, called idol (from the Greek eidolon, image). There was no need to house crowds of worshippers, since the function took place in the open air; neither was there any need for numerous inner partitions required for ceremonial purposes.

The plan of the temple (Fig. 378) is very simple. It is a rectangular room called cella, without windows, and there is only one door in the front. The Mycenaean megaron was its prototype. The cella is seldom double, in which case there are two doors, one at each narrow end.

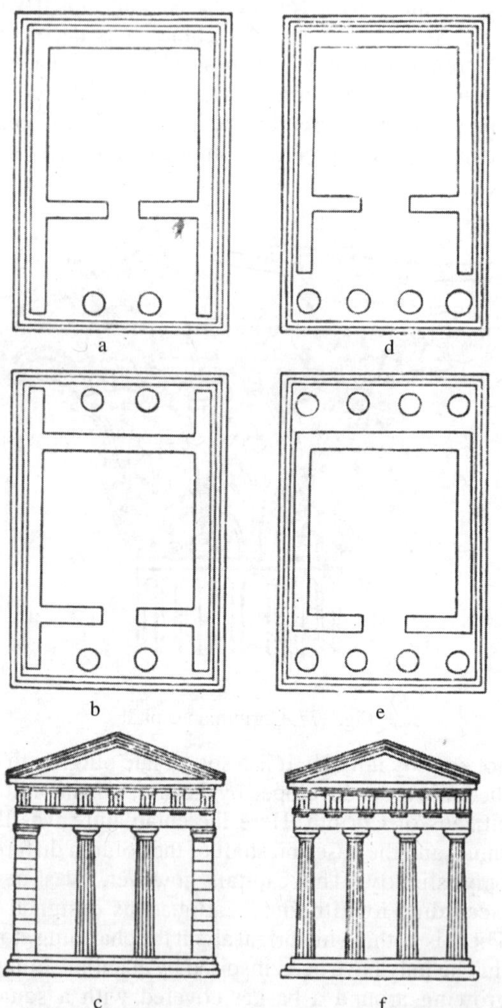


Fig.378. Greek temple plans and front elevations : *a.* in antis, *b.* double in antis, c.front elevation of *a* and *b*, *d.* prostyle, *e.*amphiprostyle, *f.* elevation of *d* and *e.*

In its most elementary form, the side walls of the cella extend in front, and two columns are set between their extremities, to form a portico or verandah. This type is called distyle in antis, or simply in antis (distyle, two columns; in, between; antis, the projecting walls). The Greeks liked this little portico with the two columns so much, that they repeated it at the back of the building, although no door led to the cella from this rear portion. This plan with two porticoes is known as the double in antis.

Later, although they kept the in antis walls, they set a row of columns along the entire front of the cella. This type is called prostyle, meaning that it has columns in the front. When they are repeated at the back of the building, it is called amphiprostyle.

The effect produced was so beautiful, that they soon surrounded the whole temple with them. A building of the in-antis or prostyle type, when surrounded by a row of columns, is called peripteral (Fig. 380*b*). Later, even two rows were placed round the building; in this case it is called dipteral.

During the early period, the Doric order was used. One of the oldest examples is the Heraeum (temple of Hera) at Olympia, built about 620 B.C. As already mentioned, according to Pausanias, it had wooden columns originally, but when these deteriorated, they were replaced by stone ones, of which some remain. At Paestum, a flourishing Greek colony in south Italy, two temples still exist: *the temple of Hera*, formerly known as the temple of Poseidon or the so-called Basilica, (c. 540 B.C.) and the *temple of Demeter* (c. 520 B.C.) Both are of the Doric order, unadorned, giving an impression of austere dignity. The *Apollo temple* at *Corinth* (540 B.C.), is another Doric example of the early style. Here the columns are sturdy, and the echinus projects considerably and is more rounded in outline. Details are as yet somewhat coarse in workmanship. More refinement in their proportions, with more slender columns and less heavy pediments appear in the *Aphaia temple* (c. 490 B.C.) on the island of *Aegina*, and the *temple of Zeus*, (c. 460 B.C.) at *Olympia*.

The development of architecture was paralyzed for a time by the Persian Wars. The invasions of Darius, and later of his successor Xerxes, occupied the Greeks too much to enable them to think of anything but self-defence. In 480 B.C. the Persians captured and burned Athens. But soon after they were defeated on sea and land, and Greek art could enter its classical period.

One city-state rose powerful and glorious from the calamities of war, and that was Athens. As the head of the Delean League, and under the leadership of Pericles (461-429 B.C.), it entered its most glorious period, the Golden Age. Much had to be done : the Persians had laid Athens in ruins. The first endeavour of Pericles, after the consolidation of his political power, was the reconstruction of the city's most sacred shrines on the Acropolis.

The Acropolis (Fig.379), meaning high city,

Fig.379. Acropolis : A. Parthenon, B. Erechtheion, C. temple of Nike Apteros, D. Propylaea, Athens.

was the upper fortified part or citadel of Athens. It stood on the top of an abruptly rising hill, which they had crowned with their most sacred building, the Athena temple. It was built of a stone called poros. Its length was a hundred Attic feet (hekatompedon), or about 30½ metres. For these reasons it was called poros-hekatompedon. The Persian invaders destroyed this old shrine. But the Greeks did not think merely of restoring it. With their characteristic energy and enthusiasm, they started something entirely new, much better than all that they had built before. Up to this time Greek architecture had developed slowly, but now it acquired an incredible speed and reached its highest perfection. Within a few years, with the help of the most eminent artists, and not sparing expenditure, the most beautiful buildings were erected:—the Parthenon, which replaced the old temple of Athena; the Erechtheion, the temple commemorating the mythical contest between Athena and Poseidon; the Propylaea or majestic gateway ; and near it the temple of Nike Apteros (wingless victory). These few buildings, of which the Parthenon is the only one somewhat larger in size, are the glory of the Periclean Golden Age because of their perfect proportions and refinement. By studying these buildings, we can learn all that is essential in Greek architecture.

The Parthenon (P1. 22.3 ) or temple of Athena, is the culmination of the Doric order. According to the ancient historian Plutarch, Pericles entrusted its planning to the architects Ictinos and Callicrates; but probably the main artistic direction was given by Pericles, to his great friend, the sculptor Phidias, who was responsible for the sculptural decoration. In less than ten years, between about 447 B.C. to 438 B.C., it was erected all in white marble brought from the quarries of Pentelikos. It does not stand on the same place as the old one, but near the southern crest of the hill, dominating by its height and size all the other buildings of the Acropolis. It measures 69 metres 50 cm. by 30 metres 78 cm. on the top of the stylobate.

The plan of the Parthenon (Fig.380*b a*) is double-celled. The bigger and more important one

Fig. 380*a*. Parthenon : front elevation Acropolis, Athens.

facing east, was given the same size and name as the old sanctuary, namely hekatompedon, out of respect for the traditional measure, because the whole building was planned much bigger. Here stood the famous gold and ivory (chryselephantine) statue of Athena. The other smaller room, facing west, was called Parthenon (the maiden's room). Its use is not very clear. Some think that it was set aside for the Athenian maidens, or perhaps it contained the treasury. At any rate, it gave its name to the whole building. Both cellas are prostyle; that is, they have a row of columns in front of them. In addition, the colonnade completely surrounds the building, forming a peripteral plan. On the two narrow sides, the ends of the sloping roof form the pediment or tympanum. There are eight columns on each of the narrow sides; and seventeen on the long ones. The proportions between the height and width of the columns, the restricted almost straight-sided echinus, the entablature much reduced in size, and the proportions of all the details between each other are perfect. The shallow grooves on the shaft, casting soft shadows in the glowing sun, alternate with the sharp lines of the arris that accentuate the upward (vertical) movement of the columns. The latter stand out clearly from the dark background before the cella. The almost imperceptible entasis seems to give elasticity to the hard marble. The eye is guided without abrupt transition from the capitals to the entablature, where the geometrical rigidity of lines is enlivened by sculptural decoration. There are carvings on the metopes, alternating with the vertical lines of the triglyphs, a long running frieze on the cella wall, and above all the sculptures of the pediments. The rising raking cornices at the ends of the sloping roof form a low triangle; and, accentuated by the central akroteria (the highest decoration), outline this dominating building on the Acropolis against its background of blue sky.

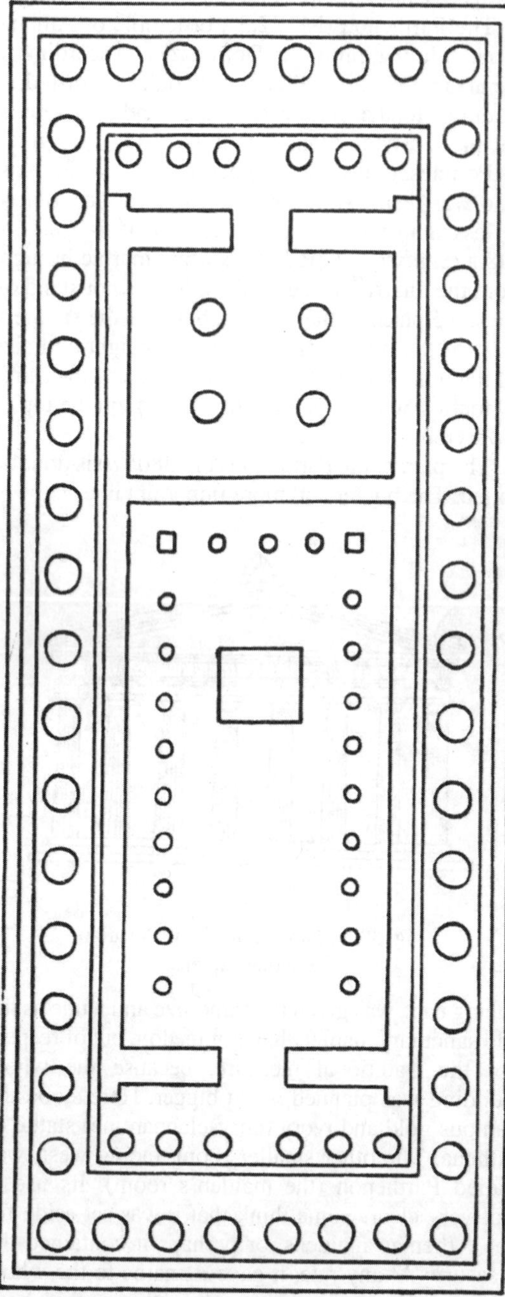

Fig. 380*b*. Parthenon : plan, Acropolis, Athens.

The later history of the Parthenon is one of sad decay, although during centuries it maintained itself in more or less good condition. When Greece became Christian, it was used as a church. In 1456, after the invasion of the Turks, it was changed into a mosque. In 1687, during a war, it was almost ruined because they had used it to store gunpowder, which exploded when the building was hit by a shot. In 1801 the Turkish government allowed Lord Elgin to take a large part of the remaining sculptures to England. They became the property of the British Museum in 1816, and are known as the Elgin marbles. Greece became an independent kingdom in 1831; and its greatest historic monument and most precious artistic gem is still the Parthenon, in spite of its damaged condition.

The Erechtheion or Erechtheum (Pl. 22.4 ) is the second temple on the Acropolis built during the Golden Age, between 420-303 B.C. It stands north of the Parthenon, near the place where the old temple of Athena stood. The temple was designed by Mnesicles, and shows a curious irregularity in plan (Fig. 381), not seen elsewhere. The building was not levelled as the Greek temples usually were. There is a difference of 3 metres 20 cm. between the two levels of the structure. There are two separate façades, one on the eastern and the other on the northern side. Both porticoes are formed by graceful Ionic columns. On the southern side is the beautiful *Caryatid* or *maidens' portico*, where in place of the columns, statues of young maidens carry the architrave on their heads (Fig.382). According to Pausanias, this temple stood on the

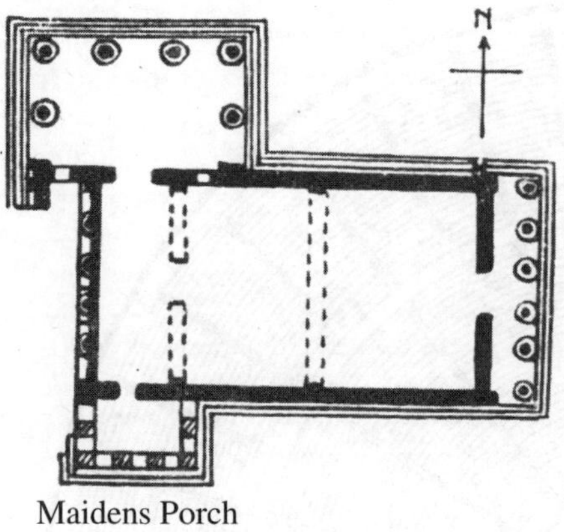


Fig. 381 Erechtheion : plan, Acropolis, Athens.

traditional place of the mythical contest between Athena and Poseidon : the place of the olive tree, which was said to have appeared when Athena

Fig. 382. Caryatid, maidens' porch, Erechtheion Acropolis, Athens.

touched the soil with her spear, and where the salt well supposedly sprung up when Poseidon struck the rock with his trident. This temple also contained the Xoanon, or primitive statue of Athena Polias carved in olive wood, since Athena, as a result of the contest, became the patron goddess of the city (polis).

The *temple of Nike Apteros* (Fig379 c), also calledAthena Nike, is the third temple of the Golden Age on the Acropolis. It was built on the south-western side in Ionic style by Callicrates, around 426 B.C. As already mentioned, Nike Apteros means the wingless victory. Generally the Greeks personified this idea by a young maiden with wings, to show that until the end of a battle, success may be on any side. The Athenians thought that they could keep it in their city by depriving it of wings. This small temple—from the stylobate of which they could see Salamis, Aegina, Corinth, and the mountains of Megaris—was built to commemorate the Persian War, as is clearly seen on its famous frieze. Here, instead of the usual representations of mythical combats, which were indirect allusions to political struggles, the actual fight is represented in its final issue at Plataea. In 1687 the Turks destroyed this temple by using its stones to build a battery on the Acropolis. This in turn was demolished in 1836; but the archaeologists were able to reconstruct the temple with the recovered stones.

To complete the description of the buildings erected during the time of Pericles on the Acropolis, and which altogether formed one composition, we have to turn to another type of building : the stately gateway or propylaea (pro, in front; pyle, gate) of which the most famous was the Propylaea (Fig.379d) on the Acropolis. It was built by Mnesicles somewhere between 437-432 B.C. A winding road led up its steep ascent. Its beautiful colonnades were built on different levels. At both ends, the lowest and the highest, the entrance porticoes were in Doric style. The interior path, on the contrary, was bordered with Ionic columns. The whole had the same perfection and splendour as the other buildings of the Acropolis.

Hence, although the Greeks centred their main artistic interest on the temple, they had other types of buildings which merit mention. The stoa (plural: stoae or stoas, meaning porch or portico) was a long building with a wall at the back and a colonnade in the front, which opened on a public place like the agora or market. It served as a roofed promenade, but could also be used as a meeting place. This was the case with the *stoa poikile* (decorated) in the agora of Athens, the walls of which were decorated with frescoes. It was here that the philosopher Zeno lectured to his disciples, hence their name Stoics.

The Greeks invented the open air theatre (Fig. 383) (theatron, a place affording a view). It had three parts. The theatron proper or auditorium, greater than a semi-circle in plan, had rising tiers of seats which were hewn out in concentric curves from the rocky hillside. Below these, was the round orchestra for the performance of the actors and the chorus. In the centre there was an altar to Dyonisus. Later on they added the skene, a building behind the orchestra and facing the theatron, which served as a booth for the actors and at the same time as a background for the play. From it projected the proskenion or proscenium, which became a small platform used by the performers.

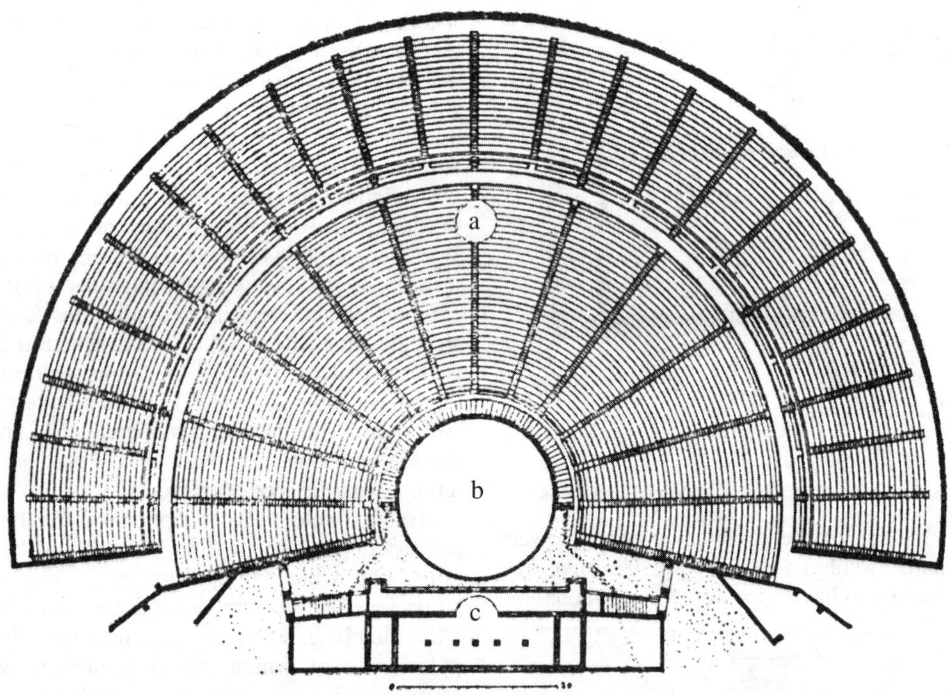


Fig. 383. Theatre : *a*. theatron ; *b*. orchestra; *c*. skene with proskenion; Epidaurus.

For athletic contests, the Greeks built stadia (singular: stadium) for foot races, and hippodromes (hippo, horse; dromos, course) for horse races. The extensive track, oblong in shape, was divided in the centre by what was called a spine. All around were tiers of seats for the spectators. Chariot races were common during the Panhellenic games. Each competitor stood on a small two-wheeled chariot, guiding four horses. The palaestra (a place for wrestling) and gymnasium (for physical exercise) were meant for individual physical exercises and bathing. They were composed of courts, chambers and bathing pools. They also had exedrae (ex, out of; hedra, seat) or semicircular seats in tiers for spectators, since they were sometimes used for public entertainments and recitations.

The most developed type of Greek house had a garden in the centre, surrounded by a peristyle or colonnade that connected the various rooms.

In early times, graves were simple and were marked by steles, or commemorative stone slabs decorated with sculpture. Monumental tombs were rare ; some were built in Asia Minor. The most important of them was the *mausoleum* of *Halicarnassos* in *Caria*, erected to king Mausolos by his widow Artemisia in 354 B.C. Upon a square base stood the cella, surrounded by thirty-six columns and covered by a pyramidal roof, the top of which was surmounted by a colossal marble quadriga (a car with four horses driven by Mausolos). Open-air altars were common in Asia Minor during the later period. The most famous of them was the *altar* of *Pergamon*.

## SCULPTURE

It was in sculpture that the Greeks excelled. They were the first to attain perfection in carving statues of the human body, both in relief and in the round, at rest and in motion. Their ideal of perfection of physical qualities was achieved by athletic exercises for the full development of bodily beauty. The result was their magnificent physique, and sculptors found splendid models among the competitors for the games.

In the beginning they used wood, then limestone and tufa (poros), but soon the splendid marbles of Greece, very suitable for carving, became popular. Metal sculpture, especially bronze, was practised. Gold was combined with ivory for the chryselephantine statues. These were hollow, with an inner framework of iron and an outer shell of wood. On this were laid thin plates of ivory, covering the exposed parts of the flesh, and finely-beaten plates of gold covering the draped parts.

The themes of Greek sculpture were varied and not limited to any one aspect of local life; they were religious, civil, domestic and sepulchral, as the need arose. The largest and most important class was religious, and was usually connected with architecture, chiefly the temple.

On it the sculptor could exercise his imagination and skill, giving the highest proof of his art. Central in position and importance was the statue of the deity housed in the cella. The rest was architectural embellishment. The carving of the capitals required much skill and delicacy of taste. The metopes and friezes in relief had to be clearly seen from below and at a distance. The discontinuous character of the metopes was more suited for episodes, like the labours of Heracles (Hercules), contests of gods and giants, of Greeks and Amazons; whereas the continuous nature of the friezes lent itself to the reproduction of processions, as in the Parthenon, and also of assemblies and battles. Finally, the most important of the architectural embellishments were the pedimental sculptures which at the same time presented the greatest difficulties. Their subjects were always related to the patron divinity of the temple.

As was the case with architecture, the Greeks attained perfection in sculpture only after a long period of experimentation and slow development. During the archaic period, from about 650 B.C. to about 480 B.C., the interest centred mainly on two subjects. The male athelete type was developed by the Dorians residing in the Peloponnesus. This gradually gave them the knowledge of human anatomy. The robed feminine type originated in Ionia. The artists thereby discovered the beauty of drapery. These two experiences combined, and formed in the fifth century the beautiful Attic style.

The Hera of Samos (Pl. 23.1 ) now in the Louvre in Paris, is an example of the Ionian feminine statues. It was found on the island of Samos, in a temple built about 550 B.C. and dedicated to Hera, the queen of the gods. The whole figure has the form of a column; therefore we say it forms a cylindrical mass. It probably evolved from earlier wooden statues carved from tree trunks. The goddess stands in a rigid frontal position, feet together, the right arm held tightly against her side, the left arm bent to her breast. It probably held some attribute, which is now broken away. The head is also missing. The statue is compact, with no limbs or parts spreading away from it. Like all the Greek feminine representations before the fourth century, this one is clothed. The artist used the folds to create a decorative pattern. The long undergarment is composed of small parallel lines indicating the folds that flow out at the bottom to join the base, leaving only the toes of the feet uncovered. The woollen upper garment sweeps in broader folds diagonally across the chest, forming a strong curve at the bottom which repeats the outlines of the shoulders. Although there is nothing realistic in this statue, the compact outline and the exquisite decorative pattern of the folds make it an outstanding masterpiece.

Several athletic figures of young men from the archaic period have been preserved. They are often called by the Greek word *kouros* (Pl.23.2) (plural kouroi). Some authors call them Apollo statues, but this designation is less precise because there is no sure indication that they represent this god. These early examples of standing athletes resemble the Egyptian pose, with the left foot forward, the broad shoulders, the rigid attitude of head and arms, and the four-sided organization. The anatomy is indicated by shallow grooves and ridges. The long hair is extremely conventionalized, although it is not a wig. These kouroi show the characteristic way of representing features in the archaic age. The shoulders are much too wide in comparison with the hips. The hair style is conventionalized, as also the ears which, as in many statues of the period, are put too high. The eyes bulge out like balls. The artist was not able to control the facial expression: the upturned corners of the mouth produced the so-called ' archaic smile '— the result, it appears, of the difficulty of making the transition between the lips and the cheeks.

The feminine type, as in the Hera of Samos, developed slowly. This is seen on the maiden statues or *kore* (Fig.384) (plural, korai). Towards the end of the archaic period, figures of noble maidens were set up on the Acropolis of Athens. Thrown down and mutilated by the Persians during the sack of the city, they were simply buried like rubble behind the new walls during the reconstruction work of Pericles. A great variety of them have since been excavated.

Fig. 384. Kore, from Acropolis, Athens

Their posture is still rigid, but they are more life-like than the Hera of Samos. Usually the right forearm is raised and held out. This was carved out of a separate block of stone and fitted into a socket hole. The hair is still stereotyped, as well as the folds of the garments, the hem of which forms a broken zig-zag line. However, the facial expressions of all these statues differ from each other. They still have, in a greater or lesser degree, protruding eyes and the archaic smile, but they show a greater mastery and more naturalistic execution.

From the pre-classical period, about 500-450 B.C. we have the *charioteer* of *Delphi* (Pl.23.3), a bronze statue in the Delphi Museum. This beautiful and noble youth belonged to a chariot group, probably erected to commemorate a victory. Except for some fragments, the other figures have been lost. The charioteer is shown after winning the race, and presenting himself to the public. He stands erect with both feet firmly on the ground, and slightly turned to the right. His long robe with deep folds is gathered by a high belt. The reins of the horses, of thin bronze, which he clasps with his right hand, can still be seen ; but his left arm is missing. Straps passing around the neck and under the arms hold up the folds of the dress to give him ease in movement. The eyes of the beautifully modelled face are made of glass paste. To keep it from getting in his way, the hair is held by a band above which the curls are shown in the conventional manner, but below it they hang down in naturalistic tufts. The work is imbued with archaic austerity. The erect posture and deeply-folded robe make us think of a fluted column. Yet these heavy pleats are required to catch the light and cast the necessary shadows in order to bring out the lines, which, due to the dark colour of the bronze, would not be seen otherwise. The whole statue gives the impression of a living body, under the conventional dress. It is a portrait statue, but with no individual features, because the Greeks of this period aimed at generalization of an idealized type of charioteer who, although he stands calm and poised, has all the capacity, strength and flexibility of body needed for chariot racing.

The *Doryphoros* (Pl. 23.4), or lance bearer, was another athletic bronze statue, made by the sculptor Polycleitos, but only marbie copies of it remain. Here all the rigidity and conventional details of the archaic kouroi have disappeared. We see an entirely life-like body in which a graceful rhythmic movement is obtained by concentrating the weight on one leg only, the other being raised so that the foot touches the ground slightly at one point.

The *Discobolos* (Pl. 23.5 ), or the discusthrower, by the sculptor Myron, is another famous athletic statue. The original, now lost, was made of bronze, but many marble copies of it exist. It shows the athlete in the typical position of balancing his quoit before hurling it. His right hand, which holds the discus, is raised up backwards; and the whole body, bent for this action, forms an S curve. In spite of this intense movement, the face—as in all these figures—shows no emotion, no efforts; it is impersonal and generalized according to the Greek ideal of the fifth century.

One of the greatest problems for the Greek sculptors was the sculptural decoration of the temple pediments, in other words, the filling with statues of the triangular field at the front and back, formed by the sloping sides of the gable-roof. They struggled with this difficulty from the earliest times, and the climax of their success is seen in the fifth century B.C. in the Parthenon. The chief problem was caused by the triangular shape of the pediment, which has a high central axis and narrow corners. To fill such a place with a group of statues, where each figure takes the posture required by the action it performs, and not by the mere limitations the narrowing space imposes, is not an easy task. In the archaic period the sculptors were more or less unsuccessful. The best of these early experimentations are seen on a group from the old Athena temple on the Acropolis where the coiling tail of a three-bodied monster filled the corner. The pedimental figures of the *Aphaia temple* on the *island of Aegina*, from about 500 B.C., show an advance. Those of the eastern pediment probably represent a scene from the Trojan War. In the centre stands Athena wearing her breastplate over the long peplos (Doric robe for ladies). Her left arm is stretched out ; the right holds a spear. Fighting groups are arranged symmetricaliy. Nearest to her, on each side, stands a fighter with helmet, shield and sword. Beside him is a falling warrior, with his comrade bending down to help him. Next there is a kneeling archer, and the corners are filled with wounded soldiers stretched on the ground. The pediment figures of the *temple of Zeus* (Pl.23.6) at *Olympia* represent a great progress in artistic achievement. The *western pediment* shows a battle between the Lapiths and the Centaurs (mythical monsters, half human, half animal, who carried away the wives of the Lapiths). Apollo stands in majestic calm in the centre, stretching out his right hand. On both sides of him are groups, each consisting of a Centaur fighting against a Lapith and his wife, first in standing, then in kneeling position, until finally lying figures fill in the corners. A pulsating vitality animates the groups, and their violent movements carry them in a dynamic rhythm from the centre to the corners. The perfection of the pedimental sculpture, as we shall see, was achieved on the Parthenon.

Phidias, undoubtedly the greatest Greek sculptor of the classical period and of all times, was charged by Pericles with the sculptural decoration of the Parthenon. When he undertook this grandiose work, he had already acquired great artistic fame with two statues, both erected on the Acropolis. One was the *Athena Promachos* (Athena who fights in the front), a colossal figure in bronze, placed on the Acropolis about 450 B.C., between the Erechtheion and the Propylaea. About 7 metres high, its gilded helmet and lance were visible from afar to sailors entering Piraeus, the Athenian harbour. The original is lost ; but from coins on which it is represented, we can see that Phidias, who showed the goddess in an attitude of majestic calm, had abandoned the old manner of representing her in a fighting posture. The other statue, the *Athena Lemnia* (Fig. 385), was ordered by some Athenian citizens who were about to leave for the colony on the island of Lemnos, as a token of gratitude to the patron goddess of their city. The statue, showing Athena without the usual helmet, was especially loved for its great beauty. Here again the original is missing. It is known only from copies.

Fig. 385. Phidias (?). Athena Lemnia.

Phidias applied all his artistic genius to give the *Parthenon* a sculptural decoration worthy of its architectural perfection. As usual, these sculptures were distributed over the eastern and western pediments and the metopes. But an unusual feature was added in the form of a long frieze on the cella wall, high up near the roof.

In chronological order, the first finished were the metopes, because they had to be dropped between the trygliphs during the building operations. From accounts we know that they were worked upon in 447 B.C. In 438, at the opening festival of the Parthenon, the frieze was also in place; and the famous chryselephantine statue of Athena Parthenos (Fig.337) stood ready in the cella for the admiration of the Athenians. Within the next six years the eastern and the western pedimental figures were finished. Plutarch, the ancient historian, remarked that the speed with which these masterpieces were made was even more marvellous than their beauty.

The *metopes* were originally ninety-two in number: thirty-two on each long, and fourteen on each narrow or pedimental side. They represented mythological combats: on the east the fight between the gods and giants, on the west the battle between the Greeks and Amazons. The northern metopes have been too much damaged to identify their scenes. The best-preserved are those of the southern side, where the *fight between the Centaurs and Lapiths* (Pl.24.1) is represented in high relief. There is no repetition of groups, however. Each one is different. At one time the Centaur is trampling on a Lapith or raising his arm to crush him; in another—and this is seen more often—the Lapith is strangling the Centaur by attacking him either from the front or from the rear. These square slabs carved in high relief and alternating with vertical triglyphs all around the temples, enliven the entablature. Because of the great speed with which these sculptures had to be finished, it was physically impossible for Phidias to do them all by himself, although the compositions may have been his ; but some of the executions show lower quality and seem to have been made by his helpers.

The wonderful *frieze* that encircles the top of the cella wall is 99 cm. high, and was originally some 160 metres long. It represents the most solemn ceremony which the Athenians performed in honour of their patron goddess. Every four years, during the summer, the Panathenaic festival was held in Athens with the greatest pomp. It lasted several days, and included musical and oratorical contests, athletic games, chariot races. The last and most outstanding act was the great procession, composed of the magistrates, the noble young ladies and youths of the city, to offer to the maiden Athena the new saffron robe woven and embroidered by the Athenian girls. An idealized form of this procession is represented on the frieze. On the western side, the procession is forming: young riders are ready to mount; others are already on their horses. The procession is on the move on the southern and northern sides, appearing as if it had divided into two streams that meet once again on the east. Some citizens lead sheep and cattle to be sacrificed, some ride chariots. A number of them carry water jars, but the most beautiful are the youths on horseback. It is here that the artistic inventiveness of Phidias seems inexhaustible. Toward the middle, the movemen quickens, but at the corners it slows down again and marshalls direct the procession. On the eastern side the gods are seated awaiting it arrival, the first-comers are the magistrates and the noble *Athenian maidens* (Fig. 386)—beautiful, modest and dignified—who are coming from both sides. Throughout this frieze there is anendlessvariety of figures in different actions

Fig.386. Athenian maidens, frieze, Parthenon. Louvre, Paris.

and in most beautiful positions. Thus the long, narrow space is filled in a pleasing and interesting way, without crowding. The noble manner in which the citizens are represented shows them conscious of the fact that only by self-control can liberty have a cultural value.

The two pediments on the east and west were finished last, after the solemn opening of the temple. This work took another six years. It has been much damaged, but from the remaining fragments and drawings made by a seventeenth century Frenchman named Carrey, we can somehow reconstruct the subject.

The eastern pediment represents the birth of Athena, the goddess of thought and intelligence. She is represented in Greek mythology as coming from the forehead of her father Zeus, full-grown and clad in armour, and crowned at once by the winged victory. Though this central part of the pediment is lost, the remaining statues from the two sides and Carrey's drawings give us some idea. On the left side *Artemis* (or Hebe), is hastening towards her companions who are sitting, probably *Demeter* and *Persephone*. The heads of all three are missing. Next to them is the beautiful reclining figure of *Dionysus* (Pl. 24.2) which is one of the most superb statues of the Parthenon. On the right side there is another seated group, usually called the Three Fates (Pl. 24.3 ), but representing probably Hestia, Dione and her daughter Aphrodite. Here also the heads and arms are broken away. The one at the left turns somewhat towards the centre. The one next to her is bending over the third, reposing on her lap. There is serene majesty in this triad, clad in graceful chitons (Ionic garments for ladies). The undulating lines formed by the folds converge towards the corner, into the narrowing space of which they marvellously fit with the greatest ease. Perhaps the most interesting groups of the eastern pediment are the two corner figures, which represent dawn, the time of Athena's birth. It shows the rising of Helios, the sun-god, and the sinking of Selene, the moon-goddess, who both, according to mythology, daily race across the sky in horse- drawn chariots. On the left corner we see the snorting head of Helios's charger rising out of the sea, and on the right the weary *head of Selene's steed* (P1. 24.   ) sinking beneath the waves. The latter is one of the most wonderful representations of a horse's head ever executed in art.

On the western pediment the contest on the Acropolis between Athena and Poseidon for the land of Attica and supremacy over the Athenians was represented. In the centre stood Athena with her lance and Poseidon with his trident, both vehemently engaged in the competition. The figures on both sides may have represented—according to general opinion—the local earth deities, of which the best-known and most remarkable figure is Ilissus, the personification of the river of Athens.

The work for which Phidias was the most praised by his contemporaries was the famous cult statue of the Parthenon, the *Athena Parthenos* (Fig.387) made of gold and ivory, which stood

FIg. 387. Phidias (?). Athena Parthenos.

in the hekatompedon or cella. For it the whole building was erected. It is now lost, and known only from copies and descriptions. Colossal in size, it was more than ii metres high. The pedestal on which it stood was of dark marble, decorated with reliefs representing the birth of Pandora on the front, and on both sides Helios with his rising horses and Selene with hers sinking back into the sea. Athena stood majestic and serene, clad in the Doric peplos, and bearing her emblems. The right foot rested on the ground, whilst the left knee was slightly bent so that the tip of the foot just touched the floor. This gave the body a beautiful curve and brought out in pleasing contrast the folds of the robe. On her helmet, three winged horses and crouching sphinxes formed the triple crest. A golden plait of hair hung in front over each shoulder. She wore a breastplate, on the centre of which was carved the head of a Gorgon (a snake-haired monster). Her left hand rested on her shield, on which the battle between the Greeks and the Amazons was represented in relief. Phidias was suspected of having represented himself and his friend Pericles among the various figures. His enemies regarded this as a sacrilegious act, for which he should be banished from Athens. On the inner side of the shield, the battle between gods and giants was painted. From beneath the shield emerged the coiling body and head of the snake Erichtonius. In her right hand, Athena held the statue of Nike (victory) placed on a column. As we have seen, the inner core of the figure was made of wood. To this were attached sheets of ivory for the flesh (face and arms) and gold for the dress, hair and ornaments. According to an ancient document, about 1,152.62 kg. of gold were used. The costliness of the material itself made a great impression on the Greeks, and together with its artistic quality, it must have been splendid indeed. Phidias left Athens soon after having finished his works on the Acropolis. He was probably banished through the jealousy of his enemies. He went to Olympia where he made his second chryselephantine statue, representing *Zeus* in a seated position. This statue, now lost, was his most splendid achievement according to the ancient writers, who showed the greatest admiration for it.

As a result of the Peloponnesian War, Athens began to decline politically; the old idea of empire was abandoned, the Greeks grew more interested in the individual man; scepticism regarding the ancient deities and religion in general developed ; the individual became more important as a resuit of Socrates' doctrine of the supremacy of man's own reason. As art is usually the reflection of the thought of the period, there was a change in the character of sculpture. Instead of the fifth century generalized type, with impersonal facial expression, we find something more personal; emotions and peculiarities are depicted, and there is a growing love of human grace and loveliness. The chief sculptpors of the fourth century were Scopas, Praxiteles, and Lysippos.

About the life of Scopas very little is known except that he came from Paros, and that he was actively at work by 320 B.C. About 350 B.C. he was in Halicarnassos busy with the carvings of the mausoleum. He probably spent his last years in Asia Minor. No statue remains that can with certainty be attributed to him. Around the mausoleum at *Halicarnassos* some battered *heads* (Fig.388) were unearthed. Art scholars generally attribute them to Scopas.

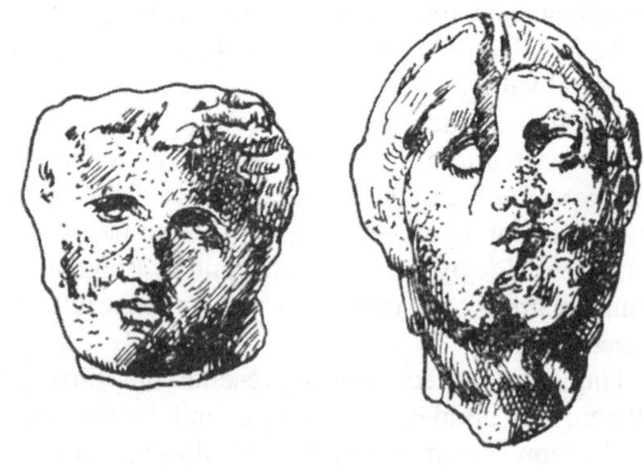

Fig. 388. Scopas (?). Heads from Halicarnassos.

The sad facial expressions, obtained by means of deep-set eyes and upturned gaze, reveal mastery in the portrayal of deep feelings and passions.

Praxiteles was an Athenian. He was the central figure of Greek sculpture in the fourth century B.C. Nearly fifty of his works are mentioned by ancient authors. He excelled in portraying the grace of youth, as is proved by his Hermes, Young Satyr, and Eros of Thespias. The statue of *Hermes* (Fig. 389), carrying the youthful

Fig. 389. Praxiteles. Hermes with infant Dionysus (detail), Olympia.

Dionysus, was found at Olympia in 1877. It is an original, not a copy; and archaeologists almost unanimously attribute it to Praxiteles. Hermes is shown leaning nonchalantly on a short stump with his left arm. This posture gives an easy curve to the body. On this leaning arm, from which his mantle falls in rich folds, sits the infant Dionysus, who stretches out his little hands for something that Hermes raises high in his right hand. Since this arm is missing, we can only guess that it may have held a bunch of grapes, an allusion to wine, since Dyonisus was the god of wine. The marble is finished with the utmost delicacy, and the statue shows a masterly expression of individual character. Praxiteles rendered in marble the softness of the flesh, the gloss of the hair and the moisture of the eyes, so that we are more aware of the human personal charm of the figure than of the marble from which it is carved.

Lysippos was the most important sculptor of the generation following Scopas and Praxiteles, namely of the second half of the fourth century B.C. He worked at the court of Alexander the Great, through whose conquests Greek art was widely spread. This period is the beginning of the Hellenestic Age. There are some statues which archaeologists attribute to Lysippos, but we are not sure whether they are really his work. One of these is the *Apoxiomenos* (P1. 24.5). It is so called because it represents an athlete scraping himself. The Greeks used to oil their bodies before contests. Naturally it became caked with sand during the fight; so after the combat, they cleaned themselves with a wooden scraper, called strigil, before they took a bath. Unlike the sculpture of the fifth century B.C., that showed the human figure in a generalized and idealized manner—this one represents an individual performing a commonplace action, an unimportant passing moment in life. Again, while the previous images could be viewed satisfactorily only from the front, and perhaps from one side, this one is artistic from any viewpoint. Lastly, the proportions also differ from the established canon of Polycletus, according to which the head was a little less than one-seventh of the total height. That of the Apoxiomenos is about one-eighth of the total height.

After the death of Alexander, his empire crumbled into small kingdoms, of which the capitals, Pergamon, Antioch, Seleucia, and Alexandria became the centres to which artists migrated from the old Greek towns, which lost their power. The chief patrons were the Hellenistic princes, the heirs of Alexander. The sober and balanced classical taste gave place to brilliance and theatrical display. Art became even more naturalistic and emotional, showing strong human feelings and violent movements. This can be seen on the *frieze* of the *altar* of *Pergamon* (Pl. 24. 6) which represents a battle between the gods and the giants. Famous statues of the age are those of *Laocoon and his sons*, of *Niobe and her daughters*, of the *Nike of Samothrace* (Pl. 24. 7), and others. Because of the realistic tendency, the subjects of sculpture became more varied. We see representations of every-day life—sometimes charming, sometimes trivial or even repulsive.

## PAINTING AND MINOR ARTS

Though Greek literary sources tell us that their schools of painting flourished as much as those of sculpture, all the monumental works of this kind, for which they were said to be famous, have disappeared. According to the writers of that time, the stoae at Athens had remarkable murals by a contemporary of Phidias, namely the great painter and sculptor Polygnotus. In them he commemorated the victories of the Athenians over the Persians. Aristotle often mentions his appreciation of Greek painting in his Poetics, whereas he hardly refers to sculpture. Zeuxis and Parhasius were famous during the fifth and fourth centuries B.C.; and Protogenes and Apelles at the time of Alexander the Great.

In the so-called house of the faun in Pompeii, there is a mosaic which is believed to be a copy of a Greek painting, and which could therefore give an idea of their great work. It seems to represent the Battle of Issus, fought between Alexander the Great and Darius.

Greek pottery decoration might also give a faint reflection of what the great monumental paintings may have been like. Earthenware became very important when increasing exports created a demand for containers for oil and honey. The potters' quarters in Athens, known as the keramikos, from which the present word ceramics is derived, became one of the most important parts of the city.

Greek vases have a double interest. They are valued for their graceful and proportionate shapes, as well as their exquisite decorations. The number of forms which they used is unexpectedly small in comparison with the extent of pottery-making. As in architecture, they worked out a few forms, each suited to its requirements as a container, then developed them, refining the contours, proportions and decoration. The chief forms (Fig.390) included the two-handled amphora

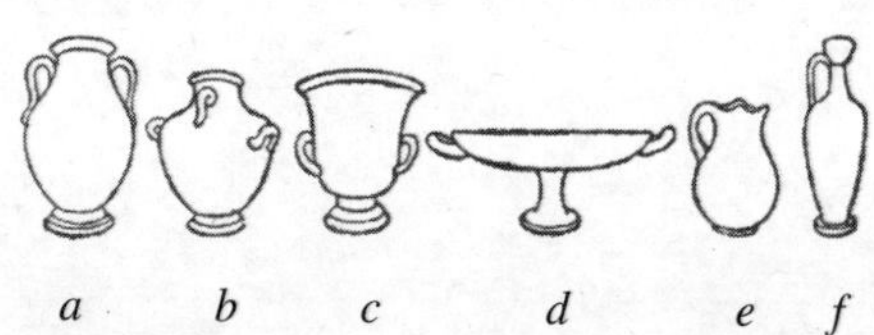


Fig. 390. Greek vases : *a*. amphora, *b*. hydria, *c*. crater, *d*. cylix, *e*. oinochoē, . lecythos.

(amphi, on both side phoreus, handle) which was used for storing wine, honey, corn and oil, and which had an opening large enough to admit a ladle; the hydria, a water-jar with three handles, two for lifting and one for carrying ; the crater, a bowl with a large mouth for mixing wine ; the cylix, a drinking bowl; the oinochoë, a wine-jug, with lip pinched into a trefoil shape to facilitate pouring ; the lecythos, an oil flask with long narrow neck to allow slow pouring of the oil, used chiefly for funeral rites. On vases before the fifth century B.C., the figures were painted in black on the natural red clay of which they were made. The details were incised with a hard, pointed instrument to expose the red beneath, and touches of white or purple were added. This was called the black-figured style. In the fifth century B.C., the images were red on a black background. The painter first polished the red clay, incised the design on the surface, and coloured the outline thus marked. He then painted the details, and filled in the background with black glaze. This was called the red-figured style. The brush lines gave the painter more freedom in showing the finer points than the incised line of the black-figured ware afforded. Between the sixth and fourth centuries B.C., the clay was covered with a coat of white glaze, on which the pictures were painted. This process was used chiefly for the funeral lecythos.

Except in the early periods, the human figure was used by the Greeks to decorate their pottery ware, where it appears much oftener than in the ceramic art of other peoples. They seemed especially fond of and skilled in representing the human body. The subjects of their vase decorations were mostly mythological scenes and pictures of every-day life, such as banquets, dances, men working or filling their hydrias at the fountain, or drawing wine and pouring it into cylixes.

The *amphora* painted by *Exekias* (Pl. 24. 8), in the Vatican Museum, is a typical example of the black-figured style. The decoration does not cover the whole body of the vase, which is black except for an ornamental band at the base, the handle, and the panel on which the figures are painted. They represent Achilles and Ajax playing draughts ; the heroes' names and the words of their conversation are written beside them. Ajax calls out three and Achilles four—he has won.

An example of the red-figured style is a *cylix* painted by *Duris*, representing a school scene. On the left side sits a boy holding a lyre, which he is learning to play from a master seated in front of him, who is also fingering an instrument. On the right side, the teacher holds an inscribed scroll, while a pupil stands in front of him.

On a *lecythos from Attica*, now in Berlin, the lamentations over the dead are represented.

# 4. ROMAN ART

## GENERAL SURVEY

The Italian peninsula is a long strip of land jutting far into the Mediterranean. The coastline is regular, with only a few deep bays or sheltered harbours; and the Alps separate it from the rest of Europe. This protected it from invasion. The surface was suited for unification : from north to south run the Apennine mountains, with great fertile plains to the west. The long one in the north is watered by the river Po and its tributary streams. In the central regions, the Arno passes Florence, and meets the sea at Pisa; while the Tiber runs through the city of Rome to its harbour Ostia, some eighteen miles westward. Sicily, a triangular-shaped island in the south, is separated from Italy by the straits of Messina, a channel only two miles wide in its narrowest parts. The climate varies. In the north, the summers are hot and the winters cold; the central part is noted for its brilliant sunshine and beautiful azure sky ; the south is almost sub-tropical.

The Italians, another Indo-European people, began to occupy this peninsula when the Greeks started invading the Peloponnesus. They had complete possession of it by around 1000 B.C. Among them, the best known and most important tribe were the Latins, who settled near the mouth of the river Tiber. Later they founded Rome.

Though the early development of the Hellenes and Romans started about the same time, the former progressed more quickly because Greece was closer to the cultured Near-East. The Romans, suffering from many internal struggles, lagged far behind; but they rose in power when the brilliant civilization of classical Greece began to decline, after the fifth century B.C.

From a village, Rome slowly grew into a city-state. Then it united the peninsula politically, and gradually expanded into a vast empire, absorbing not only the Latins, Etruscans, Greeks and Celts in Italy itself, but also the powerful Carthaginian empire, the Hellenistic east, and much of northern Europe. These conquests were much slower than Alexander's, but more thorough. The subject peoples often became proud of Roman citizenship, adopting the official Latin language and the beliefs of the conquerors, because they brought them more security, peace, prosperity, justice and uniform legislation. They were also tolerant of the laws and customs of others, adapting themselves to their cultures and spreading them. Their road system helped to preserve unity and promote communication between the various peoples. Wherever Roman power was established, cities grew up with fine buildings and good water supply; and irrigation made the deserts bloom. But too much security and luxury brought enervation and corruption—a kind of cultured barbarism. Dearth of industrious men and precious metals (drained off to the east, especially India, to buy oriental luxuries) were among the chief causes of its downfall in the fifth century A.D.

In the development of Roman civilization, the Etruscans had played an important part. Little is known of their origin, since their numerous inscriptions have not yet been deciphered. They probably came from the east, and settled in central Italy, or Etruria. From this comes the modern name Tuscany. Active in trade and industry, they subjected the agricultural Italians, and helped them to build up their civilization. Commerce with the east gave them contact with Greek culture.

Although their art kept its strongly native character, Hellenic influence on it is quite obvious. The structure of their wooden temples resembled the Greek, except for the pronaos (a deep entrance porch supported on pillars) and a peculiarly Etruscan cella. They used the Tuscan order, a modification of the Doric. Their tombs were both excavated and structural. Generally they consisted of one chamber, with the roof either gabled or slightly arched. The interior walls were covered with frescoes, on which they imitated the designs of the numerous vases imported from Greece, but with a primitive narrative spirit peculiarly their own. They built their cities on the tops of hills (as we can see at Fiesole, Arezzo, Cortona and Chiusi), and surrounded them with enormous walls made of huge stone blocks. Some still exist, as well as their gateways, erected with wedge-shaped pieces of the true arch type. They were also skilful in clay and bronze sculpture.

But it was especially the Greeks who helped in shaping Roman civilization. They began to colonize southern Italy and Sicily at the time when Etruscan culture was at its height in central Italy, and when the new city of Rome was still confined within the narrow limits of its hills beside the banks of the Tiber. But these early colonists did not have as much influence as the Hellenes whom the Romans subjugated centuries later. The Greek slaves dominated their masters oy cultural superiority: as the Roman poet Horace expressed it, ' It was captive Greece that took Rome prisoner'.

The Romans were a practical, earthly-minded people, whose interests were centred chiefly in the family and home. Their worship resembled a legal bargain in which the gods were expected to do their part if man performed the rites according to fixed regulations. There was nothing very elevating about their beliefs, which held out no future hope for the individual. Their ideas of the gods were vague. Most of them were divinities of the household and daily occupations. Every home had a shrine to the family gods (Lares). They also worshipped their ancestors. Janus, the two-faced god, was the guardian of the door, the frontiers of the state and the new year (January). The highest honours were given to Vesta, the goddess of the family and imperial hearth. Her fire was kept alight by the young girls in the home, and by the vestal virgins in her temple on the forum, the centre of the empire. To their own religious practices they added those borrowed from other nations. For instance, their belief in omens (like the flight of birds and the reflex movements of the entrails of animals newly slain) was also common among the Etruscans. Little by little they adopted the Greek gods, giving them Latin names : the chief god Zeus was called Jupiter, his wife Hera became Juno, Athena Minerva, Poseidon Neptune, Dionysus Bacchus, Aphrodite Venus, and Nike Victoria. Worship became more and more a state affair, and during the empire they introduced from the east the deification of the emperors. But education and contact with other cultures made many of the Romans dissatisfied with their religious ideas. Scepticism undermined belief in their demoralizing mythologies. Many adopted Greek philosophies like Stoicism, which had some spiritual flavour. Others looked for satisfaction in Mithraism, a mystery cult from Persia. Around the time when this spiritual restlessness began, when the Roman republic was turning into an empire under Augustus, Jesus was born in Palestine, one of the most insignificant territories conquered by Rome shortly before. His followers increased rapidly over all parts of the known world and among all classes, because they found in him the fulfilment of the deepest and noblest yearnings of the soul.

## ARCHITECTURE

During the republican age, building activity was rather limited, and bore an Etruscan and Greek impress. The glorious period of Roman architecture began under Augustus, the first emperor, who is quoted as saying, ' I found Rome a city of bricks, and I shall leave it a city of marble '. The vast number of constructions that sprang up throughout the extensive empire was the result of a long period of peace and security, increasing wealth from commerce, the government's concern for the welfare of its citizens, and their own love of comfort and magnificence.

Italy was rich in building materials. From Tivoli, near Rome, came a good hard stone called travertine; and from Carrara, a glittering white marble. They also had good clay for brick ; and for concrete they used pozzolana (a clean sandy earth) and lava, of volcanic origin. From their colonies they imported great quantities of coloured marbles and alabaster.

They adopted the three Greek orders (Doric, Ionic, and Corinthian), and added the Tuscan and Composite. The Tuscan resembles the Doric, but is even more severe: it has a column with a base, an unfluted shaft, and a simply-moulded capital carrying a plain entablature. The composite order (Fig. 391) combines the

Fig. 391. Roman composite capital.

Corinthian and Ionic capitals. It is more ornate, and was used chiefly in triumphal arches.

While the Greeks erected comparatively small structures and concentrated their architectural skill on the temple, the Romans, with their vast empire, needed greater variety and larger buildings. That is why several new types developed, both religious and secular, most of them much larger than had ever yet been attempted.

Their desire for great meeting halls made them look for a method of roofing that would leave a large open inner space, unobstructed by supports. The post and lintel system was unsuited, since it needed many columns which took up much room, as in the hypostyle hall at Karnak. To avoid this, the Roman builders generally used another structural system, the arch.

The arch system (Fig. 392a) is an architectural device in which a number of separate tapering or wedge-shaped stones (called voussoirs) are so fitted together that they bridge the space between two supports, usually in the form of an arc, curve or semi-circle. The central block (the keystone) is the last to be inserted. It holds all the pieces together once it has been firmly put into place. To build an arch, a rounded wooden scaffolding, called centering (Fig.392*b*), is needed in order to hold the voussoirs in place until the keystone has been put in position and the mortar has set. Until then it cannot be removed. The arch permits the spanning of wide distances with small blocks. With the stone lintel no more than 6 metres can be bridged ; but with the arch the Romans covered a space of 43¼ metres over the Pantheon. Its power to bear great weight is another advantage. The wedges are squeezed closer together when pressed from above, because they are wider on the top than at the bottom. This is also the reason why they do not fall. But at the same time, the more the blocks of the arch proper are held together, the more each one tends to force out the one beside it. Thus the lowest pieces slowly move outwards until there is enough space for the wider part of the voussoirs to fall down, and then the whole arch collapses (Fig.392c). This spreading, called lateral thrust, is the great disadvantage or weakness of the arch. It can be remedied by counterpressure, for instance by building masonry masses (called buttresses) against the sides, preventing the blocks from moving outwards.

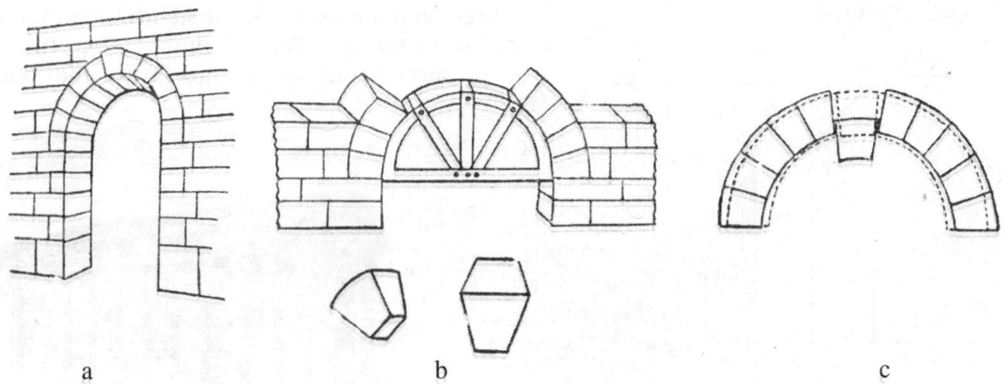


Fig. 392 *a*. the arch, *b*. centering to hold the arch during its construction, *c*. lateral thrust or weakness of the arch.

A vault (Fig.393) is an arched roofing of stone or brick. If an arch is extended in its depth, it resembles a tunnel. This is called the barrel or waggon vault (Fig.393 *a*). Since it is an extended arch, it exerts an outward pressure throughout its length. The walls on which it rests must therefore be very thick to resist both the downward and outward pressure, or lateral thrust. Another disadvantage is that the window openings must be cut below the beginning of the

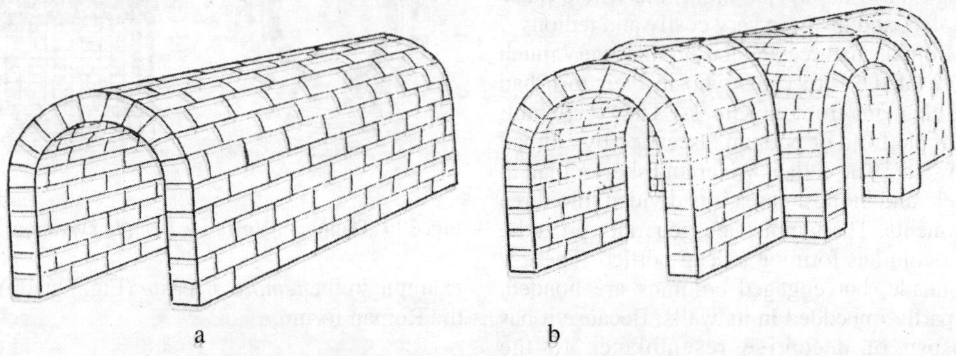


Fig. 393 The vault: *a*. barrel vault, *b*. groin vault.

vault, which reduces the inner lighting. With regard to beauty, or from the aesthetical point of view, such a long, uninterrupted, arched ceiling looks rather monotonous (Fig 394a).

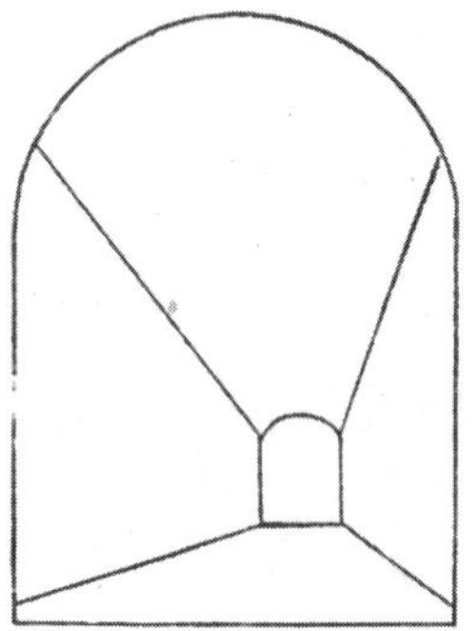

Fig.394. Interior : *a*. with barrel vault, *b*. with groin vault (bath of Caracalla).

The groin or cross vault (Fig.393b) was developed by the Romans to overcome some of these disadvantages. This type is formed by the intersection of two barrel vaults at right angles. The line of crossing is called a groin, hence the name. The advantage of such vaulting is that the pressure is exerted only at the points where the groins meet. So to keep it from collapsing, it is enough that buttresses are built at right angles against the outer wall, just at the points of intersection inside. Thus the wall itself can be thinner and lighter. The windows can also be cut even as high as the vault itself, instead of being below the place where the arch begins (i.e. the springing line), as was the case with the barrel vault. Because of its more varied aspect, this kind is also much more pleasing to the eye (Fig. 394b). Yet, since both types are really one big arch vault, the centering had to be erected along the whole place to be roofed, and this was very costly and tedious.

The Romans had rectangular temples very much like those of the Etruscans, who in their turn had adopted elements from the Greeks. They were built on a high platform or podium, ascended by a broad flight of steps. The cella is wider and shorter than in the Greek, and in most cases it is divided into three compartments. The temples are generally prostyle, the front columns forming a deep portico. There is no colonnade, but engaged columns are bonded, that is, partly imbedded in its walls. Because it has an illusory or deceptive resemblance to the perypteral, this type is called pseudo-perypteral. The best-known example in Rome is the *temple of Fortuna Virilis*, dating from the republican age, and almost intact. It stands on a high platform, and has Ionic columns. But the best-preserved and most graceful is the *Maison*

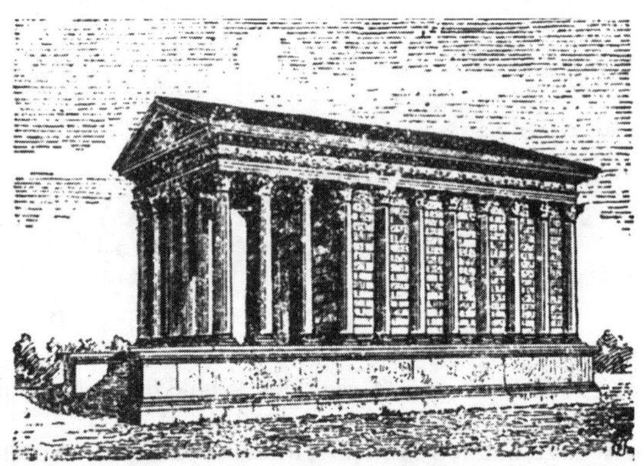

Fig. 395. Maison Carrée, Nîmes, France

*Carrée** (Fig.395) in Nimes, France, from the first century B.C. It has one cella, and Corinthian columns support the richly-carved entablature. The name by which it is now known is a French expression meaning square house.

Circular temples were common in Rome, and probably derived from Etruscan prototypes. In the more usual forms, called monopteral, the round cella is encircled by columns, as for

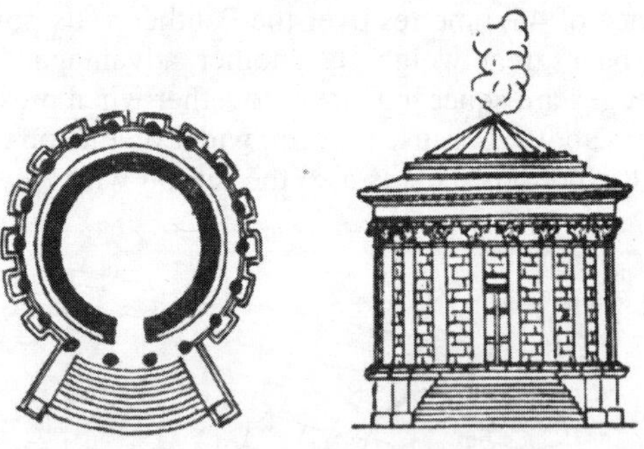

Fig. 396 Temple of Vesta : *a*. plan, *b*. elevation, Rome.

example in the *temple of Vesta* (Fig.396a, b) in the Roman forum.

* pronounced may-zon caray

Of all the circular temples, the *Pantheon* (Pl. 25.1, 2; Fig. 397) is the most magnificent. It is also one of the best-preserved of Rome's ancient monuments. The emperor Hadrian built it early in the first century A.D. An immense hemispherical dome, 43¼ metres

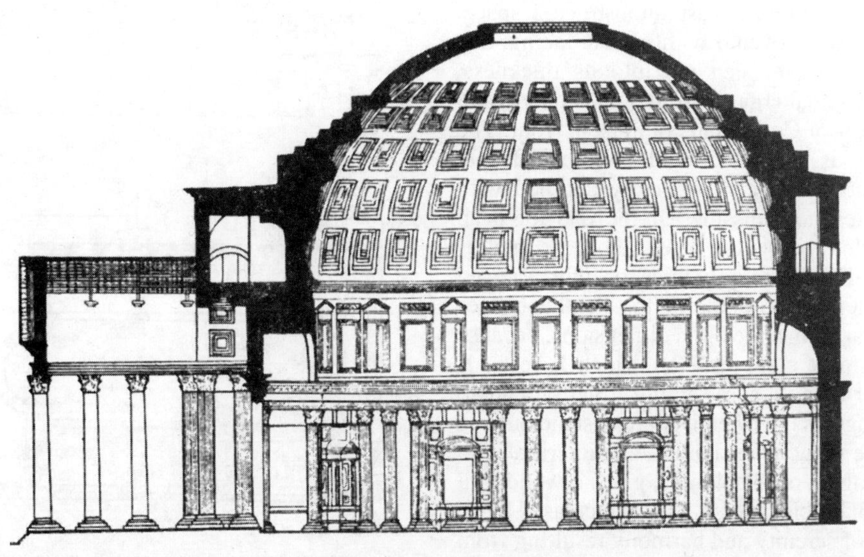

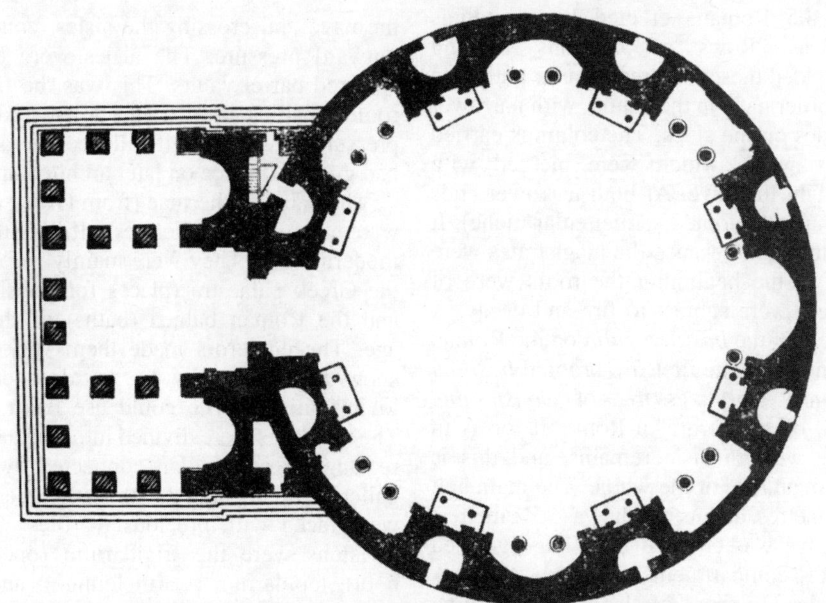

Fig. 397. Pantheon : cross section (above), plan (below), Rome.

across, is supported by a high wall, six metres thick. Attached to it, at the entrance, is a gable-ended portico with sixteen monolithic columns, similar to the front of a Greek temple. Its entablature and pediments were originally decorated with bronze sculpture. There is only one ingress through this portico with the still-existing original bronze doors. The interior is a vast unobstructed space. The round wall is covered with marble facing, and seven recesses have been cut into its thickness. These niches are alternately round and square, and each has a pair of Corinthian columns in front. The arched dome is decorated with coffered (deeply sunk) ornamental panels, originally adorned with bronze rosettes, now missing. On the very top is an opening, called the oculus (eye), about 8½ metres in diameter. This is the only inlet for light. Viewed from the exterior, the dome of the Pantheon does not look so large, in spite of its dimensions, because the thick, almost plain wall on which it rests, is raised higher than its base, hiding it partly, and so not permitting this huge hemisphere to stand out and dominate the view as it should. The interior, with no obstructing piers or columns, gives a wonderful impression of spaciousnesss. This is increased by an atmosphere of serenity and harmony resulting from the equal diffusion everywhere of the light coming from the one source above.

For their public business, judicial as well as commercial, the Romans erected big buildings called basilicas. Rows of columns running lengthwise divided these long rectangular halls into a wider and loftier nave in the centre, with narrower and lower aisles on the sides. The columns carried the clerestory walls, which were pierced with windows to light the nave. At both narrower ends there was an apse (a domed semicircular niche). It was called a tribunal, because the magistrates were seated there. In the beginning the roofs were of wood, but these were subject to fire and decay. A good example was the *basilica Julia* on the Roman forum, now in ruins. The first fire-proofed *basilica* with a masonry vault was that of *Constantine* (Fig.398) also on the forum in Rome. It too is in ruins, but the western aisle remains, and this is enough to form an idea of the whole. The main hall was 99 by 26 metres, and its height was 35½ metres. The central nave was covered by a huge groined vault of three compartments. Arched openings led to the aisles. In front of the pillars carrying these arches stood monolithic columns, which, being at the meeting point of the groins, carried the downward pressure of the vault. Behind the pillars, buttressing walls, at right angles to

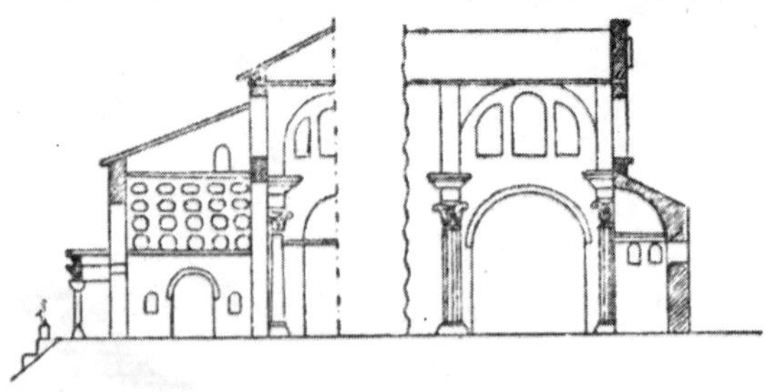

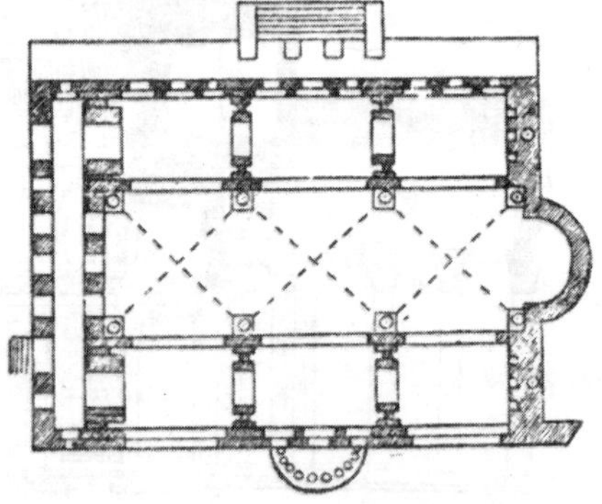

Fig. 398. Basilica of Constantine : half cross section (above left), part of longitudinal section (above right), plan (below), Rome.

the nave and crossing the aisles, counteracted the outward pressure. The aisles were covered with coffered barrel vaults. This was the first masonry-roofed basilica, in which the downward and outward pressures were scientifically counteracted. Thus it had great influence on later architecture.

The baths or thermae (from Greek thermos, hot) were magnificent structures fulfilling the role of our modern clubs. They were mainly a combination of the Greek palaestra (places for physical exercise) and the Roman balnea (baths) of the republican age. The emperors made them very luxurious to show their liberality to the decadent, pleasure-loving citizens who could use them free of cost. The buildings were divided into a sequence of halls, rectangular or circular, connected by long arched galleries, all decorated with statuary; and their walls were faced with precious marbles. The principal divisions were the frigidarium (open swimming pool), tepidarium (warm lounge), and calidarium (hot water bath). There were also small bathing cubicles for individuals or families, drawing rooms, places for physical exercise and games, courts, inner peristyles, beautifully laid-out gardens, halls for literary entertainments, libraries with reading rooms, sometimes even a small stadium. This necessarily included the service areas and water reservoirs required for such luxurious establishments. The ruins in *Rome* of *Caracalla's thermae* (Fig.399) (2II A.D), and *Diocletian's thermae*

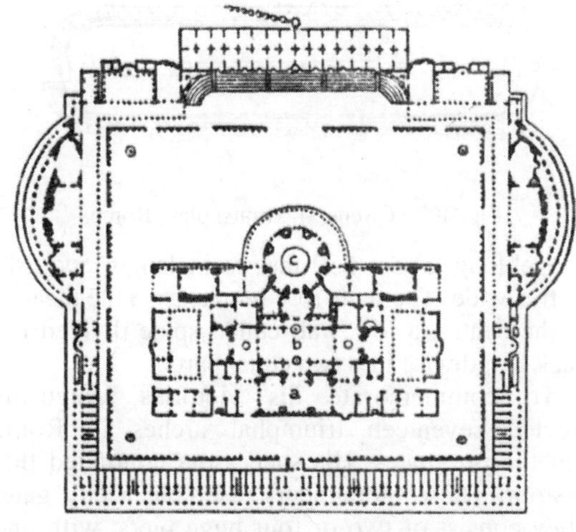

Fig. 399. Thermae of Caracalla, Rome.

(305 A.D.), give us some idea of how magnificent these buildings must have been.

Their theatres and amphitheatres were constructed according to the Greek plan, semicircular in form with rising tiers. But instead of hollowing out a hillside for this purpose, the Romans erected the entire building with concrete vaults and steps and high surrounding walls. The ground floor or orchestra, which the Greeks had reserved for the chorus, now became a part of the auditorium set aside for the members of the senate and other dignitaries. A good example of this is the theatre of Marcellus in Rome (23-13 B.C.).

The amphitheatre, as the meaning of the word itself denotes (amphi, double or on both sides), is a combination or joining together of two semicircular Greek theatres to make a round or oval shape. Thus the rising tiers of seats entirely surrounded the place for the performance, called arena, meaning sand. This was thrown on the ground to absorb the blood shed during the spectacles, which consisted of gladiatorial combats and wild beast shows. Caverns for the gladiators and beasts honeycombed the substructure under the arena and seats.

The *Colosseum* or *Flavian amphitheatre* (Pl. 26.1; Figs. 400 ab, 401) is the greatest example of the kind. In spite of its ruined condition, it is one of the most monumental landmarks of *Rome*. Elliptical in shape, its external circumference is 537 metres. The huge surrounding wall, more than 46 metres high, is built of travertine, the best and hardest building stone of Rome, and the inner vaults are of concrete and tufa. Inside, tiers of seats rose up to the highest gallery. They were divided by horizontal passage-ways, to which led numerous stairways hidden under the high vaulting which supported the upper tiers of seats. The outer wall is

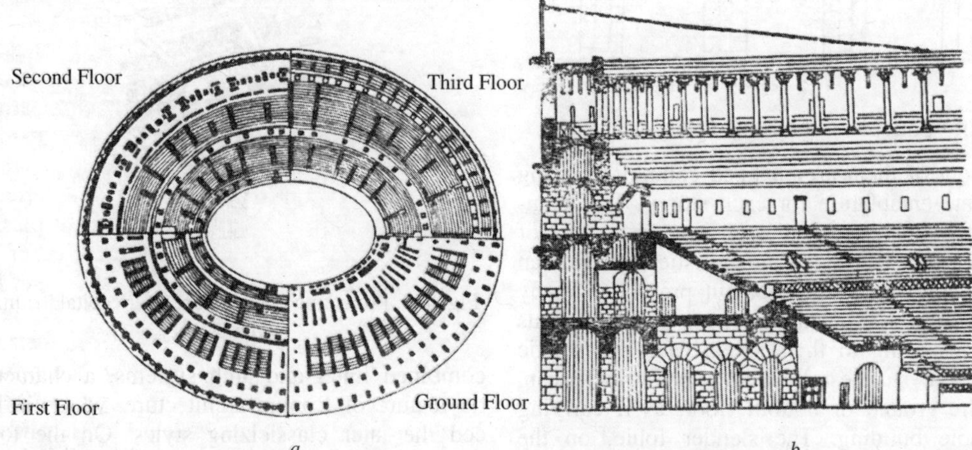


Fig. 400. Colosseum : *a*. plan, *b*. part of inner elevation, Rome.

divided into four storeys. Three of them are arcades, the arches alternating with wide piers.

Fig. 401. Colosseum, elevation of outer wall, Rome.

In front of them are engaged columns carrying a separate entablature for each storey. This combination of the lintel and arch systems is one of the most outstanding characteristics of Roman architecture, best seen here, but present in many other buildings. The arrangement of the various orders according to their levels has an aesthetic appeal. The sturdiest looking, the Doric-Tuscan, is on the ground or bottom floor, as if carrying the whole building. The slender Ionic, on the storey above, carries less weight; and the delicate Corinthian is the highest of the three. The fourth level has a plain wall, decorated with Corinthian pilasters Around the summit are sockets to hold posts for the immense awning formerly stretched over the spectators to protect them against sun and rain.

The *Roman* circus was a race course, probably derived from the Greek hippodrome. The most celebrated was the *Circus Maximus* (Fig. 402). It

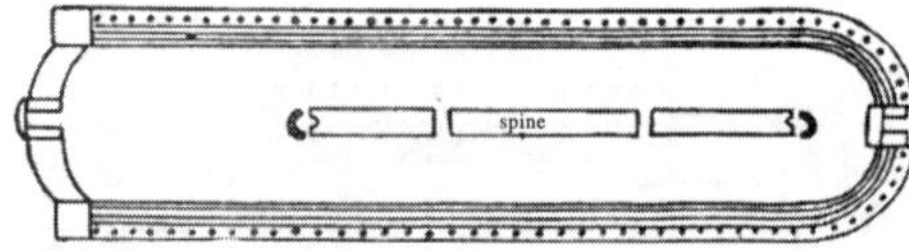


Fig. 402. Circus Maximus, plan, Rome.

was oblong, about 550 metres in length and 183 metres wide. The seats rose in tiers as in the theatre. In the centre, a low wall called spine divided the track lengthwise into two equal parts.

To commemorate his victories, Augustus erected seventeen triumphal arches in Rome and the provinces. His successors continued this custom. These monuments resemble a city gate. They consist of two or four huge piers, with one or three arched passages in between. In front of the piers, and attached to them, stand columns with composite capitals. The entablature with its architrave, frieze and cornice is broken in its horizontality by following the protruding members. These projections (Fig. 403) are like the

Fig. 403. Projecting entabalature over capital, triumphal arch, Rome.

combined lintel and arch systems, a characteristic feature of Roman architecture, which influenced the later classicizing styles. On the top of the entablature is a solid half-storey (called an attic), which carried sculptural groups. Reliefs commemorated the victorious campaigns for which they were erected. Most of them stood on the forum or near the triumphal way, through which passed the procession, with the conqueror in a chariot, en route to the Capitol. The *arch of Titus* (Pl. 26.2, ; Fig. 404a) (71-82 A.D.) on the Via Sacra, between the forum and Colosseum, is the simplest of the single arch type, and is well-preserved. It celebrates the capture of Jerusalem in a.d. 70. The capitals on the engaged columns are the earliest known examples of the Composite order. The *arch of Septimius Severus* (Fig.404b) (204 A.D.) in the forum, commemorating a victory over the Parthians, and the *arch of Constantine* (Fig.404c) (330 A.D.) near the Colosseum, recording the battle of the Milvian bridge, both have triple passages.

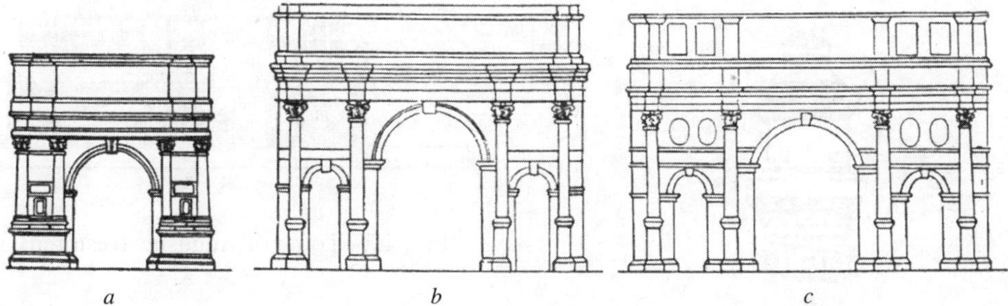


Fig. 404. Triumphal arches: *a*. arch of Titus, *b*. arch of Septimius Severus, *c*. arch of Constantine, Rome.

Victories were also honoured by memorial columns. Those of Trajan and Marcus Aurelius can still be seen in *Rome*. From the base of each a band of low reliefs winds upwards around the shaft, representing different episodes of the wars. T*rajan's column* (Fig.405) (114 A.D.) is Tuscan-Doric. Its pedestal gives entrance to his tomb, where his ashes were preserved in a golden urn. A staircase winds up the inside of the column. His statue, no longer there, once stood at the very top. The spiraling band, perhaps reminiscent of an unwinding parchment scroll, is over 244. metres long and 1.67 metres wide. Its 2500 figures represent his Dacian campaign. Columns erected for naval victories were decorated with the rostra or prows of captured ships.

The residences of the wealthy were called palaces when they stood within the city walls, and villas when they were in the country. The most luxurious was Nero's *Domus Aurea* (golden house) in *Rome*. The most famous *villa* was that *of Hadrian* at Tibur or Tivoli.

The dead were usually cremated, but sometimes they were buried. At times there are in the same tomb both urns with ashes and sarcophagi (singular: sarcophagus) or stone coffins. Since Roman law forbade interment within the city walls, the dead were buried along the main roads, generally between the first and third milestones. Customarily they had family or congregational tombs. The middle classes used subterranean passages and caverns, called caemetaria (sleeping or burial chambers), from which the word cemetery is derived. Into the walls were cut niches or columbaria similar to pigeon holes, hence the name (columba means pigeon). In these they put the urns. These sepulchres were decorated with paintings. Great families erected more imposing tombs on both sides of the highways, of which those along the Old Appian Way are the most famous. Often they resembled little temples, with a prostyle portico. The *tomb of Cecilia Metella* is round, on a square foundation. Emperors were buried within the city of *Rome*. Outstanding examples, both near the Tiber and similar in shape, are the *tomb of Augustus* (Fig. 406), a heavy circular tower standing on a massive square base, and *Hardian's mole* (or mausoleum), also called the Castello di Sant'Angelo.

The Romans were excellent engineers, and their public works were not only enduring but artistic as well. The *Pont du Gard** (Fig. 407) in Nîmes, France, is one of their famous bridge-aqueducts (water conduits). Well-known also are the arched *aqueducts* in the *Roman Campagna*. Excellent roads led to the capital from every

* pronounce: pon-dū-gar

direction of the empire. This helped the centralization of power. Until the invention of

Fig. 405. Trajan's column, Rome.

railways in the nineteenth century, many of these Roman highways remained the chief means of communication. The heart of *Rome* was the *forum* at the foot of the Capitol hill. At first it was a simple market-place lined with shops ; later it developed into the centre of public life, with a large open space, a platform for orators, and sculptural decorations. Around it were the

Fig. 406. Tomb of Augustus (restored), Rome.

Fig. 407. Pont du Gard, Nîmes, France.

chief public buildings. Near by the emperors erected *imperial forums,* the largest of these being *Trajan's.*

## SCULPTURE

Roman architecture surpassed its sculpture, in the beginning they had little appreciation for this art. Towards the end of the republic, after the sack of Corinth in 146 B.C. and the defeat of Athens in 86 B.C., they brought back to Rome shiploads of Greek statues. It became a fashion for the rich to own them; but since there were not sufficient originals, many copies were made, and it is through these that many originals, now lost, are still known to us. Many Greek sculptors migrated from their desolated country to serve their new overlords. Even the Roman statues of this time reflect strong Greek influence. Gradually this gave place to more indigenous works.

The Romans decorated their buildings with relief sculpture commemorating historical events and victories in wars. These suited their practical minds, and became a common means for the emperors to record their famous exploits in stone. The finest specimens are found on the walls around the *Ara Pacis* (Fig. 408), an altar set up in 13 B.C. to honour Augustus for the peace he had brought to the Roman world. The procession scene, showing the emperor as

Fig. 408 Relief from Ara Paris Augustae, Rome.

a high priest, with members of his family and high officials, reveals especially the native seriousness and calm dignity. The band or reliefs winding up the shaft of *Trajan's column* (Fig.405) (98-116 A.D.) is an interesting ancient document of military history. The story is told according to the continuous narration method (already explained in Early Indian Sculpture, though there is no connection whatever between the two). The emperor is represented more than seventy times.

The portrait was the greatest Roman contribution to sculpture. Their sense of realism helped them to excel in this art. In contrast to Greek idealism and generalization, they aimed at reproducing physical features truthfully, even if they were ugly. Their custom of keeping in their homes wax masks of their ancestors aided them in developing this naturalistic tendency.

A typical example is the head of *an unknown Roman* (Fig. 409), in the Museum of Fine Art,

Fig. 409. Head of an unknown Roman.

Boston. Full of vivid realism, it is the portrait of a man of the early republic—dominating, stern and strong-willed. His character is revealed by the well-shaped head, the typically Roman, strongly-curved aquiline nose, the loose skin below the chin, and the lines betraying individual characteristics. It dates from the first century B.C.

The portraits of contemporary women show less naturalism and personal character. Yet some lovely examples of fresh realism do exist, as for instance the head of a *young girl* (P1.27.1 ), sculptured during the transition period between the republic and the empire, and preserved in the Chiaramonti Collection in the Vatican. It shows an adolescent, gazing wide-eyed at the new world opening out before her, with a mingled expression of wonder and melancholy. The spontaneity of the face contrasts with the artificial curls and the small grandmotherly bun on the top of the head.

The statue of Augustus (Pl. 27.2) in the Vatican Museum, is of a different type. The emperor stands in an easy pose. He wears a linen tunic, covered with an ornate metal cuirass fringed with leather. A military cloak hangs over his left arm. The different textures of the rigid metal, the tough leather, and the soft, heavy cloth are convincingly represented. He is pointing his right arm in the direction towards which he is looking, and holding a sceptre in his left. The face shows no individual characteristics because Greek influence in Rome was at its height during the Augustan age. The features resemble the impersonal types of fifth century B.C. Greek sculptur.

The Roman sculptors had a real gift for portraying children. They skilfully represented their smooth, tender skin and childish features. The secret of their success was a sympathetic understanding of the child mind, which enabled them to seize the moment of wavering between laughter and tears betraying itself in quivering lips. The portraits of child aristocrats are excellently done, and show their genuine feelings. A good example is the marble *bust of a child* (Fig. 410) from the first century A.D., the original of which is now in the Museum of Fine Arts, Boston.

The head of the *emperor Vespasian* (Fig. 411) in the Thermae Museum, Rome, shows a hardened soldier with keen, sharp eyes, tight lips and firm chin ; but it is not as detailed or clear-cut as the republican portraits. The sharp, linear quality of the latter has been replaced by a blending of details reminding us of the Flavian reliefs.

The bust of emperor *Caracalla* (Pl. 27.3) in Berlin Museum, is the most life-like of all. The fleshy shoulders and arms, the head turned slightly sideways, the hair roughly massed over the smooth face, the grim lines of the mouth, and the deep-set eyes shadowed by heavy, frowning brows, give an immediate impression of cunning, merciless brutality and cold cruelty.

Fig. 410. Head of a Roman child.

Fig. 411. Emperor Vespasian.

## PAINTING

Wall-frescoes, like those found at Pompeii and Herculaneum, as well as in Rome, were the principal kind of painting. Some of these consisted of painted architecture with picture panels inserted, showing windows and pillars in perspective, thus giving an appearance of depth. Those at *villa Item*, near *Pompeii*, depict only a shallow space, but the light figures against a dark background look like reliefs, so cleverly are volume and structure suggested by means of shading. Generally the figures represent mythological or literary scenes, or genre. Portraits from real life are rare ; but a striking example of these is *Paquius Proculus and his wife* (PI. 27.4 ). On the walls of *villa Livia in Rome* is a naturalistic painting of a garden with different tints of green and blue, with brightly-coloured birds and flowers. It seems to be separated from the room by a low fence. These are more proofs of the Roman love of reality in art.

## MEDIEVAL ART

# 5. EARLY CHRISTIAN ART

### GENERAL SURVEY

Early Christian art, coinciding in time with Late Roman art, covers the period chiefly between 200 and 700 A.D., when the Roman empire declined and disintegrated politically and economically. Meanwhile, however, it had received a new spiritual vigour and inspiration whose influence had the most far-reaching effect.

Rome of the third century A. D. was the scene of civil wars between rival emperors, and of increasing numbers of officials, leading to political corruption and intolerable taxation. A terrible pestilence ravaged the population. Stronger emperors tried to hold on to power by tyranny and insistence on emperor-worship. The latter was one of the chief reasons for the persecution of Christians, who could not in conscience comply. In spite of this, the new faith spread among all classes. Though Diocletian tried to stamp it out completely, it continued to grow. Early in the fourth century, Constantine gave it toleration and recognition. Only then church architecture could develop. Shortly after, Rome lost its position as centre of the empire, when Byzantium, near Asia Minor, was made the capital, since it was easier to defend against the barbarian tribesmen who started pouring over the extensive borders. Early in the fifth century they sacked Rome itself, and many art treasures were destroyed. Finally, in 476, the Roman government fell into barbarian hands.

The preservation of the Roman cultural heritage and its spread among the barbarians is largely due to the early Christians, for when the emperors practically abandoned the western part of the empire, the people looked for protection to the newly-established Church.

Early Christian art reflects the history of the Church at this time. During the persecutions, it was confined chiefly to painting in the cata-combs for funeral purposes. In technique and style it remained Graeco-Roman. Much use was made of symbolism. The expressions of the face and eyes of human figures, as seen in the veiled orante, show a calm trust, despite deep suffering, derived from close communion with God. These first Christians had embraced the new faith only on the strongest convictions, since they had to be ready to lose everything, even life itself, and often under torture. This firm faith, that could arouse such courage in thousands—men, women and children—to face any loss or pain, came from the certainty that all their deepest needs and yearnings, for perfect security in the understanding and love of another, had been fulfilled by God Himself, who had adopted man's nature and lived on earth as a human being shortly before, and within the boundaries of their own empire, in order to invite mankind to share His intimate Life of unlimited Joy. They believed that God came on earth to prove His love, and to show them the way by His own example and words. From these words they had learned that God wants to share with each one His inner Life of perfect unity in Knowledge and Love. They were persecuted by the decadent society of the imperial period because their lives, modelled on God's holiness, were a reproach to vested interests and evil consciences.

Early Christian art was primarily a spontaneous, popular expression, not immediately encouraged by religious leaders, who feared a return to image-worship. Symbols were first used; but gradually figure representations developed, chiefly for didactic purposes, because in those days of political and economic insecurity, education was neglected, and many people were illiterate. The subjects were drawn from the record of God's merciful relations with human beings, namely the Bible. It shows how the coming of Jesus fulfilled man's expectation of a Saviour. So the Old Testament stories which looked forward to his coming, as well as the principal events of his life, as recorded in the New Testament, especially the Gospels, were depicted.

These stories were so often repeated that they acquired traditional names, which are recognized at once in every age : the annunciation, when God's messenger announced to the virgin Mary that she was to be the mother of the Redeemer; the visitation, when she went to assist her cousin Elizabeth and was revealed as the Saviour's mother to both Elizabeth and her unborn son; the nativity, meaning the Redeemer's birth ; the presentation, when he was offered to God in the temple at Jerusalem ; the crucifixion, representing his death at the hands of his enemies; the resurrection, showing how he proved the truth of his claim to be the Son of

God by coming back to life after three days in the tomb ; the ascension, his rising to heaven after entrusting to his followers his work of making known the Gospel, namely the good news of God's merciful invitation to all creatures to share in the divine Life.

Early Christian art aimed at giving visible expression to these sublime truths, simply enough for anyone to understand, but so beautifully that the most cultured were inspired. Through their contemplation of these scenes, the people grew familiar with the Saviour's personality and life: his intimate union with the Father, his helpful compassion for anyone in misfortune, his readiness to help others by his divine power, his absolute holiness and truth, so great that even his enemies could find no factual accusation against him, his calm courage in the face of the cruellest torture, and his entire unselfishness even in his own sufferings, thinking of others and forgiving his very tormentors.

## PAINTING IN THE CATACOMBS

Catacombs are underground cemeteries in Rome. The early Christians followed the Roman custom of having communal sepulchres. Like the poorer classes, they also used the subterranean galleries outside the city walls, between the first and third milestone. Begun in the first century A.D., they were in use up to the end of the fourth. These numerous and intricate passages, real labyrinths, formed almost a subterranean town. The long, and generally narrow and low galleries (ambulacra), were mostly dark, and only occasionally lit by light shafts. The sepulchres (loculi) (Fig. 412 a) were in the walls. Since it was customary for the Christians to bury their dead, the niches had to be long and deep enough to contain the body, instead of being small like the Roman columbaria. They were cut in the wall lengthwise, in tiers, on both sides of the gallery. After the burial, the niche was

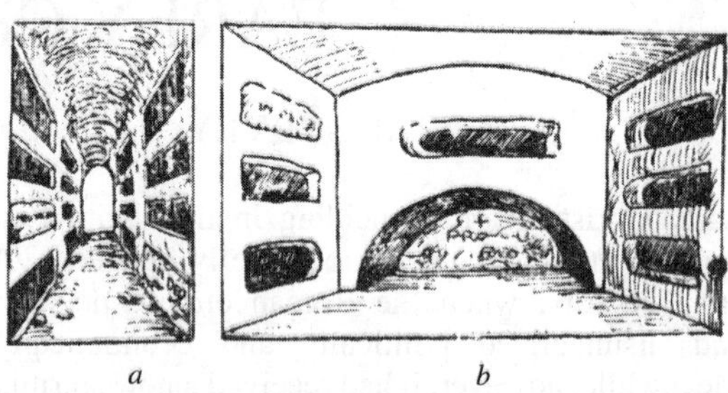

*a* *b*

Fig. 412. Catacombs : *a*. gallery with loculi ; *b*. arcosolium, Rome.

sealed hermetically with a marble or stone slab, on which the name of the deceased was written. Sometimes a more important tomb was cut out in the form of an arch (arcosolium) (Fig. 412 b); and a larger place in front of it, the cubiculum, served as a funeral chapel. The catacombs grew in importance during the persecutions, because the tombs of martyrs who were buried there became objects of special honour.

Mural paintings, decorating the walls of the catacombs, show how Early Christian art hardly differed from Roman sepulchral paintings, for many existing forms and symbols, which harmonized with their beliefs, were adapted. Thus the grapevine, a common Roman decoration, was used to illustrate the text 'I am the vine, you are its branches', showing the close union the Saviour wants to establish with the soul. The dove (Fig. 413) represents the candour and innocence of the soul of the deceased, and the Holy Spirit of Truth and Love. The lamb was the most frequently used symbol of the Redeemer. It is found in Sacred Scripture as well as in the Christian literature of the time, and is often represented in sacred art. It is an image

Fig. 413. Early Chrisitan symbols : *a*. dove ; *b*. lamb ; *c*. fish and anchor ; *d*. fish carrying a basket of bread. *e*. anchor and cross

of the divine patience, God allowing Himself to be ill-treated by His own free creatures in the hope of raising them from their attraction to brutal selfishness to true divine greatness, which, instead of seeking revenge, freely does more than is asked. The fish, or the Greek word for it, IXTUS, is an acrostic for the name and titles of the Redeemer : Jesus Christ, Son of God, Saviour. The fish was also used to signify the believers who are born into the divine life by the baptismal rite, which ordinarily includes the use of water. Perhaps the oldest specifically Christian symbol, not found on other tombs, is the anchor, which stands for hope and salvation, as well as for the cross. Christians have always respected the latter as the sign of God's greatest proof of His love, and as a reminder of the corruptive effect of evil. But since crucifixion was, at that time, a punishment reserved for the worst criminals, it was rarely shown directly until Constantine made it an emblem of victory.

Among the figure representations, one of the most frequent was the orante, signifying the soul in prayer. Generally it was a standing figure in long robes with outstretched arms. Sometimes the face was a real portrait of the departed. The *veiled consecrated virgin* (Pl. 28,1),in the catacomb of Priscilla, is a very striking example. The orante was often associated with the Good Shepherd, and with pastoral symbolism, widespread in ancient society. It was easily adapted, since it is also frequent in Sacred Scripture, especially to show how the Saviour is ready to give his life for souls, and that He goes in search especially of the stray ones, and is overjoyed at their return. In the cubicula, the orante and Good Shepherd were often connected with pictures of the seasons, representing orderly growth and spring-time resurrection. The same motif is shown in relief on the oldest stone tombs and statues before the fourth century.

Scenes were chosen from Sacred Scripture commemorating instances where God helped His friends, to inspire trust in His unlimited power and goodness, and in His promise of unending life and peace. They are like prayers on the tombs, asking the same merciful protection for the deceased. In fact, they seem to be a pictorial representation of the prayers for the dying, which go back to the very first centuries. ' Liberate his soul, Lord, as You saved Noah from the deluge, as You freed Job from his sufferings, as You delivered Moses from the hands of Pharaoh, Daniel from the claws of the lion, the three young men from the fiery furnace, as You protected Susanna from her false accusers'. To these scenes were added others from the Gospels (literally, God's story), in which similar examples of divine generosity are shown : the annunciation, the Saviour's miracles especially the raising to life of Lazarus after he had been four days in the grave. Most of these paintings originated probably at the end of the second, but mostly in the third century. The dominant idea of all is the last part of the creed, ' I believe in the communion (mutual unity through service) of saints, the forgiveness of sins, the resurrection of the body, and life everlasting.'

The finest fresco is the *seated Virgin* (Pl. 28.2) in the catacomb of Priscilla. In face, figure and clothing, it reflects the classical models. This is the first known picture of the Madonna (my Lady—a title given to the virgin Mary). The movements of the infant Saviour on her lap seem very life-like. Nearby stands the prophet Isaias, pointing to a star over Mary's head, since he had foretold, ' For men abiding in a land where death overshadowed them, light has dawned'. The picture is impressionistic, with contrasting light and shade. There is also a representation of the annunciation in the same cemetery.

Unlike the Romans, who considered manual work as fit only for slaves, the Christians also pictured the various trades in which they were engaged, since they had been shown the sanctity of labour by the example and words of the Saviour (My Father has never stopped working, and I too must be at work). All the pictures on the walls and ceilings are like a continued communion of the soul with God. Though the style and some of the symbols are borrowed from Hellenistic art, all the scenes are reduced to their simplest elements.

## ARCHITECTURE

During the persecutions, the Christians could not develop architecture. Their meetings for the commemoration of the Last Supper, or the breaking of bread, as it was called, were kept secret and held in private houses or sometimes in the catacombs. Only in the fourth century, when they were free to worship in public, did they begin to develop buildings suited to their needs. Naturally they used Roman forms as a model.

The Christian house of worship is called a 'church' (from a Greek root that means belonging to the Almighty). For various reasons the basilicas, the judicial and commercial halls of the Romans, seemed the most suitable models for buildings destined for congregational worship.

Certain elements, like the atrium, the main part of a private Roman house, were added.

The Early Christian basilica (Figs. 414 & 415), as churches of those times are usually called, had

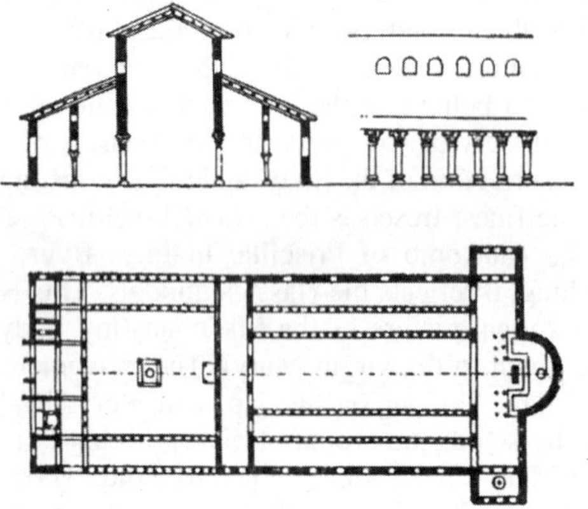

Fig. 414. Old St. Peter's basilica: plan (below); cross section (above left); part of longitudinal section (above right), Rome.

Fig. 415. Early Christian basilica.

the same long rectangular form as the Roman prototype, with only one apse, on the eastern side. On the western narrow side was the entrance, preceded by the atrium, a· gathering place, with a closed court surrounded by roofed arcades along the walls, and usually with a fountain in the centre. Its quiet atmosphere was conducive to meditation, and separated the basilica from the noisy street. The entrance porch was on its western extremity.

A roofed vestibule (the narthex) gave entrance to the basilica proper through three or five doors, according to the number of aisles. The inner space was divided lengthwise, by parallel rows of columns, into a larger and loftier central part, the nave, and one or two lower aisles on each side. The rows of columns stood quite near each other. They were bridged over with horizontal architraves or round arcades, on which rested the high clerestory (sometimes called triforium wall) pierced with windows which flooded the nave with light. These long colonnades (rows of columns) seemed to converge at the end of the building and led the eye inevitably to the focal point of the basilica, namely the altar (from aita res, high object or place). It was made of stone, and usually had the form of a table, asa reminder of the Last Supper. On this was offered the Holy Sacrifice. To make the altar predominant, it stood on a raised platform, with one or more steps leading up to it. Over it was the ciborium (Fig. 416), a

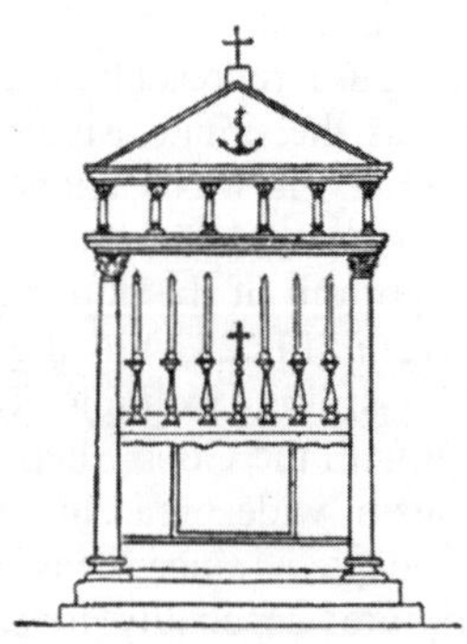

Fig. 416. Ciborium.

canopy upheld by marble pillars ; under it was the tomb of a martyr (confessio—Greek and Latin words meaning one who bore witness to Truth). Behind the altar, the building ended in a semi-circular apse roofed by a half-dome or hemisphere. In the middle of this apse stood the bishop's chair or cathedra (Fig. 417). It was surrounded by seats for the priests or presbyters

Fig. 417. Cathedra.

(hence presbyterium, the name of this part of the church). It is also called bema (step or platform), because it was raised higher than the floor, and steps led up to it.

Later on, between the nave and the apse, there was added the transept or transversal aisle, which sometimes extended beyond the width of the church. This gave the ground plan the form of a cross. Across the end of the nave, at the meeting point with the transept, there was an arch (called triumphal arch), symbolic of the passage to eternal life. The building had a timber roof with visible rafters (which later, during the Renaissance period, were often cased by gilded coffers). Only the apse had a masonry roof. The pavement was of marble inlay. On the whole, the outside of the Early Christian basilica was relatively unadorned in contrast with the interior, which was richly decorated with coloured mosaics, scintillating with gold as well as the rarest and most precious marbles, porphyry, onyx and other costly materials. It created a mystic atmosphere of calm sublimity, as if the exterior of the basilica symbolized the sufferings of earthly life, while the interior signified the enraptured beauties of the inner spirit.

Two new kinds of buildings were needed for ceremonial or liturgical (literally, the activity of prayer) purposes : the campanile and baptistery. They belonged to the basilica, but were detached from the main building. Bells were used for calling the faithful to public worship. They had to be high to be heard from afar, so towers, called campanile (Fig. 415) were built in storeys and pierced with windows.

While baptism (literally dipping, or assimilation into the divine life) was given in the form of immersion, a separate building was needed, called a baptistery (Fig. 418). It was circular or

Fig. 418. Baptistery.

octagonal, sometimes covered with a dome, or merely roofed with wood. A large marble basin was sunk in the centre of the floor, with steps leading down to it. There was usually one such baptistery close to the atrium of the chief basilica in each city until the sixth century A. D., when they were replaced by the baptismal font in the church vestibule.

The first example of the Early Christian basilica was the *old St. Peter's basilica*, (Pl. 28.3, Fig. 414) in *Rome*, built by Constantine shortly after 333. It stood till the end of the fifteenth century, when it was pulled down to make way for the present edifice. Ancient representations make it possible to reconstruct its general arrangement. It followed the different parts of the Early Christian basilicas, but it was erected with a magnificence befitting the memory of the chief of the apostles. A flight of thirty-five steps led up to a propylon (ante-porch), and the atrium court, which measured more than 64 ½ by 71 ½ metres. It was surrounded by colonnades, and a fountain stood in the centre of the open space. Under a roof of gilded bronze, supported by eight porphyry columns, was a huge bronze pine-cone— still preserved in the della Pigna garden in the Vatican—from which water fell into a square basin. Five doors opened from the narthex into the church. It was divided into a central nave and four side aisles, two on each side. The columns supported horizontal architraves, and above them light came from the clerestory windows. The triumphal arch at the end of the nave was decorated with mosaics, showing Constantine presented by Saint Peter to the Saviour, and offering Him a model of the church. The semicircular apse was adorned by another mosaic, showing Jesus with Sts. Peter and Paul. In the centre of the apse was the cathedra, surrounded by seats for the clergy. Between the apse and nave was a long transversal aisle. The altar stood in the centre or focal point of the whole building. Under it was the confessio, with the relics of St. Peter. On one side of the building were two baptisteries.

The *basilica of St. John Lateran* in *Rome* gets its name from a palace, in or close to which Constantine founded this church which he gave to Pope Sylvester I. It is the cathedral of the bishop of Rome, namely the pope. The present building, however, was altered in later times, so that very little can be seen of the original, except the position of the nave and aisles, and two columns near the entrance. The interior gives an impression of austerity and grandeur.

The *basilica of St. Paul* outside the walls of *Rome* (Pl. 28.4.), was begun in the late fourth century, on the site of the church Constantine built over St. Paul's tomb. It was much like old St. Peter's, and, until the great fire in 1823, the finest example of a basilica in Rome. Contributions for its reconstruction came from all over the world. The size, plan and splendour of the old church were retained as much as possible. It is most beautiful in its simplicity. There are two aisles on each side. A series of portraits in mosaic, along the frieze of the aisles and nave, represent the popes who succeeded St. Peter.

The *basilica of St. Mary Major* (Pl. 29.1. ) in *Rome*, is also known as Our Lady of Snows, since, according to an old legend, a miraculous fall of snow in summer showed the ground plan of the proposed church. The story of its origin is told in a series of mosaic pictures on the old façade, now masked by the arcades of the later one. This church is the best example of the form of the classical basilica. The spacious interior, the long rows of stately Ionic columns in white marble, and the softened tones of ancient mosaics, produce a sense of beauty and unity. Later additions and changes did not erase the main features of the early church, especially its columns and mosaics.

Two other examples are worth mentioning. *Santa Maria in Cosmedin* (Pl. 29.2), in *Rome*, is very simple, with a plain exterior. The interior shows the development of liturgy: the choir for the singers, with its two pulpits, fills half the nave. The pillars have different designs and sizes, since the ruins of Roman temples were used for building materials, and often they came from different sites. If they were too short, they were raised on blocks. *San Clemente, in Rome* also has a simple plan : only one aisle on either side of the nave, no transept; and the choir with the pulpits occupies half the nave in the centre.

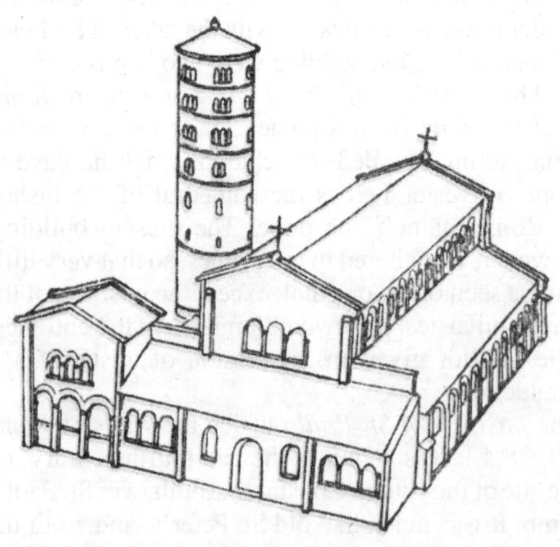

Fig. 419. Church of Sant' Apollinare in Classe, near Ravenna, Italy.

*Sant'' Apollinare Nuovo in Ravenna*, and *Sant' Apollinare in Classe* (Fig. 419), near Ravenna, closely resemble each other, and are typical examples of the old type of basilica. The outside appearance is austere and unattractive, in contrast to the brightness, peace and richness of the interior. The campanile of the latter is one of the earliest examples : a plain, cylinder-shaped structure, standing apart from the church. These free-standing campaniles remained a characteristic feature of the Italian churches even in later times.

## SCULPTURE

The wealthier Christians buried their dead in sarcophagi. In the beginning they resembled those of their neighbours, but gradually the subjects of the sculptural decorations became similar to the wall paintings in the catacombs. The earliest examples have figure carving in the corners and cèntre only; the rest of the space is filled with lines undulating in an S curve. In the fourth century they were ornamented with a continuous frieze in relief. Later there was a double row of decorations one above the other, A representation of the deceased appeared in the centre, framed in a conch shell. After the fourth century, the different subjects were separated by columns. In the Vatican Museum in Rome, there is a *sarcophagus* with figures *of the Good Shepherd* and vines; and another, the so-called *theological sarcophagus*, has scenes from Scripture. One of the later examples, preserved in the Vatican Grottoes, is the richly-carved *sarcophagus of funius Bassus* (Pl. 29.3), who died in 359. It has ten panels in a two-storeyed arrangement. The scenes, divided by columns, are taken from the Old and New Testaments : in the upper row (left to right) the sacrifice of Abraham, the imprisonment of St. Peter, Christ enthroned as the Ruler of the universe between St. Peter and Paul, Christ before Pilate (in two scenes). In the lower row : Job's sufferings, the fail, the entry into Jerusalem, Daniel in the lion's den, St. Paul led to his martyrdom.

Sculpture in the round also made its appearance. In the Vatican Museum there is a statue of the *Good Shepherd* (Pl. 29.4) carrying a lamb. Its probable model was the calf-bearer, a common figure among Greek statues. It is not surprising that it was used as one of the first representations of the Saviour, whose parable of the shepherd searching for the lost sheep emphasised so eloquently God's merciful care even for the worst. There is also a small marble statue of a seated adolescent figure, according to the Greek type. It too was probably meant to represent the Saviour.

## MOSAIC

The tremendous building activity that followed the official recognition of Christianity created a great demand for decoration in order to give the basilicas a splendour and magnificence worthy of the house of God. This decoration appeared first on the inside of the churches, where fresco painting gave place to mosaics. The mosaic, well-known among the ancient Romans, *now* assumed a new and unequalled importance and splendour.

The mosaic is a branch of pictorial art, or of flat surface decoration, made by inlaying figures or patterns with small bits of coloured stones or other materials. These pieces are called tesserae (singular : tessera). Generally they are cut into little e cubes, sometimes in shapes to fit one another accurately. For the background or clothing they are comparatively big; but they are very minute, particularly for the face. The pieces are rough on the lower surface in order to adhere firmly to the cement in which they are imbedded. The word mosaic (or musivum) comes from the Greek mouseios (pertaining to the muses), which shows the high esteem this art had attained during antiquity. Among the Romans it was used chiefly for pavement decoration. This continued during the Early Christian period, but its use was extended to the walls and vaults of the apse, and the triumphal arch at the end of the nave. Later on it was also used on the clerestory walls.

The Romans had used coloured marbles for their tesserae. The Christians continued to employ marble chiefly for floor decoration, but coloured glass tesserae were more general for the walls. The translucency and reflective capacity of glass, which could be coloured in every possible hue and shade, permitted the artist to get beautiful colour effects. A rich glitter was added to the whole by the use of golden tesserae, obtained by spreading gold leaf over a dark background. Colourless or coloured glass was fused over it to protect the gold leaf, while allowing it to shimmer through. The sheet was then cut into pieces. The coloured and glided tesserae have an intensity and brilliance that surpasses the effect of any other method of painting. To increase the jewel-like sparkle of these mosaics, the artist laid the piéces somewhat unevenly into the cement so that the rugged surface scintillates as the light moves over it. An inscription in the church of St. Agnes in Rome states that the daylight seemed to be imprisoned in those bright mosaics.

The *mosaics* on the aisle vaults of the circular church of *Santa Costanza* in *Rome* are the earliest examples of their use by Christians. They are blue on a white ground, and show birds and cupids among naturalistic, interlaced, vinebranches. In the centre is a medallion with a portrait. On the borders, cupids are seen engaged in vintage work. As yet there is nothing in the designs that reflects Christian ideas.

The earliest *mosaic* with a Christian theme is on the half-dome of the apse in the *church of Santa Pudenziana* in *Rome*. In the centre there is a majestic representation of the Saviour, with a long beard, and robed in a gold-bordered toga. He is seated on a purple cushion on the imperial throne, like a king proclaiming the new law of truth and love to the apostles. By his side are Sts. Peter and Paul, who are being crowned by two figures, generally identified as St. Pudentiana and her sister St. Praxedes. At the sides are their father, the senator Pudens, and other members of his family. According to tradition, St. Peter lived in Rome with the senator, whom he converted, together with many others. The monuments behind these figures image the heavenly Jerusalem (city of peace). In the sky there is a jewelled cross with symbolic emblems on either side. The *mosaics* in *Saint Mary Major* in *Rome* date from the fifth century. On the triumphal arch the childhood of Jesus is represented.

These Early Christian mosaics show how the naturalism of classical art, especially the Hellenistic influence, was gradually replaced by a more conventional stylized art. Hardly any indication of place was given by appropriate backgrounds. There was an increasing flatness in the representation of the human figures, although the Hellenistic modelling by means of light and shade was retained. Byzantine art, which emphasized this reaction to realism with its abstract manner of showing the human figure and the golden backgrounds, influenced later Roman mosaic art.

# 6. BYZANTINE ART

## GENERAL SURVEY

Byzantine art belonged principally to the Eastern Roman empire, with its magnificent centre, Constantinople (modern Istanbul). In the year 330 A.D., the emperor Constantine transferred his capital from Rome to the site of the ancient Greek colony called Byzantium, to which he now gave his own name: Constantinople (the city of Constantine). It lies at the southeastern tip of Europe where the sea of Marmora meets the Straits of Bosphorus. Only a narrow strip of water separates it from Asia Minor. Strategically it was a very important place. Being in the centre of the great Roman empire, the government there had an ideally commanding position. Commercially it was at the crossroads of two important trade or commercial routes: between Europe and Asia, and between the Mediterranean and Black Sea. Aesthetically its position was outstandingly beautiful.

Built on an almost triangular projection of land or peninsula, it is girded on three sides by water : by the sea of Marmora to the south and east, and by the Golden Horn to the north. This is a narrow inlet that pierces deep into the land and secures an excellent harbour. On the western or landward side the city was protected by walls. Like Rome, it was also built on seven hills, and for more than a thousand years it was a great cultural centre, the richest and one of the most splendid cities in the world. It contained within its precincts palatial buildings, beautiful parks and courts, and the famous hippodrome. Constantinople was the seat of the patriarch, whose spiritual authority extended over many souls. Thus it contained many sacred buildings and churches, and religion had a great influence on the life of the citizens.

Byzantine art began with the foundation of the city by Constantine. According to a fourth century historian, this emperor himself traced the line of the walls of his city, and practically finished the building of his capital before his death, adorning it with all kinds of art works.

In the sixth century, Byzantine art reached its maturity, in the short but brilliant period called the First Golden Age, under Justinian (527-565 a.d.). The glory of this epoch was the building of the greatest and most splendid Byzantine church, known as the Hagia Sophia (Holy Wisdom). Of the many other churches of this period, two deserve special mention : San Vitale, in Ravenna, Italy (the western stronghold of Byzantium reconquered from the barbarians by Justinian), and the church of the Holy Apostles in Constantinople, which was destroyed in 1463 to make room for a Muslim mosque. Between 726 and 843, the Iconoclast (image-breaking) controversy, a protest against religious pictures, paralyzed the development of art, and many treasures were destroyed. These persecutions, together with the Spread of Muslim power, forced many Byzantine artists into exile in Italy and northern Europe, especially England, thus spreading their art to the west.

The Second Golden Age began under Basil I in 867, and lasted until the fourth crusade in 1204. The churches of this age were rather small. Generally, they had the form of a Greek cross within a square plan. Around the central dome, set on a high drum and pierced with windows, there were four smaller domes at the four corners of the square, but exteriorly they were concealed under the roof. The church of the Holy Redeemer in Constantinople is of this type. During this age, the activity passed from Constantinople to Greece, the Balkans, and lastly to Russia. In Italy, Byzantine art had flourishing centres in Ravenna, Genoa, and especially in Venice. The most outstanding church of the Italo-Byzantine art of this age is the world-famous St. Mark's in Venice.

In 1453 the Ottoman Turks captured Con-stantinople. They turned the Hagia Sophia into a mosque. The conqueror, Mehmet II, started without delay to build a new mosque, entrusting the work to a Byzantine architect, who drew his inspiration from the Hagia Sophia. This building became the official model for the Turkish mosque architecture, which consequently is an offspring of Byzantine art. Byzantine architecture itself, although its building activity ceased in Constantinople, continued in the neighbouring lands belonging to the Greek rite, especially Russia. Byzantine art has fulfilled a glorious function, and its influence is incalculable in the east and in the west.

## ARCHITECTURE

Byzantine architecture was predominantly an ecclesiastical or church art; for although contemporary writers mention the splendour of royal palaces, the secular buildings that have survived are few and rather unimportant. The Byzantine church is of a central type, i.e., it is square or polygonal in plan, in contrast to the longitudinal type of the Early Christian basilica.

The most typical feature in Byzantine architecture is the hemispherical dome surmounting a square or octagonal base. The reason for the preference of domed roofing was its dignified and prominent appearance, very fitting for a building consecrated to the worship of God. The dome represents the vault of the sky or heaven.

As we saw in the Pantheon in Rome, the great hemispherical dome rested directly on the circular wall (Fig. 420a), which presented no special difficulty in the construction, since the round wall had the same shape as the round base of the hemispherical dome which had to rest on it. But the building of a round dome over a square base, made up either of four walls that enclosed a square space (Fig. 420b), or of four pillars standing in the four corners of a square (Fig. 420c), required first the construction of a transitional masonry to transform the square into a round base on which the dome could rest. That piece of masonry which was needed to effect this transformation was a curved, or spherical, triangle called the pendentive (Fig. 420d & 421). One of these rose from each corner of the square. Four were needed to carry the dome. They formed four semicircular arches between the piers, and met at the top to form a round base on which the dome could be built. During the First Golden Age, the lower portion of the dome was pierced with windows (Fig. 422a). In the Second Golden Age, the dome surmounted a circular wall called a drum, in which the windows were cut (Fig. 422b). These were the chief

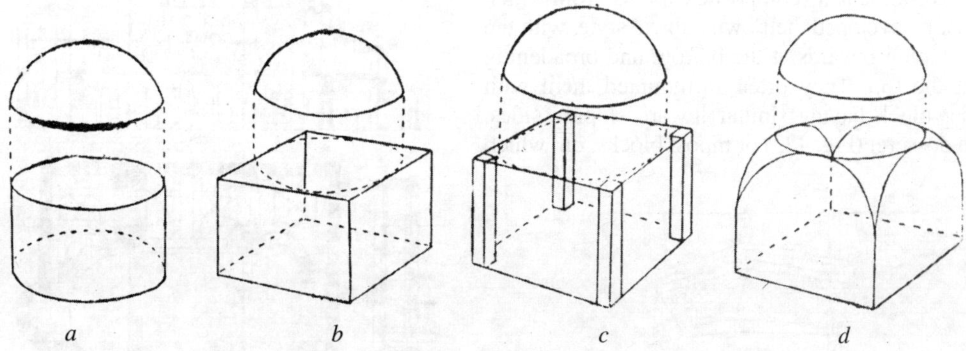


Fig. 420. Domes over round and square compartments.

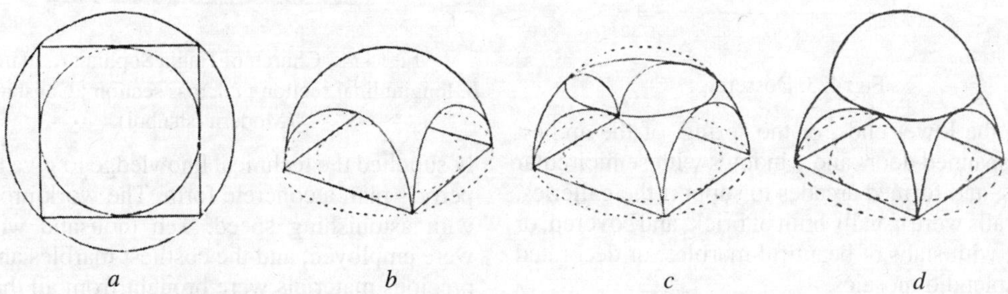


Fig.421. Geometrical analysis of the pendentive : *a.* square over which the dome has to be erected; outer circle, base of the ½ sphere to which the spherical triangles (forming the pendentives) belong ; inner circle, base of the smaller dome to be superimposed on the round base formed by the pendentives ; *b.* perfect transition from the square base to the round dome, but too low ; *c.* pendentives forming a round base for the dome; *d.* pendentives with a smaller dome superimposed.

source of illumination in the interior. This diffused light from above gave a wonderful effect.

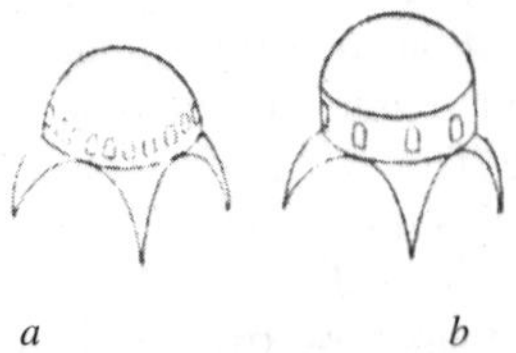


Fig. 422. *a*. dome without drum, with windows pierced around the base ; *b*. dome on a drum, with windows pierced in the drum.

The columns were monoliths, that is, they were cut from a single stone. The Byzantines used the Ionic, Corinthian and composite capitals, from which they soon developed their own cubical style, with the sides sloping inwards at the bottom and broadening out at the top. They often surmounted them with another block having similar inward sloping sides, called dosseret (Fig. 423) or inpost blocks, on which

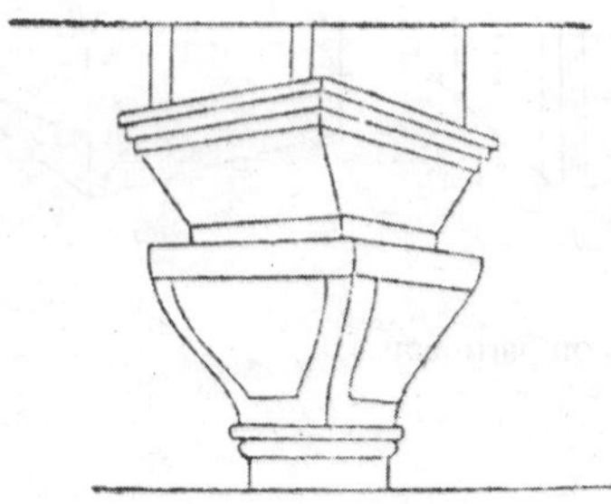

Fig. 423. Dosseret.

rested the lower ends, or the spring, of the arches. They spanned doors and windows with semicircular arches, and formed arcades to support the galleries. The walls were usually built of brick, and covered, or faced, with slabs of beautiful marbles, or decorated with splendid mosaics.

The *Hagia Sophia* (Pl. 30.1, & 2.)Figs. 424 a, b, c), in *Constantinople*, is the largest and most famous of all the Byzantine churches. It replaces two former ones which had burned down, the first of which, a wooden-roofed basilica, had been planned by Constantine himself. The present Hagia Sophia was begun in 532 during the First Golden Age, the emperor Justinian himself directing every detail. The whole building was due to his initiative, He Anthemius of Tralles and Isidore of Miletus, mere-

set up temporary quarters there to be able to supervise the work closely. The two architects,

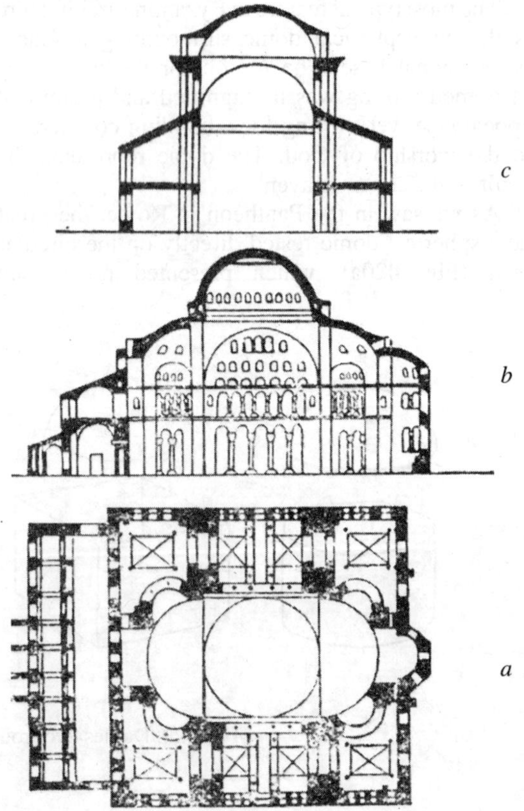


Fig. 424. Church of Hagia Sophia : *a*. plan ; *b*. longitudinal section ; *c*. cross section ; Constantinople (Modern Istanbul).

ly supplied the technical knowledge to give the emperor's plan a concrete form. The work proceeded with astonishing speed. Ten thousand workmen were employed, and the costliest marbles and most precious materials were brought from all the provinces and used lavishly. In six years the building was completed, and on the 27th of December 537, the consecration ceremony took place in the presence of the emperor, who, accompanied by the patriarch of Constantinople, entered with great pomp, gazing around the vast edifice. He thanked God for having permitted him to complete such a great project, and remarked, 'O Solomon, I have surpassed you'. (Solomon king of the Hebrews, built the first temple at Jerusalem). The Hagia Sophia, damaged by repeated earthquakes, had to be repaired several times, and massive but unpleasing buttresses were added to its exterior. When the Turks conquered Constantinople in 1453, many mosaics were destroyed, others were covered with whitewash. Four tall minarets were erected around it. In 1929 it was converted into a Byzantine museum, and much has been done for its repairs and the cleaning of its mosaics.

The Hagia Sophia is almost square in plan (Fig. 424 a), about 76 × 67 metres. It keeps the basilican divisions of a nave, flanked by two- storeyed aisles. The apse, in which originally stood the altar, is at the eastern end. At the western side is a double narthex with three doors, and an atrium of which the columns have been destroyed. The nave ends at both sides in a round apse. Each apse is flanked by two smaller ones called exedra (plural : exedrae).

The greatest achievement in the building is its roofing (Pl. 30.1 ; Figs. 424 b, c). The nave is surmounted by an immense dome in the middle; on each side are half-domes or semi-domes of the same diametre, but on a lower level. Still lower and much smaller half-domes cover the four exedrae or niches. The great dome is about 32½ metres in diameter, and rises 55 metres high. It is ribbed and encircled at the base with some forty windows. Four huge pendentives, springing from four enormous piers, form the base on which the dome rests. They are buttressed on the eastern and western sides by the semi-domes, and on the north and the south with huge transverse arches that cross the aisles. These are roofed with groin vaults, and they carry the arcaded upper storey or gallery. Lofty columns flank both storeys between the aisles and the nave. The clerestory wall, which fills in the round arches of the pendentives on the northern and southern sides, is pierced with windows.

From outside (Pl. 30.2 ) the great central dome looks rather flat, because later on they added an outside drum which covers about a third of the dome. The windows, which encircled the base of the dome inside, were pierced through this drum. Buttresses and other later additions, as well as the four minarets and other constructions added by the Muslims, have also detracted from the original beauty of the exterior ; yet even from the beginning, the magnificence of the interior was far greater than that of the exterior. It is one of the most splendid interiors ever produced in architecture. On entering (Pl. 30.1 one is overwhelmed with an indescribable impression of vast spaciousness and height. The gradually increasing semi-domes curve majestically upwards into the bigger ones, until they reach the enormous dome hovering in a mysterious half-light, whilst the light streams in through the circle of windows around its base. It looks like an awe-inspring canopy over the vast, unobstructed space of the nave, as it tries to express in stone the infinite unity and majesty of the Almighty.

This first impression of vastness is followed by one of colourful richness. The monolithic piers, the sheathing of the walls, and the patterns on the floor are all in beautiful marbles : dull red, emerald green, soft green with dark veining, rose-red, rich red. on white, warm yellow, black on white—all arranged with an eye to colour-harmony and polished to a bright lustre, so that they reflect the glittering gold backgrounds and vivid colours of the mosaics on the walls and domes. These superb mosaics, hidden under layers of whitewash since the fifteenth century, were not only the main splendour of the whole interior, but also the most precious religious representations of this sacred building, as contemporary descriptions tell us.

As the Hagia Sophia is the greatest example of the First Golden Age of Byzantine art in eastern Europe, so *St. Mark's* in *Venice* (Pl. 30. 3 & 4 ; Fig. 425) is the most renowned example of the Second Golden Age in the west. Venice was inhabited by fugitives from the barbarian invasions, who sought shelter in the marshy lands or islands amid the lagoons at the mouth of the river Po. Protected as it was by the Byzantine empire and by its lagoons, Venice prospered by expanding its trade far and wide, and by developing into the most important commercial centre between east and west. Continuous connections with Byzantine culture left a great impress on Venetian life and art.

In the early part of the ninth century, the relics of St. Mark were brought to Venice from Alexandria. They were placed in a basilica that occupied the same place as the present cathedral. Fire destroyed it partially in the later tenth century. The rebuilding took place between about 1042 to 1085, and it was only natural that the Venetians called in Byzantine artists to accomplish this work. The model they aimed at reproducing was Justinian's famous Holy Apostles' church in Constantinople, which had five domes surmounting a plan in the form of a Greek cross (a cross with arms of equal length). To transform the long nave of the old Venetian basilica into this shape, it was necessary to lengthen the sanctuary and to build a transept which, extending on both sides, formed the arms of the cross. The whole building has been

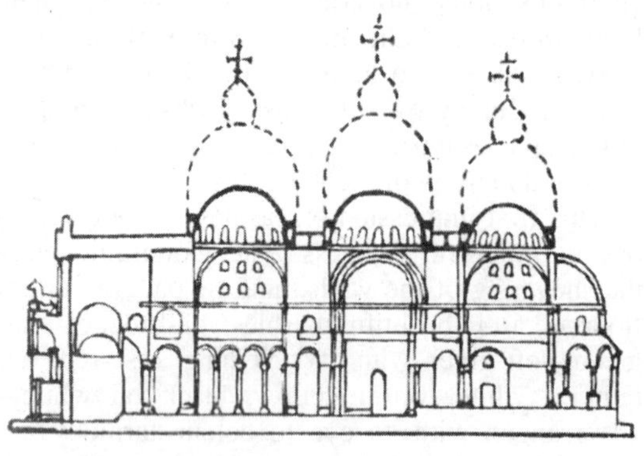

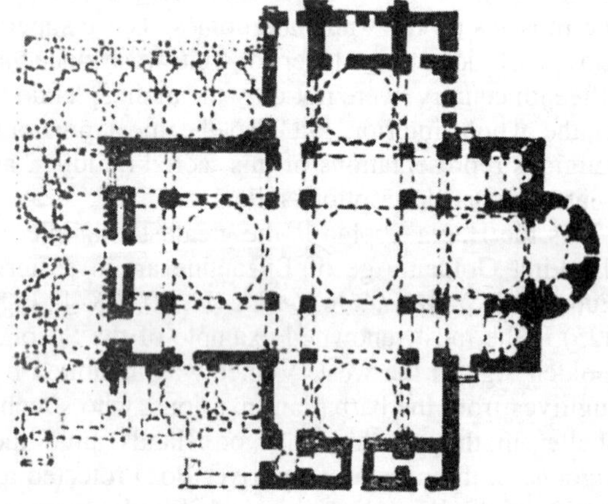

Fig. 425. S. Mark's basilica: plan (below); longitudinal section (above); Venice, Italy.

roofed with five domes on pendentives without drums : one over the centre, and one over each of the four arms of the cross. Wide arches unite the four piers between the domes, on which each of them rests. There are arcaded galleries that connect the piers with the extremities of the nave and transepts. The sanctuary ends with three apses. The narthex in the front was extended, somewhat later, around the sides.

The interior (Pl.30.3), which even today preserves its typical Byzantine aspect, is profusely decorated with rich-coloured marbles and brilliant glass mosaics with glowing gold backgrounds, covering vaults and domes, and relating in a continuous picture-story man's creation and fall, and his redemption, the Saviour's miracles, and legends of saints. If we add to this all the magnificent work in gold with enamels and jewels, especially the world-famous Pala d'Oro, a retable (from retro, behind; tabulum, altar) or reredos set up behind the main altar, we get some idea of this splendid interior.

The exterior (Pl. 30.4) shows many later additions not executed in Byzantine style. The high gilded cupolas in wood were built over the domes to get the conspicuous effect of domes on drums. The upper part of the facade was added in late Gothic style. Over the central door stand the bronze horses taken from Nero's triumphal arch. But all these details, with the richly-coloured and glittering white marbles and golden mosaics, blend harmoniously. This resplendent building faces the Piazza di San Marco or St. Mark's Square, the centre of Venetian city life.

## SCULPTURE

We know from literary sources that the emperor Constantine took many celebrated statues from ancient monuments to adorn his new capital and that, in the forum of Constantinople, he set up a representation of the Good Shepherd and another figure of the Redeemer near the imperial palace. Other emperors and military leaders had their images in various public places. Only one of these still exists, namely the colossal one in bronze of the emperor Heraclius.

We can study Byzantine sculpture from the numerous decorative carvings still existing in the churches, which were very ornate. Although mosaics, paintings, and coloured marble sheathings on the walls had a larger part than carving, the latter still had an important role. The horizontal bands and cornices separating the different storeys, the arcades, capitals, and stone railings were richly carved. Although intricate in design, they did not stand out in high relief. The sculptors used the drill more than the chisel. They bored many holes in between the incised carvings, thus giving the surface a lace-like effect. The motifs used were vines and rosettes ; and the capitals were decorated with foliage, basket-work, and monograms. The acanthus leaf was very common, but it was conventionalized, having very pointed leaves.

The best knowledge we can get of Byzantine sculpture is through the numerous small ivory carvings in relief, mostly on panels. When two small carved panels are attached to each other, we call them diptychs. A triptych has a central one, with two small side-panels or wings. Sometimes these panels represent the coronation of an emperor and empress. The Saviour stands in the middle and places a crown on the head of the imperial couple standing beside him. This signifies that their imperial power comes from God. The most favoured subject of these small ivory or stone panels is, perhaps, the virgin Mary represented either as mother, queen, or orante—that is, standing with hands raised in prayer. A very typical Byzantine representation is the so-called Deesis : the Redeemer, standing or seated in the centre, listens to the virgin Mary and St. John the Baptist, who stand on either side of him in an attitude of supplication or prayer for mankind, of which a good example is seen in the *Haberville triptych* (Pl. 31.1), in the Louvre, Paris,

One of the most important ivory carvings that have come down to us is the so-called *chair of Maximian* (Pl. 31.2), in the Archiepiscopal Palace, Ravenna. It is a cathedra or throne for a bishop, belonging to the sixth century. It is made of pieces of delicately carved ivory, finely joined.

## MOSAICS AND PAINTING

The Byzantine artists showed their greatest originality and accomplishment in pictorial representations on flat surfaces, namely with mosaics, wall-paintings, manuscript illuminations and icons. It was they who realized best the splendid possibilities of mosaic work. This art, well suited to the decoration of churches, became their principal means of creating rich colour effects. Their chief concern was spirituai rather than physical vision. Material details were ignored. This is why they preferred to concentrate on pictorial rather than sculptural art. Exact anatomy and perspective were disregarded. Instead of using the landscapes of the classical style as a background, the figures wore surrounded by golden light as if they are outside of space and time. Garments are heavy and stiff, with stylized folds. They cover thin, elongated, seemingly weightless bodies. Instead of employing light and shade, they made clear outlines by means of vivid colours, and stiffly stylized gestures, often repeated. The figures are shown in front view; the three-quarter view being abandoned. Perspective is not confined to one vanishing point : the same composition may include views on the eye-level, above it, or below. Sometimes reverse perspective is used in place of the right one. Not physical position but spiritual importance determines the size of the figure.

Everything is deeply solemn, according to their conception of the Almighty. The whole church was intended to symbolize heaven. This is reflected in the mosaic decorations, the subjects of which were almost always religious, although sometimes historical personages are also shown. These scenes were intended to teach religion and arouse devotion. For each part of the church, the subject-matter to be represented was specified. The mosaic scenes were arranged according to a traditional law. The church at Daphne near Athens, dating from the eleventh century, may serve as an example. In the dome of the naos is a huge bust of the Saviour as universal Ruler (Pantocrator), surrounded by prophets (those who speak for God), who are shown making known the Almighty Creator and Redeemer by what is written on their scrolls. In the conch of the apse in the sanctuary, the virgin Mary is represented as a queen, with angels (God's messengers) around her. A cycle of scenes from the Saviour's and Virgin's life are shown in the narthex and the pendentives under the dome and the walls of the naos, where they form a threefold ring. In each chapel beside the apse is a figure of a martyr or saint.

The most splendid examples of mosaics were those in the churches of Constantinople. When this city fell, its churches were mutilated and whitewashed. Fortunately this art had already spread, and beautiful mosaics in the Byzantine style are preserved, among others, in Ravenna.

A pair of mosaic panels in the choir of the church of San Vitale in Ravenna commemorate the personal presence of Justinian and the empress Theodora at the opening ceremonies of this church. On the panel *Justinian and his retinue*, the emperor is seen carrying a sacramental vessel. Beside him are the archbishop, courtiers and soldiers. Although it represents an earthly event, the background is still golden ; the figures are stiff, and there is so little consideration for physical relationships, that they are actually stepping on one another's toes. The second panel shows *Theodora with her attendants* (Pl. 31.3 ). At her left stand ladies-in-waiting, and at her right are two other personages, one of whom is drawing back the curtain from the door. These mosaics reproduce the pomp of a Byzantine court, its rich tapestries and furnishing, the crown, jewels, and long mantles worn by the figures.

In the later ninth century, during the reign of Basil I, there was another flowering of mosaic art in Constantinople. One example, which adorns the narthex of Hagia Sophia, shows the *Madonna and Child enthroned, with Constantine and Justinian*. The Madonna, seated on a throne in the centre, has the Child Jesus on her knees. Constantine, holding a model of Constantinople, stands at their left ; while Justinian, with the Hagia Sophia, stands at their right. The figures are placed symmetrically against the gold background. They are flat, and the folds of their rich garments, instead of suggesting volume, form a decorative pattern.

Wall painting developed simultaneously with mosaics. It became especially popular during the Second Golden Age and in the fourteenth century. It was used chiefly in monastic centres outside Constantinople, in Asia Minor, especially Cappadocia, and in the Balkans, where art reflected ordinary human feelings rather than rigid court formalism. Especially when Byzantine power declined, this popular art replaced more and more the costly mosaics, and the new style had great influence on later art in the west.

Manuscript illumination or miniatures also flourished in Byzantium. This art began in Alexandria, Egypt, in the Hellenistic period. The Byzantine artists, however, as in most of their art, adopted a stylized form. Their work was especially popular for illustrating liturgical books, to help explain the meaning of difficult scriptural passages. Sometimes they were painted on gold, silver or purple backgrounds. The drapery outlines and lettering of the text were done in gold. The figures stressed the spiritual by emphasizing the heads and eyes more than the bodies. They were arranged in rhythmic patterns. These miniatures are a precious heirloom of Byzantium, from where it spread westward.

Icons or devotional pictures for piety, with no particular story to tell, also became more and more popular. They represented the Saviour, the virgin Mary and Saints. The ground was a wooden panel, often covered with thin cloth. On this were painted the figures. The pigments were mixed with egg-white to make them adhere.

From Constantinople, icon painting passed into the Balkans and Russia, where the people were very fond of these pictures. In the fourteenth century, the iconostasis was introduced in the churches. It is a wooden screen dividing the sanctuary from the nave, on which the icons are hung in rows. They are also treasured in private homes.

One of the most famous of these icons, known as the *Vladimir Madonna* (Pl. 31.4 ), is considered one of the greatest religious paintings in existence. It seems to have been made in Constantinople in the 11th or 12th century, and taken to Russia shortly after, where it is now preserved in the Historical Museum, Moscow. Meticulous cleaning has restored it almost to its delicate original colouring. Here religious respect and tender sympathy are beautifully blended, in the lovely faces of the Child and Mother, and the intimate tenderness that unites them, expressed by the gentle embrace, and the eloquent eyes that seem to speak to each other.

# 7. ROMANESQUE ART

## GENERAL SURVEY

Romanesque art flourished especially during the tenth and eleventh centuries, but its beginnings go back to the Carolingian period, the time of Charlemagne, in the late eighth and early ninth century. The name is related to the literary term romance, meaning in the Roman manner. Although this name is not as incorrect as those of many other art periods, it does express the complex origins of this style ; since in addition to the influence of Roman art which dominated here and there, Byzantine and local influences played their parts too. In order to understand Romanesque art, we need to glance briefly at the history of the preceding centuries.

For various reasons, the Roman empire gradually weakened. Within a century, from 378 to 476 A.D., all its western provinces, including Rome itself, were occupied by waves of barbarian tribes from the east and north. In the process many art treasures were destroyed, and the former Western Empire was broken up into different states under barbarian rulers. Feudalism developed when the central government was no longer able to provide security against the continual invasions (which lasted until nearly 1000 A.D.), so the people turned for protection to strong leaders.

The new peoples respected the Graeco-Roman culture of which they became the heirs. Amidst the political anarchy of feudalism, they longed for unity and order. These they found only in the Church, which was already well-established when the empire fell. Its external organization, modelled on Roman lines, was firm and orderly. It united Europe into what is called Christendom (the closest union it has ever known) by giving it a common belief, language and culture. Among the war-like barbarians, it developed a new code of chivalry, based on respect for faith, women, and the defenceless. A new civilization arose, by a fusion of Graeco-Roman culture, barbarian vigour, and the Christian ideal which the Church tried to diffuse, since its monasteries were almost the only medium of education during those turbulent ages.

Monasteries were the chief agencies for the preservation and spread of culture. The Christian monastic system was started in the east Mediterranean region by hermits who found community life more beneficial for spiritual perfection than solitary life. This spread to the west; and during the early barbarian invasions, St. Benedict infused into it the Roman genius for organization. By combining a life of prayer, contemplation, and work, both intellectual and manual, the monks became the great social reformers of the time. Their example taught the wandering tribesmen the benefits of an orderly peaceful life, and the dignity and fruitfulness of labour, for they usually settled in some barren forest and swamp-land which they turned into fertile farms and gardens. They also built roads and bridges, encouraged fairs and commerce, and used the income from their farms to help the needy. There was no other organized charity in those days. They built hospitals, and gave to all who wished free board and schooling in the liberal arts or crafts. Each monastery supplied its own needs by workshops of all kinds. In their libraries they preserved the classics, both sacred and secular, of which they made laborious hand-copies, and which they beautified with paintings, called miniatures. They also cultivated music, architecture, sculpture, and the minor arts, of which they were almost the only custodians.

A general idea of a medieval monastery may be gathered from a *manuscript plan* (Fig. 426)

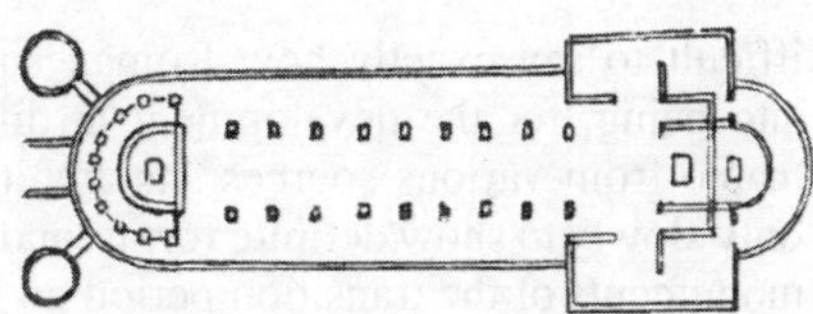

Fig. 426. Double-apsed church plan, detail from a monastery plan, manuscript, St. Gall.

(dated A.D. 819) ascribed to Charlemagne's biographer Einhart, and preserved in *St. Gall,* Switzerland. It shows a systematized arrangement of a monastic building complex in the Carolingian period. In its centre is the most imposing building, the church, of the longitudinal basilican type, ending on both sides in an apse (Fig. 116). This double-apsed church plan had a great influence on Romanesque architecture, especially in the German Rhineland. Attached to one side of it is the cloister, an open courtyard surrounded by arcades similar to the Early Christian atrium. Nearby are the living quarters of the monks: chapter house or meeting room, dormitories, refectory, kitchen, bakehouse, store rooms, and workrooms for different craftsmen: the goldsmith, who made the sacred vessels, the carpenter, blacksmith, and fuller. Guest-houses, hospitals and schools were built to serve the people. It was a self-supporting community, which needed little contact with the outside.

The Carolingian period, in which Romanesque art had its roots, is named after Charlemagne (Carolus Magnus, or Charles the Great). During the half century of his reign (768-814), he established peace and order from the borders of Spain to central Europe. Learning and the arts were revived by his personal patronage. He was a typical Frank (a Germanic tribe that settled in what is now northern France and southern Germany), but he also loved Roman culture. In *Aachen* (Aix-la-Chapelle), his capital city, he built his *palace* and the famous *Palatine chapel*. He gathered there the learned of his time from Italy, Ireland, England and Spain. He wanted all the children to be educated in the monastery and cathedral schools. Thus France became the centre of a new culture. But Charlemagne was ahead of his time. At his death his domains were again divided, and feuds and invasions followed for another two centuries. Only when peace and security were fairly restored, around the turn of the millennium, could artistic activity revive.

## ARCHITECTURE

It is difficult to say exactly how Romanesque art came into being, for the development in different places came from various sources. Its architecture began only slowly to show definite forms, and many of the monuments of the transition period no longer exist. After the year 1000, a great building activity began all over what was once the Roman empire—in Italy, Germany, Spain, England, but especially in France, where the movement began. It is this art, of eleventh to twelfth century Europe, which is called Romanesque. Its forms show a great variety, due to the differences in local needs, available building material, difficulties in transport and communication, but most especially the separation of the people into countless small political units; for medieval Europe was not then made up of nation-states as now.

The Romanesque builders generally used the longitudinal plan of the Eariy Christian basilica, but with certain changes or modifications. The transept, which originally extended only a little, was lengthened. The apse too became longer in order to provide more place for the clergy to chant the divine praises together; and for this reason it was called the choir. These extensions made the plan more markedly cruciform, i.e. in the shape of a Latin cross. Another innovation was made in France at the eastern end: the apse was surrounded by an ambulatory (walk), flanked with radiating chapels on the outer wall. The whole was called chevet*. The circulation of pilgrims paying their devotions to the relics of saints was thus made easier, and the chapels provided also for more altars. The excavations of the old sanctuary of *St. Martin* of *Tours*

Fig. 427. Plan of apse with ambulatory and radiating chapels, church of S. Martin Tours, France.

(Fig. 427) show that it was used already in the Carolingian age. It was developed in France during the Romanesque and Gothic periods. Central plans were rarely used for churches, but they were employed for baptisteries.

The Romanesque builders used various kinds of stone for construction, supplied by different local quarries. This gave the buildings variety.

Suitable roofing was their greatest problem, Wooden roofs were rarely used since they were not durable. They tried all the known masonry vaults: the barrel or tunnel, groin or cross. In places where Byzantine influence was felt, they also used the dome. To counteract the downward and outward pressures of these heavy vaults, the walls had to be very thick, and the windows small. The naves were necessarily narrow and the vaults low. To overcome these disadvantages, they made various experiments to make the churches not only durable, but light and spacious as well, with large windows and lofty ceilings.

This period, therefore, is only a transitional chapter in the evolution of the longitudinal church type. It started already during Early Christian times, and culminated in the splendours of thirteenth century Gothic. Its glories are not so much final results, but continuous efforts, full of vitality and ingenuity, to solve great problems. In time they were crowned with wonderful success. Almost all the elements, the ensemble of which formed Gothic art, were

* pronounce shö -vay

invented and attempted, now here, now there, during the Romanesque period. Some of the more advanced inventions, which led up to the Gothic constructional achievements, can be seen in the church of Sant' Ambrogio, in North Italy. *Sant' Ambrogio* (Pl. 32.1 Fig. 428) in *Milan,* is a sturdy, robust church built by the Lombards, a Germanic tribe who settled in Italy probably in the eleventh century. In plan it resembles the Early Christian basilica. The atrium, which disappeared from the churches in the Romanesque period, still exists here. The narthex (vestibule) has a two-storeyed arcading, giving entrance to the central nave and two side aisles. There is no transept (transversal aisle). On the opposite side to the entrance, the nave and aisles end, each one in an apse; so there are three apses.

The whole building is roofed with masonry vaulting. The construction of the vaults, and the necessary provisions made to carry the weight or downward pressure and the thrust or outward pressure, led to important innovations. With regard to groined aulting, we saw how troublesome it was for the Roman architects to build the wooden centering under the whole place to be vaulted. To avoid this inconvenience, the Lombards first built arches at intervals from one side of the nave wall to the other, thus obtaining square compartments that could be vaulted separately—because the four sides of the vaults had a firm resting place—two on the nave walls and two on the arches crossing the nave. By centering one compartment at a time, they could easily build the vault. This first innovation is called division into bays. (Fig. 429a)

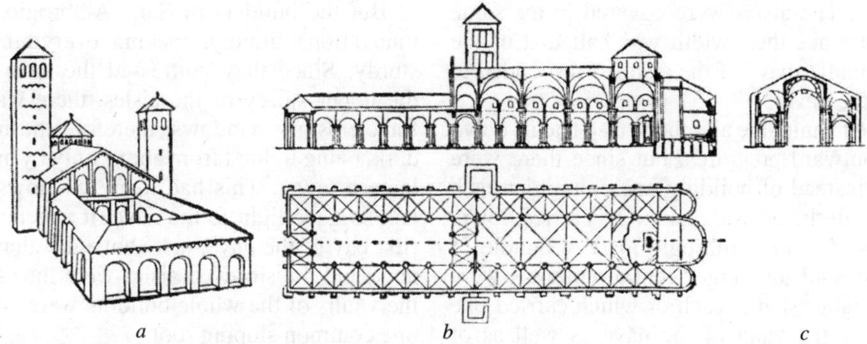


Fig. 428. Church of Sant' Ambrogio : *a*. bird's eye view ; *b*. (bottom) plan, (top) longitudinal section ; *c*. cross section ; Milan, Italy.

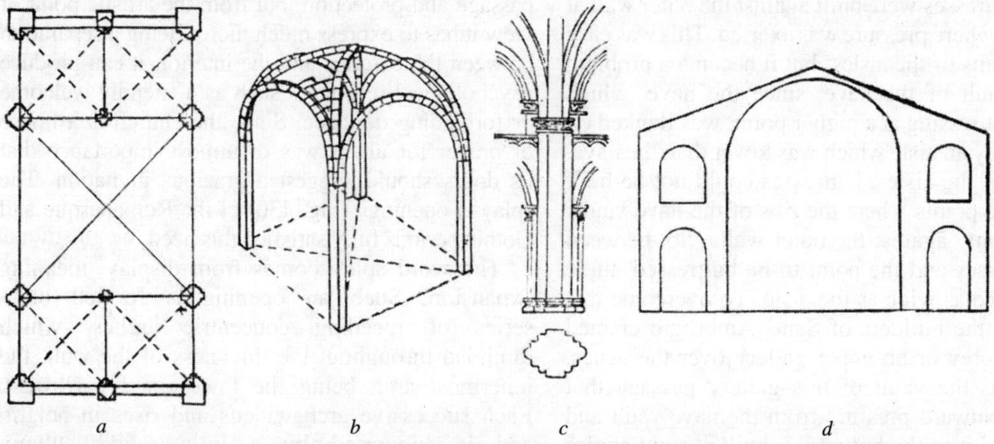


Fig. 429. Innovations in the church of Sant' Ambrogio ; *a*. division into bays (with alternating system); *b*. ribbed vaulting ; *c*, clustered column ; *d*. buttressing system.

A further step was the erection of diagonal arches (ribs) across the corners of the square bay, along the lines of the groins of the vaults to be built. The ribs became a sort of skeleton or framework for the vault which they supported, so that the latter could now be made of thinner stone panels, called the field of the vault. This innovation is known as ribbed vaulting (Fig. 429 b). The aisles were covered in the same manner, but since their width was half that of the nave, two smaller bays of the aisle corresponded to one bay of the nave.

The ribbed vault, like all others, also had its down ward and outward pressures; but since there were many ribs, instead of building one column at each point where all the pressure had to be carried down, the builders of Sant' Ambrogio made a bundle of columns. Around the bigger central columns were clustered smaller shafts, each of which carried one of the ribs of the vault of the nave as well as of the aisles. This combination of bigger and smaller columns, where each support had its separate task, is called the clustered column or compound support. (Fig. 429 c).

Since the bays of the nave were twice as big as the bays of the aisles, the number of ribs to be carried was not equal for each column. At the corners of the nave bays, where ribs of the nave bays as well as of the aisle bays met, big clustered columns were needed with many shafts. In between, where only the aisle ribs had to be carried, smaller clustered columns were sufficient. So in the nave, big and small clustered columns alternated. This is called the alternating system (Fig. 429a).

To counteract the outward pressure of the ribbed vaults, buttresses were built against the outer wall at the points where pressure was exerted. This was easy for the vaults of the aisles; but it became a problem for the vault of the nave, since the nave, which needed buttressing at a higher point, was flanked on each side by an aisle which was lower than the nave. Because of the aisles, buttresses could not be built against the points where the ribs of the nave vaults met, but only against the outer walls. So, between the buttresses and the point to be buttressed, there was a space as wide as the aisle. To overcome this difficulty, the builders of Sant' Ambrogio erected another storey or an upper gallery over the aisles, and it was the vault of this gallery passage that took the outward pressure from the nave vault and transmitted it to the buttresses, built at right angles against the outer wall and exactly at the points where buttressing was necessary (Fig. 429 d).

The division of the nave into bays, the ribbed vaulting, the clustered columns, the alternating system and the transmitting buttressing system were the great innovations which laid the foundations for the skeleton framework architecture of the Gothic period, where the parts are related in their functions to each other, just as in the skeleton system of living beings.

But the builders of Sant' Ambrogio used these innovations timidly, making everything low and sturdy. Since they buttressed the nave vault with the upper storey of the aisles, there was no place for clerestory windows; therefore the interior was dark, being lighted from above only by an octagonal lantern tower. This had many windows around it, and so gave light to the nave. It was built over the first bay of the nave, just above the altar. Since the nave and the storeyed aisles were the same height, the vaults of the whole building were covered with one common sloping roof.

More common than these daring constructional innovations, seen at Sant' Ambrogio, were the following decorative elements.

The most characteristic feature in Romanesque art, by which the style is generally recognizable, was the abundant use of the round arch, not only for the vaulting or crossing arches of the nave, but everywhere: on doors and windows, in arcadings and mouldings.

Doors and windows* always play an important role in architecture, and their form reflects in a special way the characteristics of the whole style. This is especially true of the two great medieval styles, the Romanesque and the Gothic. From the mechanical point of view a door is simply an opening in the wall, serving as a passage and protection; but from the artistic point of view it has to express much more. Being a separation between the exterior and the interior, it can produce psychological responses such as a friendly welcome or forbidding defiance. Since the church is a house of prayer for all, it was of utmost importance that its doors should suggest a gracious invitation. The splayed openings (Fig. 430) of the Romanesque and Gothic periods fully satisfied this need.

The word splay comes from display, meaning expansion. Such an opening is formed of a series of receding concentric arches, which diminish throughout the thickness of the wall, the innermost arch being the lowest and narrowest. Each successive arch widens and rises in height, and is supported by a little round column

*This idea is well explained in Talbot Hamlin's *Twentieth Century Architecture, Vol. 1.*

of its own. These columns were often connected by a continuous abacus, and each had a

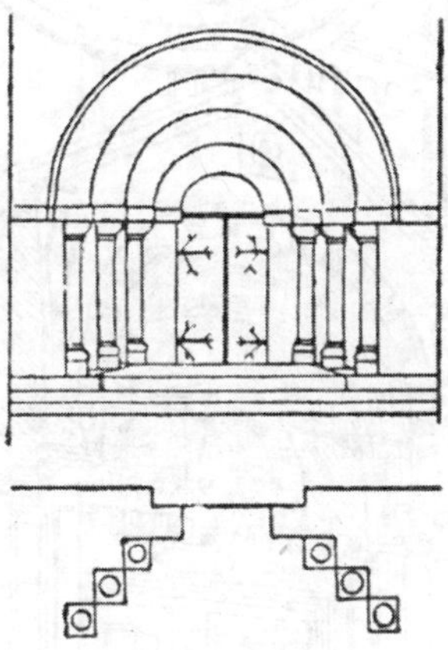

Fig. 430. Splayed door.

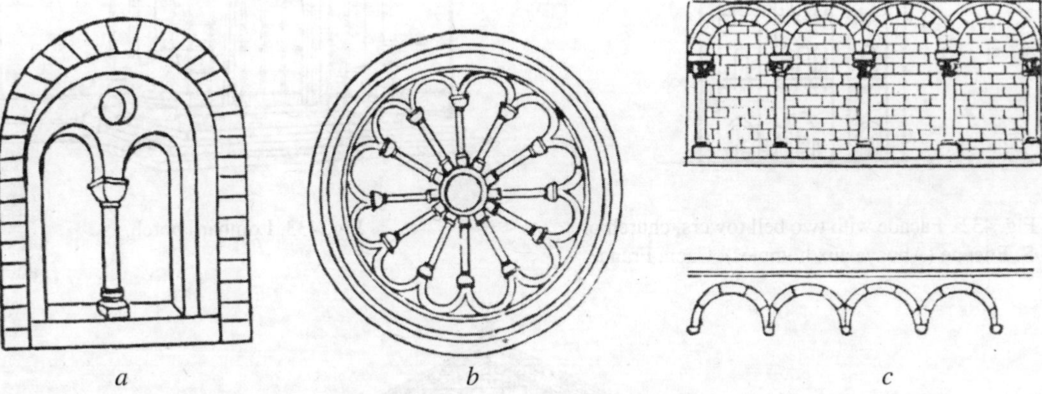

Fig. 431. *a*. twin windows; *b*. rose or wheel window; *c*. (top) blind arcade, (bottom) arched string courses or corbels.

little base. The same principle is shown here as in the clustered coloumns : i.e., every particular member has its own task. Aesthetically, the splayed doorway with its arched extensions is both imposing and pleasing.

The windows too were splayed, in harmony with the doors. These, as well as the gallery openings inside (but not the doors), had twin openings formed by a compound arch, i.e., two little arches enclosed by a bigger one, and resting in the centre on a colonnette (little column) (Fig. 431a). On the façade or front of the churches was the rose or wheel-window (Fig. 431 b), ornamented with tracery separations similar to rose petals or spokes on a wheel.

The walls were often decorated with blind arcades (Fig. 431c, top) and with arched string courses or corbels (Fig. 431 c, bottom). In France small brackets were used for supporting some weight.

The bell tower became a typical church symbol in the Romanesque period, though it originated earlier. Its vertical lines pointing upwards help to turn the soul to God and noble aspirations. In Italy it remained freestanding but became more ornate (Fig. 428 a); in the north, it was incorporated into the building (Fig. 432). Often a pair of towers adorned the façade. Sometimes the so-called lantern towers were erected over the crossing of the nave and transept to permit light to penetrate into the church, for they resembled eightsided lanterns with windows around.

Italian Romanesque was varied, and generally laid greater stress on decorative effects than constructional systems. The innovations of Sant' Ambrogio were not carried any further even by the Lombards who originated them. They decorated the wall surfaces with corbels. A rose window enlivened the plain façade, and they often liked to build a projecting porch in front of the door, whether or not it was splayed. The porch roof was supported by small columns held up by figures of crouching lions resting on a low basement on each side. This is known as the *Lombard porch* (Fig. 433). There is an interesting group of Italian Romanesque buildings at Pisa (Pl. 32. 2), where the façade of the cathedral, as well as the eight storeys of the famous *leaning tower*, are decorated with blind arcades. In Tuscany, the plain church façade was faced with black and white marble inlay, as seen on the church of *San Miniato* in *Florence*. (Fig. 434).

Fig. 432 . Façade with two bell towers, church of S. Etienne (Abbaye aux hommes), Caen, France.

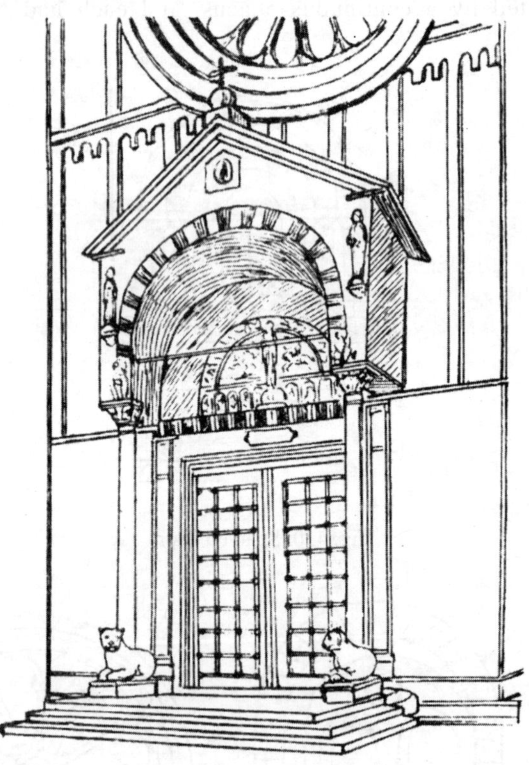

Fig. 433. Lombard porch.

Fig. 434. Church of San Miniato, Florence, Italy.

In Germany, along the Rhine valley (a trade route between northern and southern Europe) there was great building activity from the time of Charlemagne onwards. Several Carolingian or Pre-Romanesque traditions lingered on there even in Romanesque times, especially the long naves ending on both sides in an apse (Fig. 426), and also in the general design of the churches*. But they also have some special characteristics which make them typically German Romanesque. A good example of these sturdy buildings is the early Romanesque church of *St. Michael* at *Hildesheim* (Fig. 435). It has two apses, one on

Fig. 435. Church of St. Michael at Hildesheim, Germany

the east and the other' on the west. On both ends there is a transept surmounted by a square lantern tower. A slender stair tower adjoins the exterior of each transept. Between these almost symmetrical extremities is a long nave flanked by aisles. The main entrance is not at the western end as was the usual custom, but through two doorways at the northern aisle. Each of the later German Romanesque churches adopted some of these characteristics, but not all. The style reached maturity in the 12th century through influences from Burgundy and Lombardy. From the latter the Germans borrowed the external wall decorations with arcaded galleries, flat strips (called pilaster strips), and the Lombard corbels. The *cathedrals* of *Mainz*, *worms* (Pl. 32.3,), *Speier*, and *Bamberg* arc some of the most outstanding examples.

France has the greatest amount and variety of Romanesque architecture. It developed some ten different kinds.

In southern France, especially Provence, where many Roman buildings were preserved, artists naturally drew inspiration from these models. This region has some of the finest sculptured portals, e.g. at *St. Trophime* in *Arles* (Pl 32.4 ).

A Byzantine influence, unusual in France, is seen in Aquitaine, in the west-central part of the country. The cathedral *St. Front* at *Périgueux* is a central type, its plan forming a Greek cross, roofed with five domes on pendentives ; it is an imitation of St. Mark's in Venice (Fig. 425). But churches of the longitudinal types were also covered with a series of domes on pendentives as seen in the *cathedral* of *Angoulême.*

In Burgundy, there were the great mother-abbeys of the Benedictines at Cluny, and of the Cistercians at Citeaux. The *abbey church* of *Cluny*, almost entirely destroyed during the French Revolution, was the biggest church in its time. It was about 196 metres long. Reconstructions in drawing and models give us some idea of what it may have been. The school of Burgundy was also renowned for its fine sculpture, as can be seen at *St. Madeleine* at *Vézelay* and *St. Lazare* at *Antun.*

Pilgrimages were very popular and helped to unite the people. The chief places visited were the Holy Sepulchre at Jerusalem, St. Peter's in Rome, and Santiago (St. James) de Compostela in Spain. The pilgrims walked in groups on the main roads, along which at intervals of about a day's journey (some 32 km.) monasteries were built to provide hospitality. The churches in these places were spacious, to receive great crowds. Their side aisles surrounded the transept and apse, both of which were flanked with chapels, so that the people could walk all around. Some five churches of this interregional type can still be identified. The abbey-church of *St. Sernin* at *Toulouse* (Fig. 436), in Languedoc, south-western France, is a good example of the big churches along the pilgrimage road to *Santiago* de *Compostela* in Spain.

In Normandy, in northern France, sturdy buildings were erected with two heavy towers in the front, and a lantern tower over the crossing. The Normans took the style to England after

*The design of these German Romanesque churches is similar to that of Pre-Romanesque monastic church of *Centula* or *St. Riquier*, near Abbeville.

the Conquest in I066, where the best example is the *Durham cathedral*. The Normans were

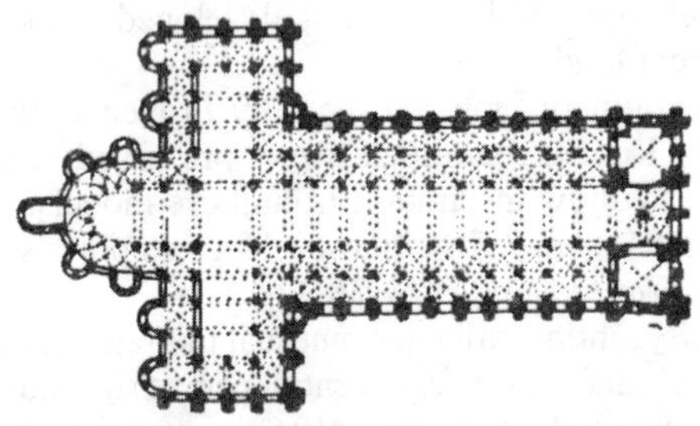

Fig. 436. Abbey-church of St. Sernin, Toulouse, France.

influenced by the Lombards, to whose structural innovations they were able to give further development, and this prepared the way for the Gothic style. The two churches at *Caen: Abbaye aux Hommes** (S. Etienne) (Fig. 432) and *Abbaye aux Femmes*** (S. Trinité), (built by William the Conqueror and his wife Matilda) are the most advanced buildings of this type in Burgundy.

## SCULPTURE

The resurgence of architecture during the Romanesque period was followed, at the end of the eleventh century, by the restoration of monumental sculpture. This art had been neglected for about six centuries, and, like architecture, its revival shows great regional differences. To appreciate its somewhat confusing aspect, we need to understand the Romanesque sculptor's aims and difficulties. A work of art is not generally something entirely new, because man always depends on existing things and ideas, to which he gives another arrangement by using his own artistic talent.

Romanesque sculptors got their inspiration from monastery workshops, where long before the revival of monumental sculpture, minor arts, like manuscript illumination, ivory carvings and metal Work, were practised. All these arts combined classical, Byzantine and barbarian influences.

Romanesque sculpture was meant for architectural ornament. It was centred mainly on the portals, which, being splayed, offered a particularly suitable field for the artist's imagination. Figures stood either against or between the door jambs. When the door was wide, it was divided by a central pillar called trumeau* (post in the centre), in front of which stood the statue of the most important figure. The door-opening was bridged by both an arch and a lintel, each of which was decorated. They enclosed the round field of the pediment, where the principal scene was represented. Inside the church, mainly the capitals were sculptured, often with storied representations.

The form of sculpture was relief, stylized and conventional, in harmony with the decorative scheme of the whole. The artist did not reproduce the human and animal forms as they are in nature. His aim was didactic. At a time when no books were printed and the majority of the people were illiterate, religious stories were told in stone, in a clear and intelligible way. To express his ideas, the sculptor used conventional signs: a disc of light encircling the head (round halo) meant holiness ; while a cross inside the halo was reserved for representations of God. To distinguish one from the other, the different saints were shown with representative symbols. In picturing a story, they used a kind of sign language to indicate the details that could not he carved out: wavy lines for water, curved or zigzag lines for the sky, a leafy stem for a tree or forest, a tower with battlements for a city, and heaven with the addition of an angel on top. Often the blessed were shown as little figures resting against Abraham's heart, protected by the folds of his robe, to signify the carefree security and affectionate recognition of each soul in heaven. The entrance of hell was represented by the open jaws of a huge monster, like a crocodile, into which the devils, with big forks, threw those who had chosen to act like them instead of growing in the generous likeness of God. The manner of representation, of course, is a highly imaginative, somewhat immature way of indicating deep spiritual and psychological realities.

The finest examples of relief sculpture on doorways were produced in Provence and Burgundy, in France. On the portal of the *Church* of *Sain Trophime* at *Arles* (Pl. 32.4 ) in Provence, the *Last Judgment* is represented. The richly-carved portal projects from the rugged wall of the church. It is composed of a plain base on both sides of the door, on which stand figures of saints separated from each other by columns. These columns carry a sculptured

* Pronounce A-bay-oz-omm.
** Pronounce A-bay-o-fumm.

* Pronounce true-mo.

frieze which runs horizontally throughout the whole portal. It turns inward in the centre, so as to pass over the recessed splayed doorway. The Last Judgment is carved in the central pediment and on the frieze. In the middle of the pediment is the seated figure of the Judge, with his right hand raised, and holding a book in his left, to denote that ' it is the message I have spoken that will be his judge at the last day.' He is entirely surrounded by a mandorla (an almond-shaped aureole of light). Around him are four symbolical figures taken from the Apocalypse or Book of Revelations. In medieval times, these winged animal forms were usually identified with the four evangelists, because of a relationship with the beginnings of the Gospels : Luke begins with a sacrificial offering, for which calves were sometimes used; Mark introduces John the Baptist as a ' voice crying in the wilderness', like a lion ; Matthew starts with the Redeemer's human genealogy, so he is represented by a man ; while John begins with His eternal generation in the Godhead, so the eagle, which was supposed to be able to gaze into the sun and to fly the highest, was assigned to him.

The end of the world and the final public judgment of all mankind was foretold by Jesus Christ and was recorded in the Gospels, ' when the Son of man shall come in his majesty all nations shall be gathered together before him and he shall separate them one from another ' and ' say to them that shall be on his right hand, (the just): Come ye blessed of my Father, possess the kingdom prepared for you from the foundation of the world. For I was hungry and you gave me to eat; I was thirsty and you gave me to drink; I was a stranger and you took me in ; naked and you covered me ; sick and you visited me ; I was in prison and you came to me. Then shall the just answer him saying: Lord when did we see thee hungry and feed thee, thirsty and gave thee drink? And when did we see thee a stranger, and took thee in ? Or naked, and covered thee ? Or when did we see thee sick or in prison and came to thee ? And the king answering shall say to them : Amen I say you, as long as you did it to one of these my least brethren, you did it to me'. Christ will then speak to those on his left, that is to the wicked. He will condemn them to everlasting punishment because they have failed in charity towards their fellow men.

The scenes on the sides of the sculptured frieze show the fulfilment of the judgment, which depends on our treatment of others (You should love one another as I have loved you .... Be true sons of the Most High, generous like him .... The measure you give to others is the measure that will be given to you). To the right of the Judge are the merciful going to heaven, and to his left the unjust, selfish ones going to their self-chosen doom.

The pediment of the *church of St. Lazare* at *Autun* in Burgundy also shows the *Last Judgment*: Here the influence of illuminated manuscripts is evident. The slender proportions, and entirely stylized representation of human figures, sometimes in distortion, are more like splendid decorative line compositions than an organic representation of human bodies.

The pediment of the *church* of *St. Pierre* at *Motssac* (pl. 33.1 ) from about 1120 A.D., is an example where manuscript illuminations, ivory carvings and metal work influenced the sculptor. It is one of the most interesting sculptural interpretations of the *adoration of the Creator*, as recorded in the Apocalypse. The sculptor tries to represent Him under the symbol of a wise ruler, in a long embroidered robe, and wearing a crown. He is surrounded by the four symbolic beings (identified with the evangelists), full of eyes, souls who are completely open to His Truth, desirous and able to see Him with their spiritual powers and His own revelation (Seek and you will find). They can also, in the light of God's eternal Truth, look before and after, i.e. beyond all the limits of time. Their wings indicate their spiritual energy and activity, which is not confined by matter, but free to penetrate into the nature and meaning of material arrangements and beyond them to their Author. Behind them are two seraphim (spirits closely united to God). Around these central figures are the twenty-four elders or priests representing those who accept God's message or word, who understand its meaning as an invitation or sharing in the fullness of God's own life, and thus, by their knowledge and love, they unite to Him all created things, by which God speaks to us. The whole is a limited attempt to represent the symphony of all creation praising and thanking God for His unbounded Goodness and Power, for which He alone is really worthy of all worship. Since He is unlimited, He has nothing to gain or lose from creation, which is an overflow of His generous, abundant joy, as an artist's work is not essential to his nature as man, but an attempt to share his inmost feelings with others, to help them see and feel what gives him happiness. God is essentially Truth and seif-giving Love, therefore entirely trustworthy, attractive, and lovabie.

Many sculptured scenes adorn the capitals, where, despite the unsuitable place, compositions are handled with great dexterity. There is also a large variety of purely decorative sculpture on lintels, jambs and arcades, which give a rich aspect to these Romanesque churches.

A minor detail in itself, but of special interest to Indian students, is the fact that the elephant, with the howdah on his back—probably imported through designs on textiles—is seen in several Romanesque churches, as for example St. Pierre d'Aulnay, Montierneuf at Poitiers, and L'Isle Barbe near Lyons. The howdah being interpreted as a tower, the artist in the church of Ste. Trinité (Abbaye aux Femmes) at Caen developed the theme thus conceived, and represented a whole castle on the back of his elephant!

## PAINTING

The origins of Romanesque wall painting are very remote, but much was destroyed. The earliest known examples (in Reichenau, Germany) go back to about the tenth century.

The Romanesque painters had huge wall surfaces at their disposal, which they could fill with frescoes. The sculptors, on the contrary, had little space, yet, in spite of this, they produced great art. The paintings, however, show a pronounced uniformity in subjects, figures and attitudes. The designs are flat, strongly geometrical in character, and rhythmic in line. Here also the influence of illuminated manuscripts is seen. Examples of Romanesque painting can be found in Italy, England, the German Rhineland and France. The most outstanding of these are, perhaps, in the church of *St Martin* at *Worms*, and at *St. Savin* near *Poitiers.*

Manuscript illumination, as we have seen, flourished in Byzantium ; but it was also widely practised in the monasteries of western Europe. Here both the writing and decorating of books was a fine art.

Every monastery had a scriptorium or writing room where the monks copied manuscripts. Before the invention of printing all books were written by hand, and the custom goes far back in human history. Egyptians, Greeks and Romans used long scrolls with a stick fastened at each end. The lines were written horizontally, from the left to the right, either throughout the length of the scroll, or they were divided into columns. The continuous unrolling with one hand and rolling with the other, which necessarily accompanied reading, was a tedious affair, however; so before long the scrolls were folded along the columns, cut and bound, as is still done with our modern books. This form was called a codex.

The material used was mainly parchment (prepared from sheepskin) and vellum (from calfskin). Paper was introduced from China through the Arabs, only shortly before the invention of printing in the fifteenth century. Since it is made of vegetable fibers, it was named after the Egyptian papyrus reed, which had also served as a writing material. Pens were usually made of goose quills, shaped somewhat like an artist's cut-point pen, a little blunted at the end. The medium used was gouache (water colour mixed with white of zinc) combined with gold or silver.

Writing itself became an art, called calligraphy, the writer being called a calligraphist. Beauty was obtained by the regular and proportioned formation of the letters. But soon the text was decorated also, and pictures were inserted. This is called miniature painting or book illumination. In the beginning, the first letter of each paragraph was decorated with intricately interlaced patterns called tracery. The name given to the work was miniatures, meaning to colour with red lead. Later it was called illumination. Modern book illustrations developed from this. In early medieval times, it was practised by monks. The Irish were especially noted for this art. Their most famous works are the *Book of Kells* and the *Lindisfarne Gospel*, dating from about 700 A.D. They are renowned for their interlaced tracery motifs. During the Carolingian period, manuscript illumination developed greatly, and human figures reappeared in the decorations, chiefly as illustrations of the Gospels.

# 8. GOTHIC ART

## GENERAL SURVEY

Gothic is the culmination of the ideals and artistic forms of mediaeval Christian art. Its cradle is in the heart of Franee : the Ile de France (literally island of France), the smallest and most central of its northern provinces with Paris as its capital. Its most noble and refined manifestation dates from 1200 to 1275. A century later it spread through Europe, to become an international style which lasted well into the middle of the sixteenth century, and even later.

The name Gothic was given to the style by the late Renaissance critics, as a term of contempt, denoting barbaric, because it did not conform to the classical ideals, which were the only ones they accepted. This criticism is not only prejudiced and narrow-minded, but shows also a lack of historical knowledge. In the thirteenth and fourteenth centuries, people called it opus modernum (modern work or style), being the newest in their time; or opus francigenum (French work), which is the most correct name with regard to its origin, but not its extensions. Art critics, ever since the Renaissance, declare this style to be one of the highest accomplishments of the human mind, and the finest artistic achievement of France. It is on a par with Greek art for originality.

The first reason why Gothic art could reach its perfection was the great progress in economic conditions. Three factors, intimately interrelated, contributed to this : namely the growth of towns, commerce, and industries. About 1000 A.D., trade was revived, towns grew up, and various handicrafts were developed. The Norsemen did much to stimulate commerce. From pirates and robbers, they changed into settlers in Normandy, Denmark and England, with trade as their chief occupation. They established contacts even with Constantinople by passing through Russia. The crusades restored relationships between the east and west. The Italian cities of Venice, Pisa and Genoa became flourishing ports, trading with the east and holding sway over the Mediterranean. Commerce was carried on overland by means of the old Roman roads. Rivers became the chief commercial arteries, along which towns sprang up. Money and credit began to replace barter, because coins were an easier medium of exchange than goods in kind. Out of this grew modern capitalism and banking. Increased trade and industry made the cities free communities with legal privileges. The citizen of a town (-burg, -borough) was independent of the feudal lords. Merchants united in associations called guilds for protection against robbers and pirates, and for mutual aid and negotiations.

The different handicrafts also formed guilds of their own, whereby the interests of the workmen as well as of the consumers were protected by insistence on good quality of the finished product. Laws were based on equality and justice. They required the master craftsman, at the head of the workshop, to treat those who worked or learned under him (journeymen and apprentices) as members of his own family. Between employer and employee there was thus greater equality and understanding, since both had the same interests. Prices, wages and profits were regulated, as well as working hours and conditions of labour, to ensure the rights of all. Profiteering, hoarding, black-marketing and competition were forbidden. There was careful supervision so that laws were enforced. Any offender could be punished by confiscating his goods to help the poor, by public disgrace, expulsion from the guild, or even loss of citizenship. Generally there was not then so wide a difference between rich and poor.

The guilds were greatly responsible for the artistic achievements of that time. Usually all the various crafts co-operated, at least with donations, to the building of the great cathedrals of their cities. Often they contributed the stained-glass windows; and to show the dignity of their work, they wanted their own craft represented. The guilds were like technical schools where artisans were trained to be artists ; and the products of these unlettered townsmen, who learned to express the best that was in them and to make useful objects beautiful as well, are still the admiration of modern art-lovers.

The social uplift of the masses was thus effected, for men found joy in creative work. This is proved by the wonderful finish of their work, even in places which only the birds could see. Nor did they work for fame, since the name of most of these artists is unknown. Within the town they co-operated to produce the best in a harmonious whole, and with the other towns there was a creative rivalry which helped to educate their tastes. Each town tried to surpass the other in the beauty of its churches.

The noble ideals of chivalry were inspired by

the model of Christian womanhood, Mary, the Saviour's mother. In a chapel dedicated to her, a squire passed a night in prayer before he became a knight. Many of the great French cathedrals were named Notre Dame (our Lady) in her honour.

With the growth of towns arose new religious societies, known as friars (brothers). By their learning they influenced the new universities, and by their example of poverty they showed people of all classes that happiness does not depend on riches. The founder of the Franciscan friars, Francis of Assisi, had belonged to the merchant class, but he identified himself with the poor by calling the members of his society Friars Minor (little poor brothers). His charming life had a considerable influence on the development of art, especially painting. His great love for God's creative work paved the way for observation of nature. After his death, commemorative fresco paintings, to illustrate his life, were in demand. The artists had in this case no traditional models which they could imitate, as before, but had to find new inspiration from their own surroundings ; and this required new techniques and inventions.

A new intellectual class arose when greater peace, prosperity and leisure were restored. The present university system came into being early in the twelfth century with that of Paris. It was organized like the guilds or labour unions, except that its trade was the arts, taught by a master of arts. A university was a federation or union of masters and students. The name means corporation, and precisely, in this it differed from other schools. The beginnings of modern science were then laid by outstanding thinkers.

Unity was the highest ideal of medieval man. This was reflected in the guild organizations, universities, encyclopedias of knowledge, and in architecture. Medieval men found the fulfilment of this ideal mainly in religion. It gave them one sure aim in life, guaranteed by God's Word, namely that the purpose of this life is an invitation to every one to intimate union with God Himself. Thus a common standard of truth, goodness and beauty was established, for all shared the same aim, the same model of activity in the Saviour's own example, and unity of worship.

## ARCHITECTURE

The beginning of Gothic art is usually considered to be the rebuilt choir of the *royal abbey church* of *St. Denis* the chevet (Fig. 437 ) with its

Fig. 437. Chevet, Church of St. Denis, near Paris.

ambulatory and radiating chapels, and pointed rib vaults. The reconstruction of this church near Paris, which served also as the burial place of the French kings, is due to the initiative and energy of abbot Suger. Its consecration took place in 1144, in the presence of king Louis VII, the queen, nobles and clergy. It is here that the elements that make up the essence of Gothic architecture are present for the first time.

This new idea sparked off a great architectural activity. The reason for this was not only the need for new buildings, but the necessity to rebuild several Romanesque churches where the vaults had collapsed because they had been erected without sufficient scientific knowledge. Others had been destroyed by fire.

The initial phase of this building activity, during the second part of the twelfth century, is called Early Gothic (1140-1194). Among its monuments is the famous *Cathedral of Notre Dame*, Paris*.

The architecture of the thirteenth century forms the classical phase called High Gothic (1194-1248). The most outstanding example is the *cathedral of Chartres* (PI. 33.2 ,4 & Fig- 438, a, b, c). The place was from very remote times a centre of pilgrimage, for its sanctuary contained a venerated statue of the virgin Mary. The early sanctuaries destroyed by invasion or fire, were followed in 1020 by the fourth one, built by bishop Fulbert. This Romanesque

*It may interest the Indian student that Gandhiji visited this cathedral as a young student. He describes his impression in his autobiography as follows: 'The ancient churches of paris are still in my memory. Their grandeur and their peacefulness are unforgettable. The wonderful construction of Demo and the elaborate decoration of the interior with its beautiful sculptures cannot be forgotten. It felt then that those who expended millions on such divine cathedrals could not but have the love of God in their hearts.'

church had a narthex. Between 1134-1170, two towers were erected in front of the building, but separated from it. Some years later, the façade of the narthex was taken, stone by stone, to be inserted between the two towers.

In 1194, when Gothic art reached its maturity, a terrible fire destroyed the whole Romanesque building, except the two towers and the newly-inserted façade. The glorious Gothic cathedral was the almost immediate reaction of the

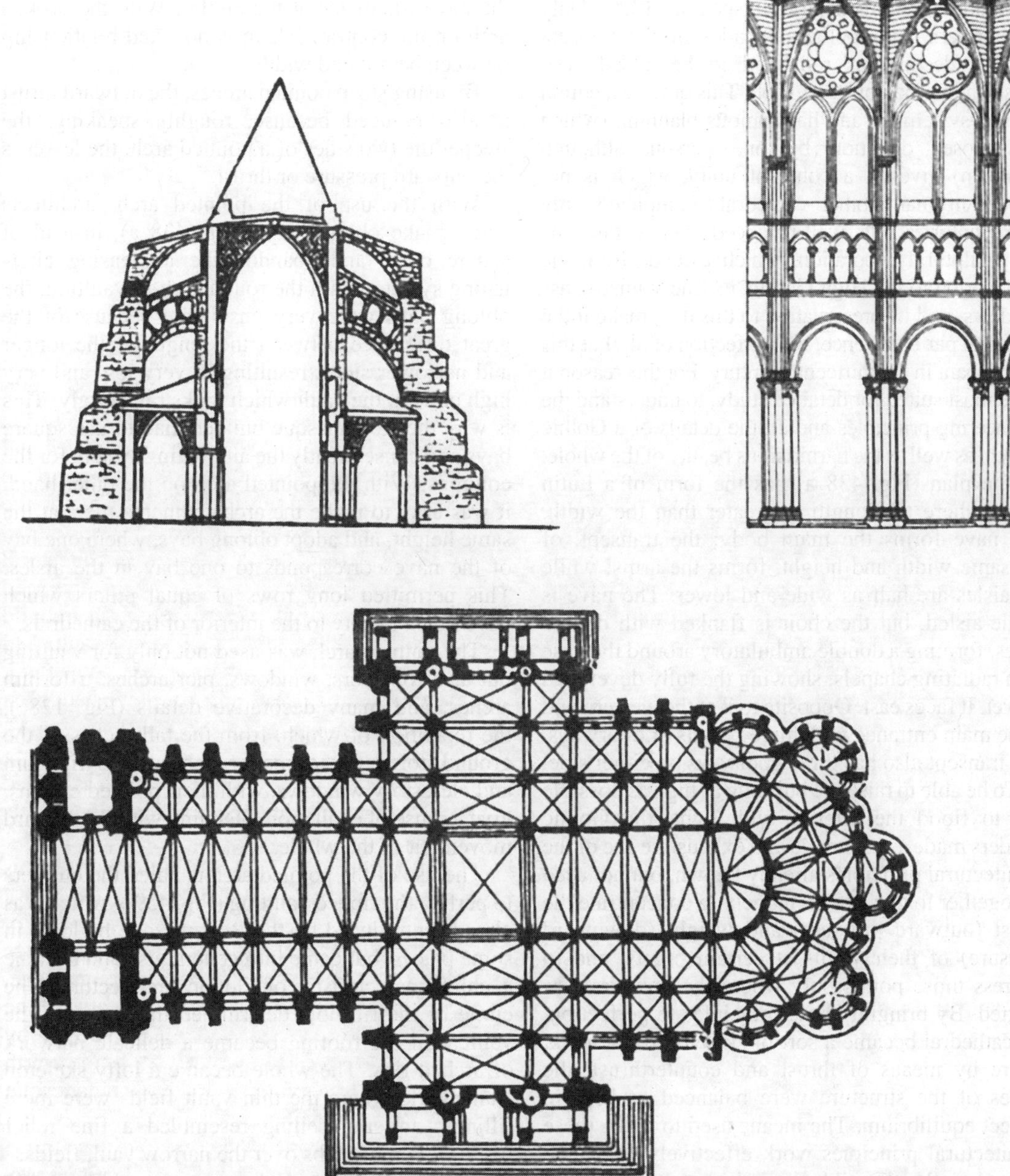

Fig 438. Cathedral of Chartres: *a*. plan (bottom); *b*. cross section (top left); *c*. longitudinal section, detail (top right).

population to this terrible disaster, when, accord-ding to the old chronicler, rich and poor, princes and simple citizens, all contributed to the rebuilding of their beloved sanctuary not only with donations but by manual labour, carrying blocks of stone from the quarry up to the cathedral. It was due only to this enthusiastic co-operation by everyone that the rebuilding was practically finished in 1220. Only the northern and southern façades of the transept and the decorations remained to be added. The consecration took place in 1260. This quick execution of such systematic and harmonious planning (which presupposes direction by one person, although unknown) gives it a coherent unity, which is not present in many other cathedrals completed only after centuries. Its well-balanced architecture, its rich sculptural decoration, which extends from the early period to the High Gothic, its fine stained-glass windows, and its preservation to this day, make it the cathedral par excellence, the perfection of all that this word meant in the thirteenth century. For this reason it is the most suited for detailed study, to understand the engineering principles and all the details of a Gothic church, as well as the harmonious beauty of the whole.

The plan (Fig. 438 a) has the form of a Latin cross, where the length is greater than the width. The nave forms the main body; the transept, of the same width and height, forms the arms; while the aisles are half as wide and lower. The nave is single-aisled, but the choir is flanked with double aisles, forming a double ambulatory around the apse with radiating chapels, showing the fully developed chevet. It faces east. Opposite to it at the western end is the main entrance with three portals or doorways. The transept also has three doorways on either side.

To be able to raise the building as high as possible and to flood the interior with light, the Gothic builders made a systematic and exhaustive use of the architectural principles already known, but not used all together to this extent, namely to concentrate the thrust (outward pressure) and weight (downward pressure) of their vaults at certain points, and to buttress those points only where the pressure was exerted. By bringing these principles to perfection, the cathedral became a sort of skeleton framework, where by means of thrust and counterthrust, the forces of the structure were balanced or kept in perfect equilibrium. The means used to make these architectural principles work effectively were: the pointed arch, the ribbed vaulting, the clustered column, and the flying buttress.

The pointed arch, (Fig. 438 b, c) rightly called by the French arc-brisé* (broken arch) is formed of two segments of a round arch, butted against each other without keystone. Its use for vaulting permitted the Gothic builder to raise the height of the building. The height of a semicircular vault (radius of the circle) can be only half the width of the nave (diameter of the circle). With the broken arch on the contrary, there is no fixed relationship between height and width.

By using steep pointed arches, the outward thrust is also reduced because, roughly speaking, the steeper the two sides of a pointed arch, the lesser is the outward pressure or thrust.

With the use of the pointed arch, architects could make oblong bays (Fig. 438 a), instead of square ones, and abandon the unpleasing alter-nating system. With the round arch in vaulting, the oblong bays were very unsuitable because of the great difference between the length of the longer and narrower sides, resulting in very low and very high parts in the vault which looks rather ugly. This is why the Romanesque builders had to use square bays and consequently the alternating system for the columns. With the pointed arch on the other hand, it was easy to make the arch segments meet at the same height, and adopt oblong bays, where one bay of the nave corresponds to one bay in the aisles. This permitted long rows of equal pillars which gave much beauty to the interior of the cathedrals.

The pointed arch was used not only for vaulting but also for doors, windows, pier arches, triforium arches, and many decorative details (Fig. 128c), the repetition of which, from the tall arches of the ground storey, to the smaller arches of the triforium and clerestory windows, with their pointed crowns, give a sense of exaltation, blending with the upward movement of the whole.

The use of the pointed arch enabled the builders to perfect the ribbed vaulting (Fig. 439)» which was already introduced by the Romanesque builders in some places, but came into general use and became a chief characteristic of Gothic architecture. The curve of the rib now determined the shape of the vault, and the roofing became a delicate network of arched ribs. The whole became a lofty skeleton framework, where the thin vault fields were mere fillings; and the ceiling resembled a fine relief tracery of arched ribs over the narrow vault fields.

Moreover, the weight (downward pressure) of the stone roof was concentrated merely on

* pronounce: arc-bree-say.

clustered columns (Fig. 438c), where each weight had its own support, each rib of the vault being

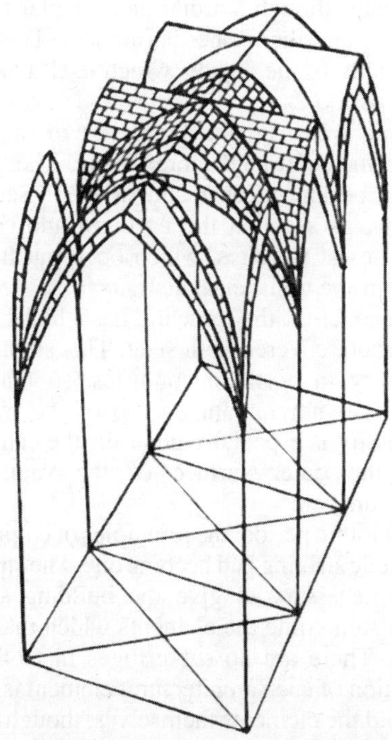

Fig. 439. Gothic ribbed vaulting.

carried by a separate little column. These clustered columns, essentially functional though they are, add greatly to the decorative design and soaring character of the interior. Their grouping of slender lines rises in a swift, almost unbroken verticle sweep from floor to roof, and is the most insistent note in the soaring rhythm.

One of the French builders' most brilliant achievements, was the invention of the flying buttress to counteract the outward pressure of the vault. At the points where the clustered columns carried the downward pressure, the outward thrust needed a counterpressure at the side. The difficulty already felt, but not adequately solved during the Romanesque period, was the difference between the height of the lower aisle and the higher nave. Buttresses could be built outside the walls of the aisles, the vault of which they supported; but to reinforce the vault of the higher nave was the great problem which the Gothic builders overcame by building half-arches from the outer buttress, passing above the roof of the aisles to bridge the intervening space. These half arches sprang from the outside buttress and leaned on the nave wall like so many arms, to strengthen the weak points : namely those at the base of the arch (where it has the tendency to move sideways, which would result in the collapse of the arch), and those at about 1/3 the height of the curve of the arch, called the haunch. If there is not enough weight on the arch at this point, this haunch may move outward and the centre of the arch may droop. At Chartres the flying buttresses (Fig. 438b) are double and are united by small sturdy columns. The higher row of flying buttresses was added only in 1316. The pier buttresses are simple, but in later cathedrals they are topped with pinnacles decorated with crockets and finials (Fig. 440).

Fig. 440. Flying buttress, with pier buttress topped with a pinnacle decorated with crockets and finials.

The interior design of the cathedral is formed by the combination of vertical lines and pointed arches. Each bay (Fig. 438c) forms a unit in three storeys. Its design is repeated in every bay, which forms the triple division of the interior from floor to roof, namely the nave arcade, the triforium, and the clerestory. The nave arcade is formed of the clustered columns (also called compound piers), and the pointed arches which they carry. The triforium is a delicately arcaded shallow gallery above the nave arcade, forming the middle storey of the interior design. Triforium means thrice-perforated, because originally it had three arches, but later it often had more. It really replaces the gallery or upper storey of the aisles in Romanesque architecture. At Chartres it is a blind arcade, i.e., it has a solid wall behind it. Later the wall was perforated with windows. The clerestory is the highest division, where— since the Gothic cathedral has become a sort of skeleton framework— practically the whole wall, from one clustered pier to another, is filled with windows.

These spacious windows, that flood the nave with light, are filled with richly-tinted glass, the vivid colours of which contrast with the quiet grey of the stone on which they play throughout the day. The stained-glass window, like the mosaic, is made up of small pieces of glass to form the design ; but whereas in mosaic they are embedded in cement and can only reflect the rays of light, in the stained-glass window they are held in frames in the window openings, so that light is transmitted directly in brilliant, moving colours, from dawn till evening. The hues also vary with the light of every season.

The pieces of coloured glass are cut into shapes to form a picture. They are held together by strips of lead, but this is too soft and pliable for larger windows, which must be reinforced with iron crossbars. These are fixed in the windows, and the lead is fastened to them.

At Chartres the clerestory has double, pointed arched windows surmounted by a wheel or rose window (Fig. 438c). Bigger rose windows of the same design grace the façade and the two transept ends. The ornamental masonry work of these windows is called tracery. At Chartres the early type was used, namely plate tracery, where the decorative pattern was cut through the stone plate. In later cathedrals where the windows became very large, they were subdivided by masonry verticals called mullions. On the top of the window the tracery was worked out piece by piece to the required shape and joined together. This is called bar tracery (Fig. 441)., All this tracery work, filled with coloured glass sparkling in the sun, is the most effective decoration of the cathedrals.

The façade, or front, of the cathedral is flanked by two mighty towers that divide it vertically into three sections ; namely the two towers on the sides, and the central space in between. At Chartres (PI. 33.2) this central space consists of a triple portal, with three lancet windows (pointed like a lance) above it, and higher up, the rose window, and an arcade with rows of statues of kings. The two towers, which once stood separately, were integrated into the Gothic building after the fire. Their bases are symmetrical, but not their spires. The southern spire was of stone, the northern of wood. This latter was struck by lightning in 1506, and the present one was then erected in the late Gothic style. The southern or old tower, though sturdier and simpler than the more ornate northern one, harmonizes better with the simplicity of the façade, which itself belongs to the early period.

As time went on, the' façade es of the cathedrals became more and more ornate. The porches especially became deeper and richer in sculptural decoration, as seen on the northern and southern side porches at Chartres, which open out from the two ends of the transversal aisles.

On the exterior, the cathedral has a high- pitched roof of wood, covered with slate. This sloping roof is necessary in northern countries, so that snow and rain will not remain on top of the building. The necessity is especially great for the cathedrals, because the outer surface of the vaulting is, naturally, uneven.

In the Gothic period, the principles of engineering and aesthetic striving had become one. The structural elements necessary to give the building stability are at the same time the elements which make it so beautiful. There are no subterfuges in Gothic art. The function of each architectural element is clearly shown, and the elements themselves, though refined and beautified to the utmost, are definitely made to fulfil their purpose.

Thus the flying buttresses (pl. 33.4 ) are frankly revealed on the outside of the building with the obvious aim of supporting the lateral thrust of the vault inside; and inside, the ribs and clustered pillars show clearly their role of supporting the downward pressure; and it is exactly the soaring verticals of these supports and the graceful curves of the flying buttresses that make these cathedrals so beautiful. An ornamental effect is achieved out of the actual structure, a feature never surpassed, and equalled only by the Greeks. The aim of architecture is to free itself from its materials, and this was never so realized as in Gothic, with its high and airy construction, its free and slender supporting skeleton. The Gothic builders always combined utility and beauty.

We can see the simple elements of Chartres cathedral developed further in the two other most famous buildings of the High Gothic, namely those at Reims and at Amiens. The *cathedral of Reims* (pl: 34.1 ) was the coronation church of the French kings. As at Chartres, the erection of the Gothic cathedral was due to an enormous fire in 1210 that destroyed the old Carolingian building. With the same fervour as the population of Chartres, the people of Reims started the rebuilding, but the reconstruction of this huge edifice lasted about two and a half centuries. The plan at Reims is similar to that of Chartres, except that the eastern end is expanded to the width of the transept, due to the need of space for coronation ceremonies. The most splendid part of this cathedral is its western façade, with its rich sculptural decoration of about five hundred and thirty statues. It has the usual, but deeply splayed, triple doorway, which here projects far beyond the thickness of the wall.

The sculpture in each pediment of the doors is in this case replaced by a rose window. The archivolts have the usual figure decorations. The gables that surmount these arches are profusely carved. The central one contains a scene of the coronation of the virgin Mary, and the northern one the crucifixion. The next horizontal division above the portals contains the huge rose window (Fig. 441), more than 12 metres in

Fig. 441. Rose window, western façade, cathedral of Reims.

diametre, made with bar tracery, which is exquisite. On each side of it are twin windows. The next division is the famous gallery of the kings, where each figure stands in a canopied niche.

While Reims is most renowned for its beautiful façade, the cathedral of Amiens presents the most harmonious arrangement in the elevation of the nave (PI. 34.2 & Fig. 442), the height of which reaches up to $41\frac{1}{2}$ metres, exceeding those of Chartres and Reims.

The rest of the thirteenth and fourteenth centuries is the period of Refined Gothic, of which the most illustrious example is the *Sainte Chapelle* in *Paris*, which was the royal chapel on the island of the city, formed by the river Seine. It was built between 1244 and 1247 by St. Louis IX, to house the relic of the Saviour's crown of thorns, that he brought back from the Holy Land. This small two-storeyed edifice, of which the upper storey dominates, has no side

Fig. 442. Elevation of the nave (one bay), cathedral of Amiens.

aisles, but only the nave, since it was for the king's private use. For this reason it has no flying buttresses. It is perhaps the finest example of the almost entire elimination of the walls, the vault being carried by delicate pillars adjoining strong buttresses. The wall-space is entirely occupied by huge stained-glass windows,

$41\frac{1}{2}$ metres wide and 15 metres high, giving the impression of a spacious house of glass. Of the *cathedral of Beauvais* (1225-1568) only the choir and transept have been built, the rest has remained unfinished. It marks the last step in the effort to obtain soaring heights. Its vauilt of 48 metres was the highest of all, but it col- lapsed a few years after completion in 1272, and had to be rebuilt.

The establishment of a central government in France was the chief reason why Gothic cathedrals were bulit all over the country. Although they present many local differences, on the whole they show a much more unified aspect than the Romanesque churches did.

The Late Gothic period of the second half of the fourteenth and of the fifteenth centuries is also called flamboyant (flaming), because the tracery imitates the form of flames (Fig. 443).

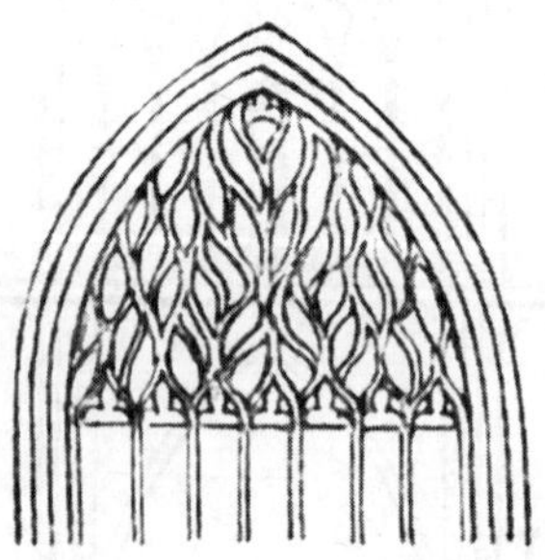

Fig. 443. Gothic window with flamboyant tracery.

During this period the surface ornament became, most profuse, and the stone carving technique reached its perfection of finish. This period is also characterized by openwork (perforated, lace-like stone carving), of which the most characteristic manifestations are the high pointed gables, which are no longer a front wall to the roofs of the projecting door, but pierced high- pointed triangles, surmounting the outer arches of the splayed doors like decorations.

Although the Gothic style is seen to best advantage in the cathedrals, yet it was adapted to many other kinds of buildings according to the growing needs of historical development. An interesting study of this is the evolution of the castle into a palace. During the feudal period, fortresses were usually built at strategic places, and their plan was determined by the terrain, often an elevation difficult of access and affording a wide view. In the twelfth to thirteenth centuries, the crusading nobles who could afford it replaced the former simple fortifications of wood by expensive stone fortresses similar to those they had seen in Constantinople. The first defence was often a ditch or moat, with a bridge that could be raised or lowered according to need. Then came the walls, supplied with towers, which were bigger at the corners; then an outer court or bailey, with a number of fortified residences and a chapel for the lord and his soldiers. In the centre, standing by itself, was the keep or donjon, round or square in shape, with very thick walls, and a platform on top for look-out. If the enemy forced the moat or walls, the defenders would retire to the donjon, which was easily defended but hard to capture. The donjon of the *castle of Coucy* in France, built about 1230, was a good example; but it was destroyed in World War I. When there was less need for defence, the castles became more residential; and when the introduction of gunpowder in the fourteenth century made them useless for defence, they were turned into palaces or country houses, though some of the old features were retained for decorative purposes. The walls were pierced by windows both into the courtyard and out, and the towers gradually disappeared.

There were also Gothic *city walls* and *gates*, especially at *Carcassonne* and *Avignon*, with their crenellated battlements; beautiful town halls; monasteries and cloisters like Mont St. Michel on a cliff in Brittany; town houses, like that of Jacques Coeur in Bourges, hospitals and many other charitable institutions; bridges and markets; barns and houses in the country and city, forming picturesque streets with their high gables, rich carving, arched doors and windows, and half-timbered facing.

After France, it was in England that Gothic art flourished most and longest. Most of England's Gothic cathedrals were, in the beginning, monastic churches. This explains why many English Gothic cathedrals are built in lonely quiet places amidst trees. Their beautiful setting contrasts with the setting of the French cathedral, soaring out of congested city quarters. England also has more literary remains of medieval times, so many of the builders' names are known, in contrast with the anonymity of French builders.

British cathedrals were usually built over a period of time covering different centuries; and so only a few, like the cathedral of Salisbury (PI. 34.3 Fig. 144) present a homogeneous Gothic character. This lovely Gothic building, contemporary with Amiens cathedral, was begun in 1220 and finished within forty years. Although belonging to the Early English period, it shows all the main characteristics of English Gothic. The plan is long (146 metres), and relatively

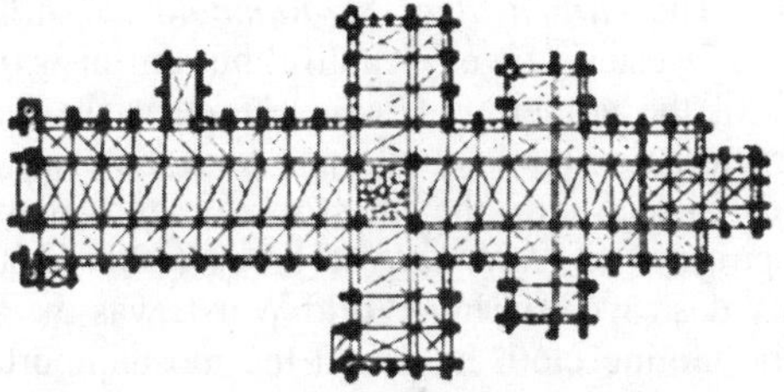

Fig. 444. Plan of the cathedral of Salisbury.

narrow, with two transepts. The eastern end, which is square, has no ambulatory or chapels, only windows. The vaults are low. The windows are of the lancet type, of fine proportions, with two or three grouped together. The main feature of the exterior design is a central tower above the crossing of the nave by the transept. It serves as a lantern internally, for light streams into the church through its windows. The form of the tower is square. It is rich with elegant decoration. Here at Salisbury, and at a few other places, it ends in a lofty spire; but English towers do not usually end in a spire. The façade forms a sort of screen, with arcadings much less imposing than the great French splayed doorways, and with little or no relation to the interior.

In England (as in France) the development of tracery forms characterize the later styles. The decorated style has wider windows, divided on the top by tracery decoration resembling the contemporary French windows. The more typically English is the perpendicular style, with its huge windows divided vertically by mullions (upright bars, like perpendicular lines) strengthened by transoms (horizontal bars) and ending in the four-centred Tudor arch. A typicalexample is the great window of St. George's chapel at Windsor.

Another peculiarity of English Gothic is the vaulting, which in its great variety and exuberant richness, contrasts with the uniform French vaults. The ornamentation of the vaulting began by adding intermediary ribs called tiercerons (Fig. 445 a) between the cross and diagonal ribs, but springing from the same points. Later, smaller ribs called liernes (Fig. 445b) were introduced, forming a link between the other ribs and producing star patterns or stellar vaulting. Bosses or rosettes were put at the confluence of the ribs. Fan vaulting was formed by many ribs springing from the same support, and having the same curve. These multiple ribs lost their structural value, and became merely decorative.

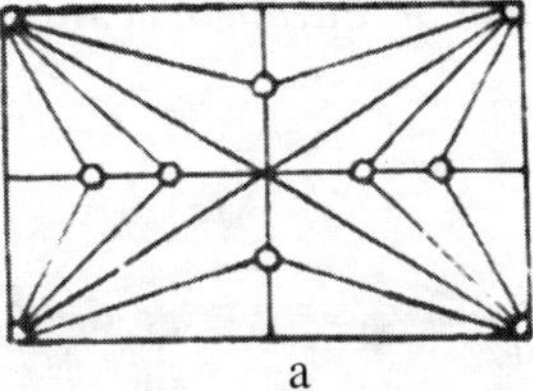


Fig. 445 *a*. Tiercerons ribs.

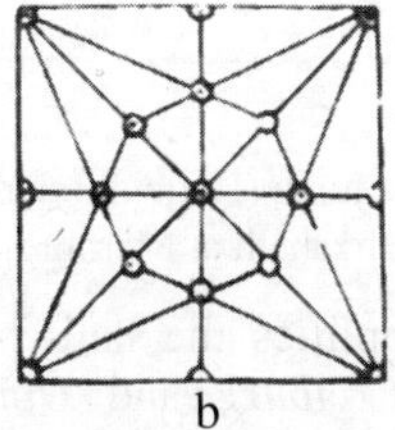


Fig. 445 *b*. Liernes ribs missing

German Gothic did not develop from German Romanesque, but was imported from France. Even after the Gothic pointed arch was introduced, the round arch of the Romanesque continued for a long time, because it suited the tastes of the people better. German Gothic lasted from 1220-1530. The first was probably the *cathedral of Cologne (Kōln)*. It was modelled after Amiens and Beauvais. German Gothic however, did not remain a mere imitation of French models. It made several original contributions, of which the most typical is the so-called hall-church (Hallenkirche) (Fig. 446). Here the side aisles were raised to the height of the nave. This required several changes in the building system. The equal height of the aisles and the nave excluded the possibility of a triforium and clerestorey, and obliged the builders to raise the pier arches and the side walls of the aisles according to the needs of this new arrangement. The whole interior aspect was no longer dominated by the nave, but became a spacious hall-like interior. On the outer walls, flying buttresses were no longer needed, since nave and aisles were of the same height, and so buttresses could be built directly against the wall. Another special feature of German Gothic was the single western tower, which replaced the splayed doorways extending throughout the wide façade of the French cathedrals. Naturally this gave an entirely different external aspect to the entrance.

The church of *St. Elizabeth* at *Marburg*

Fig. 446. Hall-church (Hallenkirche), church of St. Elizabeth at Marburg.

(Fig. 446) exemplifies the hall-church ; and the *cathedrals* of *Freiburg* and *Ulm* illustrate the single western tower. For both hall-church and single tower (although not at the western entrance), the *cathedral of St. Stephen* in *Vienna*, Austria, is a good example. Here the three aisles are almost the same height; the building has no triforium or clerestorey, and its vaults are covered with a single pitched roof. There are three entrances: the front has octagonal turrets and a single door. The two branches of the transept are transformed into entrance porches. One of these is topped by a huge tower, about 125 metres high. The transition from the square base of the tower to the octagonal, ending in a lofty spire, is a masterstroke.

German Gothic has also produced a great number of secular buildings : castles, city gates, town halls (Rathhaus), guild halls, as well as dwellings of citizens (Bürgerhaus), of winch Nüremberg has numerous examples. These houses, with their high-pitched roofs, stepped or traceried gables, balconies decorated with openwork, and turrets placed at the corners, give a very picturesque aspect to these old German cities.

Formerly Belgium and Holland were united, and together were known as the Netherlands. These two countries were influenced by their neighbours, according to their geographical position. Gothic art came to Belgium from France; while Holland was influenced more by Germany.

In Belgium, architectural activity was much greater than in Holland. Its first purely Gothic edifice was the *church of Ste. Gudule* (1225) in *Brussels*. The vast *cathedral of Antwerp* (1352-1422), has seven aisles. The *cathedral of St. Rombaut* at *Malines* has one western tower, beautiful but unfinished. In spite of the numerous Gothic churches, the really characteristic Flemish buildings were the town and guild halls, usually the finest monuments of these old cities. The *cloth hall* of *Ypres* (1200- 1304), partly destroyed during World War I, was the first of the Gothic cloth halls and the most important. Bruges, an important city of the Hanseatic League (a powerful merchant union) had the earliest town hall (1377). It has traceried windows on the façade, and niches in the walls containing statues of the counts of Flanders. The *town hall* at *Louvain* (Plate 34.4 ) (1448) is richly carved, and has three turrets at each of its narrow ends. In Holland, building activity during the Gothic age was much less intensive. Among its Gothic buildings, mention can be made of the *town hall* of Middelburg which resembles the Belgian.

Gothic art penetrated early into Italy, but its structural principles were never really accepted, nor did the style ever become wholeheartedly Italian. There were two main obstacles to the acceptance of Gothic art. First, the climatic conditions differed greatly from the north. For the hot, almost semi-tropical climate and radiant sunshine of certain parts of Italy, cool interiors with thick walls and small openings were needed to keep out the sun; while in northern Europe they wanted more sun, provided by the large stained-glass windows. Secondly, the classical influence in Italy remained strong, and the classical principle of balance between horizontals and verticals stands in direct opposition to the verticality of Gothic art. Since there is very little or no snow in central and south Italy, high-pitched roofs were not needed, so they remained flat. The western façade was also quite different. The campanile remained free-standing, so the front did not have the two bell-towers characteristic of French Gothic. The façades in Italian Gothic became decorative screens, often concealing the aisle roofs ; but they had one feature in common with the northern façades—the rose window. The small windows of the naves and aisles had no tracery; nor did the walls have mouldings ; instead, they were often decorated with strips of different kinds of marbles. Flying buttresses were almost always absent; and buttresses had no pinnacles. The big wall surfaces were frequently adorned with frescoes, or inlaid with mosaic decorations, or overlaid with panels of coloured marble, especially in Tuscany.

The monastic orders, especially the Cistercians, introduced Gothic art into Italy ; and the Franciscans and Dominicans built churches with ribbed vaulting and pointed arches. The *Church of San Francesco* in *Assisi* is the first Franciscan church in the Gothic style. It is two-storeyed. The walls are covered with beautiful frescoes illustrating mainly the life of St. Francis. The *cathedral of Orvieto* is most famous for the colour-effects produced by brilliant mosaic pictures on the façade. The *cathedral of Siena* has a beautiful exterior façade. Its walls are decorated with courses of alternating black and white marble. The effect is impressive but monotonous. *S. Maria dei Fiori* (PI.36.3 ) (Saint Mary of the flowers), the cathedral of *Florence*, usually called ' il Duomo ' by the Italians, was begun in 1296 by Arnolfo di Cambio. It was continued by Giotto and Talenti. Its sumptuous dome belongs to the Renaissance period. Far more important, artistically, is the beautiful *campanile* (bell-tower) which stands beside the duomo. It was designed by Giotto, and shows all the best characteristics of Italian Gothic. It is decorated with inlays and mosaics, alternating with relief and statues in niches. The windows have graceful traceries. Panels of dark and white marble adorn the walls of the duomo, the campanile, and the baptistery in front of them.

Italian secular architecture also produced many famous buildings during the Gothic period. The most famous are the public halls, called either palazzo del consiglio, or palazzo communale, or palazzo publico. The most famous of them is the council-hall of *Florence*, the *Palazzo Vecchio* (old palace) (1255). It is like a fortress, with a strong battlemented, projecting cornice upheld by a row of powerful corbels, on which rests the mighty tower rising to 94 metres above the ground. The Italians also liked loggias, or open halls with an arcade in front. The most famous is the Loggia dei Lanzi in Florence, before the Palazzo Vecchio. It has round semi-classic or Romanesque arches, surmounted by a horizontal cornice. It is Gothic only in its minor details.

The civic buildings in *Venice* are characterized by numerous openings, like traceried windows and balconies. The *Doge's Palace* has, on the western and southern sides, two storeys of superimposed arcades, built in 1354, which stood free at that time. In 1423-1438 the building was widened, and the heavy walls of the upper storey were built over the arcades. The *Ca d' Oro* (golden house), facing the Grand Canal, is famous for its loggia in traceried work.

Gothic architecture in Spain developed mostly under French influence, but always has a strong local character, showing Moorish influence. The Gothic building activity in Spain closely followed the victorious campaigns which finally drove the Moors entirely from the peninsula. The need of churches in the liberated places was a great incentive for building activity. Among its famous *cathedrals*, like those of *Granada*, *Toledo*, and *Valencia*, that of *Seville* is the largest.

## SCULPTURE

During the Gothic period in France, the sculptural decoration of the cathedrals was mainly centred on the façades, especially around the porches. There were usually three entrances (each with three porches): the main entrance on the western side, with the main façade ; and the two entrances ending the transept on each side, assuming sometimes the same importance.

In the Early Gothic churches the porches were cut in the thickness of the wall, but later they projected, forming real porticoes with separate roofs and gables, and the richness of their decoration increased notably. There was a great difference in the sizes of the numerous statues used in the decoration. The biggest were the so- called jamb figures, placed in rows in front or between the nook-shafts of the splayed doors. They stood on pedestals, often formed of symbolic figures, and their heads reached the capitals of the nook-shafts. On the trumeau in the centre stood the main statue. The jamb figures were statues in the round, first imitating the form of a column, later becoming more and more naturalistic. The pediments had relief sculpture on a smaller scale; and the mouldings of the receding arches of the splayed doors consisted of carved figures that followed the lines of the arches with the greatest ingenuity.

On the main façade high up was the so-called gallery of the kings, a row of figures standing in niches. As time went on, decoration became richer and richer until almost every part of the exterior was covered with it.

Although sculpture was meant for decoration, its chief aim was to teach. The cathedral of Chartres will serve as an illustration. The carving of the old western façade shows the earliest Gothic sculpture on its triple doorways, called royal portals. (PI. 33.3)· These western portals symbolized the gateways of the Heavenly Jerusalem. The sculptural decoration of these three portals presents a summary of Christian teaching. On the right portal the God-Man's birth as a poor human child is represented. In the pediment the infant Saviour and his virgin mother are shown in majesty. The lintel below is divided into two zones, the lower of which shows the annunciation, the visitation, and nativity. The upper zone has only the presentation. On the splayed archivolts are symbolic figures of the seven liberal arts, which were the compendium of medieval learning. They represent man's search for truth, which leads him to the Truth. The left portal shows the Saviour's ascension into heaven. His rising figure is seen in the pediment between two angels. The lower horizontal zone contains the row of the seated apostles, gazing upwards ; and angels are descending to them in the next zone. The cosmic and terrestrial world are symbolized by the signs of the zodiac and the various labours of the twelve months, shown in archivolts. The last scene on the central doorway represents the fulfilment of creation, with the God-Man's appearance in his divine glory at the end of the world. Here the arrangement is similar to the Romanesque style. The seated Judge in the mandorla or almond-shaped glory is surrounded by the four symbolic figures of the Apocalypse, in which medieval men saw the symbols of the Gospel writers. Below are seated apostles, each head fitting into a tiny arch, and a column between every group of three. In the archivolts are the twenty-four elders of the Apocalyptic vision.

On the capitals of the nook shafts of the three doorways, running through the whole façade like a continuous frieze, are scenes of the Saviour's life and sufferings. In front of the nook shafts stand big statues of kings and queens, the ancestors of the Redeemer's mother. The statues are elongated, and have the forms of columns. They are, perhaps, the most exquisite examples of architectural sculpture. They fit marvellously into their architectural frame ; and on close observation, the first impression of rigidity vanishes, and one sees not only their clothing in contemporary style, but each face shows a lively and distinctively realistic expression.

Religious teaching is shown again in a more ample way throughout the whole cathedral. Here sculptors and stained-glass workers combined their efforts on some ten thousand figures, giving a comprehensive picture-representation of Christian teaching. On the northern side are the prophecies of the Saviour's coming. In the rose windows the figures of the virgin Mary and child Jesus are surrounded by the ancestors and the prophets who foretold this event. The windows below develop the same theme.

The eastern apsidal windows represent the Saviour's personal appearance in human history ; the windows show the scenes from his adoption of human nature. In the southern rose windows his coming at the end of the world is shown, according to the symbolic vision in the Apocalypse. On the western façade, the rose window represents the last immediate sequel of the second coming of Christ, that is, the Last Judgment. The sculpture on the northern porch teaches the onlooker that a virtuous life is possible with divine help ; whilst the sculpture of the southern porch shows the effects of a good or bad life, namely joy or pain.

The northern and southern portals, ending the transept, dating from the thirteenth century, represent the mature phase of Gothic sculpture. The big row of jamb figures are more realistic, standing out like statues in the round. They are placed between the nook-shafts, each on a separate pedestal. On the northern portal, the annunciation and visitation groups can be mentioned. On the trumeau of the southern portal is a figure of the Saviour as teacher. Among the statues of saints, the most beautiful is that of St. Theodore, dressed as a soldier. Spirituality radiates from the gentle expression of his face.

In the Ile de France, sculptors made rapid progress in the observation of nature. The height of classical perfection was reached in the thirteenth century. The porch of the Virgin at Notre Dame de Paris is one of the best examples. Here is a blend of impressiveness with vision and poise, of a saintliness at the same time earnest and tender. The sculptural decoration of Reims cathedral can be considered as the climax of Gothic sculpture. The group of the visitation is considered to approximate to the perfection of the Parthenon statues. The upturned gaze of *Saint Paul's* statue (Pl. 35.1) on the northern portal shows, to a degree never perhaps seen at any other time in a stone carving, the joy of the soul immersed in God's love. In the representations of the Saviour, the accent is especially on the divine mercy.

In many cathedrals the statue of Christ is placed on the trumeau at the separation of the door. The most wonderful and popular is the Beau Dieu* (beautiful God) (PI. 35.2.) of Amiens cathedral, a name lovingly given by its

* Pronounce: bow-dew,

population. It seems life-like, representing the figure of Christ in a majestic and sublime way. Simplicity and dignity are the characteristics of this portrait, which represents his divinity glimpsed through his humanity. It shows how the Gothic sculptor was able to unite naturalistic observation with the noble spirituality of revelation. The Saviour holds the book of life (divine revelation) in one hand, and lifts the other in blessing. His eyes are slightly raised, and the face has an indescribable expression of divine goodness. As usual in Gothic sculpture, Christ stands on symbolic figures, representing the prophetic lines of Psalm 90, ' You shalt tread upon the adder and the basilisk; the lion and the dragon shall you trample under foot' (Fig. 447). Under the

Fig. 447. Symbolic figures under the feet of the statue of Christ (Beau Dieu), cathedral of Amiens.

Saviour's feet are a lion and dragon, representing the powers of evil. Somewhat lower on the pedestal are the symbolic animals: the basilisk, a mythical cock-headed reptile, represents death ; and a dragon-like adder is shown pressing one ear to the ground and closing the other with the end of its tail. It symbolizes the stubborn soul who willfully refuses to respond to God's Word of invitation, since it is unwilling to give up its selfish life.

Another well-known statue at Amiens cathedral is La Vierge Doree* (Pl. 35,3) (Golden Virgin), since it seems that the statue was originally gilded. It shows the virgin Mary with the child Jesus on her arm. Her lovely smile expresses especially motherly tenderness and graciousness.

At Straşsburg cathedral, the two famous statues, the Church and the Synagogue (Pl.35.4 are near in style to Chartres, especially in the drapery, but influences of Paris and Reims are also present.

During the Gothic period the storeyed capitals of Romanesque art were abandoned. The capitals were carved in a naturalistic way. The crocket type gave place first to open leaves, which later became naturalistic branches with foliage and flowers. The sculptor's fancy was left free for such details as gargoyles or water spouts, the grotesqueness of which shows the tendency of the imagination to the fantastic unless controlled by reason and divine revelation. At the end of the thirteenth century, real portraits were seen in funerary statuary. In the fourteenth century, statues began to lose their architectural character by being detached from the columns. Carving became more conventionai. At the end of the medieval period, Claus Sluter, whose most famous work was Moses' Well, infused new vigour into the art of sculpture through characteristics derived from his Flemish character.

## PAINTING

In northern Europe, the Gothic period did not offer great wall surfaces to the painter to develop a monumental kind of wall decoration such as the Italians produced in their mosaics and frescoes, for the evolution of this art aimed ever to eliminate the wall by reducing the structure to a framework of piers and vaulting, and by filling the open spaces with stained-glass windows, the great mural decorations of the north. Hence the northern painter's activity in this age was confined chiefly to painting miniatures and illuminations, unless one includes also the stained glass windows, which is handling of colours, though not with the brush.

A great number of illuminated manuscripts have been preserved from the Gothic age, when it was a flourishing art. Paris, famous for its university, became more and more the centre of book-making, until it was almost its monopoly. The types of books produced were psalters and

* Pronounce : vee-airj-door-ay.

Books of Hours (official prayer books) painted in gouache on vellum, and very richly adorned. These were ordered by people of high society. Book illumination reached its highest perfection in the thirteenth century, a period noted for its finely-executed small pictures. They are set in an architectural frame, in a way somewhat similar to the Gothic builder's making of niches to contain the statues. The best example is the beautiful psalter of St. Louis (1256). The long slender figures are set between arches with rose windows, as for example in *the trumpets of Jericho.* During this period the picture was subordinated to the scheme of the whole page.

From the fourteenth century, a very elegant type of illumination can be seen in the *Belleville breviary* of Jean Pucelle. At the end of the fourteenth century, the Flemish influence brought new life to the art of the illuminator. The most interesting manuscript of the early fifteenth century is the *trēs riches heures du due de Berry** in the Musée Condée at Chantilly. The Book of Hours derives its name from the regular hours of monastic prayer; but these expensive books were meant for the private use of people in the world. In addition to the prayers, a calendar was usually added, and tables to find the date of Easter. The calendar is the most interesting part of this Book of Hours : each month has a separate page ; above, the dates are written in a semicircle; below is a natural scene showing the country work during that particular month. For each background, the duke asked to have a painting of one of his royal castles, like the Louvre in Paris, the castles at Vincennes, Mont St. Michel, and others. It is simply the combination of a rural scene with a building behind it; but in reality these did not go together. These miniatures give us a fairly complete picture of the customs and costumes of the age.

In the fifteenth century, the miniaturists made exact and vivid pictures of nature and of society. At this time easel painting developed from manuscript illumination, and artists turned from the gouache medium of the illuminators to the use of oil. This development was most notable in Flanders.

# RENAISSANCE ART

# 9. ITALIAN ART

## GENERAL SURVEY

The art of the Renaissance (meaning rebirth i.e. a renewed interest in classical Greek and Roman culture) started in Italy, where admiration for the glorious past of the Roman empire never ceased, nor the desire to revive it. Since the invasion of the Goths broke up that empire, they were inclined to consider the products of northern Europe as barbarous, as we saw in the naming of Gothic art; and the period between the fall of the empire and the Renaissance was called the Middle Ages, meaning an insignificant time between two glorious periods.

The Renaissance movement started with what is known as humanism, or an admiration for ancient Greek and Roman literature. These books were now eagerly sought in the libraries of monasteries and cathedrals, where they had been preserved and copied during the Middle Ages. Many now also learned Greek. This literary movement was stimulated by the poet Petrarch (1304–1374). He also sawin the old Roman ruins the glory of Italy's past, and roused the interest of his fellow citizens in them; for in preceding ages, these old monuments were often used as stone quarries.

The economic and political conditions of Italy influenced the development of art. The country was wealthy, since it got the trade monopoly with the East when Byzantium declined; but it had no political unity. In the north of Italy were the duchies of Savoy and Milan. The cities of Florence, Venice, Genoa, and Siena were powerful republics. Most of central Italy formed the Papal States. In the south was the kingdom of Naples and Sicily. For centuries the country had suffered from foreign invasions and local rivalries. Sometimes rich powerful families overcame the republics. These often became patrons of art; and through a rivalry between them, each tried to get the best artists, art collections, and libraries. The most renowned were the Visconti and Sforza of Milan, the Gonzaga of Mantua, the Montefeltre of Urbino, the Malatesta of Rimini, the Este of Ferrara, but especially the Medici* of Florence, who were its leading bankers and rulers. Cosimo de' Medici was a remarkable man who successfully combined many political, financial, artistic and literary activities. He financed many famous buildings, and had the best artists to decorate them. His grandson, Lorenzo the Magnificent (1469–1492), favoured all the great talents of the Renaissance and tried to keep peace in Italy. During this period, artists began to assert their individuality. In contrast to medieval anonymity, individual artists now became more important.

The Italian names given to the late medieval or proto-Renaissance periods are: Dugento[1] (thirteenth century) and Trecento[2] (fourteenth century); to the early Renaissance time, Quatrocento[3] (fifteenth century), when art was centred in Florence; and to the High Renaissance, Cinquecento[4] (sixteenth century), when Rome was the centre of artistic activities. The seventeenth century, known as Seicento,[5] was the period of Baroque art. The origin of the word Baroque was probably the Portuguese word barocco, meaning an irregularly shaped pearl. Formerly the meaning was contemptuous, as it implied something over-ornate, peculiar, and of lavish extravagance—and even of bad taste. Baroque art is a natural outgrowth of the Renaissance classical styles, just as Hellenistic and Roman grew out of classical Greek art. The eighteenth century was dominated by the Rococo style. This century is called Settecento.[6]

## PROTO-RENAISSANCE
(Late Medieval)

### SCULPTURE

In the thirteenth and fourteenth centuries, sculpture flourished mainly in Pisa. Classical influence showed itself. It was introduced by Nicola Pisano (about 12060–1278), who was

Pronounce:
* med-ee-chy.
1 doo-gen-to.
2 tray-chen-to
3 kwat-tro-chen-to
4 chin-kway-chen-to
5 say-chen-to
6 set-tay-chen-to

trained in Apulia, southern Italy, where a strong classical revival was going on. He was famous for his pulpits.

Giovanni Pisano[1] (about 1250-1320), his son, shows much more dynamism. His statues were imbued with Gothic naturalism and linealism.

In the fourteenth century, sculptural activities started in Florence also. Another Pisano, Andrea[2] (1290–1348), was called to make a pair of bronze doors (*south doors*) for the *baptistery* in *Florence* with representations from the life of St. John the Baptist. He ingeniously divided the doors into 28 panels, framing his low reliefs with a Gothic decorative pattern. His compositions are simple, and their smoothly flowing lines harmonize admirably with the whole.

A native Florentine sculptor, Lorenzo Ghiberti[3] (1378–1455) produced the two other doors of this baptistery. For his first doors, (*north doors*) he used the same division into 28 panels and the geometric frames of Andrea Pisano. Twenty of them illustrate scenes from the New Testament and four represent doctors of the church.

But Ghiberti's masterpiece was the *eastern doors*. When Michelangelo first saw them, he exclaimed, 'They are fit to adorn the entrance to Paradise'; and from that time, the name *gates of Paradise* (Pl. 36.1) clung to them. They are also double doors, each containing in rectangular panels five scenes from the Old Testament. They are wonderfully naturalistic, and show Ghiberti's strong feeling for the picturesque. The figures are mostly in low relief, yet an effect of perspective has been cleverly given by moulding the figures in the foreground in higher relief, while the figures in the background flatten out gradually as they recede.

In his figure style, Ghiberti belongs to the Gothic. But he also belongs to the Renaissance, for it was he who discovered how to represent convincingly depth in space, to produce effects of far vistas.

## PAINTING

During medieval times Italian painting, under Byzantine influence, was conventional and stylized. Even Romanesque painting maintained this influence strongly. But during the thirteenth and fourteenth centuries the Gothic artists broke away from this two-dimensional stylization. They used the three-dimensional form and painted in a more naturalistic way, to express the new emotional content of religious art, resulting from the influence of Saint Francis of Assisi, who preached the love of God and His creation. It is he also who stimulated the beginnings of the vernacular tradition in Italian literature. These new trends in painting first appeared in Florence.

Giotto* di Bondone (1266–1336) was the first artist inspired by this spirit to break away from the traditional Byzantine art, and to display a changed attitude towards painting. He was born near Florence, and spent most of his life in that city. This Florentine was the real initiator of what was to become, a century later, Renaissance art, for he laid down the artistic principles and ideas which have guided painters since his time right up to modern times. Giotto was a pupil of Cimabue (c. 1240–1302), another Florentine, who also showed a new spirit in his work, but Giotto's naturalism probably came to him more from the realism displayed in the Roman mosaics of Cavallini, than from his master. Giotto attempted to depict convincingly human figures and actions, which were not only visually but also psychologically true to life; and he wished to represent form and space in three-dimensions on the flat canvas or wall. Naturally, he failed to solve these problems completely; but his achievements were striking considering the enormous step forward he had to take from the stylized and artificial Byzantine art. For almost a hundred years, no artist was able to improve on him. What Masaccio was able to achieve a century later was largely due to the beginnings made by Giotto, who had managed to give at least an impression of actuality, based upon what he himself saw, in direct contrast to the formal abstractions of the art of his own age.

In his religious paintings, Giotto gave his figures human emotions and dramatic force. We can see this exemplified in his twenty-eight great frescoes in the upper church in *Assisi,* which depict the *life of St. Francis.* However, some art scholars have attributed them to his disciples. But they are closely related to his other acknowledged frescoes, in their concentration on essentials rather than minor details, and in their monumental forms. His greatest work is in the *chapel of the Scrovegni* family (also called Arena chapel) in Padua. This consists of thirty-eight scenes from the life of Jesus and Mary. There are three rows of rectangular panels on the side walls, and a painting of the Last Judgment on the

Pronounce:
[1] jo-vanni pi-sa-no,
[2] un-dray-a pisano.
[3] lo-ren-tso ghee-bear-ty.
* jotto,

entrance wall. Personification of virtues and vices appear below the narrative scenes. These frescoes, following one after the other, are given a certain unity by means of the blue sky, similar in all. In the *lamentation* (Pl.36.2), the figures are composed in a monumental group round the dead Saviour. Deep sorrow is expressed by dramatic gestures and by the expressions on each face, especially on that of the virgin Mary, who bends over her Son. Even the angels in the sky reflect thiş human sadness. The composition is arranged on a diagonal line, emphasized by the long narrow rock. The *obsequies of St. Francis* (1320), in the *Bardi chapel* of the Santa Croce church, *Florence*, is one of a series of frescoes, again dealing with the life of St. Francis. The figures are here placed before a straight wall, as if in a stage setting. The composition is based on verticals and horizontals. The upward lines are formed on both sides by standing friars; whilst in the centre, the body of Francis lying in state, corresponds with and is emphasized by the horizontal line of the wall above. This strict geometrical pattern is relieved by the dramatic postures of the mourning friars who surround the dead saint. In this fresco the work is more mature and nearer to perfection than in his earlier paintings.

## EARLY RENAISSANCE

### ARCHITECTURE

The architects of the Early Renaissance in Florence, during the Quatrocento, were the first to turn their interest to Graeco-Roman architecture, and to apply the forms of antiquity to their buildings. The first to adopt classical Roman conceptions was Filippo Brunelleschi* (1377–1446), a Florentine architect and sculptor, who at the beginning of his career went to Rome with his friend Donatello. There he spent his time among the classical ruins (drawing ground plans, vaults, cornices and mouldings). After his return to Florence he was commissioned with the erection of the *dome of* the Gothic *cathedral* (Pl. 36.3), which had to be built over the crossing of the nave and the transept, and which became his greatest achievement. It was a gigantic work, the dome being 42¼ metres in diameter. It is not a true dome in the structural sense, but octagonal, with a double shell. Eight mighty ribs connect its sides, and the top is crowned by a lantern which rises to a height of 105 metres and dominates the whole city.

But it is with the building of the *foundling hospital* in Florence that Brunelleschi set a landmark for Early Renaissance architecture. The façade, fronting the square is faced with an arcade supported by fine graceful Corinthian columns which carry the upper floor. In the spandrels (spaces between the arches and the angles of the outer frame) are Andrea della Robbia's famous terracotta bambini (little children, representing those who were given refuge in the foundling hospital).

In the *Pazzi chapel* (Pl. 37.1), a small building in the cloisters of the church of Santa Croce, Florence, Brunelleschi erected a dome over the square interior. On the façade of the vestibule, he applied all the classical motifs he could. Six Corinthian columns carry a horizontal entablature, on which small twin Corinthian pilasters repeat their vertical uplift in a quicker rhythm, according to the classical balance of horizontals and verticals. Classical mouldings are also amply used.

The palaces were the most remarkable architectural type of the Quatrocento in Florence. The merchant families, who depended mainly on cloth trade, united in their palaces office and warehouse on the ground floor, with living quarters on the first and second floors. Because of periodic revolts and insecurity, these buildings had to be semi-fortified. The walls on the street were built of heavy blocks of stone with few doors. The ground floor, being for storage, had small mezzanine openings, but on the first and second floors there were rows of windows. These palaces, with usually three storeys, had an open courtyard inside surrounded on the ground floor with an arcade carried on columns, the vaults of which had to support the rooms of the second and third floors.

One of the typical examples is the *Medici Riccardi palace* (Fig. 448) built by Michelozzo** (1396–1472) for Cosimo de'Medici; and Lorenzo the Magnificent also kept his brilliant court here. It still bears on one corner the coat of arms of the Medici, but it is now named after the Riccardi, who later inhabited it. The cortile, with its colonnade, is reminiscent of the Greek or Roman villas, which had the peristyle inside and were closed from outside. From the courtyard, a grand staircase led to the piano nobile (the floor of the noble apartments). The façade is built of huge blocks of stone. The strong unbroken mouldings divide it into three storeys. On the ground floor, the outer surface of the stone was left in its natural roughness. This is called rusti-

* Pronounce: fee-lip-po broo-nel-les-kee

** mee-ke-lozzo.

cation. On the next floor, the front of the stone is dressed, but the joints are strongly bevelled.

Fig. 448. Medici Riccardi palace, detail, Florence.

The top floor is made with ashlar walling, i.e., the dressed stones join, forming a smooth surface. The ground floor has big arched doorways; most of them were later transformed into windows. The second and third floor windows, without base, rest on the horizontal moulding. They are twin windows, surmounted by an arch, reminiscent of the Gothic traceried windows. They do not project beyond the wall, but are level with its surface. The whole façade is crowned with a bold cornice, one-tenth of the height of the building, and projecting almost 2½ metres. It is held up by a row of consoles (brackets), and decorated with classical mouldings (dentils, egg and dart, and acanthus leaves).

The *Pitti palace*, now one of the famous picture galleries of Florence, was probably built after the plans of Brunelleschi, but is less successful than the Palazzo Medici. The *Strozzi palace* (Florence) built in 1490 by Benedetto da Maiano and Cronaca, is one of the noblest and most refined palaces of the Quatrocento. The *Rucellai palace*, (Fig. 449) (Florence) by Leon Battista Alberti (1404–1472), was made more ornate with classical decoration. Alberti, inspired by the superimposed orders (Doric, Ionic, Corinthian) on the Colosseum, applied them the first time on a palace façade in the form of pilasters between the windows.

He also built two famous churches. The design of the façade of the church of *San Francesco at Rimini* (Fig. 450) was inspired by the Roman triumphal arches, and *Sant" Andrea at Mantua* (Fig. 451) by the basilica of Constantine and other Roman buildings. The latter is important because it became the prototype of many Renaissance churches. Leon Battista Alberti

Fig. 449. Rucellai palace, detail, Florence

Fig. 450. Church of San Francesco, Rimini.

was a universal genius like his fellow-Florentine, Leonardo da Vinci: he was a humanist scholar, painter, sculptor, and especially a theoretician and writer, as well as an architect. He wrote treatises on architecture, sculpture and painting.

## SCULPTURE

The greatest of the Quattrocento sculptors was Donatello (1386–1466), whose statues of saints and exquisite representations of youth show a keen appreciation of character. Donatello was full of the Renaissance spirit of eager search for

Fig. 451. Church of Sant' Andrea, Mantua.

novel ways of expressing new ideas. With Brunelleschi, he had studied the classic remains in Rome. He learnt from them to make observation of nature the basis of his work. The vivid naturalism that characterizes his portraits is seen in his early work, *St, George* (Pl. 37.2), shown as a young knight, his slim figure alive with ardent vitality. The head is slightly turned, and there is a corresponding swing in the body towards the direction in which he is gazing with puckered brow. The texture of the cloak, knotted below the shoulder, and its naturalistic folds, contrast with the rigidity of the armour. The contour of the statue is simplified by the shield, on which rest the sensitive fingertips of the youthful saint; and the flowing cloak stresses the rhythm which sweeps through the whole figure. As Vasari said, 'life seems to move within the stone.'

On the campanile of the cathedral of *Florence* stand the figures of four prophets. The first of these is that of *Habacuc* (sometimes known by the nickname *Zuccone*) (Pl. 37.3). Donatello's understanding of character is seen, for the posture and sad eyes of the old man reflect his sorrow at human cruelty, yet the strongly-marked features of the ascetic face and the general attitude show the hidden strength and vitality that came from his implicit trust in God's unlimited goodness and power. The shape of the throat, right arm and shoulder shows a careful study of the human figure for the purpose of expressing character. A heavy mantle covers the rest of the body, falling in deep folds. The general attitude of the statue, though passive and meditative, gives the impression of concealed dynamism and strength.

The *Gattamelata* (Pl. 37.4) is another fine work by Donatello. It is an enormous bronze statue of a mounted rider, standing on a high oval base, in the square of the basilica of St. Antonio in *Padua,* Gattamelata (honeyed cat) was the nickname given to the rider, General Erasmo di Narni. Here again the artist's gift for depicting character is evident. He portrays a commanding personality, power mingled with diplomatic cunning; the suspicious eyes seem capable of piercing through all subterfuges of the enemy, and his whole appearance gives the impression that his victories are won more by ruse than by open battle.

Besides statues in the round, Donatello carved many low-reliefs. A sense of depth and perspective is given by the fact that the figures in the background become smaller and flatter as they recede.

*Herod's feast*, a bronze relief on the baptismal font in *Siena* cathedral, represents the tragic moment when the head of John the Baptist was brought to Herod on a plate, at the request of Salome. Having pleased the king by her dancing, she was promised whatever she desired. At the instigation of her mother Herodias, who hated John for having condemned her unlawful relation ship with Herod, Salome asked for the head of the prophet. The architectural background of this bronze relief is particularly interesting, because of the illusion of depth achieved by arcades, which suggest the existence of an inner hall.

The *mule before the Host* (Pl. 37.5) a bronze relief on the altar of Sant' Antonio in *Padua*, is a later work. The scene has an architectural background, inspired by the ruins of the basilica of Constantine in Rome. The arches divide the nave into three compartments. The movement of the crowd seems to press towards the centre on both sides, but is contained within the side arches, which permit the miracle in the centre to stand out: St. Antony is shown holding the Host, and the mule bends its knees in reverence, ignoring the oats men offer it.

The *cantoria* (Pl. 38.1) is the railing of one of the singing galleries of *Florence* cathedral.

Early dismantled, it is now preserved in the museum of the cathedral. It has a frieze of running and dancing children behind a series of twin columns. Donatello's understanding of children's physiognomy and their grouping in animated movement is remarkable.

The *annunciation* (Pl. 38.2), in the church of Santa Croce in *Florence*, is an early high relief in marble. It is a beautiful work, exquisitely set off in a sculptured framework; and is a typical production of the Florentine Quatrocento. It represents the invitation sent by God to the virgin Mary, through His angelic messenger, to cooperate in giving a human nature to His Eternal Word, to fulfil His promise of a Saviour, who would restore to mankind the true understanding of His essential Goodness and loving care even for the least. The artist tries to show the uncertainty of the pure and humble Mary, who did not know what to make of this great honour shown her, nor how to reconcile it with her resolution of giving herself totally to God, both body and soul, until the angel enlightened her about the entirely spiritual nature of this mystery of God's loving condescension. The messenger's face reflects the respect he has for one so intimately united to God. Delicate Renaissance decorations give a pleasing background and frame for this admirable group. The relief appears to be touched with colour, because delicate and varying shades of gold have been used to bring out the play of light and shade.

Besides Donatello, Luca della Robbia (1400–1482) is one of the most outstanding sculptors of the Quatrocento. He first worked in marble. His *cantoria,* the second singing gallery of Florence cathedral, represents, in relief work, groups of singers divided into panels. The work was ordered to pair Donatello's sculpture. Now both are in the cathedral museum. Luca's carvings are finer and more graceful, but they do not convey the bold rhythmic movement of Donatello's work.

Luca's great popularity lies in his glazed terra-cotta works which he used first. Terra-cotta was not costly and could be coloured. The intense blues, yellows, greens, purples and ivory whites made his works famous. A good example is the *Virgin adoring the infant Jesus* (Pl. 38.3) in the Philadelphia Museum of art. Luca's work was continued by his nephew Andrea della Robbia and his sons.

The best work of Andrea del Verrocchio* (1435–1488) is his *equestrian statue* of the Florentine prince, general *Colleoni* (Pl. 38.4) in *Venice* The figure is an interesting contrast to the Gattamelata, whose easy position in the saddle and calm bearing show quiet power. Colleoni is seated in a stiff, tense attitude, half-rising from the saddle, while his feet press hard on the stirrups. The impression is one of impetuous, violent energy, increased by the sharp turn of the body, the hard face and penetrating eyes, and by the angularity of the whole composition. Andrea Verrocchio was also a painter, and master of Leonardo da Vinci.

## PAINTING

Masaccio** (c. 1401–1428), whose full name was Tommaso di Giovanni di Simone Guidi, was the most important painter of the early Quatrocento. He spent the greatest part of his short life in Florence, visited Rome, and probably died there at the age of twenty-seven. His achievements during such a short space of time were almost incredible. At a time when other painters were still trying to discover how to represent three-dimensional space on a flat surface, Masaccio solved the problem. He managed to represent three-dimensional figures, as if really standing in space, and correctly related to the background. Light and shade were the means he used to model them. Thus he improved upon Giotto, and developed his monumental use of space and form.

All this wonderful achievement of Masaccio can be seen today only in a few works, for we have little more than the frescoes in the Brancacci chapel in the church of Santa Maria del Carmine in Florence. These include the *expulsion from Eden*, a dramatic scene full of vitality, and episodes from St. Peter's life : *St. Peter healing the lame man by his shadow, St. Peter baptizing, the distribution of alms, the cure of the ruler's son*; and especially the *tribute money* (Pl. 38.5). In the centre of this last fresco, the disciples are shown gathered around the Saviour. A tax-collector, standing in the foreground with his back to the spectators, has asked for his due. Jesus works a miracle to show the need of giving good example by complying with just laws. He tells Peter to go and fetch the required coin from the mouth of a fish. On the left he is shown finding the money as directed, whilst on the right he gives it to the tax-collector. The three scenes together form a continuous narrative, but the central group attracts the eye with its grandeur. The people look real, men of flesh and blood.

* Pronounce : un-dray-a del verrokio.

** Pronounce : ma-za-t'cho.

Their anatomy is correct. There are no needless details. The light coming from the right models them clearly: they appear large and rounded. Though the heads are all on the same level, Jesus has been made to stand out as the centre of the group. Individual figures, especially the tax-collector, show life and energy. For, as Vasari said,' Masaccio made his figures stand upon their feet.' On the whole they convey a sculptural effect. The landscape in the background gives an impression of deep space, which is accentuated by the architecture on the right. Unity between the foreground and the distance is attained by a consistent fading away of light and colour, which shows that Masaccio had already a faint idea of the existence of aerial perspective.

In the church of S. Maria Novella in Florence, Masaccio painted what is considered to be the greatest monumental fresco of the Quatrocento, the *Holy Trinity*. For the representation of the Holy Trinity, he adopts the traditional method of using symbols to express spiritual realities, the only possible way in visual arts. It is the mystery of three divine Persons united in the divine Nature of the One True God, the intimacy of God's inner life of infinite Thought and infinite Love. In Masaccio's fresco, God the Father is symbolized by the figure of a venerable old man, since the human figure is the most noble in the world ; and the Holy Spirit appears in the form of a dove, a reference to the scene of Christ's baptism in the Jordan. Christ, the second Person of the Holy Trinity, incarnate, is shown hanging on the Cross. Below this stands Mary, indicating ' the Mystery ' with a gesture ; and on the opposite side stands St. John. The two donors are seen kneeling to the extreme right and left of the picture. What is extraordinary about this painting is that Masaccio employed a characteristic piece of Renaissance architecture as a setting. This was a sensational innovation in his time. The Holy Trinity is represented in a chapel roofed with a coffered barrel vault which reflects Brunelleschi's perspective theory.

Although Masaccio's works are few in number, they had a great influence on the development of Renaissance art. Inspired by his innovations and led by the eager spirit of inquiry at the time, a group of painters in Florence tried to find scientific solutions for ever more convincing representations in art. Studies in anatomy were intensified to get a better knowledge of bodily structure. To give a greater impression of volume or three-dimensions, the effects of light and shade were investigated further. To relate the figures more correctly to space, the laws of perspective were carefully studied.

Some of the so-called scientific group of painters were Paolo Uccello* (1397–1475), Andrea del Castagno (1421–1457), Alesso Baldovinetti (1425–1499), Antonio Pollaiuolo** (1432–1498), Andrea del Verrocchio (1435–1488), and especially Piero della Francesca*** (1415–1492), of Umbrian origin but a Florentine in his artistic training.

Contemporary with Masaccio was the artist Fra Angelico, or Fra Giovanni da Fiesole (1387–1455), who represented another trend of Quatrocento art, one that was still impregnated with the spirituality inherited from the Gothic tradition, though he was well aware of the innovation brought into art by Masaccio, and into architecture by Michelozzo. He was born in the city of Vecchio, and called Guido di Pietro. He changed his name to Giovanni when he became a Dominican friar in Fiesole. But he is best known as Fra Angelico, a name given to him because of his pure, saintly life. His art reflects his contemplative soul. One of his sayings was, 'To be able to paint well, one must pray well.' His subjects were always religious. He had probably learnt to paint before entering the monastery, though we know nothing of his master. His technique is excellent, for his altarpieces are still well preserved. Their charm lies chiefly in the colouring.

When Fra Angelico was exiled with the other Dominicans of Fiesole, he went to Foligno near Assisi. There he came into contact with Giotto's works ; and amidst the lovely hills of Umbria, he acquired his love for nature, which was to figure so largely (in an idealized manner) in the backgrounds of his paintings. In 1418 the Dominicans returned to Fiesole, where Fra Angelico painted several altarpieces. In these, we already see the artist's love of light and brilliant colours, with gold dominating ; and for spirituality in the facial expressions, which was to become one of his most characteristic traits.

Of these altarpieces, the *crowning of the Virgin* (Pl. 39.1) in the convent of San Marco in Florence, is one of his most famous pictures. It is in tempera, painted on wood, with colours well preserved. This is a human, material representation of a great spiritual reality. Scripture often speaks of the eternal reward as a crowning, though of course the real reward is life with God, infinite Truth, Goodness and Beauty, which it is impossible to picture. Since God chose the virgin Mary to be the mother of Jesus, the Son of God, her dignity is much greater than that of any

* Pronounce : pawlo oo-chello. ** untohnio po-lie-you-ohlo. *** pee-airo della frahn-ches-kah.

other creature, and hence this picture represents the Saviour crowning his mother. Both are seated on clouds, encircled with golden rays, and surrounded by angels and saints who form a descending semicircle on both sides. Some of the angels hold long slender trumpets. The colouring is characteristic of Fra Angelico: lovely light pinks, greens, reds and blues, which stand out against the golden background.

In 1436, Cosimo de' Medici gave the Dominicans of Fiesole the old convent of San Marco in Florence. Michelozzo was the architect charged to restore the building; while Fra Angelico, with the help of others, painted frescoes in the chapter house, cloisters and cells. His best work is to be found among these wall-paintings.

In one of the cells the *annunciation* is represented : Mary, kneeling in a humble attitude, receives the angel's message; the Dominican, St. Peter the Martyr, appears behind some columns, lost in ecstasy as he contemplates the scene. The composition and background are simple, with no brilliant colours : pale pink, white, cream, pale mauve, with only the monk's mantle in black—as if Fra Angelico wanted to use the least of this material world to express spiritual realities.

The *crowning of the virgin Mary* (Pl. 39.2 ), a wall-painting in another cell, tries to convey a glimpse of heaven. The Saviour and his mother are shown seated on a cloud, symbolic of mystery. Both are painted only in white and cream, to indicate purity and holiness. Mary bows humbly to her divine Son, who crowns her in turn. A row of saints surrounds them in a half circle.

The *annunciation* (Pl. 39.3 ) (on the corridor wall just in front of the steps leading up to this floor) shows how Fra Angelico was influenced by the innovations then sweeping Florence. The gold backgrounds, characteristic of his altarpieces, are now replaced by a landscape. Before the annunciation scene, set on a verandah with Renaissance arcading and columns, there is a delightful garden in vivid colours, with the freshness of the flowers, grass and trees adding to the exquisite delicacy of the composition.

Fra Angelico was called to Rome by the Pope in 1445, to decorate two chapels, one of which is still standing, that of Nicholas V, with its frescoes from the lives of Sts. Stephen and Lawrence. These compositions show his advanced knowledge of Renaissance art, yet the spirituality of his painting remains unchanged. He died in Rome, and was buried in the Dominican church Santa Maria Sopra Minerva. Nicholas V himself composed his epitaph.

The fusion of medieval with Renaissance forms is also seen in the works of Fra Filippo Lippi (about 1406–1469), and was continued by Filippino Lippi (about 1457–1504), Benozzo Gozzoli (1420–1497), and Domenico Ghirlandaio* (1449–1494).

Another famous painter of the Quatrocento was Botticelli** (1444–1510), whose full name was Alessandro di Mariano Filipepi, a Florentine. He was first apprenticed as a goldsmith, but later studied under Filippo Lippi, whose influence led him to adopt the ideal manner of Fra Angelico in his paintings. The naturalism of Masaccio also affected his work. This combination of idealism and naturalism was one of his greatest qualities as a painter, and the chief reason for his great influence on other artists. During the year 1481–1482 he worked in Rome; but from 1483 to 1500 he was employed by the Medicis and other important families in Florence. Very careless about money, he lived mostly in poor circumstances. Although personally never inclined towards frivolity, his paintings, at times, reflect the worldliness and superficiality of his age ; but the influence of Savonarola brought him back to a more serious frame of mind, and this is also reflected in his work.

It is very difficult to place Botticelli's paintings in any chronological order, for he never dated or signed them. But they may be loosely classified as those dealing with religious subjects and those that depict mythological and other scenes. Of the former, we have his great frescoes on Biblical subjects in the Sistine chapel. In 1481 Pope Sixtus IV gathered together a group of painters to decorate this new chapel with scenes from the life of Moses and of Christ, two of which were painted by Botticelli.

But his Madonnas are the most charming and popular of his religious pictures. The facial expression is their most striking aspect. The look of the infant Saviour's face is thoughtful and sweetly winning. The mother's look shows tenderness mingled with reverence, and a certain sadness at the knowdedge of coming sorrow'. In the *magnificat* (Pl. 40.1) (Uffizi Gallery, Florence), the child Jesus, sitting on his mother's knees, seems to guide her hands as she writes the words of the Magnificat, her joyful song of praise and gratitude to God. Angels surround them, one supporting the book in which she writes, the other two holding up a crown. Like many of his

* Pronounce: doh-men-ee-co geer-lun-die-yo.

** Pronounce : botty-chelly

Madonnas, this is a circular picture, known as tondo (round). Another of these, also in the Uffizi Gallery, is called the *Madonna with the pomegranate.* Here again the main figures are surrounded by angels. A famous tondo in Berlin is the *Madonna enthroned.* Botticelli's mythological and allegorical paintings include the *birth of Venus* (Pl. 40.2 ) (Uffizi Gallery, Florence), based on a poem of the period, which depicts the classical myth of Venus being born at sea and then wafted in a shell towards the shores of Cyprus. His *Springtime* (Pl. 40.3 ), or *Primavera* (Uffizi Gallery, Florence), is an allegory set in an orange and olive grove, with a lawn in front, covered with flowers of more than thirty-five different types, which are painted with the greatest exactitude. Venus is in the centre of a group ; whilst Zephyr, in the trees, is driving Spring forward. *A* flying cupid shoots arrows, as Flora scatters flowers before Spring. To the right of Venus are the three Graces dancing; Mercury leads the whole procession, driving away with his right hand the remaining shades of winter.

The *calumny* (Uffizi Gallery, Florence), is an attempt to reconstruct a lost picture of the Greek artist Appelles, with the help of classical literature. It shows the victim of envy and calumny in the company of deceit and treachery, being brought before a judge. Suspicion and ignorance are seen whispering in the ass's ears. Truth, to the left of the picture, protests as she appeals to the equity of divine justice, in contrast with the futility of man's ; she is seen only by remorse, as the others are too engrossed in their fury. The setting is an antique Roman hall of justice. The outstanding qualities of this picture are grace and dignity.

The ninety *illustrations* of Botticelli, which he designed *for Dante's Divina Commedia*, are another triumph for the artist. Many of these are mere sketches, but they show once again Botticelli's interest in the contemplative expressions of human faces and in the dramatic aspect of human action. His sensitive feeling for line is also seen in the execution of these drawings.

Botticelli's eariy employment as a goldsmith seems to have left its imprint on his artistic work. As a colourist he is often fanciful. He uses gold to heighten the lights on foliage, texture, and even hair, which often seems stiff like golden threads. He is meticulous in his attention to details: embroidery and other decorations are delicately and carefully depicted. The outlines are stiff, especially in his later phase. His interest in linear rhythm is one of the outstanding traits in his works.

Among the north Italian painters of the Quattrocento, Andrea Mantegna* (1431–1506) was certainly the greatest. Born at Isola di Carturo between Vincenza and Padua, he was adopted in early youth by Francesco Squarcione, a painter whose greatest talent lay in an excellent ability to organize. His workshop was in Padua, an old Roman colony with numerous archaeological remains and a university. At that time it was a centre of classical learning, which so captivated Mantegna that the archaeological setting of his pictures are even more correct than those of the Florentine painters.

His major works were the six frescoes in the apse of the Ovetari chapel of the church of the Eremitani at Padua (1449–1454), which he painted together with two other disciples of Squarcione. They represented *stories* of the *apostle St. James the Elder* and *St. Christopher.* Unfortunately, during the Second World War, a bomb destroyed them almost entirely. Photographic reproductions show how scrupulously Mantegna tried to recreate the classic style. Antique buildings, costumes, the armour of soldiers and the human form are accurately reproduced. He had a correct feeling for perspective and foreshortening. These frescoes are equal in importance to those of Masaccio in the Brancacci chapel of the church Santa Maria del Carmine at Florence. Original though he was, he received influences from many sides: that of Florence through Fra Filippo Lippi and Paolo Uccello; but especially from Donatello, who worked a long time in Padua on his equestrian statue, the Gattamelata. He also received Venetian inspiration through Jacopo Bellini, whose daughter Nicolosia he married in 1454. In 1456 he left Squarcione, and two years later entered the service of Lodovico Gonzaga, whose ducal court was at Mantua. He served him for more than 40 years, until his death. Here he not only got ample scope for his artistic talent, but received the title of nobleman, and became a noted humanist and eminent scholar of antique art. He also became a friend of the Florentine architect Leon Battista Alberti, who was called to Mantua to build the church of Sant' Andrea.

His two most famous series of works (1468–1474) at *Mantua* were the frescoes on the wall and ceiling of the nuptial chamber (*camera degli sposi*) of the duke's residence at Mantua ; and the cartoons, called Triumphs of Julius Caesar (now in the British Royal Collection at Hampton Court), originally made for theatre decorations

* Pronounce : mun-tay-nya.

in the Mantua palace. The frescoes around the walls of the camera degli sposi are the first efforts at illusionistic painting. Though the room is surrounded by walls, the frescoes give the on looker the impression that he is in an open loggia or roofed gallery with columns instead of walls. The centre of the *ceiling* (Pl. 40.4), which opens out to the sky, looks like the oculus of the Pantheon. Reality and painting mingle. For instance, the actual capitals seem to rest on painted pilasters, and between these pilasters is painted the open sky, and curtains which seem to he fixed on rods. The ends of these curtains seem to fall over the doors, which are real. The best-known part of this fresco is the group of Lodovico Gonzaga, his wife, and members of his family—some twenty persons in all. But the most astonishing thing is the ceiling: with a sure grasp of perspective, Mantegna painted a balustrade with figures, with correct foreshortening, and a sky which seems to open above it. Today these frescoes no longer make such an impression on us, because during the Baroque age, in the seventeenth century, this device was constantly used, but at the time of Mantegna, however, it was new and sensational.

Mantegna had a great influence in north Italy especially in Venice, and even outside. We know that the German painter Albrecht Dürer came to Italy to study Mantegna's work.

Venice was always famous for its painting. The city was in close contact with the East during this period; and her own romantic site, which cut her off somewhat from the rest of Italy helped to shape the Venetian type of painting. It was characterized by love of colour and gaiety. Venetians loved pleasure, fine clothes, and social gatherings. All this finds expression in their art, which retained Byzantine and Gothic elements later than Florence. However, it did receive certain strong influences from other Italian cities, especially Florence; though it kept its own Venetian character in essentials. Oil painting, invented by the early Flemish painters, was introduced, but at first only to give surface lustre to paintings in tempera (pigment mixed with white of egg).

Jacopo Bellini (d. 1470) was the first to introduce a new spirit into Venetian painting. Joy in nature and a fanciful imagination are apparent in his drawings. He had obviously been influenced by the naturalistic movement and the growing interest in antiquity.

His son, Giovanni Bellini (c. 1430–1516) helped to create the typically colourful effects and romantic feelings of the art of his native city. His work represents all phases of this art, from the early style to the later more finished one. His best-known work is perhaps his *Madonna* (1488), in the *church of the, Frari, Venice*. The Madonna sits on a high throne in the apse of a church, with two saints standing and facing her from either side. This picture represents the splendour of Venetian painting by its rich harmonious colours, use of strong chiaroscuro, and depiction of expensive and sumptuous brocades and textures.

## HIGH RENAISSANCE

### ARCHITECTURE

In the Cinquecento or sixteenth century, the centre of building activity changed from Florence to Rome, where a famous group of architects (including Bramante, Raphael, Antonio da Sangallo, and Michelangelo) worked mainly for the papal court, but for the Roman nobles also. Here the building of palaces continued. A typical palace exemplifying the High Renaissance style is the *Farnese palace* (Fig. 452). Antonio

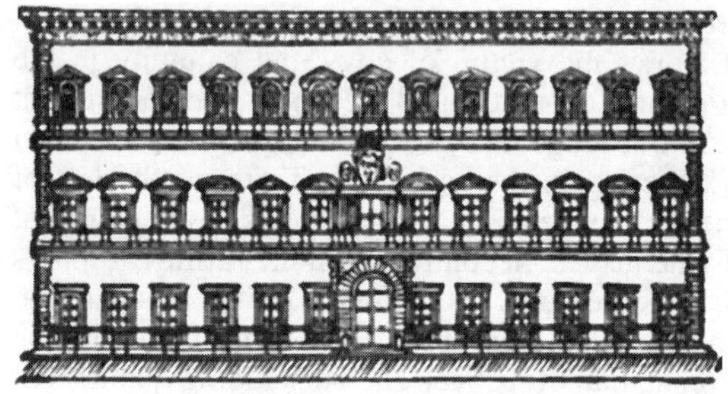

Fig. 452. Farnese palace, Rome.

da Sangallo and Giacomo della Porta worked on it; but what is most important to remember is that Michelangelo designed the cornice. It has three storeys, like the Florentine palaces. The walls are smooth, but the corners are framed by rusticated quoins on both sides, and by a heavy cornice on top. The centre is accentuated by a rusticated arch doorway, with a balcony above and the coat-of-arms of the Farnese family. This framing of the sides and accentuating of the centre is a step forward in palace building, not to be found in the Florentine palaces. The windows stand out in relief and are no longer flush with the walls. Each window is framed by two columns, and an entablature with a pediment. However, on the ground floor they have no pediments. On the first storey, or piano nobile, triangular and curved pediments alternate;

whilst the top storey has triangular ones only. The inner court is in the typicai Renaissance style, and has super-imposed columns : Doric on the ground floor, Ionic on the second floor, and Corinthian pillars on the third floor.

A more eiaborate style of palace architecture was evolved by Bramante. Raphael (architect as well as painter) continued this style with some changes. All these features were eagerly taken over by the Venetians.

Donato Bramante (1444–1514) worked in Rome during the earlier years of the High Renaissance. Admiring the circular temples of classical Rome, he built a small round church, the *tempietto di San Pietro*, not far from the Vatican. It is covered by a dome resting on a tall drum and surrounded by a colonnade. This little temple had a far-reaching influence on Renaissance architecture and contained in germ Bramante's grandiose idea for the rebuilding of St. Peter's. Bramante's influence on the history of classical revival in Rome can be compared to that of Leon Battista Alberti at Florence.

The greatest achievement of church architecture during the High Renaissance was *St. Peter's basilica* in *Rome* (Pl. 40. 5; Fig. 453). The emperor Constantine had erected the first basilica over the tomb of St. Peter, following the model employed in Early Christian churches. Throughout the Middle Ages, this edifice was a centre of Christian life. But the venerable building seemed ready to collapse, and plans were formed to erect a new one. Juiius II (1503–1513) decided to replace it with the most splendid church in Christendom. The present basilica dates from the sixteenth century. At least ten architects worked on the plans and construction during a period of a hundred and twenty years. In 1546 Michelangelo was made architect, and at the time of his death in 1564, he had completed the building as far as the top of the drum. The dome was finished according to his drawings. Between 1606 and 1626, the nave was lengthened and the façade built; in 1656–63 the colonnades were added. The present dimensions are: interior length 187½ metres; height of dome to summit of cross about 133 metres; and its diameter 42 metres.

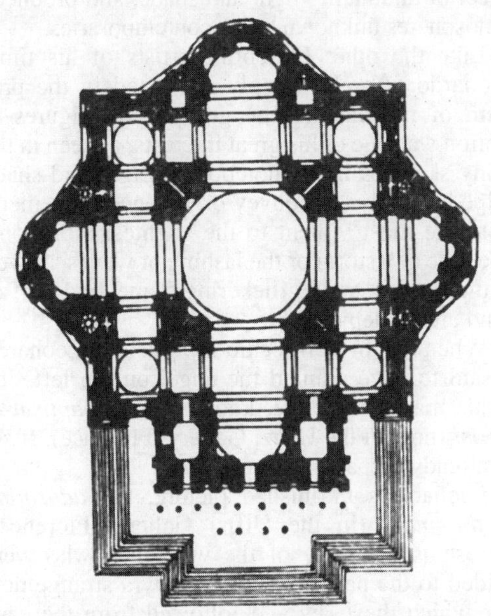

Fig. 453. Michelangelo's plan for St. Peter's basilica, Rome.

The central building roofed with a dome was the Renaissance ideal. Domes had been built centuries earlier. The Pantheon and the Hagia Sophia, as we saw, were very effective from within, but rather inconspicuous from the exterior. Brunelleschi's dome in Florence made a wonderful exterior impression, dominating the whole city; but the interior had little effect, because the long nave had to be traversed before one was able to see the interior of the dome. In St. Peter's, Bramante who designed the first plan, as well as Michelangelo at a later date, wished to create a perfect central building in the form of a Greek cross crowned with a dome, of which both the exterior and interior were equally effective. A later addition of a long nave altered their plans. But the original beauty of the exterior can stili be seen from the back of the basilica.

The whole structure is a skilful unification of geometric volumes: cube (the body of the basilica), cylinder (the drum of the dome) and a half-sphere (the dome). The body of the building is broken by pilasters, cornices and windows. Throughout the whole of the great structure we feel the rising movement, balanced by the restraint of the horizontal. The pilasters furnish the vertical lines, halted by the horizontal row of carved capitals, and especially the deep shadow cast by the cornice. Above the latter, the pilasters continue the vertical lines and with the curves of the apses lead directly into the base of the drum. Here columns, grouped in pairs, and projecting far out, catch the light and cast deep shadows, setting up a rhythm around the base. At the same time, their vertical lines lead to the curvea ribs of the dome, which rise uninterrupted up to the lantern. Here the motif of the double columns is repeated on a smaller scale, leading up to the terminating ball and the cross.

## SCULPTURE AND PAINTING

The many-sidedness of the Renaissance artists make it difficult at times to separate the different branches of art.

Three geniuses stand out in the High Renaissance: Leonardo da Vinci, Michelangelo and Raphael. Each of them means a culmination in his own art.

Leonardo da Vinci* (1452–1519), although he lived the greater part of his long and active life during the fifteenth century, is considered to be the first painter of the High Renaissance, because he gave an entirely new vision in his paintings.

He was born at Vinci, between Florence and Pisa. His father, a notary, perceiving his son's aptitudes, sent him in 1470 to Verrocchio's bottega or workshop in Florence. He became a sculptor, architect, engineer, scientist, musician, but he was above all a painter. The myriadmindedness of the Renaissance is personified in him. In a letter to the Duke of Milan, Lodovico Sforza, to whom he offered his services, he listed his various abilities : he could build bridges and canals, works of military engineering and engines of war, and he was unrivalled in the arts. From his notebook of five thousand pages, illustrated with sketches, we know that his interests were unlimited. His intellectual curiosity drove him to all manner of experiments; and his notes included references to painting, sculpture, architecture; mathematics, hydraulics and military engineering; botany, zoology, all kinds of physical and mechanical sciences; Latin and Italian grammar; the structural, emotional and intellectual aspects of man; and finally poetry and music. Many of his scientific observations were well ahead of his time. His contemporaries never knew of these, for his notebook was written in a secret code, the key of which was not discovered until long after. In his treatise on painting, when protesting against specialization in art, he wrote: 'Do you not see how many and how varied are the actions which are performed by men alone ? Do you not see how many different kinds of animals there are and also of trees and plants and flowers? What variety of hilly and level places, of springs, rivers, cities, public and private buildings; of instruments fitted for man's use, of diverse costumes, ornaments and arts?'

Leonardo's aim in painting was to portray not only the physical appearance of man, but also the spiritual aspect. He also wrote in his notes: 'A good painter has two chief objects to paint: man and the intention of his soul. The former is easy, the latter is hard, for it must be expressed by gestures and movements of the limbs.' He was always concerned with human values, with the emotional and intellectual life of man; and his great desire was to express the deepest passions of the soul. He had very subtle aesthetic sensibility, and a special love for grace and dignity.

His use of light and shade, or chiaroscuro as it was called in Italian, was one of the most striking features in his art. He believed that modelling with light and shade was the very heart of painting. Michelangelo and other artists also used chiaroscuro, but with the idea of obtaining a greater sculptural effect by the prevalence of light over shadow; whereas, for Leonardo, light and shade were means to create the effects of atmosphere as seen in twilight or mist. A veiled, diffused light bathed everything in his pictures, the background as well as the features of the faces. He once wrote: 'Towards evening or in bad weather, I have noticed the features of men and women in the streets, and remarked what grace and softness can be seen thereon.' And so he used washed outlines and smoky shadows to soften the facial features. This method of painting was called sfumato (smoke or vapour). Thus he achieved the effect of undulating light and shade, and produced atmospheres unknown to his contemporaries.

Like the other Florentine artists of his time, Leonardo was also deeply interested in the problem of movement. The grouping of figures in motion was one of his great interests, as seen in the many sketches in his notebooks. Light and shade helped him also to convey or enhance movement, from the most violent to the slightest vibrations. The rage of a storm or the lashing of waves, as well as the fleeting smile, flickering flame, and puff of wind are all depicted.

When still in Verrocchio's workshop, Leonardo is said to have painted the angel on the left side of his master's picture, known as *the baptism of Christ* (now in the Uffizi Gallery, Florence). If so, he already surpassed Verrocchio.

Leonardo's unfinished picture, the *adoration of the magi* (in the Uffizi Gallery, Florence), represents the story of the wise men who were guided to the new-horn Saviour by a strange new star which they saw and followed from the east. The Jewish people had been carried off as war

* Pronounce : lay-o-nardo dah vin-chy.

prisoners by the Assyrians and Babylonians; and their prophecies of a redeemer-king, who would be born of the Jewish race, were spread among the peoples of the Orient. This is shown by the question they asked of the Jewish ruler, Herod: 'Where is he that is born king of the Jews?', and by their presents of gold, incense and myrrh which symbolized the kingship, divinity and humanity of the Saviour. From the word magi, we gather that they were probably Medes, Persians or Parthians.

In the picture, the child Jesus sits on the lap of his mother, who regards him tenderly as he holds out his little hand to accept the gift offered by the kneeling figure on the right. The other two bow in adoration at the left. There is both psychological and formal unity in the group of figures in the centre foreground, for the attention of all is so clearly fixed on the Madonna and Child. The background is filled with half-finished architecture, horse riders and other halfformed shapes, indicating Leonardo's love of experiment, and the unlimited capacity of his imagination. Horsemen, trees, ruined buildings and landscapes are fantastically painted in an unearthly, yet strangely beautiful combination. The central tree, however, helps to create unity between this background and the figures in front. There is a symmetrical triangular basis in the construction of the Madonna and the figures, about her. Around this triangular composition is a great variety of curved shapes pressing towards the centre. The whole picture is full of suggestiveness, and it is one of the most extraordinary works of Leonardo.

The picture, the *Virgin of the rocks* (Pl. 40.6) (at the Louvre, Paris), shows the three interesting features of Leonardo's work: the mysterious background, his theory of light and shade, and his famous triangular arrangement. The background is a scene of shadowy rocks and trees, with the gleams of cascades falling into a misty pool. The triangular pattern, characteristic of his pictures, is formed by the figure of the virgin Mary in the middle, stretching her left hand over the child Jesus seated on the ground beside her, with an angel sitting close behind him; while her right arm rests lovingly on the shoulders of the boy John. Leonardo's extraordinary skill in portraying children in difficult postures together with their beauty and grace is here shown. The womanly tenderness and charm of the Madonna is also typical, for his portraits of women are always ideally beautiful. In this picture, Leonardo has also created a magical effect by his use of light and shade. He painted the most important parts in bright lights, which gradually fade to darker tones in the portions that recede into the background. This gives the figures the effect of being placed in a flood of light.

Leonardo's triangular arrangement is also well exemplified in another famous picture, the *Virgin and Child with St. Ann* (also in the Louvre, Paris).

In late 1481 or in early 1482 Leonardo left Florence for Milan, where he entered the service of Lodovico il Moro. During his stay there, he painted for the Dominican convent, Santa Maria delle Grazie, his world-famous picture.

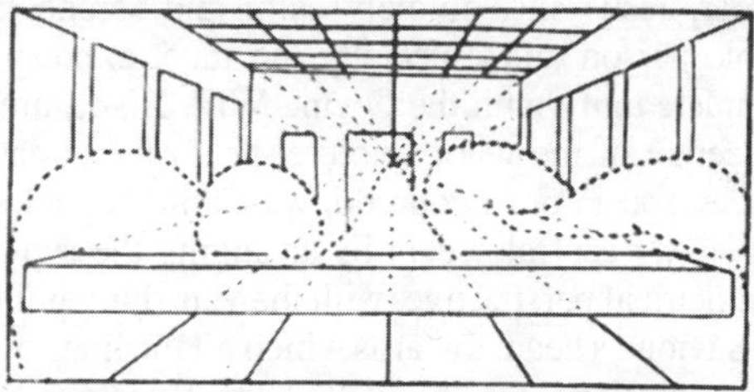

Fig. 454. Lineal organization of the Last Supper.

the *Last Supper* (Pl.41.1 & Fig. 454). This event, so important in the Saviour's life, was represented over and over again during the preceding centuries, even among the paintings in the catacombs. It had become the custom to have the scene painted in convent dining rooms. Several of these paintings have endured, especially from the Quattrocento. But Leonardo provided the classical representation of the scene, and in such a convincing manner, that ever since his picture has become the accepted interpretation of the Last Supper.

It was painted on the northern wall of the monastery refectory. Its length is 9 metres, its width 4½. Jesus and the apostles are seated or standing about a supper table, to celebrate the passover meal, the annual commemoration of God's liberation of the Jews from Egyptian slavery. The Saviour is about to give the greatest proof of his personal love, as recorded in the intimate dialogue after the supper, and the total gift of himself to those who love him, though he knows he will be cruelly murdered the following day, betrayed by one of his closest friends. The picture shows his natural grief when he foretold, 'One of you will betray me', and the various reactions—the surprise and wonder who it could be. On his right, the fiery Peter beckons to John, who had been leaning on the Saviour's breast, to ask who was meant. Between them is the traitor Judas, clenching a money bag. He has overturned the salt in his bewilderment that his treachery is already known. Beyond these three, there is another trio on the extreme right of Christ. These may be identified as Bartholomew, standing, and eagerly leaning over the table; James the Less; and Andrew, with his hands raised in protest against such baseness. Close to the Master on his left, Thomas raises a finger as if to ask, 'Is it I, Lord?'; James the Greater, with outstretched arms; and Philip, inclining pleadingly. The last group includes Mathew, Thaddaeus, and Simon, also greatly troubled and agitated.

In the centre of all this excited indignation and uproar, Jesus sits, divinely calm and serene. The whole person and especially the face, express his complete unity with the Divine Will. His figure, in the centre of the whole picture, holds the attention of the spectator. Leonardo was able to achieve this strong central accent by arranging the room in symmetrical perspective, with the vanishing point at the Saviour's head, towards which all the lines of the room converge. On the walls hang tapestries, four on each side. At the back there are three rectangular openings, the central and biggest one, with a round tympanum above it, frames the figure of Christ, which stands out clearly against the pale background of landscape and sky seen through it. So the eye is immediately carried towards the quiet and dignified figure of the Master. The symmetrical grouping of the apostles in threes, on both sides of him, also creates a strong impression of unity and balance. This close grouping of the twelve on only one side of the long narrow table—far too inadequate for such a number—not only emphasizes this physical and psychological unity, but also avoids the monotony of thirteen diners sitting in a row.

The whole painting, so dramatically alive with intense emotion and meaning, took Leonardo four years to complete. It still exists, but since the original plaster was unsuitable, and dampness penetrated through the wall, it is badly damaged. For centuries, pealing and fading of the colours went on. In spite of many attempts at restoration, it has continued to decay. During the Second World War, the whole refectory was destroyed except the wall where the Last Supper is painted.

On his return to Florence from Milan, Leonardo produced his famous portrait of the wife of Francesco del Giocondo, known as *Mona Lisa* or *La Gioconda* (Pl. 41.2 ) (now in the Louvre Museum, Paris). It has come to symbolize for many the mystery of woman. The enigmatic smile of this Italian lady is perhaps the most striking aspect of this psychological portrait. As Wölfflin has written, it is 'only a very faint smile in the corners of the mouth and an almost imperceptible trembling across the features. Like a breath of wind rippling the water, the soft planes of the face are moved, and the light and shadow play across it in whispered dialogue to which we never tire of listening.' The extremely high smooth forehead, and complete lack of eyebrows were fashionable at the time. The glance of the brown eyes is veiled; and the brown hair falls loosely under the thin, delicate veil covering her head. She sits upright, even somewhat stiffly, in an armchair, at an angle of forty-five degrees. Her head is held high as she turns it slightly towards the spectator, at whom she seems to be looking. The delicate hands and fingers are beautifully modelled, with an extraordinary sensitiveness. She is dressed in a green, pleated satin gown with yellow-brown sleeves.

The mysterious personality of Mona Lisa is reflected in the panoramic landscape which serves as a background. The dominant colours are brown, blue-green, and the blue of the sky seen between two columns and over a parapet, before which Mona Lisa sits. The landscape is rather fantastic and unusual. Great labyrinths of mountains, with lakes and rivers lying between them, fade away into the distance. They are only vaguely executed ; and the result is a dreamlike atmosphere which helps to make the apparent solidity of the human figure stand out all the more. This panorama, with its fading of colours in the distance, is a very good example of aerial perspective, which Leonardo was the first to apply in a conscious manner to painting; though, as we saw, Masaccio had some glimpses of its possibilities. Leonardo wrote about it in a treatise on painting; and his theories were successfully put into practice in his Mona Lisa.

Leonardo was called to France by king Francis I. He lived in the royal castle near Amboise, always much admired and patronized, but he became sickly, paralyzed in his right hand. He died there in 1519, leaving behind him a great reputation and many followers. None of them, however, were worthy of their master. Leonardo had sought above everything else to express moral life through his art, and to reveal the secret emotions of the soul by the fleeting tremors of facial expression. Not all of his pupils understood his genius. Most of them imitated his style only by vulgarizing the obscure and mysterious tones of his pictures, and copying with affectation the delicate gestures of his feminine types and the famous smile.

Italian sculpture of the Cinquecento or High Renaissance was dominated by the genius of

Michelangelo Buonarroti* (1475–1564), a Florentine, who was also a painter, architect, and poet. He brought Renaissance sculpture to its highest development. His special medium was the glittering white Carrara marble. He could visualize in the unhewn the human figures that seemed to be enclosed there in and which he could release with his chisel. 'His interest was in sculpture. Even when he painted, he handled light and colour so as to obtain a sculptural effect in his figures. He made light diffuse everywhere in the same way. This uniform diffusion of light occurs very rarely in nature. By using it, the painter is able to reveal exactly the shape and form and makes the convexities and hollows conspicuous. This gives the impression of three-dimensional figures, like sculptures, instead of being veiled in atmosphere like Leonardo's. And when he was commissioned with architecture, his organization of forms showed the genius of a sculptor. His chief interest was the human figure, wherein he saw the most perfect form in creation.

Michelangelo was born in Caprese of a distinguished Florentine family. From his infancy he wanted to do nothing but draw. In 1488, his father admitted him to the bottega of the painter Domenico Ghirlandaio, where he could learn all the technical skill necessary for his art; but the easy style of his master had no attraction for him: he preferred to draw his inspirations from Giotto, Masaccio and Donatello. In 1489 he entered the workshop of the sculptor Bertoldo, a pupil of Donatello, who was also the guardian of Lorenzo de' Medici's collection of antique statues. There the young Michelangelo worked in an atmosphere of admiration for the antique and for the art of Donatello. Like Leonardo, he was not satisfied with second-hand knowledge of anatomy. He made his own researches by dissecting bodies and drawing living models until he had perfectly mastered the secrets of representing the human body. Unlike the many-sided Leonardo, to whom anatomy was only one of his countless experiments, Michelangelo maintained this singleness of purpose: to make the human body the means of his aesthetic expression. His talent attracted the attention of the Medici, who became his patrons. Lorenzo the Magnificent took him into his household and put him in touch with poets and humanists, and very soon he found himself in the midst of the brilliant life of the Renaissance.

The *Pieta* (pity) (Pl. 41.3 ), a sculptured group, is one of the most beautiful works of his youth. It is now in a side chapel in St. Peter's basilica. This statue represents the Saviour's lifeless body resting on his mother's lap after it had been taken down from the cross. Often represented in Christian art, the scene takes on an unusual beauty and power in Michelangelo's handling of it. For the first time in sculpture, he applied Leonardo's triangular device. Mary's head is bent, contemplating her Son's wounds with piteous but restrained grief, for as the artist himself said, ' The mother of God does not weep like any earthly mother.' The gesture of her hand indicates entire resignation in her deep sorrow. Her face has an extraordinary delicacy. She looks much too young for a mother of a thirty-three year old son. Michelangelo gave the reason to a friend of his, ' A woman of perfect purity would keep her youth for ever.'

The garment ripples down the virgin's bosom and falls in heavy folds over her knees, spreading out widely until it forms the base for the triangular shape of the group. The size of Christ's body is reduced so as not to appear too heavy on his mother's lap. His finely-carved limbs fall inert to the ground. The contraction of the tendons marks the first attempt to produce the spasmodic energy of muscles and joints, typical of the grand statues of Michelangelo's maturity. But the slender grace and smooth shining surface are typical of the fifteenth century.

The statue of *David* is another youthful work of Michelangelo. It was carved out of a block of marble spoiled some time earlier by Agostino di Duccio in trying to make the figure of a prophet. Several artists were asked to produce a new statue of this disfigured block, but only Michelangelo accepted the task. He finished the new statue without mending or adding a piece. This colossal figure, which was placed before the Palazzo Vecchio in Florence as a symbol of the city's liberty, made the young artist widely known.

The *Holy Family* is the only easel painting accepted as Michelangelo's work. It is a devotional picture, it has no story to tell like a narrative painting. The artist could arrange his figures as he liked, his purpose being to arouse devotion in the onlooker. This picture represents the child Jesus, his mother Mary and his foster-father St. Joseph. Here Michelangelo has made the figures look like statues by the uniform diffusion of light.

In 1505, commissioned by Pope Julius II to make his tomb, Michelangelo conceived a great project, involving a considerable number of statues. With immense enthusiasm, burning

* Pronounce: mee-kel-jello boo-ohna-roty

with artistic inspiration, he himself went to Carrara, the finest marble quarry of Italy, to choose the most beautiful blocks. He spent some time there in the mountains. One can picture the master-artist among the shining white marble blocks, longing to change the whole mountain-side into living forms. But suddenly the pope abandoned this project in order to replace the old St. Peter's basilica, which was falling into ruin and becoming too small for the needs of Christendom. Wishing to build a much bigger and more splendid basilica, the pope needed all his resources for such an ambitious plan. To Michelangelo this was a tragedy, for he had to abandon his cherished ideas for the tomb. Deeply embittered, he fled to Florence; but the pope recalled him, and all his successors patronized Michelangelo and kept him at work. But the failure of the scheme for Julius' memorial was one of the greatest disappointments of his life. The tomb, in a considerably reduced form, was finished in 1545. The statue of *Moses* (Pl. 41.4 ), which was originally to be a detail of the complete monument, is the central statue of the tomb in its present form. It represents the great leader through whom God saved the Jewish people from Egyptian slavery, and to whom He gave a written law on Mount Sinai. This gigantic statue shows Moses seated ; but the apparent immobility is charged with restrained dynamic energy. The head turns left, giving the impression of authority and vision. The two horn-like projections on the head are supposed to represent the radiance which shone from his face after speaking with God. The long beard, twisting and curling, is held up by his right hand, and the muscles and protruding veins are clearly marked on the arms. The left leg is pulled back sharply. Everywhere one sees spiral movements which are confined, but not dominated, by the planes of the original block. This statue shows Michelangelo's style in his maturity, when he liked to represent gigantic figures in difficult postures. The portrayal of muscles and veins indicates a restrained yet dynamic energy. This statue is now in the church of St. Peter's Chains in Rome.

Later, Pope Julius II asked Michelangelo to decorate the *ceiling* of the *Sistine chapel* (Pl. 42.1 & Fig. 455) of the Vatican in Rome. The task was a tremendous one as Michelangelo could foresee, for the main portion of the space to be covered measured 13 by 36½ metres. He returned to the pope, begging him to let Raphael do the work, but he was refused. Where-upon he insisted on building his own scaffold, to do it properly; and no one was to be allowed into the chapel until the painting was finished, because he wanted no interference with his

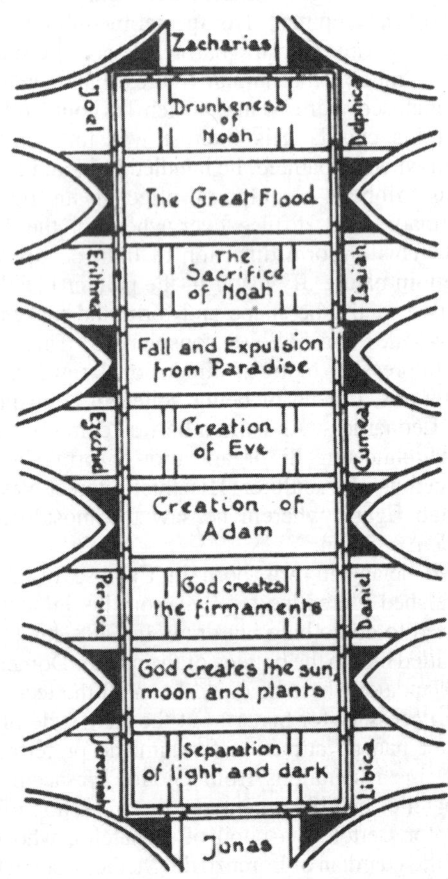


Fig. 455. Disposition of the various compositions, ceiling of the Sistine chapel, Vatican.

plans. The pope agreed, and near the end of 1508 the tremendous task was begun with the greatest vigour.

The question was how to handle the great barrel vault, some 24 metres high. The vast surfac was divided by means of painted arches and cornices, to give the impression of architecture and to section off the ceiling for his various compositions depicting man's creation and his fall. God is represented in human form to symbolize the fact that He is a living, personal being with intelligence and free will, though of course He has none of man's limitations, such as a physical body.

The first shows the creation of light, represented by the *Almighty separating light from darkness* with a movement of His arms.

Next He divides this light into lesser lights, the *sun and moon*, symbolized by His right hand touching the sun and His left the moon, while He bids the earth to bring forth life, namely plants and trees.

In the following panel He *creates the firmaments*.

When He has finished man's home and its furnishings, He *creates Adam* the first man. God is shown stretching out His hand and infusing spiritual life into Adam's body, lying lifeless on the ground.

Then with the *creation of Eve,* He gives him companionship, by calling the first woman from his side.

The next panel of the *fall and expulsion* shows on the left side the entrance of evil: Satan (the enemy) is shown twisting like a serpent (representing a harmful, hidden influence) round the tree (symbolic of free choice) of the knowledge of good and evil. Satan tempts Eve into flouting God's warning against the deadly fruit (figurative of a corruptive result) by a deliberate misrepresentation of God's essential Goodness. (God had planted a garden of delight, in which he now placed the man He had formed. Here, at the bidding of the Lord God, the soil produced all such trees as charm the eye and satisfy the taste.... And this was the trust which the Lord God gave the man, You may eat your fill of all the trees in the garden, except the tree which brings experience of good and evil; if ever you eat of this you will die .... The serpent said, What is this command God has given you, not to eat the fruit of any tree in the garden?.... What is this talk of death ? God knows well that as soon as you eat this fruit your eyes will be opened, and you yourselves will be like gods, knowing good and evil). In the second part of the same panel, Adam and Eve, having allowed themselves to be deceived, and freely chosen to experience evil and death, have their choice ratified: they are shut out of the garden of delight God had prepared for them; God lets them have their own way.

The seventh panel, *the sacrifice of Noah*, shows him preparing a thank-offering to God for having saved him and his family from the great flood. It is really a sequel to the one that follows.

In the latter is shown the oppression and destruction of men by *the great flood*, for having oppressed and destroyed each other by murder. (The earth was full of men's iniquities, and the whole frame of their thoughts was set continually on evil.... There lay the world, corrupt in God's sight, full of oppression; no creature on earth but had lost its true direction.... Man has all the thoughts and imaginations of his heart, even in youth, so bent on evil). The ark or ship God had asked Noah to build as a refuge from the flood, is seen in the background. Below it, an overcrowded boat is in danger of being upset. People flee up the rocks, in terror of the rising water.

The last panel shows the various attitudes of *Noah's* sons to his *accidental intoxication*: Cham makes fun of him, while Sem and Japhet cover him respectfully.

The arches separating these panels are enlivened by the decorative figures of *thoughtful youths,* who represent mankind contemplating the course of history. They reveal the artist's genius in depicting poses hard to reproduce in art. Lower down, seated on either side of the vault, are *seven* Biblical *prophets and five sibyls* (prophetesses in classical mythology), alternating with each other. They symbolize the great seers who foretold the coming of the Saviour who would restore to mankind the full truth of God's essential Goodness and Power. Each of these colossal figures is typical of Michelangelo's unique dynamic imagination.

In most of these figures, one is struck by their inherently sculptural quality. Michelangelo himself says, in a letter written while discouraged and depressed about the ceiling, 'This is not my profession, I waste time without any results. God help me.' For, in the medium of painting, he was moved by the same desire as in sculpture: to organise the figures into a complex arrangement in space. This usually involves strongly-contrasted movements, which produce a feeling of restlessness or even violence. There is no tranquillity in this artist.

One of the most beautiful compositions of the ceiling frescoes is the *creation of Adam* (Pl. 42.2 ). It is divided into two masses, which stand out clearly against the flat background. Adam, on a hillside, is just awakening to life. The physical potentialities of the reposing figure are suggested by the broken, jagged contours of the setting. This comparatively quiet figure is contrasted with the other group, namely the Almighty and His messengers, full of vigorous movements. The two are united by the joining of hands: God's hand full of creative power, while Adam's is still limp and lifeless. The contrast between God's life-giving finger symbolic of His creative power, and Adam's inert finger, is one of the most wonderful features of the whole composition.

The ceiling of the Sistine chapel was finished in 1512; the following year Pope Julius II died.

Some years later, cardinal Giuliano de' Medici, who became Pope Clement VII, ordered the building of the new sacristy of San Lorenzo at Florence for the burial of the members of the Medici family. Already on the opposite wing, Brunelleschi had built the so-called old sacristy for the same purpose. Michelangelo was charged with the architectural as well as the sculptural execution of the *tombs of Giuliano de' Media,* (Pl. 42.3) duke of Nemours, and of *Lorenzo de' Medici*, duke of Urbino, both nephews of Lorenzo de' Medici. The sculptural groups of each of these tombs have a pyramidal shape: the representation of the deceased, seated in a niche, forms the apex, and a sarcophagus with a reclining figure on either side makes the base. The portraits of the deceased are idealized, and are generally believed to symbolize action, in the tomb of Giuliano, and thought in that of Lorenzo. The reclining figures represent dawn and twilight on the latter, and day and night on the former. The work remained unfinished when Michelangelo returned to Rome.

Pope Paul III asked him to paint the *Last Judgement* on the wall above the altar of the Sistine chapel. With feverish passion, Michelangelo executed this gigantic composition, 48 feet high and 44 feet wide, from 1537 to 1541. It contains vast numbers of figures, and was designed to serve as an epilogue to the history of man which he had painted on the ceiling. This is the largest fresco composition in the world. It is divided into three zones. In the top area, heaven is represented, with the Saviour enthroned as judge of mankind, surrounded by the virgin Mother beside him, with an arc of apostles on the right, patriarchs on the left, and two martyrs at the lower end to complete the circle. Above the Judge, in the lunettes, Michelangelo painted throngs of angels with the instruments men used to torture and kill the Saviour: principally the cross and the pillar to which he was tied for the scourging. Opposite these, the wail is filled with prophets, saints, and martyrs on the right, and with Biblical women, holy virgins, and sibyls on the left. Michelangelo called the middle area 'the realm of those who have been judged.' To the right of the Judge he showed the 'ascent of the elect,' to His left 'the fall of the damned.' In the centre, angels blow their trumpets. The lowest area is the realm of death and demons. The space directly over the altar is filled with the resurrection of the dead and the arrival in hell. Each figure on this wall is engaged in some form of concentrated action, but the whole conception lacks the dynamism of the ceiling frescoes.

Next, Pope Paul III commissioned him to improve the Farnese palace, in which he made some fine cornices; and gave him work to do on other buildings. At the age of seventy, he was charged to continue the building of St. Peter's basilica. Michelangelo changed the schemes of Sangallo, and succeeded in making the wooden model of the beautiful and harmonious dome. He showed himself as great in architecture as in sculpture and painting, but he was essentially a sculptor: even a architect of St. Peter's, he treated his building as a mass to be modelled and sculptured.

Michelangelo had always been an untamed spirit. He lamented being lame, and having been 'deprived of a beautiful human face' by a blow on the nose. In spite of his famous acquaintances, he preferred more and more to live alone and shut himself up in his thoughts. He had always been sickly, but lie worked until his last day despite great weakness. He died in Rome in 1564, and was buried in Florence. Michelangelo's influence upon later artists was very great.

Another eminent painter of the Italian High Renaissance was Raphael, or Raffaello Sanzio or Santi (1487–1520). According to Vasari, his father, Giovanni Santi, took him to the artist Perugino (Pietro Vanucci) in Perugia; but the boy was only twelve when his father died, and Perugino was not in Perugia at that time. He was probably entrusted, in his own home town, Urbino, to a pupil of Francesco Francia, the gay and charming Timoteo Viti. His painting was, however, influenced by Perugino.

The earliest picture we have by Raphael, painted when he was about fifteen, is the *knight's dream,* a delightfully fresh and graceful work, now in the London National Gallery. On either side of the sleeping knight stand figures of pleasure and virtue, each inviting the young knight to follow her own path.

About 1499, Raphael seems to have gone to Perugia to study under Perugino, who was then decorating the Collegio del Cambio. He immediately assimilated his master's style. The *betrothed of the virgin* (Pl. 43.1) (now in the Brera Museum at Milan), painted in 1504, when Raphael was twenty-one, is apparently similar to Perugino's picture on the same subject, although the superiority of Raphael's talent is evident. Both Raphael's and Perugino's pictures represent the engagement of Mary and Joseph before the Jewish high priest. Both pictures are set in an outdoor scene, with Renaissance buildings in the background. The figures are shown in the sixteenth century clothing. Perugino's composition is crowded and flat, and the central Figures do not stand out. Raphael's composition reduces the number of spectators and places them farther back, so that the central figures stand out more clearly. The slightly inclined figure of the high priest avoids the rigid central position given by Perugino. Although Raphael's faces still show the stereotyped character of his master's compositions, his figures are composed with greater skill and grace. The small sixteen-sided temple in the background, crowned with a central dome, shows the new architectural taste.

About the beginning of 1505, the young painter went to Florence. There he found Michelangelo, Leonardo da Vinci, Fra Bartolommeo, and others. Up to this time, Florence had been the great art-centre. During the four years he spent there (1505–1508), Raphael painted a series of pictures, principally of the Madonna, which still possess an exquisite delicacy. They are admirable representations of maternal affection; the faces are gentle and lovely, with refined regular features; and the figures are well-proportioned and graceful.

Among these, we can mention only the most famous. The *Madonna del Gran Duca* (Madonna of the grand duke) (Pl. 43.2 ) was painted in 1505 for the Medici family, and is now in the Pitti Gallery, Florence. It is one of Raphael's loveliest paintings. Mary is standing, and holds the child Jesus in her arms. Motherly love, tenderness, and religious respect characterize this picture. The face is extraordinarily beautiful. The grand duke of Tuscany was so fond of this picture that he could never separate himself from it. From this fact, the picture derives its title.

The *Madonna del cardellino* (Madonna of the goldfinch), painted about 1506, is in the Uffizi Gallery, Florence. This picture shows the child Jesus with his mother and cousin, St. John the Baptist. The setting is an Umbrian iandscape, tranquil and spacious. The picture is grouped according to Leonardo's pyramidal device.

La *belle jardinēre* (the fair gardener), painted in 1507 and now in the Louvre, Paris, shows the same triangular grouping. Michelangelo's influence is seen in the restless twisting pose of the infant Jesus.

The *Madonna della sedia* (Madonna of the chair) was painted during Raphael's stay in Rome in 1509, and is now in the Pitti Gallery, Florence. The virgin Mary is dressed like an Italian peasant woman of the Renaissance.

In course of time, his madonnas became more dignified and noble. The *Madonna di San Sisto* (Pl. 43.3), his last, painted about 1516, gets its name from the convent of St. Sixtus at Piacenza, Italy, for which it was ordered. Behind a raised curtain appears a wonderful vision: the divine Child is carried in the arms of his virgin mother, who appears in the clouds, serenely earnest. Her bare feet rest on the globe of the earth, and Pope St. Sixtus III and St. Barbara kneel at the sides. Two little angels lean over the frame, gazing in rapture. This picture, which had been in the Gallery of Dresden, Germany, was taken to Moscow during Worid War II. It is undoubtedly one of Raphael's most beautiful works.

In 1508, upon the recommendation of Bramante, Raphael came to Rome, where he remained for the rest of his life. He was called there to collaborate in the decoration of the Borgia apartments in the Vatican. When Julius II saw Raphael's sketches, he commissioned him at once. The decorations were begun by several artists, but soon the remarkable value of Raphael's work was recognized, so that most of the other artists' work was removed to leave room for his paintings. These rooms are now called the Stanze di Raffaello. In the most famous, the Stanza della Segnatura, we find the two great frescoes representing allegories known as the Disputa del Sacramento and the School of Athens. In the lunettes over the windows are the frescoes, the Parnassus and Jurisprudence. The idea was to represent in a single composition the Church's protection of philosophy, theology, science and the arts.

The *Disputa del Sacramento* (Pl. 44.1 ) represents 'the communion of saints.' It is in three divisions, two showing heaven, and the third the earth. In the former, there is a symbolic representation of the Holy Trinity. In the highest curve of the arch, God the Father is represented under a traditional symbol of human paternity. Only the upper half of the figure is seen, clothed in tunic and mantle. The rest is covered by clouds to show that it is supposed to symbolize a divine mystery. Rays spread out through an atmosphere of delicately-toned sky. Youthful angels are seen against a background of stars. Other angels support a fringe of cloud. Six lovely winged seraphs (representing love) are floating in the air.

In the second division, God the Son, the Saviour, is shown seated, with a white cloth draped around him in such a way that the wound in his side is clearly seen. His hands are uplifted. The expression of his face, as well as those of his mother and John the Baptist, reflect the story of the redemption.

Flying cherub-heads, signifying knowledge of divine mysteries, surround this central group, which is completed by a symbol of the Holy Spirit just below the Saviour, to show that He has been sent to be the continual friend of human souls, to help them understand the true meaning of God's message. As the Saviour came to give men the right knowledge of God by his actions and words, so the Holy Spirit is sent to help each one understand this manifestation correctly and to apply it to his own milieu. Since the true knowledge of God through the Saviour is recorded in the Gospels, four angels, or messengers of God, are shown holding the volumes. The whole assembly rests on a semicircle of clouds, at the extreme ends of which are seated Sts. Peter and Paul, and between them appear Adam, Abraham, the apostles James and John, Moses and Daniel, Sts. Stephen and Lawrence, Jeremias and Judas Maccabeus.

Earth is represented in the third section of this huge fresco. It shows an assembly of the faithful and Doctors of the Church, all turned to the altar, where God continues His visible communion with mankind through the Sacred Host raised high to form a connecting link between heaven and earth. A group of people are contemplating it, while a boy is walking up to join them. Pointing towards him is Bramante, the designer of the new St. Peter's basilica, who is shown on the front left, leaning on a stone balustrade. The Church Doctors (or eminent teachers) near the altar include Sts. Jerome, Gregory, Ambrose and Augustine. The figures represented all around are historical portraits of Dante, Savonarola, Innocent III, and others. Their names are written in each nimbus encircling their heads, unless they are so well-known that names are unnecessary.

The allegorical fresco, the *school of Athens*, (Pl. 44.2 ) shows a scene on the steps going up to a spacious Renaissance building, the architectural design of which is reminiscent of the new St. Peter's basilica, then in course of construction by Bramante. The group of philosophers and students is so well arranged that each figure seems to lead to the two philosophers in the centre : Aristotle, pointing to earth, and Plato to heaven. Disciples are grouped on each side. Raphael's artistic ability is evident from the arrangement of the philosophers and the inimitable manner of portraying persons, forms, drapery, and characters. Raphael himself and Perugino are shown. Raphael seems to have taken the spirit of Giotto, Ghirlandaio, Leonardo and Michelangelo, and then tempered it with his own nobleness and grace. He shows here a balance of charm, a broader style of execution, more striking balance of light and shade, and a greater richness of harmonious colour than he had achieved before. The surface of this painting has since been badly damaged, the architecture has become worn, and some of the figures are almost unrecognizable. A fissure cuts into the head of Diogenes, and a much deeper and longer one divides the figures of Aristotle and Plato. This fresco broke the' last link which bound Raphael to the art of the Quattrocento. Crowe and Cavalcaselle say, 'It is simply the finest, best balanced, and most perfect arrangement of figures that was ever put together by the genius of the Italian Revival, and the scene in which it is set is the most splendid display of monumental architecture that was ever made in the sixteenth century.'

In 1515 Pope Leo X asked Raphael to prepare cartoons for tapestries which were to adorn the Sistine chapel. A cartoon is a full-scale design drawn on paper to serve as a model for tapestries. Raphael made magnificent cartoons, from which the tapestries were then woven in Brussels. The subject was the Acts of the Apostles. Seven of the original ten are today in the Victoria and Albert Museum, London.

The *transfiguration*, now in the Vatican Gallery, Rome, was one of Raphael's last works. He died on Good Friday, the sixth of April, aged thirty-seven, and was buried in the Pantheon. Despite his short life, there is great variety in his work. Until his death his technique progressed. In his youth he painted charming figures in luminous landscapes. At Florence he perfected his drawing. After he arrived in Rome for the decoration of the halls of the Vatican, his style suddenly took on an unexpected grandeur; it is there that his greatest achievement is found.

In Venice two pupils of Giovanni Bellini were to bring the painting there to its maturity by their introduction of new elements. They were Giorgione and Titian.

Giorgione, or Giorgio Barbarelli (1478–1510), left but few paintings, and there is very little known of him, for he died young. But his importance is undoubted. His *Castelfranco Madonna*, ordered about 1504, shows a Bellini-like Virgin between St. Liberal and St. Francis. She is seated on a lofty throne, and behind her is an exquisite landscape glowing in mellow light. The modelling is soft, and the calm figures are remarkable for their graceful, slightly hesitating outlines. It is a serene and beautiful picture. The *storm*, in the Giovanelli palace, Venice, is a still more striking picture. Black clouds threaten rain; and the trembling trees reflect a sensitiveness to nature that is almost modern. It is no longer a stylized landscape, meant to be an idyllic decoration forming a background to religious scenes. The shadows and lights, the thunders and winds themselves inspire the artist. The figures, which appear to have no connection with each other, are of very little importance. It is the natural surroundings which are made predominant.

Titian, or Tiziano Vecellio (1477–1576), was the leader of this brilliant Venetian school, and one of the greatest masters of painting. He lived for almost a hundred years. He was born at Pieve di Cadore at the foot of the Dolomites, one of the loveliest places in the world. Amid this glorious scenery he spent the first ten years of his life, and ever after he showed a special love for these landscapes of his childhood. At an early age he came to Venice, and at first followed rather closely the style of Giorgione, as can be seen in the *concerto*, in the Pitti Palace, Florence. This may have been painted in collaboration with Giorgione.

*Christ and the tribute money* (Pl. 45.1 ) shows the Gospel scene where his enemies tried to put him in a dilemma, to get him into trouble either with his own countrymen or the Roman authorities, by asking if it was right to pay taxes to the latter. The Saviour countered by asking them to show one of the coins they used. It bore the inscription of the Roman emperor. Then came the supreme answer of Christ: ' Render to Caesar the things that are Caesar's and to God the things that are God's.' From this he raised them to the right sense of justice and values. Since the money bore the emperor's image it belonged to him; but man's soul bears the image of God, and so it belongs to Him. Titian obtained magnificent expressiveness by contrasting the uprightness of Jesus, his frank, open countenance, with the sombre, evident cunning of the hypocritical enquirer.

Another masterpiece of Titian's youthful period is the famous picture known as *sacred and profane love*, in the Borghese Gallery, Rome.

The painting of the *assumption of the Virgin* (1581), in the church of Santa Maria dei Frari, Venice, is Titian's first great religious picture. It shows the virgin Mary being taken up to heaven, surrounded by angels. God the Father is seen above, and the apostles are watching from the earth. This is the first oil painting in which the figures are as big as those in the largest frescoes. The apostles measure nearly three metres. The colours are vigorous and bold.

For the *entombment of Christ* (in the Louvre, Paris) and for the *Madonna of the Pesaro family* (in the Santa Maria dei Frari, Venice), the means employed were such as to achieve the pomp and splendour so popular with the Venetians. Deep, rich colour masses, warm and cool, light and dark, harmonize and contrast, giving a sumptuous effect. Such surfaces were achieved by a long and patient building-up, usually on the tempera ground painting, of layer upon layer of thin coats of pigments, mixed with oil. Some of these were transparent, others thick; and at every stage there were bleachings in the sun.

Titian also painted excellent portraits, in which he expressed the very depths of character by means of the essential physical traits. He painted some of the most important personages of his day, such as *Paul II* (now in Naples), and *Charles V* (in the Prado Museum, Madrid).

Tintoretto, or Jacopo Robusti (1518–1594), was another great artist of the same school. His father had been a dyer in Venice. This gave the painter his nickname, of il Tintoretto or ' little dyer'. His aim in painting, which he wrote on the wall of his room, was 'the drawing of Michelangelo and the colour of Titian.' Having begun to paint at an early age, he sought even from the first to portray energy. This corresponded with his own passionate and independent nature which merited him the surname il furioso (the furious). He liked dynamic compositions with dramatic use of contrasts of light and shade, white and black, day and night.

In his *Last Supper* (1594), in San Giorgio Maggiore, Venice, he uses contrasts of light and darkness. By means of highlights, the eye of the spectator is carried from the two figures in the lower left hand corner of the picture, across the foreground to the group of angels at the back. Thus he also achieves an impression of deep space. There is a sense of impetuous movement and dramatic action in this picture. His *miracle of St. Mark* (Pl. 45.2 ) (1548), in the Academy, Venice, is also full of swinging movement and rhythm. There are again the same contrasting spots of light and dark colouring against a quiet and paler background.

Paolo Caliari Veronese (1528-1588) was born in Verona, but came to Venice in 1554. He exaggerated all the splendour already existing in the various arts in Venice, so that his marble porticos were not only whiter but also higher than those of others. The people he painted were more splendid, their jewels more brilliant than ever before. The *feast in the house of Levi* (1573), in the Academy, Venice, shows great animation in the portrayal of the figures which move within a massive framework of imposing architecture.

Corregio, called thus from his birthplace, but whose real name was Antonio Allergi (1494–1534) passed his short but productive life mostly in Parma. His great achievements were his ceiling frescoes in which he made use of daring perspectives, free movement of figures; and of light. In all these traits he showed himself taking the first steps towards the Baroque style. For though he belonged to the Mannerist period, he was not a Mannerist in his art. His works, especially those in Parma, inspired the decorative and illusionistic style of the seventeenth century. In the church S. Giovanni Evangelista, we can see on the main dome his *Christ in glory*, with its bold foreshortenings and vigorous movements. It is one of the great works of Italian art.

## BAROQUE

### ARCHITECTURE

Baroque architecture started in Rome at the end of the sixteenth century, and spread to the rest of Italy and other countries of Europe. It lasted until half way through the eighteenth century; but it was during the seventeenth century that this rich and decorative art flourished. It aimed at all that was grandiose and magnificent. Each building was one great unit centred round a dominating theme, so that the various architectural parts lost their independence; for there was an organic relationship between them. Architecture, sculpture and painting were no longer separated: but almost without distinction these visual arts were used in order to create one total effect of plastic forms and colour, and to stir up a great variety of sensations in the spectator, overwhelmed before such massive grandeur. There was an almost plastic handling of exterior and interior wall surfaces, often undulating and treated sculpturally. Ornamental forms became much greater in their proportions : pilasters and giant columns were heavier and higher than ever before. The decorations on the walls included twisted columns, great mouldings, huge scrolls, broken and contorted pediments, lavish plastic ornaments creating strong light and shade effects, which were often enhanced by light from invisible sources. Polychromy replaced monochrome treatment of the walls and decorations. The general impression was change and movement, colour and light, pompous, often sombre splendour—all tending towards the creation of a picturesque illusion. Even in the exterior planning of these buildings, the open space around was arranged and organized so as to obtain a similar magnificence. Yet in spite of all these powerful effects and decorations, Baroque architecture in Rome was never smothered by ornament, as it was sometimes elsewhere. The final and total effect was never merely sensational, for the great Roman architects of the period controlled their desire for the grandiose.

This period in Rome was one of church building. And this new style was first seen in the *Gesù* (Church of Jesus), by Vignola and Giacomo della Porta. It is built on the simple basilican plan, with a Baroque type of façade decorated with pediments and great scrolls. But the most important examples of Baroque architecture are seen in the work of Lorenzo Bernini. The greatest architectural project of the time was the completion of St. Peter's basilica, which had not been finished by Michelangelo and his successors. The original building, having been found lacking in space, had a long nave added to it by Carlo Maderna, who also built the façade.

Lorenzo Bernini (1598–1680), the great architect, sculptor and painter of this Baroque period, built the famous *colonnade* in *front* of the *basilica of St. Peter's.* From a sketch drawn by him, we learn that he wished the wide, curved colonnades surrounding the great piazza to symbolize the arms of Christ stretched out on the cross to embrace all mankind. Bernini deliberately gave the piazza an oval shape, instead of the more stable circle, in order to create the visual illusion of great depth: for the eye, expecting a circle, unconsciously transfers to the depth of the piazza the same greatness as is obvious in the width: The attention is at once directed to the façade of the building, past the obelisk and two fountains, as the eye is carried forward by the graceful sweep of the continuous entablature to the basilica, of which the piazza is only the prelude. Within the basilica Bernini built the great bronze *baldacchino* (Pl. 45.3 ) over the main altar, which stands above the tomb of the apostle, St. Peter. This is a mingling of architecture and sculpture, with its spiral columns and curving decorations.

Another very typical Baroque church is that of *San Carlo alle quattro fontane*, *Rome*, built by Francesco Borromini (1599–1667) This oval-shaped building is surmounted by an oval dome; and its outer surface is not straight but undulating.

During the Baroque period, Rome became a city not only of magnificent churches, but also of splendid palaces which reflect the same grand style. These were enhanced by new streets and squares, by lovely sculptured fountains with their water playing in the Roman sunshine. These splendours have not passed away; and today they help to create an exterior setting worthy of 'the Eternal City', as the Romans like to call it.

## SCULPTURE

Baroque sculpture, as we saw, was closely related to the architecture. Hence its shape and colour scheme was often determined by the larger architectural unit of which it was a decorative part. The style in sculpture was also illusionistic: wood was often treated as marble, whilst the latter was made to express movement and emotion. The dominating figure in Baroque sculpture was Bernini, as Michelangelo had been of the century before. His *throne of St. Peter* and the so-called *glory* above it, in the apse of St. Peter's basilica, are typically Baroque. The latter frames a window, with the dove a symbol of the Holy Spirit. It is a stucco decoration. Bernini's *altar of St. Teresa*, in Santa Maria della Vittoria, is in white marble. With great intensity, it represents the saint's ecstasy. He developed a new type of *tomb*, as seen in those of *Pope Urban VIII* (1642) and of *Alexander VII* (1673), with their theatrically-modelled symbolic skeletons. Among his portrait busts, the one of his patron, *cardinal Scipione Borghese,* has captured the mobility of the human features and is clearly expressive of personality. He sculptured, among others, the *Triton fountain* in Rome. As a sculptor, Bernini had a profound influence on the European style of the time; his manner became almost universal during the rest of the seventeenth century.

## PAINTING

The development of Baroque painting was much more complicated than that of architecture and sculpture. Art scholars are not yet agreed as to its origins. Two trends are clearly distinguishable: the more traditional one followed by Annibale Carracci and his Bologna Academy; the more revolutionary one of Caravaggio. The creative activity of the Italian School of the Renaissance had been unequalled for almost three centuries, whilst the great masters drew their inspiration either from observation of nature or from antiquity. Each of these great geniuses had their followers and imitators, who grouped themselves into schools, but they were unable to achieve anything worthy of their masters. On the other hand, there was a group of artists who consciously revolted against the classical ideals of the High Renaissance. These were known as Mannerists. Their work was characterized by elegance and intellectual complexity. Stress was laid on exaggerated and distorted proportions and movements, and sensuous lines. Both Carracci and Caravaggio reacted against Mannerism, though they did so in quite different ways.

Annibale Carracci (1560–1609), with his elder brother Agostino (1557–1602) and their cousin Lodovico (1555–1619), founded an academy in Bologna in 1595. This was a school for fine arts, which aimed at leading artists back to the traditional rules of art, by teaching what was best in the methods of the great masters, of which they had a thorough knowledge. The art they promoted was of a finished and sophisticated type ; and their many students filled the churches and palaces, especially in Italy, with paintings of this kind. The art of this Bolognese school was continued by Guido Reni (1575–1642). His *head of Christ* is a very good example of the pathos and grief, poignantly depicted, which was a characteristic of the Baroque period.

Caravaggio (1573–1609), whose full name was Michelangelo Merisi da Caravaggio, is one of the great revolutionaries in Italian art, for he had a large share in promoting the development of Baroque, whilst at the same time he may be considered the initiator of modern realism in art. In open revolt against the aesthetic tastes and intellectualism of his own time, he returned to the world of physical and emotional phenomena. He was born near Milan, the son of a mason. At an early age he was apprenticed as an artist in Milan, and at sixteen he went to Rome ; but in later life his disorderly conduct forced him to flee to Naples. Since the academicist painting was hardly known there, he became influential, not only in southern Italy, but also in Spain, the Netherlands, and France. He introduced a rough realism, which, nevertheless, had nothing vulgar about it, and which replaced the ideal classical forms and rules. Whilst the Caraccis painted the portraits of high class people, Caravaggio chose peasants and workers. He favoured dramatic themes and compositions, expressed by gestures and facial expressions. To achieve his strikingly sensational effects, he used foreshortenings and strong contrasts of light and shade. His undertones were conveyed by means of black and earth-brown colours. At times his backgrounds were steeped in darkness and the shades of night. Therefore he and his imitators are often called Tenebrists (tenebrae, darkness). All these qualities are seen in his *entombment* (Pl. 45.4), in the Vatican. By the gestures and facial expressions of the friends who are laying the Saviour in the tomb, he conveys their great sorrow. Before a completely dark, plain background, the figures are modelled in the strong light which flows in from the left.

During this period, ceiling painting developed greatly, since Baroque art combined the different visual arts into one synthesis. Sculpture and painting were closely allied to the architecture of the time. We can see this in the *ceiling* of the *Farnese palace* in Rome, painted by Annibale Carracci. The *ceiling of the church of Gesù* in Rome, painted by Giovanni Battista Gaulli, or Baciccio (1639-1709), is one of the most daring of these frescoes. Sculpture and painting are used to create on the vault of the nave the illusion of an unlimited vista in the sky, which opens up towards heaven.

The last phase of ceiling painting, in the Settecento or eighteenth century, can be seen in the work of Giovanni Battista Tiepolo (1696–1770), the greatest of the Rococo decorative painters. He was born in Venice, and worked there, as well as in Padua, Vicenza, Milan, Verona, Würzburg in Germany, and also in Spain, where he died. His art was rhetorical in subject, and tremendously theatrical in execution. Its characteristics were a flamboyant extravagance, light and airy colouring, and an easy graceful technique. His brilliant and fantastic paintings decorated a great number of churches and palaces.

# 10. FLEMISH ART

## GENERAL SURVEY

Flanders, originally part of the united Netherlands, is now included in modern Belgium, which became independent in 1830.

The country is bordered by the North Sea. Its coast is not far from the south-eastern end of England. The northern and western parts are plains, and the southern area belongs to the lower mountain ranges of central Europe. The soil is rich. In the mountains there are mines, and stone and marble quarries.

Centrally situated between northern and southern Europe, it became, as early as the eleventh century, a focus of great foreign commercial expansion. The most active traders were the Flemish weavers and the Walloon iron workers.

From the fourteenth to the sixteenth centuries, much was achieved for the unity of the country. The reign of the dukes of Burgundy was rich in artistic creativity. Flanders was prosperous. At Bruges, the leading seaport, Philip the Good set up his sumptuous court. Jan van Eyck became his court painter and chamberlain. The greatest ruler of the Burgundian line was Charles V, who became sovereign lord of the Low Countries, Spain, Naples, Milan, the Franche Comté, the New World and finally the Empire.

In the sixteenth century, Antwerp became the leading port. It took over the sea traffic from Bruges, and became the most important financial centre in Europe.

The University of Louvain was founded in 1425. It became the centre of literary and scientific learning.

After the middle of the sixteenth century, the disintegration of the seventeen provinces of the Netherlands set in. Philip II, king of Spain, son of Charles V, had from the first moment of his accession incurred the dislike of his subjects in the Low Countries because of the tactlessness of the governors who represented him. The open rift in the Low Countries ended in the division in which the Catholic Low Countries, which later became the kingdom of Belgium, separated from the northern United Provinces, today the Kingdom of Holland or the Netherlands.

## ARCHITECTURE

Gothic architecture flourished in Flanders long after Renaissance elements began to appear in other arts like painting. In no other country, perhaps, were there so many civic buildings such 11 as cloth halls, town halls and guild halls, as in Belgium; and with the Renaissance, their number and splendour increased even more. From the sixteenth century onwards, although the buildings were somewhat similar in character to those in France, those of Belgium showed more details and picturesqueness. This was partly due to the use of stone and bricks on the same building. The Ardennes mountains supplied good building stone. The palace of the old Chancellory, now part of the *Palais de Justice* in *Bruges*, is a good example of the first penetration of Renaissance details reflecting Italian influence. But soon, around 1550, native imagination started producing decorative forms which were less monumental and more fanciful; as for instance ribbon-like details and cartouches, belonging more to metal work than to architecture.

Even with the new style, they still used the stepped gables for their houses. This is seen in the central part of the *town hall* at *Antwerp*. The *guild houses* at Grande Place in *Brussels* are perhaps the most imaginative of their kind. They were built by the archers, skippers, carpenters, mercers, butchers, brewers, tailors and painters. *Le béguinage* at *Bruges*, in its poetical situation near the Lac d' Amour, shows a typically Belgian organization, where individual houses were grouped around a closed courtyard, with a Church inside and a big porch forming the entrance. This permitted the Béguines to live in piety and seclusion. Among the churches, the façade of *S. Michel* in *Louvain* shows the Baroque elements as understood in the country: with broken cornices and tympanons, and decorative scrolls on the sides. Inside many churches, the white and black marble from the Ardennes was used for altars and choir screens; and the excellent timber of the forest permitted the wood-carvers to make richly-decorated church furniture, such as choir stalls, confessionals, and pulpits.

## PAINTING

Suddenly, in the early fifteenth century, painting on a major scale appeared in northern Europe, and the Flemings were the first to make noteworthy advances. Jan van Eyck and his older brother Hubert freed painting from being a means of illustrating books, and thus created easel painting. In their work especially we see the transition from miniature art to that of the painter. In their pictures they used the oil technique.

Although they did not invent it, they certainly were the first to make a successful use of it.

They produced the great masterpiece, the *Mystic Lamb* (Pl. 46.1; Fig. 456), in the cathedral dral S. Bavo in *Ghent*. It is a folding altarpiece, with one pair of wings, painted on both sides. When closed, it presents the annunciation in the centre; and below, on both sides, and on the same scale, are the kneeling figures of the donors, between whom are the two Saints, John the Baptist and John the Evangelist, in grisaille. In the lunettes above the annunciation are the prophet Zacharias and Erythrean sibyl (left), with the prophet Michaeas and Cumean sibyl (right).

When open, the lower panels represent the final beatitude of all believing souls, in a radiant landscape. It is a picture of all the saints, frequent in medieval art, inspired by the liturgy of this feast, the Apocalypse, and the Golden Legend. The procession of the blessed, coming in groups from all directions to worship the Mystic Lamb, emblem of the Saviour, who shed his blood for all mankind, is the subject of the composition. The Lamb stands on an altar in the middle of a meadow. From the wound in the heart, streams of blood flow into a chalice. Angels kneel around: those in the back hold the instruments of the passion, the two in front swing thuribles with incense. The fountain of life in front of it, surrounded by kneeling aposties, represents redemption. From the four corners, groups of martyrs, holy virgins, patriarchs and prophets, holy bishops and confessors approach the centre in order to worship. Over the altar is the dove, the symbolic figure of the Holy Spirit. In the two left panels are the knights of Christ and the just judges; and in the two right ones, pilgrims and hermits. The countryside of the central panel extends into the side ones. It is fertile, full of vines and rosebushes. The meadows are dotted with colourful wild flowers, such as daisies, cowslips and violets. In the distance are wooded hills and rivers; and the Gothic spires, rising above the towns spread out beneath them, point towards a morning sky.

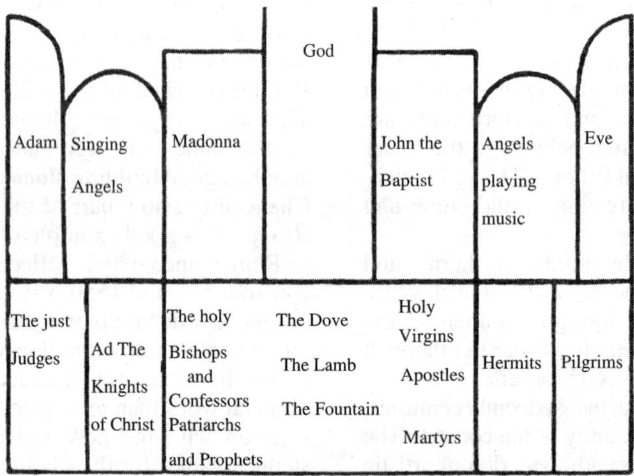


Fig. 456. Disposition of the various compositions, the Mystic Lamb, van Eyck brothers, St. Bavo cathedral, Ghent.

In the upper central panel is a majestic figure representing God, wearing a triple crown or tiara, and robed in a richly-bordered red mantle. Because of the symbolic pelicans painted behind him, the figure has sometimes been taken as a representation of Christ as king. The crown at his feet, as well as the border of the mantle, are brilliant with gold and precious stones: rubies, topaz, and pearls. These are painted with keen attention to detail. The panel to the right shows the seated figure of St. John the Baptist clad in pale green. Mary is seen reading in the left hand panel. She is dressed in dark blue, and the border of her robe is of black brocade and gold. From beneath her richly-jewelled crown, her hair falls loosely. In the whole picture, all the details are painted with painstaking exactness, as befits the work of a miniaturist. These three central panels are flanked on both sides by a panei of angel musicians, and the two outermost panels show the figures of Adam and Eve.

When compared to Italian art, what strikes one most about these Flemish paintings is their fidelity in representing objective appearances, and their minute attention to details. Yet in spite of ail the details and varieties of textures, unity is achieved by a marked sensitivity in the general use of line and colour: the surface is smooth, the colours deep, and the linear quality strong.

The van Eycks dsed oils for painting in order to create intense realism. They perfected this technique, by exploiting the interplay of successive layers of translucent colour.

Hubert van Eyck died before the completion of the Mystic Lamb. His brother Jan finished it, and continued to paint many other pictures, of which only the most outstanding can be mentioned here.

The *Madonna of the chancellor Rolin* (PI. 46.2) (in the Louvre, Paris), is typically Flemish in its concept. The setting is a loggia, with a triple arcade, tiled floors, and crown glass windows, opening out on a landscape. In the foreground is the infant Jesus on his mother's knees, raising his little hand in blessing. The Madonna, seated towards the right, wears a richlv-bordered mantle with heavy folds. Her long hair covers her shoulders. A small angel hovers in the air, holding up an elaborate gold crown. The donor, chancellor Rolin, kneels with folded hands at a prayer-desk on the left, contemplating the scene before him. His head is a naturalistic portrait. He is clothed in rich brocade; and the prayer-desk is covered with heavy drapery. The tiles on the floor lead the gaze out into the garden, and beyond it to the landscape, divided in the middle by a river. Far away on the horizon, is the pale silhouette of a range of mountains. There is a rich colour-harmony in the picture. The painter has taken care to add the minute details, and to render faithfully the different textures such as tiles, glass and textiles. Yet the artist has been able to coordinate all into a unity.

The *Madonna of the canon van der Paele* (in the Museum of Bruges) is another devotional picture, with the figure of the donor also represented. Here the religious scene has less familiarity about it. The infant Jesus with the Madonna is depicted in the centre, within a narrow circular sanctuary, on a throne covered with drapery, a baldachin above and an oriental carpet on the floor. They are flanked on either side by a saint, on the left, St. Donatian, the titular saint of the church and St. George on the right. The latter is presenting the donor, who is dressed in clerical robes and kneels with a prayer book in his hand. Here too the face is a naturalistic portrait. But van Eyck was to go even further in his search for realism.

In *Amolfini and his wife* (Pl. 47.1 ) (in the National Gallery, London), he painted the standing portraits of an Italian banker settled in Flanders, and Jeanne Cenami, also of Italian descent, to whom he was betrothed. Arnolfini, with dark clothes and a big hat, stands at the left of the picture. His right hand is raised to take the oath, and his left holds the right hand of his bride. She wears a white headdress that falls to her shoulders, and a green, white-bordered dress with heavy folds.

The room is a typical Flemish interior, with a curtained bed on the right and a casement window on the left. In the centre, a many-branched candelabra is hanging from the ceiling. On the back wall, a mirror with an elaborate frame reflects the figure of Jan van Eyck himself. Written in Latin on the wall are the words, 'Jan van Eyck was here.' There is nothing beautiful about Arnolfini's face, nor his bride's; nor even the little dog in front; still, what a wonderful picture van Eyck made of them. We notice the unifying light that floods the room, the atmospheric quality that fills the air, and the patterns he created by repeating and contrasting lines and shapes.

Roger van der Weyden (1400-1467) came from Toumai, the Walloon country, fie received his artistic inspiration from sculpture, as the van Eycks had received theirs from manuscript illuminations. Their interests were also widely different. The van Eycks liked the myriad little details of the material world and observed minute things that perhaps nobody else would have seen. Roger van der Weyden's interest on the contrary was in man. He simplified the material world for the sake of the human figure. But even in man it was his inner life that interested him most. He felt deeply, and expressed emotions to which no other painter was able to give such a tangible form.

From these two sources were to flow the dominant streams of Flemish art, though the emotional intensity of van der Weyden was to have much more influence on his countrymen than the way of painting of the van Eycks. It was the former who created the traditional Flemish style, as seen later in the work of Dirck Bouts (d. 1475) and Hugo van der Goes (d. 1482). The art of Jan van Eyck had perhaps been too far advanced for his time, for only Petrus Christus (d. 1472 or 1473) tried to carry on his style, whilst slightly Italianizing it.

Van der Weyden showed a keen sympathy

for pain. With deep compassion he represented the Saviour's sufferings. His masterpiece, the *descent from the cross* (Pl. 47.2) (in the Prado Museum, Madrid), resembles a group of figures often seen on the front of sculptured altarpieces. They are rounded like carvings in low relief, and their shadows are projected on the plain background. Van der Weyden's linear, specifically rhythmical style, conveys great depth of feeling, which is emphasized by the dramatic portrayal of the figures. Nicodemus and Joseph of Arimathea hold the Saviour's body as it is lowered from the cross. The figure of the Virgin- mother, supported by St. John, repeats symmetrically the posture of her son's body, to represent her compassion. Mary Magdalen on the right and John on the left both incline in an S curve at the edges of the picture.

The most popular Flemish painter of the second half of the fifteenth century was perhaps Hans Memling (Memlinc), born about 1430 in Mainz, Germany. He came to Flanders, and settled in Bruges in 1466. Here he assimilated the Flemish style. He painted refined, elegant figures, by means of gentle modelling ; and he gave an extraordinary suavity to the facial expression. This gave charm and sweetness to his pictures, which never degenerate into sentimentality. His figures have an unaffected simplicity, and convey a sense of deep faith, which had great devotional appeal. He borrowed from both van der Weyden and the van Eycks, yet his own artistic talent transformed these elements into his own personal style. Though Memling was not an innovator, yet his delicate and meticulous manner is a contribution in itself. His best works were done in Bruges, where most of them are preserved in the small museum of the hospital of St. John.

The most imposing of these pictures is the big altarpiece representing the *mystic marriage of St. Catherine* (Pi. 48.1). The setting is in a chapel, with a beautiful brocade hanging and an oriental carpet on the floor. A typical Flemish scene appears behind the numerous columns. The child Jesus, on the knees of his mother, seated in the centre, is placing a ring on the finger of St. Catherine, as a sign of her complete union with God. Hers is the most graceful figure in the picture; her left hand and fingers are exquisitely portrayed. She is dressed in a white bodice over a red velvet blouse; and her skirt is of gold brocade with darker designs. She wears a crown, and the veil falling on her forehead is so transparent, that it can hardly be seen. Her facial expression has an indescribable delicacy. Beside her is a broken wheel, the emblem of her martyrdom. On the other side is St. Barbara, absorbed in a book, and beside her is a small tower, representing her imprisonment for her faith. A relatively small angel kneels on either side of the Madonna, and two others, smaller still, hover above, holding a crown. The angel on the right plays a harp; the other holds a book in which Mary is reading. Placed symmetrically at the back, stand the protectors of the hospital: St. John the Baptist with his emblem, the lamb; and St. John the Apostle holding a chalice. On the side wings of this altarpiece are episodes from the lives of these two saints.

During the sixteenth century, there were two main currents in Flemish art: one followed the native tradition, the other sought to imitate Italian art. Among the former, Hieronymus Bosch carried the love for the fantastic and grotesque to its highest point. He painted several versions of the temptations of St. Anthony.

One of the greatest figures of the Flemish native traditional art was Pieter Brueghel the Elder (1525-1569), the first of a long line of painters in his family. His realistic folk-scenes earned him the nickname, the Droll or Peasant. In 1551 he became a member of the guild of painters in Antwerp; then he travelled to Italy, where he made many nature drawings. He assimilated the intellectual training of Italian art, without in any way abandoning his own native genius. This made him one of the most original folk painters of Flanders.

The *hunters in the snow* (Pl. 48.2), in the Gallery at Vienna, shows how well he adapted for his own uses the Italian power of selecting and organizing the elements in a picture, as well as his mastery over linear and aerial perspective. In this wonderful picture, he reduced the dominating colours to a cold blue, green and white, with dark, almost black details added, and a few small touches of warmer colours, in the hunters, dogs and fire. From the hill on the left to the valley below, bordered by mountains on the horizon, he leads the eye, diagonally into the depth, by means of the movements of the hunters and dogs, as well as by the lines of the landscape, from the snow-covered areas and frozen lake to the snow-capped peaks of the mountains.

In his paintings of peasant life Brueghel showed his native genius best. In the *wedding dance*, painted in 1566 (now in the Detroit Institute of Arts), he shows realistic peasant types in the front line, giving themselves in care-free abandon to the whirling movements of the dance. This seemingly unorganized dancing crowd really follows an undulating movement, going to the right and backwards, then forward and to the left, until it returns and disappears to the left. Two other important pictures of Brueghel are *the return of the herd*, painted in 1560 (now in Vienna), and *the blind leading the blind*, painted in 1577, (now in Naples). It is rather a crude realistic painting of peasant life.

Peter Paul Rubens (1577-1640) was the greatest painter of the Baroque period in Flanders. He almost dominated the Flemish school of the seventeenth century. His pupils and imitators were able to grasp only certain aspects of his genius. He was born in Germany, where his father was in exile, but the family returned to Antwerp, where he spent most of his life. He was educated in this city, and learnt eight languages. At the age of twenty, he was admitted into the painters' guild of Antwerp. His first journey to Italy was in 1600, when he visited Venice, Florence, Rome, and Genoa. He lived for several years at Mantua, as the court painter of the duke, who sent him on commissions to Spain and elsewhere. In 1608 he returned to Antwerp, and there became court painter of the Spanish governor of Flanders, the archduke Albert. In the same year he married Isabel Brandt. His studio became the centre of great activity. He had a large number of pupils. Unable to cope with all the orders received, he was assisted by his apprentices, especially by van Dyck and by others whom he trained for special tasks. The master himself designed the whole picture and painted the principal figures. Then Snyders, for example, would paint in the details and animals, whilst van Thulden did the landscapes and backgrounds. But Rubens was there giving advice, and it was he who finally retouched the painting, so that the whole picture bore the touch of his genius. After the death of his wife in 1626, he entered the diplomatic service, and made several trips to France, England and Spain. After four years he married a beautiful young girl, Helena Fourment. He spent his later years at his castle in Steen near Brussels, where he died.

Rubens' paintings deal with all kinds of subjects: religious, mythological, and folk themes. They also included portraits and landscapes. His early style was a combination of carefully chosen elements from the old masters, such as Michelangelo, Raphael, Titian, Tintoretto, Veronese, Correggio, Barocci, and his contemporaries, the Carracci and Caravaggio. From these various elements he formed his own individual style, which was ideally suited for the decoration of churches and great palaces. His figures were plastically treated, by a bold use of light and shade, in the manner of Caravaggio. We can see this in his two masterpieces in the cathedral of Antwerp, the *erection of the cross* (1610), and especially in the *descent from the cross* (1611-1614). In both, the composition is emphasized by the physical activity: of setting up the cross in the former, and of bringing down the Saviour's body after the crucifixion in the latter. The diagonal line is accentuated in both pictures, enhancing this dynamic effect. In the latter picture he obtains a strikingly pathetic effect by the use of a strong but rather artificial light.

As his style became more mature, his pictures were filled more and more with dynamic movement, which ended sometimes in an almost feverish twisting and writhing of bodies. In the great commissions received from various rulers he made use of mythological and symbolical representations, depicted in the most sumptuous manner. These were the methods he used to glorify his patrons. One of the most grandiose series is that which includes the twenty-one huge canvases, representing the *life of Marie de Medici*, for the Luxembourg palace, but now hanging in the Louvre, Paris.

After his second marriage, the young wife became his ideal of beauty. He painted her several times, but none of his later paintings surpassed that of Helena Fourment in her bridal attire (Pl. 149.1), now in Munich. The picture is full of Venetian reminiscences. He used scintillating dots to paint her rich brocade and velvet dress. Her bright eyes look directly at the beholder. The gold-pink of the dress is contrasted by the draped curtain hanging behind and framing the seated figure. It is a deep purple, a colour he used frequently in his later pictures.

One of Rubens' attractive pictures is the *head of a child*, in the Lichtenstein Gallery, Vaduz. It is believed to be the portrait of one of his daughters. Simplicity is the characteristic of this representation of a child, who seems to live on the canvas; for Rubens has achieved a most wonderful impression of vitality. This is probably the result of his bold but delicate use of light, to indicate the modelling of the face and hair.

During his last years, when he lived almost in retirement, he painted more intimate and personal subjects. From this period dates his thirty or so landscapes, as well as several other family portraits of his wife and children. Here his style is more colourful, richer and lighter than in his earlier works. He was able to obtain wonderful colour effects, as well as to represent textures in a strikingly vivid manner, by using transparent layers of paint or glazes. This he did by painting one layer over the other, so that the colour of the lower layers plays through the successive ones; and this mingling brings out extraordinarily rich effects. This technique was first used by the van Eycks, from whom Rubens borrowed, but it was lost after him. Rubens had a great influence on later painters, especially in England, where he inspired Gainsborough and Constable, and in France where he influenced Watteau.

Anthony van Dyck (1599-1641) was the most famous among Rubens' collaborators. He came of a merchant's family in Antwerp. He was already known as a painter when he entered the studio of Rubens. He assimilated so thoroughly the style of his master, that it is almost impossible to distinguish his work on a picture from that of the latter. In 1620, he went to England; but his stay was short, for after a few months, he returned to Antwerp. Shortly after, he left for Italy, where he worked four years in Genoa. In 1632 van Dyck settled down in England, where he became the court painter of Charles I. Here he made a great number of portraits; and received greater favours than any artist in England had ever received before. Having been knighted and loaded with honours, he married the daughter of a Scottish earl. He was only forty-two when he died in London.

Although he painted some religious pictures, his main work was portraits. He did literally hundreds of them, especially of his royal and aristocratic sitters in England. He created rich surface effects by depicting the costly dress of his subjects, such as silks, fine lace, feathers, and jewels. His psychological insight was such that he not only conveyed the individual personalities, but he recreated the general environment in which they lived. Among his numerous portraits of the king and the royal family, the best known is that of *Charles I* (Pl. 49.2) (1633), in the Louvre, Paris, showing the monarch in hunting dress.

# 11. GERMAN ART

## GENERAL SURVEY

Germany has widely different names in the different languages. The English word was the name of one of the Germanic tribes most familiar to the Romans. The Germans themselves call their country Deutschland. To the south of the country rises the tall, wide chain of the Alps, whose deep valleys fostered small communities, which became independent in the Middle Ages and now form the German-speaking part of Switzerland. To the north, a sandy and marshy plain reaches to the North Sea. This is the Low German region. In between, a broad upland (plateau) runs like an arc from south to northwest. This is the High German region, rich in minerals, industry and agriculture. Its language is now the official language of the country, very different from Low German. South-east of this plateau is the valley of the river Danube, a natural trade route from the Black Sea and the east since pre-historic times. Another famous river, the Rhine, flows through Germany to the North Sea.

The Romans had occupied the Danube valley and Rhineland, leaving behind numerous monuments of their civilization in southern Germany. However, German history begins with Charlemagne in the eighth century. He set its boundaries against the Scandinavian north and the Slavic east, and gave it its first political unity. With the help of English missionaries, he also gave it religious unity, and linked it with Rome and its civilizing influence. After his death, it was separated from what is now France. The Saxon kings, of whom the greatest was Otto I, who ruled in the tenth and eleventh centuries, and who linked it with Italy and Greece by conquest and marriage, brought another impetus to learning and art, and encouraged the growth of cities. Under them the German states came to be known as the Holy Roman Empire of the German Nation. This title was chiefly an honour; but politically the country remained weak. The kings were elected by dukes, who had the real power. The former remained poor and weak because of short periods of reign and frequent change of ruling houses. This disunity and weakness was an invitation to aggression by strong neighbours.

Many of the emperors were more interested in Italian than in German affairs. Under the Hohenstaufen in the early thirteenth century, there was peace and prosperity, the cities became rich, and some of the finest buildings were erected. Art took its themes from life; and literature and science flourished. St. Albert the Great might easily be called ' the Father of modern science ' for his experimental methods and wide interests. But Hohenstaufen rulers prepared the way for political disintegration by giving many rights and possessions to their vassals, so that in the following period, the Interregnum, the country was at the mercy of robber knights. To protect themselves, the merchants of the towns formed a powerful League (Hansa towns), thus forming an aristocracy of wealth, which for a century acquired great riches and power from trade all over northern Europe. The Habsburgs, who had acquired extensive domains by means of fortunate marriages, were elected emperors in 1273, and the title remained with them afterwards. They too were more interested in Italy than in Germany. They destroyed the castles of the robbers, which are now picturesque ruins along the old trade routes and the Rhine. One of them, Charles IV of Bohemia, was a great patron of art and learning, and built the first German University in Prague. In the fifteenth century, printing was introduced in Nuremberg, which was one of the richest and most advanced cities in Germany, with Cologne close behind,

Near the beginning of the Renaissance, the German empire reached its greatest extent under Charles V; but the country came to be torn by terrible civil wars and foreign attacks from many sides. The lot of the peasants became even worse after the failure of their revolt. The Turks were besieging Vienna. The greatest disaster in German history was the Thirty Years' War (1618-48), which began as a civil war, but soon Germany was the battlefield of various European powers. Its population was reduced to a fraction, cities became villages, and the countryside was completely devastated. Politically it became a meaningless jig-saw-puzzle of hundreds of tiny principalities. The people were so demoralized, that cultural stagnation set in, from which it did not recover for more than a century. In the first part of the eighteenth century, Germany gave an impulse to archaeology through the work of Winckelmann, who lived in Rome, and whose studies gave him a deeper understanding and appreciation of Greek and Roman art than the Renaissance enthusiasts had had. His writings influenced the art critic Lessing, who taught that art should grow out of a living culture. In

Germany, art found its highest expression in great music. Another scholar, Schlegel, started the study, of India's languages by the comparative method. Napoleon's invasions ended the Holy Roman Empire, but aroused national patriotism which led to political unity under Prussia in the later half of the nineteenth century.

## ARCHITECTURE

Germany, like the other north European countries, continued with Gothic architecture long after the Renaissance had begun in Italy. Renaissance forms penetrated very slowly, first, not in actual architecture, but in wood-cuts, copper engravings and paintings, where artists liked filling in their backgrounds with Renaissance palaces. Towards the second half of the sixteenth century, Renaissance ornaments were applied on constructions based entirely on Gothic principles, with their typical high gables.

These Renaissance forms varied throughout the country because they came from different sources. While southern Germany was more directly influenced by northern Italy, northern Germany got its ideas secondhand from France, Flanders and Holland. Nor was the assimilation of Renaissance principles thorough; the rigid classical rules never suited the German temperament, which is more inclined to the picturesque and irregular. That is why the German architects showed a special love for decorative forms derived from the minor arts, which they applied profusely on their buildings. Just the contrary happened in Italy, where the monumental forms of architecture were impressed on furniture and other objects of the minor arts. In Germany, for instance, the columns and pilasters on the façades of buildings imitated the forms of candelabra (candlesticks) or balusters (supports of a railing). Decorations applied on walls had often the forms of metalwork, like twisted columns or ribbon ornaments. Sometimes these forms came from woodwork decorations, imitating ribbons and scrolls (Fig. 457). German

Fig. 457. Decoration imitating scrolls.

artists were fond of the telamon (from Greek 'bearer', plural telamones), a column in the form of a male figure (Fig. 458), similar to the Greek

Fig. 458. Telamon.

atlantes or the caryatids. Often these supporting figures were only torsos, trunks with heads but no limbs, set on a downward tapering pillar that was decorated in various ways. Their correct name is terminal figures (a term was a stone post originally used for indicating a boundary line).

During the sixteenth and seventeenth centuries, many guild and town halls (Rathhaus), as well as palatial houses for wealthy citizens and castles for the nobility, were erected. Good examples of this kind of architecture are the *Peller house* in *Nuremberg,* and the group of buildings forming the *Heidelberg castle*. The Thirty Years' War (1618-1648) interrupted the building activities. After defeating the Habsburg emperor with the help of the French Bourbons, the countless petty German princes, who thus gained absolute power in their domains, now modelled their courts on the Versailles pattern. The southern Germans remained under the influence of Italian Baroque. The gradual merging of the two foreign elements by the native genius produced around 1730 the Rococo style in its typically German form, with its profusion of rock and shell ornament, and iteration of the telamones. The *Zwinger pavilion* in *Dresden* (1711-1722), built by Matthaeus Daniel Poppelmann, is a typical example of German Rococo. This style became famous also for church architecture.

## SCULPTURE

The Germans always preferred to express personal feelings and individual tastes rather than ideal forms and generalized types. This is seen especially in their sculpture. In it, as in architecture, the late Gothic style gave way only slowly to Renaissance forms. Although they used stone and bronze, German sculptors favoured wood, which was abundant in their country, and in which they produced their most famous works. This sculpture was usually polychrome.

Especially numerous and famous are the carved reredos or altarpieces, dating from the fourteenth to the sixteenth centuries. Unlike the Flemish painted altarpieces, the German ones were generally sculptured. The figures in the centre were often carved in the round; the panels on the wings were in bas-relief. Only the outer sides of the wings were painted. Around and above the different panels there was an intricate late-Gothic architectural framing, which also surmounted the entire altarpiece and reached sometimes to the ceiling. Of the numerous sculptors of altarpieces, two names stand out: Veit Stoss (1440-1533), and especially Tilman Riemenschneider (1468-1531), who worked in Wurzburg. Peter Viscfler of Nuremberg (c. 1460-1529) deserves special mention for having revived the technique of bronze sculpture. The figures of his famous *shrine of St. Sehaldus* in *Nuremberg* reveal Renaissance influence.

## PAINTING

During the early period, there were numerous German art schools, of which those of Cologne and Bohemia were the most outstanding ones in the fourteenth century. In the following century, the Flemish influence of the Van Eycks was strongly felt in northern Germany.

The greatest painter of this period was Stephan Lochner (c. 1405–1451) of the Cologne school. Early in life he had come there from his native Meerseburg, near Lake Constance, and remained till his death. His greatest work is *the adoration of the Magi*, a folding altarpiece, painted for the chapel in the town hall of Cologne (now in the cathedral). In the central part, the Magi are almost life-size. One of the side panels represents St. Ursula and her companions, and the Ovher St. Gereon and his soldiers. Lochner's most charming picture is the *Madonna in the rose garden* (Pl. 49.3), in Wallraf Richart's Museum, Cologne. It is a simple devotional picture, showing the virgin Mary with the child Jesus sitting before a rose trellis. They are surrounded hy tiny angels, some playing musical instruments. In the background, two angels are holding a delicate curtain, to secure privacy. Above this are symbolized figures of God the Father raising His hand in blessing, and a dove, the symbol of the Holy Spirit.

In contrast to Lochner's gentle delicacy, the southern German Conrad Witz (c. 1400-1447) has a harder, more sculpturesque style. He worked chiefly in Basel. In his youth he followed his father, a painter at the Duke of Burgundy's court in France and Flanders, where he was able to study the masters of his time. His extraordinary talent for landscape painting is well seen in *the miraculous draught of fishes*, at the Musée d'Art et d'Histoire in Geneva. The scene reveals the tender courtesy of divine pardon. Some of the apostles have fished all night, but caught nothing. Dawn breaks. Someone on the shore is taking a friendly interest in them, so they obey his bidding and cast their net in again at the right side of the boat. Soon it is filled to overflowing. John tells Peter that it is the Lord. Impetuous as ever, Peter cannot wait for the boat to land but jumps into the water and wades ashore. It is this moment that Conrad Witz has caught in his picture. The other apostles, still in their boat to the left middle distance, balance with their mass the majestic figure of Jesus, on the right side of the front plane. There is a touch of continuous narration, since Peter is seen twice, in the boat and in the water. Thus his figure is emphasized for the special significance this meeting had for him. The Lord's hand is stretched out to receive him, for he has come to show his love to his disciples. He will not mention their cowardly desertion in his hour of greatest need. To Peter, the self-assured braggart who had three times denied him so shamefully in his very presence during the passion, he does not deny the office of chief steward and shepherd of his flock ; but rather he confirms him in it after a triple profession of love to make up for the denial. The lake in the middle occupies about half the picture. The reflections of the scenes on the surface of the water reveal the artist's exact understanding of refraction. To the right is the city of Geneva, and in the far distance are the Alps. This shows the premature comprehension Witz had of perspective, for this was unknown in Europe at the time.

Until modern times, there was little admiration for the great artist, Matthias Grunewald (c. 1485-c. 1530), who produced one of the most outstanding masterpieces of painting in world art, the

*Isenheint altarpiece*. It is not known exactly when and where he was born, nor where he got his artistic training. In 1501 his name is mentioned in the archives of Aschaffenburg; around 1514 he became court painter of cardinal Albert of Brandenburg, elector of Mainz. He painted various pictures, but the quintessence of his talent is revealed in the above-mentioned reredos. It was made for the Antonine convent at Isenheim in Alsace. Now it is in Colmar, in the Unterlinden monastery, which was transformed into a museum. It is a great altarpiece or polyptic, having on either side double wings or hinged panels that can be opened and closed.

Grünewald painted all the panels. Those that flank the sculptural figures in the middle, when the panels are completely open, represent scenes from the life of St. Anthony the hermit. When these first wings are closed, we see from left to right the annunciation, the nativity and the resurrection. Finally, when the second or last wings are entirely closed, there appears the most important scene, the famous crucifixion. This is just the contrary to the usual way of arranging the panels, where the main scene used to be on the inner side and a preparatory event on the outer one.

The *annunciation* scene is represented in an oratory (prayer room) in Late Gothic style. Light streams in from the traceried windows, and fills the atmosphere. The humble virgin, with hands clasped before her open prayer-book, receives the heavenly message from the majestic angel, who points towards her. Mary's youthful face is filled with awe and holy fear. Here as elsewhere, colour is Grünewald's greatest means of expression. He uses different warm and cold tonalities of reds, greens and yellows to secure extraordinary effects.

The *nativity* (PI. 49.4) is represented in the centre, and is divided into two distinct scenes. On the right, the nativity proper is shown, but in a rather unusual way. There is no stable nor crib; the scene is laid in a garden, where necessary things, like cradle, pail and a small cup have been taken. The virgin mother sits in the centre, tenderly embracing her divine Child, and gazing at him with heavenly bliss. Behind her, the yellow-green landscape culminates in bluish snow-covered peaks of mountains, whose oblique cliffs carry the eye up to the left corner where heaven opens out into a radiant glory in which the symbolic figure of God the Father is more suggested than actually seen. The brilliant glory that surrounds him and flows down to earth consists of thousands of scintillating angels that flicker around in the most delightful attitudes. Their colours change from gold to pinks and blue-greens as they come down to tell the shepherds the good news of the Saviour's birth. This descent, from the radiant yellows of heaven through the pinkish-grey clouds and the bluish-white mountains, to the Infant held on a white cloth in the arms of the seated virgin, dressed in red with a blue-green cloak over her shoulders, produces a strong diagonal movement that creates the impression of the streaming down of heavenly grace. But even more outstanding is Grunewald's ability to express so much spiritual beauty in a face that lacks physical beauty.

The dark curtain, which ends the picture in a strong vertical line, connects it with the left scene, where before the same curtain stands a chapel in Late Gothic style, with most striking colours. The interior is filled with lovely angel-musicians in different sizes and colours, on the floor or hovering in the air. The tallest of them is outside playing his violoncello whilst gazing in rapture at the mother's bliss. But the eye is drawn to the figure kneeling at the entrance of the chapel, draped in a blue-green mantle and wearing a red dress, the sleeves of which melt in the circle of glory that surrounds her head and shoulders, which from concentric red and yellow dissolves almost into a glowing white. The beautiful head is crowned with a diadem of flames. It is worth while stopping a second to find out the meaning of this mysterious figure. Going back to the nativity scene, we see that Mary is surrounded with objects of well-known symbolic meaning: the fruit-bearing olive tree, the wall behind which signifies that she is in the enclosed garden, the pure waters that are like a stainless mirror, the mystic rose are all familiar emblems of her stainless purity. Above the kneeling figure in the circle of glory, angels descend with sceptre and crown, whilst above them the symbolic figure of God the Father appears again. Between the Gothic tracery of the chapel, appear in sculptural representations, two of the prophets who foretold the coming of Christ, in order to indicate the reason for such spotless purity. Everything seems to point to the fact that Grünewald made allusion to the Immaculate Conception in this mysterious figure, which is probably the youthful Mary in the temple.

The last scene at the extreme right shows the Saviour's *resurrection*. Grünewald shows Jesus rising triumphantly out of his tomb, whilst the frightened guards are lying senseless around. Here also Grünewald's great means of expression is colour. A round circle of bright light surrounds Christ's head in the same way as it surrounds Mary's figure in the temple; but here the outer circle is blue instead of red. The shroud draping the Redeemer's figure floats in the air beneath him, part of it still trailing in the tomb, and it changes in colour, until it reproduces all the tints of the rainbow.

In the *crucifixion scene* (PI. 50.1), Grünewald showed clearly that he did not search for forms of beauty; his only aim was, like that of all religious art during the Middle Ages, to convey through his pictures the teaching of religious truth. He used all the extraordinary aesthetic means that the subject, forms, and colours could give him, to express with the greatest intensity all the cruel horrors of suffering. The tortures of the cross have twisted the dying body of Christ. Thorns from the scourging are imbedded in the wounds with which they have covered him. The deadly green of the flesh stands out against the dark clotting blood. The expression of the face and the upturned hands proclaim by what torments the Redeemer offered his sacrifice for the salvation of the world. The sorrowful expressions of the surrounding figures harmonize with the whole atmosphere. Especially expressive are the gestures of the hands. The palms and fingers of the Crucified are turned upwards, as in a gesture of a priest offering the sacrifice. His mother's hands are clasped in firm resignation, as she sinks into the arms of the beloved disciple in her deep sorrow. Those of Magdalen, kneeling at the foot of the cross, are interlocked convulsively. Opposite to this group, on the other side of the cross, St. John the Baptist is pointing to the Saviour in a gesture suited to his character, and the words he once spoke, 'He must increase and I must decrease are written above him so as to make no mistake about the lesson intended. Below him are other symbols of his words, 'Behold the Lamb of God From the wounded side of a lamb carrying a cross, a stream of blood flows into a chalice, symbolizing the Holy Sacrifice of the Mass. Like other painters, who showed the importance of a figure by its relative size, Grünewald also emphasized the body of Christ by making it larger than the others.

His art is most characterized by the expression of intense feeling, by the choice of tragic subject matter, portrayal of gestures, and use of colours. It is hard to believe that the same artist, who could show the crucifixion with all its horrible sufferings more realistically than any other, should at the same time be able to express the heavenly joy of the most tender motherly love, as in the nativity scene. But it is exactly in this that the greatness of Grünewald lies.

The most famous German artist, Albrecht Dürer (1471-1528) was born in Nüremberg in the second half of the fifteenth century. At that time Nüremberg was the most famous art centre in Germany. Craftsmen eager for fame came there from different parts of Europe. Among them was a goldsmith, a native of the Hungarian village Ajtós ('ajtó' means door, as does also the German word 'türe' or 'Düre', hence probably the name Dürer). After wandering about the Netherlands for a number of years, he settled down in Nüremberg. Albrecht Dürer was the third of his eighteen children. After his schooling, he was apprenticed to his father's workshop. This early training as a goldsmith had two important effects on his later career. First of ail, a goldsmith's most important tool is the graver or burin, and by learning to use it on metals, Dürer was prepared for his famous copper engravings: for the process of engraving a picture on a copper plate is very much like engraving a monogram or design on gold or silver objects, with the difference that an engraving has to be multiplied by a printing press. The picture has, therefore, to be engraved in an inverted position on the copper plate—in other words, the right on the left and the left on the right. Secondly, the father himself had been trained in the Netherlands with the great masters, according to Dürer's own family records. Thus the son learned to respect the traditions set by the van Eycks.

His great talent for drawing showed itself early, as his self-portrait at the age of thirteen (1484) testifies. It was made, during his apprenticeship in his father's workshop, with a silverpoint, a very difficult method allowing no alteration. Yielding to the boy's manifest inclination for drawing, his father consented to apprentice him at the age of fifteen to the most famous workshop in Nüremberg, that of Michael Wohlgemuth, a painter and woodcutter. Here Dürer was instructed in ail the branches of art, and learnt to use pens and brushes, to copy and draw from life, to do landscapes in guache and water colour, and to paint with oils. Most important of all, he learnt how to make a woodcut. Wohigemuth was especially noted for his woodcuts, the technique of which Dürer improved.

Three years later, Dürer became a journeyman, who, according to the custom of that time, wandered about to perfect his art by learning from different masters in different places. Thus he stayed in Colmar, Basel and Strassburg. He returned to Nüremberg to marry. In 1494 he made his first trip to Italy where he studied especially the works of Mantegna. He made many interesting and exquisite drawings during this journey. After his return, he opened his own workshop and started to produce many woodcuts and engravings, drawings, and paintings. He visited Italy a second time in 1505, staying for a time in Bologna and Venice where he met Giovanni Bellini, who was very kind to him according to Dürer's own account. In Nüremberg, Dürer associated with important people: scholars, scientists, aristocrats, princes and bishops. He was able to discuss mythology and mathematics; he composed treatises on fortifications, the theory of human proportions, and three books on descriptive geometry.

In 1512 he was asked to work for the emperor Maximilian I, as designer-in-chief of an enormous series of woodcuts assembled in the form of a triumphal arch. He also made the marginal pen drawings in a prayer book for the emperor, who died shortly after. So in 1520 Dürer had to go to the south Netherlands in order to ask the new emperor, Charles V, to continue the yearly allowance that Maximilian had granted him. During this visit he had great success. The painters of Antwerp gave him a splendid reception and banquet in the painters' guild hall, where he was honoured not only by them but also by" the great personages of the city. He returned home successful; but broken in health. He died in 1528. Dürer's many-sided and productive artistic activity may be classified into his woodcuts, engravings, drawings, paintings, and writings.

In his woodcuts and engravings, he set up new standards of perfection. Through his work, Germany's illustrated printed books became universally renowned.

The origin of the woodcut is not known for certain. It started around the early fifteenth century, and was probably invented in Germany. The earliest known woodcuts were merely strong outlines, with blank spaces between which were often coloured by hand. These cheap pictures were pasted on walls, panels, boxes, etc. Around the middle of the fifteenth century, an explanatory text was carved on the bottom of the pictures, which were bound together into the so-called block-books, The woodcut really developed when it was used for book illustrations, and the impressions made by hand were replaced by printing presses. Woodcuts were first used to illustrate printed books during Düker's childhood, around the year 1475.

To make a woodcut, a block of wood has to be sawed along the grain. The surface is then covered with white paint, and on this the artist draws his design. After this, the block has to be cut, i.e., the wood has to be removed from both sides of the lines so that high ridges—like the letters on a rubber stamp —are left on the block. These outstanding parts are then inked, i.e., they are covered with printer's ink, made of soot mixed with oil. The block is then pressed against the paper. But since the impression will be in reverse of the design on the block, the latter has to be drawn backwards to get the right result. The woodcut is a relief printing process, because the parts that stand out are the ones that print.

The first of Dürer's great woodcut sets, which gave him a great reputation and which is still the most famous, is the *Apocalypse series*. It is ranked with the world's great masterpieces of art. It consists of fifteen huge woodcuts, the first of which illustrates the martyrdom of St. John, and the other fourteen are illustrations for the text of the Apocalypse, or the Book of Revelations. These woodcuts were printed without any inscription on the front side of the pages; the text was printed on their backs. These pages were then bound in the form of a book. This was the first time that an artist designed and printed a book all by himself in his own workshop.

Perhaps the most famous design in this series is *the four horsemen* (Pl. 50.2,). It represents conquest, and the evils that usually come in its train. Conquest is shown aiming an arrow; War has a drawn sword; Famine is personified as a fat war-profiteer, who feeds on the want of others; and Death, seated on a small, lean horse, is holding a trident. The figures are riding roughshod over the citizens: men and women, rich and poor—all alike are victims of the horrors of war.

These pictures, drawn with great precision and vigour, show Dürer's earlier interest in the unusual, the fantastic, and the narrative. The Apocalypse series shows the intense movement and intricate design characteristic of Late Gothic. His other woodcut series are the two sets of *the passion of Christ*, and the *life of the Virgin*. These later drawings are more simple, clear and natural, or as he termed it, 'more according to the original effect of nature.'

Soon Dürer turned to another graphic process, namely metal engraving, which was something new in Nüremberg at that time. We have already seen how he was trained for this during his apprenticeship as a goldsmith in his father's workshop. The process of engraving is the reverse of the wood-cutting process; for the woodcut stands out in relief, while the engraving is cut in. Thus the printer's ink is held by the outstanding parts in the woodcut, and in the cut-in-lines of the engraving. Like the wood-cutter, the engraver must first prepare his drawing on paper. Then he must transfer this design to a highly-polished metal, usually copper plate, with a burin (a sharply-pointed chisel with a handle). Holding the handle in his palm, he incises or cuts in the lines, moving from right to left. First he must do the outlines, then he fills in the details by finishing, one at a time, small areas of one or two square inches. While the burin is pushed forward to cut the line, it turns up little furs or rough edges on the plate, which have to be smoothed away or polished. The plate is then inked, and wiped clean so that the ink remains only in the depressed lines or grooves. Finally the plate is pressed very hard on a sheet of moist paper, which soaks up the ink from the lines, and so receives the print.

One of Dürer's most famous copper engravings is *St. Jerome in his study* (Pl. 50.3 ). The saint is represented as a typical scholar and writer. The austerity of his hermit life is lost in the homely atmosphere of the study in which Dürer has put him., The warm sunshine streaming in through the large small-paned windows, gives even the skull on the window-sill a friendly rather than grim appearance. The furnishings are orderly and simple, including the necessary articles and small comforts of a scholar : a large table with inkpot and crucifix, and a small desk on top of it, at which the saint is busy writing at the far end of the room. This itself increases the air of intimate seclusion and peaceful security. His only companions are a big lion whom the saint befriended, lying near the door, contented and drowsy, yet keeping a suspicious eye outside, and a very sleepy little dog who is resting his feet on the lion's paw. A balance of movement and peace is produced by the use of light, shade, and space.

Another engraving by Dürer is *Melancholia* (Pl. 50.4 ). The artist himself intended it as to St. Jerome a study in contrast in his study; for he almost always gave away the two prints together. Melancholia is represented as a winged woman, who, weary of her independent search for knowledge, sits cowering in a cold and lonely place far from the sea. She is glowering into space, while her clothes, hair, and instruments are in a wild disorder; and her neglected child sits by itself sulking and glum. Melancholia shows the futile unrest of man divorced from God, whose efforts at creation end in frustration and unhappiness to himself and others; while St. Jerome, who seeks inspiration from the crucifix and sacred writings, has found peace and happiness, reflected in the warm, bright, orderly, and home-like surroundings. Even the animals are contented in his company. Thus Dürer shows that life in union with God brings peace, order, happiness, and security; while apart from God life is restless, futile, and unhappy.

Dürer's paintings show the influence of the Italian Renaissance more strongly than his woodcuts and engravings. One of his most famous paintings is *the adoration of the Magi* (Pl. 51.1 ), which was originally the central panel of an altartriptych, or folding altar-piece, in the palace church at Wittenberg. It is now in the Uffizi Gallery in Florence. Dürer's composition, like Leonardo da Vinci's, is arranged in the shape of a pyramid. The outstanding figures are the child Jesus, who, enthroned on his mother's knees, accepts the present of the old king kneeling before Him. The Child and his mother, dignified yet familiarly human, are shown in profile. In the centre stands the second king. After the manner of Leonardo da Vinci, his body is shown in front view, while the head is in profile. Nearby, to the right side, stands the Moorish king, whose rich colours are set off by the bright landscape in the background. The ruins around the group form a kind of frame. Near the top on the left hand corner, the dark vegetation growing on the old ruins stands out against the bright sunlight behind it. Towards the lower right, a servant is seen in the yard, unpacking presents. Further back, framed by a gateway, are more followers of the kings, still seated on their horses. Behind them in the distance is a typically German scene : a hill crowned by a castle and a clear blue lake; and far away, mountains and clouds against a dim horizon. The rich colours and use of real gold, and the golden-brown frame of the ruins, show the jeweller's son in the artist, who in this case did not aim at realism, as he did in his engravings. Dürer used the Flemish, oil technique with its enamel-like surface.

Dürer's *self-portrait* (Pl. 51.2 ), dated 1500, is preserved in the Pinakothek in Munich. It is the most famous of his numerous self-portraits. The custom of making self-portraits, now centuries old, makes this seem natural to us; but in Dürer's time it was rather unusual. Painters used to be regarded as simply other craftsmen until the time of the Renaissance, when they became self-conscious of their talents and were given an important position in society, as was the case with Dürer. His self-portrait of 1500 shows him at the age of twenty-nine. He has taken a specially solemn attitude, in the strictest and most symmetrical front view, against a dark background. The wide-open eyes dominate the beautiful face, which is framed by long wavy hair. The same rich brown tone runs through the hair, the furlined coat, and darker background. The direct frontal view and symmetry are most unusual, for they are rare in the West, and do not occur in any other of Dürer's portraits. This majestic pose and idealized portrait of himself made some art critics believe that he tried to show himself as he ought to be or as he would be if he were filled with the Spirit of Christ, or as St. Paul expresses it 'another Christ'.

Dürer also painted many landscapes and nature studies in water colour. One of the most lovely of these is *the large piece of turf in* which he shows his exact observation of the beauty of ordinary things in nature, commonly not noticed. By his skill in selecting and arranging his subject, to bring out the graceful delicacy of common weeds, he has created a masterpiece. He presented these weeds as if looking at them from their own level, that is, as if lying on the ground. The colours and arrangement of various grasses and their ears of seed show an equal perfection. This picture was painted in 1502, and is now in the Albertina Museum in Vienna.

Another outstanding, painter Hans Holbein the Younger (1494-1543), was born in Augsburg, a rich merchant city which had frequent relations with Italy. He belonged to an artist family, and was trained in painting by his father, known as Hans Holbein the Elder. He soon became familiar with both the northern and the Italian styles. His first centre of activity was Basel in Switzerland, where he met Erasmus, the great Dutch scholar, whose book he illustrated, and of whom he painted several portraits.

He was over thirty when he painted his most beautiful religious picture, *the Virgin with the family of burgomaster Meyer* (Pl. 51.3 ) Arranged in the traditional fashion, the burgomaster and his family are shown kneeling devoutly on both sides. In the centre is the Madonna, standing calmly and majestically in a niche of classical design, holding in her arms the divine Child, who raises his hand in blessing. The Madonna and Child reflect the harmonious beauty of the Italian Renaissance, especially that of Giovanni Bellini and Raphael. However, the two groups of donors : the burgomaster with a boy and a child before him to the right of the Madonna, and to her left his first wife in burial clothes and his living wife, have more northern characteristics as, for example, the attention to fine details and the realistic faces. In 1526 Holbein went to England where he was introduced by a letter of recommendation from Erasmus to Sir Thomas More, the chancellor of king Henry VIII. Sir Thomas received him with great favour, and Holbein painted many portraits of him, his family, and many of his friends. Later, when More lost the king's favour and was executed, Holbein spent some time among the German merchants at the Steelyard where they had their headquarters in London. The best-known portrait of this period is that of *George Gisze*, painted in 1532, which is now in Berlin. The merchant is shown standing before his office table, holding a letter just received. Account books, letters, a money-box, and especially the steelyard or scale for weighing money—the sign of the merchant guild—shows how busy he was with affairs. Later Holbein became the court painter of Henry VIII. He painted portraits of the king and his household. As a portraitist he was a keen observer, with a great ability for selecting some linear motifs to which he could subordinate everything. Holbein was the greatest portrait painter of his time.

He was also a famous designer of woodcuts. From 1523 to 1526 he made his famous series of forty-one woodcut designs to illustrate *the dance of death*. This subject or theme, sometimes called the dance macabre, became popular in the late Middle Ages and Early Renaissance. Increased communication with the East brought to Europe luxuries which led to worldliness, against which the people had to be warned by the reminder that some day all must be left behind. It also brought terrible plagues and diseases previously unknown, so that during the Black Death, the population of Europe was reduced to one-quarter of what it was before. So the death against which they were warned became a fearful reality, which spared no classes or ages.

The early 'dances macabres' were dramatic representations of sermons. Men and women of every condition were shown as they were in life and as they would be in death. They were often represented in long rows, hand in hand. The sadness of the living was contrasted with the gay dancing pose of the dead. Holbein changed the whole subject and its manner of representation. Instead of showing a monotonous dancing procession of living persons with their dead bodies in various stages of decay, he composed for each individual whom he wanted to represent, a separate picture with picturesque scenes, like a beautiful field with long furrows, and the setting of trees and clouds, or the interior of a room, and so on. Secondly, he personified death as a very active skeleton, always busy mocking and tricking those who are alive, leading them away from life, For instance, in one picture death is shown guiding an old man, all absorbed in the music death is playing for him, and not realizing that he has been led to the graveyard, where he is just stepping into an open tomb. In a second picture, death is helping the labourer to trace the last furrow, whilst in a third he is fighting a mock duel with a warrior, using a bone as his weapon. In still another, he is gathering the money on the miser's table, whilst the latter raises his hands in despair.

Very little is known about the early life of Lucas Cranach the Elder (1472-1553). In 1503 he went to southern Germany and Austria, where he made long journeys through the lands around the Danube. He was fascinated by the views of old forests which he painted with romantic feeling, and into them he set figures to harmonize with the scenery. The *repose on the flight into Egypt* (Pl. 51.4, ), formerly in the Kaiser Friederich Museum in Berlin, is a lovely picture of the Holy Family during its escape from king Herod, who wanted to kill the Child. They are seen resting near a spring in a mountainous region. Mary, draped in a long red dress, is seated towards the right side holding the child Jesus. Behind them, St. Joseph is standing in front of a huge pine tree, which is in the central axis of the picture. His dark blue robe contrasts with his big red shawl. He is holding his hat and walking stick. Tiny idyllic angels are busy serving and amusing the weary refugees. This intimate portrayal of the Holy Family, as well as the setting amidst the beautiful, weathered trees of an old German forest, the peaceful valley, and the snow-capped mountains in the distance, reveal the deep poetic feeling of the German soul.

In 1505 Cranach became the court-painter at Wittenberg of the prince elector of Saxony. He painted many portraits, for which he became famous. His association with Humanists led him to paint mythological and allegorical subjects. He directed a large studio of painters. Many of the pictures dated after 1510 were made either by his sons, Lucas the Younger and Hans Cranach, or by his apprentices.

# 12. DUTCH ART

## GENERAL SURVEY

The country, which we now know as Holland, was one part of a group of provinces called the Lowlands or Netherlands. The people are known as the Dutch, because their language is related to German (Deutsch). Lying in the delta of the Meuse and Rhine rivers, it is the hub of busy trade routes by sea, river and land. By means of dykes and dams, this hard-working people not only protected itself against floods, but conquered from the sea fertile pastures and fields, called polders. Thus the country is able not only to support itself comfortably—though its population per square mile is much greater than India's—but also to export cheap food to other parts of Europe. Most of the industry was directed to commerce and ship-building.

The history of Holland was similar to that of Flanders, the other part of the original Netherlands, until it revolted against Spain and became independent. Its subsequent efforts to expand trade and to create a colonial empire involved it in wars with France and England.

In the 16th century it sought new trade routes everywhere—through the Mediterranean, across Africa, and northern Russia. Failing to find a suitable route to the East Indies across the seas north of Europe, it succeeded in wresting the trade monopoly to the East Indies from Portugal. As a result, the country became very wealthy, and took a cultural lead in the north during the Renaissance. Dutch universities became famous in Europe; and the newly-invented art of printing was greatly encouraged.

The most urbanized Europeans after the Italians, the townsmen were predominantly rich, practical middle-class merchants and industrialists, who beautified the cities with their clean, comfortable homes. World trade gave the Dutch towns a cosmopolitan atmosphere; and Holland was the first to advocate international law based on morality and freedom of the seas. Its citizens enjoyed comparatively more civic liberties than those of people elsewhere in Europe. The culture of the country was determined by the middle class, not by the nobility as in other countries. Therefore in their paintings they preferred the familiar scenes of city and country life, landscapes, their homes, and still-life subjects.

## ARCHITECTURE

In Holland only a few outstanding buildings, mostly town halls, were produced in the Renaissance style. The town hall of The Hague (1565), with its stepped gable, decorated with turrets and statues, was one of the first buildings in this style. In the seventeenth century Holland was one of the few countries which resisted the Baroque style. In their buildings they kept to the classical purity of form and proportion. The building material was mainly brick, due to a lack of stone in the country. An outstanding example of seventeenth century building is the *Mauritshuis* (Fig. 459) in The Hague(1643),

Fig. 459. Mauritshuis, The Hague.

built in brick, stone being used only for the pillars and mouldings around the windows to accentuate them. The burgher houses in Holland also deserve special mention. They are entirely built in brick, with high-pitched roofs and stepped gables; their interior consists of small panelled rooms, often with windows of crown glass.

## PAINTING

Soon after the Dutch had won their independence in the seventeenth century, the first group of great painters appeared. They expressed the new aspirations and ideals of their country. Frans Hals (c. 1580-1666) was an outstanding figure among them. Born in Antwerp, he went as a youth to Haarlem, where he spent his laborious life. He was a painter of group and single portraits, and genre scenes. His portraits usually give the impression of overflowing vitality and joy; but his own personal life was full of struggles and worries, and ended in misery. The most remarkable achievement in his portraits was the variety and subtlety of his studies in fleeting expressions, especially that of laughter, which he showed in all its gradations. He caught these changing expressions, not by careful analysis, but by wonderful flashes of insight into his characters, which required a quick technique on the part of the artist. He handled the brush with great technical skill, in such a way that the strokes can be distinguished on the canvas. The brush seemed to obey all his artistic impulses. Like Velasquez, he looked for essentials, adding only those details that were necessary for characterization. This method had a great influence on the Impressionist artists of the later nineteenth century.

The individual portraits done in his earlier years were mostly of laughing urchins and jolly care-free people, as for example that of the *laughing cavalier* (1624) (in the Wallace Collection, London). Here we see a gallant, self-confident soldier with a quizzical expression on his face, against a quiet bluish-grey background. The great black hat, the gorgeous coat, richly embroidered with red-browns and yellows, and white lace collar and cuffs, stand out clearly. Towards the end of his life, however, he concentrated mostly on portraits of old people, withered and broken, such as that of *Malle Bobbe* (Mad Babbe).

He painted a number of group or guild portraits, very much in vogue then in Holland, but hardly found elsewhere. These life-size portraits of members of the various guilds or societies reflect the bourgeois spirit of the time. *The banquet of the officers of the guild of the archers of St. George* (Pl. 52.1 ) (Haarlem Museum) shows a group of men sitting and standing around a banqueting table. Two of them wear plumed hats. The draped curtain and two banners form the background. Those gathered around the table are engaged in lively conversation. Each figure is equally visible, and each head is an individualized portrait. The velvet and satin textures of the clothes, the wide slashed sleeves, the white cuffs and lace ruffs are all vividly portrayed. The figures are not combined in a real composition, but form only a sort of loose pattern; yet the artist manages to give the impression of unity.

As time went on, he gradually used less and less colour, so that the tones harmonized and blended, until in the later pictures there are only various steel-grey shades. This is seen in his last two pictures (1664), painted just two years before his death, which show the *men* and *women regents* of the hospital for old men in Haarlem (Haarlem Museum). The characters are shown with a grave dignity and strength.

In the field of painting, Rembrandt van Rijn (1607-1669) was the greatest genius of the Low Countries. He was born in Leyden in 1607, the son of a well-to-do miller who lived on the bank of the Rhine. His name Rembrandt van Rijn may be connected with that fact. His first work was done in Leyden. At twenty-five he settled in Amsterdam, a wealthy commercial centre of international importance. There he made portraits and other pictures of the rich merchants and burghers. Almost at once he became the foremost painter in Amsterdam. Three years later he married a wealthy girl, Saskia van Uylenborch, who was the centre of his life until she died seven years after. Art became his consolation in the later period, when his existence was overshadowed by sorrow and misfortune. Some of his most attractive paintings are the happy portraits of various members of his family, including many of his wife, others of his son Titus, and of his mother. In the most famous of these, called *Rembrandt and his wife* (Pl. 52.2 ) (in the Dresden Gallery), the artist is gaily dressed, holding his wife on his knee. One hand is on her waist, whilst with the other he raises a glass of Rhine wine, as though drinking to their happiness.

Besides individual portraits, he also painted groups for the various corporations of the city. The first of these was done in his youth; it is the so-called *lesson in anatomy* (Pl 52.3 ) (now in the Mauritshuis, The Hague). At the order of the surgeon's organization, he represented Dr. Tulp, the anatomist, dissecting a human body before seven of his Amsterdam associates. The picture remained in the hall of the surgeons till 1818.

About the year 1639, Rembrandt was asked to paint the portraits of the members of a company of arquebusiers of Amsterdam; and the result was the famous picture known as the *night watch* (Pl. 53.1 ) (in the Rijksmuseum, Amsterdam). In reality, it represents them leaving their quarters at midday. Only two members are treated fully : the captain, Frans Banning Cock, in a black costume with a red scarf; and his lieutenant, Willem van Ruytenburch, in yellow. Of the other fourteen members of the company whose portraits had been ordered, most are more or less recognizable; but only two sergeants with halberds, the ensign, and the arquebusier in red loading his weapon, are really portrayed. The others are reduced to actors whose role is made more important than their individuality. Rembrandt tried to get a mass-effect of many more men, because only these sixteen figures represented the entire company. A number of heads, only partly visible, appeared behind the fully portrayed members. Glorious sunshine emphasizes the central part of the scene, where the shadow of the commander's outstretched hand falls on the bright uniform next to him. The captain orders the lieutenant to let the company march : everything seems to depend on this command. The arquebusiers come through the gate in groups. The sunlight, striking the ground from the left, gives depth to the painting. At the back, the light is reduced considerably more than in actual sunshine, but Rembrandt did not want to stress reality so much as the company's basic ideals : alertness and soldierly spirit. For this reason he painted them with their equipment and official costumes. There is variety of dress and movement to show that everything seems to happen at the very moment of the alarm. This provides the dynamics and romance of the masterpiece, further emphasized by the spatial build-up, with the endlessness of the deep, dark gateway in a grandiose classical style, the product of Rembrandt's imagination. This picture, valued today above all his other works, was not understood at the time. It was simply ridiculed, and resulted in a loss of reputation for the artist. Even the title of the picture is only a nickname given in derision.

In his old age, Rembrandt painted another masterpiece, a portrait group of the *syndics of the cloth hall* (Pl. 53.2 ) (in the Rijksmuseum, Amsterdam). They are assembled around a table in their office. Centuries have passed, and people have changed in many ways, but these men with their sober garments and hats remain an undying memorial of life in Rembrandt's time.

Rembrandt also painted many religious pictures based on the Bible, both the Old and the New Testaments. Those of the Old Testament depict typical Jewish types, which is not surprising, as the artist himself lived in the Jewish quarter of Amsterdam. The most moving of these pictures is that of *Saul and David* (in the Mauritshuis, The Hague), where we see on the left king Saul, who unfaithful to God, was tormented by the evil spirit, whilst young David, on the right side, plays on his harp in order to bring some relief to the disordered soul of his king.

But his pictures of incidents in the New Testament are even more touching in their deeply religious spirit. One of the earliest of these is that of *Simeon in the temple* (Pl. 54. 1 ) (in the Mauritshuis, The Hague). Here we see in a kind of Gothic Church, the virgin Mary and St. Joseph, who have come up to the temple of Jerusalem to present the infant Jesus to the Lord God. Simeon, an honest old man who longed for the fulfilment of God's promise of a Saviour, was led by His Spirit into the temple just at that moment. Full of the Holy Spirit, he recognized the Child, and was able to take Him in his arms, thanking God for allowing him to see His light which has the power to save the world. He also told the Child's mother that many would refuse to accept this light.

The *supper at Emmaus* (Pl. 54.2 ) (in the Louvre, Paris) represents the recognition of the risen Saviour by two disciples who had offered him hospitality for the night. They themselves had been in spiritual darkness after he was crucified, for all their hopes seemed crushed. They had expected that he would use his miraculous power to bring them political liberty, and instead he had allowed their own spiritual leaders to hand him over to the Roman overlords to sentence him to death as a criminal, on false charges. They were still more confused by reports of those who had been to the tomb, who saw angels who said he had risen, and in fact his body was not to be found. While they were discussing these things, he himself had joined them, but they did not recognize him, even when he explained all the passages from Sacred Scripture which had foretold the sufferings and resurrection of the promised Redeemer. Only when they had invited him into their home, when he accepted the bread they offered and shared it with them in turn, a typical gesture of his generosity with which they had become familiar, did they recognize the risen Saviour in their guest. He had come to liberate them, not from social tyranny, but to raise the human mind from its false ideas of God, by giving tangible proofs of His limitless liberality, and therefore His absolute trustworthiness and lovableness. Once this light of spiritual recognition had dawned in their hearts, he disappeared from their physical view. Rembrandt represents this dramatic moment in his picture. Jesus sits at the table, like an embodiment of loveliness, surrounded by an aureole of light, with all the highlights concentrated on him. Before him is a white tablecloth, on which his hands, holding the bread, are resting. This same brilliant light illuminates also the hands of the disciple on the left, which are folded in adoration, as well as on the face and hands of the second disciple on the right, filled with the dawning joy of recognition, and the face of the serving-boy who stands in amazement, puzzled by the whole scene. On both sides of this closely-knit group are deep shadows, which contrast with the central highlights. The dominant colours of the picture are warm yellows and cool greys.

His more than sixty *self-portraits* reveal the artist's physical and psychological development, from happy youth to sad old age. The later ones are touching revelations of great suffering. The whole series resembles an autobiography—in picture form.

In the graphic arts, he was one of the great masters. He made copper engravings; but most often he used the method called etching (which literally means to eat in). This is another intaglio process. Here the copper plate is first covered with a layer of wax. In this the artist draws his design with a needle. Then the copper plate is immersed in acid, which eats into the copper wherever the wax has been removed by the designing needle. When the lines are deep enough, the acid and wax are removed, and the plate is then ready for printing, in the same manner as in copper engraving.

Rembrandt made many etchings. One of the most famous is the *hundred guilder print*, a title probably derived from the price paid for it. It represents the Saviour healing the sick. Another interesting etching is a landscape called the *three trees.* They are shown on a grassy slope or polder on the foreground to the right, and are balanced by the massed clouds and dark streaks in the sky to the left. A city is silhouetted against the sky in the background.

Rembrandt was an incomparable master of light and shade. He created a light all his own, which is possible without being real. In his early pictures, it was a warm yellow light, which became more intense later, plunging all nature into a bath of gold. The air seemed to be filled with luminous atoms. In the *Jewish bride,* for instance, he obtained an indescribable shimmering by applying thick paint with light brushstrokes. In the *man with the golden helmet*, almost the whole picture is in shade except the helmet, face, and a part of the right shoulder. To get highlights, as in this picture, he often applied patches of thick yellow paint.

He worked constantly. For every picture, he made numerous preliminary sketches. Unlike Leonardo da Vinci, he did not bother his head about theories, nor did he write treatises or histories of art. He simply painted, drew and etched, enveloped in the light of his golden atmosphere. He left no artistic successor to continue his work: no one could reproduce his vision.

There was a group of artists known as the Little Dutchmen, contemporaries of Rembrandt and Hals, who painted small pictures for private houses, showing everyday scenes of their homes and gardens, streets and markets, still-life and city activities, and portrait characters. This realistic treatment of familiar scenes from everyday life is called genre art. These artists gave such subjects both popularity and refinement.

Pieter de Hooch (1629–1677), in *the bedroom* (Pl. 54.3 ) (Staatliche Kunsthalle, Karlsruhe) shows a typical Dutch interior. Light streams through the window and open door at the left. A little girl, evidently just come from the garden shown in the background, holds the latch with one hand and a fruit in the other, as she sheepishly looks up at her mother, who is engaged in arranging a bed. It is a homely, human scene. There is a contrast between the bright light outside and the subdued light of the interior.

Gerard Ter Borch (1617–1681) was an expert in showing various textures, especially velvet and satin, the effect of which he heightened by contrast with other textures, and the use of various lights. *The concert* (Pl. 54.4 *)* is a good example. Here two women are absorbed in their music. The ability of the artist is shown in the shiny texture of the satin dress of the lady seated in the foreground, with her back towards the onlooker.

Jan Vermeer van Delft (1632–1675) was the greatest of this group. His father was an art dealer. His scenes are usually simple and realistic, but the rich colours are strikingly contrasted. He is admired by the modern Impressionists for showing only the first impressions that strike the eye, and omitting all distracting details. Another technique of his they admire is his use of natural light, or the plein-air method, to give unity to his composition. In most of his pictures the room is lit up by a window to the left. This is well exemplified by his *girl with a pearl necklace* (Pl. 55.1, in Berlin. A young lady, standing before a table, is putting on a necklace. The light from the window falls on her yellow, ermine-trimmed jacket. The warm tones of the background contrast with the cool deep blues and dark brown in the foreground.

A small portrait of unusual beauty, the youthful, fresh-complexioned face of a *young girl with a turban* (in the Mauritshuis, The Hague), shows the artist's technical ability to vary his brushwork. The turban is painted with firm strokes, but the face is perfectly smooth, with not a trace of brushstroke. The colour combination of white.

pale blue and ochre yellow is characteristic of Vermeer. The *painter in his studio*, another of his pictures, is a classic of European painting.

The Dutch started to paint landscapes realistically and for their own sakes, not merely as backgrounds. Seascapes, warships and fishing fleets, river and canal scenes were popular. What is most remarkable about them is the sensitive awareness of changing light and of the moods of nature. One of the greatest landscape artists was Jacob van Ruisdael (c. 1628-1682). He brought out the essentials of Dutch landscapes and towns. In his famous *view of Haarlem* (in the Mauritshuis, The Hague), two-thirds of the picture is occupied by a wonderful interpretation of the cloudy Dutch sky. In the foreground is a peaceful country scene. The city of Haarlem forms the horizon.

*The mill at Wijk* (Pl. 55.2 ) (Rijksmuseum, Amsterdam) shows a typical feature of the Dutch landscape, the windmill standing on a hill. It contrasts with a castle rising behind it in the distance. On the right foreground, three women, wearing the national coif, seem to watch for the landing of the yellow-sailed boat on the riverbank. As in many of these landscapes, the sky takes up most of the picture, forming a suitable background for a windmill.

Another important Dutch artist of landscapes and city views is Meindert Hobbema (1638–1709). He studied under Jacob van Ruisdael. His landscapes and city views have a quiet homely atmosphere about them, achieved by the presence of watermills, canals, and houses. The *avenue of Middelares* (Pl. 55.3 ) (National Gallery, London) shows a rutted country road running straight through the middle almost to the horizon. The high, slender trees bordering it are stripped of their branches almost to their crowns. The dark silhouette contrasts with the clouded sky-scape, which occupies almost two-thirds of the picture. In the distance on the left, a tower rises from a hill. A cottage occupies the middle right. The two sides of the picture are balanced by trees and foliage.

# 13. SPANISH ART

## GENERAL SURVEY

Spain is geographically isolated from the rest of Europe. It lies on the south-western end of the continent. On the east it faces the Mediterranean, and on the west the Atlantic. The lofty Pyrenees cut it off from its northern neighbour, France. The country itself is varied, but even more varied are its people, who were often subject to foreign conquerors, of whom the Muslim Moors left a very deep impression on Spanish character and history. For eight centuries its history was a long struggle to regain independence from the Umayyad Caliphs, whose capital was Cordova. Under Ferdinand of Aragon and Isabella of Castille, Spain was finally united, the last Moorish stronghold in Granada was taken, and Spain began its colonial empire through the discovery of America by Columbus. It became very powerful when Charles V, a Habsburg, the grandson of Ferdinand and Isabella, was also elected Holy Roman Emperor, and as such ruled over central Europe, much of Italy, as well as the growing colonies. These reached their greatest expansion under his son Philip II, who got possession of Portugal and her colonies as well. When the Spanish Habsburg line died out in the early eighteenth century, the Bourbons took their place as rulers of Spain.

## ARCHITECTURE AND SCULPTURE

When the Renaissance penetrated Spain, its influence on architecture was mingled with native elements. The first style thus evolved is known as the Plateresque (platero, silversmith), since its delicate ornamentation resembled the work of a silversmith. Examples of this are seen on the *town hall* of *Seville* and the *entrance* to the *university of Salamanca* (Pl.56.1 ). This style is characterized by a wealth of decoration around the doors and windows, contrasted with the plainness of the other wall-surfaces. It lasted only for about half a century, for Philip II thought it too ornate. He allowed only a severely classical style. The best example of this is the *Escorial* (Pl.56.2 ) or royal monastery he had built near Madrid. This big quadrangular building, subdivided into sixteen inner courtyards, included a church, monastery, palace, library, gallery, and tomb. The walls are decorated with simple Doric and Ionic pilasters. This style is called Herreran, since its architect was Juan de Herrera (1530-97). It did not please the Spanish taste, so in the next century there appeared a new, richly ornamented style, called Churrigueresque, after its initiator, Jose Churriguera (1650-1723). This type is characterized by detailed ornamentation around the outside of the doors, and of the retables or altar screens inside. The Spanish love of splendour expanded these *altar pieces* from wall to wall, and from floor to ceiling. A most outstanding example is that of *Seville cathedral*.

In Spain, sculpture remained, on the whole, an integral part of architecture, as it had been in the Middle Ages. The most common material was wood, carved and richly painted. They tried to make their sculpture look as natural as possible. The wooden *statue of Saint Francis*, by Pedro de Mena (1628-1688) (Toledo Cathedral), shows an unusual restraint, in the plain habit and hood covering the calm figure. But the asceticism of the face is typically Spanish. The statue keeps the roundness of the wood out of which it was shaped.

## PAINTING

As was the custom all over Europe at that time, the royal courts of Spain, especially under the Emperor Charles V and King Philip II, patronized foreign artists, of whom several came from the Netherlands. Charles V appointed one of them, Anthony Mor (known in Spain as Antonio Moro), as court painter. But it was mainly Italian art that influenced Spanish painting. Of the Italian painters, Titian, who painted Charles V repeatedly, was most admired for his deep, warm colours and great artistic imagination. He became a source of inspiration to the greatest Spanish painters. Another influence, that of Caravaggio, came through Naples, then part of the Spanish empire. Two Spanish painters, Francesco Ribalta (1551-1628), and especially his pupil Jusepe de Ribera (1588-1652), both ardent followers of Caravaggio, worked practically all their lives for the Spanish court in Naples, and spread his style, with its strong lights and shadows. Spain produced outstandingly great artists, the first of whom, El Greco, though a foreigner by birth, was truly Spanish in his artistic expression.

El Greco (1541-1614), whose real name was Domenikos Theotokopulos, was a Greek, born on the island of Crete, where he got his early training in art from monks who painted icons or religious pictures in the Byzantine style. Since at that time Crete was a colony belonging to the republic of Venice, he went there to complete his training as a pupil of Titian; but the works of Tintoretto influenced him more. He also stayed in Rome for a short time, but later passed on to Spain, settling in Toledo until his death. He became known to art as El Greco (the Greek). His early paintings show the influence of the Venetian school, especially Tintoretto's manner of producing dramatic action by the use of light and shade. His later pictures, however, stress mystical experiences by means of distortions and rhythmic upward movements resembling the rising dance of flames. He tried to give actuality to spiritual truths by means of lines and colours.

A good example of the combination of the two styles is *the burial of the count of Orgaz* (Pl. 56.33) (Church of Santo Tome, Toledo). This painting, done in 1586, was intended for the church of St. Thomas in Toledo. El Greco chose for his subject a story connected with the funeral of Don Gonzales Ruiz, who had generously helped to restore this church in the fourteenth century, and who was buried within it. In the lower part of the painting, he showed the noble friends and churchmen looking with awe upon the deacon St. Stephen and the bishop St. Augustine, Ruiz's favourite saints, who, according to legend, appeared at the funeral and lowered his body into the grave. A representation of heaven is attempted in the upper part of the huge canvas. An angel carries up the transfigured soul, shown as an infant, while the virgin Mary and St. John the Baptist pray for it to the Redeemer, enthroned in glory amid the angels.

The Italian masters, like Raphael and Titian, tried to express spiritual reality under the form of material things ; El Greco, on the other hand, wanted to show it as if seen in a vision, laying stress on the fact that it is really something that lies beyond the material world. He did this by representing the group on earth in a natural manner, and the heavenly one as in a supernatural, visionary world. On the level of earth, we see more than twenty realistic portraits. Though El Greco was not a Spaniard, he caught in the faces of these noblemen the characteristic Castilian piety of that time. Under the calm aristocratic reserve, there burns a living faith in those thin, ascetic faces, watching the burial of one of their number, on whose features joy begins to gleam from his approach to God. On the whole, the lower part is solemn and dark, with clearly defined colours. There is a rhythmic spacing of quiet vertical lines produced by contrasting the white ruffs and cuffs with the black clothes of the mourning nobles. Sts. Stephen and Augustine in the centre produce in contrast a vibration of bright splashes of colour with their rich vestments, and a rhythm of simple curves as they bend over the limp corpse. The upper part of the picture, with its winding lines of floating clouds and draperies, creates a pulsating movement which leads the eye from the virgin Mary and John the Baptist, who kneel on clouds just over the earthly figures, far up to that of the Saviour. Here the colours gleam and glance in transparent fluidity. God's attraction is represented as liberating the earthly forms from the weight and shapes characteristic of material things.

The *Resurrection* (Pl.56.4, ), (in the Prado Museum, Madrid) shows the saviour's triumph over death, as the passion had demonstrated his victory over the cruelty of evil or sin. These, more than his many other miracles, proved his divine goodness and power, in order to win complete trust in his true love. According to his own repeated predictions, he rose again from the dead on the third day after his crucifixion, despite the sealed tomb and the guards placed there by his enemies, who wanted to make sure that his body would not be stolen. El Greco has omitted any natural setting of sky and earth, or of a rock-cut tomb in a garden. There is only the ascending figure of the risen Saviour, holding the banner of victory. The soldiers who had guarded his tomb shrink from the bright light streaming down from the Redeemer's glorified body. The forms, lengthened beyond their natural proportions, are arranged in a rhythmic upward movement, which is increased by the flickering white light, that is more unearthly than even the most spiritual conceptions of Rembrandt. It is this rising movement of light which gives El Greco's pictures their air of mysticism. The colouring is very effective. Separating the picture from the frame are patches of black, white and pink, that increase the visionary effect. Despite the unearthliness of the whole composition, the spatial relationship of the figures is subtly observed.

Among his last great works, in which this characteristic mystical expression is especially prominent, is the *storm over Toledo* (Pl. 57.1 5) (in the Metropolitan Museum of Art, New York). Of European paintings, this is among the first in which a landscape is represented for its own sake rather than as a background for human figures. Again the lines and colours give it an energy rarely found in this type of art. The hill on which Toledo is built is shown in a series of whirling curves, which are repeated in the stormy sky above. The colours are at once subdued and strong, and on the whole sombre. The various greens of the trees and grassy hillsides, with small patches of earth in grey-browns, shade off into darker greys towards the background. The more distant hills are somewhat lighter and shot with steel-blue; but towards the right they are crowned with white buildings. The pattern of colours in the sky is vaster and stronger, but reflects the white of the buildings and the blues of the hills and river. Of the buildings represented, some still exist; and the view of the city, looking down upon the Tagus river, still bears much the same impression.

It is a Spanish custom to give a child the family names of both father and mother. Since the mother's name comes last, the famous painter Don Diego Rodrigez de Silva y Velasquez (1599-1660) is known the world over by his mother's name. He was born at the end of the sixteenth century in Seville, in southern Spain. The dignity, courtesy, and discipline shown in his pictures reflect the noble birth which he always cherished. Intending him for some high official post, his father gave him a good education, but finally allowed him to study art because of the great talent he showed for drawing even in childhood. During his thirteenth year, he studied under Herrera, whose rude manners caused him to go to Pacheco, a lesser artist, but a good draughtsman, with a thorough knowledge of art, which is shown by his book on painting. He studied there for five years, and married one of Pacheco's daughters. His father-in-law did his best to promote his career. Through patrons of art who were influential in court, he soon got a chance to paint the portrait of Philip IV. So pleased was the king, that he appointed the young man as court painter, a post he kept almost forty years, until his death. He did not seem to have any of the difficulties of temper or fortune that weighed so heavily on other great artists. Like Raphael's, his career was constantly marked by success, without a hard beginning or a decline in old age.

In 1628 the young Velasquez met the world-famous Flemish painter Rubens, who had come to the court at Madrid on a diplomatic mission. As a result of the meeting, the king reluctantly gave in to Velasquez's great desire to study in Italy. At the king's expense he remained there for two years, staying a short time in Milan on his way to Venice. There he was most interested in Tintoretto's works. The king sent him to Italy a second time, between 1649-1651, to buy pictures for the royal art collection. Again he stayed for a long time in Venice. During a visit to Rome, great honours were paid to him, and he painted a portrait of Pope Innocent X. On his return, the king put him in charge of the palace and his art collections, but he was overworked by these official responsibilities. He died in 1661 at the age of sixty-one.

His artistic development began in Seville, with the then popular bodigones (kitchen studies), so called because they show the ordinary life of peasants. The colours are dark, with strong contrasts of light and shade in the manner of Caravaggio. One of the best examples of this early period is the *house of Martha and Mary* (National Gallery, London).

The general human attitude is shown by another picture of his, painted just after his appointment at court, which greatly increased his reputation. This painting (in the Prado Museum, Madrid) is variously known as *the topers*, the Drinkers, or the Triumph of Bacchus. The Greek god of wine is shown surrounded by a group of poor but healthy and merry peasants, in the act of crowning one of their number with a wreath of vine leaves. In this picture, mythology is only an excuse for the vigorous and sympathetic representation of Spanish peasant life.

As court painter, his main duty was painting portraits of the royal household—a difficult task since most of his subjects were not very attractive, and the fashions of that time were inelegant and stiff. Only a genius like Velasquez could succeed in making immortal art out of such material; and this he did with entire objectivity, reproducing exactly what he saw without trying to prettify anything. The king, whom he painted very often, is seen slowly changing from a prematurely serious, long-faced and timid youth, to a disillusioned ruler of a hard-pressed people, and finally to a worn-out old man, broken by the desertion of those he had done so much to help, and by the defeat of the once glorious empire.

After Velasquez's stay in Italy, his dark tones gave place to light and colour. Space and atmosphere were now his greatest interests. Although he tried to show reality from the first, he gradually realized that our vision has its limitations, for it does not perceive things exactly as they are. The eye sees clearly only what it looks at directly, whereas things beyond the immediate circle of observation become blurred in outline and paler the more they recede from this conscious point of attention. Atmosphere also affects sharp outlines and strong colours, since it increases in density in proportion to distance from the eye.

The *surrender of Breda*. (Pl. 57.2 ) (in the Prado Museum, Madrid) is one of the world's finest historical paintings. It commemorates Spain's victory over the Dutch Republic in the early part of the Thirty Years' War. It was painted only ten years later, after Velasquez's first Italian trip. The fact that he had travelled to Italy with Spinola, the Spanish general who won that battle, helped him get first-hand information to represent an event at which he himself was not present. It is at once evident, by the facial expressions and gestures, who are the victors and the vanquished of the two armies, which occupy the plain in the foreground of the picture. Since our eyes have become habituated to observing from left to right in a clock-wise movement, he placed the Dutch army on the left so that the eye would finally come to rest on the victors to the right. The effect of victory and defeat is brought out most strikingly by the position of the weapons. Among the Dutch we see a few scattered pikes and halberds, whereas about two-thirds of the sky-line is occupied by some thirty Spanish lances, smartly reared in dense vertical lines. The effect is so striking that the Spaniards call the picture Las Lanzas, or the lances. In the centre, between the two armies, the Dutch commander is shown handing over the keys of the city of Breda to the Spanish general, Spinola. Here Velasquez expressed that self-control and gracious courtesy, so characteristic of himself and of the ideal of chivalry. Surmounting all feelings of hatred or anger, the victor appears more like a sympathetic friend, or a guest politely accepting a kindness, rather than as a conqueror. To give a feeling of spaciousness, the picture opens out between the two commanders into the deep vista of a valley with smoking ruins. This is an example of Velasquez's mastery of space and atmosphere, for the forms and colours blur and fade in proportion to their distance from the observer. The colours and outlines of the two generals and the soldiers in the front line are strong and clear. The part of the army which is further away is shown in paler tones and in less distinct outlines, and finally the colours shade off into vague greenish-greys in the far distance.

An even subtler expression of this problem of space and atmosphere is found in the interior scene pictured in *las meninas* or the maids of honour (Pl. 58.1 ) painted in 1650, (in the Prado Museum, Madrid). It shows Velasquez's studio, to which the little infanta (Spanish for princess) Margarita paid an informal visit with her suite. She stands in the middle, surrounded by her maids of honour, dwarfs, and a big pet dog. A courtier is looking through the open door at the back. Velasquez, who showed himself working at a large canvas to the left, is gazing out of the picture, presumably at the princess's royal parents, whose figures are reflected in a mirror on the back wall. The scene itself is a casual everyday affair, but Velasquez has given it the true optical impression of an interior flooded with natural light. The outlines and colours have the right relation to the light and atmosphere. One can almost feel the air in the room. The princess and her attendants in the front are bathed in the radiance streaming in from the window at the right. Their outlines are clear, and the colours intense and strong. A second window at the back of the room illumines the mirror and the wall on which Velasquez's pictures are hung. The depth of the room is conveyed by the decreasing clarity of outline and intensity of colour. The courtier outside the door, although standing in full light, is smaller according to perspective, and his outlines are less clear through the increased density of atmosphere. The reflection of the king and queen in the mirror, who are the most distant visually, is shown in still paler colours and in less distinct outlines than the rest.

In the year of his death, Velasqusez again painted the same princess, the *infanta Margarita* (Pl. 58.2 ) (Prado Museum, Madrid) now some ten years older. Her face looks even more sickly than in her childhood, and her dress and hair style are stiff and unbecoming ; yet for all that, Velasquez made a masterpiece of his portrait. Here we see the final development of his technique, known as the abridged manner, since it consisted of bold, quick touches, for which he probably used long brushes, applying his strokes to the canvas standing at a distance. The colours have a pearly sheen. The dominating tones are pink, white, and particularly his unique greys. The whole picture seems flooded with real light, which gives that natural impression that the Impressionist school of the later nineteenth century admired so much. The picture is a harmony of light and colours.

The most outstanding of his religious pictures is the *Crucifix* (Pl. 58.3. ) (in the Prado Museum, Madrid). It is one of the noblest representations of the Saviour's redemptive sacrifice. Unlike many contemporary artists, he did not aim only at showing the natural effects of physical pain but, true to his own restrained manner and character, he showed the divinely majestic calm of Jesus which triumphed over suffering. This resembles somewhat the same peaceful dignity, despite the tortures of the body, which we see on the negatives made of the stains imprinted by the wounds of Christ on the winding sheet preserved in Turin, Italy. Velasquez also showed the suffering, by means of the bleeding wounds, but the beautiful face of Jesus is tranquil; the head, encircled by a small halo, is bent forward; the brown hair hangs down, covering half the face, on which is expressed a noble acceptance, and divine love, speaking of forgiveness to His creatures whose cruel rejection of Him cost Him so much suffering.

Spanish art reflects the diversities and contrasts of the country itself and its various national types. Thus El Greco's active mysticism, Velasquez's objective and aristocratic realism, and Murillo's charming, tranquil optimism are each in their own way true pictures of the Spanish temperament.

Like Velasquez, Murillo (1618-1682) too was born in Seville, and is known chiefly by his mother's name—his full name being Bartolome Esteban y Murillo. At an early age he lost both his mother and father, who was a poor artisan. He was brought up by an uncle. He was able to follow his artistic bent by being admitted into the workshop of a painter who, though not a great artist, was a good teacher. The young pupil earned his living by painting cheap religious pictures, which he sold in Seville's slum market, known as the Macarenas. Since he could not afford fine canvas on which to paint, he had to use a rough material called saga cloth, which did not allow delicate outlines but only broad strokes. This did not satisfy him, however, especially when a friend, who had been abroad, told him about van Dyck's technique of soft lighting and refinement of colouring. After saving enough money, he set out for Rome by way of Madrid, where he wanted to get a letter of recommendation from his fellow Sevillian, Velasquez, who was then at the height of his fame. With his usual kindness, Velasquez not only gave the poor young man hospitality in his own home, but secured for him admission into the royal art galleries, where for three years Murillo studied and imitated the masterpieces and techniques of Titian, Veronese, Tintoretto, and of Velasquez himself. Though the latter urged him to proceed to Rome, Murillo preferred to return to his native Seville.

At that time, the Franciscans, though poor, desired paintings for their cloisters. By accepting the contract, which did not bring him much in the line of pay, Murillo started on the road to fame and wealth by the eleven compositions he made. Soon after, he married a wealthy lady of a good family, and his home became a centre of art and culture. He spent the rest of his pure and happy life as a member of the Third Order of St. Francis in his own Seville.

There is a sympathetic realism in his pictures of the common people of southern Spain, with whom he became intimateiy acquainted by his early experiences in the Macarenas. He has made the little Andalusian street boys known and loved the world over by such pictures as the *cake-eaters* and the *fruit-sellers*, but particularly by his pictures of the *Holy Family*, where the child Jesus and St. John the Baptist are shown as typical children of Seville's poor.

In fact, in almost all his pictures we find these popular types, either in their crude realism, or transfigured by holiness and grace, as in the Christmas scenes. His deep pity or compassion are shown whenever he pictures the miseries of life. Nowhere is this expressed better than in a famous composition *the return of the prodigal son* (Fig. 460), painted in 1671, for the Caridad (hospital for the poor). This painting is now in the National Gallery in Washington, U.S.A. The simplicity and loving mercy, which are the keynotes of the Gospels, Murillo has admirably reflected in this illustration of one of the parables of Jesus. These stories are meant to teach spiritual truth by means of human, earthly examples.

Fig. 460. Murillo: the return of the prodigal son, detail, National Gallery, Washington.

In this case, God's tender merey to a repentant sinner is shown by the story of a young man, who after wasting his inheritance, decides to return to his father as a servant rather than die of hunger. He finds, to his surprise, that his father has been anxiously waiting for his return and treats him better than ever before, because of his joy in finding him again. Murillo shows the son, dirty and ragged, kneeling before his father to beg forgiveness. The expression on his face shows sorrow and shame, but at the same time great trust and hope. Most touching, however, is the figure of the good father, who tenderly embraces his unworthy child, not only forgiving him, but reinstating him fondly as his beloved son, and full of joy at finding him again, calling for a feast with music and dancing. The preparations for the celebration are shown, and new clothes are brought in. This was an appropriate picture for a hospital, to give confidence in their heavenly Father to those from whom death was about to take away all their earthly inheritance. Murillo had a special talent for bringing out the reality of religious truths by showing their practical application to familiar life. He saw how everything is penetrated by God. His pictures are convincing, because they are inspired by his own deeply religious life. His realism is not impersonal, as Velasquez's tended to be, but he adds to the objectivity of his figures and scenes something of his own living faith and tender love.

Murillo's most popular works were his paintings of the Purissima or *Imaculada* (Pl.59.1, ), a favourite devotion in Spain, especially in Seville. Representations of this mystery were therefore in great demand; and a traditional manner of visualizing it had been established in numberless paintings by earlier artists. Murillo himself produced about twenty different pictures of this subject, but each one was new and original. To present a soul completely open to God, irradiated by His Truth and transparent to His pure Love is a task beyond any artist, but Murillo came as near the ideal as possible. Mary is shown as a young Andalusian maiden, with light, flowing hair, in a white dress and blue mantle. The body, free of the law of gravity, rests lightly on a white cloud or orb, with the crescent moon beneath her feet. Tiny angels hover all around. Enraptured by God, Mary's gaze is turned upward, and her hands are folded in prayer.

Murillo's artistic development can be seen by comparing his first and later paintings. At first the outlines are heavy and the figures stiff like statues. The Spanish call this the frio, or cold style. Later the outlines become more delicate, the figures are more curved, and the colours warmer and more transparent. This is known as the calido, or warm style. In his fully-developed technique, the outlines fade in an airy blending of light and shade. This is the vaporoso, or ethereal style. A good example of this last-named is the Purissima, painted for the Capuchin Franciscans between 1674-76, and now in the Louvre in Paris.

Murillo also painted some famous pictures of saints in ecstasy, such as *St. Anthony of Padua*, enraptured by the appearance of the child Jesus in his arms. The best of this type, however, is the *vision of St. Francis* (Pl. 59.2 ). This saint, called 'the mirror of Christ , because his life was dedicated to the most perfect imitation of Jesus, is shown standing on a globe with one foot, in token of his liberation from what the world has to offer, and reaching up instead to embrace the crucified Saviour, who in turn has freed his right arm from the nail and tenderly bent over to embrace the saint. Francis is looking up full of compassion on the face of Jesus, who looks down on Francis with an expression that shows the greatness of his suffering, yet the look is serene. In accordance with the Gospel, he shows the Redeemer as more concerned with the welfare of others rather than with his own pain. The picture seems to refer to one of the saint's favourite requests to share in the sufferings of Jesus, which was answered towards the end of his life when his own hands and feet and side were miraculously marked by deep, painful wounds.

An unruly character living in a disorderly age, Francisco Goya y Lucientes (1746-1828) reflects in his art a spirit far different from his predecessors, though his technique was influenced by Velasquez. Dissolute himself, he naturally concentrated on the corruption of court life before the French Revolution, and the brutality that followed it.

Born near Saragossa in Aragon, his riotous conduct forced him to seek safety for a time in Madrid, and then in Rome. He returned to Madrid, where he married the sister of the court-painter Bayeu, by whose influence he was engaged to paint cartoons for the royal tapestries destined for the Prado, the crown-prince's residence. He made about twenty of them between 1776-1780. These compositions of his youth, the subjects of which he was free to choose, are cheerful on the whole, showing the brighter side of life. They also reveal his keen observation, in a great variety of realistic scenes of everyday life in streets, villages, and fields. Lacking religious faith, he put all his power of expression into a fleeting momentary impression. The colours are bright, the movements graceful, much in the style of Venetian Rococo. One example is *the blind guitarist* (Prado Museum, Madrid). Between the golden sky and a group of gailydressed young people, who seem ready to start dancing, there runs a dark diagonal line drawn from the poor musician in the left-hand corner, to a man on horseback, towards the top right of the group of soberly-clothed men, who gaze rather sadly at the blind singer.

Goya himself was a court painter for much of his life, serving under four rulers. With his own decline in morality, his cynicism came more and more to the fore. This is shown in his cruel analysis of the characters in the royal court, in such pictures as *the family of Charles IV* Pl. 56.3, ) (Prado Museum, Madrid), painted in 1800. The problem of space is somewhat reminiscent of Velasquez's picture, the Maids of Honour, but in treatment it is very different. For while Velasquez never showed his personal feelings, Goya's contempt is clearly visible; and how he got away with it can be explained only by the king's weakness of character, shown so well in the picture. The masterful queen is the dominant figure. Around them are their relatives, whose elegant clothes contrast all the more with their graceless faces. Like Velasquez, whose works he had studied deeply, Goya here showed a similar realism, and relationship between shape and colour, light and atmosphere. He also painted himself working on a canvas in the background. But there are also many differences. While Velasquez showed a casual, everyday scene, where the little groups blend naturally with the atmosphere, Goya's life-size figures, which occupy most of the space, are more or less posed. Again, Velasquez's painting is general and inclusive, while Goya's is focused on one group only, and reveals the character of each individual. Velasquez's lighting is soft and delicate; Goya's strong lighting makes the colours flash and the jewels glint. Against the background of the quiet spacious room, the lights and shadows play on the textures, which quiver with light and colour. By the use of different strokes, he could imitate the surfaces of silks, laces and velvets, and the gleam of jewels. Whereas Velasquez gave the impression of third dimension by means of colour shading, Goya's colours are almost uniform in hue and shade. He produced the impression of third dimension by means of the relationship of planes, or, as he expressed it himself, by showing projections and hollows, near and distant surfaces. He did not see lines or details in nature, but only lighted and unlighted forms. This is the basis of his realism, and herein lies the originality of his technique. Thus he produced his effect, not by strong outlines or shading, but by patterns of lights and surfaces, so that his paintings are spotted with colour and dappled forms rather than with clear-cut and linear details. But he did not apply this technique throughout the picture. The total effect was a mass shaped by colour rather than by lines. He worked with great speed, often finishing a portrait at one sitting. It is said that he kept his paints in tubs, and used anything that was handy, even a broom or rug, to dab on the colours. Thus he was able to produce a gallery of portraits of his famous contemporaries.

In several series of etchings, known as Caprices and Proverbs, he satirized the people of his own time. In the grim humour of *until death,* he pokes fun at vanity which tries to escape age by dressing in youthful clothes, and as a result appears the worse by contrast.

A versatile artist, Goya also used the graphic hand process method developed in the eighteenth century, known as the aquatint, since the final effect resembles a wash drawing. The surface of an etching is smooth and uniform. In the aquatint, a rough surface is obtained by covering the copper plate with various thicknesses, according to need, of powdered resin. The acid, eatirg through the space between the resin grains, leaves a rough surface, which when inked, produces a washed effect. This is often used in combination with etching proper, as Goya did in Disasters of War. The satire in Caprices was not clearly directed at any one in particular, but in Disasters of War it was; therefore this series was not published till long after his death. Here he shows with terrible horror some of the gruesome details relating to the Spanish rebellion against the Napoleonic occupation. With a few strokes and a powerful pattern of black on white, he produces strong characterization, and brings out the meaning at once, so that captions are unnecessary.

Goya, however, was not just critical. He could be sympathetic, as we see in many childcharacters, and especially in the warmly tender portrait of his wife, *Fosefa Bayeu* (Pl. 59.4, ) (in the Prado Museum, Madrid). In this picture, his technique of handling the colours is the same as in his other pictures, but the dignified and sympathetic representation shows that his cynicism was superficial, that deep down in his heart he cherished noble ideals, which lay buried under the weight of his own weakness and that of his contemporaries.

# 14. ENGLISH ART

## GENERAL SURVEY

England is the southern, largest and richest part of the island of Great Britain. The northern part, Scotland, is poorer, but picturesque with its mountains, woods, deep lakes and inlets. The western part of England is mountainous. Towards the east the gently undulating countryside has a variety of rich tree or hedgelined fields and meadows, ideal for the pleasant landscape paintings with which England has enriched world art. The climate is humid, with frequent mists and rain, but the winters are mild, considering the latitude.

For four hundred years, the Celtic inhabitants, known as Britons, were subject to Rome, which gave many names to English cities. When the Romans left in the fifth century, the country was conquered by Germanic tribes, one of which, the Angles, gave their name to the country. England means land of the Angles. They became Christian about a century later; and gave their country a rich heritage of numerous saints and scholars, as also missionaries to their kinsmen, the Germans on the continent.

In the eleventh century, the country was conquered by the Norman-French, who brought with them French words and cultural influences. Nationalism developed with the loss of England's French possessions after the Hundred Years' War; and at the same time national unity was realized after the civil Wars of the Roses, when the Tudors came into power in the later fifteenth century. Explorations led to the establishment of a commercial and colonial empire, and England became a great world power, especially on the seas. Near the end of the sixteenth century, the crowns of England and Scotland were united under the Stuarts. With the development of trade and colonies, great social changes took place within the country. In the cities, the middle class merchants and industrialists became rich and powerful. In the country, the squires enclosed the common lands in order to produce more, and built palatial country houses in parklike surroundings. But the peasants, dissatisfied with their new lands, sold them and crowded into the cities for a livelihood. Fortunately at that time new inventions and machinery led to the creation of factories so that they found employment, though conditions at first were very poor until factory laws were passed.

It was at this period that the English ' classical ' civilization reached its peak, although confined to the upper classes. In all branches of art and culture, England was then blessed with fertile genius. A majority of the artists of the time reflected the contentment of the cultured upper classes; but one or two, such as Hogarth, exposed the darker side of life to a society still too ignorant of the social problems created by the changes in agriculture and industry, and too ready to assume that England had reached perfection of political and social organization, which required only to be preserved. At the same time, the changes in agriculture had made the English landscape unique in all Europe, and at this period of greatest picturesqueness, it was mirrored for all time and nations by the genius of Gainsborough, Constable, and Turner, the founders of the movement for naturalistic landscape-painting, not only in their own country, but all over the world.

## ARCHITECTURE

Britain's island position, which always has an isolating effect, as well as its long adherence to Gothic art which it put to so many uses, are the reasons why England was the last among the northern countries to accept the classic influence of the Renaissance. From the sixteenth century onwards, attempts were made to introduce Renaissance forms, but they were not assimilated, since the master-masons of England continued to erect their buildings in the Late-Gothic style, on which foreigners applied some Renaissance decorations. This was the Tudor style, a combination of both, and thus a transition.

The acceptance in England of the classic style is due to Inigo Jones (1573-1652), who caused the Palladian architecture to be generally adopted in England after his visit to Italy, particularly Vicenza, Verona and Venice. Palladio's symmetrical and harmoniously proportioned buildings based on classical theories, but adapted to modern needs, suited the English taste. Inigo Jones adopted all the elements of Palladio's buildings for the *banqueting hall* (Fig. 461) in Whitehall, London, which is his great achievement. The walls of this two-storeyed building are decorated with pilasters in superimposed orders, that is, the pilasters of each floor are one above the other, and the entablatures of each floor project over each pillar. The windows belong to the High Renaissance type, having alternating pointed and round pediments on the ground floor, and horizontal cornices held up by

Fig. 461. Banqueting hall, detail, Whitehall, London.

scroll consoles on the upper floor, which has also a fruit-and-flower-garland decoration on the wall above the row of windows. On the top of the building there is a balustrade. This hall revolutionized British architecture, and in the time of the Georges, or early Hanoverian kings, Palladio's four books were the standard texts for architecture in Britain and America.

Sir Christopher Wren (1632-1723) was England's second famous architect. He was also under Italian influence. His talents were varied, for he was an astronomer, mathematician, and charter member of the Royal Society. In 1666 many of London's medieval buildings were destroyed by the great fire which raged for a week. To rebuild them, Wren drew up a plan which even modern city planners could not surpass; but the people were too conservative to accept the innovation. The rebuilt *St. Paul's cathedral* (Pl. 60.1, ) is his masterpiece. He maintained the long nave and short transepts and choir of the medieval church; but over the crossing he erected a huge dome. His plan had to take into account the position of the church in London's crowded centre, with no open space surrounding it. He realized that a building in such a place and in such a foggy city required a bold design to make it dominate. The dome is double: it rests on the drum, which is surrounded by a colonnade. There is a tower on each end of the façade. From the outside, the building looks as if it had two storeys. Begun in 1675, it was not completed till 1710. When Wren died in 1723, he was buried in this church.

## PAINTING

In the first half of the sixteenth century, Henry VIII made Holbein the Younger his court painter. There exist many portraits in the so-called Holbein style. Not much is known about them, but it is believed that they were made by his English pupils. A century later, Rubens and van Dyck were brought to England by Charles I, who had knowledge and taste for art. In the eighteenth century, English painting came into its own with original artists. William Hogarth (1697-1764), a Londoner, was England's first important painter. He began his artistic career as an engraver. His independence, determination, humour, and realism are typically English. He had an intimate knowledge of middle-class society in early Georgian London, and he could capture and comment on the vices of his day in order to cure them. To, achieve his aim, he made series of moralizing paintings. These he multiplied also in cheap engravings, which made his works very popular. The profitable income from these inexpensive prints enabled him to live a carefree life, independent of the patronage of wealthy men. For this reason he could show up the foibles and vices of the rich.

In *the rake's progress* (Sir John Soane's Museum, London) he shows, in a series of eight pictures, how a miser's son wastes all the wealth his father gathered so carefully. His greatest success, however, was *marriage ā la mode* or the marriage of fashion (Tate Gallery, London), in a series of six pictures. It was meant to bring out the sad effects that come from contracting a marriage merely for money or social position. The first picture shows an aristocrat exchanging his proud title for a tradesman's wealth. While their marriage is being settled like a business affair, the nobleman's son and tradesman's daughter angrily turn away from each other. Such a beginning does not promise a happy future. The second picture, *shortly after the marriage* (Pl. 60.2 ), shows the young couple, bored with each other's company, wasting their money looking for happiness elsewhere. The young wife sits yawning at the breakfast table, whilst the clock indicates midday. In the room beyond, card-tables and burning candles show how the young husband, now slouching on a chair, has spent the night. The steward is seen at the left, leaving with a pile of unpaid bills, with an expression of despair at the irresponsibility of his master. The other pictures reveal the tragic outcome of such a marriage. The spacious splendour of the interior setting is equal to any of the Flemish paintings. So faithfully does Hogarth reproduce the early Georgian styles and furnishings, that his paintings have also great historical value.

Hogarth is a moralist who wants to show the good or evil results of certain actions, much more than a satirist who delights in showing up the follies or weaknesses of others. About a year after the series which showed the bad effects of an unworthy marriage contract, he started a series to show a happy marriage, but it was not finished or engraved. Hogarth was a child of his age, for the eighteenth century was much taken up by moral problems. It was the period of England's greatest satirical writers, and the beginning of the novel. Each of his pictures is, in fact, like a chapter in a novel, and his series read like story books. However, each of his pictures is a work of art in itself. His satire is most evident in the four pictures of the *election series* (Sir John Soane's Museum, London) ; and this is the beginning of the political cartoons so much in vogue even today, especially in the English-speaking countries.

His true artistic ability is best shown in *the shrimp girl* (Pl. 60.3, ) (National Gallery, London), where he did not try to moralize, but caught with an exquisite vividness the character of a typical cockney peddling her basket of seafood along the streets of London. Though he used only a few colours, this lively portrait has a delightful freshness, and foreshadows in certain respects the Impressionistic paintings of the nineteenth century. There is a vivacious use of browns, yellows, pale pinks and lively greens, applied with strong, swift brush strokes.

English painting in the Georgian period was devoted chiefly to portraits. Sir Joshua Reynolds (1723-1792) was the first among England's important portrait painters. He came from Plymton near Plymouth. His talent for painting showed itself early. His polished manners attracted the attention of Commodore Keppel, who gave him the opportunity of seeing the Mediterranean lands by offering him a free voyage on his ship, which was then being repaired in Plymouth. Thus he could visit Rome, staying there for three years to study the works of Michelangelo, whom he admired for the rest of his life. He also saw Florence, Venice and other cities in Italy, passed through Paris on his return to England, and made his home in London in 1753. He became the leading painter in a short time; and social distinction depended for many years on having been painted by Reynolds. He had many students and several assistants. His spacious house contained studios and an exhibition hall. He collected paintings by old masters, partly because it was considered a requirement in those days in order to be fashionable, and partly because he needed them for his artistic work.

His pictures include scenes from history and portraits. He painted the important people of his time. Due to his efforts, the artist became socially acceptable, and he was admitted freely into high aristocratic society as well as literary circles. The portrait of his friend Dr. *Samuel Johnson* (Pl. 60.4, ) (National Gallery, London), the great literary leader of that time, is an excellent character study. This picture has none of the usual pompous paraphernalia of broken columns, sweeping drapery, and landscapes. Against a simple, dark, and entirely plain background, Reynolds placed the heavy figure of Dr. Johnson, whose weighty intellectuality he portrayed perfectly.

He had a special love for children, and painted many delightful child portraits. The *age of innocence* (Pl. 61.1, ) (Wallace Collection, London) is a lovely picture of his little grandniece. In *angel heads*, he represents the young daughter of Lord William Gordon, seen from different angles.

Many of his pictures are badly preserved. This is due to his love for the deep, rich colours of Venetian painters. By using bitumen, he got this rich effect at once, but the pigment does not dry, and in the sun it sometimes melts and begins to run down.

The foundation of the Royal Academy by George III was due largely to the influence of Reynolds. It was meant to be a school for art students, and to give a yearly exhibition in order to sell pictures. Its presidents were to be the outstanding men of art and letters. The first to hold this office was Reynolds himself, and for the next twenty-four yearly elections, he was kept in office. The king knighted him and made him his first painter. His Discourses on Painting are a collection of the addresses he delivered each year to the students of the Royal Academy, in which he expressed the theory underlying his practice, namely that style is a composite of the best to be found in the great masters. He called this ideal the 'grand style'. He analyzed carefully the works of Rembrandt, the great Venetians, and a number of French artists, and borrowed ideas from them for his own work. He was delighted when people recognized his allusions to the great masters. This was the eighteenth century practice in the other arts, like literature. This period, called by its contemporaries the Enlightenment or the Age of Reason, did not encourage originality or creative imagination ; but some of Reynolds' paintings do reveal these qualities, when he forgot about the styles and theories of his age, and allowed himself to be himself.

Thomas Gainsborough (1727-1788) came from Sudbury in Suffolk. His mother was a flower painter, and his contact with the beauty of nature in his lovely Suffolk increased his sensibility and encouraged him to be a landscape artist. But in his time nature was not popular, and he had to paint portraits in order to make a living; for that was the only form of art then in demand. First he worked in Ipswich, but in 1758 he went to Bath, the health resort of the wealthy. He painted the aristocrats who flocked to his studio. In the aristocratic country-houses round about, he could study old masters, since picture galleries of ancestors were considered essential by the nobles, who were proud of their family-trees. These masterpieces, especially the ones in the tradition of Rubens and van Dyck, taught him how to harmonize colours.

His fame grew steadily; and in 1774 he moved to London, where he remained until his death. His studio was frequented by the important personages of his time: aristocrats, statesmen, soldiers and actors. His fame began to rival that of Reynolds, who had reached the height of his position. While the latter was the more intellectual of the two, Gainsborough was the greater artist. There is more strength and freshness in his colours, more life in his figures. Both painters associated with high society; but while Reynolds loved it, and struggled to be accepted by it, Gainsborough was disgusted with his fashionable models. His natural romantic bent—he was a man of feeling and a lover of music and nature—did not incline him to admire that stiffly artificial life then in fashion among the higher classes. Their houses were not homes, but palaces which required stately furnishings and portraits. Reynolds and Gainsborough competed with each other at the exhibitions in the Academy, and often painted the same persons. On his death-bed, Gainsborough asked Reynolds to visit him in order to reconcile their differences. Reynolds attended his funeral and gave a whole discourse at the Academy in praise of Gainsborough. He did not, however, acknowledge him as a portrait-painter, but referred to him as a landscape artist.

The *blue boy* (Pl. 61.2 , ) or Master Jonathan Buttal (Huntington Art Gallery, San Marino, California) shows the direct influence of van Dyck, especially in the reproduction of the texture of shimmering silks, the pearly sheen of satins, the use of cool colours and soft silver-grey shadows. In 1778 Reynolds had advised the students of the Academy not to mass blue together in a painting. The Blue Boy was Gainsborough's answer, and his great success proved that Reynolds was wrong. *The Honourable Mrs. Graham* (National Gallery, Edinburgh) is a good example of Gainsborough's stately portraits. It was in the Venetian style: with a column, and masses of trees in a distant landscape as a background. Fabrics like satin and lace, and the soft plumes, are handled with great mastery and ease. The figure is surrounded by an atmosphere of light and air. Gainsborough excelled in the painting of atmosphere and fabrics.

*The painter's daughters* (National Gallery, London) is an early portrait of Mary and Margaret Gainsborough. It was made in Bath shortly after the family had moved there. The simple features and wistful expressions of the girls are portrayed realistically. Only the faces are completed. Thus the character is revealed, while the unfinished condition of the rest of the picture gives a touching intimacy to the composition. This is perhaps one of his best portraits, for it shows his natural spontaneity and dislike of formality when he was not obliged to flatter the great in order to make a living. His predilection, however, was outdoor scenery. He probably deserves the title of father of English landscape painting, for his nature studies surpassed his portraits. Unfortunately he was ahead of his time, and his natural bent could not find a remunerative outlet. This explains, perhaps, the rather melancholy tone of his later works. The aristocratic society of his time was artificial, and he had to cater to its tastes ; while he loved nature, like the common people from whom he had sprung. Romanticism, with its emphasis on feeling, nature, and the past, came into its own only around the turn of the century.

He loved the memories of his native Suffolk; and even when he was forced to paint portraits in London, he contrived landscape models with pieces of cork, coal, sand heaps, moss and clay, and broccoli to represent trees and shrubs. These gave a charming, poetic warmth to his paintings. It is not the realism, but the romantic relationship which he created between man and nature, which constitutes his greatness as a landscape artist. At his death, his house was full of landscape paintings, which people had admired but never bought, since they were not yet in fashion.

Today Constable and Turner are universally recognized not only as the greatest English landscape painters, but also as the greatest painters of any kind that England has produced. In their time, however, it was not so. Although Turner was the most popular painter during his lifetime, Constable, only a year his junior, had to struggle with misunderstanding throughout his life, and only after his death was he fully appreciated by his fellow countrymen.

John Constable (1776-1837) was born in East Bergholt, Suffolk, where his father owned a windmill. The boy grew up helping his father in the mill and painting. He was sent to London for some time to learn art. Finishing his studies after a very short time, he concentrated entirely on landscape painting—mostly rural and rustic scenes of his native country-side. He felt he could best paint his own familiar scenes. At Flatford, and especially in Dedham, where his father owned water-mills, he admired the beautiful country-side with its trees and the calm river flowing past graceful willows, spilling over the mill dam, and wearing away the wood and brickwork of the mills. His aim was to be a ' natural painter' By this he meant reproducing only the beauties of nature, without introducing any historical or legendary allusions as the painters of his time used to do. Pure landscape as an art in itself, or nature for nature's sake, was not yet recognized by the public. Constable, however, did not want artificially-composed scenes, but nature in her actual form of artlessness. He knew that spontaneity and freshness can be obtained only by direct contact with nature. He aimed not merely at painting places topographically exact, but at showing nature in her fulness, bathed in light and atmosphere.

Contrary to the custom of contemporary painters who worked only early in the morning or late in the afternoon so as to avoid strong lights, Constable painted throughout the day, reproducing sun and rain most convincingly. Instead of using the dull colours previously employed for landscapes, Constable painted nature in all its freshness by introducing the greatest possible variety of shades of green. To increase the light in his pictures, especially of the shiny grass and bright sky, he used complementary colours in little patches, such as red near green or orange near blue. His pictures are filled with a sense of movement. He loved the flying clouds and swaying trees. He tried to show the dancing lights on the leaves when a breeze plays among the branches or the reflection of the moving clouds on the surface of water. To catch these transitory movements of nature, he made little oil sketches outdoors, which could be compared to snapshots. These sketches have made art critics declare that Constable's style is Impressionistic. To get vibrating colours, and to increase the sensation of movement on the surface of things, he applied little spots of thick paint to strengthen the colour of a larger surface. For instance, the specks of light falling on the bark of a tree trunk are shown by white flecks. He often used these little white spots, especially to represent the sparkling leaves after rain. People jocularly referred to them as Constable's snow. He was among the first to reproduce natural light realistically. No one before him rendered the effects of sun or rain more naturally. Although we see Constable's love for truth in nature even in his earliest works, only gradually, by tireless efforts to improve, did he rise to the highest level of his achievement. Want of appreciation did not hinder his efforts; conscious of his pictures 'shall be valuable to posterity,' even if he did 'not reap the benefit of them.'

For years, only his friends bought his pictures. In 1821 he exhibited his famous painting, the *hay wain* (Pl. 61.3, ) (now in the National Gallery, London) at the Royal Academy, but he met with little success. Fortunately, a French art collector exhibited the same picture three years later in Paris, at the so-called English Salon or Salon Anglais, where it created a sensation. Seeing Constable's picture, Delacroix, the leader of the French Romantic painters, who was exhibiting his Massacre of Chios, took his own picture back home and retouched it with the liveliest and purest colours. A whole group of landscape painters, the Barbizon School, came into being through the inspiration of Constable's landscapes.

In 1825 he painted the *leaping horse*, which is generally considered to be his masterpiece. As he usually did for his more important pictures, Constable made for this one also a six-foot preparatory sketch, painted outdoors directly from nature. After this, he made the final picture in his studio. Luckily this preparatory sketch is preserved in South Kensington Museum in London. It shows a much fresher and more natural vigour than the painting itself, although the latter has more refinements of design.

An interesting combination of landscape and architecture is seen in his *Salisbury cathedral* (Victoria and Albert Museum, London). This old Gothic cathedral, at one time the abbey church of a monastery, is situated in a beautiful, solitary setting far from the crowded city. Constable loved it so much that he painted it a number of times, at different periods. He chose different moments of the day in order to get various lighting effects. In the above-mentioned version, a natural pointed arch is formed by trees on both sides and meeting in the fore-ground, through which the cathedral is seen in the background bathed in brilliant sunlight. Thus the light spreads out from within the picture, and appears only in broken patches towards the front, as it filters down through the foliage above.

Joseph Turner (1775-1851) is the greatest English landscape painter. Through his influence, landscape painting was accepted by the public as an art equal to the highest achievements in portraits and historical representations. Turner was born in the London slums, where his father was a barber. Early in life he was deprived of the care of his mother.

The boy's artistic taient showed itself while he was still young. Two of his father's customers were painters, and when they saw the boy's drawings, they urged the father to let his son study art. At the age of eleven he was sent to the Soho Academy, where he got a good training in drawing and perspective. At fifteen he joined the school of the Royal Academy, where he stayed four years. From the start, he could exhibit his works there. In order to help support himself during his studies, he was asked by architects to paint landscape backgrounds to enhance their drawings, and to colour prints for an engraver. This gave him practice in the technique of water colour. The thorough training that he got in his youth, in learning and applying the rules of drawing, helped him later to keep his passion for colours and space under control, so that his works did not lose touch with reality and intelligibility. When he was seventeen, he was employed by the publishers of a magazine to do a series of topographical drawings. This gave him the chance to make his first sketching tours.

The most characteristic feature of his artistic life, later on, was his hurried touring all over Europe, especially in the Rhineland and the Alps, where he sketched the tall castles, mirror-like lakes, and forbidding mountains, in the still warm atmosphere of sunset or the foreboding of a rising storm. The Italian landscapes, however, had the most decisive influence on his work. The development of Turner's artistic talent was long, and though a strict division cannot be made, it is convenient to divide it into three. During his earliest period, his colours were cool and his drawings minutely careful. Soon he became interested in the effects of light, mist, and early dawn. In his search, he turned not only to nature but to older masters like Claude Lorrain, Watteau, and the Dutch painters. His interest in the first-mcntioned is most characteristic of his second period. He liked the way Lorrain handled light and atmosphere; for by the light he gave to his pictures, he not only reproduced what he saw outdoors, but also aroused feeling—whether by the freshness of dawn or the sadness of an episode. In the last period, Turner showed his own genius most perfectly. He changed his technique in 1819, after his return from Italy. He said, 'Now I am going to begin to be Turner'.

His aim was to produce atmospheric effects. For this reason he studied light and colours more closely. His forms were often mere vapoury shapes, whose colours seemed to melt away into the shadows. He produced an imaginary world of vast spaces of light and indefinite forms. His subjects were the grandeur of space bathed in light, the majesty of the sky and sun, and the power of the sea in its various moods.

His popularity, in the beginning, was due to the fact that he started with water colours, used in the eighteenth century technique. Once he was known, people continued to accept his higher achievements. But when he reached his highest perfection in the third period, the public could not understand him any longer and even his friends believed him mad. He remained popular only as a result of the praises given him by the great art critic, John Ruskin, who understood Turner's outstanding talent.

He was a rather odd character—sad, and keeping to himself in a miserable lodging. But he had great energy and worked untiringly. When he died, he left to the country three hundred and sixty-two oil paintings, nineteen hundred drawings, and a large sum of money, partly to be used for the education of poor artists in the Academy. His last wish was that two of his best pictures be hung in the National Gallery between two paintings by Claude Lorrain. The *founding of Carthage*, painted in 1815 and now in the London National Gallery, was one of the pictures which he desired to be placed near Lorrain's painting, the Embarkation of the Queen of Sheba. Here he used the same balance of composition and light colours as the French artist, but he tried to outdo him with a more glorious sky. This is the highest achievement of his second period.

*The Fighting Temeraire towed to her last berth*

*to be broken* (Pl. 62.1, ) (National Gallery, London) is a good example of Turner's romanticism. It symbolizes the passing of one epoch and the birth of another. The Temeraire was a heroic relic of the battle of Trafalgar in 1805. Some thirty years later, it was towed to its last anchorage in order to be broken up. The once tall and stately ship, whose billowing white sails were driven by the clean sea breezes, is shown stripped of its beauty, and emptied of its valiant crew. A puny steam-tug, black and smoky, is towing it along. Turner painted the picture around 1838 or 1839 to show the contrast between the beauty of the elemental forces, that were beginning to be displaced by the ugliness of the machine or industrial age. This contrast is also shown by the sky in the background. The setting sun glows like a fire behind the puffing, smoky steam-tug, shedding upon it its last lurid rays. But to the left, behind the old sailing ship, the sky is already dark and the crescent moon looks like the bright, full sail of an unseen boat driven across the sea of space. The warship itself is silvered by the soft moonlight. Around the steam-tug on the right, the sea seems to be on fire, as the red and gold of the sky is caught in the waves. To the left the sea is blue-green, cool and glassy. The brilliance of his reds and yellows is believed to be the result of the after-touches which Turner gave his paintings whenever he saw another picture in the Academy exhibition which might rival his own in brilliance.

Rain, steam and speed (National Gallery, London) represents a train crossing a viaduct during a heavy rainstorm. Turner, however, blurs the solid objects into dreamlike phantasms of steam and smoke, so as to give only a general abstract impression of powerful movement, rather than a concrete, realistic picture. The engine is merely a dark blur around the glowing heart of its furnace. There is a general onward thrust in the long line of the tall viaduct, the clouds of smoke and steam that sweep on and on, and finally merge with the storm-drift touched with, rainbow tints by the light of the setting sun. The greenish- gray of the river glimmers through its border of high trees far under the bridge, near the bottom of the picture. Nothing in the painting is clear or distinct; it merely gives the impression of the blurred view one gets when travelling at great speed.

# 15. FRENCH ART

## GENERAL SURVEY

A comparatively large country of Europe, France has a varied geography and many neighbours: England just across the channel, Belgium and Germany to the north, Switzerland to the east, Italy to the south-east across the Alps, and Spain to the south-west across the Pyrenees. In the centre of the country is a high plateau, branching out in high mountain chains to the east, and in less rugged mountains to the west, between which lie low river basins like the valley of the Seine, where Paris is situated. Its climate is also varied, from the stormy Atlantic coast in the south-west, the humid shores around the North Sea, the cold plains of the north and the mountain regions, to the delightful Mediterranean shores. The country is devoted chiefly to agriculture, which is highly developed, and to the production of fine articles of luxury.

The people are also varied. Marseilles on the Mediterranean was a Greek colony. The Gauls, a Celtic people, were conquered by the Romans, who gave the country great prosperity and a higher culture. It was also overrun by various Germanic tribes, the chief of which, the Franks, gave the country its present name. In the eighth century, Charles Martel defeated an Arab attack on France. His grandson was Charlemagne or Charles the Great, under whom France was united with Germany, but after his death disunity set in. Normandy, in the north, was conquered and settled by Norsemen. The Capetians again started to reunite the country. The greatest of this dynasty was St. Louis IX, a model ruler. France suffered much during the Hundred Years' War, but was saved by a young girl, Joan of Arc. During the time of Louis XI, France again became great, but his successors started on foreign conquests. One of these, Francis I, brought Italian Renaissance ideas and artists from Italy, of whom the most important was Leonardo da Vinci. With the Bourbon line came peace from long civil wars, and the establishment of absolute monarchy. Under Louis XIII (Louis Treize), Italian influence became stronger in France, because the two French artists Nicholas Poussin and Claude Gellée worked in Rome. The classical ideas of the former became the basis of the art theories of the French Academy under Louis XIV (Louis Quatorze), the most powerful of the Bourbons, whose frequent foreign wars and excessively expensive Palace of Versailles gave France an outward splendour, but made her almost bankrupt. During his reign, all branches of art—architecture, sculpture, painting and minor arts—were centred on the glorification of the king. Jules Hardouin Mansart was appointed official architect, and Le Brun, the chief painter, was given the duty of preparing the designs. Official control over the arts was tightened by the establishment of academies, such as the Academy of Painting and Sculpture in 1648, the French Academy at Rome in 1666, the Academy of Architecture in 1671, and by the setting up of the Gobelin furniture and tapestry factory in 1662.

Rococo art began under Louis XV (Louis Quinze). The name comes from the French word rocaille, a spiral seashell, because the motifs used for decorating the walls of eighteenth century French palaces were based on this shape (Fig. 462). This style, characterized by delicacy

Fig. 462. Rococo motif.

and intimacy, the expression chiefly of an idle nobility, contrasted with the grandeur and magnificance of art under Louis XIV. Revolt against this parasitic form of aristocracy and its tastes led to the French Revolution in politics, and to severe classicist ideals in art, both inspired by the rebellious intellectuals. For example, Jacques Louis David (1748-1825) used art to arouse the people against oppression. This classical art continued until the early nineteenth century, when the Romantic movement replaced it. The latter was an expression of the common people, and was characterized by individual subjectivity, emotion and gay colours. It introduced new themes and inspiration, but the technique remained basically traditional. Modern art, largely inspired by France, is revolutionary not only in subject matter but also in method.

## ARCHITECTURE

In the reign of Francis I, when castles were no longer needed as military fortresses, but were being converted into more comfortable palaces, Renaissance art penetrated into France. At first, decorative motifs were rather superficially applied to the castles, while some features of the Medieval castles persisted, such as the battlements and towers. The *château* at *Blois*, especially the wing built by Francis I, is an example of this transitional style. The same combination of Medieval and Renaissance elements is seen in the *château* of *Chambord*, which is typical of the early Renaissance castles.

The *Louvre* in Paris, formerly the royal palace until Napoleon III abdicated, and today the world's finest art gallery, known as the Louvre Museum, is an outstanding example of French Renaissance architecture, especially the façade in the *square court* (Fig. 463) and on the eastern wing.

Fig. 463. Square Court, detail, eastern wing, Louvre, Paris.

The former is the work of the architect Pierre Lescot, and the sculptor Jean Goujon, during the reign of Henry II. In its well-balanced proportions, its delicate and graceful design and decoration, it is typically French. Superimposed Greek orders are used. On the first floor, pilasters separate the windows, which are surmounted with curved and angular pediments supported by consoles. The pointed roof is characteristically northern. Louis XIV brought the great artist Bernini from Italy to remodel the *eastern façade* (Pl.62.2, ) but national opposition caused him to be dismissed, and the work was confided to a French amateur, Claude Perrault who made it one of the finest masterpieces of French architecture.

But it was the building of the *palace of Versailles* (PI. 63.1, ) which absorbed the artistic energies and interests of Louis XIV. Versailles is a town about ten miles from Paris, where his father, Louis XIII, had built a small château. This he left intact, but ordered a great palace to be built around it. However, he himself always had his bedroom in the original building. Le Vau and J. H. Mansart were the architects of the new palace; Le Brun supervised the interior decorations, of which the finest arc to be found in the *galerie des glaces* (glass corridor). The gardens, planned by Le Nôtre, are magnificent, but artificial and formal, with their great avenues, terraces, clipped hedges, statues and fountains. The building of this palace, one of the biggest in the world, lasted from 1660 to 1710.

## SCULPTURE

In the sixteenth century, two parallel trends are observable in French sculpture. Michel Colomb maintained the Franco-Burgundian tradition; while Germain Pilon, and Jean Goujon, the famous sculptor of the Louvre façade, adopted the Italo-classical style.

Seventeenth century French sculptors in general resisted the temptations of Baroque and continued in the tradition of Goujon and Pilon. The most individual of them all was Pierre Puget, the French Michelangelo, who had contacts with the schools of Genoa and Milan. Coysevox and Girardon were the best among the sculptors at work on the statues of Versailles. Apart from these works, and others executed for the glorification of Louis XIV (the sun king) and his courtiers, French sculpture of the period produced excellent funerary monuments, the reserve and refinement of which is in marked contrast with the pomp of Roman tombs.

The greatest eighteenth century sculptor in France was Jean Antoine Houdon, a direct artistic descendant of Goujon. His portraits and terra-cotta busts are full of life. For instance, his colossal statue of *St Bruno* (PI. 63.2 )

(Church of Santa Maria Degli Angeli Rome) represents the monk deep in joyful contemplation, with his arms crossed over his breast.

The continuous development of French sculpture in one tradition during this long period was nowhere better exemplified than in the equestrian statues of the kings, impressive symbols of absolutism; but all the examples of this type were destroyed at the time of the Revolution.

## PAINTING

From the time of the Renaissance, French painting was influenced by Flanders and Italy, as exemplified, in the fifteenth century, by Jehan Clouet and Andrea del Sarto respectively. In the time of Louis XIII, Simon Vouet (1590-1647) introduced the Bolognese idiom, which became an official style of painting under the increasing royal absolutism. Louis XIV had it firmly established into an art school, headed by a pupil of Vouet, Charles Le Brun (1619-1690).

Fortunately, some French artists, living in Rome, isolated from official regimentation, preserved individual creativeness. The greatest of these was a contemporary of Vouet, the classicist Poussin.

Nicolas Poussin (1594-1665) came from a Norman peasant family. He got his first art lessons from a local artist, Varin. At eighteen he went to Paris, where he worked successively in the studios of Ferdinand Elle, a painter from Flanders, and of L'Allemand, an artist from Lorraine. In the royal collections he was able to study prints of Raphael and Giulio Romano. Twelve years later he left for Rome, where, except for a short visit to France, he lived till his death.

He immersed himself passionately in the study of antiques, so that he could idealize and beautify nature according to Graeco-Roman standards. He studied ancient sculpture with the greatest care, measuring the statues and modelling reliefs. So perfectly did he assimilate their proportions and attitudes, that his knowledge is always reflected in his figures. He also learned perspective and anatomy. The only painter of his time whom he esteemed was Domenichino, in whose studio he worked for a time. To develop a better style, however, he turned to the great classic masters. His admiration was given first to Titian, of whose works he made copies and whose glowing colours he tried to reproduce. The influence of Raphael, in whom he saw a follower of classic antiquity, was more intellectual. Poussin admired his rhythmic designs, his exactly planned compositions, his stress on the meaning of the subject as being of greatest importance. 'If there is no action in a painting', Poussin remarked, 'the lines and colours are ineffective.' Although he borrowed figures and gestures, he did not remain a mere imitator, but worked out a style of his own.

Several of his pictures represent mythological subjects, others are religious. Louis XIII, who wanted him to decorate the long gallery of the Louvre, called him to Paris. He stayed there from 1640-1642, making the series of the *labours of Hercules* for the Louvre, the *Last Supper* for Versailles, and eight *cartoons* for the *Gobelin tapestries*. His stay in Paris was unhappy, so after a short time he returned to Rome.

In the later part of his life, the human figures, hitherto so important in his paintings, were gradually reduced and almost lost in the scenery, while landscapes grew ever more prominent. Nevertheless his mind arranged what he saw according to his own logical patterns or ideals. He did not picture the passing, accidentai things, but the iasting essentials. The light in his pictures is calm, the forms are clearly and evenly illuminated. His art remained always in the service of the noble and beautiful. This love of rational order in Poussin is typically ciassical and French. For this reason, perhaps, he had great influence on later French artists.

The *Arcadian shepherds* (PI. 63.3 ) (about1638) (in the Louvre Museum, Paris) is one of his most popular pictures. The French classical painters regarded it as the embodiment of their ideals. In a calm southern landscape bathed in golden light, three shepherds and a shepherdess have gathered in front of a tombstone. Engraved on it are the Latin words ' Et in Arcadia ego ' meaning death is to be found even in Arcadia. The shepherd on the left is kneeling to read the inscription. A companion stands behind him, leaning his left arm on the tombstone. The shepherd on the right is pointing at the writing as he turns towards the shepherdess, who stands there silent and thoughtful. The figures, modelled with light and shade, have a strongly plastic character like statues. Their grouping is simple, but the simplicity reveals artistic knowledge and intellectual effort. With the typical restraint of classicism, Poussin has given only the essentials in the most dignified manner, and deliberately left out every unnecessary detail. It is an idyllic meditation on the shortness of life. Poussin's thinking was always accompanied by deep feeling. The work has the same elevated style as the tragedies of the contemporary French dramatists, Racine and Corneille.

The *Ordination* (1647), now owned by the Earl of Ellesmere and loaned to the National Gallery of Scotland, is one of the second set of seven pictures representing the Sacraments. It was painted after Poussin's return to Rome The scene shows the Saviour after his resurrection confirming St. Peter as chief shepherd of his followers. This picture shows Raphael's influence, in the carefully composed and well- balanced composition, and in the expressive yet controlled gestures of the figures. Unlike Raphael, Poussin gives greater importance to the landscape and classical buildings.

*Diogenes and the cup* (in the Louvre, Paris) is a good example of his later pictures, where the landscape becomes the chief interest. The purpose of the picture is still the story content, as the custom of the time required, but the two figures who are meant to tell the story have become very small indeed. Diogenes, the philosopher, seeing a boy drinking water from his hand, considered his cup a luxury, and threw it away. What captures the attention, however, is the beautifully arranged landscape, the majestic trees and surrounding shrubs of different greens, a group of buildings to the right, a hill to the left, and the winding river beside it, which carries the eye to the distant light of the horizon.

Claude Lorrain (1600-1682), the landscape painter, whose real name was Claude Gellée, was given that name because he came from Lorraine. Not only was his family poor, but at the age of twelve he was left an orphan. A merchant brought him to Rome. Here he was employed as a pastry cook by Agostino Tassi, a painter of harbour scenes. On discovering his servant's artistic talent, Tassi taught him painting. He progressed rapidly. Like many other artists of his time, he came under the influence of the Fleming Paul Brill and the German Adam Elsheimer, both of whom painted Italian scenes in a romantic landscape style which they had developed in Rome. After years of travel and changing fortunes, he returned to Rome, where he remained for the rest of his life. He made many sketches of the Campagna, the plains around Rome encircled by mountains, and rich in classical remains. These sketches show his talent for realistic portrayal. For his finished pictures, however, he used only dream-like scenes, by which he could express a certain mood. He was also a master of perspective. His chief study was light—its various conditions and effects. According to biographical notes left by a fellow painter, Sandrart, he went out before daybreak and sunset to make long studies of the glowing sky as he lay in the fields.

Although his work was appreciated, and he was interested only in nature and the beauty of light, he did not dare to paint pure landscapes, for in his time they were not yet understood. Like his contemporaries—Poussin, for instance, who also lived in Rome at about the same period—Claude gave his pictures nominal story subjects, such as classical buildings and small human figures, but these are so insignificant that they can be identified only after careful observation, and they have nothing to do with the real understanding of the pictures. He was not in the least interested in the figures, for he would say, 'I sell my landscapes and give away the figures in them.' Sometimes he allowed other painters to fill in the figures for him.

His usual method of composition was to arrange trees and buildings in a dark mass in the fore-ground, and again in the middle distance to make a kind of frame for a great space of light beyond. Like Velasquez* he realized the changing effect of atmosphere on light. This understanding of tonality enabled him to give very realistic impressions of receding views. His technique was to make little strokes with a full brush, so that his colours seemed to move with a change of light or position.

Claude is outstanding for his bright stretches of sky and sea which seem to dissolve in the distance like a pictorial representation of infinity. He could be called the first of the romantic painters, for he tried, by means of light, to give an impression of the different periods of the day and the feeling which they are apt to produce. So great was the admiration for his paintings, that travellers judged the beauty of natural scenes according to Claude's pictures, and English art lovers used them as models for their landscape gardens.

The dates of many of his paintings can be learned from his Liber Veritatis, wherein he collected drawings of his finished pictures, some two hundred in all, perhaps to keep a record of what kind of paintings he had sold.

The landscape with *Amor and Pysche* (PI. 63.4, ) (Wallraf-Richartz Museum, Cologne) typifies his method. Love and the soul are personified as little figures, almost lost in a vast scene with dark trees on both sides, with a luminous sky in the centre.

The most famous of his harbour views is *the embarkation of the queen of Sheba* (1648), which is in the National Gallery in London. The

* Note:—Claude and Velasquez were contemporaries, and during the letter's visit to Italy, Claude was in Rome, but it is nor known whether they ever met.

Renaissance building with colonnaded porticos, and the trees on either side of the open sea, form a kind of balanced stage scenery for the ships, small boats, and human figures. The horizontal lines, receding and vanishing in the glowing sunset sky, which is reflected in the rippling sea, naturally draw the attention to this, the chief interest of the picture. So beautiful is this sky and the sparkling water, that it has inspired landscape artists ever since.

The brothers Le Nain, Antoine (1588-1648), Louis (1593-1648), and Mathieu (1607-1677), painted scenes from the ordinary life of peasants and workers in the manner of the Little Dutchmen. A good example is *the peasant family* (in the Louvre Museum, Paris) (1642), by Louis Le Nain. He did not insist on minor details nor on the changeful expressions of atmosphere and light, but painted solid figures on a larger scale, and harmonized them into firm and simple compositions. In an aristocratic age, they showed the quiet dignity of country people, and thus prepared the way for the popular painters, and for those masterpieces of peasant life by Jean François Millet.

While most French painters of the eighteenth century reflected the ways of aristociacy in the courts, a few great artists devoted their genius to the life of the common people. Among the greatest of these was Jean Baptiste Chardin (1699- 1779), a Parisian. For a time he worked under the direction of the court painter Van Loo at Fontainebleau, but he did not like the nobles. He decided to carry on the example set by the Little Dutch Masters and the brothers Le Nain of the previous century. His subjects are humble and modest, based on daily life. The interiors are often middle class. Having rejected the empty show and artificiality of the Versailles court, Chardin became the greatest interpreter of the gentle and wholesome beauty of family life. He revealed the simple charm of the commonplace, because he retained an unspoiled, childlike heart. Nonetheless, his drawings have the refinement and balance of contemporary French painters. Moreover, his colours are mellow and rich, and his forms have a true innate dignity. His portrayal of common people is even more serious and respectful than that of previous genre painters, and he was the first to win popular appreciation. *Saying grace* (PI. 64.1 ) (1740), in the Louvre Museum, Paris, is one of his most charming pictures. It became popular at once; and to satisfy the people, he painted several versions of it. The setting is a small middle- class room, modest but not poor. The mother is bending over the round dining table, as she watches her little daughter asking God's blessing on the meal. The way this little girl in pink clasps her tiny hands, a bit clumsily as yet, and looks up from her low stool at her mother, is simply delightful. The older daughter, just big enough to sit on a chair, looks down on her younger sister from her superior position. The mother's face is delicate; she is plainly but tastefully dressed, like a typical middle class matron. Light streams in, presumably from an open door on the left, shining upon the gleaming white table cloth, the mother's muslin shawl and cap, and the little girls. The background is dark. The warm brown of the ground, the stripes of yellow-green and rose of the upholstered chairs, and the bright colours of the children's dresses, are balanced by the cool grey- blue of the mother's skirt and apron.

The *still life* (in the Louvre Museum, Paris), shows Chardin's ability to bring out the beauty of the simplest objects. It shows an open suitcase arranged diagonally, a pipe stem, and several cylindrical objects in a play of shadows. In the harmonized unity of the picture lies its chief value.

The greatest French painter of the Rococo period, Antoine Watteau (1684-1721), was born at Valenciennes, near the Belgian frontier. His childhood was one of hardship; for his father a poor village carpenter, stopped every financial help, when, against his wish, the son began to learn painting. He went to Paris at eighteen; but he almost starved there, thus undermining his already weak health. Finally Claude Gillot, a stage designer who painted theatrical scenery, took him into his studio. After some time Watteau had to leave this place, but the effect of the stage remained in his work. The greatest influence, however, came from his stay in the Luxembourg palace in Paris, where he was employed by its keeper, Claude Audran, who also painted decorative work. At that time the Luxembourg gardens had not yet been laid out, and the park still had its natural, wild beauty. This attracted the young Watteau towards landscapes. It inspired him to paint those lovely tree clumps which characterize the backgrounds of his idyllic country scenes. Besides, in the picture gallery of the Luxembourg palace, Watteau could study a series of paintings by Rubens, representing Marie de Medici's life (now exhibited in the Louvre). He maintained the influence of Rubens's vigour and realism, but he refined on them.

He returned to Paris in the hope of getting the Prix de Rome, which would have enabled him to go to Italy to study art, but he failed to get the scholarship. He came into contact with the rich banker Antoine Crorat, an art critic, who had a great collection of drawings and paintings by the Venetian artists. Their influence, especially that of Titian and Paolo Veronese, perfected Watteau's talent. He was admitted in 1717 as a member of the Academy, but shortly after he got tuberculosis. He lived in the country house a picture-merchant, Gersaint, lent him, in the hope of regaining his health. Instead, it declined rapidly. He now devoted himself to the welfare of his soul, and his last picture was a *crucifixion* for the parish priest. A touching anecdote of the last days shows Watteau's natural generosity and goodness. Angry because his pupil Jean Pater had copied his subjects and style, he had sent him away. But when he was ill, Watteau remembered how the jealousy of older artists had made him suffer when he himself was young. To make up for what he now considered an injustice and unkindness, he insisted that Pater should return, and he spent his last week giving him all the help and advice he could. At the age of thirty-seven, Watteau died in Gersaint's arms.

Watteau is the greatest and most representative painter of the Rococo style of eighteenth century France. This style is a reaction to the seventeenth century style, which held severely to Graeco-Roman examples and classic mythology. Only Venus and cupids remain in Rococo. In Watteau's pictures, the former appears mostly as a garden statue, and the latter in the form of little children. The aim of the painters also differed greatly. In the seventeenth century they had to glorify the ruler of the state, and produce huge canvases or tapestries to decorate vast halls. In the eighteenth century, paintings were meant for more intimate rooms, where a gay and shallow society passed its time in amusements. So the pictures were small; and the subject matter reflected the aimless, empty life of the leisurely class. Watteau was the first to paint this type of picture. In his youth, his subjects were scenes from rural and military life. As a result of his contact with the theatre, he painted stage representations of actors. But he owes his greatest fame to his garden pictures, which show the idle life of contemporary high society. It is characteristic that the Academy received him as a member under the title Painter of Fêtes Galantes (fashionable revelry). Since the Academy required that all new members should hand in a painting as a voucher of their election, Watteau produced for this purpose his masterpiece, *the embarkation for Cythera* (Berlin).

Watteau's paintings represent a dream world of the aristocratic society of his age; but his figures are drawn from minute observation of reality. The handling of his colours is masterful. Rarely are these two perfections of drawing and colouring found in the same artist. He excels in the landscapes which are the setting of most of his pictures. The blurred haze of the foliage of his trees, single or in groups, lit by mellow sunlight and surrounded by open spaces, is masterful. Gainsborough's leaves and soft shadows on the trunks of trees show Watteau's great influence on him.

Playing among these lovely trees are young aristocrats in fine silks of delicate but gay colours, painted with such fine touches that they seem to shimmer and melt in the sunny air. His original method of painting was admired already by his contemporaries. He put a vague, heavy layer of colour over his canvas and on this he filled in details of landscape and figures by little touches that produced an effect of sparkling movement. By his use of different shades and the harmony of complementary colours, he gave a lead to the later French romantic and Impressionist painters.

There is a touch of melancholoy in the gaiety of his pictures. Some art critics attribute it to sadness over his illness, but it may also show a deep psychological insight on the part of Watteau, who realized that the frivolity of this pleasure- seeking cannot be a real, lasting happiness, for that can come only from unselfishness. What he pictured was a momentary self-deception, that cannot fill or satisfy the human heart which is made for lasting, endless joy. For instance, his painting, called *Gilles*, (PI. 64.2, ) in the Louvre, Museum, Paris represents an unknown, thoughtful-looking actor in a white costume, standing full-length on an embankment. What passes through his mind seems to be suggested by the background. On the left the sky predominates, and the colours are subdued, but the young man at the bottom, who seems just to have come in from the country on donkey-back, grins cheerfully; while the gaily-dressed group at the right, seated in a bright autumnal garden, look melancholy by contrast. *The conversation* (in the Fitzwilliam Museum, Cambridge) is another typical example. Despite the artificial, idyllic style of his day, he gave this picture a wonderul realism. A soft note of sadness broods over the fairy-like gaiety of his colouring. L'*indifférent* (in the Louvre, Paris) is the portrait of an aristocrat, dressed in the brightest silks, and playing with an air-top (diaholo). The nonchalant pose, against an indefinite background, reveals his boredom.

Jean Baptiste Greuze (1725-1805) painted popular subjects, and reflected the new emphasis on morality, which arose as a reaction to the themes of the Rococo age. It was, unfortunately, accompanied by an exaggerated emotionalism. Greuze moralized on lower middle class virtues. Not only was he didactic and sentimental, but his stories seemed to have more importance than the pictures themselves.

Jacques Louis David (1748-1825) was a painter active in politics during the French Revolution and Napoleonic period. In 1774 he received the Prix de Rome. Thus he came into contact with Winckelmann's theories, resulting from the excavations in 1738 and 1748 of Herculaneum and Pompeii respectively, the two resort towns suddenly covered by Vesuvius under a stream of lava in the year 79. Many examples of Roman art and architecture were thus recovered, and increased the enthusiasm of the learned men of that time for classical types. Under this influence, David established his classical teachings, which became very influential not only in France, but throughout Europe. According to these theories, originality was frowned upon, for the classics were regarded as the only standards of beauty and taste ; and reason alone, not imagination, inspired art. A work of art had to be impersonal, for the artist was not supposed to reveal his own temperament or feelings. Ideas rather than sensations were to be expressed. Anything that went beyond the range of the human mind was ruled out, for instance anything indefinite or mysterious. Atmosphere, which makes contours indistinct or destroys them altogether, was banished, because forms had to have a clear outline. Colour played an unimportant role. Suggestions of action or movement were considered a danger to settled order. These severe standards, supposedly derived from ancient Rome, were for David a protest against the wanton frivolity of the aristocratic regime; and when the Revolution came in 1789, he became its wholehearted supporter. The revolutionaries liked his classical pictures, for they considered themselves as inspired by the Greek and Roman political ideals. David put an end to the Royal Academy in 1793, though he had belonged to it for twelve years. He was a member of the National Convention, and as such voted for the king's death. Robespierre was his friend. The Directory made him one of the first members of the fine arts section of the Institute of France, which replaced the old academies of the monarchy. After this, David became the dictator of French art.

After the Revolution, he worked for Napoleon, who made him court painter in 1804. His pictures of *Napoleon crossing the Alps* and *Napoleon distributing the eagles to his army* aimed at glorifying his patron. When Napoleon was defeated at Waterloo in 1814, the Bourbons, who were recalled to the French throne, exiled David for His revolutionary activities, especially for having voted for the king's execution.

Although the Neo-classical movement was not actually begun by David, yet he is usually credited with being its founder, and he gave this style so much authority, that it dominated realistic tendencies, and opposed originality in art in the beginning of the nineteenth century. The *oath of the Horatii* (in the Louvre, Paris) is David's most famous picture, painted in 1784 during the old regime under Louis XVI. It was very successful because of its political import, for it was an allegory of the rising opposition to monarchy. Though based on Roman history, the theme was inspired by a dance or ballet, which in turn was based on Corneille's drama Horace. Three brothers of the Horatian family are shown preparing for a deadly duel against three representatives of an enemy town. At the right are their weeping sisters, who are married to their brothers' enemies. The idea of putting country over family was something quite unheard-of in the earlier part of the century. In contrast to the many lines of Rococo, David makes the figures move in parallel lines to the plane of the picture, against a classical architectural background with three arches. The outlines are clear, and so modelled with light and shade, that the picture gives the effect *of* a sculptural low-relief.

David did not, however, always strictly adhere to his classical theories. In his portraits, which are his best work, he shows a strong realism, as seen in the *death of Marat* (Musée Moderne, Brussels). *Madame Recamier* (in the Louvre Museum, Paris) is his best-known portrait. The young woman is seated on a graceful Empire sofa. The painting is not finished, because the sitter left David's studio before he could complete it, in order to have her portrait made by his pupil, Gerard. A few years later she returned to David, begging him to finish it. He told her that artists are as perverse as women, and asked her to let him leave the picture as it was.

Jean Auguste Ingres (1780-1867) was the most talented painter among David's pupils, but instead of being neo-classic, he was classic in the sense that the word is applied to Raphael, Poussin or Cézanne. During the first half of the nineteenth century the was the most prominent of

France's conservative painters. From 1834-1841, Ingres was director of the French Academy. He imposed his artificial theory of beauty so rigidly, that the official art of this period was barren, since it hampered real artists, and permitted many untalented painters to hide their lack of imagination and genius under the classical garb. His themes were taken from classic mythology, the Renaissance, and modern subjects. Like the romanticists, he was also attracted by the East.

His true greatness lay in portraits done in hard pencil or silver point. *Madame Roche* (in the Groult Collection, Paris) is a pencil drawing. There is a fine sensitiveness in the line around the face and neck. There is little shading, which gives the whole portrait fulness in contrast to the delicate outline. His large compositions seem cold and empty because they lack imagination. The *Apotheosis of Homer* (Louvre Museum, Paris), an example of his classical ideal, lacks movement, and the colours are unattractive. The picture represents great geniuses in history, who pay tribute to Homer. Behind him is a Greek temple. This picture shows the immobility which his contemporaries of the French Academy believed to be typical of classic art. A group of muralists adopted this style for official buildings.

Théodore Géricault (1791-1827) is generally considered to be the first Romantic painter of France. After a short stay in Paris, he went in 1816 to Italy, where for three years he studied the old masters and antique art. He returned to Paris just when the wreck of the ship Medusa was causing great criticism. He immortalized the tragedy in his masterpiece, the *raft of the Medusa* (Louvre Museum, Paris). After a long series of sketches, he finally worked out the design of the rocking pyramid which he used. From the bottom to the top of the picture, there is created an impression of a crescendo of emotion from the terrible despair of the dying, lying amongst their dead comrades, to the frantic hope and excitement of the men who are holding up a negro to wave at a ship which they have seen in the distance. The dramatic effect is heightened by means of highlights and dark shadows.

Géricault managed to get this painting exhibited in the Salon of 1819, without its having passed the jury. Otherwise, it would never have been accepted. The fictional title, a nautical scene, deceived nobody. It aroused great excitement in the academic circles, and it is considered as the beginning of the Romantic revolt. There was nothing in the technical aspect of the picture which could offend the contemporary standards and traditions of the Academy, except for the broader and darker shadows. The cause of the indignation was the theme. Instead of a classical subject of the past, it depicted not only a contemporary event, but a tragedy due to official neglect. Its vivid portrayal of violence and suffering, which appealed strongly to the emotions, was at variance with the demands of the Academy which insisted upon restraint, and upon a subject which appealed rather to the mind than to the heart.

He went for a time to England where he was successful as an artist, especially with his painting of horses and their riders. He himself had a great love of horses, and died at the age of thirty-three as a result of a fall from one. His career as an artist lasted for only fifteen years ; but the quality of his works was remarkable—though many of them were left unfinished.

Eugene Delacroix (1798-1863) was the most typical of the French Romantic painters, and leader of the movement after Géricault's death. His childhood days in Marseilles gave him that love of bright colours and sunshine that later characterized his work. Of a wild, reckless nature, he feared nothing and no one. This was seen clearly in many of the exciting adventures of his boyhood. With such a character, it is no wonder that he did not respect social conventions, and that excitement played so great a role in his life and paintings. His famous journal and published letters show his intelligence and versatility. He was well acquainted with literature and music, and wrote critical estimates of writers, artists and musicians. Although a typical Romantic in temperament and work, he strangely enough considered himself a classicist. He did not appreciate Romantic poets like Lamartine ; and he preferred Mozart, the classic musician, to Beethoven. Because of the opposition of Ingres, and in spite of his high social position, he became a member of the Academy only at the age of sixty, when he was too old to hold a professorship at the Ecole des Beaux Arts.

In 1822 he exhibited in the Salon his painting, *Dante and Virgil in hell* (now in the Louvre Museum, Paris). The Classicists of the time thought it ridiculous to paint a picture of a fourteenth century poet—a period which they held in little esteem. The tortured figures of the damned also appeared to them ugly and exaggerated. In 1824 Delacroix developed the style of his maturity. He was exhibiting his *massacre of Chios* (Louvre Museum, Paris) in the famous Salon Anglais, where Constable's Hay Wain was shown at the same time. On seeing Constable's brilliant colouring, we are told, Delacroix took his picture home and repainted it in the most vivid colours possible. The subject of the Massacre of Chios was taken from a contemporary incident. In 1821, during the Greek War of Independence, the Turks massacred all but nine hundred of the one hundred thousand Greek inhabitants of the island of Chios. The purpose of the picture was to raise sympathy for the Grecks. Like Géricauh's Raft of the Medusa, it was a protest against cruelty. Their sufferings are depicted in the most grim and realistic manner. In order to strengthen the emotional impressions of the picture, Delacroix unbalanced the composition, and used such violent colouring that critics declared it had been painted with a drunken broom. Even Le Gros, who until then had sympathized with him, declared the picture was a ' massacre of painting.' These clear vibrant colours were in striking contrast to the heavy impasto (the thick application of a pigment to a canvas) of Le Gros, and even to his own earlier work. It was this factor which was regarded as revolutionary. Delacroix had learnt from Constable that what seems uniform in nature is in fact made up of a shimmering multitude of touches. Thus he was the first Frenchman who prepared the way for Impressionism. Preoccupation with colour made him enthusiastic about Titian.

In 1831, Delacroix painted his last political protest picture, *liberty leading the people* (Louvre Museum, Paris), usually called La Barricade. This is an allegory reflecting the events of the Revolution of 1830. Due to certain powerful influences, the Government purchased the picture; but it was hung facing the wall, as it might have proved politically dangerous. After this period, his painting took another direction.

In 1832 Delacroix was sent to Spain, Morocco and Algeria on a diplomatic mission. His imagination was stirred by the colourful scenes, the people, and the exotic animals. He painted vivid, exciting studies of them, as for example his *Arab rider attacked by a lion* (in the Art Institute, Chicago). It is a compact composition: the horse rears on its hind legs as the lion bites into its left foreleg. The Arab, almost unseated from the horse, plunges his sabre into the lion's neck. The dominant colour is a reddish-brown, with the bright red of the Arab's cloak and the harness of the white horse standing out. The work was done with great speed, and resulted in bold work, which seems coarse when compared to the refinement of his former paintings. His last great works were a series of important mural commissions. He decorated many of the most important buildings in Paris—as for example, the Palais Bourbon, the Luxem- bourg Palace, the Gallery of Apollo in the Louvre, and the church of St. Sulpice.

A group of painters, called the Barbizon school, were important both for their landscapes and their influence on Impressionism. Barbizon is the name of a village near the forest of Fontainebleau, where most of them lived at one time or another, due mostly to financial misery. They initiated landscape painting in France, influenced by Constable and other British and Dutch artists. But they also belonged to the Romantic movement, because they expressed their own personal impressions and feelings in their work. Their leader was Theodore Rousseau (1812-1867), the greatest master of landscape paintings amongst them. Jean Baptiste Corot (1767-1875) was quite well off in contrast with the others. Because he was always ready to help anyone of them in their needs, he was commonly called Papa Corot. He is best known for his sunny landscapes full of romantic feeling; though he also painted urban scenes, especially Italian ones. Jean François Millet (1814-1875), one of the most popular of this group, depicted the difficult life of the peasants, which was brightened by their intense faith. *The angelus* (PI. 64.3 ) is a good example of this. Here we see a poor French peasant and his wife after a hard day's work, standing in prayer as the bell rings from a distant church, to remind them how God became one with men, in their labours, hardships and sufferings. Unfortunately this popular picture was destroyed by a recent fire.

# 16 MODERN ART

## ARCHITECTURE

Industrialism, its needs and possibilities, gave birth to modern architecture. Railway stations and train sheds, factories and exposition halls, department stores and offices required spacious buildings with wide spans and good lighting. Mass production of iron and steel made this possible. Wrought iron is ten times stronger than wood and a hundred times more resistant than stone, while cast iron has twice the strength of wrought iron. Steel is strong not only under compression but also under tension, and being malleable it can be pressed and rolled. The invention of steel frames made heavy wails unnecessary. The Americans first exploited steel for architecture after it became possible to mass-produce it with the Bessemer process in the middle of the nineteenth century. Gradually *iron and steel frames* replaced traditional brick or stone walls. Not only did they provide more space but through mass production they were cheaper and more easily erected. They reduced the weight-bearing function of walls, which became mere 'curtains' for privacy and protection against the weather.

Fires in Chicago, New York and Boston in the 1870's showed that iron frames were more fire resistant when encased in masonry. Moreover concrete can be easily cast in any shape by means of wooden frames. However, though it has great compressive power, it lacks tensile strength. To overcome this disadvantage, experiments led to the' invention and perfection of *reinforced concrete* which combines the compressive strength of concrete with the tensile power of steel, thus providing modern architecture with its favourite structural material. Since the resistance of steel and concrete can be exactly calculated, trial and error in laboratories and research stations replaced trial and error on the job.

*Glass* became another favourite modern building material around the middle of the nineteenth century, together with steel and concrete. Like concrete, glass had been used by the ancient Romans who built glass walls for sun rooms in public baths. In the Middle Ages the builders of the Gothic churches, such as Chartres and La Sainte Chapelle, produced masterpieces of lacy stone filled with coloured glass. Since steel and concrete walls permit any size of opening in the walls, glass façades with a minimal frame became more and more common and experiments with mass-produced glass led to plate glass in ever larger sizes, glass bricks for walls and roofs, and polarised glass as a protection against heat. Not only does glass improve lighting and views for exhibition halls and stores, but it helps to improve health and efficiency in offices, factories, hospitals and schools. With their changing play of reflections, giass walls have added aestheti value.

Among *other new materials* for walls and roofs are asbestos which was found to be fire-resistant in 1877, aluminium panels (introduced around 1890), plastics, light metal alloys, plywood which does not warp in large sheets, and synthetic wallboard. These prefabricated materials help to solve one of the pressing problems of modern cities with their housing shortages.

To meet the needs of industrialisation. *engineers were the first to make creative use of the new materials*. Some of them even created masterpieces of a new beauty based on simple lines, honest expression and unornamented grandeur, resulting from rhythm, contrast and scale. They developed the structural principles and materials of modern architecture and opened new horizons of creative possibilities. The bridges, exhibition halls and railway stations of nineteenth century engineers foreshadow much that has become typical of twentieth century architecture though in their time they were not recognized as architecture since they conflicted with accepted ideas. Today engineering and architecture have become inseparable.

The possibilities of modern architecture derive from early *practical constructions* such as the first cast-iron bridge in 1775 with its visible frame of elegant lines in transpicuous tracery. Bulkiness disappeared. The first suspension bridges, round 1796, held in tension by chains and later by wire ropes, reduced the mass still more, being freed of all unnecessary material. They have a simple grandeur and beauty. In 1801 appeared the First edition of later high-rise buildings – a seven-storey mill with iron frame and beams. This and similar utility buildings started a new way of construction with iron and glass, but most of them showed more technique than taste. The cast- iron columns in St. Anne's Church in Liverpool instance the first use of this material for ecclesiastical architecture. During the early part of the nineteenth century French engineers experimented with iron vaulting, such as cupolas and arcades, producing ever wider spans without the need of buttresses or tie bars.

In the *Bibliotheque Ste. Genevieve* (1842-50; Paris) *H. Labrouste* frankly revealed its cast- iron skeleton. Slender columns resting on concrete pedestals support the iron roof arches. Though the new material transformed the traditional masonry arch in a beautiful way, architects still showed contempt for this 'engineer's architecture'.

With *Sir Joseph Paxton's Crystal Palace* in *London* (1850-1) engineering and manufacture successfully invaded architecture, revolutionising it and introducing an entirely new style, method and beauty. Here for the first time industrial technology was applied to architecture on a large scale, demonstrating how a vast space could be enclosed not only quickly and economically but also aesthetically. Sir Joseph Paxton was a gardener who experimented with buildings made of metal, glass and wood. Within nine months he accomplished the incredible – covering a huge rectangie of eighteen acres, even a big tree, with 300,000 panes of glass upheld by cast-iron beams and arches and 3,300 iron columns. He eliminated not only solid external walls but also the need of extensive foundations to support them. The walls became no more than light curtains of glass, as a protection against the weather, merging the interior with the exterior through their transparency. The building heralded a new style of architecture, light and airy, erected with ease and speed. It is an early example of the right use of mass-production and pre-fabrication, with standardised parts of cast-iron and panes of glass assembled at the site, thus saving time, cost and upkeep. Demand for pre-fabrication is one of the urgent problems of modern critics. Without imitating any style, Sir Joseph Paxton showed his originality in the repetition of a single structural element, thus producing an elegant work much more valuable than any of the exhibits it sheltered in that exhibition of 1851.

After steel could be mass-produced in the second half of the nineteenth century, French engineers experimented with it in conjunction with concrete and showed what these materials could do in the *Pairs* exhibitions of 1867, 1878 and 1889. The masterpieces of this last exposition were *Containin's Galerie des Machines* and the Eiffel tower. The wide span of the former, without intermediate supports, brought to a climax the nineteenth century experimentation with wide space. All the lines of forces are transferred to the ground in the most direct and economical way by nearly parabolic arches hinged at the base and apex. These supported great sheets of glass which bathed the exposition in light. Its beauty lies in the poising of forces which seem ready to spring into movement, giving the space an expanding rather than static appearance, and thus providing a new aesthetic ideal.

*Eiffel's Tower*, built between 1887-9, has become the symbol of modern Paris. With its varied pattern of metal frames, it provides a new spatial view of fields of force, and its molecular design of weight-bearing elements paved the way for B. Fuller's modular coordinates. This functionless piece of engineering also heralds modern sculpture which tries to create something altogether new without imitating anything in nature. Eiffel had tested the new lattice-beam which he developed for this in the viaduct he erected in the French mountains and in a bridge in Portugal. He also evolved the wind tunnel.

Other examples of artistic engineering include the *Clifton Suspension bridge at Bristol*, England, built by *I. Brunel* in 1836. Like his French colleague *E. Freyssinet* who built the *Dirigible Hangar* (1916-24) at *Orly*, near Paris, the Swiss engineer *R. Maillart* won the admiration of artists, sculptors and architects by combining the logic of engineering with the insight of an artist thus raising engineering to a fine art. By aiming at stylistic purity and structural unity of form, Maillart's slender reinforced concrete structures, such as the *Schwandbach Bridge* near *Berne* (1933) combine harmonious poise and strength, with all the parts integrated in the structural function, and all with the greatest economy of materials. On the vaulted shell of the *Cement Industries Hall* for the Swiss Exposition, *Zurich* (1939), he showed the strength of the 6 cm thick reinforced concrete. In 1908 he also invented mushroom slabs – most important for high structures, ensuring a light elegant appearance and flexibility with an economy of materials.

By the end of the nineteenth century architects started to use the work of engineers to create a new architecture. They used long steel *cantilevers* reaching out from only one support, such as concrete piers, in order to support floors and roofs. While flat roofs can cover any shape of building, they need more careful insulation against heat and treatment with bituminous products against rainwater. The introduction of roofs suspended by tensile steel members freed architecture from rectangular shapes and the limitations of flat roofs. These light-weight steel cables can support great loads, as demonstrated by suspension bridges. The saddle-shaped shell vaults of these *suspended roofs,* supported by cable lattices, gives them a rigid form and prevents movement, vibration or buckling through wind or self-weight. One of the first known of these roofs appears on a *hall* erected in *Raleigh, N. C.,* U.S.A. by *Deitrick* and *Nowicki.* This gave rise to a new type of architecture. Steel ropes hung from a pair of parabolic arcs carry the roof. The *Federal Reserve Bank,* constructed by *Berkets* in *Minneapolis,* U.S.A. in 1972 has a pair of massive end towers upholding cables on a catenary curve which carry the floors below in suspension, thus leaving an open space beneath as an urban amenity. In the same year *F. Orei* made a tent-like *model for the Olympic Stadium* in *Munich,* Germany, which, like the Crystal Palace, may become the prototype of a new style. Though appearing light and airy, its free spans of steel in tension are really very strong.

Concrete, of which the ancient Romans had made expert use, is very strong under compression and can be easily shaped. Around 1844 German and French engineers started experimenting with *re-inforced* or *ferro-concrete* whereby the tensile strength of steel is added. At the same time the concrete keeps the cage of steel bars embedded in it from rusting. These steel rods must be placed exactly where the tensile stresses will come. This requires an exact knowledge of forces in all parts of the building. Unevenly loaded columns, arched roofs and spiral stairs thus involve very complicated mathematical problems. Wooden shuttering holds the mix till it hardens. This versatile ferro-concrete answers to the freedom of composition of modern architecture.

*Hennebique* made the first use of ferro-concrete in the *mill* he built in 1895. Two years later *A. Baudot* made unconcealed and honest use of it for erecting the *Church of St. Jean-de-Montmartre.* In 1903 *A. Perret's apartment house* in *Paris,* his most innovative building, was the first ferro-concrete structure in the modern style, with the new material used as a skeleton frame without the normal façades of the time. The ground floor has a flexible plan. In his buildings Perret showed the suitability of reinforced concrete for post and lintel structures. He continued to explore the potentials of this material, especially to make his constructions as light as possible. His numerous ferro-concrete buildings inspired European architects, including Le Corbusier. Perret's *Church of Notre Dame Le Raincy,* in the early 1920's, is a masterpiece of twentieth century architecture with its elegant design, dignity, technical refinements, precision and delicacy of proportion and detail, and its harmony of rhythm and proportions. He economised the formwork by means of a system of columns and beams, with latticed walls of concrete and coloured glass. Though a limited budget forced him to use poor material, he produced a beautiful decorative effect with the rough concrete left completely exposed. He was an expert and lucid structural designer.

Other pioneers in the use of ferro-concrete include *T. Garnier* who in 1907 designed a *model town* of this material, which was later partly realized in Lille, France. In 1912 *M. Berg* first used this material for a large-span roof, instead of a steel frame, in the *Centenary Hall* in *Breslau.* Four years later *Freyssinet* built the *Orly Hangars* by pleating the reinforced concrete to make the thin membranes rigid and by using parabolic curves to reduce tensile stresses. He also erected some of the most daring and elegant bridges of reinforced concrete. In the same year *F. L. Wright* built the earthquake-proof *Imperial Hotel* in *Tokyo*, Japan, which was among the few large structures remaining intact in the great tremor of 1923. In 1922 *L. Mies* first demonstrated *stanchions* set back from the façade which supported floors by means of cantilevers. This was widely adopted some years later. In the same year *Bauersfeld and Dischinger* made the first practical use of *shell concrete* in *Jena,* Germany. Since then it has developed quickly. Though very thin it resists bending because of its curved shape—on the principle of egg shells or of paper which becomes strong when rolled. Four years later pre-stressed concrete was invented. It is even thinner and stronger and lends itself to more slender shapes. Later it was used for the underground Basilica of St. Pius X in Lourdes, France. In 1934 *B. Baroni* introduces shells *of hyperbolic paraboloids* in the iron foundry he built in

Milan. Italy. This too found much imitation later. A warehouse erected in Ferrara, Italy, in 1938 assumed the shape of an upturned umbrella. Shell concrete, with its sculptural possibilities, is now used for every kind of architecture. For his *Exhibition Hall* in *Turin*, Italy, *L. Nervi* employed undulating pre-fabricated units of this material on a large scale, thereby reducing the weight while increasing the resilience and tensile strength.

Despite its great variety of materials and shapes, modern architecture may be divided into two *basic forms*, depending on the ground plan. One is *symmetrical* at least along one axis, and it has pure geometrical form, as in the architecture of Mies, Nervi and B. Fuller. The other form is *asymmetncal*, open in all directions to the environment, merging with the landscape or with rows or groups of houses, often of contrasting or mixed shapes, able to expand, not restricted by rules. Examples of this type are Gropius' Bauhaus, Wright's Falling Water, Le Corbusier's Note Dame du Haut, the Opera House in Sydney, Australia, and Moshe Safdie's Habitat.* The *Prototype* of this style is *P. Webb's Red House* built for William Morris** in *Kent*, England, in reaction to the impersonality of industry. With its multi-axial ground plan it influenced a major advance in building, namely the interconnection of rooms at different levels and the interpenetration of elevation, with its open ground plan reaching out in all directions. The planning started from inner comfort and convenience rather than from formal outward appearance.

The *symmetrical* style, *modelled on* the *Crystal Palace*, reduces a building to the barest essentials. Its beauty rests in its lightness and strength – in what it can do without. Quickly erected of pre-fabricated material, it can be as easily dismantled, producing a feeling of impermanence. This is increased by its interchangeable functions – it can be used for different purposes. With its large size it is more concerned with the impersonal collective than with the individual. The temporary nature of exhibition halls makes them more useful for experimentation.

The steel and ferro-concrete frame constructions introduced a basically different kind of building. Since these carry all the loads, the walls become mere curtains as in Paxton's Crystal Palace, and their location is determined by functional and aesthetic requirements. This results in *free planning*, thus changing the traditional idea of a building with rooms rigidly enclosed. Moreover, these slender frames with light-weight walls make high-rise building possible and thus save much outlay. Nor do they need to be rooted in the ground since the weight is transferred to the base only at a few small points by slender, delicate supports which gives the buildings the appearance of floating, and the space under the building can be left open for public amenities. Through glass and sliding walls, the building interpenetrates with the landscape. The interior too has a radically changed plan, with movable partitions. Everywhere function, which does not depend on stylistic conventions, determines the form.

Adaptability, lightness, poise and elegant proportions characterise the better modern constructions. Because the architect has nothing to imitate and since he is usually tied to the needs and wishes of his patron, he requires much discrimination, sensibility and aesthetic taste in designing his buildings to avoid vulgarity. The architect's vision appears in the beauty of his work. He needs not only efficiency but imagination disciplined by good taste.

The beauty and elegance of modern architecture lies in its *simplicity*. Everything unnecessary is eliminated, even ornament such as sculpture and mouldings, lest the basic beauty be obscured. The basic structure is frankly demonstrated on the facade, as for example, on King's Cross Station, London, built in 1851. The function is honestly shown as well as the natural qualities of the materials. There is an unsentimental, open-minded return to the first principles of utility and beauty, to which stability and support have become subordinated. Only the size of the buildings answers to the human desire for the grandiose. Dignity and beauty come rather from an economy of means, from the subtle precision finishes obtained by means of machines, through proportion and contrast, over-all rhythm and the harmony of light and shadow, mass and volume, as well as the relationship of surface and line. Architecture, the art of meaningful, measured space, requires a union of thought and feeling, of technique and aesthetic sense.

Modern architecture often comes from the *joint work* of different artists, as for example in De Stijl and the Bauhaus, as we shall see later. This results in cross-fertilisation, a combination of different art forms containing the resonance of several styles, both personal and regional –

---

* *M. Safdie's Habitat,* displayed at the Montreal Expo in 1967, was composed of independent, box-like units of pre-fabricated concrete modules, and resembled children's building blocks whimsically put together.

** W. Morris, like Ruskin, shifted the stress from style to design. Both wanted to relate art to everything and to make everyone an artist.

one of the important features of twentieth century architecture.

The seeds of modern architecture, first planted in England and France, grew very tall in *America* which developed the first *skyscrapers*. Inflated land prices after the fire in Chicago in 1871 made it more profitable to build high in the crowded areas. The newly improved lifts or elevators in the 1850's as well as other equipment made this practicable. After the fire they discovered that buildings could be made more fire-proof by sheathing the metal frames with brick or masonry. For these high buildings architects began to accept engineering structures. Motivated chiefly by practical considerations they broke with tradition—but only with regard to die skyscrapers. In America itself this style (of the so-called Chicago School) did not find acceptance for non-commercial buildings until the 1930's. Yet they pointed the way to a new type of construction which other countries took up, especially Germany and Holland, who eventually brought it back to America.

Functional planning, especially for utility buildings, had been native to American architecture. In fact Gropius and Le Corbusier had praised the simple beauty of the grain elevators and found in them inspiration for modern architecture. The charm of the early skyscrapers lies in the regular, over-all rhythm of the metal frame, with the spaces between filled with big windows for light and air. This smart simplicity of rhythm became the outstanding characteristic of American commercial architecture. *W. Jenney's* ten-storey *Home Insurance Building* (1883-5) was the first notable skyscraper in Ghicago. The *Tacoma Building*, erected by *Holabird and Roche* in 1887, had the first riveted skeleton and its foundations rested on a concrete raft. Its projecting bay windows, with the glass in three panels, served as a protection against the wind while providing more light and fresh air. In *Burnham and Root's Reliance Building (*1890) the glass is almost level with the spandrels, thus reducing heavy shadows—a work of art that points to future developments. These early skyscrapers do not as yet have the apparent weightlessness and refinement of modern buildings. Those of New York, with their greater stress on a variety of detail, lack the daring simplicity of their Chicago counterparts.

*H. Richardson*, the first American architectural genius, combined his own personal style with the heavy round arches and masonry walls of Romanesque, of which he was very fond. His strong forms show the greatest discipline and unity among the nineteenth century constructions in America. His most important creation is the *Marshall Field Warehouse* (Fig. 464; 1885-7; later demolished), which more than any other

Fig. 464. Marshall Field Warehouse, Chicago, H. Richardson.

building of the time showed that good architecture comes from honest construction. Its form was simple, without ornament; and though it echoed historical styles, it did not imitate them. It occupied a whole city block, stressing long horizontal lines and solidity. Its large glass arcades point to future walls of glass. The sincerity of this masterpiece of his, as Well as numerous other buildings especially in New England, helped to free American construction from the trivia of prevalent fashion and purified the less sure taste of Sullivan.

*L. Sullivan*, the leading American representative of the over-decorative Art Nouveau,* also led the way in search of new styles. His fame rests on the refinements he introduced in designing skyscrapers and on helping to develop the organic theory of architecture, i.e., in using the

* Art Nouveau, inspired by he increased use of metal in architecture, used flowing ornaments to suggest movement, in reaction against straight lines and right angles. Though it prepared the way for a freer outlook, it degenerated into fantasy and succumbed to its very freedom by becoming just another brief period style. Examples of Art Nouveau are V. Horta's hotels in Brussels, Belgium, and A. Gaudi's buildings in Barcelona, Spain, with their irregular, exaggeratedly sculptured forms resembling nature's apparent randomness.

structural needs and available materials as the point of departure for creation. Richardson's example helped him to discipline to some extent his natural bias for elaborate ornament. He was the first really modern American architect and through him the skyscrapers evolved into distinguished architectural forms. The greatest among the Chicago School builders, Sullivan brought more artistic rhythms into their practical logic. The *auditorium* cum hotel cum offices, built in *Chicago* (1886-9), brought his talents as a designer into focus. Its interior ranks among the most original examples of planning and decoration in American architecture. The skyscrapers he designed in 1890—the Wainwright Building in St. Louis, the Bayard Building in New York and the *Gage Building* in *Chicago*—were the most modern American commercial structures until the 1930's. The last-named stands out for its beautifully proportioned windows. The open ground floor of the *Guarantee Buildings Buffalo,* N.Y. (1894-5), points to the later piers and pilotis. The upper storeys stress the verticality of the building rather than trying to disguise it, as had been the tendency before. Terra-cotta covers the vertical members between the large windows, and the building still retains a cornice.

In 1896 Sullivan published an article 'The Tall Office Building Artistically Considered' which enunciated his slogan '*form follows function*'. He aimed at a flexible relationship between the various parts of the building, somewhat like the union between the bones and tissues of the hand. He wanted architecture to be organic, with the parts in harmonious relation to the whole and to its specific function, as found in natural organisms. In a building the parts must be integrated into a concordant unity and express their purpose by emphasising the lines of stress, support and thrust. This theory goes back as far as the ancient Greeks who based the proportions of their temples on the human figure. Far-sighted, Sullivan saw a new inspiration in this commercial architecture, but in the exhibition of 1893 in Chicago the authorities refused to accept it, and so America lagged behind with classic and collegiate Gothic architecture, instead of taking the lead.

*F. L. Wright*, though ignored in his native country for almost half a century, became the only American architect who became universally recognized. Through the publication of his writings in Berlin in 1910, his domestic architecture became very influential in Europe, particularly in Germany and the Netherlands. The functional simplicity of his work appealed to the younger architects abroad, and within the next fifteen years led to the International Style and to the destruction of Art Nouveau. However his ideas were either not completely understood or accepted—they loved his vigorous forms and the apparent simplicity, particularly his new use of walls and treatment of space. Later he rejected the International Style—the European outgrowth of his inspiration.

Wright's Celtic imagination was instinctive rather than intellectual, and his native Wisconsin gave him a love of nature and the land. From his play in a Froebel kindergarten he had learnt to see in basic geometric forms the alphabet of organic architecture. He studied Ruskin, and from Viollet le Due he imbibed rationality of structure. He was influenced by Richardson, and by his own teacher and employer Sullivan, his 'dear master' in Chicago while the latter was erecting his first skyscrapers. In Chicago Wright produced his most original work, namely his city and *prairie houses* which had such great influence in Europe. Himself an engineer and a contemporary of Perret, Wright pioneered with reinforced concrete houses in America.

His architectural career extended over seventy years, and owed much to what he said and wrote. He showed his originality in the wide range of geometrical forms he produced till the end of his life: rectangular till 1925, then varied angles, circles and spirals—thus setting unusual styles which however were not always apt. Very personal, he did not imitate styles— he created them. An idealist, urged by the idea of constant progress, he tended to escape from social and technical problems. He designed a great number and variety of buildings in his long life, always trying to produce something newer and better.

For him the machine was something to be dominated, rather than imitating it as the early Le Corbusier did. For Wright the machine was a tool to make a building resemble nature. Though he stressed the natural qualities of materials and the use of indigenous ones, he was also concerned with good craftsmanship. He disliked the reflecting surfaces of the International Style, its skeleton constructions and box-like appearance. He called such buildings 'boxes on stilts'. He refused to follow both academic rules and sophisticated fashions.

In America he was the first to experiment with the free plan, as Webb had done in England. He evaluated every part of the house, and liberated the wall according to its function, using it for protection only where required, so that the plan was open, with the interior divided according to need. From the central hub, usually the fireplace, it radiates out in sweeping asymmetrical, horizontal lines that emphasize the form of the ground. Terraces and pathways extend the building to the garden, letting the inside out and bringing the outside in.

Of all the exponents of organic architecture, Wright was the most daring and consistent. For him the house and garden together constitute one work of art. Utility and efficiency were secondary to harmony with nature obtained through the unity of the plan, structure and materials with the site. Basic to this organic unity are the flexible relationships of the pans to the whole, that is the continuity of the component parts—floors, walls and ceilings—which interrelate like the organs of the body, like the bones and tissues. To harmonise with the form of the ground, he used predominantly horizontal lines for the caves and windows, so that the house seems to hug the land, becoming part of the site like trees and shrubbery as necessary and pleasant. As in Japanese architecture his houses look as if they grow out of the earth.

The first of such houses (1889), built according to these organic principles, contrasted with the stiff formality in vogue at the time. At the turn of the century his prairie houses in the state of Illinois started revolutionising American domestic architecture with their combination of primitive and modem ideas, their stress on informal, undivided inner space instead of massiveness, their lack of ornament, posts or columns. Continuous roof planes, at times cantilevered, follow the cross-axial plan with L, T or X shapes. The low windows run in long bands under the projecting eaves. In 1902 he built a house without a wasteful attic or basement and related its proportions to human size. *Robie House*, built in *Chicago* in 1909, seems to float in the air—with its cantilevered roofs reaching far beyond the walls; and its Cubist* interior, with sharp planes meeting at odd angles, shows the application of twentieth century design to domestic architecture. Parapets and terraces at each end anchor the house to the ground. The long sweeping lines of its wandering asymmetrical plan reflect the flat prairies of the American mid-West. It has no façade—its entrances are hardly perceptible. Masses and voids are balanced, with the screen walls emphasising space. For his *own house* in *Taliesin*, *Wisconsin* he used the local limestone and adapted its shape to its hillside location.

From 1916-22 Wright built the *Imperial Hotel* in *Tokyo*, Japan. He balanced the floor slabs over central supports to reduce the shocks of earth tremors. After 1920 he became extremely idiosyncratic, reacting against the Cubist regularity of the International Style and the machine idea of a house advocated by Lc Corbusier. Instead he adopted rather exotic influences from other cultures or followed his own poetic bent.

His most famous building and one of the most beautiful twentieth century houses is his *Falling Water* or *Kaufmann house* (1936), reaching out over a little waterfall at *Bear Run* in the isolated woods of Pennsylvania. The rectangular terrace parapets, firmly gripped by cantilevers from vertical stone walls which seem part of the rock ledge, seem to hover over the cascade with a sophisticated calm often lacking in his work. The abstract levels overlap and bypass each other.

In the same year he built the *S. C. Johnson Administrative Building* in *Racine*, Wisconsin, one of the costliest offices, wherein he combined the organic, naturalistic features of his design with the machine-like refinement of the modern European movement. At that time the principal leaders of the International Style, Gropius and Mies, came to America, and together with Wright made America the leader in world architecture after World War II. This office forms one big room made of red brick alternating with bands of glass tubes to stress the horizontal look. The vertical rhythm results from the free-standing internal columns renowned for their unusual shape. They rise from metal shoes, slender at the base and widening gradually till they spread out at the top like great lotus leaves on the ceiling, supporting the pyrex tubes between to form the rest of the roof. The light filtering through these tubes has an extraordinary effect, as if the office were a huge fish-pond with the light penetrating softly between the lotus-like columns. These columns are made of hollow concrete reinforced with wire mesh. The building shows a subtle use of varied materials. Some years later he added the *Research Laboratory Tower*, with alternating square and circular floors cantilevered from a central cylinder with a stair and lift shaft and other utilities. Here polarised

* Cubism, which stressed the simple geometrical forms behind appearances, was naturally more suited to architecture than painting. It became the basis of the International Style. By laying stress on basic functions it makes the new architecture appear styleless, since style itself is considered an unnecessary ornament.

glass was first, used as a protection against the heat.

In 1937 he designed the *Usonian Houses*, his most practical creations. To eliminate the need of a basement and to provide heat, he embedded metal coils in a concrete mat. A brick-walled kitchen at the centre of the L form plan rises through the roof in a stack which contains utilities and provides light through clerestory windows. The other walls are made of planks or plywood. The flat roofs are cantilevered to provide trellises and car ports to replace the garage. The living room of his *Pew House*, in *Madison*, Wisconsin, seem to leap off the hillside, upheld in mid-air by a stone pillar.

Only in the 1940's did he get widespread recognition in his own country. At that time he had just built *Taliesin West*, his own winter house in the *Arizona* desert. Made of large rough blocks of local rock, round which he poured the concrete, and covered with a canvas roof, its low thick wails resemble caves, and from a distance the structure has the profile of cactus silhouetted against the horizon. He used bright colours to go with the intense desert light.

His last work, the *Guggenheim Museum* in *New York* city (1956-9; Fig. 465) resembles a huge sea-shell—a spiralling cylinder expanding

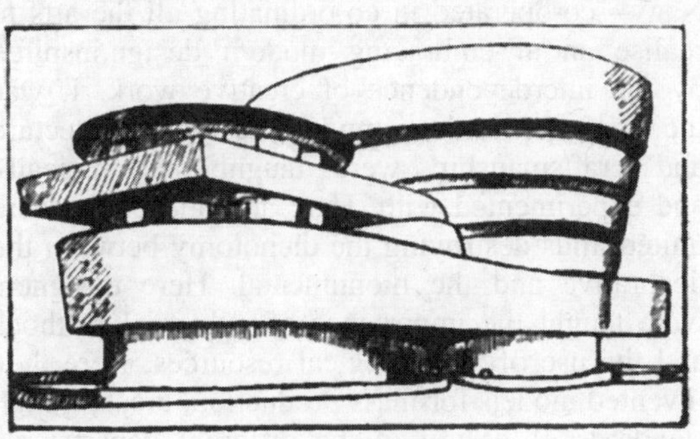

Fig. 465. Guggenheim Museum, New York, F.L. Wright.

with the height. The visitors ascend by lifts and descend by a gently sloping ramp which forms an unbroken gallery round a circular well of space ninety feet deep lit by a glass dome. Here the curved elements provide his characteristic dynamic continuity of the inner space. But the building turns in on itself, as if providing a shelter from the disagreeable city; and the closed rounded form does not harmonise with the rectilinear urban ensemble. The outer wall serves for the display of the pictures. This museum, his testament to art, reveals his distaste for the impersonal character of the International Style. In his poetic love of nature and desire to serve human needs he revolted against the oversimplified abstractions fashionable at the time.

The seed of modern architecture, planted by England and France, had grown very tall with the American skyscrapers but the Americans in general were still unwilling to accept the new ideas for anything other than commercial architecture. Young architects in the Netherlands and Germany, enthusiastic about the practical innovations, especially by the freedom of planning inspired by English and American architecture, became the leaders of the movement until they were forced into exile in America.

The formation of the *Werkbund* in 1907 started *Germany* on the way to play a leading role in modern architecture. This association of designers and craftsmen provided the opportunity for applying the new ideas through the close collaboration of artists, workers and industrialists. For the first time modern artists were thus familiarised with the new industry. The Werkbund arranged exhibitions to make their work known. When through its influence *P. Behrens* was appointed in 1909 by A.E.G., the leading German electrical firm, to handle its designs, architecture and advertisements, the Werkbund established the success of its ideas.

P. Behrens became the leader of modern architecture in Germany until the first world war, and he was one of the first twentieth century architects to meet the requirements of industrialisation. He started industrial design with simple yet rich, functional and unadorned shapes, created by his classical, rational temperament. Thus he moved away from Art Nouveau or Jugendstil. The German General Electrical Company (A.E.G.) employed him to make sure that what they produced would be artistic as well as functionally efficient—that is to humanise technology. In 1909 he built the *A.E.G. Turbo Factory* in *Berlin*—the first glass and steel structure in Germany, leaving the steel stanchions framing the huge windows frankly exposed. He showed thereby that even factories could be made beautiful with the new simple geometrical forms which he designed without imitating other styles, but returning rather to the basic principles of form and technique. He planned numerous other factories as well as flats for workers in his mathematically severe, strong and sober style. His greatest fame, however, rests in his more renowned pupils—Gropius, Mies and Le Corbusier who were with him between 1907 and 1911.

After the war, in 1919, far-sighted and capable architects were needed in Germany to plan tor actual social needs. The German Republic laid out many *big housing projects* on the example of Vienna, Austria, with settlement blocks spaced and aligned to make the best use of the sun. The settlement blocks, among the greatest building plans in history, provided good experience for modern architects as well as meeting the needs of impoverished post-war Germany. An unusual feature of German architecture was its link not only with industrial but also with municipal housing right from the very beginning. *W. Gropius* designed a number of these housing projects, for example the *Siemensstadt Housing Estate* near *Berlin* (1929) which he provided with cross ventilation and gardens in between the houses. These designs had a wide influence.

In 1904 the casual freedom of English domestic architecture, which contrasted with the formal symmetry in vogue on the Continent, became known in Germany, but the Germans made the romantic design of the English more rational. By 1914 the modern methods were no longer confined to isolated individuals or small groups like the Werkbund, but stimulated by each other's experiments, engineers and architects started out on an international movement, with Germany taking the lead in the 1920's and 30's in perfecting and spreading Sullivan and Wright's 'form follows function' to produce works combining both utility and beauty.

*W. Gropius*, another great pioneer of modern architecture, descended from generations of architects. After leaving Behrens be built the *Fagus Factory* in 1911, carrying on the traditions of his master. An industrial reformer and humanist, he believed that social needs must be the basis of architectural design. With A. Loos* he formed a synthesis of the new architectural ideas in Europe and distilled the essentials of modem design. His restraint and simplicity, rectitude and reserve make him a classic modern whose architecture is severely logical and unemotional. The beauty of his buildings lies in the precision of his work and the purity of his lines. He rejected all ornament. With patience and imagination he carried on consistent research on function and aesthetics, uniting crafts with fine art. He ranks among the most advanced thinkers and creative artists of the twentieth century. His architectural design can be adapted to the needs and traditions of different countries and to the personal tastes of individual artists, his work being capable of imitation and development. He was adventurous regarding the use of new materials and saw the great importance of industrial production in modern design. He believed in the intelligent use of standardisation and pre-fabrication through machinery. However, for him the machine was subservient—no more than a complicated hand tool.

More than anything else Gropius valued the importance and need of team-work in modern building. For him it symbolised community living and intelligent social integration. He encouraged collaboration in designing, building and furnishing. He put this ideal of teamwork to most fruitful use when in 1919 he succeeded H. Van de Velde as head of the Weimar School of Applied Arts which he transformed into *the Bauhaus*—a university for design which became an intellectual centre and source of inspiration for modernisation in central Europe. Here the best artists, designers and technicians—such as Klee, Kandinsky and Moholy Nagy—co-operated in co-ordinating all the arts to realise an all-embracing modern design,inspired by the interdependence of creative work. It was the first school where modern design, architecture and craftsmanship were taught systematically and experimented with. Here arts and crafts were united, thus destroying the dichotomy between the decorative and the monumental. Here designers were taught the importance of industrial methods and the use of technological resources. Here they invented models for mass production, creating high standards of design in the different departments of the school, which had units for prefabrication, furniture and textiles as well as architecture, in order to meet all the aesthetic, commercial and technological requirements of modern conditions. Industrialists adopted these Bauhaus designs for mass production, and many of the utilities now in common use, such as light fixtures and furniture, derive from models created at the Bauhaus.

Students and teachers worked in close collaboration. They had first to experiment with different materials in order to discover their aptitudes and latent potentials for creativity before choosing their major line of work. Before

* *A. Loos*, who designed the first flat-roofed modern urban dwelling, *Steiner House* in *Vienna* in 1910, saw the danger in all new movements of becoming ends in themselves, and of modern design congealing into just another period style. He believed in utter simplicity, since 'ornament masks defects'.

using the tools they had to understand the qualities of the various materials. They studied handicrafts and techniques as well as the aesthetic theories of designing. They received experience in building and interior decoration and were encouraged to experiment. Students of design worked in relation to machines and everyone received a good, all-round training to master industrial processes.

In 1925 *the Bauhaus* was moved to *Dessau* where Gropius designed the new building which became the earliest great masterpiece of modern European architecture. Here glass was first used on a large scale for an industrial building. The huge shimmering glass curtains show how functional need can be put to aesthetic use. Between the glass are slabs of clean white concrete surfaces. A bridge over the road, containing offices and a club, connects the three rectangular wings of the building with the workshop, school of design and hostel. These connected asymmetrical wings serve the need both for segregation and circulation. They push freely outward, completely liberated from traditional planning. There is no front or back—each part is perfectly co-ordinated and vital to the whole. The starkly simplified geometrical form, severely rational, as well as thoroughly and rhythmically designed, has a noble dignity all its own. Gropius's fame as an architect rests chiefly on this building. It combines the logic of his ideas with the actual work of both staff and students. Later on a colony, labour exchange and housing establishment were added to the institution.

As an architect he was one of the chief innovators in using glass walls. Instead of anchoring his structures in massive foundations he poised them lightly but firmly on the ground. He had an excellent sense of proportion and precision of lines. Other examples of his work include the *Total Theatre* in *Berlin* (1927), with seats revolving in sections to adjust the building to different uses, and the dual-purpose *Impington Village College* built while he was temporarily in exile in England in 1936, designed to serve both as school and community centre.

In 1928 Gropius resigned from the Bauhaus to concentrate on housing. The same year he built the *Dessau Employment Office*, perhaps his most perfect work. In 1937 he became professor of architecture and chairman of the department at Harvard, Boston, U.S.A., until 1952. With former students he designed the *Graduate Centre* for *Harvard* in 1949; and with Breuer, one of his first students at the Bauhaus, he built *residences around Boston*, combining American traditions with the International Style.

*L. Mies van der Rohe* brought the International Style to its highest refinement and sophistication. Precise and thorough by temperament, Mies learnt to appreciate values and order from his study of the Scholastics, especially St. Thomas Aquinas, at the Cathedral and trade schools in his native Aachen, Germany. From his father, a mason and stone-cutter, he acquired a deep understanding of the qualities of building materials and craftsmanship. Though he could not afford specialised training in architecture he learnt from the school of life and graduated as one of the four greatest architects of the twentieth century, with Wright, Gropius and Le Corbusier. For some time he worked as a designer of classical stucco ornaments, then with a decorator and furniture producer. He gained the greatest experience during the three years he spent in Behrens' office, where he met Gropius and Le Corbusier, Behrens increased his love of disciplined design and precise detail. In fact Mies spared no trouble in his attention to detail, for, to quote his own words 'God lives in the details'. In Behrens' work he first saw the beauty of glass façade with frankly exposed metal frames and he appreciated the serenity and proportions of his structures, especially their neoclassical forms. Like Wright he became interested in Japanese art, but he admired most those ancient buildings which transcend time and style, which have a value beyond all art.

Mies loved order and perfection, making sure that the means suit the ends exactly. He concentrated on the post and lintel system and chiselled it to a refinement and elegance in comparison with which much other modem architecture appears amateurish. His smoothly finished crystalline rectangles, either standing or reclining, have sublime classical proportions like well-balanced mathematical equations. Their simplicity gives them an austere nobility. He eliminated everything irrelevant on the policy that 'less is more'. The symmetry of his buildings imparts to the new materials a classic quality. He gave the steel frames nobility by letting them show their own value without trying to cover them up to look like something else. For him good architecture and engineering went hand in hand.

While the refined exteriors of his buildings have an urbane serenity, their interiors seem full of movement and space since he did not make them permanently for one use. Each occupant is free to arrange the interior according to his needs, so that there is great variety as in a street or landscape.

Among Mies' most notable works are a pair of *model skyscrapers*, fully walled with glass, which foreshadow his later work in America. The sides of the 1919 project have sharp angles to bring out the power of reflection of glass buildings. For him the glass also determined the choice of the site. The model shows the harmonious relationship between the steel and concrete frame and the glass, and points the way to refined designs in these materials, combining functional simplicity with the aesthetic possibilities of glass. The second project of 1921 has an unusual contour made of segments of circles to eliminate shadows and to allow the glass to reflect itself. It resulted from experiments with the best angles for making the glass walls self-reflecting.

In 1922 Mies first demonstrated the use of stanchions set back from the front of the building which support the floors by means of cantilevers. These found wide acceptance before the Second World War. The following year his *model of a brick country house* was a revolutionary step forward in architectural design in that he made the individual wall rather than the room the unit of composition. Instead of forming corners the walls bypass one another while some of them reach out into the landscape. The plan resembles an abstract De Stijl painting by Doesburg. The design suggests restless movement channelled by the walls. Here he experimented with space rather than substance.

The *Pavilion for the German Government* at the *Barcelona Exposition* (Fig. 466; 1929) was his first great building—a small gem of universal importance. Serving as an informal centre and rest house, it dramatised the principles of organic space as enunciated by Wright, eliminating the boundaries between exterior and Interior with its transparent, open walls. It resembles a disjointed cube with its free walls which alternately hid and revealed space, and which made no clear distinction between interior and exterior. The areas varied according to the degree of enclosure. The walls of solid marble or of transparent grey glass were subtly related to each other, allowing free movement. At both ends of the rectangular travertine base they continued around the corners. Eight regularly placed cross-shaped columns of chromium-plated steel supported the roof, which was cantilevered on both directions from the square bay system. Their structural purpose was diminished since no more than three or four columns could be seen from any one place but they gave a vertical accent to the horizontal lines of the walls. The interest and power of the building lay in the subtle placement of the walls around the sculptured court and the reflecting pools lined with black glass at the ends of the structure. Delicate details such as the famous classic chair which he also designed, as well as the beautiful materials with their rich surfaces set off the simplicity of the austere forms. The building however was suited only for one storey. This was Mies' most imaginative building. He confined his later works to strictly rational architecture. Only photographs remain of this masterpiece.

The following year he designed the *Tugendhat House* in *Brno*, Czechoslovakia, his last important building in Europe. The house was a wedding gift of a father to his daughter. It has the same exquisite materials as the Barcelona Pavilion, with one panel made of ebony. Situated on a steeply sloping site, the street level gives entrance to the top floor, while the back, with a hundred foot expanse of glass

Fig. 466. Pavilion for the German Government, Barcelona Exposition, L. Mies van der Rohe.

opening on a beautiful view, has two floors. The living rooms are designed as an interior landscape. The glass panels between the rooms could be lowered mechanically into spaces provided for them in the basement wall. Every part of the lower floor, even the furniture, served to channel space. The building answers to the urban need for spaciousness and the informality of modern ways. Its free plan helped to inspire modern architecture.

That same year Mies, at Gropius' suggestion, succeeded him as head of the Bauhaus where he remained until it had to close in 1933. In 1937 he came to Chicago and was appointed director of the architectural department of the *Illinois Institute of Technology*, which enabled him to spread his modern ideas among the younger architects. He designed several buildings for this Institute, especially the *new campus* of IIT which became a model for the 1950's with its cool, archetypal and elegant geometry.

Another work of art of great influence was *Farnsworth House* near *Chicago* (1946-51), a small, white, glass-walled villa beside the lake. Steel columns, which bypass the floor and roof planes which they uphold, give the impression that the building is held up by magnetism—an original invention. With its order, dignity and superb refinement of detail it is one of the finest expressions of the machine aesthetic of the sophisticated International Style.

Mies' first actual high rise buildings, based on his 1919 and 1921 models, were the pair of rectangular blocks of *apartments* on *Lake Shore Drive*, *Chicago* (1957)—masterpieces of precise engineering which had great international influence. Like Sullivan, Mies stressed the vertical rhythm and unity of the building. Mies added steel mullions to the frame right to the top not only to brace the glass walls but to provide a pattern of light and dark which changes according to the angle of view. This was widely imitated later in vertical buildings. Unadorned, these apartments derive their beauty from subtle proportions and precise finish. While Le Corbusier designed his apartments both inside and outside, the regular façade of Mies' apartments conceals individual homes which each tenant can arrange according to his needs and tastes. Mies did not pre-plan the interiors but merely provided the framework.

The next year he finished his first and most important office, the *Seagram Building*—a masterpiece—the most exquisite and yet austerely simple in form of the *New York* offices. It stands on stilts two storeys in height, each of them backed by elevator shafts. The frame of bolted steel is covered with concrete and faced with bronze to harmonise with the brown glass curtain wall used to cut the sun's glare. All the storeys have luminous ceilings.

Through his creative work Mies aimed at creating order out of the confusion of our time. His simple and self-sufficient building forms stand like unchanging monuments amid the restlessness of their surroundings. The beautiful proportions and crystal clarity of his constructions grew out of his patient working on each problem so that every part is perfectly related to the whole and the whole is much greater than the sum of its parts. Herein lies his distinction. In this discipline architects can discover a way of solving almost any problem of planning. His works represent a triumph of the human spirit over matter.

Mies is one of the most influential architects because his ideas can be taught and adapted by others with success. In the United States he exercised the greatest authority, and the company of *Skidmore, Owings and Merrill* used his style and that of Le Corbusier in many of their big buildings, most notably in *Lever House, New York,* (1950) which leaves the land beneath the building free for a public garden, and in this way helped to give modem architecture a popular appeal and encouraged imitation. Their *Inland Steel Building* (1956), clad in stainless steel, resembles a huge mirror. Yet in spite of the efficiency, adaptability and the accessibility of his style to all talents, discordant variations of his ideas have deformed New York. For while Mies sought unchanging basic principles and tried to cherish and renew old values, many American architects sought ever new fashions and self-expression. Versions of his clear, straightforward style spread over the Western countries and as far as Japan.

*Le Corbusier*, pseudonym for the Swiss architect C. Jeanneret, became very influential through his numerous publications on architectural theory. He focussed on the more important needs of our times such as city planning, with an ordered relationship between streets and residential and working quarters. In 1922 he planned a city with tall cross-shaped crystal skyscrapers to reduce traffic and increase fresh air and light, with hanging gardens, and situated amid spacious parks. His actual buildings however differ from his writings where he stresses functionalism and dreams of architectural utopias, in fact his structures are much less functional than those of Gropius, who did a great deal more to make his buildings answer to social needs.

Though he had no formal training, Le Corbusier acquired more knowledge and experience than any university could give. He met almost all the architects from whom he could learn anything. He also travelled widely through Europe to study various kinds of architectural sites and shapes. On his own he did research in machine production and standardization as well as town planning. Since he saw a basic unity in the arts he gained training not only in architecture but in painting and sculpture as well.

His work reveals three major influences. His best work shows the imaginative use he made of the geometrical forms of Cubist painting. Secondly, the advanced technology he found in Austria and Germany where, like Gropius and Mies, he worked with Behrens made him enthusiastic about machines which he found as inspiring as nature. He admired the clear, precise forms of ships, cars and planes—entirely functional and original, not tied to any tradition. Their elegance comes from the simple expression of their purpose. Therefore he designed his early houses to be 'machines for living'—functional like those of Behrens and Gropius. To make such buildings beautiful he stressed the play of light on flat or curved surfaces in order to reveal the elegance of the geometrical forms to advantage. The third influence on Le Corbusier was A. Perret, for whom he worked in Paris and who showed him the principles of ferro-concrete design. At the time when the curves of Art Nouveau were all the rage, Perret insisted on chaste rectilinear constructions. He also believed that the tall reinforced concrete frame would be the revolutionary form of the future. Though he adopted Perret's design principles, Le Corbusier did not adopt the shape of his buildings. Instead of making the frame a part of the façade as Perret did, he made the floors extend beyond the frame and covered his buildings with smooth stucco and glass. He raised the buildings on 'pilotis' or free-standing columns so that they seem to float over the landscape which flows freely underneath. At times he left the concrete uncovered, allowing the shuttering to produce the decorative effect—a trend followed by many during the lean years between the two world wars. He also loved the smooth surfaces of machine-worked materials. For this reason he put the window frames on the same level as the wall. The precise contours of his buildings are carefully proportioned and enriched by colours to stress the coherence of the design. Dignified terraces crown his flat roofs. Most of his houses are prototypes. He did not imitate himself but left it for others to do so.

In his search for new ways, he came back to the values and principles that others had discarded. He fused rationalism with classicism in the belief that the most beautiful forms derive from traditional proportions.

His plan of the *Dom Ino House* (1914) contains the elements of his new architecture which he used for constructing his domestic buildings. Since the whole weight of the structure rests on columns, it does not require massive foundations. And since the building can be raised one or two storeys above ground, the land underneath can be used for a garden and utilities. The flat roof too can be made into a garden, thus providing not only extra space but preventing the expansion of the reinforced concrete by keeping it damp with soil and grass. Since the building requires no load-bearing walls it may be enclosed by any material and the interior may be freely planned. A cantilevered ferro-concrete stair connects the storeys. The most varied architecture can be constructed from this skeleton frame.

In Le Corbusier's *town planning project* of 1922 he wanted his skyscrapers to serve as high-rise streets or communities surrounded by healthy and beautiful parks and at a distance from city traffic. Later several American cities put his plans concerning traffic into practice; while in Chandigarh he realised his idea of a city centre.

Le Corbusier's first important masterpiece, the *Swiss Pavilion* (1930-32) rests on six mighty piers over which the steel frame of the building is cantilevered. This provides a welcoming entrance. Because of a low budget he used the shuttering to provide the decorative effect on the reinforced concrete. This set a trend during the years of scarcity between the two world wars. The need to economise made architects stress the essential and practical and brought them closer to social requirements and needs, thus providing a healthy discipline leading to a simpler appearance and more intelligent grouping. However it tende d to restrict the use of imagination and high quality materials.

Le Corbusier's most exquisite work of art

and one of the most renowned twentieth century houses is his *Villa Savoye* built in 1932 at *Poissy* near Paris, which shows the practical possibilities of his Dom Ino house project of 1914. It is one of the most beautiful expressions of the machine aesthetic of the International Cubist Style. Raised one storey above ground by slender pilotis, it resembles a gem set amid the unspoiled landscape. Unlike Wright's buildings which adapt to the surroundings, the Villa seems to crown it, though Le Corbusier shows the same love for nature. The roof terrace resembles a ship's deck. Curved screen walls serve as protection against the wind. Ribbon windows cover all the sides of the near square building. The garage, unglazed utility rooms and entrance, set far back behind the columns, are chocolate brown, while the smooth surface of the main part of the building is pale cream and the roof shelters are blue and rose. A gently sloping ramp and spiral stair lead up from the entrance. In the interior he created a landscape of his own by means of different levels, sliding glass walls, wide openings and contrasting shapes, and he introduced new amenities.

In 1933 Le Corbusier invented decorative sun screens (brise-soleil) for North African officers. Three years later he visited Brazil at the time when modem architecture became popular. Here his pure geometric forms, imaginatively combined with traditional styles, revealed new beauties in the bright tropical sunlight. Le Corbusier's influence shows in the architecture of O. Niemeyer who designed much of the new capital Brasilia, and Pampulla who built the crown-like cathedral there.

Another one of the greatest architectural achievements of the twentieth century is Le Corbusier's *L'Unités d'Habitation* (1947-52) in *Marseilles*—the result of twenty-five years of experiment to provide flats with a double- storeyed living room. The duplex apartments, which give each family maximum privacy as in a private house, overlap round a central interior passage on every third floor. The seventh and eighth floors have shopping centres, laundry, post-office, hotel and restaurant; while the seventeenth floor has a nursery school. The roof, like a ship's deck overlooking mountains and sea, is a community centre with playground, children's pool and fountains, creche, gym and running track, snack bar and sun terrace. Here fantastic sculptures mix with functional exhaust pipes. The buildings, housing 1600 people, resembles a suburb at some distance from the city, away from congested unhealthy streets. Though it was meant to house homeless workers, it is actually occupied by middle-class families.

The building stands at an angle to the main, road to fit the odd-shaped sites. A double row of mighty tapering piers raises the huge building above the ground so as not to waste precious space. Each row of columns carries a deep beam on which the whole structure rests. Utilities occupy the space between the beams. Forced by a low budget to keep the building economical, he made the rough concrete beautiful by arranging the moulds in patterns, which even unskilled workman could handle. He created beauty by contrast between the unpainted and unplastered concrete and the brilliantly coloured individual balconies, with their sunbreaks, and the smooth, machine finished interiors. The building found no imitators thus far, and the influence of his rugged exteriors declined when economic conditions improved. Unlike Wright's romantic approach, Le Corbusier's was humanist. By means of his 'modulor', he based his dimensions on human proportions.

After the Second World War Le Corbusier rejected the more rational rectilinear form of the International Style and created his inimitable sculptural architecture, which had a wide but dangerours inffiuence. This is exemplified especially by his pilgrimage chapel *Notre Dame du Haut* in *Ronchamp* ( 1950-55; Fig. 467) which lacks the universality of his earlier works. Here he reverts to thick walls. Built about the same time as Wright's Guggenheim Museum, this chapel too is more poetic sculpture than functional architecture, very personal, and outside any movement. He had first designed it with small models. The odd abstract shape of the roof brings to mind a ship's bow on a mountain—somewhat like Noah's ark come to rest on Mount Ararat after the Deluge. Struts resembling airplane wings brace the concrete roof in the interior. Small stained glass windows, deeply recessed, pierce the massive concrete wall almost at random to illumine the austere, unornamented inside of the chapel with a strange light. On the outside the sloping walls are covered with a rough stucco. Only his instinctive sense of proportions gives unity to its varied shapes.

From 1950 till this death Le Corbusier was in charge of designing the *Capitol and High Court* at *Chandigarh*, (Fig. 468), the new capital in the Punjab. Here he was able to enhance his ideas of a community centre, fusing into a harmonious unity the practical functions of

Fig. 467. Notre DAme du Haut, Ronchamp, Le Corbusier.

the ministries and law courts. Here he also realised for the first time his ideas of traffic separation and zoning by means of the gridiron layout. While using local building resources, he combined classical with freer forms. A ramp links the administrative wing to the elegantly proportioned courtrooms. The roof of cantilevered vaults resembles a parasol.

*P. L. Nervi* of Italy also produced some beautiful buildings by combining technological calculations with aesthetic intuition. An engineer without architectural training like

Fig. 468. High Court, Chandigarh, Le Corbusier.

B. Fuller, both succeed best with vast spaces where details do not count so much. Like Freyssinet and Maillart, Nervi has an extraordinary gift for obtaining geometrically beautiful designs through technological calculations and research into the nature of his materials, especially the possibilities of reinforced concrete.

Nervi made a number of valuable inventions such as ferro-cemento, produced by plastering cement on wire mesh, which could easily be made into curved forms. He improved reinforced concrete prefabrication on the building site itself by using small molds and introducing a movable kind of staging through which more varied designs could be produced on a ribbed construction. He also simplified and speeded up work by inventing hydraulic pre-stressing. He did not use the steel columns of the International Style, but managed to support concrete slabs on concrete piers by calculating exactly the lines of stress. In his love for creation and experimentation he always sought means of making his buildings lighter and thus more beautiful and economical.

Nervi's first important work, the *Communal Stadium* in *Florence* (1930-32) highlights the aesthetic potential of concrete by leaving all the structural elements exposed. In 1935 he started experimenting with roofs composed of a network of joists to bear the load. The imaginative roof of the *Exhibition Hall* in *Turin* (1948-9) one of his masterpieces, shows the results of these experiments. The undulating prefabricated units not only reduce the weight but increase the tensile strength and elasticity. Thousands of precast units compose the structural ribs and create an over-all pattern. The space below the roof remains completely free. In spite of an error in the erection of the building, which diminished the perfection of the original plan, it is the finest European exhibition hall after the Crystal Palace.

The undulating roof of the *Conference Hall of the UNESCO Building* in *Paris* (1953-7), which Nervi designed with Breuer and Zehrfuss is very modern technologically and aesthetically with its beautiful rhythm. By observing the beauty and strength of tiny insects, shellfish and flowers, Nervi applied this natural principle of power in curved surface to architecture by using corrugated textures. In 1955 he covered the *Exhibition Hall* of the *Centre National des Industries* in *Paris* with a sail-like roof.

In 1958 he used the tapering form of a tree, another natural principle of strength, for the four main stanchions of the *Pirelli Skyscraper* in *Milan* which he designed with Ponti and others. The same year he built the soaring *Palazetto dello Sport, Rome* (Fig. 469) leaving exposed its graceful lines of force, which like elegant flying buttresses, carry the lateral thrust from the ground to the vault. The huge columns of the *Palazzo del Lavoro, Turin,* resemble palm trees.

Fig. 469. Palazetto dello Sport, Rome, P. L. Nervi.

*G. Ponti*, who with Nervi designed the Pirelli Skyscraper, with its tapering sides resembling the bows of ships, helped to improve the taste of the Italian bourgeoisie by means of his writings.

Still unique in the present world of architecture, the ideas worked out by the American *Buckminster Fuller* hold out much promise for the future. He saw that new social needs require a radical change in design. Therefore he tried to bring the new technological opportunities, especially from aircraft and space developments, to bear upon mass-produced housing, to achieve the greatest results from the least amount of material. He based his design on the scientific analysis of materials and the nature of structures in tension. Largely self-trained, he is primarily a mathematician, engineer and philosopher.

In 1927 Fuller produced a model of his *Dymaxion House*, meaning *dynamic* + *max*imum efficiency. A mast of duraluminium in the centre, containing mechanical services, upholds the sun roof and the two hexagonal decks which are held in place by steel cables. Doublepane vacuum units, transparent and opaque, cover the outside. Air is sucked in from the top of the mast, warmed or cooled according to need as well as purified and humidified in the mast and then distributed. Prisms diffuse the light from the mast and mirrors reflect it. Self-contained and independent of main services, the building can be set up anywhere. Pneumatic doors, floor and beds assure quiet. This practical and literal 'machine for living', not graced by the beauty of other modern buildings of the time, brought Fuller no recognition till more than thirty years later, when the value of his geodesic domes found appreciation.

Fuller's *geodesic domes* can be made almost any size and of any material since ail the load-bearing members work together. With all the stresses evenly distributed, even plastic or cardboard facets may be used to fill the intersecting arcs. The space frames are composed of prefabricated modular units, either tetra or octohedrons. This geometrical form of the grid module distinguishes the system, and leads to a new aesthetic based on the structure of matter itself. These domical shelters can be adapted to almost any need and their uninterrupted spans, made from the least amount of material, can enclose almost any amount of space to form an artificial sky as a protection against the weather. For instance the domes built in 1958 in *Baton Rouge*, *Louisiana*, have twenty-three times the volume of St. Peter's Dome yet they are both light and economical. His ideas hold great promise for the future, especially to solve the housing problem efficiently. Fuller's work ranks with the Crystal Palace as a giant step forward in the aesthetic and economical use of prefabricated materials.

*A. Aalto* of Finland, another original modern architect, also aimed at meeting human needs and rejected irrelevant fashionable trends. Without any slavishness, he understood and respected the value of tradition and stressed his native roots. His *Workers Houses* for the *Sunila Factory* harmonise with the site, with the verticals echoing the tall slender trees behind, and the ribbon windows stressing the horizontal lines of the branches. The Frenchman *J. Prouvé,* while using economical prefabricated units, gave his glass houses a uniquely cheerful character, with a very friendly appearance. In his book 'Philosophy of Structures', the Spaniard *E. Torroja* showed that calculations merely reveal the feasibility of imagination. He was the first to use Frey-sinnet's invention of pre-stressed concrete. Opposed to materialism, he loved the asymmetrical forms of nature. Another imaginative modern architect was *E. Mendelsohn*, whose *Synagogue* in *Cleveland* repeats the rhythm of the undulating site.

The International Style owed its inspiration not only to the three outstanding architects Gropius, Mies and Le Corbusier, but also to the Dutch *De Stijl* group, notably *G. Rietveld*, whose *Schroeder House* (1923) in *Utrecht* with its smooth walls in right-angled cubes, illustrates the de Stijl principles which were influenced by Abstract and Cubist painting. This group used primary colours in flat planes against black, white or grey to set off the elements of the building from one another; and they were the first to paint the walls of the same room in different colours. The asymmetrical houses have no static axis. In his *Workmen's Houses, Hook*, Holland (1926) *J. Oud* introduced curved lines to make his buildings more beautiful.

The *International Style* grew out of the teamwork between architects of different countries In the 1920's it spread until by the 1940's it was almost universal except in the Communist world. Since social needs resemble each other everywhere, this functional style has no frontiers, but regional variations appeared as it matured due to differences in climate, raw materials, temperaments, and cultural roots. Modern communications have overcome national barriers except where insecurity expresses itself in a sentimental attachment to traditional forms. In this style each problem is approached with reason, not sentiment. The buildings express their purpose honestly, with the plan determined by the function of the building and the available space. Nonbearing partitions make the inner space flexible, to be adjusted according to need.

In the 1920's vast public projects imposed a certain uniformity on the buildings. Since the upkeep of the smooth white stucco generally used at that time is very costly, it was found more economical to replace it with natural materials from the 1950's on. In the 1930's countries under dictatorships reverted to a grand pseudo-classicism to impress people with their power. Many of the modern artists had to go into exile, notably Gropius, Mies and others from Nazi Germany; and the Constructivist plans of *V. Tatlin* and others in Russia never materialised. Tatlin had planned to erect a spiralling and rotating *monument to the Third International* in Moscow in 1920, to rival the Eiffel Tower, but it remained no more than a project. In the free countries, at the same time, architects like Wright and Le Corbusier moved away from the International Style which they considered too austere. They were followed by others in the 1960's who created more ephemeral and picturesque buildings like *Saarinen's Idlewild Airport Terminal* (1962, *New York*) which resembles a bird in flight. Now too much value is given to novelty, with artists influenced by collective fashion movements, with the result that often the same building shows different styles. American structures, with their jewel-like walls, tended to be flashy and slick, modernistic rather than modern. Now architecture is endangered by a riot of self-expression of form for form's sake. Therefore architects are needed who combine the discipline and team-spirit of Gropius and Mies with the imagination of a Wright and Le Corbusier of the earlier period. Wright never allowed his ideals to be swayed by fashion or prestige.

In building practices human values are often sacrificed for profits. Many cater to the cosy comfort of the rich, and politicians neglect their social responsibilities by failing to plan and by erecting luxury buildings where dire housing shortage prevails. An example of public-minded building is the *Museum* in *Oakland*, California, built by *Roche and Dinkeloo*, which forms a garden-like oasis in the middle of a big city, with the roofs of the lower buildings serving as landscaped terraces for the next higher level.

Modern architecture boasts of a few masterpieces, but most of the buildings show little understanding of real aesthetic creativity. The demand for useless and pretentious objects has reduced the living standard instead of raising it. It has deflected attention from the pressing problems of housing and town planning, where the least is generally considered good enough, and as a result the very good is rare. Architecture mirrors the conditions, value judgments and technological knowledge of a particular period, and our haphazard cities and towns reflect the insecurities and conflicts of our culture, which lacks any agreement that will make a more general excellence possible, unlike the Middle Ages which showed a visual harmony in daily surroundings. If it were accepted by most people, modern architecture could satisfy our human desire for beauty as well as solve our need for economical housing and town planning. But mass production, prefabrication and technology have as yet hardly touched architecture so far, and knowledge of modern architecture remains confined to professionals and intellectuals. We need, as in the Middle Ages, to make intelligent use of available materials to meet the pressing need for housing—beautiful buildings that harmonise with each other.

# PAINTING

'Modern', as applied to painting, is a blanket term, a patchwork quilt covering a strange assortment of rather incompatible bedfellows. The groups or movements enfolded by 'modern' represent different approaches and fashions which overlap each other and have no fixed dates. In most cases they react against one other, and seem to agree only on the liberty to experiment freely, unrestricted by classical subjects and Renaissance techniques.

The so-called modern movement began in and around Paris as a declaration of independence against the stronghold of official academic art which had not only survived the French Revolution but had become even more conservative and barren under the new officials. In the seventeenth century Louis XIV had set up the Royal Academy of Painting and Sculpture to impose his taste or that of his officials on his subjects. Pedantic rules shackled experiment, and originality was considered bad taste. Through Louis XIV Paris became the cultural centre of Europe, a position it maintained for almost three centuries. Thus the French academy dictated art fashions not only in France but in many other countries as well, until the United States took the lead around the Second World War. The academy imposed affected notions of classical beauty and unprogressive subjects and methods. Anyone who revolted against its absolute standards had to pay the price of ridicule and poverty since the official Society of French Artists refused to exhibit his works in the Salon, the annual art exhibition in Paris. It favoured paintings like *Gérôme's Thumbs Down* (1859) which covers an ugly murder scene with a bit of classical polish, and *Bouguereau's The Birth of Venus* (1879) where the Greek mythology hardly disguises the naked, almost pornographic sensuality. Works like these, aimed at entertaining degenerate popular taste rather than elevating it with ideals, eventually influenced the sensationalism of motion pictures. The newly-rich, less cultured bourgeoisie favoured such paintings since the classical disguise gave a sense of respectabilitiy to otherwise sentimental, sensational and sensual themes.

The artists who dared to react against such subjects by painting the heroism of real people rather than imaginary heroics based on mythology or ancient history, almost starved to death. In the 1830's and 40's writers like Balzac had drawn attention to the misery of peasants and workers as a result of rapid urbanization and exploitation for the profit motive, thus creating social and political awareness. Since painters depend on rich patrons they could not show their concern for the poor so openly. A few *democratic painters*, like Courbet, Millet and Daumier got a chance to exhibit their work between 1848 and 1851, when the Salon was opened to all after the 1848 Revolution until Napoleon III became emperor. In the 1855 World's

Fair the Imperial Director of Fine Arts labelled them as Socialists, although Millet took no interest whatever in politics. Though the public preferred nudes, *J. F. Millet* continued to paint his humble peasants ennobled by the dignity and endurance that came from their Christian faith and hope. His figures, more abstract types than realistic individuals, have a modern touch. A great competition arose between the French and Americans for his paintings after he died, though during his life he nearly starved for want of buyers for his new type of pictures.

With Millet, Corot, Daumier and Manet, *G. Courbet* formed a federation to liberate artists from government interference. He. stood for the artist's right to paint what he thinks fit, and considered every aspect of life beautiful and suited for art. He inspired the Impressionists with his method of applying large daubs of colour and unifying them with a palette knife, thus creating a rough surface. As a result the critics accused him of being primitive and careless. He died in poverty and exile.

*H. Daumier* showed more self-control than Courbet and understood his era better. A cartoonist, he had little time to paint From memory he produced abstract images of the industrial masses who flocked to the cities in search of employment when cheap machine-made goods destroyed many of the village handicrafts. For example, his *Third Class Carriage* (1862) shows a cross-section of the new population and technology that changed the aspect of the cites. With a powerful technique and sense of design he showed why people act and feel, rather than their distinctive features. A comparison between Delacroix's picture of the uprising in 1839 (Liberty leading the people) and Daumier's *The Uprising* (c. 1860) shows how the older artist still held to the fashionable literary theme while the later one used real people as the leaders of the revolt. 'Papa' Corot helped Daumier when blindness drove him to dire poverty. After his death and burial in a pauper's grave, dealers stole his paintings to make capital out of them.

Painters like Millet, Courbet and Daumier rebelled against the popular subjects imposed by the Academy and paid for their liberty with the costly price of poverty. Others began slowly to *rebel against* the *academic methods*. While the academy favoured dull, unattractive colours, *Delacroix* introduced riotous ones, considered barbaric at the time. His observation that it is 'advisable not to fuse the brush strokes as they will fuse naturally at distance; thus colour gains energy and freshness' had great influence on the Impressionists. To stress emotions he unbalanced his compositions. *Puvis de Chavannes* influenced Seurat and Gauguin with his organisation of space in the manner of Far Eastern artists, his abstracted (rather than photographic) patterned effect, high horizons, and simplified modelling of figures. But what Gauguin wanted to achieve through passion Puvis de Chavannes sought in elegant taste and tenderness, as in *The Poor Fisherman* (1881). Long before them *Goya,* a compatriot of Picasso and like him an opportunist who defied all laws of taste, had started distorting his figures, employing discordant colours to show the evil man is capable of, using simplification for suggetiveness and producing Surrealistic monsters. His example influenced Daumier, Manet and Kollwitz.

In the 1860's a group of young artists, each with a different temperament and origin, met in Paris, drawn together by the desire to free themselves from the restrictions of the official Academy and to remain in contact with nature and life away from the cities. *Impressionism* came to birth in the light and moisture-filled atmosphere of the Seine estuary and the channel beaches where Boudin, Jongkind and Monet developed their colourful, fluid and ethereal style. They refused to look at nature in the set Academic form, but observed the ever new revelation of its wonder and beauty. Jongkind's art of changing atmosphere and Boudin's reflections of light prepared the way for Impressionism. Though his younger Impressionist friends owed him a great dead, Boudin modestly considered them much greater than himself.

In *The River* (1868) *Monet* first showed the triple colour of an object—its own, and the reflections on it of other objects and of the atmosphere. In 1870, while Manet, Degas and Renoir were called to the Franco-Prussian War, Monet with Pissarro and Sisley Went to London where they discovered Constable and Turner, and where Daubigny, who was on the Salon jury, introduced them to a dealer. Two years later Monet and Pissarro painted a new kind of open-air landscape with particular emphasis on light and water. The small brush-strokes to represent the reflections of light on the water were now spread over the whole landscape. The colours became lighter and instead of using Corot's brown or grey shadows, they used pure colours which harmonised or contrasted according to the laws of complementarity. Renoir, Sisley, Manet, Cezanne and Degas were won to the light-coloured pictures.

In order to reach as many as possible, the photographer Nadar exhibited the paintings of the Impressionists in his studio in 1874. The press and academicians attacked them bitterly and few had the courage to oppose the propaganda and mockery, though one critic and some dealers and collectors did support them. The critics called the group 'Impressionists' after the title of *Monet's* painting of a harbour scene, called *Impression, Sunrise.* The pictures Were auctioned at throw-away prices. Despite dire poverty and contempt they heroically continued to produce masterpieces. In 1876 the critic Duranty published 'The New Painting' wherein he wrote of their spreading a harmony of rainbow colours on canvas. And in a periodical on Impressionism, G. Rivière remarked that while the traditional subject had been mythology, history or bourgeois conventions, the Impressionists used subjects only to picture colour itself. Ten years after the first exhibition most critics and much of the public accepted the colourful Impressionist studies which brought beauty into urban drabness. There was nothing ugly in the works of Monet and Pissarro, and their paintings were no longer considered crude or unfinished. But the official opposition persisted until more novel styles had to be attacked. Yet the Impressionists themselves began to feel that they had sacrificed too many traditional elements in order to represent passing sensations of colour, and light. The group dispersed just when they were finding recognition. Inhibited by scientific theories, Monet, Pissarro and Sisley lost their original spontaneity. In their last exhibition in 1886 H. Rousseau's primitive work was first shown and Seurat aroused the ire of the conservatives with his pointillist work.

While Manet and Degas portrayed city life—in a more agitated manner than Daumier—the other Impressionists preferred to portray rural settings. But they saw nature differently from other landscape painters—not as people contemplating nature leisurely, but as people getting flashes of scenery from moving trains. With the invention of quicker and cheaper means of travel, city people returned to nature only for outings. The Impressionists reflected the disjointed views people got of nature in rapid transit, by means of their broken colour method which they evolved, and they began to see everything else in the same flashy way. Unlike the classical artists who sought the universal and typical, the Impressionists portrayed the momentary and passing appearance of things in brilliant light. They were no longer interested in the permanent, but in the fleeting sensations of light and atmosphere.

The invention of bright *chemical pigments* enabled these painters to give up the duller earth colours, and scientific studies of light and colour made them more sensitive to nature's hues. They observed that the colour of an object is constantly modified by the kind of light in which it is seen and by the reflections of other objects falling on it. It also depends on the colours around it. For instance while rather large areas of complementary colours side by side intensify one another, in small areas the eye fuses them into a neutral tone. Moreover they noticed that shadows are full of colour. Unless modified by other factors the shadow of an object possesses something of the complementary colour of the object. For instance the shadow of a yellow object contains some violet. Two centuries earlier, Vermeer had already observed that adjacent objects cast coloured shadows on each other.

The Impressionists did not mix their pigments before applying them since they noticed, like Delacroix before them, that they could get more intense hues by putting the primary colours near each other in small dabs, as for instance by setting blue and yellow brush strokes side by side to obtain green. Distance would fuse them for the eye into brighter tones than if they combined the pigments themselves. This way of painting with little strokes is called broken or divided colour. Thus they reproduced the sparkling vibrations of light on water and foliage. The public however were irritated by the fact that these pictures had to be viewed from a distance since the object could be seen clearly only after the eye had fused the colours. At a close view they were unintelligible. Nevertheless what seemed so revolutionary in their technique was only a further development of Leonardo da Vinci's theories of colour and light which were already assimilated by artists like Velasquez, Vermeer, Rubens, Constable, Turner and Delacroix. The short, choppy brush-strokes of the Imprestionists gave people the idea that they fired their colours with a pistol, and they considered these artists as savages who were unable to finish their pictures at a time when smooth, well-outlined pictures were the fashion. Yet the Impressionist technique, despite its unfinished look, required painstaking, scientific precision. The artists stepped back for almost every spot to see its effect.

Their primary aim of reproducing the fleeting effects of light and air at a given moment made them lose sight of the three-dimensional character of forms and also of perspective. They sacrificed solidity to brilliant colour. They broke up contours and abandoned modelling and precise detail, leaving large parts of their work to the imagination. They were more concerned with technique than with the subject. Their spots of colour represent light on an object rather than forms, which are distorted in the shimmer of light and atmosphere in which they are bathed.

They replaced perspective by the fading away or blurring of distant horizons, and represented space by a fore and rear plane separated by empty middle portions, all tied together by an even atmosphere. This shows the influence of eighteenth century Japanese prints which appeared in France in the 1860's. These represented depth by means of overlapping or back-stepping planes.

*C. Monet*, the most important, skillful and daring of the Impressionists whose painting *Impression, Sunrise* gave the movement its name discovered from his on-the-spot observation of sunlight on the banks of the Seine the technical principles of the style, namely the fragmentation of colour into flickering spots. He noticed that the appearance of objects changes constantly, that a landscape is not the same at sunrise or in twilight, in spring or summer. Monet used to go in the morning with several canvases to the spot he wanted to paint. He worked on the first canvas until his eye detected a change in the light. Then he put it aside and worked on the next until he noticed another change of light. Then he began the third and so on until the end of the day. The next day he continued each canvas in the same light as on the previous day. In this way he painted twenty-six impressions of Rouen cathedral and sixteen of Waterloo bridge as well as others of haystacks, poplars and lily ponds. None before him had noticed that the fog becomes opaline around the bridges of London. He painted chiefly landscapes with water providing movement. Not only did he try to represent light but mist and wind and cold—all new ambitions at the time. He showed that no absolute colour exists in nature—only reflecttions of light. In fact light was the main character of his paintings. For him as for Manet human beings took a secondary position. He studied the reflections and shimmer of light on water, and in his study of light on snow he first noticed that shadows are coloured. By his indistinct forms he showed the difficulty of seeing objects clearly under bright sunlight. Thus his paintings portray only the surface shimmer of things under constantly changing light.

His paintings, full of light and cheerful colours, do not reflect the abject poverty under which he worked for almost ten years because he refused to abandon his discoveries in order to win official favour. For a time he and Renoir subsisted on potatoes they themselves had grown. He encouraged Renoir, and Manet came to their rescue with some help. After the hostility and ridicule subsided, wealth and fame came at last, but by then he had lost the spontaneity of his earlier works.

Monet was influenced by Boudin and Jongkind whom he knew personally. *E. Boudin* loved to paint nature in bright colours. His sky-and seascapes, bathed in light, and his reproductions of cloudy atmospheric effects give a sense of calm expansiveness. He said that painters portray not so much the world itself as the atmosphere that surrounds it, namely the splendid, warming light which the Creator spreads all over. *J. Jongkind's* quiet light-filled art does not reflect his miserable life. He anticipated Monet's experiments by showing the impressions of scenes under varied atmospheric conditions. His is above all an art of liquid atmosphere, with distant horizons, shimmering water and foliage, full of life. He represented fleeting appearances simply without any scientific theories. His open-air sketches, done with a few pencil strokes, quiver with movement. Daubigny too, who befriended Monet in London, painted atmospheric impressions.

C. *Pissarro*, the oldest of the Impressionist group, was born in the West Indies of Jewish-Creole parents. More interested in people than in atmosphere, his paintings stress form and structure, and so his paintings had a great influence on Cezanne. By using small comma-like strokes he depicted bright light without distorting the forms on which it shines. His experiments with the Impressionist and Divisionist techniques resulted in powerful yet subtle lines and rich, light colours. He loved vast stretches of green or yellow cornfields, trees in flower, delicate leaves, dappled skies and running streams, and delighted in imparting a gold or silver sheen to his work. His serene pictures reflect his joy in life. He avoided anything ugly and presented his subjects in the most favourable light. He had a tender approach towards humanity, and for nature he always advocated humility, recognizing the impossibility of an artist to reproduce its fleeting aspects. An eye complaint forced him to abandon landscapes and to depict city life instead.

Everyone loved and respected Pissarro's innate kindness and goodness. Like 'Papa' Corot who had encouraged him, he offered his help to younger painters of promise: the shy Cezanne, the sickly Van Gogh, to the Neo-Impressionists Signac and Seurat when the other Impressionists looked down upon them, and to the self-centred Gauguin who remarked that everyone took from Pissarro while they denied him. For Pissarro introduced others to the source of his own meagre income, the art dealer Père Tanguy. He had an unusal gift for teaching. As someone remarked, he could have taught a stone to draw correctly. This came partly from his repect for people— he avoided imposing his ideas on others and even humbly advised his children not to trust too much in his judgment. Free of hate and full of selfless integrity, he had the gift of reconciling enemies. Yet he was a very manly gentleman, showing tireless initiative, organizing independent exhibitions, and fighting without bitterness to support his six children.

*A. Sisley*, of English origin, surpassed Monet in retaining the structures of landscapes. He did not dissolve the forms in atmosphere. He had the same skill in representing the movement of leaves and the shimmer of light on water. Though modest and timid, he held firm to his convictions and true to his friends. *Renoir* too retained the form of his subjects by using traditional colour as the base of his paintings instead of the bare canvas.

For *E. Manet*'s scientific approach, his concern with technique to create fleeting patterns of light, human beings were no more than insignificant data, disposable robots to fit into his designs. We see this impersonal, scientific detachment in his *Bar at the Folies Bergère* (1882) where the waitress is no more than another motif among the shining bottles, like the characters in the novels of his friend E. Zola. The flat surface of the painting, with the least modelling and perspective, is covered with patches of colour. Since he insisted on painting things as he saw them, his work was consigned to the Salon des Refusés, but he continued painting unacceptable pictures. He could afford to do so since he was wealthy.

Like Manet, but unlike the other Impressionists, *E. Degas* represented urban rather than rural scenes. He preferred man-made beauty (the artificial light of theatres) to sunlight. His innovations forecast photographic techniques, such as unexpected angles of vision, looking down from above, putting the main figure off-centre, giving unexpected importance to the foreground and stressing accidental details by way of contrast, selecting aspects never observed before, the clever use of empty space to integrate the viewer into the picture, as well as cut-off compositions to make the eye move beyond the frame and thus add to the impression of motion.

Much of this Degas *learned from Japanese prints.* Japanese artists do not use eye-level perspective but either look at the subject from above or below, while at the same time standing closer to it. They exaggerate the importance and shape of the foreground, and place the chief character off-centre, seen over the heads of those in the foreground. They use abrupt foreshortening, with a sharply sloping perspective. With subtle lines and simple colouring they create a decorative abstract pattern.

Like the Impressionists Degas captured the fleeting glimpses of life. Characteristic of all his work is the photographically instantaneous effect he sought. He surprised his characters at work in their most characteristic attitudes. Unlike the Impressionists he portrayed the movement of forms rather than of light. For him too technique was most important. He arranged facts, mostly from memory or from photographs, to fit a design pattern. A rigorous draughtsman with severe academic training, he kept the density of forms except in his dancers. His approach to form was linear rather than chromatic.

Degas took only an intellectual interest in his subjects. His dancers show neither intelligence nor beauty—often they look even vulgar. He is more interested in the rhythm of their movement. The beauty of the pastels which he preferred to use contrasts with the ugliness of the subjects. A wealthy bachelor, conservative and unfriendly, he opposed the proposition to make art available to the lower classes.

*B. Morisot*, opposed to the Impressionist stress on atmosphere, used long, flexible brushstrokes to maintain form, though she retained the play of light by means of a few simple spots carefully applied. She allowed no system or ideology to interfere with the spontaneity of her art. Excluding all brutality she preferred delicate family scenes.

The inventiveness of the Impressionists influenced not only sculpture, but music and literature as well.

*Neo-Impressionism or Scientific Impressionism* tried to link art even more closely to science.

Around this time much was being written on the physiology and psychology of optics and vision, on the analysis of light and colour, based on the experiments of the physicists Rood and Helmholtz who completed the discoveries of Chevreul. In his articles on the phenomena of vision D. Sutter claimed that rules do not inhibit spontaneity, rather science liberates from all uncertainty. This appealed to the French desire for system, regularity and order, and turned the minds of artists like Cezanne to concentrate on form and structure, and paved the way to more rigid abstraction. The theoretician *P. Signac*, basing himself on Blanc's claim that colour could be expressed in rules and taught like music, proposed a recipe for good painting which anyone could use—this at a time when art and society were poles apart. He wanted to make painting more scientific by applying, the discoveries about light to colour, and to reduce to written regulations what the Impressionists had practised. This making of rules for painting, however, was foreign to the Western tradition, but more like Byzantine and Indian painting which conform to rules prescribing the necessary forms and proportions.

The Neo-Impressionists introduced the techniques of divisionism and pointillism. The former uses large, mosaic-like spots, which serve as bright decorations for dark urban interiors. Pointillism consists of tiny round dots of pure color carefully applied side by side like a laboriously stippled engraving. In 1882 *G. Seurat* began experimenting with little spots of pure color to be blended by the eye like the short Impressionist strokes. He carried these experiments with divisionism as far as pointillism, systematically distributing minute spots of colour over the white ground which remained partially exposed. This method became the forerunner of photographic engraving and colour reproduction. Two years later he founded the Salon of the Independents with those whom the official Salon had rejected. For a nominal fee anyone could exhibit. Democratically run, with no jury, it contributed to free art in France and later too in America. In 1886 his painting appeared in the last Impressionist exhibition with those of Rousseau, but Seurat found only one friendly critic. Except for Pissarro, he was mocked even by the Impressionists, their dealers and the public. Though he was never in need, Seurat died of overwork at the age of thirty-one. The seven pictures, to which he had given all his time and energy, were the only outstanding events of his brief life.

For him as for many modern artists, the method rather than the subject was the chief consideration. He concerned himself chiefly with arrangement according to rules of design, especially the laws of simultaneous contrasts and the symbolic meaning of line directions. He skilfully contrasted light and shade—his forms seem to emerge from dark shadows, and a mysterious light shines through his pencil strokes. Even his greys show an intense vitality. He managed to create a sense of depth in water but how he did it remains a puzzle. His figures, flattened to fit into the abstract design, have nevertheless a solid, three-dimensional appearance. The emotional possibilities of the figures did not interest him—they are depersonalised, abstract, used merely to create a rhythmic pattern. His scenes of contemporary French life are no more than formalised symbols of humanity.

While the Renaissance artists gave primary importance to space to which they added colour, for most modem artists colour takes precedence. Basing himself on the colour theories of Delacroix and Helmholtz, Seurat made careful studies of complementary colours. He made a detailed examination of Chevreul's law of simultaneous colour contrast—for example that yellow objects cast purple shadows. Mistaking pigment for light, he worked out the pointillist theory using tiny dots instead of the larger dabs of the Impressionists, with the result, however, that his colours look more hazy and grey than those of the Impressionists. They give an illusion of atmosphere rather than of bright colour. For his frames he used a neutral white which he stippled later on with contrasting colour.

Nevertheless his paintings have a mysterious originality. He had a distinctive way of seeing things. Despite his unemotional scientific approach he had an inborn sense of design and composition, with precise, orderly arrangement. Though he flattened the forms to fit into his decorative design, he emphasised the contours by delicate lines.

His numerous oil sketches on location, more spontaneous like the Impressionist paintings, reveal a cheerful and friendly personality which does not show through his finished works. These he worked out chiefly from memory and imagination, alone in his studio. His drawings in black and white crayon, with their delicate modulations of light and shade, are masterpieces of tone and hold a power that transcends method. Here no refining process has rubbed away the emotional content.

*Seurat's* best-known work, *A Sunday Afternoon*

on *La Grande Jatte* (Art Institute of Chicago), the second of his seven large compositions, took two years to finish (1884–6). He made seventy preparatory sketches and paintings before completing it. It shows a bourgeois crowd on a Sunday outing from the city, but it is more an exercise in arrangement than a representation. The figures are no more than designs and part of a larger composition. Three large areas simplify the complex details into smaller groups. The figures in profile, parallel to the frame in the foreground and under a dark band of shade, give a quiet tone to the setting. Behind them is a lighter strip of bright sunshine, with another dark band near the top formed by the leaves of trees. These dark and light areas lead the eye around to the centre of interest and point of rest—a full-face view of a mother and child. A back wall, parallel to the front plane, stops the movement of the eye. The horizontal shady areas and embankment in the distance, the vertical figures and trees, the diagonal shadows and shoreline, together with the transitional forms all carefully placed—curved branches, umbrellas and nails—form an over-all abstract pattern of many parts all related to each other and to the whole. Though drawn almost flat, the figures have a bas-relief quality, but the impression of depth, solidity and distance does not interfere with the design. Light serves to make the shapes stand out from their surroundings. The figures have an aesthetically harmonious relationship, without crowding or empty gaps. Each elements stands in the right relationship to the next one. This intellectual composition has the precision of a machine. The colours, not broken into fleeting patches, tie the figures together. The receding and advancing qualities of the colours give the feeling of moving in and out of the picture.

Seurat's later painting, *The Parade*, much admired by the Cubists, anticipates abstract art and points in the non-realist direction in the division of the large rectangle into smaller ones, in the stress on vertical and horizontal lines and in the sacrifice of solidity to design. The human figures look much more mechanical.

The *Post-Impressionists*, completely different in character, never united into a school. Each one isolated himself from his environment though at the same time they tried to influence the world with their art, thus demonstrating the divorce of modern artists from society. Though they did represent the emotional possibilities of ordinary things and people, they were less concerned with their actual appearance and much more with what they meant to the artist. They concentrated more on technique and method by arranging what they saw and felt into designs and symbols. Increasing mechanisation changed their art into the shattered forms of the next stylistic stage.

*P. Cezanne*, often called 'the father of modern painting' exerted great influence on all subsequent movements. In 1953 the Cubists Braque and Leger stated: 'We all start from Cezanne'. A transition artist between the realism of the nineteenth and the abstractions of the early twentieth centuries, he tried to find a new art without giving up the values of the old. He gave modern painters a new method painstakingly worked out through many years of lonely experimentation. Consciously and laboriously he tried to discover both in the great masters and through his own explorations that something which photography, even artistic photography, could not give. He had a scientific attitude to art, proving by repeated tests a hypothesis or theory. As a result he made an important discovery: the possibility of replacing modelling and chiaroscuro by colour relationships.

The son of a wealthy banker, Cezanne was finally allowed to give up law in order to devote himself to painting. He went to Paris to study art. Though not a gifted pupil he compensated for it by hard and conscientious work. Like many famous artists he was largely self-taught. In the Louvre he analysed the art of the old masters to discover the basis of art—what gave them a lasting interest. From this base he built up his own structures and designs, the expression of his own personality, his mind and feelings before the inner beauty of the world.

To arrive at this, however, Cezanne suffered much. He returned to his native Aix-en-Provence, where he lived like a hermit, struggling without advice or help, living frugally on his meagre allowance. Almost till the end of his life he sold nothing. His exhibits in 1874 and 1877 encountered much hostility. Because he had no other talent and since he perceived the importance of his art, he continued his lonely struggle till a show in 1895, eleven years before his death, made him one one of the most famous modern artists.

Without being a revolutionary, he introduced revolutionary changes. He kept a steady balance between his desire to organise and his impulsive imagination, between his love of classicism and his baroque temperament, between his wild instincts and aesthetic sense. He had the characteristic Provençal temperament: unsentimental yet endowed with deep feeling, impetuous yet controlled by laws and discipline, together with an obstinacy which kept him going despite a life of disappointments. By nature he was sensitive and shy, given to introversion and a Romantic vision. His natural reserve, increased by misunderstanding, inclined him more and more to solitude. A tireless perfectionist, his achievements never satisfied him—he always looked forward to discovering something better. This love of perfection and unity together with his clear and serene vision laid the foundation of a new classicism.

During the first ten years of his artistic career he worked from imagination, trying to imitate the sombre baroque art. Around 1873 his work became bright and airy under the influence of Pissarro who brought him into contact with nature. Though he remained good friends with the Impressionists, and though their art suited him better than the Baroque, he wanted to make their method more solid and lasting. Because he refused to use their technique he was considered incompetent. While for the Impressionists the subject served merely as a light-reflecting surface, for Cezanne it served as a means for design. For both it took a secondary place.

For Cezanne 'art should give nature the thrill of continuance'. He believed it was the artist's function to discover the enduring, permanent reality behind nature's manifold appearances. Thus he arrived at the basic shapes but he did not try to replace these by geometrical forms as the Cubists did. He never reduced natural forms to geometric abstractions but represented them in their simplest dimension, stripped of accidental, individual differences. These simple shapes, of sculpturesque relief-like texture, give an appearance of unchanging dignity and serenity.

In his desire for permanence and solidity he made even air, mist and vapour, sky and sea as substantial as houses, rocks and trees, He wanted to show nature's consistency—to represent the all-embracing atmosphere and air, but without using the shimmer of Impressionism or classical chiaroscuro. His light is not of a fleeting moment but evenly diffused all over. Because he painted from nature, not from his imagination, his work has solidity, power and integrity. Though he refused to copy nature exactly, there is great resemblance between his paintings and actual photographs of the places he had represented. He preferred to paint familiar landscapes, common objects and portraits of the humble rather than the literary subjects fashionable in his time. His art brings comfort, a sense of joy mingled with deep sympathy and reveals a deep inner faith. Through his work he wanted to share his vision of an orderly, harmonious world. In order to do so he made his contours precise and strong. His planes have a sculptured clarity and even his highlights are distinctly etched.

To him design, subtly and artfully concealed and therefore always interesting, was more important than realism. The Cubists did not understand this and thus misrepresented him. Cezanne always tried to harmonise realistic nature with aesthetic design. He worked slowly and thoughtfully, from long contemplation and deep feeling controlled by a sound mind. Aesthetic feelings were important to his view of a subject. In order to find its essence he analysed and simplified.

Instead of suggesting depth by the traditional method of perspective and chiaroscuro, he used overlapping planes as in Chinese and Japanese art. Since perspective tends to disturb the over-all design by drawing the eye in one direction and boring into the painting, Cezanne made the design guide the eye around the picture by making roads disappear behind buildings or by crossing them with horizontal shadows or by blocking them off in some way. By this criss-cross of lines and forms he made the eye wander about in the painting. Instead of making distant objects fade away he accentuated their colour and height. Unlike Baroque artists who led the eye to the back of the picture, Cezanne concentrated the attention on the centre of the painting. And by raising the line of the horizon he increased the depth.

Cezanne modelled his forms not by the use of light and shade but by the modulation of colours as the Venetian painters did. By colour intensity rather than by perspective and chiaroscuro; he created the illusion of volume and solidity as well as depth and distance. He found that the greatest intensity of colour results in the fullest forms. Therefore he painted objects in one hue only. He used colour constructionally to produce depth and volume—warm light colours have an advancing effect while cool ones seem to recede. The Impressionist division of tones he replaced by putting warm and cool tones side by side. Thus he stabilised the shifting colours of the Impressionists. He believed that visibility in nature results only from colour, and that lines do not exist in nature. As in Japanese art he divided his colours into clearly defined planes which hold the composition together. His quiet, restrained colours, though seemingly lifeless and thin at first glance, have an abiding pleasantness. He had a perfect sense of colour.

Every touch of his brush was carefully planned, though the paintings appear rough and sketchy. He created his forms by means of these short, rectangular chisel-like strokes which give them a sculpturesque appearance. Often they run parallel but at times they cross the objects rather than follow its contours. Each little dash of pigment is a coloured plane in itself, applied without prior drawing. Although guided by the mind these dense, rough grained dashes quiver with feeling.

Though he loved nature Cezanne distorted his figures at times either to portray the essence or for good design. Or to eschew monotony he distorted one side of a figure. In cases like these his suppressed baroque instinct seemed to get the better of his classical ideals and otherwise strongly balanced art. We see this also in the sloping and awkward postures, stiff limbs and squint eyes, the rickety chairs and tables, the hazardous supports of his still-lifes with their crooked jugs and vases, and the lightning-struck trees. His perspectives are ambiguous, presenting things from different viewpoints in the same picture. He did not use the unified perspective introduced during the Renaissance but combined multiple perspectives in one composition. This resulted in some distortion.

Though he painted a few portraits, Cezanne expressed himself best in landscapes and still-life. His *Boy in a Red Vest*, with egg-shaped head and metallic appearance of the body and clothes, shows the application of his technique to portraits. The geometrical colour planes occupy almost the whole composition. In *The Bathers*, which he painted not for sensuality or fashion, he merely tried to discover new forms and rhythms.

He often represented *Mont Sainte Victoire* near his home in Provence since to him it symbolised the order he sought in the world. The distant mountain, bigger than normal, stands out clearly. The sky has a gun-metal colour to keep it from getting lost in the distance. A series of overlapping planes, somewhat like the scenic wings on a stage, give depth to the space without interfering with the design. As in bas-relief, the planes flatten depth without one's being aware of it. They show that distance can be represented without the use of perspective. The pine branch crossing the foreground helps to emphasise space, which is composed of many little elements—houses and fields, roads and an aqueduct—each seen from a slightly different point of view, as a spectator does not see all these forms in the same glance like a photograph, but focuses on them one by one. As a result their relative proportions vary. The background contours receive the same emphasis as those in the foreground.

In *The Sea at l'Estaque* he gives depth to the picture by raising the horizon without the use of aerial perspective. Every part of the painting is kept up front. His *Provençal landscape* resembles a Cubist abstraction with the curving forms blocked out into facets or planes which look as if sculptured rather than painted. In *Pines and Rocks* he relates each part so harmoniously to the next that while there is repose in the over-all pattern, the picture is full of inner movement. The rock base and vertical trees give it stability while the curving and twisting branches and many lively colour areas provide continuous fascination. In his later paintings, such as *Trees by the Water* (1900–1904) he made the spectator part of the view by leaving blanks for the imagination to work on. In his spirited free drawings he also resorted to suggestion, giving only the general effect without bothering about details.

His still-life paintings served as ideal means for experimenting with the forms of unrelated objects. While horizontal and vertical lines anchor the strong major forms to the picture frame, the interplay of curving and contrasting lines provides interesting movement. For aesthetic purposes he distorted the sides of the decanter and the bowls to harmonise with the forms of the fruit whose round shapes would not go well with ovals. So he presented one bowl as seen from the front and another as viewed from above—all in the same picture, as in *Still Life with Fruit Baskets.* And by tipping objects slightly off-centre he gave them a sense of movement. Instead of trying to copy the appearances of objects he aimed at giving them an interesting design.

Modern art is based on Cezanne's design aesthetic and *Van Gogh's* expressiveness of personal emotion or feeling. Van Gogh painted in order to create a new world according to his mind and feelings, not to imitate nature or to please fashionable tastes. His emphasis on personal expression above all influenced the Expressionists. He tried to paint his feelings for things—his passion for universal love for which he found expression only in his art. He wanted to embody love in his work as all the great artists did. Into the relatively impersonal Impressionist style he infused a vital empathy with the things around him. Character interested him rather than appearances; he stressed the psychological rather than the physical, feeling his way into a personality. Into nature he projected his own ardent emotions. He taught the Expressionists to see things from the inside—this is his testament to modern art. Through his work he wanted to give humanity 'something peaceful, pleasant, realistic with emotion, something brief, unified and simplified, concentrated, full of calm and harmony, comforting like music'. His paintings reveal his basic kindness and inner beauty, free of all dross. The predominance of yellow in his paintings proclaims his emphatic love for everything: 'I want to paint men and women with that something of the eternal which the halo used to symbolise and which we seek to give by radiance and vibration of colouring'.

He imparted life and humanity even to lifeless things: the branches of trees look like outstretched arms, windows resemble eyes, and worn-out shoes are depicted with as much tenderness as if they wished to speak. The expression of his sympathies, felt rather than seen, gives enduring interest to his work. His pictures seem to smile at the onlooker with such honest friendliness that he became the first modern painter whom the public really took to heart. Despite the loud colours and rough workmanship his paintings have an appealing beauty. They rank among the sunniest and happiest in the world. In keeping with his ideal 'to be of use to the world, to be simply honest' he poured into his work all that was fine and sweet in him.

Yet Van Gogh's life was a tragedy—out of which art dealers made capital. As a child he wandered alone, uncommunicative and indisciplined, seeking companionship in the nature he loved. He supplemented his meagre education by reading. At sixteen he was employed as a salesman by his uncle, an art dealer, but van Gogh's conscience did not allow him to tell the lies required for successful salesmanship and he could not adjust to a regular, practical life. He found it hard to work with others. As a social worker among miners in Belgium he wanted to make himself poorer than the poor because of his uncompromising idealism. He tended to exaggerate and to mistake ideas for fact. A humanitarian, he loathed the squalor and ugliness of the factory towns—the civilisation of businessmen who oppressed the weak and downtrodden. The greatest sorrow came to him when his love was rejected. For a time he wandered about as a vagabond, failing in everything he tried until he took to art as a last refuge.

At twenty-seven he did not even know how to draw, but he trained himself and sought guidance. Within five years he became a professional, through sheer persistence, determination and courage. He threw himself completely into painting in order to forget his inner sorrow and to find success in art where life had brought him only failure after failure. His contact with Japanese prints and especially with the Impressionists during his two years in Paris helped to polish his work and to balance it with the critical view that he lacked. His artistic activity lasted only ten years, the last two of which he spent in Arles, in southern France. Here the sun seemed to enter into his life and work. Uninhibited, he completed one or two masterpieces daily, yet always aiming at improving his work—to discover something new and to give his paintings more and more animation and life-likeness. Almost always he painted straight onto the canvas but without any alterations or working over. His work shows fine balance and arrangement, distinct contours, almost dazzling colour and light without shadow. Instead of the divided strokes of the Impressionists, he used long streaks of colour expressive of his stronger emotional drive. At times he squeezed the tube right on to the canvas. He worked at a terrific speed without concern for detail. Though painting made him happy he overworked himself and did not take proper care of his health. An argument with his rival Gauguin, opinionated like himself, led to a nervous breakdown. Moreover he had become discouraged by his work's lack of sales. Only the help and understanding of his brother Theo, who had succeeded him as art salesman in his uncle's shop and who had befriended the Impressionists, kept him going. Starving, exhausted, ill, lonely, haunted by death and at conflict with himself and society, he got fits of melancholy similar to madness.

But Van Gogh's art is not that of a madman. Almost serene, it shows concern for reason, balance and order. Through discipline and meditation he overcame his mental disturbance. After his breakdown his paintings show a greater feeling for design, more creative originality, abstraction and subtle interest. In *Asylum at St. Remy* his wriggly brushstrokes dance all over the picture and became a part of the design itself, increasing the movement. His art now attained its highest perfection: the mountains seem to soar, the sun and stars whirl about, the olives and blue-green cypresses lick up like living flames. The rhythm has intensified, vivid colours riot with lines. The death symbols also make their appearance: sunflowers losing their petals, wheatfields agitated by the wind, and stormy skies.

Van Gogh gave himself strict aesthetic rules and thereby he controlled his impulses. Even in his illness he remained a thoroughly clearheaded artist with keen insight and love for his fellow beings. Like Cezanne he had studied aesthetics and showed a strong command of the technique of painting.

Symptoms of his illness manifested themselves in his personality rather than his art. He showed extremes not only of goodness but also of less desirable characterstics. His affectionate letters to his brother Theo and his attempts at friendship reveal a tender, refined personality with a special concern for the underdog. And into his work he poured out all that was noble and sweet in him. He longed for peace, harmony, wisdom, simplicity, kindness and gentleness—and these desires he expressed through fine proportions and curves. About everything that seemed important to him he was stubbornly uncompromising and persistent in spite of discouragement. At the same time he could be hard-hearted and selfish, making life difficult for others and himself. And this made him feel very lonely.

Several influences helped to shape his art. He liked Millet, Delacroix and Daumier and at times imitated Rubens' red boundary line. Anything primitive he considered beautiful. The influence of Japanese art appears in *The Bridge at Arles*—the division of the composition into large, simple colour areas, and the flat colours at times surounded by lines. His work in turn influenced the Fauves and Expressionists.

He used intensely loud and bright colours which express his sanguine temperament. Bright yellow sunshine and whirling suns against a blue background (symbolic of infinity) occur very often to express the beautiful. He loved blue and yellow best of all. In one portrait he exaggerated the subject's yellow hair to symbolise a star shining in the blue sky. While for him blue and yellow express beauty, and the union of complementary colours stands for love, green and red, used arbitrarily in *Night Café*, express terrible passions and convey an atmosphere of evil. The colours do not represent the people's physical appearance but their mood. Not only does he distort the colours to express himself more powerfully, but he tilts the perspective of the table to convey the nausea and delirium resulting from intoxication. With his colours he stressed form and created depth and rhythm.

Van Gogh experimented constantly with the effects of various brush strokes and of heavy paint. He used simple brush-strokes, standing out separately, to suggest wheat and grass stalks and to give his paintings texture; and his curly leaves dance across the canvas.

Van Gogh pioneered in the modern use of texture, though he still used it partly for representation while those who followed him employed it entirely for design. By means of thick paint, heavy varied brush-strokes and a subtle variation of colour he broke up the areas, rounded his forms and made solid shapes more realistic.

Though his simple design lacks the lasting subtlety of Cezanne's, Van Gogh's quivers with movement: spiralling stars blaze like fireworks and his landscapes gyrate with emotion, giving an over-all impression of pattern. With strong precise lines, and broken colours and forms he captures the essence of things and reveals his ardent feeling by distorting his forms. His abstractions are symbolic rather than geometrical: the flame-like cypresses, restless, self-consuming and straining upwards to the sky, portray his inner self. Among his many works the first and best reveal his understanding, sympathy and brotherhood with all who must work hard. He too considered himself a labourer rather than an artist. Less isolated than the other Post-Impressionists, Van Gogh was aware of his time, both its power to liberate and to enslave. He showed the greatest concern for the oppressed and painted them from an empathetic rather than aesthetic viewpoint—he painted them as they were without romanticising them, but in their simple honesty —a quality much needed in our time. He tried to feel and think as they do. In his first large work, *The Potato Eaters* (1884; Van Gogh Collection, Amsterdam) he shewed how those who produced the food had to live on boiled potatoes and tea. The painting is dark, typical of his early paintings before he met the Impressionists. His *Portrait of Dr. Gachet*, who cared for him during his last illness, has a heartbroken expression, an expression common in modem art.

The sinuous curving lines of his *Country Road by Night*, full of restless life, lead the eye round and round the picture. The serpentine road, flaming trees and spiralling stars give movement to the design, which is divided into a few simple colour areas. His *Starry Night* (1889), with its exploding stars and whirling galaxies seems like a prophetic visualisation of recent astronomical discoveries of the stupendous universe.

Cypresses rise up to this grandeur while men huddle away in fear.

*P. Gauguin*, the most eclectic of nineteenth century artists, created original work out of Eastern and Western influences. His sophisticated technique derived mostly from the advanced Egyptian, Persian and Cambodian cultures, though he sought rejuvenation in barbarism. Because he hated Greek and classical art and modern civilization, its degradation, banality, psychical tensions, its boredom and morbid, oversensitive ideas of beauty, he looked for simple, primitive subjects in the South Seas. But while he changed his subjects his style remained the same. He did not adopt the hard, angular lines of Oceanic art but used the soft flowing ones that came to him naturally. Tahiti gave him the splendid physical models that suited his aim, but the stateliness of his art, with the impassive faces and grave, rigid figures bears greater resemblances to Egyptian and Cretan than to Polynesian art. As in Egyptian sculpture he distorted the flattened forms, and as in Medieval stained glass and Byzantine enamels and Japanese prints he used broad areas of flat colours. He was also influenced by folk art and primitive woodcuts.

The greatest influence on Gauguin's art came from *E. Bernard*. After their meeting Gauguin's art was completely changed. At the age of twenty Bernard had worked out the theory of synthesism and the technique of cloisonnism. Synthesism gives greater importance to the memory than to observation. Memory simplifies what has been seen to the simplest essentials, to what is significant or symbolic to the viewer. He expressed this synthesism through the technique of cloissonism, inspired by Medieval stained glass, Japanese woodcuts and folk art. Black or blue Contours (cloissons) surround the figures like the lead partitions in stained glass; and the colours of the bold, flat surfaces try to imitate the brilliance of light passing through stained glass. Entirely unselfish and disinterested, Bernard brought recognition to lonely geniuses like Van Gogh and Cezanne at a time when he was almost alone in seeing their possibilities, thus helping them to become famous.

In his turn Gauguin influenced the Fauves (in particular Matisse's audacious colours), the colour symbolism of the Blue Rider group, and the Surrealist dream world. Gauguin's sculptures made people more ready to accept Polynesian and African fetishes.

Gauguin's interest in non-European cultures derived from his early travels. As a child he lived in Peru and France, and when he became a sailor he saw many lands, including India. For the most part he taught himself since he had little formal education. He became a successful businessman and as such he collected modern art with an inborn sophistication. At twenty-five he started painting, encouraged and taught by Pissarro who had also helped Van Gogh and Cezanne. A natural artist, he had to struggle less than these two and advanced very quickly. Bored with business, he became a full-time painter ten years later but could not sell anything. As a result his family life broke up, and he became bitter at the neglect of artists by modern society. During his stay in Britanny his style matured. Inspired by Bernard he adopted the new style of cloissonnism and symbolism, with brilliant enamellike colours. Here he worked out his principles: simple and unmodelled massive forms without shadows but with heavy contours and flat colours and designs unrelated to natural appearance. In search of the exotic and primitive he worked for a time in building the Panama Canal but malaria forced him on to Martinique where his colours became more luxurious. Sickness obliged him to return to France where Theo van Gogh put on a one-man show for him and where he met Vincent van Gogh in Arles. Finally he settled in Tahiti, disgusted by what he considered the rottenness in art and the reign of gold in industrialised countries. Though he painted assiduously his works did notsell.

Gauguin's defeat, downfall and tragic end were brought on largely by his personal weaknesses and mistakes. A slave to passion, lacking good judgment and a sense of humour, restless and erratic, intolerant and bitter yet blindly optimistic and unable by temperament to settle down for long to a routine life, he was much more tormented than Van Gogh since he lacked the latter's inner sweetness and faith. He kept returning to the civilization he despised since he could not get the appreciation and praise he wanted for his sophisticated art from the unsophisticated natives.

Gauguin's is chiefly a decorative art. Like the Symbolist poets he tried to make his subjects represent his personal emotions and ideas. But he lacked Van Gogh's emotional power and Cezanne's interesting structure. While Cezanne's work is symbolised by his sculpturesque forms and Van Gogh's by his soaring flames, the patterned flower characterises Gauguin. He aimed at creating his own beauty rather than representing what he found in nature. In spite of ridicule and neglect, he believed that he was destined to be a great artist. He refused to produce art that would sell easily but chose provocative subjects instead. He put art before everything, even his family life.

Gauguin pioneered in the abstract use of colour—green or blue horses, red dogs— to represent emotion through unexpected combinations. Instead of the minute contrasts of the Impressionists he preferred large areas of bright tropical colour since 'a metre of green is greener than a centimetre of green'. He used unusual, exotic colours emotionally selected in exciting combinations to arouse interest. While he filled his figures with the most daring colours, he usually made his backgrounds soft.

Gauguin's sensuous poster-like design is better suited for murals than pictures. He distorted his figures like his colours in order to fit into a rhythmic pattern. By different textures and slight shading he modelled them in low relief. Rejecting both perspective and recessed planes, he raised his horizons instead. His flat backgrounds give his paintings a tapestry-like appearance, leading the eye over the tastefully arranged pattern of harmonious colours. His forms lack the solidity of Cezanne's. He created a feeling of calm stability by stressing strong horizontal and vertical lines and avoiding restless diagonals. The sinuous shapes of the minor figures provide movement without interfering with the relaxed mood. The large figures in the foreground, though flattened, look natural enough but those in the distance have been distorted beyond recognition to fit into the decorative pattern. Except for emphasis he avoided extreme contrasts.

In his *Struggle between Jacob and the Angel* (1889) Gauguin increased the emotional power of the painting by combining a Biblical scene with women of his own time. The thick black flowing outlines add to the emotional power. In this and *The Yellow Christ* (1888) he introduced symbolism for the first time. In the latter he combined a representation of folk sculpture with his impression of the piety of Breton peasant women who sit at the roadside contemplating the sufferings of the Redeemer. In *The Vision After the Sermon* the figures stand out almost like silhouettes against the bright red meadow which occupies most of the space. *Beautiful Angela*, also painted in Britanny, after being refused by the subject, was bought by Degas and now hangs in the Louvre. The interweaving of sinuous lines gives a sense of movement to the calm poses of the figures in his *Maternity*. Through his sea pictures he reveals fear of the unknown and repining for the loss of liberty and love.

Balance and serenity characterise the art of the late nineteenth century Post-Impressionists. Twentieth century art became much more agitated. Political crises prior to World War I made people lose confidence in the inevitable progress premised by science and technology. This loss of confidence found expression in Existential philosophy. Since objective reality seemed insecure, obscure and fragmented, they advocated its substitution by a subjective reality, constructing an arbitrary conceit of one's own no matter how absurd. This attitude found expression in Abstract art, called 'the geometry of fear'. In their progressive retreat from a seemingly hostile reality, artists tried to find security, permanence and immediate enjoyment in art itself. Art became an end in itself—art for art's sake—an object of worship. In retreat from an increasingly inhuman mechanised civilization, artists sought aesthetic enjoyment in the ivory towers of their studios. They turned away more and more from representation to design and abstraction, and to the imitation of already successful artists. Structure and style took precedence over content and subject-matter.

While the first generation of artistic pioneers had been creative innovators, largely self-taught through study of the old masters and personal experimentation, courageous individuals who worked alone and solved their own problems, the new breed of the twentieth century developed, expanded and perfected the inventions they inherited from these leaders. They were more sophisticated and intellectual, and formed groups instead of working alone. In the art of the so-called primitives they sought new vision. The Fauves led the way in seeking inspiration from African art, followed by the Cubists, whose work reflects a fragmented, disintegrating world dominated by the machine. The effects of the war appear in Dada-nihilism, and the Surrealist retreat into dream worlds portrays the nightmares of an uneasy peace. After the war quantity far surpassed quality. Art became a succession of fashionable movements fostered by commercialisation. And the modem movement, which began largely as a reaction against academic art, has itself become academic and imitative.

As in other instances in earlier modem art, the name *Fauve*, meaning 'wild beasts', derived from unfriendly criticism. Drawn together for a short time by a desire for freedom from all rules and traditions, under the leadership of

Matisse, their work is characterised by clashing abstract colours for expressionist purposes, hence the name. Within a few years most of them toned down their violent colours. Intellectual sophistication and a classical tradition helped to balance this French form of Expressionism. Still free of repulsive subject-matter, yet chic and daring, their art appealed to the sophisticated. Their beautiful flowing lines, probably influenced by Art Nouveau, gave beauty to their work. Art Nouveau, with its linear forms, was a reaction to the ugliness of mechanisation.

The Fauves were influenced chiefly by Van Gogh's expressiveness, the spontaneity of primitive art—African festishes, Polynesian wood-carving, Red Indian textiles and sculptures and modern primitives like H. Rousseau. In their unusual colours and shapes the Fauves discovered new ways of expressing feeling.

The art of *H. Matisse* bridges the old and the new. Rooted in French tradition and academically well trained—for ten years he had made copies of the old masters for museums—he searched for new inspirations and originality especially in the simple drawings of children and the sophisticated art of Persia. Throughout his life he continued to experiment. Though he loved nature, he admired Cezanne's art not only for its colour but for giving second place to subject matter. The personification of bourgeois respectability, Matisse met the demands of the art market by producing joyous rather than tragic subjects, with cheerful colours and lively decorative designs. Simplicity, balance, serenity and clarity characterise his art. He believed that art should be relaxing. After the war his works became even more charming and his colours more fresh and lively. It is interesting to note that during his stay in Paris his work reflected the general unrest, fear and depression by his temporary adoption of the Cubist style; whereas when he moved out of the capital his paintings became more joyous, realistic and attractive. Some think that his art lacks depth and dramatic struggle, i.e. the interplay of opposition or contrast, that it is more intellectual than emotional.

Matisse had a natural sense of design and rhythm. He specialised in figure painting. Though a master of anatomy, he distorted his subjects to show the inner tension of muscles. His detached human figures serve merely to form part of the decorative design. They show expression not through the face and gestures but by means of the general arrangement. By light shading incorporated into the design he replaced modelling, and he eliminated all needless details. Sometimes he merely suggested form by filling the areas between the outlines incompletely. One of the great modern draughtsmen, he created delicate over-all patterns with no one part standing out, and with the rhythm running throughout. His drawings, done without mistake or working over in a single rhythmic line, are much more spirited than his paintings.

Gifted with a fine taste for colour, Matisse invented many new combinations, such as balancing the most brilliant pigments with quiet, delicate neutrals. By subtle accents of colour he gave his flat surfaces a three-dimensional appearance. Though not naturalistic, his colours are always harmonious and pleasing, yet strong too—squeezed right out of the tube. In *Red Room* (1908–9) he contrasted warm and cool colours as well as curving and straight lines. Various strengths of colour together with directional lines indicate a front and back. As he became older and wiser Matisse turned to religious art.

*G. Rouault* too turned to religious subjects especially after 1932. Unlike many other modern painters who occupied themselves chiefly with complicated abstract theories and decorative works, Rouault's chief concern was a passionate sympathy for human misery and degradation which he transcended by faith in the Eternal. He seldom painted motifs, but by distorting forms and colours he pointed out the social flaws, the abuse of human rights and the weaknesses of human institutions.

Like the other Fauves he used simple designs. Having been apprenticed to a stained-glass artist at fourteen, he brought the technique into his painting by using the glowing colour harmonies and by effectively imitating the lead and bar divisions by means of black lines. He was a sophisticated draughtsman.

When his anger at social evils turned to pity his works became less violent and his religious subjects more numerous. He painted children's faces and recalled the sufferings of Jesus and His mother with a touching gentleness. A warm half-light seems to radiate from the wide-eyed figures. In his large religious pictures such as *Ecce Homo* and *Miserere* which have won the esteem of all, he attained the summit of his art. He seemed to have entered into an ardent communion with his holy subjects.

*A. Derain's London Bridge* (1906) shows a sharp contrast to Monet's views of Waterloo Bridge finished only three years before. To the Fauve artist his emotional reaction counted much more than the objective representation.

For him clashing colours for expressive purposes became the subject of the painting.

Though classed among the Fauves for his strong colours and vibrant pulsating harmonies, the art of *C. Walch* shows an affectionate love for nature. Deprived of the use of one hand from birth, he found joy in exploring the countryside of his native Alsace. He painted these familiar landscapes with the humble unsophisticated inhabitants at their daily occupations—a fresh countryside full of joy, of sunshine, flowers and fruit. One example is *The Sledge* (Museum of Modern Art, Paris).

*R. Dufy* was another painter of joy usually classed among the Fauves. He too did not reject reality and was not ashamed to admit that his works were representational. In fact he advised artists not to concentrate too much on technique but like himself to continue seeking new ways of expression, keeping his paintings from getting stale from repetition by always looking for something fresh. Everyone loved this cheerful and charming man who got up daily full of wonder like a child before the great secret of creation. He did well only what he did cheerfully. For him art was not just self-expression but chiefly communication and helping others. Employment as a dyer and painter of fabrics assured him a livelihood.

Though the great masters frightened him (he avoided perspeotive and chiaroscuro), Dufy was interested in Van Gogh, the Impressionists, Matisse and Braque. He became an outstanding draughtsman. The suggestiveness of his paintings, what was left out, is the most outstanding characteristic of his work. With great skill he made effective use of the white paper background. He selected and stressed a few details to convey his meaning. By using black he gave the impression of being dazzled by the sun, and by putting a sudden halt to all that changes he created the sensation of passing time.

*A. von Jawlensky* applied Fauve influence to Russian folk art. The first world war produced a deep change in his work. He became interested only in the basic structure of the human face, his colours took on a greater delicacy, and a deep mystical sense began to pervade his pictures. For him 'art is homesickness for God'. In 1919 he painted *Visions of the Saviour*.

The Welsh artist *A. John*, also influenced by the Fauves, was another among the rare modern painters who produced pictures of sheer ecstasy, delight and spontaneous achievement—though at times he is a little formal. His landscapes, gypsies and portraits will probably outlive the popular but mannered work of some of his contemporaries who are now more fashionable.

The *Expressionists*, chiefly of northern and eastern Europe, reacted against the classical restraint of the Fauves or French Expressionists. For them the French seemed too distracted and inhibited by the analysis of technique. The Expressionists had no interest in style and form as ends in themselves, and opposed the formalism of Cezanne and Seurat, carried on by the Cubists.

Deep down Expressionism was a revolt against the dehumanisation of industrialsation and mechanisation, against the personal loneliness of urbanisation and modern social conditions. The movement flourished chiefly in Germany where sudden transition produced a kind of future shock. Until the seventeenth century Germany had been a helpless victim of aggressive neighbours. Separated into small, loosely federated states with no large urban centres, it became culturally dependent especially on Paris. Suddenly it became industrialised and rose to international importance under a highly autocratic, militarist monarchy. Till the end of the nineteenth century religion had a deep influence on the development of German culture, and the Romantic movement owed much of its inspiration to the mystical tendency of the German people.

Expressionism reveals the impact of the sudden change from the spiritual to the secular. In the search for new meaning artists turned for inspiration chiefly to Van Gogh, who became their hero. The projection of his feelings on canvas, his introspection and deliberate exaggeration to express emotion had the most powerful influence on the Expressionists. Gauguin and the Fauves too had some influence on them but the Expressionists were less sophisticated and used even more violent colours to portray their emotions. They sought ideas too from El Greco and the more impetuous Germanic artists like Grünewald, Cranach, Brueghel and Bosch rather than the gently pious art of Lochner and others like him in the fifteenth and sixteenth centuries, to whom the Romantic Germans still looked for inspiration. Children's art however had the greatest influence on them, followed by African masks and sculpture—among the most expressive of all arts—which they saw in museums rather than curio shops but which they did not understand.

They revolted against the traditional Romanticism as taught in the official German academy, symbolic of authority, and roughly distorted or even eliminated realism.

The strength of the movement comes from its human interest, its record of the varied contemporary scene, its quest for personal dignity and its frequent overtones which rise above the mood of despair and sense of doom. Its weakness comes from the symbolism which the artists locked in their minds without providing a key to its understanding, while their mystical terminology lacks meaning relative to colour and form in art. Unlike the international trend of the Paris school they favoured ethnic and individual distinctions.

Intense feeling, a most trenchant tool for an artist, predominates in their work. Modern art, in fact, has studied emotion more deeply, and this explains one of its characteristics, namely its apparent oddities and eccentricities. Even abstract art is a direct communication of an artist's emotions. The artist projects his inner feelings even onto non-human beings, colours and the direction of lines. With Germanic thoroughness the Expressionists tried to communicate their uninhibited feelings by means of distortions bordering on the grotesque. Music, the least material of arts at which the Germans excel, lends itself much better to this emotional expression. Expressionism is Romanticism in the tragic modern mode, conveying the anguished mood of our times.

Though people readily accept subjective feeling in art, they revolt when caricature usurps the place of art. Some of the subject matter of the Expressionists as well as their violent technique filled the public with distaste. The artists aimed at powerful rather than graceful expression and often neglected design. They laid the colours on thickly with furious brush strokes and broad vigorous lines.

The movement passed through three phases. The first, from 1885–1900, was dominated by the Norwegian Munch and the example of Van Gogh. At the turn of the century various Expressionist groups, such as the Bridge, the Blue Rider and O. Dix's New Objectivism were formed. During his Blue and Negro periods and again during the Spanish Civil War and World War II Picasso expressed himself in this style, especially in his violent *Guernica*. From 1935–50, the third phase, when Picasso returned to this style, saw a revival of it not only in Europe but in the Americas as well.

Expressionist art first showed itself in the work of the Dutchman Van Gogh, the Belgian J. Ensor and the Norwegian *E. Munch*. Munch was the first Expressionist to be influenced by Gauguin's colours and patterns but he showed much greater emotional force. Munch in turn influenced the German Expressionists. Through frightful colours and violently distorted symbols he revealed his inner torment and obsessions. A sense of doom oppressed him from his childhood when his mother and sister died. His own health was not strong; and often his doctor-father took him along to visit the sick in poor localities. All this preoccupied his mind with death and suffering, as well as a great loneliness. Moreover the vastness of nature filled him with melancholy and fear while the power of love haunted him with a nameless terror. Life seemed to him a poignant mystery, mirrored in his frequent self-portraits near the end of his life. Even his paint appears like tear-drops that have trickled down over his canvas. *The Cry series* (1893), his most famous work, presents a neurotic skull-headed creature running in panic through a convulsive landscape. Its vertiginous lines represent the painful anguish, tension and loneliness of modern man.

*J. Ensor's* work is haunted by the fiendish mask, symbolic of human beings trying to conceal their true self. He satirised contemporary society in the manner of a cartoonist. In his best known work, *The Entry of Christ into Brussels* (1889), a hideous crowd of masked men, unworthy to be His followers, surround the Saviour. The strident blotched colours and tonal discords represent these repulsive creatures.

In 1905 three German students, Heckel, Kirchner and Schmidt-Rottluf, founded in Dresden a federation of artists known as *The Bridge*, symbolic of their aim to span the gulf between the visible and invisible, between inner feeling and its outward expression, between human emotion and nature. Every member was an artist, especially in stained glass or engraving, and they used woodcuts as their principal medium. They rediscovered Grünewald and Cranach and turned also to Munch, Art Nouveau and African sculpture for inspiration. The most profound and eloquent of the group, in fact the most typical of Expressionism at its best, was *E. Nolde*. Despite his heavy impasto technique he was a great artist with an inborn sense of design. His work combines the spirit and vitality of Van Gogh with the powerful expressiveness of Grünewald and Bosch. His subject matter includes landscapes and large religious compositions like the *Last Supper* and *Whitsun* (both 1909) and an altar-piece in nine parts, *The Life of Christ* (1912). Solitary by nature he did not remain long with the Bridge group. After the first world war E. Heckel, turning to nature and religion, produced tenderly lyrical paintings.

*The Blue Rider* group, founded in 1911 in Munich by Kandinsky and named after one of his paintings, produced more poetic and moderate works than the Bridge group. It united a large group of young artists, more particularly Marc and Klee, and had no special aim except to demonstrate the variety of artistic expression. With brilliant symbolic colours and influenced by Cubish fragmentation, they representated principally the human condition. They used various techniques including print-making and sculpture. By basing themselves on subconscious motivation they paved the way for Surrealism. *F. Marc*, who died early in the first world war, produced charming pictures of animals in Cubist designs. *W. Kandinsky*, who turned to complete abstraction, will be found under that heading; and Klee stands unique—he does not fit any classification.

Out of the starvation, despair and inflation of post-war Germany arose anarchic movements like the *New Objectivity* founded by *O. Dix*. He distorted a person's most important features to portray the anguish and emptiness of the time. In *the workmen* (1921) he showed his sympathy for the working class. After 1933 he turned to religious subjects like *Saul and David* (1945) and *Crucifixion* (1946).

Other significant Expressionists include *L. Corinth* who became truly great after his illness brought on by hard work. The most magnificent of his religious pictures is *Ecce Homo* (1925; Basel Museum). *M. Beckman* particularly concerned with suffering and human cruelty, produced some of the most forceful Expressionist works, as for example *the departure* (1932–5), where a royal family in the centre, departs serene and resigned, from scenes of torture at the sides. Heavy black lines emphasise the relief-like quality of the distorted figures. *Grosz's punishment* (1934), which combines a reminder of the destruction of Sodom and Gomorrah with an apocalyptic vision of complete destruction by bombs, reveals a hell created by man where no human figure survives, only fiery explosions, heavy clouds of smoke and failing debris. A chaos of colours and shapes, with no coherent images left, it is almost prophetic of the potential of nuclear warfare.

Mention must be made of *K. Kollwitz*, who revived the forceful splintered lines of woodcuts (ideal to portray the intense feelings of the Expressionists) to manifest her touching sympathy for the poor, whom machines had thrown out of work, as modern means of reproduction had robbed the graphic artists of their employment. Her father had given up law to be with the poor and she and her doctor-husband lived among them. Contact with real life helped to make her one of the outstanding artists of our century.

The Belgian *C. Permeke*, unlike most Expressionists, did not make a show of despair and suffering. He paid tribute to patient and humble devotion and daily toil, generosity of heart and human pluck, in manly and whole-hearted art without any artificiality. The Russian Jew *C. Soutine*, who lived in Paris, was more expressionist than the Expressionists with his monstrous distortions and harshly clashing colours.

We have seen how modern artists turned more and more to the so-called *primitive* cultures for inspiration, seeking therein for models to meet their own aesthetic and emotional needs. Artistic society had become jaded and bored, and looked for something remote and mysterious for refreshment. They also reacted against the bourgeois conceit of having reached the summit of civilisation. Moreover, perceiving themselves in a difficult situation, they felt an instinctive kinship with the primitives.

The quality of art does not depend on scientific progress. In fact the first-known artists rank among the greatest of all time and still arouse admiration and wonder. While people may seem primitive their art is highly sophisticated, as if it had been born full-grown. For instance the *Magdalenean or Cro-Magnon cave paintings* are the most true to life before Greek art. Like all great art they are not merely imitative but show design. The animals, drawn with accuracy and skill, are delineated with sensitive rhythmic contours which seem to quiver with life. Though delicate, the lines are sure, without any working over. With little stylisation, these figures differ greatly from abstract primitive art. They show the real appearance of the animal, its lively movement or solemn poses. Art seemed to form a part of their religious cult, so they approached their subjects with reverence. Perhaps for this reason too the rare human figures appear disguised. In the contemporary *Levant style*, found in Southern Spain and Africa, more interest is shown in man and his violent actions rather than his actual appearance. Though artistic, these figures are more stylised. Animist or magic cults seem to have motivated much of this primitive art. For them the image was animated by a life of its own.

Many modern artists especially the Fauves, Cubists and Expressionists admired the grotesquely distorted *wooden figures and masks from West Africa.* They had the greatest influence on modern art. Picasso in particular adapted their technique to much of his work. For the African artists the material had primary importance—-the cylindrical shapes derive from the trunks of trees. The figures have strange proportions with long bodies and short limbs. The sophisticated design is highly simplified. Both their shape and meaning reveal terrifying depths of cruelty, based on beliefs haunted by phantoms and evil spirits. The fetishes, with sinister purport, were used in magic cults; ritual masks hid a person's identity and freed him from customary restraints; and conventionalised portraits with haunting expressions served as idols in ancestor worship. Most of them instilled a sense of terror and fatalism, but some of them show touches of odd humour, even tenderness and sympathy, expressed in sensitive but sure lines. The more decorative *Polynesian art* is less gripping than the African, but like all folk art it is full of emotional expression.

Some artists, especially Klee, took their inspiration chiefly from the *drawings of children.* Children draw what they think, not what they see. They exaggerate what seems most important to them and leave out what appears irrelevant. All of them begin drawing in the same way: first they enjoy the mere movement, then it becomes rhythmic and then begins to describe circles. Children enjoy creating as they please, expressing their feelings and imagination without inhibitions. They have an inborn sense of design and feeling for beauty of line.

The so-called *Neo-Primitives,* discovered by modern artists and collectors like Apollinaire, Picasso and Delaunay, find a natural place in the history of modern art. Their development, often logical and exacting, as in the case of Vivin and Rousseau, corresponds with the experiments of modern painters. Like them they invented their own techniques, out far from artistic and cultural contacts through the circumstances of their lives. Frequently they came to art late in life. This contributed to their profound originality and freshness. They kept intact the vision of ordinary people by their close contact with them, and expressed it without any stylistic inhibitions. Executed with humility and at times with true piety, their works show an unusual decency and serenity. These modern primitives made their appearance when craft painting came to an end. But their work differs from that of craftsmen, as well as the art of children or of the mentally deranged.

*H. Rousseau,* the first and among the most outstanding of the modern primitives, exerted great influence on contemporary art, and his naive paintings won him many admirers, including Picasso, Braque and Degas as well as Apollinaire. His work, appearing at a time when people wondered whether technolcgical civilization and mechanical distortion had suffocated human creativity, came as a breath of fresh air to bring new hope. Current art movements did not affect him. His priorities differed and he did not relinquish them in spite of ridicule. The distinction of his work lies in his childlike belief in the reality of his creations, and while painting fearful subjects he himself experienced real terror. He painted from the heart, naturally and gracefully. Like all innocent beings in whom the hope of something better never dies, he saw farther than his more sophisticated and conformist contemporaries. Since he was aware of his real gifts and accomplishments criticism never discouraged him, though he suffered much from derision and maltreatment. He accepted criticism gracefully and even cultivated his childlikeness without any affectation. He remained a child at heart, loving and gentle, and always siding with the defenceless. He looked at his world sympathetically, with a lively sensibility. His pictures mirror the kindness of his attractive personality.

Rousseau started painting only in his forties. A contemporary of the Post-Impressionists, he exhibited for the first time with Seurat's 'Grande Jatte' in the last Impressionist exhibition. He worked as a customs officer near Paris, hence he was commonly called Le Douanier. Though he did not try to hide his poverty he claimed his rights courageously.

Rousseau's works show a genuine imaginative and emotional reaction to what he observed, whereas others tried to be self-consciously primitive creators of a cult. While Gauguin's interest in the primitive, for instance, came from his inability to adjust to society, Rousseau was well adapted. And while Gauguin borrowed his exoticism from museum pieces of sophisticated cultures, Rousseau's mysterious, tropical landscapes grew out of his own unsophisticated fantasy. It is unlikely that he ever left Paris; but he had a much more powerful imagination than Gauguin. Yet his dream-world is never divorced from reality—the real and the unreal merge naturally. His vision remained close to the Romantic—before the present age of individualism took over. He always saw the freshness of the world, and he gave even the most ordinary events and the simplest things an aura of enchantment, with a feeling of drama and mystery. He painted directly from imagination and memory, but especially from the heart—he needed no effort to express emotion. Therefore his paintings, born of his simple yet deep understanding of life from his own sensitive experience and imagination, have a lasting interest.

Though self-taught, Rousseau developed his natural talent for design and his masterly colour sense through 'obstinate toil'. Yet he remained perfectly spontaneous, uninhibited by art theories. He rejected studio tricks to give his work a realistic illusion. Both perspective and chiaroscuro are subdued, and he did not trouble himself with solidity and proportions. The details in his smaller paintings did not spoil their unity. The bigger paintings he divided into large areas of delicate, even tones of colour. Sincere and unselfconscious like Van Gogh, he allowed himself to be guided by instinct and experience: 'It is not I who paint but someone else who holds my hand'. Yet he planned everything carefully—the child-like freshness and originality of his work far surpasses a child's range of accomplishment.

Rousseau's jungle and dream pictures with their rhythmic designs of interwoven lines and shapes and their unusual colour effects constitute his best work. The figures and leaves intertwine as in tapestry. By enlarging the branches and magnifying the leaves he gave his landscapes monumentality. The delicate foliage, with every species carefully distinguished, produces a subtle rhythm and pleasing decorative design, with the artistic meeting and crossing of the leaves. Generally he outlined the contours directly with his brush.

The impossible dream situation, mirroring the subconscious, of Rousseau's *Sleeping Gypsy* (1897) is one of the first examples of the Surrealist method and one of the best Surrealist paintings, even before Chirico and Chagall. Initinctively he created an endless desert landscape by using a series of planes one behind the other. And by subtle tones he gave it a dramatic atmosphere.

*A. Baushant*, sponsored chiefly by Le Corbusier, had been a market gardener before he started painting at the age of forty-six. His vibrant works, glittering with beauty, open our eyes to the wonder of creation. Amid the artistic disputes about form and colour, his paintings, bursting with the joy of nature, act like a tonic. Birds fill his skies and fish his seas, and houses and trees cover his slopes. He revelled in abundance and fertility, in flowers and fruit. Filled with the spirit of St. Francis, he opens our eyes to the wonder and harmony of God's creation in bright yet delicate colours.

*Seraphine Louis*, discovered in 1912 by the German critic Uhde, had been a shepherdess and charwoman. She never revealed the secret of the inexplicable enamelled effect that she had developed. Her colours, inspired by the stained-glass church windows, have a mysterious glow and richness. Secluded in a little room with a statue of the Virgin Mary, this poor old woman expressed the unique inner world of her lively imagination in'surrealistic, paintings of fantastic leaves, flowers and fruits. With eyes, lips or fruit appearing in the middle of the leaves they bear some resemblance to peacock feathers. These ever-fresh pictures, painted with sure precision, harmony and balance, have a soaring rhythm.

*D. Peyronnet*, a printer who started painting when he was almost fifty, gave a mysterious life to familiar things without distorting reality. He loved precision and his art transcended the present preoccupations of painters. The American storekeeper *J. Pickett* began painting landscapes at sixty-live. For years he added pigment to the same painting till he had raised it to the thickness he wanted; and he joined sand, shells or the like to the paint to imitate textures. He used a perspective of his own, giving greater importance to things that mattered more to him. He painted from the heart, and his scenes transcend space and time.

One of the most outstanding among the Neo-Primitives is *Grandma Moses*, a Scotch-Irish American who took seriously to painting only in her seventies when her hands were too lame and tired to sew. When she was seventy-eight a collector who saw her work exhibited in a pharmacy made her known. He exhibited three of them in the New York Museum of Modern Art; and of her Paris Exhibition in 1962 J. Cassou wrote that through her we are helped to understand that a bit of paradise still remains on this earth amid the most daring artistic experiments of the avant-garde. This farmer's wife, who had left home at twelve to earn her living as a servant and who died at the age of a hundred and one, regarded her long hard life 'like a good day's work ... I was happy and contented. I knew nothing better and made the best of what life offered. And life is what we make it, always has been, always will be'. These feelings she expressed in her paintings of childhood scenes and disappearing occupations. With her naive manner and fresh colours she gave her simple scenes of country life a serene innocence.

By working together, with *P. Picasso* the draughtsman trying to put colour into his painting and *G. Braque*, the Fauve colourist seeking discipline through severe forms, both sought solutions to the basic problems of painting. They looked for inspiration in primitive Iberian and African sculptures with their fierce distortions, acutely faceted surfaces and severe shapes. Cezanne and Seurat's disciplined approach appealed to them too but Picasso and Braque were more theoretical. Both reacted against the brilliant colours and sensual curves of Fauvism by using only straight lines and angles. Yet by almost completely eliminating the naturalism cultivated since the Renaissance, they brought the Fauvist ideal of complete liberation from tradition to its logical outcome. By seeking the unchanging properties of objects, their inner structure or basic pattern, they arrived at the geometrical forms supposedly inspired by Cezanne. They reduced a few simple subjects found in their studios—bottles, glasses, bowls, tables and musical instruments—to geometrical forms the originals of which could still be recognized. In their first exhibition in 1908 Matisse named their creations 'Cubes', after children's building blocks, since he preferred graceful flowing lines to the straight lines and acute angles of this new style. *Cubism* eventually influenced much avant-garde art till the second world war. This style mirrored a world shattered by increasing individualism and conflict.

Cubist painters broke down reality and rearranged it according to their own fancy. They stopped short of complete abstraction, retaining traces of reality—man-made articles rather than nature—to give unity, interest and authority to their works. These resemble oriental rugs—one must puzzle out the original subjects. Yet their originals—insignificant objects in their studios—indicate their retreat from the significant problems of their society. Instead they concerned themselves with questions of theory and technique. They lived in an ivory tower, a world of their own making, out of touch with reality. Their analytic technique challenged not only the value of art as something precious but man's spiritual character. By smashing the idol of the Renaissance humanists and creating their own festishes they implied that spirit is no more than highly organised matter which can easily be splintered like the glass on a picture, or as they shattered the perspectives of their own creations.

The Cubists tried to represent collective inner feelings by means of symbols. In primitive fetishes they looked for types to express modern emotions. The power of an image depends on its ability to communicate feeling—as if it had a life of its own. A real image, which makes us think of the original rather than the image itself, interferes with the belief that the image itself is alive. The Cubists wanted to create something new to convey the impression that it had a life of its own.

However both the modern artist and his society differ greatly from the primitive set-up. Tribal artists are fully integrated into their communities and cooperate in upholding the traditions of their conservative groups. Art is considered a means of securing the welfare of the group. Most modern artists are cut off from the mainstream of society, they have long since flouted its traditions and expressed their alienation and insecurity in symbols that few can understand. While primitive artists seek to conserve their cultures, modern artists try to escape from their cultures which have become too insecure and complex to cope with. So while primitive art is organic, firmly rooted in its culture, modern art is largely imitative, an attempt to transplant exotic cultures into alien soil.

The Cubist claim to art lies in the interesting design of its paintings, the imaginative orchestration and interaction of colours, shapes and textures. However their sharp angles and straight lines inhibited the quality of their designs and their forms have much less variety and interest than natural shapes. Cubism is characteristically angular.

Cubism passed through several phases. During the groping *Cezanne phase* (c. 1907–9), inspired by his chisel-like brush strokes, the Cubists imitated sculpture in paint and used monochromes. During the extreme *analytical period* (c. 1910–12) Picasso and Braque imitated the heavy, squat Iberian sculptures of ancient Spain. They produced grotesque forms which bore little resemblance to human beings, since they broke up the shape in order to present all aspects at once, as they exist in the mind rather than as observed by the eye. The forms resemble anatomical studies, with the different organs, interior and exterior, taken out of their natural relationship and spread out side by side like laboratory specimens. This method is called simultaneity. This desire to show the whole of material reality differentiates the Cubist style.

At the same time *Léger* developed his *Block Cubism*, as seen in his *Seamsrtess*, who looks as if she had been cut out with a saw. An example of *Analytical Cubism is Picasso's Accordionist* (1911), composed of intersecting planes. The highly intellectual theories of this phase of Cubism became an artistic strait jacket, allowing little individuality so that the works of the different painters have practically no distinctive style. In 1909 Picasso developed his jewel-like *Facet Cubism* but the tangled complexity makes it an unsatisfactory means of representing human features. His *Head of a Woman* (1908–9) and *Portrait of Braque* (1909) make the originals practically unrecognisable. The eyes, only obscurely suggested, have slipped out of their place and the features coalesce with the background.

Picasso and Braque, realising the danger of art completely cut off from reality, started the next, widely publicised phase which ended the analytical. Actually they turned an ancient children's game into an art form by pasting real materials—newspapers and tobacco wrappers, sand and glass, cards and matchboxes—onto the canvas to excite the senses. The process is called *papiers collés* or *collages*.

In 1913 *Léger* started *Synthetic Cubism*. He never accepted the analytical method because he realised that showing the same object from many different points of view at the same time made it hard to understand and interfered with the rhythm of the design. In Synthetic Cubism the complexity is reduced by showing fewer views of the same object and the over-all design is given more importance. The colours become stronger and brighter and a few curves make their appearance. With greater freedom given to expression an enormous quantity of such paintings made their appearance. Later the Spaniard *J. Miró* taught all the Cubists, including Picasso, that curved lines are just as fascinating as straight and angular ones. Thus he introduced *Curvilinear Cubism*.

Though the 'New York Times' in 1913 stated that the Cubists made insanity profitable, yet from the viewpoint of Einstein's four dimensions of space-time, their art becomes more intelligible. They tried to show things as a spectator, who does not perceive everything at one glance, might remember what he had seen.

The first world war scattered the pioneers of Cubism. In 1921 *Picasso* produced his *Three Musicians*. The distorted shapes, in bright but flat colours, seem to move against the dark background to the dissonant syncopation of modern music. The forms, tending to rectangular shapes, resemble playing cards. In 1931 he developed Stained-glass Cubism.

Picasso's life, character and work are intimately connected. This precocious son of an art teacher had become a competent realistic painter at the age of fifteen. With his art he combined a clever business sense which made him aware of the currents of fashion—what the sophisticated wanted. This brought him wealth and fame. At twenty-three when he came to Paris he did not realise that the modern trend was basically opposed to representation, so he began with sad figures of the outcasts of society, the poor and sick. To stress the tragic mood he elongated and narrowed the figures in the manner of El Greco and painted them in an almost monochrome blue—hence the name *Blue Period*—outstanding both in quality and quantity.

In his attempt to find the secret of modern art he met with such artists as Braque, Gris and Derain, and especially with the collector and writer Apollinaire who made him famous. Soon thereafter he became the leader of avant-garde painters in Paris. His constant experimentation and exploration of new ideas appealed to social climbers who popularised any bizarre escape from boredom for the moneyed classes.

From the Blue, Picasso changed radically to the *Pink Period*, characterised chiefly by morbid-looking harlequins. These almost flat, distorted figures resemble Japanese paintings of phantoms. During this time he was influenced to some extent by Impressionism and Cezanne, but the forms are much more geometrical. After this he turned for inspiration to African festishes then being introduced into Europe. He was the first to recognise the design possibilities of African art and the emotional expressiveness of their crooked noses, gawking eyes and jacknifed legs. Under their spell he invented abstract but powerfully emotional forms, and thus in 1906 he became fully modern, interested in creating forms rather than representing reality. In his mask-like *Portrait of Gertrude Stein* the two sides of the face do not match, with the near side almost in profile— this became one of his pet tricks. In imitation of the African figures he broke up the features into interlocking planes. With his *Demoiselles d' Avignon* the Cubist revolution really began with the arbitrary break-up of the natural appearance into jagged planes in hard colour areas. He twisted and dislocated the human figures into grotesque gesticulating forms and violently distorted the faces. The flat composition lacks unity, for while the three faces on the left imitate Iberian sculpture, the two on the right, done later, resemble African masks. They appear from different points of view. The smaller facets of *Head of a Woman* (1908) suggests a ceremonial mask from the Congo. In the *Portrait of Braque* the edges of the small planes cut into each other like facets of a diamond or broken glass. Here the planes showing various features seem to have slipped out of place with one eye up and another down. In later pictures he made the planes overlap. In *l'Arlesienne*, the first example of simultaneous vision, the front and side views are superimposed one above the other.

From this point he began to enter into the objects in his studio, showing them from all angles at once, even turning them inside out. He represented his intellectual analysis of things. Though this should have given more solidity to objects, it actually resulted in the opposite. Cubism lost its power by being cut off from reality. The studio became a kind of laboratory where the subjects were handled unfeelingly like scientific specimens. The forms of dreary subjects, in dull colours, predominate too much.

In 1911 Picasso gave up the analytic method for more subjective imaginary form. *The Violin* (1912), where he reorganises the shapes into a rhythmic pattern, shows his skill as a designer. Around this time he began the collage technique where pasted additions for texture became the most important elements of the design, with the rest painted in. Thus painting moved into the province of sculpture and construction. In *Still Life with a Chair* (1911–12) he introduced different textures by combining manufactured articles with abstract shapes in paint. A frame of rope increased the sculpturesque impression.

As soon as Picasso found others imitating him he turned away in 1913 from the austere Cubist abstraction to *Rococo Cubism*, using strident colours, some curves and fewer angles. But the straight line still dominated. In the 1920's, influenced by his compatriot Miró, he started *Curvilinear Cubism*, with straight lines used only as contrasts to the now predominant curves. In the late 1920's he contrasted flat and sharp curves. At the same time he passed through a *Romantic Period*, with pictures of bullfights and portraits, inspired by Graeco-Roman art. Soon after he investigated *Surrealism*, but instead of following the poet Breton as the other Surrealists did, Picasso tried to portray his own subconscious, producing fantastic, meaningless shapes. The *Seated Bather* (1929), with its distant horizon, somewhat solid figure and hint of danger, shows the influence of Surrealism. At the same time he tried his hand at the *Expressionist* method with bright colours and heavy sweeping lines. In the 1930's nothing became too fantastic to express his emotions. His large allegorical mural *Guernica* painted in black and white for the Spanish Pavilion of the Paris International Exposition in 1937, in protest against the bombing of a town by that name during the civil war in Spain, is considered one of his masterpieces. Unlike Goya or Delacroix, he did not represent the scene, but by violent distortions and contrasts of light and shade and a tumultuous design of merging planes he tried to express the horror of war. These hideous forms, with their barbarously tortured bodies reflect the growing violence of human society. His portraits of children after World War II reveal an underlying tenderness. He engaged in many other artistic activities. His last important work was a mural for the UNESCO in Paris (1952).

Thus Picasso shifted suddenly from one style to another. He tried almost 'everything and introduced many sensational innovations. His work recapitulates most of the important trends and techniques of modern art.

On the whole, except for his Guernica and *Charnel House* (1945) his work also reveals the divorce of many modern artists from social concerns. Yet he contended that artists should be leaders of society and that art should be subversive. This reveals one of the many contradictions in his character. In spite of wealth and fame he continued toiling like a slave, to absorb whatever he could in order to fill his inner emptiness, always looking for happiness and finding only frustration since he tried to find this fulfilment in his dominant passion—to recreate the world according to his own desires. He wanted absolute freedom from all rules and conventions, restraints and limitations. He believed only in himself and his own omnipotence, and wanted to express himself in any way even if it took hideous and hurting forms. An anarchist and nihilist at heart he wanted to transform the world of reality into his own strange and fragile creation, based primarily on his wild instincts.

He delved into his own unconscious to find the symptoms of the psychic ailments of his time, its tensions and conflicts which led to persecution and wars. Out of this exploration come his haunting images, the horrible nightmares that lurk in the human collective unconscious. Picasso was particularly obsessed with the eye. Instead of giving mankind hope and joy, his works speak of hopeless torment and of revolt against reality, namely his own rebellion against the inevitable. Even the occasional mask of facetiousness did not conceal his sarcastic sneers and blasphemies. Though he produced a great deal he never aimed at creating works of lasting worth, and much of it remains an esoteric language understandable to very few. His natural abilities which surpassed those of his contemporaries seem to have been wasted on ephemeral work to suit the present mania for fashionable novelties. He became so preoccupied with technique that his works lost their human appeal.

Though *G. Braque* had developed the Cubist method before Picasso their meeting acted like a catalyst. Very inventive, he worked out the technique of collages. From his house-painter father he had learned how to simulate the textures of wood and marble. Later he went on to papiers collés (pasted papers), as in his *Package of Tobacco*. His recognition that an art completely divorced from the real world would become merely decorative gave the impetus to this method of stressing the textures of actual objects.

Both as a man and artist he differed very much from Picasso although they worked together until the first world war separated them. Well-balanced and manly, with an inborn sense of prudence, discipline and simplicity, he did not misuse his freedom and led a blameless life. He disliked excess of any kind— a riot of colours, turbulent lines and contrasts, rough or casual workmanship. Though he did not let method become a tyrant, he planned and worked carefully—delighting in doing things the hard way. His elegant, precise and subtle works have more rhythm and harmony and unity than Picasso's. He had an innate sense of design and colour. By subtly combining tones, even the dullest and least attractive colours took on a vibrant glow and blended into beautiful harmonies.

Braque preferred to paint landscapes. His *at l'Eitaque* (1907), like Picasso's *Demoiselles d' Avignon* which appeared in the same year, ushered in the Cubist movement, but Braque's work shows a subtler colour harmony and a more lively touch. He always preferred analysing to devising forms of his own, so he did not go on to the synthetic phase. After serving at the front during the war he worked on his own, turning to more realistic work with more cheerful colours and light, and fewer angles. His technique became more relaxed and graceful, more classic and balanced, without losing the freshness of his inspiration. Though he treated his subjects with more respect, and gave up the dull colours and artificial geometric figures and static design of Cubism in order to be more true to the lively pulsations of reality, he retained some features of Cubism such as simultaneous vision.

*F. Léger* produced precise, machinc-like forms called *Tubism or Block Cubism*, as seen in *The Seamstress* (1910). His human figures resemble the robots popularised in the literature of the time, notably K. Capek's R.U.R. (1923). He liked machines and modern city life, as seen in *The City* (1919) where the harsh colours of the posterlike painting with its division into abstract sections conveys the turmoil of our mechanised urban civilisation. The three women in *The Luncheon* (1921), shown from three points of view, have blank faces and rigid cylindrical limbs which make them resemble machines. Later he turned to religious themes.

While *A. La Patellière* adhered strictly to the Cubist principles—simple forms, plain tones, rejection of the picturesque and the use of light to convey rhythm—and though artist-friends admired his work, it is generally not given the value it deserves because he refused to conform to this nonconformist art by retaining his respect for nature and giving his paintings a quiet, meditative sense of mystery. He deserves a higher place than is generally accorded him at present. *A. Gleizes* had adopted the simplified forms and colours of Cubism and remained faithful to the Cubist method, but the first world war deepened his insight and from that time he wanted to put his art at the service of his Creator and courageously painted modernised versions of subjects popular during the ages of faith—majestic figures of Jesus, His mother and the saints. He influenced many young artists by his paintings, example and writings such as 'Homocentricity, or Return to Christian Man' (1932), and 'Form and History' where he showed the pre-eminence of art based on religious symbolism. He tried to work out a scientific technique which could be easily taught to give artists the means of praising God. The fifty-seven etchings to illustrate Pascal's 'Pensées' were his last important work. *L. Feininger*, though influenced by Cubism, developed his own architectural style while working at the Bauhaus, with clearly ordered planes and precise organisation.

*Abstract art* sprang up in widely separated countries but with the rapid modern communications they kept in close contact. Abstract or unrealistic art flourishes in a climate of fear, anxiety or disillusion, from a feeling of alienation in' a seemingly arbitrary world at the mercy of forces beyond one's control. Realistic or naturalistic art, on the contrary, reveals a happy, confident, and sympathetic relationship with the world. Motivated by faith which gives meaning and dignity to existence, naturalistic art accepts even the tragic aspects of life. It grows out of a basic love of the Creator and His creation. This unified point of view led to the discovery of perspective. This life seems like a window through which we look out at a brighter, freer world, a world of order, with clear distinctions between good and evil, truth and error, beauty and ugliness, unity and disorder. The art developed during the ages of faith, with its technique of modelling in light and shade reflects this attitude, and pictures were made to look like windows to something more beautiful than the here and now. One of the abstract artists, Gabo, expresses this difference when he states that if he were one of the lucky believers he would naturally produce socially realistic paintings, landscapes or portraits, but to enter into the world of abstraction one has to be a different person. And B. Hepworth, who produced both kinds of art, stated that realistic work recharges one's love of nature, mankind and life, while abstract work appears to liberate one's personality and stimulate one's perceptions. She advocated an alteration between the two in order to find renewal at the sources of all forms.

Abstract art began in 1910 when the danger of war hung over the world. Militarism, political and social tensions, boredom from hedonism, disillusionment with the promises of technology which dehumanised man and put him at the mercy of his own inventions, insecurity and loss of faith, a world of pragmatism and individualism led to the search for order and clarity in art, in a reality of one's own making. Men sought in art something unchanging and absolute, an escape from the depersonalisation of industrialism, and liberation from an apparently arbitrary existence. They wanted to create a new simple reality of order and harmony to escape from the complexity, discords and impending destruction.

In 1910 the half-Asiatic Russian *W. Kandinsky*, born near the Chinese border of Siberia, created the first completely non-representative art with colour spots dynamically juxtaposed, and wrote a book on the basics of abstract art. He had been a co-founder of the Expressionist Blue Rider group. He carried on research into the psychological and emotional values of lines, their direction and relationship. While Gauguin and the Fauves had divorced colour from its natural representation, Kandinsky dissociated art completely from all relationship with reality, not even making any allusion to it in his titles, unlike Klee. By scientific study he also tried to discover the laws of colour and their emotional impact. He retained the bright colours and flowing lines of Fauvism, but rejected the planes and facets typical of Cubism. Thus he gave modern art a new direction.

While Cubist art was guided by the intellect, Kandinsky's issued from his instinctive sense of design and uninhibited personal emotion. He called his sketches *Improvisations* and his finished works *Compositions*. They represent moods and feelings rather than objects. The colours and lines of his *Little Balls* (1921) seem to dance across the canvas.

Because climatic and political conditions weighed upon the Russian temperament and gave it a melancholy tendency, it took the lead in abstract art movements, such as Larionov's *Rayonism*, resembling the drapery folds in Russian ikons, the *Constructivism* of Tatlin and the Pevsner brothers, and *Malevich's Suprematism*, standing for the supremacy of feeling in art. Malevich came into touch with the work of Matisse and Picasso through collectors who brought it to Moscow. He worked with purely geometrical forms. In 1915 he issued the manifesto of the Suprematists. His off-white square, slightly tilted on a larger white Square, is the ultimate in delicacy and simplicity. Only the modulation of cool against warm white, the size and position, distinguish the squares. In 1926 the Bauhaus published his book on non-representational art. He tried to distill art into the aesthetic relationship of the basic geometrical forms. Since his art denied the sufficiency of material reality, the Soviet government banned it, for it contradicted the ideology of dialectical materialism as much as did religion which believes in an after-life.

Abstract art also flourished in Holland where the Calvinist faith in predestination and austerity gave it nourishment. *P. Mondrian*, who came into touch with Cubism during his visit to Paris in 1911, brought it to its logical conclusion. After five years of research he reduced all lines to horizontals and verticals and all colours to the primaries, together with the neutrals, black, white and grey. Only a select few, even among the sophisticated, can understand this mathematical art. To avoid monotony he varied the proportions but no one part has more value than the others. All the lines meet and cross at right angles—the only constant. He created the illusion of movement by balancing the unequal yet equivalent parts. All forms and colours that aroused feeling were strictly avoided. The appeal of this purely intellectual art lies in the severe classicism and subtlety of design, and in the precise and aesthetically balanced proportions. His *Pier and Ocean*, (1914) composed of plus and minus signs, derives from a natural scene; and his *Composition* (1921), characteristic of his later work, shows a delicate balance of thrusts and checks. Black lines of different thickness cross the white background to form rectangles of different proportions, filled at times with primary colours or grey to produce a rhythmic effect of advancing or receding movement.

The enterprising *T. van Doesburg*, who surmised the value of Mondrian's work, made him known through his writings. In 1917 he started the review 'De Stijl' and in 1922 he organised the *De Stijl* movement. Thereby he wanted to create an international style to express the deepest and universal desire for pure beauty, to manifest 'the universal force in everything, identical with what was known in the past as divinity, and as indispensible to us poor mortals, in search for an equilibrium in our lives since... external matter is hostile.' He wanted to create this pure beauty by means of pure colours and the pure relationships of lines, in keeping with his Puritan or Calvinist background. By means of asymmetrical balance these simple relationships were given a feeling of movement.

Also called *Neo-Plasticism*, De Stijl art influenced the Bauhaus with its asymmetrical plan and precise geometric order and design. Allied to engineering, this mathematical art inspired Rietveld's Schroeder House in Utrecht, among others. Already the ancient Greek philosopher Plato had seen the intrinsic beauty of lines and shapes and colours, a geometry which helps contemplation by minimising the feelings. Through the interplay of these simple elements the artist creates a dramatic movement and interest.

Abstract art exerted a valuable influence on the useful arts, not only architecture but also on furniture design, posters, typography and the decorative arts.

The American *M. Russell* turned from abstract art which always runs the risk of becoming a decorative intellectual formalism or an academic vulgarisation, to deeply religious figurative art, referring to his early abstract work as his 'kindergarten period'. He produced a number of large Biblical works.

As a classical reaction both against extreme abstraction and the capricious Rococo Cubism, *Le Corbusier* and *Ozenfant* developed *Purism* in 1918. Without distorting the subject, they simplified the forms, giving them the appearance of architectural designs with the parts carefully joined. They favoured equivocal space by making the line of one form serve as the boundary of another. Through their serenely austere art they joined in the general aim of that time to discover the basic artistic principles applicable to all times and nations.

Just before the first world war the short-lived *Futurist* movement appeared in Italy, with the aim of revolutionising the very foundations of art. In 1909 the poet Marinetti issued the first of the blatant manifestos of this movement, wherein he stated that 'art can be nothing but violence, cruelty, injustice'. The following year the sculptor Boccioni, with Balla, Severini and others proclaimed in the second manifesto that they intended 'to glorify war' which they considered 'the only health-giver of the world'. They also sang the praises of militarism, anarchism, 'the beautiful ideas that kill', aggression, everything modern—science, machines, especially speed. At the same time they publicised their contempt for tradition and custom, for morals and women, for 'the canker of professors and archaeologists', for art critics whom they considered useless or harmful, and for museums and libraries which they wanted to destroy. They idolised machines and made speed their aesthetic rule. Marinetti considered racing cars more beautiful than classical Greek art. For the Futurists the machine was the ideal of beauty.

Considering the static quality of Cubism foreign to the dynamism of modern times and too intent on pleasing the moneyed public, they reacted against its lack of social significance and emotive power. While the Impressionists had captured one moment of time, the Futurists tried to portray all moments. They believed that juxtaposing forms would have the same effect as the Impressionist method of making adjoining colours influence each other. They tried to represent movement by showing the limbs or wheels a number of times in different stages of progress or by stretching the object in the direction of the movement like magnetic lines of force. Yet the effect remains static—one does not get the impression of movement. They could do no more than represent symbols of movement, not movement itself. In the arts only the interaction of opposing volumes indicates motion. A basic rhythm gives unity to their compositions. The best-known and most amusing Futurist painting is *G. Balla's Running Dog* (Fig. 470), which resembles a slow-motion film. The static body of the animal, with its twenty legs and eight tails, reveals the deficiency of the method. In Boccioni's sculptures the Futurist movement produced its best work. The Dada artist *Duchamp* expressed their ideas

Fig. 470. G. Balla: Running Dog.

much better in his *Nude Descending a Staircase* (c. 1912), which became one of the most influential modern works. It has the effect of still photos of an action placed closely together. At this time motion pictures, which give the impression of motion by the rapid movement of stills, were being introduced. Like the Cubists, Duchamp divided the figure into planes.

*G. Severini's Pan-Pan at the Monico*, an outstanding Futurist painting, made the Cubists adopt brighter colours. He returned to classicism after he studied the monk Pacioli's work (1509) on the ideal relations between magnitudes, which had influenced many masterpieces. The Cubists too had used this constant to organise their paintings mathematically. Later Severini adorned a number of churches with mosaics and frescoes.

Like Abstract art, the *Dada* movement appeared at widely different places almost at the same time especially in Zürich, Switzerland, the neutral refuge of pacifists, political exiles and revolationaries like Lenin, who was there when the movement began during the first world war. Defeated post-war Germany became fertile ground for Dada anarchism. The name of the movement probably derives from the random opening of a dictionary.

Hatred gave birth to the Dada anti-art—loathing for the war, dissatisfaction with victory in France and despondency in defeated Germany, post-war social unrest and inflation, the debasement of values brought on by the war, the destruction of the earth through mechanisation. They opposed the sham and hyprocrisy of the time, the all-pervasive greed and materialism, the hollow sophistry of modern civilization. Culture seemed to have lost its reason. This frustration aroused a violent and bizarre emotional reaction, a blind revolt against the status quo and every value. They tried to fight senselessness, futility and destruction with greater senselessness, futility and destruction. They organised meetings only to abuse and insult their audiences; and their demonstrations, to show that culture had gone mad, became ever more insane. By every possible means they tried to undermine the traditional foundations of social order and culture. They took as their slogan 'destruction is also creation'. To destroy reason they introduced deafening music and feigned madness.

The first Dada manifesto ridiculed not only philosophy, science and psychology but art as well. They declared that 'Dada is against everything, even Dada'. This anti-artistic counter-revolution wanted to destroy the distinctions between painting and sculpture, and to declare that 'all is art'. Above all they wanted to shock. For the intellectualism and discipline of Cubism and abstract art they substituted intuition, expressing themselves in fantastic and absurd creations. They stretched artistic permissiveness, basic to modern art, to the point of utter degeneracy.

In the process, however, they did show up the aesthetic sophistries of our century. The great amount of writing needed to explain modern art and the Cubist double-talk disgusted them, as well as the indiscriminate worship of Art by the public, and their sheepish following of art fashions. They revolted against all pretense.

Like many modern artists they used the weapon of caustic wit and irony against the society they hated. They made pictures out of commonplace, manufactured objects, even rubbish, raising them to the dignity of art. Of objects and materials not considered of aesthetic value at the time they showed the artistic potentials. For emotional expressiveness they brought back perspective and chiaroscuro as well as literary connotations, but they continued to include design, whereas the Surrealists neglected even this. In spite of their destructive aims they retained some of the essentials of art. They adopted the collage technique of the Cubists, not only for texture, however, but for subject matter, preferably combined in unusual ways. Often their collages, to which they added almost anything, lack order and good taste. They created nothing really new. Most of their work is macabre and ephemeral.

The Frenchman M. Duchamp, living in New York, sacrificed his real abilities as an artist (as seen in 'Nude Descending a Staircase') to assume the leadership of the anti-aesthetic Dada movement. In his iconoclastic revolt against the artistic cult, he invented satirical ready-made objects, but he combined careful craftsmanship with his farcical subjects. As elements of design he incorporated the shadows of his ready-made objects.

*K. Schwitters* and J. Arp turned to' more real values. Schwitter's collages, called *Merzbilder* (commercial pictures) show sensitivity to design and texture, colour and form. Like a child he collected everywhere and playfully transfigured refuse by combining it in meaningful relationships. Thus he showed that nothing is contemptible if properly related. Out of chance forms *J. Arp* created austerely sober collages resembling bas-reliefs. He is noted especially as a sculptor.

The *Bull's Head* made out of the handlebars and seat of a bicycle and attributed by many to *Picasso* shows how two objects can be brought into an unexpectedly new relationship by creative imagination.

The Dada movement, which began when the war had dispersed the Cubists, disintegrated with the emergence of a Surrealist faction which opposed this basically nihilistic and revolutionary trend. With improved social conditions Dada became outdated. United only by hatred of the situation of the world at a particular time, it destroyed itself by internal disputes, and Surrealism arose out of its ashes.

*Surrealism*, apparently the last of the 'isms,' negates the chief principles of modern art by its neglect of design and re-introduction of realistic subject-matter. In this it differs from all other modern movements and takes back modern art to where it left off, namely academic realism, which it resembles in many ways. With Surrealism the creativity of modern art comes to an end, since no important new discoveries have emerged since then. Surrealism itself contributed no real innovations, except that it tried to penetrate into the hidden world of the subconscious and represent its contents in fantastic dream symbolism.

From this standpoint of subject-matter Surrealism passed through *two stages*. Before the first world war H. Rousseau, G. Chirico and M. Chagall, contemporaries of the Cubists, had produced fantastic paintings that reveal a romantic escape mechanisms into memory and imaginations together with expressions of psychotic fear. After the war the French poet Breton, who had learned Freud's ideas from his study of neurology, started the second, more sophisticated stage and gave it much cleverly organized publicity through his manifesto of Surrealism (1924) which held out the attraction of absolute liberty. He wanted to free the imagination from all inhibitions or morality, reason, religion and artistic conventions. As the Surrealist M. Ernst put it, 'Any conscious control of reason, taste or will are out of place in Surrealism'. They carried this liberty as far as license and anarchy in their attempt to penetrate into depth psychology and the world of dreams.

Like many other modern movements, Surrealism was an escapist art, a mad escape from a mad world, a romantic retreat into a world of dreams. It expressed in plastic forms the sadism and grossness stimulated by militant political ideologies and shadowed forth the degeneracy of dictatorships. The spiritual decay of the time, resulting in cynicism, futility and fear, was fertile soil for its growth. From Dada it inherited pacifism, a popular attitude between the wars, and took refuge in dreams. Although the Communist countries rejected Surrealism, these romantic materialists looked to Marxism for inspiration.

As literature had inspired nineteenth century Romanticism, so poets took the lead in the Surrealist movement. The artists merely translated their ideas into the language of shape and colour. In their search for new imagery the poets combined words without any logic, appealing not to reason but to the imagination by means of nonsense. By breaking through the barrier of the conscious to the unconscious and subconscious of psychological research, they wanted to create a new world of fantasy, a new mythology, a super or surreality more real than reality by combining the psychological levels. They looked at human psychology rather than the anatomy of human physiology which occupied the Cubists. The subjective rather than the objective interested them. They considered it to be their role to organise the hidden impulses of the subconscious, generally considered till then to be no more than baseless fantasies, and thus effect the destruction of traditional values that the Dada movement had failed to achieve. Art for them served to deepen their scientific knowledge, not as an object of contemplation or enjoyment. They ridiculed the artist's special gift or genius, declaring that it was within everyone's reach. The later Surrealists, engaging in questionable self-examination, tried to discover why people act the way they do. To give some authority to their claim that through the subconscious they could attain a more authentic reality than by conscious thought, they joined Freud's psycho-analysis to art, making frequent use of erotic symbols—as in much modern art. They tried to represent their private subconscious feelings, which are hard to communicate, by creating new symbols through the combination of the abstract and concrete, such as the connotations attributed to certain geometrical signs or to natural things like snakes and fire. To give greater credibility to their super-reality they combined the techniques of academic realism (modelled figures, depth and the distant horizons of perspective) with their fantastic subject-matter. But they ignored both design and the laws of harmony.

At first they tried to free the artistic creativity of the subconscious from reticence and the conscious control of reason by means of hypnotism, seances and automatic techniques—leaving things to chance. For instance they let the pencil wander idly without rational control, or they produced banal group pictures, with one person drawing a part, then folding the paper for the next one to draw something else. They also made collages without any regard for design but only to shock, startle and amaze. Thus they produced disturbingly nightmarish and depressing work. To open the beholder's mind to novel impressions, they tried to deprive him of traditional standards and ideas. By juxtaposing the familiar and unfamiliar (during the second period) they made things appear as in a dream. The extremely detailed figures are characteristic of pictures produced by the insane. While the manner of painting, with modelling and perspective, was realistic, the subject-matter was unrealistic.

Similar fantastic art had been produced before particularly in situations like those faced by these modern artists. H. Bosch, living in the warn-torn times between the fifteenth and sixteenth centuries, used techniques resembling those of the Surrealists, who lack however his religious belief. To him the future life was as real as the present and he combined them in a superreality which makes Dali's work pale in comparsion. Later in the sixteenth century Arcemboldo concealed faces in landscapes long before Dali, and made heads out of fruits, flowers and animals. Like Dali too, other painters of that time made figures out of furniture. In the next century Desiderio produced frighteningly mad and nightmarish pictures. Piranesi in the eighteenth century painted frenzied prison scenes and large staircases spiralling to nowhere. A contemporary of Cezanne, Redon, produced weird dream fantasies. Even great artists like Leonardo da Vinci, Botticelli, Brueghel, Goya and Blake indulged in fantasies but in a restrained and salutary manner, to heal not to destroy.

Surrealism flourished between the two world wars, side by side with Cubism and Abstract art. Its paciflsm and escape from reality into a world of dreams was one of the first war casualties, while the more robust Cubism and Abstract Art took on new vigour during the war.

While the Surrealist followers of A. Breton tried self-consciously to fabricate a cult out of Freud's psycho-analysis, the fantasies of the *pre-war Surrealists* Rousseau, Chirico and Chagall sprang spontaneously from their personalities. We have seen how the Neo-Primitive Rousseau reacted genuinely to the fearful real-unreal images that his lively imagination conjured up. Chirico too combined the possible and impossible in his dream pictures, while Chagall's fanciful symbolism was called surnatural as far back as 1912.

*G. Chirico* started *Metaphysical Painting* as a reaction to the idolisation of everything modern by his Futurist compatriots. He wanted to revive an appreciation for the art of the past, to produce a nostalgia for the infinite by his long perspectives, and in his own words to, sanctify reality. . . Around me the gang of modern painters was making a foolish commotion in the midst of worn-out formulae and sterile systems. I glimpsed an art more complete, deep and metaphysical'.

On returning to Italy from Greece where he was born, Chirico was inspired by the sculpture and architecture in Turin, especially the arcades and porticos with their beautiful arcs which leave room for imagination. The long vistas of the blank white architecture of Ferrara inspired his extreme perspectives, composed of repeated diminishing arches of Italian palaces and squares. His visit to Paris in 1911 brought him under Cubist influence.

Chirico's paintings convey a mysterious, dream-like, enigmatic impression with an atmosphere of foreboding, probably influenced by the political crises and general insecurity just prior to the first world war. Shadows are thrown by absent figures or go in the wrong direction, a little girl rolls her hoop towards the shadow thrown by an unseen statue. These long shadows effectively bring to mind the past and future. Towers rise to disturbing heights and lonely silent streets stretch to weary lengths, accentuated by a few small figures in the background. A strange romantic half-light adds to the dream-like atmosphere.

Chirico's *Souvenir of Italy, The Joys and Enigmas of a Strange Hour* (1913) illustrates his combination of past, present and future as if a person in the time of locomotives were trying to return to the past while the setting sun casts a long slanting shadow before. The medieval tower, the long stretch of loggia and street, and the large restlessly sleeping classical sculpture in the foreground recall the past, and contrast with the tiny people and locomotive in the background, who bring us to the present while the shadow seems to point to the future.

Unlike the Surrealists, Chirico did not work according to elaborate theories but from an innate artistic sense. At first they made him popular by their loud publicity but when in the 1930's he gave up metaphysical painting and repudiated his former work in favour of the classical style, they abused him so much that when he noticed a Surrealist approaching he made the sign of the cross.

Another Metaphysical artist, *G. Morandi*, produced the sense of mystery with a few simple lines and only three tones. Of him Chirico wrote, 'He sees with the eyes of a man who believes, and the inner framework of things ... appears to him under its most comforting aspect, under the eternal aspect'. Faced with new problems after the war, he turned to nature. His work ranks among the best in modern Italian art.

Eastern Jewish mysticism and memories of his early years in a Russian village with its simple pleasures, troubles and persecutions, constitute the subject-matter of *M. Chagall's* colourful and fantastic dream pictures. While studying and working in Paris, Berlin and New York he adopted the sophisticated methods of Expressionism and Cubism but he was not ashamed of retaining his romantic fancy. From the Cubists he learned the value of design but he turned more and more from abstraction to realism. By the naturalistic handling of his figures he gave his blithely mad dream-pictures the appearance of reality. Instead of breaking down forms like the Cubists, he broke up memories, while retaining the essentials of the Cubist method. Rather than by formal composition, he expressed design by emotions. Like Matisse he had an inborn sense of fluid composition, with a natural feeling for rhythm and colour. But the Cubist influence confined the original flow of his imagination and restricted it to planes and angles. His shimmering iridescent Fauvist colours, born of his fantasy rather than representative of nature, have an emotional purpose. Their beautiful harmonies give him a place among the great moderns. He used the free brushwork of the Expressionists to reveal his Russian individualism. He adopted a primitive manner and employed familiar symbols which express his joy in creation. His cheerful motley subjects need no explanatory title—they fascinate without it. In his prolific imagination he made lovers—usually representing himself and his wife—fly through the air or caress amid a bowl of flowers. Unlike Klee he usually saw things bigger than life, with giants stepping over roofs. Though he was dubbed 'surnatural' twelve years before the Surrealists issued their manifesto, his works show none of their inhumanity, their preoccupation with sex or their pleasure in seduction for its own sake. With the dry, pathetic humour that characterised him, he painted from a good heart that had suffered, caring nothmg about theories which he considered nonsense.

Deeply touched by persecution and war, Chagall started introducing religious and social issues into his art in 1935. His *Crucifixion* (1943) demonstrates the importance of faith which brings hope and courage in the midst of cruelty and terror. Over the small pathetic human figures and the village in the background appears an angel, the scroll of the Jewish scriptures and the rabbi-like figure of Christ on the cross. Chagall's engraved illustrations of the Bible show his outstanding understanding of ancient times. He decorated a number of French churches and designed a dozen stained-glass windows for the synagogue of a hospital in Jerusalem in 1962.

One of the founders of the later Surrealist movement, *M. Ernst*, exerted great influence by the techniques he introduced , such 'frottage', which bear some resemblance to the Rorschach test used in psychiatry. He coated a piece of paper with paint, placed another paper on top, and made a sandwich of them. After separating the sheets he selected the most suitable one, leaving it as it was or working on it. His fantastic imagination discovered landscapes in the most ordinary things like floorboards. Like Arp and Schwitters, his innate taste and sense of beauty got the better of him despite his destructive aims. His compositions have balance, with attractive colour and texture. But there is something uncanny about his work. Rather than super-real it is infra-real, stygian instead of elysian.

The Spaniard *S. Dali* joined the Surrealist group only in 1929 but he soon became their greatest technician and most famous member. To his baroque temperament he added studies of the seventeenth century Dutch realist masters, but Freud's research into psychological illness was the chief inspiration in his development of a new way of painting which he called 'paranoic-critical activity'. It consisted of creating startling effects by combining the unreal with the real. In order to make the unreal appear more real he painted in the precisely detailed manner of the miniaturists. In this way his paintings resemble hallucinations. He seemed to have an obsession for multiple images, a kind of optical pun, whereby he made the buildings and foliage in many of his landscapes take on the shape of faces or heads. Consciously he composed fantasies which came to Bosch instinctively. Although he claimed that he produced them in a state of delirium, the detailed technique and orderly composition seem to belie this. Amid the many poses and masks he put on it is difficult to discover his real personality. He collaborated in the making of Surrealist motion pictures and was a clever writer, but even the educated public find him hard to understand because of the pseudo-scientific expressions he employed.

Dali's best-known work is *The Persistence of Memory* (1931). This grim allegory of the end of time reveals the different aspects of his technique. Flabby watches, indicating that time is not absolute but contingent, hang from the dead branch of a tree, over a rectangular ledge and on a shapeless dormant monster in the foreground. Moreover ants and flies, symbolising decay, are devouring the precise metal instruments made by man. Here we see the combination of real and unreal—ants eating metal. The painting shows the persistence in Dali's own memory of the landscape of his native Catalonia, so dear to his childhoold and which to him seemed the most beautiful in the world. The expanse of sandy shore, bleached by the sun, gives a personal touch to his annoying fads.

Later when Dali returned to religion and a more realistic classicism, the Surrealists disowned him as a reactionarv. His most famous later works are a *Crucifixion* (1951; Glasgow Art Gallery),often reproduced, where the Saviour's figure hangs suspended over the world, and a *Last Supper* (1955), in the National Gallery, Washington.

Another Spaniard, *J. Miró*, is an instinctive Surrealist without artificiality, with no scorn for his art or professional inhibitions either by traditional convenience or by the studied exaggerations of the avant-garde. Experiments, artistic pretense and grandiloquence weary him. He does not use the current aesthetic jargon, nor try to invent painting anew or rival anyone, or propose a new style or school. He holds a unique place in modern art with his whimsical elementary forms resembling amoeba, larvae, germs or filaments. Like a primitive man or child he invents his own decorative style with basic curved forms and sparing colours, without concern for modelling or composition. Often he uses the automatic technique. For his collages he tears papers haphazardly, scatters the fragments and then gives permanence to the accidental shapes.

*Y. Tanguy's* fantasy, free of Dali's obsessions, has a humorous, good-natured charm. His semi-abstract figures stand out clearly against the deep perspective, as seen in his *Mama Papa is Wounded* (1927). *Berman's The Gates of the City* and *Night, Fall* show better design and composition than the Belgian *R. Magritte* who is considered the most typical Surrealist. An example of his work is *Mental Calculus*.

*Neo-Romanticism*, started shortly after Surrealism, influenced the latter with its greatly exaggerated perspective—even more than Chirico's. In reaction to the psychotic absorption of much modern art and against Cubist and abstract formalism, it did not make its forms resemble machines or architecture. Therefore it was more comprehensible. But it too was an escapist art with a mood of melancholy and languid futility. Often its figures sleep or hide in the darkness with a fixed stare and overcome by tedium.

*P. Klee*, a great modern artist who cannot be classified, rivals Picasso in original creativeness and rhythmical imagination, interest and quality and varied inventiveness. He was nonconformist without being self-centred—always gentle and calm, sensitive and sensible, studious and serious, intimate and modest in his work rather than excitable and exciting like Picasso. Unique in his personality and work, be did not change styles like Piccasso or associate himself with any movement, but was fully himself from the start. One of the greatest adepts of magical fantasy, he contributed a great deal to modern art. While the German Expressionists approached fantasy, they took themselves and the world too seriously. Though he owed nothing to the Paris school, he had a wider influence than Picasso. Instead of confining himself to present trends and fashions, Klee's art points to the future. In spite of his literary titles he pioneered in abstract art, and thus led ten years later to the movements started by the Russian abstract movements. He also influenced Surrealism. His work was entirely novel without his borrowing from anyone.

Born in Switzerland of a Bavarian father and French-Swiss mother, and educated in Germany, he hesitated for a while between music and art as a career. This interest gave his painting a musical quality. Like Cezanne he was convinced that the heart of nature lies in the depths, not in superficial appearances. His visit to Tunisia added colour to his fine draughtsmanship—'Now colour and I are one'. In 1920 he joined the Bauhaus as a teacher. Though he found ideas for design in African art and understood it thoroughly, he did not imitate it but created his own fancy. He also studied the pathetic paintings of the insane which often show beautiful design. The art of children however inspired him most. He made himself see like a child, sharing its wonder and delight in exploring a most enchanting world. With his characteristic 'Einfuehlung' he entered into the feelings of children, making them his own and understanding their problems. Thus his paintings resemble those of children much more than any other artist could reproduce them. Yet withal, his works are those of a great artist, showing good judgment and sophisticated composition despite the apparent simplicity. At first glance his art appears childish but on closer observation it gradually reveals a hidden world of mystery populated by figures that appear one by one. His paintings resemble children's drawings especially in his observation of unexpected, meaningful details, their charming simplicity and playfulness and their dainty lines. Examined carefully, they appear like the gradual narration of a fairy-tale. Like a child lying on the ground and looking up at the sky he painted the continual movement in the sky. Of this child-like aspect of his work he wrote: 'As a child plays at being grown up, so the painter imitates the play of those forces which created and still are creating the world'.

Guided by intuition rather than technique, he entered into his subjects, became one with them to discover their secret, for as he stated, 'An ultimate mystery lies behind the ambiguity which the intellect fails miserably to penetrate'. This enabled him to see and perceive what others overlooked, such as the numerous design possibilities contained in a shell or feather. He entered into the feelings of dying flowers or of the helpless amoeba quivering in the dark water, and into the mind of the cat waiting to pounce on its prey. To fleeting things like smoke and foam he gave form and to puzzling shadowy things he imparted substance. He was the first modern artist to show interest in the pre-conscious or subconscious depths of the human psyche and to the collective unconscious spring of somewhat grotesque myths, fantasies and fairy tales. His metaphysical art reveals an inner, more wonderful world waiting to be explored, a world transcending our limited ordinary perceptions which naturally turn outward. By combining his outward observations of nature with his inner empathy and imagination he created a new world of fantasy, a merry world of kindly wistful humour, a world of discovery of the beauty and joy of creation, set off by an occasional touch of melancholy. This world of his imagination with its mysterious creatures hidden in meadows and pools and its villages scattered among the stars had its own laws of logic and perspective.

Klee believed that art produces a wholesome effect on society through these fantasies or symbols born of the instincts since these instincts have greater power to stimulate than the other faculties. Actually his paintings reflect his sensitive reaction to our world. His fantastic creations personify human foibles and follies, but with a gentle irony. More than any other modern painter he touches our wounds, but softly in order to heal. Through his apparently naive paintings, this 'primitive of a new sensibility', as his biographer called him, actually addressed himself to the sophisticated public.

Klee insisted on giving his own titles to his paintings to make sure that others did not see in them what he did not see. Humorous at times but never facetious, these titles add to the enjoyment of the pictures. In modern paintings, especially non-representational works, titles are important to identify them in catalogues as well as to indicate the artist's purpose. Picasso's titles give the names of his almost unrecognizable subjects, while the other Cubists pointed to their original themes. The Abstract artists used simple titles to go with their subject-matter, such as Kandinsky's 'improvisations' and 'compositions'. The Dada titles illustrate their own disillusionment rather than their pictures, and like the Surrealists they tried to shock with buffoonery which has little or no relation to the picture.

Through much drawing Klee added depth to his exquisite draughtsmanship and sense of design. His sketches from nature reveal keen insight and individuality. Thorough like Kandinsky's, Klee's precise designs show more warmth and colour. The charm of his jewellike paintings comes partly from their intimacy and the humility of his approach. He perceived things smaller than in reality and usually worked on a small scale on small canvases or papers. In spite of lack of show because of their size and simple subject-matter, his paintings possess great depth and meaning that gradually unfolds itself to the imaginative spectator. By obeying natural rules and using the correct technical means, he created great art. Through contrast and balance, associations and interruptions he gave his fantasies the musical rhythm characteristic of his work. With much skill he employed different media, combining ink with colour and gouache with oil. Water colour and spryly moving lines were his speciality. The fine brisk lines of his etchings and pen drawings are sensitively done with great importance given to their direction, and the speed and rhythm of their curves. He often used arrows to point to the inner vitality of his subjects—village houses hugging each other, growing plants and dancing flames, comings and goings on roads and waves falling and rising. As a background to his lines he used many kinds of interesting textures. Always he searched for new ways of expression. For him every work was a new birth, an attempt to give abstract shape to his memories, and in the process of giving birth he gave no thought to method. His subtle colours give rhythm to his paintings, of which they form an integral part. He created an effect of movement and distance by superimposing iridescent colours over neutrals. The colours on the surface express inner power and depth.

Klee's *The Twittering Machine* (1922) pokes subtle fun at our mechanical age. Though the contraption works, real birds sing much better than this ridiculous wire gadget. The picture may also be a pointer to human mortality. The metallic heads, resembling the four temperaments, may serve to lure living birds into the trough-like trap below. Like many others, Klee felt that technology could also be destructive. Like his fellow Swiss K. Jung, Klee believed in the collective unconscious which reveals itself in primitive symbols and shapes. His almost psychiatric *Fool in a Trance* shows symptoms of our modern social disorder. But unlike lunatic art which revolves around a fixed point, Klee's interests remained wide and deep.

Klee, Mondrian and Kandinsky all died during World War II, while Picasso, Braque, Matisse, Miró and Léger carried on with the abstract art that gained in popularity during the war. But since that time nothing really original in the line of creativity has arisen, so that modern art itself has become academic and outdated. After the war the centre of art shifted to the United States of America and art has become big business promoted through advertisements by dealers and commercial galleries, with artists no more than piece workers for the fluctuating art market, with artificial fashions as the criteria rather than real artistic value.

As the first world war bred the nihilistic Dada revolt, so destructiveness characterises much of the art following the second world war, as the art critic and promotor of Cubism, G. Stein had noted: 'Everything destroys itself in the twentieth century'. The shattered images of Cubism reflect this. Ugly decomposition started ever more to usurp the place of beauty in art. Man, almost idolised by Renaissance humanism, came to be considered as insignificant and vile, no more than a statistical digit, an infinitesimal particle in a stupendously expanding universe, threatened by atomic annihilation.

In a world of wars hot and cold, where goodness, truth and beauty were the greatest casualties, artists turned in more and more upon themselves, seeking enjoyment in unrestricted creativity. They broke down the dividing walls between the media and the arts. Only the frame controlled the bitterly defiant colouring of the *Abstract Expressionists*, each of whom expressed himself in an abstract, incommunicable language of his own. *J. Pollock's* brash *Action Painting* stressed the uncontrolled process of applying colours over the content. He let the paint, mixed with impasto, sand or broken glass etc., drip on the huge canvases as he walked over them. In his own way he tried to imitate the Red Indian pictograms on sand' and the continuous movement of Chinese and Japanese paintings which, unlike Western art, have no fixed underlying forms. But while the art of these ancient cultures depends on intellectual concentration and perfect control of movement, Pollock's restless lines show no express aim, but mirror the rootlessness of his time, his craving for absolute freedom. *W. De Kooning* slashed and defaced his figures. M. *Rothko's* tranquil, meditative paintings, on the other hand, show the influence of Zen. An oft-recurring subject in *F. Bacon's* work is a human being imprisoned in a box by a glittering web of uncanny rays of light.

The *Pop* artists of the late 1950's reacted against the extreme inwardness of the Abstract Expressionists and Action Painting by turning outwards to the popular mass culture. Pop art started in London with the Independent Group composed of painters, sculptors, architects, designers and critics. Collages, composed of photos of popular culture, were enlarged into mural proportions. Others cast in bronze are banal, throwaway objects for the information of future generations. The *Op art* of the 1960's created complex geometric designs of contrasting materials, forms and colours. The optical vibrations produced by these patterns tire the eyes. Such designs can be produced mechanically by computers. *Psychedelic art* followed soon after, with unendurably brilliant colours produced under the influence of drugs. About the same time *Process and Conceptual* art introduced the audience into electronically controlled sensory perceptions. Thus by using electronic equipment, drugs, computers, ready-made objects and photography to produce his work, the artist makes himself more and more superflaous since his creativity depends on other media, not on his own genius. Critics feel that the so-called modern period has exhausted itself since nothing really original is being produced.

While the pioneers of modern art struggled in poverty and obscurity, the academic artists were popular and their art was considered fashionable. Later the tables were turned and the academic artists were ridiculed and ignored. So it may be that in spite of present fashions, artists now working in obscurity are creating great work. Thus *M. Prendergast*, one of the most original American painters, gained recognition only very late. Like a counterpoint, the mosaic-like touches and tones of his surfaces seem to answer each other, and the structures of his child-like paintings look flat and multidimensional at the same time. He liked to portray children at play. An example of his work is *Central Park* (1901), in the Whitney Maseum, New York. *C. Dufresne*, who had great influence over young painters with his passionate, sweeping rhythms, reacted against the fragmentation of subjects and had the courage to paint religious themes. *Lion Hunt* (1932) in the Lew Fox Collection, Chicago, exemplifies his work. *A. Dunoyer* produced joyful work free of the contemporary restlessness. At the risk of being outdated, he refused to give in to the pressures of fashionable theories, but retained unity and harmony in his work. *J. Pougny*, of Russian origin, had a technique of his own which eludes analyis. He ranks among the best in suggesting atmosphere and feeling by simple touches of colour. *G. Sutherland*, a leader among modern English painters, designed the tapestry of *Christ in Majesty* for the restored Coventry cathedral (1962). The Brazilian *C. Portinari* abandoned what he learned in Paris in order to paint the mystery and inner joy of the 'forgotten men' who taught him what is most authentic. He produced the large panels of *War and Peace* (1953–5) given to the UNO, and decorated churches designed by O. Niemeyer. These, and some among the numerous amateur artists of our time, may some day be raised from their present obscurity, as the first modern artists finally gained recognition.

A new art always begins with the discoveries of geniuses who refuse to imitate the fashionable styles of their times, but it always takes time for people to overcome their preferences for modes to which they have become conditioned especially through the mass media. After them come the minor artists who perfect their work. But once a style reaches perfection it deteriorates into academic imitation and conventionalisation, as the history of art demonstrates over and over again. So it happened with Renaissance art, which perfected naturalism by means of chiaroscuro and perspective, but could not hold its own against the quicker and more economical photography. But even before the invention of photography Renaissance art had gradually degenerated through the over-emotional Baroque, the frivolous Rococo, the sentimental Romanticism and the political propaganda of Neo-Classicism. Photography gave it the death-blow, so to say. So too modern art, which started as a reaction against the academy, has itself become academic by consolidating into movements. Critics now expect artists to belong to some movement before they are given recognition. Moreover the mass media have made the public more and more conformist to current fashions and the complexity of modern conditions has led to ever greater collectivisation.

Public standards of taste and opinion are now moulded largely by the commercialised mass media which reduce rather than raise the popular taste by pandering to human weaknesses—our desires for sensation, thrills, change and novelty. Whereas the classical Greeks perfected a few simple elements, the degenerate Greeks always looked for something new, to be avant-garde as many in our present society. Through advertisements people are brainwashed with the fear of being outdated and the craving for status by being sophisticated and high-brow. Dealers, concerned with commercial rather than aesthetic values, dictate art fashions as in the clothing business. In no other period of art history do we find style-shoppers like Picasso and Matisse, and shifting ephemeral modes as in the modern period. Van Gogh had remarked that many of the blasé rich as well as speculators purchase costly paintings because they are fashionable, not for their artistic value. Thus art has been prostituted to money and affectation. It has been reduced to a market commodity. As academic art, popular with the rich bourgeoisie, did not represent the best of its time, so now it is questionable whether the collections in museums and galleries made by moneyed backers represent the choice productions of our time. To earn a livelihood in this competitive set-up, artists too resort to questionable methods of promoting their work, trying to shock in order to get attention.

Before the invention of photography in 1826 and the introduction of mass education later in the century, the representational artists had rendered a very useful service to society both as visual memory and as one of the chief means of educating the illiterate. As the invention of the printing press all but destroyed the fine arts of calligraphy and manuscript illumination, and as mechanisation caused many artistic handicrafts to die out, so cameras, or machines for making pictures, and education by means of abstract written symbols instead of pictures, forced artists to turn their talents from the represenation of nature and life to discover new subjects beyond the reach of this new invention, such as the contents of the human psyche—the emotions, the mind, the instincts, the imagination and the subconscious. More and more they turned to design itself, to impose an order of their own making on the chaotic condition of society, and to seek in abstraction a basic simplicity and structure in an increasingly complex and insecure world. To express their inner experience without the use of images, they invented abstract symbols of their own, a new personal language which only an initiated elite could understand. As a result they failed to communicate with the majority of the new democratic society, forming aesthetic aristocracies or bohemian castes that reacted against each other in order to catch the attention of the dealers. Whereas the strict discipline required by the representational arts had attracted only the really gifted to this profession, the modern movements drew very many to the trade by their professed freedom from all restrictions. Unlike other workers who gradually formed unions to obtain their rights, artists remain more or less isolated or form small groups. They no longer have a sense of community—of people with and for whom they work, and so they have no exact standards answering to social needs. They became more and more divorced from society, escaping into the ivory towers of their studios, producing still-lifes and nudes and cultivating unintelligibility, speaking to themselves and a small coterie of 'elites'.

Europe's most original and glorious artistic creation was also born, like modern art, in France, especially in the vicinity of Paris, and in its time it was also called modern or French work. During the Renaissance it was contemptuously dubbed Gothic or barbarian by those who reverted to the ancient Graeco-Roman ideals. Unlike modern art, Gothic was truly democratic, everyone contributing his best. Artists formed an integral part of the free society of the new towns and they agreed on beauty, as philosophy and religion agreed on truth. Though feudalism divided them politically, they were united in faith which gave each one the same dignity as children of the heavenly Father; and the guilds, a form of worker's union, provided them with economic security. W. Morris and the Bauhaus tried to revive the spirit of the guilds but they failed because the unifying power of faith has been gradually abandoned in favour of individualism and self-interest. The Bauhaus had employed painters like Klee to train designers, because Gropius and his followers believed that painting had outlived its utility. By streamlining useful objects, modern artists did away with old-fashioned ornaments and designs. Thus they made artistic experimentation useful as scientific research leads to technological improvements. By bringing artists together with business men, the Werkbund and the Bauhaus integrated art into the age of machines and destroyed the barrier between the fine and applied arts. They helped artists find an outlet for their gift for design in creating beautiful and useful things for present needs instead of retreating into ivory towers of non-intelligibility.

In the 1920's the Mexican government too encouraged artists by welcoming everyone to the capital, where artists worked in solidarity and real friendship with the other workers and received the same wages. Though the press and public attacked them furiously, they carried on under the leadership of D. *Siqueiros*. He opposed art for art's sake and stressed that art should have a social function. Lack of government interest in the next decade however turned artists away from the people to serve the tourist trade instead. The Federal Art Project during the Depression in the United States gave artists relative economic security and a feeling of being a part of society. As a result artists adopted a more communicable artistic language and produced a more healthy art, very different from the individualistic approach before this. Unfortunately the project was given up.

## SCULPTURE

*A. Rodin,* the greatest of nineteenth century sculptors and of international renown, used the *Impressionist technique* in his work, making the surfaces catch and disperse light. This use of light in sculpture makes the solidity of the figures dissolve in a visual diversion. Seeing the expressive power in Michelangelo's unfinished works he left some of his figures incomplete and thus pointed the way to the later fragmentation of the human body in modern sculpture. His ideal was no longer beauty but vitality. He refused to idealise or to make his figures completely realistic like those in a wax museum. Rather he preferred to suggest, such as successive positions at the same time.

The son of a French bureaucrat, Rodin did not do well at school and three times the principal art school in Paris refused to accept him. He did hackwork until he was almost forty. Through obscurity, unpopularity and depreciation he worked himself up to world-wide fame. *The Age of Bronze* (1877) was his first exhibited work.

Though he admired Michelangelo who believed that a true sculptor should cut away from a block, Rodin was essentially a modeller like many modern artists. The art of cutting, which is much more difficult, is almost lost. Rodin rarely carved his own marbles and never cast his bronzes, but handed his models over to assistants. His bronzes retain the squashy thumbmarks of his swiftly finished clay models. One of his most moving works is the bronze group *The Burghers of Calais* (1886; Rodin Museum, Paris) recalling the siege of that town by Edward III of England. The inhabitants finally surrendered after a heroic resistance of several months. Angered by the long delay, Edward had determined to raze the city to the ground but six of the leading citizens offered their lives to save it. Moved by the pleadings of his queen, Edward spared both them and the city. Rodin's work shows the citizens approaching the conqueror. Their threadbare clothes reveal how the siege emaciated their bodies. Still more significant are their facial expressions and gestures as, each in his own way, they face what they regard as certain death.

Rodin's *Monument to Balzac* (1897) shows daring distortions and emphases. The sketchlike features are merely suggested. After a number of studies Rodin chose to clothe his subject in the loose-fitting robe that Balzac often wore while working. When displayed it was dubbed 'bear in a bag' or 'snowman'. But by enveloping the short fat body and stretching it into an altogether grander one he makes the author of 'The Human Comedy' appear in a most significant pose. Thus Rodin became a leader in sculpture.

*The Gates of Hell* (1900), commissioned by an American, does not illustrate the doom of Dante's 'Inferno' as much as worldly despair and exhaustion. Rodin's famous *Thinker* was originally intended to be Dante sitting over the doorway in the centre composing his great epic. The aggressively projecting figures on the doorway, with their sudden changes of scale, speak of disorder and frustration. *The Kiss* was intended to be part of this group.

Through his sculptures of dancers and horses, the painter *Degas* wanted to experiment with form and movement. His best-known work, *The Little Dancer of Fourteen* (Fig. 471) shows his desire to catch the realities of daily life. This was the only sculpture he exhibited in his lifetime.

*A. Maillol* opposed Rodin's fleeting effects of broken planes and light. An admirer of Gauguin, he tried to simplify his figures and modelled them smoothly so that they reflect the light evenly. *A. Hildebrand,* among the few who stressed direct cutting, had a good effect on the technical development of sculpture. *W. Lehmbruck,* influenced by Rodin's later distortions, made his figures very thin and long. *M. Rosso's* violently dynamic style influenced the *Futurists,* whose best work is seen in the sculptures of *U. Boccioni.* His *Anti-Graceful* (1912), representing his own mother, shows a wide

Fig. 471. E. Degas: The little dancer of fourteen.

range of facial expressions, according to the viewpoint. The head is composed of a series of intersecting curves. The shapes of distant houses combine with the form of the head. His highly original *Development of a Bottle in Space* (1912) anticipates Picasso's 'Glass of Absinthe' by two years. Through rhythmic spiral forms he represents the inner space of the bottle to suggest the transparency of the glass. Boccioni's most famous work, his *Unique Forms of Continuity in Space* (1913) comes nearest to the Futurist ideal. The figure, made of surging forms, strides forward boldly. With its broken contours and surface and its expanded form, it gives the impression of the blurred glimpse of a swiftly moving object. The artists stresses the dynamic movement rather than the appearance of the figure. Superficially it resembles the Nike of Samothrace.

*Picasso's* bronze *Head of a Woman* (1909) was the first attempt to translate analytical Cubism into sculpture. The basic planes, which eliminate the play of light and shade, reinforce the solidity of the form. *The Glass of Absinthe* (1914: Fig. 472), with a real spoon balanced on top, was the first example of an assemblage. By mixing varied objects he moved away from the abstract forms of Cubism. In the 1920's Picasso popularised Russian Constructivism but he always kept the human touch in his own work. His iron figures resemble the totems or fetishes of animistic cults. This animistic tendency or *Vitalism* became one of the chief features of modern sculpture. Amid the dehumanisation of the machine age, the creators of this sculpture seek a sense of superiority over the machine by endowing it with the 'magic' power to arouse collective emotions or to give them an outlet. During this same period

Fig. 472. P. Picasso: The glass of absinthe.

other magical tribal arts, like jazz and rock music and dances, were revived in the urban asphalt and concrete jungles. Picasso's *Iron Head Construction* (1930) was his first totem with magical intention. By reconstructing figures out of scrap iron pieces, they seemed to come to life with a magically new personality while keeping the origins visible in order to emphasise the transformations. In 1930 he also invented wire space cages. By enclosing space within outlines of wire, he completely transformed the traditional idea of sculpture as characterised by solidity and weight. In his 'transparent sculpture' he tried to show both the outside and inside of an object. In 1931 he invented statuettes resembling long sticks.

*Matisse's* four figures called *The Back*, one made in 1909 in the style of Rodin and the last in 1929 after the Cubist fashion, reveal the great change in sculpture during that short period. By constant simplification and elimination of details Matisse became a master of suggestion. He exaggerated and distorted in order to stress the inner tension of the muscles.

Influenced by Picasso's three-dimensional collages which he saw in Paris in 1913, the Russian *V. Tatlin* decided to apply engineering techniques to sculpture by eliminating all representation and all recognizable objects. Thus he created the first completely abstract sculpture, called 'constructions', and started the influential *Constructivist* or *Suprematist* movement. In 1920 Tatlin exhibited his spiralling *Model for a Monument to the Third International.* An iron and concrete framework supported a body consisting of a glass cylinder, cone, pyramid and cube, all suspended on a dynamic asymmetrical axis like a leaning Eiffel tower. It was intended to be twice the size of the Empire State Building, and the three main sections (for cultural, scientific, administrative and political activities) were to revolve at various speeds, ranging from one revolution daily to one yearly. Russia, however, could not afford the luxury of art for art's sake, and because the masses could not understand abstract art, the government banned it in 1922. Tatlin gave up art to engage in productive engineering. The others chose artistic freedom and some of them joined the Bauhaus.

The brothers *A. Pevsner* and *N. Gabo* left Russia in search of artistic freedom. They used modern materials to make their work more relevant for our industrialised culture. Gabo, a bold originator, used plastics and nylon to allow space the freedom to pass through the transparent material. In his *Linear Construction* (1950), made of plastic and nylon thread, he tried to represent the world of nuclear physics where solids and voids, ambiguously related, seem no more than mathematical expressions. *Construction in Space* (1953) shows the crystal-like precision so characteristic of his work. To the dimension of space he also tried to add that of time or movement with his *Kinetic Sculpture* (1920) where he created 'volume' by vibrating an upright metal rod by means of an electric motor.

The ideals of abstract Constructivist art, which applies engineering techniques to sculpture, correspond with those of the International Style. Like architecture it is an 'art of hollows'. For Le Corbusier a house was a 'machine for living'; Constructivist 'sculptures' may be described as 'machines for contemplation', though the emphasis of their forms is not necessarily on beauty but on dynamism—of the parts interrelated in perfect tension. These constructions in space, which have no useful purpose, do represent an optimistic and positive reaction to the general disillusionment and anxiety of the modern world, a search for a new civilisation founded on an affirmative view of life. Gabo's aim in his constructions was to represent good as against evil, order against chaos, life against death. He believed that humanity, with the poison of hate as its daily food and having learned to kill with ease, was mortally ill. Through his art of unity and harmony he wanted to relieve the pain and prevent despair, to remind the world that it can be different and to combat the mass neurosis that afflicted mankind since the fifteenth century. Thus Constructivist art, unlike most other modern movements, was based on a sense of public responsibility instead of being an escape from reality. The Constructivists carried on research into the basic physical elements in order to discover the functional and aesthetic possibilities of the new industrial materials like plexiglass, and thus they had great influence not only on architecture but especially on domestic articles like furniture. Thus their art was related to the crafts and engineering.

Unlike Gabo's kinetic sculpture which required a motor, the American *A. Calder* produced the first *mobiles*, so delicately balanced that the slightest breeze could play with the parts according to a pattern. Witty and sprightly like the paintings of Klee and Miró, they are generally non-representative. His gracefully precise *Horizontal Spines* (1942) is made of fine steel wires, which combine and contrast in continuously changing relationships with pointed flat shapes. The Swiss *J. Tinguely's Painting Machine* (1959) poked fun at the Abstract Expressionist paintings of the time by showing how they could be produced mechanically.

The Hungarian L. *Moholy-Nagy* produced the first plexiglass and chromium sculpture in 1943, and did much to develop the interweaving of shapes. Very inventive, he studied colour transparencies and for this reason he started using plexiglass to replace pigments with coloured light. Like some of the Russian Constructivists he joined the Bauhaus.

The son of a Rumanian peasant, C. *Brancusi* settled in Paris where despite his love of seclusion, his relatively few works and rare exhibitions, he became one of the foremost modern sculptors who exercised a wide influence. His works, free of anxiety, show the beauty of simplicity and clarity of form. He liberated the beauty of balance and symmetry from the extravagant tendencies of vitalism. His works reflect the austerity and simplicity of his own life. They show not only vitality but order. He paid careful attention to refined surface finish, proportions and contours. The vitality of his art came from the child-like qualities which he treasured. He stated, 'When we stop being children we're already dead'. He believed that one arrives at simplicity naturally 'as one approaches the real meaning of things'. For him shapes had to be perfect in order to be worthy of the human spirit. He established one feature of modern sculpture—respect for the qualities of materials. From this comes purity of shape, the perfect harmony between content and form. He had an exact knowledge of the structure and laws of materials. To him the lengthened ovoid form seemed the most natural. All his later sculptures are variations on this basic shape. His forms, which are types rather than individuals, derive from living things—he kept close to nature. Universal harmony was his ideal. He wanted architecture to become 'inhabited sculpture'. The two examples of *Sleeping Muse* (1906, 1909) shows the rapid evolution of his art towards simplification and the ovoid shape; similarly his *bird* (1912) and *Bird in Space* (1919). In the latter the ideas of form and flight are exquisitely combined, and he succeeds much better than the Futurists to realise their aim to represent pure movement. The form gives the impression of the bird's upward dart and has the streamlined shape inspired by aerodynamics. His 'thinking hand discovering the thoughts of materials' inspired Barbara Hepworth. For her, Brancusi and Moore, the ideal form was the human. Brancusi belonged to no movement or school.

Despite his *Dada* affiliation, the Alsatian *J. Arp* shared with Brancusi a love of natural simplicity, perfection of form and lack of artificiality. To the frenzied age of machines his works bring a soothing calm spiced with humour. In his sculptures called *Concretions* he imitated the processes of nature. The other Dada sculptors produced machines with no other function than to mock technology and science.

One of the most important *Expressionist* sculptors and playwrights, *E. Barlach* is noted chiefly for his soul-stirring *War Memorial for Gūstrow Cathedral* (1927). He depicts the human soul hovering between earth and heaven, about to open its eyes on eternal life. The plain, abstracted form of the body directs the attention to the exquisite face, where the distress of war gives way to freedom from anguish through the hope of salvation. Rarely has this theme been expressed as poignantly as in this piece of sculpture. Barlach was a sculptor in the actual sense of the word—he believed in carving. He took his inspiration from the intensely spiritual and unsophisticated Nordic tradition, where realism did not complicate the abstract shapes. His sharp-featured but smoothly finished forms show intense expression and action, deeply filled with religious belief. Other Expressionist sculptors include *G. Marcks* and *K. Kollwitz*. The latter's sculptures, such as *The Complaint* (1938) shows the same compassion as her graphic works.

With his *Woman Combing her Hair* (1915) the Russian *A. Archipenko* showed that hollows can act as powerfully as the solids hitherto associated with sculpture. The arm raised over the torso outlines the shaped or 'negative' or empty space where the head should be. The Englishman *H. Moore* used this *technique of meaningful hollows* very much in his work. By carving holes through sculpture he tried to shape stone as nature does by erosion. These hollows represent 'the mysterious fascination of caves in hillsides and cliffs' and give the impression of letting space into the composition. He felt that a hole can have as much shape and meaning as solid mass. Sometimes the hole in the stone represented the intended form. His most characteristic sculpture is based on this: his 'biomorphic' forms seem eroded away like smallscale models of time-worn landscapes. He also studied the formation of stones, trees, shells and bones to see nature's way of shaping things. He found that the contours of stone depend on their inner structure and cohesion and that symmetry does not enter into its nature. This led to his using the forms and textures of his materials as suggestions for his representations. Like Brancusi and Arp, he respected nature and tried to form his conceptions in the shapes natural to the materials with which he worked. But unlike them he was less simple. In natural objects he discovered universal forms with human connotations and based his work on the shapes suggested. The human figure interested him most because in the urban culture of our times, man and his work take on greater importance. He distorted the human figures, however, in order to show their relationship to the natural formations. His first concern was the material (its texture, hardness, structure and reaction to erosion and tools) rather than the subject, though he retained an instinctive respect for the dignity of the human figure. His sculptures look as if they had been shaped by nature's energy, eroded by the weather or tunnelled into by wind and water. He tried to form a bridge between the ancient traditions of pre-historic, Egyptian and Mexican art through his deference to the material which should retain its identity rather than resemble living flesh. After 1930 this respect for the material made him represent it as if it were propelled by an inner energy of its own. This led him to open up the sculptural mass more and more. But however much he eroded the mass, weight was his point of departure. Gravity came first for him. He always thought from the ground upwards. In some of his works his figures rise like mountains from a low point of view.

Moore did not aim at beauty which pleases only the senses but at the deeper level of spiritual vitality. He wanted to penetrate to life's meaning in order to arouse greater courage for living. His works have a pent-up power as in primitive sculptures. Because he wanted his art to inspire people, not just for decoration, he preferred to have his sculptures in the open for all to see rather than in museums. Two or three archetypal forms—reclining figures, mother and child, and the family—fascinated him so much that for many years he used these motifs over and over again. From his first *Reclining Figure* of 1929 to the last in 1963, the long series of forms do not vary much, only the materials, method, scale, surface and accent. All these, with one exception, are female figures. They always prop themselves up to show their inherent energy, the immanent spiritual essence behind the outer appearance. He saw this not only in the human form but in the growth of crystals and in erosion by wind and water. His intimate *Mother and Child* (1960) combines strength and protectiveness, power and tenderness. This theme suited his love for asymmetry, the counterpoint of void and mass, the interaction of masses and interlocking of forms. His *Madonna and Child*, commissioned for St. Matthew's church, Northampton, combines calm gentleness, repose and ease with a noble, austere dignity and grandeur. His works in general show little anxiety. In his *Glenkiln Cross* (1955) he humanised the cross which stands on a deformed pedestal.

Moore preferred carving in stone, wood or cast concrete, but later he also turned to terracotta. After 1945 he worked chiefly in bronze.

His colleague, *Barbara Hepworth,* who showed a similar understanding and love for natural materials and forms, found that 'working realistically replenishes one's love of life, humanity and the earth' while 'working abstractedly seems to release one's personality and sharpen one's perceptions'.

The *Surrealist* sculptors selected objects found in rubbish for their 'magical' potency. They did not refer to them as sculpture but as 'objects'. They also constructed precise machines which had no purpose except to disturb. *Oppenheim's Fur Lined teacup* (1956) shows the illogical Surrealist combination of things, like Dali's drooping watches. During his Surrealist phase, *A. Giacometti,* a Swiss living in Paris, produced sad figures revealing an inner emptiness that nothing can fill. It could seek some relief only in an imprecise symbol to represent the emptiness. He preferred to use plaster since, according to Sartre, 'through plaster he creates emptiness out of fulness'. During the 1940's Giacometti turned away from Cubism and Surrealism to representative art. His touching figures mirror the alienation, confusion and bewilderment of modern man. The famous bronze *City Square* (1948) shows a group, each intent on his own thing, each walking abstractedly and never meeting the other. It reveals how only a short distance separates lonely individuals from others in a crowd. Thus it points to the modern individualism and alienation. The very long, pencil-thin figures become so narrow at certain angles that they almost disappear to show how people fade away from others without anyone noticing them. A comparison with Rodin's 'burghers of Calais' shows how greatly the artistic interpretation of man changed in half a century.

The period after the second world war has been called the 'new iron age' because modern civilisation relies much on metals for its machines and because most of the sculptors turned to *metal work*, which is less expensive and more lasting than wood or stone as well as being more quickly and easily adaptable to any shape. Like some architects, they make use of its rough qualities rather than giving it finish. Picasso put *J. Gonzalez* on the way to become the creator of iron sculpture by asking him for technical assistance in welding metal pieces. Until that time Gonzalez had not succeeded as a painter for many years. After this he became very influential through his many experiments with new materials and methods. He used the human figure as the starting point for his abstractions which resemble Abstract Expressionist paintings. D. *Smith* preferred the new stainless steel. He aimed at divorcing art entirely from the human element and to demonstrate the power and cruelty of metal. *R. Blanden* wanted to do away even with the artist and his signature. His *X*, intended to be made of iron, dominates the surroundings with its tremendous black form. *Cesar* produced his stack of compressed auto bodies by employing the machinery of demolition squads. Such rough, bleak shapes with their aggressive spikes have no other aim but to terrify the collective unconscious as they stand against the bare walls of functional architecture or in parks, for sculpture is meant for public display. Yet the public is not ready to accept such art. At present there is no natural exchange of appreciation and inspiration between the people and the artist. In all great art periods, this mutual exchange had been fundamental, but in modern times there is a divorce between the artist and the public leading to inspirational sterility or illegitimacy. In the classical tragedies the evil powers of hate and aggression in the human psyche were overcome by heroism which frees the soul of the dark powers within. The modern sculptors, however, irritate and wound rather than cure and heal. For instance *G. Richter's The Bat* (1952) shows a sinister natural form in the process of decay.

*E. Paolozzi* called some of his functionless constructions 'idols' because he intended them to become mechanical fetishes, as entrancing as those of a witch-doctor in order to free people from the increasing influence of functioning machinery. In his environmental *Pop art*, *Segal* brings the beholder into the situation represented by rough but realistic plaster figures associated with actual furniture, whereby he shows the isolation and spiritual alienation of modern man with great poignancy and a minimum of artifice.

All great art grows out of a unifying ideal. Faith in a loving God who helps man transcend himself inspired the great Gothic art, while the loss of faith liberated the worst in man. Absolutist rulers who put their faith in Humanism which idolises man, sacrificed human lives to feed their ambitions. The laissez-faire Liberalists who idolised money, sacrificed the welfare of their workers (called 'hands') to profits. Modern Individualists who idolise themselves, sacrifice everything to their self-interest, leading to chaos both in life and in the arts that mirror it. Artists try to escape from this outer chaos in the worship of art for art's sake, trying to find immediate sensuous enjoyment and permanence in the fetishes of their own making, to create order without restricting the liberty of their instincts, to better the world without trying to better themselves. Alienated from the Creator as never before in history, man becomes alienated from the rest of creation as well. Through a vague fear of losing his liberty and dignity, man turns against the One on whom human liberty and dignity depend—the God who made man in His own image in order to share His infinite life of selfless love. Modern artists distort this image of man given by the Creator and try to remake man in the image of their own fragmented and distorted vision. The injustices and wars that . bedevil human relationships reveal the evil powers that can take possession of man, the selfishness and cruelty of which man is capable. The vivid realism of art such as Grünewald's, *Crucifixion*', reveals the terrible cruelty of man let loose upon the God-Man, who came to liberate man from evil by giving him another Model and life. But among popular modern artists there is no Grünewald—they add to the torment of man but offer no cure.

To judge the value of anything, art included, we must discover its purpose, and this purpose depends on man's own purpose. Art, a distinctively human creation, must serve man's purpose, as man, the greatest work of art (his creativity reflects the Creator) must serve the purpose of his Creator. A work of art that does not turn out according to the artist's wish is discarded. Art for art's sake is as meaningless a slogan as man for man's sake—which ends in the enslavement of the weak to the whims of the strong.

As science should enlighten the mind with certain aspects of truth so art should cheer the heart with beauty, uplift it with hope of something better and help man to transcend the limitations of this life. It should illustrate, that is literally, throw light to help us see better, to make us more sensitive, to brighten everything with understanding, wonder, admiration and contemplation of the immanence of the Divine in creation and His transcendence of all earthly limitations, so as to become a continuous pledge of joy and love and peace. Art should refine and contribute to human progress. According to Ruskin, the most genuine artists give permanence to the things we should always like to see without getting perturbed, since real works of art bring peace rather than excitement through their unity, harmony and rhythm. They arouse wonder and admiration. The value of art comes from the balanced, well-proportioned arrangement of colours and forms, whereas inferior works of art rely on emotion. Art should please by its absorbing fascination and enduring beauty.

# GLOSSARY

*(The Indian terms are printed in italics.)*

Abacus: (plural, abaci) in classic architecture, a flat slab or block, forming the crowning member of a capital; in the Greek Doric order, a flat square block resting on the echinus; in the Ionic order, a thin slab resting on the volutes; in the Corinthian capital, it has concave sides; in Romanesque and Gothic art, it has different forms. The word is applied to other styles: in Indian art, the round abaci of the Asokan columns; in south India, its equivalent is the *palagai*.

*Abhaṅga*: a standing posture with a slight bend, the weight of the body resting more on one leg than on the other; the commonest of flexed poses, especially used for female figures.

*Abhaya mudrā*: gesture of protection or reassurance; the open palm is held outwards and the extended fingers point downwards; often seen in representations of the Buddha.

Acanthus: a plant with large, deeply indented and sharply pointed leaves, growing in the Mediterranean countries, used as a conventionalized decoration in Greek, Roman, Byzantine, Romanesque and Neo-classical art.

Acropolis: (from Greek: akros, highest; polis, city) the top of a Greek fortified citadel, e.g., the Acropolis of Athens.

Acrostic: (from Greek: akros, extreme; stiohos, order, line) a composition, often in verse, in which the first letters taken in order form words, e.g. the IXTUS symbol of the Early Christians.

Acroterium: (plural, acroteria) block for the pedestal of a statue, on the top and lower corner of the pediment of a Greek temple; also the ornament or statue resting on these pedestals.

Aesthetics (in Greek: aisthetikcs, perceptive, sensitive) the part of philcsophy dealing with the beautiful.

Agora: (literally, an assembly) an open-air place in Greek cities for assemblies, usually surrounded by public buildings and colonnades. Its equivalent in Rome is the forum.

*Ain-i-Akbari*: a triple volume of work dealing primarily with a code of Akbar's regulations in all departments; including, besides some extraneous matter, a valuable and minute statistical account of his empire with historical and other notes.

Aisle: (in Latin: ala, wing) the side division in a building where the interior is divided by rows of columns or piers; usually lower and narrower than the central nave.

*Aiwan*: a hall surrounding the courtyard of an Islamic house.

*Akṣamālā*: prayer beads.

*Akṣasūtra*: string of beads.

*Alambana* (Ālambana): the base of the *vedikā* on which the *thāba* rests.

*Alidha* (Ālidha): pose of a warrior, with right leg bent forward and left leg drawn back.

*Alidhanṛtta* (Ālidhanṛtta): dance pose of Śiva seated in the *ālidhāsana.*

*Alidhāsana* (Ālidhāsana): the pose of archer in action, right knee is thrown in front while the left leg is retraetcd.

Altar: an elevated structure, usually a table, for purposes of worship.

Altarpiece: an ornamental screen behind the altar, either painted or sculptured, also called retable or reredos.

Ambulacra: long, generally low galleries in the Roman catacombs.

Ambulatory: literally, a place where one can walk, like a cloister or covered arcade; or in Gothic churches, the aisles surrounding the apse forming the chevet.

*Aml:* in Mughal painting; the filling of the existing *tarrah* or sketch with colour.

*Amman shrine*: a small pavilion for the ceremonial reception of the goddess or *amman*, the consort of the deity to whom the temple is dedicated.

Amphiprostyle: a building having a row of columns on both ends, front and back, but not on the sides.

Amphitheatre: (from Greek: amphi, on both sides; theatron, theatre) in Roman art, a building like two theatres facing each other; from the arena in the centre, tiers of seats rise against a huge protecting wall; used for combats, races and athletic contests.

Amphora: (from Greek: amphoreus:amphi, on both sides, phoreus, bearer) a jar or vase with two handles, an oval-shaped body and a narrow cylindrical neck; used for storage purposes.

*Amlā* or *āmalaka*: (in Sanskrit: the fruit of the Indian gooseberry—phyllantus emblica) a huge flattened ribbed disc of that shape, which forms one of the crowning elements of north Indian temples.

*Aṇḍa:* (Sanskrit for egg) the solid hemisphere forming the body of the *stūpa*

*Andhakāsuravadhamūrti*: Śiva destroying the demon of darkness —the *Andhakāsura.*

*Anga śtkhara*: miniature replica of the śikhara, clustered round it.

*Anguliya*: ring or toe-ring.

*Aniyoṭṭikkal*: a main central shaft of a pillar surrounded either by a series of small columns or with large animal sculpture; characteristic of the Vijayanagar period.

*Anjali mudrā*: a gesture of salutation, with hands folded palm to palm.

*Antarāla*: (in Sanskrit: intermediate space) the narrow vestibule in the Hindu temple, connecting the inner shrine with the *maṇḍapa.*

*Antevāsika*: apprentice, student.

Anthropomorphic: representation or conception of God under human form, with human attributes and affections.

*Anurāha-pāga*: in Orissan architecture, the projection near the *rāha-pāga* on the *gāṇḍī ,* in the saptaratha *temple.*

*Anuratha-pāga*: in Orissan architecture, the projection on the *gāṇḍī* between the *rāhā-pāga* and konaka-pāga*, in the pañcharatha temple.*

*Apsarā*: (from Sanskrit, meaning 'one who came from the water') female semi-divine being.

Apse: a recess, mostly semicircular, sometimes polygonal, projecting from the end of a building; usually roofed by a semi-dome. First used in the Roman civil basilica. In the Early Christian basilica, it contained the bishop's throne and seats for the clergy. In the Early Christian and Byzantine churches, it was decorated with beautiful mosaics.

Aqueduct: (from Latin: aqua, water; ductus, a leading) channels to conduct water from a spring or river through tunnels in hilly countries, and high bridge-like arches over valleys and rivers to the required places. Especially famous are the Imperial Roman aqueducts, and the Pont du Gard near Nîmes, France.

Arcade: a series of arches supported by columns or pillars, carrying a roof, an upper storey or a clerestory wall.

Arcading: rows of small arcades, used especially during the Romanesque period for decoration, usually built against a wall.

Arch: an architectural device to span an opening with small wedge-shaped stones (voussoirs),
capable of supporting a superimposed load; usually round, though the shape is of no importance.

Architect: (from Greek: archi, chief; tekton, workman) a person skilled in architecture, who makes plans and designs for buildings, and supervises the construction.

Architecture: the knowledge and skill of building edfices for public and private needs; different methods and styles of building; building construction in general.

Architrave: chief beam; in Greek and Roman architecture, the lowest part of the entablature; the lintel or beam resting on the capitals of the columns.

Archivolt: a moulding on the face of an arch, which follows its curved contour.

Arcosoiium: in the catacombs, an important tomb with an arch above.

Arcuated: a system of architecture, where the building is supported on arches, in contrast with the trabeated system, where vertical posts carry horizontal beams.

*Ardha- maṇḍapa*: (from Sanskrit: *ardha.* half, *maṇḍapa* hall) a pillared hall, usually smaller in size than the *maṇḍapa* in the Hindu temple: also entrance porch.

*Ardhoruka*: knee-lenth lower garment.

Arena: (from Latin; sand, sandy place) in Roman amphitheatres, the lowest open space where the combats took place, spread with sand to absorb blood.

Arris: sharp edges formed by the meeting of two curved surfaces, e.g. the flutings of the Doric columns.

*Arydka* (Āryaka): sacred pillars symbolizing the five Dhyāni Buddhas as seen in Amaravati.

*Asana* (Āsana): seat, usually with a sloping back.

Ashlar: a masonry walling, where the blocks of stone are carefully cut into squared blocks, and the smooth surfaces laid in regular courses with fine joints.

*Aśhram* or *Aśrama* (Āśrama): (from Sanskrit; *śrama,* to remove fatigue) hermitage.

*Aṣtapartvārālaya*: a central shrine, surrounded by eight sub-shrines, disposed both in the cardinal and corner directions.

Astylar: (literally, without columns) a treatment of façade or other important positions without columns; as opposed to columnar, with columns.

*Atibhaṅga*: (from Sanskrit: *bhaṇga*, bent; *ati*, very much) greatly bent—the tribhaṅga pose greatly emphasised.

Atrium: a small open court in the centre of Greek and Roman houses; in Early Christian basilicas, the open court surrounded with covered cloisters in front of the entrance of the church.

Attic: in classical monuments, a small storey built above the cornice of the entablature; it may be a mere blank wall as on the Roman triumphal arches, or it may have windows; popularly the part of a building directly under the roof.

Aureole: (also aureola) see halo.

*Avadāna*: (literally, 'heroic deed') an anthology of legends describing the heroic and pious works of Buddhist saints; stories of past and present lives of Buddhist saints.

*Avalokitesvara*: the *Bodhisattava* who presides over the present era.

*Ayaka* (Āyaka) or *āryaka:* five columns, standing on the projecting platforms on the four sides of some *stūpas*, e.g., stūpa of Amaravati.

*Ayudha* (Āyudha): weapon, emblem of the deity above the *kalaśa* on the *śikhara* of the Hindu temple.

*Bāda*: in Orissan architecture, the cubical portion of the *rekhā deul* enclosing the sanctuary *or* garbhagriha.

*Bagh*: an Islamic garden.

*Bāhuvalaya*: bracelet on upper arm above elbow.

Bailey: a court enclosed by the outer wall or bail in a medieval castle,

Baldacchino or baldaquin: in Christian churches, a canopy suspended over the altar, or episcopal throne, e.g. Bernini's bronze baldacchino in St. Peter's Basilica, Rome.

Balnea: in Latin: baths.

*Bāndhanā*: in Orissan architecture, moulding on the *jāṅgha,* which divides it into the *tala jāṅgha* and ūpar jāṅgha.

*Bangaldār*: a Bengali type of vaulted roof.

Baptistery: a building containing a baptismal font; during the Early Christian period, when Baptism was being administered by immersion, a marble basin was sunk into the floor, e.g. the baptistery of Constantine near the Lateran Basilica in Rome.

*Baradari*: pillared rooms in an Islamic garden palace.

*Bāramāsa*: (literally the twelve months') a cycle of poems which illustrates the behaviour and feelings of lovers during each of the twelve months.

*Baraṇḍa*: in Orissan architecture, the topmost moulding of the *bāda,* separating it from the *gāṇḍī*

Barrel-vault: an unbroken, tunnel-like, arched roof of masonry.

Basilica: in Roman architecture, an oblong budding with nave and aisles for business transactions and the administration of justice; in the Early Christian church, with nave and aisles ending in an apse, with an altar at the end of the nave.

Bas-relief: French term for low relief.

Bastion: usually a rounded projecting part of a fortification.

Battered: a decisive slope or slant in a wall.

Battlement: the parapet wall in a medieval fortification, built with indentations or embrasures alternating in higher and lower parts so that the archer may be sheltered by the higher part (merlon) whilst discharging his arrow over the lower part (crenel) of the parapet; the whole also called crenelation.

Bay: a compartment or section into which the nave of a building is divided.

Beam: a large, long timber, like a squared tree trunk; in architecture, it can be of any material;
used as a horizontal structural member placed on two or more supports.

*Beki*: in north Indian temples, the recessed circular portion on the top of the tower on which the *āmlā* rests.

Bema: a step, a raised place; in Greece, the platform for Athenian orators; in Early Christian basilicas, the raised sanctuary.

*Bhadra*: in Orissan and central Indian temples, flat horizontal markings on the face of the *śikhara* or tower.

*Bhadrāsana*: a sitting posture, with legs crossed and toes held by the hands.
*Bhavan*: house, mansion.
*Bhikshu* or *bhikku*: Buddhist mendicant or monk.
*Bhitti*: the principal wail between the basement and entablature of south Indian temples.
*Bhoga maṇḍapa*: in Orissan architecture, the hall of offerings.
*Bhujaṇga valaya*: bracelet in the form of a snake.
*Bhūmi*: (from Sanskrit: plane, storey) in Orissan architecture, the sections into which the *gāṇḍī* of the *rekhā deul* is divided; in south Indian architecture, the diminishing stcreys of the pyramidal tower of the *vimāna*.
*Bhūmi āmlā*: in Orissan architecture, the small sectional *āmlā* which crowns the *bhūmis*.
*Bhūmi sparśa mudrā*: earth-touching attitude, with the right hand touching the ground; the Buddha's earth-touching gesture, to call earth to witness all his good deeds.
*Bhūtas*: (from Sanskrit bhûta, meaning 'a being') goblins.
*Bihari Lal*: a 16th century Mathura poet who composed the *Sat* Sai, or seven hundred couplets on the Krishna legend.
*Bisama*: (from Pali, meaning 'not equal') the flat square slab, which closes the *śikhara* of the Hindu temple.
Blind arcade: an arcade used merely as decoration before a wall; therefore it cannot be seen through.
*Bodhisatva*: an enlightened being who has acquired *bodhi* (enlightenment) and *satva* (its very essence) but does not enter into *nirvāṇa* as he wishes to guide mankind to the true path.
Boss: (from French; bosse: bump, swelling) in Gothic architecture, a knob-like carved block of stone at the intersection of the ribs of a vault.
Bottega: an artist's workshop in Italy, where training was also given to apprentices.
Bracket: a projecting member from a wall or column to support weight; also named corbel in medieval architecture.
Bracket capital: see *potikā*.
Brise soleil: sunbreak.
Broken pediment: whilst the normal pediment has the form of a low triangle with unbroken lines, in the broken pediment the apex is omitted, as often seen in Baroque architecture.
*Burj*: towers at the corners of the Islamic garden enclosure.
Buttress: a masonry support built vertically at intervals against the outer face of a wall to resist the outward pressure or thrust of a vault, or sometimes merely to strengthen a wall.

Calidarium: in the Roman thermae, the room with the hot water bath.
Calligraphy: (Greek: kaios, good; graphein, to write) fair writing, decorative handwriting.
Campanile: bell tower; in Italy they are separate from the church building; elsewhere they form part of it; in France, the two towers of the façade led to specially beautiful developments of the latter.
Canopy: see baldacchino
Cantilever: a projecting member supported only on one end.
Capital: (from Latin: capitalis, belonging to the head) the upper part of the column, wider than the shaft of the column, to take the weight from the entablature, to which it forms the transition; their manner of carving and decoration distinguishes the styles to which they belong.
Cartouches: a scroll-shaped ornament.
Caryatid: (from Greek: karyatides, the attending maidens of Artemis at Caryae in Laconia) in architecture, draped standing figures of maidens supporting the entablature in place of columns, e.g. the Maiden's Porch of the Erechtheion, in Athens.
Castle: (from Latin: castellum; diminutive of castrum, a fort) in French, chateau; in Italian, castello; a strong building mainly used as a means of defence in the medieval period.
Catacomb: (from Greek: kata, down; kumbe, a hollow) underground cemeteries, consisting of galleries, with niches on the sides for burial purposes.
Cathedra: a chair; the seat of a bishop in a cathedral.
Cenotaph: (from Greek: kenos, empty; taphos, tomb) a funeral monument erected for someone who is not buried there.
Centering: a temporary framework needed for the building of a masonry arch or vault.
Ceramic: pottery or earthenware.
*Chaitya* arch: an arch shaped like a horseshoe, usually fronting the entrance of a chaitya temple.

*Chaitya* hall: a sanctuary, the place of religious worship for the Buddhists, containing the *stūpa.*
*Chajja* or *chhajja*: overhanging eave or sunshade.
*Chandra-śilā*: (literally, a moonstone) lowest doorstep before the shrine.
Chapter house: a place for common assembly in a monastery.
*Char bagh*: an Islamic garden laid out according to a square plan and divided into four sections.
*Chatra* or chhatra: umbrella, parasol.
*Chatrāvali* or *chhatrāvali*: row of honorific umbrellas, e.g. those set on the top of the *stūpa.*
*Chattri* or *chhattri*: in Islamic architecture, a colonnaded pavilion with a dome.
*Chatulatilakamaṇi*: jewel in the centre of the turban.
*Chatura* mode: similar to the *lalita* mode, but with both legs bent and both feet resting on the ground. The left foot is used to beat time to the music.
*Chatura mudrā*: both arms bent and hands brought close to each other in front of the chest, with thumb touching the middle finger and the little finger at 90° to the other fingers.
*Chaturmukha*: (literally, four faces) shrines of a *vimāna* which has entrances on all the four sides.
*Chatustala*: (from *chatus*, meaning four, and *tala*, meaning storey) four storeys.
*Chaurapañcāsika:* (literally, fifty stanzas of secret love) a poem in Sanskrit written by Bilhana, a Kashmiri poet (1100 A.D.), illustrating his secret love for the king's daughter.
*Chauri*: a fly whisk; an insignia of royalty.
Chevet: (from Latin: capitium, head covering) the sanctuary—usually the eastern end of a Gothic church, with the apse surrounded by one or two ambulatories and flanked with radiating chapels.
Chevron folds: folds in the drapery shaped like the Greek letter Omega'.
*Chihra-numa*: portrait, in Mughal painting.
Chiton: a Greek garment.
Choir: (from Latin; chorus; French: choeur) in architecture, the part of the church reserved for the singers
*Choli*: blouse, short-sleeved bodice.
Chorus: the group of singers or dancers in Greek dramas.
Chryselephantine: a special method in Greek sculpture, combining thin plates of ivory to represent the skin and finely beaten plates of gold for draperies, fixed on an inner framework; e.g. Phidias' Athena Parthenos at Athens and the Zeus of Olympia.
*Chūḍāmaṇṇi*: crest jewel worn on the head by women.
Chute: a narrow sloping passage by which water falls from a higher to a lower level.
*Cin* or *chin mudrā*: gesture to signify instruction by silent contemplation; the thumb and forefinger touch to form a circle with the other three fingers kept open, while the palm faces outwards.
Ciborium: liturgical cup with a cover, for keeping the Holy Eucharist in reserve; in Early Chris tian art, a masonry canopy upheld by four columns above the high altar, later called baldaquin or canopy.
Circus: in Roman art, an oblong race course, semicircular at one narrower end, with a straight ending at the other entrance side, and a long low dividing wall, called spine, in the centre; around the track seats rose in tiers.
Citadel: a defense fortress, especially the one dominating a city.
Clerestory or clearstory: a way of lighting the interior of a building from above, by raising the roof of some parts over the neighbouring parts, and cutting windows in the vertical wails between the two levels of the ceiling.
Cloister: (from Latin: claudere, to close) a covered passage, usually around an open court, with arcades On the side of the court, and walled on the opposite side.
Clustered column: a column formed of several shafts joined or clustered together, each support having its separate task; especially used in Romanesque and Gothic art; also called compound support or compound pier.
Codex: a manuscript, where the pages are cut and bound together into a book.
Colonnade: a row of columns placed at regular intervals, usually carrying an entablature.
Column: a vertical architectural member, usually consisting of a base, shaft, and capital; gene rally circular in plan, often tapering upwards; at times polygonal or square at the base.
Composite order: a Roman architectural order, where the capital is a combination of the Ionic and Corinthian capitals; the upper part having the Ionic volute and the lower part the acanthus leaves of the Corinthian order.
Compound pier: see clustered column.

Compound support: see clustered column.
Corbel: see bracket.
Corbelling: a method of construction, where each successive block of stone projects a little beyond the one below, resembling an inverted step.
Cornice : the upper portion of the entablature in a classical building.
Crater: in Greek pottery, a jar with a wide mouth, large body and two small handles, used for mixing wine and water.
Cross vault: see groin vault.
Cubiculum: a large place in front of the arcosolium in the catacombs.
Cupola: a spherical or semi-circular roof resembling an inverted bowl, over angular or round supporting walls.
Curtain wall: an enclosing wall that gives no structural support.
Cyclopean walls: walls constructed out of massive uncut blocks of stone, as in the walls of the *city of* Rajgir.
Cylix: in Greek pottery, a drinking cup with two handles, a very large mouth and shallow body on a stand.
Cymatium: the crowning element of the entablature in a classical building.

*Dalan*: verandah of an Islamic house.
*Deccan*: plateau or tableland, c. 2000 feet altitude, covering much of peninsular India.
Decorated period or style: the phase in English Gothic following the Early English period, when the lancet windows of the latter were replaced with wider windows, divided on the top with mullion and tracery decorations resembling the contemporary French style.
*Devanagari script*: (from Sanskrit: *deva*, gods; *nagara*, of the city or people) the script generally used for writing Sanskrit as well as various vernacular languages of northern, western and central India. It is the literary type of the group of scripts known as *Nagari.* The characters are written below the horizontal line.
*Devas*: (from Sanskrit: *deva*, to shine) the shining ones or gods.
*Dhammila*: referring to any kind of hairstyle in which the hair is flat in the front and decorated with jewellery at the back.
*Dharmachakra*: Buddhist wheel of law.
*Dharmachakrapravdrtana mudrā*: gesture of preaching the Buddhist law, with both hands held before the chest, the right in *chin mudrā* and the left with palm facing inwards.
*Dhruva beras*: shrine images in the Hindu temple.
*Dhoti*: lower garment worn by men.
*Dhyāna mudrā*: gesture of meditation, with one hand resting on the other in the lap.
*Dhyāni Buddhas*: meditative Buddhas.
Diptych: (from Greek: diptychos, folded, double) in ancient Rome, two wax tablets with hinges for folding them to protect the writing; large painted tablets for altarpieces, etc., with hinges for folding; in Byzantine art, the small ivory carvings in relief on two hinged tablets.
*Diwani-i-Am*: hall of public audience in an Islamic palace.
*Diwani-i-Khas*: hall of private audience in an Islamic palace.
Donjon: the central fortified place in a medieval castle (usually a round tower).
Dome: a masonry roof built on a circular plan, usually hemispherical in shape, forming arches both in the horizontal and vertical directions.
Dosseret: a square block, larger at the top than at the bottom, with sides sloping inwards surmounting the similarly shaped capitals in Byzantine art.
*Dravida*: South Indian.
Drum: in architecture, one of the cylindrical blocks of stone of which a column is built up when it is not monolithic, as in Greek architecture; a round or polygonal wall, on which a dome is built.
Dry masonry: stones laid without mortar in a building.
*Dvitala*: (*dvi*, two; *tala*, storey) two storeys.

Eave: the part of a slanting roof which projects beyond the wall on which it rests.
Echinus: in the Doric capital, the round cushion-like member supporting the abacus; so named from its resemblance to the sea-urchin, called by this name.

*Ekatala*: (*ek*, one; *tala*, storey) one-storeyed.
*Ekāralī*: single-stringed chain.
Engaged columns: columns around a wall into which they are bonded or built in, sometimes to half their diameter; usually only for decoration without any structural function, as in the Roman pseudoperipteral temples.
English bond: a method of construction in which a course of stretchers alternates with a course of headers. Entablature: in classic architecture, the horizontal superstructure carried by the vertical columns consisting of three members: the architrave, frieze and cornice.
Entasis : a slight, almost imperceptible swelling or outward curving at about the middle of the shaft of a Doric column, giving the hard marble the impression of elasticity.
Exedra: (from Greek: ex, out; hedra, seat) an outdoor bench or seat in a gymnasium; later applied also to recesses in the walls, semi-circular or rectangular, and to apses or niches in churches.

Façade: usually the front elevation of a building; sometimes applied to side elevations also.
Faience: glazed pottery.
Fan vaulting: a special vaulting characteristic of the English Perpendicular Gothic style, where all the ribs start from the same impost, and radiate with the same curve, forming an inverted cone resembling the ribs of a fan.
Fillet: a small flat moulding like a band, usually not decorated, and meant to separate two other mouldings.
Finial: a carved decoration on the top of a pinnacle, spire, or gable; in general, a crowning architectural ornamentation.
Flamboyant: flame-like tracery in later Gothic art.
Flue: an enclosed passage directing a current of air, gases etc.
Fluting: grooves or channels with curved sections formed in parallel lines, used as architectural decorations especially on columns, as in Greek and Roman architecture, of which there are two categories: the Doric fluting, shallow, elliptical in section, and separated by an arris; and the Ionic, deeper, circular in section, with a narrow fillet between.
Flying buttress: a great invention of the Gothic period; a half arch, passing from the pier buttress over the roof of the aisle, to abut the nave vault, in order to counteract its outward pressure.
Forum: in Roman cities, the central open public square surrounded by public buildings, used for meetings and markets.
Fresco: a method of painting on a freshly plastered surface before it sets, so that the colours unite with it chemically and will not peel.
Frieze: in classic architecture, the central part of the entablature between the architrave and cornice; in the Doric order, it is vertically divided into triglyphs and metopes; in the Ionic order and in other applications, it is a continuous band, usually ornamented.
Frigidarium: the cooling room in the Roman thermae with a cold bath or an open swimming pool.

Gable: the vertical triangular part of the wall at the end of a building, enclosed by a sloping or pitched roof, corresponding to the pediment or tympanon of classical art; also seen over the gable roofs of the projecting doorways in Gothic art.
*Gajahasta*: a hand position, with the right or left arm crossing the body diagonally, with hand relaxed and fingers pointing down; usually found in figures of the dancing Śivas.
*Gaja pṛṣthakara*: (literally, the form of the back of an elephant) a shrine with a rounded end re sembling an elephant's back; e.g. *Sahadevaratha*, Mamallapuram.
*Gāṇḍī*: in Orissan architecture, the curvilinear tower resting on the *bāda* and supporting the *mastaka.*
*Gandharvas*: semi-divine beings.
*Garbhagṛha* or *garbhagriha*: inner apartment; inner sanctuary of a Hindu temple.
*Garuḍa*: (literally, a white-breasted eagle) Viṣṇu's mount or *vāhana* (vehicle), half-man, half-bird.
*Ghaghra*: a skirt, usually very profusely embroidered, worn by Rajasthani ladies.
*Ghantha*: (in Sanskrit: bell) an enormous bell-shaped, member on top of the *beki* on the Orissan *pidhā deul.*
*Gita Govinda*: (literally, the 'song of the herdsmen') a poem in Sanskrit by Jayadeva describing the love life of Krishna, the estrangement and finally the reconciliation.

*Gopī*: Cowherd.
*Gopura*: gatehouse; storeyed structure used as a gatway to the temple.
*Grantha*: script used to write Sanskrit.
Greek cross: a figure produced by the intersection in the centre and at right angles of two bars of equal length.
*Grīvā*: (literally, neck) the constricted part on top of the south Indian *vimāna*, carrying the *śikhara* or the rounded or octagonal cupola with finial.
Groin vault: a type of vault formed by the intersection of two barrel vaults at right angles.
*Gūdha maṇḍapa*: the maṇḍapa in front of the temple shrine in Gujarat.
*Gumbad*: the dome over an Islamic tomb chamber.

Halo: bright rays or rings pictured as encircling the head or body of holy or illustrious persons; also called aureole.
*Hāra* (architecture): string or row of miniature shrines surrounding each terrace of the storeyed south Indian *vimānas.*
*Hāra* (jewellery): a necklace.
*Hārāntara*: lengths of cloisters which connect the various *hara* elements, like the *kūta, śālās* and *pañjaras.*
*Haram* or *zanana*: apartments of women in an Islamic house.
*Hārmika*: a sort of finial on the flattened top of the *stūpa,* in the centre of which the shaft of the honorific umbrella is fixed, surrounded by a low railing.
Haunch: in architecture, parts of an arch at the two sides of the crown, at about one-third of the height of the curves.
*HawaMahal*: in Islamic achitecture, a palace with airy halls and upper terraces open to the wind.
*Hīnayāna*: (from Sanskrit: *hīna,* lesser; *yāna,* vehicle) an early form of Buddhism, also known as the Lesser Vehicle.
Hippodrome: (from Greek: hippos, horse; dromos, course) an arena or track, oval in shape and surrounded by tiers of seats, especially for horse and chariot races.
*Holi*: spring festival in which people spray each other with coloured water.
*Hrnmāla*: long necklace.
*Hujra*: an Islamic tomb chamber, surmounted by a dome *(gumbad),* with the cenotaph in the centre.
Hydria: a water jar with three handles, two on the sides for carrying, and one higher on the neck for pouring.
Hypostyle: (from Greek; hypo, under; stylos, resting on pillars) a building whose roof is supported by rows of pillars or columns; a construction whose columns are the only support for the roof.

Iconoclasm: (from Greek: eikon, image; klan, to break) the destructive opposition to religious images.
*Idgah*: (the Persian word for the *musalla* or praying place) a long wall with niches, and at times a palpit, where congregational prayers are offered at the two chief Muslim festivals.
Illuminations: initial letters, page borders and pictures decorated with gold leaf and bright colours, especially in the hand-written books of the Middle Ages.
Impost: an architectural member, either a pillar or a wall, on which the arch is supported.
In antis: in Greek architecture, the simplest form of the temple, with the side walls extended in the front, and columns set in between their extremities, forming a portico.
Intaglio: a technique in which all the parts must stand out in relief when the seal has been pressed upon a soft material like clay or wax; a recut into its surface.
Intercolumniation: the spacing between columns.

*Jagamohana*: the maṇḍapa in Orissan architecture.
*Jagati*: a wide terrace on which the temple stands, as in central India.
*Jāli* windows: (literally, 'net') lattice or perforated windows.
*Jama or jamah*: (from Persian, meaning garment) the long cotton tunic or gown worn by north Indian Muslims.

Jamb: the side of a doorway or window frame; usually projecting.
*jāṅgha*: (in Sanskrit, shin) in Orissan architecture, the portion of the *bāḍa* between the *pābhāga* and the *barāṇḍa*; sometimes divided by the *bāndhanā* moulding into the lower or *tala jāṅgha,* and the upper or *ūpar jāṅgha.*
*Jaṭābandha*: turban-like headdress of matted hair.
*Jaṭabhāra*: a manner of arranging matted hair around the head.
*Jāṭā makuta*: matted hair piled up high above the head of Śiva or his forms.
*Jātā valaya*: a turban-like way of twisting matted hair.
*Jātaka*: legends of the supposed previous births of the Buddha; chief inspiration of Buddhist iconography.
*Jaṭāya*: the bird that attempted to rescue Sita from Ravana.
*Jati vimāna*: a *vimāna* with three or four storeys.
*Jatila*: a person with matted hair.
*Jauhar*: the self-sacrifice of Rajput ladies to preserve their chastity.
*Jawab*: (literally, an answer) an Islamic building made to resemble another for the sake of symmetry.

*Kakṣāsanas*: stone seats having sloping back rests in Hindu temples.
*Kakṣyabandhana*: a sash tied around the waist, falling in decorative folds at the sides.
*Kalośa*: water pot; a vase-shaped member on top of the *khapuri* of the north Indian *śikhara.*
*Kalyāṇa maṇḍapa*: hall of marriage; in south Indian temples, a pillared hall with a platform in the centre.
*Kamaṇḍalu*: water vessel, sometimes with a spout, usually carried by *rishis.*
*Kaṇkaṇa*: a bracelet or thick coil tied around the wrist.
*Kaṇṭha*: (literally, 'neck') a moulding on the basement of south Indian temples.
*Kanṭhī*: flat necklace around the neck, thicker at the centre.
*Kanṭhikā*: single chain with a single *rudrākṣa* seed.
*Kapilavastu*: birthplace of the Buddha.
*Kapōta*: cornice.
*Karaṇḍa makuṭa*: short headdress tapering to the top, resembling an inverted *'Karaṇḍa'* or basket.
*Kartarī mudrā* or *kartarī mukha*: a gesture in which the third finger and thumb touch each other, with fore and middle fingers stretched out and held apart in order to hold any attribute.
*Kaṭaka hasta*: a gesture in which the thumb and forefinger bend and touch each other, and the other three fingers bend. Usually this is a gesture to hold any attribute. Also known as *simhakarna hasta.*
*Kaṭaka mudrā*: hand poised to hold a flower.
*Kaṭibandha or kaṭisutra*: elaborate girdle in three strings, with a decorative clasp and loops at the sides from which drapery folds fall.
*Kaṭṭu*: an intervening portion, either octagonal or polygonal, between the top and bottom section of a Pallava pillar.
*Kaṭyāvalambita*: relaxed posture, with one hand placed on the hip.
*Kāyabandhana* or *kākṣyabandhana:* sash used as girdle, falling in decorative folds at the sides.
Keel arch: an arch shaped like the keel of a ship.
Keep: see donjon.
Keramikos: see ceramic.
*Kesava Das*: a Hindi poet whose favourite theme was the *Nayikās* and *Bārāmāsa*, which are profusely illustrated in Rajput paintings.
Keystone: the stone at the centre or crown of the arch, holding the others in place.
*Keyura*: armlet, worn just above the biceps by both men and women. It developed into elaborate patterns in the Chola and Hoysala periods.
*Khana*: an Islamic house laid out around a courtyard.
*Khapuri*: (from Sanskrit: *kapāla*, skull) a flat bell-shaped member above the *amlā* of a north Indian śikhara.
*Kharoshti*: script used by the ancient Persians and by Ashoka; written from right to left.
*Kilivāsal*: equivalant to *nāsikā,* referred to generally in Kerala temples.
*Kiṅkanis*: small bells attached to anklets.
*Kinnaras*: mythological beings, half-human and half-bird.
*Kirīta makuta*: conical headdress, usually worn by Visnu.
*Kīrti toraṇa*: (literally, victory gate) a decorative archway in front of a temple in west India.

*Konaka-pāga* or *kanika-pāga*; in Orissan architecture, the corner projections of the *gāṇḍī*.
Krobylos: same as *uṣṇīṣa*, from the Greek, meaning a tuft of hair on top of the head.
*Kṣhudra nāsikā*: usually an arched opening supported between pilasters and found on the front face of the *harāntara*.
*Kubera*: god of wealth; chief of the *yakṣas* and also guardian of the north.
*Kūḍu*: (Tamil for nest) a small horseshoe-shaped ornamentation derived from the chaitya window on the convex cornice separating the storeys of the south Indian *vimāna.*
*Kuḍya stambha*: a pilaster.
*Kumbha*: a bulbous member of the capital over the *kalośa.*
*Kuṇḍa*: temple tank in Gujarat.
*Kunḍala*: ear ornament.
*Kūrmāsana*: the ordinary cross-legged seated pose.
*Kushk*: Islamic garden palace.
*Kūṭa*: shrine with a square plan, domical roof, and one finial, e.g., those surrounding the different storeys of the south Indian *vimāna.*
*Kūṭāgāra*: in Dravidian architecture, the simple hut-type structure, with a domical roof and one finial, e.g. Draupadi ratha, Mamallapuram.

*Lakṣaṇa* or *lakshana*: a bodily mark which distinguishes a Buddha, a *Tirthankara* etc.
*Lalita mode*: one of the many dance poses of Śiva, with the left leg slightly bent and the foot resting on the ground, while the right foot is partly raised with the toes beating time to the music.
*Lalitāsana*: a sitting pose, with one leg hanging down and the other resting on the cushion on which the person sits.
Lancet window: narrow pointed windows in the Early English Gothic style.
Lantern: in architecture, a small structure on top of a dome or over the roof of a nave, for decoration or to give light.
Latin cross: the intersection at right angles of two lines, so that one line is longer than the other three which are of equal size.
Lecythos: a vase for oil, with a long narrow neck, used chiefly in Greek funeral rites.
Lierne: in Gothic vaulting, a short rib which forms a link between the tierceron ribs.
*Linga*: a phallic form of Śiva worshipped in the sanctum.
Lintel: a beam of wood or any other material, laid across an opening like a door or window, to hold up the superstructure.
*Liwan*: the colonnaded cloister round three sides of the open courtyard of a *mosque.*
Loculi: burial niches cut into the walls of the catacombs.
*Lokapāla*: (literally 'king') Lokapālas are also guardians of the eight directions—the four cardinal points and their intermediaries.
Lotiform: lotus-shaped.
Lunette: semi-circular or crescent-shaped opening.

*Mardana*: apartment for men in an Islamic house.
*Madrasa*: an Islamic theological college.
*Mahabharata*: an epic poem on the great war of the *Bharatas*, describing the struggle between the sons of two brothers, the *Pandavas* and *Kauravas*, for the kingdom of *Hastinapuri* in which the Kauravas were defeated.
*Mahal:* in Islamic architecture, a mansion or house of the rich.
*Mahā maṇḍapa*: a large *maṇḍapa* or hall in front of the main shrine of the Hindu temple.
*Mahā nāsikā*: a pillared niche surmounted by a cornice, over which is a *kūḍu* arch-shaped member.
*Mahā piṣṭha*: a supporting basement peculiar to the temples of Rajasthan, equivalent to the *jagati* of central Indian temples.
*Mahdrājalitāsana*: (position of royal pleasure) sitting posture with right leg bent on the floor, and left knee bent up with the left arm resting on it.
*Mahāyāna*: a development of Buddhism when the anthropomorphic form of the Buddha was introduced; also known as the Great Vehicle.

*Mahiṣāsuramardinī*: the goddess *Durgā* killing the buffalo demon *Mahiṣāsura.*
*Majlis-khana*: an assembly hall; e.g. the building to the east of the Taj Mahal.
*Makara*: a mythological creature shaped like a crocodile, symbolising the River Ganga.
*Makar a kuṇḍala*: ear-omament with crocodile pattern.
*Mālasthāna*: looped garland decoration on the shaft of a pillar, immediately below the capital.
*Mānasāra*: ancient Indian text-book on image-making.
*Maṇḍapa*: an open or closed pillared assembly hall, in front of the shrine of a Hindu temple.
*Maṇḍovara*: in the temples of Gujarat, the principal wall surface rising up to the entablature, equivalent to the *bāda* of the Orissan temples.
*Maqbara*: the mortuary chamber of the Islamic tomb, below the tomb chamber.
*Masjid* or *mosque*: (literally, place of prostration) the Islamic place of worship.
*Mastaka*: (literally, head or skull) in Orissan architecture, the crowning member of the temple resting on the *gāṇḍī*.
*Medhi* or *methi*: circular or square base on which the *stūpa* is built.
*Mehman-khana*: a guest house, e.g. that at the eastern side of the Taj Mahal.
*Mekhala*: girdle.
Merlon: in the parapet of a battlement, the solid block between the crenels.
*Mihrab*: the niche in the back wall of the prayer hall of a *mosque*, showing the direction of Mecca.
*Mimbar*: a pulpit in the sanctuary of a mosque.
Miniature: (from Latin: miniare, to colour with vermilion) an illumination or colourful painting of manuscript books; a little picture, usually a portrait on ivory or parchment.
*Mithuna*: an amorous pair.
Moat: a body of water, generally artificial, around a fortification or castle, to make access difficult.
Monochrome: (from Greek: monos, single; chroma, colour) a drawing or painting made with one hue, or the method of doing so.
Monogram: (from Greek: monos,single; gramma, letter) a name represented by the combination of letters, usually two, sometimes more.
Monolithic: made of one block of stone, e.g. a large piece of sculpture, a pillar, or monument.
*Mudrās*: symbolic hand gestures signifying various actions of the Buddha and Hindu deities, like the *abhaya mudrā* (gesture of protection), *dharmachakra mudrā* (preaching gesture), *varada mudrā* (charity), and others.
*Mukha maṇḍapa*: the first of several ma*ṇḍ*apas in front of Hindu temples.
*Mukhya vimānas*: larger vimānas having up to sixteen storeys or *pañcha talas*.
Mullion: vertical masonry bars dividing a window into several sections.
Mural: (literally, 'wall') a form of painting on walls, either decorative, informative or descriptive.

*Nagara*: north Indian.
*Naṇdi*: name of the bull which serves as a vehicle and attendant of Śiva.
Narthex: a narrow vestibule in front of a church.
*Nāsikā*: (literally, 'nose') an arched opening which is projected.
Naṭarāja: Śiva as Lord of the dance.
Naṭya maṇḍapa: dance hall.
*Navaraṅga*: a *maṇḍapa* which has a square bay at the centre formed by the pillars, flanked by eight smaller bays forming in all a total of nine.
*Navaratha*: in Orissan architecture, a temple with four projections in each side of the *bāda*, dividing it into nine vertical sections.
Nave: (from Latin: navis, ship—often used as a symbol of the church) in architecture, the central part of the church between the aisles, which are generally lower.
*Nāyaka-Nāyikā Bheda*: classification of heroes and heroines or lovers, arranged according to their conduct towards each other.
*Nida*: a miniature shrine, apsidal in plan and forming one of the elements of the *hāra*; same as *pañjara.*
*Nirandhara*: a temple plan having no circumambulatory passage around the shrine.
*Nṛttamūrti*: dancing Śiva.
*Nūpura*: anklet.

Obelisk: usually a monolithic tapering pillar with four sides, terminating like a pyramid.
*Oḍhani*: a veil or transparent drapery worn by the Rajasthani ladies.

*Oma*: the base of a pillar.

Orchestra: the round space before the proscenium, used by the chorus or group of singers in ancient Greek theatres; in ancient Rome, the space had seats for important persons.

Overdoor: a lintel surmounting the opening of the doorway, and extending beyond the side parts to give extra strength and stability.

*Pābhāga*: (from Sanskrit: *pada*, foot; *bhāga*, portion) in Orissan temples, the base moulding of the *bāda.*

*Pādajalaka*: oval-shaped ornament worn just below the anklet and resting on the foot.

*Pādasaras*: anklets.

*Padmabandham*: a broad decorative band between rows of lotus petals, separating the shaft from the capital of a pillar.

*Padmapāṇi:* a popular Bodhisattva in the Buddhist pantheon, whose symbol is the lotus.

*Padmāsana*: a sitting posture—cross-legged with both soles facing up, and resting on the opposite thigh; often seen in seated Buddhas.

Palisade: a fence of stakes, as for defense.

*Pañcaratha* or *pañcharatha*: in Orissan architecture, a temple with two projections on each side of the *bāda* dividing it into five vertical sections.

*Pañchatala*: five-storeyed.

*Pañcāyatana* or *pañchāyatana*: a Hindu temple with the main shrine surrounded by four shrines at the corners.

*Pañjara*: *see nīda*.

Papyrus: a tall grass-like marsh plant or sedge, found in thick tufts in the Nile valley, the pith of which was cut into slices and pressed into a kind of paper in ancient times.

Parchment: (from Latin: pergamenus, pertaining to Pergamum, an ancient city in Asia Minor) a material for writing, prepared from sheep or goat skins.

*Parīnirvāṇa*: the death of the Buddha.

*Paryaṅka* pose: ordinary cross-legged sitting pose, with feet tucked below.

*Pāśupatāstra*: a terrible war weapon given by Śiva to Arjuna for his devotion and skill as an archer.

*Patākā mudrā*: (literally, 'flag') a hand gesture with five fingers outstretched and held together.

*Patrakuṇḍala*: round ear disc, modelled on palm leaves.

*Paṭṭa*: a median band on the face of a corbel.

*Phalaka*: abacus on top of the pillar supporting the corbel.

Pediment: in classical architecture, the triangular gable formed by the horizontal cornice and the two raking cornices; from the Renaissance onwards, used as a decoration over windows and doors.

Pendentive: a piece of masonry in the form of a spherical triangle to transform a square compartment into a round base for a dome.

Peripteral: a building surrounded by a colonnade.

*Piḍhā*: the horizontal planks, which in diminishing series, compose the roof of the Orissan *piḍhā deul.*

*Piḍhā deul*: the *jagamohana* or *maṇḍapa* of the Orissan temple, with a pyramidal roof composed of *piḍhās.*

Pier: a support, like the column, but usually larger in width and more complicated in structure.

Pilaster: (from Latin: pila, pillar) in architecture, a vertical rectangular member projecting from the wall, usually having a base shaft and capital like a column.

Pillar: a vertical, long, but very narrow support, or monumental shaft.

*Piṣta* or *pishta*: platform on which the Orissan temple is built.

Polychrome: (from Greek: polys, many, chroma colour) many-coloured.

Porch: a projecting entrance, partly enclosed, with a roof of its own.

*Potala*: in Orissan architecture, a group of *pīḍhās* on the *pḍhā deul,*

*Poṭīkā*: corbel.

Pouncing: tracing either on wall or paper.

*Pradakṣiṇa* or *pradakshiṇa pātha:* (from Sanskrit: pradakṣiṇa, circumambulation from left to right;' *pātha*, path) the circumambulatory passage around a sacred monument, e.g. the Buddhist *stūpa.*

*Prajnāpāramita*: one of the twelve virtues of perfection.

*Prākāra*: enclosure wall; e,g. that of the south Indian temple.

*Prāsāda*: palace; also shrine.
*Prasara*: entablature.
Proscenium: in the Greek theatre, a small platform projecting from the skene, and used by the performers.
Prostyle: (literally, a column in front) a building with a row of columns in front, forming a portico.
*Pūrṇakalaśa*: (literally, 'vase of plenty' symbolised by a pot of foliage) a capital of north Indian temples.
*Puṣpapoṭikā*: an elaborate form of corbel, characteristic of the Vijayanagar period.

*Qabr:* the real grave in the mortuary chamber of the Islamic tomb.
*Qibla:* in Islamic art, direction for prayer indicated by the *miḥrāb*.
*Quoins*: cornerstones at the angle of a building, either rounded or polygonal.

Rafter: a piece of timber, commonly one of the sloping members of a roof.
*Rāhā-pāga*: in Orissan architecture, the central projection on the *gaṇḍi.*
*Rakshasas*: demons having grimacing faces.
*Ramayana*: epic poem describing the adventures of *Rama* in quest of his wife *Sita*, whom *Ravana* the evil king of Ceylon, had carried away.
Rampart: a broad sloping structure for defence, usually of earth.
*Rang maḥal*: a richly painted hall in an Islamic palace.
*Rangamezi*: the colouring of the figures in Mughal painting.
*Rāsamañjari*: (literally, 'a posy of delights') a Sanskrit poem by Bhanu Datta, analysing varieties of lovers.
*Ratnakuṇḍala*: ear ornament encrusted with gems.
*Rauza*: in Islamic architecture, a mausoleum or tomb, surrounded by a garden, e.g. the Taj Mahal.
*Rekhā deul*: (from Sanskrit:*rekhā,*line;*deul*—from *devālaya*—abode of the gods) in Orissan architecture, the shrine with its tower rising in one continuous line.
Reredos: see altarpiece.
Rib: in Romanesque and Gothic architecture, the diagonal arch of the vault, built across the bay.
*Rishi*: sage.
Rose or wheel window: the round window on the façade, of many Romanesque and Gothic churches with tracery resembling the petals of a rose or spokes of a wheel.
*Rudrākṣa*: prayer beads used by Śaivites.
Rustication: a method of stone-work where the outer surface of the stone is left with its natural roughness; or dressed stones, with strongly bevelled angles.

*Sabhā maṇḍapa*: in the ground plan of Gujarati temples, a detached assembly hall in front of the *gūdha maṇḍapa.*
*Saḍāṅga*: having six parts.
*Saduram*: in south Indian architecture, the basal and top section of a pillar, separated either by an octagonal or polygonal section.
*Sālā*: shrine with an oblong plan, roofed by a barrel vault, with a row of finials on the ridge; e.g. those surrounding the different storeys of the south Indian *vimāna.*
*Samabhaṅga*: erect pose; frontal, upright position, reserved for gods in a state of complete spiritual equilibrium.
*Sāndhara:*a temple plan having a circumambulatory passage around the shrine.
Saṅgha: Buddhist order of monks.
*Saṅghārama*: (from Sanskrit:*saṅgha*, community, *ārāma*, garden) habitation of the Buddhist community.
*Saṅghai*: robe worn by Buddhist monks.
*Saptaratha*: in Orissan architecture, a temple with three projections on each side of the *bāda*, dividing it into seven vertical sections.
*Sarai*: in Islamic architecture, a royal palace having many courts, with halls built around them.
Sarcophagus: originally a lime-stone used by the Greeks for making coffins, since corpses were soon reduced by it; a stone coffin.
*Sardab* or *takhana*: underground room in an Islamic palace, for use in the hot dry season.
*Sarpakuṇḍala*: ear ornaments shaped like snakes, worn by certain forms of Śiva.

*Sati*: (from Sanskrit, meaning faithful wife) the cremation of an Indian widow on her husband's funeral pyre.
*Sat Sai*: seven hundred couplets on the Krishna legend.
Scriptorium: the place or room in a monastery for writers or copyists.
Sculpture: the art of shaping hard and soft substances into statuary or ornaments.
*Senis*: corporations or guilds of builders.
Shaft: in architecture, the round part of a column between the base and capital.
*Shish mahal*: a hall in an Islamic palace reserved for festive occasions and decorated with mirrors.
*Sihn*: the open courtyard of a *mosque,*
*Śikhara*: (in Sanskrit: top, summit of a mountain) the tapering tower surmounting the inner shrine of a Hindu temple.
*Śilpa*(*sastra*): manual containing rules on art.
*Śilpin*: mason, artisan.
*Simhāsana*: lion throne, meant especially for the royalty.
*Simhakarṇahasta*: see *Kaṭaka hasta.*
*Skandhamālā*: jewelled bands on shoulders, commonly used in the Hoysala period.
Skene: the Greek wordfor a stage, tent, or covered place.
*Sopāna*: steps,staircase.
*Sopasaryana:* sitting posture with both feet down.
Spandrel: the space between the outside curve of an arch and the rectangular frame; or the space between the outside curves of adjacent arches and the line running horizontally above them.
Spire: the tapering or pyramidal roof of a tower.
Spring: in architecture, the plane or line where the curve of an arch or vault begins from the impost. Square headed doorway: a doorway having a square frame.
Squinch: a method by which a square plan is transformed by projecting diagonal arches at the comers to carry the dome.
Stadium: in ancient Greece, an arena for foot races, with tiers of seats around.
Staggered: not in line, especially doorways for privacy in Mughal architecture.
*Stambha*: (Sanskrit for pillar) very common in India through all the ages, the most famous being the stambhas of Ashoka on which his edicts were engraved.
*Sthapatis*: the guild of builders in Hindu art; master craftsmen.
*Stava*: attitude of praise.
Steatite: soapstone.
Stoa: a roofed porch or colonnade in Athens; a sheltered walk or promenade, with a colonnade in front anda wallat the back.
Struts: wooden, stone or iron architectural members meant to bear weight or pressure.
Stucco: a kind of plaster of cement for coating surfaces; especially utilised for moulded decoration.
*Stūpa*: (from Sanskrit:*stūp* to heap, to pile up) originally a simple burial mound, it became a sacred monument for the Buddhists, although the Jains also used it. It enclosed either body relics *(śārika)* or personal belongings *(pāribhogika)*of the Buddha or Buddhist teachers, or marked places sacred to Buddhists (*uddeśika*). It became the symbol of the decease (*parinirvāṇa*) of the Buddha.
*Stūpi*: the finial of the *vimāna* or *gopura,* or of any other structure.
*Sūci*(sūchi): needle or pointed blade; the flattened horizontal bar of the *vedikā.*
*Sūchi mudrā*: used to threaten or to point out something, with the index finger stretched out while the others are bent.
*Śukha nāsi*: name given in Hoysala architecture to the *antarāla*, here a very small vestibule.
*Śukha nāsikā*: an arched projection from the lower storey of the *vimāna*, roofing the vestibule in front.
*Sukhāsana*: (from Sanskrit:*sukha*, comfortable;*āsana*, posture); sitting posture, with right foot hanging down and left foot up facing right knee; position of ease and comfort.
*Surat*: figure drawing in Mughal painting.
*Surdas*: one of the great Hindi language poets who illustrated the life of Krishna in his poems.
*Swastika*: (from Sanskrit: su, good:*asti*, being) a hooked cross symbolising well-being.

*Tāḍi*: a cushion-shaped member of the capital, between the *kalośa* and *kumbha*.
*Tokhana*: see sardab.

*Takri*: a cursive alphabet used for writing dialects in the Punjab hills.
*Talā jāṅgha*: see *jāṅgha.*
Tapestry: a heavy wall hanging, furniture cover, or carpet woven by hand, usually adorned with figures.
*Taraṅga*: wavy roll ornament, on the face of the corbel of the Pallava period.
*Tarjani mudrā*: gesture of threatening, with one finger outstretched in a menacing attitude.
*Tarrah*: in Mughal painting, the first sketch of a picture.
Telemon: (from Greek: bearer) a column in the form of a male figure, or half a column and a torso, used in German Renaissance architecture.
Tempera: painting with pigments mixed with egg white.
Tepidarium: in the Roman thermae, the warm lounge-room.
*Thāba*: (from Sanskrit:*stambha)* the upright posts of the *vedikā.*
Thermae: in ancient Rome, public bathing establishments.
*Tirthankaras*: Jaina saints who represent the highest ideal of ascetism or self-denial.
Toga: in ancient Rome, the loosely draped outer garment worn by citizens for public appearance.
*Toraṇa*: arched doorway, e.g. those attached to the *vedikās* around the *stūpas.*
Trabeate system: post and lintel system of construction, as distinct from the use of arches.
Tracery: ramified or branch-like ornamentation in stone, filling the upper part of Gothic windows; interlaced lines for decoration, resembling tracery.
Transom: a crossbeam; a horizontal piece in a building, e.g. a lintel, the transverse bar of a cross; in architecture, horizontal bars placed across a window, as in late Gothic.
Transversal: (from Latin : trans, across; vertere to turn) intersecting or cutting across.
Tread: the upper horizontal part of a step on which the foot is placed.
*Tribhaṅga*: thrice bent pose, with the body bent to the right, then to the left, and again to the right, or in reverse; the Naṭarāja pose.
Triforium: in Gothic architecture, a small arcade on the nave wall between the nave arcade and the clerestory; a gallery, often with three openings at each bay; upper storey to a church nave.
Triglyph: a tablet in a frieze of the Doric order, rectangular in form, projecting a little, with vertical grooves.
*Tri-kūṭa*: a Hoyasala temple with three *vimānas*, with their *antarālas* opening into the same *navaraṅga.*
*Tripatākā mudrā*: the thumb and little finger are bent and the three middle fingers are outstretched and held together.
Triptych: a picture or a carving having three sections, the central one usually twice the size of the two wings, which can be folded over to cover it.
*Triratha*: in Orissan architecture, a temple with one projection on each side of the *bāda*, dividing it into three vertical sections.
*Tritala*: three-storeyed.
Triumphal arch: a free-standing arch, often across an important street, to commemorate a great victory; usually rectangular in form, with one or three arched passages; in the latter case, the middle is much bigger than the flanking ones.
Turret: a small tower rising above a castle or large building.
Tympanum: the triangular field of a gable.

*Udarabandhana*: waist-band worn only by men.
*Uparjāṅgha*: see *jāṅgha.*
*Upavīta*: manner of wearing the sacred thread or garment, —e.g. a saree—under the right arm and over the left shoulder.
*Urṇa*: jewel or lock or tuft of hair between the eyebrows of the Buddha, to represent his superhuman quality.
*Urudāmas*: 'U'-shaped loops of pearls hanging from the girdle to the thighs.
*Uruśṛṅga*or *ūruśringa*: the *anga-śikhara*on the central Indian temple towers.
*Uṣṇiṣa* or *ushnisha*: turban with frontal protruberance, Indra's characteristic headdress; protuberance on the head of the Buddha; the coping stone of the *vedikā.*
*Utkulikāsana*: sitting with knees bent, heels close to the rump and the back slightly curved, as in the figures of *Kevalanarasimha.*
*Utsava maṇḍapa*: a pillared hall where the deity is displayed during festivals.
*Utsava mūrti*: the temple idol made of metal which is taken out in processions during festivals (*utsava*).
*Uttariya*: cloth worn by men on the upper part of the body.

*Vaikuṇṭha*: the heavenly abode of Viṣṇu.
*Vajrapāṇi*: one of the *bodhisattvas*, an emanation of the Dhyāni Buddha Aksobhya. His symbol is '*vajra*' (thunderbolt),
*Valayas*: bangles.
*Varada mudrā*: gesture of bestowal, with palm facing outwards, fingers outstretched and the hand held below the waist.
*Varāha*: (literally, 'boar') the third incarnation of Viṣṇu in the form of a boar, to save mother earth from the depths of the ocean.
*Vāstu* or *śāstra*: manual containing rules on architecture.
*Vaṭa patraśaya*: Krishna sleeping on the banyan leaf.
Vault: a masonry structure based on the arch system, generally forming the roof or ceiling.
*Vedī*: in Sanskrit, altar.
*Vedikā*: railing around the Buddist *stūpa* or any other sacred monument in India.
Vellum: the fine-grained skin of lamb, kid, or calf, specially prepared for writing or bcok-binding; also a manuscript made of it.
*Vesara*: a type of southern *vimāna*, classified by the southern *Śilpa* and Āgama texts as having a circular, ellipsoidal or apsidal plan from the base to the apex.
Vestibule: a passage hall or ante-room, usually between the *maṇḍapa* and the main shrine in the Indian temple plans.
*Vihāra*: the dwelling place of the *bhikshus*.
*Vimāna*: in south Indian temples, the entire sanctuary from the base to the finial, consisting of the basement, pillars, walls, entablature, *griuā*, *śikhara*and finial.
*Viṇā*: stringed musical instrument.
*Vipralabdha Nāyika*: 'she who vainly awaits her lover'.
*Virabhadrānugrha*: a fierce-looking form of Śiva, with four arms,three eyes, side tusks and a garland of skulls.
*Virāsana*: sitting posture with left foot on right thigh, and left thigh on right foot; the same as the padmāsana except that the right foot is under the left thigh.
*Vismaya mudrā*: gesture of surprise, with the forearm raised, the fingers outstretched and the palm facing inwards.
Volute: the whorl-like capital of the Ionic order, resembling a spiral sea-shell.
Votive *stūpas*: small stūpas made as an offering by the devotees, also erected over the ashes of the members of the *saṇgha.*
Voussoirs: tapering or wedge-shaped stones, used for the construction of a true arch.
*Vyālas*: (Vyālas) leonine figures.
*Vyālāvari* (Vyālāvari): a decorative frieze, with leonine faces, either on the basement or on the entablature.
*Vyākhyāna mudrā*: gesture of exposition, with right thumb and index finger forming an O.

Wheel window: see rose window.

*Yakṣa* or *yaksha*: (from Sanskrit: yaj, to worship, worthy of worship) nature spirit; male semidivine being.
*Yakṣiṇi*: female counterpart *of yaksha*.
*Yajñopavita*: sacred thread worn by the higher castes of Hindus.
*Yāli*: mythological monster, part lion, horse and elephant, used as Chalukyan temple ornament.
*Yaṣti*: stick or staff fixed on the top of the *stūpa* to hold the chatra or honorific umbrella.
*Yogāsana*: sitting posture with legs crossed as in the padmāsana pose, but the knees are slightly raised and supported by the yogapatta, a narrow band.
*Yogi*: male ascetic who undertakes disciplined meditation.
*Yogini*: one of the sixty-four mother goddesses.

*Zanana*: see *haram*.
*Zarih*: in Islamic architecture, the empty tomb in the centre of the tomb chamber.

# BOOKS SUGGESTED FOR FURTHER READING

## INDIAN ART


Agarvala, V. S., *Indian Miniatures,an Album,* Department of Archaeology, 1961.
Agarvala, V. S., The *Heritage of Indian Art,* New Delhi, Government of India.
Anand, Mulk Raj, The *Hindu View of Art,* Bombay, 1954.
Archer, W. G., *Indian Miniatures,* 1960.
Archer, W. G., *Indian Painting in Bundi and Kotah,* 1959.
Appasamy, Jaya, *Abanindranath Tagore and the Art of his times,* Lalit Kala Akademy.
Appasamy, Jaya, *Sailoz Mukerjee (a monograph),* Lalit Kala Akademy, 1966.

Bacchofer, Ludwig, *Early Indian Sculpture,* Vols. I & II, Paris, 1929. Reprint—1973—Munshiram Manoharlal.
Balasubramanyam, S. R., *Early Chola Art,* Asia Publishing House, 1966.
Banerji, R. D., *Eastern Indian School of Medieval Sculpture,* Archaeological Survey of India, 1933.
Barrett, Douglas, *A Guide to Karla Caves*, Vols. I & II, Bombay, 1957.
Basham, A. L., *The Wonder that was India*, London, 1954.
Brown, Percy, *Indian Painting Under the Mughals*, London, 1924.
„ „ *Indian Architecture*, Vol. I, *Buddhist and Hindu*, Vol. II, *Islamic Period*, Bombay, Taraporevala.
„ „ *Indian Painting, The Heritage of India Series*, Calcutta, Y.M.C.A. Publishing House, 1949.
*Buddhist Shrines in India*, New Delhi, The Publication Division, Government of India, 1951.
Burgess, James, and Fergusson, James, *The Cave Temples of India*, Oriental Books Reprint Corporation, 1969.
Bussagli, Mario, *Indian Miniatures*, Hamlyn Publishing Group, London, 1969.

Coomaraswamy, A., *The Arts and Crafts of India and Ceylon*, London, 1913.
„ „ *An Introduction to Indian Art*, Adyar Theosophical Publishing House, 1956.
„ „ *History of Indian and Indonesian Art,* New York, Dover Publications, 1965.

Deva, Krishna, *Temples of North India*, National Book Trust, India.
Dhama, B. D., and Chandra, S. C., *Khajuraho*, New Delhi, Archaeological Survey of India.
Douglas, Barret and Basil Gray, *Treasures of Asia.*
Douglas, Barret and Basil Gray, *Painting of India*, 1963.
Dubreuil, Jouveau, D.,*Dravidian Architecture*, Bharat Bharati, 1970.

Fergusson, James, *History of Indian and Eastern Architecture*, Vols. I & II, Delhi, Munshiram Manoharlal, 1967.
5000 *Tears of Indian Architecture*, New Delhi, The Publications Division, Govt. of India, 1951.

Gangoly, O. C.,*Indian Art and Heritage*, Calcutta, Oxford Book and Stationary Company.
Goetz, Dr. Hermann, *India,Art of the World Series*, London, 1959.
Gopinath Rao, T. A.,*Elements of Hindu Iconography*, Indological Book House, Varanasi, 1971.
Goswami. A. *Indian Temple Sculpture.*
Gray, Basil, *Rajput Painting,Faber Gallery of Oriental Art,* London, Faber & Faber Ltd.
Grousset, Rene, *The Civilization of the East*, Vol. II, London, Hamish Hamilton, 1932.
Gupte, R. S., and Mahajan, B., D. *Ajanta and Ellora,* Taraporevala, 1962.

Havell, E. B., *The Art Heritage of India,* (comprising Indian sculpture and painting and Ideals of Indian Art) Revised Edition, Bombay, Taraporevala, 1964.
*History of the Deccan,* Vol. I, Part VIII: Fine Arts, London and Bombay, Oxford University Press, 1952.

*History and Culture of the Indian People*, Bombay, Published by Bharatiya Vidya Bhavan.

Vol. I. *Vedic Age.*
Vol. II. *The Age of Imperial Unity.*
Art : A. Architecture—S. K. Saraswati.
B. Sculpture—Nihar Ranjan Ray.
C. Painting and other Arts—Nihar Ranjan Ray.
Vol. III. *The Classical Age.*
Art : A. Architecture—S. K. Saraswati.
B. Sculpture—Nihar Rajan Ray.
C. Painting and other Arts—Nihar Rajan Ray.
Vol. V. *The Struggle for Empire.*
Art : I. Architecture—S. K. Saraswati.
II. Sculpture—Nihar Ranjan Ray.
III. Painting—Nihar Ranjan Ray.
Vol. VI. *The Delhi Sultanate.*
Art : S. K. Saraswati.
I. Introduction.
II. Delhi or Imperial Style.
III. Provincial Styles.
Vol. VII. *The Mughul Empire.*
Ch. XXIII. Mughul Architecture—S.K. Saraswati.
Ch. XXIV. Mughul Painting—Ashok Kumar Das.

*Indian Art Through the Ages,* New Delhi, The Publications Division, Govt. of India, 1948.
Iyer, K., Bharatha, *Indian Art,A Short Introduction*, Bombay, Asia Publishing House, 1958.

Kail, Owen, C.,*Buddhist Cave Temples of India*, Taraporevala, 1975.
*Kanchi, an Introduction to its Architecture*, New Delhi, The Publication Divisions, Govt. of India.
Kapur, Shiv, S., *Hussain* (a *monograph*), Lalit Kala Akademi, 1961.
Kar, Chintamoni, *Classical Indian Sculpture*, 300 B.C. to 500 A.D., London, Alec Tiranti Ltd.
,, ,, *Indian Metal Sculpture*, London, Alec Tiranti Ltd.
Khandalwala, Karl, *The Origin and Development of Rajasthani Painting*, Marg XI, No. 2.
Kramrisch, Stella, *Indian Sculpture*, Calcutta, 1933.
,, ,, *Art of India*, London, 1954.
Krishna, S. A., K. *Sreenivasulu*, (a *monograph*), Lalit Kala Akademy, 1966.

Longhurst, A. H., *Pallava Architecture,* Vols. I—III, Memoirs, Archaeological Survey of India, 1924, 1928, 1930.

Mahalingam, T. V., *The South Indian Temple Complex,* Director, Kannada Research Institute, 1970.
Mehta, J. Rustom, *Konarak,* D. B. Taraporevala, 1969.
Michell, George, *The Hindu Temple, An Introduction to its Meaning and Forms*, B. I. Publications, 1977.
Mitra Debala, *Ajanta,* New Delhi, Archaeological Survey of India, 1956.
,, ,, *Bhubaneswar*, New Delhi, Archaeological Survey of India,1956.
,, ,, *Sanchi,* New Delhi, Archaeological Survey of India.
,, ., *Buddhist Monuments,* Shishu Sahitya Samaj, 1971.
Monod-Bruhl, Odette, *Indian Temples,* Oxford University Press, 1952.
Munshi, K.M., *Saga of Indian Sculpture,* Bombay Bharatiya Vidya Bhavan, 1957.

Nihar Ranjan Ray, *'The Rajput Styl' in the Panorama of Indian Painting,* The Publications Division, 1971.

Rao, S. R.,*Lothal and the Indus Civilisation,* New York, Asia Publishing House, 1973.
Rawlinson, S. G., & Others, *Indian Art,* London, Sidgwick & Jackson Ltd., 1966.

Rowland, Benjamin, *The Art and Architecture of India*, Buddhist-Hindu-Jain, Britain, 1953.
Saraswati, S.K, *Survey of Indian Sculpture,* Calcutta, 1951.
Sastri, Hiranda, (Dr.), *A Guide to Elephanta,* 1934.
Sivaramamurti, C.,*Mahabalipuram,* New Delhi, Archaeological Survey of India, 1952.
,, ,, *The Chola Temples*, New Delhi, Archaeological Survey of India, 1960.
,, ,, *Indian Sculpture,* Bombay, Allied Publishers, 1961.
,, ,, *Indian Bronzes,* Bombay, Marg, 1962.
,, ,, *The Art of India,* New York, Harry N., Abrams, 1977.
Sivaramamurti, C., and Mario Bussagli, 5000 *Years of Indian Art,* New York, Harry N. Abrams.
Smith, Vincent, A., *History of Fine Arts in India and Ceylon,* 3rd edition, Bombay, Taraporevala, 1962.
Srinivasan, K. R., *Cave Temples of the Pallavas,* New Delhi, Archaeological Survey of India, 1964.
,, ,, *Dharmaraja Ratha and Its Sculpture: Mahabalipuram,* Abhinava Publications, 1975.

Vogel, J. Ph., *Buddhist Art in India,Ceylon and Java,* Oxford, Clarendon, 1936.
Volwahsen, Andreas, *Living Architecture: India,* Oxford and I.B.M. Publishing Company, 1969.
,, ,, *Inde Islamique,* 1971.

Wheeler, Mortimer, *The Indus Civilisations*, Cambridge, 1953.
Wilkinson, J. V. S., *The Mughal Painting,* Faber Gallery of Oriental Art, London, Faber & Faber Ltd.

## WESTERN ART

*Art Treasures of the World,* An Illustrated History in colour, London, Paul Hamlyn, 1964.

Bazin, Germain, *A Concise History of Art,* London, Thames & Hudson, 1958.
Berti, Luciano, *Raphael*, London, Weidenfeld & Nicolson.
Braham, Allen, *Dūrer*, London, Spring Art Books, 1966.

Descargues, Pierre, *German Painting from the* 14th *to* 16th *Centuries,* London, Thames & Hudson, 1961.

Faulkner, Ray & Others, *Art Today,* Holt, Rinehart and Winston, New York, 1962.

Fernan, Joachim, *Encyclopedia of Old Masters,* London, Thames & Hudson, 1958.
Fletcher, Banister, *A History of Architecture of the Comparative Method*, London, Batsford, 1956.

Gardner, Helen, *Understanding the Arts,* Harcourt, Brace and Company, New York, Chicago, 1932.
,, ,, *Art through the Ages,* 4th Edition, New York, 1948.
Gaunt, William, *Everyman's Dictionary of Pictorial Art*, Vols. I-II, London: J. M. Dent & Sons Ltd., New York: E. P. Dutton & Co. Inc. 1962.
Gettings, Fred, *The Golden Pleasure Book of Art,* London, Paul Hamlyn, 1963.
Goldscheider, Ludwig, *Michelangelo,* London, Phaidon Press, 1964.
,, ,, *Leonardo da Vinci,* London, Phaidon Press, 1964.
Gombrich, E. H., *The Story of Art,* London, 1956.

Hamlin, A. D. F. (A.M.), *A Textbook of the History of Architecture,* Toronto, Bombay, Calcutta, Madras, 1925.

Janson, Dora Jane & Janson, H. W.,*The Picture History of Painting,* from Cave Painting to Modern Times, New York, Harry N. Abrams, Inc. 1957.

Kielty, Bernardine, *Masters of Painting, Their Works, Their Lives, Their Times,* New York, Doubleday & Co., Inc., 1964.

Leicht, Hermann, *History of the World's Art,* London, Spring Books, 1965.

Milton, A. Henry, *Key Monuments of the History of Architecture,* New York, Prentice-Hall, Inc, Englewood Cliffs, N. J., and Harry N. Abrams, Inc.

Murray, Peter & Linda, *A Dictionary of Art and Artists,* Penguin Books, 1962.

Myers, Bernard, S., *Modern Art in the Making*, London, New York, 1950.

„ „ *Encyclopedia of Painting,* London, Hutchinson, 1956.

Orpen, Sir William, *The Outline of Art,* London, Newnes, 1964.

Pijoan Joseph, *History of Art,* Vols. I-III, Barcelona, Salvat, 1927.

Robb, David M.,*The Harper History of Painting,* The Occidental Tradition, New York, Harper Brothers, 1951.

Robb, David M. & Garrison, J. J., *Art in the Western World* (4th edition), New York and Evasion. Harper & Son, 1963.

Roose, Frank J., *An Illustrated Handbook of Art History,* Revised ed., New York, Macmillan.

Schmidt-Degener, *The Teach Yourself History of Painting*, based on the original works, edited by William Gaunt,

The Italian School I, Volume I.
The Italian School II, Volume II.
The Flemish School, Volume III.
The Spanish School, Volume IV
The German School, Volume V
The Dutch School, Volume VI.
The French School, Volume VII.
The British School, Volume VIII.
The XlXth Century, Volume IX.
The XXth Century, Volume X.
London, English Universities Press Limited, 1954.

Sewall, John Ives, *A History of Western Art,* Revised Edition, New York, Holt, Rinehart & Winston, 1961.

*Time Life Library of Art, The World of*: Bernini, Brueghel, Cezanne, Delacroix, Duchamp, Dürer, Gainsborough, Giotto, Goya, Leonardo, Manet, Matisse, Michelangelo, Picasso, Rembrandt, Rodin, Rubens, Turner, Titian, Van Gogh, Velasquez, Vermeer, Watteau, Whistler, Winslow Homer.

Upjohn, E. M., Wingert, P. S. & Mahler, T. G. *History of World Art*, New York, 1954.

Upjohn, E. M., Sedgwick, Jr. J. P., *Highlights,an Illustrated History of Art*; New York, Chicago, San Francisco, Toronto, London, Holt, Rinehart & Winston, 1963.

Van der Meer, Dr. F.,*Atlas of Western Civilization,* Amsterdam, Elsevier Publishing Company, 1945.

Van der Meer, F. & Mohrmann, Christine, *Atlas of the Early Christian World,* New York, Nelson, 1959.

Venturi, Adolfo, translated by Hutton, Edward, *A Short History of Italian Art,* London, 1926.

Ware, Dora & Beatty, Betty, *A Short Dictionary of Architecture,* London, George Allen & Unwin Ltd., 1946.

*World Architecture:* An Illustrated History, Hamlyn Publishing Group, London, 1963.

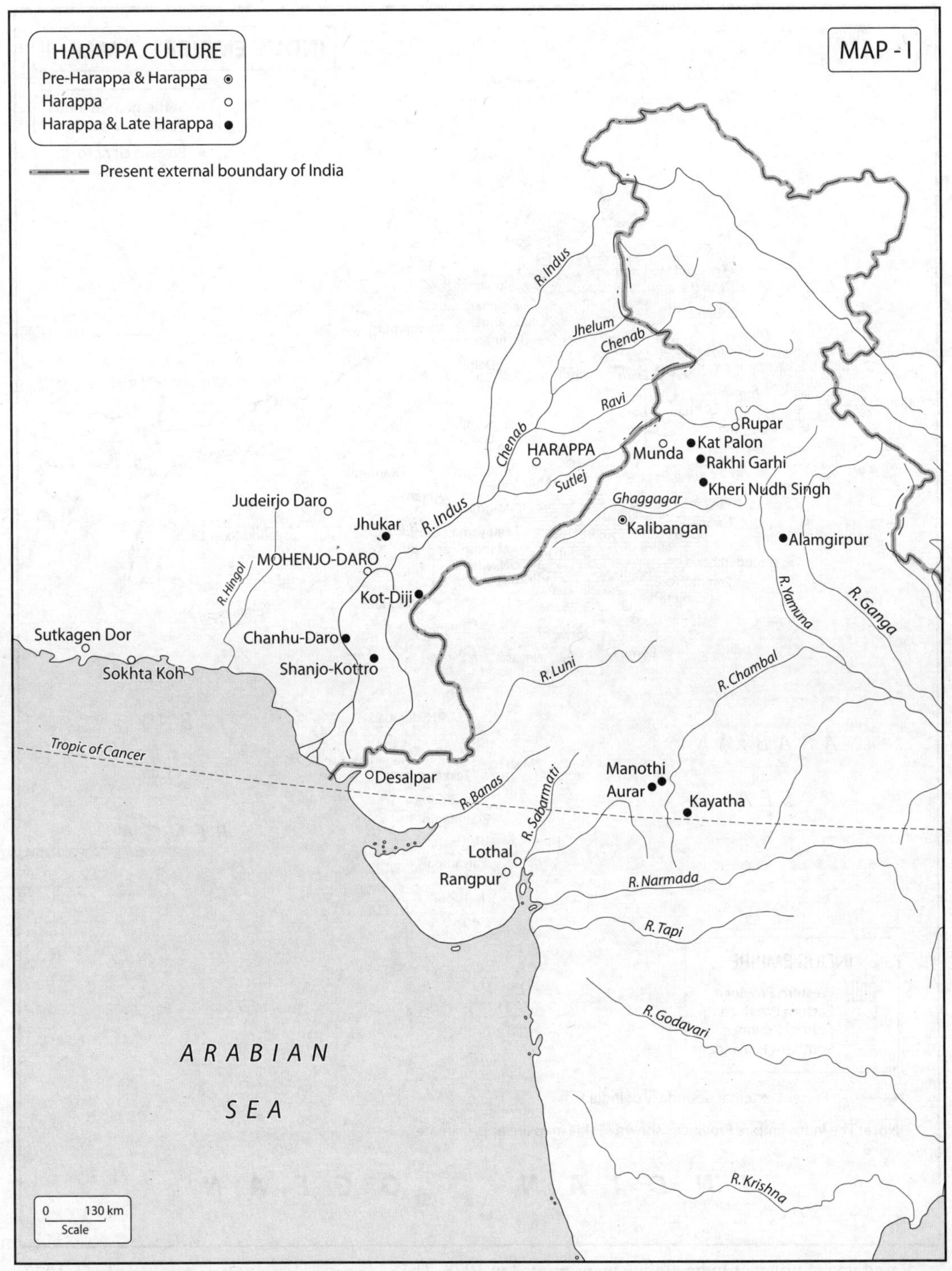


Based upon Survey of India outline maps printed in 1978. The territorial waters of India extend into the sea to a distance of twelve nautical miles measured from the appropriate base line

1:13,000,000

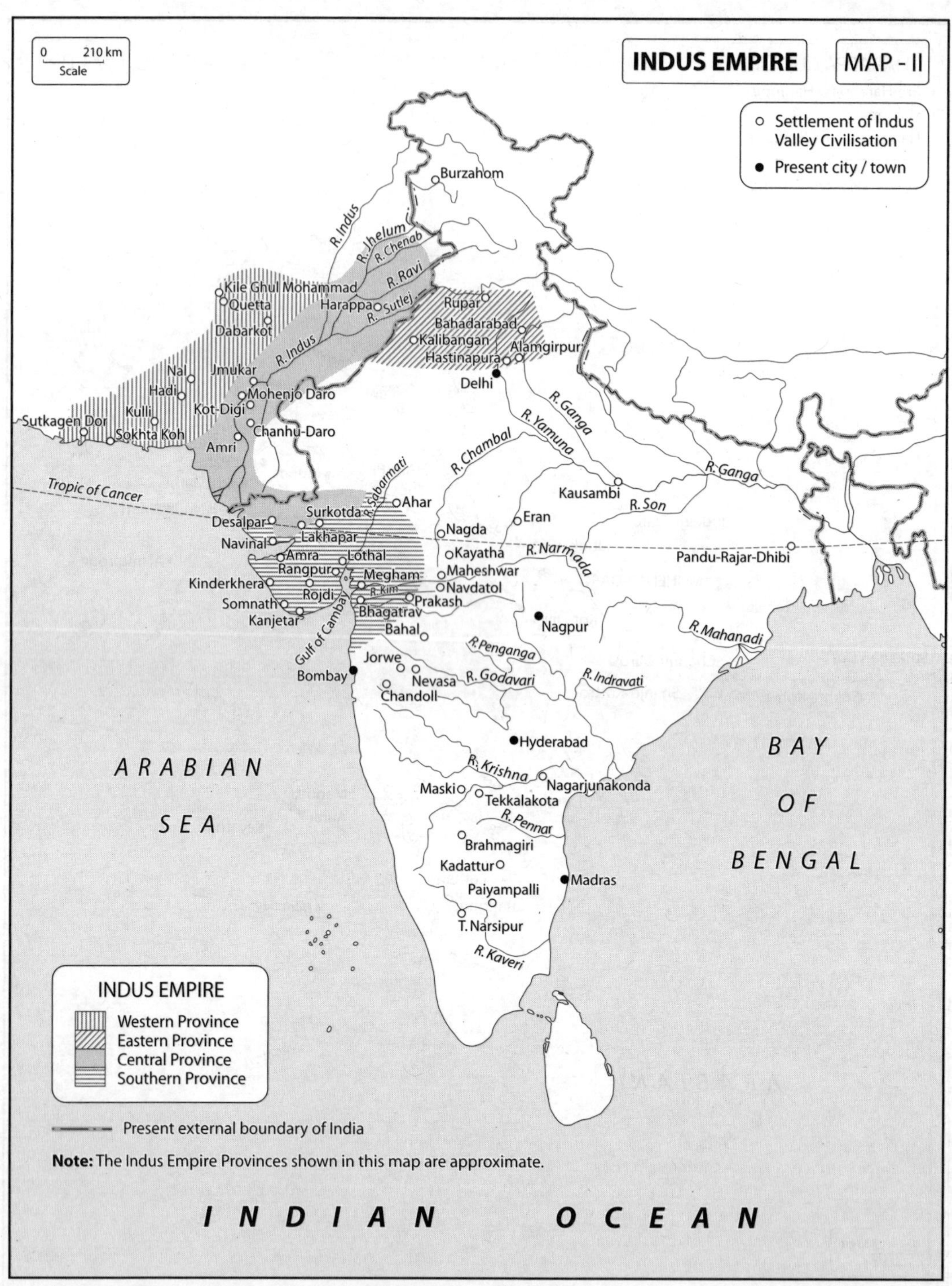


Based upon Survey of India outline maps printed in 1978. The territorial waters of India extend into the sea to a distance of twelve nautical miles measured from the appropriate base line

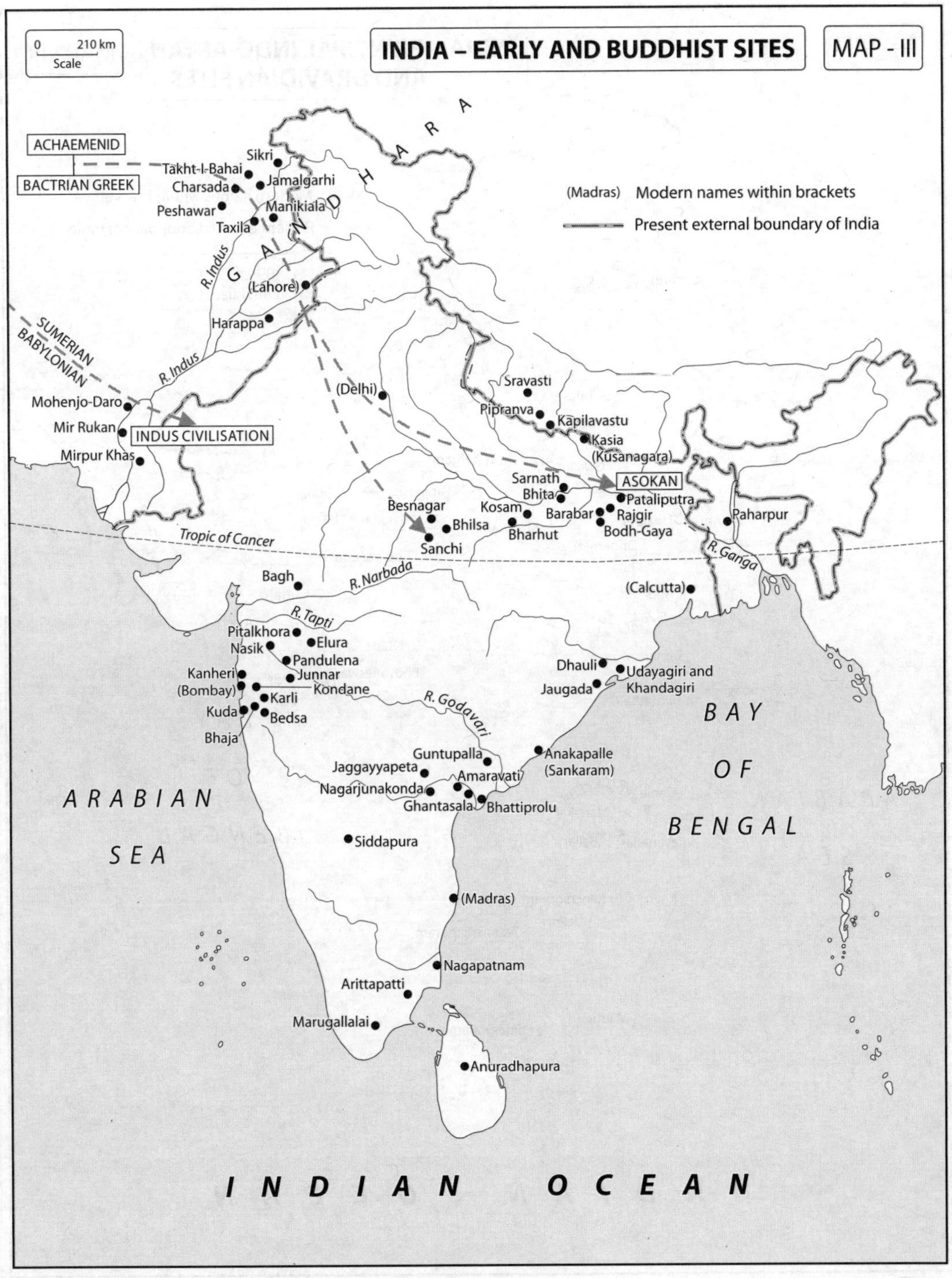


Based upon Survey of India outline maps printed in 1978. The territorial waters of India extend into the sea to a distance of twelve nautical miles measured from the appropriate base line

1:21,000,000

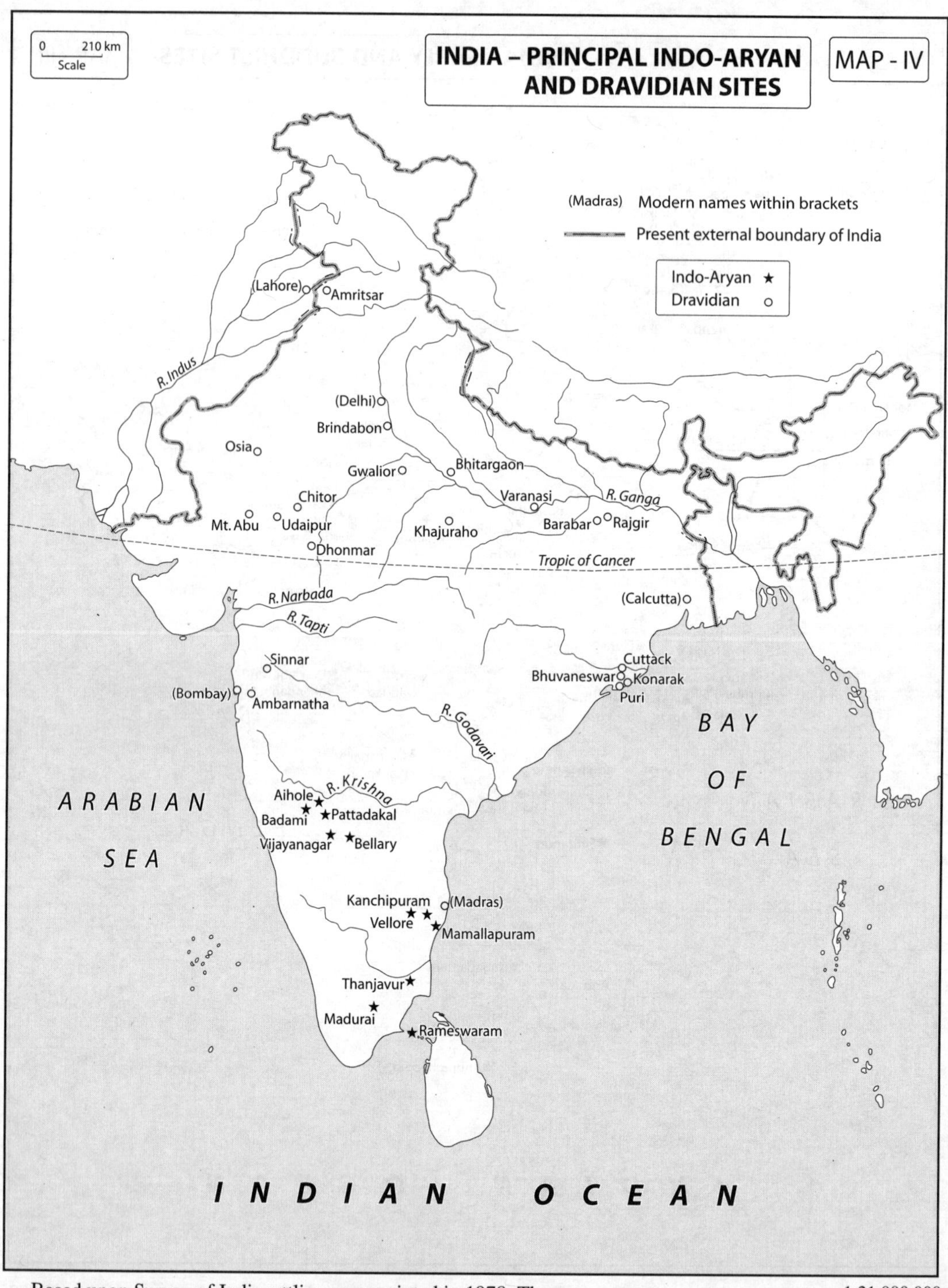


Based upon Survey of India outline maps printed in 1978. The territorial waters of India extend into the sea to a distance of twelve nautical miles measured from the appropriate base line

1:21,000,000

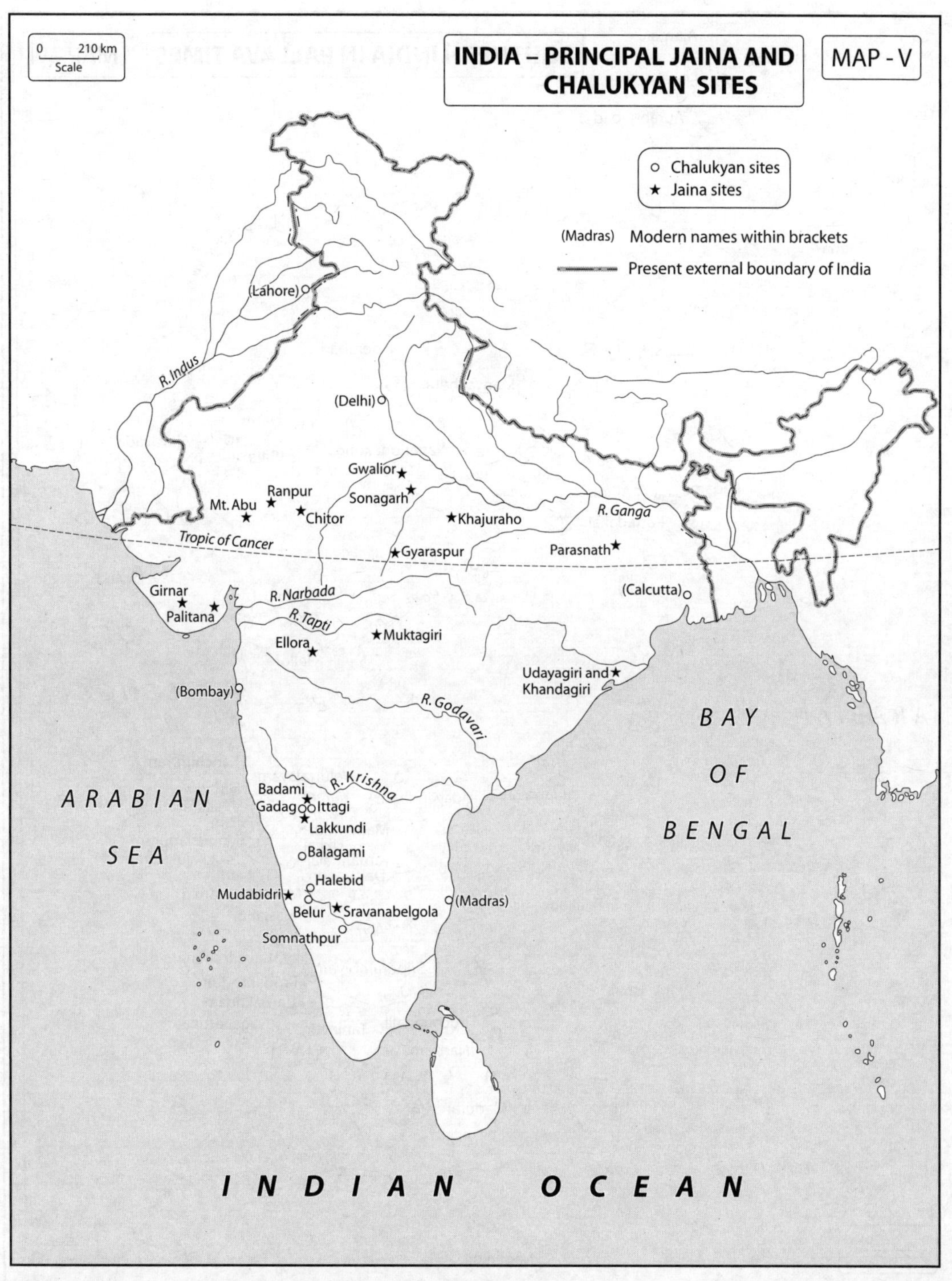


1:21,000,000

Based upon Survey of India outline maps printed in 1978. The territorial waters of India extend into the sea to a distance of twelve nautical miles measured from the appropriate base line

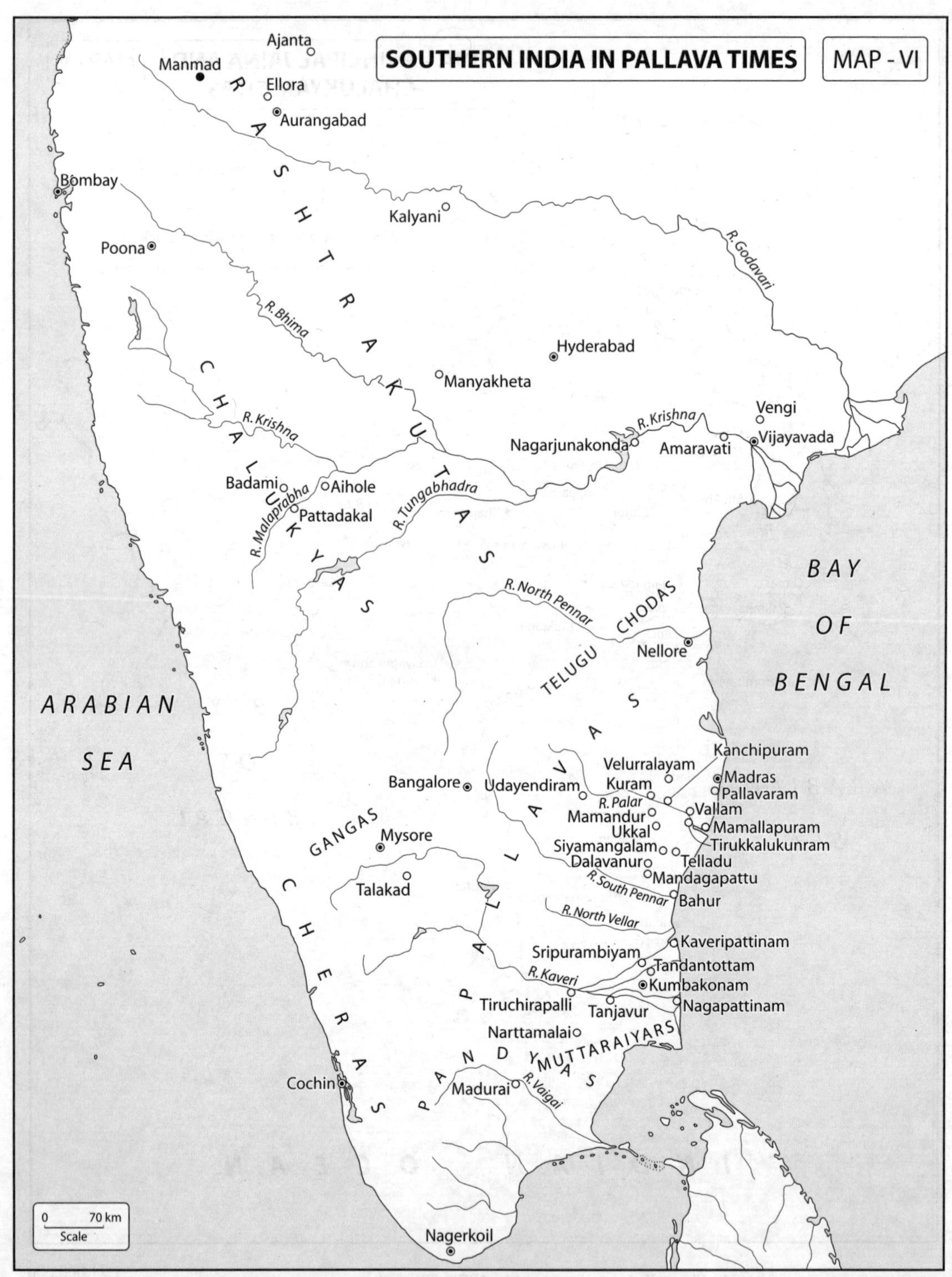


Based upon Survey of India outline maps printed in 1978. The territorial waters of India extend into the sea to a distance of twelve nautical miles measured from the appropriate base line

1:7,000,000

1:3,000,000

Based upon Survey of India outline maps printed in 1978. The territorial waters of India extend into the sea to a distance of twelve nautical miles measured from the appropriate base line

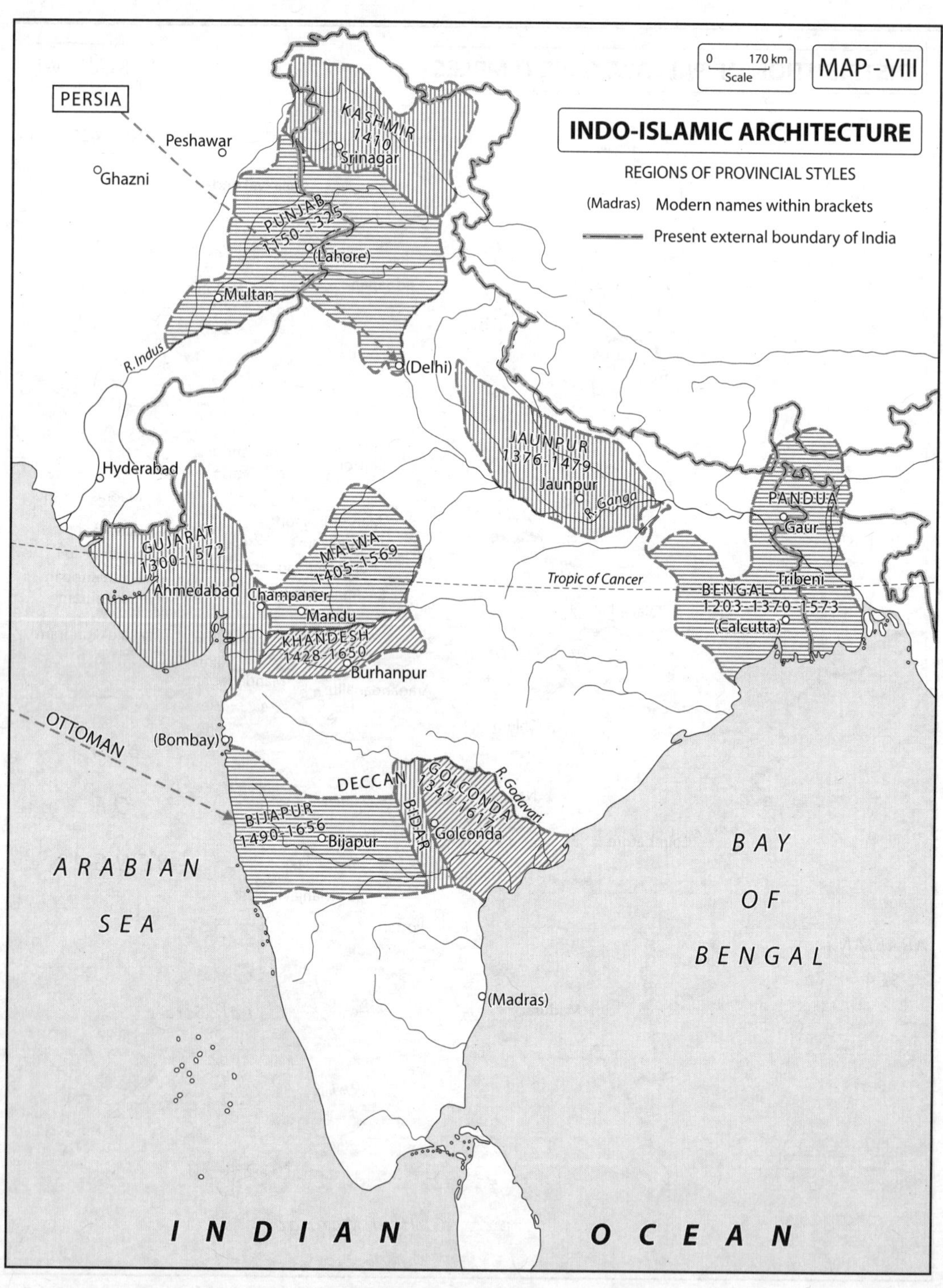


Based upon Survey of India outline maps printed in 1978. The territorial waters of India extend into the sea to a distance of twelve nautical miles measured from the appropriate base line

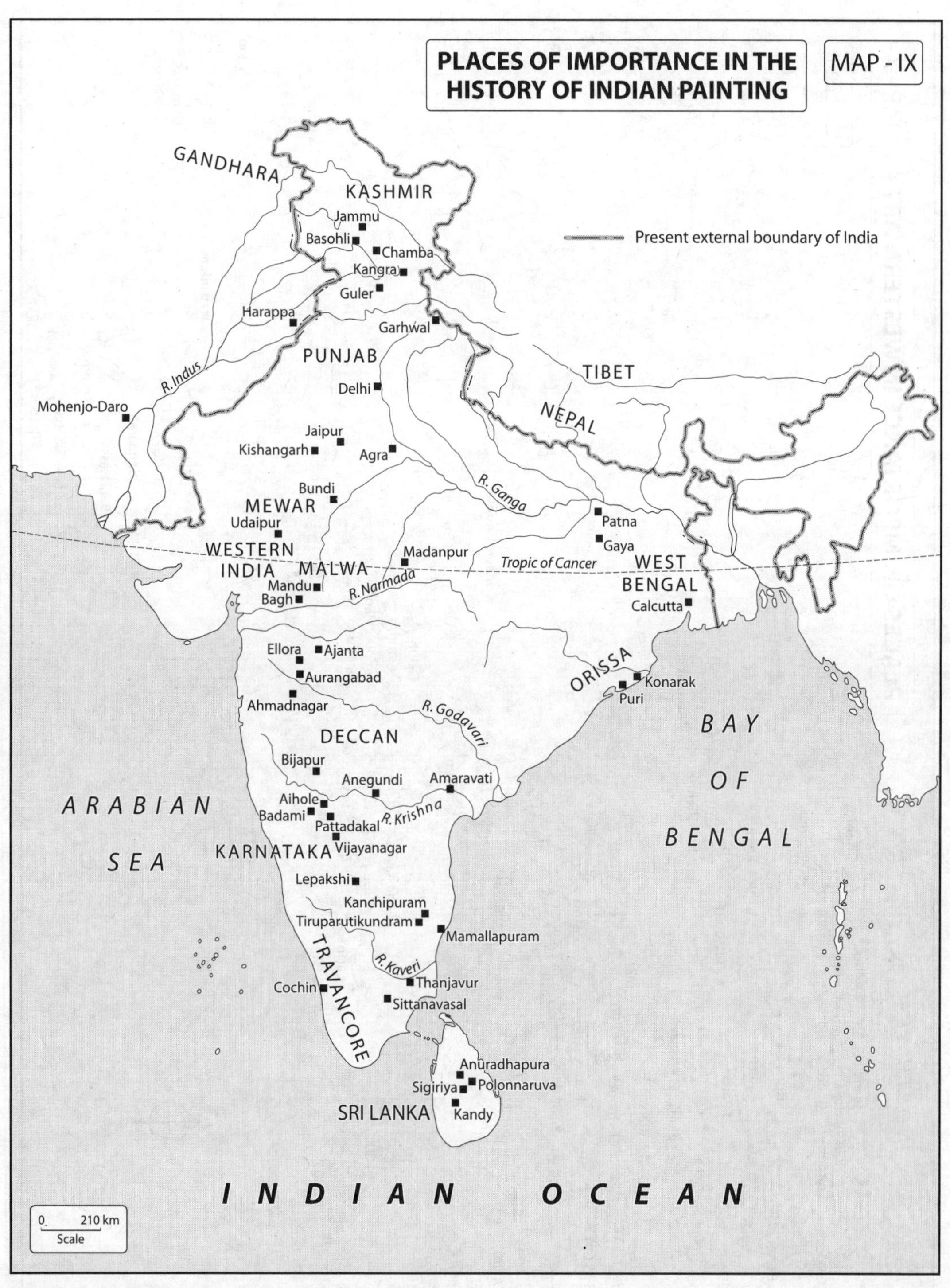


Based upon Survey of India outline maps printed in 1978. The territorial waters of India extend into the sea to a distance of twelve nautical miles measured from the appropriate base line

1:13,000,000

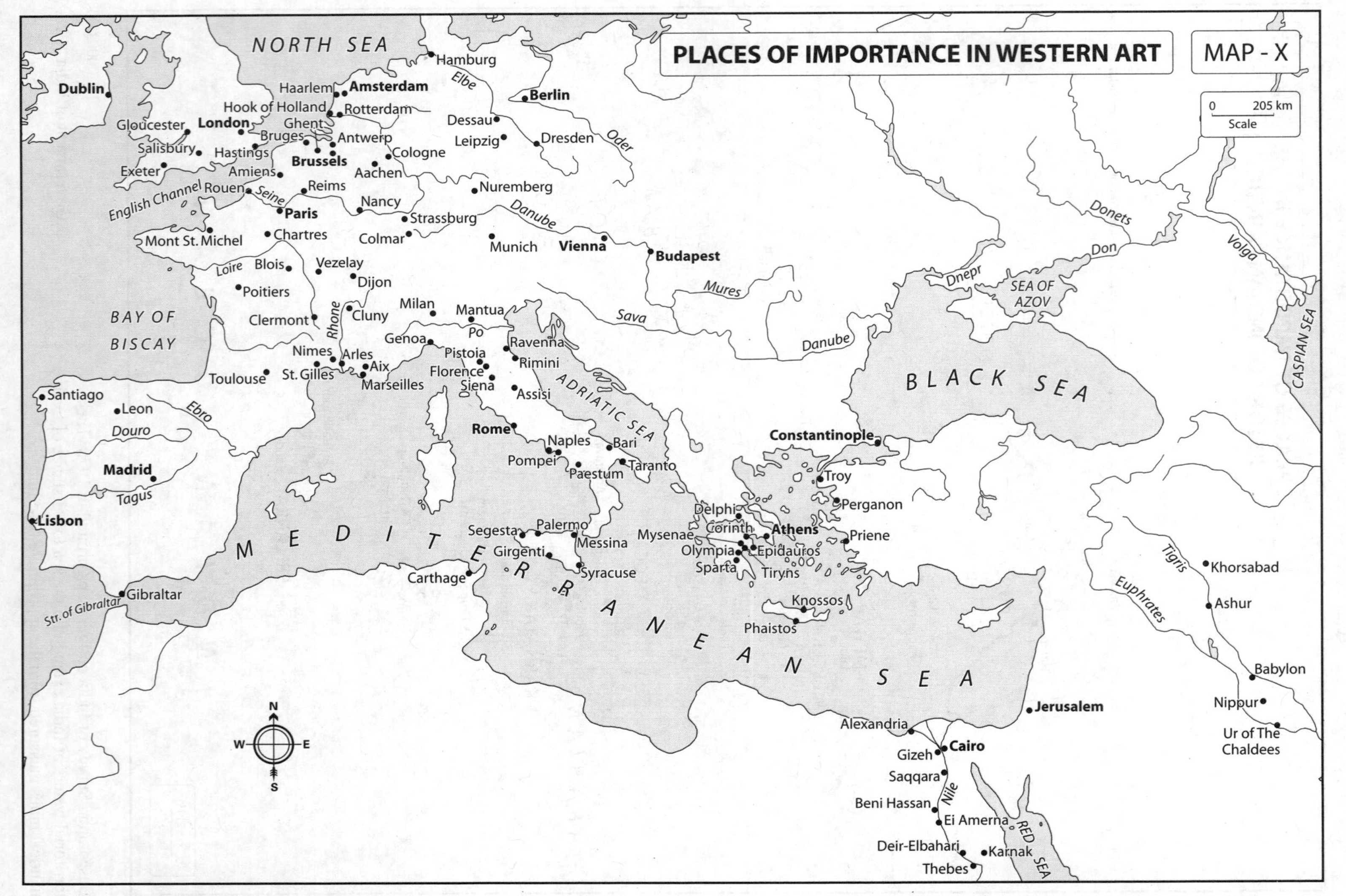
PLACES OF IMPORTANCE IN WESTERN ART
MAP - X
0 205 km
Scale
NORTH SEA
BAY OF BISCAY
MEDITERRANEAN SEA
ADRIATIC SEA
BLACK SEA
SEA OF AZOV
CASPIAN SEA
RED SEA
English Channel
Str. of Gibraltar
Dublin
Gloucester
London
Salisbury
Hastings
Exeter
Haarlem
Amsterdam
Hook of Holland
Rotterdam
Ghent
Bruges
Antwerp
Brussels
Cologne
Aachen
Amiens
Rouen
Reims
Paris
Nancy
Strassburg
Colmar
Mont St. Michel
Chartres
Blois
Vezelay
Dijon
Poitiers
Cluny
Clermont
Nimes
Arles
Aix
St. Gilles
Marseilles
Toulouse
Hamburg
Berlin
Dessau
Leipzig
Dresden
Nuremberg
Munich
Vienna
Budapest
Milan
Mantua
Genoa
Pistoia
Florence
Siena
Ravenna
Rimini
Assisi
Rome
Naples
Pompei
Paestum
Bari
Taranto
Segesta
Palermo
Messina
Girgenti
Syracuse
Carthage
Santiago
Leon
Madrid
Lisbon
Gibraltar
Constantinople
Troy
Perganon
Delphi
Corinth
Athens
Mysenae
Olympia
Epidauros
Sparta
Tiryns
Priene
Knossos
Phaistos
Jerusalem
Alexandria
Gizeh
Cairo
Saqqara
Beni Hassan
Ei Amerna
Deir-Elbahari
Karnak
Thebes
Khorsabad
Ashur
Babylon
Nippur
Ur of The Chaldees
Elbe
Oder
Seine
Loire
Rhone
Po
Danube
Sava
Mures
Dnepr
Don
Donets
Volga
Ebro
Douro
Tagus
Tigris
Euphrates
Nile
N
S
E
W

PLATE 1

1. Great Bath, Mohenjo-Daro.

3. Stūpa I, Sanchi.

2. Stambha, Laurya-Nandangarh.

PLATE 2

1. Northern Toraṇa, stūpa I, Sanchi

2. Chaitya, interior, Karle

4. Cave I, Ajanta (wooden model)

3. Ajanta caves, general view

PLATE 3

1. Mukteśvara Temple, Bhuvaneshvar

2. Lingarāja Temple, Bhuvaneshvar

PLATE 4

1. Kandaryā-Mahadevā Temple, Khajuraho

2. Sūrya Temple, Osian

3. Sūrya Temple Modhera

PLATE 5

1. Five Rathas, Mamallapuram

3. Brihadiśvara Temple, Tanjavur

2. Dharmarāja Ratha, Mamallapuram

5. Southern gopura, Minakshi Temple, Madurai

4. Vitthala Temple, Vijayanagar

PLATE 6

1. Kailāsa, Ellora

2. Keśava Temple, Somnathpur

PLATE 7

2. Alai Darwaza, Delhi

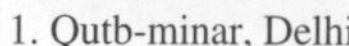

1. Qutb-minar, Delhi

3. Humayun's tomb, Delhi

PLATE 8

1. Jami Masjid, Fatehpur-Sikri

2. Buland Darwaza, Fatehpur-Sikri

3. Taj Mahal, Agra

PLATE 9

1. Bull capital from Rampurva, National Museum, Delhi

2. Lion capital from Sarnath, archaeological Museum, Sarnath

3. Yaksa Supavasa, Bharhut stūpa, Indian Museum, Calcutta

4. Parts of vedikā and eastern toraṇa, Bharhut stūpa, Indian Museum, Calcutta

PLATE 10

1. Chaddanta Jātaka, Southern toraṇa, stūpa I, Sanchi

2. Siege of Kuśinagara, Southern toraṇa, stūpa I, Sanchi

3. Great departure from Kapilavastu, Eastern toraṇa, stūpa I, Sanchi

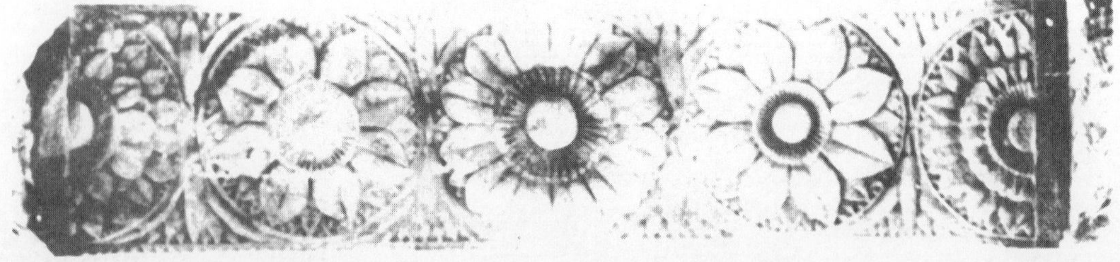

4. Lotus frieze, northern toraṇa, stūpa I, Sanchi

PLATE 11

1. Standing Buddha from Hoti Mardan

2. Seated Buddha from Takht-i-Bahai, Berlin museum

3. Standing Bodhisatva, Museum of Fine Arts, Boston

4. Seated Bodhisatva, Indian Museum, Calcutta

1. Great renunciation, Indian Museum, Calcutta

2. Parinirvāṇa, Indian Museum, Calcutta

# PLATE 13

1. Kanishka, Archaeological Museum, Mathura

2. Buddha dedicated by bhikṣu Bala, Archaeological Museum, Sarnath

3. Drum slab with stūpa representation from Amaravati, Government Museum, Madras

PLATE 14

1. Veneration of the Buddha's begging bowl from Amaravati, Government Museum, Madras

2. Standing Buddha from Mathura, National Museum, Delhi

3. Seated Buddha from Sarnath, Archaeological Museum, Sarnath

4. Nagaraja, Cave 19, Ajanta

1. Descent of the Ganga or Kirātārjunīya, Mamallapuram

2. Rāvana shaking Mount Kailāsa, Ellora

3. Siva Maheśamūrti, Elephanta

1. Horse court, Ranganathaswami temple, Srirangam

3. Vrsabhavahana from Tiruvengadu, Art Gallery, Tanjavur

2. Siva Nataraja from Tiruvalangadu, Government Museum, Madras

# PLATE 17

1. Bodhisatva Padmapani, Cave 1, Ajanta

2. Mother and Child, Cave 17, Ajanta

3. Apsaras, Cave 17, Ajanta

4. Akbar trying to control a wild elephant (from the Akbarnama)

PLATE 18

1. Akbar receiving the news of Salim's birth

2. Emperor Jahangir celebrating the festival Gulab Pashi.

3. The turkey-cock (from Jahangir's memoirs), Indian Museum, Calcutta

4. Emperor Shah Jahan on the peacock throne, Baron Rothschild collection, Paris

PLATE 19

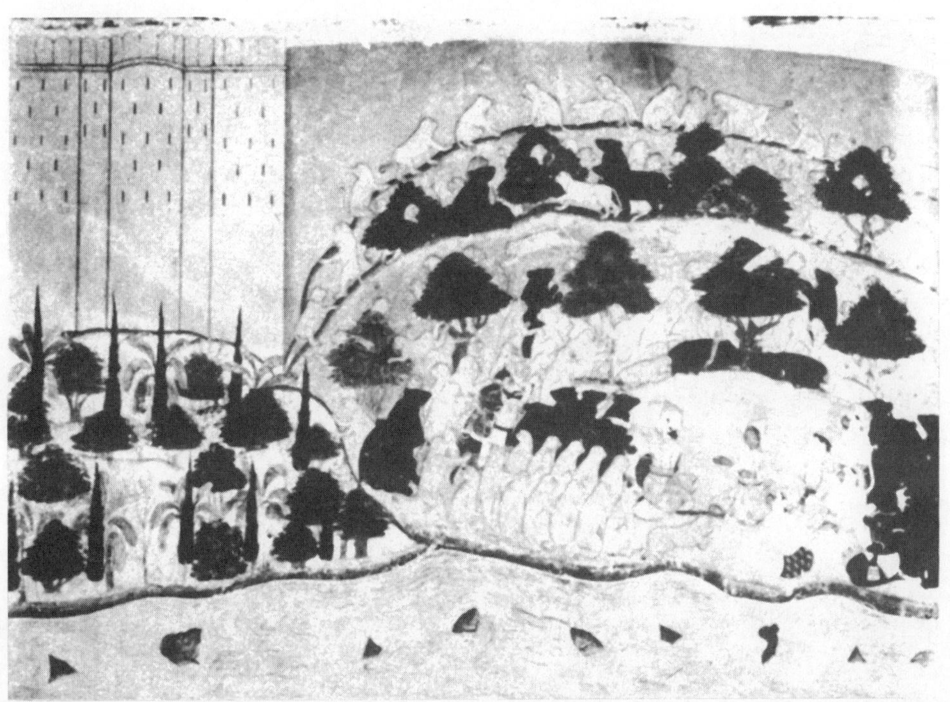

1. Arrest of the first spies, Museum of Fine Arts, Boston

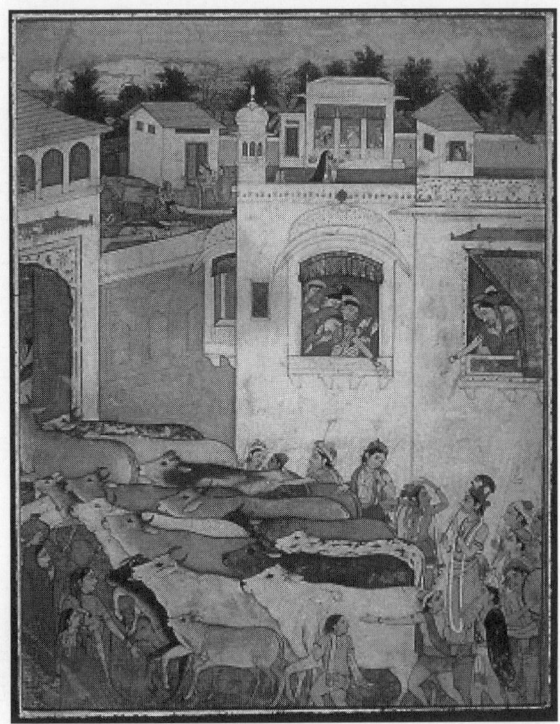

2. Hour of cowdust,
Museum of Fine Arts, Boston

PLATE 20

1. Along the roadside

2. Around the campfire

3. Krișņa subduing Kalya Naga, Metropolitan Museum of Art, New York

PLATE 21

1. Pyramid and Sphinx, Gizeh

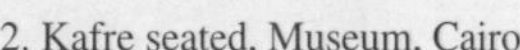

2. Kafre seated, Museum, Cairo

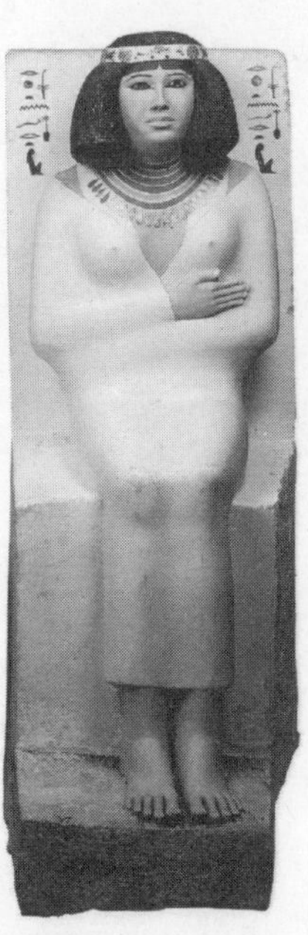

3. Rahotep and Nofret, Museum, Cairo

4. Sheik el-Beled, Museum, Cairo

5. Seated Scribe
Louvre Museum, Paris

1. Memnon statues at Luxor

2. Sunk reliefs, Temple, Edfu

3. Parthenon, Acropolis, Athens

4. Erechtheion, Acropolis, Athens

PLATE 23

1. Hera of Samos, Louvre Museum, Paris

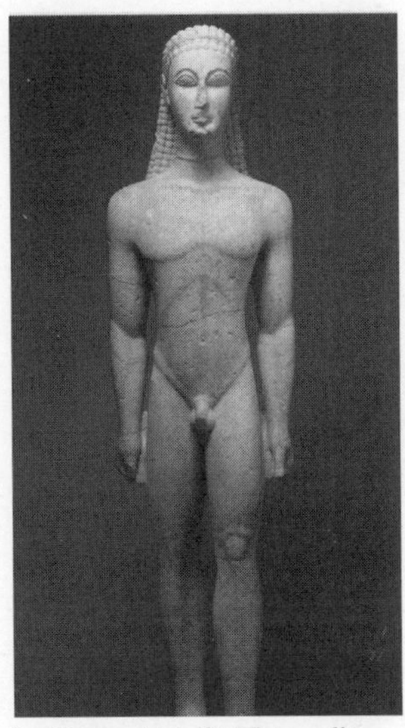

2. Kouros (detail), Metropolitan Museum of Art, New York

3. Charioteer of Delphi, Museum, Delphi

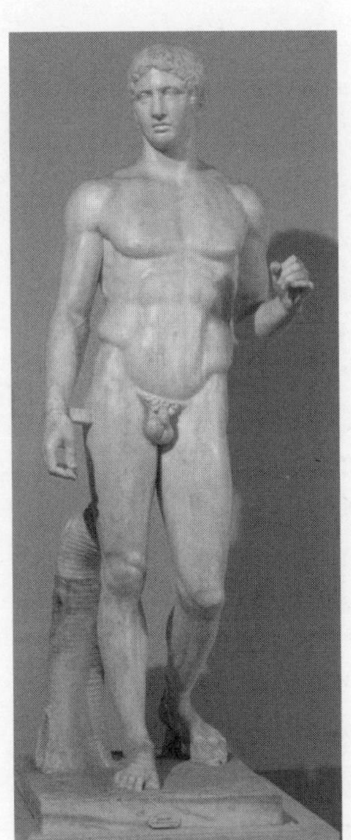

4. Polycleitos: Doryphoros, Vatican Museum, Rome

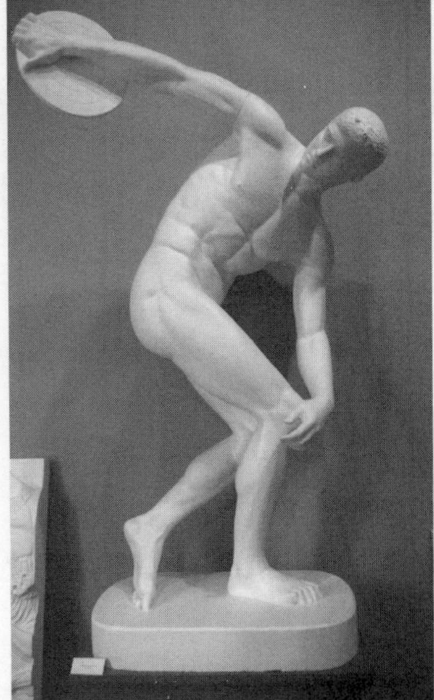

5. Myron; Discobolos, Vatican Museum, Rome

6. Western pediment, Temple of Zeus, Olympia

# PLATE 24

1. Centaur and Lapith, Parthenon, Athens, Louvre Museum, Paris

2. Dionysus, eastern pediment, Parthenon, Athens, British Museum, London

3. Three Fates, eastern pediment, Pathenon, Athens, British Museum, London

4. Head of Selene's steed, Eastern pediment, Parthenon, Athens, British Museum, London

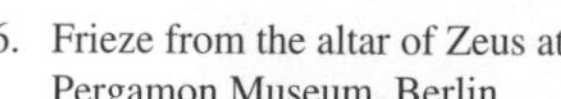

6. Frieze from the altar of Zeus at Pergamon Museum, Berlin

7. Nike of Samothrace, Louvre Museum, Paris

5. Lysippos: Apoxiomenos, Vatican Museum, Rome

8. Amphora, painted by Exekias, Vatican Museum, Rome

# PLATE 25

1. Pantheon, exterior, Rome

2. Pantheon, interior, Rome

1. Colosseum or Flavian Amphitheatre, Rome

2. Arch of Titus, Rome

# PLATE 27

1. Young girl, Chiaramonti collection
Vatican Museum, Rome

2. Emperor Augustus, Vatican Museum, Rome

3. Emperor Caracalla, Berlin Museum

4. Paquius Proculus and his wife

# PLATE 28

1. Orante, the veiled consecrated virgin, Catacombs of Priscilla, Rome

2. Seated Virgin, Catacombs of Priscilla, Rome

3. Model of old St. Peter's Basilica, Museo Petriano, Vatican

4. St. Paul's Basilica, interior,. Rome

# PLATE 29

1. Basilica of St. Mary Major, interior, Rome

2. Santa Maria in Cosmedin, interior, Rome

3. Sarcophagus of Junius Bassus, Vatican

4. Good Shepherd, Vatican Museum, Rome

PLATE 30

1. Hagia Sophia, interior, Constantinople (Istambul)

2. Hagia Sophia, exterior Constantinople (Istambul)

3. St. Mark's, interior, Venice

4. St. Mark's, exterior, Venice

PLATE 31

1. Deisis, Haberville triptych, Louvre Museum, Paris

2. Chair of Maximian, Archiepiscopal palace, Ravenna

4. Vladimir Madonna, Historical Museum, Moscow

3. Theodora with her attendants, Mosaic, San Vitale, Ravenna

1. Sant Ambrogio, interior, Milan

2. Cathedral, leaning tower and baptistery, Pisa

3. Cathedral of Worms

4. Church of St. Trophime, Arles

# PLATE 33

1. Pediment, Church of St. Pierre, Moissac

2. Facade, Cathedral of Notre Dame, Chartres

3. Royal portal, Cathedral of Notre Dame, Chartres

4. Cathedral of Notre Dame, (bird's eye view), Chartres

# PLATE 34

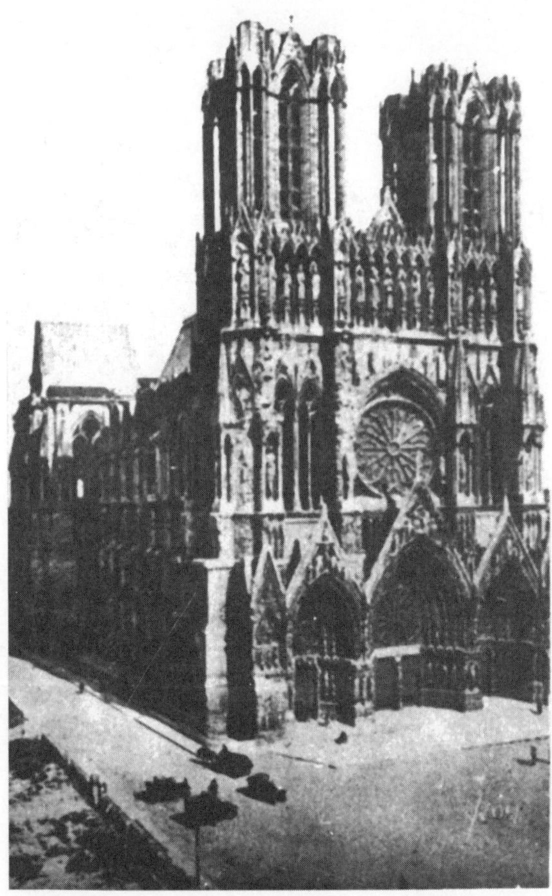

1. Cathedral of Rheims, exterior

2. Cathedral of Amiens, interior

3. Cathedral of Salisbury

4. Townhall, Louvain

PLATE 35

1. St. Paul, Cathedral of Rheims

2. Beau Dieur, Cathedral of Amiens

3. La Vierge Doree, Cathedral of Amiens

4. The Synagogue, Cathedral of Strassburg

PLATE 36

2. Giotto: Lamentation, Scrovegni chapel, Padua

1. Ghiberti: Gates of Paradise, eastern doors, baptistery, Florence

3. Cathedral of Florence

PLATE 37

1. Brunelleschi: Pazzi chapel, Florence

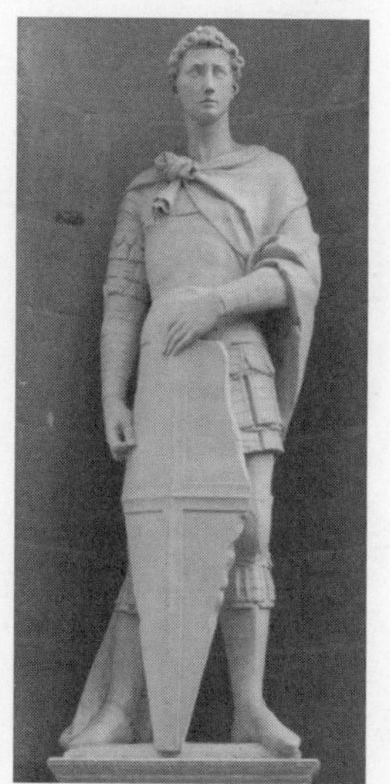

2. Donatello: St. George, originally on the exterior of Or San Michele, National Gallery, Florence

3. Donatello: Zuccone campanile, Florence

4. Donatello : Gattamelata, Erasmo di Narni, Padua.

5. Donatello: Mule before the Host, altar of Sant Antonio, Padua

PLATE 38

1. Donatello: Cantoria, Museum of Florence Cathedral

2. Donatello: Annunciation, Santa Croce. Florence

3. Luca della Robbia: Virgin adoring the Infant Jesus Philadelphia Museum of Art

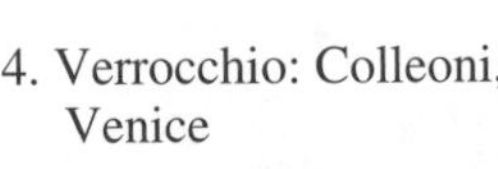

4. Verrocchio: Colleoni, Venice

5. Masaccio: Tribute money, Brancacci chapel, Church of Santa Maria del Carmine, Florence

PLATE 39

1. Fra Angelico: Crowning of the Virgin, altarpiece San Marco, Florence

2. Fra Angelico : Crowning of the Virgin, wall painting, San Marco, Florence

3. Fra Angelico: Annunciation, wall painting, San Marco, Florence

PLATE 40

1. Botticelli: Magnificat, Uffizi Gallery, Florence

2. Botticelli: Birth of Venus, Uffizi Gallery, Florence

3. Botticelli: Springtime, Uffizi Gallery, Florence

4. Mantegna: Ceiling of the camera degli sposi, castello, Mantua

5. St. Peter's Basilica, Vatican

6. Leonardo da Vinci: Virgin of the rocks, Louvre Museum, Paris

PLATE 41

1. Leonardo da Vinci:
Last Supper, refectory of Santa Maria delle Grazie, Milan

2. Leonardo da Vinci,
Mona Lisa, Louvre Museum, Paris

3. Michelangelo: Pieta, St. Peter's Basilica, Vatican

4. Michelangelo: Moses, Church of St. Peter's Chains, Rome

# PLATE 42

1. Michelangelo: Ceiling of the Sistine chapel, Vatican

2. Michelangelo : Creation of Adam Sistine chapel ceiling, Vatican

3. Michelangelo: Tomb of Giuliano de' Medici, new sacristy, San Lorenzo, Florence

PLATE 43

1. Raphael: Betrothal of the Virgin, Brera Museum, Milan

2. Raphael: Madonna del Gran Duca, Pitti Gallery, Florence

3. Raphael : Madonna di San Sisto, gallery, Dresden

PLATE 44

1. Raphael: Disputa del Sacramento, Stanza della Segnatura, Vatican

2. Raphael: School of Athens, Stanza della Segnatura, Vatican

# PLATE 45

1. Titian: Christ and the tribute money, gallery, Munich

2. Tintoretto: Miracle of St. Mark, Academy, Venice

3. Bernini: Baldacchino, St. Peter's, Vatican

4. Caravaggio: Entombment, gallery, Vatican

1. Hubert and Jan van Eyck: Mystic Lamb, Cathedral of St. Bavo, Ghent

2. Jan van Eyck: Madonna of the Chancellor Rolin, Louvre Museum, Paris

# PLATE 47

1. Jan van Eyck: Arnolfini and his wife, National Gallery, London

2. Roger van der Weyden: Descent from the cross, Prado Museum, Madrid

1. Memling: Mystic marriage of St. Catherine, Hospital of St. John, Bruges

2. Brueghel the Elder: Hunters in the snow, Kunsthistorisches Museum, Vienna

PLATE 49

1. Rubens: Helene Fourment in bridal attire, Alte Pinskothek, Munich

2. Van Dyck : Charles I, Louvre Museum, Paris

3. Stephan Lochner Madonna in the rose garden, Wallraf-Richartz Museum, Cologne

4. Grunewald: Nativity, Isenheim altarpiece, Untemnden monastery, museum, Colmar

PLATE 50

1. Grünewald: Crucifixion, Isenheim altarpiece, Unterlinden monastery, museum, Colmar

2. Dürer : Four horsemen, woodcut

3. Dürer: St. Jerome in his study engraving

4. Dürer : Melancholia, engraving

PLATE 51

1. Dürer: Adoration of the Magi, Uffizi Gallery, Florence

2. Dürer : Self-portrait, Alte Pinakothek Museum, Munich

3. Holbein the Younger: The Virgin with the family of Burgomaster Mever Hessisches Landes Museum Darmstadt

4. Cranach the Elder : Rest during the flight into Egypt, former Kaiser Friedrich Museum, Berlin

1. Hals: Archers of St. George, Frans Hals Museum, Haarlem

2. Rembrandt: Rembrandt and his wife, Dresden Gallery

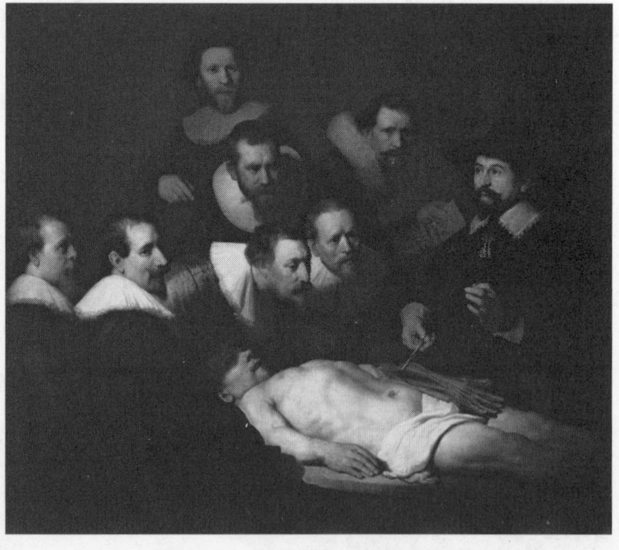

3. Rembrandt: Lesson in anatomy, Mauritshuis, The Hague

PLATE 53

1. Rembrandt: Night watch, Rijksmuseum, Amsterdam

2. Rembrandt: Syndics of the cloth hall, Rijksmuseum, Amsterdam

# PLATE 54

1. Rembrandt: Simeon in the temple, Mauritshuis, The Hague

2. Rembrandt: Supper at Emmaus, Louvre Museum, Paris

3. Pieter de Hooch : In the bedroom, Staatliche Kunsthalle, Karlsruhe

4. Ter Borch: The concert former Kaiser Friedrich Museum, Berlin

# PLATE 55

2. Ruisdael: The mill at Wijk, Rijksmuseum, Amsterdam

1. Vermeer: Girl with a pearl necklace, former Kaiser Friedrich Museum, Berlin

3. Hobbema
Avenue of Middelares,
National Gallery,
London

PLATE 56

1. Entrance to the University of Salamanca

2. Escorial, near Madrid

3. El Greco the burial of the Count of Orgaz, Church of Santo Tome, Toledo

4. El Greco : Resurrection, Prado Museum, Madrid

PLATE 57

1. E1Greco : Storm over Toledo, Metropolitan of Art, New York

2. Velasquez: Surrender of Breda, Prado Museum, Madrid

1. Velasquez: Las Meninas, Prado Museum, Madrid

2. Velasquez: Infanta Margarita, Prado Museum, Madrid

3. Velasquez: Crucifix, Prado Museum. Madrid

PLATE 59

1. Murillo: Immaculada, Louvre Museum, Paris

2. Murillo: Vision of St. Francis

3. Goya : The family of Charles IV, Prado Museum, Madrid

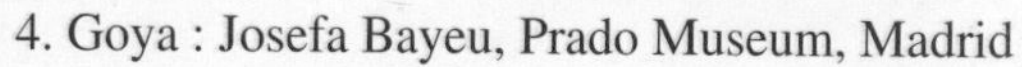

4. Goya : Josefa Bayeu, Prado Museum, Madrid

PLATE 60

1. Wren: St. Paul's Cathedral, London

2. Hogarth: Marriage a la mode, 2nd scene, Tate Gallery, London

4. Reynolds: Dr. Samuel Johnson, National Gallery, London

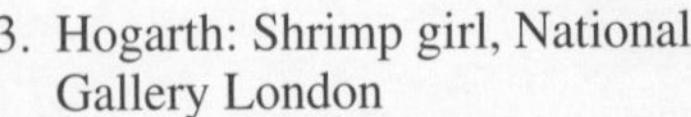

3. Hogarth: Shrimp girl, National Gallery London

PLATE 61

1. Reynolds: Age of innocence, Wallace Collection Landon

2. Gainsborough : Blue boy, Huntington Art Gallery, San Marino, California

3. Constable : Hay wain, National Gallery, London

PLATE 62

1. Turner: Fighting Temeraire, National Gallery, London

2. Perrault: Eastern facade, Louvre, Paris

PLATE 63

1. The Palace of Versailles

2. Houdon: St. Bruno, Church of Santa Maria degli Angeli, Rome

3. Poussin: Arcadian shepherds, Louvre Museum, Paris

4. Claude Lorrain : Landscape with Amor and Psyche, Wallraf Richartz Museum, Cologne

PLATE 64

2. Watteau: Gilles, Louvre Museum, Paris

1. Chardin: Saying grace, Louvre Museum, Paris

3. Millet: Angelus (destroyed by a recent fire)

# MUDRAS

## HAND POSTURES

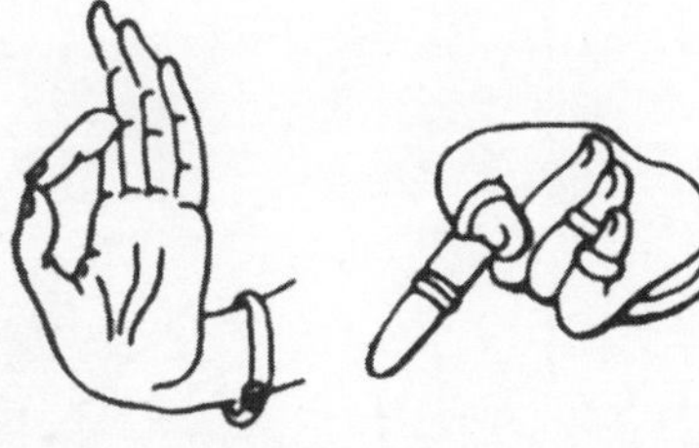

Fig. 473. Chin mudra.

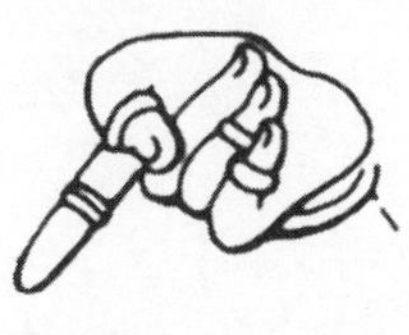

Fig. 474. Suci mudra.

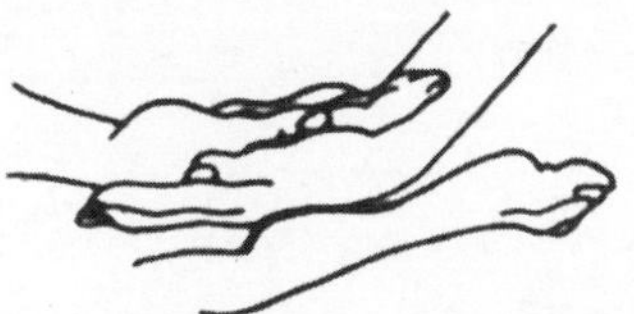

Fig. 475. Dhyana mudra.

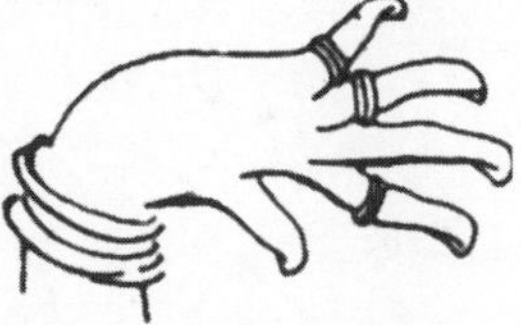

Fig. 476. Vismaya mudra.

Fig. 477. Varada mudra.

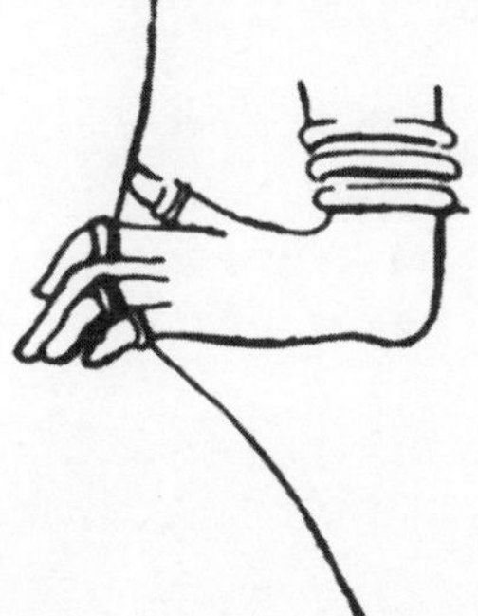

Fig. 478. Katyavalambita.

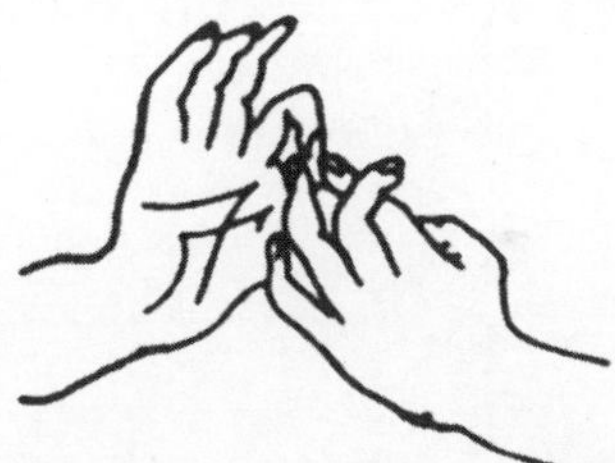

Fig. 479. Dharmachakra mudra.

Fig. 480. Katakamukha.

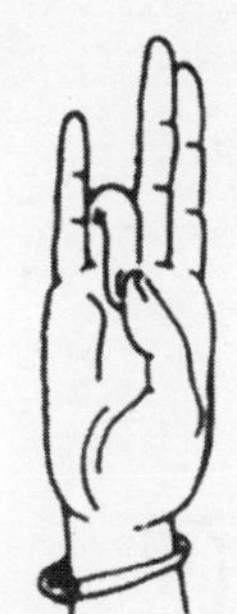

Fig. 481. Kartarimukha.

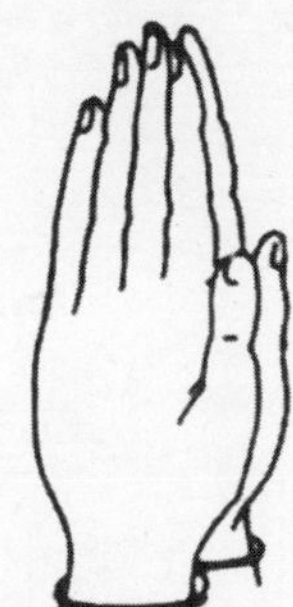

Fig. 482. Anjali.

Fig. 483. Pataka mudra.

Fig. 484. Tripataka mudra.

Fig. 485. Abhaya mudra.

Fig. 486. Chatura mudra.

# ASANAS

## SEATED POSTURES

Fig. 487. Sukhasana.

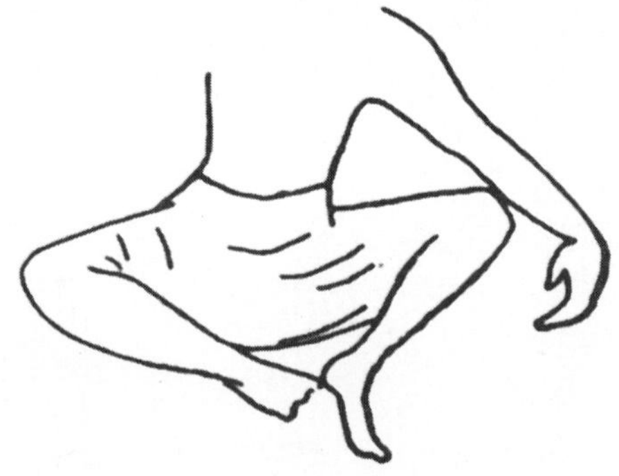

Fig. 488. Maharaja-Lilasana.

Fig. 489. Sopasaryana

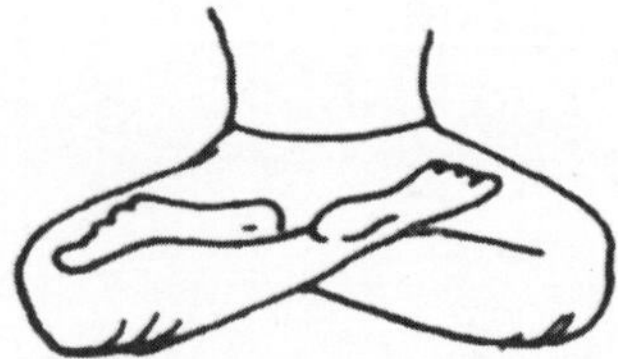

Fig. 489. Padmasana.

Fig. 491. Kirita makuta.

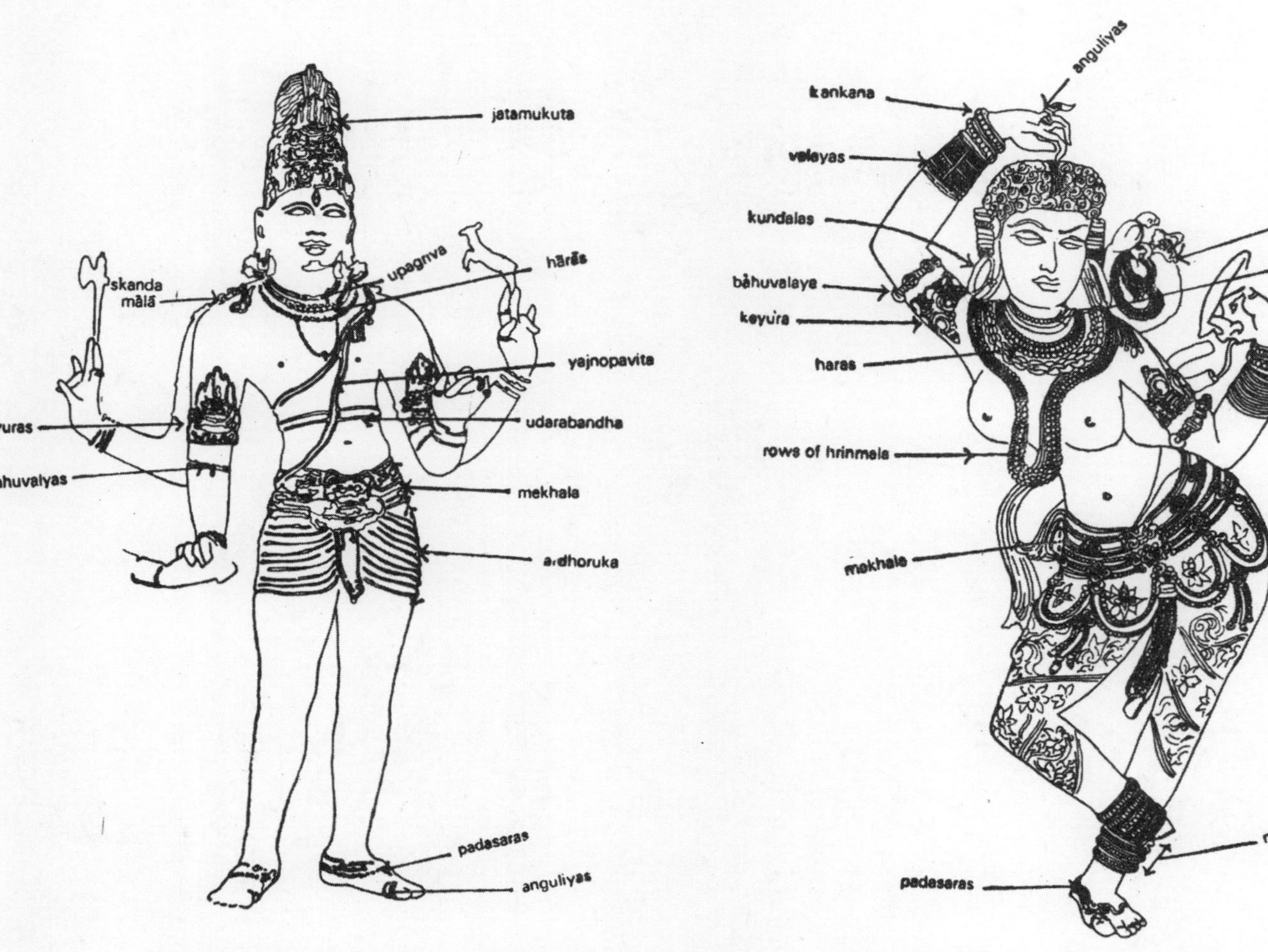


Fig. 492. Jewellery worn by a male figure in sculpture.

Fig. 493. Jewellery worn by a female figure in sculpture.

# BHANGAS

## STANDING POSTURES

Fig. 494. Atibhanga.

Fig. 495. Tribhanga.

Fig. 496. Sama bhanga

# INDEX

## A

## B

## C

## E



## F

## G

## H

## I



## J

## K

## L

## M

## N

## O



## P

## Q



## R

S

U



V

**W**



**X**



**Y**



**Z**